W9-DCA-862

The Professional Chef

John Wiley & Sons, Inc.

The Professional Chef

8th Edition

The Culinary Institute of America

PRESIDENT Dr. Tim Ryan
VICE-PRESIDENT, CONTINUING EDUCATION Mark Erickson
DIRECTOR OF INTELLECTUAL PROPERTY Nathalie Fischer
MANAGING EDITOR Kate McBride
EDITORIAL PROJECT MANAGER Mary Donovan
EDITORIAL PROJECT MANAGER Lisa Lahey
EDITORIAL ASSISTANT Margaret Otterstrom
PROJECT ASSISTANT Patrick Decker
RECIPE TESTERS Alexis Jette-Borggaard, Scott Kupferschmidt, Rachel Toomey, Lynn Tonelli, Danny Trotter

This book is printed on acid-free paper. ∞

Copyright © 2006 by The Culinary Institute of America. All rights reserved

Published by John Wiley & Sons, Inc., Hoboken, New Jersey
Published simultaneously in Canada

No part of this publication may be reproduced, stored in a retrieval system, or transmitted in any form or by any means, electronic, mechanical, photocopying, recording, scanning, or otherwise, except as permitted under Section 107 or 108 of the 1976 United States Copyright Act, without either the prior written permission of the Publisher, or authorization through payment of the appropriate per-copy fee to the Copyright Clearance Center, 222 Rosewood Drive, Danvers, MA 01923, (978) 750-8400, fax (978) 646-8600, or on the Web at www.copyright.com. Requests to the Publisher for permission should be addressed to the Permissions Department, John Wiley & Sons, Inc., 111 River Street, Hoboken, NJ 07030, (201) 748-6011, fax (201) 748-6008, or online at http://www.wiley.com/go/permissions

Limit of Liability/Disclaimer of Warranty: While the Publisher and the author have used their best efforts in preparing this book, they make no representations or warranties with respect to the accuracy or completeness of the contents of this book and specifically disclaim any implied warranties of merchantability or fitness for a particular purpose. No warranty may be created or extended by sales representatives or written sales materials. The advice and strategies contained herein may not be suitable for your situation. You should consult with a professional where appropriate. Neither the Publisher nor the author shall be liable for any loss of profit or any other commercial damages, including but not limited to special, incidental, consequential, or other damages.

For general information about our other products and services, please contact our Customer Care Department within the United States at (800) 762-2974, outside the United States at (317) 572-3993 or fax (317) 572-4002.

Wiley also publishes its books in a variety of electronic formats. Some content that appears in print may not be available in electronic books. For more information about Wiley products, visit our Web site at www.wiley.com.

LIBRARY OF CONGRESS CATALOGING-IN-PUBLICATION DATA:

The professional chef / the Culinary Institute of America.— 8th ed.
   p. cm.
 Includes index.
 ISBN-13: 978-0-7645-5734-7 (cloth)
 ISBN-10: 0-7645-5734-3 (cloth)
 1. Quantity cookery. I. Culinary Institute of America.
 TX820.P738 2006
 641.5'7—dc22

           2004027110

Printed in the United States of America

10 9 8 7 6 5 4

Cover and interior photography by Ben Fink
Cover and interior design by Vertigo Design, New York City

Acknowledgments

The common wisdom says "Leave well enough alone." It is because the following people at The Culinary Institute of America knew that "well enough" isn't the same thing as "as good as we can make it" that this revised edition came into being: Tim Ryan, CMC; Mark Erickson, CMC; Victor Gielissse, CMC; and the Institute's associate deans Eve Felder; Gregory P. Fatigati; Ron Desantis, CMC; Thomas E. Peer, CMC; Anthony Ligouri; Robert Briggs; Thomas L. Vaccaro.

The heart of this book is the detailed explanation of cooking methods in words and images, as well as an amazingly diverse collection of recipes. For their dedication to excellence in several areas (reading and critiquing the text, testing and reviewing recipes, and being the hands you see in the photographs), the following individuals are also to be congratulated and thanked: Mark Ainsworth '86, C.H.E.; Olivier Andreini, C.M.C., C.H.E.; Clemens Averbeck, C.E.C.; David J. Barry '95; Frederick C. Brash '76, C.H.E.; Elizabeth E. Briggs, C.H.E.; David J. Bruno '88, P.C. II/C.C.C., C.H.E.; Kate Cavotti, C.M.B., C.H.E.; Shirley Shuliang Cheng, C.W.C., C.H.E.; Howard F. Clark '71, C.C.E., C.W.C., C.H.E.; Richard J. Coppedge, Jr., C.M.B., C.H.E.; Gerard Coyac, C.H.E.; Phillip Crispo; Philip Delaplane, C.W.C., C.H.E.; John DeShetler '68, C.H.E.; Joseph W. DiPerri '77, C.H.E.; Alain Dubernard, C.H.E.; Stephen J. Eglinski, C.H.E.; Anita Olivarez Eisenhauer, C.H.E.; Joseba Encabo, C.H.E.; Martin Frei, C.H.E.; Richard T. Gabriel '77, C.E.C.; Michael A. Garnero, C.H.E.; Lynne Gigliotti '88, C.H.E.; Peter Greweling, C.M.B., C.H.E.; Thomas W. Griffiths '80, C.M.C., C.H.E.; Carol D. Hawran '93; Marc Haymon '81, C.M.B., C.H.E.; James W. Heywood '67, C.H.E.; George B. Higgins '78, C.M.B., C.H.E.; James Michael Jennings '93; Stephen J. Johnson '94; Lou Jones, C.H.E.; David Kamen '88, P.C. III/C.E.C., C.C.E., C.H.E.; Morey Kanner '84, C.H.E.; Eric W. Kastel '90, C.H.E.; Thomas Kief '78, C.H.E.; Joseph Klug '82, C.H.E.; Todd R. Knaster, C.H.E.; John Kowalski '77, C.H.E.; Prem Kumar; Pierre LeBlanc, C.H.E.; Xavier Le Roux, C.H.E.; Alain L. Levy, C.C.E., C.H.E.; Anthony J. Ligouri, C.H.E.; Dwayne F. LiPuma '86, C.H.E.; James Maraldo, C.H.E.; Hubert J. Martini, C.E.C., C.C.E., C.H.E., A.A.C.; Bruce S. Mattel '80, C.H.E.; Alison McLoughlin '93; Francisco Migoya; Michael Pardus '81, C.H.E.; William Phillips '88, C.H.E.; Katherine Polenz '73, C.H.E.; Heinrich Rapp, C.H.E.; Charles Rascoll, C.H.E.; John Reilly '88, C.C.C., C.H.E.; Theodore Roe '91, C.H.E.; Jose Sanchez, C.E.C., C.H.E.; Paul R. Sartory '78; Giovanni Scappin; Eric L. Schawaroch '84; Thomas Schneller, C.H.E.; Dieter G. Schorner, C.M.B., C.H.E.; Johann Sebald, C.H.E.; Michael Skibitcky, C.E.C., C.H.E.; David F. Smythe, C.C.E., C.E.C., C.H.E.; Rudolf Spiess, C.H.E.; John J. Stein '80, C.F.B.E., C.H.E.; Jürgen Temme, C.M.B., C.H.E.; Daniel Turgeon '85, C.H.E.; Alberto Vanoli; Gerard Viverito, C.E.C., C.H.E.; Frank Vollkommer, C.M.P.C., C.H.E.; Hinnerk von Bargen, C.H.E.; Stéphane Weber, C.H.E.; Jonathan A. Zearfoss, C.E.C., C.C.E., C.C.P., C.H.E.; Gregory Zifchak '80, C.H.E.

For the professional chef there are many subjects to master. A special thank you to those who helped develp and review chapters dedicated to world cuisines, management, food safety and nutrition: Marjorie Livingston, R.D., C.H.E.; Marianne Turow '83, R.D., C.H.E.; Richard Vergili, C.H.E.; Robert Danhi; Michelle Graas; Rachel Toomey; Amy Townsend.

The images in this book were created in the Institute's studios and kitchens. Many thanks to photographer Ben Fink, whose expertise and artistry are the perfect complement to the text, techniques, and recipes. A debt of gratitude to Shannon O'Hara and Frank Lopez for their assistance during the photo shoots. Thanks to those CIA staff members without whom carrying through the photo shoots would have been a near impossibility: Edward Bakter, James Creighton, Michael Murphy, and Paul Wigsten. Our thanks also to Villeroy & Boch for supplying most of the dishes and props used in the photography.

Thanks to the book's designer, Alison Lew (Vertigo Design, NYC), who brought it all together beautifully, and to the Senior Production Editor at Wiley, Leslie Anglin, for her tireless attention to every detail, large and small. And finally, thank you to Senior Editor Pam Chirls, for her overall guidance and vision.

Contents

Recipes

CHAPTER TWENTY
Grilling and Broiling, Roasting and Baking

Grilling and Broiling

Roasting and Baking

CHAPTER TWENTY-ONE
Sautéing, Pan Frying, and Deep Frying

Sautéeing

Pan Frying

CHAPTER TWENTY-TWO

Steaming and Submersion Cooking

CHAPTER TWENTY-THREE

Braising and Stewing

CHAPTER TWENTY-FIVE

Cooking Vegetables

CHAPTER THIRTY-ONE

Sandwiches

CHAPTER THIRTY-TWO

Hors d'Oeuvre and Appetizers

CHAPTER THIRTY-THREE

Charcuterie and Garde Manger

Introduction

Becoming a chef is a career-long process. Cooking is a dynamic profession—one that provides some of the greatest challenges as well as some of the greatest rewards. There is always another level of perfection to achieve and another skill to master. It is our hope that this book will function both as a springboard for future growth and as a reference point to give ballast to the lessons still to be learned.

By nature of its encyclopedic subject coverage, this text is suited to a variety of curricula, whether as part of an existing program or through independent study. An instructor may choose to use all or part of its contents; the student may use it to advance his or her learning by employing it as a broad, basic text or as a reference tool to answer specific questions about a particular technique. The techniques as explained in this book have all been tested in the Institute's kitchens. Each represents one of many possible variations. The fact that all variations are not included in this text does not imply that other methods are incorrect. Experience will teach the student many "tricks of the trade." The title of this work should not put it into the rarified category of books to be used only by those working in restaurant or hotel kitchens. The basic lessons of cooking are the same whether one prepares food for paying guests or for one's family and friends. Therefore, we hope that those who look to cooking for a creative outlet will come to regard this book as a valuable tool.

The Professional Chef is suited to a variety of teaching situations because the material is arranged in a logical, progressive sequence. Chapter One covers the history of cooking as a profession and examines the skills and attributes of a professional chef and other members of the foodservice profession. (For more information about table service and dining room operations, consult At Your Service or Remarkable Service.)

Since foodservice is a business, some of the elementary aspects of food costing are discussed in Chapter Two, as well as how to adapt recipes, from this book or any other, for use in a specific professional kitchen. Knowing how to adapt recipes is useful for scheduling, controlling costs, and improving quality. (For more details about culinary math, consult Culinary Math.) Nutrition and food science have become part of the everyday language of the professional kitchen, and Chapter Three reviews some basic concepts of nutrition and science, particularly as they relate to cooking. (For more information about nutritional cooking, consult The Professional Chef's Techniques of the Healthy Cook, Second Edition.) Food and kitchen safety are of increasing concern in all foodservice operations, and Chapter Four presents fundamental concepts and procedures for assuring that safe, wholesome food is prepared in a safe environment.

Another elemental base of information that benefits every professional chef is a basic understanding of the origins and cultures surrounding the foods we consume. This understanding will not only encourage respect for other foods and cuisines around the world, but will also help to bring about creative play that will lead to the development of new foods and cuisine. Part Two is devoted to exploring a few of the most influential cuisines around the world.

Counted among the basics in the kitchen is the ability to seek out and purchase the best possible ingredients. Part Three is a catalog of the ingredients and tools used in the professional kitchen and includes information regarding product specifications, purchasing, and such processing concerns as trim loss. Separate chapters are devoted to meats and poultry; fish; fruits, vegetables, and fresh herbs; dairy products and eggs; and nonperishable goods such as oils, flours, grains, and dried pastas. The information is presented in such a way that it can act as a quick reference to quality, seasonality, and appropriate cooking styles or techniques.

Cooking is not always a perfectly precise art, but a good grasp of the basics gives the chef or student the ability not only to apply the technique, but also to learn the standards of quality so that they begin to develop a sense of how cooking works. Part Four is devoted to stocks, sauces, and soups. The part opens with a chapter covering such basic mise en place techniques as preparing and using seasoning and aromatic combinations (bouquet garni and sachet d'épices), thickeners (roux and arrowroot), and mirepoix.

Part Five presents the techniques used to cook meats, poultry, and fish. This part covers the basic fabricating methods for familiar cuts of meat, poultry, and fish and then demonstrates how to grill, roast, sauté, pan fry, stir fry, steam, poach, stew, and braise. These important lessons are presented in clear step-by-step photographs, with explanatory text and a model recipe.

In Part Six, chapters concentrate on preparation techniques for vegetables, grains and legumes, pasta and dumplings, and potatoes. Part Seven covers breakfast and garde manger, with chapters covering eggs, salad dressings and salads, sandwiches, and garde manger items such as pâtés and terrines. (For further information on these subjects, consult *Garde Manger: The Art and Craft of the Cold Kitchen*.) Baking and pastry is presented in Part Eight, with attention paid to the preparation of breads and rolls; cakes and cookies; pastry doughs and crusts; and a variety of fillings, icings, and glazes.

The recipes included in this book are an example of the wide range of possibilities open to the student once the basics are mastered. It should be noted that these recipes have both metric and American measurements. The recipe yields reflect real-life cooking situations: some items, such as stocks and soups, are prepared in large quantities, while others, such as sautés and grills, are prepared à la minute, for a few portions at a time. Larger roasts, braises, stews, and side dishes generally have yields of 10 or 20 servings; any marinades, sauces, or condiments included in the recipes that are prepared in advance are normally given in quantities to produce a yield of 10 servings. These yields may not always suit the student who is using the book outside of a professional kitchen. In most cases, they can be reduced or increased in order to prepare the correct number of servings. Baking recipe yields are based on specific weight ratios, however, and must be followed exactly.

The new look of this edition reflects the way we think about teaching cooking. We learn best when we understand not only how to do something, but why we should do it that way. From this grounded approach, students at any level can confidently take new directions in their cooking careers.

Part One

The Culinary Professional

Chapter One

Introduction to the Profession

Evolving into a professional culinarian is a lifelong journey full of learned details and years of experience. It is challenging and demanding. Specific techniques and acquired knowledge are continually tested and improved upon. The specialized training required is intricate and precise. Deciding where to begin your study is just as important as the process of learning.

Becoming a Culinary Professional

A sound and thorough education emphasizing the culinary fundamentals is the first step to becoming fluent in the trade. Aspiring professionals will find formal training at an accredited school an excellent beginning. Other training alternatives include taking part in special apprenticeship programs or self-directed courses of study. The process involves advancing from kitchen to kitchen by learning at the side of chefs who are involved in the day-to-day business of running a professional kitchen. The goal is to ensure a thorough understanding of basic and advanced culinary techniques, regardless of the type of training received.

Creating a network of professional colleagues and industry contacts is important for future development. The avenue of growth that includes working with others, sharing information, and communicating regularly will help to keep your own work fresh and contemporary. An established network also makes it much easier for you to find a new position or qualified employees.

Learning new skills to gain a competitive stance and encourage creativity should be an ongoing part of your career development. Beneficial and rewarding opportunities result from attending continuing education classes, workshops, and seminars. Remain up to date with the following informative resources:

- Magazines
- Newsletters
- Instructional videos
- Web sites
- Government publications
- Books

The Attributes of a Culinary Professional

Each member of a profession is responsible for the profession's image, whether he or she is a teacher, lawyer, doctor, or culinarian. Those who have made the greatest impression know that the cardinal virtues of the culinary profession are an open and inquiring mind, an appreciation of and dedication to quality wherever it is found, and a sense of responsibility. Success also depends on several character traits, some of which are inherent, some of which are diligently cultivated throughout a career. These include:

- **Commitment to service**—The degree to which a foodservice professional can offer a quality product, as well as thorough customer satisfaction, is the degree to which they will succeed in providing excellent service.

- **Sense of responsibility**—The responsibility of a culinary professional includes respecting not just the customer and his or her needs but also the staff, food, equipment, and facility.

- **Sound judgment**—The ability to judge what is right and appropriate in each work situation is acquired throughout a lifetime of experience; good judgment is a prerequisite for becoming and remaining a professional.

The Chef as a Businessperson

As you continue your career, you will move from positions where your technical prowess is your greatest contribution into those where your skills as an executive, an administrator, and a manager are more clearly in demand. This does not mean that your ability to grill, sauté, or roast foods to the exact point of doneness is less important than it was before. It does mean that you will be called on to learn and assume tasks and responsibilities that are more managerial, marking a shift in the evolution of your career.

Become a good executive. Executives are the individuals who develop a mission or a plan for a company or organization. They are also the ones responsible for developing a system to allow that plan to come to fruition. As an executive, you must shoulder a large portion of responsibility for the success or failure of your establishment. Executives don't operate in a vacuum, however. Nor do they emerge full-blown one day out of the blue. Even before you wear a jacket embroidered with "Executive Chef," you will have begun to exercise your abilities as an executive.

Become a good administrator. Once an overall goal or plan has been laid down, the next task is to implement and track that plan. Now your hat becomes that of an administrator. Some administrative duties may not sound at all glamorous—preparing schedules, tracking deliveries, computing costs, and so forth. If a restaurant is small, the executive and administrator will be the same person. That same person also might be the one who dons a uniform and works the line.

The best administrators are those who can create a feeling throughout the entire staff that each person has a stake in getting things done correctly. When you give people the opportunity to help make decisions and provide them with the tools they need to perform optimally, you will see that it is easier to achieve the goals you have established on an executive level.

Learn to use the important tools of your business; budgets, accounting systems, and inventory control systems all play a role. Many organizations, from the largest chains to the smallest one-person catering company, rely upon software systems that allow them to efficiently administer a number of areas: inventory, purchases, losses, sales, profits, food costs, customer complaints, reservations, payroll, schedules, and budgets. If you are not using a system capable of tracking all this information and more, you cannot be as effective as you need to be.

Become a good manager. Managing a restaurant, or any other business, is a job that requires the ability to handle four areas effectively: physical assets, information, people (human resources), and time. The greater your skills in managing any of these areas, the greater your potential for success. Many management systems today stress the use of quality as a yardstick. Every aspect of your operation needs to be seen as a way to improve the quality of service you provide your customers. As we look at what you might be expected to do in order to manage effectively, the fundamental question you need to ask, over and over, is this: How would a change (or lack of change) in a given area affect the quality of service or goods that you are offering your customer? Competition continues to increase, and unless your establishment is different, better, faster, or unique in some way, there is every chance that it may not survive, let alone prosper.

Managing Physical Assets

Physical assets are the equipment and supplies needed to do business. In the case of a restaurant, these might include food and beverage inventory, tables, chairs, linens, china, flatware, glassware, computers and point-of-sale systems, cash registers, kitchen equipment, cleaning supplies, and ware-washing machines. When we talk about managing physical assets, we are considering how anything that you must purchase or pay for affects your ability to do business well.

The first step in bringing the expenses associated with your physical assets under control is to know what your expenses actually are. Then you can begin the process of making the adjustments and instituting the control systems that will keep your organization operating at maximal efficiency.

One of the biggest expenses for any restaurant will always be food and beverage costs. You or your purchasing agent will have to work hard to develop and sustain a good purchasing system. The information found in Part Two of this book can help. Because each operation has different needs, there are no hard-and-fast rules, just principles that you will apply to your own situation.

Managing Information

You may often feel that you can never keep current in all the important areas of your work. Given the sheer volume of information being generated each day, you are probably right. The ability to tap into the information resources you need, using all types of media and technology, has never been more important.

Restaurants, menus, and trends in dining room design have all been dramatically impacted by such societal trends as busier, on-the-go lifestyles and increasing interest in world cuisines. Prevailing tastes in politics, art, fashion, movies, and music do have an effect on what people eat and where and how they want to eat it.

Information gathering can become a full-time task on its own. To make use of the information available, you must be able to analyze and evaluate carefully to sift out the important material from useless data.

Managing Human Resources

Restaurant operations rely directly on the work and dedication of a number of people, from executives and administrators to line cooks, wait staff, and maintenance and cleaning staff. No matter how large or small your staff may be, the ability to engage all your workers in a team effort is one of the major factors in determining whether you will succeed or not.

Your goal should be to create an environment in which all staff feel they have a distinct and measurable contribution to make within the organization. The first task is establishing clear criteria, otherwise known as a job description. Training is another key component. If you want someone to do a job well, you first have to both explain and demonstrate the quality standards that you expect to see. You need to continually reinforce those standards with clear, objective evaluation of an employee's work through feedback, constructive criticism, and, when necessary, additional training or disciplinary measures.

The management of human resources includes several legal responsibilities. Everyone has the right to work in an environment that is free from physical hazards. This means that, as an employer, you must provide a workspace that is well lit, properly ventilated, and free from obvious dangers, such as improperly maintained equipment. Employees must have access to potable water and bathroom facilities. Beyond this bare minimum, you may offer a locker room, a laundry facility that provides clean uniforms and aprons, or other such amenities.

Workers' compensation, unemployment insurance, and disability insurance are also your responsibility. You are required to make all legal deductions from an employee's paycheck and to report all earnings properly to state and federal agencies. Liability insurance (to cover any harm to your facility, employees, or guests) must be kept up to date and at adequate levels.

You may also choose to offer additional forms of assistance as part of an employee benefits package. Life insurance, medical and dental insurance, assistance with such things as dependent care, adult literacy training, and enrollment in and support for those enrolled in substance abuse programs are all items of which you should be aware. In an increasingly tight labor market, a generous benefits package can make the difference in the caliber of employee you are able to attract and retain.

You must keep a properly completed I-9 form on file for every employee, and you should be familiar with the regulations that could affect you or those you employ. The Immigration and Naturalization Service (INS) will provide the necessary information.

Managing Time

It may seem that no matter how hard you work or how much planning you do, the days aren't long enough. Learning new skills, so that you can make the best possible use of the time you have, certainly ought to be an ongoing part of your career development. If you look over your operation, you will see where time is wasted. In most operations, the top five time wasters are: no clear priorities for tasks, poor staff training, poor communication, poor organization, and missing or inadequate tools to accomplish tasks. To combat these time wasters, use the following strategies.

Invest time in reviewing daily operations. Consider the way you, your coworkers, and your staff spend the day. Does everyone have a basic understanding of which tasks are most important? Do they know when to begin a particular task in order to bring it to completion on time? It can be an eye-opening experience to take a hard look at where the workday goes. Once you see that you and your staff need to walk too far to gather basic items or that the person who washes the dishes is sitting idle for the first two hours of the shift, you can take steps to rectify the problem. You can try to reorganize storage space. You may decide to train the dishwasher to do some prep work, or you can rewrite the schedule so that the shift begins two hours later. Until you are objective about what needs to be done and in what order, you can't begin the process of saving time.

Invest time in training others. If you expect someone to do a job properly, take enough time to explain the task carefully. Walk yourself and your staff through the jobs that must be done, and be sure that everyone understands how to do the work, where to find necessary items, how far each person's responsibility extends, and what to do in case a question or emergency comes up. Give your staff the yardsticks they need to evaluate the job and determine if they have done what was requested, in the appropriate fashion, and on time. If you don't invest this time up front, you may find yourself squandering precious time following your workers around, picking up the slack, and handling work that shouldn't be taking up your day.

Learn to communicate clearly. Whether you are training a new employee, introducing a new menu item, or ordering a piece of equipment, clear communication is important. Be specific, use the most concise language you can, and be as brief as possible without leaving out necessary information. If tasks are handled by a number of people, be sure to write each task out, from the first step to the last. Encourage people to ask questions if they don't understand you. If you need help learning communication skills, consider taking a workshop or seminar to strengthen any weak areas.

Take steps to create an orderly work environment. If you have to dig through five shelves to find the lid to the storage container you just put the stock in, you haven't been using your time wisely. Planning work areas carefully, thinking about all the tools, ingredients, and equipment you need for preparation and throughout service, and grouping like activities together are all techniques that can help you organize your work better. Poor placement of large and small tools is a great time waster. Use adequate, easy-to-access storage space for common items such as whips, spoons, ladles, and tongs. Electrical outlets for small equipment ought to be within reach of everyone. While you may be forced to work within the limits of your existing floor plan, be on the lookout for products or storage strategies that can turn a bad arrangement into one that works smoothly and evenly.

Purchase, replace, and maintain all necessary tools. A well-equipped kitchen will have enough of all the tools necessary to prepare every item on the menu. If you are missing something as basic as a sieve, your cream soups won't have the right consistency. If you have a menu with several sautéed appetizers, entrées, and side dishes, are you and your line cooks waiting around while the pot washer scrambles to get you restocked with sauté pans? If you can't purchase new equipment, then think about restructuring the menu to even out the workload. If you can't remove a menu item, then invest in the tools you need to prevent a slowdown during service.

Career Opportunities for Culinary Professionals

Culinary professionals are needed not just in hotel dining facilities and traditional restaurants but in a variety of settings—public and private, consumer-oriented and institutional. An increased emphasis on nutrition, sophistication, and financial and quality control means that all settings, from the white-tablecloth restaurant to the fast-food outlet, offer interesting challenges.

Hotels often have a number of different dining facilities, including fine-dining restaurants, room service, coffee shops, and banquet rooms. The kitchens are large, and there will often be separate butchering, catering, and pastry kitchens on the premises.

Full-service restaurants, such as bistros, white-tablecloth establishments, and family-style restaurants, feature a full menu, and the patrons are served by trained wait staff.

Private clubs generally provide some sort of food service. It may be as simple as a small grill featuring sandwiches, or it may be a complete dining room. The difference is that the guests are paying members, and the food costs are generally figured differently than they would be for a public restaurant.

Many corporations operate *executive dining rooms.* The degree of simplicity or elegance demanded in a particular corporation determines what type of food is offered, how it is prepared, and what style of service is appropriate.

Institutional catering (used in schools, hospitals, colleges, airlines, and correctional institutions) often demands a single menu and a cafeteria where the guests serve themselves, choosing from the offered foods. Menu selections are based on the needs of the institution's guests, the operating budget, and the administration's expectations. Many institutional catering operations are run by large corporations, which frequently offer benefits and the opportunity for career advancement within the corporation.

Caterers provide a particular service, often tailored to meet the wishes of a special client for a particular event, whether it be a wedding, a cocktail reception, or a gallery opening. Caterers may provide on-site services (the client comes to the caterer's premises), off-site services (the caterer comes to the client's premises), or both.

Home meal replacement (carry-out) food service is growing in importance as more busy couples, single professionals, and families try to enjoy meals at home without having to spend time preparing them. These establishments prepare entrées, salads, side dishes, and desserts that are packaged to be taken home. Many supermarkets now offer this service to their customers.

The Kitchen Brigade System

The brigade system was instituted by Escoffier to streamline and simplify work in hotel kitchens. It served to eliminate the chaos and duplication of effort that could result when workers did not have clear-cut responsibilities. Under this system, each position has a station and defined responsibilities, outlined below. In smaller operations, the classic system is generally abbreviated and responsibilities are organized so as to make the best use of workspace and talents. A shortage of skilled personnel has also made modifications in the brigade system necessary. The introduction of new equipment has helped to alleviate some of the problems associated with smaller kitchen staffs.

The chef is responsible for all kitchen operations, including ordering, supervision of all stations, and development of menu items. He or she also may be known as the *chef de cuisine* or *executive chef.* The *sous chef* is second in command, answers to the chef, may be responsible for scheduling, fills in for the chef, and assists the station chefs (or line cooks) as neces-

sary. Small operations may not have a sous chef. The range of positions in a classic brigade also include the following:

The **sauté chef** *(saucier)* is responsible for all sautéed items and their sauces. This position is often considered the most demanding, responsible, and glamorous on the line.

The **fish chef** *(poissonier)* is responsible for fish items, often including fish butchering, and their sauces. This position is sometimes combined with the saucier position.

The **roast chef** *(rôtisseur)* is responsible for all roasted foods and related jus or other sauces.

The **grill chef** *(grillardin)* is responsible for all grilled foods. This position may be combined with that of rôtisseur.

The **fry chef** *(friturier)* is responsible for all fried foods. This position may be combined with the rôtisseur position.

The **vegetable chef** *(entremetier)* is responsible for hot appetizers and frequently has responsibility for soups, vegetables, and pastas and other starches. (In a full, traditional brigade system, soups are prepared by the soup station or *potager,* vegetables by the *legumier.*) This station may also be responsible for egg dishes.

The **roundsman** *(tournant)* or *swing cook* works as needed throughout the kitchen.

The **cold-foods chef** *(garde-manger),* also known as the *pantry chef,* is responsible for preparation of cold foods, including salads, cold appetizers, pâtés, and the like. This is considered a separate category of kitchen work.

The **butcher** *(boucher)* is responsible for butchering meats, poultry, and, occasionally, fish. The boucher may also be responsible for breading meat and fish items.

The **pastry chef** *(pâtissier)* is responsible for baked items, pastries, and desserts. The pastry chef frequently supervises a separate kitchen area or a separate shop in larger operations. This position may be further broken down into the following areas of specialization: **confiseur** (prepares candies,petits fours), **boulanger** (prepares unsweetened doughs,as for breads and rolls), **glacier** (prepares frozen and cold desserts),and **décorateur** (prepares showpieces and special cakes).

The **expediter** or **announcer** *(aboyeur)* accepts orders from the dining room and relays them to the various station chefs. This individual is the last person to see the plate before it leaves the kitchen. In some operations,this may be either the chef or sous chef.

The **communard** prepares the meal served to staff at some point during the shift (also called the family meal).

The **commis,** or apprentice, works under a station chef to learn how the station operates and its responsibilities.

The Dining Room Brigade System

The dining room, or front-of-the-house, positions also have an established line of authority.

The **maître d'hôtel,** known in American service as the dining room manager, is the person who holds the most responsibility for the front-of-the-house operation. The maître d'hôtel trains all service personnel, oversees wine selection, works with the chef to determine the menu, and organizes seating throughout service.

The **wine steward** *(chef de vin* or *sommelier)* is responsible for all aspects of restaurant wine service, including purchasing wines, preparing a wine list, assisting guests in wine selection, and serving wine properly. The wine steward may also be responsible for the service of liquors, beers, and other beverages. If there is no wine steward, these responsibilities are generally assumed by the maître d'hôtel.

The **head waiter** *(chef de salle)* is generally in charge of the service for an entire dining room. Very often this position is combined with the position of either captain or maître d'hôtel.

The **captain** *(chef d'étage)* deals most directly with the guests once they are seated. The captain explains the menu, answers any questions, and takes the order. The captain generally does any tableside food preparation. If there is no captain, these responsibilities fall to the front waiter.

The **front waiter** *(chef de rang)* ensures that the table is properly set for each course, that the food is properly delivered to the table, and that the needs of the guests are promptly and courteously met.

The **back waiter** or **busboy** *(demi-chef de rang* or *commis de rang)* is generally the first position assigned to new dining room workers. This person clears plates between courses, fills water glasses and bread baskets, and assists the front waiter and/or captain as needed.

Other Opportunities

In addition to the kitchen and dining room positions, a growing number of less traditional opportunities exist, many of which do not involve the actual production or service of foods.

Food and beverage managers oversee all food and beverage outlets in hotels and other large establishments.

Consultants and **design specialists** will work with restaurant owners, often before the restaurant is even open, to assist in developing a menu, designing the overall layout and ambience of the dining room, and establishing work patterns for the kitchen.

Well-informed salespeople help chefs determine how best to meet their needs for food and produce, introduce them to new products, and demonstrate the proper use of new equipment.

Teachers are essential to the great number of cooking schools nationwide. Most of these teachers are chefs who are sharing the benefit of their experience with students.

Food writers and **critics** discuss food trends, restaurants, and chefs. It will always mean more, of course, if the writer is well versed in the culinary arts. Some prominent members of the food media, such as James Beard, Craig Claiborne, and Julia Child, have been influential teachers and have written landmark cookbooks in addition to contributing to newspapers and magazines and appearing on television.

Food stylists and **photographers** work with a variety of publications, including magazines, books, catalogs, and promotional and advertising pieces.

Research-and-development kitchens employ a great many culinary professionals.

These may be run by food manufacturers who are developing new products or food lines, or by advisory boards hoping to promote their products. Test kitchens are also run by a variety of both trade and consumer publications.

Challenges aside, the foodservice industry is rewarding and spontaneous. It requires stamina, drive, and creative influence. Those who have made the greatest impression know that virtues such as open communication, efficient organization, proper management, innovative marketing, and thorough accounting are necessary to prosper. In due time, your knowledge and experience will gain worthy recognition.

Chapter Two

Menus and Recipes

Menus are used in the dining room to give both wait staff and guests important information about what the establishment offers. Recipes give detailed instructions to aid kitchen staff in producing menu items. But, more than that, carefully designed menus and comprehensive recipes can help the professional chef streamline kitchen operations and control costs.

Menus

A menu is a powerful tool. It is a marketing and merchandising vehicle. It establishes and reinforces the total restaurant concept, from the style of china and flatware to staff training needs. It can assist the chef in organizing the day's work, ordering food, reducing waste, and increasing profits.

The way a menu is developed or adapted, as well as the way menu prices are established, is a reflection of how well the operation's concept or business plan has been defined. Sometimes the menu evolves as the business plan is refined. In other scenarios, the concept comes first and the menu comes later. In still others, the menu may be the guiding principle that gives a particular stamp to the way the restaurant concept evolves.

Menus tell the kitchen staff vital things, such as whose responsibility it is to prepare the dish's components or to plate and garnish it. The preparation of certain garnishes, side dishes, sauces, or marinades may be organized so that all components of a recipe are prepared by each chef or cook for that station, or it may be that prep cooks prepare some of the components. À la carte and banquet menus call for certain types of advance work to help the chef adjust to the workflow. Even if a written menu is not provided to the guest, some form of menu list in the kitchen is essential to the smooth operation of a professional kitchen.

Consult the menu, determine which items you and each staff member are responsible for, and then read the recipes for those items carefully so that you understand all the tasks that must be performed in advance of service as well as at the time of plating and serving the food. In this way service should proceed without difficulty.

Recipes

A recipe is a written record of the ingredients and preparation steps needed to make a particular dish. The form a recipe takes depends on who will ultimately use the recipe and the medium in which the recipe will be presented.

Before starting to cook from any recipe, the first step is always to read through the recipe in its entirety to gain an understanding of exactly what is required. This step will alert you to any surprises that the recipe might contain, such as requiring an unusual piece of equipment or an overnight cooling period. This is also the point at which you must decide if any modifications to the recipe are in order. Perhaps the recipe makes only ten portions and you want to make fifty, or vice versa. You will have to convert the recipe (see page 14). While increasing or decreasing the yield, you may discover that you need to make equipment modifications as well to accommodate the new volume of food. Or you might decide that you want to omit, add, or substitute an ingredient. All of these decisions should be made before any ingredient preparation or cooking begins.

Once you have read through and evaluated or modified the recipe, it is time to get your mise en place together. In many recipes, the ingredient list will indicate how the ingredient should be prepared (e.g., parboiling or cutting into pieces of a certain size) before the actual cooking or assembling begins.

Measuring Ingredients Accurately

Accurate measurements are crucial to recipes. In order to keep costs in line and ensure consistency of quality and quantity, ingredients and portion sizes must be measured correctly each time a recipe is made.

Ingredients are purchased and used according to one of three measuring conventions: count, volume, or weight. They may be purchased according to one system and measured for use in a recipe according to another.

Count is a measurement of whole items as one would purchase them. The terms *each, bunch,* and *dozen* all indicate units of count measure. If the individual item has been processed, graded, or packaged according to established standards, count can be a useful, accurate way to measure ingredients. It is less accurate for ingredients requiring some advance preparation or without any established standards for purchasing. Garlic cloves illustrate the point well. If a recipe calls for two garlic cloves, the intensity of garlic in the dish will change depending upon whether the cloves you use are large or small.

Volume is a measurement of the space occupied by a solid, liquid, or gas. The terms *teaspoon (tsp)*, *tablespoon (tbsp)*, *fluid ounce (fl oz)*, *cup, pint (pt)*, *quart (qt)*, *gallon (gal)*, *milliliter (mL)*, and *liter (L)* all indicate units of volume measure. Graduated containers (measuring cups) and utensils for which the volume is known (such as a 2-ounce ladle or a teaspoon) are used to measure volume.

Volume measurements are best suited to liquids, though they are also used for solids, especially spices, in small amounts. Tools used for measuring volume are not always as precise as necessary, especially if you must often increase or decrease a recipe. Volume measuring tools don't conform to any regulated standards. Therefore, the amount of an ingredient measured with one set of spoons, cups, or pitchers could be quite different from the amount measured with another set.

Weight is a measurement of the mass or heaviness of a solid, liquid, or gas. The terms *ounce (oz)*, *pound (lb)*, *gram (g)*, and *kilogram (kg)* all indicate units of weight measure. Scales are used to measure weight, and they must meet specific standards for accuracy. In professional kitchens, weight is usually the preferred type of measurement because it is easier to attain accuracy with weight than it is with volume.

Standardized Recipes

The recipes used in each professional kitchen are known as *standardized recipes*. Unlike published recipes, standardized recipes are tailored to suit the needs of an individual kitchen. Preparing well-written and accurate standardized recipes is a big part of the professional chef's work in all foodservice settings, as they include much more than just ingredient names and preparation steps. Standardized recipes establish total yields, portion sizes, holding and serving practices, and plating information, and they set standards for cooking temperatures and times. These standards help to ensure consistent quality and quantity, permit chefs to monitor the efficiency of their work, and reduce costs by eliminating waste.

They also allow the wait staff to become familiar with a dish, so they can answer guests' questions accurately and honestly. For example, the type of oil used in a dish may matter very much to a guest, especially if it is an oil to which he or she has an allergy.

Standardized recipes can be recorded by hand or electronically, using a recipe management program or other computerized database. They should be recorded in a consistent, clear, easy-to-follow form and should be readily accessible to all staff members. Instruct kitchen staff to follow standardized recipes to the letter unless instructed otherwise, and encourage service staff to refer to standardized recipes when a question arises about ingredients or preparation methods.

As you prepare a standardized recipe, be as precise and consistent as you can. Include as many of the following elements as possible:

- Name/title of the food item or dish

- Yield information, expressed as one or more of the following: total weight, total volume, total number of portions

- Portion information for each serving, expressed as one or more of the following: a specific number of items (count), volume, weight

- Ingredient names, expressed in appropriate detail, specifying variety or brand as necessary

- Ingredient measures, expressed as one or more of the following: count, volume, weight

- Ingredient preparation instructions, sometimes included in the ingredient name, sometimes expressed in the method itself as a step

- Equipment information for preparation, cooking, storing, holding, and serving

- Preparation steps detailing mise en place, cooking methods, and temperatures for safe food handling [see Hazard Analysis Critical Control Points (HACCP), page 32]

- Service information, describing how to finish and plate a dish, add side dishes, sauces, and garnishes, if any, and listing the proper service temperatures

- Holding and reheating information, describing procedures, equipment, times, and temperatures for safe storage

- Critical control points (CCPs) at appropriate stages in the recipe to indicate temperatures and times for safe food-handling procedures during storage, preparation, holding, and reheating

Recipe Calculations

Often you will need to modify a recipe. Sometimes a recipe must be increased or decreased. You may be adapting a recipe from another source into a standardized format, or you may be adjusting a standardized recipe for a special event, such as a banquet or a reception. You may need to convert from volume measures to weight, or from metric measurements to the U.S. system. You will also need to be able to translate between purchase units and recipe measurements. In some circumstances, you may be called upon to increase or decrease the suggested portion size for a recipe. Or you may want to determine how much the food in a particular recipe costs.

Using a Recipe Conversion Factor (RCF) to Convert Recipe Yields

To adjust the yield of a recipe to make either more or less, you need to determine the recipe conversion factor. Once you know that factor, you first multiply all the ingredient amounts by it. Then you convert the new measurements into appropriate recipe units for your kitchen. This may require converting items listed originally as a count into a weight or a volume, or rounding measurements into reasonable quantities. In some cases you will have to make a judgment call about those ingredients that do not scale up or down exactly, such as spices, salt, and thickeners.

$$\frac{\text{Desired yield}}{\text{Original yield}} = \text{Recipe conversion factor (RCF)}$$

NOTE: The desired yield and the original yield must be expressed in the same way before you can use the formula. If your original recipe says that it makes five portions, for example, and does not list the amount of each portion, you may need to test the recipe to determine what size portion it actually makes. Similarly, if the original recipe lists the yield in fluid ounces and you want to make 3 quarts of the soup, you need to convert quarts into fluid ounces before you can determine the recipe conversion factor.

The new ingredient amounts usually need some additional fine-tuning. You may need to round the result or convert it to the most logical unit of measure. For some ingredients, a straightforward increase or decrease is all that is needed. For example, to increase a recipe for chicken breasts from five servings to fifty, you would simply multiply 5 chicken breasts by 10; no further adjustments are necessary. Other ingredients, such as thickeners, aromatics, seasonings, and leavenings, may not multiply as simply, however. If a soup to serve four requires 2 tablespoons of flour to make a roux, it is not necessarily true that you will need 20 tablespoons (or 1¼ cups) of flour to thicken the same soup when you prepare it for forty. The only way to be sure is to test the new recipe and adjust it until you are satisfied with the result—and then be sure to record the measure!

Other considerations when converting recipe yields include the equipment you have to work with, the production issues you face, and the skill level of your staff. Rewrite the steps to suit your establishment at this point. It is important to do this now, so you can uncover any further changes to the ingredients or methods that the new yield might force. For instance, a soup to serve four would be made in a small pot, but a soup for forty requires a larger cooking vessel. However, using a larger vessel might result in a higher rate of evaporation, so you may find that you need to cover the soup as it cooks or increase the liquid to offset the evaporation.

Converting Portion Sizes

Sometimes it will happen that you also need to modify the portion size of a recipe. For instance, say you have a soup recipe that makes four 8-ounce portions, but you need to make enough to have forty 6-ounce portions. To make the conversion:

1. Determine the total original yield and the total desired yield of the recipe.

   Number of portions x Portion size = Total yield

   Example: 4 x 8 fl oz = 32 fl oz (total original yield)

   40 x 6 fl oz = 240 fl oz (total desired yield)

2. Determine the recipe conversion factor and modify the recipe as described above.

   Example: $\dfrac{240 \text{ fl oz}}{32 \text{ fl oz}} = 7.5$ (recipe conversion factor)

Confusion often arises between weight and volume measures, when ounces are the unit of measure. It is important to remember that weight is measured in ounces, but volume is measured in *fluid* ounces. A standard volume measuring cup is equal to 8 fluid ounces, but the contents of the cup may not always weigh 8 ounces. One cup (8 fluid ounces) of cornflakes weighs only 1 ounce, but one cup (8 fluid ounces) of peanut butter weighs 9 ounces. Water is the only substance for which it can be safely assumed that 1 fluid ounce equals 1 ounce. For all other ingredients, when the amount is expressed in ounces, weigh it; when the amount is expressed in fluid ounces, measure it with an accurate liquid (or volume) measuring tool.

Converting Volume Measures to Weight

You can convert a volume measure into a weight if you know how much 1 cup of an ingredient (prepared as required by the recipe) weighs. This information is available in a number of charts or ingredient databases. (See Weights and Measures Equivalents, page 1169.)

You can also calculate and record the information yourself as follows:

Prepare the ingredient as directed by the recipe—sift flour, chop nuts, mince garlic, grate cheeses, and so forth.

Set the measuring device on the scale and reset the scale to zero (known as *tare*).

Fill the measuring device correctly. For liquids, use graduated measuring cups or pitchers and fill to the desired level. To be sure that you have measured accurately, bend down until the level mark on the measure is at your eye level. The measuring utensil must be sitting on a level surface for an accurate measurement. Use nested measuring tools for dry ingredients measured by volume. Overfill the measure, then scrape away the excess as you level off the measure.

Return the filled measuring tool to the scale and record the weight in either grams or ounces on your standardized recipe.

Converting between U.S. and Metric Measurement Systems

The metric system, used throughout most of the world, is a decimal system, meaning that it is based on multiples of 10. The gram is the basic unit of weight, the liter is the basic unit of volume, and the meter is the basic unit of length. Prefixes added to the basic units indicate larger or smaller units. For instance, a kilogram is 1,000 grams, a milliliter is 1/1,000th of a liter, and a centimeter is 1/100th of a meter.

The U.S. system, familiar to most Americans, uses ounces and pounds to measure weight, and teaspoons, tablespoons, fluid ounces, cups, pints, quarts, and gallons to measure volume. Unlike the metric system, the U.S. system is not based on multiples of a particular number, so it is not as simple to increase or decrease quantities. Instead, either the equivalencies of the different units of measure must be memorized or a chart must be kept handy (see page 1167).

Most modern measuring equipment is capable of measuring in both U.S. and metric units. If, however, a recipe is written in a system of measurement for which you do not have the proper measuring equipment, you will need to convert to the other system.

Calculating As-Purchased Cost (APC)

Most food items purchased from suppliers are packed and priced by wholesale bulk sizes, such as by the crate, case, bag, carton, and so on. Yet in kitchen production, the packed amount is not always used for the same purpose and may often be broken down and used for several items. Therefore, in order to allocate the proper prices to each recipe, it is necessary to convert purchase pack prices to unit prices, which are expressed as price per pound, each, by the dozen, by the quart, and the like.

If you know the cost of a pack with many units, calculate the cost per unit by dividing the as-purchased cost of the pack by the number of units in the pack.

$$\frac{\text{APC total}}{\text{Number of units}} = \text{APC per unit}$$

If you know the unit price of an item, you can determine the total cost by multiplying the as-purchased cost (APC) per unit by the number of units.

APC per unit x Number of units = Total APC

Calculating the Yield of Fresh Fruits and Vegetables and Determining Yield Percent

For many food items, trimming is required before the items are actually used. In order to determine an accurate cost for these items, the trim loss must be taken into account. From this information, the yield percent will be important in determining the quantity that you need to order.

First, record the as-purchased quantity (APQ) from the invoice, or weigh the item before trimming or cutting:

Example: APQ = 5 lb (or 80 oz) carrots

Trim the item and cut as desired, saving trim and edible portion quantity in separate containers. Weigh each separately and record their weights on a costing form:

As-purchased quantity (APQ) – trim loss = Edible portion quantity (EPQ)

Example: 80 oz carrots (APQ) – 8.8 oz carrot trim = 71.2 oz sliced carrots

Next, divide the EPQ by the APQ:

$$\frac{\text{Edible portion quantity}}{\text{As-purchased quantity}} = \text{Yield percent}$$

Example: $\dfrac{\text{71.2 oz sliced carrots (EPQ)}}{\text{80 oz carrots (APQ)}} = 0.89$

To convert the decimal to a percent, multiply by 100:

Yield percent = 89%

NOTE: For more information on any of the above culinary math topics, refer to Culinary Math, 2nd edition, by Julia Hill and Linda Blocker.

Calculating the As-Purchased Quantity (APQ) Using Yield Percent

Because many recipes assume the ingredients listed are ready to cook, it is necessary to consider the trim loss when purchasing items. In this case, the edible portion quantity must be converted to the as-purchased quantity, which, when trimmed, will give the desired edible portion quantity. The yield percent is used as a tool when ordering.

$$\frac{\text{EPQ}}{\text{Yield percent}} = \text{APQ}$$

Example: A recipe requires 20 pounds of cleaned shredded cabbage. The yield percent for cabbage is 79 percent. When the 20 pounds is divided by 79 percent (0.79), the result = 25.3 pounds, which will be the minimum amount to purchase.

Generally, the as-purchased quantity obtained by this method is rounded up, since the yield percent is an estimate. Some chefs increase the figure by an additional 10 percent to account for human error as well.

It should be kept in mind that not all foods have a loss. Many processed or refined foods have a 100 percent yield, such as sugar, flour, or dried spices. Other foods have a yield percent that depends on how they are served. If, for example, the ingredient is to be served by the piece (half a cantaloupe), or if a recipe calls for it by count (15 strawberries), the yield percent is not considered; the correct number of items must be purchased in order to create the correct number of servings. However, if you are making a fruit salad and you know you need 2 ounces of cubed melon and 1 ounce of sliced strawberries per serving, you must consider the yield percent when ordering.

Calculating Edible Portion Quantity (EPQ) Using Yield Percent

Sometimes it is necessary for you to determine how many portions can be obtained from raw product. For example, if you have a case of fresh green beans that weighs 20 pounds and you need to know how many

4-ounce servings are in the case, what you need to do first is determine the yield percent for green beans, either by referring to a list of yield percent values or by performing a yield test. Once you know the yield percent, you can compute the weight of the green beans after trimming.

$$APQ \times \text{Yield percent} = EPQ$$

Example: 20 lb green beans (APQ) x 0.88 (yield percent) = 17.6 lb green beans (EPQ)

The edible portion quantity (EPQ) would be 17.6 pounds. The second step would be to compute how many 4-ounce servings are in 17.6 pounds. If necessary, convert the portion size (here, 4 ounces) to the same unit of measure as the edible portion quantity (here, 1 pound). There are 16 ounces in 1 pound; 1 portion is equal to ¼ (or 0.25) pound.

$$\frac{EPQ}{\text{Portion size}} = \text{Number of servings}$$

Example: $\dfrac{\text{17.6 lb green beans (EPQ)}}{\text{0.25 lb serving size}} = \text{70.4 servings}$

You would be able to obtain seventy full servings from the case of green beans. You should round down any partial number of portions since it would not be plausible to serve a partial portion to a guest.

Calculating Edible Portion Cost

As discussed earlier, recipes often assume ingredients are ready to cook, so when it comes to costing a recipe, the edible portion cost (EPC) per unit can be calculated from the as-purchased cost (APC) per unit, as long as the edible portion is expressed in the same unit of measure as the cost unit.

$$\frac{APC}{\text{Yield percent}} = EPC$$

Example: $\dfrac{\text{\$0.106/oz carrots (APC)}}{\substack{\text{0.75 (yield \% for} \\ \text{tournéed carrots}}} = \substack{\text{\$0.141/oz} \\ \text{tournéed carrots} \\ \text{(EPC)}}$

$$EPQ \times EPC = \text{Total cost}$$

Example: 4 oz tournéed carrots (EPQ) x \$0.141/oz tournéed carrots (EPC) = \$0.564 per serving (total cost)

Calculating the Value of Usable Trim

Often, some of the trimmings from a food may be used to prepare other foods. For example, if you have tournéed a carrot, rather than cutting it into dice or rounds, you can use the trim to prepare a soup, purée, or other dish. Using the information from your yield test, you can calculate the value of the trim. First, determine the use for the trim, then find the cost per unit and yield percent for that ingredient, as if you had to buy it to prepare the dish. For instance, if you use the trim from carrot tournées to prepare a soup, the food cost for the carrot trim is the same as for a carrot that has been trimmed and chopped.

Example:
\$0.106 (As-purchased cost of carrots per ounce) = \$0.119 (value of usable carrot trim for soup per ounce)

0.89 (Yield percent for chopped carrots)

Some products produce trim that can be used in a variety of ways. For example, a strip loin produces trimmings that can be used in several recipes. The chef may use some of the trim to prepare a clarification that might otherwise require ground meat, and more of the trim to make a filling for fajitas. Finding additional uses for trim reduces costs and helps to eliminate waste.

Using Recipes Effectively

In the professional kitchen, a recipe can be used to improve efficiency and organization and to increase profits. When you know the approximate yield percent for onions and carrots, you can get the right amount for a recipe in a single visit to the walk-in. If you understand the difference between the price you paid per pound for a whole beef tenderloin and how much you are actually paying per pound for the trimmed meat you serve, you can be more effective at reducing loss and decreasing the operation's overall food costs. Learning to read recipes carefully and using them more productively is an important step in developing your professional skills.

The Butcher's Yield Test

The purpose of a butcher's yield test is to find the accurate costs of fabricated meats, fish, and poultry. This is done to determine the amount of usable meat and trim from a particular fabrication, and to calculate the value of all edible cuts, including not only the portion of meat served to the guest, but also the value of bones used for stock and of trim used for ground meat, pâtés, soups, or other dishes.

General Procedures

Select the item to be tested and record the as-purchased weight. (Make sure you use the same scale for the entire test.) Fabricate the item to desired specifications. Keep all parts (bones, fat, usable cuts, usable trim) in separate tubs or trays, and record all weights.

Use current prices for the meat item as purchased. Use market values for fat, bones, and usable trim. For instance, if you save the lean meat to make ground meat, the value of that part of the trim is the price you would have to pay to purchase ground meat.

1. **Determine the As-Purchased Cost (APC)**
   As-purchased weight x As-purchased price per lb = APC
   Example: 28 lb x $1.30/lb = $36.40 (APC)

2. **Fabricate the Meat**
   Example: #103 beef rib trimmed to #109 beef rib (roast ready)

3. **Determine the Total Trim Weight and Value**
   Fat trim weight x Market price per lb = Trim value (fat)
   + Bones trim weight x Market price per lb
   = Trim value (bones)
   + Usable trim weight x Market price per lb
   = Trim value (trim)

Total Trim Weight	Total Trim Value
Example: 3 lb fat x $0.10/lb = $0.30	
+ 4 lb bones x $0.30/lb = $1.20	
+ 5 lb usable trim x $1.30/lb = $6.50	
12 lb Total trim weight = $8.00 Total trim value	

4. **Determine the New Fabricated Weight (NFW)**
   As-purchased weight − Total trim weight = NFW
   Example: 28 lb As-purchased weight − 12 lb Total trim weight = 16 lb (NFW)

5. **Determine the New Fabricated Cost (NFC)**
   APC − Total trim value = NFC
   Example: $36.40 − $8.00 = $28.40 (NFC)

6. **Determine the New Fabricated Price per Pound (NFPP)**
   $$\frac{NFC}{NFW} = NFPP$$
   Example: $28.40 ÷ $1.77/lb (NFPP) = 16 lb

7. **Determine the Cost Factor (CF)**
   $$\frac{NFPP}{\text{As-purchased price per pound}} = CF$$
   Example: $1.77/lb ÷ 1.36 (CF) = $1.30/lb

8. **Determine the Yield Percentage**
   $$\frac{NFW}{\text{As-purchased weight}} = \text{Yield percent}$$
   Example: 16 lb ÷ 57% (Yield percent) = 28 lb

9. **Determine the Number of Portions of Final Product from the Fabrication**
   NFW x 16 oz = Total number of ounces
   $$\frac{\text{Total number of ounces}}{\text{Portion size}} = \text{Number of portions}$$
   Example: How many 12-oz portions can be obtained from 16 lb of trimmed meat?
   16 lb x 16 oz = 256 oz
   $$\frac{256 \text{ oz}}{12 \text{ oz}} = 21.33, \text{ or } 21 \text{ portions}$$

10. **Determine the Cost per Portion**
    $$\frac{NFPP}{16 \text{ oz}} = \text{Cost of 1 oz}$$
    Cost of 1 oz x Portion size = Cost per portion
    Example: What is the cost of one 12-oz portion?
    $$\frac{\$1.77/lb}{16 \text{ oz}} = 0.1106, \text{ or } 11.06 \text{ cents/oz (cost of 1 oz)}$$
    0.1106 x 12 oz = $1.327 (cost per portion)

Chapter Three

The Basics of Nutrition and Food Science

Nutrition refers to the study of diet and health. It is through the comprehension of this study that we as foodservice professionals can accommodate and enrich various dietary preferences and restrictions. Meeting the dietary needs of today's lifestyles involves an understanding that people eat or don't eat certain foods for different reasons. The concerns of customers have moved beyond just the flavor and texture of food and now extend to a healthy diet full of nutritious high-quality foods.

Nutrition Basics

Above offering flavorful options, the foodservice professional will benefit from understanding how energy and nutrients work. To begin, energy and nutrients are used for growth, maintenance, and repair of our bodies. Energy, counted in calories, comes from carbohydrates, proteins, fats, and alcohol. The first three are considered primary nutrients, while alcohol is not. Any food source that has a good supply of nutrients in relation to the number of calories it contains is considered *nutrient-dense*.

Carbohydrates

Carbohydrates provide energy for muscle movement and red blood cells, and play a role in the regulation of fat metabolism. Composed of smaller units known as *simple carbohydrates* and *complex carbohydrates*, these are necessary for the body to work efficiently and to fulfill its energy needs. Simple carbohydrates are found in fruits, juices, dairy products, and refined sugars. Complex carbohydrates are found in plant-based foods like grains, legumes, and vegetables. Foods containing complex carbohydrates are also usually good sources of other important components of a healthy diet, such as vitamins and minerals.

Protein

Protein is a nutrient essential for the growth and maintenance of body tissues, hormone, enzyme, and antibody production, and the regulation of bodily fluids. The basic building blocks are referred to as *amino acids*. There are nine *essential amino acids* that must be supplied through the diet because the body does not produce them. All protein-rich foods contain some or all nine.

All protein foods are categorized as either complete or incomplete, depending on the presence or lack of the essential amino acids. A complete protein is any food that provides all nine amino acids in the correct ratio for the adult human body to support the production of other proteins. Meats, poultry, and fish are good sources of complete proteins.

The United States Department of Agriculture suggests the following for daily caloric intake:

55 to 60 percent of calories from carbohydrates

12 to 15 percent of calories from protein

30 percent or less of calories from fat

The nine essential amino acids are as follows:

Histidine	Phenylalanine
Isoleucine	Threonine
Leucine	Tryptophan
Lysine	Valine
Methionine	

Incomplete proteins, such as vegetables, grains, legumes, and nuts, do not contain all the essential amino acids. However, each of these food groups contains some of the essential amino acids that, when combined with other incomplete proteins, can become complete proteins. When following a vegetarian diet, the following combinations offer a sample of non-meat-based complete proteins:

Lentils and rice

Pasta and beans

Tortillas and beans

Tofu and rice

Hummus and pita

Fat

Fat is often a significant concern of those watching what they eat. While it is true that excess fat in the diet is unhealthy because it raises the risk of coronary heart disease, obesity, and certain cancers, it is still an essential nutrient that provides energy and fulfills bodily functions. Current dietary advice places emphasis on the type of fat as well as the amount of fat in the diet. Most of the daily intake of fat should come from mono- and polyunsaturated sources. Although consuming more than the recommended limit of fat is often associated with weight gain and obesity, excess total calories are the root of that problem.

Cholesterol is a fat-related compound; the two types are dietary and serum. Dietary cholesterol is *only* found in animal foods. Serum, or blood, cholesterol is found in the bloodstream and it is essential to life. It is not necessary to consume food cholesterol, because humans are capable of producing it from other dietary components. Foods high in cholesterol tend to have high amounts of fat. Regardless of how many calories are consumed daily, it is recommended that cholesterol intake not exceed 300 milligrams.

Vitamins and Minerals

Needed in smaller quantities than protein, carbohydrates, and fat, vitamins and minerals are noncaloric essential nutrients. Vitamins are classified as either water-soluble or fat-soluble. Water-soluble vitamins dissolve in water and are easily transported throughout the body in the bloodstream. Fat-soluble vitamins are stored in fat tissues. Both forms of vitamins, as well as minerals, are found in a variety of food sources. Because no food contains every essential nutrient in the correct proportions and no single pill or supplement can compensate for a poor diet, eating a well-balanced diet composed of a variety of foods is the healthiest way to meet normal nutrient requirements. For a listing of vitamins and minerals with food sources and functions, refer to the table on page 22.

Menu Development and Nutrition

When the diet offers balanced nutrition, obtaining the necessary amount of energy and nutrients is easy. Although it is impossible to know what a customer has consumed before entering your establishment, by predicting the combinations of courses that your customers are likely to order, you can design your menus to ensure they receive delicious and nutritious well-balanced meals.

As the recommended dietary guidelines continue to change, one thing remains the same—portion control is essential to maintaining a healthy weight. Portion size depends primarily on the individual's daily caloric requirements, resulting from age, size, build, and level of physical activity. Fats, oils, and sweets are suggested in very limited quantities. Choosing a diet rich in grain products, vegetables, and fruits; low in fat, saturated fat, and cholesterol; and moderate in sugars, salt, and sodium is a sufficient means of following a healthy plan.

Because consumers have grown increasingly conscious of the need to make well-balanced meal choices, the professional chef has been given the opportunity to make a difference. Developing healthy, flavorful, and satisfying menu items is both easy and worthwhile.

The following is a set of principles developed for practicing healthy cooking. The guidelines are meant as a reference for food selections, cooking techniques, and beverage offerings. They should be regarded as ways to explore the possibilities of flavor and healthy cooking.

- Select ingredients with care.

- Store and prepare all foods with the aim of preserving their best possible flavor, texture, color, and overall nutritional value.

- Incorporate a variety of plant-based dishes in the menu in all categories.

- Manage the amount of fat used both as an ingredient and as part of a preparation or cooking technique.

- Serve appropriate portions of food.

- Use salt with care and purpose.

- Offer a variety of beverages, both alcoholic and nonalcoholic, that complement the food menu.

Vitamins: Their Function and Common Sources

NAME	FUNCTION	FOOD SOURCE
WATER-SOLUBLE VITAMINS		
B-complex (thiamin, riboflavin, niacin, folate, biotin, pantothenic acid, B6, B12)	Allow for proper release of energy in the body	Grains; legumes; vegetables; animal protein (B12 only found in animal foods)
Vitamin C (ascorbic acid)	Increases body's absorption of iron; aids in growth and maintenance of body tissue; boosts immune system; contains antioxidant properties	Fruits and vegetables (berries, melons, tomatoes, potatoes, green leafy vegetables)
FAT-SOLUBLE VITAMINS		
Vitamin A	Aids in proper vision, bone growth, reproduction, cell division and differentiation; regulates immune system; maintains surface linings	Animal protein such as liver and eggs; the precursor—beta carotene—is found in orange, deep yellow, and dark green leafy vegetables
Vitamin D	Aids in proper bone formation	Milk; some cereal and breads; fatty fish; egg yolks
Vitamin E	Protects body from damage by free radicals; contains antioxidant properties	Nuts; seeds; seed oils; avocados; sweet potatoes; green leafy vegetables
Vitamin K	Aids in proper blood clotting	Dark green leafy vegetables, such as spinach, kale, broccoli
MINERALS		
Calcium (body's most abundant mineral)	Used in the development of bones and teeth; regulates blood pressure; aids in muscle contraction, transmission of nerve impulses, and clotting of the blood	Dairy products (milk, yogurt); broccoli; green leafy vegetables
Phosphorus	Plays a key role in energy-releasing reactions; used in conjunction with calcium for maintaining bones and teeth	Animal protein; nuts; cereals; legumes
Sodium and potassium (electrolytes)	Aid in the regulation of bodily functions; help to maintain the body's normal fluid balance; involved in nerve and muscle functions	Sodium is plentiful in many foods; potassium is found in virtually all fruits and vegetables
Magnesium	Promotes healthy teeth and bones; muscle contractions; nerve transmission; and bowel functions	Green vegetables; nuts; legumes; whole grains
Fluoride	Helps to prevent tooth decay; may help to prevent osteoporosis	Community water; saltwater fish; shellfish; tea
Iodine	Essential for the normal functioning of the thyroid gland; helps to regulate metabolism, cellular oxidation, and growth	Table salt; cod; grains
Iron	Helps to carry oxygen from the lungs to cells; involved in cellular energy metabolism	Liver and red meat; whole grains; legumes; green leafy vegetables; dried fruit

Healthy Substitutions

By making simple modifications to already existing recipes, healthier versions are within reach.

ORIGINAL	MODIFIED
1 egg	2 egg whites
Sauté in butter	Sauté in broth/stock
1 cup mayonnaise	½ cup mayonnaise plus ½ cup nonfat yogurt
1 cup sour cream	1 cup nonfat yogurt plus 1 to 2 tbsp buttermilk or lemon juice plus 1 tbsp flour per 8 oz yogurt
1 cup heavy cream	1 cup evaporated skim milk

Your establishment will find it rewarding to offer a variety of options. Continually striving to meet the expectations of those who walk through your door should be an ongoing challenge for you and your staff. Consult The Culinary Institute of America's *Techniques of Healthy Cooking* for a more thorough discussion of nutrition, innovative recipes, and specialized techniques.

Food Science Basics

There are dozens of scientific principles at work during the cooking process. As an introduction to the topic of food science, this section provides an overview of the most basic of these principles. For more information on any of the following subjects, refer to Readings and Resources (see page 1190) for a list of food science references.

Heat Transfer

Cooking is the act of applying heat to foods to prepare them for eating. When foods are cooked, changes in flavor, texture, aroma, color, and nutritional content occur during the process.

There are three ways that heat is transferred to foods. *Conduction* is the direct transfer of heat between adjacent molecules. An example of conduction is cooking on a flattop range. Heat is transferred from the molecules of the hot range surface to the molecules of the adjacent pan bottom, then from the pan bottom to the pan sides and the food contained within the pan. The pan must be in direct contact with the range for conduction to occur.

Some materials are better conductors of heat than others. Generally, most metals are good conductors, while gases (air), liquids, and nonmetallic solids (glass, ceramic) are not. Because it relies on direct contact, conduction is a relatively slow method of heat transfer, but the slow, direct transfer of heat between adjacent molecules is what allows a food to be cooked from the outside in, resulting in a completely cooked exterior with a moist and juicy interior.

Convection is the transfer of heat through gases or liquids. When either of these substances is heated, the portions of the gas or liquid closest to the heat source warm first and become less dense, causing them to rise and be replaced by cooler, denser portions of the gas or liquid. Convection, therefore, is a combination of conduction and mixing.

Convection occurs both naturally and through mechanical means. Natural convection is at work in a pot of water placed on the stove to boil. Conduction transfers heat from the stove to the pot to the water molecules in contact with the interior of the pot. As these water molecules heat up, convection causes them to move away and be replaced by cooler molecules. This continual movement results in convection currents within the water. If a potato is added to the water, the convection currents transfer heat to the sur-

Understanding how food reacts under certain conditions is essential to becoming a professional chef. From creating a flavorful dish to developing an innovative shortcut, chefs face challenges every day. The six basic principles of food science are as follows:

Caramelization	Denaturation
Maillard reaction	Coagulation
Gelatinization	Emulsification

face of the potato, at which point conduction takes over to transfer heat to the interior of the potato.

Mechanical convection occurs when stirring or a fan is used to speed and equalize heat distribution. When you stir a thick sauce to heat it faster and keep it from scorching on the bottom of the pan, you are creating mechanical convection. Convection ovens use fans to rapidly circulate hot air, allowing them to cook foods more quickly and evenly than conventional ovens. (Natural convection occurs in conventional ovens as air in contact with the heating element circulates, but the majority of heat transfer in a conventional oven is the result of infrared radiation.)

Radiation is the transfer of energy through waves of electromagnetic energy that travel rapidly through space. Radiation does not require direct contact between the energy source and food. When the waves traveling through space strike matter and are absorbed, they cause molecules in the matter to vibrate more rapidly, increasing the temperature. Two types of radiation are important in the kitchen: infrared and microwave.

Sources of infrared radiation include the glowing coals of a charcoal grill or the glowing coils of an electric toaster, broiler, or oven. Waves of radiant energy travel in all directions from these heat sources. Foods and cookware that absorb the energy waves are heated. Dark,

Induction Cooking

Induction cooking is a relatively new cooking method that transfers heat through a specially designed cooktop made of a smooth ceramic material over an induction coil. The induction coil creates a magnetic current that causes a metal pan on the cooktop to heat up quickly, yet the cooktop itself remains cool. Heat is then transferred to the food in the pan through conduction. Cookware used for induction cooking must be flat on the bottom for good contact with the cooktop, and it must be made of ferrous (iron-containing) metals, such as cast iron, magnetic stainless steel, or enamel over steel. Cookware made of other materials will not heat up on these cooktops. Induction cooking offers the advantages of rapid heating and easy cleanup because there are no nooks on the smooth surface of the cooktop in which spilled foods get stuck, nor do spilled foods cook on the cool surface.

Egg Structure and Uses

The egg is composed of two main parts, the white and the yolk. Various membranes help keep the yolk suspended at the center of the white and help prevent contamination or weight loss through evaporation.

Whole eggs, as well as whites and yolks separately, play a number of important culinary roles. Whole eggs are used as the main component of many breakfast dishes and can be prepared by scrambling, frying, poaching, baking, or in custards. In baked goods, whole eggs are used as a glaze and to add nourishment, flavor, and color.

The egg white consists almost exclusively of water and a protein called albumen. Its ability to form a relatively stable foam is crucial to the development of proper structure in many items, such as angel food cakes, soufflés, and meringues. Egg whites are a key ingredient in clarifying stocks and broths to produce consommé. They may also be used as a binder in some forcemeats, especially mousselines made from fish, poultry, or vegetables.

The yolk contains protein, a significant amount of fat, and a natural emulsifier called lecithin. The yolk also has the ability to foam. This function, plus its ability to form emulsions, makes egg yolks crucial to the preparation of such items as mayonnaise, hollandaise sauce, and génoise (sponge cake). Yolks are also responsible for providing additional richness to foods, as when they are included as a liaison in sauces or soups.

dull, or rough surfaces absorb radiant energy better than light-colored, smooth, or polished surfaces. Transparent glass permits the transfer of radiant energy, so conventional oven temperatures should be lowered by approximately 25°F/–4°C to offset the additional energy transfer that occurs when using glass baking dishes.

Microwave radiation, produced by microwave ovens, transfers energy through short, high-frequency waves. When these microwaves are absorbed by foods, they cause the food molecules to vibrate faster, creating heat. Microwave radiation cooks foods much faster than infrared radiation because it penetrates foods several inches deep, whereas infrared is mainly absorbed at the surface. Depending on their composition, foods react differently to microwaves. Foods with high moisture, sugar, or fat contents absorb microwaves best and heat up more readily.

Microwave cooking has a few drawbacks, however. It is best suited to cooking small batches of foods. Meats cooked in a microwave oven lose greater amounts of moisture and easily become dry. Microwave ovens also cannot brown foods, and metal cannot be used in them because it reflects the microwaves, which can cause fires and damage the oven.

Effects of Heat on Starches and Sugars: Caramelization, Maillard Reaction, and Gelatinization

As discussed previously in this chapter, carbohydrates come in various forms, and each form reacts differently when exposed to heat. The two forms of carbohydrates that are of interest from a basic food science perspective are sugar and starch.

When exposed to heat, sugar will at first melt into a thick syrup. As the temperature continues to rise, the sugar syrup changes color, from clear to light yellow to a progressively deepening brown. This browning process is called caramelization. It is a complicated chemical reaction, and in addition to color change, it also causes the flavor of the sugar to evolve and take on the rich complexity that we know to be characteristic of caramel. Different types of sugar caramelize at different temperatures. Granulated white sugar melts at 320°F/160°C and begins to caramelize at 338°F/170°C.

In foods that are not primarily sugar or starch, a different reaction, known as the Maillard reaction, is responsible for browning. This reaction involves sugars and amino acids (the building blocks of protein). When heated, these components react and produce numerous chemical by-products, resulting in a brown color and intense flavor and aroma. It is this reaction that gives coffee, chocolate, baked goods, dark beer, and roasted meats and nuts much of their rich flavor and color.

Though the Maillard reaction can happen at room temperature, both caramelization and the Maillard reaction typically require relatively high heat (above 300°F/149°C) to occur rapidly enough to make an appreciable difference in foods. Because water cannot be heated above 212°F/100°C unless it is under pressure, foods cooked with moist heat (boiling, steaming, poaching, stewing) will not brown. Foods cooked using dry-heat methods (sautéing, grilling, or roasting) will brown. It is for this reason that many stewed and braised dishes begin with an initial browning of ingredients before liquid is added.

Starch, a complex carbohydrate, has powerful thickening properties. When starch is combined with water or another liquid and heated, individual starch granules absorb the liquid and swell. This process, known as gelatinization, is what causes the liquid to thicken. Gelatinization occurs at different temperatures for different types of starch. As a general rule of thumb, root-based starches (potato and arrowroot, for instance) thicken at lower temperatures but break down more quickly, whereas cereal-based starches (corn and wheat, for example) thicken at higher temperatures but break down more slowly. High levels of sugar or acid can inhibit gelatinization, while the presence of salt can promote it.

Denaturing Proteins

At the molecular level, natural proteins are shaped like coils or springs. When natural proteins are exposed to heat, salt, or acid, they denature—that is, their coils unwind. When proteins denature, they tend to bond together, or coagulate, and form solid clumps. An example of this is a cooked egg white, which changes from a transparent fluid to an opaque solid. As proteins coagulate, they lose some of their capacity to hold water, which is why protein-rich foods give off moisture as they cook, even if they are steamed or poached. Fortunately, some heat-induced denaturation is reversible through cooling. This is why roasted foods should be allowed to rest before carving; as the temperature falls, some of the water ("juice") that was forced into spaces between the proteins is reabsorbed and the food becomes moister. Denatured proteins are easier to digest than natural proteins.

Function of Cooking Fats

Depending on their molecular structure, some fats are solid at room temperature, while others are liquid at the same temperature. Liquid fats are known as oils. Solid fats soften and eventually melt into a liquid state when exposed to heat.

In addition to being a vital nutrient, fat performs a number of culinary functions. It provides a rich flavor and silky mouthfeel or texture that most people find very enjoyable and satisfying. Fat also carries and blends the flavors of other foods, and makes available to us flavor compounds and nutrients that are soluble only in fat. Fat provides an appealing visual element when a food appears to be moist, creamy, fluffy, or shiny, among other things. During the baking process, fat performs a multitude of chemical functions, such as tenderizing, leavening, aiding in moisture retention, and creating a flaky or crumbly texture. In cooking, fat transfers heat to foods and prevents them from sticking. It also holds the heat in food, emulsifies or thickens sauces, and creates a crisp texture when used for frying.

One important aspect of fat is its ability to be heated to relatively high temperatures without boiling or otherwise breaking down. This is what allows fried foods to brown and cook quickly. If heated to high enough temperatures, however, fat will begin to break down and an acrid flavor develops, effectively ruining anything cooked in it. The temperature at which this occurs, known as the smoke point, is different for each type of fat. Generally, vegetable oils begin to smoke around 450°F/232°C, while animal fats begin to smoke around 375°F/191°C. Any additional materials in the fat (emulsifiers, preservatives, proteins, carbohydrates) lower the smoke point. Because some breakdown occurs at moderate temperatures and food particles tend to get left in the fat, repeated use of fat also lowers the smoke point.

States and Function of Water in Cooking

Water is the primary substance in most foods. Fruits and vegetables contain up to 95 percent water; raw meat is about 75 percent water. At sea level, pure water freezes (becomes solid) at 32°F/0°C and boils (turns to water vapor or steam) at 212°F/100°C. Boiling leads to evaporation, which makes reduction possible.

Water is a powerful solvent. Many vitamins, minerals, and flavor compounds are soluble in water. When salt or sugar is dissolved in water, the freezing point is lowered and the boiling point is raised. An important aspect of solutions is their pH, which is a measure of their acidity or alkalinity. Pure water, which is neutral, has a pH of seven. Anything above seven indicates an alkaline (basic) solution; a pH below seven indicates an acidic solution. Practically all foods are at least slightly acidic. The pH of a solution affects the flavor, color, texture, and nutritional quality of foods.

Forming Emulsions

An emulsion occurs when two substances that do not normally mix are forced into a mixture in which one of the substances is evenly dispersed in the form of small droplets throughout the other substance. Under normal conditions, fat (either liquid oil or solid fat) and water do not mix, but these two substances are the most common ingredients in culinary emulsions.

An emulsion consists of two phases, the dispersed phase and the continuous phase. An emulsified vinaigrette is an example of an oil-in-vinegar emulsion, meaning that the oil (the dispersed phase) has been broken up into very small droplets suspended throughout the vinegar (the continuous phase). Temporary emulsions, such as vinaigrettes, form quickly and require only the mechanical action of whipping, shaking, or stirring. To make an emulsion stable enough to keep the oil in suspension, additional ingredients, known as emulsifiers, are necessary to attract and hold together both the oil and liquid. Commonly used emulsifiers include egg yolks (which contain the emulsifier lecithin), mustard, and glace de viande. Natural starches, such as those in garlic, or modified starches, such as cornstarch or arrowroot, are also used.

Chapter Four

Food and Kitchen Safety

The importance of food and kitchen safety cannot be overemphasized. Few things are as detrimental to a foodservice establishment as an officially noted outbreak of a food-borne illness caused by poor sanitary practices. In addition to providing a sanitary atmosphere and adhering to procedures for safe food handling, it is also important to ensure a safe working environment. This chapter covers the causes of food-borne illnesses and prevention procedures and also includes checklists to help the staff achieve sanitary and safe kitchen conditions.

Food-Borne Illness

Foods can serve as carriers for many different illnesses. The most common symptoms of food-borne illnesses include abdominal cramps, nausea, vomiting, and diarrhea, possibly accompanied by fever. These symptoms may appear within a matter of hours after consumption of the affected food, although in some cases several days may elapse before onset. In order for a food-borne illness to be declared an official outbreak, it must involve two or more people who have eaten the same food, and health officials must confirm it.

Food-borne illnesses are caused by *adulterated* foods (foods unfit for human consumption). The severity of the illness depends on the amount of adulterated food ingested and, to a great extent, on the individual's susceptibility. Children, the elderly, and anyone whose immune system is already under siege generally will have much more difficulty than a healthy adult in combating a food-borne illness.

The source of the contamination affecting the food supply can be chemical, physical, or biological. Insecticides and cleaning compounds are examples of *chemical contaminants* that may accidentally find their way into foods. *Physical contaminants* include such things as bits of glass, rodent hairs, and paint chips. Careless food handling can mean that even an earring or a plastic bandage could fall into the food and result in illness or injury.

Biological contaminants account for the majority of food-borne illnesses. These include naturally occurring poisons, known as toxins, found in certain wild mushrooms, rhubarb leaves, green potatoes, and other plants. The predominant biological agents, however, are disease-causing microorganisms known as *pathogens,* which are responsible for up to 95 percent of all food-borne illnesses. Microorganisms of many kinds are present virtually everywhere, and most are helpful or harmless, if not essential; only about 1 percent of microorganisms are actually pathogenic.

Food-borne illnesses caused by biological contaminants fall into two subcategories: intoxication and infection. *Intoxication* occurs when a person consumes food containing toxins from bacteria, molds, or certain plants and animals. Once in the body, these toxins act as poison. Botulism is an example of an intoxication.

In the case of an *infection,* the food eaten by an individual contains large numbers of living pathogens. These pathogens multiply in the body and generally at-tack the gastrointestinal lining. Salmonellosis is an example of an infection. Some food-borne illnesses have characteristics of both an intoxication and an infection. *E. coli* 0157:H7 is an agent that causes such an illness.

Food Pathogens

The specific types of pathogens responsible for food-borne illnesses are fungi, viruses, parasites, and bacteria. *Fungi,* which include molds and yeast, are more adaptable than other microorganisms and have a high tolerance for acidic conditions. They are more often responsible for food spoilage than for food-borne illness. Fungi are important to the food industry in the production of cheese, bread, wine, and beer.

Viruses do not actually multiply in food, but if through poor sanitation practice a virus contaminates food, consumption of that food may result in illness. Infectious hepatitis A, caused by eating shellfish harvested from polluted waters (an illegal practice) or poor hand-washing practices after using the rest room, is an example. Once in the body, viruses invade a cell (called the host cell) and essentially reprogram it to produce more copies of the virus. The copies leave the dead host cells behind and invade still more cells. The best defenses against food-borne viruses are good personal hygiene and obtaining shellfish from certified waters.

Parasites are pathogens that feed on and take shelter in another organism, called a host. The host receives no benefit from the parasite and, in fact, suffers harm or even death as a result. Amebas and various worms, such as *Trichinella spiralis,* which is associated with pork, are among the parasites that contaminate foods. Different parasites reproduce in different ways. An example is the parasitic worm that exists in the larva stage in muscle meats. Once consumed, the life cycle and reproductive cycle continue. When the larvae reach adult stage, the fertilized female releases more eggs, which hatch and travel to the muscle tissue of the host, and the cycle continues.

Bacteria are responsible for a significant percentage of biologically caused food-borne illnesses. In order to better protect food during storage, preparation, and service, it is important to understand the classifications and patterns of bacterial growth.

Bacteria are classified by their requirement for oxygen, the temperatures at which they grow best, and their spore-forming abilities. *Aerobic bacteria* require the presence of oxygen to grow. *Anaerobic bacteria* do not require oxygen and may even die when exposed to it. *Facultative bacteria* are able to function with or without oxygen.

Bacteria reproduce by means of fission—one bacterium grows and then splits into two bacteria of equal size. These bacteria divide to form four, the four form eight, and so on. Under ideal circumstances, bacteria will reproduce every twenty minutes or so. In about twelve hours, one bacterium can multiply into sixty-eight billion bacteria, more than enough to cause illness.

Certain bacteria are able to form endospores, which serve as a means of protection against adverse circumstances such as high temperature or dehydration. Endospores allow an individual bacterium to resume its life cycle if favorable conditions should recur.

Bacteria require three basic conditions for growth and reproduction: a protein source, readily available moisture, and a moderate pH. The higher the amount of protein in a food, the greater its potential as a carrier of a food-borne illness. The amount of moisture available in a food is measured on the water activity (Aw) scale. This scale runs from 0 to 1, with 1 representing the Aw of water. Foods with a water activity above 0.85 support bacterial growth.

A food's relative acidity or alkalinity is measured on a scale known as pH. A moderate pH—a value between 4.6 and 10 on a scale that ranges from 1 to 14—is best for bacterial growth, and most foods fall within that range. Adding highly acidic ingredients, such as vinegar or citrus juice, to a food can lower its pH and extend its shelf life.

Many foods provide the three conditions necessary for bacterial growth and are therefore considered to be potentially hazardous. Meats, poultry, seafood, tofu, and dairy products (with the exception of some hard cheeses) are all categorized as potentially hazardous foods. Foods do not necessarily have to be animal-based to contain protein, however; vegetables and grains also contain protein. Cooked rice, beans, pasta, and potatoes are therefore also potentially hazardous, as are sliced melons, sprouts, and garlic-and-oil mixtures.

Food that contains pathogens in great enough numbers to cause illness may still look and smell normal. Disease-causing microorganisms are too small to be seen with the naked eye, so it is usually impossible to ascertain visually that food is adulterated. Because the microorganisms, particularly the bacteria, that cause food to spoil are different from the ones that cause food-borne illness, food may be adulterated and still have no "off" odor.

Although cooking food will destroy many of the microorganisms present, careless food handling after cooking can reintroduce pathogens that grow even more quickly without competition for food and space from the microorganisms that cause spoilage. Although shortcuts and carelessness do not always result in food-borne illness, inattention to detail increases the risk of creating an outbreak that may cause serious illness or even death. The various kinds of expenses, such as negative publicity and loss of prestige, related to an outbreak of food-borne illness are blows from which many restaurants can never recover.

Avoiding Cross Contamination

Many food-borne illnesses are a result of unsanitary handling procedures in the kitchen. Cross contamination occurs when disease-causing elements or harmful substances are transferred from one contaminated surface to another.

Excellent personal hygiene is one of the best defenses against cross contamination. An employee who reports for work with a contagious illness or an infected cut on the hand puts every customer at risk. Anytime the hands come into contact with a possible source of contamination (the face, hair, eyes, and mouth) they must be thoroughly washed before continuing any work.

Food is at greatest risk of cross contamination during the preparation stage. Ideally, separate work areas and cutting boards should be used for raw and cooked foods. Equipment and cutting boards should always be cleaned and thoroughly sanitized between uses.

All food must be stored carefully to prevent contact between raw and cooked items. Place drip pans beneath raw foods. Do not handle ready-to-eat foods with bare hands. Instead, use suitable utensils or single-use food-handling gloves.

Cross contamination icon   Hand washing icon

Proper Hand Washing

To reduce the chances of cross contamination, wash your hands often and correctly. Hands and forearms should be washed using soap and 110°F/43°C water for no less than twenty seconds. Be sure to wash your hands at the beginning of each shift and each new task, after handling raw foods, after going to the bathroom, sneezing, coughing, and so forth, and after handling any nonfood items.

Keeping Foods out of the Danger Zone

An important weapon against pathogens is the observance of strict time and temperature controls. Generally, the disease-causing microorganisms found in foods need to be present in significant quantities in order to make someone ill, with the exception of *E. coli* 0157:H7. Once pathogens have established themselves in a food source, they will either thrive or be destroyed, depending upon how long foods are in the so-called danger zone.

There are pathogens that can live at all temperature ranges. For most of those capable of causing food-borne illness, the friendliest environment is one that provides temperatures within a range of 41° to 135°F/5° to 57°C—the danger zone. Most pathogens are either destroyed or will not reproduce at temperatures above 135°F/57°C. Storing food at temperatures below 41°F/5°C will slow or interrupt the cycle of reproduction. (It should also be noted that intoxicating pathogens may be destroyed during cooking, but any toxins they have produced are still there.)

When conditions are favorable, pathogens can reproduce at an astonishing rate. Therefore, controlling the time during which foods remain in the danger zone is critical to the prevention of food-borne illness. Foods left in the danger zone for a period longer than four hours are considered adulterated. Additionally, one should be fully aware that the four-hour period is cumulative, meaning that the meter starts running again every time the food enters the danger zone. Therefore, once the four-hour period has been exceeded, heating, cooling, or any other cooking method cannot recover foods.

Receive and Store Foods Safely

It is not unheard of for foods to be delivered to a food-service operation already contaminated. To prevent this from happening to you, inspect all goods to be sure they arrive in sanitary conditions. Check the ambient temperature inside the delivery truck to see that it is adequate. Check the temperature of the product as well as the expiration dates. Verify that foods have the required government inspection and certification stamps or tags. Randomly sample items and reject any goods that do not meet your standards. Move the items immediately into proper storage conditions.

Refrigeration and freezer units should be regularly maintained and equipped with thermometers to make sure that the temperature remains within a safe range. Although in most cases chilling will not actually kill pathogens, it does drastically slow down reproduction. In general, refrigerators should be kept between 36° and 40°F/2° and 4°C, but quality is better served if certain foods can be stored at these specific temperatures:

Meat and poultry: 32° to 36°F/0° to 2°C

Fish and shellfish: 30° to 34°F/−1° to 1°C

Eggs: 38° to 40°F/3° to 4°C

Dairy products: 36° to 40°F/2° to 4°C

Produce: 40° to 45°F/4° to 7°C

Separate refrigerators for each of the above categories are ideal, but if necessary, a single unit can be divided into sections. The front of the unit will be the warmest area, the back the coldest.

Before storing food in the refrigerator, it should be properly cooled, stored in clean containers, wrapped, and labeled clearly with the contents and date. Store raw products below and away from cooked

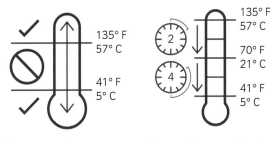

Danger zone icon   Time and temperature icon

foods to prevent cross contamination by dripping. Use the principle of "first in, first out" (FIFO) when arranging food, so that older items are in the front.

Dry storage is used for foods such as canned goods, spices, condiments, cereals, and staples such as flour and sugar, as well as for some fruits and vegetables that do not require refrigeration and have low perishability. As with all storage, the area must be clean, with proper ventilation and air circulation. Cleaning supplies should be stored in a separate place.

Hold Cooked or Ready-to-Serve Foods Safely

Keep hot foods hot and cold foods cold. Use hot-holding equipment (steam tables, double boilers, bain-maries, heated cabinets or drawers, chafing dishes, etc.) to keep foods at or above 135°F/57°C. Do not use hot-holding equipment for cooking or reheating. Use cold-holding equipment (ice or refrigeration) to keep cold foods at or below a temperature of 41°F/5°C.

Cooling Foods Safely

One of the leading causes of food-borne illness is improperly cooled food. Cooked foods that are to be stored need to be cooled to below 41°F/5°C as quickly as possible. This should be completed within four hours, unless you use the two-stage cooling method. In the first stage of this method, foods must be cooled to 70°F/21°C within two hours. In the second stage, foods must reach 41°F/5°C or below within an additional four hours, for a total cooling time of six hours.

The proper way to cool hot liquids is to place them in a metal container in an ice water bath that reaches the same level as the liquid inside the container. Stir the liquid in the container frequently so that the warmer liquid at the center mixes with the cooler liquid at the outside edges of the container, bringing the overall temperature down more rapidly.

Semisolid and solid foods should be refrigerated in single layers in shallow containers to allow greater surface exposure to the cold air. For the same reason, large cuts of meat or other foods should be cut into smaller portions, cooled to room temperature, and wrapped before refrigerating.

Reheating Foods Safely

When foods are prepared ahead and then reheated, they should move through the danger zone as rapidly as possible and be reheated to at least 165°F/74°C for a minimum of fifteen seconds. As long as all proper cooling and reheating procedures are followed each time, foods may be cooled and reheated more than once.

Food should be brought to the proper temperature over direct heat (burner, flattop, grill, or conventional oven) or in a microwave oven. A steam table will adequately hold reheated foods above 135°F/57°C, but it will not bring foods out of the danger zone quickly enough. Instant-read thermometers should always be used to check temperatures.

Today's consumer is well aware of the potential for food-borne illness through eggs. Therefore, we will look first at basic rules for safe handling of eggs and foods containing eggs.

- All eggs in the shell should be free from cracks, leaking, and obvious holes.

- Raw egg yolks are a potentially hazardous food, due to the possible presence of Salmonella enteritidis bacteria. Salmonella bacteria are killed when the eggs are held at a temperature of at least 140°F/60°C for a minimum of 3H minutes. The bacteria are also killed instantly at 160°F/71°C. Fried eggs or poached eggs with runny yolks should be prepared only at customer request.

- Any foods containing eggs must be kept at safe temperatures throughout handling, cooking, and storage. Cooling and reheating must be done quickly.

Thawing Frozen Foods Safely

Frozen foods may be safely thawed in several ways. The best—though slowest—method is to allow the food to thaw under refrigeration. The food should still be wrapped and should be placed in a shallow container on a bottom shelf to prevent possible contamination.

If there is not time to thaw foods in the refrigerator, covered or wrapped food may be placed in a container under running water of approximately 70°F/21°C or below. Use a stream of water strong enough to wash loose particles off the food.

Individual portions that are to be cooked immediately may be thawed in a microwave oven. Liquids, small items, or individual portions may also be cooked without thawing, but larger pieces that are cooked while still frozen become overcooked on the outside before they are thoroughly done throughout. Never thaw food at room temperature.

Hazard Analysis Critical Control Points (HACCP)

HACCP stands for Hazard Analysis Critical Control Points, which is a scientific state-of-the-art food safety program originally developed for astronauts. HACCP takes a systematic and preventive approach to the conditions that are responsible for most food-borne illnesses. It is preventive in nature, anticipating how food safety problems are most likely to occur, and taking steps to prevent them from occurring.

The HACCP system has been adopted by both food processors and restaurants, as well as by the FDA and USDA. At this time, there are no particular mandates that all foodservice establishments must use HACCP. However, instituting such a plan may prove advantageous on a variety of levels. The heart of HACCP is contained in the following seven principles:

1. **Assess the hazards.** The first step in an HACCP program begins with a hazard analysis of the menu item or recipe. Every step in the process must be looked at by first designing a flowchart that covers the period from "dock to dish." The types of hazards of concern are biological, chemical, and physical conditions. The biological hazards are typically microbiological, which include bacteria, viruses, and parasites.

2. **Identify the critical control points.** The next decision to make, after you have established a flow diagram and identified the potential hazards, is to identify the critical control points (CCPs). One of the most difficult aspects of putting an HACCP program together is not to overidentify these critical control points. A critical control point is the place in the utilization of the food where you have the ability to prevent, eliminate, or reduce an existing hazard or to prevent or minimize the likelihood that a hazard will occur. To quote the 1999 FDA Food Code, a critical control point is "a point or procedure in a specific food system where loss of control may result in an unacceptable health risk."

3. **Establish critical limits and control measures.** Critical limits are generally standards relating to control measures for each critical control point. Many have already been established by local health departments. For example, an established critical limit for the cooking step in preparing chicken is a 165°F/74°C final internal temperature. If you were to hold this chicken on the line before actual service, it would have to be kept at 140°F/60°C to prevent pathogenic microbes. Holding would be a critical step in this process. Control measures are what you can do ahead of time to facilitate the achievement of your critical limit.

4. **Establish procedures for monitoring CCPs.** Critical limits for each critical control point have to identify what is to be monitored. You must also establish how the CCP will be monitored and who will do it. Monitoring helps improve the system by allowing for the identification of problems or faults at particular points in the process. This allows for more control or improvement in the system.

5. **Establish corrective action plans.** If a deviation or substandard level occurs for a step in the process, a plan of action must be identified. Specific corrective actions must be developed for each CCP, because each food item and its preparation can vary greatly from one kitchen to the next.

6. **Set up a record-keeping system.** Keep documentation on hand to demonstrate whether the system is working or not. Recording events at

CCPs ensures that critical limits are met and preventive monitoring occurs. Documentation typically consists of time/temperature logs, checklists, and forms.

7. **Develop a verification system.** This step is to establish procedures to ensure that the HACCP plan is working correctly. If procedures are not being followed, try to find out what modifications can be made.

Serving Foods Safely

The potential to transmit food-borne illness does not end when the food leaves the kitchen. Restaurant servers should also be instructed in good hygiene and safe food-handling practices. Hands should be properly washed after using the restroom, eating, smoking, touching one's face or hair, and handling money, dirty dishes, or soiled table linens. When setting tables, never touch the parts of flatware that come in contact with food, and handle glassware by the stems or bases only. Carry plates, glasses, and flatware in such a way that food contact surfaces are not touched. Serve all foods using the proper utensils.

Cleaning and Sanitizing

Cleaning refers to the removal of soil or food particles, whereas *sanitizing* involves using moist heat or chemical agents to kill pathogenic microorganisms. For equipment that cannot be immersed in a sink, or for equipment such as knives and cutting boards during food preparation, use a wiping cloth, soaked in a double-strength sanitizing solution, to clean and sanitize between uses. Iodine, chlorine, or quaternary ammonium compounds are all common sanitizing agents.

Small equipment, tools, pots, and tableware should be run through a ware-washing machine or washed manually in a three-compartment sink. After sanitizing, equipment and tableware should be allowed to air-dry completely, because using paper or cloth toweling could result in cross contamination.

Careful sanitation procedures, proper handling of foods, and a well-maintained facility all work together to prevent a pest infestation. Take the necessary steps to prohibit the potential harboring of various pathogens caused by pests.

Kitchen Safety

In addition to the precautions necessary to guard against food-borne illness, care must also be taken to avoid accidents to staff and guests. The following safety measures should be practiced.

Health and Hygiene

Maintain good general health with regular checkups. Do not handle food when ill. Keep any burn or break in the skin covered with a clean, waterproof bandage. Cover the face with a tissue when coughing or sneezing and wash hands afterward.

Keep hair clean and neat, and contain it if necessary. Keep fingernails short and well maintained, with no polish. Keep hands away from hair and face when working with food.

Fire Safety

It takes only a few seconds for a simple flare-up to turn into a full-scale fire. Grease fires, electrical fires, or even a waste container full of paper catching fire when a match is carelessly tossed into it are easy to imagine in any busy kitchen. A comprehensive fire safety plan should be in place and a standard part of all employee training.

The first step to take in avoiding fires is to make sure that the entire staff is fully aware of the potential fire dangers. Be sure that all equipment is up to code. Frayed or exposed wires and faulty plugs can all too easily be the cause of a fire. Overburdened outlets are another common culprit. Thorough training is essential. Everyone should know what to do in case of a fire. Instruct your kitchen staff in the correct way to handle a grill fire and grease fire.

Have fire extinguishers in easily accessible areas. Proper maintenance of extinguishers and timely inspections by your local fire department are vital. Above all, make sure you never try to put out a grease, chemical, or electrical fire by throwing water on the flames.

Everyone should know where the fire department number is posted. The exits from all areas of the building should be easy to find, clear of any obstructions, and fully operational. Your guests rely on you and your staff for guidance.

Dressing for Safety

The various parts of the typical chef's uniform play important roles in keeping workers safe as they operate in a potentially dangerous environment. The chef's jacket, for instance, is double-breasted, which creates a two-layer cloth barrier between the chest area and steam burns, splashes, and spills. The design also means that the jacket can be rebuttoned on the opposite side to cover any spills. The sleeves of the jacket are long to cover as much of the arm as possible. Pants should be worn without cuffs, which can trap hot liquids and debris.

Be it a tall white toque or a favorite baseball cap, chefs wear hats to contain their hair, preventing it from falling into the food. Hats also help absorb sweat from overheated brows. Neckerchiefs serve a similar sweat-absorbing role.

The apron is worn to protect the jacket and pants from excessive staining. Most chefs use side towels to protect their hands when working with hot pans, dishes, or other equipment. Side towels used to lift hot items must be dry in order to provide protection.

Hard leather shoes with slip-resistant soles are recommended because of the protection they offer and the support they give your feet.

Jackets, pants, side towels, aprons, and shoes can harbor bacteria, molds, and parasites. Use hot water, a good detergent, and a sanitizer, such as borax or chlorine bleach, to remove bacteria and grime.

Regulations, Inspection, and Certification

Federal, state, and local government regulations work to ensure the wholesomeness of the food that reaches the public. Any new foodservice business should contact the local health department well in advance of opening, to ascertain the necessary legal requirements. Some states and local jurisdictions offer sanitation certification programs. Regulations and testing vary from area to area. Certification is often available through certain academic institutions.

The Occupational Safety and Health Administration (OSHA)

OSHA is a federal organization that was instituted in 1970 and falls under the purview of the Health and Human Services Administration. It helps employers and workers to establish and maintain a safe, healthy work environment.

Among OSHA's regulations is the mandate that all places of employment must have an adequate and easily accessible first-aid kit on the premises. In addition, if any organization has more than ten employees, records must be kept of all accidents and injuries to employees that require medical treatment.

OSHA concentrates its efforts on providing services where the risk to worker safety is greatest.

Americans with Disabilities Act (ADA)

This act is intended to make public places accessible and safe for those with a variety of disabilities. Any new construction or remodeling done to a restaurant must meet ADA standards. This includes locating telephones so that a person in a wheelchair can reach them, and providing toilets with handrails.

Drugs and Alcohol in the Workplace

One final topic that is of great importance in the workplace is the right of all workers to be free from the hazards posed by a coworker who comes to work under the influence of drugs or alcohol. The abuse of any substance is a serious concern because it can either alter or impair one's ability to perform his or her job. Reaction times are slowed, inhibitions are lowered, and judgment is impaired. The responsibilities of a professional working in any kitchen are too great to allow someone suffering from a substance abuse problem to diminish the respect and trust you have built with your customers and staff.

Part Two

World Cuisines

Cuisine, like any cultural element of a society, has geographic, religious, and many other influences that shape its development. However, a cuisine—once developed—exerts influence on the culture of its land of origin as well as on any outside cultures in which it may come in contact. Elements of the cuisine may shape events or celebrations that become cultural norms, or assimilate into another culture, become intrinsic to it, and then work to shape or drive agricultural demands and practices.

In this context, any meal is more than mere sustenance; for today's chef, or a student of the culinary arts, this information can be of value. Identifying some of the basic foods and preparation techniques that translate across cuisines, cultures, and continents is an important part of the culinary profession. Any cuisine is a reflection of more than just a collection of ingredients, cooking utensils, and dishes from a geographic location. These elements are undoubtedly critical to establishing a culinary identity. But they are not, all on their own, a cuisine.

Shared traditions and beliefs also give a cuisine a particular identity. A cultural cuisine is an important element in developing and maintaining a group's identity. And perhaps most relevant from today's perspective, a system of governance and trade that encourages the "migration" of foods and dishes from one place to another strongly influences cuisine. The presence or absence of a shoreline has a tremendous impact on a developing cooking style. The climate and soil, as well as farming techniques, also have a strong influence.

A cuisine also gives us a way to express and establish customs for meals (what is eaten when and with whom), from simple meals to celebrations and ritual meals. By taking a look at some of the world's major religions, it is easy to see their influence on cuisine. Edicts favoring or prohibiting certain foods, as well as a calendar of feasting, fasting, and celebrating rituals, are often widespread enough in an area to color the way that a cuisine evolves and what is widely held to be authentic. For example, Hinduism, with its proscription against eating meat for certain castes, has contributed to a cuisine with a strong tradition of meatless dishes.

There has probably never been a time when the "migration" of foods from one part of the world to another has not been a factor in a developing cuisine. While these exchanges are more rapid and frequent in modern times, they have always been apparent. Sometimes these exchanges had a great deal to do with the conquest of lands by an invading force. Other times, trade and its associated activities played a major role.

Whether benign or aggressive, a system of culinary exchange is part of any cuisine's story. New ingredients find their way into traditional dishes. Over time, the new ingredient becomes so firmly entrenched, we may even forget that the earliest culinarians would not recognize it as authentic. A clear example of this can been seen with the adoption of many ingredients that were native to the Americas, such as the tomato. Today, who could imagine Italian cuisine without the tomato? It is so imbedded in the country's cuisine that anyone could easily mistake Italy as its land of origin.

Techniques are also a window into the cooking of a specific cuisine. As you might expect, a technique can have a different name as you travel from one region to another. Certain cooking styles are popular in a given region of the world because they are suited to the lifestyle and living conditions; others may remain virtually unknown.

The study of any single cuisine is a multifaceted undertaking. Cuisines have never developed in a culinary vacuum. As you probe more deeply into the historical origins of the recipe in your hand today, you may find ingredients that traveled from East to West or from the Old World to the New World in place of an earlier option. Traditional methods of cooking a dish may have changed with the times or to meet the special challenges of cooking for large groups or in a restaurant setting. Knowing the classic techniques and cuisine of a culture (whether France, India, or beyond) is always helpful when you choose to modernize or change a traditional recipe. Read cookbooks, visit restaurants and other countries, and keep an open mind in order to experience a wide variety of world cuisines.

Chapter Five

The Americas

American cuisine finds its identity in the diversity of its origins. The blending of indigenous ingredients and foodways with those of a constant flow of explorers, conquerors, and immigrants has led to the development of a cuisine that shows the imprint of many cultures.

The United States

For culinary purposes, it's helpful to view the United States regionally, and to take into account the different cultures and ethnicities of each area.

The New England States

New England is composed of six states: Maine, Vermont, New Hampshire, Massachusetts, Rhode Island, and Connecticut. With the exception of Vermont, the New England states have at least one border on the Atlantic Ocean. Maine, Vermont, and New Hampshire also share a border with Canada. New England is known for having four vastly different seasons, including balmy summers and frigid, icy winters.

Early settlements by the British, French, Dutch, and Scandinavians heavily influenced later New England cooking. One of the biggest cultural influences on New England cookery came from the British in Boston. Because of their dislike of fanciful French cooking, the Puritan Bostonians favored extensive use of boiling, braising, baking, roasting, and stewing.

Each New England state has its own cultural influences aside from the larger New England traditions. Scottish and Welsh settlers in Maine, New Hampshire, and Vermont influenced the cooking there. The French moved down through Canada and into much of Maine as well. Maine and Massachusetts saw many German settlers move in. The Irish had a lasting influence on Massachusetts cooking, and the Portuguese have left their mark on Rhode Island cookery.

Present-day New England cooking features many of the preservation techniques that were once crucial for early settlers battling the harsh New England winters. To ensure no meat would rot and become unusable, the settlers stored surplus meat in salt barrels. This resulted in salt pork, salt cod, and corned

beef becoming the mainstays of colonial New England meals. Aside from salt, other common meat preservatives in New England were smoke and snow or ice. Fruits and vegetables also underwent preservation measures and were used in sweet pies, which became staples during the winter months. Apple pie with cinnamon and nutmeg was standard. Maine settlers, on the other hand, favored blueberry pie as berries were, and still are, plentiful in Maine. Meat pies, including chicken pot pie, were also common, especially at social gatherings.

The settlers in New England adapted their own traditional recipes to incorporate native, local ingredients, such as wild game (venison, rabbit, hare), turkey, duck, salmon, flounder, clams, lobster, cod, scallops, strawberries, cranberries, corn (including popcorn), beans, squash, maple syrup, and fiddlehead ferns. The flavor profile of New England comprises cured pork, corned beef, sweet and sour relishes, pickles, maple syrup, molasses, baked beans, warm spices, and traditional Thanksgiving meal items.

The Mid-Atlantic States

The Mid-Atlantic states include New Jersey, Delaware, Washington, DC, Maryland, Pennsylvania, Virginia, and West Virginia. New York state is often considered a Mid-Atlantic state as well. Some of these states sit on the eastern seaboard, while others are situated next to Great Lakes. The seasons of the Mid-Atlantic states vary even within some of the states. For example, the winter in New York City is quite different from the winter of Buffalo, New York, which is situated on Lake Erie and has heavy snowfall every year. Additionally, a state like Virginia has a much milder winter than a state like Pennsylvania.

The Dutch were the first to colonize much of the Mid-Atlantic region, followed by the Swedes and Finns, who were attracted to the rich farmlands. The impact of farms on the cooking from this region is immense. The farming influence runs the gamut from the international sophistication of major cities (New York and Philadelphia, for example) to the lesser-known specialties of Pennsylvania's farm country, including Amish and Shaker cooking.

Common New England and Mid-Atlantic Ingredients

Vegetables, Fruits, and Legumes		Poultry	Lobster
Apples	Fiddlehead ferns	Turkey	Oysters
Beans	Squash		
Blueberries	**Meat**	**Fish and Shellfish**	**Sweeteners**
Corn	Beef	Clams	Maple syrup
Cranberries	Venison	Cod	Molasses
		Flounder	

The Southeastern States

The cuisine of the southeastern states (Kentucky, North Carolina, South Carolina, Tennessee, Alabama, and Georgia) was originally influenced by the French, Scots, Irish, English, Spanish, Native Americans, and Africans. For many immigrants, the foods of their native countries played an important role in providing a tangible way to retain cultural identity in a foreign land. Even today, Southerners take great pride in their region and history. Recipes are often carefully handed down through the generations to preserve tradition.

Pork and corn were the mainstays in the diet of the area's earliest settlers, and they still play a major role in much of the cuisine today. Barbecuing in the Southern tradition originated with the Native Americans, who taught settlers how to cook over an open flame. Today, barbecuing is taken very seriously in the South, resulting in each subregion's variety of sauces, mops, and wet and dry rubs. Additionally, soul food is thought to have been developed in this region, and its prevalence on the area's menus gives evidence to that claim.

Seafood plays a dominant role in the coastline cuisine. Game animals are also important in Southeastern cooking. Sweet potatoes and peanuts are distinctive ingredients that are found in Southeastern favorites such as sweet potato pies and peanut soup. The South also produces one of America's most familiar alcoholic beverages—bourbon—and has perfected its own cocktail, the mint julep.

Common Southeastern Ingredients

Grains and Legumes

Green beans

Rice

Vegetables and Fruits

Apples

Berries

Black-eyed peas

Broccoli

Cherries

Collards

Corn

Cucumbers

Eggplant

Figs

Melons

Okra

Onions

Peaches

Pears

Persimmons

Potatoes

Spinach

Squash

Tomatoes

Turnip greens

Turnips

Meat

Bear

Beef

Goat

Ground hog

Mutton

Opossum

Pork

Raccoon

Squirrel

Veal

Venison

Poultry

Chicken

Fish and Shellfish

Bluegill

Crabs

Crappie

Crawfish

Flounder

Mullet

Oysters

Scallops

Shrimp

Trout

Barbecue

Barbecue is one example of a distinctive cooking technique that developed in the South. A distinction must be made between the American barbecue grill used for cooking in backyards and the type of food known as *barbecue*.

Barbecuing involves using a wet or dry rub or "mop" applied to a piece of meat before it is slowly cooked over an open fire pit. Many different types of meat can be used for barbecuing. Pork is primarily used in the Southeast, but beef, chicken, and game are good for barbecuing as well.

Dry and wet rubs vary from house to house, restaurant to restaurant, and person to person. Some examples of different dry rub ingredients are salt, sugar, paprika, garlic, pepper, onion, and herbs, while the ingredients for a wet rub might include oil, herbs, spices, vinegar, wine, citrus juice, and tomato paste.

The Gulf Coast

The portions of the states that border the Gulf Coast (Florida, Mississippi, Louisiana, and Alabama) are mostly wet, swampy marshlands. The food from this region is typically associated with the cuisine of New Orleans, with the rest of Louisiana, Mississippi, Alabama, and Florida playing a smaller role. The lush green waterways that spread across the region teem with indigenous life. The state of Florida is a peninsula, with borders on both the Gulf of Mexico and the Atlantic Ocean. A portion of Alabama sits next to Florida and also borders the Gulf. Continuing westward, Mississippi sits between Alabama and Louisiana, and the Mississippi River divides Mississippi and Louisiana in two parts. These states all share similar terrain: wet, soggy fens and lea areas. However, progressing northward, lush fields are encountered, before ultimately running into the southern end of the Appalachian highlands. Growing seasons are long and prosperous, thus the climate is ideal for a myriad of crops and agriculture.

Within fifty years of Christopher Columbus's arrival in the Bahamas, Cuba, and Santo Domingo in 1492, the Florida coast and Mississippi River became sought-after areas for France and Spain. The Spanish spent forty years trying (unsuccessfully) to colonize Florida. The French efforts proved to be more fruitful: By the end of the early 1700s, the French had settled what are the present-day regions of Mississippi, Alabama, and Louisiana. The culture of these states is an intriguing blend of Native American, Spanish, French, and African cultures.

Southern Florida is distinct from the rest of the state in its cuisine, which incorporates local seafood and tropical flavors commonly associated with the Caribbean Islands. For this reason, the food is referred to as "Floribean." The cuisine also has a distinct Latin flavor due to the prevalence of Spanish settlers and the proximity to Cuba. Many different types of sea creatures, including snapper, grouper, cobia, shrimp, wahoo, and conch, are featured in "Floribean" cuisine, as well as island spice, rum, tropical fruits, and jerk variations.

Florida leads the rest of the United States in its citrus production. From late winter through the early spring, Florida oranges and grapefruits are harvested and distributed throughout the States.

Mississippi and Alabama are similar in their topographical and cultural makeup. The Choctaw Indians played a key role in the states' culinary history, contributing things such as the beehive oven (an early predecessor to the wood-burning stove) and hominy. The two states enjoy long growing seasons and heavy rainfall, which contribute to their high proportion of fertile land. Through the early 1900s, cotton was the main crop of these states until the boll weevil virtually destroyed the cotton industry. Today, soybeans, corn, rice, and wheat are a few of the crops that provide the livelihood for farmers in these states.

The diversity of Louisiana's founding settlers is still apparent today in the spoken languages, the social and cultural celebrations, and the food preparations. Louisiana is a hodgepodge of Spanish, African, German, Italian, French, English, and Native American cultures. Louisiana inhabitants of Caribbean, African, Native American, and Spanish descent came to be known as Creole, a term that likely came from the Spanish word *criollo* meaning "native to a place." In the mid-eighteenth century, the Acadians (French settlers in Canada) were forced out of Canada by the English. Many traveled to the Bayou region of Louisiana and New Orleans and settled there. They brought their language and cooking techniques, which were blended with Native American ingredients to make a new style of cooking. The name "Acadian" eventually became "Cajun," and their culture shaped our understanding of the Bayou country today. There are several components to Cajun cooking that make it unique: iron skillets, stock (usually a combination of meats and seafood to make one hearty stock), roux (usually golden to dark brown), herbs, the "trinity" (onions, green peppers, and celery), and liqueurs.

The Gulf States are perhaps best represented by the city of New Orleans, Louisiana. This region boasts a mixture of Cajun and Creole cuisines and their flavors. Heavily spiced Cajun cuisine incorporates the region's indigenous foods, including crayfish, roots, herbs, and rice. French influence can be seen in the frequent use of cream and roux-type sauces. Creole cuisine is complex, with the Spanish influence demonstrated in the use of peppers, seafood, and spices. One of the most popular dishes in New Orleans is gumbo. The cultural makeup of the region is directly reflected in the ingredients of the different types of gumbo. From the French comes the roux base; from the French and Spanish comes the trinity; okra is an African-American influence; from the Native Americans there is filé; from the Germans come sausage and pork products; and from the Italians the gumbo gets tomatoes and herbs. The many different varieties, including Cajun, Creole, cowboy, seafood, and game gumbos, incorporate all or some of these elements.

The Midwest and Southwest

The Midwestern and Southwestern states are known as the heartland of America, and many of the plains states are referred to as the breadbasket of the world. The states in these regions include Ohio, Indiana, Illinois, Missouri, Arkansas, Oklahoma, Texas, New Mexico, Kansas, Iowa, Wyoming, Michigan, Wisconsin, Nebraska, South Dakota, and North Dakota. Rolling hills dot the Midwest-

Common Gulf Coast Ingredients

Vegetables, Fruits, Nuts, and Legumes		Meat	
Artichokes	Okra	Beef	Conch
Black-eyed peas	Pecans	Pork	Crawfish
Chicory	Persimmons		Frog legs
Coconuts	Red beans	**Poultry**	Oysters
Cushan (crookneck squash)	Rice	Chicken	Pompano
Figs	Sassafras leaves		Red snapper
	Sugarcane	**Seafood**	Shrimp
	Sweet potatoes	Alligator	Snails
		Catfish	Turtle

ern plains, and heavy forests flourish in many areas. The climates vary greatly among these states. There are the dry dusty ranches of Texas contrasted against the cold mill towns of Michigan.

The Midwest

Western expansion began soon after the United States won its independence from England. Most of the Midwestern states were settled during the 1800s. But even despite the gold rush of 1849, the Great Plains were mainly traversed on the way westward rather than settled. The areas became truly inhabited by settlers only after the American Civil War.

People came to the Midwest from the eastern United States, bringing their methods of hearth cooking, one-pot meals, and food preservation methods for the long, often harsh, winters. The settlers came from many parts of Europe. Scandinavians, with their smoked fish and hearty stews, settled around the Dakotas and Minnesota. The Germans and Polish moved into Wisconsin and Illinois, bringing with them a taste for and knowledge of sausages, beer, and cheese. Irish, English, Russians, and Italians also came to this region, adding their influences to the amalgam of cultures and cooking traditions. The culinary profile of this region includes tastes of smoked fish, meat and potatoes, jerky, smoked meats, boiled foods, and in general hearty foods. The present-day Midwestern states comprise huge cattle ranches, grain farms, and their fair share of large and growing metropolitan areas.

The Southwest

The Southwestern states are known for a mixture of cuisines developed by the Native Americans and Mexicans, who inhabited this region for hundreds of years, and by the pioneers, who ventured west in search of less populated land. Seasoning is typically spicy, but can be complex and contain cumin, coriander, cinnamon, onions, and garlic, as well as oregano and chiles. Chiles, both dried and fresh, can be found in almost all dishes from this region. Corn is also a ubiquitous element in Southwestern cooking. The popular condiment *salsa* originated in this region. Indigenous foods include snake, antelope, fowl, rabbit, trout, bass, cactus, pine nuts, squash, corn, beans, and chiles.

The heart of the American Southwest is a mostly uninhabitable region of deserts, plateaus, and rugged mountains. Native peoples such as the Pueblos, Hopi, and Navajo adapted their societies to the land long before explorers came in the sixteenth century.

Texas cuisine is as diverse as the state is large, boasting four distinct styles: Northern Texas shares characteristics found in the Old South. Eastern Texas favors food similar to that of the Gulf region. Central Texas cuisine has its roots in the Anglo and German settlers' heritage. Southern Texas has strong Mexican influence (characterized by food commonly known as Tex-Mex). Texas ranchers throughout the state enjoy their steaks and a distinctive style of barbecue (influenced by both Mexican immigrants and former slaves).

Common Midwest and Southwest Ingredients

Grains and Legumes	Vegetables and Fruits		Poultry
Barley	Apples	Potatoes	Chicken
Beans	Berries	Summer squash	
Oats	Cactus	Turnips	Fish
Sorghum	Chiles	Winter squash	Bass
Soybeans	Corn		Trout
Wheat	Peaches	Meat	
	Pears	Beef	
	Plums	Lamb	
		Pork	
		Rabbit	

California, Oregon, and Washington

The Pacific coastline of California, Oregon, and Washington spans approximately 2,000 miles (3,218 kilometers), from the Canadian border to Baja, California. The climate varies greatly in this region, from the plains where wheat and corn are grown, to the high Rocky Mountains. Spanish missionaries settled California in 1769 and the discovery of gold in the mid- to late-1840s brought international prospectors to this region. Many of these pioneers were English, German, Scandinavian, Chinese, and Japanese. The cuisine of this region shows the influence of these European, Asian, and Native American cultures. Each state within the region has its own cultural influence as well. New Englanders, Southerners, and Midwesterners settled in Oregon. Today, Oregon's cuisine reflects German, Basque, Scandinavian, Russian, and French ancestry. The coastal Native Americans taught early settlers about many native foods and techniques for salmon fishing and preparation.

Today, these states provide a bounty of food for the nation and the world. In Washington the salmon and shellfish industry remains a major economic force. Cultivation of fruits and berries such as plums, pears, prunes, cherries, blueberries, and hazelnuts, which were grown by the first settlers in Oregon, continues today. California has developed into the largest agricultural state in America. The small organic farms and large agribusinesses in California produce much of the fruits and vegetables, as well as wine, consumed in this country and around the world. The cooking in California reflects a desire to use fresh, local ingredients in a variety of ethnic preparations. The flavor profile for this region includes fresh fruits and vegetables, light sauces, and shellfish and saltwater fish.

Common California, Oregon, and Washington Ingredients

Vegetables and Fruits			Fish and Shellfish
Apples	Figs	Pistachios	Clams
Artichokes	Garlic	Tomatoes	Crabs
Berries	Grapes	Zucchini	Oysters
Cherries	Hazelnuts		Salmon
Chiles	Melons	**Meat**	Saltwater fish
Fennel	Olives	Beef	
	Onions	Lamb	
	Pears		

Alaska

Alaska is divided into three major regions. The top third of the state is located in the Arctic Circle. The Japanese current warms the south-central region, where two thirds of Alaskan produce is grown. The Aleutian Islands, where sheep and cattle are raised, stretch into the Bering Strait.

The indigenous population is made up of Eskimos, Aleuts, and North American Indians. Before contact with Europeans, these people survived on salmon, whale, seal, caribou, polar bear, mountain goat, berries, and edible native plants. Russian culinary influences are still seen today, as are Dutch, German, and Scandinavian. The Klondike gold rush brought different foodstuffs to the region, including sourdough starter, pork, lard, coffee, and tea.

Today, the mainstay of the Alaskan economy is the fishing industry, which focuses on salmon, halibut, and crab. The central region of Alaska is home to the Matanuska Valley, which began produce farming in 1935 as a direct result of the Homesteader's Act. The long hours of sunlight and cold nights across the state produce vegetables of incredible size and intense flavor. Typical preparations and foods consumed in the Alaskan diet today include pot roasts and stews, potatoes, vegetables, beans, pickles and relishes, sourdough bread, and fruit pies.

Common Alaskan Ingredients

Grains	Vegetables and Fruits	Root vegetables	Reindeer
Barley	Blueberries	Strawberries	Venison
Oats	Cabbage		
Rye	Gooseberries	**Meat**	**Fish and Shellfish**
Winter wheat	Huckleberries	Caribou	Dungeness crab
	Kale	Elk	Halibut
	Raspberries	Moose	King crab
			Salmon

Hawaii

Hawaii is made up of eight main islands and many smaller formations. The main islands are Hawaii, Maui, Oahu, Kauai, Molokai, Lanai, Nihau, and Kahoolawe.

The islands have the most multi-ethnic population in the United States. The Polynesians were the first to arrive in the sixth century. In 1776, Captain Cook arrived from Britain and subsequently told the world about the islands, which he named the Sandwich Islands in honor of the Earl of Sandwich. Immigrants from New England brought the supplies for Yankee cooking to Hawaii. This was the beginning of the incredible array of ethnic cooking styles that characterize Hawaiian cooking today.

In the early 1800s, the sugarcane crop created a need for plantation labor, which led to a second wave of immigration. The Chinese and Japanese came first and introduced rice, stir-fry, and Szechwan dishes into the Hawaiian diet. Koreans brought Korean-style barbecue and *kimchee*, with its hot and spicy profile. Filipinos contributed adobo stews, while the Vietnamese and Thai introduced their ingredients and cooking styles. In more recent years, a European style has emerged as French chefs arrived to command the kitchens of many of the resort hotels.

Many cooking styles have merged into what is modern Hawaiian cooking. The food profile for the Hawaiian islands now includes roasting, steaming, and stir-frying techniques of Asian cuisine, the charcoal broiling and grilling of the Japanese, the hot and spicy flavors of the Koreans, fish stews and bean dishes from the Portuguese, and the luau of the native Polynesians.

Common Hawaiian Ingredients

Grains	Citrus	Pineapples	Seafood
Rice	Coconuts	Sugarcane	Bonito
	Guava	Tamarind	Crab
Vegetables and Fruits	Lychee	Taro	Flounder
	Macadamia nuts	Yams	Shrimp
Arrowroot	Mangos		Swordfish
Avocados	Papaya	**Poultry**	Tuna
Bananas	Passion fruit	Chicken	
Breadfruit			

The Caribbean

The Caribbean, also referred to as the West Indies, has a rich and tumultuous cultural history. The natives on the islands, the Lucayans, Arawaks, and Quechua, were generally peaceful tribes from Peru. The Spanish, English, Dutch, and French were the first to forge settlements on the Caribbean islands. Later, the Irish, Portuguese, Chinese, and Indians came as indentured servants to participate in the coffee, sugarcane, and tobacco industries.

The islands share the same basic staples, but there are preparations that vary from island to island. The staples include sea creatures, such as shrimp, conch, grouper, snapper, and tilapia, as well as tropical fruits, corn, and cilantro. Pork and chicken are popular and every island has a version of the rice-and-beans dish. The islands' terrain ranges from flat to hilly. There are volcanoes, coral reefs, rain forests, and sandy beaches. The soil on most islands, especially volcanic ones, is rich; both indigenous and introduced crops flourish.

Caribbean cuisine is as multicultural and intense as the islands themselves. Its influences can be seen in the foods of the many regions that lie close to it.

Mexico and South America

The culinary development and traditions of Mexico and South America have many similarities and can be linked in several important ways, including geographically. The landmasses that form Mexico and South America stretch from the southern border of the United States to the southern tip of Argentina—nearly 7,000 miles (11,263 kilometers). Together, this vast region is more than three times the size of the United States and contains a total combined population of over 500 million. The terrain and climate have fostered the development of varied cuisines. The landscape of Mexico and South America has divided and isolated areas within, leading to a regional diversity of crops, customs, and cuisines. Both areas are dappled with mountain ranges, highlands, plateaus, grasslands, and tropical rain forests. The land ranges from some of the most arid and mountainous to some of the world's best and most arable farmlands.

Mexico

Northern Mexico
Northern Mexico is comprised of Baja, California, Sonora, Chihuahua, Coahuila, Nuevo Leon, Tamaulipas, Durango, and Sinaloa. These areas are known as "the frontier." Settlement has proven difficult due to the wide-open deserts, deep canyons, and two mountain ranges. The Apache, Ute, Chichameca, and nomadic tribes were native to the area. Because the frontier provided little in the way of subsistence, the people literally lived off the land, utilizing insects, wild game, and cactus in their meals. The mountains provided easier farmland, and inhabitants on the mountains raised corn, squash, and chiles. These foods are typically found in the regional foods today. Additionally, a Spanish influence is seen from the Spanish settlers who forged into the region centuries ago.

The lifestyle of the region's inhabitants had a large impact on the development of the cuisine. Sheepherders and *vaqueros* (cowboys) cooked on the open range over fire pits; fajitas and enchiladas are prime examples of the cooking borne of this culture. Fresh salsas and guacamole accompanied the food, utilizing garlic, cilantro, tomatillos, lime, and chiles native to the region. In later years, the immigrants from southern Mexico introduced corn-based dishes to the regional diet, but their preference for heavy sauces was not incorporated. Fresh, uncooked salsas still dominate, as do fiery, smoky dishes such as fajitas. In the coastal areas, fish is a large part of the diet, and inland, freshwater fish abounds. The flavor profile of the region includes smoky, rich yet lean, spicy dishes, garlic, wheat, and corn.

Central Mexico

Mexico City and its surrounding states (Puebla, Tlaxcala, Hidalgo, and Morelos) make up the area known as central Mexico. This region encompasses the mountain ranges of the four Sierras. The Tehuacan Valley, located in the central plateau of Mexico, is surrounded by these highlands: the Sierra de Pachuca Mountains are to the north, the Sierra de Ajusco Mountains lie to the south, the Sierra Nevada range is to the east, and the Sierra de las Cruces range lies to the west. The rainy season lasts

CLOCKWISE FROM TOP CENTER: cilantro, corn, tomatoes, dried epazote, cornmeal, Mexican chocolate, jalapeños, poblanos, Anaheim chiles, potatoes (top center), kidney beans (center, in bowl)

five months, from May to September, in the Sierra de las Cruces range. The remaining months are somewhat dry with occasional rain showers.

Historically, Mexico's population has been centered in this region. The early inhabitants in the area were hunter-gatherers who occasionally worked small fields of maize. Teotihuacan, an ancient city, grew up on the Mexican highland around 2 B.C.E. It was the largest center of trade and civilization in the New World before the 1519 arrival of Cortez, who conquered and all but wiped out the native population. The Aztec inhabitants of Teotihuacan had vast markets where they sold fresh produce and wares. They had orchards of avocados, coconuts, and pineapples, prickly pears, red and green tomatoes (tomatillos), and chiles. After the Spanish arrived, the native people incorporated many Spanish elements into their diets, including pork, chicken, olives, rice, cinnamon, radishes, grapes, sugarcane, stone fruits, wheat, chickpeas, melons, and onions.

The food of this area has evolved over time and the inhabitants now utilize the ingredients we recognize as Mexican. There is a wide variety of fresh and dried chiles. Numerous meats are used (chicken, beef, pork, and goat) as well as fish. Fresh produce, such as limes (Key limes), mangos, tomatoes, corn, prickly pears, and tomatillos, is also incorporated into the cooking. Herbs such as epazote, hoja santa, avocado leaves, cilantro, and Mexican oregano are used in many dishes. Cheeses, such as queso fresco, are used as a seasoning and a topping.

Southern Mexico

Southern Mexico comprises the Yucatan, Chihuahua, Quintana Roo, Campeche, Veracruz, Oaxaca, and Tabasco. The Neovolcanica mountain range runs east-west across the country. This region includes active volcanoes, Pacific lowlands, and highlands featuring dense jungles and a tropical climate. The tip of the peninsula is an arid desert-like region, which offers a vast coastline, making seafood dishes abundant in the area. The diverse geography and isolated locations led to the development of very different cultures and, therefore, cuisines. For example, Oaxaca, a very remote southern region, still retains much of its native heritage and is noted for its *moles,* which can be green, brick red, yellow, or even black, and are used in many celebrations. Oaxaca is also noted for its coffee and *mezcal* (a tequila-like beverage made from the blue agave plant) production.

Veracruz, unlike Oaxaca, was highly influenced by European settlers. Because of its location on the Gulf of Mexico, it was a port of choice for explorers as well as invaders. Veracruz was strongly influenced by Spanish, African, and Caribbean culinary traditions. Nowhere is this demonstrated more simply than in snapper Veracruzana, a specialty that blends indigenous flavors and ingredients with those of the Mediterranean—combining the use of olive oil, garlic, onions, capers, and green olives with New World ingredients like jalapeños and tomatoes.

South America

South American countries have a range of climates. Some countries are virtually landlocked, while others have long shorelines. Early groups that settled South and Central America developed a culture and cuisine that relied heavily upon seafood, meat, grains, root vegetables, fruits, and corn.

Prior to European influence, South America contained one major civilization: the Incas. The Incan civilization cultivated the fringes and valleys of the Andes Mountains of Peru. These northern Andean people constructed rock-faced terraced landscapes to provide suitable arable land. Their staple food was the potato. However, they also farmed other vegetables and grains, such as quinoa, a high-protein grain well suited for agriculture in the rough terrain of the Andes. The remainder of the continent consisted of hunter-gatherer societies until the advent of European exploration in the sixteenth century.

CLOCKWISE FROM LEFT: chihuahua, cotija, queso fresco, sardo

LEFT TO RIGHT, FROM TOP TO BOTTOM: **taro root, bananas, green and red peppers, mango, avocado, papaya, starfruit, dried habañeros, malaguetas, tomatillos, plantains, chipotle en adobo, tamarind, pepitas**

South America today can be broken into four geographic regions:

Guyana Subregion

The countries of Guyana and Suriname make up the Guyana subregion, which is divided from the Amazon River Basin by the Guyana Mountain range on the southern border and on the north by the Atlantic Ocean. The agriculture in the Guyana subregion is largely based on rice and sugarcane.

Andean Subregion

The Andean subregion encompasses Bolivia, Columbia, Ecuador, Peru, and Venezuela and includes an important geographic feature—the Andean Mountains. The climate in this region is quite varied. Here, cacao and coffee are the chief cash crops. However, a variety of native products, such as maize and beans, tubers, roots, and grains are also grown in this region; they are not typically grown for export, but for subsistence.

The terrain of landlocked Bolivia falls from the rugged Andes Mountains, with a highland plateau (Altiplano), to the hills and lowland plains of the Amazon Basin. Its climate varies with altitude from humid and tropical to cold and semiarid. Bolivian subsistence farmers grow barley, potatoes, and even some wheat, which is not a typical crop for the terrain of this region. Alpacas and llamas are raised for wool.

Colombia's geography is composed of flat coastal lowlands, central highlands, high Andes Mountains, and eastern lowland plains. The general high altitude of Colombia keeps temperatures cool except along the coast and eastern plains, where the climate is tropical. Besides cacao and coffee, Colombia also exports bananas, rice, and sugarcane. The large cattle ranches in the region are called *estancias*.

Ecuador encompasses not only the coastal plain, the Andean central highlands, and the jungle, but also the Galapagos Islands. The climate in this country is cooler inland at higher elevations and tropical along the coast and in the Amazonian jungle lowlands. Agriculture is the most important activity in Ecuador's economy. Bananas, cacao, coffee, rice, and sugarcane are grown in the coastal lowlands, while inland farmers produce potatoes, beans, corn, and coffee. Ecuador was the birthplace for beef jerky, originally called *charqui* in Quechua. Both European and Native Indian influences can be seen in Ecuadorian food. Food preferences differ in the coastal and inland areas. People from the coast tend to eat fish, beans, and plantains, while inhabitants farther inland eat meat, rice, and potatoes.

Peru has had a major influence on the cuisine of South America. Peru is dominated by dry deserts, snowcapped mountains, and hot, humid rain forests. Cities and agricultural lands have developed in the narrow coastal plains. Native cultural roots are strong here, where the Incan language, *Quechua*, is still spoken in many villages. Subsistence farms grow peanuts, potatoes, sweet potatoes, rice, plantains, and corn. In Peru there is cuisine from the sea, as well as from the land. The dishes today are based on the food of the pre-Columbian natives, along with elements borrowed from the Spanish. Aside from the expected culinary influences in Peru, there is also an Asian influence in the preparation of shellfish and fish.

Venezuela's chief geographical features include the Andes Mountains and Maracaibo Lowlands in the northwest, and the central plains (*llanos*) and Guiana Highlands in the southeast. The climate ranges from tropical, hot, and humid to more temperate in the highlands. Venezuela has seen a reduced output of traditional food crops such as yucca (cassava) and potatoes. This is primarily due to the migration of farmers to more urban areas. Farmers in this region grow a number of different crops, from vegetables to fruits and even spices.

Brazilian Subregion

The country of Brazil is considered a region unto itself; it is the fifth largest country in the world. Brazil represents 42 percent of the total area of South America and is only slightly smaller than the contiguous United States. Brazil's topography includes mostly flat to rolling lowlands in the north and plains, hills, mountains, and a narrow coastal belt (the Brazilian highlands). The climate is mostly tropical, hot, and humid, but temperate in the south. Brazil produces many crops for export: coffee, sugarcane, coconuts, wheat, maize, rice, and soybeans. Brazil is also a major producer of fruits: tropical, such as bananas and melons in the north, and citrus and grapes in the more moderate southern climate. There is a strong Portuguese influence throughout Brazil, as the Portuguese were "given" Brazil when Spain received the rest of South America. The Spanish have also had an impact, as have the West Africans who have maintained their culture despite years of slavery in the country. The West African influence on cuisine can be seen in the major crops that have been assimilated, such as bananas, coconuts, yams, okra, many beans, spices, and a small hot chile called a malagueta. Rice became a staple food early on and has persisted. The cuisine is also influenced by the Italians, Dutch, Germans, Middle Easterners, French, Asians, and even U.S. Southerners.

Southern Subregion

The final region on this large continent is the southern subregion, which includes Argentina, Chile, Paraguay, and Uruguay.

Argentina is the largest of the countries in this region. The plains of the Pampas in northern half are rich in agriculture. The climate in the flat to rolling plateau of Patagonia in the south and in the rugged Andes along the western border ranges from cold to sub-Antarctic. The country produces wheat and cereal grains for export along with fruit, sugarcane, and wine grapes. A large percentage of land is also devoted to pasture and raising livestock such as cattle, sheep, and pigs. Argentinean cuisine has its roots in Italian and Spanish cooking. The diet is heavily focused on meats such as lamb, goat, and especially beef. Pork has also gained in popularity; traditional favorites also include rabbit, venison, boar, llama, and *cuy* (guinea-pig-size dog).

Chile, with low coastal mountains, a fertile central valley, and the rugged Andes in the east, has many different climates, from temperate to hot, arid desert in the north, Mediterranean climate in the central region, and cool and damp in the south. Agriculture produces wheat, corn, beans, sugar, and potatoes. Grapes and apples are also widely grown. Cattle, sheep, and other livestock are raised.

Paraguay's climate is subtropical to temperate, with substantial rainfall in the eastern portions, becoming semiarid in the far west. Grassy plains and wooded hills characterize the land east of Rio Paraguay, while the Gran Chaco region west of Rio Paraguay is mostly low, marshy plain near the river, and dry forest and thorny scrub elsewhere. Paraguay is slightly smaller than California, and produces manioc, potatoes, and beans.

Uruguay has a warm, temperate climate; freezing temperatures are almost unknown. Its landscape is mostly rolling plains and low hills, with some fertile coastal lowlands. Uruguay's greatest natural resource is its rich agricultural land, almost 90 percent of which is devoted to raising livestock. Cattle, sheep, horses, and pigs are the major livestock animals. Grains for cattle fattening and human consumption make up the bulk of the harvested crops. Rice is the major food crop, followed by wheat and sugarcane.

Common Latin American Ingredients

Grains, Beans, and Nuts

Amaranth
Black beans
Cacao
Kidney beans
Maize
Peanuts
Pecans
Pepitas (pumpkin seeds)
Pinto beans
Rice
Quinoa
Sesame seeds

Herbs and Spices

Achiote
Avocado leaves
Banana leaves
Cilantro
Epazote
Hoja santa
Mexican oregano
Piloncillo

Vegetables

Broccoli
Cactus paddles (*nopalitos*)
Chard
Chiles
Corn
Eggplant
Kale
Lettuce
Okra
Onions
Spinach
Sweet peppers
Tomatillos
Tomatoes
Turnips
Zucchini

Tubers and Squash

Arracacha
Cassava
Chayote
Jícama
Malanga
Potatoes
Pumpkins
Squash blossoms
Sweet potatoes

Taro
Yucca

Fruits

Avocados
Bananas
Breadfruit
Cherimoya
Grapes
Guanabana
Guava
Kiwi
Limes
Mangos
Oranges
Papaya
Pineapples
Plums
Prickly pears
Quince
Tamarind

Meat

Beef
Cavy (guinea pig)
Goat
Lamb
Llama
Pork
Rabbit

Poultry

Chicken
Duck
Turkey

Fish and Shellfish

Mussels
Salmon
Sea bass
Shrimp
Snapper
Squid

Dairy Products

Crema
Goat cheese
Queso anejo
Queso chihuahua
Queso fresco
Queso ranchero

Chapter Six

Asia

Asian cuisine differs from the rest of the world in that this region more than any other developed with minimal influence from outside. With this said, it is also important to note that when cultural exchange did occur, the inhabitants embraced ingredients from the outside world and assimilated them into their cuisine. This cuisine also has a greater diversity of ingredients and techniques than any other.

China

Chinese cuisine is characterized by four distinctive cooking styles: northern (Beijing/Peking style), southern (Cantonese style), eastern/coastal (Shanghai style), and western/inland (Szechwan style)—with numerous variations of each style within each region.

Situated in the eastern part of Asia, China encompasses an area larger than 3 million square miles (8 million square kilometers). With miles of mountainous terrain, the spacious territory is home to many rivers, thousands of lakes, and a long coastline on the Pacific Ocean. China is one of the largest countries in the world, with a population of more than one billion people.

Only 10 percent of China's land is used for cultivation purposes. At times, dramatic shifts in temperature and climate wreak havoc on its generally abundant agriculture. The ever-growing population and expanding cities threaten to inhabit even more of the already inadequate space. Raising animals such as cattle and sheep is made difficult due to insufficient pastureland.

Considering that China is roughly the size of the United States, it isn't hard to imagine its diversity. Each of its regions—northern, southern, eastern (coastal), and western—have different climatic and geographical characteristics, and as with any territory, changes in terrain and weather conditions determine the crops that inspire each region's culinary development and preferences.

Regional Cuisines

Northern China

In the north, China is relatively cold and arid, with a typically dry, level terrain. The Beijing/Peking province sees frigid winter weather, leading to a growing season that is much shorter than that of other regions.

Having been the site of the Imperial Court, the northern cuisine exemplifies creativity, ingenuity, and sophistication. The lavish and traditional three-course Peking duck, served with spring onions and hoisin sauce, is an example of the area's culinary refinement. This region makes use of intense seasonings in a simple, delicate manner, but is also well known for its pungent, sweet-and-sour dishes.

Typical crops include wheat, corn, soybeans, bok choy, napa cabbage, root vegetables, eggplants, persimmons, pomegranates, peaches, pears, apples, grapes, and jujube dates. Chestnuts, walnuts, and peanuts are

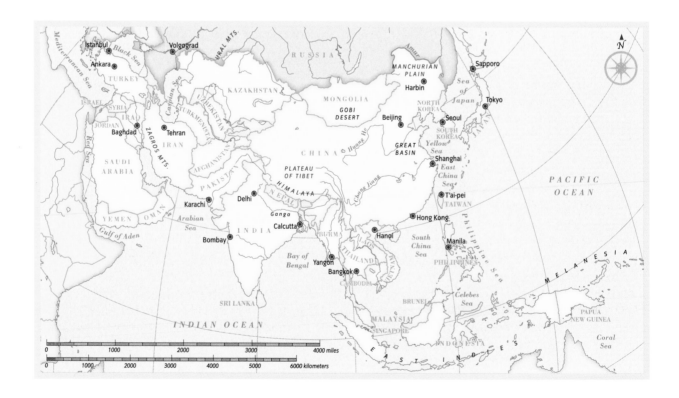

also grown in this area. These ingredients, along with garlic, green onions, and dark soy sauce lend distinct flavor principles to the area. Wheat items such as noodles, breads, dumplings, and pancakes are common.

Mongolian influences are also still apparent in the region's dishes, specifically the use of lamb and mutton, the commonality of barbecued meat dishes, and fire pot specialties (one-dish meals reminiscent of fondue). Hotpot meals include custom-blended condiments for each diner and platters of meat and vegetables. Diners use chopsticks to dip the food items into simmering liquid (broth, oil, etc.) and then place the food into their bowls, to which they can add flavorings and/or condiments. Mongolian barbecue is similar, except the ingredients are grilled and placed in buns for eating.

Southern China

The hills and low mountains of the southern region are scattered with a number of rivers, lakes, and streams. With a small portion of the land flat enough for row cropping, the heavy rainfall and abundant sunshine in and around the Cantonese province welcomes a long growing season, including two rice harvests per year.

The southern Cantonese style of cooking is a display of succulence with its masterly blend of different flavors. It is the most known style of Chinese cooking among westerners. Cantonese dishes use little seasonings; they are flavored in a simple manner featuring a minimal level of spiciness.

The principal crops of this region are rice, sugarcane, mulberries, and freshwater fish. A variety of exotic fruits, including lychee, longan, loquats, citrus, olives, guava, bananas, papayas, pineapples, and coconuts, are also produced in this area. Vegetables such as snow peas, Chinese broccoli, taro, tiger lily, bamboo shoots, lotus roots, lotus seeds, water chestnuts, squash, pumpkins, mushrooms, and beans are grown throughout the region.

Hoisin, plum, oyster, and light soy sauces are typical cooking condiments, along with garlic. Seafood is commonly used, as well as blanched vegetables, and whole suckling pigs. The Cantonese prefer quick cooking styles such as stir-frying and steaming to highlight the natural flavor, color, and texture of the fresh ingredients. Additional cooking techniques used in the Cantonese region are barbecuing, roasting, and simmering. Foods are oftentimes undercooked to bring out the natural flavors. *Dim sum* and lacquered meats are popular preparations in the area.

Eastern China

The mild climate of the eastern/coastal region results from hot, humid summers and short, moderate winters. The low, flat terrain in the Shanghai province provides for productive agriculture and ample fishing.

In the eastern region along the coast, Shanghai and its neighbor, Fukien, rely heavily on soy sauce, sugar, and ginger for flavoring agents. Fukien is known for producing the most highly regarded soy sauce in China. Natural flavors are accentuated by keeping dishes light and delicate. To emphasize the fresh ingredients, eastern chefs prefer stir-frying, steaming, "red" cooking (see page 56), and blanching. Pickling and curing are often used to preserve meat and vegetables.

This "land of fish and rice" is abundant in freshwater and saltwater fish and seafood, specifically carp and crabs. Livestock is also commonly raised here, including chickens, ducks, pigs, and cattle. The primary food crops include rice and wheat. Barley, corn (maize), and sweet potatoes are the region's secondary crops. Additionally, a variety of bamboo shoots, beans, melons, gourds, squashes, and leafy vegetables, as well as peaches, plums, and grapes are cultivated in eastern China. Shaoxing wine (yellow grain wine), Chinkiang vinegar (Chinese black vinegar used as a dipping sauce and condiment), and Jinhua ham (smoky cured ham) also commonly contribute to the cuisine's flavor profile.

Western China

The western region of China sees very little rainfall, while the inland areas of this region experience monsoon conditions. Depending on the location, agriculture can be very productive, with a growing season lasting nearly all year. In the western parts, the landscape mainly consists of mountainous ground or enclosed desert basins. With extremely dry conditions, little farming is achieved. Irrigation is essential to successfully make use of the land.

The western/inland region of Szechwan is revered for its highly seasoned dishes. The most prominent dishes are hot and sour and are often oily, a possible influence of neighboring India and Pakistan.

The area encompassing the Szechwan province raises a significant amount of poultry, as well as the largest number of cattle and pigs in China. Rice, corn, and sweet potatoes are produced here, along with wheat, rapeseed, sorghum, barley, soybeans, millet, sugarcane, citrus fruits, tung nuts, and tea.

The area's condiments and spices are quite strong. The chile, for example, appears in several forms: roasted with salt and ground, fresh, in pastes, and infused in oil. Onions, garlic, dried citrus peel, ginger, dried black mushrooms, and fungus (cloud ear or wood ear), as well as sesame oil and fermented broad bean paste, contribute to the cuisine's characteristic flavors. Beef, lamb, chicken, and fish are prepared throughout the region. Although the Szechwan cooking style makes use of all techniques, stir-frying and steaming are most popular.

Cooking Techniques

Red stewing/red cooking (*hung-shu*)—This technique is unique to Chinese cooking. The process involves cooking the food (usually pork, beef, ham, chicken, duck, or carp) in large quantities of soy sauce and water. It is similar to stewing. The soy sauce contributes to the rich taste and reddish-brown color created by using this technique.

Velvetting—A process in which meat, fish, or seafood is coated with cornstarch, egg whites, rice wine, and salt. This is done to retain moisture, producing a succulent dish. The coating also allows for sauce to adhere better to the finished dish.

Lacquer roasting—A technique performed in the Cantonese region. The food item, such as poultry, ribs, pieces of beef, or back bacon, receives several coats of a high-sugar mixture (honey, corn syrup, maltose, or sugar with an oil or soy sauce). After roasting, the meat has a glossy, crispy finish with a subtle sweetness.

A Meal in China

As in the West, traditional family meals and formal dinners are quite different from each other. Family-style meals include a staple ingredient (rice, noodles, steamed breads, or pancakes). This provides the bulk of the meal. The secondary items are prepared in small quantities and consist of meat or poultry, fish or seafood, a vegetable, and soup (served as the beverage). When presented, the items are served together and diners help themselves to each dish. The meal nears completion when the rice bowls are empty. At this point, they are filled with soup to indicate the meal is over.

In contrast, dining at a restaurant or banquet involves ten to fourteen courses. The organized affair presents each course in a particular order, beginning with a cold platter. Dishes that pair well with wine are the next to arrive, allowing for a time to drink and to toast. The main dishes (*da cai*) are elaborate and usually involve meat, fish, or poultry served whole. Dishes meant to accompany rice, such as vegetables or tofu, are served next. The meal also involves a variety of soups or pastries if it is a conventional affair. These items are meant to cleanse the palate, preparing the diner for the next dish.

LEFT TO RIGHT, FROM TOP TO BOTTOM: Thai cilantro, lotus root, rau rum, chrysanthemum greens, rice paper, nori, water chestnuts, Thai eggplant, bok choy, Thai red bird chiles, dried Thai red bird chiles, *kim chee*, lychee nuts, soba noodles, arame (top), kelp (bottom), wakame, star anise, azuki beans, jasmine rice, coconut milk, shiitake mushrooms, mung beans, soybeans, enoki mushrooms, dried shiitake mushrooms, rice flour, five-spice powder, ground Sichuan peppers, dried black mushrooms

LEFT TO RIGHT, FROM TOP TO BOTTOM: sushi rice, green onions, soy sauce, rice wine, ginger, sesame oil, tofu, garlic

Equipment

Tools for Chinese cooking are fairly basic. For centuries, China's cooks have invested a great deal of time and effort achieving certain results with minimal utensils. The principal implements are as follows:

Wok—All-purpose cooking vessel developed by the Chinese. The wok has a round bottom with high, sloping sides. It is available in a variety of sizes and is made of materials such as cast iron, rolled steel, anodized aluminum, and stainless steel. Woks typically have one (Peking or northern style) or two handles (Cantonese or southern style) and are usually accompanied by a ring-shaped stand and a dome lid. The wok can be used for stir-frying, smoking, steaming, deep fry-ing, braising, and poaching. Its shape makes tossing ingredients easy and offers an extended cooking surface.

Chopsticks (*phai-tzi*)—These cooking and eating utensils were created in China and are widely used in Asia, specifically China, Japan, Korea, Vietnam, and Thailand. They range in sizes and materials (bamboo, ivory, plastic, or lacquered wood). Long chopsticks are used for stir-frying or deep frying. Shorter varieties of chopsticks are best suited for eating and for mixing batters, sauces, or marinades.

Cleaver (*dai doh; tsoi doh*)—A versatile instrument, the cleaver is used for cutting, tenderizing, and flattening. The Chinese cleaver comes in several sizes: light, used in chopping

Common Chinese Ingredients

Grains

Barley

Corn

Millet

Rice

Sorghum (*gaoling*)

Wheat

Staple Ingredients

Millet

Rice

Soybeans

Wheat

General Flavor Profile

Garlic

Ginger

Green onions

Soy sauce

Condiments and Cooking Liquids

Bean sauce

Broad bean paste

Chili paste

Chinese rice vinegar (white, red, and black)

Duck sauce

Hoisin sauce

Hot bean paste

Oyster sauce

Plum sauce

Rice wine (Shaoxing)

Salted black beans

Sesame oil

Sesame paste

Soy sauce (light/thin, dark/thick, mushroom)

Sweet-salty sauce

Seasonings

Anise seeds

Chiles

Cinnamon

Dried shrimp

Fennel seeds

Fermented black beans

Five-spice powder

Garlic

Ginger

Green onions

Star anise

Szechwan pepper (*fagara*)

Fresh, Dried, and Pickled Fruits and Vegetables, and Beans and Legumes

Adzuki beans

Bamboo shoots

Bean sprouts (mung and soybean)

Carrots

Chinese broccoli

Chinese cabbage (bok choy)

Chinese celery

Chrysanthemum greens

Daikon radishes

Dried black mushrooms

Dried citrus peel (orange and tangerine)

Dried fungus (cloud ear and wood ear)

Lotus roots and seeds

Melons (fuzzy and winter)

Mung beans

Mushrooms

Mustard greens

Napa cabbage

Onions

Potatoes

Pumpkins

Seaweed (*zicai*, kelp, agar agar, and *facai*)

Taro

Tiger lily buds

Spinach

Sweet potatoes

Water chestnuts

Watercress

Proteins

Fowl (chicken, duck, goose, pigeons)

Freshwater fish (carp, catfish, perch, salmon, shad, trout)

Game (armadillos, cranes, deer, hare, partridge, raccoons, roe-bucks, quail, tortoises, wild ducks)

Meat (including organ meats; beef, lamb, mutton, pork)

Seafood (clams, crabs, fish, lobster, prawns, oysters, scallops, shrimp, squid, cuttle fish)

Soybean (bean curd (tofu), dried, fermented, fresh, paste, milk, sauce, sprouts, *tempeh*)

Wheat gluten

Sweeteners

Brown sugar

Rock sugar

vegetables and seasonings; medium, used in cutting various ingredients; and heavy, used in cutting through tough, dense items. Cleavers are available in carbon steel and stainless steel.

Bamboo steamer (*jing loong*)—This type of steamer efficiently absorbs steam, creating a very hot container without condensation. The food remains free of excess moisture and cooks quickly and evenly even when stacked high with many levels. The traditional Chinese bamboo steamer has two layers and a lid.

Mongolian fire pot or hot pot (*ho go*)—A pot created specifically for all fire-pot cooking. Fire-pot cooking is similar to fondue, allowing diners to cook their own food. Fire pots are available in brass, copper, and steel. The two most common types both require a heat source. The first includes a chafing dish that holds the hot cooking liquid and is heated by either a Sterno or an alcohol lamp. The other, more impressive, hot pot includes a device that holds charcoal. A chimney is attached to a ring-shaped pan containing the boiling cooking liquid.

Clay pot/sand pot—Made from a mixture of clay and sand, this heavy pot is used for braising, stewing, and casserole cooking. It is ideal for slow cooking because it distributes heat efficiently and can withstand direct heat. It is available in a variety of shapes and sizes.

Cultural Influences on Chinese Cuisine

The Chinese have been intrigued with the art of cooking for centuries, from the proper selection of ingredients to the use of specific methods and tools. Nearly 3,000 years ago, the fascination became apparent when China's first "recipes" were conceived. Today, it has been estimated that at least 80,000 dishes have been created.

Attention to detail is an integral part of preparing a Chinese dish. The food is expected to appeal to both the eye and the palate. The colors should be aesthetically pleasing, the fragrances should arouse the senses, and the ingredients should be uniform in size. And all of these elements should be aimed toward creating balance.

These tenets to the approach of Chinese cuisine can be traced back to historical events as well as religious and philosophical systems that have been in place in China for centuries.

The importance of cuisine in China is evident as early as the Tang dynasty (618–907 A.D.) with creation of both the first known cookbook and nutrition text. During the Song dynasty (960–1279 A.D.), China experienced a significant height in prosperity. The abundant economic and cultural growth resulted in spurring interest in cuisine. Chinese food writers, cooks, nutritionists, merchants, and wealthy consumers took part in creating a style of cooking and eating. Tradition was maintained while experimentation was encouraged. Food needed to be appealing, both to the eye and to the palate. In the Ming (1368–1644 A.D.) and the Ching dynasties (1644–1911 A.D.) Chinese cuisine as we know it today began to develop. This period of "imperial China" heavily influenced the cuisine, demanding more time, care, and attention be given to dishes.

In 1911, China became a republic when the dynastic system was overturned. Western influences flourished by the 1920s, bringing such delicacies as French-style custard tarts, ice cream, and European utensils and appliances.

By the end of the 1970s, China strove to regain the culinary brilliance it had once experienced during the centuries of imperialistic regime. The depression of civil war and devastation never destroyed China's interest in the quality of food and its preparation. With indigenous ingredients, as well as those introduced from other societies, China has enhanced its distinct cuisines.

Foreign trade, war, and invasion introduced foodstuffs to the Chinese palate that were traditionally unavailable. Trade during the Tang dynasty introduced items such as eggplant, spinach, pumpkin, dill, nutmeg, saffron, and peppercorns. Peaceful times experienced during the Ming and Ching dynasties influenced numerous voyages and extensive foreign trade. Explorers were sent westward along the spice routes. They passed through Persia, Turkey, the greater Middle East, North Africa, the Balkans, and Rome. Other expeditions took voyagers to India and Southeast Asia. A variety of items were brought into China through these

A Note on MSG (Monosodium Glutamate)

Developed by Japanese scientists, MSG was introduced to China in the 1930s. MSG (glutamic acid) can be manufactured through several different methods, including microbial fermentation, hydrolysis of proteins such as gluten, and synthesis. Free glutamic acid, however, naturally occurs in many common foods such as mushrooms and tomatoes. MSG enlivens the flavor of bland food and can mask undesirable flavors in processed foods. Chefs tend to frown upon its usage, while skilled eastern chefs will use it in moderation just like salt or sugar.

How Does It Affect Flavor?

Only recently has it been recognized that the tongue not only perceives sweet, sour, salty, and bitter, but a fifth taste sensation called *umami,* roughly translated as "savory" or "meaty." It was Professor Kikunae Ikeda of the University of Tokyo who first used the term *umami* in 1908. He is credited with isolating glutamate in the Japanese stock dashi; it was refined from the *Laminara japonica*—also known as *kombu*—the kelp used in the preparation of dashi.

To affect flavor, glutamate must be "free"—that is, not bound to other amino acids—as it often occurs naturally. The amount of free amino acids in a food increases as fruit ripens, meat ages, and through fermentation, improving flavor. Glutamate harmonizes especially well with foods that contain sour and salty components.

travels. Foreign trade brought new ingredients such as snow peas from Holland, watercress from Portugal, and tomatoes, corn, potatoes, and chiles from the New World.

Through the centuries, religion has also proved to be a powerful force in the formation of Chinese cuisine. From Taoism and Confucianism, to Buddhism and the teachings of Islam, the influence of religion on food is apparent in the expression of the goals of finding balance and inner peace, and displaying respect, which are all integral to the recurring theme—creating harmony.

Due in large part to the religious influences in China, Chinese cuisine has developed a legacy of ingredients and recipes that continue to affect the world of vegetarian cuisine. Although Buddhism cannot be held accountable for the beginnings of alternative forms of protein such as legumes (especially soybeans and mung beans), it did lead to the development of various legume, wheat gluten, and soybean substitutes for meat. Buddhist chefs mimicked the rich and savory taste and mouthfeel of pork, beef, chicken, and duck with the use of these products. Among the meat substitutes that created the strongest impact was bean curd (tofu) made from soybeans. With soybeans already an integral part of the Chinese diet, Buddhism further stimulated its use throughout the country.

India

Throughout history, India's borders have seen the passage of many in search of its distinctly aromatic spices. From cardamom to turmeric, the spices of India have led to the creation of one of the world's most flavorful cuisines. As a nation of twenty-eight states, distinct regional cuisines showcasing seasonal ingredients and unique cooking techniques can be found from the wheat-bearing north to the rice-laden south. Each section boasts particular culinary preferences shaped by agricultural, historical, and religious influences.

Standing as the second most populous country in the world on 1.3 million square miles (3.4 million square kilometers) in southern Asia, the peninsula of India extends into the Indian Ocean, with the Arabian Sea to the west and the Bay of Bengal to the east. Bordering countries include Pakistan, China, Bangladesh, Nepal, Bhutan, and Myanmar (Burma). With the exception of the Himalayas in the northern territory, the majority of India is relatively flat. There are three main river systems that trail through the country, including the sacred Ganges. The climate is dictated by the country's intermittent rains that bring three weather conditions to nearly all of the country: hot, wet, and cool.

More than half of India's land is used for cultivation purposes. Nevertheless, the country has relied on importation to feed its ever-increasing population. Through improved farming techniques, widespread irrigation usage, and high-yield grains, India has recently been able to supply its citizens with more product than ever before. Principal crops include grains, pulses (legumes), sugarcane, fruits, vegetables, tea, coffee, and specialty crops such as chiles, spices, cashew nuts, and betel leaf (*paan*).

With strong religious taboos against the ingestion of meat in some areas, livestock is limited. Animals do, however, play a crucial role in agriculture assistance, transportation, dairy products, leather, wool, and dung for fuel and fertilizer. Fish supplied from the surrounding seas and rivers add variety to the cuisine.

Regional Cuisines

The many similarities between the culinary regions of India are highlighted with an exquisite use of spices and flavorings. These range from cardamom, cumin, cloves, fennel seeds, and garlic to ginger, chiles, fenugreek, saffron, and turmeric. Spice mixtures, or *masalas*, are a crucial element of Indian cuisine. Whether fresh or dried, *masalas* make use of local ingredients and are prepared daily, along with grains, pulses, and vegetables.

While meat, poultry, fish, and seafood dishes are offered throughout India, most vegetarian specialties are found in the central and southern regions. For an added dimension of flavor, a variety of fruits are served fresh or pickled, such as chutney and relish. Dairy products, such as clarified butter (ghee), cheese (*paneer*), yogurt, milk, and buttermilk (*moru*), are used as ingredients and condiments. *Raita* is a popular chilled yogurt condiment garnished with chopped fruit or vegetables and spices.

Dal preparations (dried legumes and pulses) are at the center of Indian meals. When combined with grains, they provide an inexpensive source of essential protein. *Dals* are prepared whole and puréed and are generally served with vegetables and meat, where accepted. In the northern regions, thick and hearty stew-like dals are eaten with bread, while the thinner preparations of the south are best suited for rice. *Channa dal* or gram lentils are the most widely grown *dal* in India. Used both as protein and starch, garbanzos and lentils supply the base for breads, crêpes, and thickeners for curries. Other types of *dals* commonly eaten include peas, kidney beans, mung beans, and split peas.

Served at nearly every meal, vegetables are one of India's most significant ingredients. India's perfected vegetable cookery offers rich and flavorful dishes, ranging from appetizers and side dishes to entrées and condiments. Vegetables are frequently baked, deep fried, roasted, braised, sautéed, puréed, and stuffed. Dairy products, fruits, nuts, spices, and seasonings are used to embellish greens (*palak*), eggplant, gourds, roots, and squash, while caramelized onions and tomatoes provide the foundation for many sauces and stews. Cauliflower and potatoes (*alu gobi*), peas and potatoes (*alu mattar*), peas and cheese (*mattar paneer*), and spinach and cheese (*saag paneer*) are popular vegetable combinations.

From breads to rice-based dishes, grains and starches are present at each meal as well, commonly served alongside curries, meats, seafood, dals, vegetables, and condiments. In the northern states, bread is primarily made of wheat flour. The central and southern areas use flour made from ground lentils, garbanzos, mung beans, corn, or rice. See Breads (*Rotis*) sidebar, page 64.

There are several types of rice grown and eaten in India, from long-grain and medium-grain to glutinous and wild. While basmati is generally reserved for special occasions, plain boiled rice is served with everyday meals, especially in the southern areas. One-pot rice dishes, such as *biryani,* a combination of basmati rice, meat or seafood, vegetables, and expensive spices, and *pulao* (pilaf), a slow-cooked dish of vegetables, spices, nuts, fruits, and meat, seafood, or yogurt are oftentimes prepared for celebrations and religious festivals.

North India

The rich and hearty fare of the north is found in several states, including Kashmir, Punjab, Delhi, Rajasthan, Gujarat, and West Bengal. In the north, bread provides a fundamental element of most meals. Muslim-inspired meat dishes and the area's predominantly dry curries feature goat, lamb, and sheep. *Masalas* make use of dry spices, which are ground and pan fried before they are added to a dish. *Garam masala,* or "hot spices," is a pungent seasoning used in small quantities to flavor meat, poultry, and rice. Rarely used to flavor fish and vegetables, the potent spice mixture often includes bay leaves, black cardamom, black pepper, black cumin, cinnamon, cloves, mace, and nutmeg. In the north, sauces are enhanced with cream and nuts. Ghee is used to cook meat and mustard oil is sometimes used to prepare vegetables. Principal cuisines include *tandoori* and the Moghul-influenced Moghlai.

Beginning in the northern state of Kashmir, mountainous land and colder temperatures provide ideal growing conditions for wheat, nuts (almonds, walnuts), fruits (strawberries, cherries, apricots, pears, pomegranates), vegetables (turnips, tomatoes, beans, peas, cabbage), and cumin. Saffron, one of the world's most expensive spices, has been cultivated here since the third century B.C.E. and features prominently in Kashmiri dishes.

Dried fruits, vegetables, and nuts add flavor and texture to food and supply nutrients during long winters when fresh produce is limited. Rice is used in a

Curry: Not Just an Indian Specialty

Research indicates that curry has existed in India since before the birth of Christ. However, it wasn't until many years later that curry was used in other cuisines. In the nineteenth century, Indians traveled to foreign lands for trade and labor. When Indian cooking techniques and recipes were combined with local ingredients, outsiders eagerly adopted India's distinct cooking styles and flavor preferences. Today, curries are prepared all over the world, from Thailand, South Africa, and Britain, to Indonesia, Trinidad, Japan, and the United States.

To many, the word *curry* is considered a mistranslation of the word *kari* or *kaari,* meaning "sauce." Those who believe this theory conclude that the spelling changed to "curry" when the British moved to the area. Although curry is often thought of as a hot and spicy dish, in India it refers to any dish accompanied by a sauce that is used to moisten grains or enhance flatbreads. Curry sauces come in a variety of colors, depending on the primary ingredient (red: tomato; yellow: turmeric and cumin; green: spinach, mint, cilantro or green chiles; and white: coconut), and consistencies (wet and dry). The order that ingredients and seasonings are added during the cooking process determines the consistency. Because spices release their flavor and aroma at different stages, timing is essential.

For wet curries, seasonings are generally added at the end of cooking. Dry curries, on the other hand, usually require cooking the spices and flavorings together first. To finish a dry curry, the main ingredients are added to the seasonings and the sauce is reduced. This results in a flavorful coating that clings to the food items. Examples of dry curries include marinated *tandoori* dishes and *tikka* kebabs (grilled pieces of marinated meat).

Breads (Rotis)

Many types of bread are made throughout India. In the northern states, they constitute an essential part of every meal, supplying fundamental nutrients and a utensil to eat with. Ranging from deep fried to *tandoor* baked, Indian breads can be soft and warm or thin and crisp. They provide the ideal accompaniment for saucy vegetarian curries and chunky meat dishes. The following breads are a sample of the varieties found in India.

Chapati—Thin, light-textured unleavened bread made from whole wheat flour. Common in central and southern India, *chapati* is prepared on a hot griddle known as a *tava*. *Chapati* dough is used to prepare a number of *rotis*, common daily breads. This pita-like bread is best served with spicy curry dishes.

Kulcha—Leavened white flour bread with a potato stuffing, brushed with ghee, and baked in a *tandoor* oven.

Naan—Soft and puffy leavened flatbread traditionally made of wheat flour and fermented yogurt. Contemporary recipes use other types of leaveners, such as yeast, baking soda, or self-rising flour. Additional ingredients (onion, garlic, etc.) are added for flavored varieties. Baked on the walls of a hot *tandoor* oven, the light texture of *naan* complements any dish.

Paratha—Flat and flaky unleavened bread similar to *chapati*. Unlike *chapati*, *paratha* is enriched with ghee, resulting in a richer flavor. To create puffy, pastry-like bread, the dough is rolled and folded several times prior to shallow frying. Plain *parathas* are eaten with many dishes; stuffed varieties are generally served as snacks.

Poori (*puri*)—Puffy bread made from firm *chapati* dough. To prepare, the dough is rolled into small circles and fried in oil one at a time. While frying, each circle of dough is covered with oil so that it results in a steam-filled pocket of bread. Spices can be added for variety. Traditionally served for breakfast, *poori* can be eaten any time of the day.

Poppadum (*pappadam*)—Thin, crispy wafers made from dried beans or split peas. Spices are often included. *Poppadums* are rolled paper thin, dried in the sun, and served either deep fried or grilled. Similar to crackers, they provide the perfect accompaniment to vegetarian dishes and are ideal for snacking.

variety of sweet and savory preparations, and breads such as *kulchas* (leavened and enriched wheat-flour bread) are common. Heavily influenced by Moghlai cuisine, the dishes found in Kashmir are rich and flavorful, displaying a lavish use of lamb and ghee. *Rogan josh* (lamb curry stewed with tomatoes and yogurt) is a perfect example of this.

Punjab, located south of Kashmir, is home to one of India's most abundant grain-growing regions. Wheat, barley, corn, and millet are plentiful, as well as vegetables, mustard, and sugarcane. Punjab's vast farm country also produces a significant amount of milk, yogurt, and ghee. The area's predominantly vegetarian Sikh population and the renowned *tandoori*-style cooking shape the cuisine of Punjab. At the heart of *tandoori* cuisine is an open, barrel-shaped clay oven known as a *tandoor*. While bread was the first item ever baked in a *tandoor*, meat has become a common *tandoori* preparation. This is found in *raan mussalam,* a tender roasted leg of lamb marinated with yogurt and papaya. Today, Punjab is known for its variety of oven-baked breads including *naan* and other *tandoori rotis*.

The national capital territory of Delhi is situated directly south of Punjab. Once the center of the grand Moghul dynasty, Delhi cuisine is a mix of traditional Moghlai cooking and Punjabi food. The lavish Moghlai cuisine blends Hindu- and Muslim-influenced foods with Persian techniques and ingredients, such as saffron, nuts, and cream. Tomatoes are combined with browned onions to create Moghul curry sauce. *Paalag gosht* (lamb with spinach) and Moghlai-style kebabs commonly feature lamb, a favorite of Moghul cooking. Garlic, ginger, almonds, and pistachios add flavor and texture to numerous dishes.

Moghlai's elaborate preparations have greatly influenced the cooking styles of northern India, as seen in *biryanis, pulaos,* and *kormas.* Like *biryani, korma* is a dish commonly served at banquets and parties. A *korma*-style dish blends meat or seafood with exotic spices and nuts in a thick and creamy yogurt-based sauce. Today, the internationally known Moghlai specialties are a lighter version of the traditional favorites, using less ghee, cream, and nuts.

The dry and arid state of Rajasthan is found southwest of Delhi along the Pakistan border. Similar to Moghlai cuisine, the cooking of Rajasthan includes elaborate rice and meat dishes made with chicken, lamb, and pork. Traditional dishes include skewered and grilled meats marinated in yogurt and spices. Dried ingredients (vegetables and pulses) used in *dal* preparations add to the Rajasthan diet. Flour made from dried chickpeas or dried mung beans is used to prepare steamed or sun-dried dumplings. The dumplings are then sautéed and served with a spicy, yogurt-based sauce.

Located in central India, along the northwest coastline, the state of Gujarat is situated between Mumbai (formerly Bombay) and the Pakistani border. Crops grown in this semiarid state include millets, wheat, and a moderate cultivation of rice. Gujarat's cuisine combines cardamom, saffron, jaggery (palm sugar), almonds, pistachios, yogurt, and buttermilk. For the vegetarian Jainist society, vegetables are lightly stir-fried with mustard seeds and chiles, and curries are served with pungent green chutneys. Among the Muslims and Christians, meat dishes are commonplace. *Dal dhokli, Gujarati* split pea soup, combines whole wheat noodles with *toovar dal* (split peas) and tomatoes. Chickpea flour is used to make crisp noodles, a popular snack food. The northeastern state of West Bengal lies to the west of Bangladesh in central India. With little Moghul influence, the area's distinct cuisine includes a creative use of spices, unique seafood preparations, local produce (rice, mustard, coconut, and bananas) and an array of milk-based sweets. *Panchphoran* ("five spice"), a blend of cumin, fennel seeds, fenugreek seeds, mustard seeds, and onion seeds, is used to flavor many Bengali dishes.

Ground mustard, as well as mustard seeds, are added to vegetarian, meat, and poultry specialties, while mustard oil is commonly used for frying. Coconut appears in both sweet and savory preparations. Bananas are enjoyed during all stages of ripeness, eaten both raw and cooked. West Bengal's most notable culinary contribution is its decadent milk-based sweets made from *chenna,* a curd preparation similar to cottage cheese. *Rasmalai* (small, flattened

cheese patties boiled in sugar syrup and served in a rich cream sauce), *rosogolla* (cheese balls cooked in flavored syrup), and *sandesh* (creamy cheese candy made from sugar and other flavorings) are among the wide range of sweets available.

Calcutta, West Bengal's capital, features an Anglo-Indian cuisine established by the British Raj in the nineteenth century. Raj-influenced dishes include subtle curries, such as *mangsho jhol* (lamb cooked with tomatoes, yogurt, mustard seeds, baby potatoes, and shallots), egg dishes, and preserved chutneys.

South India

Southern India's bountiful spice plantations, tropical vegetation, and dominant Hindu faith have contributed to a fiery vegetarian cuisine. Tropical ingredients (coconut, bananas, mangos, limes, jackfruit, and drumsticks—a type of long bean) flourish along the coastline. Rice is the area's staple ingredient, served with nearly every meal and used to make *dosas* (rice and lentil paper-thin pancakes), *idlis* (steamed rice cakes), and freshly made noodles. The Arabian Sea and the Bay of Bengal render ample amounts of seafood.

Unlike in the northern states, masalas are produced from fresh spices that are blended with a liquid, and mixed with a mortar and pestle to form a paste. Dried spices and dried vegetables are not frequently used. Curries are infused with coconut, while tamarind imparts a pleasing sourness to dishes, and ghee is often replaced with coconut and sesame oil. *Achar,* a type of relish/pickle, is made from fruits, vegetables, and chiles preserved in oil. *Sambar* (a liquidy dal-like preparation of vegetables and lentils), *rasam* (a clear spicy soup), and *pachadi* (the southern version of yogurt-based raita) accompany most meals.

Cooking techniques common to the north (the inclusion of cream and/or yogurt, flavoring with saffron, and grilling marinated meats) are not often found in the south. Rather, the cuisine of the south is light and spicy, making use of coconut milk to thicken curries and chiles to enliven dishes. The cooking styles of Goa, Kerala, Tamil Nadu, and Andhra Pradesh best represent the bold flavors of the south.

Goa, the smallest state in India, is located along the Arabian Sea on the western coast of India. Its warm weather, tropical beaches, and Portuguese-influenced past have created a distinct and uniquely flavorful cuisine. Bay leaves, chiles, cinnamon, cloves, and coconut grow locally and can be found in many Goanese specialties. Mackerel and pomfret add to well-known fish curries flavored with ground chile paste, turmeric, and vinegar. The use of cashews, onions, tomatoes, and pork comes from a state once controlled by Portuguese rulers. *Vindaloo,* a hot and spicy stew-type curry made of pork (or duck or lamb), chiles, garlic, and vinegar is Goa's most notable culinary contribution.

The narrow state of Kerala lies below Goa along the southwest coast. Kerala's tropical environment blends lakes, rivers, and lagoons with dense vegetation and world-renowned spices. Primary crops include cashews, coconut, coffee, tea, and spices (black pepper, cardamom, cinnamon, cloves, curry leaves, ginger, tamarind, and turmeric). Spice mixtures flavor curries and *dosas*. The cuisine of Kerala offers bountiful seafood preparations and thick stews. Depending on the religious influence, various meats are eaten throughout the state, including beef, lamb, pork, and veal. Kerala is the only state that has legalized the sale of beef.

Resting on the eastern tip of India, the highly industrialized state of Tamil Nadu lies on the Bay of Bengal. Like much of the south, fertile land, warm temperatures, and sufficient rainfall provide ideal growing conditions for rice, coconuts, spices, coffee, tea, and tamarind, as well as mustard, peanuts, and sesame. The Tamili diet, based on a dominant Hindu faith, is structured around vegetables and legumes.

Vegetables are braised, steamed, and stir-fried (*poriyal*) and *dals* are often prepared with red lentils (*masoor dal*). Rice, several vegetables, *dal*, chutney/relish, and yogurt (*pachadi*) constitute most vegetarian meals. Chiles, coriander, cumin, garlic, ginger, mint, onions, and turmeric flavor both vegetarian and meat dishes. Honey, sugar, and raisins add an element of sweetness. *Kormas* are braised with coconut milk rather than yogurt. Baked, fried, and steamed seafood flavored with coconut and tamarind showcase a variety of fish (grouper, mackerel, pomfret, sole) and shellfish (crab, lobster, mussels, shrimp).

The state of Andhra Pradesh curves along the east coast above Tamil Nadu. Its cuisine is considered to be the hottest and spiciest in India, with red chiles and peppercorns producing the distinguished heat. Strong Moghul ties are found in the capital city of Hyderabad. Moghul-influenced dishes (*pulaos, biryani, kormas,* kebabs) are accented with southern spices and ingredients. Traditional Hyderabadi food is flavored with cinnamon, cumin, curry leaves, jaggery, mustard seeds, peanuts, sesame seeds, and tamarind. Common preparations include *shorva* broths (lamb or poultry broth seasoned with vegetables, coriander, mint, and spices), *nihari* (lamb and lentil stew), *samosas,* pickles, chutneys, and a variety of breads.

Cultural Influences on Indian Cuisine

Indian cookery is rich in history and tradition. Its journey has been long and tumultuous, filled with periods of religious campaigns, ruling empires, and persistent European spice traders. In tracing India's culinary origins, one could look to the Aryans, nomadic tribesmen who migrated to northern India from Central Asia in the second millennium B.C.E. As the ancient ancestors of today's Hindus, the Aryans brought about the spread of vegetarianism throughout southern India. However, it was not until Hinduism took shape during the Vedic era (1500–800 B.C.E.) that India's general aversion to meat consumption emerged and the Aryans changed their meat-eating ways. As the Aryans moved southward, they brought with them Hindu beliefs and practices. This movement forever changed India. To this day, the heaviest concentration of vegetarians can be found within India's southern states.

In discovering that over 80 percent of India follows the Hindu faith, it is not surprising to learn the impact that it has had on India's overall food practices. With an emphasis on the spiritual significance of food, Hinduism suggests that only a pure diet can maintain purity of mind and body. In this case, a "pure" diet translates into a vegetarian diet. Hindus have grown to revere the cow, looking upon it as a sacred gift. It is morally unacceptable to consume its flesh, although its products (milk, ghee, etc.) are praised for their health and religious properties.

Religion

Hinduism does not concern itself with the art of cooking. Rather, it stresses the moral investment and ritualistic practices of food. These customs are observed through life stages and a socially defining caste system. Beginning at birth and ending after death, there are particular foods prescribed at each stage. These ritualistic customs are compounded with the caste, community, and sect that each Hindu is born into. Each component has its own etiquette and taboos connected with food. The intent is to maintain caste purity. Today, the caste system is beginning to diminish, although there are still a great number of Hindus that follow these age-old customs.

While the formation of Hinduism helped to firmly establish the vegetarian lifestyle by the fourth century B.C.E., it was the Buddhist and Jainist introduction in the sixth century B.C.E. that put the vegetarian doctrine into effect. Considering that both religions supported nonviolence and the avoidance of meat consumption, they melded well with Hindu beliefs. Their powerful impact helped to keep vegetarianism the prominent cuisine for thousands of years.

The turning point came with the introduction of Islam in the eighth century A.D. When the Muslim invaders brought their teachings to the northern regions, the acceptance of meat consumption began to reappear. As observed today, Islamic followers do not ingest pork. They do, however, consume other forms of meat, especially *jhatka* (kosher) varieties. Contrary to Hinduism, Islam emphasizes the enjoyment of food. Because of this, Islam has given India exquisite Middle Eastern dishes. This period of lavish cooking can be observed during the reign of the Moghul Empire.

Conquerers, Colonizers, and Trade

Prior to the Moghuls acquiring power, Muslim rule began with the Afghans during the eleventh century A.D. With Delhi as the capital, Muslim control was concentrated in the northern regions of India. This Muslim power brought about the spread of Islamic influence in the twelfth century. By the sixteenth century, the Muslims had established several kingdoms throughout northern India. It was a conqueror by the name of Babar that brought these kingdoms together under one rule in 1562. Babar was the first Moghul emperor to reign over north India. Showing considerable distaste for Hindu society, Babar and his successors transformed Indian civilization throughout the next 300 years.

As the Moghuls embarked on changing India's food, culture, and people, they looked to Persian influences to set the standard of living. When these Persian inspirations evolved in India's Moghul society, they merged with Hindu traditions to create a unique culture. This marked the beginning of the Moghlai cuisine. From this point forward, Indian cooking changed a great deal. With the use of traditional Indian spices and ingredients, Persian additions included meat dishes cooked with cream, dried fruits, and nuts; kebabs, *pulaos*, *biryanis*, and sweets; and elaborate garnishes, such as sheets of silver and gold for banquet platters. One of the most noteworthy Muslim contributions to Indian cookery is the heavy use of lamb. Even during the Moghul decline in the eighteenth century, Muslim-inspired creations remained a major part of Indian cuisine.

The Muslims were not the first foreigners to venture into India. Due to its rich bounty of valuable spices, individuals had been making the journey to India for centuries, beginning with the Romans and Greeks in the first century A.D. Before the Suez Canal opened in 1869, traders had a difficult time finding a convenient route to India. Arab merchants took advantage of this in the seventh century A.D. by monopolizing the spice trade. As the prices soared, spices soon became luxury items only available to the wealthy. This caused endless frustration for the Europeans, who continued to search for a direct route to India. In 1498, Portuguese explorer Vasco da Gama discovered the way and opened the first sea route to India. Bringing an end to the Arab monopoly, trading outposts appeared throughout India in the sixteenth century. The Portuguese seized Goa along the southwestern coast.

This revolutionized the cooking styles of the western and southern states when they introduced chiles, vinegar, cashews, papayas, pineapples, tomatoes, and potatoes to the cuisine. The British, French, Dutch, Danes, and Spanish also contributed to India's culinary evolution with new ingredients, cooking techniques, and the organization of tea and rice cultivation. Along with the formation of Asian contacts with China, Indonesia, Cambodia, Burma, and Malaysia, India's increase in trading caused a surge of foreign conquests for power.

Of all the European spice traders, the British have left the deepest impression on Indian cuisine. As soon as the Suez Canal opened, the journey to India significantly decreased. In the beginning, the British held just as much influence as anyone else. But in the early eighteenth century, they acquired the most power in the spice trade with the formation of the British East India Company in Calcutta. As the British gained more and more control, they found themselves preoccupied with food. At the time, there was little entertainment available, so food became the subject of interest. It was not uncommon for a typical dinner of the elite to include fifteen to sixteen meat dishes followed by dessert. The British reveled in decadence.

By the middle of the nineteenth century, the British had defeated their European rivals and established an empire known as the British Raj. This period left a tremendous mark on the eating habits of middle-class Indians with the introduction of cutlery and dining tables. With Indian regional cuisines well established, the British created their own style of cookery, combining Indian ingredients and cooking techniques with their own. This included the Victorian fad for French food. While the British enjoyed experimenting with other forms of cooking, they grew quite fond of curry. They were, in a sense, responsible for the popularization of curry overseas. Even with the demise of the British Raj in 1947, their fondness for Indian cuisine never faltered. This can be observed in the countless Indian restaurants found throughout Britain today.

When British rule came to an end, the people of India began to travel more freely, around their own country as well as abroad. The average citizen was given the opportunity to sample dishes originally reserved for the upper class, including a variety of cuisines from other countries. With a new set of flavors and styles of cooking made available, India saw an increase in the desire to eat outside the home. The once nearly nonexistent restaurant industry experienced a boom in the twentieth century. Prior to this time, the few restaurants that existed had mainly catered to the British. But, as more restaurants opened and specialized cuisines became commonplace, the number of Indians dining out increased significantly. Today, the restaurants of India range from regional cuisines to Chinese, Mexican, and Thai. Through the evolution of its cookery, the flavors that characterize Indian food have endured. Even during centuries of merging cuisines, the food of India has managed to remain distinctly Indian.

Garam Masala

Garam masala is one of a large family of spice mixtures or *masalas* that are used widely in Indian cooking.

The variations of this mixture are too numerous to count. The exact mixture of spices contained in a garam masala is individual to the household or chef. The roasted spices quickly lose their potency and for this reason it is made often and held only for a short period of time.

To gain the full advantage of its full and robust flavors, the most traditional use of this spice mixture is to add it to a dish at the end of cooking or to sprinkle it over the surface of a dish just before serving. Less commonly it is added to a dish at the start of cooking for a more subtle flavor. However it is introduced, add it judiciously as its flavors can easily overpower the other flavors.

Used in the northern, colder regions of India, the literal Hindi translation for *garam masala* is "hot spice," which in Western language is something of a misnomer. The mixture of spices that constitutes *garam masala* does not contain many "hot" spices; rather it contains spices that are considered warming to the body.

Some of the spices more commonly contained in *garam masala*:

Black cardamom pod
Black pepper
Cinnamon
Cloves
Green cardamom seed
Nutmeg

LEFT TO RIGHT, TOP TO BOTTOM: ground cardamom, *garam masala*, cumin, black kakom, cardamom, ground cumin, ground cinnamon, ginger root, ground ginger, ground cloves, cloves, mint, garlic, Indian red chiles, tamarind, ground pomegranate seeds, cinnamon sticks, coriander, tamarind paste, tamarind pulp, turmeric, zatar, cayenne, saffron, poppy seeds, curry powder, asafetida

LEFT TO RIGHT, TOP TO BOTTOM: cauliflower, peas, mango, coconut, onion, potatoes, limes, shredded coconut, paneer, black lentils, brown lentils, honey, jaggery, yogurt, green lentils, Bhutanese red rice, cashews, ghee, basmati rice, mango chutney, coriander chutney

Cooking Techniques

Baghar (*tadka*; *tarka*)—Seasoning technique used for *dals*, vegetables, meat, and fish. Seasonings and/or spices are heated in ghee or oil to intensify their flavor. Typically, four to five spices are used, both whole and ground. This technique is performed either at the beginning of a dish or at the end.

Bhuna—Form of stir-frying that involves cooking ingredients over high heat with small amounts of water. The resulting dish is browned with a reduced sauce clinging to the ingredients.

Dum—Type of steam cooking that evolved during the Moghul period in the sixteenth to nineteenth centuries. Food is prepared inside a heavy pan with a tight-fitting lid. Traditionally, the pot is sealed shut with a sticky dough made of flour and water and cooked fully while encased in embers.

Korma—Braising technique that traditionally features meat as the main ingredient. *Kormas* often use expensive ingredients and are prepared for banquets and parties.

Tandoori—Type of cooking method used for baking, grilling, and roasting. The food is cooked on a spit inside the *tandoor*. The high heat produced from the clay oven and burning charcoal results in moist, juicy items with a distinctly earthy flavor.

Common Indian Ingredients

Grains

Barley

Corn

Millet

Rice

Sorghum

Wheat

Staple Ingredients

Dairy products

Fruit

Pulses

Rice

Spices/seasonings

Vegetables

Wheat

General Flavor Profile

Chiles

Coconuts

Garlic

Ghee

Ginger

Masalas (spice mixtures), dry and paste

Onions

Saffron

Tamarind

Turmeric

Yogurt

Condiments and Cooking Liquids

Achar (relish/pickles)

Chutney

Coconut oil

Mustard oil

Raita or *pachadi* (yogurt condiment)

Sesame oil

Vinegar

Seasonings

Anise seeds

Asafetida

Bay leaves

Black pepper

Cardamom

Chiles

Cinnamon

Cloves

Coriander

Cumin

Curry leaves

Fennel seeds

Fenugreek

Garlic

Ginger

Mace

Mint

Mustard (ground and seeds)

Nutmeg

Onion seeds (*nigella*)

Pomegranate seeds, dried

Poppy seeds

Saffron

Shallot

Tamarind

Turmeric

Fresh, Dried, and Pickled Fruits and Vegetables

Apricots

Bananas

Betel leaves

Cabbage

Cauliflower

Cherries

Coconuts

Eggplant

Gourds (bitter, bottle, snake, wax)

Greens (mustard, kale, spinach)

Jackfruit

Lentils (yellow, red, green, black, brown)

Limes

Mandarin oranges

Mangos

Melons

Okra

Onions

Papaya

Pears

Peas

Pineapples

Pomegranates

Potatoes

Tamarind

Tomatoes

Turnips

Squash

Strawberries

Proteins

Beans (garbanzo, kidney, mung)

Eggs

Fish and shellfish (mackarel, pomfret, grouper, sole, crab, lobster, mussels, shrimp)

Meat (beef, buffalo, chicken, goat, lamb, pork)

Nuts (almonds, cashews, pistachios, walnuts)

Pulses and grains

Dairy

Buttermilk

Cheese (*chenna*, *paneer*)

Cream

Ghee

Milk

Yogurt

Sweeteners

Fruit (dried and fresh)

Honey

Jaggery (palm sugar)

Talana—Deep-frying technique that's performed in a *karhai* (heavy cast-iron pan shaped like a wok). Ingredients such as meat, fish, and vegetables are coated in a batter made of besan or gram flour and deep fried.

Cooking Equipment

Chakki—Type of mill used for grinding grains and spices. It is made of two stone disks stacked on top of each other. Grains or spices are poured into holes in the center of the top stone. A wooden handle is turned, causing the top stone to move and grind ingredients into flour or powder.

Chula—Square hearth or stove fueled with charcoal, dried cow-dung cakes, or firewood.

Degchis—Silver-lined brass saucepans. They are without handles and are available in different sizes and depths.

Earthenware pots—Used for specific dishes that require long cooking times with low, even heat.

Karchi—Long-handled iron ladle.

Karhai (or *kadhai*)—Pan used for deep frying. Generally made of cast iron, it resembles a deep and narrow wok. *Karhais* lend a smoky flavor to foods.

Kodai—Handle-free frying pan.

Mortar and pestle—Used for grinding spices.

Tambakhash—Long-handled flat iron disk that is often perforated. It is used for frying, stirring, and removing ingredients from hot oil.

Tandoor—Barrel-shaped open clay oven fueled with charcoal. *Tandoors* are designed to spread heat evenly with temperatures ranging from 700° to 800°F/371° to 427°C. Ovens come in several sizes from small clay and iron domestic varieties to large commercial styles made of bricks or iron.

Tava—Heavy iron pan used for cooking some types of flatbreads.

Thali—Round and shallow individual serving trays made of stainless steel or brass for everyday eating and silver for special occasions.

A Meal in India

Eating styles in India vary according to location, religious affiliation, and dining occasion. The type of event, be it an everyday meal or a large feast involving many people, greatly affects the style of service and the number of dishes served.

Traditionally, women are responsible for preparing and serving meals. It is customary for the men and guests to receive their meals first, followed by the children and women. In India, presenting food to family and guests is considered both a pleasure and a privilege.

A typical meal includes a staple preparation (rice, bread or both), *dal*, vegetables, curry, side dishes, and condiments, such as *poppadums*, *raitas*, and relish. Everything is served at the same time on individual serving trays known as *thalis*. *Thalis* are ideal for daily meals and small gatherings, but for larger celebrations, banana leaves and earthenware bowls are commonly used and thrown away after the meal. Each tray, or banana leaf, holds a portion of rice and/or bread and several small bowls of each dish. Because most people eat with the fingers of their right hand, it is considered unclean, or impure, to share food amongst individual *thalis*.

At the end of the meal, diners are presented with a bowl of water to wash their hands and an assortment of ingredients to make *paan*. Commonly chewed after meals as a breath freshener and digestive aid, *paan* consists of betel leaves, betel nuts, and lime paste in its basic form.

Japan

Consisting of over 3,000 islands, and home to nearly 127 million people, Japan is positioned within the east coast of mainland Asia 500 miles (805 kilometers) from China and 100 miles (161 kilometers) from Korea. The East China Sea, the Japan Sea, and the Pacific Ocean surround it. Active volcanoes, high mountains, hills, forests, short river valleys, and small lowland plains make up Japan's diverse landmass.

The four main islands of Japan stretch over 1,200 miles (1,931 kilometers) and are, from north to south: Hokkaido, Honshu, Sikoku, and Kyushu. Honshu, the largest of the four and the most heavily populated, is home to the major cities of Tokyo, Kyoto, Osaka, and Kobe. Within the main islands, there are seven regions. With the exception of northern Hokkaido and the northern and eastern portions of Honshu, the islands host four distinctly regular seasons, each fairly mild. Winters are cold, summers are hot and humid, and precipitation is heavy. Monsoon rains in the summer are essential for the cultivation of rice, Japan's staple crop.

Regional Cuisines

The long, cold winters found on the northern island of Hokkaido bring heavy snowfall that lasts nearly half the year. Mountain ranges in the center of the island do not allow for extensive arable land, although rice, potatoes, corn, onions, squash, asparagus, and melons are cultivated. The rice grown in Hokkaido is mainly used for the production of *sake* (rice wine). Salmon, crab, clams, squid, scallops, and shrimp flourish along the beds of *kombu* that line the coastal ocean floor.

Shifts in terrain, weather, and climate are seen throughout the vast island of Honshu. In the northern section, the harsh winters are long and the mountain ranges are massive. Despite the cold climate, fruits and vegetables are not in short supply. The area is famous for its Fuji apple and Japan's top brand of rice, known as Sasanishiki. The mountains provide *sansai* (wild mountain vegetables) and mushrooms. Beef, pork, and an assortment of seafood are widely available.

Tokyo, the capital city, and its surrounding areas have exceptional weather conditions. The mountains in the north protect the large, lowland area from the cold while the warm current maintains a fairly mild and comfortable environment. This southeastern portion of Honshu has access to countless seafood items, such as *katsuo* (bonito or skipjack tuna), sardines, *nori* (seaweed), and various other fish and shellfish. A generous amount of local produce is grown in the west, including daikon, taro, burdock, and *nashi* pear. The area is known for its numerous soybean products: *natto* (fermented soybeans), *shoyu* (soy sauce), and *miso* (fermented soybean paste).

The central region of Honshu is home to the highest mountains in Japan. It is an area that fluctuates greatly in geography, climate, and produce. In the north, rice, taro, and squash are abundant. Strawberries and tea production flourish in the south, along with cattle rearing. The coast offers several unique varieties of seafood, as well as the infamous *fugu* (puffer fish). Crab, *katsuo,* abalone, trout, lobster, mackerel, and eel are a sample of the region's rich supply of sea product.

Flat terrain and a warm climate supply the cities of Osaka and Kyoto with generous amounts of produce. This portion of Honshu shares many similarities with the far western region and the island of Shikoku. Beef, sea products, rice, vegetables (*kabura*—large turnip, *matsutake* and *shiitake* mushrooms), and fruits (plums, persimmons, *nashi* pears, and citrus) provide an assortment of diverse ingredients for this area.

The subtropical island of Kyushu, located in the southern portion of Japan, offers citrus fruits, strawberries, grapes, pineapples, papaya, passion fruit, and mangos. Vegetables include onions, shiitake mushrooms, and lotus root. There is sufficient access to seafood such as mackerel, squid, and fugu. Beef, pork, and wild boar make up the livestock.

Cultural Influences on Japanese Cuisine

Historically influenced by China and Korea, Japan's cuisine first evolved during the Aristocratic period (twelfth to third centuries B.C.E.). The Heian era (1185–794 B.C.E.), in particular, was characterized by a rich court life, with a display of great wealth and a preference for elaborate food. From the Chinese, Japan acquired new foodstuffs (tea, soybeans, noodles, and fruit) and adopted and transformed prominent Chinese culinary techniques and equipment. Those included confectionery production and preservation methods (such as the procedure for making fermented soybean paste/miso) and ceramic cooking utensils, chopsticks, and rice bowls.

Religious influence from Korea brought Buddhism, which complemented the existing religion, known as Shintô. Buddhism not only became the official religion of the court, it popularized tea drinking and reinforced Japan's fondness for vegetables and its aversion to meat.

The aristocratic system crumbled in the twelfth century B.C.E., when the samurai established control. This era known as the Middle Ages/Samurai period lasted until 1868. While in power, the frugal samurai promoted a simple cuisine referred to as *shojin ryori*. The vegetarian fare, featuring small portions, was heavily influenced by the Chinese Buddhist style of dining, placing specifications on color symbolism and the five flavors.

The sixteenth century marked two significant events in Japan's history: the evolution of the tea ceremony and the first appearance of European visitors. Stemming from the Zen Buddhist philosophy of serenity and simplicity, the tea ceremony quickly formed into an elaborate ritual. Its strong Chinese influence represented a cultural ideal that sought to find harmony in nature and with one's self. As a result of the tea ceremony, the grand cuisine of *cha kaiseki* was formed (see sidebar, page 75). Its foundation was the vegetarian *shojin ryori* cuisine.

When the Portuguese arrived in Japan in the mid-sixteenth century, the Western world had yet to make an impression on Japan. Once presented with new foodstuffs (sweet potatoes, peppers, sugar, corn, chicken, and potatoes), styles of cooking (baking and deep-fat frying/*tempura*), Christianity, and firearms, the Japanese immediately embraced the foreign offerings. Not long after their arrival, the Europeans began to meddle in Japan's political and religious affairs. Feeling threatened by their presence, Japan expelled all Westerners during the Edo era (1600–1868). The self-imposed seclusion resulted in the development of food customs uninfluenced by outside forces. Japan's merchant classes poured money into restaurants and drinking establishments, bringing recognition to local specialties. Traveling throughout Japan became commonplace, contributing to the birth of the *obentô* (box lunch) and the beginnings of *sushi*.

Japan reentered the world in 1853, when the country was forced open to foreign trade. International dealings brought about further discoveries, including a taste for meat. The Modern period (1868–present day) saw an increase in meat production and restaurants featuring nonvegetarian dishes. Eating meat was seen as a show of "modernity."

Political upheaval led to significant changes. As the Modern period saw the collapse of the samurai and the reinstatement of the emperor, conflict with neighboring countries led to the occupation of Korea in 1910. War broke out with China in 1936, and in 1941, Japan attacked Pearl Harbor, resulting in the country's participation in World War II. From a culinary standpoint, it wasn't until Japan withdrew from the war in 1945 that additional Western foods were eagerly welcomed.

The British introduced curried rice, and the consumption of bread and meat grew increasingly popular. Dairy products, especially milk, became part of the modern Japanese diet. Coffee drinking grew in popularity, along with grape wine from Europe and beer from Germany and Holland. The United States made its contribution with ice cream, toast, fried eggs, ham and cheese sandwiches, and fast food restaurants. With Japan's active participation in international trade and importation, the country remains heavily influenced by Western foods.

Cuisine

From the vegetarian *shojin ryori* and the tea ceremony's *kaiseki*, to the elaborate court cuisine of the Aristocratic period and the influence of China and the New World, Japan has developed an exquisite culinary repertoire. Emphasizing the natural, Japan's philosophy of food preparation strives to retain the organic taste of food, while using a minimum amount of artificial processes. Food is meant to speak for itself. It is not meant to hide behind heavy sauces and overbearing flavors. Seasonality provides the basis for a balanced meal, while food is artfully presented with patience and consideration.

Wabi Sabi: Japan's Guiding Principle

Japan is known for its creative food presentation. The artful gestures are much more than a well-balanced and beautiful selection of items. The basis is far more involved, stemming from an aesthetic system known as *wabi sabi*. Its set of values is grounded in Zen Buddhism, providing a strong and uniquely Japanese tradition, free of outside influences. From *wabi* (quiet and simplicity) *sabi* (understated elegance), Japan has found its guiding principles in everything from culture to food.

The Tea Ceremony

Japan's *cha-dou* (tea ceremony) is a social custom that evolved from Zen Buddhism. It began as a refinement of tea drinking that became popular in the sixteenth century. Japanese tea masters were appointed to prepare tea for the country's rulers and court. The attire, manner, and etiquette of the tea masters raised the event to a fine art, combining place, garden, poetry, music, food, and atmosphere. The tea ceremony came to dictate the standards of Japanese society. Grounded in firm tradition, today's formal event still involves many steps and guidelines.

At the heart of the tea ceremony lies the *matcha* (powdered green tea) and its ritualistic preparation. Other guidelines include ensuring the ideal environment and setting, a specific number of guests, presentation style, and the quality of food selected. Depending on the type of tea ceremony performed, the event can last several hours and may involve a mere confection or an elegant, yet simple meal.

A traditional *cha-kaiseki* (formal tea ceremony meal) originally consisted of only rice, soup, and several side dishes. Today, the meal often includes rice, soup, hors d'oeuvre, a couple of simmered and grilled dishes, clear soup, a main dish, salted vegetables, hot water, and sake.

Tea cooking is known as *kaiseki ryori*. It is the grande cuisine of Japan, with many restaurants specializing in the *kaiseki* style of cooking. *Kaiseki* offers a range of sensations for the eyes, nose, and palate, placing special emphasis on color combinations. The proper selection of flavorings and seasonings is essential. Ideally, ingredients are locally obtained to ensure perfect seasonality. Food complements the containers and utensils it is served with.

Rice

Often consumed plain, short-grain Japanese rice (*gohan*) is slightly sticky and moist. Among the many rice-based dishes, sushi is one of the most popular. Flavored steamed rice (*takekomi gohan*) often accompanies Buddhist vegetarian dishes. Rice balls (*onigiri*) are filled with a variety of stuffings. Soup and gruel feature rice, as well as rice-bowl dishes known as *donburis*. *Sekihan* (red rice) is produced for celebratory occasions, combining adzuki beans with sticky rice.

Within the seven regions of Japan, there are specialty dishes and products; however, each region shares common preparations and ingredients. Short-grain rice, the indispensable soybean, and products of the sea constitute Japan's staple ingredients. Key flavors include soy sauce (*shoyu*), fermented soybean paste (*miso*), rice vinegar (*yonezu*), cooking wine (*mirin*), fish stock/broth (*dashi*), wasabi, and ginger pickle.

Fresh seafood dominates much of the cuisine, which is showcased in preparations such as *sushi* (which simply indicates seasoned rice and may include raw fish, raw or cooked shellfish, or pickled vegetables served with any number of accompaniments), and *sashimi* (thinly sliced raw fish). The vast, yet minimalist, cuisine of Japan is highlighted with soups, noodles, vegetables, seafood, meat and dairy, one-pot dishes, condiments, and an occasional sweet.

Soups and Starters

The base of most soups, as well as many Japanese dishes, begins with *dashi*, an all-purpose fish stock made from water, *kombu* (dried kelp), and dried bonito flakes. Common varieties of soup include *misoshiru* (miso broth with tofu and green onions) and *suimono* (broth with sliced mushrooms). Other types of starters include *otsumani* (Japanese tapas), sashimi, *gyoza* (fried dumplings), *edamame* (unripe soybeans cooked in the pod), and *sunomono* (vinegar-tossed "things"). *Sunomomo* usually consists of raw, crisp vegetables, cold cooked fish or shellfish, and a light dressing of rice vinegar, *dashi*, sugar, and *shoyu*. *Edamame* is typically eaten as a snack or as an accompaniment to drinks. The boiled soybean pods are served with a light sprinkling of salt.

Noodles

Noodles (*menrui*) are very popular and are eaten any time of the day. They vary in thickness, texture, and color. In most instances, Japanese-style noodles are made of wheat or buckwheat, are eaten in soup or with a dipping sauce, can include toppings such as meat, seafood, and vegetables, and are served hot or cold. Among the most common are *udon, soba,* and *somen*. The thick cream-colored *udon* is made of wheat and is popular in western Japan, particularly the Kansai region of Osaka, Kyoto, and the surrounding area. *Nabe udon* is a classic winter stew made with udon, vegetables, meat, egg, and soup. Thin buck-

wheat noodles known as *soba* are brownish-gray in color and are most prevalent in the cool regions of northern Japan, the eastern Tokyo region, and the central mountainous region of Shinshu. Similar toppings for *udon* and *soba* include tempura, fried tofu, meat, and mountain vegetables. Somen are thin wheat noodles that resemble vermicelli. They are most frequently served cold in the warmer months.

Vegetables and Soybeans

Vegetables play a vital role in the Japanese diet, from leafy greens and roots to legumes and seaweed. Some of the most frequently used items are the daikon radish, the soybean, and a variety of seaweeds. The very popular daikon often serves as a garnish, a pickled condiment, an ingredient in sauces and salads, and as an accompaniment to numerous braised and grilled dishes. Pickled daikon (*takuan*) belongs to a variety of products known as *tsukemono* (salt-pickled vegetables). Adopted from Korean's infamous *kimchi*, *tsukemono* is a popular condiment served with meals.

The soybean is one of Japan's most valued items. Prepared in a multitude of ways, much of the Japanese kitchen is built around its many by-products, specifically tofu, miso, and *shoyu*. These versatile ingredients serve to enhance the flavor, and in the case of tofu, the texture and nutritional value of dishes. Miso is an integral part of the Japanese diet, providing a rich, deep flavor to soups, marinades, dressings, sauces, and a number of dishes. The thick paste, ranging in flavors and colors from white and light (*shiro-miso*) to deep red and strongly flavored (*aka-miso*), is available in three basic varieties: *mame miso* (soybeans), *kome miso* (soybeans and rice), and *mugi miso* (soybeans and barley). *Shoyu* and miso are also used in many dipping sauces, such as *ponzu* (rice vinegar, mirin, *shoyu*, *dashi*, and *yuzu* citrus), which is often served with sashimi and beef and seafood dishes.

Seaweeds provide rich sources of minerals and vitamins. Of the numerous varieties, *nori*, *kombu* (kelp), and *wakame* are among the most commonly used in Japanese cuisine. While some types of seaweed are found wild in the ocean, *nori* is cultivated in sheltered coves along the coastline. Tokyo Bay, in particular, is known for its high-quality *nori*. The paper-thin, greenish sheets of seaweed are oftentimes found encasing a rolled sushi known as *norimaki,* crumbled, cut into thin strips as a garnish over rice and noodles, or rolled around stuffed rice balls. In Japan, the hard, black sheets of *kombu* are harvested between July and September. *Kombu* plays a vital role in the production of *dashi* and also serves as a flavoring additive and as a garnish. *Wakame* is mainly used in salads, soups, noodle dishes, sashimi, and simmered dishes. Depending on the conditions in which *wakame* is grown, it can be hard or soft, thick or thin. The long, curling strands of seaweed are most often sold dried and are reconstituted in water, but are now commonly found fresh in U.S. markets.

Seafood and Meat

Seafood, be it fresh or dried, is prominently featured in many dishes. Since ancient times, raw fish and seafood have been consumed in Japan (see sidebar for information on sushi and sashimi). Seafood also appears in countless soups, stews, and one-pot dishes, is frequently broiled, braised, tempura-fried, steamed, and simmered, and supplies Japan with several by-products essential to the cuisine. Prepared seafood by-products for cooking include bonito flakes (*katsuobushi* and *surimi*). Bonito flakes are made from dried and preserved *katsuo* fillet that has been smoked, sun dried, and shaved into flakes. They are often used as the basis for *dashi* and as a flavoring additive or salad garnish. *Surimi* is a shredded fish paste that closely resembles flaked crabmeat. Made from the flesh of white fish, it is formed into different shapes similar to mock shellfish varieties found in the United States. It is widely manufactured in Japan and is featured in many dishes.

Meat dishes and dairy products have become increasingly prominent in the Japanese diet. Other than the popular one-pot dishes featured below, beef, chicken, pork, and duck are prepared in a variety of ways. Beef, especially very tender breeds such as the famous Kobe cattle, are highly prized and sometimes eaten raw, sashimi style. Other preparations include hamburgers, sausages, and steamed buns. *Negimayaki* is a popular dish of beef rolled around green onions and broiled. Beef and chicken are commonly broiled teriyaki style. Chicken, duck, and other poultry are often served raw, grilled on bamboo sticks in *yakitori*, and used as an ingredient in many dishes. Pork is highlighted in a national favorite known as *tonkatsu*. The breaded pork cutlet is deep fried, cut into bite-size pieces, and served with a special sauce and shredded raw cabbage. Eggs are used in different preparations,

Raw Fish

The Japanese believe that fish is best served fresh and eaten raw, ensuring the most premium taste and texture. The roots of this theory can be traced back before the modern era of refrigeration, when residents living close to shore would ingest raw fish and seafood to guarantee freshness. For those living farther away, products needed to be preserved. The process involved fermenting fresh fish in boiled rice. Once sufficiently preserved, the decomposed rice was discarded, leaving behind a mildly soured fish. In the fifteenth century, both the fish and rice became edible when the fermentation period was condensed, making sushi a popular snack food. Several hundred years later, sushi was prepared without the use of fermentation, and soon afterwards, it was presented with sashimi in the hand-rolled formed *nigiri-sushi* (oblong fingers of rice topped with various ingredients). *Nigiri-sushi* is perhaps the most famous Japanese food. Sushi chefs (*itamae*) devote ten to fifteen years to the art of preparing this type of sushi, from mastering rice cooking and intricate cutting techniques, to forming sushi and learning all there is to know about fish.

The difference between sushi and sashimi is the presence, or presentation, of rice. Sashimi is most often served by itself, highlighting delicately sliced fresh seafood presented with shisô leaves, flowers, or sprouts and *shoyu* flavored with a small amount of wasabi. Sushi, on the other hand, involves countless variations, each generally consisting of vinegar-flavored rice and raw fish wrapped in rolls (*maki*) and cones (*temaki*), or formed in a wooden box as "pressed" sushi (*oshizushi*). Sesame seeds, *tobiko* (flying fish roe), and shisô leaves often provide additional flavor, texture, and color. Condiments served with sushi include soy sauce, pickled ginger (*gari*), and wasabi. *Norimaki* (rice and seasoned vegetables rolled in sheets of *nori*) and *inari-sushi* (a sweet type of sushi consisting of rice balls soaked in a light syrup and rolled in fried sheets *yuba tofu*—a soybean product made from simmered soybean milk) are just a couple of the many sushi variations.

such as *chawan mushi* (food steamed in egg custard) and *tamagoyaki* (rolled omelette often prepared for sushi and accompanied by grated daikon and *shoyu*).

Dishes and Desserts

One-pot dishes known as *nabemono* fall into two categories: dishes cooked in a pot in the kitchen and cook-your-own preparations. Generally, hearty soups, stews, and casseroles make up the first category. Regional preferences make use of local ingredients such as seafood, meat, vegetables, rice, and noodles. A sample of these dishes includes *kamameshi* (rice stew), a Tokyo favorite known as *oden* (winter root stew featuring fish cakes, potatoes, taro, greens, and tofu), *yosenabe* (seafood soups), and *kairi raisu* (a curry dish topped with an assortment of ingredients). The simmered beef dishes of *sukiyaki* and *shabu-shabu* are the most common cook-your-own styles of

nabemono. They are very similar to the Mongolian hot pot. *Sukiyaki* entails quickly braising beef and vegetables in a sweetened soy sauce broth. *Shabu-shabu* is a plainer version of *sukiyaki*, with diners blanching the ingredients in simmering water. The water is then cooked into a rich broth and noodles are added to complete the meal.

Ending a meal with fresh fruit rather than a rich dessert is most common in Japanese society. Sweets are not nearly as decadent as they are in the Western world, containing far less sugar and fat. Items such as pastries, cakes, confections, and ice creams are frequently eaten as snacks. Sticky rice and doughy buns paired with nuts and sweetened bean paste are common, as well as delicate soups and gelatin flavored with red beans. Confections oftentimes accompany the tea ceremony, along with dainty cookies.

Sake—Kanpai! ("Bottoms Up!")

For over 2,000 years, the fermented rice beverage known as *sake* has been brewed in Japan. Related to many rituals and ceremonies, *sake* is an alcoholic beverage highly revered in Japanese society. Originally made of rice, water, and a rice mold used for fermentation (*koji*), many *sake* producers began adding alcohol during periods of rice shortages. In effect, there are two broad categories of *sake* available today: *honjozo-shu* (alcohol added) and *junmai-shu* (pure *sake*). Each type comes in a variety of flavors and colors, from dry to sweet and transparent to golden. Grades of *sake* are classified by the amount of hull polished from the rice grain. Extensive polishing results in a more expensive, higher quality product. Grades are as follows:

futsu-shu (ordinary *sake*)
gingo-shu (premium *sake*)
daigingo-shu (ultra-premium *sake*)

Sake is often used in cooking, especially in marinades and sauces and in fish and seafood preparations. It adds flavor and helps to increase protein coagulation during the cooking process. When used as a beverage, it is generally served warm (not hot)—a practice that evolved as a means of disguising the flavor of lower quality *sake*. Premium varieties are best served chilled. Presented in a *tokkuri* (vase-like bottle) with small cups known as *choko* (or *o-choko*), traditional etiquette states that, unless you are alone, you should never pour *sake* for yourself. When purchasing, the fresher the *sake*, the better. Unlike wine that increases in flavor and value over time, *sake* does not. It is best stored in a cool, dry environment. Once opened, it retains its quality for about a week in the refrigerator.

Common Japanese Ingredients

Grains

Barley

Corn

Rice

Wheat

Additional Dry Ingredients

Agar-agar (dried red algae)

Panko (bread crumbs)

Starches (arrowroot, corn, potato)

Staple Ingredients

Rice

Seafood/seafood products

Soybeans

Wheat

General Flavor Profile

Fish stock (*dashi*)

Ginger

Rice vinegar (*yonezu*)

Rice wine (*mirin*) and *sake*

Sesame

Soybean paste (*miso*)

Soy sauce (*shoyu*)

Wasabi

Condiments and Cooking Liquids

Chile-bean sauce (*toban jiang*)

Pickled ginger (*wari*)

Ponzu

Rice vinegar (*yonezu*)

Rice wine (*mirin*) and *sake*

Sesame oil

Soybean paste (*miso*)

Soy sauce—light to dark (*shoyu*)

Teriyaki sauce

Tsukemon (pickled vegetables)

Wasabi

Seasonings

Black pepper

Bonito flakes (*katsuobushi*)

Dried red chiles (*akatogarashi*)

Garlic

Ginger

Mustard

Pickled green plums

Sansho (similar to ground black pepper)

Sesame seeds

Shichimi togarashi ("seven-spice powder"—dried chiles, *sansho* pepper, poppy seeds, hemp seeds, sesame seeds, dried orange peel, and *nori*)

Shisô (*perilla*)—green and red varieties

Sugar

Worcestershire sauce

Fresh, Dried, and Pickled Fruits, Vegetables, and Roots

Apples

Asparagus

Bamboo shoots

Bean sprouts

Burdock (*gobo*)

Carrots

Chinese cabbage (*hakusai*)

Citrus fruit—hybrid (*yuzu*)

Daikon

Eggplant (*nasu*)

Gourds (*kanpyo*)

Grapes

Green onions

Green plums (*ume*)—prized for cooking rather than eating raw

Greens—*mizuna, mitsuba* (three leaves), fiddlehead ferns, chrysanthemum greens (*shungiku*), pepper-tree leaves (*kinome*)

Japanese cucumbers (*kyuri*)

Lotus root

Mangos

Melons

"Mountain vegetables" (*sansai*)—spring greens including ferns and ground wort

Mushrooms—*enoki, shiitake, matustake, nameko, shimeji, kikurage*

Onions—white bulb

Papaya

Passion fruit

Pears—*nashi*

Persimmons (*kaki*)

Pineapples

Potatoes

Snowpeas

Squash (*kabocha*)

Sweet peppers

Sweet potatoes/yams

Taro

Turnip—large (*kabura*)

Proteins

Beans (adzuki, soy)

Beef, wild boar

Chicken, duck, pheasant

Fu (gluten cakes)

Nuts and seeds (chestnuts, gingko, sesame)

Pork

Seafood and sea products (clams, crab, eel, flounder, *fugu, katsuo*, mackerel, octopus, oysters, red snapper, roe, salmon, sardines, sea urchin, shrimp, trout, tuna, yellowtail)

Cooking Techniques

Shioyaki—This quick and simple method of salt broiling is often used for fish. The fish is salted, reserved for up to thirty minutes, and then placed in the broiler skin side up. It cooks until the skin is golden brown.

Teriyaki—Meaning "shining broil." Teriyaki uses a marinade made of *shoyu* and mirin. This method results in a mild and delicate product that is sweet and flavorful. The marinade not only serves as the flavoring agent before broiling, it also serves as a basting sauce during cooking, provides a glaze to complement the dish, and is sometimes used as a dipping sauce after the item is prepared.

Nimono—This method involves boiling a variety of foods in seasoned liquids, such as strongly flavored stocks and mild, lightly seasoned broths. The *nimono* category of cooking is vast and includes at least fifteen major subdivisions. Each subdivision is distinguished by the boiling liquid used and the items prepared.

Sukiyaki—Meaning "broiled on the blade of a plow." In ancient times, food prepared using this technique was broiled over an open fire. Today, *sukiyaki* fits under two categories: prepared at the table (*nabemono*) or by simmering in seasoned liquids (*nimono*).

Umani—This division of *nimono* entails boiling food in a sweet liquid.

Mushi—Ingredients are lightly seasoned with salt prior to steaming. The end result is a delicately flavored dish that highlights the natural flavor of the ingredients. *Mushi* dishes are commonly served with several dipping sauces.

Chawan mushi—Prior to steaming, ingredients are properly seasoned, placed in a special lidded ceramic cup, and covered with an egg custard. Dipping sauces are not commonly served with this dish.

Mushiyaki (steaming and broiling)—This process does not use water or additional liquid; the steam is supplied by the food's own moisture.

Horakuyaki—Items are prepared in a *horoku* (thick, unglazed pottery bowl). The ingredients (meat, seafood, vegetables, etc.) are placed over a layer of salt preheated in the cooking vessel, the pot is covered, and returned to the heat. The items cook in the steam created.

Tempura—Ingredients such as shrimp, chicken, fish, and vegetables are coated in a light batter made of egg, ice water, and flour. Cornstarch and/or rice flour can be added for a lighter and crispier end product. For best results, prepare the batter at the last moment, taking care not to overmix it. Dredge the items lightly with flour, and serve with dipping sauces immediately after frying. A traditional tempura meal will feature at least six ingredients, chosen for their color, shape, and texture.

Cooking Equipment

Cooking utensils are highly regarded in Japan. They are oftentimes shown the same respect as the ingredients themselves. Special knives have been created for the slicing of raw fish, vegetables, and tofu. A sample of Japan's most commonly used tools are listed below.

Bamboo skewers (*kushi*)—Used for many grilled dishes, such as *yakitori*.

Cooking chopsticks (*ryoribashi*)—Typically fourteen inches long, cooking chopsticks can be used to mix, stir, pick up various items, and assist in cutting.

Earthenware casseroles (*donabe*) and iron pots (*tetsunabe*)—These cooking vessels are essential for hot-pot preparations.

Graters—Steel graters (*oroshigane*) and porcelain graters (*oroshiki*) are mainly used to grate wasabi, ginger, and daikon.

Japanese knives (*hocho*)—There are numerous varieties of knives available, each made for specific tasks.

Mortar and pestle (*suribachi* and *surikogi*)—The serrated, ceramic mortar and cypress wood pestle provides unique grinding implements. Applications include the production of pastes and dressings.

Omelet pan (*tamagoyaki-ki*)—A unique pan that is rectangular and ranges from six to seven inches in length.

Portable gas stove (*takujo konro*)—Made for use at the dining table; large pots are used in conjunction with the stove to cook ingredients, such as hot-pot dishes.

Rice cooker (*sokuseki tsukemono-ki*)—This electric appliance cooks different varieties of rice while maintaining the temperature of the rice for long periods of time.

Rice spatula (*shamoji*)—This implement is generally made of wood or bamboo and is used to prepare, stir, and handle cooked rice. Spatulas range from nine to twelve inches in length.

Steamers (*mushiki*)—Bamboo steamers are of Chinese origin, while the metal versions are of Western influence.

Sushi mat (*makisu*)—Made of bamboo, the flexible mat assists in rolling sushi.

Sushi mold (*oshizushi no kata*)—This rectangular mold is made of wood and used in the preparation of "pressed" sushi.

Sushi tub (*hangiri*)—A large, wooden tub with a level bottom used in the preparation of sushi rice. The wood absorbs moisture and retains heat.

Wok—Mainly used for stir-frying, the wok has been adopted from China.

A Meal in Japan

In Japan, a typical meal consists of rice, soup, protein (usually fish), several vegetable side dishes, pickled vegetables, and *sake*. Unlike Western meals that revolve around a main dish, each component serves to complement, rather than outshine the other. In formal settings, the meal is a sequential event, similar to that found in China. Soup and rice are presented toward the end of the meal, before dessert and tea. Everyday meals, on the other hand, are a simultaneous affair. The various courses are served at the beginning of the meal on individual trays for each diner. Lacquered chopsticks (*hashi*) are the preferred implements, while spoons are not commonly used. Japanese etiquette approves of diners sipping liquid, such as soup, directly from the bowl. It is quite acceptable to hold bowls and plates close to the mouth.

Korea

Korea's mountainous peninsula is located just below Manchuria in northeastern China. It lies between the Sea of Japan and the Yellow Sea. Extending over 600 miles (965 kilometers) in length and over 130 miles (209 kilometers) in width at its narrowest point, Korea is similar in size to the state of New York. The varied coastline ranges from straight and rocky along the eastern edge to low and mudflat-laden along the western area. Korea's small plains are situated among mountains, forests, and short, shallow rivers.

The country's four seasons contribute to a wide variety of available foodstuffs and a native appetite for hearty meals. The typically humid climate changes drastically over its seasons, particularly during the winter and summer. The north experiences cold winters, while the southern areas remain warmer. Typhoons in late summer and early autumn hit the country from the south and east.

Regional Cuisines

The political division of Korea, from the north to the south, is clearly represented by its change in terrain, climate, and agriculture. The two sections combined see minimal farming, with only 20 percent arable land. Half of this limited farmland is used to cultivate rice. Most of Korea's productive cropland is located in the southeastern and western lowlands. The lowland fields provide an abundant amount of grains and vegetables, while the uplands offer wild and cultivated mushrooms, roots, and greens.

South Korea has grown into a highly industrialized society. This has resulted in small farms with relatively low crop yields. Rice is the most significant crop in the area, found mainly along the southwest Honam plain. Potatoes, barley, soybeans, fruits, and vegetables are among the other leading crops. The coast provides a prosperous fishing industry. South Korea is one of the world's major deep-sea fishing nations. The main livestock found within the area includes pigs, cattle, and chicken.

North Korea relies heavily on its summer crops, considering the winters are long and cold. In this communist society, the majority of cultivated land is in state-controlled collective farms. The once low-yielding crops have improved due to irrigation projects, an increase in cultivated land, and the use of fertilizers and mechanization. The most abundant crops are rice, corn, potatoes, soybeans, and wheat. Fishing and deep-sea fishing are prominent, supplying a variety of seafood including oysters, cod, herring, sardines, pollack, and mackerel. As in the south, cattle, pigs, and chickens are raised in areas not beneficial for crop farming.

Cultural Influences on Korean Cuisine

The roots of Korean cuisine have developed through years of Chinese and Japanese influence, as well as imperial rule. From very early on, Korea has served as the cultural mediator between these two neighboring countries. Their effects can be felt throughout the entire Korean peninsula, from introduction of food items to the impact of political and religious events. Dynastic rule, beginning as early as the Three Kingdoms era (37 B.C.E. to 935 A.D.) and ending with the Choson period and Yi dynasty (1392–1910), brought about many changes as well, specifically in farming, culinary refinement, and available foodstuffs.

In the Three Kingdoms era (Koguyro, Paekche, and Silla dynasties), fermentation became a means of preserving foods and advancements were made in rice cultivation in regard to land use and farming techniques. Seafood items were harvested as a result of highly developed shipbuilding skills. Further developments in rice production were made during the Silla dynasty, while barley, millet, sorghum, soybeans, red beans, mung beans, and buckwheat grew in production. Buddhism arrived from China and brought with it dietary restrictions.

During the Koryo dynasty (918–1392) cattle was raised, even though a significant portion of imperial members and commoners avoided the consumption of beef. Not only was it frowned upon within Buddhist society, it was also quite rare and expensive. As a result, pickled fish and shellfish appeared as side dishes. In 1231, Mongols invaded Korea and brought with them the hot pot and the hot brasier to grill meats.

The Chinese influence continued as Korea entered the Choson period under the rule of the Yi dynasty. Confucianism slowly replaced the majority of Buddhist practice, bringing with it a new set of standards affecting politics, family structure, rituals, and ceremonies. As Buddhism weakened, Korean society saw an increase in the consumption of meat products such as beef, pork, chicken, and pheasant. Foodstuffs from abroad arrived, including chiles, pumpkins, sweet potatoes (from Japan), white potatoes (from China), corn, and tomatoes. The Yi dynasty, in particular, supported the expansion of foreign trade. Korean cuisine continued to expand, specifically within the imperialistic association.

Lasting over 500 years, the Yi dynasty ended with the annexation of Korea by Japan in 1910. Until this point, Korea remained untouched by the effects of Western influences that had spread throughout Asia. As Japan made its mark on Korea, it also contributed to the country's daily diet by supplying the people with sashimi and tempura. Liberation from Japan occurred in 1945. In 1953, as a result of World War II and the Korean War, Korea was politically divided into the communist north and the noncommunist south. To this day, however, the people of Korea view themselves as a single nation, one that shares a similar cultural heritage.

Beliefs and Traditions

Confucianism made a profound impact on Korean society. The rigid system entailed following specific holiday rituals. This included food preparation in relation to nutrition and seasonality. Foods such as rice-cake soup, dumpling soup, and cakes made of glutinous rice all served as holiday fare and were considered nourishing and harmonious. Red bean porridge, for example, was described as ensuring good health, preventing colds, and driving away ghosts if eaten on the day of the winter solstice. Many of these practices are still followed today. A sample of foods still considered symbolic includes noodles (representing long life) and various kinds of rice cakes.

In relation to the Chinese philosophy of *yin* and *yang*, the four seasons play a crucial role in the Korean diet. Creating a nutritional meal entails combining a variety of available foods. Seasonal foods provide the balance needed to meet the body's nutritional requirements. Many Korean festivals are seasonally focused as well, with an emphasis on the lunar calendar. The food that is served during these occasions is symbolically tied to the season.

The occasion, the main dish, and the number of side dishes determine table settings and etiquette. To gain a sense of peace and well being, foods are presented in a particular order. Side dishes are placed in the middle of the table, while individual bowls of rice are placed in front of each diner. The classification of Korean table settings is as follows: 3-*cheop*, 5-*cheop*, 7-*cheop*, 9-*cheop*, and 12-*cheop*. The word *cheop* (or chop) corresponds to the number of side dishes served. Items such as rice, soup, and stew are eaten with spoons, while drier side dishes are eaten with chopsticks. Contrary to Chinese and Japanese custom, it is considered impolite in Korea to raise bowls or plates from the table.

Cuisine

Korea's intensely flavored food is a cross between a once intricate court cuisine and a less fanciful cuisine of the common people. Red chiles, garlic, soy, sesame, ginger, and green onions play an integral role in building the country's rich flavor profile. Fermented foods such as *kimchi*, pickles, soy sauce, hot red chile paste, and soybean paste build character, create a unique texture and flavor through the five tastes (sweet, salty, hot, sour, and bitter), and add nutrients to each meal. Boiled short-grain rice provides the foundation of each meal.

In general, more than half of the Korean diet is comprised of carbohydrates, mainly rice, noodles, dumplings, and pancakes. Noodles are generally cut long and served in a soupy liquid. They are made of wheat, buckwheat, rice, soy, mung beans, and sweet potatoes. Dumplings served in Korea are very similar to the Japanese *gyoza* variety. Uniquely seasoned, they are prepared by steaming, pan frying, or boiling and are accompanied by a garlic-laden soy sauce. The most popular pancake, *pa jon*, is made by pouring a batter on top of green onions and seafood and is often prepared at home, in restaurants, and by street vendors. Pancakes can be vegetarian, contain meat or seafood, and vary in size and shape. Batters are made of wheat flour, glutinous rice, or buckwheat flour, as well as water and an occasional egg.

Served in ample quantities, soup (*kuk* or *guk*) accompanies nearly every meal. The basic broth (*changguk*) is made from quality meat and dried seafood. *Changguk* is served as a light soup or as the base for other soups and dishes. Traditionally, soup was made from the water used to wash the rice. It also provided the only liquid served at meals. Today, there are countless recipes for this ever-present meal accompaniment. Porridges (*chuk* or *juk*) contribute intense flavors and tend to be served in smaller quantities. Ingredients for porridge (grains, nuts, and vegetables) are toasted, sautéed, and simmered in water and stock until soft and creamy.

Fish and seafood play a significant role in the Korean diet by providing much needed protein. In general, the wide variety of fish, seafood, seaweed, and crustaceans are prepared similarly to common Japanese dishes: grilled or char-grilled, tempura fried, and used as flavoring for soups and casseroles. Raw fish is enjoyed in the form of sashimi. This Japanese-influenced dish is sliced thicker in Korea and is seasoned with red chiles. Sushi tends to be much sturdier than the delicate Japanese version, although it is served in the same manner with chopsticks, soy sauce, and wasabi.

North Koreans, especially along the Chinese border, often prefer pork because it is easy to raise and readily available. Beef, rather than pork or chicken, is favored in South Korea. This is particularly the case in areas around the capital of Seoul. It is featured prominently in many of the area's distinctive dishes, including *kalbi* or *galbi* (ribs) or *kalbi* or *galbi jjim* (beef rib stew), *bulgogi* (barbecued beef), and *yukgaejang*

(spicy beef soup). The very popular barbecued beef is grilled over a hot brazier known as a *hware*. Items are marinated in a spicy, slightly sweet sauce prior to being grilled. *Bulgogi* is often accompanied by lettuce leaves, raw garlic, and green onions. *Bibimbap* is a dish first established as a means of utilizing leftovers. It consists of rice topped with beef, vegetables, egg, and chili sauce served alongside *kimchi* and condiments. Diners add the ingredients to a large bowl, stir them together, and season to taste.

Fermented sauces and pastes are used extensively in Korean cooking. Whether they are added as an ingredient or used simply as a condiment, they help to create the bold character and unique flavor of this distinctive food. Hot red pepper paste (*koch'ujang*), soy sauce (*kanjang*), and soybean paste (*toenjang*), a by-product of soy sauce, are the three main flavoring agents. Traditionally, each fermented product was made once a year and stored in earthenware crocks. Today, these essential sauces and pastes are widely available as store-bought products.

There are a number of royal dishes that are still found throughout Korea, such as *gujeolpan* and *shinselo*. *Gujeolpan* is a nine-sectioned royal platter featuring pancakes accompanied by eight ingredients, such as dried mushrooms, stir-fried matchstick carrots, and marinated shredded beef. *Shinselo* comes in a brass pot similar to the Mongolian hot pot and is served with blanched walnuts and fried ginkgo nuts. *Teuk-byeol yori* ("specialties") is an elaborate à la carte presentation of foods ranging from appetizers to rice cakes and cookies.

Garnishing

The art of garnishing (*komyng*) in the traditional Korean kitchen once required following a strict set of rules involving ingredients, color, size, and shape. Today, garnishing is still taken quite seriously, especially when prepared for ancestral ceremonies, weddings, and formal dinners. The goal is to have the food appear natural, "like gardens left unattended." Ingredients with intense colors are preferable when presenting the two traditional garnishes (three-color and five-color). The three-color garnish is comprised of yellow (egg yolks), white (egg whites), and green (Korean watercress). The five-color garnish also includes red (red pepper threads or *sil koch'u*) and black (jet-black stone-ear mushrooms). Today's current garnishes range from gingko nuts and toasted seaweed crumbles to lemon wedges and edible flowers.

Cooking Techniques

Before gas and electric stoves became commonplace, food in Korea was prepared over a wood fire. Earthenware pots and steamers were and still are widely used, as well as cast-iron kettles for rice cooking. A traditional bamboo strainer known as a *chori* is used to separate sand and stones from rice. It is considered a symbol of good fortune, sifting the good from the bad.

As in China and Japan, the art of preparing food is very important. An example is the preparation of ingredients, specifically cutting and slicing food into small pieces for quick cooking, chopstick use, and presentation. Diagonal cuts, domino shapes, ribbon cuts, diamonds, strip cuts, matchstick or julienne, slivers, threads, and strings are among the many shapes used. Cooking techniques are similar as well, with a focus on grilling. Additional techniques include, but are not limited to, pan frying, broiling, steaming, and braising. Most food preparation requires the use of little oil, particularly vegetable or sesame oil. A sample of general techniques is listed below.

Pokkŭm—The most common method of vegetable cookery. It involves pan frying or sautéing the vegetable in oil with seasoning. A wok is not used with this technique.

Tetch'im—A process of briefly blanching the vegetable in acidulated water.

Chŏlim—The technique of salt curing. The liquid of vegetables is extracted to preserve their original flavor and increase the firmness of their texture. Following this procedure, a mixture of spices is added and the vegetables are fermented. *Kimchi* is an example of this process.

Tabletop hot-pot cookery (chŏngol)—Resembles Mongolian hot pot and Japanese sukiyaki or *shabu-shabu*.

Kimchi

Kimchi, or *kim-chee*, is a pickled product that is a staple of the Korean meal. Its history dates back nearly 2,000 years, when the process of fermentation proved useful in preserving fresh vegetables during the long winters. In the beginning, *kimchi* only contained a few ingredients, mainly Chinese cabbage (napa cabbage). After the sixteenth century, other items were introduced to the fermentation process: radishes, red peppers, garlic, eggplant, cucumbers, leeks, green onions, fruit, fish, and seafood. Today, there are an estimated 200 varieties. Additional flavorings range from ginger, vinegar, sweeteners, sesame seeds, and sesame oil. Although most varieties include Chinese cabbage, red peppers, garlic, and radishes, there are regional preferences involving the addition of fish and seafood. Southern regions favor salted anchovy; the northern areas prefer various kinds of fish; and the residents of Seoul add salted shrimp for their distinct flavor.

The region and season determines the process in which *kimchi* is made. The busiest time of the year is in the fall, when *kimchi* making is at its height. The *kimchi* ritual is referred to as *kimbang*. It is a time-consuming, communal task that is shared among neighbors, friends, and relatives. Each family has a unique recipe and flavor. The basic process involves salting the ingredients, adding a mixture of spices, and fermenting the ingredients. Traditionally, *kimchi* is packed in earthenware jars and buried in the ground during the winter months. Today, many residents own refrigerators made specifically for *kimchi*.

Pan-fried dishes (*chŏn or jŏn*)

Grilled dishes (*kui*)—The item to grill is sliced very thinly, marinated, and quickly grilled.

Preserved dishes (*chaban*)—Appetizers, side dishes, flavor enhancers, and garnishes.

Salting or sun drying (*maru˘n panch'an*)

Chorin—Cooking items slowly in a spicy sauce until the liquid is absorbed and the contents are caramelized.

Cooking Equipment

With the exception of a few specialty items (some are listed below), most of the cooking equipment used in Korean cooking is very common and consists of things such as heavy skillets for frying and casseroles for hot-pot dishes. Also very common, as for most Asian cuisines, is an electric rice cooker.

Earthenware crocks—Fermented foods are typical in Korean cuisine. These crocks keep the foods from spoiling.

Firepot—This unique cooking vessel is used in firekettle meals. A chimney stands in the center of a bowl, which is filled with different bite-size foods. Hot broth is poured into the bowl to warm the food, and hot coals are placed in the chimney to keep the broth warm.

Jangdokdae—This is the place, typically outside near the kitchen, where pots are stored for fermented foods.

Tabletop grill—Many people use these grills at home to prepare Korean barbecue dishes such as *galbi*.

Wok—Mainly used for stir-frying; adopted from China.

Ginseng

Koreans have always been intrigued with the medicinal properties found in certain items, such as herbs and roots. This fascination dates back over 5,000 years, when China began to experiment with herbal medicine. Ginseng (*insam*), Korea's indigenous root, soon became recognized for its rejuvenating properties. Originally found in the remote mountains of the north, it is now widely cultivated throughout all of Korea. There are two varieties, white and red. Red ginseng is regarded as the highest quality. In Korea, ginseng is consumed in a number of manners, from pills and candies to teas and sweet and savory dishes. When used in cooking preparations, it commonly appears in soups, stews, side dishes, and desserts.

Dining Out

In Korea, as well as in the United States, many Korean restaurants are featured as specialty shops. These establishments focus on preparing only particular types of dishes. Listed below is an example of a few of the specialty shops available.

Barbecue restaurant (*bulgoki-jip*)
Dumpling kitchen (*mandoo-jip*)
Sushi bar (*saengsan-hweh-jip*)
Noodle counter (*poonsik-jip*)
Tapas bar (*sul-jip*)

Common Korean Ingredients

Grains

Barley

Corn

Rice

Sorghum

Wheat

Staple Ingredients

Ginseng

Kimchi

Rice

Soybeans

General Flavor Profile

Chiles

Garlic

Ginger

Green onions

Sesame

Soy

Condiments and Cooking Liquids

Barley malt (*yŏtkirum*)

Hot red pepper paste (*koch'ujang*)

Rice vinegar (*ch'o*)

Rice wine (*ch'ŏngju*)

Sesame oil (*kkae*)

Soy bean paste (*toenjang*)

Soy sauce (*kanjang*)

Seasonings

Bean paste

Black pepper

Chiles (*gochu*)

Cilantro

Cinnamon

Citrus (preserved or fermented lemons)

Garlic

Ginger

Ginseng

Honey

Perilla (*shisô* or Japanese basil)

Sesame (oil and seeds)

Vinegar

Fresh, Dried, and Pickled Fruits, Vegetables, and Roots

Apples

Aralia roots

Asian pear (*nashi*)

Bamboo shoots

Bean sprouts

Bellflower root (*toraji*)

Bracken (fiddlehead fern or fern tip)

Burdock

Carrots

Cherries

Chinese cabbage (napa cabbage)

Crown daisy (chrysanthemum)

Cucumbers

Daikon radishes

Eggplant

Ginger

Gourds

Grapes

Green onions

Jujubes (dried red dates)—used dried, in preserves, as stewed fruit and candy. Used in savory dishes for flavoring. Also combined with cinnamon and to make a tea garnished with pine nuts

Kimchi

Korean chiles (*gochu*)

Korean watercress (*minari*)

Leeks

Lemons

Lettuce

Lotus root

Melons

Mugwort (*moxa*)—resembles chrysanthemum leaves. Used extensively, particularly in rice cakes and soups. It is supposed to increase energy and ward off disease. Rice cakes with mugwort paste are traditionally served at the Tano festival

Mushrooms (shiitake or oak mushrooms)

Oranges

Peaches

Peppers

Pears

Persimmons

Plums

Potatoes

Radishes

Spinach

Sprouted beans

Squash

Sweet potatoes

Turnips

Proteins

Beans (soy, adzuki, mung)

Beef

Chicken

Nuts and seeds (chestnuts, gingko nuts, pine nuts, walnuts, pumpkin seeds, sesame seeds, sunflower seeds)

Pork

Seafood and shellfish (abalone, anchovies, algae, clams, cod, cuttlefish, eel, flounder, fluke, herring, mackerel, octopus, pollack, sandfish, sardines, seaweeds, shrimp, squid, tuna, whitefish)

Sweeteners

Brown sugar

Honey

The Middle East

Native peasant and nomadic foods, coupled with thousands of years of unifying empires, have given commonality to Middle Eastern cuisine, despite regional differences. Traditional foods have changed little since ancient times, and today similar dishes are served throughout the Middle East, often with regional accents.

Generally speaking, the Middle East contains four culinary regions: the Arab World, including countries of the Arabian Peninsula, as well as Iraq, Syria, Lebanon, Jordan, and Egypt; the Persian food of Iran; foods of the Near East, including Turkey and other bordering countries outside the Middle East; and Israel, distinctive because of its Jewish settlers, who brought their foodways from Europe. This section focuses on Arab-Persian foods, highlighting them with a look at the cuisines of Iran and Saudi Arabia.

The name "Middle East" comes from a European perspective, as the region lies between Europe and the Asian Far East. Geographically, it can be broken into two rough areas—those countries bordering the eastern and southeastern edge of the Mediterranean Sea, and those countries in southwestern Asia with no Mediterranean coastline. The former, relatively fertile region borders the Mediterranean, and so utilizes many Mediterranean foodways. The latter region will be the primary focus of this section. (For the first region, see The Mediterranean, pages 120–123.)

The Middle East is generally thought to cover Egypt, Iran, Iraq, Israel, Jordan, Kuwait, Lebanon, Oman, Qatar, Saudi Arabia, Sudan, Syria, Turkey, the United Arab Emirates, and Yemen. These countries span 3,743,000 square miles (9,694,370 square kilometers), with a population of about 262 million, most of whom are Arab, with a significant minority population including Persians, Turks, Kurds, and Jews.

To the east, the region is bordered by Pakistan and Afghanistan. To the west, the Mediterranean Sea borders the northern region, while the southern region is flanked by the Red Sea, separating it from Egypt. Northern bordering countries of the Middle East are, from east to west, Turkmenistan, Azerbaijan, Armenia, and Georgia. The Caspian Sea sits north of Iran; the Black Sea is north of Turkey.

Generally, the region's climate is hot and often arid, but there is a range of temperatures and terrains within this vast area—from cold, snowy mountains to blistering deserts, to the temperate Mediterranean coast.

Agriculture

The Middle East is one of the least agriculturally self-sufficient regions in the world, with only 10 percent of the land useful for cultivation. There is more than a 50 percent deficit in food, except for Syria, running below the 50 percent mark, and Turkey and Lebanon, which actually grow a surplus.

Yet agriculture began in the Middle East, most likely in Kurdistan (now Iraq and Turkey), with farmed species of lentils, barley, peas, and wheat, grown as early as 10,000 B.C.E., and 2,000 years later, the addition of the domestication of goats, pigs, and sheep. And today, wheat and lamb remain integral components of Middle Eastern cooking.

By 6,000 B.C.E., the area between the Tigris and Euphrates Rivers, in Mesopotamia (now Iraq), was dubbed "The Fertile Crescent." The region's population soared because of its productive land. This resulted in what has been called "The Birthplace of Civilization," because the region developed the building blocks of a civilized society, including writing, recipe recording, and sophisticated foodways.

Until as late as the 1900s, Middle Eastern people lived in farming villages and as nomads. But although this lifestyle still exists, by the mid-twentieth century many people had migrated to the cities.

Common Middle Eastern Ingredients

Grains

Grains are a common staple, including traditional barley, often neglected for wheat, and the most prized grain—rice, especially Basmati rice. Cracked wheat is available in a variety of sizes, including precooked (bulgur), commonly used in salads. Bread, invented in the

Middle East, is prepared both leavened and unleavened, usually as flatbreads, such as pita and lavash. Semolina wheat is prepared as "Israeli" (large) couscous. Wheat gruels are still eaten as they were in ancient Arabia. Cornmeal, kasha, and even millet are available, although less common. Grains, wheat, barley, or even bread are combined with meat for the universal Islamic dish eaten to celebrate the New Year.

Beans and Legumes

Beans and legumes are commonly used and more affordable than meat. Staples include lentils, chickpeas, and favas, which are cooked in numerous ways, such as in thick soups or rice dishes. Chickpeas are also ground and fried to make *falafel* and puréed to make hummus.

Meat, Chicken, and Eggs

Meat is eaten as often as it can be afforded and generally cooked until well done. Traditional animal proteins include lamb (most prized), goat, sometimes camel, and commonly less-expensive chicken and eggs. Beef, although available, especially in Iraq, is generally not common, as cows require too much fertile grazing land. Pork is taboo for Muslims, who make up the majority of the population.

Middle Eastern cooking techniques are simple. Stews, a regional staple, are traditionally fried, then long simmered and finished with oil or butter. Meat and poultry are also roasted, stuffed with rice, meats, nuts, and aromatics. Spit roasting is sometimes done with whole animals, but more often with kebabs, a skewered meat dish invented in the Middle East, presumably by nomads and now a popular vendor food.

Ground lamb is frequently used in stuffings or to make *kofta*, a traditional mixture of ground meat and wheat, shaped and cooked in numerous ways throughout the region. A more recent invention is thinly sliced and marinated meats, rotisserie grilled, sliced vertically, then piled high and served with flatbread, now a popular street food.

Dairy

Traditionally, fresh camel milk was a Middle Eastern staple. Today, butter, *sumna* (a clarified butter similar to Indian ghee), simple goat and sheep cheeses, and yogurt are common dairy foods. Yogurt—fresh, plain, or flavored, often combined with mint, as well as drained and dried—is used as a cooking component or accompaniment. *Dooghs*, yogurt-based drinks, are served as a sweet or savory beverage.

Vegetables

A wide variety of vegetables are grown in the Middle East, including traditional cucumbers, garlic, zucchini, onions, sweet peppers, leeks, okra, romaine lettuce, and artichokes, as well as popular tomatoes and even potatoes—both additions from the New World.

Grape and cabbage leaves, as well as vegetables including peppers, zucchini, artichokes, and even pumpkins, are often stuffed with rice, meat, dried fruit, or nuts. *Mezze*, pickles, and salads are common. Spinach and eggplant are staples, with the latter served in numerous ways, including smoked, roasted, fried, or mashed, as a "poor man's caviar."

Fruits and Nuts

Middle Eastern cuisine includes a vast array of fruits and nuts, served together or separately, in sweet and savory dishes. Fruit is the most common dessert, including fresh fruits such as citrus and melons. There is a strong cultural emphasis on dried fruit, particularly dates, but also other fruits, such as apricots. Nuts are popular, including almonds sought by medieval crusaders, as well as hazelnuts, walnuts, and pistachios.

Fish and Seafood

Fish and seafood are consumed along the many coasts of the Middle East, including the Persian Gulf, and are cooked in simple ways, similar to meat and poultry. The colder waters of the Caspian Sea also provide world-famous caviar. Some traditional dishes use fish pounded and cooked in clarified butter. Even inland, in Iraq, fried freshwater fish is popular. Increasingly, farmed fish is available.

Sweets

Middle Easterners traditionally eat fruit to finish a meal, but enjoy sweet desserts as well. The word *candy* comes from the Farsi (Iranian) word for sugar. Pastries often include honey, nuts, and dried fruit and layered phyllo dough (such as the well-known baklava).

Hot Beverages

Coffee, long served by the Bedouin tribes, is often the stimulant of choice. Sweetened teas, particularly mint flavored, are a day-long Middle Eastern staple.

Arab-Persian Foods— Highlighting Iran and Saudi Arabia

Together, Arab-Persian foods personify much of Middle Eastern cooking. In this section, we examine two countries whose roots lie in these cuisines—Iran, previously Persia, whose cooking techniques and use of ingredients have been embraced since antiquity, and Saudi Arabia, a country with simple Arab culinary traditions, where the Islamic religion originated, which is a key component in all Middle Eastern cooking.

Iran

The Iranian influence on Middle Eastern cooking cannot be overstated. Its relative sophistication brought a new level to Middle Eastern cooking that has become part of the vocabulary of the region's foods.

Known as Persia until 1935, Iran is located in southwestern Asia, rimmed by mountains and water, with 1,640 miles (2,639 kilometers) of coastline—the Caspian Sea to the north and the Persian Gulf and Gulf of Oman to the south, both sources of fish and seafood. The country spans about 630,000 square miles (1,631,700 kilometers), and is bordered by Iraq to the west; Turkey, Armenia, Azerbaijan, and Turkmenistan to the north and northwest; and Afghanistan and Pakistan to the east and southeast. Much of Iran is a vast plateau, but the country's terrain ranges from snow-capped mountains to fertile valleys and large hot deserts.

With a population of about 70 million, 64 percent live in cities and 37 percent in rural communities, with the majority settled on the slopes of the surrounding mountains. About two thirds of Iranians are descendents of Asian Aryans. Most Iranians are Muslims, of which 90 percent are Shi'a Muslims.

Only a small part of Iran's economy comes from agriculture. Chief products include a large production of dates and pistachios, as well as wheat, sugar beets, rice, barley, potatoes, cucumbers, tomatoes, and watermelons. The primary livestock are sheep, goats,

cattle, and chickens. Interestingly, in a region where water is critical, Persians have used sophisticated irrigation techniques since ancient times, including ways to harvest ice from its mountains.

A range of climates makes for a long harvest season, with a wide variety of fruits and nuts grown, including melons, grapes, mulberries, peaches, apricots, nectarines, pomegranates, persimmons, oranges, figs, lemons, hazelnuts, and almonds.

Iran's most fertile and only rice-producing region is around the Caspian Sea, which also yields world-famous caviar. The southern region has some fertile oases with date trees and sweet oranges. Its warm waters yield both fish and seafood, such as shrimp. Viviculture has been used since ancient times.

Cultural Influences

Persia dates back 5,000 years, stretching north to include parts of Russia, Egypt in the south, Greece in the west, and India in the east. Persia adapted foods from many of its colonies and, in turn, spread its eclectic cuisine.

The ancient Silk Road, a trade route from China to Syria, ran through ancient Persia. Treasures from the east included spices, important eggplant, now a primary vegetable in the Middle East, and essential rice, still the key ingredient in Persian and all Middle Eastern cooking.

Two centuries of Arab occupation brought Arabian cooking components to Persian foods, along with Islam. Alexander the Great brought the flavors of India, as did the British, many centuries later, along with a vocabulary of Indian culinary words. Although the easy travel and the global economy have long integrated international and regional foods into Persian cooking, its distinctive cuisine lives on.

Cuisine

Persian cuisine has permeated the region since antiquity, so today it is difficult to completely extricate Persian dishes from the other foods of the Middle East. But Persia did introduce two distinctive features, which will be the focus here—its rice dishes and use of sweet and sour flavors.

Rice, grown in the Caspian region and imported from Pakistan, is the staple food of Iran. Basmati-style rice is most prized, famous for its aromatic, light, fluffy nature. There are three stages to the famous Persian rice-cooking technique: The rice is first rinsed, then boiled, then steamed. *Chelow*, a classic steamed rice dish, is often dressed with saffron and butter, and is usually served with a stew or grilled meat, as in the national lamb and rice dish, *chelas kebab. Polou,* similar to what we call a rice pilaf, is a rice dish steamed with other ingredients, such as meat, herbs, vegetables, sour fruit, and pulses, except that a polou has a prized crisp crust (*tah-dig*) at the bottom of the cooking vessel. *Rahchin* is rice beaten with eggs, yogurt, and saffron, steamed with layers of meat and eggplant or spinach, an ingredient indigenous to Persia. Sweet rice puddings are also popular.

A rice dish is often served with a stew, which is first simmered, and then finished with vegetables, herbs, and often fruit. Distinctive Persian stews are often seasoned with sweet and sour flavors, such as the famous combination of walnuts and pomegranate juice, or the use of fresh and dried citrus, barberries, tamarind, rhubarb, quince, unripe plums, and grapes (*verjus*).

Leavened bread, usually relatively flat, is another staple. Lavash, almost identical to the Lebanese bread of the same name, is one of six traditional breads, and is now widely used in American wrap-style sandwiches.

Saudi Arabia

The term "Arabian food" refers to the foods of the Arabian Peninsula, including its largest country, Saudi Arabia. Both foods and styles of the Arab western Mediterranean and Egypt, including *mezze* and classic street foods, are popular in Saudi Arabia.

Saudi Arabia, located in the southern region of the Middle East, covers 830,000 square miles (2,149,700 square kilometers), three quarters of the Arabian Peninsula. It is bordered by the Persian Gulf and the United Arab Emirates to the east; Oman and Yemen to the south; the Red Sea to the west; and Jordan, Iraq, and Kuwait to the north.

The Saudi landscape is mostly barren, a largely desert climate with little rain and hot summer months, but pleasant winter temperatures. Most of the central area is a plateau, Najd, with some fertile oases. Deserts hem the plateau to the east, north, and south. The coastal plains and mountains are in the eastern part of the country.

Sunni Muslims make up 90 percent of the country's 23 million inhabitants. The majority is of Arab tribal ancestry, with a minority of immigrants descendents from African slaves, diverse Muslim pilgrims, and the former ruling Ottoman Turks. A quarter of the population is made up of the largest number of foreigners in the Middle East, mainly the result of the oil industry. Before the mid-twentieth century, most Saudis lived in rural areas, but 83 percent now reside in urban cities.

Crops grow on only 1 percent of Saudi land. Primary growing areas are Asir in the southwest and scattered oases in central and eastern regions. Chief products are barley, dates, millet, sorghum, tomatoes, and wheat. Vegetables include citrus fruits, watermelons, potatoes, cucumbers, grapes, and onions. Sheep, goats, camels, chickens, and some cattle are standard livestock.

Cultural Influences

Bedouin Arab cooking, the ancient Arabian dominance of the spice trade, and Muslim culinary traditions are Saudi Arabia's key culinary influences. (For Islamic influences, see Islam, page 93.)

Trade links brought foods and seasonings from Africa, India, Mesopotamia (now Iraq), and the Mediterranean. With the rise of Islam, which originated in the Saudi Arabian city of Mecca, Mohammad's successors, the ruling *caliphs,* conquered much of the known world, bringing Islamic culinary laws and their cultural traditions. The Ottoman (Turkish) Empire brought its cuisines, as well as the foods of its vast holdings. Additionally, today's diverse population of immigrants and expatriates contribute their varied foodways.

Although the number of true Bedouin nomads is in decline, their food culture, based on the simple scarce elements of the region, has survived to greatly influence the more settled populations of the Middle East, especially in the more arid areas of the region.

For thousands of years, these nomads survived in their arid climate, settled near oases, and herded sheep and goats in desert pastures. The domestication of the camel allowed transportation of goods and supported a nomadic lifestyle. They also depended on the camel for food and drink. Bedouin foods are based originally on milk, dates, and occasional meat. Sheep and goat were favored over camel meat, since camels were more valuable for transport and milk, except for bull calves and sick or injured beasts. Larger meat cuts were cooked in a stewpot with rendered animal fat or *samna,* a kind of clarified butter, sometimes flavored and also used in commerce. Small game was thrown on the fire to cook and eat in its entirety. Coffee was served to the men, while the women prepared the food. Other staples included dates, wheat, unleavened bread, yogurt, and later rice.

Regional Empires

In addition to the spice trade, simple, nomadic, and peasant foods of the Arabs, combined with culinary jewels culled from the region's vast historical empires, form the foundation of Middle Eastern cooking. The Middle East has spawned many civilizations, each bringing its own culinary identity to the region, but the strongest may have been the Persians, Greeks, and Arabs.

The Persian empire of c. 550 B.C.E. was the earliest to envelop the Middle East, enriching spare nomadic Arab foods with a more sophisticated cuisine. Alexander the Great's vast Greek empire influenced the region with Hellenistic foods of the Mediterranean and encouraged the mingling of Persian and Indian foods.

The Islamic empire began with the conquest and conversion of the region following the death of Mohammad in 632 A.D. Its empire also stretched across the Middle East, as well as to North Africa, Spain, Italy, and Portugal. Baghdad, now the capital of Iraq, was one of its capitals and, for at time, the center of the culinary world, renowned for its variety of foods and lavish feasts.

The Abbasid Arabs, who at one time ruled this empire, came from a simple Bedouin tradition featuring foods of the desert and oases. They were dazzled by the sophisticated brilliance of the Persians, who they had conquered, and absorbed their culinary traditions into the culture.

Since the times of the Islamic caliphs, little has changed in traditional Middle Eastern cooking, except the influence of New World foods, such as tomatoes.

When the Turkish Ottoman Empire took hold of the region, capped by the conquest of Constantinople (now Istanbul) in 1453, the Turks, whose traditions were nomadic as well, absorbed culinary heritage from their vast holdings. *Topkapi,* the palace of the Sultans, became the hub of high Ottoman cooking, with unparalleled cultural mixing, some from the Balkan countries, and a distinctive Ottoman style. Today, despite the citified air of many Middle Eastern countries, these basic underpinnings of cultural influences remain.

Cuisine

Arabian cooking is typified by the countries of the southern peninsula, as well as Iraq, Syria, Lebanon, Jordan, and Egypt to the east. The foundation of Arabian foods is the simple Arab Bedouin traditions (see sidebar), characterized by a hospitality to guests. The use of coffee, with its accompanying rules for consumption, dates back to ancient times and is still an integral part of traditional Arabian culture. A strong roast is usually seasoned with cardamom and sometimes served with dates. Sweetened tea is also extremely popular.

When affordable and available, the main dish is centered on meat, chicken, fish, or local prawns, cooked in a sauce or roasted, baked, or grilled, as in kebabs, with rice or rice accompaniments. Simply dressed salads, often including peppery cress, are common. Flatbread, yogurt, and pickles accompany meals. Cucumbers are especially popular.

The Gulf waters teem with fish and prawns, which are traditionally baked or cooked over coals but are also fried or stewed. Lamb is the most popular meat. *Khouzi,* a whole, spit-roasted lamb stuffed with chicken, eggs, and spiced rice, is the national dish. Arabian seasoning is varied. During ancient times, Arabs traded their own cardamom, coriander, and cumin for cinnamon, nutmeg, hot chiles, ginger, pepper, turmeric, and saffron. Today, the famous Arabian spice mixture *baharat* is made from black pepper, coriander, cloves, cassia (Arabic cinnamon), cumin, cardamom, nutmeg, and paprika. Tree-dried limes (*loomi*), whole or ground into a powder, are used in meat dishes and also served in tea. Tangy tamarind is still used, but is now commonly replaced with tomato. Onions, herbs, and greens (mostly parsley, mint, coriander, spinach, and cress) are staples. Aromatic flavors frequently used include olive oil, garlic, saffron, mint, marjoram, rosemary, and rose water.

Dates are commonly used in sweet and savory dishes. In fact, date cultivation goes back at least 4,000 years, with the largest date palm oasis in the world, 50,000 acres, in Saudi Arabia. Date molasses (*dibs*) is extracted from dry dates and used in desserts.

LEFT TO RIGHT, TOP TO BOTTOM: olive oil, flat-leaf parsley, dill, eggplant, spinach, grape leaves, garlic, mint, okra, cucumber, zucchini, lemon, quince, bulgur, hazelnuts, dates, dried apricots, dried figs, couscous, pistachios, almonds, raisins, olives, pine nuts, honey

Cultural Influences on Middle Eastern Cuisine

Islam, the spice trade, and a procession of vast regional empires all have played a unifying culinary role in developing similar flavors and eating customs throughout the region, much of which wasn't divided into separate countries until the twentieth century.

Islam

Today, more than 90 percent of the Middle East is Muslim, and since Islam's birth, in the 600s A.D., Islamic powers have bound the region's culinary culture. Islam's prophet, Mohammed, stressed that food was a divine blessing that should be appreciated, but also initiated strict culinary taboos. Islamic dietary rules forbid ingesting alcohol (even in cooking), pork, and blood. Although there are levels of compliance, Middle

LEFT TO RIGHT, TOP TO BOTTOM: tahini, ground cardamom, sesame seeds, cardamom pods, ground cumin, cloves, ground cloves, cumin seed, ground cinnamon, sumac, zatar, coriander, cinnamon sticks, rose water, saffron, turmeric, pomegranate molasses, fenugreek, orange water

Easterners generally cook meat thoroughly, shun pork in favor of lamb or goat, and do not drink.

In Muslim culture, the mixing of the sexes is generally discouraged, and this carries over to its foodways. Traditionally, except in wealthy homes, where a male cook may be hired, women prepare the food. In observant homes, or when guests are invited, men and women may dine separately; males may eat before women and children.

Muslims fast from dawn until dusk during the month of Ramadan, a time of self-discipline, medita-tion, and prayers, thought to revitalize many of the teachings of the *Qu'ran*, the holy book of Islam. Ramadan meals are eaten before sunrise (*suhoor*) and after sunset (*iftar*). Each country, and often each family, has their own culinary traditions that determine how the fast is broken at sunset. Many do so with dates, followed by prayer and a meal, in the manner of Mohammed. With the arrival of the new moon to signal the end of Ramadan, there is a final, prolonged feast, *Eid Ul-Fitr*.

Common Middle Eastern Ingredients

Herbs and Spices

Allspice

Baharat (see Saudi Arabia, page 91)

Black pepper

Cardamom

Carob

Cassia (a form of cinnamon)

Cloves

Coriander

Cumin

Dill

Dried fruit, sweet and sour

Fenugreek

Garlic and garlic chives

Ginger

Lemon basil

Mace

Marjoram

Mastic (bitter-tasting resin)

Mint (fresh and dried)

Orange water

Parsley

Poppy seeds

Rosemary

Rose water

Saffron

Sesame seeds

Sumac

Tahini

Tamarind

Tarragon

Turmeric

Vegetables, Fruits, Nuts, and Legumes

Almonds

Black beans

Chickpeas

Eggplant

Fava beans

Hazelnuts

Lemons

Lentils

Limes (dried, powdered, and whole)

Navy beans

Olives

Oranges

Peppers

Pickled vegetables

Pine nuts

Pomegranate seeds

Purslane

Red beans

Rice

Walnuts

Meat

Lamb

Dairy

Feta cheese

Goat's milk cheese

Yogurt (fresh, flavored, and dried)

Fats

Butter

Olive oil

Vegetable oil

The Spice Trade

The seasoning in Middle Eastern food has its roots in ancient times, when Arabs were the middlemen in the caravan spice trade. Through the great east–west Silk Road, they brought spices from India across the Middle East to the Mediterranean and Europe.

Middle Eastern cooking, greatly enhanced by the spice trade, became a model for both civilized eating and unusual ingredients in Medieval Europe. Valuable spices were also a way to show off wealth, and Europeans paid at least ten times and often forty times what they cost at their source. This system of trade not only spread foodways throughout the "known" world, but also assisted the growth of modern capitalism, as Arab traders enriched both themselves and the city-states of Italy, such as Venice and Florence.

Cooking Techniques

Middle Eastern cooking techniques are simple, as many of them are rooted in nomadic tribal traditions and a lack of kitchens. The common threads that run throughout Middle Eastern cuisine are best exemplified by how ingredients are used.

Grains—Rice is commonly steamed with other ingredients. Wheat is steam dried and cracked to make bulgar wheat, which is prepared by soaking in hot water.

Beans—The chickpea is probably most commonly used. It is soaked and ground to make preparations such as *falafel*, or cooked and puréed into a paste-like sauce, known as *hummus*.

Meats—Commonly cooked on kebabs or roasted in large pieces on a spit. Stews are also common.

Dairy—Yogurt is used often and by a number of different preparation methods. Draining yogurt for an hour or so is common because it is often not thick enough to use in food preparation. It may also be drained for 12 hours or more with light seasoning to make yogurt cheese (*labni*). Cooked yogurt (*laban matboukh*) is also common.

Grape leaves—Commonly stuffed, rolled, and braised or grilled with any number of fillings, including meats, grains, or even sardines or smelts.

The Tandoor Oven

The *tandoor* is an ancient clay oven of Middle Eastern/Indian origin, shaped like a large pottery jar, with an opening toward the bottom for fuel. It can be inserted into a wall; outdoors, it is used as a freestanding structure, with the addition of more clay to form a beehive shape. Bread is slapped onto the vertical walls, where it bakes swiftly from both radiant and convection heat.

Traditionally, Middle Easterners often made their own bread, and then brought it to a community oven to be baked. After bread baking was done, the residual heat was used to bake casseroles and other dishes. Skewered meats were also roasted in the oven over burning coals. More recently, many Arab countries are losing their taste for *tandoor*-cooked breads in favor of European brick oven breads.

A Meal in the Middle East

Traditionally, the Middle East is not a restaurant culture but a society of female home cooks, although roadside restaurants were always available for travelers, and vendor food has always been popular. Today, city restaurants abound.

As in the United States, dining practices depend on locale, class, and lifestyle. But Arab hospitality has been legendary since the ancient Bedouins, with codified rules for both host and guest. A large midday meal was the custom, but a three-meal-a-day eating pattern is now common.

Classically, Middle Easterners ate on the floor, on a carpet with pillows at a low table. They ate without utensils, often with bread as a scoop. A strict code of cleanliness required using the right hand only. Today, tables and chairs and utensils are common.

Southeast Asia

Southeast Asia includes Brunei, Cambodia, Indonesia, Laos, Malaysia, Myanmar (formerly Burma), the Philippines, Singapore, Thailand, and Vietnam. Food is such a socially important part of Southeast Asian daily life that many people in these countries greet each with a version of, "Have you eaten yet?" The Thais actually say, "Have you eaten rice?" and, while eating, it is common to discuss what the next meal will bring. With its many miles of coastline, Southeast Asia has served as a point of entry to the Asian world and has thus felt the influence of many cultures, all leaving a trace of their distinct cuisines to form a unique variety of fusion cooking across Southeast Asia. Indigenous spices have helped to create vibrant flavors that help shape a unique cuisine. More than twenty distinctly different languages are spoken in these ten countries, and there are in excess of twelve major religions practiced.

Southeast Asia includes the mountainous regions of northeast Thailand, the expansive coastline of Vietnam, and Indonesia's volcanic belt of nearly 17,000 islands that stretch from the west of the Malaysian peninsula across to the north of Australia. Tropical rain forests, mountains, islands, coastal stretches, flat plains, and highlands create a landscape that is as diverse as its cuisines. However, recent industrialization is transforming much of this land to high-rises, gated communities, industrial parks, and business centers.

The extensive network of fresh waterways and expansive coastlines throughout Southeast Asia has created cuisines that are heavily reliant on the seafood. Southeast Asians consume twice as much freshwater fish and seafood than any other animal protein source. The Mekong, Salween, Chao Phraya, and Red rivers feed the streams and lakes that supply fresh fish and allow for large-scale aquaculture; most of the world's farmed shrimp come from Southeast Asia. The prolific Mekong begins in Tibet, meanders through southeastern China, divides Laos and Myanmar, continues to flow south between Thailand and Myanmar, and ends by spreading out into a massive delta in southern Vietnam. The abundance of seafood has also led to the development of a wide variety of condiments to go with it. Fish sauce is used heavily in Thai, Vietnamese, Cambodian, Filipino, and Laotian cuisines, while fermented shrimp paste is used more frequently in Malaysia, Singapore, and Indonesia.

There is a remarkably diverse climate across the region, beginning at sea level in the tropical rain forests and climbing up to Myanmar's Hkakabo Razi on the Chinese border, which towers to just below 20,000 feet above sea level. Rice is cultivated on terraces in the mountains and hill areas and in rice paddy fields in the low-lying coastal areas and plains. Temperatures range from a scalding 100°F/38°C or more to 50°F/10°C in the mountains. A majority of Southeast Asia has long, hot, and humid days that are peppered with heavy downpours of welcome rain. Monsoon seasons, with floods and storms, are part of daily life and most would say that there is not a bad time to visit the area; when one region is wet, another is dry and sunny.

The southern Area of Malaysia, Indonesia, and the Philippines were once referred to as "the Spice Islands" since they possessed many indigenous spices, primarily pepper, cloves, cinnamon, and nutmeg. Looking to control the spice trade, the first Portuguese voyage reached the small Malaysian port of Malacca in 1509, although it took until 1511 until the Portuguese finally took control of the bustling trading port. Until then, black pepper was the only "heat" in Thai cuisine. The Portuguese introduced chiles from South America and now chiles have become an essential part of Malaysian, Thai, and other Southeast Asian cuisines. The berries of the indigenous peppercorn plant are used primarily in two forms—black and white peppercorns. The black peppercorns are riper and the white peppercorns have the outer husk removed. Indonesian cloves, the dried bud of an evergreen bush, are used throughout the region in savory dishes.

Many other native agricultural resources have become integral components of the cuisine. The large family of palms native to the area is relied upon to produce palm sugar, palm oil, coconuts, and palm vinegar. Coconut milk is a staple across Southeast Asia, especially in the southern areas of Thailand, all of Malaysia, Singapore, and Indonesia. Most cooks in America turn to canned coconut milk, yet it is still common to make your own coconut milk in Southeast Asia—they do, however, often go to a local vendor who shreds fresh coconut for them. One can make coconut milk by grating the white coconut flesh, adding some warm water, giving this mixture a quick massage, and then squeezing out the coconut milk. This first liquid would be referred to as thick coconut milk. Add some more water and squeeze again to obtain thin coconut milk. Do not confuse it with coconut water in the middle of the coconut; this is often used as a chilled beverage or as a simmering liquid for meats and seafood.

Indigenous bamboo is made into cages for small farm animals, woven into baskets for field fresh produce, crafted into steamers for the kitchen, and split into shards for chopsticks. A specific bamboo species is harvested early for its young, edible shoots. Dried bamboo leaves are also commonly used to wrap dumplings. In Malaysia, one might even have the chance to taste rice that has been wrapped in banana leaves, stuffed into a hollow piece of bamboo, and grilled over charcoal.

The myriad unique fruits found in the region could fill a book of its own, since many that are indigenous to the area are still not readily available in other parts of the world. Travelers and the like quickly adapt to many of the fruits, such as lychee, star fruit, rambutan, mangosteen, and numerous varieties of bananas.

The banana tree yields banana leaves, blossoms, hearts, and the fruit—all used in popular dishes. Banana leaves are used as a plate, to wrap items before they are steamed, grilled, and pan fried, or simply as an ornate garnish. If using fresh banana leaves, pour hot water over them to make them pliable before trying to fold them. The banana blossom is used for its astringent flavor, most often in salads. The blossom can be cut into large chunks and cooked in a curry. In Burma, they have devised a fish stew that uses the core of the main "trunk," although botanically, the banana plant is an enormous herb, not a tree.

Then there are those fruits that take a bit more adventure to appreciate. Durian, known as "the King of Fruits" throughout Southeast Asia, has hard thorns outside and creamy, sweet flesh that is reminiscent of pineapple and fermented sweet onions—one of those delicacies you must taste to understand! This stinky fruit is actually banned from rental cars, hotels, and buses because of the strong scent that some find offensive, but tigers are said to love.

Cuisine

The pantry of ingredients used in Southeast Asian cooking are almost identical in each country, yet the way in which they are combined and the regional cooking techniques create distinct cuisines. Each region has developed unique combinations to create a distinctive cuisine. The Vietnamese are known for their copious use of fresh herbs and how guests assemble many of their foods tableside, layering textures and flavors. The Thais are famous for coconut-laden sauces, hot and sour soup, and crispy green papaya salad. Indonesian-inspired satay with peanut sauce could be considered an icon of Southeast Asian cuisine. However, in many instances, regional foods are becoming blurred, as modernization has all but eliminated strictly regional traditional cuisines in most developed countries.

Curries

Curries can be found on dining tables in every country of this region. Curry is an oft-misunderstood term; the term *curry* was derived from the Indian term *Kari*, which simply means "sauce" or indicates any dish simmered in sauce. The Thais utilize the word *kaeng* (sometimes spelled *king*) to designate a spice paste–seasoned liquid. They further categorize this into thickened (such as a red curry) and thin liquids (as in broth-based soups). Thai curry pastes are based on the same fundamental ingredients: lemongrass, galangal, shallots, garlic, peppercorns, kaffir lime rind, fermented shrimp paste, and salt. Then each variety may have an ingredient that makes it unqiue: Green curry contains the addition of coriander roots and green chiles, and yellow curry incorporates turmeric. The curries of Indonesia, Singapore, and Malaysia are based on a *rempah*. Literally translated as "spice," the term is popularly used to describe a pounded paste of aromatic ingredients. Many rempahs contain garlic and shallots, and also lemongrass, galangal, chiles, and shrimp paste, and are often the primary thickener for stews and soups.

Sambal is another sauce or sauce base that is found in several countries—primarily in Malaysia, Singapore, and Indonesia. A sambal is broadly defined as a chile-based condiment. The most common ingredient list for a sambal would contain chiles, garlic, shallots, and sugar, and may contain vinegar, shrimp paste, salt, and tamarind. *Sambal* can be served cooked or uncooked, depending on the cook and region.

Rice

Any discussion of Asian food without the mention of rice would be preposterous. Actually, it is thought that central Thailand is the first site of cultivated rice. Currently, fragrant jasmine rice is one of their chief exports. Most of this region relies on a long-grain variety called *indica,* as well as the lesser-used *javanica,* a medium- to long-grain subspecies. Most often, rice is cooked by mixing water and rice together, bringing them to a boil, and simmering until the rice absorbs the moisture; salt is rarely added. This type of rice is served at almost every meal. Many countries have also developed an infatuation for "glutinous" rice, this actually being a misnomer as there is no gluten in rice. Instead, the term denotes its chewy character, so that the rice is also commonly referred to as sticky rice. It is first soaked and then steamed in specialized conical bamboo steamers.

Long-grain rice is used in many different specialties throughout Southeast Asia. It is commonly combined with water and coconut milk and cooked to create the foundation for *nasi lemak,* which translates into English as "coconut rice." This dish brings many Malay specialties to one plate. The coconut rice is often presented in the center of a banana leaf surrounded with a sampling of dry beef curry (beef *rendang*), shrimp *sambal,* hard-boiled egg, chicken curry, sliced cucumber, deep-fried peanuts, and fried *ikan billis* (a variety of anchovies). This dish is most often enjoyed from the local food stalls for breakfast. Hainanese chicken rice, a Singaporean specialty, is a dish in which gently poached chicken is paired with a special rice that is mixed with chicken fat, fried garlic, and ginger before cooking. The chicken and rice are paired with a tangy chile-garlic sauce and sliced cucumbers.

Noodles

Noodles trail close behind rice in their importance in Southeast Asian cuisine. Round, flat, thick, thin, dried, fresh, chewy, silky, or tender noodles are found throughout the region. Although rice noodles, egg noodles, and mung bean noodles are all common, it was inevitable that rice noodles would be some of the most commonly used, because of the abundance of rice. Rice noodles are usually prepared from a batter, as opposed to the firm doughs used in the prepartion of egg noodles. Dried rice is soaked and ground or rice flour is combined with water to create a batter that can be formed in a multitude of ways. Some chefs add

tapioca starch or wheat starch for elasticity. Traditionally, a pot of boiling water is topped with a thin sheet of cloth, the batter is ladled on top, and the layer is steamed to create a sheet of rice noodle. These sheets are used fresh or dried, cut into strips for noodles. Today, much of this has been mechanized, yet the same principal ingredients are used—rice and water.

Fresh rice noodles, referred to as *kway teow* in Malaysia and Singapore, are most commonly used in the preparation of a dish called *char kway teow,* in which a scorching hot wok is used to fry bean sprouts, green onions, coarsely chopped garlic, and rice noodles until they begin to brown and get a bit chewy, when they are tossed to one side of the wok. The wok is then coated with oil and an egg is broken and fried in it before being tossed together with the browned noodle mixture. Dried, thin rice noodles are most often labeled as *vermicelli, rice sticks, mee hoon, bihon,* or (when ultra thin) *bun hoi.* Dried rice noodles that are ¼ in/6 mm wide are easily recognized in the famous *pad thai* dish of stir-fried noodles with bean sprouts and peanuts.

Wheat flour noodles are also a large part of the local cuisine. Wheat flour, water, and salt are combined and kneaded into a dough and formed into noodles. Some of the wheat-based noodles have the addition of eggs or egg yolks. With the inclusion of pure starches like tapioca and wheat starch, a wide range of textures is achieved—some are more resilient and others are chewy. Although there may be many different names by which egg noodles are known, most of the doughs are prepared similarly to Italian pasta, and then formed into noodles ranging from $\frac{1}{16}$ to ¼ inch/1.50 to 6 mm thick. Dried wheat noodles are not used as often, but, as in the United States, having them on hand can help a chef out in a pinch.

It is not unusual to see an Italian-style pasta machine strapped to the side of the cart of a street vendor in Malaysia for *wonton mee,* a common example of an egg noodle dish. It is a Chinese-inspired dish, in which very thin egg noodles are boiled quickly, tossed with soy sauce, cooked greens, and white pepper, piled on a plate, and topped with slivers of Chinese roasted pork. These soy-slathered noodles are always served with a bowl of light chicken broth with a few floating wontons. *Khao soi,* thought to be an import of Myanmar (Burma) is a northern Thai specialty; in the city of Chiang Mai, the chefs have become expert at preparing the curried coconut broth with egg noodles and chicken, pork, or beef garnished with crispy egg noodles and a squeeze of fresh lime juice. The aroma will haunt you until you are able to make it back for another taste. Indonesia is where *mee goreng* originated. The spaghetti-size egg noodles are stir-fried with sliced onions, lots of garlic and shrimp, shredded cabbage, bean sprouts, and green onions. Some chefs like to use *trassi*—a fermented shrimp paste—to give the dish additional depth of flavor.

Usually imported from China, another popular noodle is made from mung bean starch, and they are sometimes referred to as glass or cellophane noodles. The Thais take advantage of their signature transparent noodles in their *yam woon sen*, in which the cooked noodles are tossed in a dressing of lime juice, fish sauce, sugar, and red chiles. Although each chef has their own version, ground pork, cilantro, and green onions usually find their way into this salad as well.

Soups

Soups are the ultimate comfort food to those that have grown up in this area. Served during the meal, rather than as a separate course, they can be used to quench the heat of a spicy dish or used to spice up steamed white rice. The Malaysian island of Penang is known for its tamarind-based *asam laksa,* a fish broth that is filled with rice noodles and garnished with strips of pineapple, cucumber, mint, and laksa leaves—known in Vietnam as *rau ram,* and often referred to as Vietnamese coriander. *Pho* (pronounced "fuh") *bo* is consumed for breakfast, lunch, or as a snack, and originated in northern Vietnam, where it is considered to be a national dish. To make this aromatic soup a rich beef broth scented with cinnamon, star anise, and charred ginger and onions is poured on top of cooked rice noodles, thinly sliced onions, and beef. Various cuts of beef are combined with different cooking techniques to achieve an array of textures and flavor. The beef may be slowly simmered gelatinous beef tendon that is sliced thinly, poached beef brisket that is then cut into thin slabs, or shaved raw beef placed on top of the bowl, where it cooks almost instantly as the hot broth is ladled over it. In step with the Vietnmese trademark of finishing the dish at the table, each diner adds his or her own garnishes of Asian basil, saw-leaf herb, cilantro, bean sprouts, green chile slivers, and a twist of fresh lime juice. As this dish migrated south, *pho ga* has emerged—a chicken-based version of similar flavors and service.

Vegetables

Vegetables are treated with respect. Some are grown underground, like potaoes, lotus root, taro, jicama, radishes, and tapioca (also known as cassava or manioc). Green leafy bok choys, Chinese broccoli, water spinach, cabbage, or mustard greens are preferred bright green and crisp after cooking. Green mung beans are sprouted and tossed in at the last moment to stir-fries. Eggplant, actually indiginous to the area, comes in a variety of colors and shapes—one in Thailand is a small, white oval, which is perhaps why the English term "eggplant" originated. Snow peas, Chinese long beans, pea shoots, and the unique tree-grown stink beans are all commonly utilized. Mushrooms are also included prominantly in Southeast Asian cooking—*straw mushrooms* gain their name from the rice straw they are grown on.

Desserts and Sweets

Desserts are not a large part of the traditional daily Southeast Asian culture. Although sweets can be found at all times of the day, they are savored and served most typically on holidays and at celebrations. Commonly referred to as cakes, most Westerners would not recognize the rice flour, palm sugar, coconut milk, and *pandanus* (scented aromatic slender green leaf, sometime referred to as Southeast Asian vanilla) concoctions that are commonly eaten with afternoon tea. Ovens are still not used often in average home kitchens; instead, cooks steam these dense sweets. Sticky rice often finds its way into desserts, in which rice flour may be used to bind and thicken or the rice may be soaked, steamed, and sweetened, then served with sliced ripe mangos, as they do in Thailand. The Nyonyas of Malaysia are known for their *kueh* or cakes. One of the most illustrious is *pulut seri kaya*—steamed sticky rice packed into a tray, topped with a coconut-egg custard, and steamed until set. Cooled briefly, it is cut into diamonds before being displayed at the local market. The Filipinos commonly make a version of flan.

No country quite focuses on sweets as the Thais do. They lead the way in the sweets category they refer to as *kanom.* They have perfected the Portuguese-influenced "Golden Strands," in which egg yolks, sugar, and jasmine essence are cooked in a sugar syrup, creating fine strands of glistening, deep yellow threads that are gathered into bundles. *Kanom krok* is an illustration of how Thais sometimes balance sweetness with a hint of salt. A thin batter of coconut milk, rice, tapioca flour, sugar, and salt are cooked in a skillet that has 1-in/3-cm divots. While the batter is cooked over a charcoal fire, kernels of corn or slivers of green onions are added with a drizzle of sweetened batter. When these half spheres are turned out, they have a crispy surface and a velvety, sweet and salty, custard consistency.

In Indonesia, one might find *pisang goreng,* baby bananas that are battered and deep fried until crispy. Some cooks like to add sesame seeds to the batter so the seeds toast as they fry. Gelatinous sweets are held together with agar agar, a seaweed-based "gelatin" that is used as the setting agent since it does not dissolve in the warm tropical heat. Rice, coconut, palm sugar, pandanus, and eggs form a large part of the pantry for Southeast Asian sweets.

Cultural Influences on Southeast Asian Cuisine

Led by Admiral Cheng Ho in the early 1400s, the Chinese took control of the area and brought with them chopsticks, woks, noodles, and soy sauces. Primarily, the men came to Malaysia and many found Malay wives, where they formed the group that is known as the *Paranakan.* The males are referred to as the *Babas* and the women as *Nyonyas*; these families developed a sophisticated culture and cuisine that is well revered in the area. Their *po piah,* or fresh spring rolls, are a clear example of how the Chinese tradition of spring rolls was transformed into a truly Malaysian delight. The wrapper in Malaysia is prepared similarly to a crêpe. The bulk of the filling is made from cooked jicama, with a locally fermented soybean paste and traditional Chinese soy sauce. *Pong teh* is another example of how Chinese ingredients and Malay techniques are combined flawlessly. Dried Chinese mushrooms, the same variety that is often called shiitake, are cooked with dark soy sauce, potatoes, and chicken. The Malaysian technique of using a pounded mixture of shallots and garlic as the primary thickener makes this truly a fusion dish.

Hundreds of years of Chinese rule in Vietnam have left an indelible stamp on the people and cuisine.

Eating Implements

Westerners often incorrectly assume that Asians eat all of their food with chopsticks. The use of chopsticks in Southeast Asia comes from the Chinese, yet in this area of the world they reserve the use of chopsticks for dishes in which they are most effective, such as in Thailand, where chopsticks are primarily reserved for noodle dishes. The European influence on these countries regularized the use of the fork. However, one might be surprised by the unique use of the spoon and fork together. In this region, the fork is usually used to push the food into the spoon, collecting the various elements of the meal to create the ideal combination of flavors and textures. Using one's hands while eating is not restricted to the young; they are used with grace to dip sticky rice in fragrant curries in northern Thailand and eat coconut rice off banana leaves in Singapore.

The name *Vietnam* is actually derived from two words: *viet* is Chinese for "clan" and *nam* means "south," hence Vietnam—the southern clan (from China). Chinese-style clay pot cooking is still a part of contemporary Vietnamese cuisine. One signature dish combines caramelized sugar, fish sauce, shallots, black pepper, and fish sauce with seafood. This mixture is simmered until the sauce becomes a deep golden syrup.

The influence of nearly a century of French occupation can been seen in Vietnamese cooking implements and preparations as well as lifestyle. Vietnamese are often found in the kitchen with a sauté pan as well as a wok. The penchant for coffee consumed in cafés along the streets of Vietnam is another remnant of the French, since missionaries planted the first crops of coffee in Vietnam in 1857. Now, Vietnam is one of the world's leading producers.

Beliefs and Traditions

The influence of the Chinese is also apparent in Southeast Asia because the Chinese religion Taoism is based on the principle of Yin and Yang, where a harmony is achieved by the proper blending of complementary opposites. This concept can be clearly seen in the kitchens and on the tables of Southeast Asia, as many of the cultures believe that food possesses the power to heal and is often used as medicine. Foods that are *yang* are considered "hot" and those that are *yin* are "cold" and are thought to have the ability to regulate the body's temperature and organ functions. Ingredients are broken into two main categories: those that are *yin*, such as sugar, soy sauce, white vegetables, and salt, and others that are *yang*, such as chiles, garlic, ginger, vinegar, rice wine, and Szechwan peppercorns. This is why the classic combination of sweet and sour is so pervasive in Southeast Asian cuisines; it is a balancing sauce. Since steaming is *yin* and frying is *yang*, deep frying a steamed duck until the skin crisps is one way that chefs use cooking techniques to create a sense of balance with contrasting textures. This concept can also be illustrated through the composition of a Chinese multi-course menu; much planning goes into what dishes will be served at the same time and in which order they will be served. A mild steamed dish of Chinese bok choy may be paired with a spicy deep-fried fish.

Malaysia has felt the influence of eastern and Arabic culture for over 800 years, along with a strong presence of Chinese and Indian cultures. Today Malaysia exists as a true multicultural society with Islam as its national religion and Malaysians, Chinese, and Indians peaceably coexisting. The presence of Islam would typically have eliminated pork from Malaysian cuisine, but the strong Chinese presence, felt for hundreds of years, would not let that happen to one of their favorite and most widely used proteins. Therefore, today you will find some restaurants that cater only to those who are Muslim, serving Chinese-style food without pork. Hindus revere the cow as sacred and do not eat its meat, yet praise its other products such as milk and butter. Clarified butter, known as ghee, is used as one of their primary cooking fats and is also used in the Hindu wedding ceremony. The fusion of Chinese and Indian cultures is obvious in the dish *mee rebus,* in which Chinese egg noodles are combined with an Indian-inspired curry powder and coconut milk to create a truly unique Malaysian dish. The Indian presence has also contributed to various flatbreads.

The Spanish colonized the Philippines in the sixteenth century and left their imprint on the cuisine by bringing ingredients such as tomatoes and bay leaves. An illustration of a Spanish-influenced Philippine dish is *pancit guisado,* a combination of thin *bihon* rice noodles, fish, and soy sauces in which one might discover strips of ham, diced tomatoes, sliced red peppers, and julienned carrots. A distinctive lemon wedge is used instead of the more common lime wedge found in much of Southeast Asia.

Chapter Seven

Europe

Europeans have influenced cuisine around the world. They were the travelers—the explorers and conquerors. They brought with them the seeds of cuisine and culture from home and around the globe and planted them wherever they traveled. They brought rice to the "New World" and brought the tomato back to European soil. Who among us today could imagine Mexican food without rice or Italian food without tomatoes.

France

France can be divided into four culinary regions: the northwest, the northeast, the southeast, and the southwest. Within each region, there are provinces, twenty-two in all, which are comprised of cities, towns, and villages. Though culinary parallels can be drawn between the provinces in each region, each province has its own culinary specialties, impacted by history, terrain, and climate.

The hexagon-shaped mainland of France is located in western Europe, with other French territories spanning the globe. France is bordered by the English Channel on the northwest; Belgium and Luxembourg on the northeast; Germany, Switzerland, and Italy on the east; the Mediterranean Sea on the southeast; Spain and Andorra on the southwest; and the Bay of Biscay and the Atlantic Ocean on the west. The independent state of Monaco is located in the southeast, completely surrounded by French territory, and the island of Corsica lies in the Mediterranean Sea, off the coast of Italy.

France encompasses an area larger than 211,209 square miles (547,000 square kilometers). Generally speaking, the terrain of the north and west is flat, with rolling hills, while the south and east are quite rugged and mountainous. The climate of the country is also rather diverse, with mild winters and summers in the west, cool winters and hot summers inland, tough winters and high levels of precipitation in the mountains, and mild winters and hot summers along the Mediterranean in the south.

About 57 percent of the land in France is dedicated to agriculture, including viticulture. The diversity of climate and topography throughout the country gives way to an array of cultivated crops. The population of France, around 60.6 million people, is amply nourished with local produce, nuts, grains, cheese, wine, livestock, game, seafood, and freshwater fish, varieties depending on each specific region.

Regional Cuisines

Northwest France

The provinces in the northwest of France include Brittany, Basse-Normandy, Haute-Normandy, Pays de la Loire, and Centre (commonly known as the Loire Valley). All but Centre have miles of coastline, and therefore a maritime climate: mild winters, cool summers, and significant rainfall. The province of Centre lies entirely inland, where winters are harsher and summers are hotter.

The proximity of northwestern France to the sea is reflected in the cuisine. Brittany is the country's principal fishing region, with oysters, lobsters, clams, Dungeness crabs, skate, mackerel, and sole driving the industry. Dover or Channel sole is caught off the coast of Normandy and is prized for its firm and flavorful flesh. Lamb and goat are also popular throughout the northwest, though beef is quite popular in Normandy and Pays de la Loire. Game, such as wild boar, rabbit, and pheasant, and freshwater fish, such as trout, carp, and shad, are prevalent in Centre.

Normandy is renowned for cow's milk cheeses, such as Camembert and Pont l'Évêque, as well as superior cream and butter, which are heavily utilized in the cooking of the region. In the rest of the northwest, goat's and sheep's milk cheeses are more common. Normandy is also the land of apples, while the neighboring provinces boast a great variety of produce, especially Centre. Fruits and vegetables of this region include plums, pears, potatoes, artichokes, endive, escarole, and pumpkins. Wheat is the preferred grain of the northwest, though barley and corn are widely consumed in Centre, along with walnuts.

Northeast France

Northeast France encompasses the provinces of Nord Pays de Calais, Picardy, Champagne-Ardenne, Île de France, Alsace, Lorraine, and Franche-Comté. These area cuisines are influenced by the countries that border them, from north to south: Belgium, Luxembourg, Germany, and Switzerland. Nord Pays de Calais and Picardy also benefit from their location on the English Channel. The climate in these regions reflects the topography. The Vosges Mountains stretch between Alsace and Île de France, giving way to greater extremes of temperature in winter and summer months, as well as high levels of precipitation. The climate in Nord Pays de Calais and Picardy is mostly maritime, while the remainder of the northeast is made up of rolling hills and plains, resulting in a more temperate climate.

The cuisines of the northeast are particularly influenced by southern Germany. The soil of the region is quite fertile, benefiting from the Rhine River to the north. Fruits and vegetables include cherries, grapes, wild mushrooms, potatoes, beets, asparagus, and cabbage (which is used to make sauerkraut). Pork, game, foie gras, freshwater fish, escargots, and frogs are popular proteins. Pork is often used to make charcuterie items, such as sausages, terrines, and pâtés. Butter and pork fat are the preferred cooking fats and cheese is generally made from cow's milk. Wheat is the grain of choice and is used to make spätzle and egg noodles.

Southeast France

Burgundy, Auvergne, Limousin, Rhône Alps, Provence-Alpes-Côte d'Azur, and Corsica are the provinces located in southeast France. The climate in the southernmost provinces, Provence-Alpes-Côte d'Azur and Corsica, is Mediterranean, with more hours of daylight than any other province of France. This area is also known for *mistral,* a northwesterly wind that blows through the region. Inland to the east, there are the Alps, bordering Italy and Switzerland; to the west, there is the Rhône River Valley.

Lyon, the culinary capital of France, is located in the Rhône Alps. This region, like most of the southeast (with the exception of Provence-Alpes-Côte d'Azur and Corsica), features a variety of meats, including beef, pork, lamb, duck, and rabbit. Cow, sheep, and goat's milk cheeses are all popular, depending on the season. Apples, grapes, cherries, pears, and strawberries are plentiful, as are mushrooms, cabbage, potatoes, haricots verts, and cardoons. Wheat and corn are the main grains grown here. Specialties of the region include Dijon mustard from Burgundy and Le Puy lentils from Auvergne.

The cuisines of Provence-Alpes-Côte d'Azur and Corsica are distinct from the rest of the southeast. Artichokes, fennel, eggplant, tomatoes, peppers, garlic, herbs, and olives are staples of the region. Apricots, cherries, plums, and figs are eaten fresh, but also made into preserves. The region is reliant on the Mediterranean Sea for much of its sustenance; common fish include anchovies, sardines, red mullet, and monkfish. Specialties of the region include a fish stew called bouillabaisse, ratatouille, and tapenade. (See The Mediterranean, pages 120–122.)

AOC

AOC (*Appellation d'Origine Contrôlée*) can be translated to roughly mean "name of origin." AOC is an official recognition given to particular French wines, cheeses, butters, livestock, poultry, and other agricultural foodstuffs. The certification of AOC is decided by an agency known as the *Institut National des Appellations d'Origine* (INAO). The INAO ensures that AOC products are made following certain criteria and that they are not falsely labeled and sold under an AOC-restricted name.

An AOC certification ensures that a product meets the following guidelines:

- The product is always produced in the time-honored manner.

- The product is produced with raw ingredients from a specific geographical region, and is at the very least aged in this area for part of the time.

- The characteristics of the product are constant and in sequence with standards that are clearly defined (size, shape, weight, composition, color, flavor, aroma, etc.).

- The production of the product is stringently monitored by the INAO following AOC-defined standards.

The origin of the AOC can be traced back as far at the fifteenth century, though the first legal decree from Parliament did not appear until 1666, and it was based exclusively on Roquefort cheese. The official AOC seal was developed in the 1950s, and several other countries followed the system to control place names for various products. Italy instituted the DOC (*Demominazione di Origine Controllata*) laws in 1963, which were followed by the DOP (*Denominazione di Origine Protetta*) regulations (see page 116), and Spain's DO (*Denominacion de Origen*), among others.

Examples of Some French AOC Products

CHEESES	OTHER PRODUCTS
Morbier	Le Puy lentils
Camembert de Normandie	Poulet de Bresse (chicken)
Roquefort	Fleur de sel (salt)
Pont-l'Evêque	Nyons black olives
Banon	Calvados

REGION	MAJOR CITY	CHARACTERISTICS OF CUISINE
NORTHWEST FRANCE		
Brittany	Brest	Apples, strawberries, haricots verts, cauliflower, potatoes, artichokes, cider, crêpes, seafood (Belon oysters, lobster, clams, skate, mackerel, sole), salted fish, lamb, duck, turkey
Basse- and Haute-Normandy	Cherbourg, Rouen	Cow's milk (Camembert cheese), cream, butter, honey, apples, cider, Calvados, seafood (Dover sole, herring, cod, mussels, oysters, shrimp, Dungeness crab), beef (tripe), pork, lamb, duck, chicken
Pays de la Loire	Nantes	Beef, pork, duck, seafood
Centre	Orléans	Goat's milk cheese, plums, melons, pears, pumpkin, asparagus, mushrooms, mâche, endive, escarole, sorrel, wheat, barley, corn, walnuts, vinegars, game (rabbit, pheasant, wild boar), lamb, organ meats, chicken, duck, freshwater fish (trout, carp, pike, shad)
NORTHEAST FRANCE		
Nord Pays de Calais	Lille	Endive, beets, potatoes, wheat, barley, fish, pork
Picardy		Beets, potatoes, wheat, barley, fish, pork
Champagne-Ardenne	Reims, Epernay, Charleville-Mézières, Châlons-sur-Marne, Chaumont, Troyes	Beets, potatoes Champagne, wheat, rye, barley, beer, snails, seafood, lamb, pork (charcuterie), sausages, game (wild boar)
Île de France	Paris	Potatoes. Grande cuisine; not very regional
Alsace	Strasbourg	Pork fat, goose fat, plums, apples, cherries, grapes, asparagus, cabbage (sauerkraut), potatoes, wild mushrooms, grains, egg noodles, spätzle, goose (foie gras), pork, game, freshwater fish
Lorraine	Nancy	Butter, cow's milk cheese, plums, apples, cherries, grapes, cabbage (sauerkraut), potatoes, wild mushrooms, grains, egg noodles, spätzle, chicken, goose (foie gras), pork, game, freshwater fish
Franche-Comté	Besançon	Cow's milk cheese (fondue), freshwater fish (trout), frog's legs, charcuterie, chicken

REGION	MAJOR CITY	CHARACTERISTICS OF CUISINE
SOUTHEAST FRANCE		
Burgundy	Dijon	Currants, mushrooms, beef, pork, poultry, game, snails, mustard
Auvergne (Massif Central)	Valence	Grenoble apples, grapes, cabbage, potatoes, mushrooms, wheat, lentils, beef, duck
Limousin	Limoges	Apples, cabbage, potatoes, mushrooms, wheat, beef, duck, lamb
Rhône Alps	Lyon	Apricots, apples, cherries, melons, pears, strawberries, cabbage, potatoes, green beans, cardoons, herbs (thyme, rosemary, bay leaf), pork, lamb, chicken, quail, turkey, rabbit, variety meats, corn, nuts
Provence-Alpes-Côte d'Azur	Nice, Marseilles	Olive oil, garlic, tomatoes, peppers, onions, zucchini, fennel, artichokes, chickpeas, eggplant, herbs (thyme, lavender, rosemary, basil), pasta, honey, lamb, seafood (red mullet, sardines, anchovies, monkfish)
Corsica		Olive oil, citrus, figs, almonds, chestnuts, seafood, beef, goat, lamb, game (blackbirds)
SOUTHWEST FRANCE		
Midi-Pyrénées	Toulouse	Olive oil, plums, peaches, apricots, tomatoes, garlic, eggplant, cèpes, seafood (eel), pork, duck, goose
Languedoc-Roussillon	Montpellier, Perpignan, Nîmes, Carcassonne	Olive oil, plums, peaches, apricots, tomatoes, garlic, eggplant, cèpes, seafood (eel), pork, duck, goose
Aquitaine	Bordeaux	Plums, strawberries, apples, pears, peaches, garlic, chiles, tomatoes, onions, corn, broad beans, peas, wild mushrooms (black truffles, cèpes, chanterelles), seafood (oysters, mussels, crabs, squid, cod, tuna, sardines, anchovies), poultry (chicken, duck, goose, turkey, pigeon)
Poitou-Charentes		Goat's milk cheese, beans, wheat, barley, corn, almonds, chestnuts, beef, seafood (oysters, eels), snails

Southwest France

Southwest France is comprised of Midi-Pyrénées, Languedoc-Roussillon, Aquitaine, and Poitou-Charentes. These regions have much in common with Spain and Portugal, as is most evident in the Pays Basque, the area along the Spanish border. The climate in this region is mostly maritime, shaped by the Bay of Biscay and the Mediterranean Sea. The Pyrenees mountain range runs through the region, also influencing the climate.

Seafood is popular on the coast in the southwest provinces; varieties include monkfish, eel, tuna, cod, oysters, and mussels. In Pays Basque, fish soup with peppers and onion is popular, as well as jambon de Bayonne, a cured ham. Inland, poultry is most common; turkey, pigeon, duck, and the famous geese from the forests of les Landes in Gascony are popular, to name a few. Foie gras, walnuts, chestnuts, black truffles, and other wild mushrooms, such as cèpes (porcini) and chanterelles are also common fare, especially in Perigord. Cassoulet and duck confit are specialties inland. Both olive oil and duck fat are used throughout the region. As dairy cattle are scarce, goat's milk cheeses are the mainstay. For produce, plums, peaches, apricots, tomatoes, eggplant, wheat, barley, and corn are staples.

Cultural Influences of French Cuisine

Throughout its history, France has been invaded by conquerors and explorers from many foreign lands. This may be attributed to its numerous boundaries with other countries, but also because of its proximity to various bodies of water. In certain areas of the country, Celtic, British, Basque, Spanish, Italian, German, Greek, Arab, and Middle Eastern influences are evident. The Celtic Gauls invaded the area known today as France between 1500 and 500 B.C.E. The Gauls introduced farming to the area and partitioned the land into an early form of the provinces that exist today. The Romans then took over the region in 56 B.C.E., introducing cheese making, for which France is known to this day. Under Roman control, fish and game were popular. Meats were spit roasted in fireplaces, or boiled in large pots that were suspended from hooks in the fireplace.

The Moors, responsible for introducing goats to the region by way of Spain, invaded France in 718 A.D., diversifying French cooking methods and ingredients. In the Middle Ages, spices such as pepper, cumin,

LEFT TO RIGHT, TOP TO BOTTOM: Mont d'Or Lyonnais, raclette, fol de epi, roquefort, morbier, mimolette, port salut, Pyrenees, brie, petit camembert, explorateur, chaume, le ple d'angloys, tomme de savoie, rambol, epoisse, boursin, muenster, chevres, boursault

anise, ginger, galangal, cinnamon, and caraway were common, a result of the spice trade making stops at France's many ports. Arab influences were evident in the use of almonds and rice as a thickener, a result of French knights' travels to the Middle East.

In the sixteenth and seventeenth centuries, modern-day French cuisine emerged. With the marriage of Catherine de Medici to Henry II (see page 117), the foundations for Grande Cuisine were established. At the same time, the discovery of the benefits of crop rotation resulted in a greater variety, quantity, and quality of vegetables. Spices were used less frequently; since food quality improved, it was no longer necessary to cover up the taste of the raw ingredients. Two thirds of the French population were farmers in 1789, dependent on cereal crops for survival when the Bastille was stormed, leaving a large percentage of the working class impoverished, while the bourgeois class celebrated Grande Cuisine.

Today, Grande Cuisine is very much a part of French culture; however, culinary characteristics specific to each region exist. Everyday food in France, eaten at home, is not all foie gras, truffles, and the "mother" sauces. There are certain ingredients, such as chicken from Bresse, Calvados from Normandy, and geese from les Landes, that are highly esteemed throughout the country as a whole, but in the home, regional specialties abound.

Restaurant History and Evolution

The first restaurant (as we know restaurants today) opened in Paris in 1765, when M. Boulanger, a tavern keeper, served a dish of sheep's feet, or trotters, in a white sauce as a restorative. Although he was brought to court for infringing on a separate guild's monopoly, he won the case and was allowed to continue serving food. Once the precedent was established, other restaurants soon appeared.

The French Revolution (1789–1799) had a particularly significant effect on restaurant proliferation, because many chefs who previously had worked for the monarchy or nobility fled France to escape the guillotine. Although some sought employment with the noble classes in other countries, others began to open their own establishments. Restaurants became increasingly refined operations, and although they were at first frequented only by men, this would change as customs in society and in the foodservice industry as a whole changed.

Most hotels and restaurants offered a simple *table d'hôte* (or set complete meal), which provided little if any choice. The Grande Cuisine, a careful code established by Marie-Antoine Carême (1784–1833) that detailed numerous dishes and their sauces, was a cooking style well suited to royal and noble households but difficult to maintain in hotel kitchens, which usually had only rudimentary cooking equipment. When the Savoy Hotel opened in London in 1898 under the direction of César Ritz and Georges-Auguste Escoffier, the Grande Cuisine was replaced by a more refined and simplified approach referred to as *Cuisine Classique* (classic or classical cuisine).

The next major shift in French cuisine occurred gradually. Fernand Point (1897–1955) took Escoffier's message of simplification even further and laid the groundwork for the next upheaval in restaurant cooking styles. Several chefs, all influenced by Point, are credited with inventing *Nouvelle Cuisine* during the early 1970s, including such luminaries as Paul Bocuse, Alain Chapel, François Bise, and Jean and Pierre Troisgros. The end result was an entirely new approach to the selection of ingredients for a dish, cooking and saucing styles, and plate presentation. Smaller portions, more artful presentation, and the combination of new ingredients became the hallmarks of this cooking style.

Today, a growing global marketplace combined with an interest in multiculturalism and diversity has led to the popularization of many cuisines within France. Some chefs are blending cooking styles and ingredients from around the world to create new dishes (sometimes known as fusion cuisine). Other chefs are exploring the lesser-known traditions of regional and ethnic cooking styles. Still others have chosen a classical path, seeking to test their technical skills and culinary artistry against the standards of their mentors.

LEFT TO RIGHT, TOP TO BOTTOM: chervil, yellow turnip, white turnips, pears, red wine, tarragon, onions, haricots verts, apple, lemon, shallots, garlic, cream, grapes, chives, red and white endive, walnuts, lentils de puy, butter, picholine olives, dried chanterelle mushrooms, whole-grain mustard, sea salt, nicoise olives, herbs de Provence

Italy

For culinary purposes, the country of Italy can be loosely divided into the south, central, and north. Northern Italy is bordered by France, Switzerland, Austria, and Slovenia. Central and southern Italy are bordered by the Mediterranean Sea, a position that holds great historical importance in terms of exploration and trade. Though only four countries border Italy by land, culinary and cultural influences are evident from numerous other countries throughout the world, including places such as Spain, Greece, North Africa, the eastern Mediterranean, and even the Americas.

Located in southern Europe, the country of Italy covers an area of 187,176 square miles (301,230 square kilometers) and extends into the central Mediterranean Sea. The islands of Sicily and Sardinia, as well many smaller islands, are also part of the Italian territory.

The generally rugged and mountainous terrain of Italy is home to a population of 58 million people. Politically, Italy is divided into twenty regions: Abruzzi, Basilicata, Calabria, Campania, Emilia-Romagna, Friuli-Venezia Giulia, Latium, Liguria, Lombardy, Le Marche, Molise, Piemonte, Apulia, Sardinia, Sicily, Toscana, Trentino-Alto Adige, Umbria, Valle d'Aosta, and Veneto. Considering that Italy is slightly larger than the state of Arizona, the culinary diversity, specialties, and pride of each region are quite remarkable.

LEFT TO RIGHT, TOP TO BOTTOM: bucatini, olive oil, balsamic vinegar, parsley, basil, rosemary, oregano, radiatore, wheat flour, fettucine, garlic, black truffles, olives, semolina flour

Common Italian Cooking Ingredients and Terms

TERM	DEFINITION	TERM	DEFINITION	TERM	DEFINITION
Aceto	Vinegar	Contorni	Side dishes served with main course	Pesce	Fish
Aglio	Garlic			Pignoli	Pine nuts
Agnello	Lamb	Cotto	Cooked	Pollo	Chicken
Agrodolce	Sour and sweet	Crudo	Raw	Pomodoro	Tomato
Al dente	The point at which pasta is cooked, meaning "to the tooth"	Dolce	Sweet	Primi Piatti	First courses
		Dolci	Dessert	Sale	Salt
Antipasti	Food eaten "before the meal"; appetizers	Fagioli	Dried beans	Salsa	Sauce
		Farina	Flour	Scaloppine	Thin slices of meat
Battuto	Chopped vegetables and herbs that are mixed with lard or oil, used as a base for soups, sauces, stews, and braises	Finocchio	Fennel	Secondi Piatti	Main courses
		Formaggio	Cheese	Semolina	Flour made from durum wheat, excellent for making pasta
		Fritto	Fried		
		Gamberi	Shrimp		
Bollito	Boiled	Insalata	Salad	Soffrito	*Battuto* that have been sautéed
Brodetto	Soup	Latte	Milk	Sugo	Gravy
Brodo	Broth	Melanzana	Eggplant	Tartufi	Truffles
Bue	Beef	Miele	Honey	Tonno	Tuna
Carciofo	Artichoke	Misto	Mxed	Uovo	Eggs
Carne	Meat	Olio	Oil	Vitello	Milk-fed, very young veal
Ceci	Chickpea	Pane	Bread	Vitellone	Young beef
Cipolla	Onion	Pecora	Sheep	Vongole	Clams
Coniglio	Rabbit	Pepperoncini	Dried or fresh red chiles	Zucchero	Sugar

LEFT TO RIGHT, TOP TO BOTTOM: Pecorino Tuscano, grana padano, Asiago, Parmesan, cacio-cavallo, provolone, Gorgonzola, Fontina, burrini, smoked mozzarella, piave vecchio, ricotta salata, taleggio, mozzarella, ricotta

Regional Cuisines

Northern Italy

Northern Italy, considered the most prosperous area of the country, includes the regions of Valle d'Aosta, Piemonte, Lombardy, Emilia-Romagna, Trentino-Alto Adige, Veneto, and Friuli-Venezia Giulia. The thriving regions of northern Italy are the most industrialized area of the country, and their affluence is reflected in a heavier style of food. However, like the rest of Italy, each region has its own unique cuisine and customs.

Northern Italy is connected to the rest of Europe by a continuous mountain range—the Alps. The mountains greatly affect the cuisine of the regions in which they lie, such as Piemonte and Trentino-Alto Adige. The Po River runs just north of Emilia-Romagna, giving way to a rich and fertile valley and pastures of grazing cattle (see sidebar, page 116). In the east, parts of Veneto,

Emilia-Romagna, and Friuli-Venezia Giulia lie on the Adriatic Sea, while the far north and west are bordered by France, Switzerland, Austria, and Slovenia, all countries who have impacted the cuisine and culture.

The cuisine in northern Italy is dominated by meat, though seafood, eel, and cuttlefish remain popular in the Veneto region. The pastures are ideal for raising cattle, so milk, butter, and cow's milk cheeses are common: Fontina Val d'Aosta, Gorgonzola, mascarpone, and Robiola to name a few. Veal, pork, and game are also quite popular. Fresh pasta, polenta, and rice are consumed, as well as gnocchi and other dumplings, evidence of Austrian and German influences. Piemonte is the largest producer of rice in the region; therefore risotto is a staple of the people. Popular cooking techniques include boiling, stewing, and braising, though there is a special oven called a *fogher* that is used for spit roasting in the Friuli-Venezia Giulia region.

Central Italy

Central Italy encompasses seven regions: Liguria, Toscano, Umbria, Le Marches, Latium, Abruzzi, and Molise. This area of the country, as a whole, has many similarities with southern Italy because of its proximity to the Mediterranean Sea, although it is also known for its plush, rolling hills. Central Italy has a rich history. Rome, the capital city of Italy and Christianity, is located in the region of Latium. The Tuscan city of Florence is the birthplace of the Renaissance and Catherine de Medici, the woman responsible for Western Europe's transformation in modern cuisine.

The terrain of central Italy is quite diverse. Toscano, Umbria, Abruzzi, and Molise have an emblematic landscape of rolling hills, very old roads, vineyards, and olive groves. For the most part, olive oil is the preferred fat of Central Italy, although in Latium lard is quite common. The western part of Toscano possesses a beautiful coastline, much like Liguria. In these regions, food is simply prepared and often seasoned only with herbs and olive oil. Central Italy is known for its livestock, mainly beef, goat, and lamb, which are commonly grilled, spit roasted, stewed, or deep fried. Pork is also very popular, especially in the town of Umbria. The produce of the region is among the best in all of Italy, with a focus on simplicity and seasonality.

Southern Italy

Southern Italy is generally thought of as the poorest and most underdeveloped area of the country. Nevertheless, the atmosphere in much of southern Italy is laid back and the people tend to be family oriented and easygoing; perhaps this is due in part to the pleasant climate throughout most of the region. Southern Italy is comprised of six regions: Campania, Basilicata, Apulia, Calabria, and the islands of Sicily and Sardinia. Though each region has its distinct culture and cuisine, there are several similarities between them.

The terrain of southern Italy is quite rugged and mountainous, especially in Calabria, and therefore not widely suitable for cattle farming. Beef is rare and tough, as cattle are not raised for milk. Meat is not consumed often, but lamb, pork, and chicken are most common. Because there is a lack of dairy cattle, butter, cream, and cow's milk cheeses are scarce. Goat and sheep's milk are more prevalent, as well as buffalo's milk, which is used to make the renowned buffalo mozzarella. Campania and Apulia boast miles of coastline and lush plains and plateaus, yielding exceptional seafood and produce, including tomatoes, eggplant, and zucchini. Naturally, olive oil is the preferred fat of the region, as olive trees grow far and wide, especially in Sicily.

Cultural Influences in Italian Cuisine

Italy has a rich past; at one time, parts of the country were occupied and/or colonized by the Etruscans, Spanish, French, Greeks, Arabs, Austrians, and Germans. Such occupations inevitably shaped cuisine in Italy today. Before the unification of Italy in 1861 by Giuseppe Garibaldi, the country was made up of separate and disputing states, controlled by any number of the above countries.

Italy is a fairly new country; perhaps the great sense of regionalism, as opposed to nationalism, among the general population can be attributed to this fact. Each region boasts its own culture, cuisine, and even dialect, all which have been shaped by historical impacts, geography, and climate.

Northern Italy

In the second century B.C.E., Marcus Aemilius Lepidus built a road through the north called the Emilian Way, which exists today as a highway separating Emilia and Romagna (Rome). At the time, the north was occupied by the Salassi, Taurani, Rhaetians, and Veneti before the conquests of the Etruscans, Gauls, Byzantines, Lombards, and Romans. The collapse of the Roman Empire left the region divided among foreign forces, battles took place over boundaries and allegiances, and conflict existed between the emperors and popes. For this reason, there are many local vernaculars throughout the north, and certain regions even speak predominately French or German.

In Medieval times, the port city of Venice, in the Veneto region, was the center for trade with the Middle East. The prosperous city had control over the trade of rare foods of the time, such as sugar, coffee, and spices. Access to foreign lands, customs, and foods inevitably shaped the cuisine of the Veneto region, while other regions associated with Venice, such as Trentino-Alto Adige and Friuli-Venezia Giulia were heavily influenced by Austria, Germany, Hungary, and Slovenia. The regions of Valle d'Aosta, Lombardy, and Piedmont, on the other hand, have strong French and Swiss influences in their cuisine.

Emilia-Romagna

Emilia-Romagna, located in northern Italy, is considered the most important culinary region in all of Italy. This region, nicknamed "*La Grossa*" (The Fat One), is often considered gluttonous by the rest of Italy; nevertheless, the region is home to innumerable specialty products. Bologna is the governmental and gastronomic center for the region, whose provinces include Ferrara, Forlì, Modena, Parma, Piacenza, Ravena, Rimini, and Reggio nell'Emilia. In terms of acreage, the region is the sixth largest in all of Italy, with a population of about 4 million.

The terrain of the Emilia-Romagna region is the flattest in all of Italy, although coastline and mountains abound as well. The region is blessed with a rich, fertile soil that yields a large quantity of quality fruits and vegetables, most notably cherries, pears, nectarines, apples, asparagus, sugar beets, and tomatoes. Emilia- Romagna is renowned for growing durum wheat, which is used to make the pasta for which the region is celebrated, as well as breads, such as *piadini* and *ciupeta*. Popular pasta shapes throughout the region include *anolini, cappelletti, lasagna, tagliatelle, tortelli,* and *tortellini.*

The region boasts many specialty products, three of the most noteworthy being Parmigiano-Reggiano, prosciutto di Parma, and *aceto balsamico tradizionale.* All three of these foodstuffs are produced and protected under strict Italian laws called *Denominazione di Origine Protetta* (Designation of Place of Origin), which is indicated by the acronym DOP. The DOP laws control the locality, methods of production, labeling, and distribution of these and other Italian agricultural products.

According to the law, Parmigiano-Reggiano can be made only between mid-April and mid-November, when the dairy cattle are feeding on fresh grass from the pastures of the provinces of Parma, Reggio nell'Emilia, and Modena, an area of Bologna on the Reno River, and a portion of Mantua in Lombardy. The cheese is made from both the morning and evening milkings, which undergo the coagulation process and are eventually shaped into wheels weighing between 66 and 88 lb/30 and 40 kg. The wheels of cheese must be aged for at least fourteen months, though most are aged for two years or more, resulting in a more golden color, granular texture, and simultaneously nutty, sweet, spicy, and salty flavors with time. Pamigiano-Reggiano is delicious grated over soups, salads, and pasta, but it is also excellent as a table cheese, served with fruit, cured meats, or even dessert wine. The simultaneously nutty, sweet, spicy, and salty flavors make this the "mother of all cheeses."

Prosciutto, meaning "ham" in Italian, has a long and detailed history in Parma, dating back thousands of years. Prosciutto di Parma is distinguished by several processes, all dependent on the particular environmental and climatic conditions of the region. The ham shanks must be obtained from pigs weighing no less than 352 lb/160 kg each, which are raised in a designated area around Parma. After the shanks are selected, they undergo the curing process, in which only salt may be used. The hams are then aged for ten to twelve months, with the breezes from the south wind imparting flavors of chestnut and pine. The deep reddish-pink prosciutto di Parma is marbled with creamy-white fat, resulting in a silky texture. The slightly sweet and salty ham is generally served very thinly sliced with fruit and/or cheese.

Aceto balsamico tradizionale is made predominately in the province of Modena, though it is also made in Reggio nell'Emilia. This rich, dark brown, syrup-like vinegar is unlike all others. It starts out as must from the Trebbiano grape, which is reduced, decanted, and then fermented with a particular starter. The vinegar is then aged in a series of progressively smaller barrels, all made from a different type of wood, including chestnut, cherry, ash, mulberry, and sometimes juniper. This aging process takes at least twelve years, but the finer vinegars can be aged for as long as twenty, fifty, or one hundred years. The result is a fragrant vinegar with a smooth texture and a sweet and sour flavor that is used sparingly, drizzled over fruit, cheese, salads, or cured meats.

Central Italy

The early settlers of Central Italy were the Etruscans, migrating from Asia Minor as early as 800 B.C.E. The Etruscans were an advanced civilization with a major empire, spanning from the Po Valley to Campania at one time (see map, page 122). The frescoes in Etruscan tombs reveal this complex culture, illustrating what appear to be colanders, pastry cutters, cheese graters, and even wide noodles (*papardelle*).

The Ancient Romans were shepherds and small-scale farmers. The sustenance of these individuals was a mush called *pulmentum,* made from millet or spelt. Much like polenta of today, pulmentum was eaten warm as a porridge, or cooled and cut into a cake. As the society advanced, mutton, pork, and poultry were boiled and roasted. Eventually, vegetables were cultivated, including cabbage, fava beans, and chard. Fruits, such as apples, cherries, and figs, were staples of the time.

The Roman Empire flourished between the fifth century B.C.E. and the fifth century A.D., with Christianity at its core. The Romans built an extensive system of roads and a central market that housed butcher shops, fishmongers, produce vendors, cheese makers, and even wine shops. Unfortunately, the high times didn't last; Barbarian tribes invaded Rome in the third century A.D., putting a stronghold on the advancement of the cuisine.

Central Italy underwent a series of rulers over the next centuries. The crusaders set out to the Holy Land in the eleventh and twelfth centuries, returning with sugar, buckwheat, and lemons, among other ingredients. At this same time, central Italy was becoming urbanized. With this urbanization came a rise in wealth and prosperity among citizens, as well as an interest in the culinary arts. The first-ever cooking school was founded in Florence in the sixteenth century, coinciding with the start of the Renaissance.

From a culinary standpoint, the most significant family in Italy is arguably the Medicis of Florence. The Medici family is known for their elaborate menus and banquets, but even more so, they are known for Catherine. In 1533, Catherine de Medici voyaged from Florence to France to wed King Henri II, bringing with her a team of chefs and pastry chefs. These Italian specialists introduced many things that are thought of as typically French, such as crêpes, the art of pastry making, and béchamel sauce, in addition to frying and the fork. Catherine de Medici introduced gastronomy to France, a passion that has flourished to this day.

Southern Italy

As a whole, southern Italy has been greatly influenced by Greece and North Africa. The landscape is spotted with the ruins of Greek temples and Norman forts. Ancient Greek and Arab vocabulary is evident throughout the region, as are their culinary traditions.

The regional cuisine began in southern Italy with the arrival of the Greeks in 415 B.C.E. The Greeks brought with them many practices, including architecture, wine making, wheat cultivation, and bread baking. They also introduced ingredients that now epitomize the cuisine of southern Italy, such as olives, honey, and nuts. Roman rule followed, leaving much less of a culinary legacy than their predecessors; however, fava beans were the staple of the Roman diet and are still widely consumed throughout the region.

Sicily, being only about 90 miles (145 kilometers) from the African continent, was conquered by the Arabs as early as the ninth century A.D. The Arabs brought with them an array of exotic ingredients and planted citrus trees, for which the region is notorious to this day. The Arabs also introduced the notion of combining sweet and sour flavors (*agrodolce*), which is a major flavor profile in Sicilian cooking today. Saffron, nuts, rice, couscous, sugarcane, and ice cream are just a few of the contributions from the Arab world. Many of these contributions made it to the mainland; however, some did not, leaving Sicily with a distinct cuisine of its own.

The Normans moved into southern Italy in the eleventh century, although they had little impact on the cuisine, aside from introducing the salting and drying of fish as a means for preservation. The Normans handed over rule to the Spanish, who controlled much of southern Italy into the eighteenth century. In the following decades, parts of southern Italy were under Spanish, Austrian, and/or French rule. Though Napoleon was defeated in 1815, French influence triumphed among the aristocracy throughout the region. It was fashionable to throw large banquets, with a Parisian chef cooking French dishes, served on French china. In culinary terms, few things have changed throughout much of southern Italy since the unification in 1860. The city of Naples (in Campania) has become the culinary capital of the south, though many regions, mainly Sicily and Sardinia, remain somewhat autonomous.

REGION	MAJOR CITY	CHARACTERISTICS OF CUISINE
NORTHERN ITALY		
Valle d'Aosta	Aosta	Butter, cow's milk cheese, cream, gnocchi, speck, boiled meats, freshwater fish
Piemonte	Turin	Butter, gnocchi, pasta (ravioli, fettuccine), porcini mushrooms, white truffles, freshwater fish, pork, beef, veal; boiling
Lombardy	Milan	Butter, cow's milk cheese, cream, apples, pears, radicchio, saffron, rice, risotto, corn, polenta, beef, veal; boiling, braising
Emilia-Romagna		Bologna lard, butter, apples, pears, cherries, tomatoes, asparagus, beets, wheat, fresh pasta (lasagna, *tagliatelle*, tortellini, *agnolotti*), corn, balsamic vinegar, Parmigiano-Reggiano, processed pork (prosciutto, mortadella, coppa)
Trentino-Alto Adige	Trento	Butter, cabbage, potatoes, rice, polenta, gnocchi, strudel, freshwater fish, salt cod, prosciutto (San Daniele)
Veneto	Venice	Butter, olive oil, apples, pears, beets, onions, peas, radicchio, rice, polenta, pasta (*bigoli*), salt cod, eel, scampi, liver, turkey
Friuli-Venezia Giulia	Trieste	Butter, caraway, corn, potatoes, polenta, horseradish, paprika, beans, seafood, pork, venison
CENTRAL ITALY		
Liguria	Genoa	Olive oil, citrus, vegetables, herbs, pesto, wine, fresh and dried pasta (ravioli), farinata, beans, seafood, fish stews and chowders, rabbit
Toscano	Florence	Olive oil, sheep's milk cheese, melon, tomatoes, black cabbage, spinach, chestnuts, walnuts, wheat, fresh pasta (*papardelle*), unsalted bread, white beans, wine, freshwater fish, seafood, beef, game, poultry; grilling and roasting

REGION	MAJOR CITY	CHARACTERISTICS OF CUISINE
Umbria	Perugia	Olive oil, sheep's milk cheese, black truffles, porcini mushrooms, dried pasta, unsalted bread, lentils, chestnuts, freshwater fish, pork, beef, lamb, cured meat; spit roasting
Le Marches	Ancona	Olive oil, fennel, wheat, dried pasta, unsalted bread, lentils, wine, fish soups and chowders, dried cod, snails, pork, white beef cattle
Latium	Rome	Lard, sheep's milk cheese, artichokes, peas, pasta (spaghetti, rigatoni, *bucatini*, egg-based fettuccine), beef, lamb, pork, poultry; frying
Abruzzi	L'Aquila	Olive oil, sheep's milk cheese, crêpes, pepperoncini, fresh and dried pasta (*maccheroni, spaghetti à la guitarra*)
Molise	Campobasso	Olive oil, sheep's milk cheese, fresh and dried pasta (*maccheroni*)
SOUTHERN ITALY		
Campania	Naples	Olive oil, sheep's milk cheese, buffalo mozzarella, citrus, tomatoes, fennel, dried pasta (spaghetti, penne, vermicelli, rigatoni), pizza
Basilicata	Potenza	Olive oil, sheep's milk cheese, dried pasta, pepperoncini, pork, sausage
Apulia	Taranto	Olive oil, sheep's milk cheese, potatoes, almonds, wheat, fresh and dried pasta (*orechiette*), pepperoncini, beans, oysters, mussels, lamb
Calabria	Cantanzaro	Olive oil, tomatoes, eggplant, pepperoncini mushrooms, dried pasta, lamb, goat, pork, venison, freshwater fish
Sicily	Palermo	Olive oil, citrus, raisins, tomatoes, eggplant, pepperoncini, almonds, marzipan, wheat, couscous, dried pasta, wine, saffron, cinnamon, honey, sardines, anchovies, tuna, swordfish, lamb, pork, goat, sweets
Sardinia	Cagliari	Olive oil, sheep's milk cheese, herbs, chestnuts, hazelnuts, dried pasta, flatbread (*carta da musica*), lamb, pork

The Mediterranean

The Mediterranean Sea is an intercontinental sea situated between Europe to the north, Africa to the south, and Asia to the east. It covers an area of about 970,000 square miles (2,512,000 square kilometers). The Mediterranean Sea is actually not a single sea; rather it is comprised of five seas: the Aegean, the Adriatic, the Ionian, the Ligurian, and the Tyrrhenian. Almost a completely closed basin, the Mediterranean Sea's major source of replenishment and water renewal comes from continuous inflow of surface water from the Atlantic Ocean.

The area known as "the Mediterranean" refers to the countries, or portions of countries, that line the Sea. These countries, though diverse in culture, religion, language, and politics, share many similarities. For example, Mediterranean countries, as a whole, are

LEFT TO RIGHT, TOP TO BOTTOM: garlic, fava beans, olive oil, lime, lemon, feta cheese, mascarpone, dates, artichokes, olives, dried figs, apricots, capers, almonds, honey, dried bay leaves, dill, chickpeas, pistachios, hazelnuts, pine nuts

Common Mediterranean Ingredients

Grains
Bulgur

Rice

Wheat (pasta, couscous, unleavened bread, country-style bread, sweet bread)

Legumes
Borlotti beans

Cannellini beans

Chickpeas

Fava beans

Lentils

Nuts and Seeds
Almonds

Chestnuts

Hazelnuts

Pine nuts

Pistachios

Sesame seeds

Walnuts

Herbs (Dried and Fresh)
Basil

Chives

Cilantro

Dill

Lavender

Marjoram

Mint

Oregano

Parsley

Rosemary

Sage

Tarragon

Thyme

Seasonings
Anise seeds

Bay leaves

Bitter orange peel

Black peppercorns

Capers

Cardamom

Chile pepper flakes

Cinnamon

Cloves

Coriander seeds

Cumin seeds

Fennel seeds

Ginger

Nutmeg

Olives

Orange flower water

Paprika (*pimenton*)

Preserved lemons

Rose water

Saffron

Sumac

Turmeric

Za'atar

Oils
Hazelnut oil

Olive oil

Walnut oil

Vinegars
Red and white wine vinegars

Vegetables
Artichokes

Arugula

Asparagus

Broccoli

Cabbage

Carrots

Cauliflower

Celery

Chiles

Cucumbers

Curly endive

Eggplant

Fennel

Garlic

Leeks

Olives

Onions

Pimientos

Potatoes

Pumpkins

Radicchio

Romaine

Spinach

Sweet peppers

Tomatoes

Turnips

Wild mushrooms

Zucchini

Fruits (Dried and Fresh)
Apples

Apricots

Cherries

Currants

Dates

Figs

Grapes (wine)

Lemons

Limes

Melons

Oranges

Peaches

Pears

Persimmons

Plums

Pomegranates

Quinces

Raisins

Wild strawberries

Meat
Goat

Lamb

Pork

Rabbit

Venison

Wild boar

Poultry
Chicken

Duck

Guinea fowl

Quail

Rock Cornish hens

Squab

Fish
Anchovies

Mackerel

Monkfish

Mullet

Sardines

Sea bass

Tuna

Shellfish
Clams

Crabs

Cuttlefish

Mussels

Octopus

Oysters

Rock lobster

Shrimp

Squid

Cheeses and Yogurt
Buffalo mozzarella

Feta

Fresh and aged sheep and goat's milk cheeses (various shapes, marinated, wrapped in leaves, rolled in herbs, crushed peppercorns, or ash)

Mascarpone

Ricotta

Yogurt

Sweeteners
Honey

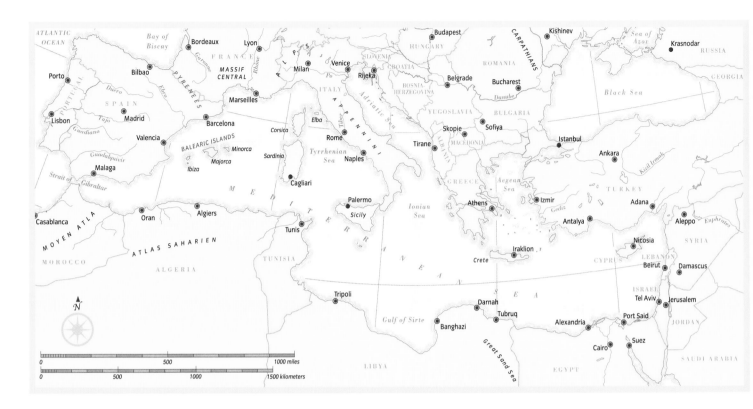

characterized by a distinct climate: cool, wet winters and warm, dry summers. Though Mediterranean cuisines are based around the fish and shellfish from the sea, this climate also proves favorable for growing a bounty of fruits and vegetables. The terrain of the inland regions, however, is quite rugged and hilly, conducive to terraced gardens as opposed to large-scale agriculture. The dry weather and rocky terrain suggest few pastures and therefore few dairy cattle and dairy produce throughout the region.

There are four large geographical regions that can be used to organize Mediterranean cuisine. The first region includes the southernmost regions of Spain and France, as well as southern and central Italy. This region includes the French island of Corsica, the Italian islands of Sicily and Sardinia, and additional smaller islands.

The second region, known as the Mahgreb, is located on the African continent. The North African coastline includes the countries of Libya, Tunisia, Algeria, and Morocco. This area has been influenced by both the Middle East and Europe, making it truly unique in culture and cuisine.

The third region includes parts of Turkey, Greece, and Slovenia, including the many small islands, as well as Cyprus and Crete. Turkey, once home to the great Ottoman Empire, was the largest territory of all the Islamic dynasties. At its height, from 1500–1917, the Empire extended deep into eastern Europe, to the borders of India, and across North Africa.

The fourth region, known as the Arab Levant, includes the countries of Syria, Lebanon, Israel, Egypt, and Jordan. This area, commonly associated with both Jewish and Arab culture and cuisine, produces exceptional fruits and vegetables, and is aptly referred to as the "Fertile Crescent."

The foods that were first associated with the Mediterranean were wheat, olives, and grapes and wine. These dominant foods have played an important role in the development of the regional cuisines, but they are by no means the only important foods. Foods that were not indigenous from the dawn of a civilization have migrated into the region and become firmly ingrained; some of the earliest arrivals from the Far East into the Mediterranean include rice, lemons, leeks, eggplant, and the ubiquitous garlic. Later on, beans, tomatoes, potatoes, and corn from the New World were introduced and assimilated.

Cooking Equipment

Traditionally, the Mediterranean region has relied on wood-fired hearths, spits, and hardwood grills for the main means of cooking. Therefore, braising, stewing, roasting, and grilling have become common methods of cooking throughout the region. One-pot cooking in *tagines*, *couscoussières*, and *paelleras* is quite popular in North Africa, Morocco, and Spain, respectively. Skewered meat, poultry, fish, and vegetables are common in eastern Mediterranean countries such as Greece, Turkey, Lebanon, and Syria.

Couscoussière—A type of ceramic, iron, or copper double boiler. A stew cooks in the bottom pot while couscous steams on top.

Tagine—An earthenware cooking vessel with a large, round base and conical lid that is used to make a stew of the same name.

Tian—An earthenware dish that is round, oval, and shallow and is used to make gratins.

Paellera—An iron, two-handled, shallow pan used to make paella. *Paelleras* are generally quite large.

Mezzaluna—A crescent-shaped rocking knife with a handle on either end that is used for chopping herbs.

Skewers—Metal or wooden and flat or round skewers that are used for grilling and roasting meat, poultry, fish, and vegetables.

Eastern Europe

Eastern Europe reaches from Poland and Hungary in the west and eastward through the vast Russian Federation, which extends across all of northern Asia. The generally cold terrain is varied, containing grassy plains, waterways, forests, and mountain ranges. The Ural Mountains in Russia roughly divide the more sparsely populated, but vast, eastern lands from the much smaller, but more densely populated, western lands. The latter is more agricultural, including Poland, and more exceptionally Hungary, the most self-sufficient countries.

In general, eastern European cuisine is typified by hearty and warming cold-climate foods. Important Slavic influences include the use of cultivated grains, preserved foods, and winter root crops. The use of grains, especially in breads and kasha (cooked cereals), as well as the preserving techniques of pickling, salting, and drying are the hallmarks of Slavic foodways, as is the custom of sour flavor profiles, using ingredients such as sour cream and *kvas* (fermented vegetable juice), enjoyed in the national soups of the region.

Meat lovers, eastern Europeans have had to make do by stretching meat in soups and stews, often by adding filling potatoes or dumplings. Where geography allows, the region's diverse waterways provide both fresh and saltwater fish, eaten fresh or preserved, as in herring. Eastern Europe's huge forests encourage foraging, especially mushroom gathering, which is popular.

The countries highlighted in this section are as follows: Hungary, the most influential cuisine of the western countries; Poland, with its large immigrant population in the United States; and the Russian Federation, by far the largest nation in both regions, and until the late twentieth century, an even larger empire, which included both of the preceding countries and many, but no independent, regional republics.

The Russian Federation

The traditional foodways of Russia are primarily Slavic, driven by the necessities of a long winter and short growing season. Generally, the drive to forage and preserve wild foods came primarily from the cold climate in the north, and the tradition of working with farmed foods from the more arable south. The northern region includes the forest belt, which supports some agriculture, as well as foraging and tree fruit in its southern region. The south includes the steppes, grassy plains reaching across Russia, used especially for farming wheat. Lands farther south include mountains, lowlands near the Caspian Sea, and the milder climate of the Caucasus.

Russia is the world's largest country, with almost 7 million square miles (18,129,917 square kilometers), almost twice as large as Canada, the second largest country. It covers much of the continents of Europe and Asia, extending from the Arctic Ocean south to the Black Sea and from the Baltic Sea east to the Pacific Ocean. Bordering eight European and three Asian countries, it has miles of diverse coastlines.

Although the Russian climate ranges vastly, it is generally cold, with snow covering more than half the country during six months of the year. This short growing season limits its crops. Only 13 percent of Russia is cropland; it does not feed itself. Even so, Russia is the world's largest producer of rye, barley, oats, and potatoes, and the third largest of wheat. Chief livestock are cattle, hogs, and sheep. Key seafoods include haddock, herring, salmon, and sturgeon, as well as prized caviar.

The population of over 143 million is largely Russian, of Slavic descent, with more than 100 ethnic groups. Two thirds of the population lives in the western region of the country, mostly in cities such as Moscow and St. Petersburg, as well as along the Volga River. The major religion is Russian Orthodox.

Russia's Regional Cuisines

For the most part, common traditional culinary staples are familiar across the nation. For clarity, this section divides Russia roughly into northern and southern regions, focusing generally on the climate and terrain that originated specific foods and their accompanying techniques.

Northern Russia

The primary characteristic of northern Russia is its cold climate, making it difficult to farm, but encouraging foraging and preserving, both great Russian passions. From its forests, foraged mushrooms and berries are a key component of the northern Russian diet. Mushrooms are marinated, pickled, and dried. Berries—including strawberries, cranberries, lingonberries, currants, bilberries, and cloudberries—wild and cultivated, are used in compotes, preserves, thick drinks (*kisel*) and sweet pastries (*pirogi*), sometimes with local honey. Preserving extends to regional fish from both the North Atlantic and local rivers, which are salted and smoked. Tree fruits, particularly apples, are grown in the southern part of the region. Warming tea, the classic drink of choice throughout Russia, is traditionally consumed in large amounts all day long.

Southern Russia

The harvest from the Steppes, located in the northern part of southern Russia, encourages a hearty diet, heavy in carbohydrates—dark bread (*corny khleb*), buckwheat groats (kasha), and ever-present potatoes. Meat is highly coveted, with favorites being beef, lamb, and chicken, but meals generally include little meat.

Grazing livestock produce dairy products, especially frequently used sour cream (*smetana*), creamy curd cheeses (*tvorog*), and, in the Caucuses, cultured yogurt. Also popular (and enjoyed throughout Russia) are sweet and savory pies, small (*pirozhki*) and large (*pirogi*), often filled with meat, fish, and vegetables, and sold in cafés and on street corners. The ultimate of these is *coulibiac* of salmon.

Traditionally, the variety of vegetables has long been limited to those that could be stored during the cold months, such as root vegetables and cabbage. The Slavic love of sour flavors is typified in pickled vegetables and their juices (*kvas*), also featured in Russian's staple soups, such as the national soup, *shchi,* which is sometimes made with pickled cabbage. Borscht, a soup also popular in the United States, pairs the sweetness of beets with this requisite sour flavor.

The Republics

For a long period, ending with the recent dissolution of the Soviet Union, what we called "Russia" included fifteen republics, of which Russia was the largest. These newly independent republics exerted an influence over the foods of what is now the Russian Federation.

To the far west, the Baltic States—Estonia, Latvia, and Lithuania, about the size of New England, fan out into the Baltic Sea. This fertile region produces many fish and seafood products, as well as milk and eggs, all with a Scandinavian influence.

To the southwest is the larger Slavic Ukraine, once the breadbasket of Russia, and home to the "Russian" dark and rye breads, as well as the famous soup, borscht.

To the south of the Ukraine are the mountainous Caucuses, including Georgia and Armenia. With per-

LEFT TO RIGHT, TOP TO BOTTOM: horseradish, red cabbage, beer, baby turnips, red and baby red beets, candy stripe beets (top), golden beets (bottom), cherries, apple, white asparagus, potatoes, carrots, cucumber, bread, plum, apricot, white mushrooms, cremini mushrooms, radishes, blueberries, blackberries, raspberries, juniper berries, whole wheat flour, spelt, steel-cut oats, caviar, kasha, caraway

Common Eastern/Central European Ingredients

Grains

Barley

Buckwheat groats

Millet

Rye

Wheat

Seasonings

Dill

Garlic

Horseradish

Mustard

Vegetables and Fruit

Apples

Beets

Berries

Cabbage

Carrots

Cucumbers

Eggplant

Mushrooms

Onions

Pickled vegetables

Potatoes

Radishes

Sauerkraut

Tomatoes

Turnips

Proteins

Beef

Chicken

Fish (often smoked, fresh, and ocean, including bream, caviar, carp, eel, herring, pike, salmon, sturgeon, and trout)

Lamb

Pork

Dairy Products

Butter

Curd cheese (*tvorog*)

European-style cheese such as Cheddar, Swiss, and feta

Kefir

Milk

Sour cream

Traditional, simple curd (*tvorog*), and cottage cheeses

Yogurt

---

haps the most diverse and savory foods of eastern Europe, this region uses a wider variety of vegetables and incorporates both eastern and Mediterranean foods into its cuisines. Pilafs and lamb dishes, such as the wildly popular *shashlick,* come from Armenia. But it is Georgia, with its well-seasoned food savored in chic Russian restaurants, that is often considered the most sophisticated of the republics.

The eastern Tatar influence of the Asian Steppes brought the introduction of noodles and dumplings.

Cultural Influences on Russian Cuisine

The early agriculturally oriented Slavs survived on gruels, and to this day, grain, especially wheat and to a lesser extent kasha, still serves as the basis for many Russian meals.

In the ninth century, the Vikings introduced the important practice of salting and drying fish and may have also influenced the dining custom of *zakusky* (see sidebar, page 127), similar to smorgasbord. The Viking trade with Constantinople exposed the Russians to Eastern Orthodox Christianity, which had a profound influence on eating habits until the twentieth century revolution. During the Orthodox Church's dominance, more than half the year, on prescribed holiday fast days, Russians gave up meat and dairy. This resulted in creative cooking, including fish with mushrooms instead of meat, and seeds and nuts instead of butter.

The Mongol occupation from the eleventh to thirteenth centuries, brought Tatar tastes and techniques from the east that are still popular today, especially tea, yogurt, curd cheese, fermented cabbage (sauerkraut), honey pastries, nuts and dried fruits, as well as a liking for skewered lamb, such as *shashlik,* still a popular street food.

Zakusky

The distinctive custom of dining on hot and cold appetizers, set out together before a meal, and often more important than the meal itself, is popular all over Russia. These *zakusky* (little bites) are self-served, lasting between one and two hours, and always accompanied by vodka, bread, and butter. The diversity of these dishes depends on the wealth of the host and the availability of ingredients. But they often include smoked fishes, sliced meats and cheeses, marinated and pickled vegetables and vegetables salads, fish roe and pancakes (*blini*), sliced cheeses, and meats.

Caviar

The world's best caviar comes from the Caspian Sea. Sturgeon roe is the most coveted, although other roe is consumed. Extracting caviar is done by hand, a time-consuming process. The roe is both fragile and perishable and it must be kept cold during the procedure. The quality and taste of caviar depends on the kind of sturgeon it comes from, in increasing order: sevruga, osetra, and beluga. Because of both pollution and poaching, sturgeon fishing is endangered.

A Meal in Russia

Although the times of meals vary with lifestyle, the Russians generally eat three meals a day, with the main meal usually, but not always, consumed at night. Breakfast might include porridge, sausages, cheese, bread, butter, and preserves. Soup is served for a midday meal with potatoes or cooked buckwheat, rarely at the evening meal.

Despite the scarcity of food and often space, much of the Russian evenings are spent socializing around long, hospitable meals, in which many people, often neighbors, are squeezed around small tables. The meal starts with five to ten *zakusky*—appetizers that are hot and cold with bread, usually white and rye. The main course (*vtoroye*) is meat, poultry, or fish, sometimes a regional specialty, with potatoes, bread, and/or kasha. The Russians are fond of sweets, such as ice cream. For dessert, tea is served with a variety of sweets, such as cakes and chocolate.

The expanding empire of the seventeenth and eighteenth centuries widened Russia's culinary exposure; by the eighteenth century, Russia encompassed much of eastern Europe, extending into Central Asia, so that eastern European food and Russian food have become synonymous. During that time, the Tsars such as Peter the Great introduced worldly foods from Europe, like white bread and sophisticated cheeses. With the Scandinavian influence, *zakusky* (see sidebar) became popular and are still enjoyed among all classes. The Tsars hired French chefs, who cooked their dishes with beloved Russian ingredients, such as sour cream in beef stroganoff. But even the Tsars cherished traditional foods, such as buckwheat porridge (kasha), and the Russian peasants ate the same way they had for centuries—on a scarcity of staple foods in a cold climate—bread, kasha, and cabbage soups. And although the Russians resisted the introduction of the potato, they learned to embrace it as a staple.

The disparity between the foodways of the rich and poor was more extreme than elsewhere in Europe. All this changed in 1917 with the Bolshevik Revolution, when women were brought into the workplace and home cooking was de-emphasized. During the Soviet era, people did not go hungry in the USSR; neither was food plentiful or nutritious, and the daily life of the average Russian might include hours of waiting on line for groceries. Still, in a culture of little culinary variety and cramped city apartments, Russian hospitality and long meals continued to be a way of life.

In the l990s, with the dissolution of the Soviet Union, significant structural and economic troubles affected the food supply. Today, new influences include Western imports, food chains, and out-of-season produce for those who can afford them. But, for the majority of Russians, scarcity and diversity of food is still prevalent. Interestingly, some restaurants now offer ethnic cuisine and nostalgic pre-revolutionary fare.

Poland

Like Russia, Poland's food is primarily of Slavic peasant origins. It is dominated by the fruits of its fertile farmland, tempered with a short growing season, and traditionally supported with foraged and hunted foods from its forests. With few exceptions, it is more united than divided by geographical differences. But all through its tumultuous past, Poland has incorporated some of its neighbor's foodways into a distinctive Polish cuisine.

Poland is located in central Europe and is about the size of New Mexico, covering 120,700 square miles (312,613 square kilometers). The south is bordered by the Czech Republic and Slovakia; the east by the Ukraine and Belarus; the northeast by Lithuania and Russia; the northwest by the Baltic Sea; and the west by Germany.

About three quarters of Poland is lowlands of the northern European plains, with forests occupying the remainder. Poland's natural borders—the Baltic Sea in the north, and the Sudete and Carpathian Mountains in the south—have changed little over the last 1,000 years. But there are no such natural borders to the east and west, resulting in enormous political and ethnic upheaval, which has influenced the tenor of Polish cuisine.

The Polish climate is marked by cold winters, necessitating warm, filling foods. Temperate summers foster typical crops on Polish farms that include grains, principally wheat, barley, and oats, but also rye, buckwheat, and millet. Vegetable crops include potatoes (second in production only to Russia), cabbage, sugar beets, and fruits, such as apples and currants. Poppies are cultivated for their seeds; rapeseed for oil; cattle, sheep, chickens, and pigs for their meat.

Today, Poland's population is about 39 million, mostly homogenous, of Slavic roots, although there are minority groups, including German. About 90 percent of Poles are Roman Catholic, and many culinary traditions center around Christian holidays.

Poland's Regional Cuisines

Polish cooking is largely shaped by its fertile farmlands and forests, tempered by a cold winter. The key features of Polish cuisine are meat, bread, and potatoes. Dill is the favorite seasoning. Poles favor pork, game, and beef, but pork rules supreme, with lard and fatback as traditional cooking components. Pork is used in numerous preparations, including popular sausages (kielbasa), ham, and breaded cutlets. Crumbled bacon (along with sour cream) is a favorite condiment. Hunted game, featured in a national dish, *bigos* (a stew), is now mostly enjoyed in restaurants. Combining meat or poultry with juniper berries or fruit, such as duck with apples or pork loin with prunes, has long been a Polish custom.

Common Polish Ingredients

Seasonings		Vegetables	Meat
Caraway	Mustard	Beets	Beef
Cinnamon	Paprika	Cabbage	Pork
Cumin	Parsley	Mushrooms	
Dill	Poppy seeds	Onions	**Dairy**
Horseradish	Vinegar		Milk
Juniper berries		**Fruits**	Sour cream
Marjoram		Apples	
		Dried fruits	

A Meal in Poland

Meal schedules vary with lifestyle, but Poles traditionally start the day with a substantial breakfast, such as bread, cheese, cold cuts, and eggs. Sometimes a second light breakfast follows, similar to an American bag lunch. Lunch is most often the main meal (*obiad*), but this is rapidly changing. *Obiad* begins with soup, which might serve as the main course, or might be a prelude to a main meat or vegetable course, with grains or potatoes. If seasonal salads are served, they become the main course. On Sundays, appetizers may start a meal. Desserts are well liked and fruit-based desserts are common.

The final meal of the day is lighter, sometimes similar to breakfast, but can include other dishes such as pancakes. Tea and coffee are served after meals; some teas may be infusions with fruits and herbs.

Staple carbohydrates, such as dense wheat and rye breads, potatoes, and grains, especially barley, as well as buckwheat groats, and noodles, have long been an integral part of the Polish diet. Bread also is used to bind stuffings and sauces and featured in dishes "a la Polonaise," an internationally recognized term meaning "with a fried bread crumb garnish," and often served with hard-boiled eggs. Hugely important to the Polish diet are potatoes, served in numerous dishes, often with sour cream. Both eggs and milk products are commonly used, especially sour cream, along with simple curd-style cheeses and butter.

During the majority of the year, vegetables are most often of the cold-weather variety, with cabbage and potatoes as favorites. Cabbages are rolled and stuffed, preserved in sauerkraut, layered in dishes, and cooked into soups. Vegetables are also sometimes seasoned with meat. During the growing season, raw salads are enjoyed. Popular Polish vegetables and legumes include carrots, celery root, beets, beans, dried peas, tomatoes, kohlrabi, cucumbers, turnips, onions, and cauliflowers.

Perhaps most of all the eastern European countries, Poles have a passion for mushrooms, foraged from their forests and used in stuffings, sauces, pickles, in brine, and dried. They are also sometimes components of the popular filled pies (*perogi*; Russian *pirozhki*), noodles, and pancakes.

Soups (sometimes served with dumplings) are essential to the Polish diet and are often soured. (See Southern Russia, page 124.) Soured Slavic foods and rye flavors are favored and traditionally, sour salt (citric acid crystals) was added to dishes to accentuate that tangy sour taste.

Fish includes eel, herring (smoked and pickled), as well as carp, pike, bream, perch, trout, and crayfish; from the Baltic Sea, cod, sole, halibut, and haddock.

Eastern Europeans love their sweets, and Poles are no exception. Honey is used as a sweetener for cakes, fruits, cheeses, and jams. Fruits, cultivated and wild, are enjoyed with meat and in soups and desserts. Fruit compotes, syrups, and juices, such as black currant juice, are popular. Jelly donuts and *babkas* (eggy, tall, yeast-risen cakes) are Polish inventions. Puddings and apple cake are also popular.

Cultural Influences on Polish Cuisine

Poland's size and shape has changed countless times in history, bringing influences from what are now its surrounding countries, and more importantly, solidifying a nationalist fervor that includes devotion to a Polish cuisine. Through all these changes, Poles have retained the essential Slavic proclivity for grains, breads and cereals, along with the use of souring food with lemon juice, sour cream, and vinegar.

From the time they converted to Christianity in 966 A.D., culinary Polish traditions have been permeated with religious meaning. Poppy seeds are used today in Polish desserts and during religious holidays, such as Christmas Eve supper. A smaller religious influence came from the Jewish minority, which until the Holocaust, was the center of the Ashkenazi branch of Jewish cooking.

As early as the thirteenth and fourteenth centuries, cookery books mention a national style of Polish cooking, and the merger of the Polish-Lithuanian royalty brought Baltic tastes to Poland, including fish and dairy preparations. The sixteenth and seventeenth centuries are considered the golden age of Poland's empire. Early in this period, the Italian princess, Bona Sforza, became Queen of Poland, bringing with her new kinds of vegetables, including still-popular cauliflower, tomatoes, and lettuce. Today, soup greens are still called "Italian things." She also introduced the Poles to pasta and the Poles gave pasta dishes their own twist. During the eighteenth century, New World potatoes were introduced and became a Polish staple.

Poland was destroyed and divided among Austria, Prussia, and Russia in 1793. Those countrymen brought their foods, including strudels, cakes, cutlets, fruit and sorrel soups, pancakes, and dumplings to Polish cuisine. French cuisine also arrived, blending with some dishes that survive today.

During the nineteenth century, Poland was forced into a Russian and German mold, and after World War II, it became a satellite of the Soviet Union until its independence in 1990. Of course, the Russian influence is apparent in the Polish diet, as they also enjoy *zakusky* (appetizers).

Despite all these influences, Polish haute cuisine is atypical in Europe, because it takes its culinary inspiration from peasants, perhaps, in part, because its monarchy descended from peasants.

Hungary

Classic Hungarian dishes and their distinctive preparation styles are enjoyed all over this small country, distinguished by offerings from its culinary regions— the Budapest area around the Danube River in central Hungary; the Great Plain, east of the Danube River; the Lake Balaton region, west of the Danube; and the Northern Mountains.

Hungary is a landlocked country in central Europe covering 35,924 square miles (93,043 square kilometers). It is bordered on the west by Austria; the southwest by Slovenia; the north by Slovakia; the north-

east by Ukraine; the east by Romania; and the south by Croatia and Serbia and Montenegro. Located in the Carpathian Basin, Hungary is rimmed by the Carpathian Mountains, the Alps, and the Dinaric Alps. The Danube River divides the country and bisects its capital, Budapest.

Hungary has four distinct seasons, with cold winters and a humid continental climate. Hungarians have traditionally made good use of their growing season, and, until the late twentieth century, more than half the population did agricultural work for home use or supplemental income. Hungary's chief crops include wheat, corn, sugar beets, barley, potatoes, apples, grapes, and sunflower seeds, with pigs, cattle, and sheep as livestock. Important food production includes paprika and salami in the Great Plain, and sauerkraut near Budapest.

The fertile Great Plain serves as Hungary's primary grain and vegetable larder, as well as home to livestock and barnyard animals. To the east, Lake Balaton is the Hungarian "sea," and its woods are ideal for mushroom gathering. The Northern Mountains are the heart of tree-fruit production, especially apples.

The country's population is about 10 million, mostly ethnic Hungarians (Magyars), with Gypsies as the largest ethnic minority. About three quarters of Hungarians are Roman Catholic and one quarter are Lutherans. Christian holidays have accompanying culinary traditions.

Hungarian Cuisine

Hungarian food is the most well-known and varied central European cuisine, exerting a strong influence over the region. It is generally characterized by soups and stews, sweet Hungarian paprika, dumplings, noodles, and fine desserts.

Beef, lamb, veal, and pork are all enjoyed, with pork the favorite, eaten both fresh and cured as bacon, salami, and sausages. Herdsmen tend cattle, oxen, and sheep. Poultry is a staple, including chicken, often raised on the Great Plain, as well as ducks, geese, turkey, and pigeons. Hungary's northern forests are the best hunting preserves in Europe, providing excellent game.

The hallmarks of Hungarian cooking are rich, meat-based soups and stews—*gulyás, pörkölt, paprikás,* and *tokány*—which are often seasoned with onion, paprika or caraway, and sour cream (see sidebar, page 132). While bacon and pork fat are traditional cooking components, oils such as sunflower and rapeseed have become more utilized.

Especially in the south, Hungary has more varieties of produce than many other Central European countries. Peppers are used generously, fresh and dried. Dried, powdered peppers—the famous Hungarian paprika—is available in a variety of intensities, with the mildest (or "sweet") the most renowned, used in a high percentage of Hungarian dishes. Cabbage dishes, notably sauerkraut, are key components in numerous meals. Potatoes, grown all over the country, are another staple, used in dishes such as soups and dumplings. Tomatoes are also popular.

All over Hungary, wheat is used in main courses, desserts, and side dishes—noodles (savory and sweet, flat and stuffed), as well as desserts, pancakes, and breads that are traditionally baked in embers, originally a specialty of the north.

Dairy products, notably sour cream, butter, and cheese are all part of the rich Hungarian diet. The country also processes a number of cheeses, from soft to semihard, made from cow, goat, or ewe's milk. These are prepared fresh, such as quark and farmer's cheese; or in the tradition of sophisticated European-style cheeses, many of them are wax coated, and some are smoked. *Liptó,* well known in the United States, is a blend of fresh cheese, butter, paprika, and caraway.

Landlocked Hungary is not a huge fish-eating nation, but its rivers and Lake Balaton provide freshwater fish, with carp the most popular. The favored fish soup is, of course, seasoned with paprika.

Many feel that Hungary's greatest glory is its desserts, both simple and homemade as well as sophisticated, as in the frequented cake shops of Budapest. There, pastries are similar to those of Germany and Austria, such as tortes with chocolate, nuts, and rich sauces. Homemade desserts include pancakes with fillings, strudel, fruit soups, and hot noodle desserts. Fruit is eaten out of hand but also preserved. In the northern region, cherries dipped in chocolate are a specialty. Poppy seeds are used in pastry; Hungarian honey as a sweetener. Coffee is the drink of choice.

Cultural Influences on Hungarian Cuisine

The primary cultural influences that shaped Hungarian foods are the nomadic Magyars, whose foodways form the underpinnings of the cuisine; ingredients and dishes brought by the Italians during the zenith of the Hungarian empire; ingredients introduced by the Turks during their rule; and the Austrian cuisine, assimilated during the period of the Hapsburgs, the Austro-Hungarian Empire.

The original Hungarians, the Magyars from the Ural Mountains between Asia and Europe, established their dynasty in 896 A.D. The food of these nomads still pervades Hungarian cuisine, including a love of meat and use of grains. Stews were cooked in heavy iron kettles (*bogrács*) over an open fire until all liquid was

Common Hungarian Ingedients

Seasonings	Vegetables		Meat
Caraway	Cabbage	Peppers	Beef
Dill	Carrots	Potatoes	Game
Onions	Cauliflower	Sorrel	Pork
Paprika	Cucumbers	Spinach	
Parsley	Kohlrabi	Tomatoes	**Dairy**
Poppy seeds	Parsley root		Milk
	Peas		Sour cream

Hallmarks of Hungarian Soups and Stews

What Americans call a "goulash" is generally one of these dishes.

Gulyás
These are beef-based soups flavored with onions and caraway, and no flour thickener; traditionally garnished with diced potatoes or dumplings. Variations include tomatoes, garlic, and hot cherry peppers. The more liquidy form is *gulyásleves* (*gulyás* soup) and the drier form is *gulyáshus* (*gulyás* meat).

Pörkölt
Pörkölt means "singed"; made with many types of meat or game or fish, these are dry stewed with onions, lard or bacon, and paprika. Variations include tomatoes and peppers.

Paprikás
Paprikás is usually made with chicken, but can also contain veal or carp. Much like *pörkölt*, it is finished with sweet or sour cream, and sometimes with flour.

Tokány
These thick stews, using lamb, veal, chicken, or game, are never thickened with flour, but braised in their juices and seasoned with onions, sometimes garlic, pepper, marjoram, and savory, with paprika in smaller amounts than in a *pörkölt*.

evaporated. When hungry, they simply added water and reheated it. Lots of liquid made *gulyás* soup (*gulyásleves*), less made a *gulyás* meat dish (*gulyáshus*). These are still key elements of Hungarian cooking, and Americans are familiar with the thicker version as goulash. The Magyars found wild boar, domesticated it, and it is still used extensively in bacon, ham, and numerous pork dishes. Techniques, such as spit roasting, cooking over fire, and thickening soured dishes with flour, milk, and egg yolk or a browned roux came from these early Hungarians.

As a great medieval power until the conquering Turks arrived, Hungary had a long affiliation with Italy, and it developed culinary characteristics partially based on the blend of Slavic and Mediterranean foods. New ingredients were introduced from southern Italy and Sicily, notably onions—the most important vegetable in Hungarian cooking—as well as domestic fowl, still widely used. The technique of cooking meat and fish in its own juices was established.

In the sixteenth century, the Turks conquered Hungary, transforming its culinary traditions. Most importantly, through the Bulgarians, they introduced paprika, for which the Hungarians are now famous. They also brought other ingredients that are still favored, including coffee, tomatoes, cherries, filo (commonly used in strudel), as well as turkey, through the New World.

From the eighteenth century until modern times, the Hapsburgs absorbed Hungary, establishing the Austro-Hungarian Empire. The upper classes were Germanized by their constant contact with the Viennese. The classic Viennese coffeehouses, pastry shops, and boutiques with ice cream established a passion for such foods, and cake shops are still prevalent in Hungary to this day.

In the nineteenth century, József Marchal, a French chef who had cooked for Emperor Napolean III and the Russian tsars, brought further sophistication to Hungarian foods by adding a French sensibility to traditional local seasonings and ingredients. Many dishes today are still "à la Marchal."

Despite subsequent Soviet rule, currently independent Hungary is still an amalgam of dominant Magyar foods with Mediterranean, Turkish, and Germanic influences.

Central Europe

The term "central Europe" is difficult to pinpoint geographically but may be more easily understood as a group of peoples and nations living in close proximity on the European continent who share a history of both cooperation and conflict. Central Europe can be said to include both Alpine and Visegrad groups of countries. The Alpine countries include (west to east) Switzerland, Germany, Lichtenstein, Austria, and Slovenia. The Visegrad group (named after the 1335 alliance of Kings) includes the Czech Republic and Slovakia. In addition to these two groups of nations, there are other countries with regions that have retained a "central European character," due to their past inclusion in kingdoms and empires such as the Holy Roman Empire, the Hapsburg monarchy, the Polish-Lithuanian Commonwealth, and Imperial Germany. These culturally affiliated areas are Western Belarus, Slavonia and Northwest Croatia, Lithuania, the Transylvania and Banat areas of Romania, the Vojvodina region of Serbia, and the Galicia region of the Ukraine. Central European culture has also been impacted by important contributions from Jewish and Roma minorities. A look into the cuisine and culture of Austria and Germany can serve as a glimpse into the cuisine and history of the Alpine countries.

Cultural Influences on Austrian Cuisine

Austrian culture has been greatly influenced by the diverse peoples who have both settled in the region or been incorporated into one of the many expanding and contracting empires that have dominated its history. The area known as Austria was first settled before 2000 B.C.E. by the Illyrians who migrated from the Balkan region. The Illyrians mined copper and salt and eventually established an agricultural economy. Other immigrant groups from present-day Germany, Scandinavia, France, and Spain began arriving in the area between 500 and 200 B.C.E. The Roman Empire was able to set the Danube as its northern border in 14 B.C.E. Austria was overrun by the Huns in 433 A.D., after which the area was dominated by Slavic and Germanic tribes. Charlemagne, the Frankish King, laid claim to the area and established the "eastern province" of Ostmark in 811. The Magyars enjoyed a period of dominance before they were defeated by Otto, the Holy Roman Emperor, at the Battle of Lechfield. Austria would then remain part of the Holy Roman Empire until its collapse in 1254. A group of nobles ruled the area until finally selecting Rudolph of the Hapsburg family as their ruler in 1273. The Hapsburg family would control much of central Europe through military might and marriage for the next 600 years. The Austro-Hungarian Empire began gaining strength in the mid-nineteenth century and exchanged cultural influences with Turkish, Swiss, Alsacian, French, Spanish, Dutch, Italian, German, Bohemian-Moravian, Hungarian, Polish, Croatian, Slovenian, Serbian, and Jewish peoples.

Generally speaking, the regional cuisine of Austria shares similarities with that of its neighbor Germany, but there are several distinct culinary regions in Austria. The Burgenland region of eastern Austria shares many culinary similarities with its neighbor Hungary. The cuisines of the southeastern Kaerrnten/Carinthia and Steiermark/Styria share Hungarian, Yugoslavian, and Italian culinary influences. Upper Austria and the Salzburg states share culinary similarities with their German and Czech neighbors. Niederoesterreich/Lower Austria's cuisine reflects its historical ties with Middle Eastern and Asian cultures. Vienna has a uniquely international cuisine that reflects its historic past as one of the most important cities in Europe.

Cultural Influences of Germany's Cuisine

Germany can be divided into three culinary regions: the northern, the central, and the southern. Culinary specialties from each of these regions are influenced by climate, terrain, as well as social status and Germany's history of localized governance through fiefdoms, kingdoms, townships, and municipalities.

Northern Germany
Major cities in northern Germany include Berlin and Hamburg. The cuisine of northern Germany is influenced

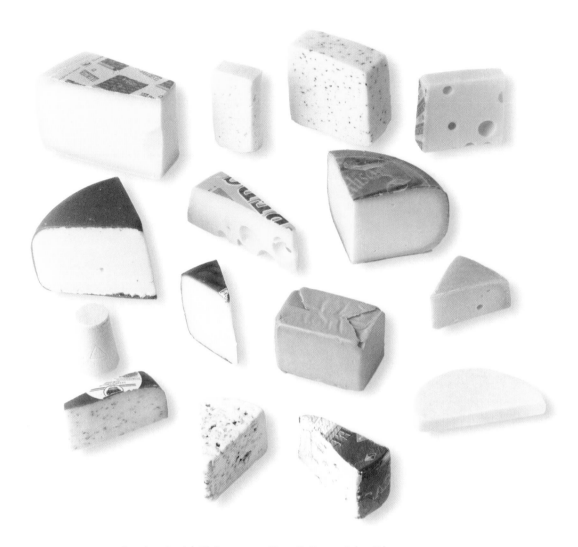

LEFT TO RIGHT, TOP TO BOTTOM: Gruyère, Danish tilsit, caraway Havarti, Emmentaler, Edam, jarlsberg, aged Gouda, sapsago, smoked Gouda, geitost, parrano, Dutch leyden, Danish blue, castello blue, Swedish farm

by its proximity to the North and Baltic Seas and shares a similarity to the cuisines of Denmark, Sweden, and Scotland. Smoked or pickled fish and meat dishes are popular and are supplemented with dishes prepared from local crops featuring potatoes, beets, cabbage, barley, hops, and rye. Pork, beef, goose, game, and lamb are also popular and often are seasoned or prepared with bacon and/or bacon grease. Sausages and cold cuts are also a staple of the northern diet with the liver sausage *Braunschweiger* hailing from the northern town of Braunshweig. Sweet and soured creamed sauces and soups are prominent in the north and meals are generally accompanied by beer or *Schnaps,* a strong liquor similar to gin flavored with juniper berries.

Central Germany

Major cities in central Germany include Frankfurt, Dresden, and Westphalia. The cuisine of central Germany can be described as hearty fare that is influenced by its prominence as an agricultural region. Pumpernickel and rye breads are produced from local grains. Dumplings are a staple, in a number of varieties made from potatoes, bread, flour, or oats. Sausages and stews, including the *Frankfurter,* which originated in the city of Frankfurt, and *Pfefferpotthast,* a beef short rib stew strongly seasoned with pepper, are popular. Westphalia is famous for its hams and pork dishes. The Rhine and Mosel river banks produce thriving vineyards from which wine is produced. The traditional Christmas bread *Stollen* is made using locally grown fruits and berries.

Southern Germany

The states of Bavaria, Swabia, Baden, and Alsace-Lorraine comprise southern Germany. The cuisine of southern Germany features many of the same staples as its northern and central neighbors, but the dishes are prepared in a "lighter" fashion. Vegetables including white asparagus, radishes, and cabbage are consumed in large quantities here and vegetable salads are popular throughout southern Germany. The cuisine of Bavaria, which is located in southeast Germany, is influenced by its proximity to Austria and the cuisine of Alsace-Lorraine, which is located in southwest Germany, has been influenced by its proximity to France. Fine wines are produced in southern Germany, but this is beer country with a historical tradition of government oversight of the brewing industry. *Spatzel*, a cross between a dumpling and a noodle is a popular side dish. Luscious desserts are prepared with such fruits as plums, cherries, apples, and berries that are grown in this region. The Black Forrest region is known for producing several varieties of mushrooms but is perhaps best known for its *schwartzwalder kirschtorte* or Black Forrest cherry cake flavored with the cherry liquor *Kirshwasser.*

German cuisine has retained many elements that are specifically German in origin, but it has also been influenced by its often tumultuous relationship with its central European neighbors. The area known as Germany was originally occupied by small Teutonic and Germanic tribes. These tribes fell under domination by the Roman Empire between 100 B.C.E. and 9 A.D., when a single tribe was able to defeat the Roman army of General Varnius and free the area from Roman occupation. Individual tribes developed into feudal kingdoms, which effectively controlled the region until they were overrun by the Huns about 375 A.D. The area was again briefly united during the reign of Charlemagne's Holy Roman Empire, but the Germans eventually organized into the five independent duchies of Bavaria, Franconia, Saxony, Scandia, and Lorraine sometime before 900 A.D. Germany sought to expand its borders and undertook a series of wars with Italy and the Catholic Church. German influence extended from the Rhine River east through Poland and Austria. The Franks and Celts controlled the territories to the west of the Rhine. After the death of Frederick II in 1250 A.D., the German states once again fell into political disunity.

With the coronation of Frederick III in 1437, the Hapsburg dynasty began a long period of supremacy. The rule of the Hapsburgs and nobles were particularly oppressive to the peasants and this period is characterized by large-scale peasant unrest and rebellion. The peasant rebellion was effectively suppressed and many of the nobles sided with Martin Luther in his Protestant movement. By the middle of the sixteenth century, the western principalities adopted Protestantism and the eastern Hapsburg monarchies retained Catholicism and sought to have it reinstated throughout Germany. The "Thirty Years' War" of the early seventeenth century was a battle between the Catholic League and the Protestant League. An early defeat of the Protestant League weakened Germany and led to the Danish and Swedish armies entering the conflict. Sweden's King Gustavus Adolphus was defeated in 1625, but French ruler Cardinal Richelieu's support of the Protestants allowed the conflict to continue until the "Peace of Westphalia" in 1638. Alsace and Lorraine adopted Catholicism, while the other German states either reverted to Protestantism or were given independence. Fear of Russian aggression caused the states of Prussia, Saxony, and Hanover to establish the League of German Princes in 1785.

The French Empire controlled much of Germany until 1806 when Napoleon relinquished his claim to them. The Napoleonic conquest of Germany brought about the collapse of the old German Empire and resulted in a weakened state that fell under Austrian control. In the years prior to 1828, the Northeast princedom of Prussia gradually became powerful enough to rule all of the German people except for those in Austria. Otto Van Bismark began uniting the disparate German principalities in 1866. Germany reacquired Alsace and Lorraine after defeating France on the Battlefield in 1871. Wilhelm I, who had been King of Prussia, was installed as the first German Kaiser, which effectively united Germany under one rule.

In southwestern Europe, the Iberian Peninsula juts out from France and the Pyrenees into the waters of the Mediterranean Sea and the Atlantic Ocean. It includes two countries, Spain and Portugal, with Spain covering more than three quarters of its landmass. The proximity of these countries, with their large coastline regions and overlapping historical influences, bind their culinary traditions.

Cultural Influences on the Iberian Peninsula

Since ancient times, waves of invasions of both Spain and Portugal, which together make up the Iberian Peninsula, have radically influenced its foods. Romans brought irrigation and olive trees; olive oil is still an essential staple in the region. In the north, Celtic and Visigothic people introduced pigs, and pork dishes remain popular today.

Arabs, who dominated the region for over 800 years, arrived with saffron and short-grained rice (vital for paella), and citrus fruits, such as Seville oranges. From the east, they brought ingredients such as almonds, eggplant, and cumin, still used today. Both Spain and Portugal utilize many Moorish ingredients and their recipes.

After Moorish rule ended, the age of exploration began in earnest in the fifteenth century, when the powerful rival ships of Spain and Portugal traveled the world in search of spices, bringing home black pepper, nutmeg, cloves, and cinnamon.

The single most important culinary influence during the sixteenth and seventeenth centuries on the peninsula, as well as all of Europe, was the arrival of New World foods, including chiles (sweet and hot), corn, beans, tomatoes, vanilla, chocolate, squash, guava, pecans, pine nuts, turkey, and potatoes. Cod also arrived from the Grand Banks off Newfoundland and dried codfish recipes are still enormously popular today.

Ingredients and prepared dishes flowed back and forth between Spain and Portugal and their vast colonies, forever influencing the cuisines of the conquerors and their conquests, which for Spain included Mexico, Cuba, Puerto Rico, and the Philippines, and for Portugal included Brazil, Mozambique, Angola, Timor (near Bali), parts of China, and India.

Today, the cuisine of the Iberian Peninsula, especially its cosmopolitan cities, is influenced by international flavors, but it still bears the strong stamp of historical foodways.

Spain

The Spanish landscape is dominated by a high plateau, the Meseta Central. It is surrounded, as well as dissected, by mountains, isolating one culinary region from another. This terrain creates distinct regional cuisines and further delineations within each region.

For culinary purposes, the country can be roughly divided into the north coast; the north interior; the central plains; the northeast; the southeast coast; the south; and the Canary Islands.

In southwestern Europe, Spain is the second largest county on the continent, with a total of 195,000 square miles (505,050 square kilometers). Continental Spain borders the Bay of Biscay, France, and Andorra in the Pyrenees to the north; the Mediterranean Sea and the Straits of Gibraltar to the east and south; the Atlantic Ocean to the southwest; and Portugal and the Atlantic to the west. It also includes the Balearic Islands in the Mediterranean, the Canary Islands in the Atlantic, three small islands off the coast of Africa, and the autonomous towns of Ceuta and Melilla on the Mediterranean North African coast of Morocco.

Generally, the Spanish climate has hot, dry Mediterranean summers and mild winters. The northern coastal region is wetter, with rainfall throughout the year and less sun, and the sunny South is prone to draught. Spain has been called "the Market Garden of Europe," because agriculture is a significant part of the economy and a major export. The world's largest producer and exporter of olive oil and oranges, Spain is also home to the largest fishing fleet in the world and has more land in grape production than any other country.

Spain's population is almost 43 million, with a combination of Mediterranean and Nordic heritages. Almost all are Roman Catholic, making Christian holidays, such as Christmas and Easter, as well as numerous smaller holidays, occasions for culinary rituals and celebrations. Castilians are the nation's ethnically dominant group, but ethnic minorities, including Basques and Catalans, offer some of the countries most celebrated cuisines.

Although distinct dishes are found within culinary regions, many are enjoyed nationally, notably *tortilla Espanola* (a thick cake of eggs and potatoes), a variety of cured hams and sausages, paella (a dish of saffron rice and various proteins), *cocidos* (brothy stews), gazpacho (a cold soup), as well as flan (a dessert custard), and almond-based desserts.

Regional Cuisines

The North Coast

Bordering the Atlantic, this cooler, wet and green region is distinguished by Basque food, which, along with Catalan, is considered Spain's most distinctive cuisine. Men's cooking societies are part of the culture, and numerous top chefs originate in Basque country. Regional cooking techniques include slow simmering in olive oil and subtle green and red sauces. Fish dishes abound, including a signature dish with hake, and very thin baby eels or *elvers,* served with hot chile oil. Sardines and anchovies are canned.

The westernmost region, Galicia, is especially well known for its superior seafood, which is often flown to Spain's inland capital, Madrid. Good grazing land supports beef and veal, and Galicia also features savory meat and fish pies, most likely of Celtic origins, as well as dishes similar to northern Portuguese cuisine.

The North Interior

Adjacent to France, the landlocked north interior is desolate in the mountain areas, with fertile regions near its rivers, which also contain trout. It is known for its simple foods, such as torn, sautéed bread, cooked with meats, vegetables, or eggs. Its most famous crop is sweet red peppers (*pimientos del piquillo*). Wheat and orchard fruit, along with white asparagus, baby artichokes, peas, beans, and potatoes are grown there.

The Central Plains

The vast central plains of Castilian Spain, with its hot summers and cold winters, contain Madrid, the sophisticated capital, featuring international foods. Some of the popular foods are flown in, such as fish, which are often served in almond sauce. But generally, because the region is inland, fish often gives way to meat, beans, and sausage, such as the commonly cooked brothy stew, *cocido,* a boiled dinner of meat, vegetables, such as potatoes or seasonal greens, and beans. The broth is eaten as a first course and its contents as an entrée. Good grazing country sustains wheat and sheep—the source of popular baby lamb and Spain's most well-known sheep's cheese, manchego. This is also the home of the famous Spanish saffron crop, used in Spanish cooking and exported all over the world. Costly saffron comes from the hand-picked pistils of saffron crocuses.

A Meal in Spain

The Spanish are notorious for eating late and often. Spaniards sometimes eat both an early and mid-morning breakfast, as well as a full lunch and dinner, also snacking on pre-lunch tapas, and pre-dinner tea with pastry or tapas.

Lunch, considered a heavier meal than dinner, is generally served at 2:00 P.M., for two to three hours, and dinner at 10:00 P.M. A full meal might begin with tapas, followed by a light first course, a main course, then dessert. Typically, restaurant menus are flexible, broken into meats, poultry and game, fish, vegetables, eggs and rice, so diners can take their own approach to ordering. As in the United States, the courses and complexity of a meal depends on income and lifestyle.

Common Spanish Ingredients

Legumes

Fava beans

Garbanzo beans

Kidney beans

Lentils

White beans

Seasonings

Capers

Cumin

Cured ham

Garlic

Olive oil and olives

Oregano

Paprika

Peppers (sweet, hot, fresh, and dry)

Saffron

Vegetables

Artichokes and cardoons

Asparagus

Cabbage

Carrots

Chard

Eggplant

Green beans

Onions

Peas

Peppers

Potatoes

Tomatoes

Zucchini

Fruit

Almonds

Apricots

Avocados

Bananas

Carobs

Cherimoyas (custard apples)

Citrus (oranges, mandarins, lemons)

Dates

Figs

Grapes

Grapes: muscatel (wine and raisins)

Kumquats

Mangos

Olives

Peaches

Persimmons

Pineapples

Plantain

Pomegranates

Strawberries

Meat

Beef

Lamb

Pork

Sausages

Veal

Poultry and Game

Chickens

Rabbits

Squab

Fish and Shellfish

Anchovy

Bream

Clams

Cod

Conger eel

Hake

Mackerel

Monkfish

Mullet

Oysters

Prawns

Sardines

Sea bass

Sole

Squid

Swordfish

Trout

Tuna

Turbot

The Northeast

This region, covering Catalonia with its mountains and green coastline, as well as the Balearic Islands in the Mediterranean, developed one of the most prized cuisines in Spain. Both complex and distinctive, Catalan foods have Roman, Visigoth, Moorish, French, and Italian roots, with a strong contemporary influence from Spanish and international restaurateurs.

Known for its unusual combinations, such as squid with pork, rabbit, and snails, and salt cod with raisins, Catalan food is closer to Spain's medieval roots than any other European cuisine, utilizing typically sweet seasonings in savory dishes and pulverized nuts to thicken sauces, such as romesco sauce.

Four dishes define Catalan cooking: *safregit,* a sautéed onion mixture used to begin a preparation; *picada,* a paste of almonds, bread, and garlic used to flavor and thicken; *allioli,* an eggless garlic and olive oil emulsion served with seafood, including salt cod; and *samfaina,* a vegetable stew used as a side dish or sauce.

LEFT TO RIGHT, TOP TO BOTTOM: eggs, Spanish olive oil, eggplant, plantain, Spanish rice, Spanish onion, peppers, orange, thyme, sherry vinegar, garlic bulbs, lemons, saffron, paprika, avocado, grapes, carobs, tomatoes

The Balearic Islands serve more peasant-style cookery. Majorca features pork, including sausages such as spicy *sobrassada* and *butifarro,* a blood sausage, as well as apricots and almonds.

The Southeast Coast

On the southeast coast, the Levante begins south of Catalonia and extends to Andalusia in southernmost Spain. Semitropical, this flat, coastal region, with a fertile delta area and tidal flatlands, is considered "the Garden of Spain," with vast citrus groves, including famous Valencia oranges, muscatel grape vineyards, vegetable farms, and a large greenhouse industry.

The Levante is also home to Spain's popular short-grain *bomba* variety of rice. The Moors introduced rice and saffron to this region. Today, Valencia is still known for its numerous rice dishes, especially paella, which utilizes both rice and saffron, and is named for its flat pan.

LEFT TO RIGHT, TOP TO BOTTOM: idiazabel, Spanish blue, manchego, iberico, tetilla, Spanish goat (round), mahon

The South

Andalusia is the most southern region of Spain, with a coastline bordered by both the Mediterranean and the Atlantic. It is the largest olive oil producing region, with abundant seafood, much of it fried in robustly flavored olive oil. The Moors, who occupied Andalusia for 800 years, greatly influenced its foods with dishes that combine lamb and dried fruit or honey. Andalusia is also known for its cured hams, serrano, and *bellota*.

Andalusia is home to two foods now popular all over Spain—tapas and gazpacho. Tapas, "little dishes" popular in bars and cafes, originated in the nineteenth century. The name derives from *tapar,* meaning "to cover," as the original tapas were simply slices of sausage or ham covering a glass of sherry. Today there are hundreds of tapas varieties, from plain olives or almonds to omelets and hot sauced dishes. Gazpacho, a cold soup traditional to this region, was originally made with bread, but is often prepared with tomatoes. It may be green, from herbs, or white, from almonds.

The Canary Islands

The Canary Islands, off the African coast, draw their culinary roots from Moorish and African influences. The terrain is ideal for raising crops brought from the New World, such as a significant portion of Spain's tomatoes, along with corn, avocados, papaya, and pineapples. The Spanish also introduced bananas, wheat, sugarcane, goats, chickens, and grapevines. Moorish sweet potatoes are used in stews. Signature flavorings include spiced *mojos,* which are green (herb) or red (sweet or hot chile) marinades.

CHEESE	KIND OF MILK	FROM	TEXTURE/TASTE
Manchego (most well-known Spanish cheese)	Sheep's milk	Central plains: La Mancha	Soft, semisoft, and mild to hard and sharp; herringbone pattern on rind depicts original wrapping
Burgos	Sheep's milk	Burgos	Fresh, soft, mild; often eaten as dessert with sugar or honey
Cabrales	Various milks	North Spain: Asturias	Smooth and strong; blue-veined cheese; wrapped in leaves
Cabrero	Cow's milk	North coast: Galicia	Firm
Idiazabal	Sheep's milk	North coast: Basque	Soft or firm; often smoked and formed into small balls
Mahon	Cow's milk	The Balearic Islands: Menorca	Semisoft and strong; sometimes preserved with oil and paprika
Roncal	Cow and sheep's milk	North Spain: The Pyrenees	Medium-hard cheese; smoked; with tiny holes
San Simon	Cow's milk	North coast: Galicia	Medium cured; strongly smoked; amber colored; pear shaped
Tetilla	Cow's milk	North coast: Galicia	Creamy and pungent; distinctive pyramidal shape

Cooking Equipment

Cazuela—Flameproof, earthenware dishes, glazed on the inside, rough on the outside. Used in numerous sizes, either shallow or deep. For a wide variety of dishes including tapas, roasts, and saucy and rice-based dishes. Earthenware heats evenly and retains heat after it is removed from the heat source.

Paella—Large, round, flat, metal cooking vessel with two or more handles that is used for rice-based dishes. The paella pan is shallow to help ensure even cooking. Paella is traditionally cooked over an open fire.

Portugal

Many of Portugal's foodways originated with its long coastline, which has fostered a passion for seafood and launched transformative culinary exploration. Its proximity to larger, neighboring Spain and its isolated rural character further defined its cuisine.

For culinary purposes, Portugal is roughly divided into regions north and north of the Tagus River, which cuts the country through its narrow middle in the east, and travels southeasterly to Lisbon and the Atlantic. Regions here include the north coast and inland provinces; the south inland and coastal provinces; and in the Atlantic Ocean, the Madeira and Azores Islands.

Set on the easternmost promontory of continental Europe, Portugal occupies about one sixth of the western coast of the Iberian Peninsula, and covers a total of 35,516 square miles (91,986 square kilometers). The population is 10.6 million and is largely homogeneous, of Nordic and Mediterranean descent. Like Spain, Portugal is almost totally Roman Catholic, and Christian holidays figure largely into culinary traditions.

With a long coastline and ten major rivers, water is a key element in Portuguese foodways. Portugal's terrain is generally mountainous north of the Tagus River, with rolling plains to the south. The climate is varied, with considerable colder weather, rainfall, and seasonal temperatures in the north, and hotter temperatures and a dryer Mediterranean climate along the southern coast.

Despite its rural character, with more country dwellers than any European nation, Portugal's agriculture does not support its people. The Portuguese coastline is home to its vital fishing industry; the Portuguese eat more fish per capita than any other European country. But today, with fish prices rising, even traditionally inexpensive salt cod (*bacalhau*), which is considered Portugal's national dish, is less accessible.

Portugal's main agricultural products are wheat, corn, rice, potatoes, grapes, and olive oil. Pastureland is scarce, but livestock includes pigs, sheep, goats, chickens, and some cattle. Traditionally, the poor have subsisted on olive oil and garlic-infused dishes made from homegrown crops, bread, and salt cod.

Regional Cuisine

Because of shared geography, climate, and overlapping history, Portuguese food is similar to the food of its larger neighbor, Spain. Still, there are important differences. Perhaps because of the influence from their colonies, the Portuguese use more varied and intense seasonings, notably more hot peppers and fresh cilantro, an herb not favored in Spanish cooking. Portugal is more rural, although less agriculturally rich, than Spain, so daily foods tend to be more "countrified," or simply prepared. Less ethnically diverse, the Portuguese don't have strong Catalan and Basque influences.

North of the Tagus River

Northern Portugal has a cold Atlantic climate and residents prefer hearty rustic recipes, some using goat and pork and pork fat, as well as the classic olive oil. Typical fish, meat, and vegetable soups and stews (see sidebar) cooked or accompanied with dense crusty breads, are often made with corn, as well as wheat or rye. Both rice and potatoes may accompany a meal.

A Meal in Portugal

The Portuguese generally eat a light breakfast, often simply a roll and milky coffee, sometimes followed by a mid-morning snack, then lunch, starting at about 1:30 and running until 3:00 or 3:30 P.M., followed by a leisurely dinner. The main meal, either lunch or dinner, varies according to income and lifestyle. Often it starts with soup—one of the most popular dishes in Portugal—followed by a meat or fish dish, heavily augmented with vegetables (as green salads are not popular). Soup is accompanied by potatoes, rice, or bread (or a combination of these), and a simple dessert, such as rice pudding or fruit and cheese. This is followed by coffee, the drink of choice in Portugal. Cake shops and tea houses thrive all over Portugal.

Common Portugese Ingredients

Seasonings

Bay leaf

Cilantro

Cinnamon

Cumin

Garlic

Mint

Olive oil

Oregano

Paprika

Parsley

Saffron

Vinegar

Wine

Vegetables and Fruits

Almonds

Grapes

Lemons

Oranges

Olives

Onions

Peppers

Potatoes

Meat

Bacon

Pork

Sausage

Smoked ham

Seafood

Clams

Mackerel

Oysters

Salt cod

In the northwestern coastal area lies Minho and Doura, covered with scenic small farms, vineyards, and forests. Minho is home to several Portuguese favorites, such as *caldo verde*—a soup of potatoes (grown in Minho and brought long ago from the New World), onions, shredded *couve,* a kale-like Portuguese cabbage, and *linguiça* sausage. *Caldo verde* is sometimes thickened with the rough, yeast-raised cornbread typical of the north. *À Minhota,* "of Minho," means that a dish contains ham, and all cuts of pork are popular in this northern province. Unusual in other parts of Europe, curry is used as a seasoning, but in minuscule amounts.

Farther down the coast is low-lying Beira Litoral, with Aveiro to its south, which contains a water lagoon with sea eels and perch. There are sardines and skate, and cod farther out to sea, which is canned and salted. Salted cod (*bacalau*) and eel broth are regional specialties. Inland, crops include olives, corn, wheat, fruit, and grapes.

To the coastal south is Estremadura, approximately in the center of the country, and containing Portugal's capital, Lisbon, where the Tagus River enters the Atlantic. Lisbon is a city with varied foods; fish and shellfish are excellent there, and the market at Cascaus is the largest in the country, displaying everything from spider crab to lobster. Shellfish bisque and fried squid are specialties. The Estremadura province is also home to *acorda de mariscos,* a popular "dry" bread soup with egg, shellfish, and fresh coriander. *Acordas,* popular all over Portugal, are based on bread, broth or stock, and whatever else is local.

Inland, the northern provinces bordering Spain include Tras-os-Montes (beyond the mountains) e Alto Doura, with Alta and Baixa Beiras farther south. This is one of the least-populated areas of Portugal, with high barren areas and well-planted, deeply cut valleys with fruit trees, vegetables fields, and vineyards. The regional mainstays are sheep and pigs, and Tras-os-Montes boasts the best cured ham in Portugal and the spiced Beiras *bocheira* sausage and suckling pig. The finest cheese of Portugal, *queijo da serra,* comes from the Beiras; cheese, honey, and olive oil are traded. Regional Beiras specialties include a boiled dinner with dried white beans, similar to Spanish *cocidos,* bread baked with eggs and meat, chestnut soup, and almond and egg confections, strongly influenced by Moorish desserts.

South of the Tagus River

Portugal's southern foodways are shaped by the region's hotter, more fertile climate. The country's wheat crop is cultivated on its wide plains and, as in all of Portugal, bread is a staple. Here, it tends to be made with white flour. Eaten out of hand, as in the north, it is also used to thicken *acorda* ("dry" soups) or thicker stews called *migras,* meaning "crumbs," both eaten with regional variations all over Portugal.

Portuguese Soups and Stews

Portugal is a big soup- and stew-eating country and soup often begins a meal or is a meal in itself.

Acordas: These "dry" soups are garlic-infused bread soups, based on stale bread and broth, often containing eggs and whatever is in season, as well as herbs. Regional versions abound. (*Migas* are drier, meatier, stewy versions, often with layered ingredients.)

Sopa Seca: This means "dry" soup; uses shreds of available meats, layered into a bowl with vegetables and bread with fresh herbs, such as mint or coriander.

Canja: Portugal's chicken soup with lemon and mint.

Sopas: *Sopas* means "soups," and these are generally chunky soups with vegetables, meats, and seafood, often thickened with potatoes. Portuguese stone soup with beans is from the Ribatejo province.

Green Soups/Sopa de Conentro: A potato-thickened fresh coriander soup. *Acordos* are sometimes also made as green soups.

Caldo Verde: A *caldo* is a clear or puréed soup. *Caldo verde* is the national soup of Portugal, with shredded kale-like cabbage, potatoes, and sausage or cured loin of pork.

Cozidos: Much like those of Spain, these are boiled dinners, where the broth is eaten separately from the other ingredients.

Fish Soups and Stews/Caldeiradas: A fish stew with regional variations, such as *moda de guincho*, a kind of grand Portuguese bouillabaisse. *Acordos* are also made with shellfish.

Just northwest of Lisbon, the Tagus River runs through the western region of the inland Ribatejo province and the northern riverbank is intensely farmed with olive groves, fruit orchards, and vineyards. Varied regional dishes include shad roe from the river, kid (goat) cutlets, hare stewed in red wine, and carrot pudding.

Farther inland, toward Spain with a small "window" on the Atlantic, lies Alentejo, covering about one third of Portugal's landmass. Alentejo is also home to both olives and almonds. Grazing land makes it hospitable to sheep. Pigs are common barnyard livestock, with pork processed into both smoked ham and garlicky sausages. A traditional ingredient is *massa de pimentao,* a red pepper paste, often blended with mashed garlic, parsley, and bay leaves, and used to season meats and poultry, including regional sausages. Another popular "dry soup," the simple *acorda a alentejo,* of bread, egg, and fresh coriander, is a common way to stretch a meager diet. Here *migas* contain layers of meat, vegetables, and bread, spinkled with mint. On the Spanish border, sweet plums preserved in syrup are considered a specialty.

From the southernmost region, Algarve, comes *piri-piri,* a hot chile sauce that became popular in Portugal in modern times. Historically, the region was commonly visted by explorers, traders, and travelers, making it a crossroads for many exotic ingredients, and the hot climate is conducive to cultivating figs, apricots, lemons, carob, almonds, sugarcane, citrus, and rice. A variety of vegetables are grown here as well and the regional fish is considered excellent. The *cataplana,* a hinged copper pan, originated in Algarve, and regional specialties include clams steamed in a *cataplana.* Desserts also bear the stamp of the Moors, with almonds, spices, and egg yolks. The tourist hotels have brought an international flavor to the region's cooking.

The Madeira and Azores Islands

In the Atlantic, on the volcanic island of Madeira, man-made terraces grow spring vegetables, tropical fruits, including bananas, and grapes. A true Madeira cake is much like gingerbread, made with molasses and spices. From the Azores come fragrant pineapples and a dish eaten all over Portugal—beefsteak with fried egg on top.

Part Three

Tools and Ingredients in the Professional Kitchen

Equipment Identification

Tools, large and small, make it possible for chefs to do their jobs well; in fact, using the right tool for the job is one of the hallmarks of a professional. Equally important is the ability to handle and care for each tool, whether it is a cutting board, a knife, a mandoline, or a stockpot.

Knives

Assembling a personal collection of knives is one of the first steps in becoming a professional. Just as an artist or craftsperson gathers together the tools necessary for painting, sculpting, or drawing, you will need to select knives that allow you to do your work in the safest and most efficient way. The knives you choose will become as important to you as your own fingers—quite literally an extension of your own hands.

1. **Handle knives with respect.** Knives can be damaged if they are handled carelessly. Even though good-quality knives are manufactured to last a lifetime, they are still prone to damage if not properly taken care of.

2. **Keep knives sharp.** Learn the proper techniques for both sharpening and honing knives. A sharp knife not only performs better, but is safer to use because less effort is required to cut through the food. There are many ways to sharpen knives. Use a stone periodically, a sharpening machine, or send them to a professional cutlery sharpener.

3. **Keep knives clean.** Clean knives thoroughly, immediately after using them. Sanitize the entire knife, including the handle, bolster, and blade, as necessary, so that the tool will not cross-contaminate food. Do not clean knives in a dishwasher.

4. **Use safe handling procedures for knives.** There are standards of behavior that should be remembered when using knives. When you are passing a knife, lay it down on a work surface so that the handle is extended toward the person who will pick it up. Whenever you must carry a knife from one area of the kitchen to another, hold the knife straight down at your side with the sharp edge facing behind you, and let people know you are passing by with something sharp. When you lay a knife down on a work surface, be sure that no part of it extends over the edge of the cutting board or worktable. Also, do not cover the knife with food towels, equipment, and the like. Be sure the blade is facing away from the edge of the work surface. Do not attempt to catch a falling knife.

5. **Use an appropriate cutting surface.** Cutting directly on metal, glass, or marble surfaces will dull and eventually damage the blade of a knife. To prevent dulling, always use wooden or composition cutting boards.

6. **Keep knives properly stored.** There are a number of safe, practical ways to store knives, including in knife kits or rolls, slots, racks, and on magnetized holders. Storage systems should be kept just as clean as knives.

The Parts of a Knife

To select a knife of good quality that fits your hand well and is suitable for the intended task, you need a basic knowledge of the various parts of a knife.

Blades

Currently, the most frequently used material for blades is high-carbon stainless steel. Other materials, such as stainless steel and carbon steel, are also available.

Although carbon-steel blades take a better edge than either regular or high-carbon stainless steel, they tend to lose their sharpness quickly. Also, carbon-steel blades will discolor when they come into contact with acidic foods. The metal is brittle and can break easily under stress.

Stainless steel is much stronger than carbon steel and will not discolor or rust. It is difficult to get a good edge on a stainless-steel blade, although once an edge is established, it tends to last longer than the edge on a carbon-steel blade.

High-carbon stainless steel is a relatively recent development that combines the advantages of carbon steel and stainless steel. The higher percentage of carbon allows the blade to take and keep a keener edge. The most desirable type of blade for general use is *taper-ground,* meaning that the blade has been forged out of a single sheet of metal and has been ground so that it tapers smoothly from the spine to the cutting edge, with no apparent beveling.

Hollow-ground blades are made by combining two sheets of metal. The edges are then beveled or fluted.

Tangs

The tang is a continuation of the blade that extends into the knife's handle. Knives used for heavy work, such as chef's knives or cleavers, should have a full tang; that is, the tang is almost as long as the entire handle. Although blades with partial tangs are not as durable, they are acceptable on knives that will be used less frequently. Rat-tail tangs are much narrower than the spine of the blade and are encased in the handle.

Handles

A preferred material for knife handles is rosewood, because it is extremely hard and has a very tight or fine grain, which helps to prevent splitting and cracking. Impregnating wood with plastic protects the handle from damage caused by continued exposure to water and detergents. The handle should fit your hand comfortably. A comfortable fit will reduce fatigue.

Rivets

Metal rivets are usually used to secure the tang to the handle. The rivets should be completely smooth and lie flush with the surface of the handle.

Bolsters

In some knives, there is a collar or shank, known as a bolster, at the point where the blade meets the handle. This is a sign of a well-made knife. The bolster helps to balance the knife and protect the hand from accidental slips. Some knives may have a collar that looks like a bolster but is actually a separate piece attached to the handle. These knives tend to come apart easily and should be avoided.

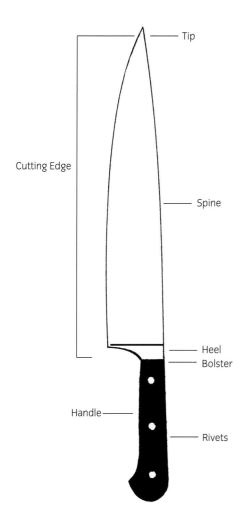

Parts of a knife

Types of Knives

A wide array of knives is available to suit specific functions. As you continue to work in professional kitchens, your knife kit will grow to encompass not only the basics—chef's or French knife, boning knife, paring knife, and slicer—but also a number of special knives. This list is intended as a guide to the knives that may be found in nearly any well-outfitted knife kit.

> **Chef's knife or French knife** This all-purpose knife is used for a variety of chopping, slicing, and mincing chores. The blade is normally 8 to 12 inches long.
>
> **Utility knife** This smaller, lighter chef's knife is used for light cutting chores. The blade is generally 5 to 8 inches long.
>
> **Paring knife** This short knife, used for paring and trimming vegetables and fruits, has a 2- to 4-inch blade.
>
> **Boning knife** A boning knife is used to separate raw meat from the bone. The blade, which is thinner and shorter than the blade of a chef's knife, is about 6 inches long and is usually rigid.
>
> **Filleting knife** Used for filleting fish, this knife is similar in shape and size to a boning knife, but is thinner and with a more flexible blade.

Types of Knives

FROM TOP LEFT: cleaver, utility knives (next two), slicer, flexible slicer, scimitar, serrated slicers (pointed and round tipped) FROM BOTTOM LEFT: French knives (first three in row), boning knife, granton-style edge French knife, paring knife, tourné knife

Slicer This knife is generally used for slicing cooked meat, and is also suitable for food such as smoked salmon. It has a long blade with a round or pointed tip. The blade may be flexible or rigid and may be taper-ground or have a fluted edge.

Cleaver Used for chopping, the cleaver is often heavy enough to cut through bones. It has a rectangular blade and varies in size according to its intended use.

Tourné knife This small knife, similar to a paring knife, has a curved blade to make cutting the curved surfaces of tournéed vegetables easier.

Sharpening and Honing

The key to the proper and efficient use of any knife is making sure that it is sharp. A knife with a sharp blade always works better and more safely because it cuts easily. Knife blades are given an edge on a sharpening stone and maintained between sharpenings by honing them with a steel.

Sharpening stones are essential to the proper maintenance of knives. Sharpen the blade by passing its edge over the stone at a 20-degree angle. The grit—the degree of coarseness or fineness of the stone's surface—abrades the blade's edge, creating a sharp cutting edge. When sharpening a knife, always begin by using the coarsest surface of the stone, and then move on to the finer surfaces.

A stone with a fine grit should be used for boning knives and other tools on which an especially sharp edge is required. Most stones may be used either dry or moistened with water or mineral oil.

Carborundum stones have a fine side and a medium side.

Arkansas stones are available in several grades of fineness. Some consist of three stones of varying degrees of fineness mounted on a wheel.

Diamond-impregnated stones are also available. Although they are expensive, some chefs prefer them because they feel these stones give a sharper edge.

Opinion is split about whether a knife blade should be run over a stone from heel to tip or tip to heel. Most chefs do agree that consistency in the direction of the stroke used to pass the blade over the stone is important.

Before using a stone, be sure that it is properly stabilized. No matter which method you use, keep the following guidelines in mind:

1. Assemble your mise en place.

2. Anchor the stone to keep it from slipping as you work. Place carborundum or diamond stones on a damp cloth or rubber mat. A triple-faced stone is mounted on a rotating framework that can be locked into position so that it cannot move.

3. Lubricate the stone with mineral oil or water. Be consistent about the type of lubricant you use on your stone. Water or mineral oil helps reduce friction as you sharpen your knife. The heat caused by friction may not seem significant, but it can eventually harm the blade.

4. Begin sharpening the edge on the coarsest grit you require. The duller the blade, the coarser the grit should be.

5. Run the entire edge over the surface of the stone, keeping the pressure even on the knife. Hold the knife at the correct angle as you work. A 20-degree angle is suitable for chef's knives and knives with similar blades. You may need to adjust the angle by a few degrees to properly sharpen thinner blades, such as slicers, or thicker blades, such as cleavers.

6. Always sharpen the blade in the same direction. This ensures that the edge remains even and in proper alignment.

7. Make strokes of equal number and equal pressure on each side of the blade. Do not oversharpen the edge on coarse stones. After about ten strokes on each side of the blade, move on to the next finer grit.

8. Finish sharpening on the finest stone, and then wash and dry the knife thoroughly before using or storing it.

Sharpening Method One

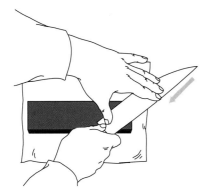

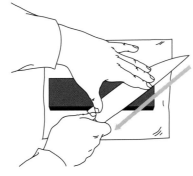

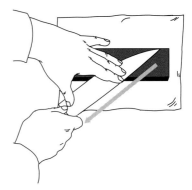

1. Use four fingers of the guiding hand to maintain constant pressure on the knife.

2. Draw the knife across the stone gently.

3. Draw the knife off the stone smoothly. Turn the knife over and repeat the entire process on the other side.

Sharpening Method Two

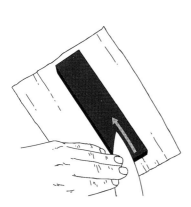

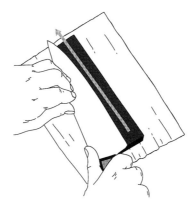

1. Push the blade over the stone's surface, using the guiding hand to keep pressure even.

2. Continue to push the entire length of the blade over the stone.

3. Push the knife off the stone smoothly. Turn the knife over and repeat the entire process on the other side.

Steels

A steel should be used both immediately after sharpening the blade with a stone and also between sharpenings to keep the edges in alignment. The length of the steel's working surface can range from three inches for a pocket version to over fourteen inches. Hard steel is the traditional material for steels. Other materials, such as glass, ceramic, and diamond-impregnated surfaces, are also available.

Steels come with coarse, medium, and fine grains, and some are magnetic, which helps the blade maintain proper alignment and also collects metal shavings. A guard or hilt between the steel and the handle protects the user, and a ring on the bottom of the handle can be used to hang the steel.

When using a steel, the knife is held almost vertically, with the blade at a 20-degree angle, resting on the inner side of the steel. The blade should be drawn along the entire length of the steel. Keep the following guidelines in mind:

1. Allow yourself plenty of room as you work, and stand with your weight evenly distributed. Hold the steel with your thumb and fingers safely behind the guard.

2. Draw the blade along the steel so that the entire edge touches the steel. Work in the same direction on each side of the blade to keep the edge straight.

3. Be sure to keep the pressure even to avoid wearing away the metal in the center of the edge. Over time, this could produce a curve in the edge. Keep the knife blade at a 20-degree angle to the steel.

4. Use a light touch, stroking evenly and consistently. Lay the blade against the steel; don't slap it. Listen for a light ringing sound; a heavy grinding sound indicates that too much pressure is being applied.

5. Repeat the stroke on the opposite side of the edge to properly straighten the edge. If a blade requires more than five strokes per side on a steel, it probably should be sharpened on a stone.

Steeling Method One

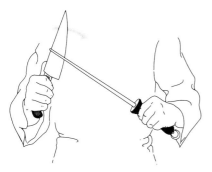  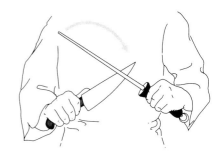

1. Start with the knife nearly vertical, with the blade resting on the steel's inner side.

2. Rotate the wrist holding the knife as the blade moves along the steel in a downward motion.

3. Keep the blade in contact with the steel until the tip is drawn off the steel. Repeat the process with the blade resting on the steel's outer side.

Steeling Method Two

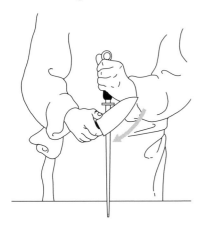 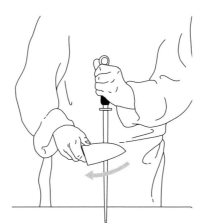 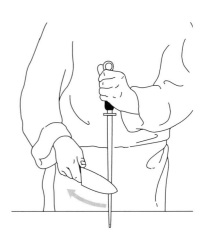

1. Hold the steel in a near-vertical position with the tip resting on a nonslippery surface. Start with the heel of the knife against one side of the steel.

2. Maintain light pressure and use an arm action, not a wrist action, to draw the knife down the shaft of the steel in a smooth continuous motion.

3. Finish the first pass by drawing the blade all the way along the shaft up to and including the tip. Repeat the entire action, this time with the blade against the steel's other side.

Sharpening Stones and Steels

CLOCKWISE FROM TOP: multisided oil stone (tri-stone), ceramic steels (white and blue), diamond-impregnated steel, hard steel, flat steel, ceramic stone, diamond-impregnated stone

Hand Tools

CLOCKWISE FROM TOP LEFT: fish spatula, kitchen fork, wide perforated offset spatula, French rolling pins (two pictured), ball bearing rolling pin, offset palette knives, balloon whips, sauce whip, swivel-bladed peelers

Hand Tools

A number of small hand tools other than knives belong in a knife kit:

Rotary or swivel-bladed peeler This is used to peel the skin from various vegetables and fruits. The swivel action accommodates the contours of various products. Because the blade is sharpened on both sides, it will peel in both an upward and a downward motion.

Parisienne scoop (melon baller) This is specifically designed for scooping out balls or ovals from vegetables and fruits.

Kitchen fork A fork with two long tines is used to test the doneness of braised meats and vegetables, for lifting finished items to the carving board or plate, and to hold the item being carved in place.

Palette knife (metal spatula) This is a flexible, round-tipped tool used in the kitchen and bakeshop for turning pancakes or grilled foods, spreading fillings and glazes, and a variety of other functions.

Whips/whisks These tools are used to beat, blend, and whip foods. Balloon whips are sphere-shaped and have thin wires to incorporate air for making foams. Sauce whips are narrower and frequently have thicker wires.

Offset spatula This is used to turn or lift foods on grills, broilers, and griddles. It has a wide, chisel-edged blade set in a short handle.

Proper Care and Cleaning of Rolling Pins

Rolling pins are made from hard, tight-grained woods, which prevent fats and flavorings used in rolled doughs from penetrating the pin. Rolling pins should never be washed with water. Doing this could ruin the integrity of the pin by warping or distorting the grain of the wood. Always use a dry cloth to wipe the pin clean directly after use. Damage to the surface of the pin will relay imperfections to the dough being rolled.

The two basic types of rolling pins are the French-style pin and the rod-and-bearing pin. The French pin is a long cylinder of wood used to roll over the dough with the palms of the hands. The second type is heavier and wider. It has a lengthwise shaft at the center of the wooden cylinder through which runs a metal rod with two wooden handles at either end.

Measuring Equipment

Measurements are determined in many different ways in a professional kitchen. This makes it important to have equipment for liquid and dry volume measures calibrated for both the U.S. and metric systems, as well as a variety of scales for accurate measurement by weight.

Among the most common and useful measuring equipment are as follows: **measuring pitchers** (used for measuring liquids); spring, balance beam, and electronic **scales** (used to weigh ingredients for preparation and portion control); instant-read, candy, and deep-fat **thermometers** (used to measure internal temperatures); and **measuring spoons.**

TOP GROUPING, CLOCKWISE FROM LEFT: **measuring pitchers, balance beam scale, spring scale, electronic scale, measuring spoons** RIGHT GROUPING, FROM LEFT: instant-read thermometers, candy/deep-fat thermometer, probe thermometer

Sieves and Strainers

Sieves and strainers are used to sift, aerate, and help remove any large impurities from dry ingredients. They are also used to drain or purée cooked or raw foods. The delicate mesh of some strainers is highly vulnerable to damage; never drop these into a pot sink, where they could be crushed or torn.

The **food mill** is a type of strainer used to purée soft foods. A flat, curving blade is rotated over a disk by a hand-operated crank. Most professional models have interchangeable disks with holes of varying fineness. The **drum sieve** *(tamis)* consists of a tinned-steel, nylon, or stainless-steel screen stretched in an aluminum or wood frame. A drum sieve is used for sifting or puréeing. The **conical sieve** *(chinois)* is used for straining and/or puréeing food. The openings in the cone can be of varying sizes, from very large to very small. The **colander,** available in a variety of sizes, is a stainless-steel or aluminum sieve, with or without a base, and is used for straining or draining foods. The **ricer** is a device in which cooked food, often potatoes, are placed in a pierced hopper. A plate on the end of a lever pushes the food through the openings in the hopper. **Cheesecloth** is light, fine, mesh gauze and is frequently used along with or in place of a fine conical sieve. It is essential for straining some sauces. It is also used for making sachets. Before use, cheesecloth should be rinsed thoroughly in hot water and then cold water to remove any loose fibers. Cheesecloth also clings better to the sides of bowls, sieves, and so forth when it is wet.

CLOCKWISE FROM LEFT: conical sieves, food mill, colander, ricer, cheesecloth

Bowls for Mixing

Most kitchens are equipped with a variety of bowls, usually made of a nonreactive material, such as stainless steel. Copper bowls are often included in the kitchen's stock of mixing bowls, because they are considered best for whipping egg whites.

Storage Containers

Foods in the kitchen may be stored raw, partially prepared, or cooked. It is crucial to have an adequate stock of containers (plastic or stainless steel) to hold foods safely in the refrigerator or freezer.

Pots, Pans, and Molds

Various materials and combinations of materials are used in the construction of pots, pans, and molds. Because form and function are closely related, it is important to choose the proper equipment for the task at hand.

Pots made of **copper** transfer heat rapidly and evenly; because direct contact with copper will affect the color and consistency of many foods, copper pots are generally lined. (An exception is the copper pan used to cook jams, jellies, chocolates, and other high-sugar items, often known as a preserving pan.) Great care must be taken not to scratch linings made from a soft metal, such as tin. If the lining becomes scratched or wears away, it may be repaired by retinning. Copper also tends to discolor quickly; its proper upkeep requires significant time and labor.

Cast iron has the capacity to hold heat well and transmit it very evenly. The metal is somewhat brittle (unless coated with enamel) and must be treated carefully to prevent pitting, scarring, and rusting. Stainless steel is a relatively poor conductor of heat, but it is often used because it has other advantages, including easy maintenance. Other metals, such as aluminum or copper, are often sandwiched with stainless steel to improve heat conduction. Stainless steel will not react with foods; for example, white sauces will remain a pure white or ivory color.

Blue-steel, black-steel, pressed-steel, or rolled-steel pans are all prone to discoloration but transmit heat very rapidly; these pans are generally thin and are often preferred for sautéing foods. **Aluminum** is also an excellent conductor of heat; however, it is a soft metal that wears down quickly. When a metal spoon or whip is used to stir a white or light-colored sauce, soup, or stock in an aluminum pot, the food may take on a gray color. Anodized or treated aluminum tends not to react with foods and is one of the most popular metals for pots used in contemporary kitchens.

Nonstick coatings on pans have some use in professional kitchens, especially for restaurants that offer foods cooked with less fat and oil. These surfaces are not as sturdy as metal linings.

When choosing a pan or mold, consider the following information:

1. **Choose a size appropriate to the food being cooked.** Be familiar with the capacity of various pots, pans, and molds. If too many pieces of meat are crowded into a sauteuse, for instance, the food will not brown properly. If the sauteuse is too large, however, the *fond* (caramelized drippings from the meat) could scorch. If a small fish is poached in a large pot, the *cuisson* (cooking liquid) will not have the proper intensity of flavor.

2. **Choose material appropriate to the cooking technique.** Experience has shown, and science has verified, that certain cooking techniques are more successful when used with certain materials. For instance, sautéed foods require pans that transmit heat quickly and are sensitive to temperature changes. Braises, on the other hand, require long, fairly gentle cooking, and it is more important that the particular pot transmit heat evenly and hold heat well than that it respond rapidly to changes in heat.

3. **Use proper handling, cleaning, and storing techniques.** Avoid subjecting pots to heat extremes and rapid changes in temperature (e.g., placing a smoking-hot pot into a sinkful of water) because some materials are prone to warping. Other materials may chip or even crack if allowed to sit over heat when they are empty or if they are handled roughly. Casseroles or molds made of enameled cast iron or steel are especially vulnerable.

Proper Care and Cleaning of Copper Pans

This technique for cleaning and shining copper cookware has been used by chefs for many years and is still favored because it is fast, inexpensive, and efficient. Mix equal parts of flour and salt, and then add enough distilled white vinegar to form a paste. The vinegar will react with the copper to erase any discoloration caused by oxidation and heat. Any other acid, such as lemon juice, would work equally well, but white vinegar is typically the most economical choice. The salt acts as a scouring agent, and the flour provides the binder. Coat copper surfaces completely with this paste, then vigorously massage them clean with a cloth. Clean the interior cooking surfaces as you would other pots and pans, with a gentle scouring pad and cleanser.

NOTE: Delicate copper serving dishes and utensils should be cleaned with a commercial cream or polish without abrasives, to avoid scratching.

Seasoning Pans

Chefs who use pans made of cast iron or rolled steel often season their pans to seal the pores. Seasoning preserves the cooking surface and creates an essentially nonstick coating. To season a pan, pour enough cooking oil into the pan to evenly coat the bottom by about ¼ inch/6 mm. Place the pan in a 300°F/149°C oven for one hour. Remove the pan from the oven and let it cool. Wipe away any excess oil with paper towels. Repeat the procedure every so often to renew the seal. To clean a seasoned pan, use a bundle of paper towels to scour salt over the surface of the pan until the food particles have been removed.

Pots and Pans for Stovetop Cooking

Pots and pans used on the stovetop may be made from a variety of materials, but they must be able to withstand direct heat from a flame. A poorly produced pot will have weak spots and will warp.

Stockpot (marmite) This large pot is taller than it is wide and has straight sides. Some stockpots have a spigot at the base so that the liquid can be drained off without lifting the heavy pot.

Saucepan This pan has straight or slightly flared sides and has a single long handle.

Sauce pot This pot is similar in shape to a stockpot, although not as large, with straight sides and two loop handles for lifting.

Rondeau This is a wide, fairly shallow pot with two loop handles. When made from cast iron, these pots are frequently known as griswolds, and they may have a single

short handle rather than two loop handles. A brasier is similar to a rondeau and may be square instead of round.

Sauteuse This shallow skillet with sloping sides and a single long handle is referred to as a sauté pan.

Sautoir This shallow skillet has straight sides and a single long handle. It is often referred to as a fry pan.

CLOCKWISE FROM BOTTOM LEFT: sauteuse (nonstick and two stainless nested), saucepan, sauce pot, rondeau, stockpot (nested inside the rondeau), wok, bamboo steamer (nested inside the wok), sautoir (with lid), fish poacher (center)

Omelet pan/crêpe pan This shallow skillet has very short, slightly sloping sides and is most often made of rolled or blue steel.

Bain-marie (double boiler) These are nesting pots with single long handles. The bottom pot is filled with water that is heated to gently cook or warm the food in the upper pot. The term *bain-marie* also refers to the stainless-steel containers used to hold food in a steam table.

Griddle A griddle is flat with no sides and may be built directly into the stove.

Fish poacher This is a long, narrow pot with straight sides and includes a perforated rack for holding the fish.

Steamer This consists of a set of stacked pots or bamboo baskets with a tight-fitting lid. The upper pot has a perforated bottom and is placed over the second pot, which is filled with boiling or simmering water. The perforations allow the steam to rise from the pot below to cook the food above.

Pans for Oven Cooking

Pans used in ovens are produced from the same basic materials used to make stovetop pots and pans; in addition, glazed and unglazed earthenware, glass, and ceramic are also used. The heat of the oven is less intense than that of a burner, making it possible to use these more delicate materials without risk of cracking and shattering. Pans are available in several gauges (*gauge* refers to the thickness of the metal). Heavy-gauge pans are usually pre-ferred because they transfer heat more evenly. Regarding heat conductivity, some metals heat faster than others. Aluminum heats quickly but is susceptible to burning food if it is a light gauge. On the other hand, stainless steel is a poor conductor of heat but works best for baking in a lighter gauge. Tin is a good conductor of heat, while materials such as glass, ceramic, and earthenware hold heat well but transfer it poorly.

Roasting pan This rectangular pan with medium-high sides is used for roasting or baking and comes in various sizes.

Sheet pan This shallow, rectangular pan is used for baking and may be full or half size.

Hotel pans These are rectangular pans, also referred to as steam table pans, that are used occasionally for preparing foods but more often as containers to hold cooked foods in steam tables, hot boxes, or electric or gas steamers. They are also frequently used to marinate meats or for refrigerated food storage. They are available in a wide range of sizes. Chafing dishes and hotel pans are usually of standard sizes, so most of them will fit together properly.

Pâté mold A deep rectangular metal mold, the mold used for pâté en croûte usually has hinged sides to facilitate removal of the pâté. Special shapes may be available.

Terrine mold The terrine mold may be rectangular or oval, with a lid. Traditionally an earthenware mold, it may also be made of enameled cast iron.

Gratin dish A shallow oval baking dish made of ceramic, enameled cast iron, or enameled steel.

Soufflé dish These round, straight-edged ceramic dishes come in various sizes.

Timbale mold This small metal or ceramic mold is used for individual portions of various molded foods.

Specialty molds These are different-sized molds that are used to achieve varying shapes.

Cake pans These pans have straight sides and are available in various sizes and shapes.

Springform pans These are similar to cake pans, but their sides have springs that can be released in order to remove the cake from the pan more easily.

Loose-bottomed tart pans These shallow pans have a removable bottom. The sides may be scalloped or straight and are generally shorter than those of pie pans.

Pie pans Pie pans are round pans with flared sides. They are deeper than tart pans.

Loaf pans These deep pans are usually rectangular. The sides may be straight or slightly flared. Pullman loaf pans have lids and produce square loaves.

Muffin tins These are pans with small, round sections for producing muffins of various sizes.

Tube pans These deep, round pans have a tube in the center and are used to create a specific effect. Some styles are similar to springform pans, having removable sides.

Kugelhopf forms These special tube pans with a fluted design are traditionally used to prepare a sweet, yeast-raised cake flavored with dried fruits and nuts.

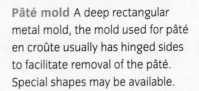

CLOCKWISE FROM BOTTOM LEFT: bundt pan, (stacked pans from bottom to top) muffin tin, loose-bottomed tart mold, and cake pans, springform pan, roasting pan, loaf pan (on top), Pullman loaf pan (on bottom), flexible silicon mold, gratin dishes, soufflé molds/ramekins (nested in the gratin molds), pâté en croûte mold

Large Equipment

When working with large equipment, safety precautions must be observed and proper maintenance and cleaning consistently done.

1. Obtain proper instruction in the machine's safe operation.

2. First turn off and then unplug electrical equipment before assembling it or breaking it down.

3. Use all safety features: Be sure that lids are secure, hand guards are used, and the machine is stable.

4. Clean and sanitize the equipment thoroughly after each use.

5. Be sure that all pieces of equipment are properly reassembled and left unplugged after each use.

6. Report any problems or malfunctions promptly, and alert coworkers to the problem.

Kettles and Steamers

Kettles and steamers enable a chef to prepare large amounts of food efficiently, since the heat is applied over a much larger area than is possible when a single burner is used. Cooking times are often shorter than when using the stovetop.

Steam-jacketed kettle This freestanding or tabletop kettle circulates steam through the double side walls, providing even heat. Units vary; they may tilt, may be insulated, and may have spigots or lids. Available in a range of sizes, these kettles are excellent for producing stocks, soups, and sauces.

Tilting kettle This large, relatively shallow freestanding unit (also known as a Swiss brasier, tilting skillet, and tilting fry pan) is used for braising, stewing, and sautéing large quantities of meats or vegetables at one time. Most tilting kettles have lids, allowing for steaming as well.

Pressure steamer Water is heated under pressure in a sealed compartment, allowing it to reach temperatures above the boiling point, 212°F/100°C. The cooking time is controlled by automatic timers, which open the exhaust valves at the end.

Convection steamer The steam is generated in a boiler and then piped to the cooking chamber, where it is vented over the food. Pressure does not build up in the unit; it is continuously exhausted, which means the door may be opened at any time without danger of scalding or burning.

Deep-fat fryer This piece of equipment consists of a gas or electric heating element and a large stainless-steel reservoir that holds the fat. A thermostat allows the user to control the temperature of the fat. Stainless-steel wire mesh baskets are used to lower and lift foods from the fat.

Ranges and Ovens

The stovetop is known as the range; the oven is usually below the range. However, there are a number of different variations on this standard arrangement. Gas or electric ranges are available in many sizes and with various combinations of open burners, flattops (not to be confused with griddle units), and ring tops. Open burners and ring tops supply direct heat, which is easy to change and control. Flattops provide indirect heat, which is more even and less intense than direct heat. Foods that require long, slow cooking, such as stocks, are more effectively cooked on a flattop. Small units known as candy stoves or stockpot ranges have rings of gas jets or removable rings in a flattop, allowing for excellent heat control. Ovens cook foods by surrounding them with hot air, a gentler and more even source of heat than the direct heat of a burner.

Open-burner range This type of range has an individual grate-style burner that allows for easy adjustment of heat.

Flattop range This type of range consists of a thick plate of cast iron or steel set over the heat source. Flattops give relatively even and consistent heat but do not allow for quick adjustments of temperature.

Ring-top range This is a flattop with plates that can be removed to widen the opening, supplying more or less heat.

Induction cooktop This type of burner relies on the magnetic attraction between the cooktop and steel or cast iron in the pan to generate heat. The cooktop itself remains cool. Reaction time is significantly faster than with traditional burners. Pans containing copper or aluminum may not be used.

Convection oven In a convection oven, fans force hot air to circulate around the food, cooking it evenly and quickly. Some convection ovens have the capacity to introduce moisture. Special features may include infrared and a convection/microwave combination.

Conventional/deck ovens The heat source is located on the bottom, underneath the deck, or floor, of the oven. Heat is conducted through the deck to the cavity. Conventional ovens can be located below a range top or as individual shelves arranged one above another. The latter are known as deck ovens, and the food is placed directly on the deck, instead of on a wire rack. Deck ovens normally consist of two to four decks, though single-deck models are available.

Combi oven This piece of equipment, powered by either gas or electricity, is a combination steamer and convection oven. It can be used in steam mode, hot-air convection mode, or heat/steam (combi) mode.

Microwave oven This type of oven uses electricity to generate microwave radiation, which cooks or reheats foods very quickly. Some models double as convection ovens.

Griddles and Grills

Two other oven/range features, the griddle and the grill, are part of the traditional commercial foodservice setup.

Griddle Similar to a flattop range, a griddle has a heat source located beneath a thick plate of metal, generally cast iron or steel. The food is cooked directly on this surface.

Grill/broiler/salamander In a grill, the heat source is located below the rack; in a broiler or salamander, the heat source is above. Some units have adjustable racks, which allow the food to be raised or lowered to control cooking speed. Some grills burn wood or charcoal or both, but units in restaurants are often either gas or electric with ceramic "rocks" that create a bed of coals, producing the effect of a charcoal grill. Salamanders are small broilers, used primarily to finish or glaze foods.

Smokers

A true smoker will treat foods with smoke and can be operated at either cool or hot temperatures. Smokers generally have racks or hooks, which allow foods to smoke evenly.

Grinding, Slicing, Mixing, and Puréeing Equipment

Grinders, slicers, and puréeing equipment all have the potential to be extremely dangerous. As these tools are essential for a number of different operations, all chefs should be able to use them with confidence.

Meat grinder This is a freestanding machine or an attachment for a standing mixer. A meat grinder should have disks of varying sizes and in general will have a feed tray and a pusher.

Blender A blender consists of a base, which houses the motor, and a removable lidded jar with a propeller-like blade in its bottom. Speed settings for the motor are in the base. Jars are made of stainless steel, plastic, or glass, and are available in several capacities. Blenders are excellent for puréeing, liquefying, and emulsifying foods.

Food processor This is a machine that houses the motor separately from the bowl, blades, and lid. Food processors can grind, purée, blend, emulsify, crush, knead, and, with special disks, slice, julienne, and shred foods.

Immersion blender This long and slender one-piece machine (also known as a hand blender, stick blender, or burr mixer) is like an inverted blender. The top part of the machine houses the motor, which generally runs at just one speed. A plastic handle with an on/off button extends from the top of the motor. A stainless-steel driveshaft extends from the motor and ends with the blade, which is immersed in the food to be puréed. The advantage of using an immersion blender over a regular blender is that large batches of food can be puréed directly in the cooking vessel.

Vertical chopping machine (VCM) A motor at the base is permanently attached to a bowl with integral blades. As a safety precaution, the hinged lid must be locked in place before the unit will operate. The VCM is used to grind, whip, emulsify, blend, or crush large quantities of foods.

FROM LEFT: mandoline, food processor, standing mixer and attachments, immersion blender, blender

Food chopper (buffalo chopper) The food is placed in a rotating bowl that passes under a hood, where blades chop the food. Some units have hoppers or feed tubes and interchangeable disks for slicing and grating. Food choppers are available in floor and tabletop models.

Food/meat slicer This machine is used to slice foods in even thicknesses. A carrier moves the food back and forth against a circular blade, which is generally made of carbon steel.

Mandoline This slicing device has blades of high-carbon steel. Levers adjust the blades to achieve the cut and thickness desired. As with food slicers, be sure to use the guard.

The mandoline can be used to make slices, juliennes, gaufrettes, and batonnets.

Standing mixer This electric mixing machine has large bowls of varying capacities (5-quart, 10-quart, 20-quart, 40-quart, etc.). The bowl is locked in place and the beater, whip, paddle, or dough hook rotates through the batter or dough.

Refrigeration Equipment

Maintaining adequate refrigerated storage is crucial to any foodservice operation; therefore, the menu and the storage must be evaluated and coordinated. All units should be maintained properly, which means regular and thorough cleaning.

Walk-in This is the largest style of refrigeration unit and usually has shelves that are arranged around the walls. It is possible to zone a walk-in to maintain appropriate temperature and humidity levels for storing various foods. Some walk-ins are large enough to accommodate rolling carts for additional storage. Some units have pass-through or reach-in doors to facilitate access to frequently required items. Walk-ins may be situated in the kitchen or outside the facility.

Reach-in A reach-in may be a single unit or part of a bank of units, available in many sizes. Units with pass-through doors are especially helpful for the pantry area, where cold items can be retrieved by the wait staff as needed.

On-site refrigeration Refrigerated drawers or undercounter reach-ins, which allow foods on the line to be held at the proper temperature.

Portable refrigeration A refrigerated cart that can be placed as needed in the kitchen.

Display refrigeration Display cases that are generally used in the dining room for desserts, salads, or salad bars.

Chapter Nine

Meat, Poultry, and Game Identification

For most restaurants, the purchase, preparation, and service of meats is one of the most expensive areas of the business—but also one of the most potentially profitable. In order to get the most value out of the meats purchased, it is important to understand how to select the right cut for a particular cooking method.

Meat Basics

The meat, poultry, and game cuts that a restaurant should buy will depend upon the nature of the particular operation. A restaurant featuring predominantly à la minute preparations—especially those with a preponderance of grilled or sautéed items—will need to purchase extremely tender (and more expensive) cuts. A restaurant that uses a variety of techniques may be able to use some less tender cuts, for example, the veal shank in a braise such as osso buco.

Meats can be purchased in a number of forms and at varying degrees of readiness to cook. The chef should consider several factors when deciding what type of meat to buy. Storage capacity, the equipment required to prepare a menu item, the kitchen staff's ability to fabricate cuts, and the volume of meat required must all be taken into consideration. Once this information is evaluated, you can determine whether it is more economical to purchase large pieces, such as whole legs of veal, or prefabricated meats, such as veal already cut into a top round or precut scaloppini.

Meats should be checked for wholesomeness and freshness. Cut surfaces should appear moist, but not shiny. The meat should have a good color, which varies by type as well as by cut. The meat should also smell appealing. Packaged meats should arrive with the packaging intact with no punctures or tears.

The tables accompanying the following sections contain key pieces of information about beef, veal, pork, and lamb adapted from The Meat Buyer's Guide by The National Association of Meat Purveyors (NAMP) including item numbers as assigned by the NAMP and an average range in size for a cut. Appropriate cooking methods for various cuts have also been included.

Storage

Meats, poultry, and game should be wrapped and stored under refrigeration. When possible, they should be held in a separate unit, or at least in a separate part of the cooler. They should always be placed on trays to prevent them from dripping onto other foods or the floor.

The chef should separate different kinds of meats; for example, poultry should not come into contact with beef, or pork products into contact with any other meats. This will prevent cross contamination.

Vacuum-packed meats can be stored directly in the package, as long as it has not been punctured or ripped. Once unwrapped, meats should be rewrapped in air-permeable paper, such as butcher's paper, because airtight containers promote bacterial growth that could result in spoilage or contamination.

Variety meats, poultry, and uncured pork products, which have short shelf lives, should be cooked as soon as possible after they are received. Meat stored at the proper temperature and under optimal conditions can be held for several days without noticeable loss of quality. However, meat can also be frozen for longer storage.

- Refrigeration: 28° to 32°F/–2° to 0°C

- Frozen: 0° to 20°F/–18° to –7°C

Inspection and Grading

Government inspection of all meats is mandatory. Inspections are required at various times—at the slaughterhouse (antemortem), and again after butchering (postmortem). This is done to ensure that the animal is free from disease and that the meat is wholesome and fit for human consumption. Inspection is a service paid for by tax dollars.

Some states have relinquished the responsibility for inspecting meats to federal inspectors. Those states that still administer their own inspections of meat must at least meet, if not exceed, the accepted federal standards.

Quality grading, however, is not mandatory. The U.S. Department of Agriculture (USDA) has developed specific standards used to assign grades to meats and they train graders. The packer may, however, choose not to hire a USDA grader and may forgo grading in favor of the use of an in-house brand name instead. The costs involved in grading meats are absorbed by the individual meat packer, not the taxpayer, since this process is voluntary.

Depending upon the particular animal, the grader will consider overall carcass shape, ratio of fat to lean, ratio of meat to bone, color, and marbling of lean flesh. The grade placed on a particular carcass is then applied to all the cuts from that animal. In beef, only a small percentage of meats produced will be graded prime. Choice and select are more often available. Grades lower than select are generally used for processed meat and are of no practical importance to the restaurant (or retail) industry.

Some meats may also receive yield grades. This grade is of the greatest significance to wholesalers. It indicates the amount of salable meat in relation to the total weight of the carcass. Butchers refer to this as "cutability." In other words, it is a measure of the yield of edible meat from each pound of the carcass.

Market Forms of Meat

After slaughtering, inspection, and grading, the animal carcass is cut into manageable pieces. Sides are prepared by making a cut down the length of the backbone. Each side is cut into two pieces to make quarters, dividing the sides between specific vertebrae. Saddles are made by cutting the animal across the belly, again at a specified point. The exact standards for individual animal types govern where the carcass is to be divided.

The next step is to cut the animal into what are referred to as primal cuts. There are uniform standards for beef, veal, pork, and lamb primals. These large cuts are then further broken down into subprimals. Subprimals are generally trimmed and packed as food service, value added, or HRI (Hotel, Restaurant, and Institution) cuts. There may be even more fabrication or butchering done in order to prepare steaks, chops, roasts, or ground meat. These cuts are referred to as portion control cuts.

The amount of butchering done in packing plants has increased over the past several years. While it is still possible to purchase hanging meat, most operations will buy what is referred to as boxed meat. This indicates that the meat has been fabricated to a specific point (primal, subprimal, or retail cut), then packed in Cryovac, boxed, and shipped for sale to purveyors, butchers, chain retail outlets, and so forth.

Kosher Meats

Kosher meats are specially slaughtered, bled, and fabricated in order to comply with religious dietary laws. In this country, only beef and veal forequarters, poultry, and some game are customarily used for kosher preparations. Kosher meats are butchered from animals that have been slaughtered by a *shohet,* or specially trained rabbi. The animal must be killed with a single stroke of a knife and then fully bled. All the veins and arteries must be removed from the meat. This process would essentially mutilate the flesh of loins and legs of beef and veal; therefore, these are generally not sold as kosher.

Beef

Beef is essential to the foodservice industry, especially in the United States. A significant source of protein, beef is featured in an array of classic and contemporary dishes. This expensive product demands special care and training. Utilizing as much of each cut to maximize the yield is an important practice to follow.

Cattle used for the beef industry are typically steers (castrated males) over one year old and heifers (female cows) that are not required for breeding. The older the bovine, the tougher the meat. Specialty beef, such as Kobe beef from Japan, Limousin beef from France, Certified Angus, natural, organic, and dry-aged beef from the United States are also available.

The eight grades of beef are in order as follows: Prime, Choice, Select, Standard, Commercial, Utility, Cutter, and Canner. Prime is usually reserved for restaurants and butcher shops.

These cuts of meat are from the primal cut known as the round: 1. Hind shank, 2. Shank stew, 3. Top round, 4. Top round tied as a roast, 5. Marrow bones.

These cuts of meat are from the primal cut known as the loin: 1. Short loin,
2. Porterhouse steak cut from the short loin, 3. Top sirloin butt, 4. Flank steak,
5. Tenderloin PSMO, 6. Trimmed tenderloin, 7. Tenderloin steaks, 8. Boneless
strip loin, 9. Portion-cut strip loin steaks.

Beef, continued

These cuts of meat are from the primal cut known as the rib: 1. Short loin,
2. Portion-cut short ribs, 3. Rib eye lip on, 4. Portion-cut rib steaks.

These cuts of meat are from the primal cut known as the chuck:
1. Trimmed shoulder clod, 2. Top blade, 3. Shoulder stew, 4. Chuck roll,
5. Brisket, 6. Skirt steak, 7. Trimmed skirt steak, 8. Tripe, 9. Oxtail.

Bovine Beef Primal Cuts

Subprimal	Common Culinary Uses
THE ROUND PRIMAL CUT	
Shank	Common cooking methods include braising and stewing. Meat often prepared ground.
Heel	Common cooking methods include braising and stewing.
Knuckle	Common cooking methods include braising and roasting. Meat often prepared as kabobs.
Top round	Common cooking methods include roasting, pan frying, and broiling. Meat often prepared as a roulade, braciola, or London broil.
Eye round	Common cooking methods include roasting and braising.
Bottom round	Braising is the most common cooking method. Meat often prepared as a pot roast or sauerbraten.
THE LOIN PRIMAL CUT	
Sirloin (top sirloin butt)	Common cooking methods include roasting, broiling, and grilling. Meat often prepared as steaks.
Tenderloin, PSMO portion-cut	Common cooking methods include roasting, broiling, grilling, and sautéing. Meat often prepared as châteaubriand, tournedos, medallions, or filet mignon.
Flank steak	Common cooking methods include broiling, grilling, and braising. Meat often prepared as London broil, butterflied, or stuffed.
Strip loin, 175 bone-in (shell); 180 boneless	Common cooking methods include roasting, broiling, and grilling. Meat often prepared as a roast or steaks (New York strip steak).
Short loin	Common cooking methods include broiling and grilling. Meat often prepared as porterhouse or T-bone.

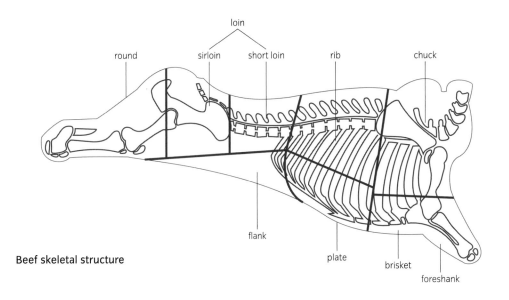

Beef skeletal structure

Subprimal	Common Culinary Uses
THE RIB PRIMAL CUT	
Bone-in export rib, 109 export	Common cooking methods include roasting and grilling. Meat often prepared as prime rib roast, bone-in ribsteak, or cowboy steak.
Boneless lip-on rib, 112A lip on	Common cooking methods include roasting, grilling, and sautéing. Meat often prepared boneless as rib eye roast or Delmonico steaks.
Short ribs	Braising is the most common cooking method.
THE CHUCK PRIMAL CUT	
Square-cut chuck	Common cooking methods include braising and stewing. Meat often prepared as chuck roast or ground.
Shoulder clod	Common cooking methods include braising, roasting, stewing, and grilling. Meat often prepared as steaks or ground.
MARKET FORMS	
Plate	Braising is the most common cooking method. Meat often prepared as short ribs.
Brisket	Braising is the most common cooking method. Meat often prepared corned and as pastrami.
Foreshank	Common cooking methods include braising and stewing. Meat often prepared ground.
VARIETY MEATS (OFFALS)	
Liver	Sautéing is the most common cooking method. Meat often prepared as forcemeat.
Tripe	Common cooking methods include braising or slow simmering in a broth or red sauce.
Kidneys	Stewing is the most common cooking method. Also often baked into a pie.
Tongue	Simmering is the most common cooking method. Meat is often prepared smoked.
Oxtails	Common cooking methods include braising and stewing.
Intestines	Used as casing for sausage.
Heart	Common cooking methods include braising and stewing.
Blood	Used to prepare coagulate sausages.

Beef HRI Cuts

Item	Product Name	Weight Range (in pounds)
103	Rib (primal)	35–40
109	Rib, roast-ready	18–22
109d	Rib, roast-ready, cover off, short-cut	16–18
112	Rib, rib eye roll	8–10
112a	Rib, rib eye roll, lip on	11–13
113	Chuck, square-cut (primal)	79–106
114	Chuck, shoulder clod	15–21
116b	Chuck, chuck roll, tied	15–21
120	Brisket, boneless, deckle off	10–12
121c	Plate, skirt steak (diaphragm), outer	2 and up
121d	Plate, skirt steak, inner	3 and up
123	Short ribs	3–5
123b	Rib, short ribs, trimmed	Amount as specified
166b	Round, rump and shank partially removed, handle on, steamship	52–70
167	Round, knuckle	9–13
167a	Round, knuckle, full	8–12
169	Round, top (inside)	17–23
170	Round, bottom (gooseneck)	23–31
170a	Round, bottom (gooseneck), heel out	20–28
171b	Round, outside round, bottom	10–16
171c	Round, eye of round	3 and up
172	Loin, full loin, trimmed (primal)	50–70
174	Loin, short loin, short-cut	22–26
175	Loin, strip loin, bone-in	18–20
180	Loin, strip loin, short-cut, boneless	7–11
181	Loin, sirloin	19–28
184	Loin, top sirloin butt	12–14

Item	Product Name	Weight Range (in pounds)
185a	Loin, bottom sirloin butt, flap	3 and up
185b	Loin, bottom sirloin butt, ball tip	3 and up
185d	Loin, bottom sirloin butt, tri-tip, defatted	3 and up
189	Loin, full tenderloin	8–10
189a	Loin, full tenderloin, side muscle on, defatted	5–6
190	Loin, full tenderloin, side muscle off, defatted	3–4
190a	Loin, full tenderloin, side muscle off, skinned	3–4
191	Loin, butt tenderloin	2–4
193	Flank steak	1 and up
134	Beef bones	Amount as specified
135	Diced beef	Amount as specified
135a	Beef for stewing	Amount as specified
136	Ground beef	Amount as specified
136b	Beef patty mix	Amount as specified

Veal

Veal is the flesh of a young calf, generally four to five months old. Because of its young, delicately tender flesh, it is considered by some to be the finest meat available. Classical preparations include, but are not limited to, Osso Buco, Vitello Tonnato, Cordon Bleu, Veal Piccata, and Veal Scaloppine. Fine veal calves are fed mother's milk or formula. Milk-fed veal is up to twelve weeks old and is believed to have the most tender meat. Formula-fed calves consume a special diet and are the standard type of veal used today; this veal is up to four months old.

Veal should be selected by color; it should be creamy white with barely a hint of pink. The six grades of veal are as follows: USDA Prime, Choice, Good, Standard, Utility, and Cull. Because the overall ratio of meat to bone is less than a full-grown bovine, there are proportionately fewer cuts of veal.

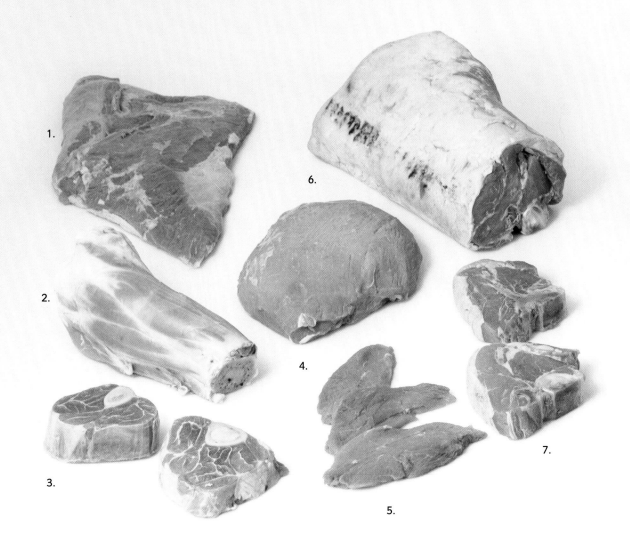

These cuts of meats are from the hind saddle: 1. Bottom round, 2. Shank, 3. Osso buco, 4. Top round cap off, 5. Portion-cut veal cutlets, 6. Trimmed loin, 7. Portion-cut chops.

These cuts of meat are from the foresaddle: 1. Rack (chop ready), 2. Frenched rack chops, 3. Breast, 4. Trimmed shoulder clod, 5. Stew, 6. Sweetbreads, 7. Liver, 8. Kidneys.

Bovine Veal Primal Cuts

Subprimal	Common Culinary Uses
THE LEG PRIMAL CUT	
Shank	Common cooking methods include braising and stewing. Meat is often prepared Osso Buco.
Heel	Stewing is the most common cooking method. Meat is often prepared ground.
Top round; Knuckle; Bottom round; Eye round; Butt	Common cooking methods include dry heat sauté, roasting, and stewing. Meat is often prepared as scaloppine, cutlets (½ in/1 cm), schnitzel (¼ in/6 mm), emince, escalope, and kabobs. Usable trim often used for stewing or prepared as forcemeat.
THE LOIN PRIMAL CUT	
Tenderloin; Sirloin	Common cooking methods include roasting and sautéing. Meat is often prepared as medallions, noisettes, and as a whole roast.
Trimmed loin; Split boneless loin (strip loin)	Common cooking methods include roasting (bone-in or boneless), sautéing, and broiling. Meat is often prepared as chops (bone-in or boneless), medallions, scaloppine, emince, escalope.
THE HOTEL RACK PRIMAL CUT	
Rack, Split chop-ready rack; Frenched rack	Common cooking methods include cut of veal roasting (bone-in or boneless), broiling, grilling, and sautéing. Meat is often prepared as frenched or crown, chops (bone-in, frenched), and medallions, scaloppine, emince, escalope.
THE SQUARE-CUT SHOULDER PRIMAL CUT	
Square-cut shoulder, boneless	Common cooking methods include roasting (boneless), stewing, and braising. Meat is often prepared ground.
Shoulder clod	Common cooking methods include stewing, roasting, and braising. Meat is often prepared ground.
MARKET FORMS	
Breast	Common cooking methods include braising, roasting. Meat is often prepared stuffed, butterflied, or as bacon.
Foreshank	Common cooking methods include braising and stewing. Meat is often prepared ground.

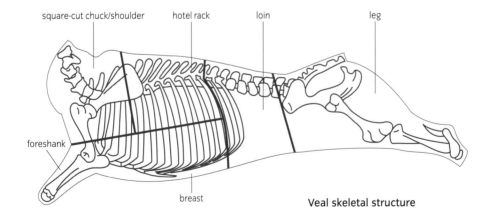

Veal skeletal structure

Subprimal	Common Culinary Uses
VARIETY MEATS (OFFALS)	
Cheeks	Common cooking methods include braising and stewing.
Tongue	Braising is the most common cooking method. Often used in the preparation of terrines.
Sweetbreads	Poaching and then sautéing is the most common method of preparation.
Liver	Sautéing is the most common cooking method.
Heart	Common cooking methods include braising and stewing.
Kidneys	Sautéing is the most common cooking method.
Brains	Poaching and then sautéing is the most common method of preparation.
Feet	Most often used in making stock.

Veal HRI Cuts

Item	Product Name	Weight Range (in pounds)
306	Hotel rack, 7 ribs	10–12
306a	Chop-ready rack	6–8
307	Rack, rib eye	3–4
309	Chuck, square-cut, bone-in primal	20–36
309B	Chuck, square-cut, boneless	19–33
309D	Chuck, square-cut, neck off, boneless, tied	18–32
310	Chuck, shoulder clod	4–7
310A	Chuck, shoulder clod, special	4–7
312	Foreshank	2–4
313	Breast	6–10
331	Loin	10–18
332	Loin, trimmed	8–14
344	Loin, strip loin, boneless	3–6
346	Loin, butt tenderloin	1–1½
334	Leg (primal)	40–70
336	Leg, shank off, boneless, roast-ready, tied	11–19
337	Hindshank	2–4
338	Shank, osso buco	13
348	Legs, TBS, 4 parts	24–32
348a	Leg, TBS, 3 parts	16–24
349	Leg, top round, cap on	8–12
349a	Leg, top round, cap off	6–8
395	Veal for stewing	Amount as specified
396	Ground veal	Amount as specified

Pork

Pork, the meat of domesticated pigs, is among the most popular meat sold in the United States. Typically high in fat, pigs have been specifically bred over many generations to produce leaner cuts of meat. Pigs are commonly slaughtered under one year of age to ensure a tender product.

Although quality grades are less frequently assigned to pork, when applied, the grades are as follows: USDA 1, 2, 3, 4, and Utility. Because USDA grading is not required for pork and federal grading must be paid for, packers will often use their own grading system. This does not necessarily mean that

various cuts of pork are not of good quality, for the grading systems used by major packers are clearly defined and are generally reliable.

These cuts of meat are from the rear half of the swine: 1. Ham prepared by smoking, 2. Fresh ham, 3. Ham prepared by curing (prosciutto), 4. Center-cut pork loin, 5. Frenched rib end of loin, 6. Baby back ribs, 7. Boneless tied loin roast, 8. Tenderloin, 9. Center-cut pork chop from the loin end, 10. Center-cut pork chop from the rib end.

These cuts of meat are from the front half of the swine: 1. Boston butt, 2. Pork picnic, 3. Spare ribs, 4. Foot.

The following are examples of prepared pork items: 5. Genoa salami, 6. Sliced bacon, 7. Kielbasa, 8. Chorizo, 9. Pancetta, 10. Italian sausage, 11. Breakfast sausage.

Swine (Pig) Primal Cuts

Subprimal	Common Culinary Uses
THE HAM PRIMAL CUT	
Shank/Hock	Common cooking methods include stewing and braising. Meat often prepared smoked or corned.
Ham (bone-in or boneless)	Fresh ham roast (bone-in, BRT); inside ham RTE, baked; thin sliced smoked ham (wet cured, half or whole, butt/shank); boiled ham (wet cured, cooked to 145°F); prosciutto ham (salted and dry cured long term); Smithfield ham (dry cured and smoked)
Top round	Sautéing is the most common cooking method. Meat is often prepared as cutlets.
THE LOIN PRIMAL CUT	
Center-cut pork loin	Common cooking methods include roasting, grilling, broiling, and sautéing. Meat often prepared as a roast (bone-in, boneless), frenched, smoked, chops (bone-in), or as Canadian-style bacon.
Boneless loin (eye muscle)	Common cooking methods include grilling, broiling, and sautéing. Meat often prepared as cutlets, medallions, or schnitzel.
Baby back ribs	Barbecuing is the most common cooking method.
Tenderloin	Common cooking methods include roasting and sautéing.
THE BOSTON BUTT PRIMAL CUT	
Boston butt (bone-in, boneless)	Common cooking methods include roasting, stewing, and sautéing. Meat often prepared as forcemeat or sausages.
Cottage butt	Common cooking methods include roasting or frying as bacon. Meat often prepared as a roast (fresh) or smoked (English bacon).
THE PICNIC PRIMAL CUT	
Picnic (bone-in or boneless)	Common cooking methods include braising and stewing. Meat often prepared as a roast (boneless, BRT, skin on, fresh), smoked, and cured (picnic ham, smoked shoulder), as tasso ham, or as forcemeat (used for cold-cut preparations).

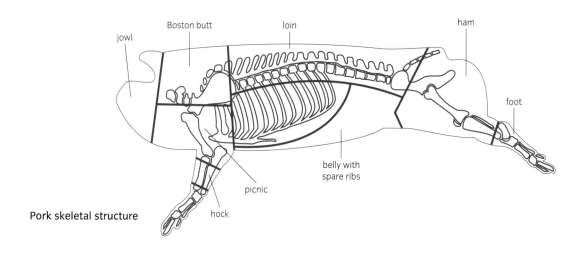

Pork skeletal structure

Subprimal	Common Culinary Uses
MARKET FORMS	
Belly (bacon, pancetta, salt pork, fresh)	When fresh, this cut is most often sautéed. Other forms are most often fried.
Spare ribs, St. Louis ribs (trimmed)	Common cooking methods include barbecuing and braising.
Fatback (fresh, salt)	Meat often prepared as lardons, confit, cassoulet, pâté, and terrines.
VARIETY MEATS (OFFALS)	
Jowl; Snout; Neckbones; Liver; Heart; Feet; Toes; Tail; Intestines; Kidneys; Caul fat	Braising is the most common cooking method. Meat is often prepared as forcemeat and as sausage.

Pork HRI Cuts

Item	Product name	Weight Range (in pounds)
401	Fresh ham	18–20
402B	Fresh ham, boneless, tied	8–12
403	Shoulder, picnic	6–8
405A	Shoulder, picnic, boneless	4–8
406	Shoulder, Boston butt	4 and up
406A	Shoulder, Boston butt, boneless	4 and up
408	Belly	12–18
410	Loin	16–18
412	Loin, center-cut, 8 ribs	8–10
412b	Loin, center-cut, 8 ribs, boneless	4–6
412c	Loin, center-cut, 11 ribs	10–12
412e	Loin, center-cut, 11 ribs, boneless	5–7
413	Loin, boneless	9–11
415	Tenderloin	1 and up
416	Spare ribs	2½–5½
416a	Spare ribs, St. Louis style	2–3
417	Shoulder hocks	¾ and up
418	Trimmings	Amount as specified
420	Feet, front	½–¾
421	Neck bones	Amount as specified
422	Loin, back ribs, baby back ribs	1½–2¼

Lamb and Mutton

Lamb is the tender meat produced by young, domesticated sheep. Its texture is a direct result of what it consumes and the age at which it is slaughtered. The milk-fed varieties of lamb are inclined to yield the most delicate meat. Once a lamb begins to eat grass, the flesh loses some of its tenderness. However, most lamb produced in the United States is finished on a grain diet and are six to seven months old. Lamb that is allowed to age over sixteen months is known as mutton. Compared to lamb, mutton is considered to have a more pronounced flavor and texture. As with other varieties of meat, lamb becomes tougher as it ages.

Lamb tends to be fatty. Its unique flavor pairs nicely with intense seasonings and accompaniments. The five grades of lamb are in order as follows: Prime, Choice, Good, Utility, and Cull.

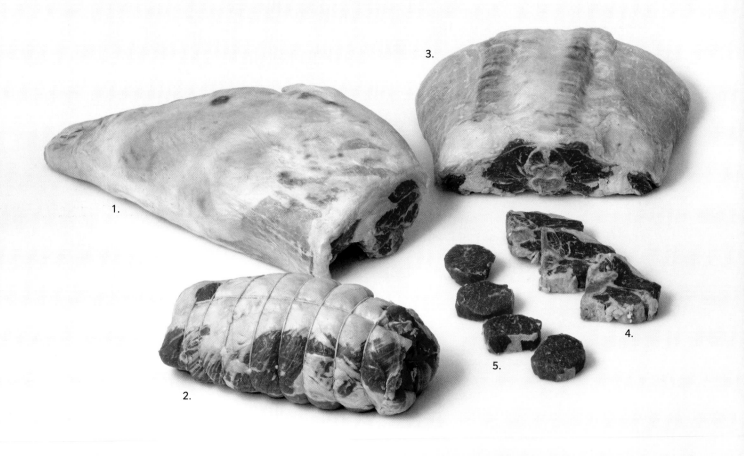

These cuts of meat are from the hindsaddle: 1. Leg, 2. Leg BRT, 3. Trimmed loin, 4. Loin chops, 5. Noisettes.

These cuts of meat are from the foresaddle: 1. Split and chined rack,
2. Frenched rack, 3. Double- and single-rack chops, 4. Square-cut chuck/shoulder,
5. Shoulder BRT, 6. Shanks.

Ovine (Lamb) Primal Cuts

Subprimal	Common Culinary Uses
THE LEG PRIMAL CUT	
Shank; **Heel; Knuckle;** **Eye round;** **Bottom round**	Common cooking methods include stewing (bone-in or boneless) and braising. Roasting is the most common cooking method. Meat often prepared as a leg of lamb or roast (bone-in, BRT, oven-ready, frenched, semiboneless).
Top round	Common cooking methods include roasting, sautéing, grilling, and broiling. Meat often prepared as steaks, scaloppine, or butterflied.
THE LOIN PRIMAL CUT	
Trimmed loin, split; **Boneless (eye muscle);** **Sirloin**	Common cooking methods include roasting (rare), sautéing, grilling, and broiling. Meat often prepared as a roast (bone-in, boneless), chops: English (single/double) or Saratoga (boneless, single/double).
Tenderloin	Common cooking methods include sautéing, grilling, and broiling. Meat often prepared as medallions or noisettes.
THE HOTEL RACK PRIMAL CUT	
Rack (split and chined)	Common cooking methods include roasting, sautéing, broiling, and grilling. Meat often prepared as a roast (bone-in, crown roast) or chops: American (single/double) or frenched.
Breast	Common cooking methods include braising and stewing. Meat often prepared as riblets or stuffed.

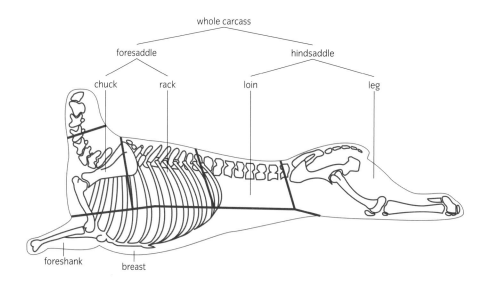

Lamb and mutton skeletal structure

Subprimal	Common Culinary Uses
THE SHOULDER SQUARE PRIMAL CUT	
Foreshank	Common cooking methods include braising and stewing. Meat may be prepared bone-in or boneless.
Neck	Common cooking methods include braising and stewing. Meat often prepared ground.
Square-cut chuck, boneless	Common cooking methods include braising, stewing, grilling, and broiling. Meat often prepared as a roast (bone-in or BRT) or chops (round or blade bone).
VARIETY MEATS (OFFAL)	
Tongue	Simmering is the most common cooking method. Meat is often smoked.
Liver	Sautéing is the most common cooking method. Meat often prepared as forcemeat.
Heart	Common cooking methods include braising and stewing.
Kidneys	Stewing is the most common cooking method.
Intestines	Used as casing for sausage.

Lamb HRI Cuts

Item	Product Name	Weight Range (in pounds)
204	Rack (primal)	6–8
204b	Rack, roast-ready, single	2–4
206	Shoulder, primal, pair	20–24
207	Shoulder, square cut, single	5–7
208	Shoulder, square cut, boneless, tied	6–8
209	Breast	7–11
210	Foreshank	2–3
231	Loin	9–11
232	Loin, trimmed	6–8
232b	Loin, double, boneless, tied	3–4
233	Leg, primal, pair	19–20
233a	Leg, single, trotter off	10–12
233b	Leg, boneless, tied, single	8–10
233e	Leg, hindshank	1 and up
241	Leg, steamship	7–9
295	Lamb for stewing	Amount as needed
295a	Lamb for kabobs	Amount as needed
296	Ground lamb	Amount as needed

Venison and Furred Game

Free-roaming and domesticated wild animals fall under the category of game. The variety of game meats has become increasingly popular due in part to customer awareness and lower fat and cholesterol content. Depending upon the area of the country, several types of furred game are available.

Game meats are categorized into two segments: large and small. Venison is the most popular large game, characterized by lean meat that is free from intramuscular fat, generally dark red in color, and suitable for roasting, sautéing, and grilling. Though venison commonly refers to deer, other members of the venison family include moose, elk, and reindeer. Buffalo and wild boar are other popular large game.

The most common of the small game is rabbit. Rabbit has mild, lean, tender, and fine-textured meat. A hare ranges from six to twelve pounds, a mature rabbit from three to five pounds, and young rabbit is generally two to three pounds. The loin is often sautéed or roasted, while legs are commonly braised or stewed.

Commercial game meats are federally inspected. The quality of the flesh is a direct result of age, diet, and the time of year that it was killed.

These cuts of meat are from a variety of game animals: 1. Venison leg/haunch, 2. Boneless venison loin, 3. Venison medallions, 4. Venison saddle, 5. Frenched venison rack, 6. Venison shoulder, 7. Boneless venison loin, 8. Rabbit.

Poultry

The word *poultry* refers to any domesticated bird used for human consumption. Once reserved for special occasions, chicken and other poultry have become commonplace in restaurants and homes. The subtle and familiar flavor of chicken lends itself well to a number of different cooking methods. Considered very nutritious, poultry entrees are among the most popular on most menus.

Similar to other meats, poultry must undergo a mandatory inspection for wholesomeness. Depending on numerous factors, such as carcass shape and the ratio of meat to bone, the grading system is as follows: USDA A, B, or C. Once inspected, the birds are plucked, cleaned, chilled, and packaged. They may be purchased whole or in parts. Poultry is classified by age. The younger the bird, the more tender the flesh.

These birds are examples of geese and ducks: 1. Buddhist duck (called a pekin duck if the head is removed), 2. Moulard duck breast, 3. Goose, 4. Moulard duck legs, 5. Foie gras.

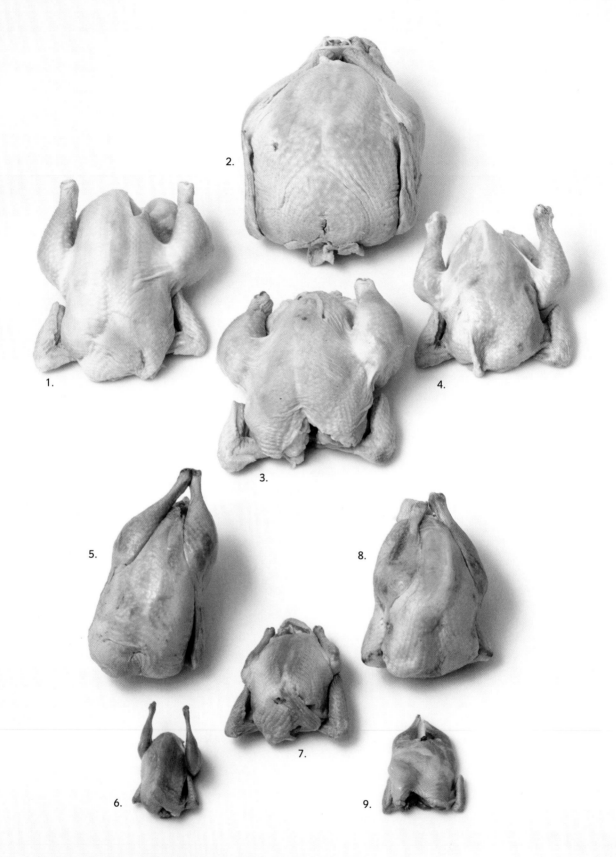

These birds are examples of the chicken family: 1. 6-pound roaster chicken,
2. Turkey, 3. Stewing hen, 4. 3-pound fryer chicken, 5. Pheasant,
6. Bone-in quail, 7. Squab, 8. Guinea fowl, 9. Boneless quail.

Poultry

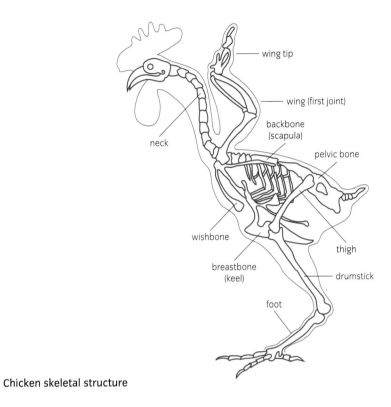

Chicken skeletal structure

Classes of Poultry

Type (description)	Approx. Age	Approx. Weight (in pounds)	Common Cooking Method
Broiler	4–6 weeks	1–3	Common cooking methods include broiling, grilling, and sautéing. Bird often prepared whole or split.
Fryer	6–10 weeks	3½–4½	Common cooking methods include roasting, grilling, broiling, and sautéing. Bird often prepared whole, split, quartered, or disjointed.
Roaster	3–5 months	7–9	Roasting is the most common cooking method. Bird most often prepared whole.
Fowl (stewing hen, female)	Over 10 months	6–8	Bird most often prepared in a soup, stock, or stew.

Type (description)	Approx. Age	Approx. Weight (in pounds)	Common Cooking Method
Poussin	3 weeks	1	Roasting is the most common cooking method. Bird most often prepared whole.
Rock Cornish hen; Cornish cross	5–7 weeks	Less than 2	Roasting is the most common cooking method. Bird most often prepared whole or split.
Capon (castrated male)	Under 8 months	7–9	Roasting is the most common cooking method.
Hen turkey (female)	5–7 months	8–20	Roasting is the most common cooking method.
Tom turkey (male)	Over 7 months	20 and up	Roasting is the most common cooking method.
Broiler duckling	Under 8 weeks	4–6	Common cooking methods include roasting, sautéing, and grilling. Often only the breast prepared. Legs often prepared as confit.
Roaster duckling	Under 12 weeks	6–8	Roasting is the most common cooking method.
Goose	6 months and up	8–16	Roasting is the most common cooking method.
Squab	25–30 days	¾–1	Roasting is the most common cooking method.
Pigeon	2–6 months	¾–1	Roasting is the most common cooking method.
Pheasant; Guinea hen	6–8 weeks	2–3	Roasting is the most common cooking method.
Quail	6–8 weeks	¼–½	Roasting is the most common cooking method.

Chapter Ten

Fish and Shellfish Identification

Fish and shellfish were once plentiful and inexpensive; however, due to increased popularity and more efficient, sophisticated fishing techniques, as well as the development and degradation of many coastal areas, demand has begun to outstrip supply. These factors have caused many countries to pass regulations limiting commercial fishing in specific waters, as well as aquaculture, or the farm raising of fish, to ensure reliable sources of fresh fish.

The increased value of seafood demands that a chef must be familiar with a wide variety of fish, shellfish, and their sources; be able to select fish and shellfish of the best quality; and understand the best cooking method or methods to use in their preparation.

Fish Basics

The health benefits of fish are becoming increasingly widely known, and although many Americans traditionally have favored red meats both at home and when they eat out, a large number are ordering fish entrées more often. The chef should be famliar with a wide variety of fish and be able to select absolutely fresh fish of the best quality. The first step in this process is assessing the purveyor or market. The fishmonger should properly handle, ice, and display the fish and should be able to answer any questions regarding the fish's origin and its qualities: lean or oily, firm-textured or delicate, appropriate for moist-heat method or able to withstand a grill's heat.

Market Forms of Fish

Fish can be purchased fresh in one of the market forms described below, as well as in frozen, smoked, pickled, or salted forms.

Whole fish This is the fish as it was caught, completely intact.

Drawn fish The viscera (guts) are removed, but head, fins, and scales are still intact.

H&G (headed and gutted) or Head-off drawn The viscera (guts) and head are removed, but scales and fins are still intact.

Dressed fish The viscera (guts), gills, scales, and fins are removed. The head may or may not be removed. Also known as pan-dressed, these fish are usually appropriate for a single serving.

Steak This is a portion-sized, cross-section cut from a dressed fish. Portion cuts from the fillets of large fish, such as tuna and swordfish, are also commonly called steaks.

Fillet This is a boneless piece of fish, removed from either side of the backbone. The skin may or may not be removed before cooking. Purveyors often sell fillets "pin-bone in," so it is important to specify "pin-bone out" when ordering.

Tranche A portion-sized slice of a fillet that is cut at a 45-degree angle to expose a greater surface area. A tranche is generally cut from a large fillet—for example, salmon or halibut.

Pavé A portion-sized, square cut from a fillet. A pavé is generally cut from a large fillet—for example, salmon, halibut, mahi mahi, or tuna.

Freshness Checks for Finfish

To ensure that fish are of the best quality, the chef should carefully inspect the fish, checking for as many of the following signs of freshness and quality as possible:

Fish should be received at a temperature of 40°F/4°C or less.

The fish should have a good overall appearance (clear slime, no cuts or bruising, pliable fins, etc.).

The scales should tightly adhere to the fish.

The flesh should respond to light pressure and not feel soft.

The eyes should be clear, bright, and bulging.

The gills should be bright pink to maroon in color, and if mucous is present, it should be clear.

There should be no belly burn—evidence that the viscera (guts) were left in the fish too long, resulting in bacteria and enzymes breaking down the flesh along the rib cage.

The fish should have a clean, sweet, sea-like smell.

Storage

Under correct storage conditions, fish and shellfish can be held for several days without losing any appreciable quality. Ideally, however, the chef should purchase only the amount of fish needed for a day or two and should store it properly, as described below:

1. Always keep fish at a proper storage temperature and handle it as little as possible. Fin fish: 28° to 32°F/–2° to 0°C; live mollusk: 35° to 40°F/2° to 4°C; live crustacean: 39° to 45°F/4° to 7°C; caviar: 28° to 32°F/–2° to 0°C; smoked fish: 32°F/0°C.

2. Check the fish carefully for freshness and quality. The fish may be rinsed at this point; scaling and fabricating should be delayed until close to service time.

3. Place the fish on a bed of shaved or flaked ice in a perforated container (such as a hotel pan with a draining pan), preferably stainless steel. The fish should be belly down, and the belly cavity should be filled with shaved ice as well.

4. Cover with additional ice; the fish may be layered, if necessary, with shaved or flaked ice. Cubed ice can bruise the fish's flesh. It also will not conform as closely to the fish. Shaved or flaked ice makes a tighter seal around the entire fish. This prevents undue contact with the air, slowing loss of quality and helping to extend safe storage life.

5. Set the perforated container in a second container. In this way, as the ice melts, the water will drain away. If fish is allowed to sit in a pool of water, flavor and texture loss will occur. The longer it sits, the greater the loss of quality.

6. Re-ice the fish daily. Even when properly iced, the fish will gradually lose some quality. To slow this loss, skim the top layer of ice from the storage container, and replace it with fresh ice.

Fish purchased as fillets should be stored in stainless-steel containers set on ice. They should not be in direct contact with the ice, however, because as it melts, much of the flavor and texture of the fish will be lost.

Frozen fish, including ice-glazed whole fish (repeatedly coated with water and frozen so that the ice builds up in layers, coating the entire fish), individually quick frozen (IQF) and frozen fillets [which are often treated with sodium tripolyphosphate (stp) to promote added water retention] should be stored at −20° to 0°F/−29° to −18°C until ready to be thawed and cooked.

Do not accept any frozen fish with white frost on its edges. This indicates freezer burn—the result of improper packaging or thawing and refreezing of the product.

Common Fish Types

The skeletal structure of fish is a useful means of separating finfish into smaller groupings. The three basic types of finfish are round, flat, and nonbony. Round fish have a middle backbone with one fillet on either side,

and one eye on each side of the head. Flatfish have a backbone that runs through the center of the fish, two upper and two lower fillets, and both eyes on the same side of the head. Nonbony fish have cartilage rather than bones. (See diagrams below.)

Fish may also be categorized by their activity level: low, medium, or high. The more a fish swims, the darker its flesh will be. Darker fleshed fish have a higher oil content and, therefore, a stronger flavor. When choosing the best cooking technique for a given fish, consider the oil content of the flesh. Low- and high-activity fish have limited cooking methods, while medium-activity fish are quite versatile. (See the tables on pages 203 to 214.)

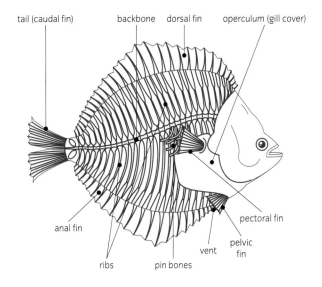

Flat fish skeletal structure

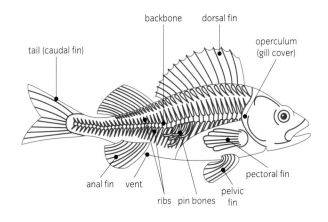

Round fish skeletal structure

Flat Fish

The characteristics of flat fish include the following: one pigmented and one nonpigmented side; either right- or left-eyed; a continuous dorsal and anal fin that stops before the caudal fin.

FROM LEFT TO RIGHT, TOP TO BOTTOM: halibut, turbot, Petrale sole, lemon sole, black-back flounder (right-eyed), fluke (left-eyed flounder), gray sole, Dover sole

Type	Description	Common Culinary Uses
RIGHT-EYED		
Gray sole/ Witch flounder	Found throughout the Gulf of Maine in deeper areas along Georges Bank; averages 24 inches and 3 to 4 pounds, with 4- to 10-ounce fillets; light, slightly sweet, delicate flesh	Baked, poached, sautéed, steamed
Winter/Black-back flounder/Mud dab	Found inshore during winter months, mostly in New York, Massachusetts, and Rhode Island; averages 1½ to 2 pounds; color ranges from reddish-brown to deep olive green; white underside; diamond shape; delicate and mildly flavorful flesh	Baked, poached, sautéed, steamed
Plaice/ Rough dab	Found on both sides of the Atlantic, called European, Irish, American or Canadian plaice depending on where it is found; member of flounder family; small, flat fish; 1 to 3 pounds average size; firm, sweet, lean flesh; considered good quality	Baked, poached, sautéed, steamed
Yellowtail flounder	Found primarily from Labrador to Rhode Island, can be as far south as Virginia; averages 1 to 2 pounds; olive brown with rusty spots; yellow tail; color mirrors the ocean floor, providing protection from predators; lean, flaky, sweet flesh	Baked, poached, sautéed
Lemon sole	A winter flounder that is a minimum of 3½ pounds, with 8-ounce fillets; white, somewhat firm, mildly sweet flesh	Baked, poached, sautéed
Rock sole	Found from the Bering Sea to California, and as far west as Japan; averages less than 5 pounds; firm and creamy white flesh	Baked, poached, sautéed
Petrale/Petrale sole	Found in the Pacific Ocean from Alaska to Mexico; the most important commercial West Coast species; averages 6 to 7 pounds; firm, white flesh; similar in eating qualities to lemon sole; sold whole or with head, tail, and pigmented skin removed	Poached, sautéed
Rex sole	Found in cold waters near and around Alaska; averages 1 to 2 pounds; elongated body; delicate, creamy, white, somewhat soft flesh; distinct in flavor	Poached, sautéed
Dover sole	Found only in European waters; pale gray to brown; small, compressed head; very small eyes; elongated body; flesh is fattier and firmer than other members of the flat fish family	Baked, broiled, poached, sautéed, steamed
Halibut	Found in the Atlantic from Greenland to southern New Jersey, must be labeled Pacific halibut if from Pacific Ocean; can be as large as 700 pounds, commonly 15 to 30 pounds; gray skin with white mottling; dense, snow white flesh; fine texture; mild taste; highest fat content of all low-activity flat fish	Baked, broiled, fried, grilled, poached, sautéed, steamed
LEFT-EYED		
Fluke/Summer flounder	Found in coastal waters from the Gulf of Maine to the Carolinas; large mouth extends below and beyond its eyes; white, flaky flesh; delicate flavor and texture	Baked, poached, sautéed
Turbot	Found in the North Sea and European North Atlantic, though mostly farmed in the Iberian Peninsula and Chile; averages 3 to 6 pounds; delicate flavor; firm texture	Baked, broiled, fried, grilled, poached, steamed, sautéed

Low-Activity Round Fish

The characteristics of round fish include the following: eyes on both sides of head; swim in upright posi-tion; firm grill plate; low, medium, or high activity.

FROM THE TOP: wolf fish, haddock, pollock, cod, white hake

Type	Description	Common Culinary Uses
Cod	Saltwater fish; thick, white flesh; mild flavor; provides weighty fillets with good shelf life; roe, cheeks, and chins are delicacies in some cultures	Shallow poached, baked, pan fried, deep fried, smoked, cured, salted, and dried
Haddock	Saltwater fish; member of the cod family; averages 2 to 5 pounds; similar to cod, but smaller maximum size; low fat; firm texture; mild flavor; available drawn or as fillets and steaks (when buying fillets, skin should be left on to distinguish from Atlantic cod)	Poached, baked, sautéed, pan fried; salted and smoked in Finnan Haddie
White hake	Saltwater fish; member of the cod family; averages 3 to 10 pounds, though can be as large as 30 pounds; soft flesh; sweeter and more flavorful than other members of the cod family; commonly sold without the head	Pan fried, smoked, baked
Pollock	Saltwater fish; member of the cod family; averages 4 to 10 pounds; darker flesh; stronger and more distinct flavor than other members of the cod family; reduced shelf life because of higher oil content; mostly sold as skinless fillets	Poached, baked, sautéed, grilled, broiled, smoked
Wolf fish	Found in North Atlantic; averages 8 to 15 pounds; big teeth, continuous dorsal and anal fins; firm, white flesh	Poached, baked, sautéed, pan fried, en papillote

Medium-Activity Round Fish

FROM LEFT TO RIGHT, TOP TO BOTTOM: walleyed pike, tilefish, grouper, yellowtail snapper, vermillion snapper, silk snapper, hybrid striped bass, black sea bass, wild striped bass

Type	Description	Common Culinary Uses
Weakfish	Saltwater fish; averages 2 to 6 pounds; sweet, off-white delicate flesh	Poached, baked, sautéed, grilled, broiled, steamed; used to make forcemeats
Walleyed pike	Freshwater fish; spiny finned; averages 1½ to 3 pounds; mild flavor; low fat content; firm texture	Broiled, sautéed, poached, steamed, baked, stewed; in soups; used to make forcemeats
Black sea bass	Saltwater fish from New England to North Carolina, very popular in Mid-Atlantic region; averages 1 to 3 pounds; white, firm flesh; delicate texture; available drawn whole or in fillets	Poached, baked, deep fried, sautéed, pickled; commonly served whole, using tableside presentation
Striped bass	Averages 2 to 15 pounds, can reach up to 50 pounds; firm flesh, large flake; flavorful flesh	Broiled, grilled, poached, baked, deep fried, sautéed, pickled; extremely versatile
Hybrid bass/ Hybrid striped bass	Farm-raised fish that hit the market in the 1980s; cross between a white bass and striped bass; averages 1 to 2 pounds; flesh cooks very white; somewhat earthy flavor	Broiled, grilled, poached, baked, deep fried, sautéed, pickled; extremely versatile
Red snapper	Found in the Gulf of Mexico and adjacent Atlantic waters; reef fish, therefore buy less than 5 pounds because of Ciguatera toxin; dorsal red skin that becomes light red or pink on belly, red eyes, long pectoral fins; firm texture	Poached, baked, sautéed, grilled, broiled, steamed
Yellowtail snapper	Saltwater reef fish; averages 1 to 2 pounds, can be as large as 6 pounds, however buy less than 5 pounds because of Ciguatera toxin; greenish-yellow stripe runs length of body; slightly sweet, white, fine, flaky flesh; good eating fish	Poached, baked, sautéed, grilled, broiled, steamed
Silk snapper	Saltwater reef fish, therefore buy less than 5 pounds because of Ciguatera toxin; similar to red snapper; reddish-pink skin, yellow underside, and yellow eyes; typically less expensive	Poached, baked, sautéed, grilled, broiled, steamed
Vermillion snapper/ Beeliner/Caribeau snapper	Saltwater reef fish; averages 2 pounds, but can be as large as 5 or 6 pounds, however buy less than 5 pounds because of Ciguatera toxin; greenish-brown and yellow along its side; often substituted for red snapper, though smaller, commercially less valuable, and less flavorful	Poached, baked, sautéed, grilled, broiled, steamed
Red grouper	Saltwater reef fish, therefore buy less than 5 pounds because of Ciguatera toxin; reddish-brown color; blotches on the skin; black dots around the eyes; few, if any, pin bones; important commercial catch; sweet, white flesh	Poached, baked, broiled, steamed, deep fried; in chowders
Black grouper	Saltwater reef fish, in deep waters; buy less than 5 pounds because of Ciguatera toxin; blackish-brown color; few, if any, pin bones; sweet, off-white flesh	Poached, baked, broiled, steamed, deep fried; in chowders
Gag grouper	Saltwater reef fish, therefore buy less than 5 pounds because of Ciguatera toxin; few, if any, pin bones; sweet, white flesh	Poached, baked, broiled, steamed, deep fried; in chowders
Tilefish	Saltwater fish; found along the entire East Coast; bass-like qualities; averages 6 to 8 pounds, can be as large as 30 pounds; colorful body; firm yet tender flesh	Poached, baked, broiled, deep fried; pan fried; available whole and drawn, or as fillets

High-Activity Round Fish

FROM LEFT TO RIGHT, TOP TO BOTTOM: mahi mahi (head off), farm-raised King salmon (Pacific salmon), Atlantic salmon, Arctic char, Rainbow trout, Spanish mackerel, Atlantic mackerel, pompano, Yellowfin tuna (loin)

Type	Description	Common Culinary Uses
Atlantic salmon	Anadromous fish; averages 6 to 12 pounds; deep pink flesh; high fat; shiny and moist; available year-round throughout the United States; because of farming, no wild catch is commercially available	Smoked, poached, baked, broiled, steamed, grilled; in dips, soups, sushi, and sashimi
King/Pacific salmon	Anadromous fish; found from the Pacific Northwest to Alaska; ranges from 16 to 20 pounds, largest of commercial salmon; wide bodied; medium to dark red flesh	Smoked, poached, baked, broiled, steamed, grilled; in dips and soups
Coho/Silver salmon	Anadromous fish; found throughout the Pacific; similar in taste and texture to Atlantic salmon	Smoked, poached, baked, broiled, steamed, grilled; in dips and soups
Sockeye/Red salmon	Anadromous fish; found in Alaskan and British Columbian rivers; averages 5 to 7 pounds; dark red flesh; glistening, silver skin	Smoked, poached, baked, broiled, steamed, grilled; in dips, soups, sushi, and sashimi; ideal for canning
Brook trout	Freshwater fish; found in the northeastern United States and eastern Canada, also farm raised; averages 6 to 10 ounces; dark, olive-green skin; cream-colored spots; delicate and buttery flesh	Poached, baked, broiled, fried, grilled, steamed, stuffed
Rainbow trout	Freshwater fish; farm raised; averages 10 to 14 ounces; dark spots on a lighter background; firm, off-white flesh with mild flavor; generally sold head on	Poached, baked, broiled, fried, grilled, steamed, stuffed
Steelhead trout	Anadromous species of Rainbow trout; farm raised in the United States and Canada; averages less than 12 pounds; similar markings to Rainbow trout; taste, texture, and color similar to Atlantic salmon	Poached, baked, broiled, fried, grilled, steamed, stuffed
Arctic char	Anadromous fish; found in Europe, Canada, and Alaska; also farm raised; averages 2 to 8 pounds; dark red to rose or white flesh; some consider it superior to salmon	Poached, baked, broiled, fried, grilled, steamed, stuffed
Albacore/Tombo tuna	Saltwater fish from Atlantic and Pacific waters; averages 10 to 30 pounds; light red to pink flesh that is off-white when cooked; mild flavor; valuable commodity in U.S. canning industry, sold as "white tuna"	Baked, broiled, grilled, sautéed
Bigeye tuna/Ahi-B	Saltwater fish from tropical, temperate waters; ranges from 20 to 100 pounds; rich, dark flesh	Baked, broiled, grilled, sautéed; much sought after for sushi and sashimi

(continued)

High-Activity Round Fish, continued

Type	Description	Common Culinary Uses
Bluefin tuna	Saltwater fish from the Atlantic and the Gulf of Mexico; among the largest of fish; can weigh up to 1,500 pounds; dark red to reddish-brown flesh; very distinct flavor when cooked	Baked, broiled, grilled, sautéed; the most sought after for sushi and sashimi (consistently high prices; most is exported)
Yellowfin tuna/Ahi	Saltwater fish from tropical and subtropical waters; flesh darker than albacore, lighter than Bluefin; yellow stripes down side and on dorsal and anal fins; widely available in the United States; less expensive than Bigeye and Bluefin	Baked, broiled, grilled, sautéed
Skipjack tuna/Aku	Saltwater fish from the Central Pacific and Hawaii; averages 7 to 12 pounds; similar in color to Yellowfin; often canned, sold as "light tuna"; often marketed frozen	Baked, broiled, grilled, sautéed
Spanish mackerel	Saltwater fish from Virginia to the Gulf of Mexico in spring and winter; averages 2 to 4 pounds; bright yellow-gold spots along its sides; lean and delicate flesh	Baked, broiled, grilled, sautéed, smoked
Atlantic mackerel	Saltwater fish from the North Atlantic; averages 1 to 2 pounds; smooth skin with vibrant hues of blue and silver; oily, dark flesh; pungent flavor; best purchased in the fall	Baked, broiled, grilled, sautéed, smoked
King mackerel	Saltwater fish from Florida in winter months; averages 10 to 20 pounds; contains more fat than Spanish mackerel; well flavored	Broiled, grilled, smoked
Pompano	Saltwater fish from the Carolinas to Florida and the Gulf of Mexico; member of the Jack family; averages 1 to 2 pounds; delicate, beige flesh, turns white when cooked; complex flavor; medium fat content; highly regarded fish; very expensive	Poached, baked, broiled, grilled, fried, steamed, en papillote
Permit	Saltwater fish; similar to pompano only in color and geography; member of the Jack family; averages 10 to 20 pounds, can be as large as 50 pounds; drier, more granular flesh than pompano (though if offered in the same weight range, flesh can be similar)	Poached, baked, broiled, grilled, fried, steamed
Greater amberjack	Saltwater fish from Gulf of Mexico, West Africa, and the Mediterranean; member of the Jack family; averages 10 to 40 pounds; dark, oily flesh; strong flavor	Baked, broiled, sautéed, smoked

Type	Description	Common Culinary Uses
Lesser amberjack	Saltwater fish from Massachusetts to the Gulf of Mexico and Brazil; member of the Jack family; weighs less than 8 pounds; lighter flesh than Greater amberjack; similar in quality	Baked, broiled, sautéed, smoked
Mahi mahi/ Dolphin fish	Saltwater fish from tropical and subtropical waters; ranges from 4 to 15 pounds, can be as large as 50 pounds; flesh is pink to light tan, turning beige to off-white when cooked; dense, sweet, moist, and delicate flesh, with a large flake	Baked, broiled, grilled, pan fried, sautéed
Bluefish	Saltwater fish from the Atlantic coast; averages 4 to 10 pounds; dark, oily, strongly flavored flesh; fine textured; smaller sizes have a more mild flavor	Baked, broiled
Shad	Anadromous fish from Florida to St. Lawrence River; female (roe shad) averages 4 to 5 pounds, but the male is smaller; off-white, sweet flesh; high fat content; roe is considered a delicacy	Baked, broiled, grilled, sautéed, smoked

Nonbony Fish

CLOCKWISE FROM TOP: sturgeon (head off), skate wings, monkfish, swordfish wheel

Type	Description	Common Culinary Uses
Swordfish	Saltwater fish from tropical, temperate waters; smooth skin, firm, dense flesh; distinctly flavored; available skinless and headless, in fillets or steaks	Baked, broiled, grilled, sautéed
Sturgeon	Anadromous fish; from northern Florida to St. Lawrence River (Atlantic sturgeon), averages 60 to 80 pounds; White sturgeon is found from California to Alaska, and farm raised, averages 10 to 15 pounds; highly regarded for their eggs, fine caviar; firm, high-fat flesh; delicate flavor	Baked, braised, broiled, grilled, sautéed, smoked
Monkfish	Saltwater fish; averages 15 to 50 pounds, with 2- to 6-pound fillets; firm, mild white flesh; also known as goosefish, anglerfish, fishing frog lotte, and bellyfish; commonly sold as tails and fillets, low yield when sold head on	Baked, broiled, grilled, fried, sautéed, pan fried; livers are popular in Japan
Mako shark	Saltwater fish from warm, temperate, and tropical waters; ranges from 30 to 100 pounds; one of the most regarded species of shark	Baked, broiled, grilled, fried, sautéed; shark fin is popular in Hong Kong and Canton China
Dog fish/Cape shark	Saltwater fish; 3 to 5 pounds average weight; smooth skin; brownish or gray topside; white underside; white/gray spots along the side of the body; sweet, pink to white, firm flesh	Poached, baked, broiled, grilled, fried, sautéed
Thresher shark	Saltwater fish from warm, temperate, and tropical waters; averages 30 to 50 pounds; easily identifiable by its extremely elongated fin; sweet, pink flesh	Baked, broiled, grilled, fried, sautéed; shark fin is popular in Hong Kong and China
Skate/Ray	Saltwater fish found in waters throughout the United States; flat creatures, related to the shark; white, sweet, firm flesh; fin is edible part of the fish, called "wings," producing 2 fillets; upper fillet is generally thicker than lower one; excellent eating fish	Poached, baked, fried, sautéed

Other Fish

Type	Description	Common Culinary Uses
Eel	Anadromous fish; American eel is slightly smaller than European eel; females are larger than males, farm raised in China; snake-like shape; high-fat, firm flesh; available alive or whole; best quality just before journey to spawn	Broiled, fried, stewed; excellent smoked
American catfish	Freshwater fish; found mostly in southern regions, though vast majority is farm raised; fillets average 6 to 12 ounces; low-fat, firm flesh; mild flavor; commonly sold headless and skinless	Poached, baked, broiled, grilled, steamed, stewed, deep fried, pan fried, and smoked
Anchovy	Saltwater fish from California, South America, the Mediterranean, and Europe; over 20 species are recognized as anchovies; best less than 4 inches in length; silver skin; soft, flavorful flesh; also marketed salt cured, canned (packed in oil), dried, as fishmeal, and bait	When sold fresh whole, commonly deep fried, pan fried, smoked, and marinated; used as a flavoring additive and garnish
Sardine	Saltwater fish; imported from Spain, Portugal, and Italy; best less than 7 inches in length; delicate fatty flesh; silvery skin; sardines are recognized as a species of small herring; available whole or dressed, salted, smoked, or canned	Broiled, grilled, deep fried, marinated
John Dory	Saltwater fish from the eastern Atlantic, Nova Scotia and the Mediterranean (referred to as St. Peter's fish in Europe); black spots with a golden halo on each side of body; firm, bright white flesh; delicately mild flavor; fine flake	Poached, grilled, sautéed
Wolf fish/ Ocean catfish	Saltwater fish from the North Atlantic (New England and Iceland); can be up to 40 pounds; member of the catfish family; large head, powerful jaws, and sharp canine teeth; feeds on mollusks, clams, and whelks; white, firm flesh of varying fat content	Shallow poached, sautéed, pan fried
Tilapia/Mud fish	Aqua-cultured around the world; native to Africa; marketed around 1 to 2 pounds; approximately 4 to 18 inches long; hybridized to achieve red, black, or golden skin; distinguished by the interruption along its lateral line; off-white to pink flesh, very mild flavor, can be musty	Poached, baked, broiled, grilled, steamed

Shellfish

Shellfish are aquatic animals protected by some sort of shell. Based on skeletal structure, they can be segmented into four distinct categories: univalves (single-shelled mollusks), bivalves (mollusks with two shells joined by a hinge), crustaceans (jointed exterior skeletons or shells), and cephalopods (mollusks with tentacles attached directly to the head).

Market Forms

Shellfish are available fresh and frozen in various forms. Fresh shellfish are available live, shucked, as tails, cocktail claws, and legs and claws. Frozen shellfish are also available shucked, as tails, cocktail claws, and legs and claws.

Shucking is the removal of a mollusk from the shell; this term also refers to the item's market form sold as meat only, along with natural juices known as liquor. Mollusks such as oysters, clams, and mussels may be available shucked; scallops are nearly always sold shucked, although there is a growing market for scallops that are live and on the half shell with roe.

Quality Indicators

When purchasing live shellfish, look for signs of movement. While lobsters and crabs should move about, clams, mussels and oysters should be tightly closed, or close when touched. As they age, they will begin to open. Any shells that do not snap shut when tapped should be discarded; this means that the fish are dead. Molluskan shellfish should have a sweet, sea-like aroma.

Storage

Crabs, lobsters, and other live shellfish should be packed in seaweed or damp paper upon delivery. If a lobster tank is not available, they can be stored directly in their shipping containers or in perforated pans at 40°F/ 4°C until they are to be prepared. Do not allow fresh water to come into direct contact with lobsters or crabs, as it will kill them.

Clams, mussels, and oysters purchased in the shell should be stored in the bag in which they were delivered or in perforated pans. They should not be iced and they should be stored at a temperature between 35° and 40°F/2° and 4°C. The bag should be closed tightly and lightly weighted to keep the shellfish from opening.

Molluskan Shellfish

LEFT COLUMN, FROM THE TOP: sea urchins, sea scallops, bay scallops
CENTER COLUMN, FROM THE TOP: Belon oysters, Kumamoto oysters,
Fanny Bay oysters, Malpeque oysters, Florida oysters
RIGHT COLUMN, FROM THE TOP: Cherrystone clams, Topneck clams, Cockle clams,
Razor clams, Geoduck clam, green mussels, blue mussels

Univalves

Type	Description	Common Culinary Uses
Abalone	Gastropod mollusk found along the Pacific coast, also farm raised in California, Chile, and Japan; farm raised averages 3 inches in diameter; encased inside round, oval shell; available whole or in steaks; fresh or frozen; shells are used for mother-of-pearl	Grilled, sautéed, marinated
Sea urchin/Uni	Found in oceans around the world; hard, dark purple shell covered with spines; averages 1 pound; harvested for its internal roe (uni); ranges from bright red, to orange, to yellow in color; firm texture that melts in your mouth; sweet flavor; considered a delicacy. Often grouped with mollusks for marketing, however are true echinoderms	Sushi, baked, as flavoring in sauces
Conch	Gastropod mollusk indigenous to the Caribbean and the Florida Keys, also farm raised in the Caribbean and Florida; older conchs have tough, dark flesh, younger conchs yield sweet, white, tender flesh; available out of shell or ground; farmed have very mild flavor; also known as scongilli	Salads, ceviche, chowders, fritters
Whelk/Channel whelk	Gastropod mollusk; found in shallow water along East Coast from Massachusetts to northern Florida; large sea snail used mainly in Europe and Korea; available fresh or cooked, preserved in vinegar, and canned	Marinated; in salads and ceviche
Land snail/Escargot	Gastropod mollusk; abundant in most parts of the world; farm raised in California; air breathing; available fresh, canned, or packaged	Baked, boiled, broiled
Periwinkle	Gastropod mollusk; found along Atlantic coasts of Europe and North America; smooth, conical spiral shell with 4 whorls; outer shell is gray to dark green with reddish bands that encircle it; common in Europe and New England	Boiled, sautéed

(continued)

Bivalves

Type	Description	Common Culinary Uses
Quahog clam	Hard-shelled clam from cold northern waters; sizes (from smallest to largest) include Littleneck, Topneck, Cherrystone, and Chowder; sold as count per 60-pound bushel	Baked, steamed, stewed; in chowder; smaller sizes eaten on the half shell
Razor/Atlantic Jackknife clam	Hard-shelled clam found in shallow waters along the East Coast; shaped like a razor with sharp edges; difficult to store out of water; quickly dehydrate, leaving shells dry and brittle	Baked, steamed, stewed, deep fried; in fritters
Soft-shelled/Ipswich/ Horse clam/Steamer	Soft-shelled clam found in shallow waters in the Chesapeake, Maine, Massachusetts, and entire Pacific coast; lengthy, gray, soft, brittle shell; neck or siphon covered by thin skin; sweet flavor; can be sandy unless depurated	Steamed, breaded, deep fried
Geoduck clam	Hard-shelled clam found along the West Coast, also farm raised in the Pacific Northwest; can reach 9 inches in length, can reach 10 pounds, though most are marketed at 3 to 4 pounds; largest clam found in North America; grayish-white, ringed shell; neck is exceptionally long in relation to shell	Baked, steamed, sautéed; in fritters, chowder, sushi, and ceviche
Manila/West Coast Littleneck clam	Hard-shelled clam found in the Pacific; slightly elongated, grayish-white shell with dark black markings; can grow up to 3 inches in length	Baked, steamed; in stews
Cockle	Commercially valuable in Asia, the United States, and Europe, large resource from British Columbia, Greenland, and Florida; small, white to green shell	Baked, steamed; too small to be used shucked
Blue mussel	Found in temperate waters of the northern and southern hemispheres; farm raised in Maine, Nova Scotia, Prince Edward Island, and Spain; dark blue shell; averages 2 to 3 inches in length; slightly sweet flavor	Baked, steamed; in stews
Green mussel	Found in coastal, tropical waters of the Indo-Pacific region, also farm raised in New Zealand; green shell; averages 3 to 4 inches in length; slightly sweet flavor; available live, half shell, and shucked	Baked, steamed; in stews
East Coast oyster	From the Northeast, Virginia, and Gulf coasts; available wild and farm raised; grown while submerged underwater; most sold oyster in the United States; smooth shell on top and bottom; varieties include Malpeque, Chincoteague, and Florida	Baked, batter fried, grilled, sautéed, steamed, roasted; on the half shell; used in soups, stews, stuffings, and appetizers

Type	Description	Common Culinary Uses
Japanese/West Coast oyster	Grown underwater at high tide and out of water at low tide; scalloped shell; Kumamoto is a popular variety	Baked, batter fried, grilled, sautéed, steamed; on the half shell; used in soups, stews, stuffings, and appetizers
European flat oyster/ Horse's Hoof	Native to Europe; seen off the coast of Maine; available wild and farm raised; round, flat shell; salty, metallic flavor; varieties include Belon, Marennes, and Helford; growing in popularity	Baked, batter fried, grilled, sautéed, steamed, roasted; on the half shell; used in soups, stews, stuffings, and appetizers
Pacific/Olympia oyster	Native West Coast United States oyster; small, less than 3 inches in diameter; less cupped than eastern varieties; distinct aftertaste	Baked, batter fried, grilled, sautéed, steamed; on the half shell; used in soups, stews, stuffings, and appetizers; in a dish called Hangtown Fry
Bay/Cape Cod/ Long Island scallop	Found from Massachusetts to North Carolina; small compared to sea variety; creamy ivory to pink in color; very sweet; bay harvesting in fall and winter; hand raked; shucked on shore; sold fresh (limited live market), not frozen; often considered the best tasting scallop	Broiled, grilled, poached, stewed, sautéed
Sea scallop/ Diver scallop	Found from the Gulf of Maine to North Carolina, also farm raised (limited market); brown shell; can be 8 inches in diameter; sweet, moist flesh, not as tender as bay variety; commonly frozen; fresh available year-round. Diver scallop indicates it was hand harvested; found in Maine; more uniform in size; more moisture and less grit than those dredged	Broiled, grilled, poached, stewed, sautéed
Calico scallop	Found in waters from Carolina to South America, on both Atlantic and Gulf of Mexico coasts; small, less than 3 inches; flesh is darker in color than bay varieties; flavor and texture inferior to bay varieties as well; available year-round	Broiled, grilled, poached, stewed, sautéed

Cephalopods

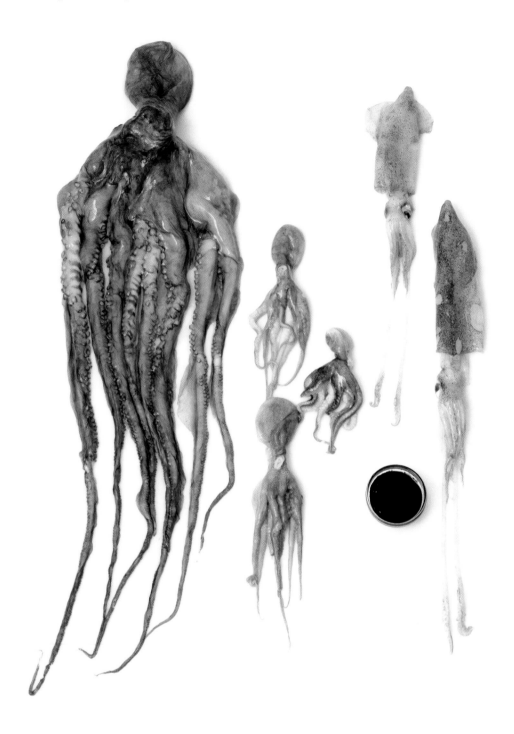

FROM LEFT: octopus, baby octopi, squid, squid ink (in bowl)

Type	Description	Common Culinary Uses
Squid/Calamari	Found along the East and West Coasts; averages 7 inches in length; slightly chewy, firm texture; mild and sweet flavor; invertebrate; changes color of skin for protection; ink used to confuse predator; available cleaned and uncleaned (dirty), fresh and frozen	Baked, boiled, broiled, deep fried, pan fried, stir fried, sautéed; ink used to color pasta and rice, and in sauces
Octopus	Found in shallow and deep waters of California and Alaska, also the Atlantic and Arctic regions from the English Channel to Bermuda; range in size from a few ounces (baby) to over 100 pounds; blue blooded; soft bodied; eyes on both sides of head; 8 arms, with 2 rows of suction cups on each; mild flavor, chewy texture	Boiled; when small they are often prepared deep fried, grilled, or sautéed
Cuttlefish	Found in shallow coastal waters from Thailand, China, India, Spain, and Portugal; 10 arms and 2 long, narrow tentacles; light brown in color with zebra-like stripes; sweet, textured, bright white	Boiled, steamed, stir fried, sushi, sashimi

Crustacean Shellfish

CLOCKWISE FROM TOP: King crab, freshwater shrimp, pink shrimp (head on), white shrimp (head off), Tiger shrimp (head off), American lobster, Snow crab claws, Jonah crab, Dungeness crab

Type	Description	Common Culinary Uses
Maine/Northern/ North American lobster	Found off the Atlantic coast of the northern United States, Canada, and in Europe (though smaller); can take 8 years to reach market size of 1 to 2 pounds; firm, sweet, delicate flesh; color of flesh is bright white with reddish streaks	Baked, broiled, grilled, poached, steamed, stir fried
Spiny/Rock lobster	Found in waters off Florida, southern California, New Mexico, Australia, New Zealand, and South Africa; all 10 legs are same size; has no claws; flesh is found in tail; firm flesh, less sweet than American lobster	Baked, grilled, poached, steamed, stir fried
Crayfish/Crawfish	Found in freshwater swamps, creeks, and bayous; farm raised in Louisiana and Florida; imported from S.E. Asia; deep red shells, bright red when cooked; sweet, white, firm flesh; available shucked, cooked meats and picked meats	Boiled, steamed
Langoustine/ Dublin Bay prawn/ Scampi	Found in European, Atlantic, and Mediterranean waters; related to Spiny lobster; slightly sweet and flavorful flesh	Poached, boiled, steamed, broiled, grilled, sautéed
Warm water shrimp	Found in tropical waters, majority of U.S. catch harvested in South Atlantic and the Gulf of Mexico; classified by shell color: pink (sweet and tender), brown (briny, firm, and inconsistent), white (sweet and mild); sold by size count per pound	Baked, broiled, deep fried, en papillote, grilled, poached, sautéed, steamed, stewed, poached
Cold water shrimp	Found in the North Atlantic and North Pacific; considerably smaller and softer than warm water varieties; sold by size count per pound	Baked, broiled, deep fried, en papillote, grilled, sautéed, steamed, stewed
Freshwater shrimp	Farm raised in Hawaii and California; up to 12 inches in length; very soft, mild flesh; sold by size count per pound	Baked, broiled, deep fried, grilled, sautéed, steamed
Tiger shrimp	Found in the South Pacific, Southeast Africa, and India; farm raised in Asia; grayish-black stripes on grayish-blue shells, although shell stripes turn bright red when cooked; white flesh with orange if cooked peeled, and red if cooked in the shell; mild, briny, slightly bland flavor; sold by size count per pound	Baked, broiled, deep fried, grilled, poached, sautéed, steamed
Rock shrimp	Hard-shelled shrimp; found from the southeastern United States to the Gulf of Mexico; flavor and texture more like crawfish than other shrimp; sold peeled, 40/50 count per pound	Baked, broiled, deep fried, en papillote, grilled, poached, sautéed, steamed, stewed, poached

(continued)

Crustacean Shellfish, continued

Type	Description	Common Culinary Uses
Blue crab	Found from Chesapeake Bay to the Gulf Coast; males have blue claws, females have reddish-blue; both have long spine on each side of dark green shell; sweet, tender, moist, buttery flesh; should be alive just before cooking	Baked, broiled, deep fried, grilled, poached, sautéed, steamed, stewed
Soft-shell crab	Blue crab that sheds its shell and is harvested when still soft; in season from April to mid-September, peak in June and early July; after cleaning, the entire crab may be eaten	Baked, broiled, grilled, deep fried, pan fried, grilled, sautéed, sushi
Jonah crab	Found from Prince Edward Island to Maine; oval in shape; has 2 strong, black-tipped claws; sweet, briny, slightly stringy, firm flesh	Baked, broiled, deep fried, grilled, poached, sautéed, steamed, stewed
King/Alaska King crab	Found in northern Pacific, most abundant in Alaska and Russia; can reach 10 feet and weigh 10 to 15 pounds; varieties include red, brown/golden, and blue	Baked, broiled, deep fried, grilled, poached, sautéed, steamed, stewed
Dungeness crab	Found along the Pacific coast, from Alaska to Mexico; averages 1½ to 3 pounds; reddish-brown shell, whitish-orange underside; flesh is mild and sweet	Baked, broiled, deep fried, grilled, poached, sautéed, steamed, stewed
Snow crab	Found in Alaska and eastern Canada; averages 5 pounds; oval shaped; 4 pairs of slender legs, 2 shorter claws in front; white flesh, tinged with pink; sweet, slightly stringy, and less flavorful than King crab	Baked, broiled, deep fried, grilled, poached, sautéed, steamed, stewed

Chapter Eleven

Fruit, Vegetable, and Fresh Herb Identification

Fruits, vegetables, and herbs have always been an important part of the human diet, but today consumers are more aware than ever of the important role these foods play in maintaining overall health and fitness. This chapter provides professional chefs with the information they need to take full advantage of the abundance of fresh produce now available, including tips on availability, determination of quality, proper storage, and culinary uses.

General Guidelines

Selection

Fruits, vegetables, and herbs should be in good condition, though what constitutes a favorable appearance varies from one item to another. In general, fruits and vegetables should be free of bruises, mold, brown or soft spots, and pest damage; they should have colors and textures appropriate to their type; and any attached leaves should not be wilted. Fruits should be plump, not shriveled. Specific information on particular types of produce is given in the sections below.

Production Methods

Foodservice operations wield purchasing power that can be used to support or discourage specific agricultural practices. You may wish to consider several agricultural production and treatment methods when purchasing ingredients.

Agricultural biotechnology includes a multitude of scientific techniques that are used to create, improve, or modify plants. For hundreds of years, scientists have improved plants for human benefit using conventional techniques, such as selective breeding. However, conventional breeding methods can be time consuming and inaccurate. Through genetic engineering, scientists are now able to isolate genes with a desirable trait and transfer them to other organisms, resulting in genetically modified organisms (GMOs) that have higher resistance to disease.

Irradiation is a food safety technology that is used to kill pathogenic organisms and extend shelf life. Similar to the pasteurization of milk and pressure cooking of canned goods, treating foods with ionizing radiation (also known as "cold pasteurization") can kill bacteria that might otherwise cause food-borne illness.

Sustainable agriculture pertains to agricultural production and distribution systems that focus on providing a profitable farm income, while promoting environmental stewardship. Key practices include renewing and protecting soil fertility and the natural resource base, improving the use of on-farm resources, and minimizing the use of nonrenewable resources. Sustainable farming strives to promote opportunities in family farming and farm communities. Sustainable practices include methods such as integrated pest management, field terracing, and stemming soil erosion.

Organic food is produced without the use of most conventional pesticides, synthetic fertilizers, sewage sludge, bioengineering, or ionizing radiation. In order for a product to be labeled "organic," a government-approved USDA certifier must inspect where the food is grown and processed to ensure that USDA organic standards are adhered to.

Hydroponic crops are grown in nutrient-enriched water rather than soil. Hydroponic growing takes place indoors under regulated temperature and light, so any growing season may be duplicated. Today, hydroponically grown lettuces, spinach, herbs, and tomatoes are all readily available. Although they have the advantage of being easy to clean, these products may have a less pronounced flavor than conventionally grown fruits and vegetables.

Availability and Seasonality

Prior to the increase in agricultural production and distribution technology, chefs were limited to locally grown seasonal fruits and vegetables. Though food establishments are no longer bound to buy local produce, it is still a favorable practice if and when possible. It is important to support the local growers. Moreover, so-called boutique farmers may have specialty produce (wild lettuces, golden beets, and yellow tomatoes) that is not available through large commercial purveyors. Another advantage to buying locally is that the flavor and condition of the foods are often superior; locally grown sweet corn, apricots, peaches, and strawberries that have not been shipped are just a few examples. Conversely, there are items that ship particularly well. Examples include asparagus, head lettuces, broccoli, apples, and citrus fruits.

Storage

Once the produce has been received, following certain storage guidelines can ensure that its quality remains high. Most foodservice establishments store produce for no more than three or four days, although length of storage depends on the business's volume, the kind of available storage facilities, and delivery frequency. It is ideal to let the purveyor handle the produce as long as possible to help ensure that you are using the freshest product possible and not to overload your valuable storage space.

With a few exceptions (bananas, tomatoes, potatoes, dry onions), ripe fruits and vegetables should be refrigerated. Unless otherwise specified, produce should be kept at a temperature of 40° to 45°F/4° to 7°C, with a relative humidity of 80 to 90 percent. The ideal situation is to have a separate walk-in or reach-in refrigerator for fruits and vegetables.

Most fruits and vegetables should be kept dry, because excess moisture can promote spoilage. Therefore, most produce should not be peeled, washed, or trimmed until just before use. The outer leaves of lettuce, for example, should be left intact; carrots should remain unpeeled. The exceptions to this rule are the leafy tops on vegetables such as beets, turnips, carrots, and radishes. They should be removed and either discarded or used immediately because even after harvesting, the leaves absorb nutrients from the root and increase moisture loss.

Fruits and vegetables that need further ripening, notably peaches and avocados, should be stored at room temperature, 65° to 70°F/18° to 21°C. Once the produce is ripe, it should be refrigerated so that it does not become overripe.

Certain fruits (including apples, bananas, and melons) emit high amounts of ethylene gas as they sit in storage. Ethylene gas can accelerate ripening in unripe fruits, but can also promote spoilage in fruits and vegetables that are already ripe. For this reason, unless they are being used deliberately as a ripening agent, high ethylene-producing fruits should be stored separately. When separate storage space is unavailable, place ethylene-producing fruits in sealed containers.

Some fruits and vegetables, including onions, garlic, lemons, and melons, give off odors that can permeate other foods. Dairy products are particularly susceptible to odor absorption and should always be stored away from fruits and vegetables. Certain fruits, such as apples and cherries, also absorb odors. They too should be well wrapped or stored separately.

Many fruits and vegetables begin to deteriorate after three or four days. Although citrus fruits, most root vegetables, and hard squashes have a longer storage life, most restaurants do not hold even these items for more than two to three weeks.

Fruits

Fruits are the ovaries that surround or contain the seeds of plants. Customarily used in sweet dishes, fruits are also excellent with savory items, such as potato latkes and grilled pork chops. Fruit is wonderful served alone as a refreshing breakfast or a finale to a meal. Dried fruits find their way into compotes, stuffings, and sauces.

Vegetables

Vegetables are the roots, tubers, stems, leaves, leaf stalks, seeds, seedpods, and flower heads of plants that may be safely eaten. Vegetables commonly include a number of foods that botanically are classified as fruits, such as tomatoes. Their culinary application is the guiding principle for placing them in this section, rather than the previous one.

Herbs

Herbs are the leaves of aromatic plants and are used primarily to add flavor to foods. Aroma is a good indicator of quality in both fresh and dried herbs. They should also have even color, healthy-looking leaves and stems, and no wilting, brown spots, sunburn, or pest damage.

Fresh herbs should be minced or cut in chiffonade as close to service time as possible. They are usually added to a dish toward the end of the cooking time. For uncooked preparations, fresh herbs should be added well in advance of serving.

In general, herbs should be stored loosely wrapped in damp paper towels and refrigerated (it is a good idea to label the herbs, so that they are easy to locate). If desired, the wrapped herbs may then be placed in plastic bags to help retain moisture and reduce wilting and discoloration of leaves.

Apples

Apples are perhaps America's favorite fruit. According to surveys from the International Apple Institute, apples account for nearly 14 percent of all tree fruits sold in this country. Apples range in color from yellow, to green, to red, and colors in between. Different varieties of apples have particular characteristics. Some are best for eating out of hand, others are considered best for pies and baking, and still others are selected for their ability to cook down into a rich, smooth purée for applesauce. For cider, a blend of apples is usually chosen, to give the finished drink a full, well-balanced flavor.

Select firm apples that have a smooth skin with no bruising, though rough brown spots are acceptable. Apples can be held in climate-controlled cold storage for many months without significant loss of quality. Dried apples, prepared applesauce, apple juice (bottled or frozen concentrate), cider, spiced or plain pie filling, and a host of other prepared items made from apples can also be purchased.

The flesh of many apples will begin to turn brown once they are cut open and come in contact with air. Dousing them in acidulated water (water with a little lemon juice) will help prevent browning but may not be desirable if a pure apple taste is important. The following table covers a selection of apple varieties.

TOP ROW, FROM LEFT TO RIGHT: **Stayman Winesap, McIntosh, Northern Spy, Cortland, Honey Crisp** BOTTOM ROW, FROM LEFT TO RIGHT: **Cameo, Gala, Golden Delicious, Granny Smith, Macoun, Cox Orange Pippin**

Type*	Description	Common Culinary Uses
Crabapple	Small; red with yellow or white; very hard flesh; tart flavor	Cooked in sauces, jellies, jams, and relishes
Golden Delicious	Yellowish-green skin with freckling; crisp, juicy texture; sweet flavor; stays white after cutting longer than other varieties	All-purpose
Granny Smith	Green skin, white flesh; extremely crisp, finely textured flesh; tart flavor; stays white after cutting longer than other varieties	Eaten out of hand; sweet and savory preparations; used in pies
McIntosh	Primarily red, streaked with yellow or green; flesh is very white; semitart	Eaten out of hand; used for sauces, cider; can be frozen
Northern Spy	Red skin streaked with yellow; crisp, firm texture, juicy; sweet-tart taste	Excellent in pies
Red Delicious	Bright red speckled with yellow, flesh is yellow-white; firm texture and sweet taste	Eaten out of hand
Rome Beauty	Bright red skin speckled with yellow; flesh is firm; mild tart-sweet flavor	Great for baking whole
Stayman Winesap	Dusty red with white spots; flesh is firm and crisp; tart and aromatic	All-purpose; used for pies, sauces, baking; can be frozen
Cortland	Smooth, shiny, and red skin; crisp texture; sweet-tart flavor; stays white after cutting longer than other varieties	All-purpose
Honey Crisp	Yellow with good amount of red blush; very crisp; very sweet	All-purpose
Gala	Peachy-red speckled with yellow; crisp and juicy; sweet and zesty	Eaten out of hand
Cameo	Dull red, splotchy, with some yellow-brown coloring	All-purpose
Macoun	Ranges from maroon to green with dull red blush, some white spots; crisp and juicy; sweet-tart flesh	All-purpose; eaten out of hand
Cox Orange Pippin	Golden brownish-orange with green tinge; crisp and juicy; slightly tart	All-purpose

*There are many varieties of apples available only within small regions. These apples share eating and cooking characteristics with those described here. If you have any questions, ask your purveyor or other reputable source for the best use for a particular variety.

Berries

Berries tend to be highly perishable (with the exception of cranberries) and are susceptible to bruising, mold, and overripening in fairly short order. Inspect all berries and their packaging carefully before you accept them. Juice-stained cartons or juice leaking through the carton is a clear indication that the fruit has been mishandled or is old. Once berries begin to turn moldy, the entire batch goes bad quickly.

When fresh berries are out of season, IQF (individually quick-frozen) berries are often a perfectly fine substitute. Dried berries are a delicious addition to winter fruit compotes, stuffings, or baked goods. The following table covers a selection of berry varieties.

TOP: blueberries, raspberries, cranberries, gooseberries (with and without husk) BOTTOM: strawberries, blackberries, currants

Type	Description	Common Culinary Uses
Blackberry	Large; purplish-black; cultivated and wild; tart when under-ripe	Eaten out of hand; in baked goods
Blueberry	Small to medium; bluish-purple with dusty silver-blue "bloom"; smooth, round, juicy flesh; sweet flavor	Eaten out of hand; in baked goods, jams, dried, and to flavor vinegars
Cranberry	Small; shiny red berry, some with white blush; hard; dry and sour	Generally cooked; in relishes; sauces, jellies, juices; in breads; dried
Gooseberry	Small to medium; yellow to green; almost transparent skin; round, smooth	Generally cooked; in jellies, pies, other baked goods
Raspberry	Clusters of tiny fruits (drupes), each containing a seed; may have "hairs" on surface; red, black, or golden; sweet, juicy fruit; Dewberry is a type of raspberry	Eaten out of hand; in baked goods, syrups, purées, sauces, cordials, syrups, and to flavor vinegars
Strawberry	Range in size; red; shiny, heart-shaped, seeds on the exterior; sweet	Eaten out of hand; served with shortcakes; in baked goods, purées, jams, jellies, ice cream
Currant	Tiny, round fruit; smooth skin; range in color from white to red to black; sweet	White and red are eaten out of hand; black currants are used to make preserves, syrups, and liquors, such as cassis

Citrus Fruits

Citrus fruits are characterized by extremely juicy, segmented flesh, and skins that contain aromatic oils. Grapefruits, lemons, limes, and oranges are the most common citrus fruits. They range dramatically in size, color, and flavor.

Select citrus that is firm and heavy in relation to its size, with no soft spots. Green hues or rough brown spots generally do not affect the flavor or texture of the fruit. For oranges, it is not necessary to select fruits with brightly colored skins, as they are often dyed. When selecting grapefruits, lemons, and limes, on the other hand, look for brightly colored fruits with a finely textured skin. Citrus can be stored at room temperature for a short time, but should be refrigerated if being held for an extended period. Citrus juice is available canned, bottled, frozen, and as frozen concentrate. The table that follows covers a selection of citrus varieties.

Type	Description	Common Culinary Uses
Navel orange	Orange skin; relatively smooth; seedless; sweet (zest may be candied)	Eaten out of hand; juiced; zested
Blood orange	Thin orange skin with blush of red; pockets of dark red flesh; aromatic and sweet	Eaten out of hand; juiced; in sauces, flavoring
Mandarin orange	Several varieties, ranging in size from very small to medium; seedless or with seeds; tangerines and clementines are Mandarin varieties	Eaten out of hand
Tangerine	Orange; lightly pebbled skin; many seeds; juicy, sweet flavor	Eaten out of hand; juiced
Tangelo	Orange; slightly pebbled skin; slightly tapered at top; sweet juicy flavor	Eaten out of hand; juiced
Seville orange	Thick, rough skin; many seeds; tart, bitter flavor, astringent	Marmalade, Sauce Bigarade, candied peel, liqueurs
Lemon	Yellow-green to deep yellow skin; seeds; extremely tart flesh	Juiced; flavoring agent; zested (zest may be candied)
Meyer lemon	Round shape; smooth skin; sweeter, less acidic juice than regular lemons	Juiced; flavoring agent; baked goods; zested (zest may be candied)
Lime	Dark green; smooth skin; seedless; tart	Juiced; flavoring agent; zested (zest may be candied)
Key lime	Small; yellowish-green; round shape; tart	Juiced; flavoring agent (most famous use is Key Lime Pie)
White, red, or pink grapefruit	Yellow skin, sometimes with green blush; flesh ranges from pale yellow to deep red; seedless varieties available; sweet-tart	Eaten out of hand; juiced; flavoring agent; zested (zest may be candied)
Uniq™/Ugli™ fruit	Hybrid citrus; yellow-green, thick, loose, wrinkled skin; pink-yellow flesh; seedless	Eaten out of hand

FACING PAGE, TOP ROW, FROM LEFT TO RIGHT: Uniq™/Ugli™ fruit, tangerine, tangelo SECOND ROW, FROM LEFT TO RIGHT: navel orange, blood orange THIRD ROW, FROM LEFT TO RIGHT: white grapefruit, pink grapefruit BOTTOM ROW, FROM LEFT TO RIGHT: Meyer lemon, lemon, lime

Grapes

Technically, grapes are berries, but because they include so many varieties and have so many different uses, they are usually grouped separately. There are varieties of grapes, both with seeds and seedless, that are available for both eating and wine making.

Grapes vary greatly in color, from pale green to deep purple. Choose grapes that are plump and juicy, with smooth skins that have a pale gray film, known as bloom. Grapes should be firmly attached to their green stems. There are varieties of grapes with skin that easily slips off the fruit (Concord), and other varieties in which the skin remains firmly intact (Thompson seedless). Grapes are also dried to make raisins and currants.

Store grapes, unwashed, in the refrigerator. Grapes should be thoroughly washed and blotted dry just prior to being eaten. Grapes are best served at room temperature. The following table covers a selection of grape varieties.

Type	Description	Common Culinary Uses
Green/Red seedless	Medium sized; green; seedless; sweet, mild flavor; e.g. Thompson	Table grape; also dried as raisins
Concord	Blue-black; thick skin slips easily from flesh; sweet; contains seeds	In juices, jams, jellies, syrups, and preserves
Black	Large; deep purple skin; with or without seeds	Table grape
Red	Light to deep red, with green streaking; thin, tightly adhering skin; with or without seeds; e.g. Red Emperor	Table grape
Champagne/ Black Corinth	¼ inch in diameter; red to light purple; seedless; juicy and sweet	Table grape

FROM LEFT TO RIGHT: champagne/black Corinth, Thompson seedless, Red Emperor, black, Concord

Melons

These succulent and fragrant fruits are members of the gourd family, as are squashes and cucumbers. They come in many varieties and range from the size of an orange to that of a watermelon. The two major categories of melons are the muskmelon and the watermelon. There are two kinds of muskmelons commonly available, the cantaloupe type and the honeydew type.

Selecting melons and determining ripeness depends greatly on the type. When selecting the cantaloupe-type muskmelons, look for heavy fruits with a "full slip"—that is, a clean break from the stem—signifying that the melon ripened on the vine. When ripe, all muskmelons should become slightly soft at the stem end and give off a sweet scent. Muskmelons must be halved and seeded before they are eaten. The mildly flavored

watermelon varieties should be symmetrical, be they oblong or round in shape. Avoid those with flat sides, soft spots, or damaged rinds. A ripe watermelon should have good ground color, without any white on the underside. Unripe melons should be stored in a cool, dark place, and ripe or cut melon should be kept under refrigeration. The following table covers a selection of melon varieties.

TOP ROW FROM LEFT TO RIGHT: honeydew, seedless watermelon BOTTOM ROW FROM LEFT TO RIGHT: cantaloupe, Cavillion, Santa Claus

Type	Description	Common Culinary Uses
MUSKMELONS		
Cantaloupe	Beige netting or veining over surface of skin; flesh is pale orange colored; smooth, juicy, very sweet, and fragrant flesh	Eaten out of hand; served with cured meats and cheeses; in chilled fruit soups
Persian	Large, dark green skin with yellow netting; bright salmon-colored flesh; slightly sweet; cantaloupe-type muskmelon	Eaten out of hand
Honeydew	Somewhat oval; creamy white to yellowish rind, smooth skin; pastel green, juicy flesh; very sweet; honeydew-type muskmelon	Eaten out of hand; in chilled fruit soups; garnish; desserts
Casaba	Skin is light green to yellow-green with thick grooves; creamy colored and juicy; mild, clean, and refreshing flavor; honeydew-type muskmelon	Eaten out of hand
Crenshaw	Large, oval shaped; yellowish-green, smooth, yet ridged skin; salmon-colored flesh; fragrant, spicy flesh, extremely sweet; honeydew-type muskmelon	Eaten out of hand
WATERMELONS		
Watermelon	Ranges from a large, oblong shape to a small, round shape; rind is green with lighter stripes; watery flesh ranges from red-pink to yellow to white; shiny black, brown, or white seeds; some varieties are seedless; sweet and refreshing	Eaten out of hand; rind is pickled, seeds are roasted

Pears

Pears are to the French what apples are to the Americans. These fruits come in many varieties, ranging from round to bell shaped, spicy to sweet, and yellow to red. Unlike many other fruits, pears ripen after they are picked. This is a positive aspect because ripe pears are extremely fragile and otherwise wouldn't ship well.

Choose pears that are fragrant and unblemished. Keep unripe pears at room temperature, but refrigerate them once they are ripe. Like apples, peeled and cut pears turn brown once they are exposed to the air. Storing them in acidulated water will help prevent browning, but may alter the true flavor of the pear. The best uses for several varieties are given in the table below.

Type	Description	Common Culinary Uses
Bartlett/William	Large pear, bell shaped; ranges from green to red in color; smooth skin; juicy flesh; sweet	Eaten out of hand; poached; in preserves; used to flavor cordials
Bosc	Large pear, long neck, squat bottom; dark, russeted skin; sweet-tart flavor	Eaten out of hand; poached, baked
D'Anjou	Large pear, squat all over; green-yellow skin with green speckles, can have a red blush; sweet flavor	Eaten out of hand; poached, baked
Seckel	Small pear; golden skin with red blush; extremely firm and crisp flesh; sweet and spicy	Poached, baked, canned
Forelle	Medium pear; golden with red blush and red speckles	Eaten out of hand; poached, baked
Asian	Round; golden orange with white speckles; firm, crunchy, and juicy flesh; mild flavor	Eaten out of hand; excellent in salads

FROM LEFT TO RIGHT: Bosc, Red Bartlett/William, d'Anjou, Seckel, Forelle, Asian, Bartlett/William

Stone Fruits

Peaches, nectarines, apricots, plums, and cherries are often referred to as stone fruits because they have one large central pit, or stone. In addition to their fresh form, these fruits are also commonly available canned, frozen, and dried. Many countries produce fruit brandies, wines, and cordials flavored with peaches, cherries, and plums.

Stone fruits need to be handled delicately because their flesh has a tendency to bruise easily. Select plump fruit that is firm, but not hard, and is without soft spots. The following table covers a selection of stone fruit varieties.

Type	Description	Common Culinary Uses
Peaches	Medium to large; fuzzy skin, white to yellow-orange to red; very juicy flesh; two classifications: freestone and clingstone	Eaten out of hand; in jams and jellies, ice cream, and desserts; canned and dried
Apricots	Medium; skin is slightly fuzzy, and yellow to gold-orange with rosy patches; drier than a peach; with a sweet and slightly tart flavor	Eaten out of hand; in jams and jellies, desserts, juice; dried
Nectarines	Large; smooth, yellow and red skin; firm, but juicy flesh; sweet	Eaten out of hand; in salads and cooked desserts
Cherries	Small; range in shades from red to black; shiny skin; firm flesh; available both sweet and sour	Sweet varieties: eaten out of hand; in baked goods and syrups; dried Sour varieties: in pies, preserves, and syrups; dried
Plums	Small to medium; oval to round; skin color ranges from green to red to purple; juicy flesh; very sweet	Eaten out of hand; in baked goods, preserves; some varieties are dried as prunes
Italian plums	Small; oval; purple skin; yellow-green flesh	Eaten out of hand; in baked goods, preserves

FROM LEFT TO RIGHT: white peach, peach, nectarine, plum, Italian plum

Other Fruits

A wide variety of fruits fall in the "others" group, as they do not fit cleanly into another category. Some of these fruits are tropical, while others are grown in more temperate climates. Many of these fruits, such as the passion fruit, can be considered rare, while others are as common as the banana. The following table provides information on these uncategorized fruits.

CLOCKWISE FROM TOP CENTER: pineapple, papaya (with cut half), rhubarb, kiwifruit (with cut half), guava (with cut half), plantains, bananas, coconut, avocadoes, mango, starfruit (with cut half)

Type	Description	Common Culinary Uses
Avocado	Pear shaped; green to black leathery skin, smooth or bumpy; yellowish-green flesh; creamy, buttery texture; mild flavor	In salads, dips (guacamole), on sandwiches, in salsa
Banana	Sweet, creamy flesh encased in a yellow or red, inedible peel	Eaten out of hand; in puddings, baked goods, and other desserts
Plantain	Larger and starchier relative of the common banana; hard, green peel; potato-like flesh when unripe and becomes increasingly sweet, soft, and mottled as it ripens	Excellent fried, baked, and mashed; eaten at all stages of ripeness
Rhubarb	Long green stalks that are tinged with red; crisp texture and sour, tart flavor	In pies, tarts, and preserves
Coconut	Round; hard, brown, hairy husk; firm, creamy, white meat; thin, watery liquid in the center; processed into coconut oil, coconut milk, and dry-packaged; sweetened or unsweetened; shredded or flaked	Eaten raw or cooked; in sweet and savory preparations such as chutney, cake, curry
Fig	Small, round or bell-shaped fruit; soft, thin skin; tiny edible seeds; ranges in color from purple-black to light green; extremely sweet flavor; most common varieties are Mission and Calimyrna	Eaten out of hand; dried; in preserves; often eaten with cheese
Guava	Oval-shaped fruit; thin skin that ranges in color from yellow, to red, to almost black when ripe; most commonly available in its green, unripe state; flesh color ranges from pale yellow to bright red; extremely sweet and fragrant; available fresh, canned, frozen, as paste	Excellent for jams, preserves, and sauces; guava paste served with cheese
Kiwifruit	Small, oblong berry; fuzzy brown skin; bright green flesh; dotted with edible black seeds; soft, sweet, tart flesh	Eaten out of hand; excellent in sauces and sorbets
Mango	Round to oblong-shaped fruit; sweet, soft, bright yellow flesh; contains a single large flat seed; skin color ranges from yellow to green and red; most common variety is Tommy Atkins; available fresh, canned, frozen, as puree, nectar, and dried	Excellent for sweet sauces and sorbets as well as in chutneys; also used in its unripe, green form in salads
Pineapple	Large, cylindrical fruit; rough, diamond-patterned yellow skin; long, sword-like leaves sprouting from its top; commonly available varieties have extremely fragrant, juicy, and sweet bright yellow flesh; also available frozen, canned, candied, or dried	Eaten out of hand; grilled, juiced; in baked goods
Starfruit	Yellow to green fruit, about 3 to 5 inches in length with 5 distinctive ribs that extend outward from the center; crosscut slices resemble stars; also called Carambola	Eaten out of hand; used in fruit salads, desserts, and as a garnish

Type	Description	Common Culinary Uses
Papaya	Pear-shaped fruit about 6 inches in length; golden-yellow skin and bright pinkish-orange flesh when ripe; contains a center cavity packed with black, round, edible seeds; fragrant, sweet, silky flesh; nectar, purée, and dried also available	Eaten out of hand, both ripened and in its green state; enzyme (papain) is used to tenderize meat
Pomegranate	Fragrant, apple-shaped fruit with bright red, leathery skin; contains hundreds of tiny, red, flesh-covered, edible seeds separated into packets by thin, cream-colored membranes; very tart and sweet, juicy flavor; juice concentrate and molasses are also available	Eaten out of hand; seeds often used as a garnish or pressed for juice
Passion fruit	Egg-shaped fruit, about 3 inches long, with dimpled skin that is dark purple when ripe; contains extremely fragrant, yellow, sweet-tart flesh, flecked with edible black seeds; available fresh or pureed and frozen; canned nectar and concentrate are also available	Excellent in desserts and beverages
Persimmon	Tomato-shaped fruit with red-orange skin and flesh; tangy-sweet flavor; smooth, creamy texture when ripe (Hachiya) or softly yielding like a tomato (Fuyu); most commonly available varieties are the Hachiya and Fuyu; available fresh or puréed and frozen	Eaten out of hand; Hachiya excellent in pies and puddings; Hachiya must be fully ripened before eaten; Fuyu good in salads, eaten crisp or soft and fully ripened
Quince	Yellow-skinned fruit that looks and tastes similar to an apple and has texture similar to a pear; contains crisp white flesh that has a dry and astringent flavor	Excellent in jams, jellies, preserves, and baked items; must be cooked before eaten

Quince

Cabbage Family

The cabbage (brassica) family includes a wide range of vegetables. Some members of this family, such as cauliflower and green cabbage, are referred to as heading cabbages. Others, such as bok choy, form loose heads, while other varieties do not form a head, but are prized for their roots. Turnips and rutabagas are also members of the brassica family, but they are more commonly thought of as root vegetables. The following table covers a selection of brassica varieties.

CLOCKWISE FROM TOP CENTER: Collard greens, bok choy/Chinese white cabbage, Napa/Chinese cabbage, broccoflower, kohlrabi (white and purple), broccoli rabe/rapini, Aspiration™, Brussels sprouts, baby bok choy, kale, broccoli, Tuscan kale, red cabbage, cauliflower, Savoy cabbage

Type	Description	Common Culinary Uses
Broccoli	Deep green crown, some have purple cast; pale green, crunchy stems	Steamed, boiled, raw, sautéed, or baked in casseroles
Broccoli rabe/Rapini	Deep green; long, thin stems with small florets; leafy; strong, bitter flavor	Steamed, braised, or sautéed with olive oil, garlic, and crushed red pepper flakes
Brussels sprouts	Small, about 1 inch in diameter; round, cabbage-shaped, light green; strong flavor	Steamed, boiled, sautéed, or braised
Bok choy	Loose head; deep green leaves, white crisp stems; tender leaves; mild flavor; baby bok choy is a small variety	Salads, stir fried, steamed, or boiled
Green cabbage	Tight, round, heading cabbage; light to medium green; crisp texture; somewhat strong flavor	Steamed, braised, sautéed, fermented in sauerkraut and kimchee; raw in salads and coleslaw
Red cabbage	Tight, round, heading cabbage; deep purple to maroon; stems on individual leaves are white, giving marbled appearance when cut; crisp texture; somewhat strong flavor	Steamed, braised, or sautéed; raw in salads and coleslaw
Napa/Chinese cabbage	Elongated heading cabbage; light yellow with green tips; soft, wrinkly leaves; mild in flavor	Steamed, braised, or sautéed; raw in salads and coleslaw
Savoy cabbage	Moderately tight, round, heading cabbage; textured, wrinkly leaves; mild flavor	Raw, steamed, braised, or sautéed
Cauliflower	White, green, or purple flowering head with green leaves; somewhat strong flavor	Steamed, boiled, raw, sautéed, or baked in casseroles
Kohlrabi/ Cabbage turnip	Round, turnip-shaped bulb with stems and leaves attached; white with purple tint; tender; mildly sweet flavor	Steamed, boiled, or stir fried
Kale	Deep green, sometimes with purple hues; ruffled leaves; mild cabbage flavor.	Sautéed, boiled, or steamed; in soups
Collard greens	Large, flat, rounded green leaves; in between cabbage and kale in flavor	Steamed, sautéed, braised, or boiled with a ham hock
Turnip greens	Broad, flat green leaves; tough, coarse texture; strongly flavored	Steamed, sautéed, or braised
Aspiration™/ Broccolini™	Bright green color; long slender stalks with small florets; crunchy texture; mild, sweet flavor; a hybrid cross between chinese broccoli and broccoli	Steamed, boiled, sautéed, or grilled
Baby bok choy/ Pak Choy	Light green tender leaves; crisp stalks	Braised, in soups, stir fried, steamed

Soft-Shell Squash, Cucumber, and Eggplant

Soft-shell squash varieties, cucumbers, and eggplants are all members of the gourd family. All these vegetables are picked when they are immature to ensure a deli- cate flesh, tender seeds, and thin skins. Soft-shell squash and egg- plant varieties cook rather quickly, while cucumbers are most often eaten raw. Select soft-shell squashes, eggplants, and cucum- bers that are on the smaller side, firm, brightly colored, and without bruising. These varieties should all be refrigerated.

FROM LEFT TO RIGHT, TOP TO BOTTOM: Pattypan squash, chayote, Japanese eggplant, zucchini, standard/purple eggplant, English cucumber, yellow squash, Kirby cucumber, squash blossom, standard/slicing cucumber, white eggplant

Type	Description	Uses
CUCUMBERS		
Standard/Slicing cucumber	Long, narrow, tapering at ends; thin green skin, sometimes with pale green spotting creamy white flesh; crisp and refreshing, mild flavor	Pickled; in salads, relish, and uncooked sauces such as Raita
Kirby	Short, chubby cylinder; green skin, white flesh; deep ridges, warts; very crunchy texture; mild flavor	Eaten out of hand; excellent pickled
English/Burpless/ Hothouse/Seedless	Long, even cylinder with some ridging; no seeds; vibrant green skin; crispy texture, mild flavor	Pickled; in salads and crudités
EGGPLANT		
Standard/Purple	Rounded or elongated pear shape; deep purple-black skin with a sheen; green calyx attached at the top; off-white flesh; can be slightly bitter, especially larger vegetables	Stewed, braised, roasted, grilled, and fried; popular dishes include Ratatouille, Baba Ganoush, and Eggplant Parmesan
Japanese	Long, narrow, cylinder shape that is sometimes arched; deep purple-black striated skin with a sheen; purple to black calyx attached at the top; tender flesh; mildly sweet flavor	Stewed, braised, roasted, grilled, and fried
White	May be long or round (egg shape); milky white, sometimes with purple streaks; tougher skin; firm, smooth flesh; slightly bitter	Stewed, braised, roasted, grilled, and fried
SOFT-SHELL SQUASH		
Pattypan	Small to medium; light green to yellow, sometimes speckled or streaked with dark green; disk shape with scalloped edge; tender; mild flavor	Steamed, sautéed, and fried
Chayote/Mirliton	Medium to large; pear shape; light green, with deep "puckers" between halves; white flesh surrounding one seed; bland flavor	Steamed, sautéed, stir fried, stuffed, and fried
Crookneck	Long, bent, narrow neck, attached to a larger base; yellow skin, sometimes with bumps; light yellow flesh; delicate flavor	Steamed, sautéed, and fried
Yellow	Elongated pear shape; yellow, with cream-colored flesh; mild flavor	Steamed, sautéed, fried, and grilled
Zucchini	Narrow, cylindrical shape; green, with flecks of yellow or white; creamy flesh with green hue; mild flavor	Steamed, sautéed, fried, and grilled; in quick breads and fritters
Squash blossoms	Soft, yellow-orange flowers with a green stem; squash-like flavor, mild	Raw in salads; stuffed, baked, sautéed, fried, as garnish

Hard-Shell Squash

Hard-shell squashes, also members of the gourd family, are characterized by their hard, thick rinds and seeds. These thick skins and yellow to orange flesh require longer cooking than their soft-shelled counterparts. Select squashes that are heavy for their size, with a hard, unblemished rind. Hard-shell squashes may be stored in a cool, dark place for many weeks without deteriorating in quality.

BACK ROW, FROM LEFT TO RIGHT: Red curry squash, Blue Hubbard SECOND ROW, FROM LEFT TO RIGHT: Kabocha, cheese pumpkin, spaghetti squash THIRD ROW, FROM LEFT TO RIGHT: Sweet Dumpling, Delicata, pumpkin, Striped Eddy, Carnivale BOTTOM ROW: Jack-be-Little pumpkins (white and orange), butternut squash

Type*	Description	Common Culinary Uses
Acorn	Acorn shape with deep ridges; dark green, usually with some orange; deep orange flesh; slightly stringy texture; sweet flavor	Baked, puréed, simmered, glazed with honey or maple syrup; in soups
Butternut	Elongated pear shape; tan skin with bright orange, creamy flesh; sweet flavor	Baked, puréed, simmered, glazed with honey or maple syrup; in soups.
Hubbard	Large, dusty green to bright orange, can also be blue; very warty skin; yellow-orange flesh; grainy texture	Baked, puréed, simmered, glazed with honey or maple syrup; in soups
Pumpkin	Wide variety of pumpkins with different uses: Pie (round, bright orange, green stem), Jack-be-Little or Mini (miniature versions, white or orange), and Cheese (large, flat, beige) are common varieties	Baked, puréed, simmered, glazed with honey or maple syrup; in soups, pies, and quick breads; seeds, known as pepitas, are roasted
Spaghetti	Watermelon shape; bright yellow skin and flesh; after it is cooked, the flesh separates into strands; mild flavor	Steamed or roasted
Delicata/Sweet potato squash	Oblong shape; yellow skin with green stripes; bright yellow flesh; extremely sweet	Steamed or roasted

*There are many varieties of hard squashes available only within small regions. See the photo on facing page for some harder-to-find varieties.

Lettuce

Each of the thousands of lettuce varieties can be classified into one of the following categories: leaf, romaine, butterhead, or crisphead. Select lettuce that is crisp, never wilted or bruised. Lettuce should not be washed, cut, or torn until it is ready to serve. Store lettuce in the refrigerator, covered loosely with damp paper towels. As with most greens, it is very important to thoroughly wash lettuce, as dirt and grit tend to hide between the leaves. Never submerge lettuce in water for an extended amount of time, and be sure that it is dried well after washing (a salad spinner is great for this). The following table covers several varieties of lettuce.

CLOCKWISE FROM TOP LEFT: Iceberg, Green leaf, Red leaf, Romaine, Boston

Type	Description	Common Culinary Uses
BUTTERHEAD		
Boston	Loosely formed heads; soft, very tender leaves, vibrant green color; mild, sweet, delicate flavor	In salads, braised
Bibb	Smaller than Boston; loosely formed heads; soft, very tender leaves, vibrant green color; mild, sweet, delicate flavor	In salads, braised
CRISPHEAD		
Iceberg	Tight heading lettuce with pale green leaves; very mild flavor	In salads (shredded or served as a wedge)
Romaine	Long, cylindrical head; outer leaves are ribbed; dark green leaves, becoming lighter on the interior; outer leaves are slightly bitter, inner leaves are mild and sweet	In salads, especially Caesar Salad; braised
LEAF		
Red or Green Leaf	May be green or red-tipped; loose heading lettuce, tender, crisp leaves; mild, becoming bitter with age	In salads
Oak Leaf	Scalloping on leaves; loose heading lettuce; tender, crisp leaves; nutty flavor	In salads

Bitter Salad Greens

Bitter salad greens are those that are tender enough to be eaten in salads, but that may also be sautéed, steamed, grilled, or braised. There are many varieties that fit into this category, from green, leafy arugula, to crimson heads of radicchio. Selection criteria and handling practices for bitter salad greens are similar to those for lettuce. The following table covers several varieties of bitter salad greens.

CLOCKWISE FROM TOP LEFT: escarole, frisée, arugula, mâche/lamb's lettuce, watercress, radicchio, Belgian endive (red and white)

Type	Description	Common Culinary Uses
Arugula/Rocket	Tender leaves; rounded "teeth" on the ends of the leaves; vibrant green; peppery flavor	In salads, pesto, and soups; sautéed
Belgian endive	Tight, oblong head; white leaves with yellowish-green or red at tips; crisp leaves, mildly bitter flavor	In salads, grilled, roasted, and braised
Frisée	Thin, curly leaves; white with yellowish-green tips; mildly bitter flavor	In salads, lettuce mixes such as mesclun
Escarole	Heading lettuce; scalloped, crinkly edges on leaves; green color; slightly bitter	In salads and soups; braised and stewed
Mâche/Lamb's lettuce	Loose rosettes; thin, rounded leaves; dark green; very tender; nutty flavor	In salads; steamed
Radicchio	Round or oblong heads; firm, deep red to purple leaves, white veining; bitter flavor	In salads; grilled, sautéed, baked, and braised
Watercress	Small, scalloped leaves; dark green, crisp leaves; mustard-like, peppery flavor	In salads, sandwiches, and soups; as a garnish

Cooking Greens

Cooking greens are the edible leaves of certain plants that are often too fibrous to eat without first being sautéed, steamed, or braised.

Selection criteria and handling practices for cooking greens are similar to those for lettuce and bitter salad greens. The following table covers several varieties of cooking greens. See the Cabbage Family table on page 243 for information on kale, collard greens, and turnip greens.

CLOCKWISE FROM TOP LEFT: Swiss chard, mustard greens, beet greens, baby Swiss chard (white and red), rainbow Swiss chard, dandelion greens, spinach

Type	Description	Common Culinary Uses
Beet greens	Flat leaves; deep green, red ribbing; mild, earthy flavor	Steamed, sautéed, and braised
Dandelion greens	Narrow, tooth-edged leaves; tender, crisp; bright green; mildly bitter flavor	Salads, steamed, sautéed, and braised
Mustard greens	Scalloped, narrow leaves; dark green; crisp; peppery, mustard flavor; also available frozen and canned	Steamed, sautéed, simmered, and braised
Spinach	Leaves may be deeply lobed or flat, depending upon variety; deep green; also available frozen	In salads and sandwiches; steamed, sautéed, braised
Swiss chard	Lobed, wrinkled tender leaves; crisp stalks; dark green leaves; stems and ribs may be white, yellow, or red; mild flavor	In soups; steamed, sautéed, braised; stalks and leaves are both eaten

Mushrooms

Mushrooms are a fungus that exists in thousands of varieties. Cultivated mushrooms, commonly available today, include the familiar White mushroom and as varieties such as the portobello, cremini, shiitake, and oyster mushrooms. Wild mushrooms, prized for their concentrated, earthy flavor, include the cèpe (porcini), chanterelle, Morel, and the truffle. Knowing your purveyor is important when you have wild mushrooms on the menu, as many varieties are poisonous. Varieties of mushrooms are available canned, frozen, and dried.

Select mushrooms that are firm, without blemishes or breaks. If using varieties such as the white or cremini, the caps should be tightly closed, as opened gills are a sign of age. Conversely, when selecting portobellos, a mature cremini, it is desirable for the gills to be open, signifying a concentration of flavor. Mushrooms that are to be cooked whole should be of equal size so that they cook evenly.

Mushrooms should be stored in the refrigerator, in a single layer, covered with damp paper towels. When you want to use them, wipe mushrooms with a damp paper towel, or very quickly rinse them in cold water and drain immediately. Mushrooms should never be submerged in water, since they absorb it like a sponge and will become mushy. See the following table for information on varieties of mushrooms.

CLOCKWISE FROM TOP LEFT: maitake, oyster, portobellos, lobster, chanterelles, morels, matsutaki, white. CENTER, TOP TO BOTTOM: shiitakes, cremini

Type	Description	Common Culinary Uses
White	White to buff colored; round cap, ranges from ½ to 3 inches in diameter; "button" refers to the smallest of this variety	Raw or cooked; marinated, in sauces, soups, stews, and stuffed
Cèpe/Porcini	Pale brown; ranges from 1 to 10 inches in diameter; smooth, meaty texture; pungent flavor; available dried	Raw or cooked; marinated, in sauces, soups, and stews
Chanterelle	Golden to apricot; trumpet shaped; chewy texture; nutty flavor	Raw or cooked; marinated, in sauces, soups, and stews
Cremini	Dark brown; round cap, ranges from ½ to 2 inches in diameter; firm texture	Raw or cooked; in sauces
Enoki	White to buff; long, slender, stalk-like mushrooms; crunchy texture; mild, fruity flavor	Raw or cooked; in salads and soups, as garnish
Lobster	Deep red, mottled color	Sautéed; in sauces
Morel	Tan to very dark brown; ranges from 2 to 4 inches in height; cone-shaped, hollow cap; firm but spongy texture; earthy flavor; available dried	Sautéed; in sauces and salads; available dried
Portobello	Dark brown; opened, flat caps; ranges 3 to 6 inches in diameter; dense, meaty texture; strongly flavored	Sautéed or grilled; in sandwiches and salads
Oyster	Creamy to silvery gray; cluster of fan-shaped mushrooms; delicate texture; peppery flavor when raw, but mellows when cooked	Sautéed
Shiitake	Tan to brown; ranges 3 to 6 inches in diameter; meaty texture; earthy flavor; available dried	Sautéed, broiled, grilled; stems used in stock
Truffle	Black or off-white; irregularly shaped, wrinkled; perfumy fragrance; earthy, garlicky flavor; available canned, frozen, and as flavored oil	Served raw over pasta; used to flavor sauces and risottos
Matsutaki	Dark brown; dense, meaty texture; nutty, fragrant flavor	Braised, grilled, steamed, and fried
Maitake/ Hen-of-the-Woods	Grayish-brown; clustered, overlapping, fan-shaped caps; white stems; chewy texture; deep flavor	Sautéed; also used as a dietary supplement

Onion Family

Onions, invaluable to any kitchen, belong to the lily family. They fall into two main categories, reflecting the state in which they are used: dry (cured) and green (fresh). Green onions include scallions, leeks, and ramps. Dry onions are categorized by size and color. They can range in size from pearl to Spanish, and from white, to yellow, to red in color.

Garlic, shallots, and onions (green and dry) all share a pungent flavor and aroma. Dry onions make up half of the most fundamental aromatic combination, mirepoix. Green onions, whether cooked (leeks) or raw (scallions), impart a sweetly subtle onion flavor. Shallots and garlic are the flavoring agents in innumerable preparations.

Select dry onions, garlic, and shallots that are heavy for their size and have tight-fitting, dry, and papery skins. Green onions should be green with white bottoms. They should be crisp, not wilted. Dry onions, shallots, and garlic should be stored in a relatively cool, dry area of the kitchen in the bags or boxes in which they are received. Green onions should be refrigerated and must be thoroughly washed before they are used (leeks tend to have dirt between each layer). Chives are also a member of the onion family, though their main culinary application is similar to that of fresh herbs. See the following table for more information on onions.

CLOCKWISE FROM LEFT: leek, green onions, sweet onion, Spanish onions, shallots, boiling onions, cipollini onions, pearl onions, red pearl onions, red globe onions, gold pearl onions, garlic

Type	Description	Common Culinary Uses
DRY		
Pearl/Creamer	Small, ¾-inch diameter, oval onions; may be white or red; mild flavor	Boiled, pickled, brined; served in stews and braises; as garnish in drinks
Boiling	Small, 1-inch diameter, round onions; white or yellow skin; mild flavor	In stews and soups; pickled
Cipollini	Small, round, flattened onions; yellow papery skin; slightly sweet flavor; also available preserved in oil	Roasted, grilled; in casseroles
Globe	Medium, 1- to 4-inch diameter, round onions; may be white, yellow, or red; pungent flavor	Stews, soups, and sauces
Spanish/Jumbo	Large, 3-inch or more diameter, round onions; yellow, red, or white; mild flavor; known as Colossal when diameter exceeds 3½ inches	Aromatic in stocks, soups, sauces, braises, and stews; component of mirepoix
Sweet	Large, sometimes flattened shape; white to yellow in color; sweet flavor; varieties include Walla Walla, Vidalia, and Maui	Salads, grilled, sautéed, fried
Garlic	Small bulb, about 2 to 3 inches in diameter; papery white or red-streaked skin, encasing ½- to 1-inch-long individual cloves, also covered with papery skin; pungent flavor; Elephant garlic: more mildly flavored, can be as large as a small grapefruit.Garlic greens are also available; they are mildly flavored and are used much like scallions	Aromatic in stocks, soups, sauces, braises, stews; also roasted and puréed
Shallots	Small, 1 to 2 inches in length; usually cloves bunched together; light brown papery skin; white-purple flesh; mild flavor	Aromatic in soups, sauces, braises, stews; fried as garnish
GREEN		
Leeks	Long, thick cylinder with flat leaves; white stem end, gradually becoming dark green at tops; tender; subtle onion flavor	Aromatic in stocks, soups, sauces, braises, and stews; component of white mirepoix; sautéed, grilled, steamed, braised, fried as garnish
Ramps/Wild leeks	Long, thin cylinder with flat leaves; white stem end, sometimes with a purple hue, gradually becoming green at tops; pungent, garlicky flavor	Aromatic in stocks, soups, sauces, braises, and stews; sautéed, grilled, steamed, braised, fried as garnish
Scallions/ Green onions	Long, thin cylinder with cylindrical leaves; white stem end gradually becoming green at tops	Aromatic in stir fries; raw in salads; as garnish

Peppers

There are two basic types of peppers—sweet peppers and chiles. Sweet peppers are sometimes called bell peppers because of their shape. Sweet peppers of various colors have similar flavors, though red and yellow varieties tend to be sweeter.

Chiles, an important ingredient in many cuisines, are available in various sizes, colors, and levels of spice. Capsaicin is the compound that gives a chile its heat, and it is most potent on the white ribs inside the pepper. Generally, the hotter chiles are those that are smaller in size. It is imperative to take precautions when handling chiles; wear gloves, wash cutting surfaces and knives, and avoid contact with sensitive tissue such as the eyes. Chiles are available fresh, canned, dried (whole, flaked, and ground), and smoked. Frequently, dried and/or smoked chiles are given a name different than their fresh counterpart (e.g., chipotles).

When selecting both categories, look for firm, heavy peppers, with skin that is tight and glossy, with no puckering or wrinkling. The flesh should be relatively thick and crisp.

CLOCKWISE FROM TOP LEFT: red, yellow, and green sweet, Manzana, red and green habanero, serrano, fresno, chipotle, jalapeño, poblano, ancho, dried and fresh red bird/Thai, Marisol, Anaheim/California

Type	Description	Common Culinary Uses
Sweet peppers	Bell shaped; 3 to 5 inches long and 2 to 4 inches wide; green, red, yellow, or purple; crisp, juicy flesh; mild, sweet flavor; roasted peppers are available canned and bottled	In salads; raw, sautéed, grilled, roasted, and stuffed
CHILES/HOT PEPPERS (listed in order from mild to hot)		
Anaheim/California	Long, narrow, tapered; green; sweet, mild flavor; red variety is known as Colorado; also available dried, called Marisol	In salsa, stuffed
Poblano	Large; tapered, flattened shape; 4 to 5 inches long, 3 inches wide; very dark green, sometimes with a black hue; mild flavor; also available dried, called Ancho or Mulato	Stuffed, as in Chiles Rellenos
Fresno	Small to medium; tapered chile; 2 to 3 inches long; deep green or red; range from mild to medium hot	In rice, salads, sauces, salsa
Jalapeño	Small to medium, tapered chile; 2 inches long, ¾ inch wide; deep green or red; range from hot to very hot; available canned and bottled; smoked and dried called Chipotles	In rice, salads, sauces and salsa; stuffed
Serrano	Small, skinny; 1½ inches long; dark green to red; very hot; also available canned in oil or pickled; dried, in whole or powdered form, called chile seco	In sauces and salsa
Thai	Tiny, thin; 1 inch long, ¼ inch wide; green to red; very hot; also available dried, called Bird chiles	In sauces and stir fries
Habanero	Small; lantern shaped; pale green to orange in color; extremely hot; a similar variety is the Scotch Bonnet; also available dried	In sauces, meat rubs, bottled condiments
Manzana	Black seeds in a pod that pull away from the flesh; available in red, yellow, and green; usually 1½ to 2 inches long; similar in heat to habanero peppers	In sauces, meat rubs, bottled condiments

Pod and Seed Vegetables

This group includes fresh legumes (peas, beans, and bean sprouts), as well as corn and okra. All varieties are best eaten young, when they are at their sweetest and most tender stage. If possible, purchase pod and seed vegetables from local growers to minimize the amount of time between picking and serving.

This is especially important with peas and corn.

Some fresh peas and beans are eaten whole, when the pods are still fleshy and tender—for example, sugar snap peas, snow peas, green beans, and wax beans.

In other cases, the peas or beans (such as limas, Scarlet runners, and black-eyed peas) are removed from their inedible pods. Select vegetables that are crisp, brightly colored, and free of discoloration.

Peas, beans, and corn are also available dried, as discussed in Chapter 13.

CLOCKWISE FROM BOTTOM LEFT: yellow Romano, Chinese long/yard long, haricots verts, green, corn, edamame, green Romano, sugar snap, fava, snow, green/English/garden peas

Type	Description	Common Culinary Uses
Corn	Papery husk surrounding silk-like hair and long, thick cobs; yellow and/or white kernels; juicy and sweet; commonly available canned and frozen	Boiled, steamed, and grilled; often cut off the cob for soups, creamed corn, succotash, and other side dishes
BEANS		
Green	Long, thin, edible pods containing small seeds; dull green color; similar varieties include a pale yellow (wax bean) or purple (Burgundy bean, which turns green when cooked); green beans are commonly available canned and frozen	Boiled, steamed, sautéed, and roasted
Haricots verts/ French green bean	Long, very thin, edible pods containing small seeds; dull green, velvety skin	Boiled, steamed, sautéed, and roasted
Romano	Wide, flat-looking string beans; edible pods; dull green color; more pronounced flavor	Boiled, steamed, sautéed, and roasted
Chinese long bean/ Yard-long bean	¼ inch thick, 1½ to 3 feet long; edible pods containing small seeds; dull green, velvety skin; flexible texture	Sautéed and stir fried
Lima	Long, large, inedible pods; large, plump, kidney-shaped beans; green pods; light green beans; known as butter beans in the southern United States; also available frozen, canned, and dried	Boiled and sautéed; puréed; served hot or cold, in succotash
Fava	Long, large, inedible green pods; large, flat, kidney-shaped beans; a light green, tough skin must be peeled away to reveal the light green bean; also available dried	Boiled and sautéed; puréed; served hot or cold
Cranberry	Large, inedible, light tan pod, flecked with red; off-white and red-splotched beans; nutty flavor; available dried	Boiled and sautéed; puréed; served hot or cold; in soup
Edamame/Green soy bean	1 to 2 inches long; fuzzy, green pods containing green beans; sweet flavor	Boiled and steamed, as a snack or appetizer
PEAS		
Green/English/Garden	Tapered, rounded, inedible green pods; small, round, shiny, light green peas; sweet flavor	Steamed and stewed; chilled and puréed in soups
Snow	Thin, flat, edible, green pod, containing tiny seeds; crisp, sweet flavor	Steamed, stir fried, and eaten raw
Sugar Snap	Plump, edible deep green pod containing small peas; crunchy; sweet flavor	Steamed, stir fried, and eaten raw

Root Vegetables

Roots serve as a food storage area for plants; therefore, they are rich in sugars, starches, vitamins, and minerals. Root vegetables (such as beets, carrots, and turnips) are directly attached to the plant via leaves or leaf stems. Roots primarily move nutrients and moisture to the tops of the plant.

Roots vegetables should be stored dry and unpeeled. If they come with greens attached, these should be healthy in appearance at the time of purchase and cut off as soon as possible thereafter. When properly stored, most root vegetables will retain good quality for several weeks.

CLOCKWISE FROM TOP LEFT: celery root, yellow turnip/rutabaga, white turnip, baby white turnips, large gold beets (with cut half), baby Candystripe beets (with cut halves), horseradish, daikon (outside), salsify, parsnips, baby carrots, Taro root (with cut half), baby gold beets (with cut half), large red beets (with cut half), baby red beets, lotus root (center)

Type	Description	Common Culinary Uses
Carrot	Long, thin, tapered root; orange, yellow, or purple, often with green feathery tops; crunchy, sweet flesh; baby carrots commonly available	Component of mirepoix; boiled, steamed, sautéed, roasted, glazed; raw in salads and crudité platters
Celery root	Light brown; bumpy, round; white flesh	Boiled or roasted; served in soups, stews, and casseroles
Lotus root	Reddish-brown skin; white flesh	Boiled, creamed, in soups
Taro	Brown rough skin; white starchy flesh	Boiled, creamed, in soups and stews
Parsnip	Carrot shaped; white skin, flecked with brown; white flesh; creamy texture; sweet flavor	Component of white mirepoix; boiled, steamed, sautéed, roasted
Salsify/Oyster plant	Long, thin, stick-shaped; black, dull skin, white flesh; mild oyster flavor	Flavoring for stir fries, soups, sauces
Turnip	Purple to white skin; white flesh; round	Steamed, boiled, sautéed; in soup; raw in salads
Purple-topped/ White turnips	Round, ranging from 1 to 4 inches in diameter; white skin with purple top, white flesh; mild, sweet flavor	Steamed, boiled, roasted, fried, puréed; popular in Caribbean cuisine
Rutabaga/Yellow turnip	Large, round, 3 to 5 inches in diameter; yellow skin and flesh; firm, sweet flesh	Steamed and boiled; mashed or puréed; popular in Caribbean, Latin American, and African cuisines
Radishes	Red skin; round; white flesh	Boiled, creamed, in soups
Standard beet	Small, round, or elongated; red, pink, purple, white, or striped; green, leafy tops (also available cello-packed without tops); crisp, peppery flavor	Boiled, roasted; served hot and cold; in salads; glazed, pickled; in soup (Borscht)
Daikon	Carrot-shaped, up to 15 inches in length, and 3 inches wide; white skin, white flesh; crisp and juicy, mild flavor	Raw in salads; grilled, baked, boiled, creamed; in soups and stews

Tubers

Tubers, which include a variety of miscellaneous vegetables such as the Jerusalem artichoke and jícama as well as the entire family of potatoes, are vegetables that are connected to the root system by an underground stem and are not, therefore, connected directly to the plant, as are roots. Tubers act to store nutrients and moisture for the plant's reproductive capability. Select tubers that are firm and the appropriate size and shape to their type. To retain quality, tubers should be stored dry and unpeeled, away from excess heat and light, and in a well-ventilated area. When exposed to moisture or heat, tubers begin to sprout and wrinkle.

The tuberous potato includes sweet potatoes/yams for culinary purposes (though of another botanical classification). Though potatoes are remarkably versatile in their cooking media, there are types that work best for each cooking method.

Potatoes are separated into categories based on starch content, and subsequently divided according to size (A,B,C) and skin color (white, red, yellow, purple). Size A potatoes range from 1⅞ to 2½ inches, size B range from 1½ to 2¼ inches, and size C must be less than 1¼ inches. New potatoes are those of any color that are recently harvested and thin-skinned. Most size C potatoes are marketed as creamer potatoes.

TOP ROW, FROM LEFT TO RIGHT: chef potato, sweet potatoes, Boniato SECOND ROW, FROM LEFT TO RIGHT: Russet potatoes (50 and 100 count), yellow potatoes, jícama THIRD ROW, FROM LEFT TO RIGHT: Cassava/Yuca, red potatoes, purple potatoes, galangal BOTTOM ROW, FROM LEFT TO RIGHT: Fingerling potatoes, white potatoes, ginger, sunchokes

Type	Description	Common Culinary Uses
Cassava/Yuca/Manioc	6 to 12 inches in length, 2 to 3 inches in diameter; dark brown skin, white flesh; sweet flavor; commonly available dried, ground (tapioca flour), and as bottled juice	Flavoring for stir fries, soups, sauces, desserts (tapioca), and beverages (tea, ginger ale); candied, pickled. Note that bitter cassava is poisonous unless properly cooked.
Ginger	Gnarled, rough rhizome; light brown skin, yellowish-white flesh; fibrous, but juicy; spicy, with subtle sweetness; commonly available dried, ground, and as bottled juice	Flavoring for stir fries, soups, sauces, desserts, and beverages (tea, ginger ale); candied, pickled
Galangal	Resembles ginger, with lighter colored flesh; very peppery and spicy	Flavoring for stir fries, soups, sauces
Jícama	Large, round; brown skin, white flesh; crisp and crunchy; mild, sweet flavor	Steamed, boiled, sautéed; raw in salads, slaws, and crudités
Sunchoke/ Jerusalem artichoke	Similar in appearance to ginger; brown skin, white flesh; crisp, sweet, nutty flavor	Steamed, boiled, sautéed; in soup; raw in salads
Boniato	Large, up to 1 foot in length; oblong shape; reddish-brown skin, white flesh; sweet flesh	Steamed, boiled, roasted, fried, puréed
POTATOES		
Chef	Ranges from 2½ to 3½ inches in diameter and 3 to 4 inches in length; firm, round; light tan skin, off-white flesh; moderate to high moisture and starch content; smooth, shallow eyes	Boiled, in potato salad
Russet/Baking/Idaho	Oblong, about 5 inches long, 3 inches in diameter; brown, coarse skin, white flesh; low moisture and high starch content	Baked, fried, puréed, mashed
Red	Red skin, off-white flesh; Huckleberry is an heirloom variety with red flesh	Boiled, roasted; in potato salad
Yellow	Yellowish-tan skin, buttery golden flesh; Yukon Gold and Yellow Finn are two varieties available	Baked, puréed; in casseroles, salads
White	Tan skin and white flesh	Baked, puréed; in casseroles, salads
Purple	Deep purple skin, off-white or purple flesh; Peruvian Purple is an heirloom variety	Salads, home fries, other preparations to showcase color and flavor
Fingerling	Small, finger-like; skin color ranges from tan to red; flesh can be off-white or yellow; Russian Banana is an heirloom variety	Boiled, roasted
Sweet potato/Yam	Tan or light to deep orange skin, moist flesh; may be rounded or tapered; dense texture; quite sweet	Roasted, boiled, puréed; used in casseroles, soups, pies

Shoots and Stalks

This family consists of plants that produce shoots and stalks used as vegetables. Artichokes (thistle-like plants that are members of the aster family), asparagus (another member of the lily family), celery, fennel, and fiddleheads (which are part of the growth cycle of a fern) are examples. The stalks should be firm, fleshy, and full, with no evidence of browning or wilting. Store these vegetables in the refrigerator, and wash just prior to cooking them.

CLOCKWISE FROM TOP LEFT: artichokes (baby and jumbo), fennel, fiddlehead ferns, asparagus, celery, white asparagus

Type	Description	Common Culinary Uses
Asparagus	Tall, slender stalks; green with purple-hued tips or white; skinnier asparagus usually more tender	Steamed, sautéed, roasted, and grilled; used in soups
Fennel	Very pale green bulb, with stalks and bright green fronds; crunchy; anise flavored	Raw in salads; sautéed, blanched, and roasted; fronds are used in salads or as garnish
Fiddlehead fern	Small, tightly wound spirals; deep green color; chewy texture; similar flavor to asparagus	Raw in salads; sautéed, steamed, and boiled
Celery	Long stalks, bunched together with leaves on top; light green color; crunchy texture; mild but distinct flavor	Component of mirepoix; raw in salads; in soups or braised; leaves are used in salads or as garnish
Artichokes	Range in size from baby to jumbo; green, tough outer leaves; heart is tender, with a creamy texture; sweet flavor; artichoke hearts are commonly available canned, packed in oil, and frozen	Jumbo artichokes: stuffed or steamed; baby artichokes: served whole, sautéed, fried, roasted, or marinated

Tomatoes

These universal vegetables are actually a fruit. They are grown in hundreds of varieties, in colors from green to yellow to bright red. Basic types include small, round cherry tomatoes, oblong plum tomatoes, and large standard tomatoes; all of which are available in various colors. All have smooth, shiny skin, juicy flesh, and small, edible seeds. Most tomatoes grown commercially are picked unripe and allowed to ripen in transit, though many chefs prefer to find locally grown varieties that are ripened on the vine. There has been a recent surge in demand for the heirloom species, such as the Cherokee Purple and Green Zebra.

Select brightly colored tomatoes that are free of soft spots and blemishes. They should be heavy for their size, but not overly firm. Tomatoes should not be refrigerated because the cold makes the texture mushy and seizes the flavor and halts ripening. Tomatoes may be purchased in numerous forms, including canned, sun-dried, purée, paste, and diced. The following table covers several varieties of tomatoes, including their relative, the tomatillo.

BACK ROW, FROM LEFT TO RIGHT: tomatillos, heirloom Aunt Ruby's German Green, heirloom Striped German, standard/beefsteak, yellow, plum/Roma, cherry FRONT ROW, FROM LEFT TO RIGHT: heirloom Purple Cherokee, yellow grape, grape, yellow pear, pear

Type	Description	Common Culinary Uses
Standard/Beefsteak	Large, round or oval; deep red or yellow; juicy; sweet	Raw in salads and sandwiches; cooked in sauces, braises, and stews
Plum/Italian plum/ Roma	Medium, egg shaped; red or yellow; greater proportion of flesh; sweet	In sauces, purées, soups, and other cooked dishes; oven roasted
Cherry	Small, 1 inch in diameter; red or yellow; juicy; sweet	Raw in salads and crudité platters
Currant/Cranberry	Very small, ½ to ¾ inch in diameter; red or yellow; crisp, sweet	Raw in salads; specialty item
Pear tomatoes	Small, pear shaped; red or yellow; juicy, sweet	Raw in salads and crudité platters
Heirloom (Brandywine, Marvel Striped, Purple Calabash)	Ranging in size and color from small, green stripes to large pinkish-purple; beautiful, often oddly shaped; juicy and sweet	Raw in salads; cooked in soups and sauces
Tomatillos	Medium, 1 to 2 inches in diameter, round; green or purple with brown papery husk; firm; tart, fruity flavor	Raw in salads and salsas; cooked in sauces; popular in Mexican and Southwestern cuisines

Herbs

FACING PAGE, CLOCKWISE FROM TOP LEFT: curly parsley, flat-leaf parsley, purple basil, mint, basil, chervil, sorrel, cilantro, Thai basil

TOP ROW, FROM LEFT TO RIGHT: chives, rosemary, curry leaves
SECOND ROW, FROM LEFT TO RIGHT: lemongrass, tarragon, lemon thyme,
sage, marjoram BOTTOM ROW, FROM LEFT TO RIGHT: thyme, dill, oregano

Type	Description	Common Culinary Uses
Basil	Small to large, oval, pointed leaves; green or purple; delicate leaves; pungent, licorice-like flavor; varieties include Opal, Lemon, and Thai basil; also available dried	Flavoring for sauces, dressings, infused oils, and vinegars; pesto sauce; popular in Mediterranean cuisine
Bay leaf/Laurel leaf	Smooth, oval leaves; green; aromatic; most commonly available dried	Flavoring for soups, stews, stocks, sauces, and grain dishes
Chervil	Small, curly leaves; green; delicate texture; anise flavor; also available dried	Component of "fines herbes"; garnish
Chives	Long, thin; bright green; mild onion flavor	Flavoring for salads and cream cheese; garnish; component of "fines herbes"
Cilantro/Chinese parsley/Coriander	Similar shape to Flat-leaf parsley; green; delicate leaves; fresh, clean flavor	Flavoring for salsa and uncooked sauces
Curry leaves	Small to medium size; pointed oval; dark green; mild, aromatic flavor	Stir fry, curry
Dill	Long, feather-like leaves; green; distinct flavor; also available dried	Flavoring for salads, sauces, stews, braises
Lemongrass	Long blades with rough surface; pale yellow green	Flavoring for soups, stocks, stir frys, or steamed preparations
Marjoram	Small, oval leaves; pale green; mild, similar flavor to oregano; commonly available dried	Flavoring for lamb and vegetable dishes
Mint	Pointed, textured leaves; pale green to bright green; leaf size and strength varies with type; varieties include Peppermint, Spearmint, and Chocolate mint	Flavoring sweet dishes, sauces, and beverages; garnish for desserts; mint jelly is an accompaniment to lamb
Oregano	Small, oval leaves; pale green; pungent flavor; Mexican and Mediterranean varieties are available; commonly available dried	Flavoring for tomato-based dishes
Parsley	Curly or flat leaves; pointed, scalloped edges; bright green; clean tasting; Flat-leaf parsley is also known as Italian parsley; commonly available dried	Flavoring for sauces, stocks, soups, dressings; component of "fines herbes"; garnish; used in bouquet garni and sachet d'épices
Rosemary	Pine needle–shaped leaves, woody stem; grayish, deep green color; strong pine aroma and flavor; commonly available dried	Flavoring for grilled foods (lamb) and marinades; popular in Mediterranean cuisine; branch-like stems are used as skewers
Sage	Thin, oval, velvety leaves; grayish-green color; musty flavor; varieties include Pineapple sage; commonly available dried, both crumbled and ground	Flavoring for stuffing, sausage, and stews
Savory	Oblong leaves; dark green; soft, fuzzy texture; commonly available dried	Flavoring for pâtés, stuffing; used to make poultry seasoning
Tarragon	Thin, pointed leaves; dark green; delicate texture; anise flavor; commonly available dried	Flavoring for Béarnaise sauce; component of "fines herbes"
Thyme	Very small leaves; woody stem; deep green color; varieties include Garden thyme, Lemon thyme, and Wild thyme; commonly available dried	Flavoring for soups, stocks, sauces, stews, braises, and roasted items; used in bouquet garni and sachet d'épices

Chapter Twelve

Dairy and Egg Purchasing and Identification

A concentrated source of many nutrients, dairy products and eggs can be found on almost any menu, both on their own and as key ingredients in many preparations. Béchamel sauce, for example, has a milk base. Cream, crème fraîche, sour cream, and yogurt are used to prepare salad dressings and in many baked goods. Butter is used as a chief ingredient in numerous baked goods and as a cooking fat. Cheese may be served as a separate course with fruit, or as part of another dish. Eggs appear on their own as well as in breakfast dishes, dessert soufflés, and numerous sauces.

Purchasing and Storage

Dairy products and eggs are highly perishable; for these reasons, careful purchasing and storage procedures are extremely important.

Milk and cream containers are customarily dated to indicate how long the contents will remain fresh. The freshness periods vary between each container; therefore, to avoid contamination, milk and cream from different containers should never be combined. Unfortunately, detecting spoilage by simply smelling or tasting unheated milk is often impossible. When used in hot dishes, milk or cream should be brought to a boil before adding it to other ingredients. If milk curdles, it should not be used.

When considering storage arrangements for dairy products, flavor transfer is a particular concern. Milk, cream, and butter should be stored away from foods with strong odors, such as onions. Cheeses should be carefully wrapped to maintain moistness, and to prevent flavor transfer to and from other foods.

Eggs should be refrigerated and the stock rotated to ensure that only fresh, wholesome eggs are served. All eggs should be inspected carefully upon delivery, making sure that shells are clean and free of cracks. Eggs with broken shells should be discarded because of the high risk of contamination.

Dairy Products

Milk

Milk is a key ingredient in most kitchens, whether it is served as a beverage or used as a component in various dishes. U.S. federal regulations govern how milk is produced and sold to ensure that it is clean and safe to consume. Most milk sold in the United States has been pasteurized. In pasteurization, the milk is heated to 145°F/63°C for 30 minutes or to 161°F/72°C for 15 seconds, in order to kill bacteria or other organisms that could cause infection or contamination. Milk products with a higher percentage of milk fat than whole milk are heated to either 150°F/66°C for 30 minutes or to 166°F/74°C for 30 seconds for ultrapasteurization.

The date stamped on milk and cream cartons can be seven, ten, or sixteen days from the point of pasteurization. It is an indicator of how long the unopened product will remain fresh and wholesome, assuming that it has been properly stored and handled.

Generally, milk is homogenized, which means that it has been forced through an ultrafine mesh at high pressure in order to break up the fat globules it contains. This fat is then dispersed evenly throughout the milk, preventing it from rising to the surface. Milk may also be fortified with vitamins A and D. Low-fat and skim milk are almost always fortified, because removing the fat also removes fat-soluble vitamins.

State and local government standards for milk are fairly consistent. Milk products are carefully inspected before and after processing. Farms and animals (cows, sheep, and goats) are also inspected, to ensure that sanitary conditions are upheld. Milk that has been properly produced and processed is labeled Grade A.

Milk comes in various forms and is classified according to its percentage of fat and milk solids. The table on page 275 describes available forms of milk and cream and their common culinary uses.

Cream

Milk, as it comes from the cow, goat, or sheep, contains a certain percentage of fat, known as *milk fat* or *butterfat*. Originally, milk was allowed to settle long enough for the cream, which is lighter than the milk, to rise to the surface. Today, a centrifuge is used to spin the milk. The cream is driven to the center, where it can be easily drawn off, leaving the milk behind.

Cream, like milk, is homogenized and pasteurized, and may also be stabilized to help extend shelf life. Some chefs prefer cream that has not been stabilized or ultrapasteurized, because they believe it will whip to a greater volume. Two forms of cream are used in most kitchens: heavy (whipping) cream and light cream. Half-and-half, a combination of whole milk and cream, does not contain enough milk fat to be considered a true cream; its milk fat content is approximately 10.5 percent. See the table on page 275.

Forms of Milk and Cream

Type	Description*	Common Culinary Uses
Nonfat or skim milk	Contains less than 0.25% milk fat	Beverage; enriching dishes
Reduced-fat milk	Contains 1 or 2% milk fat, labeled accordingly	Beverage; enriching dishes
Whole milk	Contains 3.50% milk fat	Béchamel sauce; beverage; enriching dishes
Half-and-half	Contains 10.50% milk fat	Table or coffee cream; enriching soups and sauces
Light cream	Contains 18% milk fat	Table or coffee cream; enriching soups and sauces
Whipping cream	Contains 34% milk fat	Whipped cream, cold mousses; enriching soups and sauces
Heavy cream	Contains 36% milk fat	Whipped cream, cold mousses; enriching soups and sauces
Powdered or dry milk	Milk from which water is completely removed; made from either whole or skim milk and labeled accordingly	In baked goods, charcuterie, and drink mixes
Evaporated milk	Milk that has been heated in a vacuum to remove 60% of its water; may be made from whole or skim milk and is labeled accordingly	Enriching custards and sauces
Condensed milk	Evaporated milk that has been sweetened	Candies, pies, puddings, and baked goods
Yogurt	Contains less than 0.25% to 3.50% milk fat, labeled accordingly	With fruit; in soups, sauces, baked goods and desserts
Sour cream	Contains 18% milk fat	Enriching soups and sauces; in baked goods and desserts

* The fat percentages given here are minimums required by FDA labeling regulations.
Some products, such as heavy cream, may contain a higher percentage of milk fat.

Ice Cream

In order to meet government standards, any product labeled as ice cream must contain a certain amount of milk fat. For vanilla, it is no less than 10 percent. For any other flavor, the requirement is 8 percent. Stabilizers can make up no more than 2 percent of ice cream. Frozen dairy foods that contain less fat must be labeled as ice milk. Premium ice cream may contain several times more fat than is required by these standards. The richest ice creams have a custard base (a mixture of cream and/or milk and eggs), which gives them a dense, smooth texture.

When ice cream melts at room temperature there should be no separation. The appearance of "weeping" in melting ice cream indicates an excessive amount of stabilizers.

Other frozen desserts similar to ice cream include gelato, sherbet, sorbet, frozen yogurt, and frozen desserts made with soy or rice milk. Gelato is Italian for "ice cream"; though similar, gelato contains less air than American ice cream, giving it a creamier texture. Sherbet does not contain cream, so it is far lower in butterfat than ice cream; however, it does contain a relatively high percentage of sugar in order to achieve the correct texture and consistency when frozen. Some sherbets contain a percentage of either eggs or milk, or both. Although the word sherbet is the closest English translation of the French word *sorbet,* sorbets are commonly understood to contain no milk.

Soy and rice milk frozen desserts and frozen yogurt often contain stabilizers. They may be lower in total fat than ice cream, or even fat-free, but some brands are still high in calories because of a high sugar content.

Test a variety of these products to determine which brands offer the best quality for the best price. Refer to Chapter 37 for information about preparing frozen desserts in your own kitchen.

Butter

Anyone who has accidentally overwhipped cream has been well on the way to producing butter. Historically, butter was churned by hand. Today it is made mechanically by high-speed mixing of cream that contains between 30 and 45 percent milk fat. Eventually, the milk fat clumps together, separating out into a solid mass, which is butter; the fluid that remains is referred to as buttermilk (most buttermilk sold today, however, is nonfat milk that has been cultured).

The best-quality butter has a sweet flavor, similar to very fresh heavy cream. If salt has been added, it should be barely detectable. The color of butter will vary depending upon the breed of cow and time of year, but is usually a pale yellow.

The designation *sweet butter* indicates only that the butter is made from sweet cream (as opposed to sour). If unsalted butter is desired, be sure that the word *unsalted* appears on the package.

Salted butter may contain a maximum of 2 percent salt. The salt can aid in extending butter's shelf life, but can also mask a slightly "old" flavor or aroma. Old butter will take on a very faint cheese flavor and aroma, especially when heated. As it continues to deteriorate, the flavor and aroma can become quite pronounced and extremely unpleasant, much like sour or curdled milk.

The best-quality butter, labeled Grade AA, is made from sweet cream and has the best flavor, color, aroma, and texture. Grade A butter also is of excellent quality. Both grades AA and A contain a minimum of 80 percent fat. Grade B may have a slightly acidic taste, as it is made from sour cream.

Fermented and Cultured Milk Products

Yogurt, sour cream, crème fraîche, and buttermilk are all produced by inoculating milk or cream with a bacterial strain that causes fermentation to begin. The fermentation process thickens the milk and gives it a pleasantly sour flavor.

Yogurt is made by introducing the proper culture into milk (whole, low-fat, or nonfat may be used). Available in a variety of container sizes, yogurt can be purchased plain or flavored with different fruits, honey, coffee, or other ingredients.

Sour cream is a cultured sweet cream that contains about 18 percent milk fat. It comes in containers of various sizes, beginning with a half pint. Low-fat and nonfat versions of sour cream are available.

Crème fraîche is similar to sour cream but has a slightly more rounded flavor, with less bite. It is often preferable in cooking because it tends to curdle less readily than sour cream when used in hot dishes. This product is made from heavy cream with a butterfat content of approximately 30 percent. The high butterfat content helps account for its higher cost.

Buttermilk, strictly speaking, is the by-product of churned butter. Most buttermilk sold today is actually nonfat or reduced-fat milk to which a bacterial strain has been added. Usually sold in pints or quarts, buttermilk is also available as a dried powder for baking uses.

Cheese

The variety of cheeses produced throughout the world is extensive, ranging from mild, fresh cheeses (pot cheese or cottage cheese) to strongly flavored, blue-veined cheeses (Roquefort or Gorgonzola) and hard grating cheeses (Parmigiano-Reggiano or dry Monterey Jack). Some cheeses are excellent for cooking, while others are best served on their own.

The name of a cheese can be derived from place of origin, manufacturing process, or type of milk or ingredient. Pecorino cheeses are an excellent illustration of how a cheese is named. Pecorino denotes that the cheese is made of sheep's milk; Pecorino Romano and Pecorino Mugello are sheep's milk cheeses from nearby Rome and Mugello, respectively. Cheese is made from a variety of different milks—cow's milk, goat's milk, sheep's milk, and even buffalo's milk. The type of milk used will help to determine the cheese's ultimate flavor and texture.

Most cheeses are made through the following procedure: Milk is combined with the appropriate starter (either rennet, which contains an enzyme, or an acid such as tartaric acid or lemon juice), causing the milk solids to coagulate into curds. The remaining liquid is known as the whey. The curds are then processed in various ways, depending on the type of cheese desired. They may be drained and used immediately, as fresh cheese, or they may be pressed, shaped, inoculated with a special mold, and aged.

Natural cheeses are considered "living" in much the same way that wine is considered living. The cheese will continue to grow, developing or aging to maturity (ripening), and finally spoiling (overripening). Processed or pasteurized cheeses and cheese foods, on the other hand, do not ripen and their character will not change.

Cheeses may be grouped according to the type of milk from which they are made, texture, age, or ripening process. This book categorizes cheese as Fresh Cheeses, Soft/Rind-Ripened Cheeses, Semisoft Cheeses, Hard Cheeses, Grating Cheeses, and Blue-Veined Cheeses. See the tables on pages 279 to 289.

Fresh Cheeses

These cheeses are moist and very soft. They have a flavor that is generally termed mild, but fresh cheese made from goat's or sheep's milk may be slightly tangy and strong. Fresh cheeses are unripened, high in moisture, and generally have a fresh, creamy, clean flavor. They are typically the most perishable of cheeses and are sometimes held in brines.

CLOCKWISE FROM TOP LEFT: cheese curd, soft ash goat cheese, queso fresco, feta, farmer's cheese, Boursin, ricotta, cottage cheese, mascarpone

Variety	Description	Common Culinary Uses
Chèvre	Goat's milk; white block, pyramid, button, wheel, or log; mild to tangy (depending on age), may be flavored with herbs or peppercorns; soft to crumbly (depending on age); also known as goat cheese; Montrachet is a popular variety	Spreads; fillings; in salads
Cottage cheese	Whole or skim cow's milk; packaged in containers; white curds; mild; soft, moist	With fruit; in dips
Cream cheese	Whole cow's milk, plus cream; white block; mild, slightly tangy; soft, creamy; also known as Neufchâtel in many of the United States (with a lower fat content), though Neufchâtel is a different cheese in France	Spreads; cooking ingredient; in cheesecake; in dips
Feta	Sheep's, goat's, or cow's milk; white block; tangy, salty; soft, crumbly	In salads; filling for Spanakopita
Fromage blanc	Whole or skim cow's milk; white; mild, tangy; soft, slightly crumbly	Cooking ingredient
Mascarpone	Cow's cream; formless, packaged in containers; pale yellow; buttery, sweet, rich; soft, smooth	With fruit; in tiramisu; to enrich dishes
Mozzarella	Whole or skim cow's or buffalo's milk; irregular sphere; white, greenish-yellow tint; mild; tender to slightly elastic (depending on age); may be smoked	Pizza, pasta; with tomatoes and basil in a Caprese salad
Ricotta	Whole, skim, or low-fat cow's milk; soft, white curds; mild; moist to slightly dry; grainy; often made as a by-product of cheese making by adding rennet or acid or both to the whey after heating	Cooking ingredient; desserts; filling for cannoli; makes excellent cheesecake
Farmer's cheese	Cow's milk; white, curdless; firm enough to cut; mild; grainy, spoonable	With fresh fruit and vegetables; dips, desserts, pasta
Boursin	Whole cow's milk and cream; white rounds; flavored or herbed cream cheese spread; smooth	Spreads
Queso fresco	Cow's milk; off-white to white rounds; mild, salty; similar to ricotta or farmer's cheese; crumbly, slightly grainy	Topping or filling for many Mexican dishes

Soft/Rind-Ripened Cheeses

Soft/rind-ripened cheeses usually have a surface mold. This soft, velvety skin is often edible, though some people find it too strong to enjoy. The cheese ripens from the outside to the center. When fully ripe, a soft cheese should be nearly runny, with a full flavor. These cheeses are typically sprayed or dusted with a mold and then allowed to ripen. Soft ripened cheeses are available with varying degrees of richness. For example, single, double, and triple cream cheeses have 50, 60, and 70 percent butterfat, respectively.

CLOCKWISE FROM TOP LEFT: Pont l'Évêque, Taleggio, Reblochon, Explorateur, Hudson Valley Camembert, Epoisses, Brie (in center)

Variety	Description	Common Culinary Uses
Brie	Pasteurized whole or skim cow's and goat's milk, sometimes cream; light yellow wheels; buttery, pungent; soft, smooth, with edible rind, creamy	Sandwiches, salads; table cheese
Camembert	Raw or pasteurized whole cow's and goat's milk; light yellow disk; mild, mushroom-like flavor; soft, creamy, with edible rind	Sandwiches; table cheese
Explorateur	Whole cow's milk and cream; pale yellow barrels, disks, or wheels; rich, mild; soft, creamy, smooth	Table cheese; excellent with Champagne
Limburger	Whole or low-fat cow's milk; light yellow block, brown exterior; very strong flavor and aroma, salty; soft, smooth, waxy	Table cheese, with fruit and vegetables
Pont l'Évêque	Whole cow's milk; light yellow square; piquant, strong aroma; soft, supple, with small holes and edible golden-yellow crust; washed rind	Dessert, crêpes, salads; table cheese
Taleggio	Raw cow's milk; light yellow square; tart, salty, buttery, and powerful (depending on age); has some small holes; washed rind	Salads; cooking ingredient; table cheese
Epoisses	Cow's milk; blonde, almost straw-colored disks; rich, huge flavor; pleasantly smelly, barnyard-like aroma; smooth; washed rind	Table cheese; dish accompaniment
Reblochon	Cow's milk; ivory disk; sweet, powerful, nutty; creamy, velvety; washed rind	Table cheese, with fruit or bread

Semisoft Cheeses

Semisoft cheeses are more solid than soft cheeses; while they do not grate easily, they are ideal for slicing. An inedible wax rind may be used to coat the cheese, in order to preserve moisture and extend shelf life. These cheeses are allowed to age for specific periods of time, though not quite as long as hard or grating cheeses. Semisoft cheeses may be ripened through one of three processes: wash-rind cheeses are periodically washed with any number of liquids, including beer, cider, wine, brandy, or oils, during the ripening period; dry-rind cheeses are allowed to form a natural rind during ripening; and wax-rind cheeses are sealed in wax prior to aging.

TOP ROW: Muenster (orange skin), Caciotta, Caraway Havarti, Fontina
BOTTOM ROW: Monterey Jack, Morbier

Variety	Description	Common Culinary Uses
Fontina	Whole cow's or sheep's milk; medium yellow wheel; mild, grassy, fruity, and nutty	Table cheese; in sandwiches; in cooking; in fondues; great melting cheese
Havarti	Cream-enriched cow's milk; white to light yellow blocks or wheels; very mild, buttery, often flavored with herbs, spices, or peppers; creamy, with small holes	Great on sandwiches
Morbier	Whole cow's milk; light yellow wheel with edible ash layer and a brown crust; creamy, smooth; fruity and nutty, with hay-like aroma	Table cheese
Monterey Jack	Whole, pasteurized cow's milk; light yellow wheel or block; mild (may be flavored with jalapeños)	Table cheese; great for melting
Muenster	Whole cow's milk; light yellow wheel or block, rind may be orange; mild to pungent (depending on age); smooth, waxy with small holes	Great for melting
Port-Salut	Whole or low-fat cow's milk; yellow block; orange rind; buttery, mellow to sharp; smooth with tiny holes	Table cheese paired with raw onions and beer; great for melting
Caciotta	Whole cow's milk cheese, semisoft with some curd holes, and a thick, yellowish wax; aged for 2 months; mellow and savory; available flavored with chiles or herbs. When flavored with ancho chile the cheese is aged slightly longer and may be classified as a grating cheese (see photo on page 286)	Table cheese; great for melting

Hard Cheeses

Hard cheeses have a drier texture than semi-soft cheeses and a firm consistency. They slice and grate easily. Cheeses that fall into this category are made by varying processes. One of the most common is Cheddar. The cheddaring process originated in England, but a variety of cheeses that originated in the United States are made using the same method. Some examples are Colby, Monterey Jack, and dry Jack cheeses.

LEFT TO RIGHT, TOP TO BOTTOM: Emmentaler, aged Provolone, Gruyère, Manchego, ricotta salata, aged Gouda, aged Pecorino, Antico Mugella, aged Cheddar

Variety	Description	Common Culinary Uses
Cantal	Whole cow's milk; light yellow cylinder; mild, buttery; crumbly, firm	Salads, sandwiches, with fruit
Cheddar	Whole cow's milk; light to medium yellow wheels or rectangles; mild to sharp (depending on age), sweet grassy aroma; buttery, rich	Table cheese; with beer, sandwiches; cooking ingredient; great melting cheese
Emmentaler	Raw or pasteurized, part-skim cow's milk; light yellow wheel; full flavored, nutty, fruity; smooth, shiny, with large holes; commonly called Swiss cheese	Great melting cheese; in fondues, sandwiches
Gouda	Whole cow's milk; wheel (usually coated with red wax), ranges from golden to amber (depending on age); mild, creamy, slightly nutty; smooth, may have tiny holes; may be smoked	Table cheese; great for melting; aged Gouda can be grated
Jarlsberg	Part-skim cow's milk; light yellow wheel; sharp, nutty; large holes	Great melting cheese; very popular in the United States
Manchego	Whole sheep's milk; white to yellowish wheels with brownish-gray rinds; slightly briny, nutty flavor; tiny holes	Table cheese; in salads; can be grated
Provolone	Whole cow's milk; shaped like a pear, sausage, or round balls; pale yellow with yellow to golden-brown rind; sharp; elastic, oily; may be smoked	Table cheese with olives, bread, raw vegetables, or salami; in sandwiches; for melting
Ricotta salata	Whole sheep's milk; pure white cylinder; mild, nutty; smooth but crumbly	Pasta, salads; with salami, fruit, and vegetables
Gruyère	Whole raw cow's milk; flat beige wheels with brown rind; fruity and nutty	Fondue; gratins, soups, sandwiches; cooking ingredient

Grating Cheeses

Grating cheeses are typically grated or shaved rather than cut into slices because of their crumbly texture. They are commonly used as a table or eating cheese. In Italy, these cheeses are known as Granas, or grainy cheeses, because of their granular texture. The characteristic texture of grating cheeses is due, in large part, to the long aging process that typically lasts from 2 to 7 years, although some cheeses may be aged for longer periods. They are low-moisture cheeses, making them less prone to spoilage than other cheeses.

FROM LEFT TO RIGHT, TOP TO BOTTOM: Asiago, Parmigiano-Reggiano, Grana Padano, Ancho Chile Caciotta, dry Monterey Jack (center), Pecorino Romano, Sap Sago, Spanish goat cheese

Variety	Description	Common Culinary Uses
Asiago	Whole or part-skim cow's milk; light yellow wheels with gray rind; mild to sharp (depending on age)	Salads, pasta; with fruit and bread
Parmigiano-Reggiano	Part-skim cow's milk; large drums, straw-colored interior with golden rind; sharp, nutty, salty; very hard, dry, crumbly	Table cheese; grated over pasta or risotto; in salads; rind is used in vegetable stocks
Dry Monterey Jack	Whole or part-skim cow's milk; pale yellow with a rich, sharp, slightly nutty flavor; also known as aged Monterey Jack	Table cheese; grated over pasta, in salads
Pecorino Romano	Whole sheep's milk; tall cylinders, white with thin, black rind; very sharp, salty, peppery; dry, crumbly	Table cheese; grated over pasta or risotto, in salads
Sap Sago	Skim cow's milk; light green flattened cone; piquant, sharp, sage and lettuce flavor; very hard, granular; also known as Glarner Schabzieger	Grated on noodles, salads, or soups; mixed with butter or yogurt in dips
Grana Padano	Cow's milk; drums, golden colored; mild; very hard	Grating; a less-expensive alternative to Parmigiano-Reggiano for cooking

Blue-Veined Cheeses

Blue-veined cheeses have consistencies that range from smooth and creamy to dry and crumbly. Their blue veining is the result of injecting a special mold into the cheese before ripening. After being injected with the mold, these cheeses are then salted or brined before being allowed to ripen in dark, cool, damp conditions.

CLOCKWISE FROM BOTTOM: Stilton, Roquefort, Gorgonzola, Spanish blue, Pont Reyes (center)

Variety	Description	Common Culinary Uses
Danish blue	Whole cow's milk; white blocks or drums, no rind; strong, sharp, salty; firm, crumbly	Dressings, salads; slices, spreads
Gorgonzola	Whole cow's and/or goat's milk; medium yellow wheel with blue marbling; tangy, piquant; semisoft, creamy; crumbles well	Table cheese with fruit; salads, pizza; cooking ingredient; slices, spreads
Roquefort	Raw sheep's milk; ivory cylinder with blue-green marbling; deep, full, spicy; semisoft, crumbly	Table cheese; salads
Stilton	Whole cow's milk; tall cylinder, ivory-colored paste with blue-green marbling; full, rich, cheesy, spicy aroma; firm yet crumbly	Table cheese; salads
Spanish blue	Cow's, sheep's, or goat's milk; straw-colored cylinder with veins of purplish-blue color; salty, sharp and tangy; moist, crumbly; common variety is Cabrales	Table cheese; salads
Pont Reyes	Cow's milk; bone-colored cylinder with little blue veining; full-flavored with hints of lemongrass and sea salt; creamy	Table cheese; dressings, salads
Maytag blue	Whole cow's milk; medium yellow cylinder with blue marbling; spicy, peppery, earthy flavor; hard, creamy, crumbly	Table cheese; dressings, salads

Eggs

Eggs are one of the kitchen's most important items. From mayonnaise to meringues, soups to sauces, appetizers to desserts, they are prominent on any menu. The ability to select the right egg for a particular dish (shell egg, yolks only, whites only, or pasteurized eggs) is critical to its success. To learn more about cooking eggs, see Chapter 29.

Grading, Sizes, and Forms

Eggs are graded by the U.S. Department of Agriculture on the basis of external appearance and freshness. The top grade, AA, indicates that the egg is fresh, with a white that will not spread unduly once the egg is broken, and a yolk that rides high on the white's surface. The yolk should also be anchored in place by membranes known as the *chalazae*.

Eggs come in a number of sizes: jumbo, extra large, large, medium, small, and peewee. Younger hens produce smaller eggs, which are often regarded as better quality than larger eggs. Medium eggs are best for breakfast cookery, where the cooked egg's appearance is important. Large and extra-large eggs are generally used for cooking and baking, where the whole egg's appearance is less critical.

Eggs are also sold in several processed forms: bulk or fluid whole eggs (which sometimes includes a percentage of extra yolks to obtain a specific blend), egg whites, and egg yolks. Pasteurized eggs are used in preparations such as salad dressings, eggnog, or desserts, where the traditional recipe may have indicated that the eggs should be raw. These products generally are available in liquid or frozen form.

Dried, powdered eggs are also sold and may be useful for some baked goods or in certain circumstances. For instance, on board a ship, it may not be possible to properly store fresh eggs for the duration of a voyage.

Egg substitutes may be entirely egg-free or may be produced from egg whites, with dairy or vegetable products substituted for the yolks. These substitutes are important for people who require a reduced-cholesterol diet.

Chapter Thirteen

Dry Goods Identification

Dry goods include a wide range of ingredients that are essential to almost every preparation in any foodservice operation. They must be chosen, purchased, and stored with the same degree of care as required by fresh meats or produce.

Purchasing and Storage

Dry goods are also referred to as nonperishable goods. However, these ingredients, like perishable goods, lose quality over time. Keeping an adequate stock on hand is essential to a smooth-running operation, but having too much ties up necessary space and money. Rotating dry goods and observing a rule of "first in, first out" is just as important for dry goods as it is for more perishable foods.

Store dry goods in an area that is dry, properly ventilated, and accessible. All goods should be placed above floor level, on shelving or pallets. Some dry items, such as whole grains, nuts and seeds, and coffee (if they are not vacuum packed), are best stored in the refrigerator or even the freezer.

Grains, Meals, and Flours

This broad category extends from whole grains, such as rice and barley, to cornmeal and pastry flour. Grains are versatile and universal foods enjoyed worldwide, in every cuisine and culture. While they are important sources of nutrition, it is also their subtle but satisfying flavors and textures that give them such culinary importance.

Grains are the fruits and seeds of cereal grasses. For the most part, they are inexpensive and readily available, and provide a valuable and concentrated source of nutrients and fiber. Although grains differ in appearance from other fruits (apples and pears, for example), their structure is quite similar.

Wheat and corn are of primary importance in Western countries, such as the United States and Canada. Rice is fundamental to many Asian cuisines. In fact, in many Asian languages, the word for rice is the same as that for food. Other cultures rely upon grains such as oats, rye, and buckwheat.

Whole grains are grains that have not been milled. They tend to have a shorter life span than milled grains and therefore should be purchased in amounts that can be used in a relatively short period of time: two to three weeks. Milled grains have been polished; that is, they have had the germ, bran, and/or hull removed. Although milled grains tend to last longer, some of their nutritive value is lost during the processing phase.

Milled grains that are broken into coarse particles may be referred to as cracked. If the milling process continues, meals and cereals (cornmeal, farina, cream of rice) are formed. Finally, the grain may be ground into a fine powder, known as flour.

Various methods are used for milling: crushing between metal rollers, grinding between stones, or cutting with steel blades in an action similar to that of a food processor. Stone-ground grains may be preferable in some cases, because they remain at a lower temperature during processing as compared to other types of milling and so retain more of their nutritive value. The following tables describe some of the available forms for several different grains.

Wheat

Overly abundant and economical, wheat has been cultivated for thousands of years. It is by far the most nutritious of all the staple grains, containing the greatest amount of protein. Wheat is used in a variety of savory and sweet applications. It is versatile and flavorful.

Type	Description	Common Culinary Uses
Berries/ Whole	Unrefined or minimally processed whole kernels; light brown to reddish-brown; somewhat chewy texture; nutty flavor	Hot cereal, pilaf, salads, breads
Cracked	Coarsely crushed, minimally processed kernels; light brown to reddish-brown; somewhat chewy texture; nutty flavor	Hot cereal, pilaf, salads, breads
Bulgur	Steamed, dried, and crushed wheat; fine, medium, or coarse; light brown in color; tender; mild flavor	Hot cereal, pilaf, salads (Tabbouleh)
Bran	Separated outer covering of wheat kernel; brown flakes; mildly nutty flavor	Hot and cold cereals, baked goods (bran muffins); used to increase dietary fiber
Germ	Separated embryo of wheat kernel; small, brown, pellet-like; strong nutty flavor; available toasted and raw	Hot and cold cereals, baked goods; used to increase nutritional values in food
Ebly®/ Tender	Soft, parboiled durum wheat; resembles plump grains of rice in raw state; resembles pearl barley when cooked; subtly mild flavor; available raw or cooked	Soups, salads, side dishes, entrées, desserts
Farina	Polished, medium-grind wheat; white; flour-like; very mild flavor	Hot cereal

CLOCKWISE FROM TOP LEFT:
wheat berries, Ebly® wheat, bulgur, farina flour, wheat bran, raw wheat germ, toasted wheat germ (center)

Wheat Flour

When milled into flour, wheat is generally used to produce baked items. Gluten, the substance formed from wheat's protein, provides elasticity and structure that aids in the development of baked goods, specifically bread.

Among the numerous varieties of wheat, hard (winter), soft (summer), and durum are the most common types.

CLOCKWISE FROM TOP LEFT: whole wheat flour, semolina flour, all-purpose flour, bread flour, cake flour, durum flour (center)

Type	Description	Common Culinary Uses
Whole	Hard wheat; the entire kernel is finely milled; light brown color; full, nutty flavor; graham flour is whole wheat flour with a coarser grind	Baked goods, pasta
All-purpose	Blend of hard and soft wheat; the endosperm is finely milled; off-white color; usually enriched, may be bleached	Baked goods, pasta, thickening agent
Bread	Hard wheat; the endosperm is finely milled; off-white color; usually enriched, may be bleached; also known as patent flour	Bread, soft rolls
Cake	Soft wheat; the endosperm is very finely milled; pure white color; polished soft wheat kernels; usually enriched and bleached	Cakes, cookies
Pastry	Soft wheat; the endosperm is very finely milled; pure white color; polished soft wheat kernels; usually enriched and bleached	Pie dough, muffins, biscuits, pastries
Durum	Hard wheat; the endosperm from a durum wheat kernel is finely milled	Bread
Semolina	Durum wheat; the endosperm is coarsely milled; pale yellow	Pasta, gnocchi, puddings; used to make couscous

Rice

A staple food to at least half of the world's communities, rice is an invaluable and versatile ingredient. This starchy whole grain complements nearly any flavor component with which it's paired.

Rice is commercially classified by size (long, medium, and short grain). The two main types of rice are white and brown. White rice is milled, while brown rice is unmilled, resulting in a more nutritious and fiber-packed grain.

TOP ROW, FROM LEFT TO RIGHT: **parboiled rice, rice flour, cream of rice** SECOND ROW, FROM LEFT TO RIGHT: **Carnaroli rice, Spanish rice, Bhutanese red rice** THIRD ROW, FROM LEFT TO RIGHT: **long-grain rice, long-grain brown rice, wild rice** BOTTOM ROW, FROM LEFT TO RIGHT: **Jasmine rice, Popcorn rice, Basmati rice**

Type	Description	Common Culinary Uses
Brown	Whole grain, with the inedible husk removed; light brown; chewy texture; nutty flavor; available as short, medium, or long grain	Pilaf, salads
White/Polished	Husk, bran, and germ removed; white color; mild flavor; available as short, medium, or long grain	Pilaf, salads; short grain used to make rice pudding
Converted/Parboiled	Unhulled grain soaked and steamed before the husk, bran, and germ are removed; fluffy, separated grains when cooked; very light brown color	Pilaf, salads
Basmati	Extra-long grain; fine, delicate texture; aromatic, nutty flavor; aged to reduce moisture content; available as brown or white rice; Popcorn rice is a variety of Basmati	Pilaf, salads
Jasmine	Aromatic, nutty flavor	Pilaf, steamed, rice pudding
Arborio/Italian	Very short, very fat grain; high starch content; off-white; creamy when cooked; also known as Italian rice; varieties include Carnaroli, Piedmontese, and Vialone Nano	Risotto, pudding
Calaspara	Very short, very fat grain; high starch content; off-white; creamy when cooked	Paella
Wild	Long, thin grain; dark brown; chewy texture; nutty flavor; marsh grass, unrelated to regular rice	Salads, stuffing; often combined with brown rice
Sticky/Pearl/ Glutinous/Sushi	Round, short grain; very starchy; sticky when cooked; sweet, mild flavor	Sushi
Rice flour	White rice that has been very finely milled; powdery, white; mild flavor	Thickening agent; baked goods
Heirloom	Varieties include Bhutanese Red, Forbidden Black, and Kalijira rice	Salads, stuffing; often combined with brown rice

Corn

Corn is popular in many cuisines throughout the world in numerous forms. It is often eaten fresh (on the cob), dried, or used as the foundation of many by-products (bourbon, corn oil, cornstarch, cornmeal, corn syrup).

Type	Description	Common Culinary Uses
Hominy	Dried kernels; soaked in lye to remove the hull and germ; available canned or dried	Succotash, casseroles, soups, stews, side dishes
Grits	Ground hominy; available in fine, medium, and coarse grinds	Hot cereal, baked goods, side dishes; popular in the southern United States
Masa	Dried kernels; cooked and soaked in limewater, then ground into dough; pale yellow; moist; variation: masa harina, dried and ground to a fine flour; must be reconstituted to make a dough	Used to make tortillas, tamales, and other Mexican dishes; masa harina often used in baked goods
Cornmeal	Dried kernels; ground to fine, medium, or coarse texture; colors: white, yellow, or blue; variations: corn flour (finely ground); polenta (coarse-ground)	Hot cereal, baked goods; coating items for sautéing or pan frying
Cornstarch	Dried kernels; hull and germ removed; ground to a powder; pure white	Thickening agent (slurry); baked goods; coatings

CLOCKWISE FROM TOP LEFT: grits, hominy, cornstarch, masa harina, blue cornmeal, yellow cornmeal, white cornmeal (center)

Oats

Oats are a valuable source of nutrients and fiber. They are readily available and inexpensive. Mainly consumed as a hot or cold cereal, oats are also commonly used as an ingredient in baked goods and side dishes.

Type	Description	Common Culinary Uses
Groats	Hulled, usually crushed grain, especially oats, but can be wheat, buckwheat kasha, or other cereals	Hot cereal, salads, stuffing
Rolled/Old-fashioned	Groats, steamed and flattened; very pale brown, almost white; round, flake-like; tender; also available: "quick-cooking" and "instant"	Hot cereal (oatmeal), granola, baked goods
Steel-cut/Irish/Scotch	Groats, cut into pieces; brown; chewy	Hot cereal, baked goods
Bran	Outer covering of the oat	Hot and cold cereals, baked goods
Flour	Groats, milled into a fine powder	Baked goods

FROM LEFT TO RIGHT: steel-cut oats, rolled oats, whole oat groats, oat bran

Other Grains

A wide variety of grains fall in the "others" group, as they do not fit cleanly into another category. Some of these grains are quite common, while others are rarely used. In recent years, however, chefs have begun to experiment with many of these less common varieties of grains.

TOP ROW: quinoa SECOND ROW, FROM LEFT TO RIGHT: teff, barley flour THIRD ROW, FROM LEFT TO RIGHT: millet, amaranth, kasha BOTTOM ROW, FROM LEFT TO RIGHT: spelt, pearl barley

Type	Description	Common Culinary Uses
Buckwheat	Whole or milled into flour; light brown; mildly nutty flavor	Hot cereal, pilafs; flour is used for pancakes, blinis, baked goods
Kasha	Hulled, crushed kernels (buckwheat groats); roasted; reddish-brown; chewy texture; toasty, nutty flavor	Pilafs, salads
Millet	Whole or milled into flour; bland flavor	Hot cereal, pilafs; flour is used for puddings, flatbreads, cakes
Sorghum	Commonly boiled to a thick syrup	Porridge, flatbreads, beer, syrup, molasses
Rye	Whole, cracked, or milled into flour; ranges from light to dark brown; dense; pumpernickel flour is very dark, coarsely ground rye	Pilafs, salads; flour is used for baked goods
Teff	Whole; extremely tiny; light to reddish-brown; sweet, chestnut-like flavor	Soups, casseroles; thickening agent
Amaranth	Whole or milled into flour; greens are also eaten; color ranges from white to tan, gold, or pink; sweet flavor	Hot and cold cereals, pilafs, salads
Spelt	Whole or milled into flour; moderately nutty flavor	Pilafs, salads; flour is used for baked goods
Job's Tears	Whole; small; white; slightly chewy texture; grass-like flavor	Pilafs, salads
Quinoa	Whole or milled into flour; very tiny circles; off-white; mild flavor	Pilafs, salads, puddings, soups
Barley	Hulled and Pearl (hull and bran removed); varieties: grits, flour; tan to white; nutty flavor	Pilafs, salads, soups; used to make whiskey and beer

Dried Pasta and Noodles

Dried pasta is a valuable convenience food. It stores well, cooks quickly, and comes in an extensive array of shapes, sizes, and flavors, as described in the table on pages 304–305. Pasta and noodles are made from a number of different flours and grains. Good-quality dried pastas from wheat flour are customarily made from durum semolina. Many pastas are flavored or colored with spinach, tomatoes, or squid ink.

TOP ROW, FROM LEFT TO RIGHT: fusilli, farfalle SECOND ROW, FROM LEFT TO RIGHT: penne, shells, radiatore THIRD ROW, FROM LEFT TO RIGHT: orecchiette, orzo, tubetti BOTTOM ROW, FROM LEFT TO RIGHT: couscous, Israeli couscous, acini de pepe

TOP ROW, FROM LEFT TO RIGHT: bean thread noodles, Korean sweet potato starch noodles
SECOND ROW: Japanese vermicelli (black wrapper) THIRD ROW, FROM LEFT TO RIGHT: buck-wheat/soba noodles (white wrapper), Japanese wheat noodles (purple wrapper), rice vermicelli, rice noodles BOTTOM ROW, FROM LEFT TO RIGHT: spinach fettuccine nest, capellini, spaghetti, bucatini (center, from top to bottom) linguine, fettuccine

Dried Pasta and Noodles, continued

Type	Description	Common Culinary Uses
Bucatini	Hollow, long strands; spaghetti-shaped	Served with thicker sauces
Bean thread noodles	Slender, gelatinous noodles; made from mung beans	Soups, stir-fries, salads, desserts, drinks; common to Asian-influenced dishes
Capellini	Thin, long strands; thinner version: capelli d'angelo (angel hair)	Served with broth, oil, or very light sauces
Fettuccine	Thick, long strands; flat, ribbon-shaped	Served with a variety of sauces, specifically cream sauces
Lasagne	Thick, long, flat, wide noodles; ruffled edges	Casseroles
Linguine	Thin, long, flattened strands	Served with a variety of sauces, light to heavy
Rice noodles	Various widths; long strands; made from rice flour	Common to Asian-influenced dishes
Soba noodles	Fine, long strands; ribbon-shaped; Japanese buckwheat pasta	Soups, stir-fries; common to Asian-influenced dishes
Spaghetti	Round, long strands; widths range in size	Served with a variety of sauces, light to heavy
Udon noodles	Thick, long strands; Japanese noodles	Soups, stews, stir-fries; common to Asian-influenced dishes
Vermicelli	Thin, long strands; similar to spaghetti	Broths, soups, light sauces
Acini de pepe	Small; rice-shaped	Served with a variety of sauces; soups, salads, casseroles
Casareccia	Short; rolled; twisted	Served with a variety of sauces; soups, salads, casseroles
Elbows	Short; narrow, curved tubes	Served with a variety of sauces; soups, salads, casseroles
Farfalle	Medium; bowtie-shaped	Served with a variety of sauces; soups, salads, casseroles
Fusilli	Short; corkscrew shaped	Served with a variety of sauces; soups, salads, casseroles
Orecchiette	Flat; smooth; curved rounds	Served with a variety of sauces; soups, salads, casseroles
Orzo	Small; grain-shaped	Served with a variety of sauces; soups, salads, casseroles

Type	Description	Common Culinary Uses
Penne	Short tubes; smooth or ridged; diagonally cut	Served with a variety of sauces; soups, salads, casseroles
Radiatore	Short; chunky shape with rippled edges	Served with a variety of sauces; soups, salads, casseroles
Rigatoni	Thick; ridged tubes	Served with a variety of sauces; soups, salads, casseroles
Shells	Small to large; resemble conch shells; larger shells stuffed	Served with a variety of sauces; soups, salads, casseroles
Tubetti	Small to medium; tube-shaped	Served with a variety of sauces; soups, salads, casseroles
Couscous	Small, irregular shape; grain-like; similar to coarse sand	Hot cereal, pilafs, salads
Israeli couscous	Larger than traditional couscous; pearl-like, smooth, round balls; chewy texture; sometimes toasted	Pilafs, salads, soups
Italian couscous/ Fregola Sarda	Larger than traditional couscous; irregular shape; sun-baked; golden brown color; chewy texture; nutty flavor	Salads, fish- or tomato-based soups

Dried Legumes

Commonly referred to as beans or peas, legumes are the dried seeds of pod-bearing plants. Legumes are considered to be a staple food to many cuisines throughout the world.

Legumes become drier and harder and require a longer cooking time as they age, so they are best if used within six months of purchase. When purchasing legumes, look for beans/peas that are bright and shiny and free of dust or mold. They should always be rinsed before preparing to remove any foreign, inedible debris. Discard any beans or peas that appear moldy, damp, or wrinkled.

TOP ROW, FROM LEFT TO RIGHT: French lentils, black lentils, red lentils SECOND ROW, FROM LEFT TO RIGHT: brown lentils, green split peas, yellow split peas THIRD ROW, FROM LEFT TO RIGHT: rice beans, canary beans, Great Northern beans

TOP ROW, FROM LEFT TO RIGHT: garbanzo beans, giant Peruvian beans, fava beans SECOND ROW, FROM LEFT TO RIGHT: black/turtle beans, soybeans, northern kidney beans THIRD ROW, FROM LEFT TO RIGHT: Flageolets vert, pigeon peas, cranberry beans

Dried Legumes, continued

Type	Description	Common Culinary Uses
BEANS		
Adzuki	Small; reddish-brown; available whole or powdered	Popular in Japanese cuisine; used in confections as a sweet paste or sugar-coated; savory dishes
Black/Turtle	Large; black exterior, light creamy interior; sweet flavor	Soups, stews, salsas, salads, side dishes
Canary	Slightly smaller than pinto beans; canary-yellow color	Popular in Peruvian dishes, specifically stews
Cannellini/ Italian Kidney	Medium; kidney-shaped; white; nutty flavor	Minestrone soup, salads, stews, side dishes
Cranberry	Small; round; maroon markings; nutty flavor	Soups, stews, salads, side dishes
Fava/Broad	Large; flat; oval; tan	Popular in Mediterranean and Middle Eastern cuisines; falafel, soups, stews, salads, side dishes
Flageolets	Small; kidney-shaped; pale green to creamy white	Served with lamb; braised and puréed as a side dish
Garbanzo/Chickpeas	Medium; acorn-shaped; beige; nutty flavor	Popular in many ethnic dishes; couscous, hummus, soups, stews, salads, side dishes
Great Northern	Large; slightly rounded; white; mildly delicate flavor	Soups, stews, casseroles, side dishes
Kidney	Medium; kidney-shaped; pink to maroon; full-bodied flavor	Chili con carne, refried beans, beans and rice, soups, stews, casseroles, side dishes
Lentils	Small; round; varieties include French/European (grayish exterior with pale yellow interior), Egyptian, red, and yellow	Served as an accompaniment whole or puréed; soups, stews, salads, side dishes
Lima/Butter	Medium; slightly kidney-shaped; white to pale green; buttery taste	Succotash, soups, stews, salads, side dishes
Mung	Small; round; green	Sprouted for bean sprouts; ground into flour to make cellophane noodles and bean threads
Navy/Yankee	Small; round; white	Baked beans, chili, soups, salads
Pinto/Red Mexican	Medium; kidney-shaped; beige with brown streaks	Chili, refried beans, stews, soups

Type	Description	Common Culinary Uses
Rice	Heirloom bean; plump grains resembling rice; slightly bitter taste; varieties include white, brown, Falcon, green, and Mocasin; related to kidney beans	Substitute for rice; soups, stews, casseroles, side dishes
Soybeans	Small; pea- to cherry-shaped; bland flavor; colors include red, yellow, green, brown, and black; dried version is mature bean	Soups, stews, casseroles, side dishes
Heirloom varieties (Calypso, Tongues of Fire, Jacob's Cattle, Madeira)	Range tremendously in size and color; many have stripes or speckles	Soups, stews, casseroles, side dishes, salads
PEAS		
Black-eyed	Small; kidney-shaped; beige with black "eye"	Hoppin' John, soups, side dishes
Pigeon/Gandoles	Heirloom bean; small; nearly round; beige with orange spotting	Popular in African, Caribbean, and Indian dishes
Split	Small; round; split; dried; green or yellow; earthy flavor	Split Pea Soup, salads, side dishes

Nuts and Seeds

Nuts are the fruits of various trees, with the exception of the peanut, which grows underground in the root system of a leguminous plant. Nuts are available in the shell, or shelled and roasted, blanched, sliced, slivered, halved, and chopped. Nuts are also used to produce butters, such as the ever-popular peanut butter.

Considering that nuts are somewhat expensive, storing them properly is a must. They are susceptible to turning rancid rather quickly. Nuts that have not been roasted or shelled will keep longer. Shelled nuts may be stored in the freezer or refrigerator to allow for an extended shelf life.

TOP ROW, FROM LEFT TO RIGHT: walnuts, pecans SECOND ROW, FROM LEFT TO RIGHT: cashews, almonds, macadamia nuts THIRD ROW, FROM LEFT TO RIGHT: pumpkin seeds, hazelnuts/filberts, pistachios, peanuts FOURTH ROW, FROM LEFT TO RIGHT: sunflower seeds, pine nuts, poppy seeds BOTTOM ROW, FROM LEFT TO RIGHT: white sesame seeds, black sesame seeds

Type	Description	Common Culinary Uses
NUTS		
Almond	Teardrop-shaped; pale tan, woody shell; sweet flavor; available whole in shell or shelled, blanched, slivered, sliced, split, chopped, ground; used to produce almond paste, almond butter, and almond oil	Raw, toasted, or cooked; in baked goods, confections, granola, curry dishes; eaten out of hand
Brazil	Large, triangular nut; dark brown, hard shell; white, rich nut	Raw, toasted, or cooked; eaten out of hand; baked goods
Cashew	Kidney-shaped; tan; buttery, slightly sweet flavor; only sold hulled (its skin contains oils similar to those in poison ivy) used to produce cashew butter	Raw, toasted, or cooked; baked goods, confections; eaten out of hand
Chestnut	Fairly large; round to teardrop-shaped; hard, glossy, dark brown shell; off-white nut; sweet flavor; available whole in shell, canned in water or syrup, frozen, dried, or puréed	Raw or cooked; sweet and savory dishes, roasted, boiled, puréed
Hazelnut/Filbert	Small; nearly round; smooth, hard shell; rich, sweet, delicate flavor; available whole in shell or shelled: blanched, whole, chopped	Raw, toasted, or cooked; sweet or savory dishes, baked goods, salads, cereals
Macadamia	Nearly round; extremely hard shell; golden-yellow nut; rich, slightly sweet, buttery; available shelled only	Raw or roasted; baked goods, confections; eaten out of hand
Peanut	Tan, pod-like shell; papery brown skin; off-white-colored nut; sweet flavor; available whole in shell or shelled, skinned; used to produce peanut butter and peanut oil	Raw or roasted; sweet or savory dishes, baked goods, confections, salads; eaten out of hand
Pecan	Smooth, hard, thin, oval shell; two-lobed; brown nut, cream-colored interior; rich, buttery flavor; available whole in shell or shelled, halved, chopped	Raw or roasted; sweet or savory dishes, baked goods, pie, confections, salads; eaten out of hand
Pine/Pignoli	Small, elongated kernel; about ½ inch long; light tan; buttery, mild flavor	Raw or roasted; sweet and savory dishes, baked goods, salads, pesto
Pistachio	Tan; shell opens slightly when nut is mature; green nut; subtle, sweet flavor; available whole in shell: roasted, usually salted; shells sometimes dyed red; occasionally shelled, chopped	Raw or roasted; eaten out of hand; sweet and savory dishes
Walnut	Light brown shell; thick or thin; brown nuts; grown in gnarled segments; tender; oily; mild flavor; available whole in shell or shelled, halved, chopped; pickled; used to produce walnut oil	Raw or roasted; in sweet or savory dishes, baked goods, confections, salads; eaten out of hand

Nuts and Seeds, continued

Type	Description	Common Culinary Uses
SEEDS		
Poppy	Very tiny; round; blue-black seeds; crunchy texture; rich, slightly musty flavor; available whole or ground	Filling and topping for baked goods; in salad dressings; popular in cuisines of central Europe and the Middle East
Pumpkin/Pepitas	Small; flat; oval; soft; cream-colored hulls; greenish-brown, oily interior; delicate flavor; available whole or hulled, usually salted	Raw or roasted; sweet or savory dishes, baked goods; popular in Mexican cuisine
Flax	Tiny, oval seeds; golden or dark brown; mildly nutty; used to produce linseed oil	Baked goods, hot and cold cereal
Sesame	Tiny, flat, oval seeds; black, red, or tan; crunchy; sweet, nutty flavor; used to produce oil and tahini (paste)	Raw or toasted; sweet and savory dishes, baked goods, confections, as garnish
Sunflower	Small; somewhat flat; teardrop-shaped seeds; woody, black and white shell; light tan seed; mild flavor; available whole in shell or shelled, usually salted; used to make sunflower oil	Raw, dried, or roasted; baked goods, salads

FACING PAGE, TOP ROW, FROM LEFT TO RIGHT: cardamom, cumin seed, caraway, turmeric SECOND ROW, FROM LEFT TO RIGHT: anardana (ground pomegranate seeds), fenugreek, anise seed, cloves THIRD ROW, FROM LEFT TO RIGHT: gumbo filé, epazote, black cumin seed, celery seed FOURTH ROW, FROM LEFT TO RIGHT: allspice berries, juniper berries, coriander seed, mustard seed BOTTOM ROW, FROM LEFT TO RIGHT: cinnamon sticks, star anise, nutmeg

Dried Spices

Spices are aromatics produced primarily from the bark and seeds of plants. They have long been used as flavor additives for savory and sweet applications. The pungent flavor of most spices is intense. Dried spices are available whole, ground, or as spice blends and are widely used for their assorted culinary uses.

Whole spices will generally keep longer than ground spices. Dried spices are best stored in sealed containers in a cool, dry environment away from extreme heat and direct light. Spices tend to lose their potency over time, so it is best to discard any that have lost their flavor or become stale. For best results, purchase whole spices and grind them just prior to using.

Dried Spices, continued

Type	Description	Common Culinary Uses
Allspice	Dried, unripened, pea-sized berry of the small evergreen pimiento tree; dark reddish-brown; tastes like cinnamon, nutmeg, and cloves; available whole or ground	Braises, forcemeats, fish, pickles, desserts
Annatto	Dried, small achiote seeds; deep red; nearly flavorless; imparts yellowish-orange color to foods; available whole	Popular in Latin American and Caribbean cooking; stews, soups, sauces
Anardana	Dried, sticky pomegranate seeds; muted, deep red; sour taste; available whole or ground	Popular in Indian cuisine as souring agent
Anise	Dried ripe fruit of the herb *Pimpinella anisum;* similar flavor to fennel seeds; light brown; sweet, spicy, licorice taste and aroma	Popular in Southeast Asian cooking; savory dishes, desserts, baked goods, liqueur
Caraway	Dried fruit of the aromatic caraway plant; member of the parsley family; resemble small seeds; brown; delicate flavor; similar flavor to, but sweeter than, anise seeds	Popular in Austrian, German, and Hungarian cuisines; rye bread, pork, cabbage, soups, stews, some cheeses, baked goods, liqueur (*kümmel*)
Cardamom	Dried, unripened fruit; member of the ginger family; small seeds enclosed in green, black, or bleached white cranberry-sized pod; strong aroma; sweet, spicy flavor; available as whole pod, seeds, or ground	Curries, baked goods, pickles
Cayenne	Dried, ripened fruit pod of *Capsicum frutescens;* bright red; hot; spicy; available fresh or dried	Sauces, soups, meat, fish, poultry
Celery	Dried seed of a wild celery (lovage); strong flavor; available whole or ground	Salads, coleslaw, salad dressings, soups, stews, tomatoes, baked goods
Cinnamon	Dried inner bark of a tropical tree; reddish brown; available in sticks or ground	Baked goods, curries, dessert sauces, beverages, stews
Cloves	Dried, unopened flower of the tropical evergreen clove tree; reddish-brown; spike shaped; sweet, pungent flavor; available whole or ground	Stocks, sauces, braises, marinades, curries, pickles, desserts, baked goods
Coriander	Dried, ripe fruit of the cilantro plant; small, tannish-brown seeds; unique citrus-like flavor; available whole or ground	Popular in Asian, Indian, and Middle Eastern cuisines; curries, forcemeats, pickles, baked goods
Cumin	Dried fruit of a plant in the parsley family; small, crescent-shaped seeds; three colors: amber, black and white; nutty flavor; available whole or ground and black cumin seeds	Popular in Indian, Mexican, and Middle Eastern cuisines; curries, chili

Type	Description	Common Culinary Uses
Dill	Dried fruit of the herb *Anethum graveolens*; member of the parsley family; small, tan seeds; strong, pungent flavor; available whole	Popular in northern and eastern European cuisines; pickles, sauerkraut, cheeses, breads, salad dressings
Epazote	An herb, *Chenopodium ambrosioides*; small, green leaves; pungent flavor and aroma; calms intestinal tract, antigas agent; available dried or fresh	Popular in Mexican and Caribbean cuisines; chili, beans, soups, stews
Fennel	Dried, ripe fruit of the perennial *Foeniculum vulgare*; small, oval seeds; light greenish-brown; sweet licorice flavor and aroma; available whole or ground	Popular seasoning blends of Mediterranean, Italian, Chinese, and Scandinavian cuisines; sausages, fish, shellfish, tomatoes, baked goods, marinades, liqueurs
Fenugreek	Seed pods from an annual herb; small, flat, rectangular seeds; yellowish-brown; bitter taste and pungent, hay-like aroma; available whole or ground	Popular in Indian cuisine; curries, meat, marinades, poultry, chutneys, spice blends, teas
Filé powder	Dried leaves of the sassafras tree; woodsy flavor, similar to root beer; available ground	Popular in Creole cuisine; gumbo
Ginger	Plant from tropical and subtropical regions; tan, knobby root; fibrous; sweet, peppery flavor; spicy aroma; available fresh, candied, pickled, or ground	Popular in Asian and Indian cuisines; curries, braises, baked goods
Horseradish	Large, white root; member of the mustard family; sharp, intense flavor; pungent aroma; dried or fresh	Sauces, condiments, egg salad, potatoes, beets
Juniper berries	Small, dried berry; dark blue; slightly bitter; must crush before using to release flavor	Marinades, braises, meats/game, sauerkraut, gin, liqueurs, teas
Mace	Membrane covering of the nutmeg seed; bright red when fresh; yellowish-orange when dry; strong nutmeg taste and aroma; whole or ground	Forcemeats, pork, fish, spinach and other vegetables, pickles, desserts, baked goods
Mustard	Seeds from plants within the cabbage family; three types: the traditional white/yellow (smaller; less pungent flavor), brown, and black (larger; pungent, hot flavor); available whole or powdered	Pickles, meats, sauces, cheese, eggs, prepared mustard
Nutmeg	Large seed of a fruit that grows on the tropical evergreen *Myristica fragans*; small egg shape; dark brown; sweet, spicy flavor and aroma; available whole or ground	Sauces, soups, veal, chicken, aspics, vegetables, desserts, baked goods, eggnog

(continued)

Dried Spices, continued

Type	Description	Common Culinary Uses
Paprika	Dried, ground pods of sweet red peppers; many varieties; superior from Hungary; colors range from orange-red to deep red; mild to intense flavor and aroma; ground	Popular in Hungarian cuisine; braises, stews, goulashes, sauces, garnishes
Saffron	Tiny, dried stigmas of the violet flowers of *Crocus sativus;* thread-like; yellow-orange; 14,000 stigmas per one ounce of saffron; expensive due to labor-intensive process; powdered or threads available	Popular in Paella, Bouillabaisse, and Risotto Milanese, poultry, seafood, rice pilafs, sauces, soups, baked goods
Star anise	Dried, 8- to 12-pointed pod from Chinese evergreen, member of the magnolia family; star shape; dark brown; intense licorice flavor and aroma; use sparingly; available whole or ground	Popular in Asian dishes; pork, duck, baked goods, teas, liqueurs
Turmeric	Dried root of the tropical plant *Curcuma longa,* related to ginger; shape similar to ginger; bright yellow; intense spicy flavor; powdered	Popular in Indian and Middle Eastern cuisines; curries, sauces, mustard, pickles, rice
SPICE MIXES		
Chili powder	Blend of ground spices with dried chiles as the base; can include cumin, cloves, coriander, garlic, and oregano; degree of spiciness changes with variety	Popular in Southwestern and Mexican cuisines; chili, Chili con Carne, soups, stews, sauces
Chinese five-spice	Blend of ground spices; equal parts Szechwan peppercorns, star anise, cinnamon, cloves, and fennel; pungent flavor and aroma	Popular in Chinese cuisine; meat, fish, vegetables, marinades, sauces
Curry powder	Blend of ground spices; can include cardamom, chiles, cinnamon, cloves, coriander, cumin, fennel seed, fenugreek, mace, nutmeg, red and black pepper, poppy and sesame seeds, saffron, tamarind, turmeric; degree of spiciness and color change with variety	Popular in Indian cuisine; meat, seafood, vegetables, sauces, rice, soups
Garam masala	Blend of dry-roasted spices; many variations; can include black pepper, cinnamon, cloves, coriander, cumin, cardamom, dried chiles, fennel, mace, nutmeg; warm flavor and aroma; whole or ground	Popular in Indian cuisine; fish, lamb, pork, poultry, cauliflower, potatoes
Quatre épices	French term meaning "four spices"; refers to a variety of ground spice mixtures; can include pepper, allspice, ginger, cinnamon, cloves, nutmeg	Stews, soups, vegetables

Salt and Pepper

Long valued for their preservation qualities, both salt (sodium chloride) and pepper have been prized for centuries. However, with refrigeration widely used today, they have become less important as preservatives.

Available in many forms, salt is a precious mineral that can be obtained from two different sources and processes; it is either mined or evaporated from seawater. Free of shelf life concerns, salt is best stored in a dry place. In humid weather, salt may cake together; to prevent this, mix a few grains of rice in with the salt.

Peppercorns are berries grown on trees in tropical regions around the world. The type and flavor of peppercorn depends upon when it is harvested. Whole peppercorns will retain their flavor almost indefinitely, but they must be crushed or ground in order for the flavor to be released.

Type	Description	Common Culinary Uses
SALT		
Curing	93.75% table salt, 6.25% sodium nitrate; dyed pink to differentiate from other salts	Curing meats and fish
Kosher	Flaky, coarse grains; iodine free; developed for preparation of kosher meats; preferred over table salt by many	Multipurpose flavor enhancer; cooking, canning, pickling
Iodized	Table salt fortified with iodine, a nutrient supplement to regulate thyroid; can impart bitter taste; may react with certain foods	Multipurpose flavor enhancer
MSG (Monosodium glutamate)	Food additive; derived from glutamic acid; intensifies the flavor of savory foods	Popular flavor enhancer for Asian cooking; used in many processed foods
Pickling/Canning	Similar to table salt; contains no additives; will clump when exposed to moisture; provides pure taste and clear pickling/canning liquid	Pickling, canning, substitute for table salt as flavor enhancer
Rock	Very coarse grains; inexpensive	Used in crank ice cream machines; provides bed for shellfish
Salt substitutes	Light salt; some or all sodium chloride is replaced with potassium chloride	Sodium-restricted cooking; substitute for table salt as flavor enhancer
Sea/Bay	Thin, flaky layers; produced from evaporated seawater; contains trace minerals; intense flavor; fine-grain and larger crystals available	Flavor and texture enhancer; do not use for pickling, canning, or baking

(continued)

Salt and Pepper, continued

Type	Description	Common Culinary Uses
Seasoned	Table salt combined with other flavor additives	Flavor enhancer for specific preparations
Table	Sodium chloride; two varieties: iodine fortified and nonfortified; contains added calcium silicate for anti-caking and dextrose to stabilize	Multipurpose flavor enhancer
PEPPER		
Black peppercorns	Dried, dark, shriveled berry; picked unripe and allowed to dry; strong, peppery flavor; most common of all peppers; two varieties: Tellicherry and Lampong; available as whole berries, cracked, or ground	Multipurpose flavor enhancer; curing, pickling, sachet d'épices
Green peppercorns	Soft, unripened berry; mild, slightly sour flavor; similar to capers; available freeze-dried or packed in vinegar or brine	Seasoning, flavor enhancer
Pink peppercorns	Dried berry of the Baies rose plant; rose colored; pungent; slightly sweet; expensive; available freeze-dried or packed in brine or water	Seasoning meat and fish dishes, sauces
Szechwan peppercorns/Anise pepper/Chinese pepper	Dried berry of the prickly ash tree; resembles black peppercorns; contains a small seed; hot, spicy flavor; available whole or powdered	Popular to the cuisines of China's Szechwan and Hunan provinces
White peppercorns	Ripened peppercorn with exterior skin removed; beige color; mild flavor; available as whole berries, cracked, or ground	Seasoning light-colored sauces and foods

Sweeteners

Once a symbol of wealth and prosperity, sugar is now widely used in all facets of the professional kitchen. Sugar is extracted from plant sources (sugar beets and sugarcane) and refined into the desired form. Most varieties of syrup, such as maple, corn, molasses, and honey, are derived from plants as well. The flavor intensity of sweeteners typically corresponds with the color—the darker the sugar or syrup, the more concentrated the flavor.

Sugar is responsible for the caramelization process, balancing the acidity in foods, and contributing to the appearance, flavor, and viscosity of glazes, sauces, and marinades. In the bakeshop, sugar adds sweetness, retains moisture, prolongs freshness/shelf life, aids in the creaming process, and imparts color and flavor to crusts. Selecting the proper sweetener will help determine the desired end product.

TOP ROW, FROM LEFT TO RIGHT: molasses, honey, light corn syrup SECOND ROW, FROM LEFT TO RIGHT: maple sugar, light brown sugar, dark brown sugar THIRD ROW, FROM LEFT TO RIGHT: turbinado, coarse sugar, sugar cubes BOTTOM ROW, FROM LEFT TO RIGHT: granulated sugar, superfine sugar, confectioners' sugar

Other Sweeteners

CLOCKWISE FROM TOP LEFT: sugarcane sticks, piloncillo, jaggery, palm sugar, sugarcane

Type	Description	Common Culinary Uses
SUGAR		
Artificial sweeteners	Sugar substitutes; nonnutritive values; varieties include (but not limited to): Aspartame, Acesulfame-K, Saccharin, and Sucralose	Sugar substitutes; not suggested for all baking and cooking applications
Brown	Refined, granulated sugar with some impurities remaining or molasses added; somewhat moist; two variations: light and dark; dark brown has most intense (molasses) flavor	Baking, pastry, sauces, savory applications
Confectioners'/Powdered/10X	Pure refined sugar; white; fine powder; minimal amount of cornstarch added to prevent clumping	Baking, pastry, icings, confections, decorative garnish
Granulated/White	Pure; refined cane or beet sugar; white; small granules; available in various sizes: coarse (crystal/decorating), superfine, cubes, tablets	Baking, pastry, sauces, savory applications
Maple	Maple sap; liquid boiled until near evaporation; much sweeter than granulated sugar	Baking, sweet additive to cereals, yogurt, coffee, tea
Piloncillo	Unrefined, hard, compressed sugar from Mexico; medium to dark brown; cone shaped; ¾-ounce to 9-ounce cones; two varieties: blanco (lighter) and oscuro (darker)	Substitute for dark brown sugar
Jaggery/Palm	Unrefined from palm tree sap or sugarcane; dark; available in several forms; two most popular: soft/spreadable and solid; coarse grains	Popular in Indian cuisine; spread for breads; baking, confections, sweets additive
Raw	Purified, sugarcane residue; several varieties: Demerara (white sugar crystals with the addition of molasses syrup; coarse grains), Barbados/Muscovado (moist, dark, fine-textured grains), Turbinado (steam-cleaned, light brown, coarse grains)	Coarse grains best suited for decorating and as a sweet additive; fine-textured grains used to substitute for light brown sugar
Sugarcane	Source of sugar; member of the grass family; made edible by boiling; available in stalks; less sweet than granulated sugar	Snack, garnish
SYRUP		
Corn	Liquefied sugar created by processing cornstarch; three varieties: light (clarified to remove color), dark (color added, caramel flavor), and high fructose; less sweet than granulated sugar; the darker the syrup, the more intense the flavor; inhibits crystallization	Baking, pastry, confections, spreads
Flavored	Sugar or other syrup with added flavoring; flavor varieties include fruit, nut, spice, chocolate, caramel	Baking, pastry, savory applications, beverages

(continued)

Other Sweeteners, continued

Type	Description	Common Culinary Uses
Honey	Thick, sweet liquid from flower nectar produced by bees; pale yellow to dark brown; flavor intensifies as color deepens; countless varieties; named according to specific flower; available in comb, chunk-style, liquid, whipped	Baking, pastry, savory applications, beverages, spreads
Maple	Boiled maple tree sap; golden brown; unique flavor	Accompaniment to pancakes, waffles, and French toast; baking, pastry, confections, savory applications
Molasses	Liquid by-product of sugar refining; three varieties: light (first boil), dark (second boil), and blackstrap (third boil, darkest and thickest); flavor and aroma intensifies as color deepens	Accompaniment to pancakes, waffles, and French toast; baking, pastry, savory applications

Fats and Oils

The applications for fats and oils in the professional kitchen or bakeshop are innumerable. Fat provides a rich flavor, silky mouthfeel and texture, and pleasing aroma. It also performs a multitude of chemical functions, such as tenderizing, leavening, aiding in moisture retention, and creating flaky/crumbly textures. Fats and oils act as insulators for food, transfer heat to food, prevent sticking, emulsify or thicken sauces, and create crispy textures when used for frying.

While they are similar in many ways, fat is solid at room temperature, and oil is liquefied. Oils are produced by pressing a high-oil food, such as olives, nuts, corn, or soybeans. It is then filtered, clarified, or hydrogenated to produce an oil or fat (shortening). The smoke point of a fat or oil greatly determines its appropriate use. For example, the higher the smoke point, the better suited it is for frying because it can withstand higher heat ranges.

Type	Description	Common Culinary Uses
Butter, whole	Solid fat churned from milk; 80% milk fat, 20% water and milk solids; quality based on flavor, body, texture, color, and salt; Grades: AA (finest), A, B, C	Cooking, baking, pastry, sauces, compound butters
Butter, clarified/ drawn/ghee	Purified butterfat; unsalted butter with milk solids removed; longer shelf life than butter; high smoke point	Roux, warm butter sauces, Indian cooking
Frying fats	Liquid or malleable at room temperature; blended oils or shortenings; based on processed corn or peanut oils; high smoke point; long fry life	Deep-frying
Lard	Solid; rendered pork fat; mild flavor if processed; high in saturated fat; high smoke point	Frying, baking, pastry
Shortening	Solid fat; made from vegetable oils, may contain animal fats; liquid oil chemically transformed through hydrogenation; flavorless; high smoke point	Deep-frying, baking
OIL		
Canola/Rapeseed	Light; golden-colored; similar to safflower oil; low in saturated fat; extracted from rapeseeds; bland taste	Cooking, salad dressings
Coconut	Heavy; nearly colorless; high in saturated fat; extracted from dried coconut meat	Commercial packaged goods, blended oils, shortenings
Corn	Refined oil; odorless; medium yellow color; mild flavor; high smoke point	Deep-frying, commercial salad dressings, margarine

(continued)

Fats and Oils, continued

Type	Description	Common Culinary Uses
Cottonseed	Heavy; very light to pale yellow; extracted from cotton plant seeds	Combined with other oils to produce vegetable and cooking oils, salad dressings, margarine, commercial products
Grapeseed	Light; pale color; neutral flavor; high smoke point	Sautéing, frying, salad dressings
Olive	Varies in viscosity; pale yellow to deep green (depending on type of olive and processing); quality based on acidity level (the finest being extra-virgin); two distinct classes: virgin and blended; low to high smoke point	Common to Mediterranean cuisine; low- to high-heat cooking depending on type of processing; marinades, salad dressings
Oil sprays	Light, vegetable oils; blended; packaged in pump or aerosol sprays; varieties include vegetable, olive oil, and butter-flavored	Light coating for pans and griddles
Peanut	Light; refined; clear to pale yellow; subtle scent/flavor; less-refined varieties have stronger scent/flavor; high smoke point	Deep-frying, stir-frying, commercial salad dressings, margarine, shortening
Safflower	Light; refined; colorless; flavorless; extracted from safflower seeds; high smoke point	Deep-frying, salad dressings
Salad	Blended vegetable oils; subtle flavor	Salad dressings, mayonnaise
Sesame	Two types: one is light and mild with nutty flavor, the other is dark with stronger flavor and aroma; extracted from sesame seeds; low to high smoke point	Frying, sautéing, salad dressings, flavor additive
Soybean	Heavy; light yellow; pronounced flavor and aroma; high smoke point	Common to Chinese cuisine; stir-frying, commercial margarine, shortening
Sunflower	Light; pale yellow; subtle flavor; low in saturated fat; extracted from sunflower seeds; low smoke point	All-purpose cooking, salad dressings
Vegetable	Light; refined; blended vegetable oils; mild flavor and aroma; high smoke point	All-purpose cooking, deep-frying, baking
Walnut	Light; pale to medium yellow; unrefined; delicate nutty flavor and aroma; highly perishable; refrigerate to prevent rancidity	Flavor additive in salad dressings, meat dishes, pasta, desserts; best used uncooked

Miscellaneous Dry Goods

Chocolate

Chocolate is produced from cocoa beans, which grow in a pod on the cacao tree. For the ancient Aztecs, cocoa beans served not only to produce drinks and as a component of various sauces, but also as currency. Today, chocolate is usually found in a variety of sweets, including cakes, candies, and other desserts, although it is also used in savory entrées, such as Mole Poblano, a turkey dish of Mexican origin.

The chocolate extraction process is lengthy and has undergone a great deal of refinement since the days of the Aztecs. The first stage involves crushing the kernels into a paste; at this point it is completely unsweetened and is called chocolate liquor. The liquor is then further ground to give it a smoother, finer texture, and sweeteners and other ingredients may be added. The liquor may be pressed, causing cocoa butter to be forced out. The cocoa solids that are left are ground into cocoa powder. The cocoa butter may be combined with chocolate liquor to make eating chocolate, or it may be flavored and sweetened to make white chocolate. Cocoa butter also has numerous pharmaceutical and cosmetic uses.

Chocolate should be stored, well wrapped, in a cool, dry, ventilated area. Under most conditions, it should not be refrigerated, since this could cause moisture to condense on the surface. Sometimes stored chocolate develops a white "bloom"; the bloom merely indicates that some of the cocoa butter has melted and then recrystallized on the surface. Chocolate with a bloom can still be used safely. Cocoa powder should be stored in tightly sealed containers in a dry place. It will keep almost indefinitely.

Vinegars and Condiments

Vinegars and most condiments are used to introduce sharp, piquant, sweet, or hot flavors into foods. They may be used as an ingredient or served on the side, to be added according to a guest's taste. A well-stocked kitchen should include a full range of vinegars, mustards, relishes, pickles, olives, jams, and other condiments. In general, vinegars and condiments should be stored in the same manner as oils and shortenings.

Extracts

The chef uses a variety of flavoring extracts for cooking and baking. Herbs, spices, nuts, and fruits are used to prepare extracts, which are alcohol based. Common flavors include vanilla, lemon, mint, and almond. Extracts can lose their potency if they are allowed to come in contact with air, heat, or light. To preserve flavor, store extracts in tightly capped dark jars or bottles away from heat or direct light.

Leaveners

Leaveners are used to give foods a light, airy texture. Chemical leaveners, such as baking soda (sodium bicarbonate) and baking powder (a combination of baking soda, cream of tartar, and talc), work rapidly. Baking powder is usually double acting, which means that one reaction happens in the presence of moisture, when liquids are added to dry ingredients, and a second occurs in the presence of heat, as the item bakes in the oven.

Yeast leavens foods by the process of fermentation, which produces alcohol and carbon dioxide. The gas produced is trapped by the dough, creating a number of small pockets, and the alcohol burns off during baking.

Chemical leaveners should be kept perfectly dry. Dried yeast can be held for extended periods, but fresh yeast has a short shelf life; it will last only a few weeks under refrigeration.

Thickeners

Thickeners are used to give liquid a certain amount of viscosity. The process of forming an emulsion is one way to thicken a liquid, as is the process of reduction. In addition, various thickening ingredients can be used. These include arrowroot, cornstarch, filé powder, and gelatin, to name a few.

Coffee, Tea, and Other Beverages

A good cup of coffee or tea is often the key to a restaurant's reputation. The chef should identify brands and blends that best serve the establishment's specific needs. Whereas some operations prefer to select whole coffee beans, others may be better served by buying preground, portioned, vacuum-packed coffee. Many restaurants serve brewed decaffeinated coffee, and some offer espresso and cappuccino, both regular and decaffeinated.

Teas come in many varieties, including black tea, green tea, and herbal teas. Most are blends and are available in single-serving bags or in loose form.

Although coffee and tea generally keep well, they will lose a lot of flavor if stored too long or under improper conditions. Whole beans or opened containers of ground coffee should be kept cool (ideally, refrigerated); teas should be stored in cool, dry areas, away from light and moisture.

Prepared mixes (powdered fruit drinks or cocoa mixes, for example) also should be kept moisture-free. Frozen juices and other beverages should remain solidly frozen until needed. Canned juices should be kept in dry storage. Remember to rotate stock, and check all cans, boxes, and other containers for leaks, bulges, or mold.

Wines, Cordials, and Liqueurs

A general rule of thumb for selecting wines, cordials, and liqueurs for use in cooking and baking is this: If it is not suitable for drinking, it is not suitable for cooking.

Brandies and cognacs, Champagne, dry red and white wines, port, Sauternes, sherry, stouts, ales, beers, and sweet and dry vermouth are commonly used in the kitchen. For baking purposes, the chef should keep on hand bourbon, crème de cassis, fruit brandies, gin, Kahlúa, rum, and scotch. Purchase wines and cordials that are affordably priced and of good quality. Table wines (Burgundies, Chablis, and Chardonnays, for example) lose their flavor and become acidic once opened, especially when subjected to heat, light, and air. To preserve flavor, keep them in closed bottles or bottles fitted with pouring spouts, and refrigerate when not needed. Fortified wines (Madeiras, sherries, and ports, for example) are more stable than table wines and can be held in dry storage. The same also applies to cordials, cognacs, and liqueurs.

Part Four

Stocks, Sauces, and Soups

Chapter Fourteen

Mise en Place for Stocks, Sauces, and Soups

Good cooking is the result of carefully developing the best possible flavor and most perfect texture in each dish. Basic flavoring and aromatic combinations constitute the flavor base; thickeners contribute a rich, smooth mouthfeel; and liaisons lend body in stocks, sauces, and soups.

Bouquets, Sachets, and Oignon Brûlé

Bouquet garni, sachet d'épices, and oignon brûlé are three basic aromatic preparations called for in recipes again and again. These combinations of aromatic vegetables, herbs, and spices are meant to enhance and support the flavors of a dish. They add flavor to stocks, sauces, and soups by gently infusing the liquid with their aroma. Both of these aromatic preparations are added during the cooking process. Bouquets and sachets are typically tied together for easy removal during cooking after the desired amount of flavor has been extracted, even before all of the ingredients in a dish are finished cooking.

A bouquet garni is made up of fresh herbs and vegetables, tied into a bundle. If a leek is used to wrap the other bouquet garni ingredients, it must be thoroughly rinsed of dirt first. Cut a piece of string long enough to leave a tail to tie the bouquet to the pot handle. This makes it easy to pull out the bouquet when it is time to remove it.

A sachet contains ingredients such as peppercorns, other spices, and herbs. The seasonings are often tied up in a cheesecloth bag for recipes that are not strained after cooking. A "loose" sachet, which is only the sachet ingredients added directly to a recipe without first being tied, may be used when the ingredients will be strained away after the dish has finished cooking. A standard bouquet or sachet can be modified a little (add some carrot or a garlic clove) or a lot (use cardamom, ginger, or cinnamon) to produce different effects. A sachet infuses a liquid with flavor, in the same way that a teabag is used to make a cup of tea.

For a small batch (less than a gallon), add the sachet or bouquet in the last fifteen to thirty minutes. For batches of several gallons or more, add them about one hour before the end of the cooking time. Consult specific recipes and formulas for guidance. When you add a bouquet or sachet to a stock or soup, taste the dish before and after adding it to learn its effect on the dish's flavor profile. If the aromatics have been combined following a basic formula and simmered long enough to infuse the dish with their aroma, the dish should be flavored, but not overwhelmed, by them.

Oignon brûlé (burnt onion) and oignon piqué (pricked or studded onion) are flavoring ingredients based on whole, halved, or quartered onions. An oignon brûlé is made by peeling and halving an onion and charring the cut edges in a dry skillet. It is used in some stocks and consommés to provide golden brown color. An oignon piqué is prepared by studding an onion wih a few whole cloves and a bay leaf. It is used to flavor béchamel sauce and some soups.

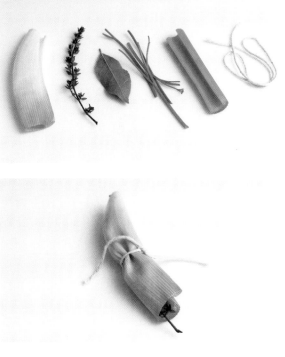

A standard Bouquet Garni, adequate to flavor 1 gal/3.84 L of liquid, includes

1 sprig of thyme

3 or 4 parsley stems

1 bay leaf

2 or 3 leek leaves and/or 1 celery stalk, cut crosswise in half

(Top) Ingredients for a standard bouquet garni

(Bottom) The finished bouquet garni

A standard Sachet d'Épices, adequate to flavor 1 gal/3.84 L of liquid, includes

3 or 4 parsley stems

1 sprig of thyme or 1 tsp/2 g dried thyme

1 bay leaf

1 tsp/2 g cracked peppercorns

1 garlic clove (optional)

(Top) Ingredients for a standard sachet d'épices

(Bottom) The finished sachet d'épices

Mirepoix

Mirepoix and similar aromatic vegetable combinations are intended to provide a subtle but pleasing background flavor, supporting and improving the flavor of the finished dish.

Mirepoix is the French name for a combination of onions, carrots, and celery, but it is not the only such combination, even within the French culinary repertoire. Onions, carrots, celery (both Pascal and celeriac), leeks, parsnips, garlic, tomatoes, shallots, mushrooms, peppers, and ginger are among the ingredients commonly referred to as *aromatics*. They may be used in various combinations, as dictated by the cuisine and the dish itself.

Even when used in relatively small amounts, aromatic ingredients make a significant contribution to a dish. For example, 1 lb/454 g of mirepoix is enough to flavor 1 gal/3.84 L of stock, soup, sauce, stew, braise, or marinade and, according to the formula on page 333, would include 8 oz/227 g onion, 4 oz/113 g celery, and 4 oz/113 g carrot.

To get the best flavor from mirepoix and similar preparations, thoroughly rinse and trim all the vegetables first. Onion skin will give a simmering liquid an orange or yellow tint, which may not be desirable, so determine whether to peel onions. Scrubbing, but not peeling, carrots and parsnips can cut down on the prep time. Nevertheless, some chefs peel all vegetables on the premise that flavor is extracted into the dish more easily; others peel them only when they are not strained out of the finished dish.

Regardless of whether or not the vegetables are peeled, cut them into pieces of a relatively uniform size, with the dimensions matching the cooking time of the dish. The shorter the simmering time, the smaller and thinner the cut; the longer the time, the larger and thicker the cut. Make larger cuts for long-simmering dishes such as pot roasts or brown veal stock. Cut mirepoix small or slice it for use in uncooked marinades, pan gravies, and dishes that simmer up to three hours. Slice mirepoix very fine for fumets and stocks that simmer less than one hour.

Basic mirepoix (left) and white mirepoix (right)

A basic formula for Mirepoix

Used to flavor a variety of stocks and soups, tomato paste or purée is often included for brown stock, gravy, stew, or soup.

2 parts onion
1 part celery
1 part carrot

A basic formula for White Mirepoix

Used to flavor white stocks and soups that should have a mild flavor and/or pale ivory or white color.

2 parts onion or the white of leeks
1 part celery root or hearts
1 part parsnips

A basic formula for Asian Aromatics

Used in many Asian stir fries, soups, and sauces.

2 parts ginger
2 parts garlic
1 part green onion

A basic formula for Cajun Trinity

Used in many Louisiana Creole and Cajun dishes, such as gumbo.

2 parts onion
1 part green bell pepper
1 part celery

A basic formula for Matignon

Sometimes called edible mirepoix, it typically includes onions, carrots, celery, and ham cut into very neat dice. Mushrooms and assorted herbs and spices may be added as desired. Used to garnish a dish as well as to flavor it.

3½ oz/99 g ham
4½ oz/128 g onion
4½ oz/128 g carrot
2 oz/57 g celery
1 sprig thyme
1 bay leaf

1. **Add the celery once the onions and carrots are browned.** Mirepoix will add a distinct aroma to a dish, even if the cut-up vegetables are simply added to the pot as it simmers. Sweating, smothering, or browning them in fat, however, significantly changes their flavor. Start by cooking onions and leeks in just enough fat to coat the bottom of the pan and vegetables, then add the carrots, and finally the celery.

White stocks or cream soups generally call for cooking the mirepoix over low heat in fat until it starts to give off some juices, known as *sweating*. If the pot is covered as the aromatics sweat, the technique is *smothering*. Mirepoix can cook until it turns a deep rich brown (sometimes referred to as caramelized), either on the stovetop or in the oven.

2. **Add tomato paste after the celery softens and color deepens.** Tomato paste or purée is often added to the mirepoix for added flavor and color. Add it, if required, once the mirepoix ingredients are partly cooked.

3. **Cook carefully until deeply browned to complete pinçage.** Cook the tomato paste until it turns rusty brown and has a sweet aroma. This technique is called *pinçage,* from the French *pincer,* "to stiffen or pinch," which is a good description of what happens to the tomatoes as they cook in hot fat.

Roux

Roux thickens sauces, soups, and stews, as well as lending those dishes a special flavor. Cooking flour in fat inactivates an enzyme that, if not destroyed by high heat, interferes with flour's thickening ability. Cooking flour also changes the flour's raw cereal taste to a toasty or nutty flavor. Both the flavor and the color become deeper the longer the roux cooks. In addition to improving raw flour's flavor and color, cooking flour in fat helps to keep the starch in the flour from forming long strands or clumps when the roux is combined with a liquid. However, it must be kept in mind that the same weight of white roux has more thickening power than a darker roux, because the browning process causes some of the starch in the flour to break down, making it unavailable for thickening. Therefore, the darker the roux, the less thickening power it has.

Although other thickeners are gradually supplanting roux in the American kitchen for various reasons (including the longer cooking time it requires to remove any taste of a raw flour and because it creates a heavier sauce), it is still used extensively, perhaps because of its European culinary heritage and its several distinct advantages. In addition to thickening a dish, roux will change the color of a sauce and lend it a nutty/toasted flavor (if a dark roux is used). For example, dark roux is particularly important in Creole and Cajun cuisines, where it gives gumbos and stews a unique character. Another advantage of using roux is that the starches present in the flour do not break down as easily as some others, creating a more stable sauce.

Roux can be prepared with any type of white wheat flour; however, the most desirable is all-purpose flour due to its starch content. Flours vary in their starch to protein ratio. Cake flour, for instance, has a higher proportion of starch to protein than bread flour and will, therefore, have more thickening power than a bread-flour roux. All-purpose flour has a thickening power between the two. Rouxs called for in this book were tested using all-purpose flour. Clarified butter is the most common fat used for making roux, but whole butter, vegetable oils, rendered chicken fat, or other rendered fats may also be used. Each fat will influence the finished dish's flavor.

Heat the fat over medium heat and add the flour, stirring to combine. The basic formula (by weight) for a roux is three parts flour to two parts fat. The roux should be very smooth and moist, with a glossy sheen; not dry or greasy. It should look "like sand at low tide." Adjust the roux's texture by adding more flour or fat. Stir the roux as it cooks to keep it from scorching and continue to cook it to the desired color. To reduce the chances of scorching, large quantities of roux may be placed in a moderate (350° to 375°F/177° to 191°C) oven to complete cooking. The four basic colors of roux are white (barely colored or chalky), blond (golden straw color with a slightly nutty aroma), brown (deep brown with a strong nutty aroma), and dark (dark brown with a pronounced nutty flavor and aroma). Once the roux is cooked to its desired doneness, it is ready to use, or it may be cooled and stored for later.

Roux can be combined with liquid in three ways. Cool roux may be added to hot liquid, cool liquid may be added to hot roux, or warm roux may be added to liquid of the sauce temperature. For any approach, though, follow these general guidelines:

- Avoid temperature extremes to prevent lumping.

- Cool or room-temperature roux can be incorporated into hot liquid more easily than ice-cold roux because the fat is not as solid.

- Very cold liquid should not be used, as it will initially cause the roux to harden.

- Extremely hot roux should be avoided, because it may spatter when combined with a liquid and cause serious burns.

The full thickening action of the roux becomes evident when the liquid has reached approximately 200°F/93°C. For a medium consistency finished product, use 15 to 16 oz/425 to 454 g of roux per gallon and for an end result with a light consistency, use 14 oz/397g of roux per gallon. Long-cooking sauces and soups are further thickened through reduction.

Roux (from left to right): white, blond, brown, dark

Clarified Butter

Clarified butter is made by heating whole butter until the butterfat and milk solids separate. When whole butter is clarified, some of its volume is lost during skimming and decanting. For example, 1 lb/454 g of butter will yield approximately 12 oz/340 g of clarified butter.

Using salted butter for clarifying is not recommended because the concentration of salt in the resulting clarified butter is unpredictable. Unsalted clarified butter can always be salted as it is used.

Clarifying Butter

The purpose of clarifying butter is to remove its milk solids and water. This makes it possible to cook with butter at a higher temperature than is possible with whole butter. Clarified butter is commonly used to make roux and because it has some butter flavor, it is often used for sautéing, sometimes in combination with vegetable oil to further raise its smoking point. Some chefs also prefer it for warm butter sauces, such as Hollandaise and Bearnaise. Ghee, which is used in some Asian cuisines, is a type of clarified butter. It has a nutty flavor because the milk solids brown before they are separated from the butterfat.

Melted butter (left) and clarified butter (right)

1. **Melt the butter and skim off the foam.** Heat the butter over low heat until foam rises to the surface and the milk solids drop to the bottom of the pot. The remaining butterfat becomes very clear. Skim the surface foam as the butter clarifies using a ladle, screen skimmer, or perforated spoon.

2. **Decant the clarified butter.** Pour or ladle off the butterfat into another container, carefully leaving all of the water and milk solids in the pan bottom. After whole butter is clarified, some of its volume is lost due to skimming, decanting, and discarding the water and milk solids. One lb/454 g of whole butter yields approximately 12 oz/340 g of clarified butter.

Pure Starch Slurries

Arrowroot, cornstarch, and other pure starches have greater thickening power, ounce for ounce, than flour and do not require an extended simmering time like roux. They also lend much less or no color at all to a final dish. However, it should be kept in mind that they do break down more quickly over time than does roux.

Arrowroot, cornstarch, tapioca, potato starch, and rice flour are all pure starches. They are made into slurries by dispersing them in cold liquid. Thoroughly blend the starch and liquid to about the consistency of heavy cream. Slurries can be blended in advance and held to use during à la minute preparations. If not used immediately, the starch will settle out of the liquid and move to the bottom of the container. Stir the slurry just before use to recombine the starch evenly throughout the liquid.

Pour or ladle the slurry into simmering liquid while stirring constantly. When added in this way, slurries quickly thicken liquid, making it easy for the chef to control the final consistency of the dish. Whisk constantly to prevent lumping and scorching. Bring the liquid back to a boil and cook just until the sauce reaches the desired thickness and clarity.

Dishes thickened with slurries have limited holding periods. Be sure to check periodically for quality if they must be held in a steam table. Various starches have somewhat different qualities but may be substituted one for the other, following the formula below.

To Substitute a Pure Starch for Roux

Weight of flour in roux (multiply weight of roux by 0.6 to determine weight of flour) × Thickening power of replacement starch (see below) = Weight of replacement starch required (estimated)

Example: To substitute arrowroot in a recipe that calls for 10 oz of roux:

10 oz roux × 0.6 = 6 oz flour
6 oz flour × 0.5 (arrowroot thickening power) = 3 oz arrowroot

Thickening Powers

Rice flour: 0.6	Cornstarch: 0.5
Arrowroot: 0.5	Tapioca: 0.4
Potato starch: 0.2	

Arrowroot Thickening power roughly equivalent to cornstarch but more translucent. Does not gel or weep when cooled.

Cornstarch Translucent. Thickens when heated, but gels and weeps upon cooling. Thickening power diminishes with excessive heating.

Tapioca/Cassava Flour Translucent. Thickening power slightly greater than cornstarch. Available from Asian-food purveyors. Moderately priced.

Potato Starch Translucent. More thickening power than cornstarch. Moderately priced.

Rice Flour Translucent. Relatively weak thickening power. Freezes well. Fairly expensive.

Liaison

The mixture of egg yolks and cream that is used to enrich and slightly thicken sauces and soups is called a liaison. A liaison is not a thickener in the same way that roux and pure starch slurries are, but the combination of cream and eggs, when properly simmered in a dish, adds sheen, smoothness, body, and flavor as well as a light golden-ivory color. Liaisons also add flavor and a smoother texture to a sauce or soup.

Liaisons add body and sheen to a dish. They are not thickeners in the same way that roux and pure starch slurries are, but the combination of cream and eggs, when properly simmered in a dish, gives more body as well as a light golden-ivory color. A liaison also adds flavor to a sauce or soup and gives it a smooth texture.

Egg yolks normally begin to coagulate at 149°F/65°C. The addition of cream raises the coagulation point to 180° to 185°F/82° to 85°C. Blend the cream and egg yolks together until evenly blended. Adding a portion of the hot liquid to the liaison avoids a drastic heat change, which could cause the yolks to curdle.

This process, known as tempering, reduces temperature extremes so the finished soup or sauce remains smooth. Gradually add about one-third of the hot liquid to the liaison, a ladleful at a time, whipping constantly.

When enough hot liquid has been added, return the tempered liaison to the soup or sauce. Return the pot to low heat and gently warm the mixture, stirring frequently, until it thickens slightly. Do not allow the mixture to go beyond 185°F/85°C or the egg yolks might curdle.

For reasons of quality, add the liaison as close to service time as possible. Hold soups and sauces thickened with a liaison above 140°F/60°C for food safety reasons but below 185°F/85°C to maintain quality.

A basic formula (by weight) for enough liaison to thicken 24 fl oz/ 720 mL liquid

3 parts cream (8 fl oz/240 mL)

1 part egg yolk (about 3 large yolks or 2½ fl oz/ 75 mL)

1. **Begin with a hot soup, sauce, or dish such as Veal Blanquette (page 660).** Egg yolks normally begin to coagulate at 149°F/65°C. The addition of cream raises the coagulation point to 180° to 185°F/82° to 85°C. Blend the cream and egg yolks together until evenly combined.

2. Slowly add some of the hot liquid to the liaison to temper it. Adding a portion of the hot liquid to the liaison avoids a drastic heat change, which could cause the yolks to curdle. This process, known as tempering, reduces temperature extremes so the finished soup or sauce remains smooth. Gradually add about one-third of the hot liquid to the liaison, a ladleful at a time, whisking constantly.

3. Add the tempered liaison back to the dish. When enough hot liquid has been added, return the tempered liaison to the soup or sauce. Return the pot to low heat and gently warm the mixture, stirring frequently, until slightly thickened. Do not allow the mixture to go beyond 185°F/85°C or the egg yolks might curdle.

Add the liaison as close to service time as possible. Hold soups and sauces thickened with a liaison above 140°F/60°C for food safety reasons, but below 185°F/85°C to maintain quality.

Chapter Fifteen

Stocks

Stocks are among the most basic preparations found in any professional kitchen. In fact, they are referred to in French as *fonds de cuisine*, or "the foundations of cooking." A stock is a flavorful liquid prepared by simmering meaty bones from meat or poultry, seafood, and/or vegetables in water with aromatics until their flavor, aroma, color, body, and nutritive value are extracted. The liquid is then used to prepare sauces, soups, and as a braising and simmering cooking medium for vegetables and grains.

Stocks

White stocks, brown stocks, and fumets are the three basic types of stock. White stocks are made by combining all of the ingredients with a cool liquid (typically water) and simmering them over gentle heat. Brown stocks are made by browning the bones and mirepoix in enough fat to produce a rich mahogany color, either by roasting in the oven or on the stovetop before simmering. Fumets (sometimes known as essences) call for sweating or smothering the main ingredients before simmering, often with the addition of a dry white wine.

For good flavor and body, use meaty bones and fish bones. They can be acquired as a by-product of meat and fish fabrication or purchased solely for stock. Bones from younger animals contain a high percentage of cartilage and other connective tissues that break down into gelatin during simmering and give the stock body. Knuckle, back, and neck bones are good for stock as well. Include any wholesome trim from fabrication, if available, to further bolster flavor. Cut bones into 3-in/8-cm lengths for quicker and more thorough extraction of flavor, gelatin, and nutritive value. If bones are purchased frozen, thaw them before simmering for stock.

Rinse all bones, fresh or frozen, thoroughly before putting them into the stockpot, to remove blood and other impurities that can compromise the quality of the stock. For brown stocks, prepare the bones and trim by roasting them first; for more information, see page 352.

Trim and cut mirepoix to a size that will allow for good flavor extraction. A ½-in/1-cm dice or slice is good for a simmering time of one hour. Cut vegetables larger or smaller for longer or shorter simmering times. The mirepoix and tomato paste called for in brown stocks are roasted or sautéed until browned before they are added to the stock.

Stocks also include a sachet d'épices or bouquet garni containing aromatics suited to the type of stock being made. Because the stock will eventually be strained, some chefs do not tie up sachet or bouquet ingredients. However, tying makes it easy to remove the aromatics if their flavor becomes too strong.

Pots used for stocks are usually taller than they are wide. This type of pot creates a smaller surface area so the evaporation rate is minimized during simmering. Some stockpots have spigots at the bottom that can be used to remove the finished stock without disturbing the bones. Steam-jacketed kettles are often used to produce large quantities of stock. Court bouillons, fumets, and essences that do not have long simmering times can be prepared in rondeaus or other wide shallow pots. Tilting or steam-jacketed kettles are often used for large-scale production. Ladles or skimmers should be on hand to remove scum from the stock as it simmers. Cheesecloth, sieves, and colanders are used to separate the bones and vegetables from the stock. A thermometer and metal containers for cooling, as well as plastic containers for storing the stock, should be on hand. Tasting spoons will also be needed.

A basic formula for 1 gal/3.84 L Meat or Poultry Stock

8 lb/3.63 kg bones and trimmings

1 gal 64 fl oz/5.76 L cool liquid (depending on the bone type)

1 lb/454 g mirepoix (page 333)

1 standard sachet d'épices or bouquet garni (page 331)

(Top) Ingredients for white stock

(Bottom) Ingredients for brown stock

A basic formula for 1 gal/3.84 L Fish or Shellfish Stock

12 lb/5.44 kg bones and trimmings

1 gal 16 fl oz/4.32 L cool liquid (sometimes including 32 to 64 fl oz/960 mL to 1.92 L dry white wine)

1 lb/454 g white mirepoix (page 333; sometimes including mushroom trimmings)

1 standard sachet d'épices or bouquet garni (page 331)

(Top) Ingredients for fish fumet

(Bottom) Ingredients for vegetable stock

1. **Combine the bones with cool liquid just to cover by two inches and bring them slowly to a simmer.** Skim as necessary. For the best flavor and clearest stock, start with a cool liquid (water or remouillage) to gently extract flavor and body. Maintain a bare simmer throughout the cooking process. Bubbles should break the surface of the stock infrequently. The French use the verb *frémir*, meaning "to tremble," to describe the action of the bubbles as the stock cooks.

2. **To produce a clear stock, skim the liquid consistently and regulate the proper temperature.** The French verb *dépouiller*, literally "to skin or peel," is used to describe the skimming process. Apart from the aesthetics of a clear stock, the impurities that leave a stock cloudy are the same elements that will quickly spoil and sour a stock. Therefore, the clearer the stock, the longer its shelf life.

3. Add the mirepoix to the stock at the appropriate time to extract the maximum amount of flavor. The right time to add mirepoix to all stocks except fish stocks and court bouillons is about 2 hours before the end of cooking time. Adding mirepoix at this point will allow enough time for the best flavor to be extracted but not so much time that the flavor is broken down and destroyed. Other aromatics such as sachet d'épices or bouquet garni should be added in the last 30 to 45 minutes of cooking. Taste the stock to determine whether it is necessary to adjust the standard formula. Since fish stocks, fumets, essences, and court bouillons do not have extended cooking times, the mirepoix ingredients are normally cut smaller and added near the beginning of the simmering time, and they remain in the stock throughout cooking.

4. Add a sachet about 45 minutes before the stock has finished simmering to obtain the most flavor. Simmer until the desired flavor, aroma, body, and color are achieved. Smell and taste the stock as it develops so that you can begin to understand its stages and to notice when it has reached its peak. Once the stock reaches that point, further cooking will cause flavors to become flat. Even the color of the stock may be slightly off if it simmers too long.

5. **Strain and use the stock immediately or cool it properly.** Pour or ladle the stock out of the pot and through a fine-mesh sieve or a colander lined with rinsed cheesecloth. Disturb the solid ingredients as little as possible for the clearest stock. Once you have removed as much stock as possible by ladling, drain the remaining stock through a colander into a bowl. Then strain the stock through cheesecloth or a fine-mesh sieve to remove any remaining impurities, if desired. Reserve the bones and mirepoix to prepare a remouillage if desired (see page 350).

6. **If not using immediately, cool the stock stirring frequently over an ice bath until it has reached 40°F/4°C.** Skim any fat that rises to the surface or wait until it has hardened under refrigeration and simply lift it away before reheating the stock for later use. Always check a stock before using it to make sure it is still flavorful and wholesome. Boil a small amount and taste it. The aroma should be appealing, not overly pungent or sour.

Evaluate the quality of the finished stock on the basis of four criteria: flavor, color, aroma, and clarity. If the correct ratio of bones, mirepoix, and aromatics to liquid has been used and the correct procedure has been followed, the flavor will be well balanced, rich, and full-bodied with the major flavoring ingredient dominating and the flavors of the aromatics unobtrusive.

The color of stocks will vary by type. Quality white stocks are clear and light to golden when hot. Brown stocks are a deep amber or brown due to the preliminary roasting of the bones and mirepoix. Vegetable stocks vary in color according to main ingredient.

General Guidelines for Stocks

Making stocks takes both time and money. If your kitchen prepares stocks, you should be sure you follow the correct procedures for cooling and storing them. Select a stock to use in a dish based upon either recipe requirements or the effect you hope to achieve, but make sure that any stock you use is flavorful and wholesome.

Remouillage

Translated from the French as "rewetting," remouillage is made by reserving the simmered bones and mirepoix from a stock and simmering them a second time. Remouillage may also be made from the clarification raft used to prepare consommé (see page 397). This secondary stock can be used as the liquid for stocks, broths, as a cooking medium, or reduced to a glace.

Glace

Glace is a highly reduced stock or remouillage. As a result of continued reduction, the stock acquires a jellylike or syrupy consistency and its flavor is highly concentrated. When chilled, a glace becomes rubbery. Glaces are used to boost the flavor of other foods, particularly sauces. When they are reconstituted with water, they may also serve as a sauce base in much the same way as a commercially prepared base. Glaces are made from different kinds of stock; the most common is *glace de viande*, made from brown veal stock, beef stock, or remouillage.

Commercial bases

Not all kitchens prepare stocks today, either because meaty bones and trim are not readily available on a consistent basis or because they do not have the space or manpower to successfully prepare and hold stocks. Commercially prepared bases are then used in place of stocks. Even in kitchens that do prepare stocks, bases are helpful to have on hand to deepen and improve the stock's flavor.

Bases are available in highly reduced forms, similar to the classic *glace de viande,* or dehydrated (powdered or cubed). Not all bases are created equal, however. Read the labels carefully. Avoid bases that rely on high-sodium ingredients for flavor. Quality bases are made from meats, bones, vegetables, spices, and aromatics. Prepare them according to the package instructions and taste each one. Judge the base on its flavor, saltiness, balance, and depth.

After deciding that a base meets your standards for quality and cost, learn how to make any adjustments necessary. For example, you might sweat or roast more vegetables and simmer them in a diluted base, perhaps along with browned trim, to make a rich brown sauce.

Cooking Times for Stocks

The following cooking times are approximate; the times will vary according to numerous factors such as ingredient quality, total volume, and the cooking temperature.

White Beef Stock
8 to 10 hours

White and Brown Veal and Game Stocks
6 to 8 hours

White Poultry and Game Bird Stocks
3 to 4 hours

Fish Stock and Fumet
45 minutes to 1 hour

Vegetable Stocks
45 minutes to 1 hour, depending on the specific ingredients and the size of the vegetable cut

Chicken Stock

Makes 1 gal/3.84 L

8 lb/3.63 kg chicken bones, cut into 3-in/8-cm lengths

1 gal 96 fl oz/6.72 L cold water

2 tsp/10 g salt

1 lb/454 g medium-dice **Mirepoix** (page 333)

1 **Sachet d'Épices** (page 331)

1. Rinse the bones under cool running water and place them in a stockpot.

2. Add the cold water and salt. (The water should cover the bones by about 2 in.) Slowly bring the stock to a simmer. Skim the surface as necessary.

3. Simmer for 3 to 4 hours.

4. Add the mirepoix and sachet and continue to simmer the stock 1 more hour, skimming as necessary and tasting from time to time.

5. Strain the stock. It may be used now (degrease by skimming if necessary), or it may be rapidly cooled and stored for later use.

NOTES
Replace 2 pounds of the chicken bones with chicken necks for an extra rich, gelatinous stock.

Add or replace aromatic ingredients to achieve a particular flavor.

For example:
    Ginger, lemongrass, and fresh or dried chiles
    Juniper berries for game stocks
    Strongly flavored herbs, such as tarragon or rosemary
    Wild mushroom stems

White Veal Stock: Replace the chicken bones with an equal amount of veal bones and simmer for 6 to 8 hours.

White Beef Stock: Replace the chicken bones with an equal amount of beef bones and simmer for 8 to 10 hours.

Brown Veal Stock

Makes 1 gal/3.84 L

2 fl oz/60 mL vegetable oil, or as needed

8 lb/3.63 kg veal bones, including knuckles and trim

1 gal 48 fl oz/5.28 L cold water

2 tsp/10 g salt

1 lb/454 g large-dice **Mirepoix** (page 333)

4 to 6 oz/113 to 170 g tomato paste

1 **Sachet d'Épices** (page 331)

1. Condition the roasting pan: Heat the pan and enough oil to lightly film the pan in a 425° to 450°F/218° to 232°C oven. Add the bones to the pan and return to the oven. Roast the bones, stirring and turning from time to time, until they are a deep brown, 30 to 45 minutes.

2. Transfer the bones to a stockpot and add all but 1 cup of the cold water and the salt. Deglaze the roasting pan with the remaining 1 cup of water and add the released drippings to the stockpot. Bring the stock to a simmer slowly over low heat. Adjust the heat if necessary to establish an even, gentle simmer and continue to cook, skimming the surface as necessary.

3. While the stock is simmering, heat a medium-sized rondeau over medium-high heat. Add enough oil to film the pan. Add the mirepoix and cook, stirring occasionally, until the onions are a deep golden brown, 15 to 20 minutes. Add the tomato paste and continue to cook, stirring frequently, until it takes on a rusty brown color and gives off a sweet aroma, 1 to 2 minutes. Add a few ladles of the stock to the rondeau and stir well to release the drippings; add this mixture to the stock after it has simmered for about 5 hours. Add the sachet at the same time.

4. Continue to simmer the stock, skimming as necessary and tasting from time to time, until it has developed a rich flavor and a noticeable body, about 1 more hour.

5. Strain the stock. It may be used now (degrease by skimming if necessary), or it may be rapidly cooled and stored for later use.

Brown Game Stock (Jus de Gibier): Replace the veal bones and trim with an equal amount of game bones and trim. Include fennel seeds and/or juniper berries in a standard sachet d'épices.

Estouffade: Replace half the veal bones and trim with beef bones and trim and add an unsmoked ham hock.

Brown Lamb Stock: Replace the veal bones and trim with an equal amount of lamb bones and trim. Add one or more of the following herbs and spices to the standard sachet d'épices: mint stems, juniper berries, cumin seeds, caraway seeds, or rosemary.

Brown Pork Stock: Replace the veal bones and trim with an equal amount of fresh or smoked pork bones and trim. Add one or more of the following herbs and spices to a standard sachet d'épices: oregano stems, crushed red pepper, caraway seeds, or mustard seeds.

Brown Chicken Stock: Replace the veal bones and trim with an equal amount of chicken bones and trim.

Brown Duck Stock: Replace the veal bones and trim with an equal amount of duck bones and trim (or bones of other game birds, such as pheasant). Include fennel seeds and/or juniper berries in a standard sachet d'épices, if desired.

Fish Fumet

Makes 1 gal/3.84 L

2 fl oz/60 mL vegetable oil

11 lb/4.99 kg nonoily fish bones

1 lb/454 g thinly sliced **White Mirepoix** (page 333)

112 fl oz/3.36 L cold water

32 fl oz/960 mL white wine

2 tsp/10 g salt

1 **Sachet d'Épices** (page 331)

1. Heat the oil in a large rondeau and add the bones and mirepoix. Cover the pot and sweat the bones and mirepoix over medium heat for 10 to 12 minutes until the mirepoix is soft and the bones are opaque.

2. Add the water, wine, salt, and sachet and bring to a simmer.

3. Simmer for 45 to 60 minutes, skimming the surface as necessary.

4. Strain the fumet. It may be used now (degrease by skimming if necessary), or it may be rapidly cooled and stored for later use.

Fish Stock: Combine the bones with the cool water and aromatics and simmer gently for 45 minutes. This is sometimes called the swimming method, to distinguish it from fumet made by the sweating method.

Shellfish Stock: Replace the fish bones with an equal amount of crustacean shells (shrimp, lobster, or crab). Sauté the shells in hot oil until the color deepens. Add a standard Mirepoix (page 333) and sauté until tender. If desired, add 3 oz/85 g of tomato paste and cook until it takes on a deep red color. Add enough water to cover the shells and simmer for 40 minutes, skimming throughout.

Vegetable Stock

Makes 1 gal/3.84 L

2 fl oz/60 mL vegetable oil, or as needed

3 lb/1.36 kg large-dice **Mirepoix** (page 333)

3 lb/1.36 kg nonstarchy vegetables (leeks, tomatoes, garlic, etc.)

1 gal 16 fl oz/4.32 L cold water

2 tsp/10 g salt

1 **Sachet d'Épices** (page 331)

1. Heat the oil in a large rondeau over medium-high heat and add the mirepoix and vegetables.

2. Cover and sweat the vegetables for 10 to 12 minutes, stirring occasionally.

3. Add the water and salt; simmer for 45 minutes to an hour, then add the sachet.

4. Strain the stock. It may be used now (degrease by skimming if necessary), or it may be rapidly cooled and stored for later use.

Roasted Vegetable Stock: Roast the vegetables in a large pan, turning to make sure all sides are evenly browned. Combine the roasted vegetables with the water and simmer for 45 minutes.

Court Bouillon

Makes 1 gal/3.84 L

1 gal 32 fl oz/4.80 L cold water

8 fl oz/240 mL white wine vinegar

2 tsp/10 g salt

12 oz/340 g sliced carrots

1 lb/454 g sliced onions

1 pinch dried thyme

3 bay leaves

12 parsley stems

½ tsp/1 g black peppercorns

1. Combine the water, vinegar, salt, carrots, onions, and herbs in a large stockpot. Simmer for 50 minutes.

2. Add the peppercorns and simmer for 10 minutes more.

3. Strain the court bouillon. It may be used now, or it may be rapidly cooled and stored for later use.

Poultry and Meat Stock (Brodo)

Makes 1 gal/3.84 L

2 lb 8 oz/1.13 kg beef shank

1 chicken fowl, excess skin and fat removed

2 lb 8 oz/1.13 kg turkey bones, cracked

2 lb 8 oz/1.13 kg chicken wings

8 oz/227 g chicken feet

1 gal 64 fl oz/5.76 L cold water

3 lb/1.36 kg roughly chopped **Mirepoix** (page 333)

5 garlic cloves, crushed

2 bay leaves

6 parsley stems

½ bunch thyme

2 tsp/10 g salt

1. Rinse all meat and bones in hot water twice. Drain.

2. Place the meat and bones in a large stockpot and cover with water by 6 in/15 cm. Bring to a simmer over medium heat, skimming as necessary.

3. Add the mirepoix, garlic, herbs, and salt. Continue to slowly simmer over medium-low heat for 6 hours, skimming often. Take care to not let the broth boil, as boiling will make the broth cloudy.

4. Strain the stock. It may be used now (degrease by skimming if necessary), or it may be rapidly cooled and stored for later use.

Dashi

Makes 1 gal/3.84 L

2 kelp (*kombu*), 3-in/8-cm squares

1 gal/3.84 L cold water

3 to 4 oz/85 to 113 g dried bonito (*katsuobushi*)

1. Slash the kombu with a knife in a few places and wipe it with a damp cloth to remove sand (do not remove any of the flavorful white powder).

2. In large stainless-steel stockpot, add the cold water and kombu. Bring it to a boil over medium heat. Just before the water boils, remove the kombu.

3. Add the bonito flakes and turn off the heat. Steep for 2 minutes.

4. Strain the dashi. It may be used now, or it may be rapidly cooled and stored for later use.

Chapter Sixteen

Sauces

Sauces are often considered one of the greatest tests of a chef's skill. The successful pairing of a sauce with a food demonstrates technical expertise, an understanding of the food, and the ability to judge and evaluate a dish's flavors, textures, and colors.

Brown Sauce

At one time the term *brown sauce* was equated exclusively with the classic sauces espagnole and demi-glace. Today it may also indicate jus de veau lié, pan sauces, or reduction-style sauces based on a brown or fortified stock.

Espagnole sauce is prepared by bolstering a brown veal stock with additional roasted mirepoix, tomato pinçage, and aromatics and thickening it with roux. Classically, demi-glace is composed of equal parts espagnole and brown stock and reduced by half or to a nappé consistency. These days, it may be made of brown stock that has additional caramelized trim and mirepoix, reduced to a nappé consistency, and optionally thickened with a starch slurry. Jus liés are made by reducing brown stocks or fortified stocks (with added flavorings if desired) and thickening them with a pure starch slurry. Pan sauces and reduction sauces are produced as part of the roasting or sautéing cooking process; thickening can be accomplished by reduction, roux, or pure starch slurries. Regardless of the approach taken, though, the end goal is the same—to make a basic brown sauce that is flavorful enough to be served as is but can also be used as the foundation for other sauces.

The ultimate success of the brown sauce depends directly on the base stock, usually Brown Veal Stock (page 352). The stock must be of excellent quality, with a rich and well-balanced flavor and aroma, and without any strong notes of mirepoix, herbs, or spices that might overwhelm the finished sauce.

Bones and trim, cut in small pieces for faster extraction, that are added to the sauce improve the flavor of the base stock. Mirepoix, cut into large dice, may also be added to the sauce base. If the stock is extremely flavorful, additional bones, trim, and mirepoix may not be necessary. Mushroom trim, herbs, garlic, or shallots may also be added to the sauce as it develops.

Roux (page 335) is one thickening option and it may be prepared ahead of time, or it may be prepared as part of the sauce-making process. The thickener of choice for jus lié is arrowroot, though another pure starch, such as potato starch or cornstarch, may be used. Arrowroot is preferable because it results in a translucent, glossy sauce.

Jus lié is generally prepared in a saucepan or pot that is wider than it is tall. This is the most effective means of extracting flavors fully and quickly into the finished sauce. You will also need a kitchen spoon, ladle, or skimmer to skim the developing sauce, and tasting spoons, fine strainers, and containers to hold the finished sauce. Additional containers are necessary for both cooling and storing the sauce.

A basic formula for 1 gal/3.84 L Brown Sauce

1 gal 64 fl oz/5.76 L Brown Stock (page 352)

4 lb/1.81 kg additional roasted bones and trim

1 lb/454 g large-cut mirepoix, well browned

Oil, for browning bones, trim, and mirepoix

3 to 4 oz/85 to 113 g tomato paste

12 oz/340 g roux (page 335) or 1 oz/28 g arrowroot or other pure starch

1 sachet d'épices or bouquet garni

1. **Brown the trim and/or bones and mirepoix.** The flavor of the base stock is usually fortified with well-browned meaty bones and lean trim meat and mirepoix, or a commercial base. Browning these ingredients will enrich the finished sauce and help darken its color. Brown them by roasting in a little oil in a hot oven (425° to 450°F/218° to 232°C) or over medium to high heat on the stovetop in the same pot that will be used to simmer the sauce. Let the bones, trim, and mirepoix reach a deep golden-brown color. Allow the tomato paste to "cook out" (pincé) until rust colored to reduce excessive sweetness, acidity, and bitterness. It also encourages the development of the sauce's overall flavor and aroma. When browning the mirepoix in the oven, add the tomato paste to the roasting pan with the vegetables. If browning the mirepoix on the stovetop, add the paste when the vegetables are nearly browned. Be careful not to let the tomato paste burn, as it cooks out very quickly on the stovetop. Deglaze the pan and add the deglazing liquid to the sauce.

(continued)

Add the brown stock to the bones and/or trim and mirepoix and simmer for 2 to 4 hours, skimming as necessary throughout the cooking time. (See photograph on page 357.) Let the sauce base simmer long enough for the richest possible flavor to develop. Skim the surface often throughout simmering time. Pulling the pot off center on the burner encourages impurities to collect on one side of the pot, where they are easier to collect.

2. **Add a sachet or other aromatics as the flavor develops.** Simmering develops flavor in two ways: extracting flavor from the bones, trim, and mirepoix and reducing the volume of liquid, concentrating flavor. Taste the sauce base frequently as it develops and adjust the seasoning as necessary by adding aromatics or seasonings. Remove from the heat once the desired flavor is achieved. (Optional: Add a prepared roux now and simmer for 3 minutes, if desired, to prepare an espagnole sauce. For jus lié, add a pure starch slurry either before or after straining, if desired, and simmer until thickened.)

for service by adding reductions, fortified wines, garnishes, and/or whole butter (see Options for Finishing a Perfect Brown Sauce, page 360).

Brown sauces sometimes develop a skin when they are held uncovered. To avoid this, use a fitted cover for the bain-marie or a piece of parchment paper or plastic wrap cut to fit directly on the surface of the sauce.

3. **Strain the sauce using a fine-mesh sieve or a double thickness of cheesecloth.** It is now ready to finish for service, or it may be rapidly cooled and stored. The texture and, to some extent, the color of a brown sauce depend on the type of thickener used. A roux-thickened brown sauce (espagnole) is opaque with a thick body. A sauce thickened with puréed mirepoix is also thick and opaque but with a slightly rougher, more rustic texture. A sauce thickened with both roux and reduction (demi-glace) is translucent and highly glossy, with a noticeable body, although it should never feel tacky in the mouth. A pure starch-thickened sauce (jus lié), as shown in the above photograph, has a greater degree of clarity than other brown sauces as well as a lighter texture and color.

Finish as desired and hold at 165°F/74°C for service. Return the sauce to a simmer and make any necessary adjustment to its flavor or consistency. If the sauce requires additional thickening, either reduce it by simmering over high heat or add a starch slurry now. If the sauce has already been thickened, with a roux, arrowroot, or by reduction, no additional thickener is necessary. Brown sauces can be finished

4. **Evaluate the quality of the finished brown sauce.** A brown sauce of excellent quality has a full, rich flavor. The initial roasting of bones, trimmings, and/or mirepoix gives the finished sauce a pleasant roasted or caramel aroma, readily discernible when the sauce is heated, and a predominant flavor of roasted meat or vegetables. The mirepoix, tomatoes, and aromatics should not overpower the main flavor. There should be no bitter or burnt flavors.

Good brown sauces have a deep brown color without any dark specks or debris, as shown above. The color is affected by the color of the base stock, the amount of tomato paste or purée used (too much will give a red cast to the sauce), the amount of caramelization on the trim and mirepoix, proper skimming, the length of simmering time (reduction factor), as well as any finishing or garnishing ingredients.

Options for Making Perfect Brown Sauce

Additional ingredients may be added as the sauce develops to improve the flavor of the base stock, such as the following: bones and trim, cut in small pieces; mirepoix, cut into large dice; mushroom trim; herbs, garlic, or shallots.

To thicken the sauce, any one of the following may be used, depending on your desired results: roux; puréed mirepoix; reduction (demi-glace); or pure starch (arrowroot, potato starch, or cornstarch). The texture and, to some extent, the color of a brown sauce depend on the type of thickener used.

Options for Finishing Perfect Brown Sauce

Some ingredients may be added to the simmering sauce after it has finished cooking:

Reductions of wine from deglazing, or that has simmered with aromatics;

Garnish of precooked high-moisture ingredients (mushrooms, shallots, and tomatoes);

Fortified wines such as Port, Madeira, or sherry; or

Butter that is cold or at room temperature.

NAME OF DERIVATIVE	FLAVOR PROFILE	TYPICALLY SERVED WITH
Bigarade	Caramelized sugar diluted with vinegar, orange, and lemon juices; finish with blanched finely julienned orange and lemon zests	Feathered game, duck
Bordelaise	Red wine, shallots, peppercorns, thyme, and bay leaf; finish with lemon juice, meat glaze, and diced or sliced poached bone marrow	Grilled red meats, fish (in contemporary cooking)
Bourguignonne	Red wine, shallots, thyme, parsley, bay leaf, and mushrooms; finish with whole butter and a pinch of cayenne pepper	Eggs or beef
Bretonne	Onions, butter, white wine, tomatoes, garlic; finish with a pinch of coarsely chopped parsley	Green Beans à la Bretonne
Charcutière	Sauce Robert finished with julienned cornichons	Smoked pork
Chasseur/Huntsman's	Mushrooms, shallots, white wine, brandy, tomatoes; finished with butter and herbs (tarragon, chervil, and/or parsley)	Beef and furred game
Cherry	Port wine, pâté spice, orange zest and juice, red currant jelly, and cherries	Duck or venison
Chevreuil	Poivrade Sauce with bacon in the mirepoix; simmer and skim while adding a little red wine; strain and finish with a pinch of sugar and cayenne pepper; use game trimmings in place of bacon for feathered game	Beef, feathered or furred game
Diane	Mirepoix, game trim, bay leaf, thyme, parsley, white wine, peppercorns; finish with butter, whipped cream, and small crescents of truffle and cooked egg white	Feathered or furred game
Financière	Madeira wine and truffle essence	Beef
Genevoise/Génoise	Mirepoix, salmon trim, red wine; finish with anchovy essence and butter	Salmon and trout
Gratin	White wine, fish, shallots, and parsley	Sole or other white fish
Italienne	Tomatoes and ham; finish with tarragon, chervil, and parsley; when preparing for fish, omit the ham	Poultry or fish
Matelote	Red wine, mushrooms, fish, parsley, and cayenne pepper	Eel
Mushroom	Mushrooms and butter	Beef, veal, poultry
Poivrade	Mirepoix, game trim, bay leaf, thyme, parsley, white wine, peppercorns; finish with butter	Furred game
Régence	Red wine, mirepoix, butter, and truffle	Sautéed livers and kidneys
Robert	Onions, butter, white wine; finish with a pinch of sugar and English dry mustard, diluted	Grilled pork
Zingara	Shallots, bread crumbs, butter; finish with parsley and lemon juice	Veal or poultry

White Sauce

The white sauce family includes the classic sauces velouté and béchamel, both produced by thickening a liquid with roux. A classic velouté, which translates from French as "velvety, soft, and smooth to the palate," is prepared by flavoring a white stock (veal, chicken, or fish) with aromatics and thickening it with blond roux. In Escoffier's time, a béchamel sauce was made by adding cream to a relatively thick velouté sauce. Today, it is made by thickening milk (sometimes infused with aromatics for flavor) with a white roux.

Stock (veal, chicken, fish, or vegetable) or milk used to make white sauces may be brought to a simmer and, if desired, infused with aromatics and flavorings to produce a special flavor and/or color in the finished sauce. Blond roux is the traditional thickener for veloutés; blond or white roux may be used for a béchamel (the darker the roux, the more golden the sauce will be). The amount of roux (page 335) determines the thickness of a white sauce.

Additional mirepoix, mushroom trim, or members of the onion family are sometimes added, either to strengthen the flavor of the sauce or to create a specific flavor profile. Cut them into small dice or slice them thinly to encourage rapid flavor release into the sauce.

White sauces scorch easily, and they can take on a grayish cast if prepared in an aluminum pan. Choose a heavy nonaluminum pot with a perfectly flat bottom for the best results. Simmer white sauces on a flattop for gentle, even heat, or use a heat diffuser if available.

A basic formula for 1 gal/3.84 L White Sauce

1 gal/3.84 L flavorful liquid (white stock for velouté; milk for béchamel)

1 sachet d'épices or bouquet garni or other aromatics (white mirepoix, minced onions, or mushroom trim, for instance) and seasonings as appropriate

12 oz to 1 lb/340 to 454 g white or blond roux

1. **Sweat the aromatics in fat.** Any meat trim included should be gently cooked with them. There are several methods of incorporating the roux into the white sauce. The first is to add flour to the fat and aromatics in the pot and cook, stirring frequently. The roux is then cooked in the pot, as part of the sauce-making process. Add more oil or butter as needed to produce a roux of the appropriate consistency. Let the roux cook for about 4 to 5 minutes or to a light blond color (as shown in the above photograph). Another method is for a prepared roux to be added to the softened aromatics. A final method is adding the liquid to the aromatics and bringing it to a simmer; later, a prepared roux is whisked into the simmering liquid. In any case, the roux should be warm when it is added to the hot stock.

Add the liquid to the roux gradually. Many chefs add cool or room-temperature stock or milk to the roux. Others prefer to bring the liquid to a simmer separately, which allows them to adjust the seasoning with salt, pepper, or other aromatic ingredients. If the liquid is preheated, it should be removed from the heat so that its temperature drops slightly, making it cooler than the hot roux. Add the liquid in stages, whisking until very smooth between additions.

2. **Add seasoning, sachet, or other aromatics and simmer for 30 minutes, stirring frequently and tasting throughout the cooking time.** Very rich stocks may not require additional aromatics. If desired, either infuse the liquid with them when preheating or add a sachet or bouquet garni once the sauce returns to a simmer. A simmering time of at least 30 minutes is long enough to cook away any raw flavor from the roux.

Using a wooden spoon, stir the sauce occasionally while simmering. Make sure that the spoon scrapes the bottom and corners of the pot to prevent scorching. Scorching is of more concern with béchamel than with velouté because milk solids tend to settle.

Taste the sauce frequently as it develops, adjusting the seasoning as necessary. To test the texture, hold a small amount of the sauce on your tongue and press it against the roof of your mouth. If the sauce is adequately cooked, there will be no tacky, gluey, or gritty sensation.

3. **Strain the sauce.** As the sauce simmers, it almost inevitably develops a thick skin on its surface as well as a heavy, gluey layer on the bottom and sides of the pot. Straining the sauce removes any lumps and develops a very smooth texture. The sauce is ready to use now, or it may be cooled and stored for later use.

Finish as desired and hold the sauce at 165°F/74°C for service. Return the sauce to a simmer over low heat, stirring frequently. Make any necessary adjustments to the consistency, and add any finishing ingredients. For white sauce derivatives, the base sauce may be flavored with a reduction or essence and garnished. White sauces are also often finished with cream.

White sauces may develop a skin if held uncovered. To avoid this use a fitted cover on the bain-marie or place a piece of parchment paper or plastic wrap to fit directly on the surface of the sauce. An excellent white sauce meets several criteria. The flavor reflects the liquid used in its preparation. The sauce should be translucent, with a definite sheen. A good white sauce is perfectly smooth, with noticeable body and no graininess. It is thick enough to coat the back of a spoon yet still easy to pour from a ladle.

Examples of Sauce Béchamel Derivatives

NAME OF DERIVATIVE	FLAVOR PROFILE	TYPICALLY SERVED WITH
Bohémienne	Tarragon; served cold	Cold fish, poached salmon
Cardinal	Truffles and lobster	Fish, truffles, and lobster
Écossaise/Scotch Egg	Eggs	Eggs
Homard à l'Anglaise/Lobster	Anchovy essence; garnished with diced lobster meat and cayenne	Fish
Huitres/Oyster	Oyster; garnished with sliced poached oysters	Poached fish
Mornay	Gruyère and Parmesan; finish with butter	Poached fish
Sauce à l'Anglaise/Egg	Eggs and nutmeg	Dessert sauce

Options for Making the Perfect White Sauce

The liquid used to make a white sauce may be different depending on the desired use and whether it is a velouté or a béchamel.

Liquid used to make velouté:
   White veal stock
   Chicken stock
   Fish stock
   Vegetable stock

Liquid used to make béchamel:
   Milk

Additional seasonings may be added depending on the desired flavor profile and the richness of the stock. Mirepoix and vegetable trim from mushrooms or onions would be added at the beginning of the cooking process while aromatics such as a sachet should be added during the last 30 minutes of simmering. When using cheese, it should be grated and stirred in after the sauce has been thickened.

   Additional vegetables
   A sachet or bouquet
   Roasted tomato product
   Grated cheese

Using different amounts of roux will allow for varying consistencies of sauce, which are necessary depending on the desired use.

For a light consistency for soups, add 10 to 12 oz/284 to 340 g blond or white roux.

For medium consistency for most sauces, increase the amount of roux to 12 to 14 oz/340 to 397 g.

For heavy consistency for a binder for croquettes, fillings, stuffings, or baked pasta dishes, increase the amount of roux to 1 lb 2 oz to 1 lb 4 oz/510 to 567 g.

A heavy béchamel must be strained by the wringing method because it is too thick to pass through a fine-mesh strainer.

Examples of Sauce Velouté Derivatives

NAME OF DERIVATIVE	FLAVOR PROFILE	TYPICALLY SERVED WITH
Albufera	Sauce Suprême, meat glaze, and pimiento butter	Poached and braised poultry
Allemande/Parisienne	Mushrooms, egg yolks, lemon	Poultry
Américaine	Anchovies, fish trim, and butter	Fish
Aurore	Tomato purée	Eggs, white meat, and poultry
Aurore Maigre	Fish trim and butter	Fish
Aux Crevettes	Fish trim, cream, shrimp shells, and butter	Fish and certain egg dishes
Bercy	Shallots, white wine, fish trim, butter, and chopped parsley	Fish
Bonnefoy	White Bordelaise with white wine and velouté instead of espagnole; finish with tarragon	Grilled fish and white meats
Bretonne	Fish trim, cream, leeks, celery, onions, and mushrooms	Fish
Chivry	White wine, chervil, parsley, tarragon, shallots, chives, and fresh young salad burnet	Poached and boiled poultry
Diplomate	Fish trim, butter, lobster meat, and truffle	Whole large fish
Normande	Fish trim, mushrooms, mussels, lemon juice, egg yolks for a wide range of applications for other fish dishes	Sole Normande; also used as base
Suprême	Mushrooms, cream, and butter	Poultry
Véron	Sauce Normande, Sauce Tyrolienne, melted meat glaze, and anchovy essence	Fish
Villeroy	Mushrooms, egg yolks, lemon, ham, and truffle	Used to coat items to be breaded
Vin Blanc	Fish trim, egg yolks, and butter	Fish

Tomato Sauce

Tomato sauces of all sorts, from simply seasoned and fresh to complex and highly seasoned, are featured in cuisines around the world. Tomato sauce is a generic term used to describe any sauce that is based mainly on tomatoes. Tomato sauces can be made several ways. They may be raw or cooked, anywhere from ten minutes to several hours. In some versions, olive oil is the only cooking fat. For others, rendered salt pork or bacon is required. Some recipes call for roasted veal or pork bones; others are made strictly from tomatoes and the desired vegetables. Some tomato sauces are puréed until smooth while others are left chunky. Escoffier's tomato sauce relied on roux as a thickener.

Good tomato sauce can be made from fresh or canned tomatoes. When fresh tomatoes are at their peak, it may be a good idea to use them exclusively. At other times of the year, good-quality canned tomatoes are a better choice. Plum tomatoes, sometimes referred to as Romas, are generally preferred for tomato sauces because they have a high ratio of flesh to skin and seeds. Fresh tomatoes may be skinned and seeded for sauce, or they may be simply rinsed, cored, and quartered or chopped. Canned tomatoes come peeled and whole, puréed, or a combination of the two. Tomato paste is sometimes added to the sauce as well.

There are many choices for additional flavoring ingredients. Some recipes call for a standard mirepoix as the aromatic vegetable component, while others rely simply on garlic and onions.

Choose a heavy-gauge pot that is made of nonreactive materials such as stainless steel or anodized aluminum because tomatoes have a high acid content. Because of the high sugar content of some tomatoes, you will need to establish an even heat without hot spots so the sauce will not scorch. Use a food mill to purée the sauce. For a very smooth texture, you may wish to use a blender, immersion blender, or food processor.

A basic formula for 1 gal/3.84 L Tomato Sauce

10 to 12 lb/4.54 to 5.44 kg fresh tomatoes or 9 lb/4.08 kg canned tomatoes

2 fl oz/60 mL oil or other cooking fat

12 oz/340 g minced onions and/or

1 oz/28 g garlic

Salt and pepper

Additional ingredients or preparations (depending on your formula or intended use): tomato purée and/or paste, carrots or mirepoix, fresh and/or dried herbs, smoked meats, stock, thickeners (roux or pure starch slurries)

1. **Cook the onions until tender and to the desired color before adding the tomatoes.** Sweat or sauté the aromatic vegetables gently to release their flavor into the fat to help the flavor permeate the sauce. The way the vegetables are cooked influences the flavor of the finished sauce: The vegetables are usually sweated in a fat until they become tender, but for a more complex roasted flavor, they may be sautéed until lightly browned.

Purée the sauce, if desired. If using a blender, a small amount of oil added during puréeing will emulsify the sauce, creating a lighter yet thicker consistency.

Check the balance and seasoning of the sauce and make any necessary adjustments to its flavor and consistency by adding salt, pepper, fresh herbs, or other ingredients as indicated by the recipe. At this point, the sauce is ready to be served, or it may be finished for service as desired (see recipes), or it may be cooled and stored.

2. **Add the tomatoes and any remaining ingredients and simmer until the flavor is fully developed.** Stir frequently, skimming and tasting throughout the cooking time. If desired, add fresh herbs just before the sauce has finished cooking. (A fresh chiffonade of basil is added above.)

Cooking time varies, depending on the ingredients, but in general, the less cooking time, the better for any sauce based on fruits or vegetables. Extended cooking diminishes the fresh flavors. Most tomato sauces should be cooked just long enough for the flavors to meld together. If a tomato sauce that is not going to be puréed is too watery, strain and reduce the excess liquid separately to avoid overcooking.

Stir tomato sauce frequently throughout preparation, and check the flavor occasionally. If it becomes necessary to correct a harsh or bitter flavor, sweat a small amount of chopped onions and carrot and add them to the sauce. If the flavor is weak, add a small amount of reduced tomato paste or purée. Too much sweetness may be corrected by adding stock, water, or more tomatoes.

Options for Making the Perfect Tomato Sauce

To develop different flavors, add any of the following ingredients at the appropriate time. Some are added early in the cooking process, while others are added near the end so they retain their individual flavor and fresh taste. Onions and other aromatics added at the very beginning of the cooking process may be sautéed until lightly browned rather than until just tender for additional depth of flavor.

Fresh and/or dried herbs
Smoked meats
Smoked ham bone or pork bone
Tomato paste or purée
Onions and carrots, sweated and chopped
Stock

When appropriate, a tomato sauce may be thickened with any of the following:

Roux
Pure starch slurries

The type of tomato product used will also have a definite effect on the final product. Any of the following may be used, some alone or in combination:

Fresh tomatoes
Canned tomatoes—whole, peeled, puréed, or chopped
Tomato paste

Depending on the desired finished consistency of the tomato sauce, it may be puréed.

A good tomato sauce is opaque and slightly coarse, with a concentrated flavor of tomatoes and without any trace of bitterness, excess acidity, or sweetness. Ingredients selected to flavor the sauce should provide only subtle underpinnings. Tomato sauces should pour easily. The sauce on the left was not puréed while the sauce on the right was puréed using the fine opening of a food mill.

Hollandaise Sauce

Since the largest part of hollandaise is butter, the success or failure of the sauce depends not only on skillfully combining egg yolks, water, acid, and butter into a rich, smooth sauce, but also on the quality of the butter itself. Hollandaise sauce is prepared by emulsifying melted or clarified butter and water (in the form of an acidic reduction and/or lemon juice) with partially cooked egg yolks. A number of similar warm egg emulsion sauces, as this group of sauces is sometimes known, can be prepared by varying the ingredients in the reduction or by adding different finishing and garnishing ingredients such as tarragon. The group includes béarnaise, choron, and mousseline sauces. Hollandaise can also be combined with whipped cream and/or velouté to prepare a glaçage, which is used to coat a dish that is then lightly browned under a salamander or broiler just before service.

Melted whole butter or clarified butter may be used in a hollandaise. Some chefs like melted whole butter for the rich, creamy flavor it imparts to the sauce, which is best for most meat, fish, vegetable, and egg dishes. Others prefer clarified butter, for a stiffer, more stable sauce, which is of particular advantage if the sauce is to be used in a glaçage. Whatever the approach, the butter must be quite warm (about 145°F/63°C) but not too hot for the sauce to come together successfully.

In general, the ratio of egg to butter is 1 egg yolk to every 2 to 3 oz/57 to 85 g of butter. As the volume of sauce increases, the amount of butter that can be emulsified with 1 egg yolk also increases. A hollandaise made with 20 yolks, for instance, can usually tolerate more than 3 oz/85 g of butter per yolk. Pasteurized egg yolks may be used for hollandaise, if desired. However, the method outlined here cooks the yolks enough that salmonella bacteria, a major concern with eggs, is rendered harmless.

An acidic ingredient is included in Hollandaise both for flavor and for the effect it has on the protein in the egg yolks. The acidic ingredient, which can be either a vinegar reduction or lemon juice, also provides the water necessary to form an emulsion. Whether to use a reduction or lemon juice is determined by the desired flavor of the finished sauce. A reduction will impart a more complex flavor, particularly if lemon juice is also used as a final seasoning.

A basic formula for a 10-portion (2 fl oz/60 mL per portion) batch of Hollandaise Sauce

4 egg yolks or an equivalent quantity of pasteurized egg yolks (3½ oz/99 g)

10 to 12 fl oz/300 to 360 mL melted whole butter or clarified butter

Reduction made from white wine or cider vinegar, minced shallots, and peppercorns

Lemon juice, salt, and hot sauce or cayenne

1. **Having all of the mise en place prepared is one of the keys to successfully making hollandaise sauce.** Unlike many other sauces, hollandaise is prepared in a single operation. It is also fragile because it is not a true mixture.

2. **Make the standard reduction for hollandaise.**
Cook dry white wine, white wine vinegar, and cracked peppercorns over moderate direct heat until nearly dry (à sec). Cool the reduction to room temperature, then strain into a stainless-steel bowl.

3. **Add the egg yolks to the reduction and whisk over barely simmering water until thickened and warm (145°F/63°C).** Be sure that the water is just barely simmering, with no visible signs of surface action, just plenty of steam rising from the surface. As the yolks become warm they increase in volume

If the yolks seem to be getting too hot and coagulating slightly around the sides and bottom of the bowl, remove it from the heat. Set the bowl on a cool surface and whisk until the mixture has cooled very slightly. Continue cooking over barely simmering water.

When the yolks have tripled in volume, fall in ribbons into the bowl, and the whisk leaves "trails" in them, remove them from the simmering water. Do not overcook the yolks or they will lose their ability to emulsify the sauce.

Add seasonings such as lemon juice, salt, pepper, and cayenne, as desired, when the sauce is nearly finished. Lemon juice will lighten the sauce's flavor and texture, but do not let it become a dominant taste. Add just enough to lift the flavor. If the sauce is too thick, add a little warm water to regain the desired light texture.

Specific ingredients may be added to produce a derivative sauce at this point. Add meat glaze (glace de viande), tomato purée, essences or juices, or other semiliquid or liquid ingredients to the sauce gradually to avoid thinning it too much. Including flavoring ingredients may mean that other seasonings and flavorings need to be adjusted again.

Some hollandaise-style sauces are finished with minced herbs. Herbs should be properly rinsed, dried, and then cut into uniform mince or chiffonade with a very sharp knife to retain color and flavor. Finely diced tomato or citrus suprêmes may also be added to certain hollandaise-style sauces; these garnishes should be properly cut and allowed to drain, so that excess moisture does not thin the sauce.

4. **Stabilize the bowl by setting it on a towel or in a pot that has been draped with a towel to keep the bowl from slipping.** Add the butter slowly in a thin stream, whisking constantly as it is incorporated. The sauce will begin to thicken as more butter is blended in. If the sauce becomes too thick, add a bit of water or lemon juice. This makes it possible to finish adding the correct amount of butter without breaking the sauce.

If the sauce does start to break, try adding a small amount of water and whisking until the sauce is smooth before adding more butter. If that doesn't work, cook another egg yolk over simmering water until thickened, as directed above, and then gradually whisk the broken hollandaise into the new egg yolk. Note, however, that a sauce restored in this manner will not have the same volume as a sauce that did not have to be rescued, and it will not hold as well. If the sauce becomes too hot, the egg yolks will begin to scramble. To correct this problem, remove the sauce from the heat and add a small amount of cool water. Whisk the sauce until it is smooth and, if necessary, strain it to remove any bits of overcooked yolk.

Some kitchens prepare batches of hollandaise to be finished to order with the appropriate flavorings and garnishes. Be sure that the storage containers are perfectly clean. Stainless-steel bain-maries, ceramic containers, or vacuum bottles with wide necks are good choices. Keep all sauce spoons and ladles meticulously clean, and never reintroduce a tasting spoon, bare fingers, or other sources of cross contamination into the sauce.

5. **Evaluate the quality of the finished hollandaise.** Butter is the predominant flavor and aroma of a good hollandaise sauce. The egg yolks contribute a great deal of flavor as well. The reduction ingredients give the sauce a balanced taste, as do the lemon juice and any additional finishing seasonings. Hollandaise should be a lemon-yellow color with a satiny smooth texture. (A grainy texture indicates that the egg yolks are overcooked or scrambled.) The sauce should have a luster and not appear oily. The consistency should be light and pourable.

Serve immediately or hold hollandaise at or near 145°F/63°C for no more than 2 hours. Most kitchens have one or two spots that are the perfect temperature for holding hollandaise, usually above the stove or ovens or near (but not directly under) heat lamps. Holding hollandaise presents an unusual challenge, however. The sauce must be held below 150°F/66°C to keep the yolks from curdling, but at this temperature the sauce hovers just above the danger zone for bacterial growth. The acid from the reduction and/or lemon juice helps keep some bacteria at bay, but the sauce should never be held longer than 2 hours.

Examples of Hollandaise Derivative Sauces

NAME	FLAVOR PROFILE	TYPICALLY SERVED WITH
Bavaroise	Crayfish butter, whipped cream, and diced crayfish tail meat	Fish
Béarnaise	Tarragon reduction; garnish with fresh tarragon and chervil	Grilled meats
Choron	Béarnaise and tomato	Grilled meat and poultry
Foyot/Valois	Béarnaise and glace de viande	Grilled meats and offal
Maltaise	Blood oranges	Asparagus
Mousseline	Whipped heavy cream	Boiled fish, asparagus
Paloise	Mint reduction and fresh mint	Grilled meats
Royal	Equal parts velouté, hollandaise, and whipped heavy cream	Poached white meats and shallow-poached fish

Options for Making the Perfect Hollandaise

Melted whole butter or clarified butter may be used in a hollandaise. Melted whole butter provides a richer, creamier texture, while clarified butter provides a stiffer, more stable sauce.

The acidic ingredient can be varied when making the sauce, depending on the desired flavor, such as:

Vinegar reduction
Lemon juice

A number of similar warm egg emulsion sauces, as this group of sauces is sometimes known, can be prepared by varying the ingredients in the reduction or by adding different finishing and garnishing ingredients:

Lemon juice
Cayenne
Minced herbs
Finely diced tomato or citrus suprêmes
Meat glaze (glace de viande), tomato purée, essences, or juices

Hollandaise can also be combined with whipped cream and/or velouté to prepare a glaçage.

Beurre Blanc

Traditionally, beurre blanc is prepared as an integral part of the shallow-poaching process, using the reduction cooking liquid (cuisson). Another common practice is to prepare a reduction separately and make the beurre blanc in a larger batch so it can be used as a grand sauce on which derivative sauces are based. As with hollandaise, beurre blanc derivatives are prepared by either varying the ingredients in the reduction or altering the garnish ingredients. Beurre rouge, for instance, is made by using red wine in the reduction.

The quality of the butter is critical to the success of a beurre blanc. Unsalted butter is best because the salt level can better be controlled to taste later on. Check the butter carefully for a creamy texture and sweet aroma. Cube the butter and keep it cool.

A standard reduction for a beurre blanc is made from dry white wine and shallots. (When prepared as part of a shallow-poached dish, the cooking liquid becomes the reduction used in the sauce; see page 610.) Other ingredients often used in the reduction include vinegar or citrus juice; chopped herbs including tarragon, basil, chives, or chervil; cracked peppercorns; and sometimes garlic, ginger, lemongrass, saffron, and other flavoring ingredients.

A small amount of reduced heavy cream is occasionally added to stabilize the emulsion. To use cream, reduce it by half separately. Carefully simmer the cream until it thickens and has a rich, ivory-yellow color. The more reduced the cream, the greater its stabilizing effect. The more stable the sauce, the longer it will last during service. However, the flavor of cream will overpower the fresh taste of the butter.

Be sure that the pan is of a nonreactive metal. Bi-metal pans, such as copper or anodized aluminum lined with stainless steel, are excellent choices for this sauce.

A whisk may be used to incorporate the butter into the sauce, but many chefs prefer to allow the motion of the pan swirling over the burner or flattop to incorporate the butter. Straining is optional for this sauce, but if you choose to strain either the reduction or the finished sauce, you will need a sieve. Once prepared, the sauce may be kept warm in the container used to prepare it, or it may be transferred to a clean bain-marie, ceramic vessel, or wide-necked vacuum bottle.

A basic formula for 32 fl oz/960 mL Beurre Blanc

1 lb 8 oz/680 g butter

Reduction made from 8 fl oz/240 mL dry white wine, 3 fl oz/90 mL vinegar, shallots, and peppercorns

4 fl oz/120 mL heavy cream (optional)

Salt

Ground white pepper

Lemon juice

1. **Prepare the initial reduction of acid, shallots, and peppercorns, which gives the sauce much of its flavor.** Other aromatics, such as shallots or bay leaves, may be added as required by the recipe. Combine the reduction ingredients and reduce over fairly brisk heat to a syrupy consistency (à sec). If preparing the sauce as an integral part of a shallow-poached dish, simply reduce the cuisson (see page 610).

Reduce the heat to low. Gradually incorporate the butter into the reduction, blending it in with a whisk (as shown above) or by keeping the pan in constant motion. The action is similar to that used in finishing a sauce with butter (*monter au beurre*). If the sauce looks oily rather than creamy or if it appears to be separating, it has gotten too hot.

Immediately pull the pan off the heat and set it on a cool surface. Continue to add the butter a little at a time, whisking until the mixture regains the proper creamy appearance. Then continue to incorporate the remainder of the butter over low heat.

If the butter takes a very long time to become incorporated into the sauce, increase the heat under the pan very slightly.

Options for Making the Perfect Beurre Blanc

Additional ingredients may be added to the reduction for flavor:

- Vinegar
- Citrus juice
- Red wine
- Chopped herbs
- Cracked peppercorns
- Garlic
- Ginger
- Lemongrass
- Saffron

A small amount of reduced heavy cream is occasionally added to stabilize the sauce. If cream is used, reduce it by half separately. The more the cream is reduced, the greater its stabilizing effect.

Straining is optional for this sauce, as the reduction ingredients can be left in the sauce for texture and garnish.

2. **Make the necessary final adjustments to flavor and texture by checking the seasoning and straining, if desired.** Alternatively, the reduction ingredients can also be left in the sauce for texture and garnish. If you did not strain the reduction earlier, you now have the option of straining the sauce. If you do choose to strain, work quickly to keep the sauce warm.

Serve immediately or keep warm. To prepare a large batch of beurre blanc and hold it through a service period, use the same holding techniques described for hollandaise (see page 375). The sauce may deteriorate over time, however, and must be monitored for quality.

The flavor of beurre blanc is that of whole butter with piquant accents from the reduction. The finishing and/or garnishing ingredients also influence the flavor. A good beurre blanc is creamy in color, although garnishes may change the color. The sauce should have a distinct sheen. The body should be light. If the sauce is too thin, it probably does not contain enough butter. Conversely, a beurre blanc that is too thick includes too much butter or cream. The texture should be frothy, and the sauce should not leave an oily or greasy feeling in the mouth.

The Purpose of Sauces

Most sauces have more than one function in a dish. A sauce that adds a counterpoint flavor, for example, may also introduce textural and visual appeal. Sauces generally serve one or more of the following purposes.

Introduce complementary or counterpoint flavors

Sauces that are classically paired with particular foods illustrate this function. Suprême sauce is based on a reduction of chicken velouté with chicken stock and finished with cream. This ivory-colored sauce has a deep chicken flavor and a velvety texture. When served with chicken, the color and flavor of the sauce complement the delicate meat and help intensify its flavor. The cream in the sauce rounds out the flavors.

Charcutière sauce is made with mustard and cornichons. This sauce is pungent and flavorful. When served with pork, the sharpness of the sauce introduces a counterpoint flavor, cutting the meat's richness and providing a contrast that is pleasing but not startling to the palate. The sauce brings out the pork's flavor but might overwhelm a more delicate meat like veal.

A sauce that includes a flavor complementary to a food enhances the flavor of that food. Tarragon heightens the mild sweetness of poultry. A pungent green peppercorn sauce highlights the rich flavor of beef by deepening and enriching the overall taste.

Add moisture or succulence

A sauce can add moisture to naturally lean foods (e.g., poultry or fish) or when using cooking techniques that tend to have a drying effect, such as grilling or sautéing. Grilled foods are frequently served with a warm butter emulsion sauce like béarnaise, with compound butter, or with salsa or chutney. Beurre blanc is often served with shallow-poached lean white fish to add a bit of succulence to the dish.

Add visual interest

A sauce can enhance a dish's appearance by adding luster and sheen. Lightly coating a sautéed medallion of lamb with a jus lié creates a glossy finish on the lamb, giving the entire plate more eye appeal. Pooling a red pepper coulis beneath a grilled swordfish steak gives the dish a degree of visual excitement by adding an element of color.

Adjust texture

Many sauces include a garnish that adds texture to the finished dish. A sauce finished with tomatoes and mushrooms enhances Chicken Chasseur, while a smooth sauce adds a textural contrast to pan-fried soft-shell crab.

Sauce Pairing

Certain classic sauce combinations endure because the composition is well balanced in all areas: taste, texture, and eye appeal. When choosing an appropriate sauce, it should be:

- **Suitable for the style of service.** In a banquet setting or in any situation where large quantities of food must be served rapidly and at the peak of flavor, choose a sauce that may be prepared in advance and held in large quantities at the correct temperature without affecting quality. In an à la carte kitchen, sauces prepared à la minute are more appropriate.

- **Matched to the main ingredient's cooking technique.** Pair a cooking technique that produces flavorful drippings (fond), such as roasting or sautéing, with a sauce that makes use of those drippings. Similarly, beurre blanc is suitable for foods that have been shallow-poached because the cooking liquid (cuisson) can become a part of the sauce.

- **Appropriate for the flavor of the food with which it is paired.** Dover sole is perfectly complemented by a delicate cream sauce. The same sauce would be overwhelmed by the flavor of grilled tuna. Lamb has its own strong flavor that can stand up to a sauce flavored by rosemary. The same sauce would completely overpower a delicate fish.

Guidelines for Plating Sauces

- **Maintain correct temperature.** Check the temperature of the sauce, of the food being sauced, and of the plate. Be sure that hot sauces are extremely hot, warm emulsion sauces are as warm as possible without danger of breaking, and cold sauces remain cold until they come in contact with hot foods.

- **Consider the texture of the food being served.** Pool the sauce beneath the food, spreading it in a layer directly on the plate if the food has a crisp or otherwise interesting texture. Spoon or ladle the sauce evenly over the top of the food if it could benefit from a little cover or if the sauce has visual appeal.

- **Serve an appropriate portion of sauce.** There should be enough sauce for every bite of the sauced food but not so much that the dish looks swamped. Too much sauce disturbs the balance between the items on the plate and makes it difficult for the waiter to carry the food from the kitchen to the guest's table without at least some of the sauce running onto the rim, or worse, over the edge of the plate.

Jus de Veau Lié

Makes 1 gal/3.84 L

2 fl oz/60 mL vegetable oil

4 lb/1.81 kg lean veal trim

1 lb/454 g medium-dice **Mirepoix** (page 333)

4 fl oz/120 mL tomato purée

1 gal 16 fl oz/4.32 L **Brown Veal Stock** (page 352)

1 **Sachet d'Épices** (page 331)

1 oz/28 g arrowroot or cornstarch, diluted with cold water or stock to make a slurry

salt, as needed

ground black pepper, as needed

1. Heat the oil in a rondeau over medium heat. Add the veal trim and mirepoix and sauté, stirring from time to time, until the veal, onions, and carrots have taken on a rich brown color, 25 to 30 minutes.

2. Add the tomato purée and continue to cook over medium heat until it turns a rusty brown and has a sweet aroma, about 1 minute.

3. Add the stock and bring to a simmer. Continue to simmer, skimming as necessary, until a good flavor develops, 2 to 3 hours. Add the sachet during the last hour of cooking time.

4. Return the sauce base to a simmer. Stir the slurry to recombine if necessary and gradually add it to the sauce base, adding just enough to achieve a good coating consistency (nappé). The amount of slurry needed depends on the batch itself and its intended use.

5. Taste the sauce and season with salt and pepper.

6. Strain the sauce. The sauce is ready to serve now, or it may be rapidly cooled and refrigerated for later use.

Jus de Volaille Lié: Replace the Brown Veal Stock with Brown Chicken Stock (page 352) and replace the veal trim with an equal amount of chicken trim.

Jus de Canard Lié: Replace the Brown Veal Stock with Brown Duck Stock (page 352) and replace the veal trim with an equal amount of duck trim.

Jus d'Agneau Lié: Replace the Brown Veal Stock with Brown Lamb Stock (page 352) and replace the veal trim with an equal amount of lamb trim.

Jus de Gibier Lié: Replace the Brown Veal Stock with Brown Game Stock (page 352) and replace the veal trim with an equal amount of venison trim.

Espagnole Sauce

Makes 1 gal/3.84 L

3 fl oz/90 mL vegetable oil

1 lb/454 g medium-dice **Mirepoix** ingredients, separate (page 333)

2 fl oz/60 mL tomato paste

1 gal 32 fl oz/5.76 L **Brown Veal Stock** (page 352), hot

1 lb/454 g **Brown Roux** (page 335)

1 **Sachet d'Épices** (page 331)

salt, as needed

ground black pepper, as needed

1. Heat the oil in a rondeau over medium heat and sauté the carrots until lightly browned. Add the onions and sauté until translucent. Add the celery and cook until browned.

2. Add the tomato paste and cook for several minutes until it turns a rusty brown and has a sweet aroma, about 1 minute.

3. Add the stock and bring it to a simmer.

4. Whisk the roux into the stock. Return to a simmer and add the sachet. Simmer for about 1 hour, skimming the surface as necessary.

5. Strain the sauce. Taste the sauce and season with salt and pepper. The sauce is ready to serve now, or it may be rapidly cooled and refrigerated for later use.

Demi-Glace

Makes 32 fl oz/960 mL

32 fl oz/960 mL **Brown Veal Stock** (page 352)

32 fl oz/960 mL **Espagnole Sauce** (page 382)

1. Combine the stock and the Espagnole Sauce in a heavy pot and simmer over low to medium heat until reduced by half. Skim the sauce frequently as it simmers.

2. Strain the sauce. The sauce is ready to serve now, or it may be rapidly cooled and refrigerated for later use.

Chicken Velouté

Makes 1 gal/3.84 mL

2 fl oz/60 mL clarified butter or vegetable oil

8 oz/227 g small-dice **White Mirepoix** (page 333)

12 oz/340 g **Blond Roux** (page 335)

1 gal 16 fl oz/4.32 L **Chicken Stock** (page 351)

1 **Sachet d'Épices** (page 331)

salt, as needed

ground white pepper, as needed

1. Heat the butter or oil in a saucepan over medium heat. Add the mirepoix and cook, stirring from time to time, until the onions are limp and have begun to release their juices into the pan, about 15 minutes. They may take on a light golden color but should not be allowed to brown.

2. Add the roux to the mirepoix and cook until the roux is very hot, about 2 minutes.

3. Add the stock to the pan gradually, stirring or whisking to work out any lumps. Bring to a full boil, then lower the heat to establish a simmer. (Use a heat diffuser, if desired, to avoid scorching.) Add the sachet and continue to simmer, skimming as necessary, until a good flavor and consistency develop and the starchy feel and taste of the flour have cooked away, 45 minutes to 1 hour.

4. Strain the sauce through a fine-mesh sieve. Strain a second time through a double thickness of rinsed cheese-cloth, if desired, for the finest texture.

5. Return the sauce to a simmer. Taste and season with salt and pepper. Finish the sauce as desired.

6. The sauce is ready to serve now, or it may be rapidly cooled and refrigerated for later use.

Suprême Sauce: Add 32 fl oz/960 mL of heavy cream and 2 lb/907 g of sliced mushrooms. Simmer the sauce, stirring and skimming the surface frequently, until it coats the back of a spoon. If desired, the sauce may be finished with 6 oz/170 g of butter. Season with salt and pepper.

Ordinary Velouté: Replace the Chicken Stock with White Beef Stock (page 351).

Fish Velouté: Replace the Chicken Stock with Fish Fumet or Fish Stock (page 353).

Shrimp Velouté: Replace the Chicken Stock with Shrimp Stock (page 353).

Vegetable Velouté: Replace the Chicken Stock with Vegetable Stock (page 353).

Béchamel Sauce

Makes 1 gal/3.84 L

2 fl oz/60 mL clarified butter or vegetable oil

2 oz/57 g minced onions

1 lb/454 g **White Roux** (page 335)

1 gal 16 fl oz/4.32 L milk

salt, as needed

ground white pepper, as needed

ground nutmeg, as needed (optional)

1. Heat the butter or oil and add the onions. Sauté over low to medium heat, stirring frequently, until the onions are tender and translucent, 6 to 8 minutes.

2. Add the roux to the onions and cook until the roux is very hot, about 2 minutes.

3. Add the milk to the pan gradually, whisking or stirring to work out any lumps. Bring the sauce to a full boil, then reduce the heat and simmer until the sauce is smooth and thickened, about 30 minutes. Stir frequently and skim as necessary throughout the cooking time.

4. Season with salt, pepper, and nutmeg, if using. Strain through a double thickness of rinsed cheesecloth.

5. Return the sauce to a simmer. Taste and adjust seasoning with salt and pepper. Finish the sauce as desired.

6. The sauce is ready to serve now, or it may be rapidly cooled and refrigerated for later use.

Cheddar Cheese Sauce: Add 1 lb/454 g of grated sharp Cheddar.

Mornay Sauce: Add 8 oz/227 g each of grated Gruyère and Parmesan. Finish with up to 8 oz/227 g of whole butter, if desired.

Cream Sauce: Add 16 fl oz/480 mL of heated heavy cream to the finished béchamel and simmer for 4 to 5 minutes.

Tomato Sauce

Makes 1 gal/3.84 L

2 fl oz/60 mL olive oil

8 oz/227 g small-dice onions

2 oz/57 g minced or thinly sliced garlic

10 to 12 lb/4.54 to 5.44 kg cored and chopped plum tomatoes

3 oz/85 g chopped basil leaves

salt, as needed

ground black pepper, as needed

1. Heat the oil in a rondeau or wide shallow pot over medium-low heat. Add the onions and cook, stirring occasionally, until they take on a light golden color, 12 to 15 minutes.

2. Add the garlic and continue to sauté, stirring frequently, until the garlic is soft and fragrant, about 1 minute.

3. Add the tomatoes. Bring the sauce to a simmer and cook over low heat, stirring from time to time for about 45 minutes (exact cooking time depends on the quality of the tomatoes and their natural moisture content), until a good sauce-like consistency develops.

4. Add the basil and simmer for 2 to 3 minutes more. Taste the sauce and season with salt and pepper if necessary.

5. The sauce may be puréed through a food mill fitted with a coarse disk, broken up with a whisk to make a rough purée, or left chunky.

6. The sauce is ready to serve now, or it may be rapidly cooled and refrigerated for later use.

Variation: Substitute 9 lb/4.08 kg of canned whole plum tomatoes for the fresh tomatoes. With canned tomatoes, it may be necessary to drain off some of the liquid first. If desired, the canned whole tomatoes can be puréed in a food mill before preparing the sauce.

Tomato Coulis

Makes 32 fl oz/960 mL

1 fl oz/30 mL olive oil

4 oz/113 g minced onions

2 tsp/6 g minced garlic

4 fl oz/120 mL tomato purée

6 fl oz/180 mL red wine

1 lb 4 oz/567 g peeled, seeded, and medium-diced plum tomatoes

16 fl oz/480 mL **Chicken Stock** (page 351)

5 basil leaves

1 thyme sprig

1 bay leaf

salt, as needed

ground black pepper, as needed

1. Heat the oil and sauté the onions until they are translucent, 6 to 8 minutes. Add the garlic and sauté it briefly. Add the tomato purée and cook for several minutes, until it turns a rusty brown and has a sweet aroma, about 1 minute.

2. Add the red wine, tomatoes, stock, basil, thyme, and bay leaf. Simmer for about 45 minutes. Remove and discard the herbs.

3. Pass the mixture through a food mill fitted with the coarse disk. Adjust the consistency if necessary.

4. Taste and season with salt and pepper. The sauce is ready to serve now, or it may be rapidly cooled and refrigerated for later use.

Bolognese Meat Sauce (Ragu Bolognese)

Makes 32 fl oz/960 mL

2 oz/57 g finely diced pancetta

½ fl oz/15 mL extra-virgin olive oil

½ oz/14 g butter

5 oz/142 g fine-dice onions

2 oz/57 g fine-dice carrots

1½ oz/43 g fine-dice celery

8 oz/227 g lean ground beef

8 oz/227 g lean ground pork

8 fl oz/240 mL white wine

1½ oz/43 g tomato paste

salt, as needed

ground black pepper, as needed

ground nutmeg, as needed

16 fl oz/480 mL **Chicken Stock** (page 351)

8 fl oz/240 mL heavy cream, heated

1. Combine the pancetta with the oil and butter in a medium stockpot. Cook over medium-low heat, stirring frequently, until the pancetta is golden brown and the fat is rendered, about 15 minutes.

2. Increase the heat to medium-high. Add the onions, carrots, and celery and cook, stirring frequently, until the vegetables are softened and the onions are translucent.

3. Add the ground beef and pork. Cook, stirring continuously, until the meat is browned, 3 to 4 minutes. Drain the fat if necessary.

4. Stir in the wine and reduce the mixture until nearly dry. Stir in the tomato paste and cook for 2 to 3 minutes, until lightly caramelized. Season the sauce with salt, pepper, and nutmeg.

5. Add the stock, bring the sauce to a boil, reduce the heat to low, and simmer uncovered for 2 hours, or until the mixture has reduced and the flavors have concentrated. Add additional stock if necessary to avoid scorching.

6. Stir in the cream just prior to service and return the sauce to a simmer. Do not allow the sauce to boil. Adjust seasoning with salt and pepper.

7. The sauce is ready to serve now, or it may be rapidly cooled and refrigerated for later use.

Hollandaise Sauce

Makes 32 fl oz/960 mL

¾ tsp/1.50 g cracked black peppercorns

6 fl oz/180 mL cider or white wine vinegar

6 fl oz/180 mL (about 8) egg yolks, fresh or pasteurized

20 fl oz/600 mL melted or clarified butter, warm

½ fl oz/15 mL lemon juice

salt, as needed

ground white pepper, as needed

pinch cayenne (optional)

1. Combine the peppercorns and vinegar in a small pan and reduce over medium heat until 4 fl oz/120 mL of vinegar remains.

2. Strain the reduction into a stainless-steel bowl.

3. Whisk the egg yolks together with the reduction and place them over simmering water. Cook, whisking constantly, until the eggs are thickened and form ribbons when they fall from the whisk.

4. Gradually add the butter in a thin stream, whisking constantly, until all of the butter is added and the sauce is thickened.

5. Taste the sauce and add the lemon juice, salt, pepper, and cayenne, if desired. The sauce is ready to serve now. It may be held warm for up to 2 hours.

Mousseline Sauce: Whip 5 fl oz/150 mL of heavy cream to medium peaks and fold it into the batch of hollandaise, or fold whipped cream into individual portions at the time of service.

Maltaise Sauce: Add 2 fl oz/60 mL of blood orange juice to the reduction. Finish the hollandaise with 2 tsp/6 g of grated or julienned blood orange zest and 1½ fl oz/45 mL of blood orange juice.

Béarnaise Sauce

Makes 32 fl oz/960 mL

¾ tsp/1.50 g cracked black peppercorns

1 tbsp/6 g dried tarragon

3 tarragon stems, chopped

3 fl oz/90 mL tarragon vinegar

1½ fl oz/45 mL dry white wine

3 fl oz/90 mL water

6 fl oz/180 mL (about 8) egg yolks, fresh or pasteurized

24 fl oz/720 mL melted or clarified butter, warm

3 tbsp/9 g chopped tarragon

1½ tbsp/4.50 g chopped chervil

salt, as needed

1. Combine the peppercorns, dried tarragon, tarragon stems, and vinegar in a small pan. Reduce over medium heat until nearly dry.

2. Add the wine and water to the reduction and strain it into a stainless-steel bowl.

3. Whisk the egg yolks together with the reduction and place them over simmering water. Cook, whisking constantly, until the eggs are thickened and form ribbons when they fall from the whisk.

Choron Sauce

4. Gradually add the butter in a thin stream, whisking constantly, until all of the butter is added and the sauce is thickened.

5. Add the chopped tarragon and chervil and season with salt. The sauce is ready to serve now. It may be held warm for up to 2 hours.

Mint Sauce (Paloise Sauce): Replace the tarragon stems with mint stems; replace the tarragon vinegar with cider vinegar; and replace the chopped tarragon and chervil with 3 tbsp/9 g of chopped mint leaves.

Choron Sauce: Stir 1½ oz/43 g of heated or cooked tomato purée into the finished sauce. Adjust the sauce's consistency with water or lemon juice as needed.

Beurre Blanc

Makes 32 fl oz/960 mL

2 tbsp/18 g minced shallots

6 to 8 black peppercorns

8 fl oz/240 mL dry white wine

2 fl oz/60 mL lemon juice

3 fl oz/90 mL cider or white wine vinegar

8 fl oz/240 mL heavy cream, reduced by half (optional)

1 lb 8 oz/680 g cubed butter, chilled

salt, as needed

ground white pepper, as needed

1 tbsp/9 g grated lemon zest (optional)

1. Combine the shallots, peppercorns, wine, lemon juice, and vinegar in a saucepan. Reduce over medium-high heat until nearly dry.

2. Add the reduced heavy cream, if using, and simmer the sauce for 2 to 3 minutes to reduce slightly.

3. Add the butter a few pieces at a time, whisking constantly to blend the butter into the reduction. The heat should be quite low as you work. Continue adding butter until the full amount has been incorporated.

4. Taste and season with salt and pepper. Finish the sauce by adding the lemon zest, if using. The sauce may be strained, if desired.

5. The sauce is ready to serve now. It may be held warm for up to 2 hours.

Red Pepper Coulis

Makes 32 fl oz/960 mL

1 fl oz/30 mL olive oil

½ oz/14 g minced shallots

1 lb 8 oz/680 g peeled, seeded, deribbed, and chopped red peppers

salt, as needed

ground black pepper, as needed

4 fl oz/120 mL dry white wine

8 fl oz/240 mL **Chicken Stock** (page 351)

2 to 3 fl oz/60 to 90 mL heavy cream (optional)

1. Heat the oil over medium heat and sweat the shallots until they are tender, about 2 minutes. Add the peppers and continue to sweat until they are very tender, about 12 minutes. Add salt and pepper.

2. Deglaze the pan with the wine and let the wine reduce until nearly cooked away. Add the stock and simmer until reduced by half.

3. Purée the sauce in a food processor or blender until very smooth. Add the heavy cream to the puréed sauce, if using. Taste and adjust seasoning with salt and pepper.

4. The sauce is ready to serve now, or it may be rapidly cooled and refrigerated for later use.

Maître d'Hôtel Butter

Makes 1 lb/454 g

1 lb/454 g butter, room temperature

2 oz/56 g minced parsley

1½ tbsp/22.50 mL lemon juice

salt, as needed

ground black pepper, as needed

1. Work the butter by hand or with the paddle attachment of an electric mixer until it is soft. Add the remaining ingredients and blend well. Taste and adjust seasoning with salt and pepper.

2. The compound butter is ready to use, or it may be rolled into a log or piped into shapes and chilled for later use.

Tarragon Butter: Replace the parsley with an equal amount of minced tarragon.

Pimiento Butter: Replace the parsley with an equal amount of minced pimientos.

Green Onion Butter: Add ½ fl oz/15 mL of soy sauce, ½ tsp/1.50 g of minced garlic, and replace the parsley with an equal amount of minced green onions.

Dill Butter: Replace the parsley with an equal amount of minced dill.

Sun-Dried Tomato and Oregano Butter: Add 1 tbsp/3 g minced oregano and 1 oz/28 g of minced sun-dried tomatoes.

Basil Butter: Replace the parsley with an equal amount of minced basil.

Pesto

Makes about 32 fl oz/960 mL

8 oz/227 g basil leaves

10 oz/284 g toasted pine nuts

1 oz/28 g garlic, mashed to a paste

1 oz/28 g salt

8 to 16 fl oz/240 to 480 mL olive oil

8 oz/227 g grated Parmesan

1. Rinse the basil leaves well, dry thoroughly, and coarsely chop. Transfer them to a food processor or mortar and pestle. Grind the basil, pine nuts, garlic, and salt together, adding the oil gradually to form a thick paste.

2. Taste and adjust seasoning with salt and stir in the Parmesan. The sauce is ready to use now, or it may be refrigerated for later use.

NOTE
Blanching the basil in boiling salted water will help prevent the pesto from oxidizing during storage and make the color more pronounced.

Rolling Maître d'Hôtel Butter

Tarragon Butter

Chapter Seventeen

Soups

A well-prepared soup always makes a memorable impression. Soups offer a full array of flavoring ingredients and garnishing opportunities. Soups also allow the chef to use trimmings and leftovers creatively, an important profit-making consideration for any foodservice establishment.

Broth

Stocks and broths are similar in technique and cooking time. Meat, poultry, fish, trimmings, or vegetables, which can be roasted or seared, are slowly simmered along with aromatic vegetables, spices, and herbs to produce a clear and flavorful liquid with some body. The major distinction between broths and stocks is that broths can be served as is, whereas stocks are used in the production of other dishes.

Meat and poultry broths have a more pronounced flavor than their stock counterparts because they are based on meat rather than bones. Fish and vegetable broths are made from the same basic ingredients as fish and vegetable stocks, so the difference between them is really one of intended end use and word choice.

If a broth's cooking temperature is carefully regulated so that it is never more than an even, gentle simmer and if the surface is skimmed as necessary, a broth can be as clear, full bodied, and rich as any consommé, without clarification.

The best broths are made from the most flavorful ingredients. Choose meat cuts from more exercised parts of the animal because the more fully developed the muscle, the more pronounced the flavor. The same is true of poultry broths, where stewing hens or more mature game birds are the best choice for deep flavor. Frequently, the meat or poultry used to prepare broths can work for other preparations, if they are cooked until fully tender and no longer. The meat can be julienned or diced to use as a garnish.

Fish freshness is of primary concern, as is the relative leanness or oiliness of the fish. It is best to use lean, white-fleshed fish, such as sole, flounder, halibut, or cod. Richer, oilier types of fish, such as bluefish or mackerel, tend to lose their flavor when their delicate oils are subjected to high temperatures for even short periods. Shellfish and crustaceans cooked in the shell in a small amount of liquid produce excellent broth. It must then be strained very carefully to remove all traces of grit or sand.

For vegetable broths, combine wholesome trim from several vegetables to make a broth, or follow a specific recipe. Consider the strength of the vegetable's flavor and how that might affect the broth's balance. Cabbage family members such as cauliflower or cabbage can become overwhelmingly strong.

Many broths begin with the simplest of all liquids: cool, fresh water. Using a stock, remouillage, or broth as the base liquid will produce what is sometimes referred to as a "double broth." Select additional ingredients to add flavor, aroma, and color to a broth. Aromatic herb and vegetable combinations such as mirepoix, sachet d'épices, or bouquet garni are traditional. Contemporary broths may call for such ingredients as dried tomatoes, lemon grass, wild mushrooms, or ginger to give the broth a unique character.

Garnishing broths adds visual and textural interest. Simple garnishes, such as a fine brunoise of vegetables or chervil pluches, are traditional. Other choices include diced or julienned meats; pieces of fish or shellfish; croutons; dumplings, quenelles, and wontons; noodles; and rice. The recipes found in this book and in many other books illustrate the breadth of possibilities.

When assembling the equipment, select a pot large enough to accommodate the broth as it cooks. There should be sufficient room at the top of the pot to allow some expansion during cooking, as well as to make it easy to skim away any impurities on the surface. The pot should be tall and narrow rather than short and wide. If available, select a pot with a spigot to make it easier to strain the broth. You will also need skimmers and ladles, storage or holding containers, strainers, tasting spoons and cups, and a kitchen fork to remove any large pieces of meat.

A basic formula for 1 gal/3.84 L Meat or Poultry Broth

10 to 12 lb/4.54 to 5.44 kg meat or poultry (including bones) to 1 gal 64 fl oz/5.76 L cool liquid

1 lb/454 g mirepoix

1 standard sachet d'épices or bouquet garni

A basic formula for 1 gal/3.84 L Fish or Shellfish Broth

10 to 12 lb/4.54 to 5.44 kg fish or shellfish, including bones or shells, to 1 gal/3.84 L cool liquid

1 lb/454 g white mirepoix (sometimes including mushroom trimmings)

1 standard sachet d'épices or bouquet garni

A basic formula for 1 gal/3.84 L Vegetable Broth

6 to 8 lb/2.72 to 3.63 kg vegetables to 1 gal/3.84 L cool liquid

1 lb/454 g mirepoix

1 standard sachet d'épices or bouquet garni

1. **Combine major flavoring ingredients, appropriate seasonings, and cool liquid to cover the ingredients completely.** Gently bring the liquid to a simmer, skimming as necessary. Gentle simmering extracts maximum flavor and establishes a natural clarification process and encourages impurities (fat and scum) to collect on the surface, where they can be skimmed away. The process of blanching meat or poultry before making a broth will help to remove impurities.

Avoid a hard boil when cooking broths, which could cook the flavor out of the ingredients. Vigorous boiling action also causes fat and impurities to be mixed back in, thereby clouding the broth.

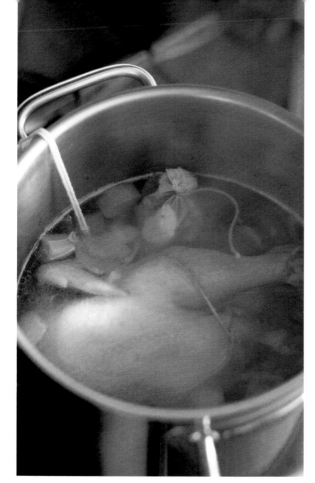

2. **Add remaining ingredients and aromatics at appropriate intervals.** Sachet d'épices or bouquet garni ingredients release their flavors quickly and are added near the end of cooking time. Rather than intensifying the flavor, continued cooking could actually cook away the delicate, volatile oils that hold their flavor essence. Simmer until flavor, color, and body are fully developed. Since the cooking times for broths vary widely, consult specific recipes for guidance. Taste the broth from time to time as it simmers to be sure that it is developing properly, and make corrections if necessary. For example, if a clove in the sachet d'épices threatens to overwhelm the broth, remove it. If there is a lack of rich, roasted flavors, add an oignon brûlé (see page 330). Final seasoning and flavor adjustments, however, are generally done after the major flavoring ingredients have given up their maximum flavor. Meat and poultry should be cooked until fork tender. Fish, shellfish, and crustaceans should be simmered briefly until just cooked through. Vegetables should be extremely soft but not cooked into shreds.

3. **Ladle, don't pour, the broth out of the pot.** To keep the soup clear, first lift the meat or chicken and vegetables from the broth before straining. Line a sieve or colander with rinsed, doubled cheesecloth. A fine-mesh sieve or a paper filter can also be used. Skim as much fat from the surface as possible before garnishing and serving or before cooling and storing rapidly.

Bring the broth to service temperature and garnish as desired. If the broth has been cooled, lift away any congealed fat and return the broth to a simmer. Prepare and heat the garnish.

4. **Evaluate the quality of the finished broth.** A good broth is clear, golden in color, rich tasting, and aromatic, with good flavor and noticeable body. The selection of fresh, high-quality ingredients, the right proportion of flavoring ingredients to liquid, careful temperature regulation, thorough skimming, adequate cooking time, and adjustments to the broth's seasoning throughout cooking time result in the highest quality broth possible. Proper handling of the soup during storage and reheating assures that the broth maintains its quality. Broths typically have a few droplets of fat on the surface, a sign of a rich, full-flavored soup.

Options for Making the Perfect Broth

To intensify the flavor of a broth, the amount of meat or vegetable may be increased. To further enhance the flavor and color of a broth, brown the major flavoring ingredients (meat and/or vegetables) before adding the liquid.

Additional ingredients may be added to develop more flavor. Add these ingredients at the appropriate time. Add some early in the cooking process to infuse flavor. Others may be added later on so that they retain their individual flavor and/or texture.

> Sachet or bouquet
> Oignon brûlé
> Fresh or dried herbs
> Aromatic vegetables

Garnishing a broth is yet another way to introduce and influence the flavor profile. Garnishing ingredients cut to the appropriate size and desired shape are added at the very end of the cooking process.

> Vegetables
> Meat, poultry, or fish
> Fresh herbs
> Cooked pasta
> Cooked grains such as rice or barley

Consommé

A consommé is a perfectly clear broth. Consommés are exceptionally rich in flavor and are crystal clear, an effect achieved by combining a high-quality stock or broth with a clarification mixture. To assure a high-quality consommé, the chef must choose ingredients carefully, keep the clarification mixture very cold until it is time to cook the consommé, and monitor the temperature of the consommé as it cooks at a slow simmer. Once the consommé has developed a rich flavor and color, it must be carefully strained and degreased to produce a crystal-clear soup, with no traces of fat, and an intense and satisfying flavor.

Stock for consommé should be of high quality and very fresh. To check for quality, bring a small amount to a boil, then smell and taste it. If there is any doubt about the quality of the stock, use a fresher batch or prepare new stock.

The clarification is a combination of lean ground meat, egg whites, mirepoix, herbs and spices, and tomato or other acidic ingredients. All of these ingredients serve multiple functions in preparing a well-balanced consommé. This mixture of ingredients produces a crystal-clear flavorful soup by removing impurities from the stock and bolstering its flavor. Whenever possible, grind the meat along with the mirepoix vegetables for the best flavor and quality in the finished consommé. Whether or not you grind the meat in-house, be sure to keep it and the egg whites refrigerated so that they remain wholesome and flavorful.

Mirepoix vegetables should be cut small or ground so that they become part of the raft and release their flavors quickly. A variety of aromatic vegetables such as onions, carrots, celery, garlic, leeks, parsnips, and mushrooms are typical. Mix the clarification ingredients (except for the acid) thoroughly and chill, if time permits, for several hours or overnight. An acidic ingredient, such as tomatoes, is added just before the stock is blended into the clarification to help the raft form properly, as well as for its flavor. Lemon juice or vinegar is an acidic option for a fish or vegetable consommé. An oignon brûlé may also be included to give additional flavor and color. Other flavoring items are used as necessary or appropriate to achieve a special flavor.

Herbs and spices are also included in the clarification mixture: sprigs or stems of tarragon, parsley, chervil, dill, thyme, or other fresh herbs; cloves, bay leaves, peppercorns, juniper berries, or star anise; and ginger and lemongrass.

The equipment needs for making consommés are the same as those described earlier for broths, with the following special considerations: The pot should have a heavy bottom to help prevent the clarification ingredients from sticking and scorching, and it should be taller than it is wide. The even heat of steam kettles and flattop ranges, if available, are ideal for making consommé.

A basic formula for 1 gal/ 3.84 L Consommé

Clarification ingredients:
1 lb/454 g mirepoix; 3 lb/1.36 kg lean ground meat, poultry, or fish; 10 egg whites; acid, such as tomatoes or lemon juice

1 gal 32 fl oz/4.80 L cooking liquid (stock or broth)

Seasonings and flavorings, such as salt and pepper, sachet d'épices or bouquet garni, oignon brûlé, or others as desired

1. **Have the clarification ingredients very cold (below 40°F/4°C) at the start of cooking time.** Some chefs prefer to grind the clarification mixture the day before making the consommé to allow it plenty of time to chill. Add the acid (tomatoes or lemon juice, for instance) just before cooking the consommé. Add enough cold stock to loosen the clarification. For large quantities the rest of the stock can be brought to a simmer separately to shorten the overall cooking time of the consommé.

2. **Bring to a simmer, stirring frequently, until the raft begins to form.** Continue to stir the consommé so that the clarification ingredients do not stick to the pot or scorch. As it heats up, the clarification ingredients begin to turn gray and coalesce into a large soft mass, which is known as a raft. This occurs at a temperature range of approximately 120° to 125°F/49° to 52°C. Stop stirring the consommé at this temperature and adjust the heat until only a few small bubbles break the surface. If there is a strong simmering or boiling action, the raft might break apart before it has sufficiently cleared and flavored the consommé. On the other hand, if the heat is too low, impurities may not rise from the bottom of the pot to the top, where they can be trapped by the raft. Add an oignon brûlé if desired.

3. **Simmer without stirring once the clarification ingredients cook together into a raft.** Basting assures that the fullest flavor will develop and prevents the raft from drying out and potentially breaking.

As the consommé continues to simmer, the meat and eggs will naturally coagulate, forming the raft. The simmering action of the soup carries impurities from the bottom of the pot to the raft, where they are trapped. This action clarifies the soup. The simmering action may also cause a small hole to form in the raft. If a small opening does not form on its own, use a spoon or ladle to gently poke through the raft so that you can taste the consommé as it develops and make any necessary seasoning adjustments. The hole should be just large enough to accommodate a small ladle.

Simmer gently until the flavor, color, and body are fully developed. Recipes usually provide a cooking guideline (generally from 1 to 1½ hours)—long enough to fortify the soup's flavor and clarify it properly. Baste the raft frequently as the consommé simmers. When the raft begins to sink slightly, assuming that this happens after a reasonable cooking time rather than because the heat wasn't adjusted properly, the consommé is properly simmered. Pour a small amount into a soup bowl or plate to assess its clarity visually.

Strain the consommé using a fine-mesh sieve, a conical sieve lined with a coffee filter, or carefully rinsed cheesecloth. Avoid breaking up the raft as you strain the consommé and don't pour the consommé and raft into a strainer, because this will release impurities. Adjust the seasoning as necessary.

4. **Carefully degrease the consommé.** Blot the consommé with absorbent paper or refrigerate it. Any fat will congeal and be easy to lift away before reheating. It should be completely fat free. The consommé is now ready for garnishing and service or to be cooled and stored.

Evaluate the quality of the finished consommé. A consommé of excellent quality has a well-balanced, rich flavor reflecting the major ingredient, and a discernible body. It is perfectly clear, completely fat free, and aromatic. The selection of fresh, high-quality ingredients, very cold clarification ingredients, the proper ratio of flavoring ingredients and aromatics to liquid, adequate cooking time, careful temperature regulation, careful skimming, and seasoning adjustments throughout cooking time result in the highest quality consommé. Careful handling of the consommé during storage and reheating assures that it maintains its quality.

Options for Making the Perfect Consommé

To enhance the flavor and color of a consommé, double the amount of ground meat in the recipe. This is known as a Double Consommé.

Additional ingredients may be added to develop more flavor. Add these ingredients at the appropriate time.

Sachet or bouquet
Oignon brûlé
Fresh or dried herbs
Aromatic vegetables

Use different acids in a consommé to produce a desired flavor or color.

Tomato
Lemon juice
Dry wine
Vinegar

Garnishing a consommé is yet another way to introduce and influence flavors. Garnishing ingredients cut to the appropriate size and desired shape are added at the very end of the cooking process.

Hundreds of classically codified garnishes for consommés exist, ranging from such humble items as neatly diced root vegetables to the esoteric edible gold leaf featured in a recipe found in Escoffier's *Le Guide Culinaire*. They draw on influences as diverse as Asian cuisines, Caribbean dishes, and Italian provincial cooking styles. No matter what the garnish may be, it is important that it be as well prepared as the consommé. Vegetable cuts should be neat and precise. Royales should be delicately set, soft, and supple in the mouth. The seasoning selected for the garnish should enhance the flavor of the consommé, not distract from it.

Consommé Brunoise
Consommé garnished with small cubes of carrot, turnip, celery, leek, and chervil

Consommé Célèstine
Consommé lightly thickened with tapioca and garnished with julienned crêpes mixed with chopped truffles or herbs

Consommé Julienne
Consommé garnished with julienned carrots, leeks, turnips, celery, and cabbage, plus green peas and a chiffonade of sorrel and chervil

Consommé Printanier
Consommé garnished with balls of carrot and turnips, peas, and chervil

Consommé Royale
Chicken consommé garnished with cubes, rounds, or lozenges of Royale (custard)

Consommé Chasseur
Game consommé garnished with julienned mushrooms and game quenelles or profiteroles stuffed with game purée

Consommé Diplomate
Chicken consommé lightly thickened with tapioca and garnished with julienned truffles and rondelles of chicken forcemeat blended with crayfish butter

Consommé Grimaldi
Consommé clarified with fresh tomato purée; garnished with diced Royale (custard) and julienned celery

Consommé Mikado
Chicken consommé with tomato, garnished with diced tomato and chicken

Hearty Broths

Hearty broths are based on clear broths or stock and have more flavor, texture, and body than clear broths. Vegetables are cut into uniform size and simmered in the soup until tender. Meats, grains, and pasta are frequently included to add body. These soups lack the clarity of broth or consommé because of the additional ingredients cooked directly in the broth. Hearty broths may also be made from a single vegetable (e.g., onion soup).

Hearty broths include vegetables chosen both for their own flavors and for their aromatic qualities. Prepare each vegetable by trimming, peeling, and cutting it into neat and even-sized pieces so that they cook uniformly and have an attractive appearance.

Some hearty broths also include meat, poultry, or fish. Trim and cut meat, poultry, or fish to suit the style of soup you are preparing. After cooking in the soup, these ingredients are often diced or julienned and returned to the soup just before it is finished.

Other ingredients might include beans, whole grains, or pasta. For a relatively clear soup, cook these starchy ingredients separately and add them to the soup as a garnish. A more rustic approach calls for these ingredients to be cooked in the broth as part of the soup-making process. Such soups tend to have more body and are sometimes referred to as hearty vegetable soups.

Clear broths, good-quality stocks, water, vegetable essences, or juices are all used as the liquid base for vegetable soups. Be sure to taste the liquid and add seasonings as necessary from the start of cooking time up to and including just before service. Refer to specific recipes for ingredient suggestions. Bring the broth to a simmer over low heat while preparing the other ingredients, along with seasonings and aromatics as needed. This will improve the flavor of the finished broth and help reduce overall cooking time, since the soup will come to the correct cooking speed more quickly.

Garnishes are as varied as the soups themselves. Croutons are common, and they may be an integral part of the preparation, as in Onion Soup Gratinée (page 432). Add other garnishes, such as pesto, grated cheese, or even beaten eggs, to vegetable soups just before service. Purées of red peppers, chiles, tomato, or sorrel may also be added at the last moment for a dash of color and flavor. Fortified wines such as sherry, vinegar, or citrus juices may be used for last-minute flavor adjustments.

Most vegetable soups cook from start to finish in a single pot. The pot should be taller than it is wide to allow the soup to cook gently and evenly at a constant simmer. Skimmers, ladles, and spoons are all used throughout the preparation time. Tasting spoons and cups should be on hand so that you can monitor the soup's flavor development. Storage or holding containers will also be needed.

A basic formula for 1 gal/3.84 L Hearty Broth

4 lb/1.81 kg of one or more main flavoring ingredients, such as vegetables, meat, poultry, fish, legumes, or pasta

1 gal 32 fl oz/4.80 L of stock or broth

Seasonings and flavorings, such as salt and pepper, 1 sachet d'épices or bouquet garni, oignon brûlé, or others as desired

1. **Cut vegetables in uniform shapes and sizes.** Cook the aromatic vegetables in fat to the desired stage, adding them at intervals to develop the best flavor, texture, and color. Onions, garlic, leeks, celery, carrots, and parsnips are basic aromatic ingredients of many vegetable soups. Sweating them in a small amount of fat begins the process of releasing their flavors into the soup. Some tender vegetables, such as broccoli florets, asparagus tips, and other delicate types are not allowed to sweat. They are added at staggered intervals, according to individual cooking times. Cooking vegetables such as onions to a deep golden brown will develop a richer flavor in the finished broth. Consult recipes for specific instructions on cooking the vegetables.

2. **Add liquid and bring to a simmer, stirring, skimming, and adjusting seasoning throughout the cooking time.** Add main flavoring ingredients at appropriate intervals. Depending upon the flavor of the broth, appropriate seasoning is also added at this point. Bear in mind that the soup will simmer for about 1 hour longer.

A slow simmer is the best cooking speed for most soups. The vegetables and meats will release the best flavor, and the appearance of vegetables will be more attractive when cooked at a simmer. A hard boil tends to cook food to shreds. Continue to add ingredients at the appropriate point so that they cook properly and develop a good flavor.

Additional aromatic ingredients, such as a sachet d'épices or bouquet garni, are also added toward the end so that they will cook just long enough to release flavor into the soup. Skim the surface as needed throughout preparation. The scum that develops on the soup needs to be removed for the best finished quality and appearance. Taste the soup frequently as it cooks and make adjustments as necessary. Once the soup has reached its peak flavor, it is ready for final seasoning, garnishing, and service. Or it may be cooled and stored.

3. **Evaluate the quality of the finished soup.** The finished soup should have a rich color, flavor, and aroma. "Clear" vegetable soups are not as clear as broth or consommé. Unlike strained soups, the vegetables are part of the soup itself and give it texture and body. When properly cooked, vegetables should have appealing colors. Meats, poultry, fish, and starchy ingredients, such as potatoes and beans, should hold their shape but have a very soft texture.

Options for Making the Perfect Hearty Broth

To intensify the flavor of a broth, the amount of meat or vegetable may be increased. To further enhance the flavor and color of a broth, brown the major flavoring ingredients (meat and/or vegetables) before adding the liquid.

Additional ingredients may be added to develop more flavor. Add these ingredients at the appropriate time. Add some early in the cooking process to infuse flavor. Add others later on so that they retain their individual flavor and/or texture.

- Sachet or bouquet
- Oignon brûlé
- Fresh or dried herbs
- Aromatic vegetables

To add body to a hearty broth any one of the following may be used, depending on the desired results.

- Meats
- Grains
- Pasta
- Starchy vegetables
- Legumes

Garnishing a hearty broth is yet another way to introduce and influence the flavor profile. Add garnishing ingredients cut to the appropriate size and desired shape at the very end of the cooking process or just before service.

- Meat, poultry or fish
- Grains or pasta
- Vegetables
- Fresh herbs, or herb pastes, such as pesto
- Croutons
- Cheese
- Plain or flavored oils
- Fortified wines, or others as desired

Additions for the Broth

Meats, Poultry, and Fish

Cuts of meat that are more mature and less tender should be added to the soup early in the cooking process so that they will flavor the broth properly and finish cooking at the same time as the other ingredients. Add fish or shellfish to hearty broths close to the end of cooking time to prevent them from becoming overcooked.

Grains and Pasta

Allow grains and pasta a little more time than would be necessary to cook in boiling salted water.

Legumes

Add lentils and black-eyed peas to the soup along with the stock so that they will cook fully. Other beans may need to be cooked separately (see pages 806–808).

Dense or Starchy Vegetables

Turnips, carrots, potatoes, winter squash, rutabagas, beets, parsnips, and potatoes cut to small dice typically require 30 to 45 minutes to fully cook.

Green Vegetables

Add peas, green beans, and leafy vegetables such as spinach or kale during the final 15 to 20 minutes of simmering time for the soup. Some chefs prefer to blanch these vegetables to help set the colors before adding them to a soup.

Tomatoes

In some cases, tomatoes may be added at the beginning of the cooking time, along with the aromatic ingredients, to act as a broth flavoring. A tomato garnish may be added during the final 5 to 10 minutes of simmering time.

Herbs and Spices

Add dried herbs and most spices to the soup along with the aromatics to flavor the broth throughout the cooking time. Fresh and dried herbs and spices may also be added in the form of a sachet or bouquet during the final 15 to 20 minutes of simmering time or before service for the freshest flavor.

Cream Soup

According to classical definitions, a cream soup is based on a béchamel sauce—milk thickened with roux—and is finished with heavy cream. A velouté soup is based on a light velouté sauce—stock thickened with roux—and is finished with a liaison of heavy cream and egg yolks. Contemporary chefs no longer draw a distinction between the two; they frequently substitute a velouté base for the béchamel in cream soups or even use the term *cream* to refer to a purée soup that has simply been finished with cream.

The main flavoring for some cream soups is often a single ingredient, such as broccoli, asparagus, chicken, or fish. When simmering poultry or fish in the soup to give flavor and body, be sure to trim, truss, or cut those ingredients as appropriate. Vegetables, whether used as main flavoring ingredients or as aromatics, should be well rinsed, then peeled, trimmed, and cut into small and uniform pieces so they cook evenly.

A well-seasoned, full-bodied broth, stock, or light velouté should be on hand. Milk or a light béchamel is sometimes appropriate. Bring the liquid up to a simmer, along with seasonings, aromatics, or other ingredients meant to provide flavor. Refer to specific recipes for guidance.

Thickeners, including prepared roux, flour, potatoes, or the natural thickening of the puréed main ingredient, give cream soups their texture. However, added thickeners are unnecessary if the base liquid is a prepared velouté. Assemble finishing ingredients, final flavoring and seasonings, and garnishes ahead of time to be ready to add at the proper time. Bring cream to a simmer before adding it to simmering soup. Blend liaisons and temper them just before serving the soup.

Pots with heavy flat bottoms, made of nonreactive materials, such as stainless steel or anodized aluminum, are a good choice for cream soups. Simmer cream soups on flattops or a heat diffuser to prevent hot spots from developing and scorching the soup. Have wooden spoons, ladles, and skimmers available throughout the cooking process. Use blenders (countertop and immersion style), food processors, and food mills singly or in combination to purée the soup. For a velvety texture in the finished soup, you may also need fine-mesh strainers or cheesecloth to strain the soup a final time.

A basic formula for 1 gal/3.84 L Cream Soup

4 lb/1.81 kg of one or more main flavoring ingredients, such as vegetables, meat, poultry, or fish

1 gal/3.84 L cooking liquid (stock, broth, or prepared velouté)

A thickening agent, if not using a béchamel or velouté sauce, such as blond roux, flour, or potatoes

Seasonings and flavorings (salt and pepper, sachet d'épices, or bouquet garni)

Finishing and garnishing ingredients as appropriate [liaison (page 341), 16 fl oz/480 mL heavy cream, diced or julienned main flavoring ingredient, or mince or chiffonade of herbs]

1. **Cook the aromatic vegetables to develop a good flavor base.** White mirepoix is a common aromatic combination for cream soups. Here it is used for the aromatic base to preserve the soup's light green color.

make any necessary adjustments. Add certain ingredients to the soup at intervals, depending upon how dense they are and the effect that extended cooking might have on them. Tender new peas will become gray and pasty if allowed to cook for too long. A sachet d'épices left in the soup too long may lose its fresh flavor. Consult individual recipes for specific instructions on when to add ingredients.

Simmer until the main ingredient is fully cooked and tender and the soup has a good flavor, stirring, skimming, and adjusting the seasoning throughout the cooking time.

Cream soups usually need 1 hour of simmering time to develop flavor and thicken properly. Stir frequently to prevent scorching. Skimming the soup removes excess fat and impurities to create good flavor, color, and texture in the finished soup. Pull the pot slightly to the side of the burner; the fat and impurities will collect on one side of the pot, where it is easy to skim them away. Taste the soup often as it develops and add additional seasonings and aromatics as needed.

2. **For some soups, the main flavoring ingredient(s) may also be added in the first stages of cooking.** Sweat the broccoli and aromatics until translucent before adding the velouté. Cook gently over low heat in oil or whole or clarified butter until the vegetables are tender and translucent and begin to release their juices. The amount of fat you use to sweat the vegetables depends on how you intend to introduce the roux into the soup. If the roux is to be made as part of the overall process (as shown here), sweat the aromatics in enough fat to also make the roux. If you intend to use a premade velouté, béchamel, or a roux, use only enough fat to smother the aromatics and keep them from burning.

Stir the flour, if using, into the fat and cook the roux just long enough for it to take on a pale golden color. If using a premade roux, velouté, or béchamel, omit this step. Add prepared roux once the soup is at a simmer. Alternatively, include a potato to thicken the soup.

Slowly whisk in the hot broth, stock, velouté, or béchamel. Bring the soup just up to a simmer, stirring frequently. Check the soup's seasoning and

3. **Purée the soup (as necessary) and strain it.** The soup must be strained and then the solids should be puréed. After that, the simmered soup base should be added back to the solids until the desired consistency is achieved.

Use a food mill, blender, immersion blender, or food processor to purée vegetable cream soups. Cream soups based upon meat, fish, or poultry are not necessarily puréed. Puréed cream soups need to be strained using either a fine-mesh sieve or rinsed doubled cheesecloth. If using a fine-mesh sieve, push the solids against the sides to extract the purée. Straining produces the velvet-smooth texture of a good cream soup by removing all fibers.

The soup should have the desired flavor and consistency at this point. Make any necessary adjustments to consistency now. The soup is ready to finish now, or it may be rapidly cooled and refrigerated for later service (or to serve as a chilled soup).

4. **Simmer the soup, checking for flavor, consistency, and seasoning before adding the cream.** For a hot cream soup, return the soup to a simmer over medium heat and add enough hot cream to enrich the soup, without overwhelming the main ingredient's flavor. Return the soup to a simmer and adjust the seasoning if necessary.

5. **Garnishes must be very hot when added to hot soup.** Reheat them in flavorful liquid to further enhance the soup's flavor. Cream soups can be finished and garnished by individual portion or by batches, according to the kitchen's needs. Cook the garnish fully and season it well. This must be done as a separate operation since garnish ingredients don't actually simmer in the soup as it cooks.

Add the heated and seasoned garnish to the soup, if desired, and serve at once in heated bowls or cups.

To finish a cold cream soup, add chilled cream to the soup. Adjust the seasoning if necessary (cold foods often need more seasoning than the same dish served hot), and add the chilled and seasoned garnish. Serve at once in chilled bowls or cups.

6. **Evaluate the quality of the finished cream soup.** Good cream soups have a rich flavor, balancing the main flavoring ingredient(s) and supporting aromatic and finishing flavors, velvety texture, and a lightly thickened consistency, similar to heavy cream. Very thick cream soups often have a pasty feel and taste due to either too much thickener or to overcooking. Disappointing flavor and color indicate that not enough of the main flavoring ingredient(s) was used, ingredients were overcooked, or too much liquid was added. Too much cream can detract from the major flavor of the soup, masking the primary taste.

Options for Making the Perfect Cream Soup

To thicken, any one of the following may be used depending on the desired results:

Blond roux
White roux
Flour
Potatoes

Additional ingredients may be added to develop more flavor. Add the ingredient at the appropriate time. Add some early in the cooking process to infuse flavor. Others may be added later so that they retain their individual flavor and/or texture.

Sachet d'épices
Bouquet garni

Garnishing a cream soup is yet another way to introduce and influence flavors. Garnishing ingredients cut to the appropriate size and desired shape are added at the very end of the cooking process or just before service. Any of the following may be used:

Liaison
Heavy cream
Diced or julienned main flavoring ingredient
Mince or chiffonade of herbs

Chowder

Chowders get their name from the French word *chaudière,* a kettle in which fisherman made their stews. Classically, chowders were made from seafood and included pork, potatoes, and onions, though it is not uncommon for any thick, rich, and chunky soup to be called a chowder. There is also a group of chowders, of which Manhattan is probably most widely known, that are prepared more like a hearty broth. The main flavoring ingredients for chowder are often shellfish, fish, or vegetables, such as corn. Vegetables, whether used as main flavoring ingredients or as aromatics, should be well rinsed, then peeled, trimmed, and cut into small and uniform pieces so they cook evenly.

A well-seasoned, full-bodied broth or stock or water should be on hand. Bring the liquid up to a simmer, along with seasonings, aromatics, or other ingredients meant to provide flavor. Refer to specific recipes for guidance.

Thickeners, including flour and potatoes, give chowders their texture. Assemble finishing ingredients, final flavoring and seasonings, and garnishes ahead of time to be ready to add at the proper time. If adding cream, bring it to a simmer before adding it to the simmering chowder.

Traditionally chowder is made employing the singer method, where the flour for thickening is cooked with the aromatics rather than separately as for velouté. For this reason more fat is necessary when cooking the aromatics; this is critical to successfully making any soup using the singer method. Because the roux will be hot, make sure the liquid to be added is cool or at room temperature, otherwise the roux will become lumpy. Add the liquid slowly while stirring constantly to further ensure that the finished liquid for the chowder will be smooth.

A basic formula for 1 gal/3.84 L Chowder

One or more main flavoring ingredients, such as vegetables or seafood

1 gal/3.84 L cooking liquid (stock, broth, or water)

A thickening agent, such as flour or potatoes

Seasonings and flavorings, such as salt and pepper, sachet d'épices, or bouquet garni

Finishing and garnishing ingredients, such as heavy cream, salt pork, bacon, small dice of the main ingredient, or mince or chiffonade of herbs

1. **Render the salt pork or bacon and add the aromatics.** It may be necessary to add additional oil or butter to the rendered fat, depending on how you intend to introduce the roux into the soup. If the roux is to be made as part of the overall process, known as the singer method (as shown here), additional fat is needed. White mirepoix is a common aromatic combination for light-colored chowders, though for other chowders a combination of vegetables, such as carrots, onions, celery, leeks, garlic, and peppers, is also used. Cook the aromatics gently in the rendered fat and/or oil over low heat, until the vegetables are tender and translucent and begin to release their juices.

If making a shellfish-based chowder (clams, mussels, oysters, etc.), before beginning, steam the main ingredient in stock or water until they open. Strain the broth through a filter or cheesecloth and reserve. Pick the meat, chop, and reserve.

2. **Stir the flour into the fat and cook the roux just long enough for it to take on a pale golden color.** Having the right amount of fat in the pan to make the roux is critical to making soup successfully using the singer method.

Be sure to fully incorporate the stock into the roux and whisk any lumps out of the soup. Slowly whisk in the reserved broth and/or stock. Bring the soup just up to a simmer, stirring frequently. Check the soup's seasoning and make any necessary adjustments. Certain ingredients are added to the soup at intervals, depending upon how dense they are and the effect extended cooking might have on them. Tender new peas will become gray and pasty if allowed to cook for too long, but potatoes need time to cook. A sachet d'épices left in the soup too long may lose its fresh flavor. Consult individual recipes for specific instructions on when to add ingredients.

3. **Simmer until all the ingredients are fully cooked and tender and the soup has good flavor.** Stir, skim, and adjust seasoning throughout cooking time. Chowders usually need 1 hour of simmering time to develop flavor and thicken properly. Make any necessary adjustments to the consistency now. The soup is ready to finish now, or it may be rapidly cooled and refrigerated for later service.

Chowders are generally finished and garnished in batches. Return the soup to a simmer over medium heat and add enough hot cream, if using, to enrich the soup, without overwhelming the main ingredient's flavor. Add the garnish or reserved main ingredient back to the chowder. Return the soup to a simmer and adjust seasoning if necessary. Serve at once in heated bowls or cups.

4. **Evaluate the quality of the finished chowder.**
Good chowders have a rich flavor, balancing the main flavoring ingredient(s) and supporting aromatic and finishing flavors, a velvety texture, and a lightly thickened consistency, similar to heavy cream. Very thick chowders often have a pasty feel and taste due to either too much thickener or to overcooking. Disappointing flavor and color indicate that not enough of the main flavoring ingredient(s) was used or too much liquid was added. Too much cream can detract from the major flavor of the soup, masking the primary taste.

Options for Making the Perfect Chowder

To thicken, any one of the following may be used depending on the desired results:

> Blond roux
> White roux
> Flour
> Potatoes

Additional ingredients may be added to develop more flavor. Add the ingredient at the appropriate time. Add some early in the cooking process to infuse flavor. Others may be added later so that they retain their individual flavor and/or texture.

> Sachet d'épices
> Bouquet garni

Garnishing a chowder is yet another way to introduce and influence flavors. Garnishing ingredients cut to the appropriate size and desired shape are added at the very end of the cooking process or just before service.

> Liaison
> Heavy cream
> Diced or julienned main flavoring ingredient
> Mince or chiffonade of herbs

Purée Soups

Purée soups are slightly thicker than cream soups and have a somewhat coarser texture. Often based on dried legumes or starchy vegetables, purée soups are usually entirely puréed, though occasionally some of the solids are left whole for textural interest. Although not necessary, finishing ingredients may include milk or cream. Purée soups are often garnished with croutons or small dice of a complementary meat or vegetable.

Many purée soups are based on dried beans: Great Northern, navy beans, black beans, lentils, and split peas, for example. Beans (other than lentils and split peas) may be soaked for several hours before cooking. The beans absorb some liquid, the overall cooking time is shortened, and the beans cook more evenly. Relatively starchy vegetables such as potatoes, squash, or celery root are often the base for other purée soups. These have to be peeled and diced or sliced. While these ingredients are puréed, relative uniformity of cut size is necessary for the ingredients to cook evenly.

Aromatic ingredients such as onions, garlic, carrots, and celery are often found in purée soups. Vegetables may be roasted or grilled beforehand for extra flavor. Consult specific recipes for preparation and cutting instructions.

Water, broth, and stock are the most frequently used base liquids. Check the freshness of broths or stocks that have been stored before using them in a soup. Many purée soups based on a legume call for a bit of rendered salt pork, smoked ham, bacon, or other cured pork products. In some instances, these ingredients should be blanched first to remove any excess salt: Cover them with cool water, bring the water to a simmer, and then drain and rinse. Consult specific recipes for guidance. An alternative is to use a ham-based broth. Besides cured pork, ingredients used to season purée soups are as diverse as chiles, dried mushrooms, hot sauce, citrus zest or juice, and vinegar. Garnishes include chopped herbs, croutons, diced meats, toasted or fried tortillas, salsas, dollops of sour cream, and so forth.

Equipment requirements for making purée soups are quite similar to those for cream soups. Look for pots that have heavy bottoms to avoid scorching or the development of hot spots. If available, a heat diffuser or other similar device should be used to keep the heat even. Tasting spoons and cups must be on hand so that you can check the flavor of the soup throughout the cooking time. Have wooden spoons, ladles, and skimmers available throughout the cooking process. Puréeing equipment such as a food mill or blender is necessary to finish the soup. You will also need containers for cooling or holding the soup.

A basic formula for 1 gal/ 3.84 L Purée Soup

4 lb/1.81 kg of one or more vegetables, such as potatoes or squash; or
2 lb/907 g dried legumes, such as lentils

1 gal/3.84 L cooking liquid (stock or broth)

Seasonings and flavorings, such as salt and pepper, 1 sachet d'épices or bouquet garni, smoked ham or pork, mirepoix, tomatoes, lemon juice or vinegar

Finishing and garnishing ingredients, such as croutons or diced ham

1. **Render the salt pork to begin the process of building a flavor base.** It also provides the fat necessary to sweat or brown the aromatics. Lightly brown the aromatic vegetables. If the recipe calls for minced salt pork or bacon, render it over low heat to release the fat. Or heat the butter or oil, and add the onions, garlic, shallots, leeks, or other aromatic vegetables. Cook over low to medium heat, stirring from time to time, until a rich aroma develops or until they take on a rich golden hue, anywhere from 20 to 30 minutes.

Stir the soup frequently as it cooks to prevent starchy ingredients from sticking to the bottom of the pan. Add more stock or other liquid as necessary during the cooking time. The starchy or dry ingredients used in many purée soups will absorb different amounts of liquid as they cook, depending upon their maturity. Skim the soup as it cooks to remove any impurities or scum, and adjust the seasoning as necessary.

2. **Add the liquid and then add the remaining ingredients at the appropriate intervals.** Simmer until the soup is well flavored and all the ingredients are very tender. Add dry, dense, tough, fibrous, or starchy ingredients (dry beans, root vegetables, winter squash, for instance) at the beginning of cooking time, usually as soon as the stock or broth has returned to a simmer. Since the soup is puréed before service, it is less critical that these ingredients not overcook than in a hearty broth, where the ingredients are intended to retain their shape during cooking and service. Add sachets or bouquets garni during the final 30 minutes of cooking time.

Many purée soups are based on legumes. These soups may call for a ham hock or similar smoked pork cut to be added to the soup as soon as the stock or broth returns to a simmer, to properly flavor the broth and the main ingredients. Remove them from the soup once they have added the desired flavor. Cut the lean meat into neat dice and reserve it to add as a garnish.

3. **Purée the soup and adjust the seasoning and consistency.** Different types of puréeing equipment will produce different textures in the finished soup. Rustic or home-style purées may be relatively coarse and may even rely simply upon the starch in the main ingredient to give the soup its thickened texture. A food mill fitted with a coarse disk can also be used for a textured purée. Food processors, blenders, and immersion blenders produce very smooth soups with a very fine consistency. At this point, the soup is ready to be finished for service or rapidly cooled and refrigerated.

4. **Evaluate the quality of the finished purée soup.** Purée soups are somewhat thicker and have a slightly coarser texture than other thick soups, but they should still be liquid enough to pour easily from a ladle into a bowl, with a consistency similar to heavy cream.

A proper balance between solid ingredients and liquid results in a soup with a pleasing, robust flavor. Optionally, for extra richness, a bit of softened butter can be swirled on top of the soup just before it leaves the kitchen for the dining room.

Bisques

Traditionally, bisques are based on crustaceans, such as shrimp, lobster, or crayfish, and thickened with rice, rice flour, or bread. The crustacean shells are usually pulverized along with the other ingredients before a final straining. The end result is a soup with a consistency like that of a cream soup.

Contemporary bisques may be based on ingredients other than crustaceans and rely on a vegetable purée or roux as the thickener. A vegetable-based bisque is prepared in the same manner as a purée soup. If the main vegetable does not contain enough starch to act as a thickener, rice, roux, or a starchy vegetable such as potato may be used to provide additional thickness. When the vegetables are tender, the soup is puréed until smooth. Consequently, the distinction between a purée and a bisque is not always clear.

Crustacean meat and shells for bisque should be rinsed well, then coarsely chopped. Shellfish should be scrubbed clean. Consult specific recipes for guidance. Check the quality of stored fumets, stocks, or broths used to prepare a bisque before use. Bring a small amount to a boil and taste it for any sour or off odors.

Peel, trim, and chop any vegetables to be used in the bisque. Chopped onion mirepoix, or garlic is generally a part of the soup. Other ingredients frequently used to add flavor and color include tomato paste, sweet paprika, brandy, and wine.

Traditionally, bisque is thickened with rice; however, more contemporary bisques may be thickened using a roux or flour. Added thickeners are unnecessary if using a prepared velouté. Cream and sherry are finishing ingredients for most bisques. Diced cooked pieces of the main flavoring ingredient commonly garnish a bisque.

The equipment requirements for making bisque are identical to those for making cream soup (see page 404) and include a heavy-gauge pot, puréeing equipment, and a strainer or cheesecloth, as well as equipment for holding, serving, and storing bisques.

A basic formula for 1 gal/3.84 L Bisque

2 lb/907 g of one or more main flavoring ingredients, such as crustacean shells (shrimp, crab, lobster, or a combination)

1 gal/3.84 L cooking liquid (shellfish stock, fumet, broth, or shellfish velouté)

A thickening agent, if not using a prepared velouté, such as blond roux, flour, or rice (whole grains or rice flour)

Seasonings and flavorings, such as salt and pepper, 1 sachet d'épices or bouquet garni, 1 lb/454 g mirepoix, tomato paste or purée

Finishing and garnishing ingredients, such as 16 fl oz/480 mL heavy cream; dice or other cuts of cooked shrimp, lobster, or crab; sherry

1. **Rinse the shells well and chop larger shells, such as crab or lobster.** Drain and dry them well. Traditional bisques get their color and flavor from shrimp, lobster, crab, or crayfish shells. Use one type of crustacean or a combination. Brown the shells in the cooking fat, stirring frequently, until they turn a bright pink or red and remove them from the pan.

2. Add the mirepoix to the pan and cook it over medium heat for 20 to 30 minutes, or until the vegetables are tender and the onions are light brown. Tomato paste is often added at this point and allowed to cook until it has a sweet aroma and a deep rust color. Add spices such as paprika to the shells and other aromatics to cook in the fat.

3. Some bisque recipes indicate the addition of flour to prepare a roux as part of the soup-making process. If necessary, add a bit more oil or butter to the shells, then stir in the roux and cook, stirring constantly, for 4 to 5 minutes. Alternatively, add a prepared roux to the shells and cook long enough to soften the roux.

A good-quality stock or broth is as important to the flavor of a bisque as the shells are. If available, a prepared light velouté (page 383) made from a shellfish or fish stock thickened with a blond roux may be used. Bring the velouté to a simmer while cooking the aromatic vegetables to make cooking more efficient. Also, a more traditional rice-thickened stock may be used as the base for the soup. In that case, there is no need to add either flour or a prepared roux.

At this point, add wine and additional herbs or aromatics, such as a sachet d'épices or bouquet garni.

4. **Taste the soup and make modifications to the seasoning or consistency during cooking.** Add more liquid, if necessary, to maintain a good balance between the liquid and solids as the soup cooks. Stir frequently and monitor the heat. A bisque, like any other soup with starchy ingredients, can scorch quickly if left unattended for even a few minutes.

A bisque takes about 45 minutes to 1 hour to cook properly. At that point, all ingredients (except, obviously, the shells) should be relatively tender, so they will purée easily. Skim the bisque throughout.

Remove and discard the sachet or bouquet before puréeing the bisque. Use a blender (immersion or countertop) to purée it to a fairly smooth and even consistency. Pulverizing the shells and puréeing the aromatic vegetables helps to release more flavor into the soup. If time allows, return the puréed bisque to a simmer for several minutes and make any appropriate adjustments to the soup's seasoning or consistency before straining.

5. **Use rinsed cheesecloth to strain a shellfish bisque.** Cheesecloth removes all traces of the shell and gives the bisque a very fine, delicate texture. This is a two-person task. First, set a sieve or colander in a clean pot. Drape the rinsed cheesecloth in the sieve or colander and pour the bisque through it. Most of the bisque will pass through the cheesecloth. Each person holds two corners of the cheesecloth and lifts the corners up in an alternating sequence (known as the milking method). When only solids remain in the cheesecloth, each person gathers his or her corners together and twists in opposite directions to finish straining the bisque (known as the wringing method). The bisque is ready to finish now, or it may be rapidly cooled and refrigerated for later service.

6. **Finish the bisque and add any garnish ingredients.** Return the bisque to medium heat and bring it to a simmer. Taste the soup and make any seasoning adjustments. Separately, bring the cream to a simmer and add it gradually to the bisque. There should be enough cream to enrich the soup and add a smooth flavor and mouthfeel, but not so much that the cream masks the main ingredient.

7. **Evaluate the quality of the finished bisque.** A good bisque reflects the flavor of the main ingredient. If adding cream to round out and mellow the soup, make sure that it does not mask the main flavor. All bisques are slightly coarse or grainy, with a consistency similar to heavy cream. A crustacean bisque is pale pink or red in color; a shellfish bisque ivory; and a vegetable bisque a paler shade of the main vegetable.

General Guidelines for Soup

Cooking

Add vegetables at staggered intervals, according to cooking times. Stir the soup from time to time throughout the cooking process, to prevent starchy ingredients from sticking to the bottom of the pot and for the best flavor, texture, and appearance. When the flavor is fully developed and all of the ingredients are tender, the soup may be finished or garnished and served right away, or it may be cooled and refrigerated. Although some soups develop a more rounded, mellow flavor if served the day after they are prepared, no soup benefits from hours on the stove. Not only will the flavor become dull and flat, but the nutritive value will greatly diminish as well.

Adjusting consistency

Thick soups, especially those made with starchy vegetables or dried beans, may continue to thicken during cooking, storage, and reheating or holding. As a rule, creams and bisques are about as thick as cold heavy cream and liquid enough to pour from a ladle into a bowl. Purées are somewhat thicker.

For a soup that is too thin, a small amount of starch slurry may be added. Have the soup at a simmer or slow boil when the slurry is added, then stir constantly and continue to simmer for 2 or 3 minutes.

Adjusting flavor and seasoning

Season soups throughout the cooking process. Meat or poultry glaze may be added to bolster a weak broth or consommé, but this will affect the clarity. Chopped fresh herbs, a few drops of lemon juice, Tabasco sauce, Worcestershire sauce, or grated citrus zest may be added to brighten a soup's flavor.

Degreasing

Some soups, especially broth-based ones, may be prepared in advance, then cooled and refrigerated. It is then easy to remove the fat, which congeals on the surface, before reheating the soup. If the soup is to be served just after it is prepared, skim as much fat as possible from the surface. Clear soups may be blotted with strips of paper towel or unwaxed brown butcher paper to remove any traces of fat before serving. Float the strips on the surface, then carefully lift them off. Consommés should be completely fat free, but broths and clear vegetable soups characteristically have some droplets of fat on the surface.

Garnishing

Garnishes may provide contrasts of flavor and texture or they may introduce a complementary flavor. They may also provide additional or contrasting color. In all cases, they should be thoughtfully selected, well prepared, and well seasoned.

Shape large garnishes, such as dumplings, wontons, or quenelles to a size that does not allow them to overwhelm the soup cup or plate selected for service. It is equally important that they not be too difficult for the guest to eat. They should be soft enough to cut through with the edge of a soup spoon.

Since service temperature is extremely important for all soups, remember to bring the garnish to service temperature before adding it to the soup. There are several ways to do this:

- Heat the garnish in a steamer or in a small quantity of broth or consommé and hold it in a steam table.

- Cut delicate items into shapes that will allow the heat of the soup to warm them thoroughly. (If they are small and relatively thin, they will not cause the soup's temperature to drop too severely.)

- Keep large items like dumplings, wontons, or quenelles warm and lightly moistened in a steam table or on the shelf over the range.

Serving

Hot soups should be served very hot. The thinner the soup, the more important this is. Since consommés and broths lose their heat rapidly, they should be nearly at a boil before they are ladled into heated cups. The more surface area exposed to the air, the quicker the soup will cool. This is one reason that consommés and other broth-style soups are traditionally served in cups rather than in the flatter, wider soup plates or bowls often used for cream soups and purées. Serving thin soups in cups also makes it easier for servers to transport the soup without spilling. Cold soups should be thoroughly chilled and served in chilled cups, bowls, or glasses.

Try to plate all soups, but especially consommés, only when the server is in the kitchen, ready to pick up the order. That way, soups will not lose heat as they sit on the line waiting for the server. Use soup cup covers, if available.

Take the time to explain to anyone involved in serving soups the importance of keeping hot soups very hot and taking them quickly from the kitchen to the guest. Show all servers or line cooks the way that a soup should look when it is served to the guest, with garnishes and additional elements such as grated cheese or fine oils, to pass or serve at tableside.

Finishing

Some soups may be prepared to a specific point and then cooled and refrigerated. Garnish clear soups just before service to prevent them from becoming cloudy and to keep the garnish fresh. Some garnishes are added, portion by portion, to heated cups or bowls just prior to service. In other cases, such as for buffet service, the garnish may be added to the entire quantity of soup.

Finish cream and liaison soups just prior to service. Do this for two reasons: The soup will have a fresher flavor, and its shelf life will be greater. Bring cream to a boil before adding it to soup to check freshness and to prevent it from lowering the soup's temperature. Temper a liaison to prevent curdling (see pages 340–342). Make final seasoning adjustments after the soup is finished. Always check the seasoning immediately before service.

Reheating

If a soup has been prepared in advance, reheat only the amount needed for a particular service period. Maintaining food at high temperatures for extended periods often has undesirable effects on flavor and texture. One good way to maintain optimum quality and minimize waste is to reheat individual portions to order. Sometimes, however, this approach is not practical. Learn the best way to make use of the equipment available for service to determine how to get foods to service temperature. Getting foods through the danger zone quickly is important.

Bring clear soup just up to a boil. Check seasoning and consistency and add the appropriate garnishes before serving. Reheat thick soups gently. Reheat the soup over low heat at first, stirring frequently until it softens slightly. Then increase the heat slightly and bring the soup to a simmer.

If a soup has already been finished with cream, sour cream, or a liaison in particular, do not let it come all the way up to a boil, or it may curdle. A temperature of 180°F/82°C is adequate for both quality and food safety concerns. Check seasoning and consistency and add any garnishes just before serving.

Check the temperature regularly for soups held in a steam table. If they consistently fall short of a desirable temperature (at least 165°F/74°C for most soups and sauces), then adjust the thermostat on the steam table, have it repaired, or learn to compensate by quickly bringing individual servings to the correct temperature over direct heat or in a microwave.

Chicken Broth

Makes 1 gal/3.84 L

6 lb/2.72 kg stewing hen

1 gal 32 fl oz/4.80 L water

salt, as needed

1 lb/454 g medium-dice **Mirepoix** (page 333)

1 **Sachet d'Épices** (page 331)

ground black pepper, as needed

1. Place the hen in a stockpot and add the cold water and salt. The water should just cover the chicken. Bring the liquid to a simmer over medium heat. Reduce the heat slightly and continue to simmer for 3 to 5 hours, skimming the surface as necessary.

2. Add the mirepoix and simmer for 30 minutes. Add the sachet to the broth and continue to simmer until the chicken is fully cooked and tender and the broth has a rich flavor and good body, another 30 to 40 minutes.

3. Remove the hen from the broth when it is fully cooked and tender. Discard the bones, skin, and tendons. Reserve the meat to use as a garnish for the broth or for other applications, if desired.

4. Taste the broth and season with salt and pepper. Strain the broth through a fine-mesh sieve or cheesecloth and degrease, if necessary. It is ready to garnish and serve in heated bowls or cups (see Notes), use as an ingredient in another dish, or rapidly cooled and refrigerated for later use.

NOTES

As shown on page 394, chicken broth can be garnished with 10 oz/284 g of the reserved chicken meat, diced; 10 oz/284 g of herbed pasta, cut into 1-in/3-cm squares and cooked; and 6 oz/170 g each of paysanne-cut carrot and celery, cooked until tender. Other options for garnishing chicken broth include julienned meat, diced or finely julienned vegetables, barley, or spätzle.

Amish Corn and Chicken Soup: Substitute chicken stock for water when making the broth. Add ¼ tsp/0.20 g crushed saffron threads with the sachet. Dice or shred the reserved chicken meat and add it to the broth along with 6 oz/170 g cooked corn (fresh or frozen), 6 oz/170 g cooked egg noodles, and 2 oz/57 g chopped parsley.

Beef Broth: Replace the stewing hen with an equal amount of beef shank, chuck, bottom round, oxtail, or short ribs.

Veal Broth: Replace the stewing hen with an equal amount of veal shank or shin, chuck, bottom round, or calf's head.

Ham or Smoked Pork Broth: Replace the stewing hen with an equal amount of ham hocks (fresh or smoked), meaty ham bones, or Boston butt.

Lamb Broth: Replace the stewing hen with an equal amount of lamb shank, leg, shoulder, or neck.

Turkey or Game Broth: Replace the stewing hen with an equal amount of necks, backs, or legs of turkey, guinea hen, duck, pheasant, goose, or other poultry or game birds.

Fish Broth: Replace the stewing hen with an equal amount of lean white fish, such as cod, halibut, hake, flounder, or pike. Use white mirepoix to keep a light color.

Shellfish Broth: Replace the stewing hen with an equal amount of shrimp, lobster, crayfish, and/or crab.

Vegetable Broth: Replace the stewing hen with 7 lb/3.18 kg nonstarchy vegetables, such as onions, garlic, leeks, shallots, celery, celeriac, carrots, parsnips, mushrooms, tomatoes, fennel, broccoli stems, or others as deemed appropriate by recipe or intended use.

Chicken Rice Soup (Canja)

Makes 1 gal/3.84 L

about 3 lb/1.36 kg stewing hen, cut into 6 pieces

2 fl oz/60 mL olive oil

8 oz/227 g rough-cut **Mirepoix** (page 333)

½ oz/14 g chopped ginger

2 bay leaves

1 to 2 Malaguetas or jalapeños, chopped

1 rosemary sprig

salt, as needed

ground black pepper, as needed

1 gal/3.84 L **Chicken Stock** (page 351)

3 oz/85 g long-grain rice, rinsed and drained

½ fl oz/15 mL palm oil

3 garlic cloves, minced

1 lb/454 g corn kernels, fresh or frozen

1½ oz/43 g cilantro, chiffonade

1. Blot the chicken pieces dry with a paper towel. In a soup pot, heat the olive oil over medium heat. Add the chicken pieces, skin side down first, and brown until golden on all sides, 12 to 14 minutes. Remove the chicken from the pot.

2. Add the mirepoix, ginger, bay leaves, and Malaguetas or jalapeños. Sauté for about 5 minutes, stirring the mixture frequently.

3. Return the chicken to the pot, along with the rosemary sprig, salt, pepper, and stock. Bring the soup to a boil while stirring and scraping the bottom of the pan. Lower the heat, cover and let simmer for 1 to 1½ hours. Be sure the chicken is tender.

4. Remove the soup from the heat, take out the chicken pieces, and strain through a fine-mesh sieve. Discard the contents of the sieve and let the strained stock sit for a few minutes so that all the fat rises to the surface. Degrease the stock and discard the fat. Reserve the stock.

5. Discard the skin and bones from the cooked chicken and cut the meat into a medium dice. Reserve it to garnish the soup later.

6. Meanwhile, cook the rice in a separate pot, drain, air-dry, and reserve for service.

7. In the soup pot, heat the palm oil and garlic over medium heat. Do not brown the garlic. Add salt and pepper and the reserved stock and bring to a boil. Lower the heat, cover, and cook for 15 minutes.

8. Add the chicken meat and the corn and continue cooking for another 5 minutes, or until the corn is tender and the chicken is heated thoroughly.

9. Add the cooked rice and adjust seasoning with salt and pepper. Garnish with the cilantro and serve the soup in heated bowls or cups, or properly cool and refrigerate it for later use.

Chicken Rice Soup (*Canja*)

Chicken Consommé Royale

Beef Consommé

Makes 1 gal/3.84 L

1 lb/454 g minced or ground **Mirepoix** (page 333)

3 lb/1.36 kg lean ground beef

10 egg whites, beaten

12 oz/340 g fresh or canned tomatoes, chopped

1 gal 64 fl oz/5.76 L **White Beef Stock** (page 351), cold

salt, as needed

1 **Sachet d'Épices** (page 331), plus 1 clove and 2 allspice berries (see Notes)

2 oignons brûlé (see page 330) (optional)

1. Blend the mirepoix, ground beef, egg whites, and tomatoes. Add this clarification mixture to the stock in a stockpot. Stir to combine thoroughly.

2. Bring the mixture to a slow simmer, stirring frequently until the raft just begins to form, 8 to 10 minutes. Create a small hole in part of the raft. Add some salt, the sachet, and the oignons brûlé, if using, to the mixture through the hole.

3. Simmer slowly for 1 to 1½ hours, or until the appropriate flavor and clarity is achieved (see page 397). Baste the raft occasionally through the opening.

4. Strain the consommé through a paper filter or rinsed double cheesecloth. Adjust seasoning with salt as needed. The consommé is ready to finish now, or it may be rapidly cooled and refrigerated for later service.

5. To finish the soup for service, return it to a boil. Degrease the hot consommé by skimming or blotting with paper towels, or lift the fat from the surface of the refrigerated consommé.

6. Taste the consommé and adjust seasoning with salt. Serve in heated bowls or cups and garnish as desired.

NOTES

If the first clarification was less than successful, clarify a second time by combining 1 gal/3.84 L cold consommé with no more than 4 beaten egg whites, a small amount of mirepoix, and ½ fl oz/15 mL tomato purée or lemon juice. Bring the consommé slowly to a boil. As the egg whites coagulate, the impurities will be trapped. This emergency measure, however, tends to remove not only the impurities but some flavor as well.

The aromatics can be added as a sachet (which will better control the flavor of the finished product), or as loose ingredients.

Chicken Consommé Royale: Substitute an equal amount of White Mirepoix (page 333) for the standard Mirepoix, ground chicken for the ground beef, and Chicken Stock (page 351) for the White Beef Stock. Simmer for 1 to 1 hour 15 minutes. Garnish the consommé with Royale Custard (recipe follows).

Royale Custard

Makes 90 1-in/3-cm rounds

3 egg yolks

1 egg

6⅔ fl oz/200 mL **Chicken or White Beef Stock** (page 351)

¼ tsp/0.50 g salt, or as needed

pinch ground white pepper, or as needed

1. Mix all the ingredients together and pour the custard into a buttered half hotel pan. The custard should be no more than ⅜ in/9 mm thick.

2. Set the pan in a hot-water bath and bake it in a 300°F/149°C oven for about 30 minutes, or until just firm throughout.

3. Using a 1-in/3-cm round cutter, cut the custard into circles. Cover and refrigerate until needed.

NOTES

To ensure that the custard has a uniform thickness, select a hotel pan that has a completely flat bottom and be sure that the rack inside the oven is level.

The Royale may be cut into various shapes, such as diamonds or squares. The yield will vary depending on the shape and size of the cutters used.

Cream of Broccoli Soup

Makes 1 gal/3.84 L

4 lb/1.81 kg broccoli

2 fl oz/60 mL clarified butter or vegetable oil

1 lb/454 g medium-dice **White Mirepoix** (page 333)

1 gal/3.84 L **Chicken Velouté** (page 383)

1 **Sachet d'Épices** (page 331)

16 fl oz/480 mL heavy cream, hot

salt, as needed

ground black pepper, as needed

1. Remove the stems from the broccoli and reserve the florets for garnish. Peel and dice the stems.

2. Heat the butter or oil and add the mirepoix. Sweat until the onions are translucent, 6 to 8 minutes. Add the broccoli stems and sweat until slightly tender.

3. Add the velouté to the pot and bring to a full boil. Reduce the heat and simmer until the soup is thickened, about 35 minutes. Add the sachet and simmer for another 25 minutes. Stir frequently and skim as needed.

4. Cut the florets into bite-size pieces, keeping their shape, and blanch in boiling, salted water until tender. Shock the florets in an ice bath and reserve for service.

5. Strain the solids from the soup and purée them until smooth. Add the strained soup back to the purée. Strain again using a fine-mesh sieve or cheesecloth. The soup is ready to finish now, or it may be rapidly cooled and refrigerated for later service.

6. Return the soup to a simmer. Add the cream and season with salt and pepper. Heat the broccoli florets in simmering stock or water and garnish individual portions or the entire batch. Serve in heated bowls or cups.

Cream of Asparagus (Crème Argenteuil): Replace the broccoli with an equal amount of asparagus stems. Garnish with blanched asparagus tips.

Cream of Lettuce (Crème Choisy): Replace the broccoli with an equal amount of shredded lettuce. Garnish with a chiffonade of Fines Herbes (page 463).

Cream of Celery (Crème Céleri): Replace the broccoli with an equal amount of celery or celeriac. Garnish with blanched small-dice celery.

Cream of Tomato Soup

Makes 1 gal/3.84 L

2 oz/57 g small-dice bacon (optional)

3 fl oz/90 mL butter or vegetable oil

1 lb/454 g small-dice **Mirepoix** (page 333)

2 garlic cloves, minced

4 oz/85 g all-purpose flour

96 fl oz/2.88 L **Chicken Stock** (page 351)

2 lb/907 g chopped plum tomatoes, fresh or canned

24 fl oz/720 mL tomato purée

salt, as needed

ground white pepper, as needed

1 **Sachet d'Épices** (page 331), plus 2 cloves

16 fl oz/480 mL heavy cream, hot

GARNISH

8 oz/227 g **Croutons** (page 921)

1. Render the bacon, if using, in a soup pot over low heat, 5 to 6 minutes. Add the butter or oil, mirepoix, and garlic. Sweat the vegetables over medium-high heat until they are tender, 8 to 10 minutes.

2. Add the flour. Cook, stirring frequently, over medium heat to make a blond roux, 8 to 10 minutes.

3. Add the stock and blend well. Add the tomatoes, tomato purée, salt, and pepper. Simmer the soup for about 25 minutes.

4. Add the sachet and simmer for an additional 25 minutes. Strain the solids out of the soup and purée them until they are completely smooth. Return the purée to the liquid and simmer slowly over medium-low heat for 8 to 10 minutes. Strain the soup through a fine-mesh sieve or cheesecloth, if desired.

5. The soup is ready to finish now, or it may be rapidly cooled and refrigerated for later service.

6. Return the soup to a simmer for service. Add the cream and adjust seasoning with salt and pepper. Garnish individual portions with croutons and serve in heated bowls or cups.

Cream of Tomato Soup with Rice: Add 1 lb/454 g cooked long-grain white rice to the tomato soup immediately before serving.

Cream of Tomato Soup

Tortilla Soup

Makes 1 gal/3.84 L

1 gal 32 fl oz/4.80 L **Chicken Stock** (page 351)

about 6 lb/2.72 kg whole chicken

2 fl oz/60 mL vegetable oil

1 lb 6 oz/624 g minced onions

2 garlic cloves, roughly chopped

10 oz/284 g plum tomatoes, charred, peeled, seeded

2 tsp/2 g epazote

salt, as needed

ground black pepper, as needed

GARNISH

2 to 4 pasilla chiles

4 corn tortillas, julienned

2 avocados, medium dice

2 limes, cut into wedges

8 oz/227 g grated Monterey Jack

1. Combine the stock and chicken and simmer for 1½ to 2 hours, until the chicken is tender and completely cooked. Remove the chicken and set it aside. Cool it slightly and then discard all the bones, skin, and cartilage. Shred or dice the chicken meat and hold it for garnish. Strain the broth and hold.

2. Meanwhile, in a sauté pan, heat the oil and add the onions and garlic. Cook them until they start to turn golden. Place the cooked onion mixture in a blender along with the charred and peeled tomatoes. Purée until very fine.

3. Pour the mixture into a stockpot and simmer for 5 minutes. Add the chicken broth and simmer for 30 minutes more. Just before serving, add the epazote and cook for 1 minute longer. Season with salt and pepper. The soup is ready to finish now, or it may be rapidly cooled and refrigerated for later service.

4. For the garnish: Toast the chiles under the broiler or salamander to just change their color—do not allow them to get too dark. Remove the stems and seeds and cut them into small dice. Reserve.

5. Deep fry the julienned tortillas at 350°F/177°C, drain on paper towels, and reserve.

6. To finish the soup for service, return it to a boil. Serve the soup in heated bowls or cups. Garnish individual portions with the diced avocados, pasillas, tortillas, lime wedges, cheese, and the reserved chicken meat. Alternatively, the garnishes may be served in ramekins or serving bowls alongside the soup.

Onion Soup

Makes 1 gal/3.84 L

5 lb/1.81 kg thinly sliced onions

2 oz/57 g clarified or whole butter

4 fl oz/120 mL Calvados or sherry

1 gal 32 fl oz to 1 gal 64 fl oz/4.80 to 5.76 L **Chicken or White Beef Stock** (page 351), warm

1 **Sachet d'Épices** (page 331)

salt, as needed

ground black pepper, as needed

1. Sauté the onions in the butter over medium heat, stirring occasionally, until browned, about 30 minutes.

2. Deglaze the pan with the Calvados or sherry and reduce until it reaches a syrupy consistency.

3. Add the stock and the sachet and simmer until the onions are tender and the soup is properly flavored, 30 to 35 minutes. The soup is ready to finish now, or it may be rapidly cooled and refrigerated for later service.

4. To finish the soup for service, return it to a boil. Season with salt and pepper and serve in heated bowls or cups.

White Onion Soup: Gently cook the onions in butter over low heat until they are limp, but not colored. If desired, add up to 6 oz/170 g flour as a thickener. The onions may also be puréed and added back to the soup, or spread on a crouton.

Onion Soup Gratinée: Garnish each portion of the soup with a crouton. Top each crouton generously with grated Gruyère (1¼ oz/35 g per serving) and brown under a salamander or broiler for 3 to 5 minutes, or until lightly browned.

New England–Style Clam Chowder

Makes 1 gal/3.84 L

60 chowder clams

96 fl oz/2.88 L or as needed **Fish Stock** (page 353) or water

4 oz/113 g salt pork, minced to a paste

4 fl oz/120 mL clarified butter

8 oz/227 g minced onions

4 oz/113 g small-dice celery

4 oz/113 g all-purpose flour

12 oz/340 g russet potatoes, peeled, small dice

32 fl oz/960 mL heavy cream, hot

salt, as needed

ground white pepper, as needed

1 tsp/5 mL Tabasco sauce, or as needed

1 tsp/5 mL Worcestershire sauce, or as needed

1. In a covered pot, steam the clams in the stock or water until they open.

2. Decant and strain the broth through a filter or cheesecloth and reserve. Pick the clams and chop and reserve the meat.

3. In a large stockpot, render the salt pork over medium-low heat. Add the butter, onions, and celery. Sweat until they are translucent, 6 to 7 minutes.

4. Add the flour and cook 5 to 6 minutes to make a blond roux.

5. Combine the reserved clam broth and enough additional stock or water to make 64 fl oz/1.92 L of liquid. Gradually add the stock to the roux and stir to incorporate completely, working out any lumps. Simmer for 30 minutes, skimming the surface as necessary.

6. Add the potatoes and simmer until they are tender. The soup is ready to finish now, or it may be rapidly cooled and refrigerated for later service.

7. Return the soup to a simmer for service. Add the reserved clams and cream. Season with salt, pepper, Tabasco, and Worcestershire. Serve in heated bowls or cups.

Conch Chowder

Makes 1 gal/3.84 L

2 lb 8 oz/1.13 kg conch meat, ground through a ⅛-in/3-mm die

2 fl oz/60 mL lemon juice

1½ oz/43 g butter

2 lb/907 g medium-dice **Mirepoix** (page 333)

1 Scotch bonnet, seeded, minced

1 lb 8 oz/680 g potatoes, peeled, medium dice

64 fl oz/1.92 L water

64 fl oz/1.92 L **Fish Stock** (page 353)

1 lb 8 oz/680 g peeled, seeded, and medium-diced plum tomatoes

2 oz/57 g tomato paste

2 bay leaves

1 tbsp/3 g chopped thyme

salt, as needed

ground black pepper, as needed

1. In a large bowl, combine the conch with the lemon juice and marinate for 30 minutes.

2. In a large stockpot over medium heat, add the butter and mirepoix and sweat the vegetables until tender, about 7 minutes. Add the Scotch bonnet and potatoes and cook for an additional 2 to 3 minutes.

3. Add the water, stock, marinated conch, tomato products, and bay leaves and simmer for 45 minutes, or until the potatoes are very tender and the soup is well flavored. Finish with the thyme and season with salt and pepper. Serve in heated bowls or cups.

Corn Chowder

Makes 1 gal/3.84 L

4 oz/113 g salt pork

2 oz/57 g butter

6 oz/170 g small-dice onions

6 oz/170 g small-dice celery

4 oz/113 g small-dice green peppers

4 oz/113 g small-dice red peppers

3⅓ oz/94 g all-purpose flour

64 fl oz/1.92 L **Chicken Stock** (page 351)

2 lb/907 g corn kernels, fresh or frozen

2 lb/907 g potatoes, peeled, small dice

1 bay leaf

8 fl oz/240 mL heavy cream, hot

8 fl oz/240 mL milk, hot

salt, as needed

ground white pepper, as needed

2 tsp/10 mL Tabasco sauce

2 tsp/10 mL Worcestershire sauce

1. In a large pot, render the salt pork and melt the butter together over medium heat, until lean portions of salt pork are lightly crisp, about 6 minutes.

2. Add the onions, celery, and peppers to the fat mixture and sweat until softened, about 5 minutes.

3. Add the flour and cook to make a white roux, about 3 minutes.

4. Remove the pot from the heat and add ⅓ of the stock. Stir until combined. Return the pot to medium heat and continue stirring to work out any lumps. Repeat with the remaining ⅔ of the stock. Bring the soup to a simmer and cook, stirring periodically to prevent scorching, until the soup thickens, 30 to 40 minutes.

5. Purée half of the corn and add it to the soup with the potatoes. Add the remaining whole corn and bay leaf and simmer, covered, until the corn and potatoes are tender, about 15 minutes.

6. Add the cream and milk to the soup, and stir to combine. Heat the soup just until it begins to simmer, about

10 minutes. Remove and discard the bay leaf. The soup is ready to finish now, or it may be rapidly cooled and refrigerated for later service.

7. To finish the soup for service, return it to a boil. Season with salt, white pepper, Tabasco, and Worcestershire sauce and serve in heated bowls or cups.

Pacific Seafood Chowder

Makes 1 gal/3.84 L

12 fl oz/360 mL dry white wine

1 sachet d'épices, containing 3 cloves crushed garlic; 1 oz/28 g peeled ginger; 5 stalks lemongrass, cut into 1-in/3-cm pieces; and 12 kaffir lime leaves

64 fl oz/1.92 L clam juice

48 fl oz/1.44 L coconut milk

8 fl oz/240 mL heavy cream, hot

2 oz/60 g **Red Curry Paste** (page 464)

1 oz/28 g cornstarch (to make a slurry)

1 lb/454 g snapper fillet, skinned, medium dice

1 lb/454 g shrimp, peeled, deveined, medium dice

3 lemons, juiced

salt, as needed

GARNISH

1 oz/28 g basil leaves, chiffonade

1. In a large nonreactive pot, combine the wine and the sachet and bring to a boil. Simmer for 10 minutes. Add the clam juice, coconut milk, and cream; return to a boil and mix in the curry paste.

2. Mix the cornstarch with some water to the consistency of heavy cream and add this to the soup. Add enough slurry to produce a light body. Cook for 5 minutes until the soup thickens. Remove the sachet. The soup is ready to finish now, or it may be rapidly cooled and refrigerated for later service.

3. To finish the soup for service, return it to a boil. Add the snapper and the shrimp and cook until the seafood is cooked through, 5 to 7 minutes.

4. Season with the lemon juice and salt. Garnish with the basil and serve in heated bowls or cups.

Pacific Seafood Chowder

Manhattan-Style Clam Chowder

Makes 1 gal/3.84 L

10 lb/4.54 kg chowder clams, washed

1 gal/3.84 L water

3 oz/85 g salt pork, minced to a paste

1 lb/454 g medium-dice **Mirepoix** (page 333)

4 oz/113 g medium-dice leeks, white parts only

4 oz/113 g medium-dice green peppers

1 tsp/3 g minced garlic

1 lb/454 g plum tomatoes, peeled, seeded, medium dice

1 bay leaf

1 thyme sprig

1 oregano sprig

12 oz/340 g russet potatoes, peeled, medium dice

salt, as needed

ground white pepper, as needed

¼ tsp/1.25 mL Tabasco sauce

¼ tsp/1.25 mL Worcestershire sauce

¼ tsp/0.50 g Old Bay seasoning

1. In a covered pot, steam the clams in water until they open, about 5 minutes. Remove the clam meat from the shells; chop and reserve. Strain and reserve the clam broth.

2. In a soup pot, render the salt pork, about 6 minutes. Add the mirepoix, leeks, and peppers and sweat until softened, about 5 minutes.

3. Add the garlic and sauté for 1 minute, until aromatic. Add the reserved clam broth, tomatoes, bay leaf, thyme, and oregano; simmer for 30 minutes over medium to medium-low heat.

4. Add the potatoes and simmer until they are tender, 8 to 10 minutes. Remove the herbs and discard. The soup is ready to finish now, or it may be rapidly cooled and refrigerated for later service.

5. To finish the soup for service, return it to a boil. Degrease the soup. Add the reserved clams and season with salt, white pepper, Tabasco, Worcestershire sauce, and Old Bay. Serve in heated bowls or cups.

Purée of Lentil Soup

Makes 1 gal/3.84 L

6 oz/170 g medium-dice bacon

1 lb/454 g medium-dice **Mirepoix** (page 333)

2 lb/907 g brown lentils, rinsed and sorted

1 gal 64 fl oz/5.76 L **Chicken Stock** (page 351)

salt, as needed

ground black pepper, as needed

1 **Sachet d'Épices** (page 331)

2 fl oz/60 mL lemon juice

GARNISH

8 oz/227 g **Croutons** (page 921)

1 oz/28 g chopped chervil

1. Render the bacon in a medium pot over low heat. Reserve the bits of bacon for garnish.

2. Add the mirepoix and cook until tender and lightly browned, about 15 minutes.

3. Add the lentils and allow them to lightly toast before adding the stock, salt, and pepper. Bring to a simmer and skim as needed.

4. Add the sachet and simmer for 30 minutes, or until the lentils are tender. Remove from the heat and discard the sachet.

5. Strain the mixture, reserving the soup broth. Purée the solids in a food processor, with a food mill, or with an immersion blender. Add enough of the reserved soup broth to achieve the proper consistency.

6. Season with lemon juice. The soup is ready to finish now, or it may be rapidly cooled and refrigerated for later service.

7. Return the soup to a simmer for service and adjust seasoning with salt and pepper. Garnish individual portions with reserved bacon, croutons, and chervil and serve in heated bowls or cups.

Purée of Split Pea Soup

Makes 1 gal/3.84 L

2 oz/57 g minced bacon

2 fl oz/60 mL vegetable oil

1 lb/454 g small-dice **Mirepoix** (page 333)

2 tsp/6 g minced garlic

1 gal 64 fl oz/5.76 L **Chicken Stock** (page 351)

1 lb/454 g potatoes, peeled, large dice

3 lb/1.36 kg green split peas

1 ham hock

1 bay leaf

salt, as needed

ground black pepper, as needed

GARNISH

1 lb/454 g **Croutons** (page 921)

1. Render the bacon over medium heat. Remove the bits of bacon and reserve for garnish. Add the oil and sauté the mirepoix until the onions become transparent, 10 to 12 minutes. Add the garlic and sauté for another minute. Do not brown the garlic.

2. Add the stock, potatoes, split peas, ham hock, and bay leaf and bring to a simmer. Allow the soup to simmer for 45 minutes, or until the peas are tender. Remove the bay leaf and the ham hock and dice the lean meat, if desired. Reserve.

3. Purée the soup using a food mill, blender, or food processor until it is smooth. Add the ham hock meat if desired. Taste and season with salt and pepper. The soup is ready to finish now, or it may be rapidly cooled and refrigerated for later service.

4. To finish the soup for service, return it to a boil. Serve it in heated bowls or cups and garnish with croutons.

Purée of Yellow Split Pea Soup: Replace the green split peas with an equal amount of yellow split peas.

Caribbean-Style Pureé of Black Bean Soup

Makes 1 gal/3.84 L

3 oz/85 g diced salt pork

8 oz/227 g small-dice **Mirepoix** (page 333)

2 lb/907 g dried black beans, soaked overnight

1 gal 64 fl oz/5.76 L **Chicken Stock** (page 351)

1 **Sachet d'Épices** (page 331)

2 smoked ham hocks

5½ fl oz/165 mL dry sherry

½ tsp/1 g ground allspice

salt, as needed

ground black pepper, as needed

GARNISH

13 oz/369 g sour cream

5½ oz/156 g peeled, seeded, and medium-diced plum tomatoes

1 oz/28 g thinly sliced greeen onions, cut on the bias

1. Render the salt pork over low heat, about 10 minutes. Add the mirepoix and sweat until the onions are translucent, 5 to 7 minutes.

2. Add the soaked beans, stock, sachet, and ham hocks. Simmer the mixture until the beans are very tender, 3 to 4 hours.

3. Remove the ham hocks and dice the lean meat to add as garnish, if desired.

4. Purée half of the beans using a food mill or food processor. Add the bean purée to the soup.

5. Finish the soup with sherry and allspice. Season with salt and pepper. The soup is ready to finish now, or it may be rapidly cooled and refrigerated for later service.

6. To finish the soup for service, return it to a boil. Garnish with the diced ham, sour cream, tomato, and green onions. Serve in heated bowls or cups.

Senate Bean Soup

Makes 1 gal/3.84 L

1 lb 8 oz/680 g dried navy beans, soaked overnight

1 gal 64 fl oz/5.76 L **Chicken Stock** (page 351)

2 smoked ham hocks

2 fl oz/60 mL vegetable oil

6 oz/170 g medium-dice onions

6 oz/170 g medium-dice carrots

6 oz/170 g medium-dice celery

2 garlic cloves, minced

1 **Sachet d'Épices** (page 331)

6 to 8 drops Tabasco sauce

salt, as needed

ground black pepper, as needed

1. In a stockpot, combine the beans, stock, and ham hocks. Simmer over medium heat for 2 hours. Strain the broth and reserve. Set the beans aside, remove the ham hocks, and dice the meat for garnish. Reserve.

2. Heat the oil in the same stockpot. Add the onions, carrots, and celery and sweat over medium heat, for 4 to 5 minutes, or until the onions are translucent. Add the garlic and sauté until it is aromatic, about 1 minute.

3. Return the beans and broth to the pot. Add the sachet. Simmer until the beans are tender, 20 to 30 minutes. Remove and discard the sachet.

4. Purée half of the soup in a blender or with a food mill. Recombine the purée and reserved ham with the remaining soup. Adjust the consistency with additional broth or water if necessary. The soup is ready to finish now, or it may be rapidly cooled and refrigerated for later service.

5. To finish the soup for service, return it to a simmer over low heat, 6 to 8 minutes, and season with Tabasco, salt, and pepper.

Potage Garbure

Makes 1 gal/3.84 L

2 oz/57 g ground salt pork

2 fl oz/60 mL olive oil

8 oz/227 g finely chopped onions

8 oz/227 g finely chopped carrots

12 oz/340 g finely chopped leeks, white and pale green parts

96 fl oz/2.88 L **Chicken Stock** (page 351)

12 oz/340 g thinly sliced potatoes

12 oz/340 g thinly sliced green cabbage

12 oz/340 g peeled, seeded, and chopped tomatoes

salt, as needed

ground black pepper, as needed

GARNISH

Croutons (page 921)

1. Heat the salt pork and olive oil in a soup pot over medium heat until the fat renders from the pork, 12 to 15 minutes.

2. Add the onions, carrots, and leeks and stir until the vegetables are coated with fat. Cover the pan and smother over low heat until the vegetables are tender and translucent, 10 to 12 minutes, stirring from time to time.

3. Add the stock, potatoes, cabbage, and tomatoes and simmer over low to medium heat until the potatoes are just starting to fall apart, 20 to 25 minutes. Skim the surface of the soup as needed during cooking time. Taste the soup periodically to monitor the cooking time and adjust seasoning as the soup simmers.

4. Purée the soup to a coarse texture. The soup is ready to finish now, or it may be rapidly cooled and refrigerated for later service.

5. To finish the soup for service, return it to a boil. Taste the soup and season with salt and pepper. Serve in heated bowls or cups and garnish each serving with a crouton.

Vichyssoise

Makes 1 gal/3.84 L

1½ fl oz/45 mL vegetable oil

1 lb 8 oz/680 g finely chopped leeks, white parts only

6 oz/170 g finely chopped onions

3 lb/1.36 kg potatoes, peeled, medium dice

96 fl oz/2.88 L **Chicken Stock** (page 351)

1 **Sachet d'Épices** (page 331)

1 tbsp/15 g salt, plus as needed

ground white pepper, as needed

24 fl oz/720 mL half-and-half

2 oz/57 g snipped chives

1. Heat the oil in a medium stockpot. Add the leeks and onions and sweat over medium-low heat until translucent, 2 to 3 minutes.

2. Increase the heat to high; add the potatoes, stock, sachet, 1 tablespoon of salt, and white pepper. Bring to a full boil, reduce the heat to medium-low, and simmer until the potatoes are soft, about 30 minutes. Remove and discard the sachet.

3. Purée the soup in batches using a blender or food mill.

4. To finish the soup for service, stir in the half-and-half and chives. Adjust seasoning with salt and white pepper. Serve in chilled bowls or cups.

Shrimp Bisque

Makes 1 gal/3.84 L

1 lb 8 oz/680 g shrimp shells

3 oz/85 g butter

1 lb/454 g onions, minced

3 garlic cloves, minced

1 tbsp/6 g paprika, or as needed

2 oz/57 g tomato paste

3 fl oz/90 mL brandy

96 fl oz/2.88 L **Fish or Shrimp Velouté** (page 383)

salt, as needed

ground black pepper, as needed

32 fl oz/960 mL heavy cream, hot

1 lb 10 oz/737 g shrimp, peeled and deveined

½ tsp/1 g Old Bay seasoning

½ tsp/2.50 mL Tabasco sauce, or as needed

½ tsp/2.50 mL Worcestershire sauce, or as needed

4 fl oz/120 mL dry sherry

1. Rinse the shrimp shells thoroughly and drain them. Sauté the shrimp shells in a medium stockpot in 2 oz/57 g of the butter over medium-high heat for 1 to 2 minutes, until the shells turn bright pink.

2. Reduce the heat to medium, and add the onions. Sauté the onions until they are translucent, about 2 minutes.

3. Add the garlic, paprika, and tomato paste and cook for 2 minutes until there is a sweet, cooked tomato aroma and the shells soften slightly.

4. Deglaze the mixture with the brandy and reduce for 2 to 3 minutes until nearly dry. Add the cooked shrimp shells back.

5. Add the velouté and simmer for 45 minutes on medium-low, until the bisque is intensely rust colored and has thickened slightly. Season with salt and pepper as the bisque simmers. Strain the bisque through a fine-mesh strainer or using the wringing method (as shown on page 421).

6. Return the bisque to a simmer and add the cream.

7. Cut the shrimp into small dice and sauté in the remaining 1 oz/28 g butter for 1 to 2 minutes over medium-high heat, until cooked thoroughly and pink. Add the shrimp to the bisque and simmer for 5 minutes.

8. Add the Old Bay, Tabasco, and Worcestershire sauce and adjust seasoning with salt and pepper. The soup is ready to finish now, or it may be rapidly cooled and refrigerated for later service.

9. To finish the soup for service, return it to a boil. Add the sherry and serve in heated bowls or cups.

Lobster Bisque (Bisque de Homard)

Makes 1 gal/3.84 L

3 fl oz/90 mL olive oil

1 lb 2 oz/510 g small-dice onions

1 lb 2 oz/510 g small-dice carrots

1 lb 2 oz/510 g small-dice celery

8 oz/227 g thinly sliced leeks

2 lb 4 oz/1.25 kg small-dice fennel

6 garlic cloves, crushed

6 lb 5 oz/2.86 kg lobster shells, cleaned, crushed, and roasted

4 oz/113 g tomato paste

2½ fl oz/75 mL brandy

12 fl oz/360 mL dry white wine

96 fl oz/2.88 L **Fish Stock** (page 353)

48 fl oz/1.44 L water

4 oz/113 g Italian rice (Arborio or Carnaroli)

5 oz/142 g **Blond Roux** (page 335)

24 fl oz/720 mL heavy cream, hot

salt, as needed

cayenne, as needed

1 fl oz/15 mL lemon juice

1 oz/28 g tarragon leaves, chopped

1. In a large soup pot or rondeau, heat the oil over medium heat. Add the onions and sweat for 5 minutes. Add the carrots, celery, leeks, fennel, and garlic and sweat for an additional 5 minutes.

2. Add the lobster shells and sweat for 10 minutes, until the shells are very fragrant and the liquid is released.

3. Add the tomato paste and cook until it turns a rusty brown color. Add the brandy and flambé.

4. Add the wine and reduce it by half, about 5 minutes. Add the stock and water and bring to a boil. Add the rice and cook, covered, for 45 minutes.

5. When the rice is very soft, strain the soup through a fine-mesh strainer, return it to the pot, and bring it to a boil.

6. Add the roux and cook 10 minutes more, until the soup thickens, stirring out any lumps.

7. Add the cream, reduce to the desired consistency, and season with salt, cayenne, and lemon juice. Pass it through a strainer again, if necessary. The soup is ready to finish now, or it may be rapidly cooled and refrigerated for later service.

8. To finish the soup for service, return it to a boil. Add the tarragon and serve in heated bowls or cups.

Wisconsin Cheddar Cheese and Beer Soup

Makes 1 gal/3.84 L

6 fl oz/180 mL clarified butter

6 oz/170 g minced onions

3 oz/85 g thinly sliced mushrooms

3 oz/85 g rough-cut celery

1 oz/28 g minced garlic

6 oz/170 g all-purpose flour

96 fl oz/2.88 L **Chicken Stock** (page 351)

8 fl oz/240 mL beer

2 lb/907 g grated Cheddar

½ oz/14 g dry mustard

8 fl oz/240 mL heavy cream, hot

Tabasco sauce, as needed

Worcestershire sauce, as needed

salt, as needed

ground white pepper, as needed

GARNISH

8 oz/227 g **Rye Croutons** (page 921)

1. In a large soup pot or rondeau, heat the butter over medium heat. Sweat the onions, mushrooms, celery, and garlic until the onions are translucent.

2. Add the flour and cook to make a blond roux, about 12 minutes. Add the stock gradually, whisking constantly

to work out any lumps. Simmer for 45 minutes, or until the soup has a good flavor and velvety texture. Strain through a fine-mesh sieve. The soup is ready to finish now, or it may be rapidly cooled and refrigerated for later service.

3. To finish the soup for service, return it to a simmer. Shortly before service, add the beer and cheese and continue to heat the soup gently until the cheese melts. Do not boil.

4. Blend the dry mustard with enough water to make a paste. Add the mustard mixture and the cream to the soup and bring the soup back to a simmer. Adjust the consistency with stock, if necessary.

5. Season the soup with Tabasco, Worcestershire, salt, and pepper.

6. Serve in heated bowls or cups with the rye croutons on the side.

Chicken and Shrimp Gumbo

Makes 1 gal/3.84 L

½ fl oz/15 mL vegetable oil

4 oz/113 g andouille sausage, small dice

8 oz/227 g boneless and skinless chicken breast, medium dice

8 oz/227 g medium-dice onions

5 oz/142 g medium-dice green peppers

5 oz/142 g medium-dice celery

½ oz/14 g minced jalapeños

3½ oz/99 g thinly sliced green onions, cut on the bias

½ oz/14 g chopped garlic

5 oz/142 g sliced okra

8 oz/227 g peeled, seeded, and medium-diced plum tomatoes

5 oz/142 g all-purpose flour, baked until dark brown

96 fl oz/2.88 L **Chicken Stock** (page 351)

2 bay leaves

1 tsp/2 g dried oregano

1 tsp/2 g onion powder

½ tsp/1 g dried thyme

½ tsp/1 g dried basil

salt, as needed

ground black pepper, as needed

1 lb 4 oz/567 g shrimp, peeled, deveined, and chopped

13 oz/369 g cooked long-grain rice

1 tbsp/9 g filé powder

1. Heat the oil over medium-high heat in a large, heavy-bottomed soup pot and add the andouille. Sauté until the sausage starts to become firm, about 1 minute, stirring occasionally.

2. Add the chicken and sear until it begins to lose its raw appearance, 2 to 3 minutes.

3. Add the onions, peppers, celery, jalapeños, green onions, garlic, okra, and tomatoes. Sauté the vegetables until they are tender and the onions are translucent, 5 to 7 minutes, stirring occasionally.

4. Add the flour to the mixture and cook for 1 minute, stirring constantly. Add the stock and stir constantly to work out any lumps.

5. Add the bay leaves, oregano, onion powder, thyme, basil, salt, and pepper. Simmer for 30 minutes.

6. Add the shrimp and rice, simmer for 2 minutes, and whisk in the filé powder. Be sure to blend well. Do not allow the soup to return to a boil. The soup is ready to finish now, or it may be rapidly cooled and refrigerated for later service

7. To finish the soup for service, return it to a simmer. Adjust seasoning with salt and pepper, if necessary. Serve in heated bowls or cups.

Gazpacho Andaluz (Andalucian Gazpacho)

Makes 1 gal/3.84 L

8 lb/3.63 kg peeled, seeded, and medium-diced plum tomatoes

1 lb/454 g diced green peppers

1 lb/454 g diced cucumbers

8 garlic cloves, crushed

8 fl oz/240 mL red wine vinegar

16 fl oz/480 mL olive oil

salt, as needed

ground black pepper, as needed

GARNISH

4 oz/113 g small-dice tomatoes

4 oz/113 g small-dice green peppers

4 oz/113 g small-dice cucumbers

1 oz/28 g small-dice bread

1. Combine all the ingredients except the garnishes; cover, refrigerate, and marinate overnight.

2. Purée the marinated ingredients in a blender or food mill, working in batches if necessary. Strain through a fine-mesh sieve. Adjust seasoning with salt and pepper.

3. Chill the soup thoroughly before serving.

4. At service, garnish the soup with diced tomatoes, peppers, cucumbers, and bread. Serve in chilled bowls or cups.

Ham Bone and Collard Greens Soup

Makes 1 gal/3.84 L

4 oz/113 g minced salt pork

3 fl oz/90 mL clarified butter or vegetable oil

8 oz/227 g small-dice onions

4 oz/113 g small-dice celery

5 oz/142 g all-purpose flour

96 fl oz/2.88 L **Chicken Stock** (page 351)

3 ham hocks

1 **Sachet d'Épices** (page 331)

1 lb/454 g collard greens, chopped, blanched

salt, as needed

ground black pepper, as needed

1. Render the salt pork over medium heat in a stockpot, 5 to 7 minutes.

2. Add the butter or oil, onions, and celery, and sweat until translucent, about 6 minutes.

3. Add the flour and cook for several minutes to make a pale roux, stirring frequently.

4. Gradually add the chicken stock to the roux, whisking out any lumps.

5. Add the ham hocks and sachet, bring to a simmer, and cook for 1 hour.

6. Add the greens to the soup. Simmer until tender, about 30 minutes.

7. Remove the hocks and sachet. Remove the meat from the hock and cut it into small dice. Add the diced meat to the soup and season with salt and pepper. The soup is ready to serve now, or it may be rapidly cooled and refrigerated for later service.

8. To finish the soup for service, return it to a boil. Serve in heated bowls or cups.

Chinese Hot and Sour Soup (Suan La Tang)

Makes 1 gal/3.84 L

2 fl oz/60 mL vegetable oil

1 tbsp/9 g minced ginger

¾ oz/21 g thinly sliced green onions

8 oz/227 g ground pork butt

1 oz/28 g black fungus, soaked, short julienne

1½ oz/43 g lily buds, soaked, short julienne

8 oz/227 g savoy cabbage, chiffonade

8 oz/227 g small-dice firm tofu

112 fl oz/3.36 L **Chicken Stock** (page 351)

2 fl oz/60 mL dark soy sauce

8 fl oz/240 mL rice vinegar

1 tbsp/15 g salt

¾ oz/21 g ground black pepper

2¼ oz/64 g cornstarch

4 fl oz/120 mL water

3 eggs, lightly beaten

1 fl oz/30 mL sesame oil

GARNISH

1 oz/28 g thinly sliced green onions

1. Heat the vegetable oil in a wok or soup pot over medium-high heat. Add the ginger and green onions and stir-fry until aromatic, about 30 seconds.

2. Add the ground pork and stir-fry until it is cooked, 4 to 5 minutes.

3. Add the black fungus, lily buds, and cabbage and stir-fry until the cabbage is tender, 3 to 4 minutes.

4. Add the tofu, stock, soy sauce, vinegar, salt, and pepper and bring the soup to a boil.

5. Mix the cornstarch and water together and slowly add the slurry to the boiling soup, stirring constantly.

6. Slowly add the eggs to the soup. Hold hot, but do not boil. The soup is ready to finish now, or it may be rapidly cooled and refrigerated for later service.

7. To finish the soup for service, return it to a simmer. Add the sesame oil. Garnish with green onions and serve in heated bowls or cups.

Spicy Beef Soup (Yukkaejang)

Makes 1 gal/3.84 L

7 lb 8 oz/3.40 kg beef bones

1 lb 8 oz/680 g beef flank, trimmed, fat reserved

1 gal 16 fl oz/4.32 L water

1 lb/454 g onions, peeled and quartered

1 oz/28 g ginger, peeled, cut into ⅛-in/3-mm slices

2 oz/57 g beef fat

1 oz/28 g all-purpose flour

1 tbsp/6 g thinly sliced green onions

4 fl oz/120 mL Korean red pepper paste

8 fl oz/240 mL Korean soybean paste

1 tsp/5 mL light soy sauce

10 oz/284 g green cabbage, chiffonade

1½ tsp/7.50 mL sesame oil

1 tsp/3 g minced garlic

3 oz/85 g bean sprouts, cut into 1-in/3-cm lengths

2 eggs, lightly beaten

salt, as needed

ground black pepper, as needed

1. In a large stockpot, blanch the beef bones and drain and rinse. Bring the bones, beef, and water to a boil, then lower to a simmer.

2. On medium-low heat, simmer the beef until tender, about 1 hour 15 minutes. When the beef is tender, remove it from the pot and plunge it into cold water for 15 minutes. Pull the beef into 1-in/3-cm strips. Refrigerate, covered.

3. Add the onions and ginger to the pot and return to a simmer. On medium-low heat, simmer for about 1 hour. At this point, the broth can be strained, rapidly cooled, and refrigerated for service. To finish the soup for service, skim the fat off broth and return it to a boil.

4. Render the beef fat, browning it slightly. Strain and transfer 1 fl oz/30 mL of the fat to a stockpot. Add the flour to create a roux, stirring over low heat for 5 minutes. Gradually add the hot broth, stirring frequently, and bring to boil.

5. Add the green onions, red pepper paste, soybean paste, soy sauce, cabbage, and reserved beef. Return the soup to a boil, stirring occasionally.

6. In a separate heavy skillet, heat the sesame oil over medium heat. Add the garlic and stir-fry until aromatic, about 30 seconds. Add the bean sprouts and stir-fry until cooked, but still firm, about 3 minutes. Add the cooked sprouts to the soup.

7. Add the eggs and stir very gently to create long ribbons. Taste and season with salt and pepper. Serve in heated bowls or cups.

Miso Soup

Makes 1 gal/3.84 L

½ oz/14 g dried wakame seaweed

1 gal/3.84 L **Dashi** (page 354)

8 fl oz/240 mL miso (*aka*/red for summer and *shiro*/white for winter)

1 lb 8 oz/680 g small-dice tofu

GARNISH

1¼ oz/35 g thinly sliced green onions, cut on the bias

1. Soak the wakame in warm water for 30 minutes. Drain it, pour boiling water over it, and plunge it into very cold water (no ice). Drain well. Trim off any tough parts. Chop the remaining seaweed roughly (½ in/1 cm maximum). Wrap in doubled rinsed cheesecloth and twist to extract excess moisture.

2. Place the dashi in a large stockpot or wok. Temper the miso into the dashi gradually, whisking constantly to combine completely.

3. Bring the dashi to a simmer, add the tofu and chopped wakame and simmer for 1 minute. The soup is ready to finish now, or it may be rapidly cooled and refrigerated for later service.

4. To finish the soup for service, return it to a boil. Add the green onions and serve in heated bowls or cups.

Miso Soup

Thai Chicken Soup with Coconut Milk and Galangal

Makes 1 gal/3.84 L

1 fl oz/30 mL vegetable oil

3¼ oz/92 g minced shallots

1½ tsp/4.50 g minced garlic

2 oz/57 g minced lemongrass

1 fl oz/30 mL Thai chili paste

1½ oz/43 g galangal, sliced ¼ in/6 mm thick

12 kaffir lime leaves, bruised

80 fl oz/2.40 L **Chicken Stock** (page 351)

1 tbsp/15 g sugar, or as needed

6 fl oz/180 mL fish sauce, or as needed

48 fl oz/1.44 L coconut milk

8 oz/227 g chicken thighs, cut into thin strips

6½ oz/184 g canned straw mushrooms, drained and halved

4 oz/113 g medium-dice tomatoes

1 fl oz/30 mL lime juice, or as needed

1 tbsp/15 g salt, or as needed

GARNISH

40 cilantro sprigs

1. Heat the oil in a soup pot over medium heat and add the shallots, garlic, lemongrass, and chili paste. Cook until aromatic, about 30 seconds.

2. Add the galangal, lime leaves, stock, sugar, fish sauce, and coconut milk. Bring to a boil, simmer 15 minutes, and strain into a new pot. Add the chicken, mushrooms, and tomatoes. Return to a simmer.

3. Add the lime juice and salt and adjust seasoning with sugar and fish sauce. The soup is ready to finish now, or it may be rapidly cooled and refrigerated for later service.

4. To finish the soup for service, return it to a simmer. Garnish with cilantro sprigs and serve in heated bowls or cups.

Thai Hot and Sour Soup (Tom Yum Kung)

Makes 1 gal/3.84 L

1 fl oz/30 mL vegetable oil

2 fl oz/60 mL **Red Curry Paste** (page 464)

shrimp shells, reserved from shrimp (below)

1 tbsp/8 g minced Thai bird chiles

1 gal/3.84 L **Chicken Stock** (page 351)

4 stalks lemongrass, bruised, cut into 3-in/8-cm lengths

1 oz/28 g galangal, sliced ⅛ in/3 mm thick

12 kaffir lime leaves, bruised

14 oz/397 g plum tomatoes, cut into eighths

1 lb 2 oz/510 g canned straw mushrooms, drained and halved

4 fl oz/120 mL fish sauce

1 oz/28 g sugar

4 fl oz/120 mL lime juice

1 lb/454 g shrimp (31–36 count), peeled, deveined, halved lengthwise

1½ oz/43 g cilantro leaves

1. Heat the oil over medium heat, add the curry paste, and cook and stir for 1 minute without browning. Add the reserved shrimp shells, chiles, stock, lemongrass, galangal, and lime leaves.

2. Simmer for 10 minutes. Strain the broth into new pot, add the tomatoes, mushrooms, fish sauce, and sugar, and bring to a boil.

3. Mix in the lime juice and adjust seasoning with fish sauce. The soup is ready to finish now, or it may be rapidly cooled and refrigerated for later service.

4. Poach the shrimp until they are opaque and cooked through, 2 to 3 minutes. Remove the shrimp from the liquid and cool on a sheet pan. (The poaching liquid can be added back to the soup.) Toss the cooled shrimp with the cilantro and reserve for service.

5. To finish the soup for service, return it to a boil. Add the shrimp and cilantro mixture to a heated bowl or cup and ladle the broth on top. Serve immediately.

Wonton Soup

Makes 1 gal/3.84 L

WONTONS

8 oz/227 g ground pork

8 oz/227 g finely chopped Chinese cabbage

1 oz/28 g thinly sliced green onions

2 tsp/6 g minced ginger

½ fl oz/15 mL light soy sauce

½ fl oz/15 mL sesame oil

½ tsp/2.50 g salt, or as needed

1 tbsp/15 g sugar

¼ tsp/0.50 g ground white pepper, or as needed

40 wonton wrappers (3-in/8-cm square)

1 egg, slightly beaten

SOUP

1 fl oz/30 mL vegetable or peanut oil

2 oz/57 g thinly sliced green onions, cut on the bias

1 tsp/3 g minced ginger

1 gal/3.84 L **Chicken Stock** (page 351)

2½ fl oz/75 mL dark soy sauce

¼ tsp/1.25 g salt, or as needed

⅛ tsp/0.25 g ground white pepper, or as needed

6 oz/170 g spinach, stemmed

4 oz/113 g ham, fine julienne

OMELET

½ fl oz/15 mL vegetable or peanut oil

4 eggs, beaten

1. To make the wonton filling, combine the ground pork, cabbage, green onions, ginger, soy sauce, sesame oil, salt, sugar, and pepper and mix well with a spoon or work by hand until thoroughly combined. Keep chilled until ready to fill the wontons.

2. To make the wontons, spoon 1 tsp/5 mL of the filling mixture into the center of each wrapper and brush the edges of the wrapper lightly with the beaten egg. Fold the wonton in half to make a triangle and then overlap the points, pressing them in place. Cook the wontons in batches in boiling salted water for 2 to 3 minutes, or until cooked through. Drain and reserve.

3. To make the soup, heat the oil in a soup pot over medium high heat. Add the green onions and ginger and sauté, stirring frequently, until aromatic, about 1 minute. Add the stock, bring to a boil, and season with soy sauce, salt, and pepper. The soup is ready to finish now, or it may be rapidly cooled and refrigerated for later service.

4. Bring a large pot of salted water to a rolling boil. Add the spinach and blanch for 30 seconds. Drain and rinse in cold water until chilled. Drain again, squeeze out the excess water, and chop coarsely.

5. To make the omelet, heat the oil in a medium skillet or omelet pan. Cook the eggs, stirring constantly, until they are set. Flatten the eggs into an even layer and roll the omelet out of the pan. Allow it to cool slightly and then cut into a fine julienne.

6. To finish the soup for service, return it to a simmer. Add the spinach, ham, and omelet to the soup. Simmer just long enough to heat, about 2 minutes.

7. Reheat the wontons if necessary and place 3 in a heated bowl or cup. Ladle the hot soup over the wontons and serve at once.

Vegetable Soup Emilia Romagna Style

Vegetable Soup Emilia Romagna Style (Minestrone alla Emiliana)

Makes 1 gal/3.84 L

8 fl oz/240 mL olive oil

4 oz/113 g butter

1 lb/454 g thinly sliced onions

1 lb/454 g small-dice carrots

1 lb/454 g small-dice celery

1 lb 2 oz/510 g russet potatoes, peeled, small dice

1 lb 8 oz/680 g small-dice zucchini

12 oz/340 g small-dice green beans

2 lb/907 g shredded savoy cabbage

1 gal/3.84 L **Brodo** (page 354)

2 Parmesan rinds, 3-in/8-cm square, cleaned

1 lb/454 g canned plum tomatoes, with juices

salt, as needed

ground black pepper, as needed

10 oz/284 g **Great Northern** or navy beans, cooked (page 808)

GARNISH

2 oz/57 g grated Parmesan, or as needed

4 fl oz/120 mL extra-virgin olive oil, or as needed

1. In a large soup pot, heat the oil and melt the butter over low heat. Add the onions and sweat until wilted and soft. Add the carrots and cook for 3 minutes.

2. Add the vegetables in the following sequence, allowing each to soften before adding the next: celery, potatoes, zucchini, green beans, and cabbage. Do not brown the vegetables.

3. Add the brodo, cheese rind, and tomatoes with their juices.

4. Partially cover and cook at a low simmer for at least 3 hours. Add more broth as necessary. The soup is ready to finish now, or it may be rapidly cooled and refrigerated for later service.

5. To finish the soup for service, return it to a boil. Taste and season with salt and pepper. Add the cooked beans and serve in heated bowls or cups with grated Parmesan and a drizzle of olive oil.

Minestrone

Makes 1 gal/3.84 L; 21 portions (6 fl oz/180 mL each)

2 oz/57 g salt pork

2 fl oz/60 mL olive oil

1 lb/454 g paysanne-cut onions

8 oz/227 g paysanne-cut celery

8 oz/227 g paysanne-cut carrots

8 oz/227 g paysanne-cut green peppers

8 oz/227 g paysanne-cut green cabbage

½ oz/14 g minced garlic

1 lb/454 g tomato concassé

1 lb/454 g **Chicken Stock** (page 351)

salt, as needed

ground black pepper, as needed

4 oz/113 g cooked chickpeas

6 oz/170 g cooked black-eyed peas

6 oz/170 g cooked ditalini

GARNISH

5 oz/142 g grated Parmesan

1. Render the salt pork in the oil. Do not brown.

2. Add the onions, celery, carrots, peppers, cabbage, and garlic and sweat until the onions are translucent.

3. Add the tomato concassé, stock, salt, and pepper. Simmer until the vegetables are tender, 25 to 30 minutes. Do not overcook.

4. Add the chickpeas, black-eyed peas, and ditalini. Simmer the soup until all the ingredients are tender, 10 to 12 minutes more. The soup is ready to finish now, or it may be rapidly cooled and stored for later service.

5. To finish the soup for service, return it to a simmer. Adjust seasoning with salt and pepper. Garnish individual portions with grated Parmesan.

Tuscan White Bean and Escarole Soup

Makes 1 gal/3.84 L

1 fl oz/30 mL olive oil

12 oz/340 g small-dice pancetta

6 oz/170 g small-dice onions

1 oz/28 g minced shallots

12 oz/340 g dried navy beans, soaked overnight

1 lb 8 oz/680 g canned tomatoes, seeded and chopped

80 fl oz/2.40 L **Chicken Stock** (page 351)

1 **Sachet d'Épices** (page 331)

4 oz/113 g small-dice carrots

salt, as needed

ground black pepper, as needed

8 oz/227 g escarole, finely chopped

8 oz/227 g tubettini pasta

olive oil, as needed

1¾ oz/50 g sliced garlic

GARNISH

20 **Croutons** (page 921)

1½ oz/43 g Parmesan, grated

1. Heat the oil in a large, heavy saucepan over medium-high heat and add the pancetta. Cook until lightly browned, stirring frequently. Remove the pancetta with a slotted spoon and drain on absorbent paper toweling. Pour off all but ½ fl oz/15 mL of the fat (reserving for later use).

2. Reduce the heat to low, add the onions and shallots, and cook for 5 to 6 minutes, until softened and slightly golden in color.

3. Add the drained beans, tomatoes, stock, sachet, and cooked pancetta. Simmer until the beans are almost tender, about 1 hour.

4. Add the carrots and cook until both the beans and carrots are tender, 15 to 20 minutes. Season with salt and pepper and reserve warm. The soup is ready to finish now, or it may be rapidly cooled and refrigerated for later service.

5. Blanch the escarole in boiling salted water (about 1 minute), shock in ice water, and reserve.

6. Cook the tubettini to al dente in boiling salted water. Shock in ice water, drain well, and toss lightly in olive oil.

7. To finish the soup for service, return it to a simmer. In a sauté pan, brown the sliced garlic in the reserved pancetta fat over medium-high heat, 2 to 3 minutes. Add the golden-brown garlic to the soup. Add the escarole and the pasta and cook until heated through, about 3 minutes. Adjust seasoning with salt and pepper. Garnish with croutons and grated Parmesan and serve in heated bowls or cups.

Part Five

Meats, Poultry, Fish, and Shellfish

Chapter Eighteen

Mise en Place for Meats, Poultry, and Fish

Bringing out the best flavor in meats, poultry, and fish is a skill that seems to come naturally to a professional chef. Another hallmark of the professional is an ability to cook meats, poultry, and fish to the perfect degree of doneness. These skills develop through concentration, practice, and a basic understanding of seasoning and cooking techniques.

Seasonings

Adding seasonings at the proper point in the cooking process is key to giving a finished dish the fullest possible flavor. The array of seasonings runs from simple to complex blends of herbs and spices or marinades, which may include oils, acids, and aromatics, such as onions, garlic, fresh or dried herbs, or spices. In every case, though, seasonings are meant to enhance flavor, not detract from or overwhelm the dish. Liquid marinades may change the texture of foods in addition to flavoring them.

Salt and pepper are taken so much for granted that some beginning cooks fail to apply these two seasonings early enough during cooking or in enough quantity to bring out the best flavor in cooked foods. Salt and pepper added before cooking bring out the inherent flavors in foods. If these seasonings are added only after the cooking is complete, the salt and pepper may take on too much significance in the finished dish's flavor. It is generally better to apply salt and pepper separately. Using the fingertips to apply salt and pepper is a good way to control the amount added, and to apply a more even coat.

Salt and pepper are fundamental, but blends, which combine various spices, herbs, and other aromatics, can create a particular flavor profile. Like salt and pepper, they may be applied directly to raw meat, poultry, or fish. To intensify the flavor of seeds and spices, toast them either on the stovetop or in a moderate oven just before grinding. Be sure to pay close attention. They can go from perfectly toasted to scorched very quickly.

To toast seeds or spices in the oven, spread them out on a dry sheet pan in a moderate oven just until a pleasant aroma is apparent. Stir often to ensure even browning. Remove immediately and transfer to a fresh pan or plate to cool.

To toast spices and seeds on the stovetop, spread them in a shallow layer in a preheated,

A cut of meat with the proper amount of dry rub on it

dry sauté pan and toss, shake, or swirl the pan until a rich, penetrating aroma arises. Transfer them to a cool pan to avoid scorching.

Fresh herbs and other ingredients such as garlic, fresh or dry bread crumbs, or grated cheeses can be blended into a paste or coating. They are sometimes moistened with oil, prepared mustard, or similar ingredients to create a texture that can easily adhere to a food, or make it easier to blend it into a dish as a final seasoning. Fresh herbs may have dirt in their leaves, so rinse them well to remove sand or grit. Thorough drying improves the flavor and texture of the blend by preventing any water clinging to the herb's leaves from diluting flavor.

When a spice blend is used as a dry rub (also called a dry marinade) to coat food, the food is refrigerated after application to allow it to absorb the flavors. Very often, these rubs contain some salt to help intensify all the flavors in the dish. Dry rubs may be left on the food during cooking or they may be scraped away first. Spice blends may also be added to aromatic vegetables as they cook during the initial stages of preparing a braise or stew. The fat used to cook the vegetables releases the flavor of the spices and infuses the dish more effectively than if the spice blend were simply added to a simmering dish. Barbecued beef and Jamaican jerked pork are several examples of dishes that may be prepared using a dry rub.

Marinades generally contain one or more of the following: oil, acid, and aromatics (spices, herbs, and vegetables). Oils protect food from intense heat during cooking and help hold other flavorful ingredients in contact with the food. Acids, such as vinegar, wine, yogurt, and citrus juices, flavor the food and change its texture. In some cases, acids firm or stiffen foods (e.g., the lime juice marinade that "cooks" the raw fish in seviche).

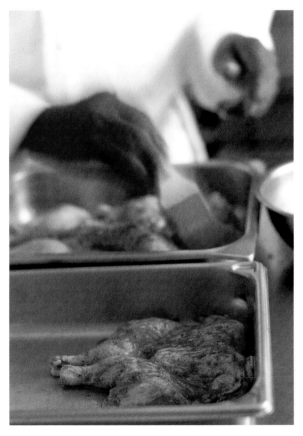

Marinade may be brushed on the ingredient or the ingredient may be dipped in the marinade to coat it thoroughly.

Marinating times vary according to the food's texture. Tender or delicate foods such as fish or poultry breast require less time. A tougher cut of meat may be marinated for days. The ratio of acid to other ingredients may also affect timing. High-acid marinades such as those used to prepare seviche produce the desired effect within 15 or 20 minutes of applying them to a food. Others are best left in contact with foods for several hours, while some require several days.

Some marinades are cooked before use; others are not. Sometimes the marinade is used to flavor an accompanying sauce or may itself become a dipping sauce. Marinades that have been in contact with raw foods can be used in these ways provided that they are boiled for several minutes first to kill any lingering pathogens.

To use a liquid marinade, add it to the ingredient and turn the ingredient to coat evenly. Cover and marinate, refrigerated, for the length of time indicated by the recipe, the type of meat, poultry, or fish, and the desired result. Brush or scrape off excess marinade before cooking and pat dry, particularly if the marinade contains herbs or other aromatics that burn easily.

Stuffings

Stuffings add flavor, moisture, and texture to a dish. The simplest stuffings are made from only herbs, vegetables, and fruits, and options include quartered or halved onions, garlic cloves, lemons or oranges, and sprigs or bunches of fresh herbs. Although these are uncomplicated, they can have a dramatic impact on flavor.

Bread and, particularly, forcemeat stuffings are more complex options. Prepare bread stuffings by cubing or breaking breads (peasant style, corn, French, or Italian style) into small pieces. They are generally flavored with aromatic vegetables (typically cooked in some fat to develop their flavor), herbs, and spices. Some bread stuffings are moistened with stocks or broths. Optionally, eggs may be included to bind the stuffing. Additional ingredients, such as cooked sausages, seafood, or mushrooms, may also be included.

Grain-based stuffings are based upon rice, barley, kasha, or other grains that have been cooked until just tender (use the pilaf or boiling methods; see pages 809 and 812). Once cooked, the grains should be allowed to cool completely before the stuffing is added to meat, poultry, or fish. These stuffings can be seasoned, moistened, and bound similar to bread-based stuffings.

Forcemeat stuffings can be prepared using any of the forcemeat methods or recipes included in Chapter 33 (pages 1024–1028). These mixtures must be handled carefully to keep them well chilled and wholesome. Keep forcemeats over an ice bath for quality as well as food safety. They are often used to fill delicate cuts of meat and fish (e.g., to fill fish fillets before they are rolled into paupiettes and shallow-poached).

Another important consideration with stuffings, along with flavor and quality, is proper handling for food safety. Any stuffing ingredients that require precooking should be cooled to below 40°F/4°C before they are combined with other stuffing elements. The finished mixture should also be chilled well before stuffing. During final cooking, stuffings must reach the minimum safe temperature for the food they were stuffed into. Stuffing in a chicken breast or leg, for instance, must reach 165°F/74°C. For this reason, whole chickens and turkeys are rarely stuffed in professional kitchens. By the time the stuffing would reach the necessary temperature, the meat would be overcooked. Instead, stuffings for whole roasted birds are more often baked separately, in which case they are known as dressings.

Standard Breading

Breading is done to create a crisp crust on fried foods. It is prepared by coating foods with flour, egg wash, and bread crumbs or other coatings. The standard breading procedure is the most efficient way to coat a number of items, using a consistent sequence.

Be sure to season the food before applying any coating, and always handle food properly for the best flavor and in such a way as to prevent cross contamination, which can lead to food-borne illnesses.

Use flour and similar meals or powders, such as cornstarch, to lightly dredge or dust foods before they are dipped in an egg wash.

Make an egg wash by blending eggs (whole, yolks, or whites) and water or milk. A general guideline calls for about 2 ounces of milk for every 2 whole eggs. Some items are dipped into milk or buttermilk before they are breaded, rather than in egg wash.

The standard breading procedure setup

Bread crumbs may be dry or fresh. Fresh white bread crumbs (called *mie de pain* in French) are prepared by grating or processing finely textured bread, such as white Pullman bread with the crust removed. Dry bread crumbs (called *chapelure* in French) are prepared from slightly stale bread that may be further dried or toasted in a warm oven.

Other ingredients may be used in place of or in addition to bread crumbs. Options include nuts, seeds, shredded coconut, cornflakes, potato flakes, shredded potatoes, grated cheese, ground spices, garlic paste, or chopped herbs. Blot the food dry with absorbent toweling and season as desired. Hold it in one hand and dip it in flour. Shake off any excess flour and transfer the food to the container of egg wash. Switch hands, pick up the food, and turn it if necessary to coat it on all sides. Transfer it to the container of bread crumbs. Use your dry hand to pack bread crumbs evenly around the food. Shake off any excess, then transfer the food to a rack set over a holding tray. Store breaded food in single layers, but if you must stack the pieces, use parchment or wax paper to separate the layers.

Discard any unused flour, egg wash, or bread crumbs. The presence of juices, drippings, or particles of the food you just coated will contaminate these products, making them unsafe for use with other foods. Even sifting the flour or crumbs or straining the egg wash will not be sufficient to prevent cross contamination and eliminate the potential for food poisoning.

General Guidelines for Determining Doneness in Meats, Poultry, and Fish

Chefs must rely not only upon a thermometer, but also on their senses when cooking. Those senses are put to a greater test in determining doneness in à la minute cooking because chefs can't actually taste what they are serving, the way they can taste a soup or a sauce. Follow these guidelines:

The way it smells. As foods near doneness, their smells change. Aromas intensify and become easier to identify. Each cooking method produces a particular aroma. Grilled and broiled foods should have a pleasing smoky, charred aroma, indicating rich, deep flavor. Poached and steamed foods have a subtler smell.

The way it feels. Foods should be easy to cut and chew. Touch foods (with a gloved finger) to gauge resistance. The less well done a piece of meat is, the softer and more yielding it will feel. Practice is needed to become adept at judging doneness by touch. Also keep in mind that texture varies in different cuts of meat.

The way it looks. As meat cooks, the exterior will change color. The interior colors also change, an important factor when determining doneness in meats cooked to customer preference (rare, medium, or well done). If the meat appears pale or even gray, it has not been properly cooked. The juices that run from the meat, although minimal, should be the correct color; the rarer the meat, the bloodier the juices should appear. Appearance is also an important factor in knowing when to turn a piece of meat. When the meat's upper surface begins to appear very moist (there may even be moisture beads), the meat should be turned. Thin pieces may start to change color at the edges when they are ready for turning.

The temperatures in the following table are final resting temperatures, based on the USDA's safe cooking temperatures. Most meats, poultry, and fish need to be removed from the pan, grill, or oven before they reach their final temperature to avoid overcooking and drying out. Heat is retained by foods even after they are removed from the heat source. That residual heat causes the food to keep cooking, a phenomenon referred to as carryover cooking. Internal temperatures taken just as the food is removed from the oven, for example, and again after resting will show a temperature difference of anywhere from a few degrees to ten, fifteen, or more. Factors that play a role in changes in internal temperature during resting include the size of the food being prepared and the presence or absence of stuffing and bones.

DEGREE OF DONENESS	FINAL RESTING TEMPERATURE	DESCRIPTION
FRESH BEEF, VEAL, AND LAMB		
Rare	135°F/57°C	Interior appearance shiny
Medium rare	145°F/63°C	Deep red to pink
Medium	160°F/71°C	Pink to light pink
Well done	170°F/77°C	Light pink with greying on the edges for medium well and no pink for well done
FRESH PORK		
Medium	160°F/71°C	Meat opaque throughout, slight give, juices with faint blush
Well done	170°F/77°C	Slight give, juices clear
HAM		
Fresh ham	160°F/71°C	Slight give, juices with faint blush
Precooked (to reheat)	140°F/60°C	Meat already fully cooked
POULTRY		
Whole birds (chicken, turkey, duck, goose)	180°F/82°C	Leg easy to move in socket, juices with only blush
Poultry breasts	170°F/77°C	Meat opaque, firm throughout
Poultry thighs, legs, wings	180°F/82°C	Meat releases from bone
Stuffing (cooked alone or in bird)	165°F/74°C	
GROUND MEAT AND MEAT MIXTURES		
Turkey, chicken	165°F/74°C	Opaque throughout, juices clear
Beef, veal, lamb, pork	160°F/71°C	Opaque, may have blush of red, juices opaque, no red
SEAFOOD		
Fish	145°F/63°C or until opaque	Still moist, separates easily into segments
Shrimp, lobster, crab		Shells turn red, flesh becomes pearly opaque
Scallops		Turn milky white or opaque and firm
Clams, mussels, oyster		Shells open

Garam Masala

Makes 2 oz/57 g

12 to 13 green or black cardamom pods

4 tsp/7 g coriander seeds

4 tsp/8 g cumin seeds

1¼ cinnamon sticks, broken into small pieces

1¼ tsp/2 g cloves

2½ tsp/5 g black peppercorns

¼ tsp/0.50 g ground nutmeg

2 to 3 bay leaves (optional)

1. Break open the cardamom pods and remove the seeds. Combine all the ingredients except the nutmeg and bay leaves (if using). Roast in a 350°F/177°C oven for 5 minutes. Remove and cool slightly.

2. Combine the spices with the nutmeg and bay leaves (if using) in a clean spice grinder and grind to a medium-fine powder.

3. Place in a tightly sealed container and use within 1 month.

Chinese Five-Spice Powder

Makes 2 oz/57 g

5 star anise pods

1 tbsp/7 g fennel seeds

4½ tsp/9 g Szechwan peppercorns

2 to 3 cloves

¼ cinnamon stick

1. Combine all spices in a clean spice grinder and grind to a medium-fine powder. Place in a tightly sealed container and use within 1 month.

2. When ready to use, measure the appropriate amount and lightly toast the powder in a dry pan without oil until you can smell the aroma of the spices. Quickly move the toasted powder to a cool pan or container so that it does not continue to cook and burn.

Barbecue Spice Mix

Makes 2 oz/57 g

½ oz/14 g Spanish paprika

½ oz/14 g **Chili Powder** (page 463), or purchased

½ oz/14 g salt

2 tsp/4 g ground cumin

2 tsp/10 g sugar

1 tsp/2 g dry mustard

1 tsp/2 g ground black pepper

1 tsp/2 g dried thyme

1 tsp/2 g dried oregano

1 tsp/3 g **Curry Powder** (page 463), or purchased

½ tsp/1 g cayenne

1. Combine all the spices.

2. Place in a tightly sealed container and use within 1 month.

Chili Powder

Makes 2 oz/57 g

1½ oz/43 g dried chiles, ground

½ oz/14 g ground cumin

1 tsp/2 g dried oregano

½ tsp/1 g garlic powder

¼ tsp/0.50 g ground coriander

¼ tsp/0.50 g ground cloves (optional)

1. Combine all the spices, including the cloves, if desired.

2. Place in a tightly sealed container and use within 1 month.

NOTES

Some commercially prepared chili powder is actually a blend similar to this one. This chili powder should not be confused with the ground chiles called for in some recipes.

Curry Powder

Makes 2 oz/57g

1½ oz/43 g cumin seeds

½ oz/14 g coriander seeds

2 tsp/8 g mustard seeds

8 dried red chiles

2 tbsp/12 g ground cinnamon

½ oz/14 g ground turmeric

2 tbsp/12 g ground ginger

1. Combine all the spices. Roast in a 350°F/177°C oven for 5 minutes. Remove and cool slightly. Split the chiles and remove the seeds.

2. Combine all spices in a clean spice grinder and grind them to a medium-fine powder. Place in a tightly sealed container and use within 1 month.

NOTE

Add paprika, cloves, or fresh curry leaves to the blend if desired.

Quatre Épices

Makes 2 oz/57 g

1¼ oz/35 g black peppercorns

½ oz/14 g ground nutmeg

1 tbsp/6 g ground cinnamon

2 tsp/4 g cloves

1. Combine all spices in a clean spice grinder and grind to a medium-fine powder.

2. Place in a tightly sealed container and use within 1 month.

Fines Herbes

Makes 2 oz/57 g

½ oz/14 g chopped chervil leaves

½ oz/14 g chopped chives

½ oz/14 g chopped parsley leaves

½ oz/14 g chopped tarragon leaves

1. Combine all the herbs and mix well.

2. Place in a tightly sealed container and refrigerate or use as needed.

NOTES

Add burnet, marjoram, savory, lavender, or watercress to the herb mixture to adjust the flavor, if desired. Fines herbes should be added near the end of cooking time because they do not hold their flavor long. Typical uses include flavoring for omelets or crêpes, or as the final addition to soups and consommés.

Red Curry Paste

Makes 2 oz/57 g

½ oz/14 g red Thai chiles

4 dried New Mexico or guajillo chiles, stemmed, cut into several pieces

½ tsp/1 g cumin seeds

1½ tsp/2.50 g coriander seeds

¼ tsp/0.50 g white peppercorns

3 garlic cloves, thinly sliced

1 to 2 shallots, thinly sliced

1 tbsp/9 g thinly sliced lemongrass

1½ tsp/4.50 g thinly sliced galangal

½ tsp/1.50 g lime zest

1 to 2 wild lime leaves, chopped

1½ tsp/1 g finely chopped cilantro root

1 tsp/2 g Thai shrimp paste

½ tsp/2.50 g coarse salt

2 fl oz/60 mL water, or as needed

1. Soak the dried chile peppers in hot water for 15 minutes. Drain and set aside.

2. Combine the cumin, coriander, and peppercorns in a small skillet. Toast over medium heat until fragrant, about 5 minutes, stirring frequently. Cool.

3. Using a clean spice grinder, grind the cumin, coriander, and peppercorns to a medium-fine powder and set aside.

4. Place the remaining ingredients, except the ground spices, in a blender and grind into a fine paste.

5. Combine the paste with the ground spices and blend together until smooth.

6. Place in a tightly sealed container and refrigerate or use as needed.

Green Curry Paste

Makes 2 oz/57 g

¼ tsp/0.50 g cumin seeds

1½ tsp/2.50 g coriander seeds

5 white peppercorns

1 to 2 shallots, thinly sliced

3 garlic cloves, thinly sliced

5 Green Thai chiles, seeds removed

1½ tsp/1 g finely chopped cilantro root

½ oz/14 g thinly sliced lemongrass

½ tsp/1 g sliced galangal

½ tsp/1.50 g kaffir lime zest

1 to 2 wild kaffir lime leaves, chopped

½ tsp/1 g shrimp paste

½ tsp/2.50 g coarse salt

1. Toast the cumin and coriander seeds until golden brown and aromatic. Transfer to a small bowl.

2. In the same pan, toast the peppercorns in the same manner and combine with the cumin and coriander.

3. Using a clean spice grinder, grind the toasted cumin, coriander, and peppercorns to a medium-fine powder and set aside.

4. Place the remaining ingredients, except the ground spices, in a blender and grind into a fine paste.

5. Combine the paste with the ground spices and blend together until smooth.

6. Place in a tightly sealed container and refrigerate or use as needed.

Yellow Curry Paste

Makes 2 oz/57 g

½ tsp/1 g cumin seeds

1½ tsp/2.50 g coriander seeds

2 white peppercorns

½ oz/14 g fresh Thai chiles, split and seeded

2 garlic cloves, sliced

2 shallots, sliced

1½ tsp/3 g ground turmeric

1½ tsp/4.50 g thinly sliced galangal

½ tsp/1.50 g kaffir lime zest

1 to 2 wild kaffir lime leaves, chopped

1 tsp/2 g Thai shrimp paste

1 tsp/5 g coarse salt

1½ tsp/7.50 fl oz vegetable oil

1. Toast the cumin and coriander seeds until golden brown and aromatic. Transfer to a small bowl.

2. In the same pan, toast the peppercorns in the same manner and combine with the cumin and coriander.

3. Place the chiles in the pan and toast very lightly until dark spots begin to appear. (Do not let them blacken.) Remove from the heat and set aside.

4. Toast the garlic and shallots in the same manner. Set aside.

5. Using a clean spice grinder, grind the cumin, coriander, and peppercorns to a medium-fine powder and set aside.

6. Place the remaining ingredients, except the ground spices and oil, in a blender and grind into a fine paste.

7. Combine the paste with the ground spices and oil and blend together until smooth.

8. Place in a tightly sealed container and refrigerate or use as needed.

Seasoning Mix for Spit-Roasted Meats and Poultry

Makes 2 oz/57 g

1¼ oz/35 g coarse salt

2 tbsp/12 g dry mustard

2½ tsp/5 g ground black pepper

1½ tsp/3 g dried thyme

1½ tsp/3 g dried oregano

1½ tsp/3 g ground coriander

1½ tsp/2.50 g celery seed

1. Combine all the spices.

2. Place in a tightly sealed container and use within 1 month.

Asian-Style Marinade

Makes 16 fl oz/480 mL

6 fl oz/180 mL hoisin sauce

6 fl oz/180 mL sherry

2 fl oz/60 mL rice wine vinegar

2 fl oz/60 mL soy sauce

½ oz/14 g minced garlic

1. Combine all the ingredients.

2. Place in a tightly sealed container and refrigerate or use as needed.

Barbecue Marinade

Makes 16 fl oz/480 mL

10 fl oz/300 mL vegetable oil

5 fl oz/150 mL cider vinegar

1 fl oz/30 mL Worcestershire sauce

1 tbsp/15 g brown sugar

2 tsp/4 g dry mustard

1 tsp/5 mL Tabasco sauce

1 tsp/2 g garlic powder

1 tsp/2 g onion powder

2 tsp/6 g minced garlic

1. Combine all the ingredients.

2. Place in a tightly sealed container and refrigerate or use as needed.

Fish Marinade

Makes 16 fl oz/480 mL

12 fl oz/360 mL olive oil

4 fl oz/120 mL lemon juice, dry white wine, or white vermouth

½ oz/14 g minced garlic

2 tsp/10 g salt

2 tsp/4 g ground black pepper

1. Combine all the ingredients.

2. Place in a tightly sealed container and refrigerate or use as needed.

Red Wine Game Marinade

Makes 16 fl oz/480 mL

6 fl oz/180 mL dry red wine

1 fl oz/30 mL olive oil

1 fl oz/30 mL red wine vinegar

1 tsp/2 g dried thyme

½ tsp/1 g juniper berries

½ tsp/1 g dried savory

½ tsp/1 g ground black pepper

1 to 2 parsley sprigs

1 tsp/3 g minced garlic

1½ oz/43 g diced carrots

5 oz/142 g diced onions

1½ oz/43 g diced celery

1 bay leaf

1. Combine all the ingredients.

2. Place in a tightly sealed container and refrigerate or use as needed.

Rosemary and Gin Marinade for Game Meats

Makes 16 fl oz/480 mL

8 fl oz/240 mL gin

8 fl oz/240 mL dry vermouth

1 bay leaf

8 black peppercorns

3 oz/85 g minced onions

1 oz/28 g minced carrots

1 oz/28 g minced celery

1 tsp/3 g minced garlic

1 tbsp/3 g chopped rosemary

1. Combine all the ingredients.

2. Place in a tightly sealed container and refrigerate or use as needed.

Lamb Marinade

Makes 16 fl oz/480 mL

4 fl oz/120 mL dry red wine

4 fl oz/120 mL red wine vinegar

2 fl oz/60 mL olive oil

1 tbsp/15 g sugar

1 tbsp/6 g dried mint

1 tsp/5 g salt

1 tsp/2 g juniper berries

2 bay leaves

2 onion slices

1 parsley sprig

1 thyme sprig

1 garlic clove, minced

pinch ground nutmeg

1. Combine all the ingredients.

2. Place in a tightly sealed container and refrigerate or use as needed.

Latin Citrus Marinade (Mojo)

Makes 16 fl oz/480 mL

9 fl oz/270 mL orange juice

4½ fl oz/135 mL lemon juice

1½ fl oz/45 mL lime juice

4½ tsp/8 g ground annato seeds

1 tsp/3 g chopped garlic

1½ tsp/7.50 g salt

¾ tsp/1.50 g dried oregano

¾ tsp/1.50 g ground cumin

¼ tsp/0.50 g ground cloves

¼ tsp/0.50 g ground cinnamon

¼ tsp/0.50 g ground black pepper

1. Combine all the ingredients.

2. Place in a tightly sealed container and refrigerate or use as needed.

Red Wine Marinade for Grilled Meats

Makes 16 fl oz/480 mL

8 fl oz/240 mL red wine

6 fl oz/180 mL olive oil

2 fl oz/60 mL lemon juice

2 tsp/6 g minced garlic

1 tsp/5 g salt

1 tsp/2 g ground black pepper

1. Combine all the ingredients.

2. Place in a tightly sealed container and refrigerate or use as needed.

Teriyaki Marinade

Makes 16 fl oz/480 mL

6 fl oz/180 mL soy sauce

6 fl oz/180 mL peanut oil

3 fl oz/90 mL dry sherry

1 oz/28 g honey

2 tsp/6 g minced garlic

2 tsp/6 g grated ginger

2 tbsp/18 g grated orange zest (optional)

1. Combine all the ingredients, including the orange zest, if desired.

2. Place in a tightly sealed container and refrigerate or use as needed.

Chapter Nineteen

Fabricating Meats, Poultry, and Fish

Meat, poultry, and fish are the most costly part of the food budget of a foodservice operation, no matter the establishment's scale. Generally, the size and scope of the operation determine the form in which it purchases meats, poultry, and fish. For operations with limited labor and storage resources, quality prefabricated boxed meats, poultry, and fish are an acceptable purchasing form.

Meat Fabrication

Chefs with the means to do so often prefer to perform many fabrication tasks in-house to control portion size and quality—important considerations when it comes to the establishment's reputation. Depending on the prevailing local market rates for food and labor, in-house fabrication may be less expensive than buying prefabricated menu cuts. As a further economic benefit, trim and bones can be used to prepare other dishes (e.g., stocks, soups, sauces, and forcemeats).

General similarities exist between cuts of beef, veal, lamb, venison, and pork if they come from the same parts of the butchered animal. The rib and the loin contain the tenderest cuts. They tend to cost more than cuts from the shoulder, which are often more exercised and tough. The leg may contain tender cuts as well as cuts that are quite tough. Proper handling during fabrication prepares meats for subsequent cooking. Most of the techniques described here do not require any special knowledge of the bones in a cut of meat or of the animal's overall anatomy, although reference to sections of Chapter 9 Meat, Poultry, and Game Identification (pages 171–198), will be helpful.

Trimming a tenderloin

Since the tenderloin is one of the most expensive cuts of meat, extra care should be taken to leave the meat as intact as possible. Use a very sharp knife and pay close attention to be sure that only silverskin, fat, and gristle are removed, not edible meat. The tenderloin contains several sections: the chain, or long side muscle, the large side muscle, and the main center cut section.

1. Lift and pull away the chain of an untrimmed tenderloin. This chain pulls away easily, and the blade of a boning knife is used to steady the tenderloin as the chain is pulled away. If necessary, use the boning knife to help remove it from the tenderloin.

2. Completely remove the membrane, collagen, and silverskin. Work so that your cuts move toward the head (the larger end of the tenderloin). This tough membrane, which gets its name from its somewhat silvery color, tends to shrink when exposed to heat and cause uneven cooking. Work the top of a boning knife under the meat and hold it tight against the meat. Glide the knife blade just underneath, angling the blade upward slightly. A tenderloin of beef is shown here, but the same techniques can be applied to pork, veal, and lamb tenderloin as well as to other cuts of meat with silverskin, including top round of beef and veal and loin cuts of venison and other large game.

Shaping a medallion

Boneless cuts from the tenderloin of beef and the loin or tenderloin of veal, lamb, or pork may be called medallions, noisettes (so named because they are like little nuts of meat), or grenadins (large cuts from the loin). The terms *noisette* and *medallion* are often used interchangeably to refer to a small, boneless, tender cut of meat weighing from 2 to 6 oz/57 to 170 g. *Tournedos* and *châteaubriand* are special terms generally used only for beef tenderloin cuts. Tournedos are typically cut from the thinner end of the tenderloin to weigh 5 oz/142 g. Châteaubriand serves two and is cut from the center of the tenderloin; it typically weighs 10 oz/284 g.

After the medallions or similar boneless cuts are portioned, they may then be wrapped in cheesecloth and molded to give them a compact, uniform shape. Not only does this give the meat a more pleasing appearance, it also helps the medallion to cook evenly. Gather the cheesecloth together and twist to tighten it around the meat. As you twist the cloth with one hand, press down on the meat firmly, with even, moderate pressure, using the broad side of a knife blade or a similar flat object. The medallions on the left have been shaped and are of a more uniform size.

Fabricating boneless meats

Meats to be sautéed or pan fried, grilled, or stewed are often fabricated from larger boneless cuts, such as rounds, loins, and/or tenderloins. These cuts are typically composed of more than one muscle. Each muscle has its own grain, or direction in which the meat fibers are arranged. Breaking a larger cut into individual sections allows the chef to cut each piece of meat properly for the recipe or menu item.

1. To divide larger cuts (veal top round shown here), follow the natural muscle seams—they act as a roadmap to define specific cuts. This makes it possible to cut each muscle against the grain and easily trim out any connective tissue or fat.

2. Using the same technique as described for a beef tenderloin, trim away the fat and silverskin. Pay attention to the angle of the knife blade. It should be angled upward to prevent removing edible meat.

3. Cutting the meat across the grain produces a cut of meat that is less tough than a piece cut with the grain.

Shredding and mincing meats

The French word for this cut is *émincé,* or "cut into slivers." Meat is cut against the grain into thin strips of a length and width appropriate for the dish. Since the meat is generally sautéed, the cut should be one of the most tender. This technique can be used for beef, lamb, or even pork. Be sure to trim the meat completely before cutting it into émincé. Once cut, the émincé may be pounded, if appropriate, using the same technique as for pounding cutlets. Blot the pounded émincé dry before cooking.

Cutting and pounding cutlets

A meat cutlet or scallop is a thin boneless cut of meat prepared from the loin, the tenderloin, or any other sufficiently tender cut of meat such as the top round. Cutlet, *scaloppine* in Italian, and *escalope* in French are different words for the same cut and are used depending on a menu's particular style. Cutlets are typically cut across the grain and on the bias.

Cutlets are often pounded to ensure an even thickness over their entire surface so that they can be rapidly sautéed or pan fried. A paillard is a pounded cutlet that is grilled rather than sautéed or pan fried. Adjust the weight of the mallet and strength of the blow to match the delicacy of the meat. Turkey cutlets (slices of turkey breast), for example, require a more delicate touch than pork cutlets. Be careful not to tear or overstretch the meat while pounding it.

1. Cut pieces of the same weight (generally 1 to 4 oz/28 to 113 g) and circumference. Using a scimitar knife is not absolutely necessary, but will help to prevent tears in the meat when cutting.

2. Place the meat in between layers of plastic wrap. Use a pounding and pulling motion to evenly thin the cutlet. Increased surface area and decreased thickness promote rapid cooking.

Cutting bone-in chops

Chops and steaks are made from bone-in cuts from the rib or loin. Large bones can be difficult to saw through, but the bones of cuts from the rib and loin of pork, lamb, venison, and beef are more manageable.

1. Cut away the backbone, often referred to as the chine bone, using a handsaw. Completely sever the bone from the rib bones without cutting into the meat muscle.

2. Using your guiding hand to hold the chine bone away from the meat, work with the tip of a boning knife to make smooth strokes along the feather bones, cutting the meat cleanly away from the bones.

3. Cut between each rib bone with a scimitar or chef's knife to make individual chops. When cutting through the meat, use even pressure to create a smooth surface on the chops.

Trimming a strip loin and cutting boneless steaks

Steaks can be purchased already portioned and trimmed, but cutting attractive, consistently sized steaks in-house can keep the kitchen's food cost down. Cuts must be made evenly to guarantee even cooking time.

1. The strip loin has a tail, sometimes referred to as a lip, running along one edge of the muscle. This heavy layer of fat is cut away first, taking care not to cut the interior loin muscle as you work. Hold this fat cover taut as you run the knife blade down the length of the loin, angling the blade up slightly. Remove 1½ to 2 in/4 to 5 cm of the fat cover.

2. A strip loin may have a section known as the chain. Once the fat cover is trimmed to the desired thickness, the chain is removed. Reserve it for another use.

3. The chef is cutting steaks from the rib end of the strip loin. The steak on the left has been cut from this end. The V-shaped streak of collagen was removed and the steak on the right was cut from the sirloin end.

While steaks cut from this end are as tender as those cut from the rib end, the collagen itself is tough, and can give the impression that the steak is tough. These steaks are sometimes referred to as vein steaks. Adjust the thickness of the cut to produce equal-sized steaks of the desired weight. Refrigerate cut steaks until ready to cook.

Trimming and boning a pork loin

A whole pork loin often costs less per pound than a trimmed boneless loin. Removing the fat and bones is relatively easy, and the bones and any lean trim can then be roasted and used to prepare a rich brown jus or stock. It may take some time at first to learn how to properly trim and bone a loin for a roast or cutlets.

1. The novice should cut slowly and stop to examine the loin between cuts. The first step when working with a pork loin is to remove the tenderloin, if it is still intact. Next, cut away the fat cover to the desired thickness. Make smooth strokes along the rib bones to free the meat, as shown here. Pull the bones away from the meat with your guiding hand to make it easy to see and prevent cuts into the edible meat. Pass the knife close to the bones, scraping them clean so that as little meat as possible is left on the bones.

2. Use the tip of the knife to cut around joints and between bones and the flat part of the blade for longer, sweeping strokes. Near the bottom of the rib bones is a knob-shaped ridge or step that must be cut around to completely remove the meat from the bone. It has an almost right angle that must be cut around. Take care not to cut into the edible meat when cutting around the step. Once the loin has been trimmed and boned, it can be used to prepare a wide variety of menu cuts including medallions, cutlets, and émincé.

Boning a leg of lamb

Although this procedure may look difficult, it is possible to do it successfully by following the steps shown in the accompanying illustrations.

The leg is covered with a layer of fat and a membrane, known as the *fell*. The fat and membrane should be removed carefully, leaving as much edible meat intact as possible.

A leg of lamb can be boned out to use in a number of different ways. It can be butterflied and grilled, or rolled, tied, and roasted. The meat can be divided along the natural seams to make small roasts, or sliced into cutlets or cubes.

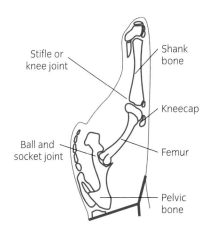

1. The leg contains the hind shank bone, the pelvic bones (consisting of the hip bone and the aitch bone), a portion of the backbone and tail, and the leg bone (also known as the femur).

2. Work the tip of the knife around the pelvic bone. As you cut into the meat to remove the bones, use an overhand grip to hold your boning knife and cut with the top of the blade as you work around bones and joints. Work the knife tip along the bone to remove as much meat as possible.

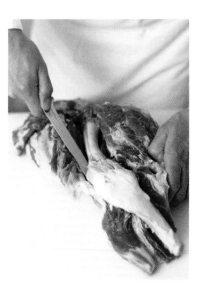

3. When the meat has been freed from the pelvic bone, lift the bone up and away from the leg.

4. Make a cut down the shank bone and cut the meat cleanly away from the bone.

5. After freeing the meat from the shank bone, cut around the femur bone to remove the bones from the meat.

Frenching a rack of lamb

This technique is one of the more complicated fabrication techniques, but it is not especially difficult to master. Trimmed and frenched racks or chops can be ordered from a meat purveyor, of course, but the chef can exercise greater control over trim loss if the work is done in the kitchen. The same technique can be used to french individual rib chops of lamb, veal, or pork. Any lean trim can be used to prepare jus or a stock.

1. Make an even cut through the fat covering all the way down to the bone. The cut should be about 1 in/3 cm from the meat's eye.

2. Set the rack on one end and make a stabbing cut between each bone, using the initial cut as a guide.

3. Use the tip of a boning knife to score the thin membrane covering the bones. This will allow them to break through the membrane easily.

4. Push the bones through the membrane. Use your fingers to stabilize the bottom of the rack while peeling away the cut membranes and pushing the bones out with your thumbs.

5. Lay the rack so that the bones are facing down. Make an even cut to sever the meat surrounding the bone ends. It should pull away easily.

Working with variety meats

In recent years, as Americans have become less squeamish about organ meats, the demand for properly prepared liver, kidneys, tongue, sweetbreads, and other kinds of variety meats has grown. Because these cuts are difficult to find in a grocery store, or even a butcher's shop, many people are uncomfortable with or unsure of proper preparation techniques.

Liver

Prepare liver before cooking by removing any silverskin, tough membranes, veins, or gristle. When subjected to intense heat, silverskin shrinks more rapidly than meat, thus making the liver pucker and cook unevenly.

Kidneys

The unique flavor of kidneys will come through as long as they are perfectly fresh and properly handled. Soak kidneys in salted water for 12 hours, then rinse well and soak in milk for another 12 to 24 hours. Rinse the kidneys, then cut them in half and remove all the fat and veins. In some cases, recipes may indicate that the kidneys be blanched first. Peel the kidneys by pulling away the membrane covering them.

Tongue

Tongue is a muscle that is quite tough. This cut of meat may be sold with the skin. It is easier to remove the skin from the cooked smoked tongue. Gently simmer the tongue in a flavorful broth or bouillon, and it will become very tender. Let the tongue cool in the cooking liquid to bolster its flavor. Once the tongue is cooled, carefully peel it to remove the skin. The skin will cling more tightly near the base of the tongue. It may be necessary to use a paring knife to remove the remaining skin from the base and underside of the tongue. It will peel away easily near the tip of the tongue using just your fingers.

Once peeled, tongue can be used in a variety of ways: It can be cut into julienne or dice and used as a garnish for sauces, soups, or pâtés. It may be sliced thinly and served hot or cold, or used as a liner for terrine molds. It is a classic part of the Alsatian dish choucroute.

Marrow

Marrow—the soft inner substance of bones—is often used as a garnish for soups, sauces, and other dishes. Certain bones, known as marrow bones, have a significant amount of marrow that is relatively easy to remove using the following technique: Submerge the marrow bones in cold, salted water for a few hours to remove the excess blood and impurities. After they have soaked, push the marrow out using your thumb.

Sweetbreads

Sweetbreads need to be thoroughly rinsed in cold water to remove all traces of blood. They are then blanched in a court bouillon, peeled, and pressed to give them a firmer, more appealing texture. The sweetbreads can then be prepared à la meunière (floured and sautéed). Sweetbreads are used to prepare terrines.

1. Sweetbreads need to be thoroughly rinsed in cold water to remove all traces of blood. They should be blanched in enough court bouillon to cover them.

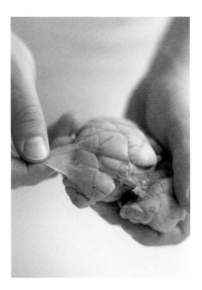

2. After blanching the sweetbreads, let them cool enough to handle easily. Pull away the membrane covering the meat.

3. Roll the peeled lobes tightly in cheesecloth to give the sweetbreads a firmer, more appealing texture. Place the sweetbreads in a perforated hotel pan (as shown), place weight on top of them, and press the sweetbreads under refrigeration for several hours.

4. The pressed sweetbreads should be firm, compact, and able to be sliced easily. The sweetbreads can be prepared à la meunière (floured and sautéed), used to prepare terrines, or utilized in other preparations.

Tying a roast

Tying a roast with secure knots that have the right tension is one of the simplest and most frequently required types of meat fabrication. It ensures that the roast will be evenly cooked and that it will retain its shape after roasting. Although simple, the technique is often one of the most frustrating to learn. For one thing, knot tying is not always easy. As long as the string is taut enough to give the roast a compact shape without being too tight, however, the result will be fine. There is one trick to keep in mind that will make initial attempts easier. Leave the string very long, so that it will wrap easily around the entire diameter of the meat. Or leave the string attached to the spool, and cut it only when the entire roast is tied. There are other methods used for tying roasts than the two shown here. If you have the chance to learn other methods, you will be better able to adapt to tying different cuts of meat with ease.

Both techniques illustrated here work for either boneless or bone-in roasts. The choice of technique is a matter of personal preference.

Technique one

For this technique, the string is left attached to the spool, rather than cut into lengths. To start tying the roast, tie the end of the string around the thicker end of the meat (any knot that holds securely may be used).

1. Pass the string around your outspread fingers and thumb so that the string crosses itself and makes an X.

2. Spread your hand open to enlarge the loop.

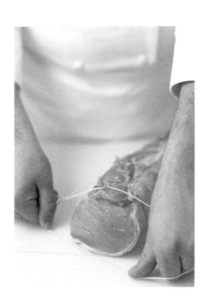

3. Continue to enlarge the loop until it is wide enough to pass easily around the thicker end of the meat, completely encircling it.

4. Encircle the meat with the loop, making sure that the knots are spaced evenly apart from one another.

5. Pull the loose end of the string until the loop is securely tightened around the meat. Note that the string has formed a "half hitch" knot at this point. Continue until the entire piece of meat has been secured with loops.

6. Turn the piece of meat over. Pass the loose end of the string through the loop, then pass it back around and underneath the loop. Pull the string tight and continue down the length of the meat.

7. Once the string has been wrapped around each loop from one end to the other, turn the meat back over. Cut the loose end and tie the string securely to the first loop.

Technique two

For this tying technique, cut several lengths of string. Each piece should be long enough to wrap completely around the meat with sufficient additional length to tie a series of double knots.

Grinding meat

Grinding meat calls for scrupulous attention to safe food handling practices (see page 30). This fabrication technique applies to meats, as well as poultry and fish. Observe the following procedures for best results:

- Unplug the grinder before assembling or disassembling.

- Clean the grinder well and put it together correctly. Make sure that the blade is sitting flush against the die. In this position, the blade cuts the food neatly, rather than tearing or shredding it.

- Cut the meat into dice or strips that will fit easily through the grinder's feed tube.

- Chill meats thoroughly before grinding. Chill all grinder parts that will come in contact with the food by either refrigerating them or submerging them in ice water.

- Do not force the meat through the feed tube with a tamper. If they are the correct size, the pieces will be drawn easily by the worm.

- Be sure that the blade is sharp. Meat should be cut cleanly, never mangled or mashed, as it passes through the grinder.

- For all but very delicate meats (salmon or other fish, for example), begin with a die that has large openings. The meat will appear quite coarse.

- Grind through progressively through smaller dies until the desired consistency is achieved.

- A final pass through a fine die gives the ground meat a more refined texture, and further blends the lean meat and fat.

The parts of the grinder. (From left to right): grinder housing or grinder body, worm, blade, different size plates, collar

Meats ground with different sized plates. (From left to right): meats ground with a coarse plate, medium plate, and fine plate

Poultry Fabrication

Poultry, always popular and readily available, is among the least costly of meats used for entrées and other menu items. Fabrication techniques are demonstrated here on a chicken, the bird most commonly used in restaurants. These techniques can be applied to virtually all poultry types, not only chicken but squab, duck, pheasant, turkey, and quail, with some modification to adapt to size (smaller birds require more delicate, precise cuts; larger or older birds, a heavier blade and greater pressure to break through tough joints and sinew).

The younger the bird, the easier it is to cut up. Young birds are usually much smaller and their bones are not completely hardened. The size and breed of the bird will also have some bearing on how easy or difficult it is to fabricate. Chickens are generally far simpler to cut up, for example, than are pheasant. The tendons and ligaments in chicken are less well developed, except in the case of free-range birds, which move freely about an enclosed pen or yard.

When fabricating, pay close attention to food safety regulations. Some kitchens use color-coded cutting boards to avoid cross contamination between meat, poultry, fish, and vegetables. Regardless of the material that cutting boards are made of (wood or plastic resin), they will remain sanitary if properly cleaned.

Preparing a suprême

A suprême is a semiboneless poultry breast half, usually from a chicken, pheasant, partridge, or duck, so named because it is the best (suprême) portion. One wing joint, often frenched, is left attached to the breast meat. If the skin is removed from the suprême, it may be referred to as a côtelette. Suprêmes may be sautéed, poached, or grilled.

To prepare a chicken suprême from a whole chicken by this technique, you must cut away the wing tip and then remove the legs. The breast meat and the first joint of the wing are cut away from the bird's carcass. Reserve the carcass for stock or broth.

1. Use the tip of a boning knife to make a cut that circles around the second joint of the wing bone. Make sure to cut through the web skin as well. Bend the wing bone at the second joint to snap it. Continue to cut through the joint until the wing tip and wing flap are removed, leaving the drumette attached to the breast.

2. Cut through the skin between the thigh and the breast.

3. Bend the leg backward, away from the body, to expose the ball socket. Then make a cut that runs along the backbone to the ball and socket, as shown. Hold the chicken stable with the heel of your knife, and pull the leg away from the body firmly and evenly. This will remove the leg and the oyster cleanly from the backbone structure. Repeat on the other side.

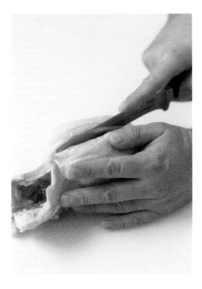

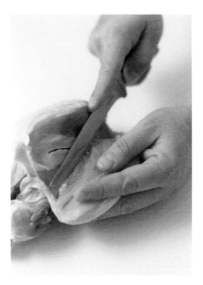

4. With the breast facing up, cut along either side of the keel bone with a knife. Use your guiding hand to steady the bird.

5. Remove the breast meat from the rib cage with delicate cuts. Use the tip of the knife to free the meat from the bones, running the tip along the bones for the best yield.

6. Trim excess skin away from the breast, making sure to keep enough skin intact to cover the chicken breast.

7. Use the blade to scrape the meat off the remaining wing bone to expose the bone completely. This is known as frenching the bone. It is not absolutely necessary to french the bone of a suprême.

8. The suprême on the left does not have a frenched bone while the suprême on the right does have the excess meat removed.

Trussing poultry

The object of trussing or tying any bird is to give it a smooth, compact shape so that it will cook evenly and retain moisture. Several different methods for trussing poultry exist, some involving trussing needles, some requiring only string. One simple way of tying with string is shown here.

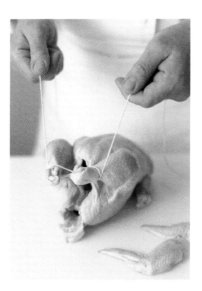

1. Cut away the wing tip and wing flap. Pass the middle of a piece of string underneath the joints at the end of the drumstick, and cross the ends of the string to make an X. Pull the ends of the string down toward the tail to loop the string around the joints.

2. Pull both ends of the string tightly across the joint that connects the drumstick and the thigh and continue to pull the string along the body toward the bird's back, catching the wing underneath the string.

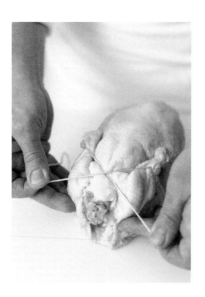

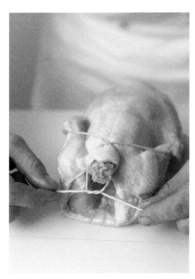

3. Flip the bird over and pull the string tight. Make an X across the wings to hold them tightly against the bird.

4. Pull the ends of the string underneath the backbone at the neck opening. Tie the two ends of the string with a secure knot.

5. The front and rear views of a properly trussed bird.

Halving and quartering poultry

Chicken and other birds may be halved or quartered before or after cooking. Smaller birds, such as Cornish game hens and broiler chickens that are to be grilled are often halved. These birds are small enough to cook through completely before the skin becomes scorched or charred. If the bones are left intact during grilling, they provide some protection against shrinkage.

In many restaurants, the ducks needed for an evening's service will be roasted in advance, then halved and partially deboned; at service, then, it is necessary only to reheat the duck and crisp the skin in a hot oven.

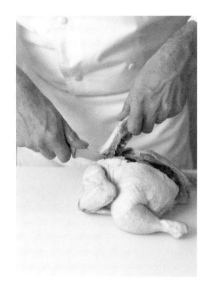

1. Cut from the tail to the neck opening down either side of the backbone. Pull upward slightly while cutting down, exerting enough pressure to cut through the rib bones.

2. Lay out the whole breast, with the bones facing up. Use the tip of a boning knife to cut through the white cartilage at the very top of the keel bone.

3. Open the breast like a book. This bending action will expose the keel bone. Grab the keel bone firmly and pull it and the attached cartilage away from the breast meat. The cartilage may break away from the keel bone. Be sure to remove the entire structure.

4. Cut the chicken into halves by making a cut down the center of the bird.

5. Separate the leg and thigh from the breast and wing by cutting through the skin just above where the breast and thigh meet.

Disjointing a rabbit

The technique for disjointing a rabbit is similar to that for a chicken. Rabbit is a relatively lean, mildly flavored meat. The loin and rib sections are leaner than the legs, in much the same way that chicken breast is leaner than the legs. By removing the legs and shoulder, you can apply two different cooking methods to one rabbit—moist heat for the legs, dry heat for the loin—to achieve the most satisfactory results.

1. Spread open the belly cavity of the rabbit and pull out the kidneys and liver. Sever any membrane attaching the liver to the cavity. Reserve the liver for another use, if desired.

2. Remove the hind legs by cutting through the joint and then through the meat to separate the hind leg from the loin.

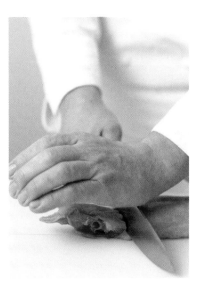

3. To separate the front legs and shoulder from the rest of the body, pull the leg away from the body and cut through the joint.

4. Cut away the hind and front portions of the loin to produce the saddle.

5. A fully disjointed rabbit is shown here, including the hind legs (top), saddle, liver, kidneys, and foreleg/shoulder sections.

Fish Fabrication

Most fish fall into one of two categories: round or flat. Time, practice, and experience will help determine which of a number of techniques to use to fabricate a particular fish. Different methods can achieve virtually the same results, and the methods shown here are not always the only way to proceed.

The basic procedure for scaling—the first step in preparing the fish before any further fabrication is done—applies to all types of fish. Methods differ slightly, however, for gutting round fish and flat fish. Similarly, the technique for filleting a round fish is different from that used for a flat fish. In determining how to fabricate a fish, knowledge of that particular fish's specific properties is important (see Chapter 9, Fish and Shellfish Identification). Other seafood, including lobster, shrimp, crayfish, and crab; shellfish such as clams, oysters, and mussels; and cephalopods like squid and octopus, also must be carefully handled to maintain quality and wholesomeness.

Scaling and trimming fish

Most fish, though not all, have scales that must be removed as a first step in fabrication. The best way to remove scales is with a fish scaler; but other tools (e.g., the dull side of a knife, a table crumber, a spoon handle) can be used if a scaler is not available. The fins and tails can be cut away at this point or later when the fish is gutted.

To scale a fish, work from the tail toward the head, gripping the fish by the tail, and allow water to flow over the fish to help keep the scales from flying around. Do not pinch the fish too tightly as this could bruise the flesh.

Gutting round fish

Frequently, fish viscera (guts) are removed soon after the fish is taken from the water, right on the fishing boat. The enzymes in the viscera can begin to break down the flesh rapidly, leading to spoilage. If a fish has not been gutted, this step should be performed right after it has been scaled.

To gut a round fish, make a slit in the fish's belly and pull out the guts. Rinse the belly cavity thoroughly under cold running water to remove all traces of viscera and blood.

Filleting round fish: straight cut method

Fillets are one of the most common fabrications for fish. These boneless and (usually) skinless fish pieces can be sautéed, grilled, baked, formed into paupiettes, or cut into tranches or goujonettes.

Round fish are fabricated into two fillets, one from each side of the fish. There are two techniques for filleting a round fish. The first technique is used on soft-boned round fish, like the salmon and trout family and Spanish mackerel. The name of the technique for soft-boned round fish is the *straight cut method*. The second, for use on hard-boned round fish, is called the *up and over technique*.

1. Lay the fish on a cutting board with the backbone parallel to the work surface and the head on the same side as your dominant hand. Using a filleting knife, cut behind the head and gill plates. Angle the knife so that the cutting motion is down and away from the body. This does not cut the head of the fish away from the body.

2. Without removing the knife, turn it so that the cutting edge is pointing toward the tail of the fish. Position the knife so that the handle is lower than the tip of the blade. This will improve the yield by keeping the knife's edge aimed at the bones, rather than the flesh. Run the blade down the length of the fish, cutting against the backbone. Avoid sawing the blade back and forth.

3. By cutting evenly and smoothly, you will split the tail, as shown. Lay the fillet skin side down on the work surface or in a hotel pan.

4. Turn the fish over and repeat the previous steps to remove the second fillet.

5. Remove the belly bones by making smooth strokes against the bones to cut them cleanly away. If necessary, cut away the remnants of the backbone by running the blade just underneath the line of the backbone.

6. To remove the skin, lay the fillet parallel to the edge of the cutting surface. Hold the knife so that the cutting edge is against the skin; pull the skin taut with your guiding hand as you cut the fillet free.

7. Locate the pin bones by running a fingertip over the fillet. Use needle-nose pliers or tweezers to pull out the bones. Pull them out in the direction of the head of the fillet (with the grain) to avoid ripping the flesh.

Up and over technique for round fish

The up and over technique may be used only on hard-boned round fish. A filet knife with a flexible blade should be used for this technique.

1. Lay the fish on the cutting board with the belly away from you and the head to your right. Cut through the belly, under the pectoral fin, and around the gill plate, making sure to get into the head.

2. Score through the skin from the head to tail using one long stroke. Continue making long, straight strokes along the back until you reach the center bone.

3. Flex your knife up and over the center bone, cutting through the pin bones.

4. Continue cutting close to the belly bones until the fillet is free from the carcass. Skinning is the same as for the straight cut method (page 493).

Gutting flat fish

All fish are typically gutted before they are shipped to market. If a fish has not been gutted, this step should be performed immediately after scaling.

1. To gut a flat fish, cut around the head, making a V-shaped notch.

2. Pull the head away from the body while twisting it slightly. The guts will come away with the head. Rinse the belly cavity thoroughly under cold running water to remove all traces of viscera and blood.

Filleting flat fish: making full fillets

Flat fish can be fabricated into two fillets, one from the top and one from the bottom of the fish.

1. To make two fillets from a flat fish, use a filleting knife to cut the flesh away from the bones, starting on an outer edge and working from the tail toward the head.

2. Adjust the direction and length of your strokes to go over the ridge of bones in the center of the fillet. Hold the fillet up and away from the bones as you work to see the bone structure. Continue cutting to the other edge and remove the top fillet in a single piece. Repeat on the other side.

Making four (or quarter) fillets of flat fish

Flat fish can be fabricated into four fillets by removing the fillet from each side of the backbone on the top and again on the bottom.

1. Position the fish with the head facing toward you and cut to one side of the center ridge.

2. Make cuts along the bones, working from the center to the edge.

3. After the fillet is removed, you can see the roe sack and the belly portion. These should be trimmed away from the fillet as part of its preparation for cooking.

Cutting fish into steaks

Fish steaks are simply crosscuts of the fish and are relatively easy to cut. The fish is scaled, gutted, and trimmed of its fins and gills. Steaks can be of virtually any thickness. *Darnes,* a French term, are thick steaks. There are few flat fish large enough to cut into steaks; instead, round fish like salmon are generally fabricated in this fashion.

Starting with a scaled, gutted, and trimmed fish (in this case salmon), use a chef's knife to make crosswise cuts through the fish to yield steaks of the desired size. Pan-dressed fish are smaller, dressed fish that are usually served whole.

Tranche

A tranche is simply a slice of the fillet. It is cut by holding the knife at an angle while cutting to expose more surface area and give the piece of fish a larger appearance. A tranche can be cut from any relatively large fillet of fish—for example salmon or halibut. Though this cut is normally associated with sautéed or pan-fried dishes, a tranche is often grilled or broiled.

Using a very sharp slicer, slice across the fish at approximately a 45-degree angle. The greater the angle of the knife, the more surface area will be exposed.

Paupiette

A paupiette is a rolled thin fillet, often—but not necessarily—filled with a forcemeat or other stuffing. Properly prepared, it resembles a large cork. Paupiettes are generally made from lean fish, such as flounder or sole, although they may also be made from some moderately fatty fish, such as trout or salmon. The most common preparation technique for paupiettes is shallow poaching.

Goujonette

The name for this cut is derived from the French name for a small fish, the *goujon*. Goujonettes are small strips cut from a fillet; they are often breaded or dipped in batter and then deep-fried. This cut has about the same dimensions as an adult's index finger. Goujonettes are normally cut from lean white fish, such as sole or flounder.

Make even, finger-sized cuts from the prepared fillet by cutting at an angle across the grain of the flesh.

Dover sole

Dover sole is handled in a special way. Many chefs like to skin the fish before filleting it. The skin is freed from the tail using a filleting knife, and then it is simply pulled away.

1. Cut away the fins with kitchen scissors.

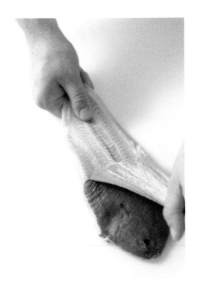

2. Make an initial cut to free the skin from the flesh of the tail. Hold the tail firmly and pull the skin away before filleting.

Shellfish Fabrication

The main shellfish categories are as follows: crustaceans, with jointed skeletons on the exterior of their bodies; mollusks, with a single (univalve) or a hinged (bivalve) shell; and cephalopods, with tentacles. Lobster, shrimp, crayfish, and crab are all crustaceans; mollusks include clams, oysters, and mussels; squid and octopus are cephalopods. They are all prepared before cooking using a variety of fabrication techniques.

Working with live lobster

Lobster is best when purchased alive. The first step in preparing a lobster to boil or steam is to kill it. Lobsters can also be split before they are broiled or baked.

1. Leave the bands on the lobster's claws and lay it, stomach-side down, on a work surface. Insert the tip of a chef's knife into the base of the head. Pull the knife all the way down through the shell, splitting the head in half.

2. Split the tail by reversing the direction of the lobster and positioning the tip of the knife at the point where you made your initial cut. Then, cut through the shell of the tail section.

Cooked lobster

The flesh of a lobster or other crustacean adheres tightly to the shell until it has been cooked. Lobster that will be served out of the shell or used in salads, stuffings, or as a garnish can be cooked whole by steaming, grilling, or deep poaching. Once the lobster is cool enough to handle, the meat can be removed from the shell easily.

The edible meat can be removed from a lobster, as shown, to produce a large tail portion and intact claw sections as well as smaller pieces from the knuckles and legs. The lobster's tomalley (liver) and coral (eggs; only in females) should be removed and used as an ingredient in stuffing, sauce, or butter.

1. Hold the tail section securely in one hand and hold the body of the lobster with the other. Twist your hands in opposite directions, pulling the tail away from the body.

2. Use scissors to cut down both sides of the underside of the lobster tail. Pull the tail meat out of the shell. It should come away in one piece.

3. Use the back of a knife or the heel of a chef's knife to crack the claws.

4. Use your fingers to pry the shell away from the meat. The claw meat should also come out in a single piece, retaining the shape of the claw.

5. Use the knife to cut through the knuckles. Pull out the knuckle meat.

Shrimp

To clean shrimp, remove the shell and then the vein that runs along the back of the shrimp, either before or after cooking. Shrimp that have been boiled or steamed in the shell are moister and plumper than shrimp that were peeled and deveined before cooking. Shrimp that will be served cold—in appetizers or salads, for example—can be cooked in the shell. Shrimp dishes that are sautéed or grilled usually call for the shrimp to be peeled and deveined before cooking. The shells can be reserved for other uses, such as making shrimp stock, bisque, or shellfish butters.

1. To devein shrimp, lay the shelled shrimp on a work surface, with the curved outer edge of the shrimp on the same side as your cutting hand. Slice into the shrimp with a paring or utility knife; make a shallow cut for deveining or a deeper cut for butterflying the shrimp.

2. Use the tip of the knife to scrape out the "vein" or intestinal tract.

3. As an alternative, to remove the vein without cutting the shrimp, hook it with a toothpick or skewer and pull it out completely.

Cleaning soft-shelled crab

A seasonal favorite, soft-shelled crabs are considered a great delicacy. They are not especially difficult to clean once their various parts are identified.

Soft-shelled crabs are commonly prepared by sautéing or pan-frying, and the shell may be eaten along with the meat.

1. Peel back the pointed shell and scrape away the gill filament on each side.

2. Cut the eyes and mouth away from head just behind the eyes, and squeeze gently to force out the green bubble, which has an unpleasant flavor.

3. Bend back the tail flap (or apron) and pull with a slight twisting motion. The intestinal vein is drawn out of the body at the same time.

4. The cleaned crab with the tail flap, head, and gill filaments removed.

Cleaning and picking crayfish

Crayfish share many similarities with lobster, but they are much smaller. (They can also be purchased frozen, whole, or as just tails.) It is relatively simple to remove the vein from the crayfish before cooking, though this may be done afterward, if preferred. If live, pick through them and discard any dead ones. Remove the vein before or after cooking. Crayfish may be boiled or steamed in the shell. They can be served as is, whole, or they can be peeled after cooking to pick out the tail meat.

Cleaning and opening oysters, clams, and mussels

Oysters and clams are sold live in the shell and already shucked, but since they are often served on the half shell, it is important to be able to open them with ease. In addition, freshly shucked oysters and clams are often used for cooked dishes.

Scrub all mollusks well with a brush under cold running water before opening them. Any that remain open when tapped are dead and should be discarded. If a shell feels unusually heavy or light, check it. Occasionally, empty shells or shells that have filled with clay or sand will be found.

Oysters

Open oysters by prying open the hinge holding the two shells together. When opening oysters (and clams), be sure to reserve any juices, which are sometimes referred to as liquor. The liquor adds great flavor to soups, stews, and stocks.

1. Wear a wire mesh glove to hold the oyster, positioned so that the hinged side is facing outward. Work the tip of an oyster knife into the hinge holding the upper and lower shells together and twist it to break open the hinge.

2. Once open, slide the knife over the inside of the top shell to release the oyster from the shell. Make a similar stroke to release the oyster from the bottom shell.

Clams

Wear a wire mesh glove to protect the hand holding the clam. Work the side of a clam knife into the seam between the upper and lower shells.

1. Place the clam in your hand so that the hinged side is toward the palm of your hand. The fingers of your gloved hand can be used to both help guide the knife and give it extra force. Twist the blade slightly, like a key in a lock, to pry open the shell.

2. Once the shell is open, slide the knife over the inside of the top shell to release the clam from the shell. Make a similar stroke to release the clam from the bottom shell.

Mussels

Mussels are rarely served raw, but the method for cleaning them before steaming and poaching is similar to that used for clams. Unlike clams and oysters, mussels often have a dark, shaggy beard. It is normally removed before cooking.

Pull the beard away from the shell. Removing the beard kills the mussel, so perform this step as close to service as possible.

Cleaning octopus and squid

Octopus and squid belong to a category of shellfish known as cephalopods. They must be properly cleaned and cut to make the most of their flavor and texture in any cooked dish. Small squid and octopi are tender and moist when properly handled, even when cooked quickly and at high temperatures. Larger ones are better prepared by braising or stewing.

Octopus

Octopus is typically sold already cleaned. However, you may need to occasionally remove the viscera and beak (sometimes known as the eye). If the octopus you purchase has already been cleaned, simply cut the head away from the legs, and cut each piece into the appropriate size. Baby octopi are typically cooked whole.

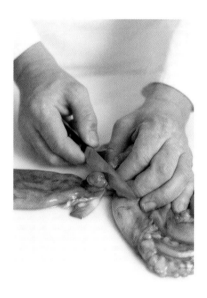

1. Use a paring knife to cut around the "eye" (beak) and lift it from the octopus.

2. Peel the skin away from the body by pulling firmly.

3. Pull the suction cups away from the tentacles if desired. The octopus is ready to use.

Squid

The squid mantle can be cut into rings to sauté, pan fry, or deep fry; or the squid may be left whole to grill or braise, with or without a stuffing. If desired, the ink sac can be saved and used to prepare various dishes, which will turn a dramatic black color.

1. Pull the mantle and the tentacles apart. The eye, ink sac, and intestines will come away with the tentacles.

2. Pull the transparent quill from the mantle and discard.

3. Pull away as much of the skin as possible from the mantle. Discard the skin.

4. Cut the tentacles away from the head by making a cut just below the eye. If desired, the ink sac may be reserved. Discard the rest of the head.

5. Open the tentacles to expose the beak. Pull it away and discard. The tentacles may be left whole if they are small or cut into pieces if they are large. Once the squid is cleaned, rinse it in cold water.

Chapter Twenty

Grilling and Broiling, Roasting and Baking

Some cooking methods rely on dry heat without fats or oils. The food is cooked either by a direct application of radiant heat (grilling and broiling) or by indirect heat in an oven (roasting and baking). The result of these cooking methods is a highly flavored exterior and a moist interior.

Grilling and Broiling

Grilling and broiling are quick cooking techniques that are used for naturally tender, portion-sized or smaller pieces of meat, poultry, or fish. By contrast, roasting and baking require a longer cooking time and are frequently used with larger cuts of meat, whole birds, and dressed fish.

Grilling cooks food with radiant heat from a source located below it. Some of the juices are actually reduced directly on the food while the rest drip away. Grilled foods have a slightly charred flavor, resulting from the juices and fats that are rendered as the food cooks, as well as from direct contact with the rods of the grill rack.

Broiling is similar to grilling but uses a heat source located above the food rather than below. Frequently, delicate foods like lean white fish are brushed with butter or oil, put on a heated, oiled sizzler platter, and then placed on the rack below the heat source instead of directly on the rods.

Tender portion-sized cuts of poultry, cuts of meat from the loin, rib, or top round areas, and fillets of such fatty fish as tuna and salmon are suited to grilling and broiling. Lean fish may also be grilled or broiled if they are coated with oil or an oil-based marinade. Some less tender cuts of meat such as hanger or flank steak may also be used if they are cut very thin.

When preparing meat for grilling or broiling, pound meats and fish lightly to even their thickness if necessary. Meat should be trimmed of excess fat and all silverskin and gristle. All meat and fish should be cut to an even thickness. Some foods are cut into strips, chunks, or cubes and then threaded onto skewers. The food itself should be seasoned and in some cases lightly oiled.

Different parts of the grill are hotter than others. Divide the grill into zones of varying heat intensity, including a very hot section for quickly searing foods and an area of moderate to low heat for slow cooking and holding foods. (If the grill is wood or charcoal fired, set aside an area for igniting the fuel, which is too hot and smoky over which to cook foods directly.) Zones may also be allocated for different types of foods, in order to prevent an undesirable transfer of flavors. Developing a system for placing foods on the grill or broiler, whether by food type or by range of doneness helps speed up work on the line.

Special woods such as mesquite, hickory, or apple are frequently used to impart special flavors. Hardwood chips, herb stems, grapevine trimmings, and other aromatics can be soaked in cold water and then thrown on the grill fire to create aromatic smoke. The sauce that accompanies a grilled item is prepared separately.

A basic formula for a single-entrée-sized portion

1 portion-size cut of meat, poultry, or fish; 6 to 8 oz/170 to 227 g

Seasonings, including salt and pepper or marinades, rubs, glazes, or barbecue sauce if desired

Other accompaniments, including compound butters, brown sauces, vegetable coulis, or salsas

1. **Brush the rods with a wire brush and then rub with a cloth dipped in vegetable oil to lubricate and clean them before preheating the grill.** Metal skewers need to be cleaned and oiled before use; wooden skewers should be soaked in water to prevent them from charring too much or catching on fire. Sizzler plates, tongs, offset spatulas, flexible spatulas, and brushes to apply glazes, marinades, or barbecue sauces should be part of the grill station's equipment mise en place, as well as all items necessary for service (heated plates, spoons, or ladles). Hand racks for delicate foods or those that might be awkward to turn easily should also be cleaned and oiled between uses to prevent meat skin from sticking and tearing.

2. **Let the food cook undisturbed on the first side before turning it over.** This develops better flavor and also lets the food's natural fats (if any) help release the food from the grill without tearing.

Place the seasoned food on the preheated grill or broiler rods to start cooking and to mark it. It does make a difference which side of the food goes onto the grill first. The best-looking, or presentation, side always goes face down on the rods first; however, the presentation side should always be face up when broiling. When the food comes into contact with the heated rods, marks are charred onto the surface of the food. To mark foods with a crosshatch on a grill, gently work the spatula or tongs under the food and give it a quarter turn (90 degrees).

Because many barbecue sauces contain sugar and burn easily, it is usually a good idea to partially cook the food before applying the sauce. That way, as the food finishes cooking, the sauce glazes and caramelizes lightly without burning. A single coat of sauce may be applied to each side of the food or, to build up a thicker, slightly crusty coat of sauce, the food may be brushed repeatedly with light coats of sauce.

3. **Remove the meat or fish when it is still slightly underdone, so it does not end up overcooked by the time it is served.** Even thin pieces of meat or fish will retain some heat, allowing them to cook after they have been removed from the heat.

Turn the food over and continue cooking to the desired doneness. Since most foods cooked by grilling or broiling are relatively thin and tender, they do not require much more cooking time once they have been turned over. Thicker cuts or those that must be cooked to a higher internal doneness may need to be moved to the cooler portion of the grill or broiler, so that they don't develop a charred exterior. Or they may be removed from the grill or broiler altogether and finished in the oven. For banquets, foods can be quickly marked on the rods of a grill or broiler, just barely cooking the outer layers of the food. Then they can be laid out on racks over sheet pans and finished in the oven. This approach allows you to expand the potential output of the grill or broiler. For food safety reasons, exercise extreme care in chilling partially cooked food quickly if it is to be held for any length of time.

Evaluate the quality of the finished grilled or broiled food. Properly prepared grilled and broiled foods have a distinctly smoky flavor, which is enhanced by a certain amount of charring and by the addition to the grill of hardwood or herb sprigs. This smoky flavor and aroma should not overpower the food's natural flavor and the charring should not be so extensive that it gives the food a bitter or carbonized taste. Any marinades or glazes should support and not mask the food's natural flavor.

Options for Making the Perfect Grill or Broil

To season the main ingredient, there are many options. Apply each one at the appropriate time, most typically before cooking.

Spice rubs

Marinades

Brines: Use a nonpreserving light brine (5 gal/19.20 L water, 1 lb/454 g salt, 1 lb/454 g sugar, and any additional aromatics)

Presalting: Massage the salt into the item before cooking to help to retain its moisture

To add additional flavor, add items to the grill fire to create an aromatic smoke, such as:

Hardwood chips
Herb stems
Grapevine trimmings

Pan Grilling

Pan grilling involves cooking foods on the stove over intense heat in a heavy cast-iron or other warp-resistant metal pan with a ridged bottom. The thick ridges in the bottom of the pan create marks similar to a grill and hold the food up and away from any juices or fat that might collect. It is important to consider, however, that pan grilling will not impart the same flavor as will traditional grilling. Grills and broilers must be well maintained and kept clean to produce a good-quality grilled or broiled entrée. Take the time to prepare the grill before, during, and after service. It is necessary to relubricate the rods throughout a service period, so keep a small container of oil and a cloth as part of the grill station mise en place.

Roasting

Roasting, whether by pan roasting, baking, smoke roasting, or poêléing, is a way of cooking by indirect heat in an oven. Spit roasting is more like grilling or broiling. Either way, the result is a crusty exterior and tender interior. The term *baking* is often used interchangeably with roasting; however, it is most typically used in relation to breads, cakes, pastries, and the like.

Rotisserie cooking involves placing the food on a rod, which is turned either manually or with a motor. The radiant heat given off by a fire or gas jet cooks the food while constant turning creates a basting effect and ensures that the food cooks evenly.

Roasting, as it is most often practiced today, is more similar to baking than it is to spit roasting or rotisserie cooking. In an oven, roasted foods are cooked through contact with dry, heated air held in a closed environment. As the outer layers become heated, the food's natural juices turn to steam and penetrate the food more deeply. The rendered juices, also called pan drippings or fond, are the foundation for sauces prepared while the roast rests. Roasting commonly refers to large, multiportion meat cuts, whole birds, and dressed fish.

Smoke roasting is an adaptation of roasting that allows foods to take on a rich, smoky flavor. The food cooks in a tightly closed environment or in a smoking setup. This can be done over an open flame or in the oven.

Tender meats from the rib, loin, and leg give the best results. Young, tender birds may be roasted whole, as may dressed fish. Trim away any excess fat and silverskin. A layer of fat or poultry skin helps to baste foods naturally as they roast. Season meats, poultry, and fish before roasting to fully develop their flavor. For additional flavor during roasting, herbs or aromatic vegetables may be used to stuff the cavity or to insert under the skin.

Foods such as whole birds, chicken breasts, and chops may be stuffed before roasting. Season the stuffing and chill it to below 40°F/4°C before combining it with raw meat, fish, or poultry. Allow enough time for the seasonings to interact with the food before starting to roast. Place fresh herbs in the cavity of a bird before trussing. Or, rub seasonings on the skin or slip them under the skin.

A good roasting pan has a flat bottom with relatively low sides to encourage hot air to circulate freely around the roasting food. Select a pan that holds the food comfortably but is not so large that the pan juices scorch. Food to be roasted may be set on a roasting rack, which permits the hot air to contact all of the food's surfaces, but good results are also possible when foods are set in very shallow roasting or baking pans elevated by aromatics, such as mirepoix. The pan should remain uncovered.

You may need butcher's twine or skewers, as well as an instant-read thermometer and a kitchen fork. Have an additional pan to hold the roasted food while a sauce is made from the pan drippings. Strainers and skimmers or ladles are needed to prepare the sauce. Have a carving board and an extremely sharp carving knife nearby for final service.

Best results are achieved when the oven is at the correct roasting temperature before the roasting pan is put into it. If searing foods in a very hot oven, heat the oven to 425° to 450°F/218° to 232°C. Roast large cuts such as prime rib or turkey at a low to moderate temperature throughout roasting; a deeply browned exterior is the result of the extended roasting time. Start smaller or more delicate foods at a low to moderate temperature (300° to 325°F/149° to 163°C) and then brown them at the very end of roasting by increasing the temperature of the oven from 350° to 375°F/177° to 191°C.

Barding and Larding

Two traditional preparation techniques for roasted foods that are naturally lean are barding (tying thin sheets of fatback, bacon, or caul fat around a food) and larding (inserting small strips of fatback into a food). The extra fat provides additional flavor and also helps keep the meat tender and juicy. Venison, wild boar, game birds, and certain cuts of beef or lamb may be candidates for barding or larding. Variations using different products are also employed to give different flavors to roasted foods. For example, a roast, rather than being larded with fatback, may be studded with slivers of garlic. The garlic will not have the same tenderizing effect as the fatback, but it will add plenty of flavor.

Today, with increased concern over the amount of fat in diets, every trace of visible fat or skin is often removed in an effort to reduce fat in the final dish, even though the amount of fat released from skin or fat layers as foods roast does not penetrate far into the meat. Fat and skin provide some protection from the drying effects of an oven without dramatically changing the amount of fat in the meat, and foods stripped of their natural protection of fat or skin can become dry and lose flavor.

A basic formula for an entrée-sized portion of meat, poultry, or fish

1 portion meat, fish, or poultry, trimmed as desired, trussed, or tied

1 oz/28 g mirepoix

Seasonings

2 fl oz/60 mL prepared pan sauce, pan gravy, or other sauce as appropriate

A basic formula for pan gravy

Stock (fortified or regular)

Mirepoix or other aromatic vegetables

A thickener such as roux or pure starch slurry. In some cases, the puréed mirepoix may be used to thicken. Reduction is used to thicken some pan sauces.

1. **Use the fat and juices released by the food itself for a traditional basting liquid.** However, a separate basting liquid, such as a marinade, glaze, or flavored or plain butter, may also be used. Sear the food (optional). Arrange it in a roasting pan, and place it in a preheated oven. Once the foods have been seasoned and tied or trussed, if necessary, they may be seared in hot fat on the stovetop, under a broiler, or in a very hot oven. Some foods are not seared, especially large cuts, since an extended roasting time will produce a deeply colored exterior even without an initial searing.

Arrange the food in the roasting pan so that hot air can come into contact with all sides of the meat, poultry, or fish. A rack will help improve air circulation. There should be enough room in the pan so that foods fit comfortably. Place it in a preheated oven. Roast, adjusting oven temperature as necessary. Baste as necessary throughout cooking time (as shown in photo above). There are several different theories regarding oven temperatures for roasting. Some items are traditionally roasted very quickly at high temperatures. Others are begun at low temperatures, then finished at a higher temperature. Still others are started at a high temperature, then finished at lower temperatures. In all cases, it is necessary to monitor the cooking speed to avoid over- or undercooking foods.

Basting returns some moisture to the food, preventing it from drying out. The basting liquid also imparts additional flavor. Alternative basting liquids such as melted butter, oil, or marinades are particularly useful if the food is lean and does not release enough fat of its own for basting.

For a pan sauce or gravy, add mirepoix or other aromatic ingredients to the roasting pan (optional). Onions, carrots, celery, garlic, or other aromatic vegetables or herbs may be added to the roasting pan to brown and roast in the drippings. They take on a deep color and absorb some of the flavor from the drippings, so that they can properly flavor and color the finished pan sauce.

2. **Use an instant-read thermometer to determine doneness in roasted foods.** To get the most accurate read, the thermometer must be inserted at least as far as the small dimple on the stem. Notice that the stem is inserted into the item's thickest part, away from any bones.

Roast foods to the correct doneness and let them rest before serving. Meats, fish, poultry, and game are generally cooked to a specified internal temperature (see page 461). When the meat is nearly done, remove it from the pan and allow it to rest. Cover the food loosely with foil to keep it moist and place it in a warm spot to rest.

Allow a resting period of about 5 minutes for small items, 15 to 20 minutes for medium items, and up to 45 minutes for very large roasts. This is done because as foods roast, their juices become concentrated in the center. A resting period before cutting into the food gives the juices time to redistribute evenly throughout. Resting also lets the temperature of the food equalize, which benefits texture, aroma, and flavor. Resting plays a key role in carryover cooking, which should be thought of as the last stage of cooking.

3. Serve roasted foods with a pan sauce based on the accumulated drippings from the food. Jus and pan gravy are the most frequently prepared pan sauces. Before preparing any pan sauce, be sure that the drippings are not scorched. Scorched drippings result in a bitter, unpalatable sauce.

To make a pan gravy, place the roasting pan on the stovetop and cook the drippings over medium heat until the mirepoix is browned and the fat is transparent and clear. The juices will have separated from the fat and cooked down to a fond on the bottom of the pan.

Degrease the pan and prepare the roux. For a pan gravy, pour off the fat, but leave enough to prepare a roux by cooking the fat and some flour together. If preparing a jus, flour is not used.

4. After the roux browns, gradually add the stock to the pan and stir constantly to work out any lumps. Be sure the liquid is not too hot or it may spatter.

Add the stock and simmer the pan gravy or jus. Cook a pan gravy until thickened, but for a minimum of 20 minutes to ensure the starch in the flour is sufficiently cooked.

To prepare a jus-style sauce, pour off all of the remaining fat and deglaze the pan, if desired, with wine or another liquid. Add a stock that suits the meat. Simmer until the flavor is well developed, 15 to 20 minutes. Skim the jus as it simmers to remove fat and particles from the surface. Adjust seasoning and strain to finish the jus. A jus may be cooked until thickened or it may be thickened using a starch slurry. To prepare a jus lié, thicken the jus with an arrowroot or cornstarch slurry just before straining.

5. Use a fine-mesh sieve to strain the pan gravy into a clean holding container for storage or into a pan to keep warm for service. Hold the finished pan gravy or jus in a steam table or water bath like any other sauce. Hold a jus by covering it with a tightly fitting lid.

Large roasted foods must be carved or cut into portions correctly to make the most of the item. The three items carved on the following pages—a whole duck, a rib roast of beef, and a ham—should be considered prototypes for other meats. For example, because they are similar in structure, a leg of lamb would be carved in the same manner as the ham.

The flavor and aroma of a food that has been well roasted contribute to an overall sensation of full flavor, richness, and depth. The color varies according to the type of food, but roasted foods in general are nicely browned. The color has a direct bearing on the flavor as well as appearance. Foods that are too pale lack eye appeal and depth of flavor. Well-roasted foods are tender and moist. The skin, if left on the food, should be crisp, creating a contrast with the texture of the meat.

Options for Preparing the Perfect Roasted or Baked Item

To develop additional flavor and color, sear the item before roasting. Once the foods have been seasoned and tied or trussed, they may be seared in hot fat on the stovetop, under a broiler, or in a very hot oven. To sear an item, it is cooked quickly in a small amount of oil but not cooked completely through. Searing is used in these cooking methods as an effective way to develop flavor and color in longer, slower cooking methods.

Basting is a technique that both adds flavor and moisture. If the food is lean and does not release enough fat of its own for basting, any one of the following may be used:

Melted butter
Oil
Marinades

Barding and larding are two techniques that will also add additional flavor and moisture.

Barding: Tying thin sheets of fatback, bacon, or caul fat around a food

Larding: Inserting small strips of fatback into a food

If roasts are drastically trimmed, an alternative "skin" should be added in the form of a coating or crust. Different ingredients may be combined with a small amount of fat and used to form this crust, such as:

Seasoned dried potato flakes
Rice flakes
Cornflakes
Cornmeal
Finely ground dried mushrooms

Items may also be glazed to add flavor. To do this, use a stock-based or fruit-based liquid.

Carving a roast duck

When a guest orders duck, this presentation is the most user friendly. Most of the bones are removed so that the leg portion has only the drumstick bone and the breast portion has a single wing bone. The two are nestled together so that the boneless breast and thigh meat overlap. The guest can simply cut into the meat without having to work around bones.

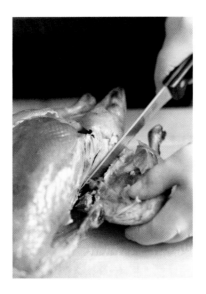

1. Cut the legs away from the body at the point where the leg meets the breast. Pulling away the leg will reveal the ball joint. Pull the leg away from the body and cut through the ball-and-socket joint to sever it completely.

2. Use the boning knife to cut along either side of the keel bone.

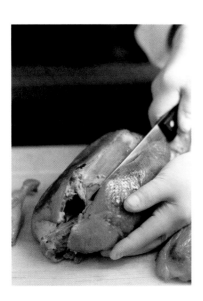

3. Carve the breast away from the rib cage with as little trim loss as possible by making the edge of the blade run as close to the bones as you can.

4. Pull the thigh bone up and away from the thigh meat. Use the knife as shown to separate the bone at the leg joint.

5. To nest the leg and breast portions for presentation, position the leg portion on the bottom and the breast portion overlapping the leg, with the drumstick bone and the wing bone on opposite sides.

Carving a rib roast

A beef rib roast is a large cut and is easiest to handle when turned on its side. This carving method can also be used for a rack of veal or venison. These smaller roasts need not be turned on their sides, and cuts are made from top to bottom between the bones. The meat can be cut away from the bones to make slices or the bones may be left in place to produce chops.

Lay the rib roast on its side. Using a slicing knife, make parallel cuts from the outer edge toward the bones. Use the knife tip to cut the slices of meat away from the bone. Store cut side up if necessary to prevent juice loss.

Carving ham in the dining room

This carving method may also be used for legs of lamb and steamship rounds.

1. After the end piece has been cut away, make parallel cuts from the shank end down the bone. Continue cutting slices of meat from the leg, cutting away from the bone to make even slices. The initial cuts are made vertically, until the bone is reached.

2. When the slices become very large, begin to cut the meat at a slight angle, first from the left side, then from the right side, alternating until the leg is entirely sliced.

Carving ham in the kitchen

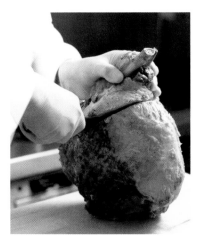

1. Stand the ham on end, with the sirloin end resting on the board. Hold the shank end with your guiding hand to keep the ham stable. Make a cut into the lean meat just below the stifle joint on the shank end and follow the natural curve of the femur bone.

2. At the ball-and-socket joint, cut around the joint. This first cut will not completely cut the meat away from the bone. Remove the top piece of meat from the aitch bone.

3. Repeat the same sequence of cuts on the second side of the bone to completely free the meat. The meat will appear to have a V-shaped notch where it was cut away from the bone.

4. Cut away the meat from the back side of the femur bone. Try to keep the pieces of meat as intact as possible.

5. Cut the larger pieces of ham into manageable pieces that can be sliced into portions.

6. Carve the ham into slices with a meat slicer as shown. The ham could also be sliced on an electric meat slicer.

Grilled or Broiled Sirloin Steak with Mushroom Sauce

Makes 10 servings

10 (10 oz/284 g) sirloin steaks

1 tbsp/15 g salt

1½ tsp/3 g ground black pepper

3 fl oz/45 mL vegetable oil

20 fl oz/600 mL **Mushroom Sauce** (recipe follows)

1. Preheat the grill or broiler.

2. Season the steaks with salt and pepper and lightly brush with oil.

3. Place the steaks presentation side down on the grill or broiler rods. Grill or broil undisturbed until halfway cooked. (Optional: Give each steak a quarter turn to achieve grill marks.)

4. Turn the steaks over and complete cooking to the desired doneness, about 5 minutes more for rare (internal temperature of 135°F/57°C), 6½ minutes for medium rare (145°F/63°C), 8 minutes for medium (160°F/71°C), 9 minutes for medium well (165°F/74°C), and 11 minutes for well done (170°F/77°C).

5. Heat the Mushroom Sauce, serve each steak with 2 fl oz/60 mL of the sauce, and serve at once.

Grilled or Broiled Sirloin Steak with Maître d'Hôtel Butter: Replace the Mushroom Sauce with 10 oz/284 g maître d'hôtel butter, piped or sliced into ten 1-oz/28-g servings. Grill the steak and top each with the butter. Heat under a broiler or salamander until the butter begins to melt. Serve at once.

Mushroom Sauce

Makes 32 fl oz/960 mL

1½ oz/43 g minced shallots

2 oz/57 g butter

2 lb 4 oz/1.25 kg sliced white mushrooms

7½ fl oz/225 mL dry white wine

32 fl oz/960 mL **Demi-Glace** (page 383) or **Jus de Veau Lié** (page 382)

salt, as needed

ground black pepper, as needed

1. Sweat the shallots in the butter over medium heat.

2. Add the mushrooms and continue to sauté until their juices have cooked away.

3. Add the wine to deglaze the pan. Cook until the wine is reduced.

4. Add the demi-glace or jus de veau lié and simmer for 5 minutes more, or until the sauce has a good consistency and flavor.

5. Season with salt and pepper. The sauce is ready to serve now, or it may be rapidly cooled and refrigerated for later use.

Grilled or Broiled Sirloin with Marchand de Vin Sauce

Makes 10 servings

10 (10 oz/284 g) sirloin steaks

1 tbsp/15 g salt

1½ tsp/3 g ground black pepper

3 fl oz/45 mL vegetable oil

20 fl oz/600 mL **Marchand de Vin Sauce** (recipe follows)

1. Preheat the grill or broiler to 400°F/204°C.

2. Season the steaks with salt and pepper and lightly brush with oil.

3. Place the steaks presentation side down on the grill or broiler rods. Grill or broil undisturbed for about 2 minutes. (Optional: Give each steak a quarter turn to achieve grill marks.)

4. Turn the steaks over and complete cooking to the desired doneness, about 5 minutes more for rare (internal temperature of 135°F/57°C), 6½ minutes for medium rare (145°F/63°C), 8 minutes for medium (160°F/71°C), 9 minutes for medium well (165°F/74°C), and 11 minutes for well done (170°F/77°C).

5. Heat the Marchand de Vin Sauce, serve each steak with 2 fl oz/60 mL of the sauce, and serve at once.

Marchand de Vin Sauce

Makes 32 fl oz/960 mL

2 oz/57 g minced shallots

2 thyme sprigs

1 bay leaf

½ tsp/1 g cracked peppercorns

16 fl oz/480 mL red wine

32 fl oz/960 mL **Demi-Glace** (page 383)

salt, as needed

ground black pepper, as needed

4 oz/113 g butter, diced

1. Combine the shallots, thyme, bay leaf, peppercorns, and wine in a medium sauté pan. Bring the mixture to a boil and reduce until syrupy, about 10 minutes.

2. Add the demi-glace and reduce until the sauce coats the back of a spoon, 8 to 10 minutes. Season with salt and pepper and strain the sauce. Finish the sauce with butter.

3. The sauce is ready to serve now, or it may be rapidly cooled and refrigerated for later use.

Barbecued Steak with Herb Crust

Makes 10 servings

HERB CRUST

2 tsp/6 g minced garlic

½ oz/14 g parsley, chopped

6 oz/170 g bread crumbs

6 oz/170 g butter, melted

1 tsp/5 g salt

½ tsp/1 g ground black pepper

STEAKS

10 (10 oz/284 g) sirloin steaks

1 tbsp/15 g salt

1½ tsp/3 g ground black pepper

1 tbsp/9 g minced garlic

3 fl oz/45 mL vegetable oil

12 fl oz/360 mL **Barbecue Sauce** (page 549)

1. Preheat the grill or broiler to 400°F/204°C.

2. Combine all of the ingredients for the herb crust and blend well.

3. Season the steaks with salt and pepper, rub with garlic, and lightly brush with oil.

4. Place the steaks presentation side down on the grill or broiler rods. Grill or broil the steaks undisturbed for about 2 minutes.

5. Turn the steaks over and complete cooking to the desired doneness, about 5 minutes more for rare (internal temperature of 135°F/57°C), 6½ minutes for medium rare (145°F/63°C), 8 minutes for medium (160°F/71°C), 9 minutes for medium well (165°F/74°C), and 11 minutes for well done (170°F/77°C).

6. Top the steaks with the herb crust and brown the topping under a salamander or broiler. Serve the steaks at once, with Barbecue Sauce if desired.

Skewered Beef and Scallions

Makes 10 servings

MARINADE

4 fl oz/120 mL soy sauce

1½ oz/43 g sugar

2 fl oz/60 mL sesame oil

½ oz/14 g minced garlic

½ oz/14 g minced ginger

1 tsp/2 g ground black pepper

BEEF

3 lb 12 oz/1.70 kg beef top butt or flank steak, cut 1 in/3 cm wide by 4 in/10 cm long and ⅛ in/3 mm thick

6 bunches green onions, cut into pieces 3½ in/9 cm long

1. Combine the ingredients for the marinade, add the beef, and marinate in the refrigerator for 3 hours or overnight.

2. Soak bamboo skewers for 10 minutes. Thread the beef on the skewers, alternating with the green onions.

3. Preheat the grill or broiler to 400°F/204°C.

4. Place the skewers presentation side down on the grill or broiler rods. Grill or broil undisturbed for about 1 minute. (Optional: Give each skewer a quarter turn to achieve grill marks.)

5. Turn the skewers over and complete cooking to the desired doneness, about 1 minute more for rare (internal temperature of 135°F/57°C), 2½ minutes for medium rare (145°F/63°C), 3½ minutes for medium (160°F/71°C), 4½ minutes for medium well (165°F/74°C), and 5½ minutes for well done (170°F/77°C).

6. Serve immediately.

Beef Teriyaki

Beef Teriyaki

Makes 10 servings

MARINADE

8 fl oz/240 mL light soy sauce

8 fl oz/240 mL sake

6 fl oz/180 mL mirin

3¾ oz/106 g sugar

2¼ oz/64 g grated apple

10 (about 6 oz/170 g) beef skirt steaks

1 lb/454 g snow peas

1 fl oz/30 mL vegetable oil

20 white mushrooms, medium-sized caps

1 lb/454 g bean sprouts

1½ tsp/7.50 g salt

1. Combine the soy sauce, sake, mirin, and sugar and bring to a boil. Add the apple, mix well, and cool completely. Pour the marinade over the steaks and marinate in the refrigerator for 8 hours, and up to overnight.

2. Cut the snow peas in 2 or 3 pieces diagonally.

3. Heat the oil in a sauté pan over medium-high heat. Add the mushroom caps, bean sprouts, and snow peas and cook until just tender. Season with salt. Reserve warm.

4. Preheat the grill or broiler to 400°F/204°C. Allow any excess marinade to drain from the beef before grilling or broiling; blot if necessary.

5. Place the steaks presentation side down on the grill or broiler rods. Grill or broil undisturbed for about 2 minutes. (Optional: Give each steak a quarter turn to achieve grill marks.)

6. Turn the steaks over and complete cooking to the desired doneness, about 5 minutes more for rare (internal temperature of 135°F/57°C), 6½ minutes for medium rare (145°F/63°C), 8 minutes for medium (160°F/71°C), 9 minutes for medium well (165°F/74°C), and 11 minutes for well done (170°F/77°C).

7. Remove the steaks from the grill and allow them to rest for 5 minutes in a warm place. Slice each steak on the bias into 5 pieces.

8. Serve immediately with the vegetables.

Grilled Rib Eye Steak

Makes 10 servings

MARINADE

16 fl oz/480 mL olive oil

½ oz/14 g ground black pepper

1 bunch rosemary, roughly chopped

13 garlic cloves, crushed

BEEF

10 (10 oz/284 g) rib eye steaks, boneless

1 oz/28 g salt

½ oz/14 g ground black pepper

1. Preheat the grill to 400°F/204°C.

2. Prepare the marinade by combining the oil, pepper, rosemary, and garlic. Marinate the meat, covered, in the refrigerator for at least 3 hours.

3. Wipe excess oil from the steaks. Season with salt and pepper. Place the steaks presentation side down on the grill or broiler rods. Grill or broil undisturbed for about 2 minutes. (Optional: Give each steak a quarter turn to achieve grill marks.)

4. Turn the steaks over and complete cooking to the desired doneness, about 2 minutes more for rare (internal temperature of 135°F/57°C), 4 minutes for medium rare (145°F/63°C), 7 minutes for medium (160°F/71°C), 8 minutes for medium well (165°F/74°C), and 9 minutes for well done (170°F/77°C).

5. Serve immediately.

Pork and Veal Skewers (Raznjici)

Makes 10 servings

MARINADE

1¾ oz/50 g thinly sliced garlic

4 oz/113 g sliced onions

4 fl oz/120 mL vegetable oil

4 fl oz/120 mL lemon juice

2 tbsp/6 g chopped parsley

2 lb/907 g veal top round, cut into 1½-in/4-cm cubes

2 lb/907 g pork loin, cut into 1½-in/4-cm cubes

1 tbsp/15 g salt

1½ tsp/3 g ground black pepper

GARNISH

12 oz/340 g thinly sliced onions

20 fl oz/600 mL **Dill Sauce** (recipe follows)

1. Combine the ingredients for the marinade, add the meat, and marinate in the refrigerator for 3 hours or overnight.

2. Soak bamboo skewers for 10 minutes. Thread the meat onto the skewers. Allow any excess marinade to drain from the meat before grilling or broiling; blot if necessary. Season with salt and pepper.

3. Preheat the grill or broiler to 400°F/204°C. Place the skewers presentation side down on the grill or broiler rods. Grill or broil undisturbed for 3 to 4 minutes.

4. Turn the skewers over and complete cooking, 3 to 4 minutes more. Brush the meat with additional marinade as it broils or grills.

5. Serve immediately with the sliced onions and Dill Sauce.

Broiled Lamb Kebabs with Pimiento Butter: Replace the veal and pork with an equal amount of boneless leg of lamb. Replace Dill Sauce with Pimiento Butter (page 388).

Dill Sauce

Makes 32 fl oz/960 mL

24 fl oz/720 mL **Chicken Velouté** (page 383)

8 fl oz/240 mL sour cream

3 tbsp/9 g chopped dill

salt, as needed

ground black pepper, as needed

1. In a medium sauce pot, warm the velouté to a gentle simmer. Temper the sour cream and add it to the sauce.

2. Stir in the dill. Return to just below a simmer, season with salt and pepper, and keep warm for service.

Grilled (or Broiled) Pork Chops with Sherry Vinegar Sauce

Makes 10 servings

10 (about 12 oz/340 g) bone-in pork chops, 2 in/5 cm thick

1 tbsp/15 g salt

1½ tsp/3 g ground black pepper

2 fl oz/60 mL olive oil

20 fl oz/600 mL **Sherry Vinegar Sauce** (recipe follows)

1. Preheat the grill or broiler to 400°F/204°C.

2. Season the pork with salt and pepper and lightly brush with oil. Place the pork chops presentation side down on the grill or broiler rods. Grill or broil undisturbed for 8 to 10 minutes. (Optional: Give each chop a quarter turn to achieve grill marks.)

3. Turn the pork chops over and grill to an internal temperature of 160°F/71°C for medium, 170°F/77°C for well done, 8 to 10 minutes more.

4. Remove the pork chops from the grill or broiler and allow them to rest for about 5 minutes.

5. Heat the Sherry Vinegar Sauce, top each pork chop with 2 fl oz/60 mL of the sauce, and serve at once.

Sherry Vinegar Sauce

Makes 32 fl oz/960 mL

4 fl oz/120 mL sherry wine vinegar

3 oz/85 g dark brown sugar

26 fl oz/780 mL **Jus de Veau Lié** (page 382) or **Demi-Glace** (page 383)

salt, as needed

ground black pepper, as needed

1. Prepare a gastrique as follows: Cook the vinegar and sugar in a saucepan over medium-high heat until the mixture comes to a boil and the sugar is completely dissolved, 4 to 6 minutes.

2. Remove the saucepan from the heat and add the jus lié or demi-glace to the gastrique. Stir to combine and return to a simmer over medium heat until reduced to a thickness that coats the back of a spoon, about 15 minutes.

3. Season with salt and pepper. Strain the sauce. The sauce is ready to serve now, or it may be rapidly cooled and refrigerated for later use.

Grilled Smoked Iowa Pork Chops with Potato Pancake (page 797), Braised Red Cabbage (page 765), Caramelized Apples, and Haricots Verts

Grilled Smoked Iowa Pork Chops

Makes 10 servings

10 (about 8 oz/227 g) loin pork chops

1 tbsp/15 g salt

1½ tsp/3 g ground black pepper

2 fl oz/60 mL vegetable oil, or as needed

20 fl oz/600 mL **Apple Cider Sauce** (recipe follows)

10 servings **Caramelized Apples** (recipe follows)

2 lb 13 oz/1.28 kg **Braised Red Cabbage** (page 765)

1. Place 6 charcoal briquettes onto a rack over the direct flame of a burner until red hot. Place the coals into a sauté pan. Place a hotel pan of ice in a cold oven.

2. Place the pork on a wire rack in the cold oven with the hotel pan of ice. Put the hot coals in the oven in another pan. Sprinkle wood chips over the coals. Close the oven door and smoke the pork for 10 to 15 minutes only. Do not oversmoke.

3. Remove the pork and refrigerate it until needed. Pour water over the coals until extinguished and dispose of them.

4. Preheat the grill to 400°F/204°C. Season the pork with salt and pepper and lightly brush with oil. Place the pork chops presentation side down on the grill. Grill undisturbed for about 2 minutes. (Optional: Give each chop a quarter turn to achieve grill marks.) Turn the pork chops over and grill to an internal temperature of 145°F/63°C.

5. Heat the Apple Cider Sauce and Caramelized Apples and serve each chop with 4½ oz/128 g Braised Red Cabbage, 2 fl oz/60 mL of the sauce, and 1 serving of the apples.

Apple Cider Sauce

Makes 32 fl oz/960 mL

8 oz/227 g pork, cut into 1-in/3-cm cubes

1 tsp/5 g salt

½ tsp/1 g ground black pepper

1 fl oz/30 mL vegetable oil

4 oz/113 g medium-dice **Mirepoix** (page 333)

16 fl oz/480 mL apple cider

1 fl oz/30 mL applejack brandy

3 thyme sprigs

5 black peppercorns, crushed

1 bay leaf

1 gal/3.84 L **Brown Veal Stock** (page 352)

Slurry (page 339), as needed

1. Season the pork with the salt and pepper. Heat the oil over medium-high heat in a large sauce pot, add the pork and cook until evenly browned on all sides.

2. Add the mirepoix to the pan and cook until caramelized. Deglaze with the cider and applejack. Reduce by half.

3. Add the thyme, peppercorns, bay leaf, and stock. Bring to a simmer and continue to cook until it reaches a nappé consistency, skimming as necessary, 2 to 3 hours.

4. Thicken with a slurry, if necessary. Strain and hold until service.

Caramelized Apples

Makes 10 servings

8 seasonal apples

2 lemons, juiced

7 oz/198 g sugar

salt, as needed

1. Peel and core the apples. Cut each apple into 8 wedges using the radial cut. Sprinkle half of the lemon juice over the apples to prevent oxidation.

2. Place the sugar in a sauté pan with the remaining lemon juice and mix well. Caramelize the sugar over high heat. Carefully add the apple slices and coat with the caramelized sugar. Season lightly with a pinch of salt. Reserve warm.

Grilled Lamb Chops with Rosemary, Roasted Artichokes, and Cipollini Onions

Makes 10 servings

MARINADE

6 black peppercorns

1 bay leaf

2 oz/57 g parsley leaves

½ oz/14 g thyme leaves

½ oz/14 g rosemary leaves

1 oz/28 g garlic cloves

24 fl oz/720 mL olive oil

CHOPS

20 (about 4 oz/113 g) lamb rib chops

3 lemons, juiced

30 baby artichokes

6 fl oz/180 mL extra-virgin olive oil

1 tbsp/15 g salt

1½ tsp/3 g ground black pepper

30 cipollini onions

2 oz/57 g sliced garlic

2 tbsp/6 g chopped oregano

3 tbsp/9 g chopped parsley

24 fl oz/720 mL **Chicken Stock** (page 351)

6 oz/170 g butter, cubed

1. Place the peppercorns, bay leaf, parsley, thyme, rosemary, and garlic in a blender. Add 2 fl oz/60 mL of the olive oil and blend until the mixture is smooth. Gradually add the remaining oil. Pour the marinade over the lamb chops and refrigerate for a minimum of 45 minutes.

2. Combine 1 gal/3.84 L of water with the lemon juice. Remove the stems and tough outer leaves of the artichokes. Cut into quarters and store in the lemon water to prevent browning. Heat 3 fl oz/90 mL, or more as needed, of the extra-virgin olive oil in large sauté pan over medium-high heat. (Use more oil than a sauté, but less than a pan fry.) Lightly brown the artichokes, without overcrowding the pan. (Work in batches if necessary.) When lightly golden, season the artichokes with salt and pepper, remove them from the pan, and place on a paper towel to drain. Reserve.

3. Bring a large pot of water to a boil and cook the onions for 8 to 10 minutes, or until ¾ of the way cooked. Shock in cold water, peel, and cut them in half. Heat a large sauté pan with 2 fl oz/60 mL of extra-virgin olive oil over medium heat. Cook the onions until they are lightly caramelized, about 8 to 10 minutes. Remove from the pan, let cool, and reserve.

4. Sauté the garlic slices in 1 fl oz/30 mL of olive oil until the edges begin to brown. Add the onions, artichokes, oregano, and parsley and adjust seasoning with salt and pepper. Add the stock and reduce by ¾. Stir in the butter and cook until the vegetables are glazed. Reserve warm while grilling the lamb.

5. Preheat the grill to 400°F/204°C. Drain off any excess marinade and season the lamb chops with salt and pepper. Wrap the bones with aluminum foil, if desired.

6. Place the lamb presentation side down on the grill or broiler rods. Grill or broil undisturbed for about 2 minutes. (Optional: Give each chop a quarter turn to achieve grill marks.) Turn the lamb chops over and complete cooking to the desired doneness, about 4 minutes more for rare (internal temperature of 135°F/57°C), 7 minutes for medium rare (145°F/63°C), 9 minutes for medium (160°F/71°C), 11 minutes for medium well (165°F/74°C), and 14 minutes for well done (170°F/77°C).

7. Serve the ragout of vegetables in the middle of the plate with 2 chops on top.

Pakistani-Style Lamb Patties

Makes 10 servings

2 oz/57 g minced onions

1 fl oz/30 mL vegetable oil

1 tbsp/9 g minced garlic

2 oz/57 g fresh white bread crumbs

water, as needed

3 lb/1.36 kg ground lamb

3 oz/85 g toasted pine nuts

2 eggs, beaten

1 oz/28 g tahini

3 tbsp/9 g chopped parsley

1 tbsp/15 g salt

1½ tsp/3 g ground black pepper

1 tsp/2 g ground coriander

2 tbsp/12 g ground cumin

1 tsp/2 g ground fennel seed

2 tbsp/18 g grated ginger

1. Sauté the onions in the oil over medium heat until translucent, about 5 minutes. Add the garlic and sauté 1 minute. Remove from the heat and let cool.

2. Soak the bread crumbs in water. Squeeze out any excess moisture. Combine with the onions and garlic.

3. Combine the bread crumb mixture with the lamb, pine nuts, eggs, tahini, parsley, salt, pepper, spices, and ginger. Mix gently but thoroughly. Shape the mixture into patties and chill.

4. Preheat the grill or broiler to 400°F/204°C. Place the patties on the grill or broiler rods. Grill or broil undisturbed for about 2 minutes. (Optional: Give each patty a quarter turn to achieve grill marks.)

5. Turn the patties over and complete cooking to the desired doneness, about 3 minutes more for rare (internal temperature of 135°F/57°C), 5 minutes for medium rare (145°F/63°C), 7 minutes for medium (160°F/71°C), 9 minutes for medium well (165°F/74°C), and 12 minutes for well done (170°F/77°C).

6. Serve immediately.

Indian Grilled Lamb with Fresh Mango Chutney

Indian Grilled Lamb with Fresh Mango Chutney

Makes 10 servings

6 lb/2.72 kg boneless leg of lamb, butterflied

MARINADE

1 tsp/2 g ground green cardamom

1 tsp/2 g ground cumin

½ tsp/1 g ground nutmeg

4 oz/113 g minced onions

¾ oz/21 g minced garlic

¾ oz/21 g minced ginger

1 tsp/2 g ground black pepper

4 fl oz/120 mL plain yogurt

20 fl oz/600 mL **Fresh Mango Chutney** (recipe follows)

1. Trim the lamb and separate it into individual muscles. Remove all interior fat and gristle. Cut the meat into long, thin strips (4 by 1 by ⅛ in/10 cm by 3 cm by 3 mm).

2. Prepare the marinade. Toast the cardamom and cumin lightly in a pan. Add the nutmeg, onions, garlic, ginger, and pepper and sauté until fragrant. Let cool. Add to the yogurt.

3. Pour the marinade over the lamb and turn to coat evenly. Marinate the lamb for 8 hours or overnight in the refrigerator.

4. Preheat the grill to 400°F/204°C. Thread the lamb onto skewers and allow the excess marinade to drain away. Place the lamb presentation side down on the grill.

5. Grill undisturbed for about 1 minute. (Optional: Give each skewer a quarter turn to achieve grill marks.) Turn the skewers over and complete cooking to the desired doneness, about 1 minute more for rare (internal temperature of 135°F/57°C), 2½ minutes for medium rare (145°F/63°C), 3½ minutes for medium (160°F/71°C), 4½ minutes for medium well (165°F/74°C), and 5½ minutes for well done (170°F/77°C).

6. Serve 3 to 4 skewers per person with 2 fl oz/60 mL of the chutney.

Fresh Mango Chutney

Makes 32 fl oz/960 mL

2 lb/907 g small-dice mangos

2 fl oz/60 mL lime juice

4 tsp/4 g chopped cilantro

2 tsp/6 g minced ginger

1 tsp/3 g minced jalapeños (optional)

salt, as needed

ground black pepper, as needed

1. Combine all the ingredients and let the chutney rest in the refrigerator for up to 2 hours, to allow the flavors to marry. Adjust seasoning before serving, if necessary, with additional lime juice, salt, or pepper.

Grilled or Broiled Chicken Breasts with Sun-Dried Tomato and Oregano Butter

Makes 10 servings

10 (6 oz/170 g) chicken breasts, boneless, skin on

1 tbsp/15 g salt

1½ tsp/3 g ground black pepper

3 tbsp/45 mL vegetable oil

10 oz/284 g **Sun-Dried Tomato and Oregano Butter** (page 388), piped or sliced into ten 1-oz/28-g servings

1. Preheat the grill or broiler to 400°F/204°C.

2. Season the chicken with salt and pepper and lightly brush with oil.

3. Place the chicken presentation side down on the grill or broiler rods. Grill or broil undisturbed for about 2 minutes. (Optional: Give each breast a quarter turn to achieve grill marks.) Turn the chicken over and continue cooking until the chicken is cooked through, 6 to 8 minutes (165°F/74°C).

4. Top each chicken breast with a serving of the Sun-Dried Tomato and Oregano Butter; heat under a broiler or salamander until the butter begins to melt. Serve at once.

Grilled Chicken Breasts with Fennel

Makes 10 servings

6 fl oz/180 mL olive oil

3 garlic cloves, crushed

¾ tsp/2 g cracked fennel seeds

¾ tsp/3.75 g salt

½ tsp/1 g ground black pepper

10 (about 5 to 6 oz/142 to 170 g) chicken breasts, boneless, skinless

2 oz/57 g butter

1 oz/28 g minced shallots

1 lb 4 oz/567 g julienned fennel

1 fl oz/30 mL Pernod

10 fennel leaves (optional)

1. Combine the oil, garlic, fennel seeds, ½ tsp/2.50 g of the salt, and ¼ tsp/0.50 g of the pepper. Add the chicken and marinate in the refrigerator for 30 minutes.

2. Preheat the grill or broiler to 400°F/204°C. Allow any excess marinade to drain from the chicken before grilling or broiling; blot if necessary.

3. Place the chicken presentation side down on the grill or broiler rods. Grill or broil undisturbed for about 2 minutes. (Optional: Give each breast a quarter turn to achieve grill marks.) Brush with the marinade and turn the chicken over. Continue to cook the chicken, brushing with the marinade periodically, until the chicken is cooked through, 6 to 8 minutes (165°F/74°C).

4. Heat the butter in a medium saucepan over medium-high heat. Sauté the shallots until they are translucent, approximately 1 minute.

5. Add the fennel and cover the pan. Cook until the fennel is tender, approximately 10 minutes. Add the Pernod and the remaining ¼ tsp/1.25 g salt and ¼ tsp/0.50 g pepper.

6. Serve the chicken breasts on a bed of fennel. Garnish with fennel leaves, if desired.

Grilled Paillards of Chicken with Tarragon Butter

Makes 10 servings

10 (about 5 to 6 oz/142 to 170 g) chicken breasts, boneless, skinless

MARINADE

2 fl oz/60 mL vegetable oil

1 tsp/5 g salt

½ tsp/1 g ground black pepper

2 fl oz/60 mL lemon juice

2 tsp/2 g chopped tarragon leaves

10 oz/284 g **Tarragon Butter** (page 388), piped or sliced into ten 1-oz/28-g servings

1. Trim and pound the chicken into paillards (see page 474).

2. Combine all the ingredients for the marinade, add the chicken, and marinate for 30 minutes.

3. Preheat the grill or broiler to 400°F/204°C. Allow any excess marinade to drain from the chicken before grilling; blot if necessary.

4. Place the chicken presentation side down on the grill or broiler rods. Grill undisturbed for about 2 minutes. (Optional: Give each breast a quarter turn to achieve grill marks.) Turn the chicken over. Continue to cook the chicken until cooked through, 6 to 8 minutes (165°F/74°C).

5. Top each paillard with a serving of the Tarragon Butter and serve immediately.

Barbecued Chicken Breast with Black Bean Sauce

Makes 10 servings

MARINADE

8 fl oz/240 mL apple cider

1 fl oz/30 mL cider vinegar

½ oz/14 g minced shallots

1 tsp/3 g minced garlic

1 tsp/2 g cracked black peppercorns

CHICKEN

10 (6 oz/170 g) chicken breasts, boneless, skin on

1 tbsp/15 g salt

1½ tsp/3 g ground black pepper

16 fl oz/480 mL **Barbecue Sauce** (page 549)

20 fl oz/600 mL **Black Bean Sauce, warm** (recipe follows)

1. Combine all the ingredients for the marinade. Add the chicken and turn to coat it evenly. Marinate the chicken in the refrigerator for 1 to 2 hours.

2. Preheat the grill or broiler to 400°F/204°C. Allow any excess marinade to drain from the chicken before grilling or broiling; blot if necessary. Season with salt and pepper.

3. Place the chicken presentation side down on the grill or broiler rods. Grill or broil undisturbed for about 2 minutes. (Optional: Give each breast a quarter turn to achieve grill marks.) Brush with the barbecue sauce and turn the chicken over. Continue to cook the chicken, brushing with a light coat of barbecue sauce periodically, until the chicken is cooked through, 6 to 8 minutes (165°F/74°C).

4. Serve the chicken on heated plates with the Black Bean Sauce.

Black Bean Sauce

Makes 32 fl oz/960 mL

9½ oz/269 g dried black beans, soaked overnight

50 fl oz/1.50 L **Chicken Stock** (page 351)

½ oz/14 g diced bacon

½ fl oz/15 mL vegetable oil

4 oz/113 g diced onions

2 tsp/6 g minced garlic

¼ tsp/0.25 g chopped oregano

½ tsp/1 g ground cumin

½ tsp/1.50 g chopped jalapeños

1 dried chile

salt, as needed

ground black pepper, as needed

½ oz/14 g chopped sun-dried tomatoes

½ fl oz/15 mL lemon juice, or as needed

1 tsp/5 mL sherry wine vinegar

1. In a medium saucepan, simmer the beans in the stock until tender over medium heat, about 1 hour. Drain the beans and reserve about 8 fl oz/240 mL of the cooking liquid.

2. In a second medium saucepan, render the bacon over medium heat until it releases its fat, about 5 minutes. Add the oil, onions, garlic, oregano, cumin, jalapeños, and dried chile. Continue to sauté over medium heat, stirring occasionally, until the onions are limp and translucent, 6 to 8 minutes.

3. Add the cooked beans to the sautéed vegetables. Season the sauce with salt and pepper and cook for 10 to 15 minutes more.

4. Remove the chile and purée a third of the beans. Add the purée back to the sauce along with the tomatoes. Adjust the consistency with the reserved cooking liquid, as needed. Season with lemon juice and vinegar.

5. Adjust seasoning with salt and pepper. The sauce is ready to serve now, or it may be rapidly cooled and refrigerated for later use.

Brazilian Mixed Grill

Makes 10 servings

MARINADE

2 fl oz/60 mL olive oil

½ oz/14 g minced Malaguetas or habaneros

1 tsp/1 g chopped thyme

1 tsp/3 g minced garlic

2½ tsp/12.50 g salt

1½ tsp/3 g ground black pepper

MIXED GRILL

5 (about 8 oz/227 g) whole chicken legs, separated

2 lb/907 g boneless pork loin

2 lb/907 g flank steak

20 fl oz/600 mL **Hot Pepper Sauce** (Molho Apimentado; recipe follows)

1. Prepare the marinade by combining the oil, peppers, thyme, garlic, ½ tsp/2.50 g of the salt, and ½ tsp/1 g of the pepper. Marinate the chicken, refrigerated, overnight.

2. Preheat the grill to 400°F/204°C and the oven to 350°F/177°C. Season the pork with 1 tsp/5 g of the salt and ½ tsp/1 g of the pepper. Grill the pork for 4 to 5 minutes per side until golden brown. Transfer the pork to the preheated oven and cook until the internal temperature reaches 155°F/68°C, about 10 minutes, depending on thickness. Remove from the oven and allow to rest for 10 minutes.

3. Season the steak with the remaining salt and pepper. Place the steak and chicken on the grill. Grill the chicken for 8 to 10 minutes per side until cooked through, rotating throughout to ensure even browning.

4. Grill the steak undisturbed for about 2 minutes. Turn the steaks over and complete cooking to the desired doneness, about 6 minutes more for rare (internal temperature of 135°F/57°C), 9 minutes for medium rare (145°F/63°C), 13 minutes for medium (160°F/71°C), 15 minutes for medium well (165°F/74°C), and 16 minutes for well done (170°F/77°C). Remove the steak and set aside to rest for 5 minutes prior to slicing.

5. Slice the pork into ½-in/1-cm portions. Thinly slice the beef against the grain. Serve 1 chicken drumstick or thigh, 2 slices of pork loin, and 2 slices of flank steak. Serve with Hot Pepper Sauce (Molho Apimentado).

Brazilian Mixed Grill

Hot Pepper Sauce (Molho Apimentado)

Makes 32 fl oz/960 mL

1 lb 8 oz/680 g small-dice onions

1 lb 8 oz/680 g small-dice peeled plum tomatoes

¾ oz/21 g chopped parsley

¾ tsp/2.25 g minced garlic

3 fl oz/90 mL vegetable oil

3 fl oz/90 mL red wine vinegar

Malagueta oil or hot pepper sauce, as needed

salt, as needed

ground black pepper, as needed

1. Combine the onions, tomatoes, parsley, and garlic in a small mixing bowl. Mix in the oil and vinegar and season with the hot pepper oil or sauce, salt, and pepper.

2. Cover and chill at least 1 hour prior to service. Adjust seasoning with salt, pepper, and hot pepper oil or sauce, if necessary.

Jerked Game Hens

Makes 10 servings

4 oz/113 g roughly chopped onions

2½ oz/71 g roughly chopped green onions

1 to 2 Scotch bonnets, stems and seeds removed, roughly chopped

4 fl oz/120 mL vegetable oil

2 fl oz/60 mL dark rum

2 fl oz/60 mL soy sauce

1¼ oz/35 g ground allspice

4 tsp/4 g thyme

1 tbsp/6 g ground cinnamon

1½ tsp/7.50 g salt

1½ tsp/3 g ground nutmeg

1 tsp/2 g ground cloves

10 game hens, butterflied

1 oz/28 g coarse salt

1. Combine the onions, green onions, Scotch bonnets, oil, rum, soy sauce, allspice, thyme, cinnamon, salt, nutmeg, and cloves in a blender. Purée to form a smooth, thick paste.

2. Using gloves, rub the jerk seasoning onto both sides of the game hens. Refrigerate, and marinate overnight.

3. Preheat the grill or broiler to 450°F/232°C. Season each hen with ½ tsp/2.50 g of the salt. Cook, presentation side down, for 12 minutes. Reduce the heat, turn the hens over, and cook for another 12 minutes, or until an internal temperature of 180°F/82°C.

4. Serve immediately.

Fillet of Mahi Mahi with Pineapple Jícama Salsa

Makes 10 servings

3 lb 12 oz/1.70 kg mahi mahi fillets, cut into ten 6-oz/170-g servings

1 tbsp/15 g salt

1½ tsp/3 g ground black pepper

2½ fl oz/75 mL lime juice

2½ fl oz/75 mL vegetable oil

20 fl oz/600 mL **Pineapple Jícama Salsa** (recipe follows)

1. Preheat the grill or broiler to 400°F/204°C.

2. Season the fillets with salt, pepper, and lime juice. Brush the fillets lightly with the oil.

3. Place the fish presentation side down on the grill or broiler rods. Grill or broil undisturbed for about 2 minutes. (Optional: Give each piece of fish a quarter turn to achieve grill marks.)

4. Turn the fish over and complete cooking until the flesh is opaque and firm, 3 to 5 minutes.

5. Serve immediately with Pineapple Jícama Salsa.

Pineapple Jícama Salsa

Makes 32 fl oz/960 mL

½ fl oz/15 mL olive oil

1½ fl oz/45 mL lime juice

salt, as needed

ground black pepper, as needed

1 tbsp/3 g chopped cilantro

6 oz/170 g peeled jicama, fine julienne

8 oz/227 g small-dice pineapple

4¼ oz/120 g minced red onions

4½ oz/128 g small-dice red peppers

½ oz/14 g minced jalapeños

1. Mix together the oil, lime juice, salt, pepper, and cilantro.

2. Add the remaining ingredients and toss to coat. Adjust seasoning with salt and pepper.

3. The salsa is ready to serve now, or it may be refrigerated for later use.

Broiled Bluefish à l'Anglaise with Maître d'Hôtel Butter

Makes 10 servings

3 lb 12 oz/1.70 kg bluefish fillets, cut into ten 6-oz/170-g servings

1 tbsp/15 g salt

1½ tsp/3 g ground black pepper

2½ fl oz/75 mL lemon juice

4 oz/113 g butter, melted

1 oz/28 g fresh bread crumbs

10 oz/284 g **Maître d'Hôtel Butter** (page 388), piped or sliced into ten 1-oz/28-g servings

1. Preheat the broiler to 400°F/204°C.

2. Season the fillets with salt, pepper, and lemon juice. Brush the fillets lightly with the butter, dip in the bread crumbs, and gently press down on the surface.

3. Place the fillets on an oiled sizzler platter and broil them until barely cooked through (flesh should be opaque and firm), 3 to 4 minutes.

4. Top each fillet with a serving of the Maître d'Hôtel Butter and pass under a broiler briefly to begin melting the butter. Serve at once.

Broiled Stuffed Lobster

Makes 10 servings

10 (1 lb 8 oz/680 g) lobsters

3½ oz/99 g butter

10 oz/284 g minced onions

5 oz/142 g minced celery

4 oz/113 g minced red peppers

4 oz/113 g minced green peppers

1 tbsp/15 g salt

1½ tsp/3 g ground black pepper

1¼ oz/35 g bread crumbs

1½ fl oz/45 mL dry sherry

2 oz/57 g butter, melted

1. Bring a large pot of salted water to a boil. Add the lobsters and parboil for 7 minutes. Allow the lobsters to cool slightly.

2. Detach the claws from the bodies. Remove the meat from the claws and dice. Reserve. Split the lobster bodies. Remove the coral and tomalley and reserve to add to the stuffing, if desired.

3. Melt the butter in a sauté pan over medium-high heat. Add the onions, celery, and peppers to the pan and cook for 5 to 6 minutes, or until the onions are translucent. Season with salt and pepper and remove from the heat. Add the reserved coral and tomalley, if using, the diced claw meat, bread crumbs, and sherry. Adjust seasoning with salt and pepper, if needed.

4. Spoon the mixture into the body cavity of each lobster. Do not place stuffing mixture over the tail meat. Season the tail meat with salt and pepper and lightly brush with butter.

5. Place the lobsters back on a rack, shell side down, under the broiler until the stuffing begins to crisp and turn golden brown, 5 to 7 minutes.

Broiled Stuffed Lobster

Fish Kebabs

Makes 10 servings

MARINADE

10 fl oz/300 mL sour cream

4 oz/113 g cashew nut paste

3 oz/85 g chickpea flour

2 tsp/4 g ajwain, crushed

½ oz/14 g finely chopped Thai chiles

1 tbsp/6 g ground fennel

salt, as needed

4½ tsp/9 g ground white pepper

1½ fl oz/45 mL lemon juice

1 tsp/3 g ground ginger

1 tbsp/9 g garlic paste

KEBABS

3 lb 12 oz/1.70 kg black cod fillets, cut into 3-in/8-cm cubes

salt, as needed

lemon juice, as needed

2 fl oz/60 mL clarified butter

20 fl oz/600 mL **Mint and Yogurt Chutney** (recipe follows)

1. To make the marinade, combine all the ingredients. Adjust seasoning with salt, pepper, and additional chiles, if necessary.

2. Season the fish with salt and lemon juice. Let it stand for 15 minutes, remove the excess moisture, and place the fish in the marinade. Marinate in the refrigerator for at least 1 hour and up to overnight.

3. Place the fish on a rack on a sheet pan and baste with the butter. Make sure there is sufficient marinade on each piece.

4. Heat the broiler on high and cook the fish for 12 to 15 minutes, or until the top of the fish is dark brown with spots of black.

5. Serve immediately with the Mint and Yogurt Chutney.

Mint and Yogurt Chutney

Makes 32 fl oz/960 mL

5½ oz/156 g cilantro stems and leaves

5½ oz/156 g mint leaves

2 tsp/4 g cumin seeds

16 Thai bird chiles

6 fl oz/180 mL lemon juice

1 oz/28 g sugar

salt, as needed

20 fl oz/600 mL unflavored yogurt, drained

1. Combine the cilantro, mint, cumin, and chiles in a blender and purée until the mixture is smooth. If necessary, add 1 fl oz/30 mL of the lemon juice when blending. The mixture should not be watery (drain if necessary).

2. Combine the herb mixture with the remaining lemon juice, sugar, salt, and yogurt. Adjust seasoning, if necessary. (The chutney should be minty, spicy, sweet, and salty.)

3. The chutney is ready to serve now, or it may be refrigerated for later use.

Standing Rib Roast au Jus

Makes 25 servings

14 lb/6.35 kg beef rib roast, bone-in

1¼ oz/35 g salt

1 tbsp/6 g ground black pepper

1 lb 8 oz/680 g medium-dice **Mirepoix** (page 333)

64 fl oz/1.92 L **Brown Veal Stock** (page 352)

1. Preheat the oven to 350°F/177°C. Season the beef with salt and pepper.

2. Place the beef on a rack in a roasting pan and roast until an internal temperature of 130°F/54°C.

3. Add the mirepoix about 30 minutes before the roast is done and let it brown.

4. Remove the roast from the pan and allow it to rest for 30 minutes.

5. While the roast is resting, place the roasting pan on the range. Clarify the fat and reduce the pan drippings. Degrease as needed. Deglaze the roasting pan with the stock.

6. Slice the beef and serve immediately with the jus.

NOTE

A standard rib roast can range from 14 lb/6.35 kg to as much as 22 lb/9.97 kg.

Beef Wellington

Makes 10 servings

4 to 5 lb/1.81 to 2.27 kg beef tenderloin

1 tbsp/15 g salt

1½ tsp/3 g ground black pepper

2 fl oz/60 mL clarified butter or vegetable oil

8 oz/227 g foie gras pâté

2 oz/57 g finely chopped truffle peelings

1 sheet **Puff Pastry** (page 1110)

3 fl oz/90 mL **Egg Wash** (page 1061)

20 fl oz/600 mL **Madeira Sauce** (recipe follows)

1. Season the tenderloin with salt and pepper. Heat the butter or oil in a large sauté pan over high heat. Sear the tenderloin on all sides and let it cool. Spread the tenderloin with the pâté and sprinkle with the truffles.

2. Roll the dough out to ³⁄₁₆ in/5 mm thick. Place the tenderloin top side down in the center of the dough. Wrap the dough around the tenderloin. Fold the ends under and place the seam on the bottom. Brush with egg wash.

3. Place the beef, seam side down, on an oiled baking sheet in a 400°F/204°C oven. Bake until the puff pastry is lightly browned, about 20 minutes. (Use a convection oven if possible.)

4. Cut into ¾-in/2-cm-thick slices. Serve immediately with the Madeira Sauce on the side.

Madeira Sauce

Makes 32 fl oz/960 mL

40 fl oz/1.20 L **Jus de Veau Lié** (page 382) or **Demi-Glace** (page 383)

12 fl oz/360 mL Madeira

salt, as needed

ground black pepper, as needed

4 oz/113 g butter, medium dice

1. Bring the lié or demi-glace to a simmer and reduce by half over medium heat.

2. Add the Madeira and simmer for 2 to 3 minutes more, or until the sauce has a good flavor and consistency. Season with salt and pepper.

3. Whisk in the butter over low heat just before serving.

Corned Beef Hash

Makes 10 servings

2 fl oz/60 mL vegetable oil or bacon fat

8 oz/227 g large-dice onions

5 oz/142 g large-dice parsnips

3 oz/85 g large-dice carrots

1 lb 8 oz/680 g red skin potatoes, peeled if desired

2 lb/907 g corned beef, cooked, cut into 1-in/3-cm dice

1½ fl oz/45 mL tomato purée

salt, as needed

ground black pepper, as needed

1. Heat a roasting pan over medium heat. Add 1 fl oz/30 mL of the oil or fat to the pan. Add the onions and sweat until they are soft, 5 to 6 minutes. Add the parsnips, carrots, potatoes, and corned beef to the pan and cover with foil.

2. Place the pan in a 375°F/191°C oven and roast for about 1 hour. Remove the foil, stir in the tomato purée, and return the pan to the oven uncovered. Cook until the tomato purée has browned, about 15 minutes. Season with salt and pepper. Cool slightly.

3. Grind the mixture through a medium grinding plate of a meat grinder. Form into patties (2 to 3 oz/57 to 85 g each) by hand or using a circular mold. Refrigerate until service.

4. Heat 1 fl oz/30 mL of the oil in a heavy sauté pan or griddle. Cook the patties until they are crispy on each side and hot in the center. Work in batches if necessary. Serve immediately.

Veal Shoulder Poêlé

Makes 10 servings

4 lb/1.81 kg veal shoulder, boneless

1½ tsp/7.50 g salt

1 tsp/2 g ground black pepper

¼ tsp/0.25 g finely chopped rosemary

½ tsp/0.50 g finely chopped basil

½ tsp/0.50 g finely chopped thyme

½ tsp/0.50 g finely chopped marjoram

2 garlic cloves, minced

2 fl oz/60 mL clarified butter

2 oz/57 g diced slab bacon or smoked ham

8 oz/227 g small-dice **Mirepoix** (page 333)

1 oz/28 g tomato paste (optional)

8 fl oz/240 mL white wine

2 bay leaves

8 fl oz/240 mL **Brown Veal Stock** (page 352)

1 tsp/3 g cornstarch, diluted in water or stock to make a slurry

1. Butterfly the veal and season it with salt and pepper. Mix the herbs and garlic together and spread this mixture evenly over the inside of the veal. Roll and tie the veal roast.

2. Prepare the matignon: Heat the butter over medium heat. Add the bacon or ham and cook for 1 or 2 minutes. Add the mirepoix; cook until a light golden brown, 10 to 12 minutes. Add the tomato paste, if desired, and cook briefly.

3. Place the veal on top of the matignon and baste with some additional butter.

4. Cover the pan and poêlé in a 300°F/149°C oven, basting every 20 minutes for about 1 hour. Remove the lid for the last 30 minutes to allow the veal to brown.

5. Check for doneness: The meat should be tender when pierced with a fork. When done, remove the veal and keep warm.

6. Add the wine, bay leaves, and stock to the pan and simmer for 20 minutes. Degrease if necessary.

7. Thicken with the slurry and reduce, if necessary. Adjust seasoning with salt and pepper.

8. Carve the veal into portions and serve with the sauce.

Pork Roast with Jus Lié

Makes 10 servings

4 lb 8 oz/2.04 kg bone-in pork loin roast

½ oz/14 g minced garlic

1 tsp/1 g minced rosemary

1 tbsp/15 g salt

1½ tsp/3 g ground black pepper

JUS LIÉ

8 oz/227 g small-dice **Mirepoix** (page 333)

4 fl oz/120 mL dry white wine

1 fl oz/30 mL tomato paste

32 fl oz/960 mL **Brown Veal Stock** (page 352)

2 thyme sprigs

1 bay leaf

1 fl oz/30 mL arrowroot slurry, or as needed

1. Trim the pork loin and tie. Rub the roast with the garlic, rosemary, salt, and pepper. Place the pork loin on a rack in a roasting pan.

2. Roast at 375°F/191°C for 1 hour, basting from time to time. Scatter the mirepoix around the pork and continue to roast another 30 to 45 minutes or until a thermometer inserted in the center of the meat registers 160°F/71°C.

3. Remove the pork from the roasting pan and allow it to rest for 20 minutes before carving.

4. To prepare the jus lié: Place the roasting pan on the stovetop and cook until the mirepoix is browned and the fat is clear. Pour off all the fat. Deglaze with the wine. Add the tomato paste and cook, stirring frequently, until it has a sweet aroma and brick red color, 30 to 45 seconds.

5. Add the stock, stirring to release the fond completely. Add the thyme and bay leaf, and simmer the jus for 20 to 30 minutes, or until it reaches the proper consistency and flavor. Add slurry to thicken the sauce enough to coat the back of a spoon. Degrease and adjust seasoning with salt and pepper.

6. Strain the jus lié through a fine-mesh sieve and keep it hot for service. Carve the pork loin into portions and serve immediately with the jus lié.

Baked Stuffed Pork Chops

Makes 10 servings

10 (8 to 10 oz/227 to 284 g) center-cut pork chops, 1½ in/4 cm thick

STUFFING

2 oz/57 g vegetable oil

4 oz/113 g minced onions

3 oz/85 g minced celery

2 tsp/6 g minced garlic

1 lb 8 oz/680 g dried bread crumbs

1 tbsp/3 g chopped parsley

1 tsp/1 g rubbed sage

2 tsp/10 g salt

1 tsp/2 g ground black pepper

6 fl oz/180 mL **Chicken Stock** (page 351), or as needed

24 fl oz/720 mL **Demi-Glace** (page 383)

1. Cut a pocket in each pork chop and refrigerate until the stuffing is properly prepared and cooled.

2. Heat half of the oil in a pan over medium heat. Add the onions and cook until golden brown, 8 to 10 minutes. Add the celery and garlic and cook until the celery is limp, another 8 to 10 minutes. Remove from the pan, spread out on a sheet pan, and allow to cool completely.

3. Combine the onion mixture with the bread crumbs, parsley, and sage. Season with salt and pepper. Add enough of the stock to make a stuffing that is moist but not wet. Chill the stuffing until it is 40°F/4°C.

4. Divide the mixture into 10 equal portions and place 1 portion into the cavity of each pork chop. Secure the chops by closing with skewers.

5. Season the chops with salt and pepper. Heat the remaining oil in a sauté pan over high heat. Sear the pork chops until golden brown on both sides. Transfer to a sheet pan and finish cooking in a 350°F/177°C oven to an internal temperature of 160°F/71°C.

6. Pour off any excess oil from the sauté pan. Add the demi-glace and bring to a simmer. Degrease the sauce if necessary. Adjust seasoning with salt and pepper.

7. Serve the stuffed pork chops with the sauce.

Cantonese Roast Pork (Char Sieu)

Makes 10 servings

4 lb/1.81 kg boneless pork butt

BRINE

1 gal/3.84 L water

4 oz/113 g salt

4 oz/113 g brown sugar

1 orange, peel only

1 cinnamon stick

1 tbsp/6 g black peppercorns

1 tbsp/6 g Szechwan peppercorns

3 star anise pods

½ oz/14 g ginger, crushed

10 dried Chinese chiles

1 bunch green onions, bruised

MARINADE

2 tsp/6 g minced garlic

1 tsp/3 g **Chinese Five-Spice Powder** (page 462)

1½ oz/43 g brown sugar

1 fl oz/30 mL mushroom soy sauce

4 tsp/20 mL hoisin sauce

½ fl oz/15 mL brown bean paste

1 tsp/5 mL sesame oil

2 fl oz/60 mL Chinese rice wine (Shaoxing)

3 fl oz/90 mL **Chicken Stock** (page 351) or **Brown Pork Stock** (page 352)

5 oz/142 g sliced green onions

1. Cut the pork into rectangles (3 by 3 by 8 in/8 by 8 by 20 cm).

2. Bring the water for the brine to a boil and add all the brine ingredients. Stir to dissolve the sugar and salt. Allow the brine to cool to room temperature.

3. Place the pork in the cool brine, cover, and refrigerate overnight.

4. The next day, remove the pork from the brine, pat dry, and discard the brine.

5. To make the marinade, combine all the ingredients. Pour the marinade over the pork, massage it into the meat, cover, and refrigerate overnight, turning the meat occasionally.

6. On the third day, remove the pork from the marinade and wipe off excess (reserve excess marinade for glazing). Place the pork in a roasting pan on a wire rack.

7. Fill a pan with water, place it in the oven, and heat the oven to 325°F/163°C.

8. Place the pork in the oven and roast, glazing every 30 minutes with the reserved marinade, until it reaches an internal temperature of 150°F/66°C, about 1½ hours.

9. Remove the pork from the oven and allow it to rest for 5 minutes before slicing. Serve garnished with green onions or chop and use to fill pork buns.

Guava-Glazed Pork Ribs

Makes 10 servings

MARINADE

8 oz/227 g chopped onions

2 oz/57 g chopped cilantro

2 oz/57 g chopped oregano

½ oz/14 g ground cumin

16 fl oz/480 mL red wine vinegar

10 garlic cloves

2 tsp/4 g ground black pepper

24 fl oz/720 mL water

13 lb/5.90 kg pork baby back ribs

24 fl oz/720 mL **Guava Barbecue Sauce** (recipe follows)

1. To make the marinade, combine all the ingredients and purée in a blender.

2. Place the ribs in a large, nonreactive container and coat with the marinade. Marinate overnight in the refrigerator.

3. Transfer the ribs and marinade to a rondeau or kettle and simmer for 30 minutes. Drain the liquid and allow the ribs to cool.

4. Heat the oven to 350°/177°C. Place the ribs on roasting racks on sheet pans.

5. Roast the ribs for 20 to 25 minutes. Brush the barbecue sauce on both sides of the ribs and bake for an additional 8 to 10 minutes. Brush the ribs with sauce again, turn, and cook the ribs for 8 to 10 minutes more, until they are well glazed.

6. Serve immediately.

Guava Barbecue Sauce

Makes 32 fl oz/960 mL

12 oz/340 g guava marmalade

2 oz/57 g tomato paste

1 oz/28 g molasses

1 oz/28 g dry mustard

1 tbsp/6 g ground cumin

¾ oz/21 g minced garlic

4 fl oz/120 mL dry sherry

1 Scotch bonnet, minced

8 fl oz/240 mL water

salt, as needed

ground black pepper, as needed

4 fl oz/120 mL lime juice

1. In a medium saucepan, combine the marmalade, tomato paste, molasses, mustard, cumin, garlic, sherry, Scotch bonnet, and water. Season with salt and pepper.

2. Simmer the sauce for 30 minutes. Remove it from the heat and set aside to cool. Add the lime juice when the sauce has cooled.

3. The sauce is ready to use now, or it may be refrigerated for later use.

Carolina Barbecue with coleslaw

Carolina Barbecue

Makes 10 servings

12 lb/5.44 kg pork butt

1 oz/28 g salt

½ oz/14 g ground black pepper

10 sandwich buns, split and toasted

10 fl oz/300 mL **North Carolina Piedmont Sauce** (recipe follows)

10 fl oz/300 mL **Barbecue Sauce** (North Carolina Western Sauce; recipe follows)

10 fl oz/300 mL **Mustard Barbecue Sauce** (North Carolina Eastern Low Country Sauce; recipe follows)

1. Season the pork butt with salt and pepper. Roast in a 300°F/149°C oven until tender, about 5 hours.

2. Remove the pork from the oven and allow it to cool slightly. When cool enough to handle, shred or chop the pork.

3. For each portion, serve about 6 oz/170 g of the pork on a toasted bun with the sauces on the side.

North Carolina Piedmont Sauce

Makes 32 fl oz/960 mL

15 fl oz/450 mL white vinegar

15 fl oz/450 mL cider vinegar

3½ tsp/7 g red pepper flakes

1½ fl oz/45 mL Tabasco sauce

1¾ oz/50 g sugar

4 tsp/8 g cracked black peppercorns

1. Combine all the ingredients and mix well.

2. The sauce is ready to use now, or it may be refrigerated for later use.

Barbecue Sauce (North Carolina Western Sauce)

Makes 32 fl oz/960 mL

1½ oz/43 g brown sugar

4½ tsp/9 g paprika

4½ tsp/9 g chili powder

4½ tsp/9 g dry mustard

1 tsp/5 g salt

¾ tsp/1.50 g cayenne

1 fl oz/30 mL Worcestershire sauce

6 fl oz/240 mL white vinegar

24 fl oz/720 mL ketchup

2 fl oz/60 mL water

1. Combine all the ingredients and mix well. Adjust seasoning with salt and cayenne, if necessary.

2. The sauce is ready to use now, or it may be refrigerated for later use.

Mustard Barbecue Sauce (North Carolina Eastern Low Country Sauce)

Makes 32 fl oz/960 mL

1 fl oz/30 mL vegetable oil

1 lb/454 g chopped onions

1½ oz/43 g minced garlic

16 fl oz/480 mL white vinegar

11 fl oz/330 mL spicy brown mustard

2 tsp/4 g celery seed

3½ oz/99 g sugar

salt, as needed

ground black pepper, as needed

1. Heat the oil in a saucepan over medium heat. Add the onions and sauté until translucent, about 4 minutes. Add the garlic and cook until aromatic, about 1 minute.

2. Add the remaining ingredients and bring the mixture to a simmer to melt the sugar. Remove the pan from the heat and allow the flavors to blend, about 30 minutes. Adjust seasoning with salt and pepper.

3. The sauce is ready to use now, or it may be refrigerated for later use.

Lacquer-Roasted Pork Ribs (Kao Paigu)

Makes 10 servings

1½ fl oz/45 mL dark soy sauce

1½ fl oz/45 mL sherry

5 pork sparerib racks, trimmed

MARINADE

8 fl oz/240 mL hoisin sauce

6 fl oz/180 mL black bean sauce

12 fl oz/360 mL ketchup

1 tbsp/9 g minced garlic

2 tsp/6 g minced ginger

1 tsp/2 g ground white pepper

½ oz/14 g thinly sliced green onions

2 fl oz/60 mL Chinese rice wine (Shaoxing)

1 fl oz/30 mL sesame oil

1 tbsp/15 g salt

3½ oz/99 g sugar

LACQUER COATING

4 fl oz/120 mL honey

½ fl oz/15 mL sesame oil

1. Combine the soy sauce and sherry and brush the mixture on the ribs.

2. Combine all the ingredients for the marinade. Pour it over the ribs, massage it into the meat, cover, and refrigerate overnight, turning occasionally.

3. Remove the ribs from the marinade and wipe off excess. Place the ribs in a roasting pan on a wire rack.

4. Fill a pan with water, place it in the oven, and heat the oven to 325°F/163°C.

5. Place the ribs in the oven and roast until they reach an internal temperature of 150°F/66°C, about 1½ hours.

6. To make the lacquer coating, combine the honey and sesame oil. During the last 20 minutes of roasting, brush the ribs with the mixture.

7. Remove the ribs from the oven and allow them to rest for 10 minutes. Cut the racks in half, or into individual ribs, before serving.

Roast Rack of Lamb Persillé

Makes 8 servings

2 (2 lb/907 g) frenched racks of lamb

1 fl oz/30 mL vegetable oil

1 tbsp/15 g salt

1½ tsp/3 g ground black pepper

1 tsp/1 g chopped rosemary

1 tsp/1 g chopped thyme

10 oz/284 g diced **Mirepoix** (page 333)

40 fl oz/1.20 L **Brown Lamb or Brown Veal Stock** (page 352)

12 oz/340 g **Persillade** (recipe follows)

1. Lightly brush the racks of lamb with oil, season with salt and pepper, and rub with the chopped rosemary and thyme.

2. Place the lamb on a rack in a roasting pan.

3. Roast at 400°F/204°C for 15 minutes, basting periodically with rendered juices and fat. Scatter the mirepoix around the lamb, reduce the heat to 325°F/163°C, and continue to roast to the desired internal doneness.

4. To make the jus: Place the roasting pan on the stovetop, and cook until the mirepoix is browned and the fat is clear. Pour off all the fat. Add the stock, stirring to release the fond completely. Simmer for 20 to 30 minutes, or until it reaches the proper consistency and flavor. Degrease and adjust seasoning with salt and pepper. Strain through a fine-mesh sieve and keep warm.

5. Transfer the lamb to a sheet pan and spread half of the persillade on top of each rack of lamb. Return the lamb to the oven until the persillade is lightly browned.

6. Cut the lamb into chops and serve with the sauce.

Persillade

Makes 12 oz/340 g

5 oz/142 g fresh bread crumbs

2 tsp/6 g garlic, mashed to a paste

1¼ oz/35 g minced parsley

3½ oz/99 g butter, melted

2 tsp/10 g salt

1. Mix all the ingredients together to make an evenly moistened mixture.

2. Place in a tightly sealed container and refrigerate or use as needed.

Roasted Shoulder of Lamb and Couscous (Mechoui)

Makes 10 servings

1 lb/454 g butter, soft

2 oz/57 g garlic, mashed to a paste with a pinch of salt

¾ oz/21 g chopped parsley

¾ oz/21 g chopped cilantro

1 tbsp/6 g dried thyme

1 tbsp/6 g ground cumin

1 tbsp/6 g ground paprika

10 lb/4.54 kg lamb shoulder, square cut, excess fat and silverskin removed

1 oz/28 g salt

1 tbsp/6 g ground black pepper

4 fl oz/120 mL extra-virgin olive oil, or as needed

8 fl oz/240 mL water, or as needed

1 tbsp/9 g cornstarch, mixed with ½ fl oz/15 mL of water to make a slurry

3 lb/1.36 kg **Couscous** (page 861)

CONDIMENT

1 tbsp/15 g coarse salt

1 tbsp/6 g ground cumin

1 tsp/2 g ground black pepper

1. Preheat the oven to 350°F/177°C.

2. Mix the butter with the garlic, parsley, cilantro, thyme, cumin, and paprika.

3. Season the lamb with about 1 tsp/5 g of the salt and ¼ tsp/0.50 g of the pepper. Coat the lamb with the seasoned butter.

4. Place the lamb on a rack in a roasting pan. Add enough of the oil and water to cover the bottom of the pan, but not touch the lamb. (The amount needed will depend on the size of pan used.)

5. Roast uncovered in a 350°F/177°C oven, basting every 15 minutes, until a deep caramel color develops, about 45 minutes.

6. Cover the lamb and continue to cook until the meat is extremely tender, 2 to 3 hours. Check the water/oil level every 30 minutes.

7. Remove the meat and keep it warm.

8. Degrease the liquid in the pan. Gradually add the slurry, whisking constantly. Adjust seasoning with salt and pepper.

9. Thinly slice the lamb and serve immediately with the couscous and condiment mix.

Roasted Shoulder of Lamb and Couscous (*Mechoui*) and
Moroccan Carrot Salad (page 953)

Roast Leg of Lamb Boulangère

Makes 10 servings

9 lb/4.08 kg leg of lamb, bone-in

1¼ oz/35 g salt

1 tbsp/6 g ground black pepper

1 oz/28 g slivered garlic

2 lb 8 oz/1.13 kg russet potatoes, sliced ⅛ in/3 mm thick

8 oz/227 g thinly sliced onions

12 fl oz/360 mL **Brown Lamb or Brown Veal Stock** (page 352), **or as needed**

20 fl oz/600 mL **Jus de Veau Lié** (page 382) or **Demi-Glace** (page 383)

1. Preheat the oven to 400°F/204°C. Season the lamb with some of the salt and pepper and stud it with the slivered garlic.

2. Place the lamb on a rack in a roasting pan. Roast it at 400°F/204°C for 1 hour, basting from time to time. Remove the lamb from the pan and pour off the grease.

3. Layer the sliced potatoes and onions in the roasting pan. Season the layers with the remaining salt and pepper. Add enough stock to moisten well.

4. Place the lamb on the potatoes. Continue to roast until the desired doneness, another 30 to 45 minutes, or until a thermometer inserted into the center registers 135°F/57°C for rare, 145°F/63°C for medium rare, 160°F/71°C for medium, 165°F/74°C for medium well, and 170°F/77°C for well done. The potatoes should be tender.

5. Remove the lamb from the oven and allow it to rest before carving.

6. Heat the jus de veau lié or demi-glace over medium heat while the lamb rests.

7. Carve the lamb into slices. For each portion, place 3 oz/85 g of potatoes and onions on a heated plate. Top with 6 oz/170 g of roasted lamb and ladle 2 fl oz/60 mL of sauce over the lamb. Serve at once.

NOTE
Leg of lamb will range from 9 to 12 lb/4.08 to 5.44 kg and can yield from 10 to 15 servings.

Roast Leg of Lamb with Haricots Blanc (Gigots à la Bretonne)

Makes 10 servings

HARICOTS BLANC

1 lb 8 oz/680 g dried haricots blancs

½ fl oz/30 mL olive oil

12 oz/340 g chopped onions

¾ oz/21 g chopped garlic

2 bay leaves

2 parsley sprigs

1 tbsp/15 g salt

1½ tsp/3 g ground black pepper

1 oz/28 g butter

1 lb 8 oz/680 g peeled, seeded, and medium-diced tomatoes

½ tsp/0.50 g thyme

LAMB

9 lb/4.08 kg leg of lamb, bone-in

½ oz/14 g slivered garlic

½ fl oz/15 mL olive oil

1 tbsp/15 g salt

1½ tsp/3 g ground black pepper

6 fl oz/180 mL boiling water

4 fl oz/120 mL dry white wine

1. Sort the beans and rinse well with cold water. Soak the beans using the long or short soak method (see page 807). Drain the soaked beans.

2. Cover the beans with water in a large soup pot and bring to a boil; skim off all the scum that rises to the top, remove from the heat and drain. In the same pot, heat the oil and add 4 oz/113 g of the chopped onions and 2 tsp/6 g of the chopped garlic. Cook over low heat until the onions begin to soften. Return the beans to the pot and add enough cold water to cover by 2 in/5 cm. Bring to a boil, add the bay leaves and parsley sprigs, cover, and simmer for 45 minutes.

3. Add the salt, and an additional 2 tsp/6 g of the chopped garlic. Cover and continue to cook for another 30 minutes or until the beans are tender but not mushy. Remove the bay leaves and parsley sprigs and adjust seasoning with salt and pepper as needed. Set aside.

4. While the beans are cooking, heat the butter in a heavy-bottomed skillet and add the remaining onions and chopped garlic. Sauté over low heat for 5 to 10 minutes, stirring until golden. Stir in the tomatoes and thyme. Cook over medium heat, stirring from time to time, for 15 minutes. Adjust seasoning with salt and pepper, and add this mixture to the beans.

5. For the lamb: Preheat the oven to 400°F/204°C. Make some incisions into the leg and slip in the slivers of garlic, rub with the oil and season with salt and pepper.

6. Sear the lamb on all sides in a roasting pan and place in the preheated oven. After the first 15 minutes, add the boiling water to the roasting pan; from time to time, baste the legs with the liquid. Roast for 1 hour or until the thermometer reads 120° to 125°F/49° to 52°C. Remove the lamb from the roasting pan and let it rest in a warm spot.

7. Degrease the roasting pan and deglaze with the white wine, reduce by half, and stir the pan juices into the beans.

8. Slice the lamb and serve it on a bed of the beans.

NOTE
Leg of lamb will range from 9 to 12 lb/4.08 to 5.44 kg and can yield from 10 to 15 servings.

Roast Leg of Lamb with Mint Sauce

Makes 10 servings

6 lb/2.72 kg boneless leg of lamb

¾ oz/21 g **Salt Herbs** (recipe follows)

½ oz/14 g minced garlic

2 fl oz/60 mL vegetable oil, or as needed

4 oz/113 g medium-dice **Mirepoix** (page 333)

MINT SAUCE

24 fl oz/720 mL **Demi-Glace** (page 383)

2 oz/57 g mint stems or sprigs

1 tbsp/15 g salt

1½ tsp/3 g ground black pepper

1 oz/28 g mint chiffonade

1. Rub the lamb on all sides with the salt herbs and garlic and marinate in the refrigerator overnight.

2. Roll and tie the roast. Rub it with oil and place it on a rack in a roasting pan.

3. Roast at 350°F/177°C for 45 minutes, basting from time to time. Scatter the mirepoix around the lamb and continue to roast another 30 to 40 minutes, or until a thermometer inserted in the center of the meat registers 135°F/57°C for rare, 145°F/63°C for medium rare, 160°F/71°C for medium, 165°F/74°C for medium well, or 170°F/77°C for well done. Remove the lamb from the roasting pan and allow it to rest.

4. To make the mint sauce: Place the roasting pan on the stovetop and cook until the mirepoix is browned and the fat is clear. Pour off all the fat. Add the demi-glace, stirring to release the fond completely. Add the mint stems and simmer for 20 to 30 minutes, or until the sauce reaches the proper consistency and flavor. Degrease and season with salt and pepper. Strain through a fine-mesh sieve. Finish with mint chiffonade.

5. Carve the lamb into portions and serve it with the mint sauce.

Salt Herbs

Makes 2 oz/57 g

1¼ oz/35 g salt

4 tsp/4 g rosemary leaves

4 tsp/4 g thyme leaves

6 bay leaves

1 tsp/2 g black peppercorns

1. Combine all the ingredients in a clean spice grinder and grind to a medium-fine powder.

2. Put them in an airtight container and let the salt herbs rest for 12 hours before using.

Roast Chicken with Pan Gravy

Makes 10 servings

5 (2 lb 8 oz/1.13 kg) chickens, wing tips removed and reserved

2 oz/57 g salt

4 tsp/8 g ground white pepper

5 thyme sprigs

5 rosemary sprigs

5 bay leaves

5 fl oz/150 mL clarified butter or vegetable oil

12 oz/340 g medium-dice **Mirepoix** (page 333)

2 oz/57 g all-purpose flour

40 fl oz/1.20 L **Chicken Stock** (page 351), hot

1. Season the cavity of each chicken with salt and pepper. Place 1 sprig each of thyme and rosemary and 1 bay leaf inside each cavity.

2. Rub the skin of the chickens with butter or oil and truss each chicken with twine.

3. Place chickens, breast side up, on a rack in a roasting pan. Scatter the wing tips in the pan.

4. Roast at 400°F/204°C for 40 minutes, basting from time to time. Scatter the mirepoix around the chicken and continue to roast another 30 to 40 minutes, until the thigh meat registers an internal temperature of 180°F/82°C.

5. Remove the chickens from the roasting pan and allow them to rest.

6. Place the roasting pan on the stovetop and cook until the mirepoix is browned and the fat is clear. Pour off all but 1½ fl oz/45 mL of the fat.

7. Add the flour and cook the roux for 4 to 5 minutes. Whisk in the stock until completely smooth.

8. Simmer the gravy for 20 to 30 minutes, or until it reaches the proper consistency and flavor. Degrease and adjust seasoning with salt and pepper. Strain through a fine-mesh sieve.

9. Cut the chickens in half and serve them immediately with the pan gravy.

Chicken Legs with Duxelles Stuffing

Makes 10 servings

10 (6 oz/170 g) chicken legs

DUXELLES STUFFING

6 oz/170 g minced shallots

2 oz/57 g butter

2 lb/907 g small-dice mushrooms

1 tbsp/15 g salt

2 tsp/4 g ground black pepper

8 fl oz/240 mL heavy cream, reduced

8 oz/227 g fresh bread crumbs

1 tbsp/9 g chopped parsley

2 oz/57 g butter, melted

20 fl oz/600 mL **Suprême Sauce** (page 383)

1. Bone out the chicken legs. Lay the meat between sheets of parchment paper or plastic wrap. Pound the legs flat with a mallet. Refrigerate until needed.

2. To make the duxelles stuffing, sweat the shallots in the butter over medium-high heat until translucent, 2 to 3 minutes. Add the mushrooms and sauté them until dry to create a duxelles. Season the duxelles with some of the salt and pepper.

3. Add the cream, bread crumbs, and parsley and mix well. If desired, the duxelles can be chilled now and reserved for later use.

4. Season the chicken legs with the remaining salt and pepper. Portion 3 oz/85 g of the duxelles onto each chicken leg. Fold the meat over the stuffing and place the stuffed legs on a rack in a roasting pan with the seam side down.

5. Brush the chicken legs with the butter. Bake in a 375°F/191°C oven, basting occasionally, until a thermometer inserted in the center of the legs reaches a temperature of 180°F/82°C, 25 to 30 minutes. The chicken legs should be a light golden brown.

6. Serve each chicken leg with 2 fl oz/60 mL of the sauce on a heated plate.

Pan-Smoked Chicken

Makes 10 servings

10 (6 oz/170 g) chicken breasts

½ tsp/2.50 g salt

¼ tsp/0.50 g ground black pepper

MARINADE

8 fl oz/240 mL apple cider

2 fl oz/60 mL apple cider vinegar

½ oz/14 g minced shallots

2 tsp/6 g minced garlic

1. Rinse the chicken, pat dry, season with salt and pepper, and place in a shallow hotel pan.

2. Combine the ingredients for the marinade and pour over the chicken, turning to coat evenly. Marinate, covered, in the refrigerator for 3 hours or up to overnight.

3. Place the chicken on a rack in a pan over lightly dampened hardwood chips. Cover tightly and heat in a 450°F/232°C oven until the smell of smoke is apparent, 6 to 8 minutes. Smoke for 3 minutes from that point. Transfer the chicken to a baking pan and finish baking (without smoke) in a 350°F/177°C oven until cooked through (165°F/74°C), 10 to 12 minutes more.

4. Serve immediately or cool and refrigerate until needed.

Breast of Rock Cornish Game Hen with Mushroom Forcemeat

Makes 10 servings

10 (1 lb 4 oz/567 g) Rock Cornish game hens

1 tbsp/15 g salt

1½ tsp/3 g ground black pepper

2 lb 12 oz/1.25 kg **Mushroom Forcemeat** (recipe follows)

1 fl oz/30 mL clarified butter

20 fl oz/600 mL **Madeira Sauce** (page 544)

1. Remove the breasts from the hens. Make them into suprêmes and remove and reserve the leg and thigh meat to prepare the Mushroom Forcemeat stuffing. Refrigerate until needed.

2. Loosen the skin from the breast meat. Season the breasts on all sides with salt and pepper. Pipe about 2 oz/57 g of the forcemeat between the skin and meat of each breast. Smooth the surface to spread the forcemeat evenly.

3. Place the stuffed breasts in a baking dish. Brush lightly with butter. Bake in a preheated 350°F/177°C oven for 20 to 25 minutes or to an internal temperature of 165°F/74°C. Baste with additional butter or any pan juices during baking time.

4. Heat the Madeira Sauce and serve 2 fl oz/60 mL with each breast (2 suprêmes). (Optional: Slice each breast on a slight diagonal into 4 slices and fan the slices out on a warm plate.)

Mushroom Forcemeat

Makes 2 lb 12 oz/1.25 kg

12 oz/340 g Rock Cornish game hens, leg and thigh meat only, small dice (see Note)

2 tsp/10 g salt

½ tsp/1 g ground black pepper

2½ oz/71 g minced bacon

1 oz/28 g butter

1 oz/28 g minced shallots

1 garlic clove, minced

10 oz/284 g minced white mushrooms

10 oz/284 g minced morels

1 thyme sprig

1 bay leaf

4 sage leaves

4 fl oz/120 mL Madeira

1 egg

5 fl oz/150 mL heavy cream

1. Season the meat with salt and pepper and refrigerate until needed.

2. Place the bacon and butter in a sauté pan over medium heat. Render the bacon until crisp. Add the shallots and garlic and sauté until aromatic. Add all the mushrooms and sweat until barely tender. Add the thyme, bay leaf, sage, and Madeira. Reduce until thickened. Remove and discard the bay leaf, thyme, and sage. Adjust seasoning with salt and pepper. Chill the mixture to below 40°F/4°C.

3. Process the diced meat and egg to a paste in a food processor, scraping down the bowl periodically. Add the cream and pulse the machine on and off until the cream is just incorporated. Transfer to a bowl. Fold in the cooled mushroom mixture. Hold chilled until ready to use.

NOTE
This forcemeat can be prepared using any lean diced poultry meat to replace the leg and thigh meat from the Cornish game hen.

Roast Duckling with Sauce Bigarade

Makes 10 servings

5 (5 lb 8 oz/2.50 kg) ducklings

½ oz/14 g salt

1 tsp/2 g ground black pepper

25 parsley stems

5 thyme sprigs

5 bay leaves

8 fl oz/240 mL **Brown Veal Stock** (page 352)

SAUCE BIGARADE

¾ oz/21 g sugar

½ fl oz/15 mL water

1 fl oz/30 mL white wine

1 fl oz/30 mL cider vinegar

3 fl oz/90 mL blood orange juice

32 fl oz/960 mL **Demi-Glace** (page 383)

16 fl oz/480 mL **Brown Veal Stock** (page 352)

salt, as needed

ground black pepper, as needed

1 blood orange

1. Rinse and trim the ducklings, removing the fat from the body cavity (reserve for other use if desired). Place the ducklings, breast side up, on a rack in a roasting pan. Season them with salt and pepper. Place 5 parsley stems, 1 thyme sprig, and 1 bay leaf into the cavity of each bird.

2. Roast the duckling at 425°F/218°C until the juices run barely pink and the thigh meat registers 180°F/82°C, about 1 hour. Remove the ducklings from the pan and rest for at least 10 minutes before carving.

3. Degrease and deglaze the pan with 8 fl oz/240 mL stock. Strain and reserve the drippings.

4. While the duck is roasting, combine the sugar and water in a saucepan. Cook the mixture over medium heat until it melts and caramelizes to a deep golden brown, about 1 minute.

5. Add the wine, vinegar, and blood orange juice. Mix them well and simmer over medium-high heat until reduced by half, about 1 minute. Stir to dissolve any lumps.

6. Add the demi-glace and 16 fl oz/480 mL stock and bring the sauce to a boil. Add the reserved pan drippings. Reduce the heat and simmer over medium heat until a good flavor and consistency develops, about 15 minutes. Season with salt and pepper. Strain the sauce through cheesecloth and reserve warm.

7. Remove the zest from the blood orange, cut it into julienne, and blanch. Cut the flesh of the orange into suprêmes.

8. Carve the duck for service by cutting away the breast from the rib and cutting the leg away from the body. Place the duck on a sizzler platter, overlapping the leg and breast portions, skin side facing up. Brush the duckling with a small amount of the sauce and reheat it in a 450°F/232°C oven, until it is crisp, about 5 minutes.

9. Pool 2 fl oz/60 mL of the sauce on each plate and place the duckling on the sauce. Garnish with the blanched orange zest and orange segments.

Roast Turkey with Pan Gravy and Chestnut Stuffing

Makes 10 servings

13 lb/5.90 kg whole turkey

1 tbsp/15 g salt

1 tsp/2 g ground black pepper

2 onions, peeled and quartered

12 to 15 parsley stems

5 fl oz/150 mL clarified butter or vegetable oil

12 oz/340 g medium-dice **Mirepoix** (page 333)

2 oz/57 g all-purpose flour

40 fl oz/1.20 L **Chicken Stock** (page 351), hot

2 lb 12 oz/1.25 kg **Chestnut Stuffing** (recipe follows)

1. Season the cavity of the turkey with salt and pepper. Place the quartered onions and parsley stems inside the cavity.

2. Rub the skin of the turkey with butter or oil and truss with twine.

3. Place the turkey, breast side up, on a rack in a roasting pan.

4. Roast at 350°F/177°C for 3 hours, basting from time to time. Scatter the mirepoix around the turkey and continue to roast another 30 to 40 minutes, until the thigh meat registers an internal temperature of 180°F/82°C.

5. Remove the turkey from the roasting pan and allow it to rest.

6. Place the roasting pan on the stovetop and cook until the mirepoix is browned and the fat is clear. Pour off all but 1 fl oz/30 mL of the fat.

7. Add the flour and cook the roux for 4 to 5 minutes. Whisk in the stock until completely smooth.

8. Simmer the gravy for 20 to 30 minutes, or until it reaches the proper consistency and flavor. Degrease and adjust seasoning with salt and pepper. Strain through a fine-mesh sieve. Carve the turkey in portions and serve it with the pan gravy and Chestnut Stuffing.

Chestnut Stuffing

Makes 2 lb 12 oz/ 1.25 kg

4 oz/113 g minced onions

4 oz/113 g bacon fat or butter

1 lb 8 oz/680 g cubed day-old bread

8 fl oz/240 mL **Chicken Stock** (page 351), hot

1 egg

2 tbsp/6 g chopped parsley

1 tsp/1 g chopped sage

8 oz/227 g peeled roasted chestnuts, chopped

1 tsp/5 g salt

½ tsp/1 g ground black pepper

1. Sauté the onions in the bacon fat or butter until they are tender.

2. Combine the bread, stock, and egg and add to the onions.

3. Add the parsley, sage, chestnuts, salt, and pepper. Mix well.

4. Place the stuffing in a buttered hotel pan and cover it with parchment paper. Bake the stuffing at 350°F/177°C for 45 minutes. Serve immediately.

Salmon Fillet with Smoked Salmon and Horseradish Crust

Makes 10 servings

3 lb 12 oz/1.70 kg salmon fillets, cut into ten 6-oz/170-g portions

2 fl oz/60 mL lime juice

2 tsp/6 g minced shallots

2 tsp/6 g minced garlic

2 tsp/4 g crushed black peppercorns

CRUMB MIXTURE

1½ tsp/4.50 g minced shallots

¾ tsp/2.25 g minced garlic

3 oz/85 g butter

5 oz/142 g fresh bread crumbs

5 oz/142 g minced smoked salmon

1 oz/28 g prepared horseradish

20 fl oz/600 mL **Beurre Blanc** (page 387)

1. Preheat the oven to 350°F/177°C.

2. Rub the salmon fillets with the lime juice, shallots, garlic, and peppercorns.

3. To prepare the crumb mixture, sauté the shallots and garlic in the butter until they are aromatic, about 1 minute.

4. Combine the sautéed shallots and garlic, the bread crumbs, smoked salmon, and horseradish in a food processor and process to a fine consistency.

5. Portion about 1 oz/28 g of the crumb mixture onto each fillet. Bake the salmon in a 350°F/177°C oven until it is opaque pink on the outside and just beginning to flake, 6 or 7 minutes.

6. Serve the salmon on heated plates with the Beurre Blanc.

Chapter Twenty-one

Sautéing, Pan Frying, and Deep Frying

The cooking techniques presented in this chapter rely on a fat or oil as the cooking medium. As the amount of fat varies from a thin film to enough to completely submerge foods, different effects are achieved.

Sautéing

Sautéing is a technique that cooks food rapidly in a little fat over relatively high heat. Certain menu items, listed as seared/pan-seared, charred/pan-charred, or pan-broiled, are essentially sautés. Those terms on a menu have come to suggest that even less oil is used than for a traditional sauté. Sautéed dishes typically include a sauce made with the drippings, or fond, left in the pan.

Searing may be a first step for some roasted, braised, or stewed foods. In other words, they are cooked quickly in a small amount of oil over direct heat. The difference between searing and sautéing is not how the technique is performed, but that these foods are not cooked completely as a result of being seared. Searing is used in these cooking methods as an effective way to develop flavor and color in these longer, slower cooking methods.

Stir frying, associated with Asian cooking and successfully adapted by innovative Western chefs, shares many similarities with sautéing. Foods are customarily cut into small pieces, usually strips, dice, or shreds, and cooked rapidly in a little oil. They are added to the pan in sequence; those requiring the longest cooking times are added first, those that cook quickly only at the last moment. The sauce for a stir fry, like that of a sauté, is made or finished in the pan to capture the dish's entire flavor.

Choose cuts from the rib or loin, as well as portions of the leg, for beef, veal, lamb, pork, or large game animals. These cuts are the most tender. Poultry and game bird breasts are often preferred for sautéing. Firm or moderately textured fish are easier to sauté than very delicate fish. Shellfish, in and out of the shell, also sauté well. Select the cooking fat according to the flavor you want to create, food cost, availability, and smoking point.

The base for a pan sauce in sautéing may vary to suit the flavor of the main item. Brown sauces, such as demi-glace or jus lié, veloutés, reduced stocks (thickened with a slurry if necessary), vegetable coulis, or tomato sauce may be used. Consult specific recipes.

A sauté pan has short, sloped sides and is wider than it is tall to encourage rapid moisture evaporation. It is made of a metal that responds quickly to rapid heat changes. Woks are used to prepare stir fries. Pan-seared and pan-broiled items are often prepared in heavy-gauge pans that retain heat, such as cast-iron pans. Have tongs or spatulas available to turn foods and remove them from the pan, holding pans to reserve foods while a sauce is prepared or finished, and all appropriate service items (heated plates, garnishes, and accompaniments).

A basic formula for a sautéed single entrée-sized portion

One boneless portion (6 to 8 oz/170 to 227 g) of meat, poultry, or seafood (adjust the portion size to account for bones, skin, or shells)

Small amount of cooking fat or oil

Salt and pepper, plus other seasonings as required

One portion (2 to 3 fl oz/60 to 90 mL) of sauce

1. **Season foods with salt and pepper, as well as spice blends or rubs if appropriate, just before cooking to build flavor into the dish.** Seasoning before cooking is more effective than simply adding salt and pepper at the end. Flour will help to absorb excess moisture, to prevent the item from sticking to the pan, and will produce a good surface color for some light or white meats, poultry, and fish. Dusting is optional. If done, be sure to coat the item evenly and shake off any excess.

Select a pan of the appropriate size; it should be large enough so that the main item will just cover the bottom of the pan without overlapping. Heating the pan before adding oil is referred to as conditioning the pan. Add enough fat to lightly film the pan, adjusting the amount to suit the food and the pan's size and surface as well as the item to be cooked. The more natural marbling or fat present in the food, the less fat needed in the pan. Well-seasoned or nonstick pans may not require any fat beyond that which is already present in the food. Bring the pan and the cooking fat to the correct temperature before adding the food. This way the cooking process begins as soon as the food hits the hot pan. To sauté red meats and/or very thin meat pieces, heat the cooking fat until

(continued)

the surface ripples and looks hazy. Less intense heat is required for white meats, fish, and shellfish as well as thicker cuts.

Immediately add the food to the pan. Place the food's better-looking side, the presentation side, down onto the heated pan first for the best-looking sautéed foods. This side will be face up when the dish is presented to the guest. Sauté on the first side until browned or golden. Make sure that each portion comes in direct contact with the fat in the pan, with no overlapping or touching. Let the food sauté undisturbed for several seconds up to a minute or two to develop the proper flavor and color in the finished sauté. The food may stick to the pan at first, but it will release itself by the time it is ready to be turned.

2. **Turn sautéed foods only once to develop a good flavor and color.** Each time the meat is turned the temperature of the meat and pan drops. Sautéed foods are usually turned only once so that the fond can develop in the pan. More frequent turning can disturb this process, although there are exceptions. Sautéed shrimp or meat cut into émincé, for example, may be repeatedly tossed or turned. Adjust the heat under the sauté pan if necessary to complete cooking on the stovetop. In some cases, sautéed food may be finished in the oven, either in the sauté pan or in a baking dish, sizzler platter, or sheet pan.

Proper doneness in sautéed foods depends upon the food itself, safe food handling, and customer preference. Be sure to allow for some carryover cooking so that foods are not overdone by the time you are ready to put them on a plate. For more information, review Guidelines for Determining Doneness (see page 460).

3. **Add a liquid like stock or wine to release the browned drippings, or fond, and to give the sauce a deep and customized flavor.** Remove the food from the pan when it is done and make a sauce with the fond. Transfer sautéed items to a warm holding area while preparing a sauce directly in the pan. To make a sauce incorporating the fond found in the sauté pan, first remove any excess fat or oil. Add aromatic ingredients or garnish items that need to be cooked. Then deglaze the pan, releasing the reduced drippings. Wine, stock, or broth are commonly used for this step. Reduce the liquid.

4. **Reduce wine or stock until it is nearly dry, or *à sec.*** The sauce base (such as a separately prepared sauce, jus lié, reduced stock, or vegetable purée or coulis) should be added to the pan and brought to a simmer. Cream, if called for, should be added along with the sauce base so that it can reduce properly along with the base. Some sauces may need to be thickened before they are served; if so, add a small amount of a pure starch slurry until the correct consistency is reached.

exterior, resulting from proper browning, which serves to intensify the food's flavor. Weak flavor and color indicate that the food was sautéed at too low a temperature or that the pan was too crowded. "Good color" depends on the type of food. When sautéed well, red meats and game should have a deep brown exterior. White meats (veal, pork, and poultry) should have a golden or amber exterior. Lean white fish should be pale gold when sautéed as skinless fillets, while firm fish steaks, like tuna, should take on a darker color.

Only naturally tender foods should be sautéed, and after sautéing they should remain tender and moist. Excessive dryness is a sign that the food was overcooked, that it was cooked too far in advance and held too long, or that it was sautéed at a temperature higher than necessary.

5. **Finish and garnish a pan sauce in one of several ways.** It may be strained through a fine-mesh strainer for a very smooth texture before adding any finishing or garnishing ingredients. Simmer finishing and garnishing ingredients in the sauce long enough for them to be properly heated. Adjust seasoning with salt, pepper, fresh herbs, juices, essences, purées, or similar items. If desired, a small amount of whole butter may be added just before serving (monté au beurre) to add both flavor and body.

After a final check to be sure the seasoning is correct, chefs often opt to return the main item (a chicken breast or veal scallop, for example) to the finished sauce briefly to coat and gently reheat the item. The sauce may be ladled in a pool on the plate and the food set on top. Or the sauce may be ladled over the food (nappé), or ladled around the food (cordon). Be sure to wipe away any drips on the plate with a clean cloth wrung out in hot water before the plate is sent to the dining room.

Evaluate the quality of the finished sautéed food. The object of sautéing is to produce a flavorful

Pan Frying

Pan-fried foods have a richly textured crust and a moist flavorful interior, producing a dish of intriguing contrasts in texture and flavor. When a carefully selected sauce is paired with a dish, the effects can range from home-style to haute cuisine. Pan-fried food is almost always coated—dredged in flour, coated with batter, or breaded. Food is fried in enough oil to come halfway or two thirds up its side; it is often cooked over less intense heat than in sautéing. The product is cooked more by the oil's heat than by direct contact with the pan. In pan frying, the hot oil seals the food's coated surface, thereby locking in the natural juices inside. Because no juices are released and a larger amount of oil is involved, sauces accompanying pan-fried foods are usually made separately.

Pan-fried food is usually portion sized or smaller. Select cuts that are naturally tender, as you would for a sauté. Rib or loin cuts, top round, or poultry breasts are all good choices. Lean fish, such as sole or flounder, are also well suited to pan frying. Trim away any fat, silverskin, and gristle. Remove the skin and bones of poultry and fish fillets if necessary or desired. You may want to pound cutlets for an even thickness and to shorten cooking time. This means that the exterior will brown without overcooking in the same time that the meat cooks through.

Ingredients for breading include flour, milk and/or beaten eggs, and bread crumbs or cornmeal. For instructions on Standard Breading, see page 458.

The fat for pan frying must be able to reach high temperatures without breaking down or smoking. Vegetable oils, olive oil, and shortenings may all be used for pan frying. Lard, goose fat, and other rendered animal fats have a place in certain regional and ethnic dishes. The choice of fat makes a difference in the flavor of the finished dish.

The pan used for pan frying must be large enough to hold foods in a single layer without touching. If the food is crowded, the temperature of the fat will drop quickly and a good crust will not form. Pans should be made of heavy-gauge metal and should be able to transmit heat evenly. The sides should be higher than those appropriate for sautés to avoid splashing hot oil out of the pan as foods are added to the oil or turned during cooking. Have on hand a pan lined with absorbent toweling to blot away surface fat from fried foods. Tongs or slotted spatulas are typically used to turn foods. Select shallow, wide containers to hold coatings, breading, or batters.

A basic formula for a single pan-fried entrée-sized portion

One boneless portion (6 to 8 oz/170 to 227 g) of meat, poultry, or seafood (adjust the portion size to account for bones or skin)

Enough cooking fat or oil to cover half to two thirds of the item being pan-fried

Standard breading, batter, or other coating

Salt and pepper, plus other seasonings as required

One portion (2 to 3 fl oz/60 to 90 mL) of sauce

1. **Bread the cutlets using the standard breading procedure described on page 458.** Blot the food dry with absorbent toweling. Any moisture left on the surface could make the coating too moist. It will also break down the cooking fat more quickly, as well as causing it to splatter. Add any seasonings before the coating. Foods are usually dipped in flour or a meal, then egg wash, followed by a coating of bread crumbs. Apply coatings such as bread crumbs just as the food is ready to go into the pan. Standard breading can be applied 3 or 4 hours in advance.

The pan and the cooking fat must reach the correct temperature before the food is added. Otherwise, the crust's development will be slowed, and it may never achieve the desired crisp texture and golden brown color. As a rule of thumb, add enough fat to come one half to two thirds of the way up the food; the thinner the food, the less fat is required. When a faint haze or slight shimmer is noticeable, the fat is usually hot enough. To test the temperature, dip a corner of the food in the fat. If the fat is at about 350°F/177°C, it will bubble around the food, and the coating will start to brown within 45 seconds.

2. **Add the food carefully to the hot fat and pan fry on the first side until a good crust and color develop.** Exercise extreme caution at this point to prevent burns. Getting pan-fried foods evenly browned and crisped requires that the food be in direct contact with the hot fat. Be sure not to over-crowd the pan, or the food may not develop good color and texture. If there is not enough fat in the pan, the food may stick to the pan and tear, or the coating may come away. When pan frying large quantities, skim or strain away any loose particles between batches. Add more fresh fat to keep the level constant and to prevent smoking or foaming.

Some foods, because they are thick or include bones or a stuffing, may need to be removed from the fat and placed in an oven to finish cooking. If they do need to go into the oven, be sure that they are not covered. A cover could cause steam to soften the crisp coating.

3. **Turn the food once and continue to pan fry until the second side is golden and the food is properly cooked.** It is difficult to give precise instructions for determining doneness in pan-fried foods. In general, the thinner and more delicate the meat, the more quickly it will cook. Pan-fried as well as sautéed and deep-fried items, even thin pieces, are subject to carryover cooking. It is thus best to slightly under-cook. For more information, review Guidelines for Determining Doneness on page 460.

Drain or blot pan-fried food on clean absorbent paper or cloth. The food is ready to serve now. Do not hold fried foods for more than a very brief period before serving. They tend to get soggy quickly. Do not cover fried foods if they need to be held for a short period of time. They should be held in dry heat on an open rack. Serve sauces for pan-fried foods under the food or separately to preserve the crust.

The object of pan frying is to produce a flavorful exterior with a crisp, brown crust, which acts as a barrier to retain juices and flavor. The color depends upon the coating, its thickness, and the food.

Deep Frying

Deep-fried foods have many of the same characteristics as pan-fried foods, including a crisp, browned exterior and a moist, flavorful interior. Deep-fried foods, however, are cooked in enough fat or oil to completely submerge them. In deep frying, significantly more fat is used than for either sautéing or pan frying. The food is almost always coated with a standard breading, a batter such as a tempura or beer batter, or a simple flour coating. The coating acts as a barrier between the fat and the food and also contributes flavor and texture.

To cook rapidly and evenly, foods must be trimmed and cut into a uniform size and shape. Select cuts that are naturally tender; some typical choices include poultry, seafood, and vegetables. Remove the skin and bones of poultry and fish fillets if necessary or desired. Be certain to season the food before adding a coating. Deep frying is also suitable for croquettes and similar dishes made from a mixture of cooked, diced meats, fish, or poultry, bound with a heavy béchamel and breaded.

Breadings and coatings are common for deep-fried foods. Standard breading can be done three to four hours ahead and items refrigerated before frying, but ideally breading should be done as close to service as possible. For Standard Breading instructions, see page 458. A batter or plain flour coating is applied immediately before cooking.

Electric or gas deep fryers with baskets are typically used for deep frying, although it is also feasible to fry foods using a large pot. The sides should be high enough to prevent fat from foaming over or splashing, and wide enough to allow the chef to add and remove foods easily. Use a deep-fat frying thermometer to check the fat's temperature, regardless of whether you use an electric or gas fryer or a pot on a stovetop. Become familiar with the fryer's recovery time; that is, the time needed for the fat to regain the proper temperature after foods are added. The fat will lose temperature for a brief time. The more food added, the more the temperature will drop and the longer it will take to come back to the proper level.

Kitchens that must fry many kinds of food often have several different fryers to help prevent flavor transfer. Have a pan lined with absorbent toweling to blot fried foods before they are served. Tongs, spiders, and baskets help add foods to the fryer and remove them when properly cooked.

A basic formula for an entrée-sized portion

One boneless portion (4 to 6 oz/170 to 227 g) of meat, poultry, or seafood

Enough cooking fat or oil to completely submerge the food

Standard breading, batter, or other coating

Salt and pepper, plus other seasonings as required

One portion (2 to 3 fl oz/60 to 90 mL) of sauce

1. Heat the cooking fat to the proper temperature (generally 325° to 375°F/163° to 191°C). The fat must reach and maintain a nearly steady temperature throughout the frying time to prepare crisp, flavorful, and nongreasy fried foods. Proper maintenance of oil will help extend its life. Old fats and oils have a darker color and more pronounced aroma than fresh oil. They may also smoke at a lower temperature and foam when foods are added. Be sure to strain or filter the oil properly after each meal period. Replenish the fryer's oil to the appropriate level if necessary.

The *swimming method* of frying is generally used for battered food. To coat prepped foods with batter, dust it with flour, then shake off the excess before dropping it into the batter. Carefully lower the battered food halfway into the hot oil using tongs. When it starts to bubble, release it and it will not sink. The *basket method* is generally used for breaded items. Place the breaded food in a frying basket and then lower both the food and the basket into the hot fat. Once the food is cooked, use the basket to lift out the food. Foods that would tend to rise to the surface

(continued)

too rapidly are held down by setting a second basket on top of the food; this is known as the double-basket method.

The choice between the two methods of deep frying depends on the food, the coating, and the intended result Use all your senses as well as a thermometer to accurately judge internal doneness. For more information, review Guidelines for Determining Doneness on page 460.

2. **Fry food until it is fully cooked and the coating is a light golden brown.** Drain on paper towels before serving. Evaluate the quality of the finished deep-fried food. Deep-fried foods should taste like the food, not like the fat used (or like other foods previously fried in the fat). Foods served very hot, directly from the frying kettle, have a better, less greasy taste. If the food tastes heavy, greasy, or strongly of another food, the fat was not hot enough, the fat was too old, or a strongly flavored food such as fish was fried in the same fat.

Well-prepared deep-fried food has a moist and tender interior, with a crisp, delicate crust. If the crust has become soggy, the food may have been held too long after cooking or, again, the oil was not at the correct temperature.

Sautéed Chicken with Fines Herbes Sauce

Makes 10 servings

10 (7 to 8 oz/198 to 227 g) boneless chicken suprêmes

2 tsp/10 g salt

1 tsp/2 g ground black pepper

3 oz/85 g all-purpose flour (optional)

2 fl oz/60 mL clarified butter or oil

¾ oz/21 g minced shallots

4 fl oz/120 mL dry white wine

20 fl oz/600 mL **Fines Herbes Sauce** (recipe follows)

4 oz/113 g **Fines Herbes** (page 463)

1. Blot the chicken dry and season with salt and pepper. Dredge in flour, if desired.

2. Heat the butter or oil in a large sauté pan over medium-high heat until it is almost smoking. Sauté the chicken on the first side until golden brown, about 3 minutes. Turn the chicken and continue to sauté until cooked through (180°F/82°C). Remove the chicken from the pan and keep warm while completing the sauce.

3. Degrease the pan. Add the shallots and sauté them until they are translucent, about 1 minute.

4. Deglaze the pan with the wine; reduce until it is almost dry, about 3 minutes. Add the Fines Herbes Sauce, simmer briefly, then strain into a clean saucepan.

5. Adjust seasoning with salt and pepper and stir in the Fines Herbes.

6. Serve the chicken immediately with the sauce or hold it hot for service.

Fines Herbes Sauce

Makes 32 fl oz/960 mL

1 fl oz/30 mL clarified butter

¾ oz/21 g minced shallots

9 fl oz/270 mL dry white wine

6 oz/170 g **Fines Herbes** (page 463)

32 fl oz/960 mL **Jus de Volaille Lié** (page 382), **Jus de Veau Lié** (page 382), or **Demi-Glace** (page 383)

9 fl oz/270 mL heavy cream

salt, as needed

ground black pepper, as needed

1. Heat the butter in a saucepan over medium-high heat. Add the shallots and sweat until translucent, 2 to 3 minutes. Add the wine and Fines Herbes and simmer until nearly dry.

2. Add the jus lié or demi-glace, bring to a simmer, and reduce slightly. Add the cream and continue to simmer the sauce to reach a good flavor and consistency, skimming as necessary.

3. Season with salt and pepper and strain the sauce.

4. The sauce is ready to serve now, or it may be rapidly cooled and refrigerated for later use.

Chicken Provençal

Makes 10 servings

10 (7 to 8 oz/198 to 227 g) chicken suprêmes

2 tsp/10 g salt

1 tsp/2 g ground black pepper

3 oz/85 g all-purpose flour (optional)

2 fl oz/60 mL clarified butter or oil

PROVENÇAL SAUCE

2 tsp/6 g minced garlic

3 anchovy fillets, mashed to a paste

12 oz/340 g tomato concassé

10 fl oz/300 mL dry white wine

24 fl oz/720 mL **Jus de Volaille Lié** (page 382), **Jus de Veau Lié** (page 382), or **Demi-Glace** (page 383)

4 oz/113 g black olive slices or julienne

1 oz/28 g basil chiffonade

1. Blot the chicken dry and season with salt and pepper. Dredge in flour, if desired.

2. Heat the butter or oil in a large sauté pan over medium-high heat until it is almost smoking. Sauté the chicken on the first side until golden brown, about 3 minutes. Turn the chicken and continue to sauté until cooked through (180°F/82°C). Remove the chicken from the pan and keep warm while completing the sauce.

3. Pour off the excess fat from the pan and add the garlic and anchovies; sauté for 30 to 40 seconds to release their aroma. Add the tomatoes and continue to sauté until any juices they release have cooked down. Add the wine to deglaze the pan and simmer until nearly cooked away.

4. Add the jus or demi-glace and any juices released by the chicken. Reduce to a good flavor and consistency. Strain into a clean pan and return to a simmer. Add the olives and basil, return to a simmer, and adjust seasoning with salt and pepper as needed.

5. Return the chicken to the pan and turn to coat it with the sauce. Serve immediately with the sauce or hold it hot for service.

NOTE

You may elect to use different kinds of olives in this dish, introduce some capers, or add other herbs, either in addition to or as a replacement for the basil: Oregano, marjoram, chives, chervil, and thyme are all good choices.

Beef Tournedos Provençal: Substitute ten 6-oz/170-g beef tournedos for the chicken and red wine for the white wine. Season the beef with salt and pepper and sauté to desired doneness, following the above method, 2 minutes per side for rare (135°F/57°C), 3 minutes per side for medium rare (145°F/63°C), 4½ minutes per side for medium (160°F/71°C), 6 minutes per side for medium well (165°F/74°C), and 7 minutes per side for well done (170°F/77°C). Remove the beef from the pan and reserve warm while finishing the sauce following the above method.

Veal Scaloppine Marsala

Makes 10 servings

3 lb 12 oz/1.70 kg boneless veal top round, cut into ten 6-oz/170-g portions

2 tsp/10 g salt

1 tsp/2 g ground black pepper

3 oz/85 g all-purpose flour (optional)

2 fl oz/60 mL clarified butter or oil

½ oz/14 g shallots, minced

6 fl oz/180 mL white wine

24 fl oz/720 mL **Marsala Sauce** (recipe follows)

5 oz/142 g butter (optional)

1. Pound each portion of veal between sheets of parchment or plastic wrap to a thickness of ¼ in/6 mm. Blot dry and season with salt and pepper. Dredge in flour, if desired.

2. Heat the butter or oil in a large sauté pan over medium-high heat until it is almost smoking. Sauté the veal to the desired doneness, about 2 minutes per side for medium (180°F/82°C). Remove the veal from the pan and keep warm while completing the sauce.

3. Degrease the pan. Add the shallots and sauté until they are translucent, about 1 minute.

4. Deglaze the pan with the wine; reduce until it is almost dry, about 3 minutes. Add the Marsala Sauce, simmer briefly, then strain into a clean saucepan.

5. Return the sauce to a simmer and adjust seasoning with salt and pepper as needed. Swirl in the butter to finish the sauce, if desired.

6. Serve immediately with the sauce or hold it hot for service.

Pork Scaloppine with Tomato Sauce: Substitute boneless pork loin for the veal and Tomato Sauce (page 384) for the Marsala Sauce.

Marsala Sauce

Makes 32 fl oz/960 mL

1 oz/28 g minced shallots

2 thyme sprigs

1 bay leaf

½ tsp/1 g black peppercorns

8 fl oz/240 mL dry red wine

32 fl oz/960 mL **Jus de Veau Lié** (page 382) or **Demi-Glace** (page 383)

8 fl oz/240 mL Marsala

salt, as needed

ground black pepper, as needed

4 oz/113 g butter, diced

1. In a saucepan, combine the shallots, thyme, bay leaf, peppercorns, and wine. Reduce by half over medium-high heat.

2. Add the jus lié or demi-glace and continue to simmer until the sauce has developed a good flavor and consistency. Add the Marsala and return to a simmer. Season with salt and pepper. Strain the sauce into a clean saucepan.

3. Finish the sauce by swirling in the butter. The sauce is ready to serve now, or it may be rapidly cooled and refrigerated for later use.

Swiss-Style Shredded Veal with Rösti Potatoes (page 798) and Haricots Verts

Swiss-Style Shredded Veal

Makes 10 servings

3 lb 12 oz/1.70 kg veal top round or tender leg cut, cut into émincé

4 tsp/20 g salt

2 tsp/4 g ground black pepper

3 oz/85 g all-purpose flour (optional)

2 fl oz/60 mL clarified butter or oil

3 oz/85 g chopped shallots

5 oz/142 g sliced mushrooms

10 fl oz/300 mL white wine

10 fl oz/300 mL **Jus de Veau Lié** (page 382) or **Demi-Glace** (page 383)

4 fl oz/120 mL heavy cream

1 fl oz/30 mL brandy

2 tsp/10 mL lemon juice

1. Blot the veal dry and season with salt and pepper. Dredge in flour, if desired.

2. Heat the butter or oil in a large sauté pan over medium-high heat until it is almost smoking. Working in batches, sauté the veal, stirring from time to time, until the desired doneness (180°F/82°C), about 3 minutes. Remove the veal from the pan and keep warm while completing the sauce.

3. Degrease the pan. Add the shallots and mushrooms and sauté them until they are softened and translucent, about 3 minutes.

4. Deglaze the pan with the wine; reduce until it is almost dry, about 3 minutes.

5. Add the jus lié or demi-glace, cream, brandy, and any juices released from the veal. Reduce until a good flavor and consistency is achieved, 1 to 2 minutes.

6. Add the lemon juice and adjust seasoning with salt and pepper, if necessary.

7. Serve the veal immediately with the sauce or hold it hot for service.

Noisettes of Pork with Green Peppercorns and Pineapple

Makes 10 servings

3 lb 12 oz/1.70 kg boneless pork leg or loin, cut into twenty 3-oz/85-g noisettes

2 tsp/10 g salt

1 tsp/2 g ground black pepper

2 fl oz/60 mL clarified butter or oil

¾ oz/21 g minced shallots

8 fl oz/240 mL white wine

20 fl oz/600 mL **Brown Pork Stock** (page 352), **Jus de Veau Lié** (page 382), or **Demi-Glace** (page 383)

5 fl oz/150 mL heavy cream

½ fl oz/15 mL dijon mustard

7 oz/198 g small-dice pineapple

1 oz/28 g green peppercorns

1. Blot the pork dry and season with salt and pepper.

2. Heat the butter or oil in a large sauté pan over medium-high heat until it is almost smoking. Sauté the pork 2 to 3 minutes per side to 160°F/71°C. Remove the pork from the pan and keep warm while completing the sauce.

3. Degrease the pan. Add the shallots and sauté them until they are translucent, about 1 minute.

4. Deglaze the pan with the wine; reduce until it is almost dry, about 3 minutes.

5. Add the stock, jus lié, or demi-glace, cream, mustard, and any juices released by the pork. Reduce to a good flavor and consistency. Strain into a clean saucepan and return to a simmer.

6. Add the pineapple and peppercorns and adjust seasoning with salt and pepper, if necessary. Return the pork to the sauce to reheat.

7. Serve 2 noisettes per serving with the sauce immediately, or hold it hot for service.

Pork Medallions with Warm Cabbage Salad

Makes 10 servings

3 lb 12 oz/1.70 kg pork tenderloin, cut into thirty 2-oz/57-g medallions

2 tsp/10 g salt

1 tsp/2 g ground black pepper

2 fl oz/60 mL clarified butter or oil

6 fl oz/180 mL dry white wine

20 fl oz/600 mL **Sherry Vinegar Sauce** (page 527)

10 servings **Warm Cabbage Salad** (recipe follows)

1. Blot the pork dry and season with salt and pepper.

2. Heat the butter or oil in a large sauté pan over medium-high heat until it is almost smoking. Sauté the pork 2 to 3 minutes per side to 160°F/71°C. Remove the pork from the pan and keep warm while completing the sauce.

3. Degrease the pan and add the wine to deglaze the pan; reduce until it is almost dry.

4. Add the Sherry Vinegar Sauce and any juices released by the pork. Reduce to a good flavor and consistency. Adjust seasoning with salt and pepper as needed.

5. Serve the pork immediately with the sauce and Warm Cabbage Salad or hold it hot for service.

Noisettes of Pork with Red Onion Confit: Sauté the pork following the above method. Replace the Warm Cabbage Salad with red onion confit. To make the red onion confit, simmer 2 lb/907 g sliced red onions with 4 fl oz/120 mL honey, 4 fl oz/120 mL red wine, and 5 fl oz/150 mL red wine vinegar until the mixture is the consistency of marmalade, about 40 minutes. Adjust seasoning with salt and pepper. Keep warm for service or cool and refrigerate for later service.

Warm Cabbage Salad

Makes 10 servings

1¾ oz/50 g minced bacon

1 oz/28 g butter

3½ oz/99 g small-dice red onions

½ oz/14 g minced garlic

2 lb/907 g savoy cabbage chiffonade

1¾ fl oz/53 mL sherry vinegar

1 oz/28 g sugar

1 tsp/2 g caraway seeds

1 tbsp/3 g chopped parsley

salt, as needed

ground black pepper, as needed

1. Cook the bacon in a sauté pan over medium heat until the fat is rendered and the bacon is crisped. Remove the bacon with a slotted spoon, allowing the fat to drain back into the pan. Reserve the bacon.

2. Add the butter to the pan. Add the onions and garlic, and sauté until they are translucent and tender, 2 to 3 minutes.

3. Add the cabbage, toss to coat evenly with the fat, and sauté until limp, stirring frequently, 6 to 8 minutes.

4. Add the vinegar, sugar, and caraway seeds, and bring to a simmer. Cook until the cabbage is very hot and tender, 3 to 4 minutes more. Add the parsley. Season with salt and pepper.

5. Serve immediately or hold it hot for service.

Pork Medallions with Warm Cabbage Salad, Broccoli Rabe
(page 757), and Spaghetti Squash (page 744)

Sautéed Medallions of Pork with Winter Fruit Sauce

Makes 10 servings

3 lb 12 oz/1.70 kg boneless pork loin, cut into twenty 3-oz/85-g medallions

2 tsp/10 g salt

1 tsp/2 g ground black pepper

2 fl oz/60 mL clarified butter or oil

8 fl oz/240 mL dry white wine

20 fl oz/600 mL **Winter Fruit Sauce** (recipe follows)

1. Blot the pork dry and season with salt and pepper.

2. Heat the butter or oil in a large sauté pan over medium-high heat until it is almost smoking. Sauté the pork 2 to 3 minutes per side to 160°F/71°C. Remove the pork from the pan and keep warm while completing the sauce.

3. Degrease the pan. Deglaze the pan with the wine; reduce until it is almost dry, about 3 minutes.

4. Add the Winter Fruit Sauce and any juices released by the pork. Reduce to a good flavor and consistency. Adjust seasoning with salt and pepper.

5. Serve immediately with the sauce or hold it hot for service.

Winter Fruit Sauce

Makes 32 fl oz/960 mL

10 fl oz/300 mL semidry white wine

3½ oz/99 g dried apricots (sulfur free)

1¾ oz/50 g dried cherries

2 fl oz/60 mL clarified butter or oil

1 oz/28 g minced shallots

5 oz/142 g small-dice Red Delicious apples

4 oz/113 g small-dice Bartlett pears

1¾ fl oz/53 mL apple-flavored brandy

24 fl oz/720 mL **Brown Pork Stock** (page 352), **Jus de Veau Lié** (page 382), **or Demi-Glace** (page 383)

2 tsp/10 mL lemon juice, or as needed

salt, as needed

ground black pepper, as needed

1. Heat the wine in a small saucepan to just below a boil. Remove from the heat and add the dried fruit. Let the fruit soak in the wine (macerate) for 30 minutes. Drain the fruit and reserve the wine.

2. Heat the butter or oil in a saucepan over medium heat and add the shallots. Sauté until translucent, 1 to 2 minutes. Add the apples and pears and sauté until lightly browned.

3. Add the brandy to deglaze the pan and let it reduce until nearly cooked away. Add the reserved wine and bring to a simmer. Add the stock, jus lié, or demi-glace and bring to a simmer again. Simmer until reduced to a good flavor and consistency. Add the macerated dried fruit and season with lemon juice, salt, and pepper.

4. The sauce is ready to serve now, or it may be rapidly cooled and refrigerated for later use.

Pork Cutlet with Sauce Robert

Makes 10 servings

3 lb 12 oz/1.70 kg boneless pork leg or loin, cut into ten 6-oz/170-g portions

2 tsp/10 g salt

1 tsp/2 g ground black pepper

3 oz/85 g all-purpose flour

2 fl oz/60 mL clarified butter or oil

4 fl oz/120 mL dry white wine

20 fl oz/600 mL **Sauce Robert** (recipe follows)

1. Pound each portion of pork between sheets of parchment or plastic wrap to a thickness of ¼ in/6 mm.

2. Blot the cutlets dry and season with salt and pepper. Dredge in flour, if desired.

3. Heat the butter or oil in a large sauté pan over medium-high heat until it is almost smoking. Working in batches, sauté the pork on the first side until golden brown, about 3 minutes. Turn the pork and continue to sauté until done (160°F/71°C), 2 to 3 minutes. Remove the cutlets from the pan and keep warm while completing the sauce.

4. Degrease the pan and deglaze with the wine; reduce until it is almost dry, about 3 minutes. Add the Sauce Robert and any juices released from the pork. Cook until heated through, stirring constantly. Adjust seasoning with salt and pepper, if necessary.

5. Serve immediately with the sauce or hold it hot for service.

Sauce Robert

Makes 32 fl oz/960 mL

2 fl oz/60 mL clarified butter or oil

2 oz/57 g finely chopped shallots

8 fl oz/240 mL dry white wine

1 tsp/2 g cracked black peppercorns

32 fl oz/960 mL **Demi-Glace** (page 383)

1 fl oz/30 mL Dijon mustard

2 tsp/10 mL lemon juice

salt, as needed

ground black pepper, as needed

4 oz/113 g butter, diced

1. Heat the butter or oil in a medium-sized saucepan over medium-low heat. Add the shallots and sauté until translucent, 2 to 3 minutes.

2. Add the wine and peppercorns, bring to a simmer, and reduce by half.

3. Stir in the demi-glace, return to a simmer, and cook for 20 minutes, stirring frequently, until the sauce has thickened. Strain the sauce into a clean pan and return to a simmer.

4. Add the mustard and lemon juice. Season with salt and pepper.

5. Finish the sauce by swirling in the butter. The sauce is ready to serve now, or it may be rapidly cooled and refrigerated for later use.

Sauce Charcuterie: Add 1½ oz/43 g cornichon julienne to the sauce along with the mustard and lemon juice.

Ancho-Crusted Salmon with Yellow Mole served with Stewed
Black Beans (page 824) and Yellow Squash Noodles (page 756)

Ancho-Crusted Salmon with Yellow Mole

Makes 10 servings

2 ancho chiles

1 tbsp/6 g cumin seeds

1 tbsp/6 g fennel seeds

4½ tsp/7.50 g coriander seeds

1 tbsp/6 g whole black peppercorns

1 tbsp/6 g dried thyme leaves

1 tbsp/6 g dried oregano

1½ oz/43 g salt

1 tbsp/6 g dry mustard

3 lb 12 oz/1.70 kg salmon fillets, cut into ten 6-oz/170-g portions

1½ fl oz/45 mL clarified butter or oil

20 fl oz/600 mL **Yellow Mole** (recipe follows)

1. Remove the stems and seeds from the chiles and roughly chop them.

2. Toast the chiles, cumin, fennel, and coriander seeds in a 300°F/149°C oven for 5 minutes or until fragrant. Remove and cool to room temperature.

3. In a spice grinder, combine the toasted spices with the peppercorns, thyme, and oregano. Grind to a coarse powder. Stir in the salt and dry mustard and reserve until service.

4. Lightly coat each portion of salmon with the crust. Heat the butter or oil in a large sauté pan over medium-high heat. Sauté the salmon on the first side, until the spices start to brown, 1 to 2 minutes.

5. Flip the salmon over and cook over medium heat, or in a 350°F/177°C oven for 4 to 6 minutes (depending on thickness of cut), until desired doneness.

6. Serve immediately with the mole or hold it hot for service.

Yellow Mole

Makes 32 fl oz/960 mL

1 fl oz/30 mL olive oil

12 oz/340 g sliced onions

1 tsp/3 g sliced garlic

1 lb 8 oz/680 g yellow peppers, seeded and chopped

5 oz/142 g chopped fennel

1 (2 in/5 cm) cinnamon stick

¼ tsp/0.50 g ground allspice

1½ tsp/3 g dried epazote

¾ oz/21 g sugar

8 fl oz/240 mL water

3 oz/85 g tomatillos, quartered

1 fl oz/30 mL lime juice, or as needed

salt, as needed

1. Heat the oil in a heavy-bottomed pot over medium-high heat. Add the onions and garlic and cook until translucent, about 8 minutes.

2. Add the peppers, fennel, cinnamon, allspice, epazote, sugar, and water.

3. Cover the pot and simmer on low heat until the peppers are soft, about 25 minutes.

4. Transfer the mixture to a blender and purée with the tomatillos until very smooth. Strain through a large-holed strainer.

5. Season with the lime juice and salt. The sauce is ready to serve now, or it may be rapidly cooled and refrigerated for later use.

Red Snapper with Grapefruit Salsa

Makes 10 servings

3 lb 12 oz/1.70 kg red snapper fillets, skin on, cut into ten 6-oz/170-g portions

1 tsp/5 g salt

⅛ tsp/0.25 g ground black pepper

4 oz/113 g all-purpose flour, or as needed

2 fl oz/60 mL olive oil, or as needed

20 fl oz/600 mL **Grapefruit Salsa** (page 989)

1. Season the snapper with the salt and pepper. Dredge the fish in the flour, shaking off the excess.

2. Heat the oil in a skillet over medium-high heat. Sauté the snapper until golden brown and cooked through, 2 to 3 minutes per side, depending on thickness of the fillet.

3. Serve immediately with the salsa.

Trout Amandine

Makes 10 servings

10 (6 oz/170 g) trout fillets

2 tsp/10 g salt

1 tsp/2 g ground black pepper

8 fl oz/240 mL milk, or as needed (optional)

3 oz/85 g all-purpose flour, or as needed

2 fl oz/60 mL clarified butter or oil

10 oz/284 g butter

5 oz/142 g slivered almonds

5 fl oz/150 mL lemon juice

2 oz/57 g chopped parsley

1. Blot the trout fillets dry and season with salt and pepper. Dip the trout fillets into milk, if desired, and dredge with flour, shaking off any excess.

2. Heat the clarified butter or oil in a large sauté pan over medium heat. Sauté the trout for 2 to 3 minutes on each side, or until the flesh is opaque and firm (145°F/63°C). Remove the fish from the pan and keep warm while completing the sauce.

3. Degrease the pan and add the whole butter. Heat the butter until lightly browned with a nutty aroma, 2 to 3 minutes.

4. Add the almonds and stir to coat them evenly with the butter. Add the lemon juice and swirl to deglaze the pan. Add the parsley.

5. Serve the trout immediately with the sauce or hold it hot for service.

Vatapa

Makes 10 servings

1 whole (1 lb 14 oz/850 g) coconut

5 fl oz/150 mL olive oil

Shrimp shells, reserved from shrimp (below)

4 fl oz/120 mL brandy

12 oz/340 g small-dice onions

3 garlic cloves, minced

2 jalapeños, small dice

2½ oz/71 g chopped peanuts

2½ oz/71 g grated ginger

2 oz/57 g tomato paste

4 fl oz/120 mL white wine

48 fl oz/1.44 L **Shellfish Stock** (page 353), **Fish Stock** (page 353), or **Chicken Stock** (page 351)

3 oz/85 g **White Roux** (page 335)

12 fl oz/360 mL heavy cream

2 lb 8 oz/1.13 kg monkfish, cut into 1-in/3-cm cubes

1½ tsp/7.50 g salt

¼ tsp/0.50 g ground black pepper

4 oz/113 g all-purpose flour

2 lb 8 oz/1.13 kg shrimp (16–20 count), peeled and deveined, shells reserved

8 oz/227 g peeled, seeded, and small-diced tomato

4 oz/113 g roasted peanuts

3 tbsp/9 g cilantro leaves

1. Split the coconut in half and reserve the water. Remove and shred the flesh. Toast 4 oz/113 g of the shredded flesh in a 350°F/177°C oven until a light golden brown; reserve. Reserve the remaining shredded coconut for the sauce.

2. Heat 1½ fl oz/45 mL of the oil in a large sauté pan over high heat. Sauté the reserved shrimp shells until pink and slightly caramelized, 45 seconds to 1 minute. Add the brandy and flambé the shells.

3. Add the onions, garlic, jalapeños, the reserved shredded coconut, chopped peanuts, and ginger to the shrimp shells and sauté for 3 minutes.

4. Reduce the heat to medium and add the tomato paste. Sauté for 1 minute, deglaze with the wine, add the stock and reserved coconut water, and bring to a boil. Reduce the mixture by half, about 10 minutes. Reduce the heat to low, add the roux, and simmer for 15 minutes longer.

5. Add the cream and reduce over medium heat to a nappé consistency, 1 to 2 minutes. Strain the sauce through a fine-mesh sieve.

6. Season the monkfish with the salt and pepper and dredge in flour. Sauté the monkfish in the remaining oil over high heat for 2 minutes, then add the shrimp. Sauté both until they are cooked through, about 8 minutes, and then add the sauce. Check the consistency and seasoning of the Vatapa.

7. Serve immediately, garnished with the tomatoes, the reserved toasted coconut, peanuts, and cilantro, or hold it hot for service.

Sautéed Trout à la Meunière

Makes 10 servings

10 (9 to 10 oz/255 to 284 g) pan-dressed trout

2 tsp/10 g salt

1 tsp/2 g ground black pepper

2 oz/57 g all-purpose flour

2 fl oz/60 mL clarified butter or oil

10 oz/284 g butter

2 fl oz/60 mL lemon juice

3 tbsp/9 g chopped parsley

1. Blot the trout dry and season with salt and pepper. Dredge in flour.

2. Heat the clarified butter or oil in a large sauté pan over medium heat. Working in batches, sauté the trout until lightly browned and cooked through, 3 to 4 minutes per side. Remove the trout from the pan and keep warm while completing the sauce.

3. Degrease the pan and add the whole butter. Heat the butter until lightly browned with a nutty aroma, 2 to 3 minutes.

4. Add the lemon juice to the pan and swirl to deglaze it. Add the parsley and pour or spoon the sauce over the trout. Serve immediately.

Bibimbap

Makes 10 servings

MARINADE

2 fl oz/60 mL Korean soy sauce

1 tbsp/15 g sugar

¾ oz/21 g minced green onions

¾ oz/21 g minced garlic

1 tbsp/9 g minced ginger

1 tbsp/9 g sesame seeds, toasted and ground

1 tsp/5 mL dark sesame oil

1 tsp/2 g ground black pepper

1 lb/454 g beef skirt steak julienne

8 oz/227 g red radish julienne

8 oz/227 g daikon julienne

8 oz/227 g carrot julienne

8 oz/227 g European cucumber julienne

10 shiso leaves, chiffonade

8 oz/227 g iceberg lettuce chiffonade

2½ fl oz/75 mL vegetable oil

10 eggs

4 lb 6 oz/1.98 kg **Steamed Long-Grain Rice** (page 832)

10 fl oz/300 mL Korean red pepper paste

1. To make the marinade, combine the soy sauce, sugar, green onions, garlic, ginger, sesame seeds, sesame oil, and pepper. Add the beef to the marinade and refrigerate.

2. Toss the vegetables together and reserve.

3. Heat 2 fl oz/60 mL of the vegetable oil in a wok over medium-high heat. Add the beef and stir-fry until barely cooked through, 3 to 4 minutes. Remove from the pan and reserve warm.

5. Heat a nonstick sauté pan with the remaining ½ fl oz/15 mL of the vegetable oil. Fry the eggs "sunny-side up."

6. For each portion, toss about 1½ oz/43 g of the stir-fried beef with about 4 oz/113 g of raw vegetables and serve them on top of 7 oz/198 g of the rice. Slide a fried egg out of the pan on top of the beef and vegetables.

7. Serve immediately with 1 fl oz/30 mL of Korean red pepper paste on the side.

Stir-Fried Squid with Thai Basil

Makes 10 servings

1½ oz/43 g sliced garlic

2 tbsp/6 g finely chopped cilantro root

1 oz/28 g minced Thai chiles

1 tsp/2 g cracked black peppercorns

2 fl oz/60 mL vegetable oil

2 lb/907 g squid tubes and tentacles, cut into large bite-size pieces

8 oz/227 g red pepper julienne

3 oz/85 g green onion julienne

2 fl oz/60 mL oyster sauce

2 fl oz/60 mL fish sauce

1 oz/28 g sugar

8 fl oz/240 mL **Chicken Stock** (page 351)

1 oz/28 g Thai basil leaves

1. Combine the garlic, cilantro root, chiles, and peppercorns in a blender and process to make a paste.

2. Heat the oil in a wok, add the paste, and stir-fry until aromatic, about 30 seconds.

3. Add the squid and stir-fry until half cooked and brown on the edges, 3 to 4 minutes.

4. Add the peppers and stir-fry about 1 minute more.

5. Add the green onions, oyster sauce, fish sauce, sugar, and stock. Cook until the squid is just cooked, 2 to 3 minutes.

6. Add the basil and toss well. Serve immediately or hold it hot for service.

Breast of Chicken with Duxelles Stuffing and Suprême Sauce

Makes 10 servings

10 (7 to 8 oz/198 to 227 g) boneless chicken suprêmes

2 tsp/10 g salt

1 tsp/2 g ground black pepper

2 lb/907 g **Duxelles Stuffing** (page 556)

5 oz/142 g all-purpose flour, or as needed

6 fl oz/180 mL egg wash, or as needed

12 oz/340 g bread crumbs, or as needed

24 fl oz/720 mL clarified butter or oil, or as needed

20 fl oz/600 mL **Suprême Sauce** (page 383)

1. Trim the chicken suprêmes and remove the skin, if desired. Butterfly each breast portion and pound between sheets of parchment or plastic wrap to even thickness.

2. At the time of service or up to 3 hours in advance, blot dry the chicken and season with salt and pepper. Fill each breast with a portion of the Duxelles Stuffing and roll the breast around the stuffing. Overlap the edges to form a seam.

3. Apply a standard breading: Dredge the chicken in flour, dip in egg wash, and roll in bread crumbs. (Refrigerate seam side down if breaded in advance.)

4. Heat about ½ in/1 cm of the butter or oil to about 350°F/177°C over medium heat. Add the chicken to the hot oil seam side down first and pan fry for 2 to 3 minutes, or until golden brown and crisp. Turn once, and finish pan frying on the second side, 3 minutes more or until it reaches an internal temperature of 170°F/77°C. (Finish cooking in a 350°F/177°F oven once the crust is properly browned, if preferred.)

5. Blot the chicken on absorbent paper towels briefly before serving with the heated Suprême Sauce.

Buttermilk Fried Chicken with Whipped Potatoes (page 790)
and Braised Collard Greens (page 764)

Buttermilk Fried Chicken

Makes 10 servings

4 (3 lb 8 oz/1.59 kg) chickens, cut into 10 pieces each

16 fl oz/480 mL buttermilk

4 tbsp/12 g minced tarragon

4 oz/120 mL Dijon mustard

1½ tsp/2 g poultry seasoning

2 lb/907 g all-purpose flour

1½ tsp/3 g cayenne

½ oz/14 g Old Bay seasoning

64 oz/1.92 L vegetable shortening, or as needed

20 fl oz/600 mL **Country Gravy** (recipe follows)

1. Combine the chicken pieces with the buttermilk, tarragon, mustard, and poultry seasoning. Mix well and marinate in the refrigerator overnight.

2. Combine the flour with the cayenne and Old Bay. Mix well.

3. Drain the chicken from the buttermilk mixture. Dredge in the flour and let sit for several minutes.

4. Heat the shortening in a large cast-iron pan. Dredge the chicken in the flour again. Working in batches, pan fry the chicken until golden brown on both sides.

5. Finish the chicken in a 350°F/177°C oven on a roasting rack placed on top of a sheet pan until it reaches an internal temperature of 180°F/82°C.

6. Serve immediately with the Country Gravy or hold it hot for service.

Country Gravy

Makes 32 fl oz/960 mL

8 oz/227 g minced slab bacon

2 fl oz/60 mL clarified butter

8 oz/227 g minced onions

2 oz/57 g minced celery

1½ tsp/4.50 g minced garlic

2½ oz/71 g all-purpose flour

40 fl oz/1.20 L **Chicken Stock** (page 351)

12 oz/340 g chicken wings, browned

1 bay leaf

salt, as needed

ground black pepper, as needed

3 fl oz/90 mL milk

3 fl oz/90 mL heavy cream

1. Render the bacon in the butter over medium-low heat until crispy, about 8 minutes.

2. Add the onions, celery, and garlic, and sweat until the onions are translucent, 4 to 6 minutes.

3. Stir in the flour and cook over medium heat to make a pale roux.

4. Add the stock, wings, and bay leaf. Season with salt and pepper.

5. Simmer the gravy for 1½ to 2 hours, skimming as necessary. Add the milk and cream and return the gravy to a simmer.

6. Strain the gravy. Adjust seasoning with salt and pepper, as needed.

7. The gravy is ready to serve now, or it may be rapidly cooled and refrigerated for later use.

Pan-Fried Veal Cutlets

Makes 10 servings

3 lb 12 oz/1.70 kg boneless veal top round, cut into ten 6-oz/170-g portions

1 tsp/5 g salt

½ tsp/1 g ground black pepper

5 oz/142 g all-purpose flour, or as needed

6 fl oz/180 mL egg wash, or as needed

12 oz/340 g bread crumbs, or as needed

24 fl oz/720 mL vegetable oil, or as needed

1. Pound each portion of veal between sheets of parchment or plastic wrap to a thickness of ¼ in/6 mm.

2. At the time of service or up to 3 hours in advance, apply a standard breading to the veal: Blot dry, season with salt and pepper, dredge the veal in flour, dip in egg wash, and roll in bread crumbs. (Refrigerate if breaded in advance.)

3. Heat about ⅛ in/3 mm of oil to about 350°F/177°C over medium heat. Working in batches, add the breaded veal to the hot oil and pan fry on the first side for about 2 minutes, or until golden brown and crisp. Turn once and finish pan frying on the second side, 1 or 2 minutes more or until it reaches an internal temperature of 160°F/71°C.

4. Drain briefly on absorbent paper towels and serve immediately or hold it hot for service.

Wiener Schnitzel: Prepare the cutlets as directed above. Heat 4 oz/113 g butter in a sauté pan until it sizzles, about 2 minutes. Add the pan-fried veal to the hot butter and turn to coat on both sides. Serve at once on heated plates with lemon wedges or slices and parsley sprigs.

Pan-Fried Breaded Pork Cutlet: Substitute an equal amount of boneless pork loin for the veal. Prepare the cutlets as directed above.

Veal Cordon Bleu

Makes 10 servings

3 lb 12 oz/1.70 kg boneless veal top round, cut into ten 6-oz/170-g portions

1 tsp/5 g salt

½ tsp/0.50 g ground black pepper

5 oz/142 g thinly sliced ham

5 oz/142 g thinly sliced Gruyère

5 oz/142 g all-purpose flour, or as needed

4 fl oz/120 mL egg wash, or as needed

8 oz/227 g fresh bread crumbs, or as needed

20 fl oz/600 mL **Mushroom Sauce** (page 521), or as needed

1. Pound each portion of veal between sheets of parchment or plastic wrap to a thickness of ¼ in/6 mm. Blot dry and season with salt and pepper.

2. Top each scaloppine with ½ oz/14 g each of the ham and cheese. Roll the veal around the ham and cheese to form a half-moon shape. Carefully pound the open edges between parchment paper or plastic wrap to seal the cordon bleu.

3. At the time of service or up to 3 hours in advance, apply a standard breading to the veal: Dredge the veal in flour, dip in egg wash, and roll in bread crumbs. (Refrigerate if breaded in advance.)

4. Heat about ½ in/1 cm of oil to about 350°F/177°C over medium heat. Add the veal to the hot oil and pan fry on the first side for 2 to 3 minutes, or until golden brown and crisp. Turn once, and finish pan frying on the second side, 2 minutes more or until it reaches an internal temperature of 160°F/71°C. (Optional: Finish cooking in a 350°F/177°C oven if preferred.) Blot the veal on absorbent paper towels.

5. Serve immediately with the Mushroom Sauce or hold it hot for service.

Veal Piccata with Milanese Sauce (Piccata di Vitello alla Milanese)

Makes 10 servings

3 lb 12 oz/1.70 kg boneless veal top round, cut into ten 6-oz/170-g portions

4 eggs, beaten

2 oz/57 g grated Parmesan

1 tsp/5 g salt

½ tsp/1 g ground black pepper

6 oz/170 g all-purpose flour, or as needed

8 fl oz/240 mL vegetable oil, or as needed

20 fl oz/600 mL **Milanese Sauce** (recipe follows)

1. Pound each portion of veal between sheets of parchment or plastic wrap to a thickness of ¼ in/6 mm.

2. Combine the eggs and Parmesan, mix well, and reserve.

3. Blot the veal dry, season with salt and pepper, dip in egg mixture, and dredge in flour. (Refrigerate if breaded in advance.)

4. Heat about ½ in/16 mm of oil to about 350°F/177°C over medium heat. Add the veal to the hot oil and pan fry on the first side for about 2 minutes. When golden brown and crisp, turn once and finish pan frying on second side for 2 minutes more or until it reaches an internal temperature of 160°F/71°C. Remove the veal from the pan and blot on absorbent paper towels.

5. Serve immediately with the Milanese Sauce or hold it hot for service.

Milanese Sauce

Makes 32 fl oz/960 mL

3 fl oz/ 90 mL clarified butter

4 oz/113 g white mushroom julienne

2 oz/57 g minced shallots

12 fl oz/360 mL dry red wine

24 fl oz/720 mL **Tomato Sauce** (page 384)

24 fl oz/720 mL **Jus de Veau Lié** (page 382)

4 oz/113 g ham julienne

2 oz/57 g beef tongue julienne

4 tsp/4 g chopped parsley

salt, as needed

ground black pepper, as needed

1. In a saucepan, heat the butter over medium heat. Add the mushrooms and shallots and sauté for about 1 minute.

2. Add the wine and reduce until nearly dry. Add the tomato sauce and jus lié. Simmer until the sauce has reduced by about one quarter to one half.

3. Add the ham, tongue, and parsley and simmer until all the ingredients are hot. Season with salt and pepper.

4. The sauce is ready to serve now, or it may be rapidly cooled and refrigerated for later use.

Fisherman's Platter

Makes 10 servings

1 lb 4 oz/567 g flounder, cut into 1-oz/28-g goujonettes

20 littleneck clams, shucked

20 oysters, shucked

20 shrimp (16–20 count), peeled and deveined

10 oz/284 g sea scallops, muscle tabs removed

2 fl oz/60 mL lemon juice, or as needed

1 tsp/5 g salt

½ tsp/1 g ground black pepper

5 oz/142 g all-purpose flour, or as needed

6 fl oz/180 mL egg wash, or as needed

12 oz/340 g bread crumbs, or as needed

16 fl oz/480 mL vegetable oil, or as needed

20 fl oz/600 mL **Rémoulade Sauce** (recipe follows)

1. At the time of service or up to 3 hours in advance, blot dry the surface of the fish, clams, oysters, shrimp, and scallops and season with lemon juice, salt, and pepper. Apply a standard breading: Dredge each piece in flour, dip in egg wash, and roll in bread crumbs. (Refrigerate if breaded in advance.)

2. Heat about ½ in/16 mm of oil to about 350°F/177°C over medium heat. Add the fish and seafood to the hot oil and pan fry on the first side for about 2 minutes, or until golden brown and crisp. Turn once and finish pan frying on the second side, 1 to 2 minutes more, or until each variety reaches an internal temperature of 145°F/63°C. (Finish cooking in a 350°F/177°C oven once the crust is properly browned, if preferred.)

3. Blot the fish and seafood on absorbent paper towels briefly. Serve 2 goujonettes, 2 clams, 2 oysters, 2 shrimp, and 1 scallop per serving with 2 fl oz/60 mL of Rémoulade Sauce.

Rémoulade Sauce

Makes 32 fl oz/960 mL

28 fl oz/840 mL **Mayonnaise** (page 936)

2 oz/57 g chopped capers

3 tbsp/9 g chopped chives

3 tbsp/9 g chopped tarragon

½ fl oz/15 mL Dijon mustard

1 tsp/5 mL anchovy paste

salt, as needed

Worcestershire sauce, as needed

Tabasco sauce, as needed

1. Combine all the ingredients and mix well. Adjust seasoning with salt, pepper, Worcestershire, and Tabasco.

2. The sauce is ready to serve now, or it may be refrigerated for later use.

Old-Fashioned Salt Cod Cakes

Makes 10 servings

1 lb 8 oz/680 g salt cod fillets

64 fl oz/1.92 L water

32 fl oz/960 mL whole milk

3 lb/1.36 kg russet potatoes

12 oz/340 g minced onions

4 tsp/12 g minced garlic

2 oz/57 g butter

3 eggs

4½ tsp/22.50 mL mustard

4½ tsp/22.50 mL Worcestershire sauce

½ oz/14 g chopped parsley

2 tsp/10 g salt

½ tsp/1 g ground black pepper

3 oz/85 g Japanese bread crumbs (panko)

1 lb/454 g thinly sliced slab bacon

16 fl oz/480 mL vegetable oil, or as needed

1. Rinse the salt cod in several changes of water. Soak it overnight in the water.

2. The next day, remove the salt cod from the water, cut into large chunks, and simmer in the milk over medium-low heat for 15 minutes.

3. Discard the milk and rinse the salt cod under cold water. Taste the cod; it should not be salty. If still salty, repeat as necessary with fresh milk. Shred or chop the cod into fine pieces. Refrigerate until thoroughly chilled.

4. Scrub, peel, and cut the potatoes into large pieces. Cook the potatoes by boiling or steaming until tender enough to mash easily. Drain and dry them over low heat or on a sheet pan in a 300°F/149°C oven until no more steam rises from them. While the potatoes are still hot, purée them through a food mill or potato ricer into a heated bowl.

5. While the potatoes are cooking, sweat the onions and garlic in the butter in a sauté pan over medium heat until translucent, 3 to 4 minutes. Refrigerate until thoroughly chilled.

6. Combine the potatoes with the salt cod. There should still be small flakes of the cod visible throughout the potato mixture.

7. Add the eggs, mustard, Worcestershire sauce, parsley, and chilled onions and garlic to the salt cod mixture and season with salt and pepper. Chill the mixture thoroughly before using.

8. Portion the cod mixture into 3-oz/85-g cakes that are approximately 2½ in/6 cm in diameter and 1 in/3 cm thick.

9. Lightly coat the cakes in the bread crumbs and then wrap a piece of bacon around the outside of each cod cake. Secure the bacon with a toothpick.

10. Heat about 4 fl oz/120 mL of the oil in a sautoir over medium-high heat. Pan fry the cod cakes until golden brown, crispy, and cooked through, 3 to 4 minutes per side. Add clean oil to the pan when necessary.

11. Drain on absorbent paper towels and serve immediately or hold them hot for service.

Pan-Fried Brook Trout with Bacon with Converted Wild Rice
Pilaf (page 828) and Glazed Carrots (page 741)

Pan-Fried Brook Trout with Bacon

Makes 10 servings

15 bacon slices

10 brook trout, trimmed, boned

2 tsp/10 g salt

1 tsp/2 g ground black pepper

16 fl oz/480 mL buttermilk, or as needed

16 fl oz/480 mL vegetable oil, or as needed

8 oz/227 g all-purpose flour, or as needed

2 lemons, cut into wedges

1. Lay the bacon on a sheet pan in a single layer. Place in a 375°F/191°C oven and cook for 15 minutes or until crispy. Cut each slice in half and reserve.

2. Season the interior of the trout with salt and pepper. Lay the trout in a buttermilk-lined hotel pan.

3. Heat the oil in a large cast-iron skillet or sauté pan over medium-high heat. Lightly dredge the trout in flour and shake off excess.

4. Pan fry the trout 4 to 5 minutes per side; lower the heat as needed to avoid scorching.

5. Blot briefly on absorbent paper towels.

6. Lay 3 slices of crispy bacon on top of each trout and serve immediately with a lemon wedge, or reserve hot for service.

Shrimp Tempura

Makes 10 servings

3 lb 12 oz/1.70 kg shrimp (16–20 count), peeled and deveined

16 fl oz/480 mL vegetable oil

8 fl oz/240 mL peanut oil

8 fl oz/240 mL sesame oil

TEMPURA BATTER

3 eggs, beaten

16 fl oz/480 mL water

8 oz/227 g ice, crushed

13 oz/369 g all-purpose flour, plus more for dredging

20 fl oz/600 mL **Tempura Dipping Sauce** (recipe follows)

1. If desired, make a couple incisions on the stomach side of each shrimp so that it stays straight. Refrigerate until service.

2. Combine the vegetable, peanut, and sesame oils in a deep pot or fryer. Heat to 350°F/177°C.

3. To make the batter, combine the eggs, water, and ice. Add the flour and mix gently. Do not overmix.

4. Lightly dredge the shrimp in flour. Pick up the shrimp by their tails and dip the bodies only in the batter to lightly coat. Immediately deep fry until crispy and white or light golden brown.

5. Blot the tempura on absorbent paper towels and serve immediately with the dipping sauce.

Tempura Dipping Sauce

Makes 32 fl oz/960 mL

16 fl oz/480 mL light soy sauce

8 fl oz/240 mL **Dashi** (page 354)

8 fl oz/240 mL mirin

5 oz/142 g finely grated daikon

1 tbsp/9 g finely grated ginger

1. Combine all the ingredients in a saucepan and warm slightly over low heat.

2. The sauce is ready to serve now, or it may be rapidly cooled and refrigerated for later use.

Crispy Tangerine-Flavored Chicken

Makes 10 servings

MARINADE

1 fl oz/30 mL light soy sauce

1½ tsp/4.50 g minced garlic

1 tsp/5 g salt

2 tsp/4 g ground white pepper

2 lb/907 g chicken thighs, cut into 1-in/3-cm cubes

32 fl oz/960 mL vegetable oil, or as needed

COATING

1 egg

4 fl oz/120 mL water

6 oz/170 g cornstarch

2 fl oz/60 mL peanut oil

1 tbsp/9 g minced ginger

1 tbsp/9 g minced garlic

½ oz/14 g thinly sliced green onions

½ oz/14 g dried tangerine skin, rehydrated and minced

2 tsp/7 g dried red chiles

8 oz/227 g white mushrooms, quartered

8 oz/227 g red peppers, cut into 1-in/3-cm squares

8 oz/227 g broccoli florets, blanched

14 fl oz/420 mL **Sweet Garlic Sauce** (recipe follows)

1. To make the marinade, combine the soy sauce, garlic, salt, and pepper. Pour the mixture over the chicken and marinate in the refrigerator for 20 minutes.

2. Heat the vegetable oil to 350°F/177°C.

3. To make the coating, combine the egg, water, and cornstarch to make a smooth paste. Drain the chicken from the marinade and cover it with the coating mixture.

4. Deep-fry the chicken until it is golden brown, crispy, and cooked through, 2 to 3 minutes. Drain briefly on absorbent paper towels and reserve warm.

5. At service, heat the peanut oil in a wok over medium-high heat. Add the ginger, garlic, green onions, tangerine skin, and chiles and stir-fry until aromatic, 15 to 30 seconds.

6. Add the mushrooms and stir-fry for 2 minutes. Add the red peppers and stir-fry 1 to 2 minutes. Add the broccoli and stir-fry 1 to 2 minutes.

7. Add the fried chicken and stir-fry to reheat, 1 to 2 minutes.

8. Slowly add the Sweet Garlic Sauce, stirring constantly to coat the chicken and vegetables in the sauce.

9. Serve immediately.

Sweet Garlic Sauce

Makes 32 fl oz/960 mL

2½ fl oz/75 mL vegetable oil

2 tsp/10 g minced ginger

1 oz/28 g minced garlic

1¼ oz/35 g minced green onions

2 tsp/10 mL hot bean paste

6 fl oz/480 mL light soy sauce

2½ fl oz/75 mL rice wine (Shaoxing)

2½ fl oz/75 mL rice vinegar

10 fl oz/300 mL **Chicken Stock** (page 351)

5½ oz/156 g sugar

2 tsp/10 mL sesame oil

2½ oz/71 g cornstarch, mixed with water to make a slurry

1. Heat the oil in a wok over medium-high heat. Add the ginger, garlic, and green onions and stir-fry until aromatic, 15 to 30 seconds.

2. Add the bean paste and stir-fry for another 15 to 30 seconds.

3. Add the soy sauce, rice wine, vinegar, and stock and bring the mixture to a boil.

4. Stir in the sugar and sesame oil and return to a boil.

5. Gradually add the cornstarch slurry to the sauce until it becomes medium thick.

6. The sauce is ready to serve now, or it may be rapidly cooled and refrigerated for later use.

Crispy Tangerine-Flavored Chicken

Shrimp in Achiote Sauce, Yucatan Style

Makes 10 servings

3 lb 8 oz/1.59 kg shrimp (16–20 count), peeled and deveined

1 tbsp/9 g minced garlic

1 tbsp/15 g salt

ACHIOTE SAUCE

3½ oz/99 g achiote paste

8 oz/227 g chopped onions

3 garlic cloves

3 dried pequin chiles

5 cloves

4 allspice berries

4 fl oz/120 mL orange juice

4 fl oz/120 mL lime juice

½ fl oz/15 mL white vinegar

salt, as needed

ground black pepper, as needed

2 fl oz/60 mL vegetable oil

10 fl oz/300 mL **Pickled Red Onions** (page 997)

1. Rub the shrimp with the garlic and salt and refrigerate for up to 2 hours.

2. To make the sauce, combine the achiote paste, onions, garlic, chiles, cloves, allspice, orange juice, lime juice, and vinegar in a blender and blend until very smooth, 2 to 3 minutes. Season with salt and pepper.

3. Pour this mixture over the shrimp and marinate for 20 minutes in the refrigerator.

4. Drain the shrimp and reserve the marinade.

5. Heat the oil in a sauté pan over high heat and sauté the shrimp until golden brown, 3 to 4 minutes. Work in batches, if necessary. Pour the reserved marinade over the shrimp, letting the contents boil for 1 to 2 more minutes. Adjust seasoning with salt and pepper, if necessary.

6. Remove the shrimp from the pan and reserve warm. Cook the sauce for 1 to 2 more minutes. Remove from the heat and pour over the shrimp.

7. Garnish with the Pickled Red Onions and serve immediately or hold it hot for service.

Flounder à l'Orly

Makes 10 servings

32 fl oz/960 mL vegetable oil, or as needed

3 lb 12 oz/1.70 kg flounder fillets, cut into ten 6-oz/170-g portions

1 fl oz/30 mL lemon juice

1 tsp/5 g salt

½ tsp/1 g ground black pepper

all-purpose flour, as needed

22 fl oz/660 mL **Beer Batter** (recipe follows)

20 fl oz/600 mL **Tomato Sauce** (page 384)

20 parsley sprigs

10 lemon wedges

1. Heat the oil to 350°F/177°C in a deep fryer or tall pot.

2. At the time of service, blot the fish dry and season with lemon juice, salt, and pepper. Dip into the flour, shaking off any excess, then dip into the Beer Batter. Place the flounder in a fryer basket, lower it into the oil, and deep fry the fish until golden brown and cooked through, 3 to 4 minutes.

3. Blot briefly on absorbent paper towels and serve immediately with 2 fl oz/60 mL of Tomato Sauce, 2 parsley sprigs, and 1 lemon wedge.

Beer Batter

Makes 22 fl oz/60 mL

10 oz/284 g all-purpose flour

½ tsp/1.50 g baking powder

1 tsp/5 g salt

1 egg, separated

16 fl oz/480 mL beer

1. Whisk together the flour, baking powder, and salt. Add the egg yolk and the beer all at once, and whisk until very smooth. Keep chilled until service.

2. At the time of service, whip the reserved egg white to soft peaks. Fold the whites into the batter and use at once.

Hanoi Fried Fish with Dill (Cha Ca Thang Long)

Makes 10 servings

4 oz/113 g rice flour

2 tsp/4 g turmeric

1 tbsp/15 g salt

32 fl oz/960 mL vegetable oil

3 lb/1.36 kg catfish fillets, cut into 2-in/5-cm squares

1 fl oz/30 mL peanut oil

4 oz/113 g green onions, julienned

30 Thai basil leaves, halved lengthwise

60 cilantro leaves

60 dill sprigs, stemmed

1 lb/454 g rice noodle vermicelli, cooked

2½ oz/71 g pan-roasted peanuts

16 fl oz/480 mL **Vietnamese Dipping Sauce** (page 991)

1. Combine the rice flour, turmeric, and salt in a large bowl. Heat the vegetable oil to 375°F/191°C.

2. Toss the fish in the flour mixture, shake off excess, and immediately deep fry until golden and crispy, 2 to 3 minutes. Drain on absorbent paper towels and reserve warm.

3. Heat the peanut oil in a wok, stir-fry the green onions for about 5 seconds. Add the basil, cilantro, and dill and stir-fry just until the herbs wilt, 30 to 45 seconds. Remove immediately.

4. Serve the fish on a bed of the noodles topped with the herb mixture. Garnish with the roasted peanuts and serve with Vietnamese Dipping Sauce.

Fried Fish Cakes

Makes 10 servings

10 Thai chiles

1½ oz/43 g shallots, peeled

2 garlic cloves, peeled

½ oz/14 g cilantro root or stem

1 tbsp/8 g galangal

3 kaffir lime leaves

1 tsp/5 g salt

1 lb 4 oz/567 g white-fleshed fish fillets, minced

1 fl oz/30 mL fish sauce

4 oz/113 g long beans, sliced into paper-thin rounds

32 fl oz/960 mL peanut oil

20 fl oz/600 mL **Cucumber Salad** (page 956)

1. Grind the chiles, shallots, garlic, cilantro, galangal, lime leaves, and salt to a paste in a food processor.

2. Combine spice paste, fish, fish sauce, and beans in a bowl and knead until well combined and the consistency is slightly tacky.

3. Shape into round, flat pucks. Refrigerate until ready to cook.

4. Heat the oil to 350°F/177°C. Deep fry the cakes until they are golden brown on the outside and they float to the top of the oil, about 3 minutes.

5. Remove the cakes from the oil and drain on absorbent paper towels.

6. Serve immediately with the Cucumber Salad or hold them hot for service.

Chapter Twenty-Two

Steaming and Submersion Cooking

Moist-heat techniques—steaming, cooking foods en papillote, shallow poaching, deep poaching, and simmering—rely on liquid and/or water vapor as the cooking medium. Monitoring cooking temperatures and times vigilantly and determining doneness accurately are key to a mastery of moist-heat methods.

Steaming

Cooked surrounded by water vapor in a closed cooking vessel, steamed foods have clean, clear flavors. Steam circulating around the food provides an even, moist environment. Steaming is an efficient and highly effective way to prepare naturally tender fish and poultry. Properly steamed foods are plump, moist, and tender; they generally do not lose much of their original volume. They often retain more intrinsic flavor than foods cooked by other methods because the cooking medium does not generally impart much flavor of its own. Colors also stay true.

The best foods for steaming are naturally tender and of a size and shape that allow them to cook in a short amount of time. Cut food into the appropriate size, if necessary. Fish is generally cooked as fillets, though there are some typical presentations of whole fish. Similarly, boneless, skinless poultry breasts, or suprêmes, steam well. Shellfish can be left in the shell, unless otherwise indicated; for example, scallops are customarily removed from the shell. Shrimp may also be peeled before steaming.

Many different liquids are used for steaming. Water is common, but a flavorful broth or stock, court bouillon, wine, or beer can also be used, especially if the steaming liquid is served along with the food. Adding such aromatic ingredients as herbs and spices, citrus zest, lemongrass, ginger, garlic, and mushrooms to the liquid boosts its flavor as well as that of the food being steamed. Sometimes food is steamed on a bed of vegetables in a closed vessel; the vegetables' natural moisture becomes part of the steam bath cooking the food. Fillings, marinades, and wrappers can all be used in preparing steamed foods. Fish is sometimes wrapped in this way to keep it exceptionally moist.

Small amounts of food can be steamed using a small insert. Larger quantities, or foods that require different cooking times, are better prepared in a tiered steamer. Remember that it is important to allow enough room for steam to circulate completely around foods as they cook to encourage even, rapid cooking.

Pressure steamers, which reach higher temperatures than tiered steamers, and convection steamers are good choices for steaming large quantities. The chef can then prepare appropriately sized batches throughout a meal period or handle the more intense demands of a banquet or institutional meal situation.

A basic formula for a single, steamed, entrée-sized portion

One portion (6 to 8 oz/170 to 227 g) of prepared meat, poultry, or fish

Enough steaming liquid to last throughout the cooking time

Salt and other seasonings for both the main item and the steaming liquid

Additional finishing and garnishing ingredients

2 to 3 fl oz/60 to 90 mL prepared sauce

1. **Bring the liquid and any additional aromatics to a full boil in a covered vessel.** Add enough liquid to the bottom of the steamer to last throughout cooking. Adding more liquid to the pot during cooking lowers the cooking temperature and lengthens the time needed to prepare steamed foods. If you must add liquid, preheat it.

2. **Place the main item in the steamer in a single layer.** If cooking more than one layer of food at a time, use a tiered steamer. Foods may be placed on plates or in shallow dishes on the rack to collect any juices that might escape.

Adjust the heat to maintain even, moderate heat. Liquids do not need to be at a rolling boil in order to produce steam. In fact, rapid boiling may cause the liquid to cook away too fast.

Replace the lid and steam until done. Since steaming is done in a closed cooking vessel, it can be more difficult than other methods to gauge how long foods need to cook. Recipes may tell how long to steam foods for the correct doneness. Still, it is important to start checking for doneness at the earliest point at which the food might be done. Remember to tilt the lid away from you as you open it so that the steam will safely vent away from your face and hands.

3. **Cooked steamed foods until they are just done and serve immediately.** Steamed foods can easily become rubbery and dry, so be careful not to overcook them. Any juices from the food should be nearly colorless. When done, the flesh of fish and shellfish loses its translucency, taking on a nearly opaque appearance. The shells of mollusks (mussels, clams, and oysters) open, the flesh turns opaque, and the edges curl. Crustaceans (shrimp, crab, and lobster) have a bright pink or red color when done. Poultry turns opaque, and the flesh offers little resistance when pressed with a fingertip.

Serve the food immediately on heated plates with an appropriate sauce, as desired, or as indicated by the recipe. Remember that steamed food continues to cook after it comes out of the steamer.

Evaluate the quality of steamed foods according to flavor, appearance, and texture. Because no initial browning of the food takes place, the flavor remains delicate. Any aromatics appropriate to the food's flavor should not be so intense as to overwhelm the main item. When properly done, the food's surface appears quite moist. Fish, especially salmon, should not have deposits of white albumin on the flesh, which indicates that it has been overcooked and/or cooked too quickly.

Cooking en Papillote

In this variation of steaming, which translates literally as "in paper," the main item and accompanying ingredients are wrapped in a parchment paper package and cooked in the steam produced by their own juices.

En papillote indicates a specific preparation, but there are similar dishes, known by regional names, throughout the world. The classic wrapper for a dish en papillote is parchment paper, but the effect is similar when aluminum foil, lettuce, plantain, grape, or banana leaves, corn husks, or similar wrappers are used to enclose foods as they cook. The wrapper traps the steam driven from the foods as they heat up—the dish is often presented to the guest still in its wrapper, and when the packet is opened, it releases a cloud of aromatic steam.

Foods prepared en papillote should be cooked until just done. This is difficult to gauge without experience, because you cannot open the package to see or feel for doneness. If the food has been cut to the correct size or if it has been partially cooked in advance, it should be done when the package is very puffy and the paper is brown. Performing a few test runs of an en papillote dish will help establish a reliable cooking time for the dish, provided that the ingredients are consistently prepared beforehand.

Cooking en papillote, like steaming, is suited to naturally tender foods, like chicken, fish, and shellfish. Trim and portion foods as required by the recipe. They may be marinated or seared as an initial step, if appropriate. Marinades can add flavor and color; searing helps to assure that thicker cuts cook more quickly and deepens both the flavor and color of the seared item. Some foods may be filled or stuffed.

Include vegetables for moisture as well as flavor, color, and texture. Cut the vegetables small, usually into thin slices, a fine julienne, or tiny dice, and sweat or blanch them, if necessary, to ensure that they will be fully cooked. Leave herbs in sprigs, cut them into a chiffonade, or mince them. Also have available a prepared sauce, reduced heavy cream, wine, or citrus juices as required by the recipe.

To cook en papillote, you will need parchment paper (or other wrappers as required by the recipe), sizzler platters or baking sheets, and service items. Cut the wrapper large enough to allow the food and any additional ingredients to fit comfortably without overcrowding.

A basic formula for a single entrée-sized portion

One portion (4 to 6 oz/113 to 170 g) of prepared meat, poultry, or fish

Up to 1 fl oz/30 mL of a cooking liquid (stock, sauce, wine) or enough naturally moist vegetables to produce steam

Salt and other seasonings

Additional finishing and garnishing ingredients as desired

1. **Assemble the packages.** Cut the parchment or other wrapper into heart or other shapes large enough to hold the food on one half, with a 1-in/3-cm margin of paper all the way around.

Lightly oil or butter the wrapper on both sides to prevent it from burning. Arrange a bed of vegetables, aromatics, or sauce on one half of wrapper and top it with the main item.

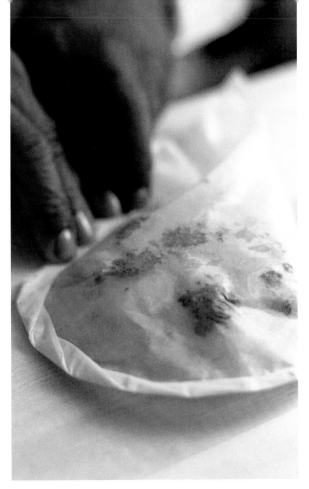

2. **Fold the other half over, then crimp the edges of the paper or foil or tie the packet securely to seal it.** Sealing the edges of the package keeps in the steam, so that it can properly cook the food.

3. **Place the package on a preheated sizzler platter or baking sheet and bake in a moderate oven until the package is puffed and the paper is browned.** The oven temperature needs to be carefully monitored because delicate foods such as fish fillets can be overcooked quickly.

As the package cools, it will begin to deflate, so serve en papillote dishes as soon as possible. For a dramatic presentation, have the server cut open the package in front of the guest.

Evaluate the quality of the finished dish. Meats, fish, and poultry prepared en papillote or by similar techniques should be cooked according to doneness standards for the kitchen or to guest preference (see the table on page 461). Sauces, cooking liquids, and other ingredients should also have a full flavor and be properly cooked.

Shallow Poaching

Shallow poaching, like sautéing and grilling, is an à la minute technique. Foods are cooked in a combination of steam and simmering liquid. Shallow-poached foods are partially submerged in liquid, which often contains an acid (wine or lemon juice). Aromatics, such as shallots and herbs, are added for more flavor. Cover the pan to capture some of the steam released by the liquid during cooking. A significant amount of flavor is transferred from the food to the cooking liquid. For maximum flavor, the cooking liquid (cuisson) is usually reduced and used as the base for a sauce. The acids give the sauce a bright, balanced flavor. Butter can be easily emulsified in the sauce; beurre blanc is often the sauce of choice for shallow-poached foods.

As for steaming, naturally tender foods of a size and shape that allow for quick cooking work best. Fish, shellfish, and chicken breasts are among the most common options for this cooking method. Trim the main item as appropriate. Remove bones or skin from fish to make fillets or from poultry to make suprêmes or boneless skinless breast portions. Fish fillets may be rolled or folded around a stuffing to form paupiettes (see page 609), with the bone side of the fish showing on the exterior. Remove shellfish from the shell, if desired.

Liquid contributes flavor to the food as well as to the sauce prepared from it. Choose rich broths or stocks and add wine, vinegar, or citrus juice as desired.

Cut aromatics fine or mince them. Other ingredients to be served along with the sauce as a garnish should be cut neatly into strips, dice, julienne, or chiffonade. These ingredients are often sweated or parcooked first to develop the best possible flavor as well as to make certain that all parts of the finished dish are fully cooked at the same time.

The sauce may be a beurre blanc or sauce vin blanc (page 612), or simply the reduced cooking liquids. Refer to specific recipes for additional suggestions or guidance.

Use a sauté pan or other shallow cooking vessel, such as a sautoir or rondeau, to shallow poach. Select the pan or baking dish carefully; if there is too much or too little space left around the food, it may over- or undercook, or there may be too much or too little liquid for the sauce. Buttered or oiled parchment or a loose-fitting lid is used to loosely cover the pan as the food cooks. It traps enough of the steam to cook the unexposed part of the food, but not so much that the cooking speed rises. You may require a strainer for the sauce. You will also need utensils for handling the poached food, such as a slotted spatula, and heated plates for service.

Filling Paupiettes

A paupiette is a thin, rolled fillet, often filled with a forcemeat or other stuffing. It should resemble a large spiral. Paupiettes are generally made from lean fish, such as flounder or sole, although they may also be made from some moderately fatty fish, such as trout or salmon. The most common preparation technique for paupiettes is shallow poaching.

After the fillets are gently flattened between plastic wrap to ensure even cooking, pipe a cold filling down the length of each fillet. Spread the filling evenly over the entire surface for paupiettes. Fillings are optional, but if used, they should be kept very cold until ready to cook.

Fillings need to be fully encased to ensure they are fully retained during cooking and do not leak out. The fish is rolled completely around the filling before transferring the paupiettes to a holding container for later service.

A basic formula for a single entrée-sized portion

One portion (4 to 6 oz/113 to 170 g) of fish or chicken breast

1 oz/30 g butter

½ oz/14 g shallots

Enough poaching liquid to last throughout cooking time (about 10 to 20 fl oz/300 to 600 mL)

Salt and other seasonings for both the food and the poaching liquid

Additional finishing ingredients, including prepared sauce and garnishes

1. **Make sure the liquid's level goes no higher than halfway up the food; generally, less is required.** If too much liquid is used, either a great deal of time will be needed to reduce it properly or only part of it will be usable in the sauce.

Lightly butter a shallow pan and add aromatics to the pan to give the cooking liquid and finished sauce a good flavor. If the aromatics can cook completely in the time required, they can be added raw. Otherwise, cook them separately beforehand by sweating lightly in the butter.

Season and place the main item on top of the aromatics, then pour the liquid around the item. It is not necessary in most cases to preheat the liquid, though for large quantities, it may be helpful to do so. Be careful not to have it at a full boil.

2. **Cover the paupiettes with buttered parchment (cartouche) before putting them in the oven.**
It is best to finish poaching foods in the oven because oven heat is more even and gentle than direct heat. It also frees burner space for other purposes.

Bring the liquid up to cooking level over direct heat, loosely covered with parchment paper, and finish in a moderate oven. On some occasions, however, it is preferable to perform the entire cooking operation in the oven. The quantity of food prepared and the available equipment will dictate what is most logical. Do not allow the liquid to boil at any time. A rapid boil will cook the food too quickly, affecting the quality of the dish.

3. **Cook shallow-poached foods until just done.**
Fish and shellfish should appear opaque and feel slightly firm; the flesh of oysters, clams, and mussels should curl around the edges. Chicken suprêmes should appear opaque and offer slight resistance when pressed with a fingertip.

Transfer the paupiettes to a holding dish and moisten with a small amount of the cooking liquid to keep it from drying out while the sauce is prepared. Cover the food loosely and keep it warm. Add the additional ingredients for the sauce to the cooking liquid as directed in the recipe.

When well prepared, shallow-poached dishes reflect the flavor of both the food and the cooking liquid. The sauce adds a rich, complementary flavor. In general, foods appear moist, opaque, and relatively light in color. Fish should not have deposits of white albumin, which indicates that it has been overcooked or cooked too quickly. Properly cooked shallow-poached foods are very tender and exceptionally moist. And because this technique is most often used with delicate foods, they have an almost fragile texture. If they are falling apart or dry, however, they have been overcooked.

4. Simmer the cooking liquid (cuisson) over direct heat to concentrate the flavor and thicken the liquid. A prepared fish velouté has been added to the reduced cuisson. Other options include reduced cream, vegetable purées, or butter.

To Make a Beurre Blanc

Reduce the cooking liquid until it is syrupy. (It may be strained into a separate pot at this point if desired.) With the reduced cooking liquid at a simmer, add pieces of cold butter a few at time. Keep the pan in motion as the butter is added, swirling it into the sauce as it melts.

To Make a Sauce Vin Blanc

Reduce the cooking liquid and add the desired aromatics and an appropriately flavored velouté. Strain the sauce if necessary and finish with cream or a liaison and any additional garnishes. For more information about preparing sauces for shallow-poached items, refer to specific recipes.

Deep Poaching and Simmering

Deep poaching and simmering call for a food to be completely submerged in a liquid at a constant, moderate temperature. The aim of deep poaching and simmering is the same—to produce foods that are moist and extremely tender. The distinguishing factors between the two methods are differences in cooking temperature and appropriate types of food. Deep poaching is done at a lower temperature and is better suited to naturally tender cuts of meat, poultry, or fish. Simmering occurs at slightly higher temperature so that the tougher cuts can become tender and moist during cooking.

Items to be deep poached should be naturally tender; those to be simmered need not be since the simmering process will tenderize them. Though portion-size cuts are often used—chicken quarters, for example—poached and simmered items also include dressed fish, whole birds, or large pieces of meat.

Wrap dressed fish in cheesecloth to protect it from breaking apart during cooking. Stuff the poultry, if desired, and truss it to help retain its shape. Stuff meats, if desired, and tie them to maintain their shape.

The liquid used in deep poaching and simmering should be well flavored. For meat and poultry, select a well-developed stock of the appropriate flavor. For fish and shellfish, use fish stock, fumet, wine, or a court bouillon. Aromatic ingredients, such as herbs and spices, wine, vegetables, vegetable juices, or citrus zest, may be added to the cooking liquid to enhance the flavor of the finished dish. See specific recipes for instructions on preparing and adding these ingredients.

Deep-poached and simmered foods are often served with a sauce that is prepared separately. "Boiled" beef, for instance, is traditionally served with a horseradish sauce, and poached salmon is often served with a warm butter emulsion sauce, such as béarnaise or mousseline. See specific recipes for sauce suggestions.

The pot used for deep poaching or simmering should hold the food, liquid, and aromatics comfortably, with enough room to allow the liquid to expand as it heats. There should also be enough space so that the surface can be skimmed if necessary throughout cooking. A tight-fitting lid may be helpful for bringing the liquid up to temperature. Leaving a lid on throughout the cooking process may actually cause the liquid to become hotter than desired.

Other helpful equipment includes ladles or skimmers, holding containers to keep the foods warm, carving boards, and slicers. An instant-read thermometer is also helpful to monitor the temperature of the cooking liquid; it can be difficult to see the difference between a liquid at a perfect poaching temperature and one that is a degree or two away from a slow boil. The difference to the food can be quite important.

A basic formula for a single entrée-sized portion

One 6-oz/170-g portion of fish, chicken, or meat

About 10 fl oz/300 mL of stock or other liquid

Assorted vegetables

Salt and other seasonings for both the food and the liquid

Additional finishing ingredients, including prepared sauce and garnishes

1. **Lower the food into fumet that has been brought to the appropriate poaching temperature (160° to 185°F/71° to 85°C).** Be sure that the pan is not overcrowded or the food will cook unevenly.

Some foods are started off in cool liquid. Poaching liquid should be at 160° to 185°F/71° to 85°C. The surface of the liquid may show some motion, sometimes called shivering, but no air bubbles should break the surface. Simmering liquid will have small bubbles gently breaking the surface and should be between 185° and 200°F/85° and 93°C.

2. **Be sure that the food is completely submerged in the liquid.** If a part of the food is above the level of the cooking liquid, the cooking will be uneven and the finished product will not have the proper delicate color.

Maintain the proper cooking speed throughout the poaching or simmering process until the item is done. Skim as necessary and adjust seasoning throughout the cooking time. If a cover is used, the cooking temperature must be monitored regularly. Covering a pot creates pressure, which raises the temperature of the liquid. Setting the lid slightly ajar is a good precaution to be certain that the liquid does not inadvertently come to a boil.

3. **Poach the food until properly done.** Tests for doneness vary from one food type to another. If a poached or simmered item is to be served cold, it may be desirable to slightly undercook it. Remove the pot from the heat and let the food cool in the poaching liquid, which will retain enough heat to complete the cooking process. Cool the liquid in an ice water bath to prevent bacterial growth. Once it has reached room temperature, remove the food for any further preparation. The liquid may be used to poach or simmer other items.

Properly deep-poached or simmered poultry and meats are fork tender, and any juices from poultry are nearly colorless. Poultry flesh takes on an evenly opaque appearance and offers little resistance when pressed with a fingertip. When whole birds are fully cooked, the legs move easily in the sockets.

When properly cooked, the flesh of fish and shellfish is slightly firm and has lost its translucency, taking on a nearly opaque appearance. Shellfish open and the edges of the flesh curl. Shrimp, crab, and lobster have a bright pink or red color.

The aromatics, seasonings, and flavorings should either bolster or complement the flavor of the food in a balanced way.

New England Shore Dinner

New England Shore Dinner

Makes 10 servings

4 oz/113 g butter

10 oz/284 g small-dice onions

½ oz/14 g minced garlic

1 tsp/2 g dried thyme

2 bay leaves

16 fl oz/480 mL **Chicken Stock** (page 351), or as needed

5 ears corn on the cob, husked and quartered

5 lobster tails, halved

60 littleneck or cherrystone clams

60 mussels, scrubbed and debearded

2 lb/907 g Red Bliss potatoes

1 lb 4 oz/567 g cod fillets

5 leeks, split and washed

30 pearl onions, blanched and peeled

10 oz/284 g sea scallops

1 lb 4 oz/567 g zucchini, thick batonnet

2 tbsp/6 g chopped parsley

1. Heat the butter in a large pot over medium heat. Add the onions and cook, stirring frequently, until the onions are tender and translucent, 2 to 3 minutes. Add the garlic and sweat until aromatic, 1 minute.

2. Add the thyme, bay leaves, and stock and bring to a simmer over low heat.

3. Arrange the ingredients on top of the onion mixture in the following sequence: corn, lobster, clams, mussels, potatoes, cod, leeks, pearl onions, scallops, and zucchini.

4. Cover the pot with a tight-fitting lid and steam over medium heat until all of the ingredients are cooked through, about 25 minutes.

5. Arrange the fish, seafood, and vegetables on a platter, or serve directly from the pot. Garnish with parsley. Strain the broth and serve separately, if desired.

Bass and Scallops en Papillote

Makes 10 servings

2 oz/57 g butter

24 fl oz/720 mL **Vegetable Stock** (page 353)

8 fl oz/240 mL vermouth

2 lb/907 g celeriac julienne

1 lb/454 g thinly sliced Red Bliss potatoes

10½ oz/315 g carrot julienne

10½ oz/315 g cucumber julienne

1 lb/454 g sea bass fillets, cut into ten 1½-oz/43-g portions

1 lb/454 g sea scallops, muscle tabs removed

5 fl oz/150 mL **Gremolata** (page 662)

1 tsp/2 g crushed black peppercorns

1. Cut 10 heart shapes out of parchment paper, large enough to enclose the fish, scallops, and vegetables. Lightly butter both sides of the paper.

2. Combine the stock and vermouth in a large saucepan and bring to a simmer. Separately blanch the celeriac, potatoes, and carrots in the stock mixture until tender. Drain the vegetables and toss with the cucumber.

3. Arrange a bed of about 7 oz/198 g of the vegetables on one half of each paper heart. Top the vegetables with 1 portion of the bass and 1½ oz/43 g of the scallops. Top with about ½ fl oz/15 mL of the gremolata and sprinkle with the peppercorns.

4. Fold the top of the heart over the fish and vegetables. Crimp the edges of the paper to seal tightly. Refrigerate until needed.

5. For each serving, place 1 parchment package on a pre-heated sizzler pan or sheet pan and bake in a 425°F/218°C oven for 7 minutes. The package should be puffy and the paper brown. Serve immediately. For a dramatic presentation, cut the package open in front of the diner.

Poached Trout Paupiettes with Vin Blanc Sauce

Makes 10 servings

20 (3 to 4 oz/85 to 113 g) skinless trout fillets

1 tsp/5 g salt

½ tsp/1 g ground white pepper

1 lb/454 g **Salmon Mousseline** (page 1030)

1 oz/28 g butter

3 shallots, minced

5 parsley stems

5 chive stems

¼ tsp/0.50 g coarsely cracked white peppercorns

8 fl oz/240 mL dry white wine

24 fl oz/720 mL **Fish Fumet** (page 353)

24 fl oz/720 mL **Fish Velouté** (page 383)

8 fl oz/240 mL heavy cream

1 fl oz/30 mL lemon juice, or as needed (optional)

1. Season the trout with the salt and pepper. Spread the mousseline in an even layer over the trout fillets and roll each piece up to make paupiettes. Place them in a hotel pan, seam side down, until ready to poach.

2. Lightly butter a shallow pan and sprinkle it evenly with the shallots. Place the parsley stems, chive stems, and peppercorns on top. Place the paupiettes, seam side down, on the bed of shallots. Add the wine and fumet.

3. Bring the liquid to just under a simmer over direct heat. Place a piece of buttered parchment (cartouche) over the fillets to cover. Transfer the entire pan to a 300° to 325°F/149° to163°C oven.

4. Poach the trout for 10 to 12 minutes, or until the flesh is opaque and gives under slight pressure.

5. Transfer the trout to a half hotel pan, cover with the cartouche, and hold warm.

6. Place the pan with the cuisson over direct heat and reduce by two thirds. Add the velouté and simmer for 1 to 2 minutes. Stir in the cream and reduce to a nappé consistency. Add lemon juice, if desired, and adjust seasoning with salt and white pepper.

7. Strain the sauce through a fine-mesh sieve into a clean saucepan or bain marie.

8. Blot the paupiettes dry on absorbent paper towels. Serve immediately with the sauce or hold hot for service.

Fillet of Snapper en Papillote

Makes 10 servings

6 oz/170 g butter

10 (6 oz/170 g) red snapper fillets

1 tsp/5 g salt

½ tsp/1 g ground black pepper

5 fl oz/150 mL **Fish Velouté** (page 383)

2½ oz/71 g minced shallots

5 oz/142 g thinly sliced green onions

5 oz/142 g thinly sliced white mushrooms

5 fl oz/150 mL dry white wine

1. Cut 10 heart shapes out of parchment paper, large enough to enclose the fillets. Lightly butter both sides of the paper.

2. Heat the butter in a sauté pan over medium-high heat. Season the fillets with the salt and pepper and sear briefly on the flesh sides only. Remove the fish from the pan.

3. Place ½ fl oz/15 mL of the velouté on 1 side of each parchment heart. Sprinkle 2 tsp/6 g of shallots on the velouté. Place the fillets, skin side down, on the parchment hearts. Sprinkle ½ oz/14 g of sliced green onions on top of each fillet. Shingle ½ oz/14 g of the sliced mushrooms on the snapper. Drizzle with ½ fl oz/15 mL of the white wine.

4. Fold the top of the heart over the fish. Crimp the edges of the paper to seal tightly. Refrigerate until needed.

5. For each serving, place 1 parchment package on a preheated sizzler pan or sheet pan and bake in a 425°F/218°C oven for 7 minutes. The package should be puffy and the paper brown. Serve immediately. For a dramatic presentation, cut the package open in front of the diner.

Fillet of Snapper en Papillote

Poached Trout Paupiettes with Saffron served with
Sautéed Spinach (page 754)

Poached Trout Paupiettes with Saffron

Makes 10 servings

20 (3 to 4 oz/85 to 113 g) skinless trout fillets

1 tsp/5 g salt

½ tsp/1 g ground white pepper

10 oz/284 g **Trout and Saffron Mousseline** (recipe follows)

1 oz/28 g butter

3 shallots, minced

2 fl oz/60 mL dry white wine

4 fl oz/120 mL **Fish Fumet** (page 353)

16 fl oz/480 mL **Fish Velouté** (page 383)

7 oz/198 g tomato concassé

2 tbsp/6 g chopped chives

10 oz/284 g spinach

1. Season the trout with the salt and pepper. Spread the mousseline in an even layer over the fillets and roll each piece up to make paupiettes. Place in a hotel pan, seam side down, until ready to poach.

2. Lightly butter a shallow pan and sprinkle it evenly with the shallots. Place the paupiettes, seam side down, on top. Add the wine and fumet.

3. Bring the liquid to just under a simmer over direct heat. Place a piece of buttered parchment (cartouche) over the fillets to cover. Transfer the entire pan to a 300° to 325°F/149° to163°C oven.

4. Poach the trout for 10 to 12 minutes, or until the flesh is opaque and gives under slight pressure.

5. Transfer the trout to a half hotel pan, cover with the cartouche, and hold warm.

6. Place the pan with the cuisson over direct heat and reduce by two thirds. Add the velouté and simmer for 1 to 2 minutes. Adjust seasoning with salt and white pepper.

7. Strain the sauce through a fine-mesh sieve into a clean saucepan or bain marie, if desired. Finish the sauce with the tomatoes and chives.

8. Blot the paupiettes dry on absorbent paper towels. Serve immediately with the sauce on a bed of spinach or hold hot for service.

Trout and Saffron Mousseline

Makes 10 oz/284 g

Pinch saffron threads, pulverized

2 fl oz/60 mL heavy cream

7 oz/198 g trout fillet scraps

1 egg white

1 tsp/5 g salt

Pinch ground white pepper

1. Combine the saffron and cream in a saucepan, heat to simmering, and let steep for 30 minutes. Chill well.

2. Place the trout scraps and egg white in a food processor with a steel blade. Process to a fine paste, scraping down the sides of the bowl as needed. Add the saffron-infused cream, salt, and pepper, pulsing the processor on and off to blend.

3. Test the mousseline by poaching a small amount in simmering, salted water. Adjust seasoning if necessary before proceeding.

4. Push the mousseline through a fine-mesh sieve, if desired.

5. The mousseline is ready to serve now, or it may be refrigerated for later use.

Sole Mousseline: Substitute an equal amount of sole for the trout. Omit the saffron.

Poached Sole with Vegetable Julienne and Vin Blanc Sauce

Makes 10 servings

10 (5 to 6 oz/142 to 170 g) flounder fillets

1 tsp/5 g salt

½ tsp/1 g ground white pepper

2 oz/57 g red pepper julienne, blanched

3 oz/85 g carrot julienne, blanched

2 oz/57 g yellow squash julienne, blanched

2 oz/57 g zucchini julienne, blanched

1 oz/28 g butter

3 shallots, minced

5 parsley stems

5 chive stems

¼ tsp/0.50 g coarsely cracked white peppercorns

8 fl oz/240 mL dry white wine

24 fl oz/720 mL **Fish Fumet** (page 353)

5 lb/2.27 kg shrimp (21–25 count), peeled and deveined

24 fl oz/720 mL **Fish Velouté** (page 383)

8 fl oz/240 mL heavy cream

1 fl oz/30 mL lemon juice, or as needed (optional)

4 tbsp/12 g minced chives

4 tbsp/12 g finely chopped parsley

1. Place the fillets skin side up and season them with salt and white pepper. Combine the peppers, carrots, squash, and zucchini. Place a generous portion of vegetables across each fillet, leaving the vegetables extending over the edge of the fillets on both sides. Roll (or fold) the fillets tail to head. Place them in a hotel pan, seam side down, until ready to poach.

2. Lightly butter a shallow pan and sprinkle it evenly with the shallots. Place the parsley stems, chive stems, and peppercorns on top of the shallots. Place the rolled sole portions, seam side down, on the bed of shallots. Add the wine and fumet.

3. Bring the liquid to just under a simmer over direct heat. Place a piece of buttered parchment (cartouche) over the fillets to cover. Transfer the entire pan to a 300° to 325°F/149° to163°C oven.

4. After 6 minutes, add 3 shrimp per portion to the pan. Poach for 4 to 6 minutes more, or until the flesh of the fish and shrimp is opaque and gives under slight pressure.

5. Transfer the sole and shrimp to a half hotel pan, cover with the cartouche, and hold warm.

6. Place the pan with the cuisson over direct heat and reduce by two thirds. Add the velouté and simmer for 1 to 2 minutes. Stir in the cream and reduce it to a nappé consistency. Add lemon juice, if desired, and adjust seasoning with salt and white pepper.

7. Strain the sauce through a fine-mesh sieve into a clean saucepan or bain marie. Mix the chives and parsley into the sauce.

8. Blot the sole rolls and shrimp dry on absorbent paper towels. Serve immediately with the sauce or hold hot for service.

Poached Sole Paupiettes Veronique

Makes 10 servings

10 (5 to 6 oz/142 to 170 g) flounder fillets

1 tsp/5 g salt

½ tsp/1 g ground white pepper

10 oz/284 g **Sole Mousseline** (page 621)

1 oz/28 g butter

1 tbsp/9 g minced shallots

8 parsley stems, chopped

4 fl oz/120 mL dry white wine

5 fl oz/150 mL **Fish Fumet** (page 353)

24 fl oz/720 mL **Royal Glaçage** (recipe follows)

10 oz/284 g green seedless grapes, peeled and heated (about 4 per serving)

1. Season the sole with the salt and pepper. Spread the mousseline in an even layer over the fillets and roll each piece up to make paupiettes. Place them in a hotel pan, seam side down, until ready to poach.

2. Lightly butter a shallow pan and sprinkle it evenly with the shallots. Place the parsley stems on top of the shallots. Place the paupiettes, seam side down, on the bed of shallots. Add the wine and fumet.

3. Bring the liquid to just under a simmer over direct heat. Place a piece of buttered parchment (cartouche) over the fillets to cover. Transfer the entire pan to a 300° to 325°F/149° to163°C oven.

4. Poach the sole for 10 to 12 minutes, or until the flesh is opaque and gives under slight pressure.

5. Transfer the sole to a sizzler platter and coat it with the glaçage. Brown under a salamander or broiler. (Reserve the cuisson for the Royal Glaçage.)

6. Serve immediately, garnished with grapes or hold it hot for service.

Royal Glaçage

Makes 24 fl oz/720 mL

5 fl oz/150 mL poaching liquid, if available

7 fl oz/210 mL **Fish Velouté** (page 383)

7 fl oz/210 mL **Hollandaise Sauce** (page 386)

7 fl oz/210 mL heavy cream

1. Reduce the poaching liquid, if available, until nearly dry. Strain it into a bowl.

2. Have the velouté and hollandaise at the same temperature (about 170°F/77°C). Add them to the reduced cuisson and fold together.

3. Whip the cream to medium peaks and fold it into the velouté and hollandaise mixture.

4. Keep warm and use as needed.

Poached Sea Bass with Clams, Bacon, and Peppers

Makes 10 servings

4 oz/113 g butter, cold

3 lb 12 oz/1.70 kg sea bass fillets

50 littleneck clams, thoroughly scrubbed

4 fl oz/120 mL dry white wine

5 fl oz/150 mL **Fish Stock** (page 353)

5 fl oz/150 mL clam juice

salt, as needed

ground black pepper, as needed

8 oz/227 g green pepper julienne, blanched

10 oz/284 g minced bacon, rendered crisp

1 tbsp/3 g chopped chives

1. Lightly butter a shallow pan with 1 oz/28 g of the butter. Add the fish, clams, wine, stock, and clam juice.

2. Bring the liquid to just under a simmer over direct heat. Place a piece of buttered parchment (cartouche) over the fillets to cover. Transfer the entire pan to a 350°F/177°C oven.

3. Poach the fish and clams until the fish is slightly underdone and the clams are barely open, 10 to 12 minutes. Remove the fish and clams and keep them warm.

4. Transfer the fish and clams to a half hotel pan, cover with the cartouche, and hold warm.

5. Place the pan with the cuisson over direct heat and reduce by two thirds. Whip in the remaining butter to lightly thicken the sauce. Season with salt and pepper.

6. Strain the sauce through a fine-mesh sieve into a clean saucepan or bain marie, if desired. Finish the sauce with the peppers and bacon.

7. Serve the fish and clams immediately with the sauce, garnished with the chives, or hold hot for service.

Boston Scrod with Cream, Capers, and Tomatoes

Makes 10 servings

3 lb 12 oz/1.70 kg scrod fillets, cut into ten 6-oz/170-g portions

1 tsp/5 g salt

½ tsp/1 g ground black pepper

4 oz/113 g butter, cold

1 tbsp/9 g minced shallots

5 fl oz/150 mL dry white wine

5 fl oz/150 mL **Fish Fumet** (page 353)

6 fl oz/180 mL heavy cream

4 oz/113 g tomato concassé

2 tbsp/30 mL capers, drained

4 oz/113 g sliced mushrooms, sautéed

1 fl oz/30 mL lemon juice, or as needed

1. Season the scrod with the salt and pepper.

2. Lightly butter a sautoir with 1 oz/28 g of the butter and sprinkle it evenly with the shallots. Place the scrod on top. Add the wine and fumet.

3. Bring the liquid to just under a simmer over direct heat. Place a piece of buttered parchment (cartouche) over the scrod to cover. Transfer the entire pan to a 350°F/177°C oven.

4. Poach the scrod for 10 to 12 minutes, or until the flesh is opaque and gives under slight pressure. Transfer the fish to a half hotel pan, cover with the cartouche, and hold warm. Place the cream in a saucepot and allow to reduce by half over medium heat.

5. Place the pan with the cuisson over direct heat and reduce by two thirds. Add the cream and simmer for 1 to 2 minutes.

6. Add the concassé, capers, and mushrooms and simmer long enough for the sauce to develop a good flavor and consistency, 3 to 4 minutes. Whisk or swirl in the remaining butter, add the lemon juice, and adjust seasoning with salt and pepper.

7. Serve immediately with the sauce or hold it hot for service.

Pescada à la Veracruzana

Makes 10 servings

10 (about 6 oz/170 g) red snapper fillets

1 tsp/5 g salt

½ tsp/1 g ground black pepper

6 fl oz/180 mL lime juice

SAUCE

3 fl oz/90 mL olive oil

1 lb/454 g minced onions

3 garlic cloves, minced

3 lb/1.36 kg peeled, seeded, and medium-diced tomatoes

15 green olives, pitted and chopped

4½ tsp/22.50 mL capers, rinsed

5 pickled jalapeños, julienned

3 bay leaves

1½ tsp/1.50 g chopped marjoram or oregano

1½ tsp/1.50 g chopped thyme

32 fl oz/960 mL **Fish Stock** (page 353), or as needed

GARNISH

4 tbsp/12 g chopped parsley

4 tbsp/60 mL capers, rinsed

30 to 40 green olives, rinsed

1. Cut a shallow crisscross into the skin of all the fillets with a boning knife. Season the fish with the salt and pepper and marinate it in the lime juice, refrigerated, for at least 1 hour.

2. Meanwhile, prepare the sauce. Heat 2 fl oz/60 mL of the oil in a saucepan over medium-high heat. Add the onions and garlic and sauté until they start to turn golden. Add the tomatoes, chopped olives, capers, jalapeños, bay leaves, marjoram or oregano, thyme, and stock. Bring the sauce to a simmer and cook until the tomatoes are soft and the flavors have blended. Adjust seasoning with salt and pepper, if necessary. Reserve.

3. Lightly grease a shallow pan with the remaining oil. Place the snapper in the pan. Pour the sauce over and around the fish.

4. Bring the liquid to just under a simmer over direct heat. Place a piece of buttered parchment (cartouche) over the fish to cover. Transfer the entire pan to a 350°F/177°C oven.

5. Poach the fish for 6 to 8 minutes, or until cooked through (140°F/60°C).

6. Serve the fish immediately with the sauce spooned over the top. Garnish with the parsley, capers, and olives.

Poached Chicken Breast with Tarragon Sauce

Makes 10 servings

10 (7 to 8 oz/198 to 227 g) boneless chicken suprêmes

salt, as needed

ground white pepper, as needed

2 oz/57 g butter

2 oz/57 g minced shallots

6 fl oz/180 mL dry white wine

4 fl oz/120 mL **Chicken Stock** (page 351)

20 fl oz/600 mL **Chicken Velouté** (page 383)

4 fl oz/120 mL heavy cream

1 tbsp/3 g chopped tarragon

1. Season the chicken with the salt and pepper.

2. Lightly butter a shallow pan and sprinkle it evenly with the shallots. Place the chicken on top. Add the wine and stock.

3. Bring the liquid to just under a simmer over direct heat. Place a piece of buttered parchment (cartouche) over the chicken to cover. Transfer the entire pan to a 350°F/177°C oven.

4. Poach the chicken for 12 to 14 minutes, or until cooked through (165°F/74°C).

5. Transfer the chicken to a half hotel pan, cover with the cartouche, and hold warm.

6. Place the pan with the cuisson over direct heat and reduce by two thirds. Add the velouté and simmer for 1 to 2 minutes. Stir in the cream and reduce to a nappé consistency. Adjust seasoning with salt and white pepper.

7. Strain the sauce through a fine-mesh sieve into a clean saucepan or bain marie. Stir the tarragon into the sauce.

8. Blot the chicken dry on absorbent paper towels. Serve it immediately with the sauce or hold it hot for service.

Farmhouse Chicken with Angel Biscuits

Makes 10 servings

10 (7 to 8 oz/198 to 227 g) boneless and skinless chicken suprêmes

salt, as needed

ground white pepper, as needed

4 oz/85 g butter

2 oz/57 g minced shallots

4 fl oz/120 mL dry white wine

8 fl oz/240 mL **Chicken Stock** (page 351), or as needed

20 fl oz/600 mL **Chicken Velouté** (page 383)

1 lb 8 oz/680 g white mushrooms

30 baby carrots, peeled and blanched

30 white turnip battonet, blanched

30 rutabaga batonnet, blanched

15 brussels sprouts, halved and blanched

20 **Biscuit Dumplings** (page 868)

4 tbsp/12 g chopped parsley

4 tbsp/12 g chopped dill

1. Season the chicken with the salt and pepper.

2. Lightly butter a shallow pan with half of the butter and sprinkle it evenly with the shallots. Place the chicken on top. Add the wine and stock.

3. Bring the liquid to just under a simmer over direct heat. Place a piece of buttered parchment (cartouche) over the chicken to cover. Transfer the entire pan to a 350°F/177°C oven.

4. Poach the chicken for 12 to 14 minutes, or until cooked through (165°F/74°C).

5. Transfer the chicken to a half hotel pan, cover with the cartouche, and hold warm.

6. Place the pan with the cuisson over direct heat and reduce by two thirds. Add the velouté and reduce to a nappé consistency. Adjust seasoning with salt and white pepper.

7. Strain the sauce through a fine-mesh sieve into a clean saucepan or bain marie. Reserve warm.

8. Heat 1 oz/28 g of the remaining butter in a sauté pan over medium-high heat. Add the mushrooms and sauté until tender. Season with salt and pepper. Reserve warm.

9. Heat the remaining butter in another sauté pan and reheat the carrots, turnips, rutabagas, and brussels sprouts. Add a little stock, if necessary. Season with salt and pepper.

10. Serve the chicken immediately with the sauce, vegetables, and biscuits. Garnish with a pinch of chopped parsley and dill.

Poule au Pot (Chicken with Vegetables)

Makes 8 servings

2 (about 3 lb/1.36 kg) broiler chickens

112 fl oz/3.36 L **Chicken Stock** (page 351)

1 **Bouquet Garni** (page 331)

1 **Sachet d'Épices** (page 331)

8 oz/227 g large-dice carrots

8 oz/227 g large-dice parsnips

8 oz/227 g large-dice celeriac

8 oz/227 g large-dice potatoes

8 oz/227 g large-dice leeks

1 tbsp/15 g salt

1 tsp/2 g ground black pepper

1 oz/28 g minced chives

1. Remove the backbones from the chickens and reserve. Cut the birds into quarters, and then halve the breasts.

2. Bring the stock to a simmer in a large pot. Place the chicken, backbones, necks, hearts, and gizzards, but not the liver, in a pot and add enough simmering stock to cover by about 1 to 1½ in/3 to 4 cm. Return the stock to a simmer over low heat. Skim carefully throughout the cooking time.

3. Add the bouquet garni and sachet. Simmer for approximately 45 minutes. Transfer the chicken legs and breasts to a clean pot. Strain the broth over the chicken and return to a simmer over low heat for another 30 minutes. Discard the bouquet garni, sachet, backbones, necks, heart, and gizzards.

4. Add the vegetables to the broth in a staggered sequence: carrots and parsnips first, celeriac after 5 minutes, potatoes after celeriac. Add the leeks last.

5. Continue to simmer, skimming as necessary, until the chicken is fork tender and all of the vegetables are tender, about 30 minutes.

6. Remove the chicken and separate the drumsticks from the thighs. Cut the breast halves in half again, on a bias. Season with salt and pepper.

7. Arrange the chicken (a breast portion and either a drumstick or thigh) in each bowl with vegetables, ladle broth into the bowl and finish with the chives. Serve immediately or hold it hot for service.

Udon Noodle Pot

Makes 10 servings

3 lb/1.36 kg dry udon noodles

1 fl oz/30 mL vegetable oil

1 gal/3.84 L **Dashi** (page 354)

20 littleneck clams

1 lb 8 oz/680 g boneless and skinless chicken thighs, cut into bite-size pieces

20 shrimp (31–36 count), peeled and deveined, blanched

2 lb 3 oz/992 g shiitake mushrooms, stemmed

1 lb 4 oz/567 g napa cabbage, blanched, chiffonade

1 lb/454 g spinach, blanched, chiffonade

1 lb/454 g carrots, cut into coins, blanched

8 oz/227 g snow peas, strings removed, blanched

10 fl oz/300 mL soy sauce

1 fl oz/30 mL mirin

2 green onions, thinly sliced on the bias

1. Bring a large pot of salted water to a boil. Cook the noodles until just tender, 6 to 8 minutes. Drain the noodles and rinse under cold water. Drain the noodles again, toss with the oil, and reserve.

2. Bring the dashi to a simmer in a large pot.

3. Place the clams, chicken, shrimp, and shiitakes in a separate pot and ladle the simmering dashi over the top. Poach until the clams are open and the chicken is cooked through (180°F/82°C).

4. Serve the clams, chicken, shrimp, and shiitakes in a bowl on a bed of the noodles with the cabbage, spinach, carrots, and snow peas. Ladle the dashi over the top and serve immediately. Garnish with the soy sauce, mirin, and green onions.

Poached Salmon with Dill Butter

Makes 10 servings

32 fl oz/960 mL **Fish Fumet** (page 353)

1 lb/454 g paysanne-cut celeriac or celery

1 lb/454 g paysanne-cut carrots

1 lb/454 g paysanne-cut leeks, white parts only

3 lb 12 oz/1.70 kg salmon fillets, cut into ten 6-oz/170-g portions

40 potato tournées, cooked until tender

5 oz/142 g **Dill Butter** (page 388) sliced into ten ½-oz/14-g portions

1. Combine the fumet and paysanne-cut vegetables and bring to a simmer over low heat. When it reaches 165°F/74°C, add the salmon.

2. Poach the salmon in the fumet until it is cooked through (140°F/60°C).

3. Serve the salmon with the vegetables and potatoes. Ladle the poaching liquid over the fish and vegetables.

4. Top the salmon with a slice of Dill Butter immediately or hold hot for service.

Beef Noodle Soup (Pho Bo)

Makes 10 servings

10 lb/4.54 kg beef marrow bones

2 lb/907 g beef shoulder clod

3 gal/11.52 L water

10 oz/284 g ginger, cut in half lengthwise, dry roasted

10 shallots, peeled, dry roasted

8 fl oz/240 mL fish sauce

7 oz/198 g sugar

6 cinnamon sticks

12 star anise pods, lightly toasted

6 cloves, lightly toasted

salt, as needed

ground black pepper, as needed

1 lb/454 g rice noodles, ⅛ in/3 mm wide

6 oz/170 g bean sprouts

1 onion, sliced paper thin

8 oz/227 g beef strip loin, slightly frozen, sliced paper thin

4 green onions, sliced thin

30 Thai basil leaves

30 cilantro leaves

30 mint leaves

30 rau ram leaves

5 Thai chiles, sliced paper thin

10 lime wedges

5 fl oz/150 mL Vietnamese chili sauce

1. Blanch the bones and shoulder. In a large pot, cover the bones and shoulder with the water. Add the roasted ginger and shallots, fish sauce, and sugar. Bring to a boil.

2. Simmer until the shoulder is tender, about 1½ hours, skimming the surface throughout the cooking time, as needed.

3. Remove the shoulder from the liquid and submerge it in a bowl of cool water for 15 minutes.

4. Add the cinnamon, star anise, and cloves to the broth and continue to simmer until their flavor is apparent, about 30 minutes. Strain the broth and season with salt and pepper. Reserve.

5. Remove the beef shoulder from the water, slice it into thin pieces, and reserve.

6. Bring a large pot of salted water to a boil. Add the noodles and cook until just tender. Serve immediately or rinse until cool, drain well, and reheat at service.

7. For each portion, place noodles in a bowl. Place some bean sprouts and onion slices over the noodles, followed by a few slices of the beef shoulder. Over the shoulder lay 2 to 3 slices of the raw beef. Ladle the boiling broth into the bowl. The broth should cover the meat by 1 in/3 cm.

8. Serve immediately garnished with the green onions, herbs, and chiles. Serve a lime wedge and chili sauce on the side.

Beef Noodle Soup (*Pho Bo*)

Corned Beef with Winter Vegetables

Corned Beef with Winter Vegetables

Makes 12 to 14 servings

10 lb/4.54 kg corned beef brisket, trimmed

96 fl oz/2.88 L **White Beef Stock** (page 351) or water, cold

2 lb/907 g green cabbage wedges

14 new potatoes, halved

30 baby carrots, peeled

14 baby turnips, peeled

1 lb/454 g pearl onions, blanched and peeled

salt, as needed

ground black pepper, as needed

1. Split the brisket along the natural seam into 2 pieces.

2. Place the meat in a deep pot and add enough stock or water to cover the meat. Bring to a boil, skimming the surface as necessary. Reduce the heat to establish a slow simmer, cover, and continue simmering until the meat is nearly fork tender, about 2½ hours.

3. Add the vegetables to the corned beef and continue to simmer until they are tender and flavorful and the corned beef is fork tender, 35 to 45 minutes. Season with salt and pepper as needed throughout the cooking time.

4. Remove the corned beef from the cooking liquid and carve into slices. Serve immediately with the vegetables or hold it hot for service.

Boiled Beef with Spätzle and Potatoes (Gaisburger Marsch)

Makes 10 servings

4 lb/1.81 kg beef shank meat, cut into ½-in/1-cm cubes

1 gal 64 fl oz/5.76 L **White Beef Stock** (page 351)

2 lb 12 oz/1.25 kg medium-dice onions

2 bay leaves

1 clove

salt, as needed

ground black pepper, as needed

12 oz/340 g medium-dice leeks

1 lb/454 g medium-dice potatoes

3 oz/85 g butter

2 lb/907 g **Spätzle** (page 866)

1 oz/28 g chopped parsley

1. Blanch the beef, drain, and combine it with the stock, 12 oz/340 g of the onions, the bay leaves, and clove. Simmer until the beef is 80% tender, 45 minutes to 1 hour. Skim as necessary and season with salt and pepper as needed throughout the cooking time.

2. Add the leeks and potatoes and cook until tender, about 20 more minutes.

3. Sauté the remaining 2 lb/907 g of onions in the butter until brown, 15 to 20 minutes. Add the sautéed onions to the broth with the spätzle and parsley. Adjust seasoning with salt and pepper.

4. Serve immediately or hold hot for service.

New England Boiled Dinner

Makes 25 servings

10 lb/4.54 kg corned beef brisket

2 lb/907 g beef tongue

1 gal/3.84 L **White Beef Stock** (page 351)

1 **Sachet d'Épices** (page 331)

VEGETABLE GARNISH

50 each Red Bliss potatoes, cut into wedges

50 each green cabbage wedges

50 each pearl onions, blanched and peeled

50 each carrot tournés

50 each parsnip tournés

50 each rutabaga tournés

50 each beet tournés

3 oz/85 g green beans, cut into 2-in/5-cm lengths

HORSERADISH SAUCE

12 fl oz/360 mL heavy cream

40 fl oz/1.20 L **Béchamel Sauce** (page 384)

6 oz/170 g grated horseradish, or as needed

salt, as needed

ground black pepper, as needed

1. Place the beef and tongue in a large pot with enough cold stock to cover them. Bring the stock to a slow simmer over medium-high heat.

2. Add the sachet and continue to simmer gently, skimming the surface as necessary, for about 3 hours, or until the meats are very tender. Remove the meats from the liquid and keep them warm and moist.

3. Salt the cooking liquid and cook the vegetables separately until tender. Place the cream in a saucepot and reduce by half over medium heat.

4. Combine the béchamel, cream, and horseradish in a saucepan and heat over medium heat. Season with salt, pepper, and additional horseradish as needed.

5. Slice the meats and serve them immediately with the vegetables and sauce or hold them hot for service.

Seafood Poached in a Saffron Broth with Fennel

Makes 10 servings

32 fl oz/960 mL **Fish Fumet** (page 353)

1 tsp/1.50 g saffron, crushed

1 **Sachet d'Épices** (page 331)

4 fl oz/120 mL Pernod

4 fl oz/120 mL dry white wine

1 lb/454 g fennel julienne

1 lb/454 g tomato concassé

salt, as needed

ground black pepper, as needed

3 lb/1.36 kg assorted seafood

1. Combine the fumet, saffron, sachet, Pernod, wine, fennel, and tomato concassé; simmer the liquid until the fennel is barely tender and the broth is well flavored, about 12 minutes. Season with salt and pepper.

2. At the time of service, bring the broth to a bare simmer. Add the seafood (see Note) and poach until it is just cooked through, 6 to 8 minutes.

3. Serve immediately with the broth or hold it hot for service.

NOTE

A variety of seafood may be used, including shrimp, monkfish, squid, shark, scallops, and lobster.

Chapter Twenty-three

Braising and Stewing

Braises and stews are often thought of as peasant dishes because they frequently call for less tender (and less expensive) main ingredients than other techniques. These dishes have a robust, hearty flavor and are often considered fall and winter meals; however, by replacing traditional ingredients with poultry, fish, or shellfish, braises and stews can be faster to prepare, lighter in flavor and color, and appropriate for contemporary menus.

Braises

To braise meat, first sear it in hot fat to the desired color, then simmer it in a covered vessel in stock or another cooking liquid. The amount of liquid used in the braise is crucial to the success of the finished dish. Be sure to have enough liquid to keep the food moistened throughout the cooking time and to produce an adequate amount of sauce to serve with the finished item. Typically, one third to one half of the main item should be submerged in the cooking medium.

One of the benefits of braising is that tough cuts of meat become tender as the moist heat gently penetrates the meat and causes the connective tissues to soften. Another benefit is that flavor is released into the cooking liquid to become the accompanying sauce; thus, virtually all the flavor and nutrients are retained. The sauce resulting from a braise also has exceptional body, as the slow cooking breaks down the tough connective tissues and causes them to release gelatin. Tender foods, even delicate fish and shellfish, can also be braised. To properly braise these kinds of foods, use less cooking liquid and cook the food at a lower temperature for a shorter period of time.

The less tender cuts of meat to be braised traditionally come from more mature and more exercised animals. These cuts are more deeply flavored than the tender foods used for sautéing and steaming. Braised foods are often, although not always, left in a single large piece that can be sliced or carved into servings. In general, it's a good idea to truss or tie the meat in order to maintain the proper shape. Food may also be wrapped in lettuce leaves or other coverings to help maintain the shape and prevent the food from breaking apart during cooking.

The cooking liquids usually consist of rich stock or a combination of a stock and a sauce (such as espagnole, demi-glace, or velouté) suited to the main item's flavor. Broths, essences, or vegetable juices may also be used. Wine is often used to deglaze the pan before adding the braising liquid.

Aromatic vegetables, herbs, and other ingredients are sometimes added to the cooking liquid for more flavor. If they are to be strained out of the sauce or puréed and added back to the sauce, peeling and uniform cuts are not so important. However, when aromatic ingredients will be used as a garnish in the finished dish, they should be peeled, cut to a uniform size and shape, and added to the dish in the proper sequence, so that all components finish cooking at the same time.

Tomato products may be included to give the finished dish additional flavor and color. Tomato concassé, tomato purée, or tomato paste can all be used.

Prepare a sachet d'épices or bouquet garni, including spices, herbs, and other aromatic ingredients, as desired or required by the recipe. A whole garlic head can be roasted with a little oil and added to give a deeper, sweeter flavor to the dish.

To thicken the braising liquid for a sauce, use roux, roux-thickened sauces, reductions, beurre manié, or a pure starch slurry. Mirepoix may also be puréed and added back to the sauce to thicken it.

Choose a heavy-gauge braising pan or rondeau with a lid, of a size and shape that best fits the meat or poultry, for slow even cooking. Use a large tilting kettle to prepare a batch suitable for volume service or banquets. Use a kitchen fork to test doneness and to remove the food from the sauce. Also have a carving knife and other equipment to finish the sauce, such as a strainer and/or immersion blender.

A basic formula for braising a single entrée-sized portion of meat, poultry, or fish

One portion (8 to 10 oz/227 to 284 g) of meat, poultry, or fish

3 to 5 fl oz/90 to 150 mL cooking liquid (brown stock, brown sauce, and/or other flavorful liquids such as wine)

1 oz/28 g prepared aromatics (mirepoix and/or other vegetables)

Salt and other seasonings (sachet d'épices or bouquet garni, for example)

Additional finishing or garnishing ingredients as appropriate

1. Trim fabricated cuts of meat of all excess fat and gristle. Meat or poultry should be seasoned with salt and freshly ground pepper, spice blends, or marinades before searing.

Properly fabricated meat improves the quality and flavor of the dish. Braising concentrates the natural flavors of the main item, cooking liquid, and added ingredients, but it is still important to season the food before beginning to cook. Long simmering times reduce the volume of liquid and make relatively small amounts of seasoning more intense. Taste and adjust seasoning throughout the entire cooking process.

2. **Sear the meat to develop flavor and a rich brown color.** Heat the pan and oil and sear the seasoned main item on all sides to a deep brown. Cook the main item on high heat, turning it as often as necessary, just until each side is well colored. Some foods are seared only until their exterior stiffens without browning for a paler dish, sometimes referred to as a white braise. After searing, the main item should be removed and the mirepoix should be cooked to the desired color.

3. **After browning the mirepoix, cook the tomato paste until it turns a deep rust color and smells sweet.** Add the aromatic vegetables to the pan and cook. Onions and leeks are typically added to the pan first and allowed to cook to the appropriate color: tender and translucent for a light-colored braise, or deep golden for a brown braise. Allow enough time to cook these ingredients properly. Add other vegetables, herbs, and spices to the pan in sequence. Acidic ingredients such as tomatoes or wine are often added to a braise. Acid helps to soften the tough tissues of some braised foods and adds a desirable flavor and color to the finished dish.

4. **Add enough stock to the pinçage to cover the item by one third to one half.** Bring to a simmer. Add the main item back to the simmering liquid, along with any additional ingredients (see sidebar). Cover the pot.

The amount of liquid should be adapted to suit the characteristics of the main item. Bring the liquid just up to a simmer (not a true boil), stirring well, especially if flour was added to the aromatic vegetables. Add the aromatics (such as roasted garlic, a sachet or bouquet, additional vegetables, or other ingredients) at the appropriate time. Add some aromatics early in the cooking process to infuse the dish with the flavor. Others may be added later on in the process so they retain their flavor or texture.

5. **Braise until the main item is fully cooked and tender.** Establish a slow simmer over direct heat, cover the pot, and finish cooking the braise in a moderate oven or over low direct heat. Stir, skim, and adjust the seasoning and amount of liquid throughout the cooking time. Baste or turn the foods from time to time to keep all surfaces evenly moistened with the cooking liquid. This helps to ensure that the food cooks evenly. Remove the lid during the final part of the cooking time. This will cause the cooking liquid to reduce adequately so that the sauce will have a good consistency and flavor. Also, if the main item is turned frequently after the lid has been removed and is thus exposed to hot air, a glaze will form on the surface, providing a glossy sheen and good flavor. Fork-tender braised foods slide easily from a kitchen fork or may be cut with the side of a fork.

Even though carryover cooking is not as big a factor for these dishes as it is for roasts, grills, and sautés, it is still easier to carve foods after they are allowed to rest for several minutes. Transfer the main item to a pan and keep it warm while finishing the sauce.

As the braised food rests, the sauce can be finished in a number of ways (see sidebar). Remove and discard the sachet d'épices or bouquet garni. Return the braising liquid to a simmer and degrease the sauce by skimming away any surface fat. Once it reaches the correct consistency, adjust seasoning as needed. Many braises include vegetables, potatoes, or other components that are cooked along with the main item. Serve these sauces unstrained. In other instances, the sauce is strained before it is served. Add any final finishing or garnishing ingredients just before serving the braise.

Evaluate the quality of the finished braise. Well-made braises have an intense flavor, as a result of the long, gentle cooking, and a soft, almost melting texture. The main item's natural juices, along with the cooking liquid, become concentrated, providing both a deep flavor and a full-bodied sauce. Braised foods have a deep color depending on the type of food. They should retain their natural shape, although a significant amount of volume is lost during cooking. When done, braised foods are extremely tender. They should not, however, be dry or fall into shreds. This would indicate that the food has been overcooked or cooked too rapidly at a high heat.

NOTE

The braise may be cooled and stored at this point for later service. Recombine the main item with the sauce to keep it flavorful and moist during storage.

Options for Making the Perfect Braise

To thicken the sauce, any one of the following may be used, depending on your desired results. Flour may be added either by dusting the main item or by adding it directly to the pan with the aromatic vegetables. To reduce a sauce, cook it over medium heat to a good consistency.

> Flour (roux)
> Starch slurry
> Puréed aromatic vegetables
> Reduction

Additional ingredients may be added to develop more flavor. Add some early in the cooking process to infuse flavor. Others may be added later on so that they retain their individual flavor and/or texture.

> Roasted garlic
> Sachet or bouquet
> Additional vegetables

The sauce for the braise may be served unstrained, containing ingredients that are cooked along with the main item, such as potatoes and other vegetables. In other instances, the sauce is strained before it is served and any additional finishing or garnishing ingredients are added just before serving.

Stews

Stews share many similarities with braises, from the cuts of meat chosen to the texture of the finished dish. They differ from braises in that the foods are cut into bite-size pieces and are cooked in more liquid.

Stews are often thought of as one-dish meals, producing a tender and highly flavored dish including not only meat, poultry, or seafood, but also a variety of vegetables in a redolent sauce. The sauce itself takes on a deeper flavor and body during stewing. It is also possible to finish a stew with cream, herbs, or a liaison of eggs and cream.

Stews are based on the same cuts of meat, poultry, or fish as a braise. Trim the food of exterior and interior fat, gristle, and sinew. Divide larger cuts along seam lines to make it easier to cut against the grain for a more tender finished stew. The size of the cut will vary according to the style of stew, but typically they are bite-size cubes. Season foods for stewing before cooking, using salt, pepper, marinades, or dry rubs to give the finished dish a good flavor. Select the cooking liquid according to the food being stewed or the recipe's recommendation. Flavorful stocks or combinations of stocks and sauces, vegetable or fruit juices, or water may be used. Stews often include vegetables, both as an aromatic component and as an integral component of the dish. Rinse, peel, and cut vegetables into uniform shapes so that they will cook properly. Keep the vegetables separated so that they can be added to the stew in the proper sequence.

Choose a heavy-gauge braising pan or rondeau with a lid for slow, even cooking. Have a ladle or skimmer available to skim the stew as it cooks. To test for doneness, use a table fork to cut a piece, or bite into a small portion.

A basic formula for a single entrée-sized portion of meat, poultry, or fish stew

One portion (8 to 10 oz/227 to 284 g) of meat, poultry, or fish

3 to 5 fl oz/90 to 150 mL of cooking liquid (stock, sauce, and/or other flavorful liquids such as wine)

1 oz/28 g prepared aromatics (mirepoix and/or other vegetables)

Salt and other seasonings (sachet d'épices or bouquet garni, for example)

Additional finishing or garnishing ingredients (see individual recipes)

1. **Heat the pan and oil and sear the seasoned main item on all sides to the desired color, or combine the main item with the cooking liquid.** Bring the cooking liquid to a simmer separately before pouring it over the prepared meat. This way the cooking liquid can be seasoned and the overall cooking time shortened. It also improves the texture of the dish.

Foods to be stewed are typically cut into bite-size pieces. Meats, poultry, and fish should be trimmed and seasoned. It may be appropriate to dust these items with flour. Peel and cut fruits and vegetables as necessary. Beans and grains may require soaking or parcooking.

Searing the main item assists in developing color and flavor. In order to develop a good color, the main item should not be added to the pot in quantities so large that the pieces are touching one another. If they are touching, the pan's temperature will be lowered significantly, hindering proper coloring. Instead, the item should be seared in batches, and each batch should be removed when it has developed good color.

(continued)

Some stews call for the main meat or poultry to be dusted with flour and then cooked in hot oil just until it starts to stiffen, with no browning. Other stews call for the main item to be cooked to a deep brown. Once the meat, poultry, or fish is properly colored, remove it from the pan and keep it warm while sweating, smothering, or browning the aromatic vegetables, if desired.

White stews, such as blanquettes, do not call for the main item to be sautéed before the cooking liquid is added. Instead, a seasoned cooking liquid is added directly to the uncooked meat. Otherwise, the stewing liquid is added to the pan with the aromatics and the main item is returned to the stew.

Stewed foods are typically completely covered with cooking liquid throughout cooking time. The amount of liquid required varies from one cut of meat or poultry to another, however. Delicate or tender foods, such as fish or shellfish, may require very little added moisture to stew successfully. Tougher cuts may need proportionately more liquid for a longer cooking time as well as to soften tough tissues. Consult specific recipes for guidance.

2. **Cover the meat completely in the cooking liquid.** Skimming improves the flavor, color, and texture of the finished dish by removing impurities and solid particles. Keep a small bowl nearby to hold the skimmed scum.

Bring the liquid to a simmer over low heat, cover the pot, and finish the stew in a moderate oven or over low direct heat uncovered. Stir, skim, and adjust the amount of liquid and seasoning throughout the cooking time. Add any additional aromatics and vegetable garnish in the proper sequence throughout the cooking time for a rich complex flavor and perfect texture. In some dishes, some or all of the garnish is prepared separately to maintain color. Add parcooked, blanched, or quick-cooking ingredients as close to service time as reasonable. Be sure to taste the cooking liquid before deciding what aromatics, if any, are needed. If the stock is very flavorful already, a bouquet garni or sachet may not be necessary.

3. **Before removing the meat to finish the sauce, check a few pieces to be sure that the meat is fully cooked and tender.** Properly cooked stewed foods should be easy to cut with the side of a table fork. (Texture contrast, when desired, may be provided by a final garnish or side dish.) Discard the sachet d'épices or bouquet garni. Stews may be prepared to this point, then cooled and stored for later service. Cooling the stew makes it easy to lift any fat from the surface.

The stewing liquid is finished into a sauce. First, remove the solid ingredients with a slotted spoon or skimmer. Moisten them with a little of the cooking liquid, cover, and keep warm. Strain the sauce if necessary and thicken by reducing it over direct heat. Add any additional thickeners, such as a prepared roux or a starch slurry, and continue to cook, skimming as necessary, until the sauce has a good flavor and consistency. Return the solid ingredients to the sauce and return the stew to a simmer.

Many stews include additional components, such as vegetables, mushrooms, potatoes, or dumplings. When these ingredients are cooked along with the main ingredient, their own flavors are improved as well as the flavor of the entire stew.

4. **Make the final adjustments to the stew's flavor and consistency.** The finished stew should have a velvety sauce, and each ingredient is fully cooked but still retains its shape. Add heavy cream or temper a liaison (page 341) into the stew as a finishing and enriching step. Adjust the consistency by additional simmering if necessary. Season with salt, pepper, lemon juice, or other ingredients. Add additional garnish ingredients to the stew either in batches or by individual servings.

Evaluate the quality of the stew. A well-made stew has a rich flavor and a soft, almost melting texture. The natural juices of the ingredients, along with the cooking liquid, become concentrated and provide both good flavor and a full-bodied sauce. The major components in a stew retain their natural shape, although a certain amount of volume may be lost during cooking. When done, a stew is extremely tender, almost to the point where it can be cut with a fork but not where it falls into shreds. This would indicate that the food has been overcooked.

Braised Oxtails

Makes 10 servings

10 lb/4.54 kg oxtails, cut into 2-in/5-cm cross sections

1 tbsp/15 g salt

1½ tsp/3 g ground black pepper

2 fl oz/60 mL vegetable oil

1 lb/454 g large-dice **Mirepoix** (page 333)

2 fl oz/60 mL tomato purée

32 fl oz/960 mL dry red wine

32 fl oz/960 mL **Brown Veal Stock** (page 352)

1 **Sachet d'Épices** (page 331)

6 oz/170 g carrot tourné or batonnet

6 oz/170 g celeriac tourné or batonnet

6 oz/170 g white turnip tourné or batonnet

6 oz/170 g rutabaga tourné or batonnet

10 oz/284 g **Deep-Fried Onions** (recipe follows)

1. Season the oxtails with salt and pepper.

2. Heat the oil in a rondeau or brasier over medium-high heat until it starts to shimmer. Place the oxtails carefully in the oil and sear until deep brown on all sides. Transfer the oxtails to a hotel pan and reserve.

3. Add the mirepoix to the pan and cook, stirring from time to time, until golden brown. Add the tomato purée and cook until it turns a deeper color and gives off a sweet aroma, about 1 minute.

4. Add the wine to the pan, stirring to release any drippings. Reduce the wine by half. Return the oxtails to the pan along with any juices they may have released. Add the stock to cover the oxtails by two thirds.

5. Bring to a gentle simmer over medium-low heat and add the sachet. Cover the pot and transfer it to a moderate oven (350°F/177°C). Braise the oxtails for 1½ hours and add the vegetables. Continue to braise until the meat is fork tender and the vegetables are fully cooked, turning the oxtails occasionally to keep them evenly moistened.

6. Transfer the oxtails to a hotel pan or other holding container and moisten with some of the cooking liquid. Keep them warm while finishing the sauce.

7. Continue to simmer the cooking liquid until it has a good flavor and consistency. Skim thoroughly to degrease the sauce. Adjust seasoning with salt and pepper and strain.

8. Serve the oxtails immediately with the sauce and vegetables or hold them hot for service. Garnish with the Deep-Fried Onions.

Deep-Fried Onions

Makes 10 servings

32 fl oz/960 mL vegetable oil

12 oz/340 g onion julienne or thin rings

5 oz/142 g all-purpose flour

salt, as needed

1. Heat the vegetable oil in a deep fryer or a deep pot to 375°F/191°C.

2. Dredge the onions in the flour and shake off any excess. Deep fry until golden brown. Drain on absorbent paper towels, season with salt, and keep warm until ready to serve.

Braised Short Ribs

Makes 10 servings

10 (about 1 lb/454 g) beef short ribs

1 tbsp/15 g salt

1½ tsp/3 g ground black pepper

2 fl oz/60 mL vegetable oil

8 oz/227 g large-dice **Mirepoix** (page 333)

2 fl oz/60 mL tomato paste

4 fl oz/120 mL dry red wine

8 fl oz/240 mL **Brown Veal Stock** (page 352)

20 fl oz/600 mL **Demi-Glace** (page 383), **Jus de Veau Lié**
(page 382), or **Espagnole Sauce** (page 382)

2 bay leaves

pinch dried thyme

3 fl oz/90 mL Madeira or sherry

1. Season the short ribs with salt and pepper.

2. Heat the oil over medium-high heat in a rondeau or brasier until it starts to shimmer. Place the short ribs carefully in the oil and sear until deep brown on all sides. Transfer the short ribs to a hotel pan and reserve.

3. Add the mirepoix to the pan and cook, stirring from time to time, until golden brown. Add the tomato paste and cook until it turns a deeper color and gives off a sweet aroma, about 1 minute.

4. Add the wine to the pan, stirring to release any drippings. Reduce the wine by half. Return the short ribs to the pan along with any juices they may have released. Add enough stock and demi-glace, jus lié, or espagnole to cover the short ribs by two thirds.

5. Bring to a gentle simmer over medium-low heat. Cover the pot and transfer it to a 275°F/135°C oven. Braise the short ribs for 45 minutes. Add the bay leaves and thyme and degrease the liquid if necessary. Finish braising the short ribs until fork-tender, about 45 minutes more.

6. Transfer the short ribs to a hotel pan or other holding container and moisten with some of the cooking liquid. Keep warm while finishing the sauce.

7. Continue to simmer the cooking liquid until it has a good flavor and consistency. Skim thoroughly to degrease the sauce. Adjust seasoning with salt and pepper and strain. Stir in the Madeira or sherry to finish the sauce.

8. Serve the short ribs immediately with the sauce or hold them hot for service.

Korean Braised Short Ribs (Kalbi Jjim)

Makes 10 servings

10 dried shiitake mushrooms

20 (about 8 oz/227 g) beef short ribs, cut into 3-in/8-cm lengths

16 fl oz/480 mL mirin

8 fl oz/240 mL light soy sauce, or as needed

8 oz/227 g onions, cut into 2-in/5-cm pieces

2 oz/57 g ginger, peeled and lightly crushed

6 garlic cloves, chopped

2½ oz/71 g Chinese red dates (jujubes)

1 lb/454 g sliced daikon

1 lb/454 g oblique-cut carrots

1 tsp/5 g salt

1 fl oz/30 mL vegetable oil

4 eggs, separated

sugar, as needed

5 oz/142 g toasted pine nuts

½ fl oz/15 mL sesame oil

1. Rehydrate the mushrooms in cool water overnight or in warm water the day of service. Cut off the stems and halve the mushrooms. Strain the rehydration water and reserve.

2. Bring a large pot of water to a boil. Blanch the short ribs for 6 to 8 minutes to remove any impurities. Skim the scum that forms on the surface; drain and rinse.

3. Place the blanched short ribs in a large pot and add the mirin, soy sauce, onions, ginger, garlic, dates, and reserved mushroom-infused water to just cover the short ribs.

4. Simmer over low heat until the short ribs are fork tender, about 2 hours, turning occasionally to keep the beef evenly moistened.

5. When the meat is fork tender, add the mushrooms, daikon, carrots, and salt and simmer for an additional 10 minutes, or until the vegetables are tender.

6. Meanwhile, heat half of the vegetable oil in a sauté pan. Cook the egg whites to make a thin omelet. Repeat with the remaining oil and egg yolks. Cut both the egg white and egg yolk omelets into lozenge shapes. Reserve.

7. Remove and discard the ginger from the cooking liquid. Add the sugar and adjust seasoning with soy sauce, if necessary. Stir in the pine nuts and sesame oil and cook until heated through.

8. Serve the short ribs immediately with the sauce or hold them hot for service. Garnish with the omelet lozenges.

Korean Braised Short Ribs *(Kalbi Jjim)*

Beef Rouladen in Burgundy Sauce

Makes 10 servings

3 lb/1.36 kg boneless beef bottom round, trimmed, cut into twenty 2-oz/57-g pieces

1 tbsp/15 g salt

1½ tsp/3 g ground black pepper

1 lb 4 oz/567 g **Rouladen Stuffing** (recipe follows)

20 gherkins

3 oz/85 g all-purpose flour, or as needed

2 fl oz/60 mL vegetable oil, or as needed

6 oz/170 g small-dice onions

1 tsp/3 g minced garlic

4 oz/113 g tomato purée

4 fl oz/120 mL Burgundy or other dry red wine

32 fl oz/960 mL **Demi-Glace** (page 383), **Jus de Veau Lié** (page 382), or **Espagnole Sauce** (page 382)

1. Pound each piece of beef between sheets of parchment or plastic wrap to a thickness of ¼ in/6 mm. Blot dry and season with salt and pepper.

2. Center 1 oz/28 g of the stuffing on each piece, top with a gherkin, roll the beef around the stuffing, and secure with toothpicks or string. Dredge the beef in the flour and shake off any excess.

3. Heat the oil over medium-high heat in a rondeau or brasier until it starts to shimmer. Place the beef rolls carefully in the oil and sear until deep brown on all sides. Transfer the beef rolls to a hotel pan and reserve.

4. Add the onions to the pan and cook, stirring from time to time, until golden brown, 7 to 8 minutes. Add the garlic and cook until aromatic, 1 minute more. Add the tomato purée and cook until it turns a deeper color and gives off a sweet aroma, about 1 minute.

5. Add the wine to the pan, stirring to release any drippings. Reduce by half. Return the beef rolls to the pan along with any juices they may have released. Add enough demi-glace, jus lié, or espagnole to cover the rolls by two thirds.

6. Bring to a gentle simmer over medium-low heat. Cover and braise in a 350°F/177°C oven for 1 to 1½ hours or until fork tender, turning occasionally to keep the beef evenly moistened.

7. Transfer the beef rolls to a hotel pan, moisten with some of the cooking liquid, and keep warm.

8. Continue to simmer the cooking liquid to a good flavor and consistency. Skim thoroughly to degrease the sauce. Adjust seasoning with salt and pepper and strain the sauce.

9. Serve the rouladen immediately with the sauce or hold it hot for service.

Rouladen Stuffing

Makes 1 lb 8 oz/680 g

2 fl oz/60 mL vegetable oil

3 oz/85 g minced onions

8 oz/227 g chopped bacon

4 oz/113 g chopped lean ham

2 oz/57 g ground beef

2 eggs, beaten

6 oz/170 g bread crumbs, or as needed

1 tbsp/3 g chopped parsley

1 tsp/5 g salt

½ tsp/1 g ground black pepper

1. Heat the oil in a sauté pan over medium-high heat. Add the onions and sauté until tender and translucent, 4 to 5 minutes. Transfer to a bowl and let the onions cool.

2. Add the bacon, ham, beef, and eggs and mix until evenly combined.

3. Add enough bread crumbs to tighten the stuffing; the mixture should hold together but still be moist. Season with parsley, salt, and pepper.

4. The stuffing is ready to use now, or it may be refrigerated for later use.

Yankee Pot Roast

Makes 10 servings

4 lb/1.81 kg beef top blade, bottom round, or eye round, trimmed

2 tsp/10 g salt

½ tsp/1 g ground black pepper

2 fl oz/60 mL vegetable oil

8 oz/227 g small-dice onions

6 oz/170 g tomato purée

8 fl oz/227 mL dry red wine

24 fl oz/720 mL **Brown Veal Stock** (page 352)

24 fl oz/720 mL **Demi-Glace** (page 383) or **Espagnole Sauce** (page 382)

1 **Sachet d'Épices** (page 331)

10 new potatoes

10 baby turnips

20 baby carrots

60 pearl onions, blanched and peeled

1. Season the beef with salt and pepper and tie it.

2. Heat the oil over medium-high heat in a rondeau or brasier until it starts to shimmer. Place the beef carefully in the oil and sear until deep brown on all sides. Transfer the beef to a hotel pan and reserve.

3. Add the onions to the pan and cook, stirring from time to time, until golden brown, 6 to 8 minutes. Add the tomato purée and cook until it turns a deeper color and gives off a sweet aroma, about 1 minute.

4. Add the wine to the pan, stirring to release any drippings. Reduce the wine by half. Return the beef to the pan along with any juices it may have released. Add enough stock and demi-glace or espagnole to come about halfway up the beef.

5. Bring to a gentle simmer over medium to low heat. Cover the pot and transfer it to a moderate oven (350° to 375°F/177° to 191°C). Braise the beef for 1½ hours, turning occasionally to keep it evenly moistened. Add the sachet and degrease the liquid if necessary.

6. Add the potatoes, turnips, carrots, and pearl onions and finish braising until the beef is fork tender and the vegetables are fully cooked, 35 to 45 minutes more.

7. Transfer the beef to a hotel pan or other holding container and moisten with some of the cooking liquid. Keep it warm while finishing the sauce.

8. Continue to simmer the cooking liquid until it has a good flavor and consistency. Skim thoroughly to degrease the sauce. Adjust seasoning with salt and pepper, if necessary.

9. Remove the string from the beef, slice it into servings, and serve immediately with the sauce and vegetables or hold it hot for service.

Sauerbraten

Makes 10 servings

MARINADE

8 fl oz/240 mL dry red wine

8 fl oz/240 mL red wine vinegar

64 fl oz/1.92 L water

12 oz/340 g sliced onions

8 black peppercorns

10 juniper berries

2 bay leaves

2 cloves

4 lb/1.81 kg boneless beef bottom round

2 tsp/10 g salt

1 tsp/2 g ground black pepper

3 fl oz/90 mL vegetable oil

1 lb/454 g **Mirepoix** (page 333)

4 oz/113 g tomato paste

2 oz/57 g all-purpose flour

96 fl oz/2.88 L **Brown Veal Stock** (page 352)

3 oz/85 g gingersnaps, pulverized

1. To make the marinade, combine the wine, vinegar, water, onions, peppercorns, juniper berries, bay leaves, and cloves in a medium saucepan and bring the mixture to a boil. Cool to room temperature.

2. Season the beef with salt and pepper and tie it. Place the beef in the marinade; refrigerate for 3 to 5 days, turning it twice per day.

3. Remove the meat from the marinade. Dry thoroughly and season again with salt and pepper.

4. Strain the marinade and reserve the liquid and solids separately. Bring the strained marinade to a boil and skim off the scum.

5. Heat the oil over medium-high heat in a rondeau or brasier until it starts to shimmer. Place the beef carefully in the oil and sear until deep brown on all sides. Transfer the beef to a hotel pan and reserve.

6. Add the mirepoix to the pan and cook, stirring from time to time, until golden brown. Add the tomato paste and cook until it turns a deeper color and gives off a sweet aroma, about 1 minute.

7. Add the reserved marinade to the pan, stirring to release any drippings. Reduce the marinade by half. Add the flour to the pan to make a roux. Cook the roux for 4 to 5 minutes.

8. Whisk in the stock and bring to a simmer. Return the beef to the pan along with any juices it may have released. Cover the pan and simmer over low heat until the beef is tender, 3½ to 4½ hours.

9. Transfer the beef to a hotel pan or other holding container and moisten with some of the cooking liquid. Keep it warm while finishing the sauce.

10. Continue to simmer the cooking liquid until it has a good flavor and consistency, 30 to 35 minutes. Skim thoroughly to degrease the sauce.

11. Add the gingersnaps and cook the sauce for 10 minutes, until the gingersnaps dissolve. Strain the sauce through cheesecloth. Adjust seasoning with salt and pepper, if necessary.

12. Remove the string from the beef, slice it into servings, and serve immediately with the sauce, or hold it hot for service.

Beef Stew

Makes 10 servings

3 lb 12 oz/1.70 kg boneless beef shank or chuck, cut into 2-in/5-cm cubes

1 tbsp/15 g salt

1½ tsp/3 g ground black pepper

2 fl oz/60 mL vegetable oil

5 oz/142 g minced onions

5 garlic cloves, minced

2 fl oz/60 mL tomato paste (optional)

30 fl oz/900 mL red wine

40 fl oz/1.20 L **Brown Veal Stock** (page 352), or as needed

80 fl oz/2.40 L **Espagnole Sauce** (page 382)

1 **Sachet d'Épices** (page 331)

1 **Bouquet Garni** (page 331)

2 oz/57 g butter

8 fl oz/240 mL **Chicken Stock** (page 351)

1 lb 4 oz/567 g carrots, large dice or battonet, blanched

1 lb 4 oz/567 g white turnips, large dice or battonet, blanched

1 lb 4 oz/567 g yellow turnips, large dice or battonet, blanched

1 lb 4 oz/567 g green beans, cut into 1-in/3-cm pieces, blanched

½ oz/14 g chopped parsley

1. Season the beef with the salt and pepper.

2. Heat the oil over medium-high heat in a rondeau or brasier until it starts to shimmer. Place the beef carefully in the oil and sear until deep brown on as many sides as possible. Transfer the beef to a hotel pan and reserve.

3. Degrease the pan, if necessary. Add the onions to the pan and cook, stirring from time to time, until caramelized. Add the garlic and tomato paste, if using, and cook until the tomato paste turns a deeper color and gives off a sweet aroma, about 1 minute.

4. Add the wine to the pan, stirring to release any drippings. Reduce the wine by three quarters. Return the beef to the pan along with any juices it may have released.

5. Add the veal stock, espagnole, sachet, and bouquet garni. Bring to a gentle simmer over medium-low heat. Cover the pot and stew the beef until tender, about 2 hours. Add more stock during cooking, if necessary. Skim and degrease the stew as it cooks. Remove and discard the sachet and bouquet garni.

6. At service, heat the butter and chicken stock in a large sauté pan over medium-high heat. Add the blanched vegetables and toss to coat until the stock has reduced and the vegetables are hot. Adjust seasoning with salt and pepper.

7. Serve the stew immediately with the vegetables or hold it hot for service. Garnish with the parsley.

Braised Pork Rolls and Sausage in Meat Sauce with Rigatoni
(*Braciole di Maiale al Ragu e Rigatoni*)

Braised Pork Rolls and Sausage in Meat Sauce with Rigatoni (Braciole di Maiale al Ragu e Rigatoni)

Makes 10 servings

5 lb/2.27 kg pork butt, thinly sliced

9 oz/255 g crustless bread, dried, cut into 1-in/3-cm cubes

12 oz/360 mL milk

1½ oz/43 g toasted pine nuts

1½ oz/43 g finely chopped parsley

1 oz/28 g minced garlic

1½ oz/43 g finely grated Parmesan

1½ oz/43 g finely grated pecorino

2¾ oz/78 g raisins

1 tsp/5 g salt

¼ tsp/0.50 g ground black pepper

4 oz/113 g thinly sliced prosciutto

4 oz/113 g provolone batonnet

4 fl oz/120 mL extra-virgin olive oil

2 oz/57 g garlic, peeled and crushed

8 fl oz/240 mL red wine

12 lb 8 oz/5.67 kg peeled plum tomatoes, passed through a food mill, with liquid

1 tsp/2 g red pepper flakes

3 bay leaves

2 lb/907 g fennel sausage

1 lb/454 g rigatoni pasta, cooked

½ oz/14 g finely grated Parmesan

½ oz/14 g finely grated pecorino

2 tbsp/6 g chopped basil

2 tbsp/6 g chopped parsley

1. Pound each portion of pork between sheets of parchment or plastic wrap into a piece 8 by 8 in/20 by 20 cm and ⅛ in/3 mm thick. Use the rough side of the mallet to tenderize the meat. Refrigerate.

2. To make the filling, soak the bread in the milk until soft. Squeeze the bread to remove excess moisture. Combine the bread with the pine nuts, parsley, minced garlic, 1½ oz/43 g Parmesan, 1½ oz/43 g pecorino, and raisins. Season with salt and pepper.

3. Cover each slice of pork with a small piece of prosciutto. Spread the filling over the slices, leaving about ½ in/1 cm at the edge. Lay a battonet of provolone over the filling on each piece.

4. Roll the pork over the filling and tie into bundles with butcher's twine. Season the outside of the rolls with salt and pepper.

5. Heat half of the oil over medium-high heat in a rondeau or brasier until it starts to shimmer. Place the pork rolls carefully in the oil and sear until deep brown on all sides. Transfer the pork rolls to a hotel pan and reserve.

6. Add the crushed garlic to the pan and cook, stirring from time to time, until golden brown, 3 to 4 minutes. Remove and discard.

7. Add the wine to the pan, stirring to release any drippings. Reduce until nearly dry, about 8 minutes. Add the tomatoes and bring the mixture to a simmer. Return the pork rolls to the pan along with any juices they may have released. Add the red pepper flakes and bay leaves. Adjust seasoning with salt and pepper.

8. Bring to a gentle simmer over medium-low heat. Cover and braise for 1 hour or until fork tender, turning occasionally to keep the pork evenly moistened.

9. Meanwhile, heat the remaining oil in a heavy skillet. Add the sausage and cook slowly over low heat until golden brown, about 15 minutes.

10. Add the sausage to the pork rolls after 1 hour and cook an additional 30 minutes.

11. Allow the braised pork rolls, sausage, and sauce to rest for 30 minutes. Degrease, if necessary.

12. Remove the strings for the pork rolls and serve immediately on a bed of rigatoni with the sausage and sauce, or hold everything hot for service. Garnish with the Parmesan, pecorino, basil, and parsley.

Choucroute

Makes 20 servings

1 lb 14 oz/851 g smoked pork loin, sliced

salt, as needed

ground black pepper, as needed

10 beef frankfurters

1 lb 4 oz/567 g garlic sausages

6 fl oz/180 mL rendered goose fat, lard, or vegetable shortening

10 oz/284 g sliced onions

1 oz/28 g minced garlic

8 oz/227 g Granny Smith apples, peeled, small dice

2 lb 8 oz/1.13 kg **Homemade Sauerkraut** (recipe follows)

16 fl oz/480 mL **Chicken Stock** (page 351), or as needed

8 fl oz/240 mL dry white wine

1 **Sachet d'Épices** (page 331), plus 6 juniper berries

1 carrot

1 lb 4 oz/567 g slab bacon, cut into slices 1 by 2 in/3 by 5 cm

3 lb 12 oz/1.70 kg russet potatoes, tourné

1. Season the pork with salt and pepper and tie, if necessary. Prick the frankfurters and sausages in 5 or 6 places to prevent them from bursting.

2. Heat the fat over medium heat in a rondeau or brasier. Add the onions, garlic, and apples and sweat them in the hot fat without browning them. Add the sauerkraut to the onion mixture.

3. Add the stock, wine, sachet, and carrot and stir. Bring the liquid up to a simmer.

4. Place the pork and bacon on top of the sauerkraut and add more stock if necessary to cover the pork by about one half. Cover the pan and braise in a 350°F/177°C oven for approximately 45 minutes. Add the frankfurters and sausages to the pan, return the cover, and continue to cook until the pork, frankfurters, and sausages reach an internal temperature of 150°F/66°C, 15 to 20 minutes.

5. Transfer the meat to a holding pan and keep warm. Remove and discard the carrot and sachet.

6. Add the potatoes to the sauerkraut and simmer until the potatoes are fully cooked, about 15 minutes. Adjust seasoning with salt and pepper.

7. Slice the pork, frankfurters, and sausages and serve immediately on a bed of sauerkraut and potatoes, or hold everything hot for service.

Homemade Sauerkraut

Makes about 2 gal/7.68 L

20 lb/9.07 kg shredded green cabbage, 2-in/5-cm lengths

8 oz/227 g salt

1. Toss the cabbage together with the salt until evenly combined.

2. Line a food-grade plastic bucket with cheesecloth. Place the salted cabbage in the bucket and fold the cheesecloth over the top. Press firmly to pack the cabbage down and create an even surface.

3. Weight the top of the cabbage and cover with plastic wrap. Label with the date. Let the sauerkraut ferment at room temperature for 10 days. Remove the weights, cover well, and refrigerate.

4. The sauerkraut is ready to serve now, or it may be refrigerated for later service. (Rinse the sauerkraut in cool running water to remove a little of the excess salt before using.)

Choucroute

Cassoulet

Makes 12 servings

BEAN STEW

96 fl oz/2.88 L **Chicken Stock** (page 351)

2 lb/907 g dried navy beans, soaked overnight

1 lb/454 g slab bacon, cut into slices ¼ in/6 mm thick

1 lb/454 g garlic sausage

2 onions

1 oz/28 g chopped garlic

1 **Bouquet Garni** (page 331)

1 tbsp/15 g salt

MEAT STEW

1 lb 8 oz/680 g pork loin, cut into 2-in/5-cm cubes

1 lb 8 oz/680 g lamb shoulder or leg, cut into 2-in/5-cm cubes

salt, as needed

ground black pepper, as needed

3 fl oz/90 mL olive oil

1 lb/454 g **White Mirepoix** (page 333)

½ tsp/1.50 g garlic, mashed to a paste

3 fl oz/90 mL white wine

8 oz/227 g tomato concassé

1 **Sachet d'Épices** (page 331)

16 fl oz/480 mL **Demi-Glace** (page 383)

32 fl oz/960 mL **Brown Veal Stock** (page 352)

1 lb 12 oz/794 g **Duck Confit** (page 657)

12 oz/340 g bread crumbs

2 tbsp/6 g chopped parsley

1. Bring the chicken stock to a boil in a large saucepot and add the beans and bacon. Return the mixture to a simmer and cook for 30 minutes.

2. Add the sausage, onions, garlic, and bouquet garni. Return the mixture to a boil and cook until the sausage reaches 150°F/66°C and the bacon is fork tender, about 30 minutes. Remove the sausage, bacon, onion, and bouquet garni. Reserve the bacon and sausage.

3. Add the salt and continue to cook the beans until they are tender, 20 to 25 minutes. Strain the beans and reserve; reduce the stock by half, until it is beginning to become a nappé consistency, about 30 minutes. Reserve the sauce for later use.

4. Season the pork and lamb with salt and pepper. Heat the oil over medium-high heat in a rondeau or brasier until it starts to shimmer. Place the pork and lamb carefully in the oil and sear until deep brown on as many sides as possible. Transfer the meat to a hotel pan and reserve.

5. Degrease the pan, if necessary. Add the mirepoix to the pan and cook, stirring from time to time, until caramelized, about 11 minutes. Add the garlic and cook until aromatic, about 1 minute.

6. Add the wine to the pan, stirring to release any drippings. Reduce the wine until nearly dry. Return the beef to the pan along with any juices it may have released.

7. Add the concassé, sachet d'épices, demi-glace, and veal stock. Bring to a gentle simmer over medium-low heat. Cover the pot and transfer it to a 275°F/135°C oven. Braise the meat for 1 hour, or until fork tender.

8. Transfer the meat to a hotel pan or other holding container and moisten with some of the cooking liquid. Keep warm while finishing the sauce.

9. Continue to simmer the cooking liquid until it has a good flavor and consistency. Skim thoroughly to degrease the sauce. Adjust seasoning with salt and pepper and strain. Pour the sauce over the meat and keep hot for service.

10. Peel the reserved sausage and slice it into slices ¼ in/6 mm thick. Cut the bacon in slices ¼ in/6 mm thick as well. Place the sausage, bacon, pork, and lamb in a casserole.

11. Cover the meat with half of the beans, then the Duck Confit, and then the remaining beans.

12. Pour the sauce from the beans over the mixture and sprinkle it with the bread crumbs and parsley. Bake the cassoulet in a 300°F/149°C oven until it is heated through and a good crust has formed, about 1 hour.

13. Serve immediately or hold it hot for service.

New Mexican Green Chile Stew

Makes 10 servings

8 oz/227 g white beans, soaked overnight

3 lb 8 oz/1.59 kg pork shoulder, medium dice

80 fl oz/2.40 L **Chicken Stock** (page 351)

1 lb 8 oz/680 g Anaheim peppers

1 fl oz/30 mL vegetable oil

12 oz/340 g small-dice onions

1 oz/28 g minced garlic

2 lb/907 g russet potatoes, medium dice

1½ oz/43 g jalapeños, seeded

2¾ oz/78 g chopped cilantro

¾ oz/21 g salt

¾ oz/21 g cilantro sprigs

1. Place the beans in a pot and cover with water. Simmer over medium-low heat for about 1 hour or until completely tender. Add more water throughout the cooking process, if necessary. Reserve the beans in their cooking liquid.

2. Bring a large pot of water to a boil while the beans are simmering. Blanch the pork for 6 minutes in simmering water to remove any impurities. Skim the scum that forms on the surface; drain and rinse.

3. Place the blanched pork in a large pot and add the stock. Simmer over low heat until the pork is tender, about 2 hours.

4. Fire-roast the Anaheim peppers for 6 to 8 minutes or until the skin blackens and the flesh is tender. Place the peppers in a bowl and cover with plastic wrap to steam. Peel and remove the seeds. Reserve.

5. Heat the oil in a sauté pan over medium-high heat. Add the onions and garlic and sweat until the onions are translucent, about 5 minutes. Add the onions and garlic to the pork.

6. Add the potatoes and beans to the pork and simmer for about 10 minutes, or until the potatoes are tender.

7. Place the roasted peppers, jalapeños, and chopped cilantro in a blender and purée until completely smooth.

Add some of the cooking liquid from the stew to facilitate puréeing. Strain the mixture through a large-holed strainer, if desired.

8. Add the purée to the stew just before serving. Simmer for 1 to 2 minutes. Add the salt.

9. Serve immediately or hold it hot for service. Garnish with cilantro pluches.

Duck Confit

Makes 1 lb 12 oz/794 g

2½ oz/71 g salt

¼ tsp/1.25 g curing salt

¼ tsp/0.50 g ground black pepper

2 juniper berries, crushed

1 bay leaf, crushed

½ tsp/1.50 g chopped garlic

1 (about 6 lb/2.72 kg) duck

24 fl oz/720 mL rendered duck fat

1. Mix the 2 salts, pepper, juniper berries, bay leaf, and garlic together.

2. Coat the duck with the seasoning mixture. Place the duck in a container with a weighted lid and press it for 72 hours in the refrigerator.

3. Brush off the excess seasoning mixture. Place the duck in a rondeau or brasier and cover it with the rendered duck fat. Stew the meat in the fat over medium-low heat until it is very tender, about 2 hours.

4. Cool and store the duck in the cooking fat. When ready to use the confit, scrape away any excess fat and broil the duck on a rack until the skin is crisp, about 2 minutes. Use as needed.

Pork in a Green Curry Sauce

Makes 10 servings

80 fl oz/2.40 L coconut milk

8 fl oz/240 mL **Green Curry Paste** (page 464)

4 lb/1.81 kg pork butt, cut into 2-in/5-cm cubes

12 wild lime leaves, bruised

4 fl oz/120 mL fish sauce

2½ oz/71 g palm sugar

1 lb/454 g Thai eggplant, quartered

50 Thai basil leaves

3 to 4 Thai chiles, fine julienne

1. Skim the thick coconut cream from the top of the coconut milk; place the cream in a large pot, and cook, stirring constantly, until the cream begins to separate.

2. Stir in the curry paste and cook until aromatic, at least 2 minutes. Add the pork and lime leaves and mix well to coat the pork.

3. Add the fish sauce, sugar, and remaining coconut milk. Bring the mixture to a simmer; add the eggplant, and continue to simmer until the pork is tender and cooked through.

4. Remove the pan from the heat, add the basil, and mix well.

5. Serve immediately or hold it hot for service. Garnish with the chiles.

Pork Vindaloo

Makes 15 servings

SPICE PASTE

1 tsp/2 g cloves

1 tsp/2 g cardamom pods

3 tbsp/6 g cumin seeds

20 garlic cloves, thinly sliced

5 oz/142 g sliced ginger

½ oz/14 g ground turmeric

1 oz/28 g coriander seeds

4½ tsp/9 g methi seeds

14 oz/397 g dried red chiles

18 fl oz/540 mL palm vinegar

3½ oz/99 g sugar

8 fl oz/240 mL tamarind pulp, strained

5 oz/142 g salt

1 tbsp/6 g ground cinnamon

PORK MARINADE

1 tbsp/6 g ground turmeric

½ oz/14 g **Chili Powder** (page 463)

2½ oz/71 g sugar

8 fl oz/240 mL palm vinegar

10 lb/4.54 kg pork butt, cut into 1-in/3-cm cubes

2 fl oz/60 mL vegetable oil

2 onions, large dice

4 oz/113 g tomato paste

4 fl oz/120 mL water

salt, as needed

ground black pepper, as needed

1. To make the spice paste, combine the cloves, cardamom, cumin, garlic, ginger, turmeric, coriander, methi, chiles, vinegar, sugar, tamarind, salt, and cinnamon. Cover the mixture and refrigerate for 1 day. Purée the mixture in a blender to make a coarse paste.

2. To make the marinade, combine the turmeric, chili powder, sugar, and vinegar. Pour the marinade over the pork, cover, and refrigerate overnight.

3. Heat the oil over medium-high heat in a rondeau or brasier. Add the onions and sauté until golden brown. Add the spice paste and cook until aromatic. Combine the tomato paste and water and add it to pot. Cook until most of the water has evaporated and the mixture is almost dry.

4. Drain the pork from the marinade and add it to the pot. Stir to cover the pork cubes with the spice mixture.

5. Bring to a gentle simmer over medium-low heat. Cover the pot and stew the pork until tender, stirring occasionally to make sure that the meat does not scorch or burn. Skim and degrease the stew as it cooks.

6. Season with salt and pepper and serve immediately or hold it hot for service.

Székely Goulash (Székely Gulyás)

Makes 10 servings

12 oz/340 g small-dice slab bacon

1 lb/454 g small-dice onions

3 lb 8 oz/1.59 kg pork leg or shoulder, cut into ¾-in/2-cm cubes

4 tsp/8 g sweet paprika, or as needed

4 lb 8 oz/2.04 kg **Homemade Sauerkraut** (page 654)

48 fl oz/1.44 L **White Beef Stock** (page 351) or **Chicken Stock** (page 351), or as needed

2 oz/57 g all-purpose flour, mixed with water to make a slurry

16 fl oz/480 mL sour cream

10 oz/284 g slab bacon, rind on, cut into thick slices

1. Render the diced bacon over medium heat in a large pot until crispy, about 10 minutes. Remove bacon from pan and reserve.

2. Add the onions to the pan and sauté over medium-high heat until translucent, 6 to 8 minutes. Remove the pot from the heat.

3. Add 1 tbsp/6 g of the paprika and the pork to the pan, cover, and cook over low heat for 30 minutes, stirring periodically. (Be careful not to cook out the moisture and burn the paprika.)

4. Add the sauerkraut to the pot. Pour enough stock over the sauerkraut mixture to cover. Bring to a simmer, cover the pot, and cook until the meat is fork tender, about 1 hour.

5. Combine the flour slurry with 8 fl oz/240 mL of the sour cream. Add the slurry mixture to the goulash and simmer for 4 to 5 minutes, or until the sauce has thickened sufficiently.

6. To make "coxcombs," make incisions (½ to ¾ in/1 to 2 cm) into the rind of each slice of bacon at intervals of ½ to ¾ in/1 to 2 cm. Sauté the bacon until crisp and brown. Dip the tips of the coxcombs in the remaining paprika and keep them warm until ready to serve.

7. Serve the goulash immediately with the remaining sour cream on top, or hold it ungarnished and hot for service. Garnish with the coxcombs.

Veal Blanquette

Makes 10 servings

4 lb/1.81 kg boneless veal breast, excess fat removed, cut into 2-in/5-cm cubes

1 tbsp/15 g salt

½ tsp/1 g ground white pepper

64 fl oz/1.92 L **White Veal Stock** (page 351), **White Beef Stock** (page 351), or **Chicken Stock** (page 351)

1 **Bouquet Garni** (page 331)

8 oz/227 g **Blond or White Roux** (page 335)

1 lb 12 oz/794 g white mushrooms, stewed in butter and/or stock until tender

12 oz/340 g pearl onions, cooked and peeled

2 egg yolks, beaten

8 fl oz/240 mL heavy cream

lemon juice, as needed

1. Season the veal with salt and pepper.

2. Heat the stock to a simmer and season with salt and pepper as needed. Place the veal in a second pot and pour the heated stock over it. Return to a simmer, stirring and skimming as necessary to remove impurities. Simmer for 1 hour and add the bouquet garni. Continue to simmer until the veal is tender to the bite, 30 to 45 minutes. Transfer the veal to a hotel pan and keep warm.

3. Add the roux to the simmering liquid, whisking to combine well, and return to a full boil. Reduce the heat and simmer, stirring and skimming as necessary, until the sauce is thickened and flavorful, 20 to 30 minutes.

4. Return the veal and any juices it has released to the sauce, along with the mushrooms and pearl onions. Simmer until hot. (The stew may be cooled rapidly and refrigerated for later service. Return cooled stew to a simmer before adding the liaison.)

5. Combine the egg yolks and cream to make a liaison. Temper the liaison with some of the simmering liquid, and add to the stew. Return the stew to a slow simmer and cook until it is lightly thickened and has reached 165°F/74°C. Add the lemon juice and adjust seasoning with salt and pepper.

6. Serve the blanquette immediately or hold it hot for service.

Braised Veal Breast with Mushroom Sausage

Makes 15 to 20 servings

About 8 lb/3.63 kg boneless veal breast

1 tbsp/15 g salt

1½ tsp/3 g ground black pepper

2 lb 12 oz/1.25 kg **Mushroom Sausage** (recipe follows)

2 fl oz/60 mL olive oil

8 oz/227 g small-dice **Mirepoix** (page 333)

2 oz/57 g tomato paste

6 fl oz/180 mL dry white wine

16 fl oz/480 mL **Brown Veal Stock** (page 352)

16 fl oz/480 mL **Demi-Glace** (page 383) or **Jus de Veau Lié** (page 382)

1. Butterfly the veal breast and pound to an even thickness. Season with salt and pepper. Center the sausage on the breast, roll the veal around the sausage with the grain, and tie to secure.

2. Heat the oil over medium-high heat in a rondeau or brasier until it starts to shimmer. Place the veal carefully in the oil and sear until deep brown on all sides. Transfer the veal to a hotel pan and reserve.

3. Add the mirepoix to the pan and cook, stirring from time to time, until golden brown, 7 to 8 minutes. Add the tomato paste and cook until it turns a deeper color and gives off a sweet aroma, about 1 minute.

4. Add the wine to the pan, stirring to release any drippings. Reduce by half. Return the veal to the pan along with any juices it may have released. Add enough stock and demi-glace or jus lié to cover the veal by two thirds.

5. Bring to a gentle simmer over medium to low heat. Cover and braise in a 350°F/177°C oven for 1 hour 45 minutes to 2 hours or until fork tender, turning occasionally to keep the veal evenly moistened.

6. Transfer the veal to a hotel pan, moisten with some of the cooking liquid, and keep warm.

7. Continue to simmer the cooking liquid to a good flavor and consistency. Skim thoroughly to degrease the sauce. Adjust seasoning with salt and pepper and strain the sauce.

8. Remove the strings and slice the veal into servings. Serve immediately with the sauce or hold it hot for service.

Mushroom Sausage

Makes 2 lb 12 oz/1.25 kg

SPICE MIXTURE

2 tsp/6 g onion powder

¼ tsp/0.75 g garlic powder

¾ tsp/4 g **Pâté Spice** (page 1044)

1 tsp/5 g salt

¼ tsp/0.50 g Spanish paprika

½ tsp/3 g anise seeds

¼ tsp/0.50 g cayenne

1 lb 12 oz/794 g veal shank or lean pork, diced

6 oz/170 g cooked rice

3½ oz/99 g minced onions

3 fl oz/90 mL heavy cream

3 egg whites

7 oz/198 g white mushrooms, diced

1. Combine the ingredients for the spice mixture, scatter over the veal or pork, and toss to coat evenly. Refrigerate until needed.

2. Grind the seasoned meat through a coarse plate. Fold the rice and onions into the ground meat and grind a second time. (Chill the meat mixture if the temperature rises above 40°F/4°C.)

3. Working over an ice bath, add the cream and egg whites and mix by hand until evenly blended. Fold in the mushrooms.

4. The sausage is ready to use now, or it may be refrigerated for later use.

Pork Goulash

Makes 10 portions

4 lb/1.81 kg boneless pork shoulder, cut into 2-in/5-cm cubes

¾ oz/21 g Hungarian paprika

salt, as needed

ground black pepper, as needed

3 oz/85 g vegetable oil or lard

3 lb/1.36 kg small-dice onions

8 fl oz/240 mL dry white wine

16 fl oz/480 mL **Jus De Veau Lié** (page 382)

16 fl oz/480 mL **Brown Veal Stock** (page 352)

Sachet d'épices, containing 2 bay leaves, ¼ tsp/0.25 g thyme, ¼ tsp/0.50 g peppercorns, 1 tsp/2 g caraway seeds, ½ tsp/0.50 g marjoram, ½ tsp/0.50 g savory, 2 garlic cloves, 1 tsp/3 g grated lemon zest

8 fl oz/240 mL sour cream

1. Season the pork with the paprika, salt, and pepper.

2. Heat the oil or lard over medium-high heat in a rondeau or brasier until it starts to shimmer. Place the pork carefully in the oil and sear until deep brown on all sides. Transfer the pork to a hotel pan and reserve.

3. Add the onions to the pan and cook, stirring from time to time, until golden brown, 6 to 8 minutes.

4. Add the wine to the pan, stirring to release any drippings. Reduce the wine by half. Return the pork to the pan along with any juices it may have released. Add the jus lié and enough stock to completely cover the pork.

5. Bring to a gentle simmer over medium to low heat. Add the sachet, cover the pot, and continue to cook over low heat, or transfer to a moderate oven (350°F/175°C). Stew the pork for 1 hour 15 minutes or until the pork is fork tender.

6. Skim thoroughly to degrease the stew. Remove and discard the sachet. Adjust seasoning with salt and pepper and strain. Serve the stew in heated bowls garnished with sour cream.

Beef Goulash: Replace the pork with an equal amount of boneless beef round or chuck.

Osso Buco Milanese

Makes 10 servings

10 (1 lb/454 g) veal shank crosscuts, 1½ in/4 cm thick

1 tbsp/15 g salt

1½ tsp/3 g ground black pepper

2 oz/57 g all-purpose flour

2 fl oz/60 mL olive oil

12 oz/340 g small-dice **Mirepoix** (page 333)

1 tsp/3 g minced garlic

3 oz/85 g tomato paste

8 fl oz/240 mL dry white wine

64 fl oz /1.92 L **Brown Veal Stock** (page 352)

1 **Bouquet Garni** (page 331)

arrowroot slurry, as needed (optional)

1 oz/28 g **Gremolata** (recipe follows)

1. Season the veal with salt and pepper and tie a string around the shanks to keep them together. Lightly dredge them in flour.

2. Heat the oil over medium-high heat in a rondeau or brasier until it starts to shimmer. Place the shanks carefully in the oil and sear until deep brown on all sides. Transfer the shanks to a hotel pan and reserve.

3. Add the onions from the mirepoix to the pan and cook, stirring from time to time, until golden brown. Add the carrots and celery and cook until barely translucent. Add the garlic and tomato paste and cook until the tomato paste turns a deeper color and gives off a sweet aroma, about 1 minute.

4. Add the wine to the pan, stirring to release any drippings. Reduce the wine by half. Return the shanks to the pan along with any juices they may have released. Add enough stock to cover the veal by two thirds.

5. Bring to a gentle simmer over medium-low heat. Cover the pot and transfer it to a moderate oven (350°F/177°C). Braise the veal shanks for 45 minutes. Add the bouquet garni and degrease the liquid if necessary. Finish braising the veal until fork tender, 1 to 1½ hours more.

6. Transfer the veal shanks to a hotel pan or other holding container and moisten with some of the cooking liquid. Keep warm while finishing the sauce.

7. Continue to simmer the cooking liquid until it has a good flavor and consistency. Skim thoroughly to degrease the sauce. If necessary, the sauce can be thickened lightly with the arrowroot slurry. Adjust seasoning with salt and pepper and strain. Keep hot for service.

8. Serve the veal shanks immediately with the sauce and Gremolata, or hold them hot for service.

Gremolata

Makes 16 fl oz/480 mL

5 oz/142 g panko bread crumbs

½ oz/14 g orange zest, blanched, minced

½ oz/14 g lemon zest, blanched, minced

4 garlic cloves, minced

½ oz/14 g chopped parsley

salt, as needed

ground black pepper, as needed

1. Process the bread crumbs in a food processor for 5 seconds and spread thinly on a dry sheet pan. Toast them in a 500°F/260°C oven until lightly browned, about 7 minutes. Transfer to a bowl and reserve.

2. Add the orange and lemon zests, garlic, parsley, salt, and pepper to the bread crumbs. Toss to combine.

3. The gremolata is ready to use now, or it may be refrigerated for later use.

NOTE

For a more traditional gremolata, combine ½ oz/14 g minced garlic, ¾ oz/21 g lemon zest, 1½ oz/43 g chopped parsley, and, if desired, ¼ oz/7 g anchovy fillets.

Osso Buco Milanese with Risotto alla Milanese (page 831)

Polish Stuffed Cabbage

Polish Stuffed Cabbage

Makes 10 servings

20 large savoy cabbage leaves (outer leaves), blanched

12 oz/340 g boneless veal breast, diced

12 oz/340 g boneless pork shoulder, diced

12 oz/340 g boneless beef bottom round, diced

1 tbsp/15 g salt

1½ tsp/3 g ground black pepper

10 oz/284 g small-dice onion, sautéed and cooled

8 fl oz/240 mL heavy cream

3 eggs

6 oz/170 g bread crumbs

salt, as needed

ground black pepper, as needed

ground nutmeg, as needed

6 oz/170 g thinly sliced **Mirepoix** (page 333)

1 bay leaf

32 fl oz/960 mL **White Beef Stock** (page 351), or as needed, hot

6 oz/170 g slab bacon, cut into 10 slices (optional)

25 fl oz/750 mL **Tomato Sauce** (page 384)

1. Bring a large pot of salted water to a boil and cook the cabbage leaves, drain, rinse in cold water, and drain once more. Remove the large vein from each cabbage leaf. Reserve.

2. Season the veal, pork, and beef with salt and pepper.

3. Grind the seasoned meat through a coarse plate of a meat grinder. Fold the onions into the ground meat and grind a second time. (Chill the meat mixture if the temperature rises above 40°F/4°C.)

4. Working over an ice bath, add the cream and eggs and mix by hand until evenly blended. Fold in the bread crumbs. Season with salt, pepper, and nutmeg. Keep this mixture chilled until ready to use.

5. For each cabbage roll, dampen 1 sq ft/30 sq cm of cheesecloth. Place the cheesecloth in an 8-fl oz/24-mL round cup. Place 2 cabbage leaves in the cup, overlap-

ping the leaves so that there are no open spaces. Place the meat in the center of the leaves and wrap them around to enclose the filling. Twist the excess cheesecloth to form each roll into a ball. Do not twist too hard or the cabbage leaves will rip.

6. Place the mirepoix and bay leaf in a rondeau or brasier. Place the cabbage rolls seam side down on top of the mirepoix. Add enough hot stock to cover the rolls by about one half and place the sliced bacon on top of the cabbage rolls, if desired. Bring the stock to a gentle simmer over medium to low heat. Cover the pot and transfer it to a moderate oven (350°F/177°C). Braise the cabbage rolls for 45 to 50 minutes, or to an internal temperature of 160°F/71°C.

7. Serve the cabbage rolls immediately with 2½ fl oz/ 75 mL of Tomato Sauce per serving, or hold them hot for service.

Braised Lamb Shanks

Makes 10 servings

10 (1 lb/454 g) lamb shanks

1 tbsp/15 g salt

1½ tsp/3 g ground black pepper

2 fl oz/60 mL vegetable oil

1 lb/454 g large-dice **Mirepoix** (page 333)

1 garlic head, halved and roasted

1 fl oz/30 mL tomato paste

2 oz/57 g all-purpose flour (optional)

16 fl oz/480 mL dry red wine

64 fl oz/1.9 L **Brown Lamb Stock** (page 352) or **Brown Veal Stock** (page 352)

1 **Sachet d'Épices** (page 331)

arrowroot slurry, as needed (optional)

1. Season the shanks with salt and pepper.

2. Heat the oil over medium-high heat in a rondeau or brasier until it starts to shimmer. Place the shanks carefully in the oil and sear until deep brown on all sides. Transfer the shanks to a hotel pan and reserve.

3. Add the onions from the mirepoix to the pan and cook, stirring from time to time, until golden brown. Add the carrots and celery and cook until barely translucent. Add the roasted garlic pulp and tomato paste and cook until the tomato paste turns a deeper color and gives off a sweet aroma, about 1 minute. If desired, stir in the flour to make a roux. Cook the roux for 4 to 5 minutes.

4. Add the wine to the pan, stirring to release any drippings. Reduce the wine by half. Whisk in the stock and bring to a simmer. Return the shanks to the pan along with any juices they may have released.

5. Bring to a gentle simmer over medium-low heat. Cover the pot and transfer it to a moderate oven (350°F/177°C). Braise the lamb shanks for 45 minutes. Add the sachet and degrease the liquid if necessary. Finish braising the lamb until fork tender, about 45 minutes more.

6. Transfer the shanks to a hotel pan or other holding container and moisten with some of the cooking liquid. Keep warm while finishing the sauce.

7. Continue to simmer the cooking liquid until it has a good flavor and consistency. Skim thoroughly to degrease the sauce. If necessary, the sauce can be thickened lightly with arrowroot slurry. Adjust seasoning with salt and pepper and strain. Keep hot for service.

8. Serve the shanks immediately with the sauce or hold them hot for service.

NOTES

To prepare braised lamb shanks in advance and finish them in batches or à la minute, cool the shanks after they have been removed from the braising liquid. Foods that are braised on the bone have a wonderful flavor and texture but may be a challenge for the guest to eat. It is sometimes appropriate to remove the bones before service. Once the shanks are cool enough to handle, pull out the shank bone. Transfer the boneless shanks to a hotel pan. Cover and refrigerate the cooled shanks.

Cool and store the sauce separately in a bain marie or other container. To complete the shanks for service, ladle a small amount of a flavorful stock, remouillage, or broth on the shanks and reheat them in the oven. To complete the dish, reheat the amount of sauce needed in a sauté pan, add the reheated shanks, simmer briefly, and adjust seasoning.

Portuguese Stuffed Leg of Lamb

Makes 12 servings

5 lb/2.27 kg boneless lamb leg

1 tbsp/15 g salt

1½ tsp/3 g ground black pepper

2 lb 4 oz/1.25 kg **Herbed Forcemeat Stuffing** (recipe follows)

2 fl oz/60 mL olive oil

12 oz/340 g small-dice **Mirepoix** (page 333)

2 fl oz/60 mL tomato paste

3 fl oz/90 mL dry sherry

48 fl oz/1.44 L **Brown Lamb Stock** (page 352) or **Brown Veal Stock** (page 352)

2 bay leaves

arrowroot slurry, as needed

1 tbsp/3 g chopped cilantro

1. Butterfly the lamb and pound to an even thickness. Season with salt and pepper. Spread the stuffing on the lamb, roll, and tie to secure.

2. Heat the oil over medium-high heat in a rondeau or brasier until it starts to shimmer. Place the lamb carefully in the oil and sear until deep brown on all sides. Transfer the lamb to a hotel pan and reserve.

3. Add the mirepoix to the pan and cook, stirring from time to time, until golden brown, 7 to 8 minutes. Add the tomato paste and cook until it turns a deeper color and gives off a sweet aroma, about 1 minute.

4. Add the sherry to the pan, stirring to release any drippings. Reduce by half. Return the lamb to the pan along with any juices it may have released. Add enough stock to cover the lamb by two thirds.

5. Bring to a gentle simmer over medium to low heat. Add the bay leaves, cover, and braise in a 350°F/177°C oven for 1½ to 2 hours or until fork tender, turning occasionally to keep the lamb evenly moistened.

6. Transfer the lamb to a hotel pan, moisten with some of the cooking liquid, and keep warm.

7. Continue to simmer the cooking liquid to a good flavor and consistency. Skim thoroughly to degrease the sauce. If necessary, thicken with arrowroot slurry. Adjust seasoning with salt and pepper and strain. Add cilantro to the entire batch or to individual servings. Keep hot for service.

8. Remove the strings and slice the lamb into servings. Serve immediately with the sauce or hold it hot for service.

Herbed Forcemeat Stuffing

Makes 2 lb 4 oz/1.25 kg

2 oz/57 g butter

8 oz/227 g fine-dice onions

3 oz/85 g fine-dice celery

8 oz/227 g fine-dice mushrooms

5 oz/142 g small-dice bread

6 oz/170 g ground beef

6 oz/170 g ground pork

6 oz/170 g ground veal

1 egg

½ oz/14 g minced parsley

½ tsp/0.50 g chopped basil

½ tsp/0.50 g minced savory

½ tsp/0.50 g minced sage

salt, as needed

ground black pepper, as needed

1. Heat the butter in a large sauté pan over medium-high heat. Add the onions and sauté, stirring frequently, until they are golden brown, 5 to 6 minutes. Add the celery and mushrooms. Continue to cook until tender and translucent. Transfer to a bowl and cool.

2. Add the bread, ground meats, egg, herbs, salt, and pepper, and mix until combined.

3. The stuffing is ready to use now, or it may be refrigerated for later use.

Lamb Navarin

Makes 10 servings

4 lb/1.81 kg boneless lamb shoulder, neck, shank, or leg, cut into 2-in/5-cm cubes

1 tbsp/15 g salt

1½ tsp/3 g ground black pepper

2 fl oz/60 mL vegetable oil

6 oz/170 g medium-dice onion

1 tsp/3 g minced garlic

2 fl oz/60 mL tomato paste

4 fl oz/120 mL dry red wine

8 fl oz/240 mL, or as needed **Brown Lamb Stock** (page 352) or **Brown Veal Stock** (page 352)

20 fl oz/600 mL **Demi-Glace** (page 383), **Jus d'Agneau Lié** (page 382), **Jus de Veau Lié** (page 382), or **Espagnole Sauce** (page 382)

1 **Sachet d'Épices** (page 331)

8 oz/227 g carrot tourné or oblique cut

8 oz/227 g potato tourné or medium dice

8 oz/227 g celery tourné or oblique cut

8 oz/227 g turnip tourné or medium dice

8 oz/227 g white mushrooms

6 oz/170 g tomato concassé

1. Season the lamb with salt and pepper.

2. Heat the oil over medium-high heat in a rondeau or brasier until it starts to shimmer. Place the lamb carefully in the oil and sear until deep brown on as many sides as possible. Transfer the lamb to a hotel pan and reserve.

3. Degrease the pan, if necessary. Add the onions to the pan and cook, stirring from time to time, until caramelized. Add the garlic and tomato paste and cook until the tomato paste turns a deeper color and gives off a sweet aroma, about 1 minute.

4. Add the wine to the pan, stirring to release any drippings. Reduce the wine by three quarters. Return the lamb to the pan along with any juices it may have released.

5. Add enough stock and brown sauce to cover the lamb, along with the sachet. Bring to a gentle simmer over medium-low heat. Cover the pot and stew the lamb for about 1 hour. Add more stock during cooking, if necessary. Skim and degrease the stew as it cooks.

6. Add the carrots, potatoes, celery, turnips, and mushrooms. Continue to stew until the lamb is tender to the bite and the vegetables are fully cooked. Remove and discard the sachet. Add the concassé and simmer until the tomatoes are very hot, 10 minutes more. Adjust seasoning with salt and pepper.

7. Serve the stew immediately or hold it hot for service.

Lamb Khorma

Makes 10 servings

MARINADE

10 fl oz/300 mL yogurt

2 tsp/4 g ground white pepper

2 tsp/4 g ground cardamom

1 tbsp/9 g garlic paste

1 tbsp/9 g ginger paste

LAMB

5 lb/2.27 kg lamb, cut into 1½-in/4-cm cubes

10 fl oz/300 mL ghee or vegetable oil

1 lb 8 oz/680 g small-dice onions

2 tbsp/12 g ground cumin

1 tsp/2 g ground cardamom

1 tbsp/6 g ground fennel

1 tbsp/6 g ground white pepper

1 tbsp/9 g chopped ginger

2 tbsp/12 g ground coriander

15 Thai chiles, minced

1 oz/28 g chopped cilantro stems

12 oz/340 g cashews, soaked in hot water, ground to a paste

8 fl oz/240 mL heavy cream

½ oz/21 g chopped cilantro

1. To make the marinade, combine the yogurt, pepper, cardamom, garlic, and ginger and mix to combine. Add the lamb and marinate for 30 minutes in the refrigerator.

2. Heat the ghee or oil over medium-high heat in a rondeau or brasier. Add the onions and sweat until translucent.

3. In 1- to 2-minute intervals over medium heat, stir in the cumin, cardamom, fennel, pepper, ginger, and coriander. When the spices are aromatic, add the chiles and cilantro stems.

4. Cook the mixture for 1 to 2 minutes and add the cashew paste, stirring to make sure nothing sticks to the bottom of the pan. Add water if the mixture becomes too dry.

5. Drain the lamb from the marinade and add it to the pot. Increase the heat and mix until the lamb is evenly covered with the spices. Bring to a simmer, cover the pan, and cook over medium-low heat for 45 minutes, stirring occasionally to prevent the meat from sticking to the bottom of the pan. Add water if the mixture becomes too dry.

6. Add the cream and adjust seasoning with salt and pepper. Mix well and continue to cook until the meat is tender.

7. Serve immediately or hold it hot for service. Garnish with the cilantro.

Chicken Fricassee

Makes 10 servings

5 (2 lb 8 oz/1.13 kg) chickens, cut into 8 pieces each

1 tbsp/15 g salt

¼ tsp/0.50 g ground white pepper

4 fl oz/120 mL clarified butter or vegetable oil

1 lb/454 g diced onions

2 tsp/6 g minced garlic

2 oz/57 g all-purpose flour

8 fl oz/240 mL white wine

16 fl oz/480 mL **Chicken Stock** (page 351)

2 bay leaves

1 tbsp/6 g thyme

8 fl oz/240 mL heavy cream

1 lb/454 g small-dice carrots, blanched

1 lb/454 g small-dice leeks, blanched

½ oz/14 g chopped chives or parsley

1. Season the chicken pieces with salt and pepper.

2. Heat the butter or oil over medium heat in a rondeau or brasier. Place the chicken pieces carefully in the pan and sauté until they stiffen slightly, but do not brown. Transfer the chicken to a hotel pan and reserve.

3. Degrease the pan, if necessary. Add the onions and garlic to the pan and cook, stirring from time to time, until the onions are translucent, about 5 minutes.

4. Add the flour and cook, stirring frequently, for about 5 minutes.

5. Add the wine to the pan, stirring to release any drippings. Add the stock, bay leaves, and thyme and bring to a simmer. Return the chicken pieces to the pan along with any juices they may have released.

6. Cover the pot and cook the chicken over low to medium heat, until fork tender and cooked through, 30 to 40 minutes.

7. Transfer the chicken to a hotel pan or other holding container and moisten with some of the cooking liquid. Keep it warm while finishing the sauce.

8. Add the cream and simmer until the sauce has thickened slightly, 5 to 7 minutes. Skim thoroughly to degrease the sauce. Adjust seasoning with salt and pepper and strain.

9. Return the chicken to the sauce, along with the carrots and leeks. Simmer for about 2 minutes and serve immediately or hold it hot for service. Garnish with the chives or parsley.

Veal Fricassee: Substitute an equal amount of boneless veal shoulder, breast, or leg meat for the chicken.

Curried Goat with Green Papaya Salsa

Makes 20 servings

about 25 lb/11.34 kg goat, cut into primal sections

1 oz/28 g salt

4 tsp/8 g ground black pepper

8 fl oz/240 mL vegetable oil

2 gal/7.68 L **Brown Veal Stock** (page 352)

8 thyme sprigs

2 habaneros, seeded and minced

½ oz/14 g **Curry Powder** (page 463)

Demi-Glace (page 383), as needed (optional)

20 plum tomatoes, peeled, seeded, medium dice

1 lb 4 oz/567 g green onions, sliced ½ in/1 cm thick

7 fl oz/210 mL lime juice

40 fl oz/1.20 L **Green Papaya Salsa** (page 989)

1. Season the goat with salt and pepper.

2. Heat some of the oil over medium-high heat in a brasier until it starts to shimmer. Working in batches, place the goat pieces carefully in the oil and sear until deep brown on all sides. Transfer to hotel pans and reserve.

3. Once all the goat pieces have been seared, return them to the brasier along with the stock and thyme. Adjust seasoning with salt and pepper. Bring to a gentle simmer over medium-low heat. Cover the pot and transfer it to a moderate oven (350°F/177°C). Braise the goat for at least 2 to 3 hours, or until very tender.

4. Transfer the goat to hotel pans or other holding containers and moisten with some of the cooking liquid. Keep it warm while finishing the sauce.

5. Continue to simmer the cooking liquid until it has reduced by half. Skim thoroughly to degrease the sauce. Adjust seasoning with salt and pepper and strain. Keep hot for service.

6. Shred the goat meat into large pieces. Heat some oil in a large rondeau over medium-high heat. Add the chiles and sweat until soft and aromatic. Add the shredded goat, curry powder, and the reduced cooking liquid. Bring to a simmer and adjust seasoning with salt and pepper. If desired, add demi-glace to the mixture.

7. Just before service, stir in the tomatoes, half the green onions, and lime juice. Serve immediately with the Green Papaya Salsa and garnished with the remaining green onions, or hold it hot for service.

Couscous with Lamb and Chicken Stew

Makes 10 servings

2 lb/907 g boneless lamb shoulder or leg, cut into 1-in/3-cm cubes

3 lb/1.36 kg skinless chicken legs (bone in), thighs, and drumsticks separated

1 tbsp/15 g salt

1½ tsp/3 g ground black pepper

4 fl oz/120 mL olive oil

8 oz/227 g diced onions

¾ oz/21 g minced garlic

1 tbsp/9 g grated ginger

½ oz/14 g ground cumin

½ oz/14 g ground turmeric

1 tsp/2 g ground coriander

½ tsp/1 g ground nutmeg

2 bay leaves

pinch saffron threads

dash ground cloves

32 fl oz/960 mL **Brown Lamb Stock** (page 352) or **Brown Chicken Stock** (page 351)

8 oz/227 g large-dice carrots

4 oz/113 g large-dice turnips

1 lb/454 g couscous

8 oz/227 g small-dice zucchini

8 oz/227 g small-dice green peppers

4 oz/113 g cooked chickpeas

2 oz/57 g cooked lima beans

1 lb/454 g tomatoes, peeled and cut into wedges

6 oz/170 g artichoke bottoms, quartered

4 oz/113 g Arabic white truffles, sliced (optional)

GARNISH

6 oz/170 g sliced almonds, toasted

6 oz/170 g raisins or currants

1 fl oz/30 mL **Harissa** (page 994)

½ oz/14 g chopped parsley

1. Season the lamb and chicken with salt and pepper.

2. Heat half of the oil over medium-high heat in the lower part of a couscousière until it starts to shimmer. Place the lamb carefully in the oil and sear until deep brown on as many sides as possible.

3. Add the onions, garlic, ginger, and spices. Add enough stock to cover the lamb. Bring the stock to a simmer and cook for 45 minutes.

4. Add the carrots, turnips, and chicken to the stew and return to a simmer over low heat. Skim and degrease as necessary.

5. Line the top of the couscousière with rinsed cheese-cloth and add the couscous. Cover and continue to cook for another 30 minutes.

6. Remove the top of the couscousière, adjust seasoning with salt, and add about 2 fl oz/60 mL of oil, working to break up any clumps. Keep hot while finishing the stew.

7. Add the zucchini and green peppers to the stew and cook for 4 minutes.

8. Add the chickpeas, lima beans, tomatoes, artichoke bottoms, and truffles, if using, and simmer the stew until all of the ingredients are tender and very hot. Adjust seasoning with salt, pepper, and spices, if necessary.

9. Mound the couscous on a heated plate or platter and place the stew in the center of the mound. Scatter with the almonds, raisins or currants, droplets of harissa, and parsley. Serve immediately.

Irish Stew

Makes 10 servings

4 lb/1.81 kg boneless lamb shoulder, cut into 2-in/5-cm cubes

1 tbsp/15 g salt

½ tsp/0.50 g ground white pepper

48 fl oz/1.44 L **White Beef Stock** (page 351)

1 **Bouquet Garni** (page 331)

1 lb/454 g pearl onions, blanched and peeled

1 lb/454 g large-dice potatoes

8 oz/227 g large-dice celery

8 oz/227 g large-dice carrots

8 oz/227 g large-dice parsnips

8 oz/227 g large-dice turnips

2 tbsp/6 g chopped parsley

1. Season the lamb with salt and pepper.

2. Heat the stock to a simmer and adjust seasoning with salt and pepper as needed. Place the lamb in a second pot and pour the heated stock over it. Return to a simmer, stirring from time to time and skimming as necessary to remove impurities. Simmer for 1 hour and add the bouquet garni and vegetables. Continue to simmer until the lamb and vegetables are tender to the bite, 30 to 45 minutes more.

3. Serve the stew immediately or hold it hot for service. Garnish with the parsley.

Chicken Tagine

Makes 10 servings

5 (2 lb 8 oz/1.13 kg) chickens, cut into 6 pieces each

1 tbsp/15 g salt

1½ tsp/3 g ground black pepper

2 fl oz/60 mL extra-virgin olive oil

30 cipollini onions, blanched and peeled

1 ginger piece (½ in/1 cm long), thinly sliced

5 garlic cloves, thinly sliced

1 tsp/2 g cumin seeds, toasted and ground

¼ tsp/0.20 g saffron

8 to 10 fl oz/240 to 300 mL water or **Chicken Stock** (page 351), or as needed

50 picholine olives

2 **Preserved Lemons** (recipe follows)

4 tbsp/12 g chopped parsley

1. Season the chicken pieces with salt and pepper.

2. Heat the oil over medium-high heat in a tagine, rondeau, or brasier. Place the chicken pieces carefully in the oil and sauté until they turn golden brown. Transfer the chicken to a hotel pan and reserve.

3. Add the onions to the pan and cook, stirring from time to time, until golden brown, 7 to 8 minutes. Add the ginger and garlic and toast until aromatic, 1 minute more. Add the cumin and saffron and cook until the mixture turns a deeper color and gives off a sweet aroma, about 1 minute.

4. Return the chicken to the pan and add the water or stock. Adjust seasoning with salt and pepper. Bring to a gentle simmer over medium-low heat. Cover and braise for 30 to 40 minutes, or until the chicken is cooked through, turning the pieces occasionally to keep them evenly moistened. (Maintain only a small amount of water or stock so the braising liquid will become concentrated.)

5. In the last 15 minutes, add the olives, lemons, and parsley. Simmer the mixture until the olives are tender and the aroma of the lemons is apparent.

6. Remove the lemons and serve the tagine immediately or hold it hot for service.

Preserved Lemons

Makes 6 lemons

6 lemons

5 oz/142 g salt

10 fl oz/300 mL lemon juice, or as needed

1. Wash the lemons very well. Cut each one in 6 wedges lengthwise and remove all the seeds. Place the lemon wedges in a very clean jar. Add the salt and the lemon juice and mix well. Add more lemon juice if necessary to just cover the lemons.

2. Cover with a lid and refrigerate. Stir the lemons every day or two to help dissolve the salt. Allow the lemons to cure for at least 1 week. Rinse under cold water before using as needed.

Chicken Tagine

Chicken and Prawn Ragout (*Mar i Muntanya*)

Chicken and Prawn Ragout (Mar i Muntanya)

Makes 10 servings

3 (2 lb 8 oz/1.13 kg) chickens, cut into 8 pieces each

1 tbsp/15 g salt

1½ tsp/3 g ground black pepper

2 fl oz/60 mL extra-virgin olive oil

1 lb 12 oz/794 g shrimp (16–20 count), deveined, with shells on

12 oz/340 g small-dice onions

1 lb 8 oz/680 g plum tomatoes

10 fl oz/300 mL white wine

16 fl oz/480 mL **Chicken Stock** (page 351)

1 fl oz/30 mL Pernod

PICADA

1¼ oz/35 g minced garlic

½ oz/14 g toasted French bread

2½ oz/71 g Mexican chocolate

1 oz/28 g blanched almonds, roasted

1 tsp/1 g chopped parsley

salt, as needed

ground black pepper, as needed

½ fl oz/15 mL extra-virgin olive oil

1. Season the chicken pieces with salt and pepper.

2. Heat the oil over medium-high heat in a rondeau or brasier. Place the chicken pieces carefully in the oil and sauté until they turn golden brown. Transfer the chicken to a hotel pan and reserve.

3. In the same pan, sauté the shrimp in their shells until bright red, about 3 minutes. Transfer the shrimp to a hotel pan and reserve.

4. Degrease the pan, if necessary. Add the onions and tomatoes to the pan and cook, stirring from time to time, until softened and slightly rust colored, about 15 minutes.

5. Add the wine to the pan, stirring to release any drip-pings. Reduce by half. Return the chicken pieces to the pan along with any juices they may have released. Add enough stock and cover the chicken.

6. Bring to a gentle simmer over medium-low heat. Cover the pot and cook the chicken until fork tender and cooked through, 30 to 40 minutes.

7. Add the Pernod and continue simmering for an additional 10 minutes. Add the shrimp and finish cooking, about 2 minutes. Adjust seasoning with salt and pepper.

8. To make the picada, crush or grind the garlic, bread, chocolate, and almonds until smooth. Add the parsley and combine well. Season with salt and pepper. Add enough oil to barely cover the picada and work it into a thick paste.

9. Stir the picada into the stew and cook for an additional 2 minutes.

10. Serve the stew immediately or hold it hot for service.

Cioppino

Makes 10 servings

1 fl oz/30 mL olive oil

12 oz/340 g finely diced onions

1 bunch green onions, sliced on the bias

12 oz/340 g small-dice green peppers

12 oz/340 g small-dice fennel

1 tbsp/15 g salt

¼ tsp/0.50 g ground black pepper

4 tsp/12 g minced garlic

4 lb/1.81 kg tomato concassé

8 fl oz/240 mL dry white wine

16 fl oz/480 mL **Tomato Sauce** (page 384)

2 bay leaves

32 fl oz/960 mL **Fish Fumet** (page 353)

2 lb 8 oz/1.13 kg Manila clams, scrubbed

2 lb 8 oz/1.13 kg mussels, scrubbed and debearded

1 lb 8 oz/680 g shrimp (16–20 count), peeled and deveined

2 lb 8 oz/1.13 kg cod, large dice

12 oz/340 g scallops, muscle tabs removed

10 **Garlic-Flavored Croutons** (recipe follows)

¾ oz/21 g basil chiffonade

1. Heat the oil in a large soup pot over medium heat. Add the onions, green onions, peppers, and fennel and season with salt and pepper. Sauté until the onions are translucent, 7 to 8 minutes. Add the garlic and sauté until aromatic, 1 minute more.

2. Add the concassé, wine, tomato sauce, bay leaves, and fumet. Cover the pot and simmer slowly for about 20 minutes. Add more stock if necessary. Remove and discard the bay leaves.

3. Add the seafood to the pot and simmer until the cod, shrimp, and scallops are cooked, and the clams and mussels are opened, 7 to 8 minutes.

4. Garnish the cioppino with a crouton and basil and serve immediately.

Garlic-Flavored Croutons

Makes 10 servings

10 thin French bread slices, cut on the diagonal

5 garlic cloves, peeled and halved

2 fl oz/60 mL olive oil

salt, as needed

ground black pepper, as needed

1. Arrange the bread slices on a baking sheet. Rub each slice with garlic and brush lightly with oil on both sides. Season with salt and pepper.

2. Brown the bread in a broiler; turn and brown on the second side. Reserve until ready to serve.

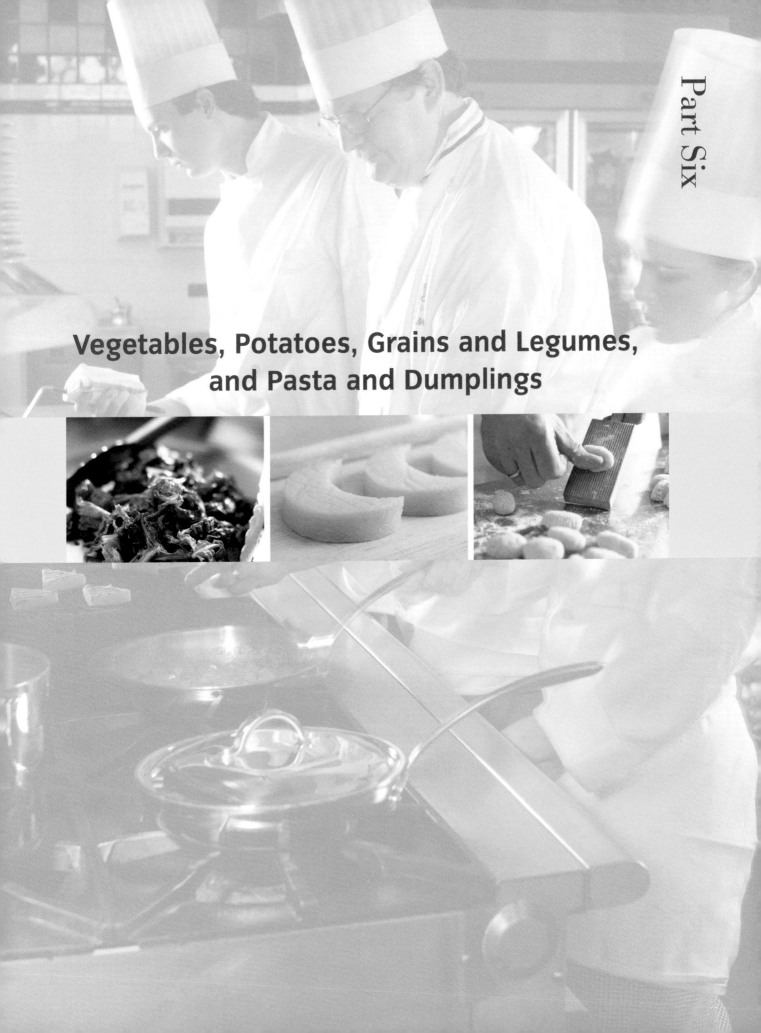

Part Six

Vegetables, Potatoes, Grains and Legumes, and Pasta and Dumplings

Chapter Twenty-four

Mise en Place for Vegetables and Fresh Herbs

From trimming and peeling to slicing and dicing, many vegetables and herbs need advance preparation before they are ready to serve or use as an ingredient in a cooked dish. Various knife cuts are used to shape vegetables and herbs. A thorough mastery of knife skills includes the ability to prepare vegetables and herbs properly for cutting, to use a variety of cutting tools, and to make cuts that are uniform and precise.

Cutting Vegetables and Fresh Herbs

Make all vegetable cuts uniform in shape and size so that they cook evenly and have a neat, attractive appearance.

The best dishes begin with the best-quality produce. Review the information about purchasing and handling produce found in Chapter 11. Handle fresh produce carefully to maintain its flavor, color, and nutritional value throughout all stages of preparation and cooking. One key to preserving quality in produce is to perform all cutting tasks as close as possible to cooking time.

Another important factor is the ability to select the right tool for the job, and to keep that tool in proper working condition. A steel should be on hand whenever you are cutting any food to periodically hone your knife blade as you work. For a review of basic knife handling, see pages xxx–xxx.

The basic knife cuts include:

Chopping

Mincing

Chiffonade (shredding)

Julienne and batonnet

Dicing

Paysanne (fermière)

Diamond (lozenge)

Rondelle, bias, oblique, or roll cuts

Your aim, whenever you cut something, should always be to cut the food into pieces of uniform shape and size. Unevenly cut items give an impression of carelessness that can spoil the dish's look. An even more important consideration is that foods of different sizes and shapes won't cook evenly.

Peeling vegetables

All fresh produce, even if it will be peeled before cutting, should be washed well. Washing removes surface dirt and bacteria and other contaminants that might otherwise come in contact with cut surfaces by way of the knife or peeler. For the best shelf life, wash vegetables as close to preparation time as possible.

Not all vegetables require peeling before cooking, but when it is necessary, use a tool that will evenly and neatly remove the skin without taking off too much of the edible flesh. Some vegetables and fruits have relatively thin skins or peels. Examples include carrots, parsnips, asparagus, apples, pears, and potatoes.

Peeling a thick-skinned vegetable such as winter squash requires the use of a chef's knife. Chef's knives are better for larger vegetables or those with very tough rinds, such as celeriac or winter squash. Remove fibrous or tough skins from broccoli and similar vegetables by using a paring knife or swivel-bladed peeler to trim away the skin; often it can be pulled away after the initial cut.

Peel vegetables with relatively thin skins or peels, such as asparagus, carrots, or parsnips, using a swivel-bladed peeler. These peelers can be used in both directions, so that the skin or peel is removed on both the downward and upward strokes. A paring knife can be used in place of a peeler in some instances. Hold the blade's edge at a 20-degree angle to the vegetable's surface and shave the blade just under the surface to remove a thin layer.

Chopping

Coarse chopping is generally used for mirepoix or similar flavoring ingredients that are to be strained out of the dish and discarded. It is also appropriate when cutting vegetables that will be puréed. Trim the root and stem ends and peel the vegetables if necessary. Slice or cut through the vegetables at nearly regular intervals until the cuts are relatively uniform. This need not be a perfectly neat cut, but all the pieces should be roughly the same size.

1. Rinse and dry herbs well, and then strip the leaves from the stems. Gather the herbs into a tight ball before slicing them, which produces a very coarse chop. Use your guiding hand to hold them in place. Position the knife so that it can slice through the pile and chop coarsely.

2. Once the herbs are coarsely chopped, use the fingertips of your guiding hand to hold the tip of the chef's knife in contact with the cutting board. Keeping the tip of the blade against the cutting board, lower the knife firmly and rapidly, repeatedly cutting through the herbs.

Mincing

Mincing is a very fine cut that is suitable for many vegetables and herbs. Onions, garlic, and shallots are often minced.

3. Finely mince the herbs by continuing to cut until the desired fineness is attained.

Green onions and chives are minced differently. Rather than cutting repeatedly, slice them very finely.

Chiffonade/shredding

The chiffonade cut is used for leafy vegetables and herbs. The result is a fine shred, often used as a garnish or bed.

For Belgian endive, remove the leaves from the core and stack them. Make parallel cuts to produce a shred. For greens with large leaves, such as romaine, roll individual leaves into cylinders before cutting. Stack smaller leaves, such as basil, one on top of the other, then roll them into cylinders and cut. Use a chef's knife to make very fine, parallel cuts to produce fine shreds.

Standard vegetable cuts

The standard cuts are illustrated on the chart on the following page. The dimensions indicated are guidelines and may be modified as necessary. Determine the size of the cut by the requirements of the recipe or menu item, the nature of the vegetable being cut, the desired cooking time, and appearance.

Before chopping or cutting vegetables, they are trimmed to remove roots, cores, stems, or seeds. They may also be trimmed by slicing away one side of a round vegetable. This makes vegetable cutting tasks safer, since the vegetable will not roll or slip as it is cut. To produce very regular and precise cuts, such as julienne or dice, cut a slice from each side and both ends of the vegetable to make an even rectangle or square.

Standard Vegetable Cuts

Fine julienne
⅟₁₆ x ⅟₁₆ x 1 to 2 in/1.50 mm x 1.50 mm x 3 to 5 cm

Julienne/allumette
⅛ x ⅛ x 1 to 2 in/3 mm x 3 mm x 3 to 5 cm

Batonnet
¼ x ¼ x 2 to 2½ in/6 mm x 6 mm x 5 to 6 cm

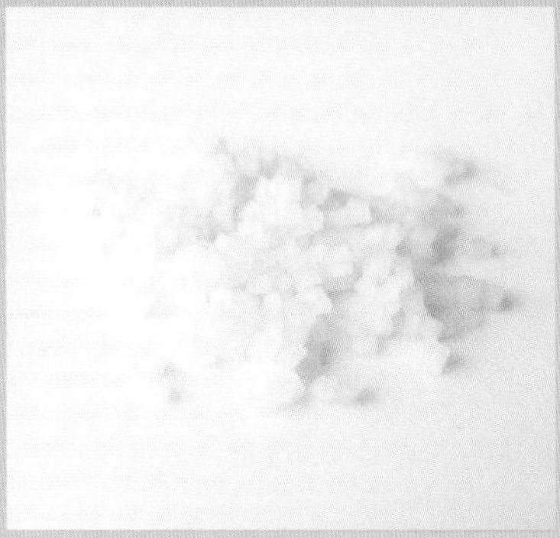

Fine brunoise
⅟₁₆ x ⅟₁₆ x ⅟₁₆ in/1.50 x 1.50 x 1.50 mm

Brunoise
⅛ x ⅛ x ⅛ in/3 x 3 x 3 mm

Small dice
¼ x ¼ x ¼ in/6 x 6 x 6 mm

Medium dice
½ x ½ x ½ in/1 x 1 x 1 cm

Large dice
¾ x ¾ x ¾ in/2 x 2 x 2 cm

Julienne and batonnet

Julienne and batonnet are long, rectangular cuts. Related cuts are the standard pommes frites and pommes pont neuf cuts (both are names for French fries) and the allumette (or matchstick) cut. The difference between these cuts is the final size.

Trim and square off the vegetable by cutting a slice to make four straight sides. Cut both ends to even the block off. These initial slices make it easier to produce even cuts. The trimmings can be used for stocks, soups, purées, or other preparations where the shape is not important.

1. After squaring off the vegetable, slice the vegetable lengthwise, making parallel cuts of even thickness.

2. Stack the cut slices, aligning the edges, and make even, parallel cuts of the same thickness for a batonnet.

Dicing

Dicing produces cube shapes. Different preparations require different sizes of dice. The names given to the different-sized dice are fine brunoise/brunoise, and small, medium, and large dice. The table to the left lists the dimensions. To begin, trim and cut the vegetable as for julienne or batonnet.

3. Gather the julienne or batonnet pieces and cut through them crosswise at evenly spaced intervals.

Other Vegetable Cuts

The vegetables shown here have been cut to precise standards for a more upscale presentation. They may be cut so that the natural shape of the vegetable is visible in each slice.

Tourné cuts (see page 691) may be the classic football shape shown here or modified to suit different vegetable types.

Paysanne
½ x ½ x ⅛ in/1 cm x 6 mm x 3 mm

Fermière
Cut to desired thickness: ⅛ to ½ in/3 mm to 1 cm

Lozenge
Diamond shape: ½ x ½ x ⅛ in/ 1 cm x 1 cm x 3 mm

Rondelle
Cut to desired thickness: ⅛ to ½ in/6 mm to 1 cm

Tourné
Approximately 2 in/5 cm long with 7 faces

Making paysanne/ fermière

Cuts produced in the paysanne (peasant) and fermière (farmer) style are generally used in dishes intended to have a rustic or home-style appeal. When used for traditional regional specialties, they may be cut in such a way that the shape of the vegetable's curved or uneven edges is still apparent in the finished cut. However, it is important to cut them all to the same thickness so that they will cook evenly.

Square off the vegetable first and make large batonnet, ¾ in/2 cm thick. Make even, parallel cuts crosswise at ⅛ in/3 mm intervals to produce the paysanne cut.

For a more rustic presentation, cut the vegetable into halves, quarters, or eighths, depending on its size. The pieces should be roughly similar in dimension to a batonnet. Make even, thin crosswise cuts at roughly ⅛-in/3-mm intervals.

Making diamond/ lozenge cuts

The diamond, or lozenge, cut is similar to the paysanne. Instead of cutting batonnets, thinly slice the vegetable, then cut into strips of the appropriate width.

Trim and thinly slice the vegetable. Cut the slices on the bias into ⅛-in/3-mm-thick strips of the correct width. Make an initial bias cut to begin. This will leave some trim (reserve the trim for use in preparations that do not require a neat, decorative cut). Continue to make bias cuts, parallel to the first one.

Making rounds/ rondelles

Rounds, or rondelles, are simple to cut. Just cut a cylindrical vegetable, such as a carrot or cucumber, crosswise. The basic round shape can be varied by cutting the vegetable on the bias to produce an elongated or oval disk or by slicing it in half for half-moons. Score the vegetable with a channel knife to produce flower shapes. Trim and peel the vegetable if necessary. Make parallel slicing cuts through the vegetable at even intervals. Guide the vegetable as you are cutting by pushing on the end of it with your thumb.

Making diagonal/ bias cuts

This cut is often used to prepare vegetables for stir-fries and other Asian-style dishes because it exposes a greater surface area and shortens cooking time. To make a diagonal cut, place the peeled or trimmed vegetable on the work surface. Hold the blade so that it cuts through the food on an angle. The wider the angle, the more elongated the cut surface will be. Continue making parallel cuts, adjusting the angle of the blade so that all the pieces are approximately the same size.

Making oblique or roll cuts

This cut is used primarily with long, cylindrical vegetables such as parsnips or carrots. Place the peeled vegetable on a cutting board. Make a diagonal cut to remove the stem end. Hold the knife in the same position and roll the vegetable a quarter turn (approximately 90 degrees). Slice through it on the same diagonal, forming a piece with two angled edges. Be sure to decrease the angle of the diagonal as the vegetable gets larger in diameter. This will ensure uniform cuts that will cook evenly. Repeat until the entire vegetable has been cut.

Decorative Cuts Using Special Techniques

Decorative cuts can be an attractive visual component of a dish. Basic tools like a paring knife or a swivel-bladed peeler (for curled or shaved Parmesan to top carpaccio or Caesar salad, for example) or Parisienne scoops or melon ballers (for balls of different sizes) can be used to create special effects. More specialized tools include a mandoline, a Japanese "turner," an apple peeler, a ripple cutter, or a box grater for hand cutting. For large-volume operations, specialized cutting machines and tools are available. Be sure to read any instructions that come with special cutters, and use all the safety guards that come with them.

Waffle/gaufrette

Use a mandoline to make waffle, or gaufrette, cuts. Potatoes, sweet potatoes, beets, and other large, relatively solid foods can be made into this cut.

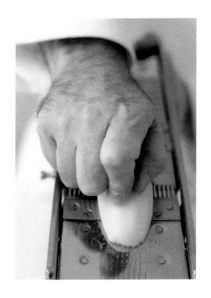 

1. The blades of the mandoline are set so that the first pass of the vegetable doesn't actually cut away a slice but only makes grooves.

2. Turn the potato 45 degrees and make the second pass to create waffle cut potatoes. Run the vegetable the entire length of the mandoline. Turn the vegetable 45 degrees and repeat the entire stroke. Repeat this procedure, turning the vegetable 45 degrees on each pass over the mandoline.

Fluting

Fluting takes some practice to master, but it makes a very attractive garnish. It is customarily used on mushrooms.

1. Hold the mushroom between the thumb and forefinger of your guiding hand. Remove the outer layer of the mushroom cap by peeling the mushroom. Start at the underside of the cap, going toward the center.

2. Place the blade of a paring knife at a very slight angle against the mushroom cap center. Rest the thumb of your cutting hand on the mushroom and use it to brace the knife. Rotate the knife toward the base of the cap while turning the mushroom in the opposite direction.

3. Finish the fluted mushroom by lightly pressing the tip of your paring knife into the top of the mushroom to create a star pattern. Turn the mushroom slightly and repeat the cutting steps. Continue until the entire cap is fluted. Pull away the trimmings. Trim away the stem.

Cutting turned/tourné vegetables

Turning vegetables (*tourner* in French) requires a series of cuts that simultaneously trim and shape the vegetable. The shape is similar to a small barrel or football. Peel the vegetable, if desired, and cut it into pieces of manageable size. Cut large round or oval vegetables, such as beets and potatoes, into quarters, sixths, or eighths (depending on the size), to form pieces slightly larger than 2 in/5 cm. Cut cylindrical vegetables, such as carrots, into 2-in/5-cm pieces.

Using a paring or tourné knife, cut the vegetables into manageable-sized pieces before tournéing them. Carve the pieces into barrel or football shapes. Try to make as few cuts as possible to create the 7 sides so that the faces of the tourné remain distinct. The faces should be smooth, evenly spaced, and tapered so that both ends are narrower than the center.

Fanning

The fan cut uses one basic, easy-to-master cut to produce complicated-looking garnishes. It is used on both raw and cooked foods, such as pickles, strawberries, peach halves, avocados, zucchini, and other somewhat pliable vegetables and fruits.

Leaving the stem end intact, make a series of parallel lengthwise slices. Spread the cut fruit or vegetable into a fan shape.

Preparation Techniques for Specific Vegetables

A typical restaurant kitchen's vegetable and herb mise en place often includes vegetables that grow in layers, have seeds, grow in bulbs, or are otherwise unique.

Onions

Onions of all types taste best when cut as close as possible to the time to be used. The longer cut onions are stored, the more flavor and overall quality they lose. Once cut, onions develop a strong, sulfurous odor that can spoil a dish's aroma and appeal.

1. When peeling an onion, take off as few layers as possible. Here, the chef is using a paring knife to remove the outer layers of skin.

Use a paring knife to cut a thin slice away from the stem and root ends of the bulb. Catch the peel between the pad of your thumb and the flat side of your knife blade and pull away the peel. Trim away any brown spots from underlying layers if necessary

before cutting the vegetable to the desired size or shape.

Leave the onion whole after peeling if you need slices or rings. To cut onion rings from a whole onion, be sure to hold the onion securely with your guiding hand. The rounded surface of the onion can slip on the cutting surface.

Cut the onion in half, making a cut that runs from the root end to the stem end in order to cut julienne or dice. The root end, though trimmed, is still intact. This helps to hold the onion layers together as it is sliced or diced. To cut julienne from a halved onion, make a V-shaped notch cut on either side of the root end.

An alternative peeling method is especially good for cutting and using the onion right away. Halve the onion lengthwise through the root before trimming and peeling. Trim the ends, leaving the root end intact if the onion will be diced, and pull away the skin from each half.

2. To dice or mince an onion half, lay it cut side down on a cutting board. Using a chef's knife, make a series of evenly spaced, parallel, lengthwise cuts with the tip of the knife, leaving the root end intact. Cuts spaced ¼ in/6 mm apart will make small dice; cuts spaced ½ in/1 cm or ¾ in/2 cm apart will produce medium or large dice.

3. Make two or three horizontal cuts parallel to the work surface, from the stem end toward the root end, but do not cut all the way through, while gently holding the vertical cuts together. Holding the previous cuts together will produce a more uniform mince.

4. To complete the dice, make even, crosswise cuts working from the stem end up to the root end, cutting through all layers of the onion. Reserve any usable trim for mirepoix.

Remove the root from the onion before making even cuts that follow the natural curve of the onion. Some chefs prefer to cut onions by making a series of evenly spaced cuts that follow the natural curve of the onion. These cuts are sometimes referred to as radial cuts. Radial cuts result in even julienne or batonnet, which can then be cut crosswise into dice if desired.

Garlic

Garlic has distinctly different flavors depending upon how it is cut. It can be purchased already peeled or chopped, but many chefs feel strongly that the loss in flavor and quality is not worth the convenience for all but volume cooking situations. Once cut, garlic (like onions) starts to take on a stronger flavor.

Mashed or minced garlic is called for in many preparations, so it is important to have enough prepared to last through a service period, but not so much that a significant amount has to be thrown out at the end of a shift. To prevent bacterial growth, store uncooked minced garlic covered in oil in the refrigerator and use within 24 hours.

To separate the garlic cloves, wrap an entire head of garlic in a side towel and press down on the top. The cloves will break cleanly away from the root end. The towel keeps the papery skin from flying around the work area.

1. An alternative to smashing the clove of garlic in order to remove the peel is to peel the garlic clove using a paring knife. To loosen the skin from each clove, place it on the cutting board, place the flat side of the knife blade on top, and hit the blade using a fist or the heel of your hand. Peel off the skin and remove the root end and any brown spots. At some times of the year and under certain storage conditions, the garlic may begin to sprout. Split the clove in half and remove the sprout for the best flavor.

Lay the skinned cloves on the cutting board with the flat of the knife blade over them. Using a motion similar to that for cracking the skin, hit the blade firmly and forcefully with a fist or the heel of your hand to crush the cloves.

2. Slice the peeled garlic cloves before chopping them.

To mash the garlic, hold the knife nearly flat against the cutting board and use the cutting edge to mash the garlic against the board. Repeat this step until the garlic is mashed to a paste. If desired, sprinkle the garlic with salt before mashing. The salt acts as an abrasive, speeding the mashing process and preventing the garlic from sticking to the knife blade. To mince large quantities of peeled garlic, use a food processor, if desired. Or crush and grind salt-sprinkled garlic to a paste with a mortar and pestle.

3. Cut the garlic slices to create roughly chopped garlic.

4. Mince garlic cloves like you would mince an onion. Mince or chop the cloves fairly fine, using a rocking motion, as for herbs.

Roasting garlic

The flavor of garlic becomes rich, sweet, and smoky after roasting. Roasted garlic can be found as a component of vegetable or potato purées, marinades, glazes, and vinaigrettes, as well as a spread for grilled bread.

Place unpeeled heads of garlic in a small pan or on a sizzler platter. To produce a drier texture place the garlic on a bed of salt. You may wrap whole heads of garlic in foil. Cut off the tip of each clove beforehand to make it easier to squeeze out the roasted garlic. Or peel the cloves first, lightly oil them, and roast in a parchment-paper envelope.

Roast at a moderate temperature (350°F/177°C) until the garlic cloves are quite soft, usually 30 to 45 minutes. Any juices that run from the garlic will brown. The aroma should be sweet and pleasing with no hints of harshness or sulfur. Separate the cloves and squeeze the roasted garlic from the skins or pass them through a food mill.

Leeks

A leek grows in layers, trapping grit and sand between each layer, and one of the biggest concerns when working with leeks is removing every trace of dirt. Careful rinsing is essential.

1. To clean leeks, rinse off all the surface dirt, paying special attention to the roots, where dirt clings. Lay the leek on the cutting board, and using a chef's knife, trim away the heavy, dark green portion of the leaves. By cutting on an angle, you can avoid losing the tender light green portion of the leek. Reserve the dark green portion of the leek to make bouquet garni or for other uses.

2. Trim away most of the root end. Cut the leek lengthwise into halves, thirds, or quarters. Then rinse the leek under running water to remove any remaining grit or sand.

Cut the leek into the desired shape. Leeks may be left in halves or quarters with the stem end still intact for braising. Or they may be cut into slices, chiffonade, julienne, dice, or paysanne-style cuts.

Tomatoes

Fresh and canned tomatoes are used in a number of dishes. Tomatoes can be cut into slices using a special tomato knife, which has a serrated blade, but a sharp chef's, utility, or paring knife also works well. Large quantities can be sliced on an electric slicer. Tomatoes have a skin that clings tightly to the flesh and the interior contains pockets of seeds and juice. When the tomato is peeled, seeded, and chopped, it is known as tomato concassé. The blanching technique for tomatoes is also used for peaches and nuts, such as almonds and chestnuts. The techniques for seeding and chopping or dicing can be used for both fresh and canned tomatoes. Whole or sliced tomatoes can be roasted to intensify their flavor and change their texture.

Preparing tomato concassé

Tomato concassé is required in the preparation or finishing of many different sauces and dishes. Only enough should be made in advance to last through a single service period. Once peeled and chopped, tomatoes begin to lose flavor and texture.

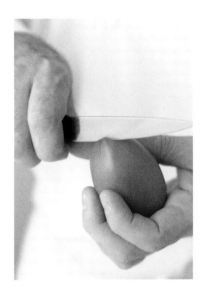

1. Cut an X into the bottom of the tomato, but be sure not to cut too deeply. Some chefs also like to cut out the stem at this point to allow for better heat penetration. Others prefer to wait until the tomato has been blanched.

2. Bring a pot of water to a rolling boil. Have an ice bath ready to shock the tomatoes. Drop the tomato into the water. After 10 to 15 seconds, depending on the tomato's age and ripeness, remove it with a slotted spoon, skimmer, or spider. Immediately plunge the tomato into very cold or ice water.

  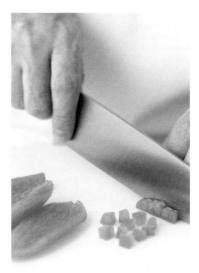

3. Use a paring knife to peel away the skin of the tomato. If the tomatoes were properly blanched, none of the flesh will be removed from the tomatoes.

4. Halve the tomato crosswise at its widest point. (Cut plum tomatoes lengthwise to seed them more easily.) Gently squeeze out the seeds. For a more precise cut, quarter the tomatoes and cut away the seeds. For a rough chop, simply squeeze out the seeds.

5. The definition of a concassé calls for a rough chop, but the peeled and seeded tomatoes can be cut as desired.

Precision cuts for peeled tomatoes

To prepare tomatoes so that they can be cut into precise julienne, dice, lozenge, or similar cuts, the tomato flesh must be trimmed so that it has an even thickness. Halve or quarter the peeled tomato, cutting from stem to blossom end.

Using the tip of a knife, cut away any seeds and membranes. This technique is sometimes referred to as filleting. It is also used for peppers and chiles. Cut the flesh into julienne or other shapes, as desired.

Tomatoes prepared in this way may be used as garnish for hot items such as soups or sauces. They may also be used in cold preparations such as salads or in the production of hors d'oeuvre, where they can be used as a base or finely chopped for a colorful and flavorful garnish. Peeled and cut tomatoes will have a tendency to weep, so when using for cold preparations be sure to cut and assemble as close to service as possible.

Fresh peppers and chiles

Peppers and chiles are used in dishes from cuisines as diverse as those of Central and South America, many Asian countries, Spain, and Hungary. As the interest in peppers and chiles has grown, many special varieties have become available, both fresh and dried. For more information about working with dried chiles, see page 705. Whenever working with very hot chiles, wear plastic gloves to protect your skin from the irritating oils they contain.

Cutting and seeding fresh peppers and chiles

Cut through the pepper from top to bottom. Continue to cut it into quarters, especially if the pepper is large.

Using the tip of a paring knife, cut away the stem and seeds. This cut removes the least amount of usable pepper. Chiles retain a good deal of their heat in the seeds, ribs, and blossom ends. The degree of heat can be controlled by adjusting how much, if any, of these parts of the chile is added to a dish.

1. You can make very fine, even julienne or dice by filleting the pepper—that is, removing the seeds and ribs—before cutting it. Cut away the top and bottom of the pepper to create an even rectangle. Roll the pepper away from the paring knife as you cut the seeds and ribs away to create a long rectangle of pepper that can be cut as desired.

2. Peel away the skin, if desired, and then cut the flesh into neat julienne or dice. For a more precise preparation, use a chef's knife to cut away a thin layer of the flesh to make a completely flat surface. This will create a more square, uniform julienne or dice. Reserve any edible scraps to use in coulis or to flavor broths, stews, or court bouillons.

Peeling fresh peppers or chiles

Peppers and chiles are often peeled before they are used in a dish, to improve the dish's flavor or texture, or both. The thin but relatively tough skin can be removed using a swivel-bladed peeler or paring knife. This approach is often taken when the peppers are to be served raw, as in a salad or salsa, or in a dish that is intended to retain the pepper's sweet, fresh flavor.

To peel raw peppers with a swivel-bladed peeler, first section the pepper with a knife, cutting along the folds to expose the skin. Then remove the core, seeds, and ribs and peel with a swivel-bladed peeler.

1. Peppers and chiles are often charred in a flame, broiled or grilled, or roasted in a very hot oven to produce a deep, rich flavor as well as to make the pepper easier to peel. To roast and peel small quantities of fresh peppers or chiles, hold the pepper over the flame of a gas burner with tongs or a kitchen fork, or place the pepper on a grill. Turn the pepper and roast it until the surface is evenly charred. Then place the pepper in a plastic or paper bag or covered bowl and let stand for at least 30 minutes to steam the skin loose.

2. When the pepper is cool enough to handle, use a paring knife to remove the charred skin after it has steamed. Have a bowl of water nearby to rinse the charred skin off of your knife as you work. To remove any bits of charred skin that remain on the pepper, rub lightly with a towel.

Larger quantities of peppers or chiles are often roasted in a hot oven or under a broiler, rather than charred individually in a flame. Halve the peppers or chiles and remove the stems, seeds, and ribs if desired. (The peppers or chiles may also be left whole.) Place cut side down on an oiled sheet pan. Place the pan in a very hot oven or under a broiler. Roast or broil until evenly charred. Remove from the oven or broiler and cover immediately, using an inverted sheet pan. Let stand for 30 minutes, to steam the peppers and make the skin easier to remove.

Mushrooms

Clean mushrooms just before preparing them by rinsing quickly in cool water, only long enough to remove any dirt. Do not allow the mushrooms to soak; they absorb liquids quickly, and an excess of moisture will cause them to deteriorate rapidly. (Some people clean mushrooms by wiping them with a soft cloth or brushing them with a soft-bristled brush; this is not always practical in a professional kitchen.) Let the mushrooms drain and dry well on layers of absorbent toweling before slicing or mincing.

Cook mushrooms as soon as possible after they are cut for the best flavor, color, and consistency in the finished dish. Avoid cutting more than needed at any given time.

Some mushrooms must have the stems removed. Shiitakes, for example, have very tough, woody stems; cut them away from the caps and save for stock or to flavor sauces. The stems of other mushrooms, such as white mushrooms, morels, and cèpes, can usually be left intact, although a slice should be cut away from the stem end to trim dried or fibrous portions.

Chestnuts

To peel chestnuts using a paring knife or chestnut knife, cut an X in the flat side of each nut just through the outer skin. Boil or roast the chestnuts just until the skin begins to pull away. Work in small batches, keeping the chestnuts warm, and pull and cut away the tough outer skin. Cooked chestnuts can be left whole, puréed, sweetened, or glazed.

If possible, rest the mushroom on a flat side to provide more stability as you slice through the mushroom. Holding the mushroom cap with your guiding hand, make slices through the cap and stem, if it has not been trimmed off. To cut a large amount efficiently, slice the mushrooms so that the slices are layered. Then cut across the slices at the desired thickness to create julienne strips. Turn the julienne strips so that they are parallel to the edge of the work surface. Make crosswise cuts to mince the mushrooms for use in duxelles or other applications.

Corn

Whole ears of corn can be boiled or steamed after the husk has been peeled away. The fine threads, known as silk, that cling to the corn should be pulled away. Once husked, cook the corn as soon as possible.

To cut the kernels away from the cob, hold the ear upright and cut downward as close to the cob as possible.

To "milk" the corn, remove the husk and silk. Lay the ear down on a cutting surface and lightly score each row of kernels. Then, use the back of a knife, a spoon, or a butter curler to scrape out the flesh and milk.

Peapods

Snow peas and sugar snap peas both have edible pods and are typically eaten raw, steamed, or stir-fried. They should be carefully selected for freshness as their quality and flavor deteriorate quickly. Their peak season is early spring to summer.

Snow peas and sugar snap peas, depending upon the variety, often have a rather tough string that runs along one seam. This string should be removed before the peas are cooked. Snap off the stem end, using either a paring knife or your fingers, and pull. The string will come away easily.

Asparagus

Young asparagus may need no further preparation than a simple trim to remove the very ends of the stalk, and a quick rinse. More mature asparagus may need to have the stalk trimmed a little more and partially peeled to remove the outer skin, which can be tough and stringy.

As asparagus matures, the stalk becomes tough. To remove the woody portion, bend the stalk gently until it snaps. Using a special asparagus peeler or a swivel-bladed peeler, peel the remaining stalk partway up; this enhances palatability and also makes it easier to cook the asparagus evenly.

Asparagus may be tied into loose portion-sized bundles to make it easier to remove them from boiling water when they are blanched or boiled. Don't tie them too tightly or make the bundles more than a few inches in diameter. Otherwise the asparagus in the middle will not cook properly.

Artichokes

Artichokes are members of the thistle family. Their leaves have sharp barbs, like thorns. The edible meat of the artichoke is found at the base of each leaf, which grows from a stem, as well as at the fleshy base of the vegetable, known as the bottom. Artichokes have a purple, feathery center—the "choke"—that is inedible in mature artichokes. The choke in baby artichokes may be tender enough to eat.

To prepare whole artichokes, first cut away the stem. The amount of stem removed is determined by how the artichoke is to be presented, as well as by how tender or tough the stem is. Cutting the stem away even with the bottom of the artichoke makes a flat surface, allowing the artichoke to sit flat on the plate. If the artichoke is to be halved or quartered, some of the stem may be left intact. Peel the stem with a paring knife. Cut off the top of the artichoke. Snip the barbs from each leaf with kitchen scissors. Rub the cut surfaces with lemon juice to prevent browning, or hold the trimmed artichoke in acidulated water (a mixture of lemon juice and water). The artichoke can be simmered or steamed at this point, if desired, or the center of the artichoke, the choke, may be removed prior to cooking. To remove the choke, spread the leaves of the cooked or raw artichoke open. The choke can now be scooped out using a spoon.

1. To prepare artichoke bottoms, pull away the leaves from around the stem and trim the stem as desired. Make a cut through the artichoke at its widest point, just above the artichoke bottom.

2. Use a paring knife to trim the tough outer leaves away from the artichoke bottom.

3. Scoop out the center of the artichoke bottom, known as the choke. Hold trimmed artichoke bottoms in acidulate water to prevent browning.

Avocados

Avocados have a rough, thick skin and a large pit. The flesh is soft enough to purée easily when properly ripened. Avocados, like potatoes, bananas, and artichokes, turn brown when they are exposed to air. To prevent browning, cut avocados as close to the time of service as possible. Citrus juices both brighten the flavor of this rich but relatively bland food and prevent the flesh from turning brown.

To remove the skin and pit from an avocado, hold it securely but gently with the fingertips of your guiding hand. Insert a knife blade into the bottom of the avocado. Turn the avocado against the knife blade to make a cut completely around it. The cut should pierce the skin and cut through the flesh up to the pit.

To slice the avocado, cut it lengthwise into wedges or slices. To dice the avocado, cut crosswise through the wedges. To dice an avocado while it is still in the skin, use the tip of a knife to score the flesh into dice of the desired size. Use the edge of a kitchen spoon to slice through the flesh. As the flesh is sliced away and lifted from the avocado, it is cut into dice. Make each layer as thick or as thin as desired.

1. Twist the two halves of a sliced avocado away from each other and pull gently to separate them.

2. Since it can be difficult to pick out the pit with your fingertips without mangling the flesh, scoop it out with a spoon, removing as little flesh as possible, or carefully chop the heel of the knife into the pit, then twist and pull it free from the flesh. To remove the pit from the knife safely, use the edge of the cutting board or the lip of a container to pry the pit free.

3. To peel the avocado, catch the skin between the ball of your thumb and the flat side of a knife blade and pull it free from the flesh. If the flesh is underripe, this may not be possible; in that case, use the knife to cut the skin away.

Working with Dried Vegetables and Fruits

Dried vegetables and fruits have always been used in many cuisines. Drying makes foods suitable for long-term storage and concentrates their flavors.

Even today, some vegetables and fruits are too perishable to transport great distances or they have a very short season. The rest of the year, they can be found only in a preserved form. The flavor of dried chiles, mushrooms, tomatoes, and fruits such as apples, cherries, and raisins are special even though those same ingredients may be purchased fresh throughout the year.

To get the most from these ingredients, recipes may often call for them to be rehydrated or "plumped" by letting them soak in a liquid. To rehydrate dried vegetables and fruits, check first for insect infestation and remove any obvious debris or seriously blemished or moldy specimens. Place the vegetable or fruit in a bowl or other container and add enough boiling or very hot liquid (water, wine, fruit juice, or broth) to cover. Let the vegetable or fruit steep in the hot water for several minutes, until soft and plumped. Pour off the liquid, reserving it, if desired, for use in another preparation. If necessary, strain it through a coffee filter or cheesecloth to remove any debris.

Other dried fruits and vegetables may be toasted or charred in a flame or on a griddle or heated pan to soften them. Some may be toasted and then rehydrated.

Toast dried chiles in the same manner as dried spices, nuts, and seeds, by tossing them in a dry skillet over moderate heat. Or pass them repeatedly through a flame until toasted and softened. Scrape the pulp and seeds from the skin, or use the whole chile, according to the recipe. Break or cut open the chile and shake out the seeds. After toasting, rehydrate the chile in a hot liquid.

General Guidelines for Vegetable and Herb Mise en Place

One of the ways to distinguish a novice from a seasoned chef is the way each one approaches the task of cutting vegetables and herbs. The goal is consistency and speed. Without practice, it is impossible to achieve either.

To better approach vegetable mise en place, start by figuring out the proper timing of the work. Make a list and prioritize tasks so that foods that can be prepared well in advance are done first, while those that lose good flavor or color when cut too early are done as close to service or cooking time as possible. Making such a list involves knowledge of the menu, of estimates for the meal periods (if known) for which the vegetables are being cut, and of standard kitchen practices for holding cut vegetables.

Think out the work carefully before beginning. Assemble all the tools needed, including containers to hold unprepped vegetables, prepped vegetables, usable trim, and trim that is not useful. Assemble the peelers, knives, and steel. Hone the knives (including the paring knife) at the start and during the work.

Wash vegetables and herbs before doing any initial trim work to avoid getting the work surface unnecessarily dirty. Spin dry leafy greens and herbs before they are cut.

Arrange the work in a logical flow, so that things are positioned within easy reach. This makes the work easier, faster, less wasteful, and more comfortable.

Keep all tools and the work surface clean and free from debris. Remove trim as it accumulates, before it has a chance to fall on the floor. Wipe down knife blades and cutting boards between phases of work. Sanitize all cutting and work surfaces when you switch from one food item to another. Wash your hands, too, and remember to use gloves if the vegetables will not be cooked before serving them to a guest.

In addition to the techniques and preparations already discussed, vegetable cookery often requires knowledge of other techniques—many of which can be found elsewhere in this book:

Preparing leafy greens (see pages 919–920)

Toasting spices, nuts, and seeds (see page 454)

Zesting citrus fruit and cutting suprêmes (see page 924)

Preparing fruits (see pages 925–926)

Marinades (see pages 455–456)

Standard breading procedure (see page 458)

Chapter Twenty-five

Cooking Vegetables

Vegetables are far more important in contemporary menu planning than simply as a side-dish afterthought. They can be the focal part of a meatless entrée. They can be selected and prepared to enhance another dish. Or they can be served as an appetizer or hors d'oeuvre. Buying vegetables that are at the peak of quality, observing proper storage and handling standards, and giving meticulous attention to the cooking process are vital to producing an appealing vegetable dish.

Boiling

Boiling is a fundamental vegetable cooking technique that can result in a wide range of textures and flavors, depending upon how the technique is applied. Vegetables may be blanched, parcooked (or parboiled), or fully cooked. Boiled vegetables can be served chilled, added to another dish such as a stew to finish cooking, glazed or finished in butter or oil, or used to make a purée. Almost all vegetables can be boiled, as long as the appropriate modifications are made to the boiling process.

Prepare vegetables for boiling by properly rinsing or scrubbing them to remove all traces of dirt. They may be trimmed and cut before cooking, or they may be cooked whole, according to the vegetable's nature as well as the intended presentation. If the vegetable has a tendency to turn brown once it is cut and exposed to the air (as artichokes do), try to cut it immediately before cooking, or hold the vegetable submerged in plain or acidulated water. Extended storage in water, once vegetables are peeled or cut, can rob them of flavor, texture, and nutritional value. Vegetables boiled whole or cut should be of a similar size, shape, and diameter to assure even cooking.

Water is the most commonly used liquid for boiling, though other liquids may be used depending on the desired flavor of the finished dish. Adding salt and other seasonings to the liquid enhances the flavor of a vegetable. Additional flavor and interest can be provided with finishing and garnishing ingredients.

Select the pot size in relation to the amount of food being prepared. It should hold the vegetables, liquid, and aromatics comfortably, with enough room for the liquid to expand as it heats. Leave enough space for the surface to be skimmed if necessary. A tight-fitting lid is helpful for bringing the liquid up to temperature, but it is not essential. Leaving a lid on throughout the cooking process may shorten cooking time, but be sure to check the vegetables periodically to avoid overcooking them.

Other useful equipment includes colanders or strainers for draining; equipment for cooling vegetables cooked in advance; holding containers to keep the vegetables warm; and spoons, ladles, or skimmers for cooking, tasting, and serving.

A basic formula for 10 servings of boiled green vegetables

2 lb 8 oz/1.13 kg prepped vegetables (weighed after trimming, peeling, and cutting)

96 fl oz/2.88 L salted boiling water

A basic formula for 10 servings of boiled root vegetables

2 lb 8 oz/1.13 kg prepped vegetables (weighed after trimming, peeling, and cutting)

Enough salted cold water to generously cover the vegetables in the pot

A basic formula for 10 servings of boiled red or white vegetables

2 lb 8 oz/1.13 kg prepped vegetables (weighed after trimming, peeling, and cutting)

Enough cold or boiling salted water to hold the vegetables without crowding

Dash of vinegar, lemon juice, or other acid

1. **Season the cooking liquid and bring it to the proper cooking temperature before adding the prepared vegetables.** The amount of liquid required varies, depending on the type and amount of vegetable and the length of cooking time. In general, there should be enough water to hold the vegetables comfortably, without excessive crowding. Add salt and any other seasonings or aromatic ingredients to the liquid.

2. **Bring the water to a rolling boil, except for dense or starchy root vegetables such as turnips and celeriac.** These vegetables are started in cold water that is then brought to a boil for even cooking.

For the best color in red cabbage, beets, and white vegetables like turnips or celeriac, return the cover to the pot. This helps retain acids that set the color in these vegetables.

Cover the pot while boiling orange and yellow vegetables (carrots and squash, for example) if desired.

If preparing a green vegetable that will cook rapidly, such as peas or spinach, return the lid to the pot to help shorten cooking time.

Denser green vegetables, such as broccoli, should be boiled uncovered for at least the first 2 to 3 minutes, to produce a good green color in the cooked vegetable.

Once the vegetables are added to the pot, bring the water back to a rapid simmer and continue to cook the vegetables to the appropriate doneness (see sidebar, page 710).

Vegetables should be removed from the water, either by draining the cooking liquid through a colander or sieve or by lifting the vegetables from the water using a spider or skimmer.

3. **The vegetables are ready to finish and season now (see Finishing and Glazing by Sautéing, page 725).** They may also be rapidly chilled to stop any further cooking, to cool them for service in a cold dish, or to hold them for later service. The procedure for cooling vegetables, sometimes referred to as either shocking or refreshing, is as follows: Once the vegetables are drained, submerge them in very cold or ice water long enough to cool them. As soon as they are cool, drain the vegetables again, place them in storage containers, cover, and refrigerate. Vegetables should not be allowed to sit in water for extended periods of time.

4. **Evaluate the quality of the finished boiled vegetable.** Taste the vegetable. It should have a good, fresh flavor. Most boiled vegetables served hot should be tender, yet still hold their original shape. The color should be appealing. Green vegetables should be a deep or bright green with no traces of graying or yellowing. White vegetables should be white or ivory. Red vegetables deepen in color, some taking on a purple or magenta color, but not blue or green.

Taste and evaluate vegetables if they are held, and replace them with a fresh batch as necessary during service time.

Determining Doneness in Vegetables

Blanched

Immerse vegetables briefly, usually 30 seconds to 1 minute, depending on type of vegetable and ripeness, in boiling water to make the skin easy to remove, to eliminate or reduce strong odors or flavors, to set the color for serving cold, and/or as the first step in other cooking techniques.

Parcooked/parboiled

Vegetables are cooked to partial doneness, to prepare them for finishing by grilling, sautéing, or stewing.

Tender-crisp or al dente

Cook vegetables until they can be bitten into easily, but still offer a slight resistance and sense of texture. (The term *al dente,* which is Italian for "to the tooth," is more accurately used to describe the desired doneness of pasta rather than vegetables.)

Steaming

Steamed vegetables are cooked in a vapor bath to produce dishes that have pure, undiluted flavors. Steaming shares many similarities with boiling as a cooking technique for vegetables. Any vegetable that can be boiled can also be steamed. It would be hard for most people to tell steamed and boiled carrots apart if they were presented side by side. But there are some differences. Since steaming cooks through direct contact with steam rather than liquid, steamed vegetables may be less soggy than some boiled vegetables. They are generally considered to have better nutritional value as well.

Prepare vegetables for steaming as you would for boiling. All vegetables should be properly rinsed or scrubbed, peeled, trimmed, and cut to shape as close to the time of service as is reasonable.

Although the most commonly used steaming liquid is water, flavorful stocks, broths, or other aromatic liquids are sometimes used to replace some or all of the water. The amount of liquid required depends on how long the vegetable will take to cook: The shorter the cooking time, the less liquid needed.

Salt, pepper, and other seasonings may be combined with the vegetables as they steam or as they are finished for service. Aromatic vegetables, spices, herbs, or citrus zest can be added to the steaming liquid to produce specific flavors. Steamed vegetables may be reheated or finished with flavorful oils, butter, heavy cream, or a sauce.

The quantity of vegetables to be steamed determines the correct equipment. Small amounts can be steamed using an insert. Larger quantities, or a combination of vegetables that require different cooking times, are better prepared in tiered steamers, pressure steamers, or convection steamers. It is important to allow enough room for steam to circulate completely around foods as they cook, to encourage even, rapid cooking. In addition to steamers, it is important to have on hand the tools needed for handling the vegetables for service or for holding. Also needed are containers to hold sauces, spoons, ladles, and other serving utensils.

A basic formula for 10 servings of steamed vegetables

2 lb 8 oz/1.13 kg prepped vegetables (weight after trimming, peeling, and cutting)

Enough cooking liquid to produce steam throughout the cooking time (2 to 3 in/5 to 8 cm)

Seasonings to add to the vegetables and/or the cooking liquid

1. Bring the liquid to a full boil in the bottom of a covered steamer. The vegetables should be arranged in a single layer on a steamer insert or tier to allow the steam to come into contact with all sides of the vegetable. Seasonings should be added to the vegetables before they go into the steamer for the best flavor development. Adding seasonings to the liquid at the beginning helps release their flavors. Before putting the steamer over direct heat, add any desired aromatics or seasonings to the steaming liquid so that they can release their flavor into the steam more effectively. As the liquid comes to a boil, it produces the steam to cook the vegetables. Cover the steamer to bring the liquid to a boil faster and trap the steam inside the vessel.

Steam the vegetables to the desired doneness. Doneness is determined by how the particular vegetable will be handled once it is steamed (see Determining Doneness in Vegetables, page 710). Steamed vegetables may be handled in the same ways as boiled vegetables.

2. **Evaluate the quality of the finished steamed vegetable.** Properly steamed vegetables should have good flavor and vibrant colors. Be sure to taste the vegetable to assess not only the flavor but also the texture. The textures may vary from very crisp (blanched vegetables) to tender enough to purée. Properly steamed broccoli, for example, should be bright green and the stem should be able to be pierced with a paring knife with little resistance. Seasonings should enhance the flavor of the dish. Unless they are meant to be served chilled, vegetables should be very hot when served to the guest.

Flavoring and Seasoning Steamed Vegetables

Vegetables are flavorful on their own, but to add additional flavor to a steamed vegetable try one or a combination of the following:

Replace some or all of the water with

Broth

Fruit juices, such as orange, apple, cranberry

Stock

Add aromatic vegetables to flavor the liquid

Carrots

Celery

Onions

Add spices and herbs to flavor the liquid

Bay leaf

Chopped fresh garlic

Chopped fresh parsley

Chopped fresh thyme

Coriander

Cracked peppercorns

Cumin

Grated fresh ginger

Pan Steaming

Pan steaming is a good à la minute technique for small batches or individual orders. Pan-steamed vegetables are prepared in a covered pot with a relatively small amount of liquid. Usually the liquid barely covers the vegetables, and most of the cooking occurs by steaming. Speed is a major advantage of this technique. Green vegetables that sometimes discolor when cooked in a covered pan (such as green beans) are done quickly enough to retain a bright color. Another advantage is that the reduced cooking liquids can be used to make a pan sauce or glaze.

Vegetables of virtually all sorts can be prepared by pan steaming. Inspect the vegetables for quality and freshness. Rinse, trim, peel, and cut the vegetable as close to cooking time as possible for the best flavor and nutrition. All cuts should be precise and uniform for the best flavor and texture in the finished dish. Hold cut vegetables covered and refrigerated when necessary.

Water is often used to prepare pan-steamed vegetables, but stocks or broths can be used for added flavor if desired. Check the seasoning of any cooking liquid, adding salt or other flavorings, including options such as wine, fruit juice, herbs, spices, or aromatic vegetables like leeks or shallots.

Sweeteners, including white sugar, brown sugar, maple syrup, honey, or molasses, can be added to glaze a vegetable if desired. If the cooking liquid will be used to prepare a pan sauce, have on hand additional seasonings or garnishes, thickeners, cream, or liaison, as indicated by the recipe.

Pan steaming is effective because vegetables cook very quickly before they lose significant flavor, color, texture, or nutritive value. To shorten the total amount of time the vegetables spend in the pan, some chefs like to have the liquid already at a simmer. In addition, this step permits the chef to steep the liquid with seasonings and aromatics such as shallots and ginger. This infuses the cooking liquid and the steam for a more flavorful finished dish.

A basic formula for 10 servings of pan-steamed vegetables

2 lb 8 oz/1.13 kg prepped vegetables (weight after trimming, peeling, and cutting)

Enough seasoned cooking liquid to last throughout cooking time (2 to 3 in/5 to 8 cm)

Additional ingredients or preparations as specified

1. **Pour or ladle enough cooking liquid into the pan to properly cook the vegetables.** Very dense vegetables or large cuts will require more liquid than tender vegetables or small cuts. For carrots, add enough liquid to nearly cover the vegetable. There may be a small amount of liquid left after cooking is complete; the pan should not cook dry, however. Check to see that the level of the cooking liquid is adequate throughout cooking time. Covering the pan with a tight-fitting lid captures the steam released by the cooking liquid. The steam condenses on the lid and falls back onto the vegetables. This means that any flavors lost to the cooking liquid are retained.

How to Pan Steam Vegetables

2. Check the vegetables periodically while they are cooking to check the doneness and maintain the proper level of heat. Pan-steamed vegetables can be cooked to a range of doneness, according to their intended use. They may be very lightly blanched, parcooked, or fully cooked (see Determining Doneness in Vegetables, page 710). To check for proper doneness, bite or cut into a piece.

3. If desired, remove the cover and let the cooking liquid continue to reduce to make a glaze or pan sauce. Leave the vegetables in the pan while the cooking liquid reduces to form a glaze. Before making a pan sauce, remove the vegetables from the pan if they are delicate or if they might overcook before the sauce is finished. Let the cooking liquid reduce until flavorful, and if necessary, add a starch slurry or beurre manié to thicken it.

Evaluate the quality of the pan-steamed vegetable. Look at the dish, smell it, and taste it. The vegetable cuts should look attractive, uniform, and neatly cut. The dish should smell appealing and reflect the seasonings and finishing or garnishing ingredients selected. The vegetables should be properly cooked and tender, flavorful, very hot, and well seasoned.

Grilling and Broiling

The intense heat of grills and broilers gives vegetables a rich, bold flavor. The main restriction governing which vegetables can or cannot be broiled is their size.

Expanding the repertoire from a relatively short list, including summer squashes, peppers, and sliced onions, chefs have experimented and succeeded at grilling and broiling such tender vegetables as heads of radicchio to such dense and sturdy vegetables as winter squashes.

Select perfectly fresh vegetables for the grill with no softening, discoloration, or wilting. Once selected, vegetables should be properly rinsed or scrubbed. Remove the peel or skin, core, and seeds if appropriate. Vegetables should be cut into uniform slices or other shapes before grilling or broiling. High-moisture or tender vegetables can be grilled or broiled from the raw state; dense or starchy vegetables may require preliminary cooking to assure thorough cooking. Among the vegetables that can be grilled from the raw state are eggplant, zucchini, peppers, and mushrooms. Those vegetables that are typically parcooked include fennel, sweet potatoes, carrots, and beets. Prepare the vegetables according to the type and desired result. Rinse, trim, peel, and cut them into even pieces. Thread the vegetables on skewers, if desired.

Soft vegetables and precooked hard vegetables may be marinated briefly (15 to 30 minutes) before grilling or broiling. Longer marinating could result in the vegetables absorbing too much moisture.

If a marinade has been used, it may be served as a sauce with the cooked vegetables. Other possible accompaniments include salsa, soy sauce, a jus-based sauce, butter sauce, or cream sauce.

Maintain grills and broilers carefully. Scour the rods well with a wire grill brush between grilling different foods, as well as after each service period, to remove any buildup of charred food particles. Rub the rods lightly with a cloth dipped in vegetable oil to lubricate them before preheating the grill and throughout the service period.

Grilled vegetables have a distinctly charred flavor. They usually have deeply browned exteriors, sometimes with marks from the rods. The interior is generally very tender with an intense flavor.

A basic formula for 10 servings of grilled or broiled vegetables

2 lb 8 oz/1.13 kg prepped vegetables (weight after trimming, peeling, and cutting)

Oil, marinade, or glaze (optional), salt, pepper, and other seasonings

Sauce and finishing or garnishing ingredients

1. **Place the prepared vegetable directly on the grill or broiler rods.** Vegetables can be seasoned with a marinade prior to grilling or broiling. Allow excess marinade to drain from vegetables to prevent flare-ups. Season vegetables during cooking by brushing on a light coat of glaze or marinade. Salt and pepper will not adhere well to all raw vegetables, but will to a vegetable that is hot from the grill or broiler. If the vegetables might stick easily to the rods or fall through, set them on a sizzler platter or in a hand-grill.

2. **Grill or broil the vegetables, turning as necessary, until properly cooked.** Use a spatula or tongs to turn grilled vegetables over after the first side has been marked or browned. To create crosshatch marks, give the vegetables a 90-degree turn after the grill rods have made an imprint; allow the rods to imprint again. Complete the cooking time on the second side to produce a well-browned exterior.

Vegetables may be grilled only enough to mark and flavor them before they are used in another dish. Thick cuts or high-starch vegetables can retain heat after they are removed from the grill or broiler. Allow time for carry-over cooking to avoid overcooking the grilled vegetables.

Roasting and Baking

Roasted or baked vegetables can be cooked whole or they may be cut to produce a browned exterior. Vegetables are roasted for many different reasons. Thick-skinned vegetables such as winter squashes or eggplant can be roasted to make a richly flavored purée. Mirepoix and other aromatic vegetables are roasted to add an extra dimension of flavor and color to stocks, sauces, and other dishes. Tomatoes or peppers can be roasted to intensify their flavor and give them a drier texture.

Thick-skinned whole vegetables, such as potatoes and other root vegetables, winter squash, and eggplant, are well suited to roasting or baking. The skins protect the interior from drying or scorching. Roasting is also excellent for halved, cut, sliced, or diced vegetables, as well as vegetables that might otherwise be difficult to peel, such as peppers. Rinse, peel, trim, and cut the vegetable, as necessary. To assure even cooking, cut vegetables into uniform pieces. Toss the vegetables with oil to prevent excessive drying and scorching.

Marinades can enhance flavor and give extra protection to vegetables as they cook in the dry heat. Add seasonings or aromatics such as salt, pepper, spice blends, or garlic. Have finishing ingredients ready (chopped fresh herbs, plain or flavored oils, whole or compound butter, reduced heavy cream, or a sauce) as desired or according to the particular recipe.

Have available roasting pans or sheet pans that can hold the vegetables with enough room for air to circulate freely, but not so much that juices from the food are likely to scorch. Some vegetables can also be set on roasting racks. For baked dishes, use hotel pans or similar baking pans or dishes.

A basic formula for 10 servings of roasted or baked vegetables

3 lb 8 oz/1.59 kg prepped vegetables (weight after trimming, peeling, and cutting)

Oil, marinade, or glaze (optional)

Salt, pepper, and other seasonings

Sauce and finishing or garnishing ingredients

1. **After piercing the skin, arrange the butternut squash cut side down in the pan to roast.** Prepare vegetables for roasting, as appropriate, by type or intended use and arrange them, cut sides down, in a baking or roasting pan. Cut or sliced vegetables may be seasoned with salt, pepper, spices, juices, or marinades. Add some liquid to the pan to steam dense vegetables and to prevent them from becoming overly brown or scorching as they roast. Set vegetables on racks over the liquid, or directly in the liquid, as preferred.

2. **Place the prepared vegetable in a moderate or hot oven and roast to the desired doneness.** Serve immediately, hold for later use, or use as an ingredient in another dish.

The longer the roasting time—a factor determined by the type of vegetable, size and thickness, diameter of the cut, and its density—the lower the temperature of the oven should be. Vegetables may be roasted on sheet pans or in roasting pans or, in some cases, directly on the oven rack to allow the hot air to circulate readily. Generally, roasted vegetables are properly done when they can be easily pierced with the tip of a knife or a kitchen fork. Vegetables should be rotated as they roast to promote even cooking because most ovens have hot spots. The placement of other items in the oven could also cause uneven cooking. Stir or turn the vegetables to keep those on the edge of the sheet pan from scorching. If the pan was covered, remove the cover or foil during the final stage of cooking to develop a rich, roasted flavor and color.

Roasted vegetables are best served immediately on heated plates with finishing ingredients as desired. If the vegetables must be held, keep them uncovered in a warm spot for the shortest possible time.

3. **Evaluate the quality of the finished roasted or baked vegetable.** The aim of roasting and baking is to create intense flavor and a special texture. Browning produces the expected roasted flavor.

The absence of added liquid means that the vegetable has a more intense flavor. The flesh of thick-skinned vegetables such as winter squash or eggplant should be soft enough to scoop out easily with a spoon. Roasted vegetables are frequently puréed for use as ingredients in other items, such as soups or sauces.

Puréeing

Vegetables are often boiled, steamed, or baked until they are soft enough to make into a purée. Some are naturally soft or moist enough, even when uncooked to make into a purée. The purée itself can be served as is or it may be used as a base for such dishes as vegetable timbales, custards, croquettes, or soufflés. It may also be used as an ingredient in other dishes or to flavor or color a sauce or soup.

Vegetables can range in texture from coarse to very smooth. If necessary or desired, cook the vegetables until the flesh is soft enough to mash easily. Cooked vegetables should be puréed while still very hot. Use a clean side towel to protect your hands as you work.

Once roasted, cut away heavy or inedible peels, rinds, stems, or roots. Scoop or squeeze out seeds. Remove as little edible flesh as possible. Break or cut the vegetable in pieces sized properly for the puréeing equipment. Select the equipment to make the purée according to the way it will be used. A food mill, ricer, or sieve will remove fibers, skin, and seeds. These tools produce purées with a rather rough texture. Food processors can make quite smooth purées from cooked or raw vegetables that have already been trimmed, peeled, and seeded. If the vegetable is fibrous, the processor won't necessarily remove the strings, so the purée will need to be pushed through a sieve. Blenders, immersion or countertop, and vertical chopping machines, can cut vegetables so fine that they produce a very smooth purée, though they, too, do not remove fibers and strings from some vegetables.

A vegetable purée can be finished by adjusting its seasoning, adding cream or butter, or blending it into other preparations. Or it may be cooled and stored for later use. Cool hot purées over an ice bath before wrapping and storing. Reheat cooled purées over gentle heat or in a bain-marie.

Sautéing

Sautéing and its related technique, stir-frying, may be used as the primary cooking techniques for vegetables as well as à la minute finishing techniques.

Boiled, steamed, or pan-steamed vegetables may be tossed or rolled in butter over high heat as a finishing step, or they may be cooked in a small amount of a flavorful liquid, sauce, or cream. Sautéed vegetables have a distinct flavor, primarily dependent upon the vegetable, but also influenced by the cooking fat that is chosen, as well as any additional finishing or garnishing ingredients.

Glazing is another finishing technique based upon the sautéing method. Add a small amount of butter and honey, sugar, or maple syrup to the vegetable as it reheats. The sugars liquefy and may be allowed to caramelize, coating the vegetable evenly to give it some flavor, sheen, and a golden color.

Rinse, trim, and peel the raw vegetable and cut it. Arugula, spinach, and other leafy greens, mushrooms, summer squashes, and onions may be sautéed or stir-fried from the raw state. Drain greens and other vegetables that can hold excess moisture. This important step assures the best flavor, texture, and color in the finished dish.

Some vegetables will not cook completely when sautéed unless they are cooked by a separate method first. In this case, just finish the vegetables by the sautéing method. If necessary, partially or wholly cook the vegetable by boiling, steaming, or roasting it first.

Select a cooking fat to complement the flavor of the vegetable. Oils such as olive, peanut, canola, corn, or safflower can be used, as well as whole or clarified butter, or rendered animal fat (lard, goose fat, bacon).

Optional seasonings and aromatics (salt, pepper, and lemon juice) can adjust or heighten the flavor. Finely mince or chop fresh herbs and add them at the last moment. Take the quantity of food to be sautéed into account when selecting the pan. It needs to be large enough to avoid overcrowding. If too much is put in the pan, the temperature will drop too quickly. On the other hand, the pan must not be too large, to avoid scorching. Certain materials are better at conducting heat with quick reaction to changes in temperature; others offer a more constant heat and do not react as quickly. There are benefits to both types of pan, and you will learn quickly which pan works best in which situation and with which food.

A basic formula for 10 servings of sautéed vegetables

2 lb 8 oz/1.13 kg prepped vegetables (weight after trimming, peeling, cutting, and blanching or parcooking; however, leafy green vegetables lose about half their weight in moisture during sautéing, so begin with 4 lb/1.81 kg to prepare 10 servings)

Small amount of oil or other cooking fat

Salt, pepper, and other seasonings

Sauce and finishing or garnishing ingredients

1. **Add the prepared vegetables to the fat and sweated aromatics in the pan.** Use only enough oil or fat to keep the pan lubricated and prevent the vegetable from burning. The cooking medium should be hot but not hazy or smoking. Vegetables require less intense heat than meat, poultry, and fish. Some vegetable sautés begin by cooking aromatic ingredients in the oil to add flavor to the finished dish.

If more than one type of vegetable is being cooked, the vegetables should be added in sequence, starting with those that require the longest cooking time and ending with those that require the least.

Do not overcrowd the pan. For most vegetables, add only enough to make a relatively thin layer in the pan. Leafy greens can be loosely mounded in the pan, as they lose volume quickly while sautéing.

Add seasonings and continue to sauté until the vegetables are fully cooked and flavorful. Some vegetables must be kept in nearly constant motion as they sauté; others develop a better flavor and color when turned only once or twice. Use offset spatulas, tongs, or stir-frying tools to turn and lift vegetables as they sauté.

2. **Evaluate the quality of the finished sautéed vegetable.** As vegetables sauté, they wilt or soften and the color intensifies. Each component of a sautéed vegetable dish should be cooked until done, very hot, and well seasoned. Be sure to check the temperature and seasoning of vegetables that are held for service in a steam table or other holding device.

Finishing and Glazing Vegetables by Sautéing

When vegetables are fully or partially cooked by steaming, boiling, or roasting, they can be sautéed just long enough to reheat them or to complete cooking them—a technique known as finishing.

Whole butter is a common choice for finishing vegetables, but other flavorful cooking fats, such as extra-virgin olive oil, infused oils, or rendered bacon, are also used to give a specific flavor to the dish. Vegetables may also be cooked instead in a small amount of heavy cream or a sauce, usually just enough to cling to the vegetables.

Heat the cooking fat, cream, or sauce over moderate heat. Add a small amount of sugar, honey, or other syrup to produce a sweet glaze, if desired. Garnishes may be added now or after the vegetables are heated through.

Add the prepared vegetables to the pan without crowding and stir, toss, or turn them until they are very hot and evenly coated. Taste them for proper doneness and seasoning, and serve at once.

A basic formula for 10 servings of stir-fried vegetables

2 lb 8 oz/1.13 kg prepped vegetables (weight after trimming, peeling, and cutting)

Small amount of oil or other cooking fat

Salt, pepper, and other seasonings

Sauce or ingredients to make sauce (optional)

1. Heat the wok before adding the oil by ladling it around the upper edge of the pan. Once the oil in the bottom of the pan is hot, add the aromatics to release their flavors. To stir-fry a combination of vegetables, add the cut vegetables in sequence, starting with the vegetables that take the longest to cook, such as carrots and broccoli. Keep the vegetables in constant motion.

2. **As the vegetables become hot, push them up onto the sides of the wok.** This allows the wok to recover its heat before making the next addition of vegetables. Continue adding the vegetables to the center of the wok and continue to stir-fry until each addition is very hot. Add vegetables like zucchini and yellow squash at the midpoint of cooking time and very tender ingredients like fresh herbs at the last moment.

3. **Evaluate the quality of the finished stir-fried vegetable.** A properly prepared vegetable stir-fry has a combination of flavors, textures, and colors. Some vegetables may become very tender (eggplant or zucchini, for instance), while others should have an almost crisp texture. A variety of seasonings and flavorings can be added to the finished stir-fry. Serve vegetable stir-fries very hot, directly from the wok.

Pan Frying

Pan-fried vegetables have a satisfying, crisp exterior that provides a pleasing contrast to the moist, flavorful interior. Pan frying is similar to sautéing, the main difference being that, in pan frying, the amount of oil used as a cooking medium is greater than for sautéing. Also, any sauce served with pan-fried vegetables is made separately. The vegetables may be breaded or coated with flour or a batter.

Rinse, peel, trim, and cut the vegetable. Wholly or partially cook the vegetable, if necessary. Bread it with a standard breading, or coat it with flour or batter.

Clarified butter, most vegetable oils, shortening, and rendered animal fat (goose fat or lard) can all be used for pan frying. The cooking fat should come about halfway up the vegetables in the pan.

Aromatics and seasonings may be added to the vegetable before or after cooking, or they may be included in the breading or batter, if appropriate. In addition, a recipe may call for finishing ingredients such as a compound butter, sauce, relish, or salsa.

The pan must be large enough to avoid overcrowding. If the pan is crowded, the oil temperature will drop quickly and a good seal will not form. If this happens, the vegetable may absorb the oil and the breading can become soggy or even fall away in places. Use tongs, a skimmer, or a spider to remove the vegetables from the oil. Have a pan or platter lined with paper toweling to blot excess oil from the vegetables before service.

A basic formula for 10 servings of pan-fried vegetables

2 lb 8 oz/1.13 kg prepped vegetables (weight after trimming, peeling, and cutting), blanched, parcooked, or fully cooked, as necessary

Coating ingredients, such as flour, egg wash, standard breading, or batter (optional)

Oil or other cooking fat

Salt, pepper, and other seasonings

Sauce and finishing or garnishing ingredients

1. **Heat the cooking fat in a heavy-gauge skillet, rondeau, or brasier.** Pan frying requires high heat. When the cooking fat appears hazy or shimmering, it is hot enough. Monitor the heat of the fat to keep it even throughout cooking time. The shorter the necessary cooking time, the higher the heat may be. For rapid cooking and for the best color, avoid crowding the vegetables in the pan. Add the vegetables gradually; too many vegetables added at once will lower the cooking temperature. Overcrowding also causes the coating to pull away from the vegetable.

2. **Cook the vegetables over medium to high heat until the first side becomes lightly browned and crisp.** Turn them and complete cooking on the second side. Remove the vegetables and blot them briefly on absorbent paper toweling to absorb any excess fat. Season with salt and pepper away from the cooking fat, to help the oil last through successive batches. Skim away any bits of coating before adding the next batch.

Properly pan-fried vegetables have a golden or brown, crisp exterior, with the interior tender to the bite and very hot. Any coating is crisp and light.

Deep Frying

Perfectly fried vegetables are light and savory, and offer the chef a range of textures and flavors to showcase in appetizers, side dishes, garnishes, accompaniments, and entrées.

When vegetables are deep fried, the results can range from crisp, fragile chips to hearty croquettes. Tempura-style deep frying pairs fresh vegetables with a light batter. (For deep-fried potatoes, see pages 785–787.)

Choose fresh and flavorful vegetables and prepare them for frying according to the recipe's requirements or the intended style of service. All vegetables must be thoroughly rinsed, and in some cases scrubbed. Trim away tough or inedible skins, peels, cores, seeds, or roots. Cut or slice as required. When necessary, the vegetables should be parcooked before frying.

Dice, mince, or purée vegetables used in a croquette mixture, and use an appropriate binder to hold them together into a batter. Options include heavy béchamel or velouté, heavy cream, fresh cheeses, eggs, or bread crumbs.

Some fried vegetable preparations call for a standard breading (see page 458) or batter. The batter should be applied just before the vegetable is fried.

Choose oils and other cooking fats for frying that can reach a high temperature without smoking or breaking down. Vegetable oils, including corn oil, canola oil, and safflower oil, have neutral flavors and high smoking points. Special oils may be used for a specific flavor. Olive oil or rendered duck or goose fat may be appropriate.

Use either a frying kettle or deep fryer. Electric or gas deep fryers maintain an even temperature throughout cooking time and are efficient for menus that produce quantities of fried vegetables and other fried dishes. Use baskets to lower some fried items into the oil and to remove them once cooked. For other fried foods, use tongs to add the vegetables to the frying fat and a spider or skimmer to remove them. Prepare a pan lined with absorbent paper toweling to blot fried foods immediately after they complete cooking.

A basic formula for 10 servings of deep-fried vegetables

2 lb 8 oz/1.13 kg prepped vegetables (weight after trimming, peeling, and cutting), blanched, parcooked, or fully cooked, as necessary

Coating ingredients, such as flour, egg wash, standard breading, or batter (optional)

Enough oil or other cooking fat to completely submerge the vegetable

Salt, pepper, and other seasonings

Sauce and finishing or garnishing ingredients

1. **Heat the oil in a deep fryer or kettle.** The best temperature for deep frying most vegetables is about 350°F/177°C. Lower breaded vegetables into the oil using a basket. Be sure to leave room between larger pieces to prevent them from sticking to each other, and do not overcrowd the basket. Batter-coated vegetables should be dipped into the batter (in some cases, they should be dusted with flour before they are coated in batter) using tongs or a spider, then immediately lowered into the hot oil.

Adding the vegetables will lower the temperature of the oil for a time (this is known as recovery time), so adjust the size of the batches added to shorten recovery time.

Transfer fried vegetables to a pan lined with paper towels to blot them. Season them with salt, pepper, or spice blends now. Seasoning should never be done directly over the fryer, since these seasonings could hasten the breakdown of the frying oil. Fried vegetables are at their peak of quality now, and should be served right away. If necessary, they may be held for up to 15 minutes in a warm place (such as under a heat lamp).

Evaluate the quality of the finished deep-fried vegetable. In general, the thinner the cut used for the vegetable, the crisper the finished dish will be. The exterior of the vegetable should be golden or brown in color, the flavor fresh and appealing. The coating, if any was used, should be an even thickness and not excessive in relation to the vegetable portion. The vegetable, as well as any coatings, should be properly seasoned and extremely hot.

2. **Fry the vegetables until fully cooked. Remove and drain. Season if necessary.** Frying times vary according to the type of vegetable fried. The vegetable (or vegetable mixture, in the case of croquettes and fritters) should be fully cooked, tender, and hot. The coating, if any, should have a golden to brown color. However, finished tempura vegetables should not be golden brown like an item fried using the standard breading procedure. Properly fried tempura vegetables should be white to light golden in color and have a crispy texture on the outside.

Vegetables coated in breading and prepared by the basket method typically stay submerged until they are fully cooked, when they rise to the oil's surface. Use the basket to lift them from the oil. Hold the basket over the fryer briefly to allow the oil to drain back into the kettle. Batter-coated vegetables fried using the swimming method may be turned as they fry to cook and brown them evenly. Use tongs, a spider, or similar tools to turn the vegetables and lift them from the oil when fully cooked.

Stewing and Braising

Vegetable stews and braises include such delicate dishes as petit pois à la française and, on the other end of the spectrum, such sturdy and robust dishes as ratatouille and braised cabbage. Stewed or braised vegetables literally cook in their own juices. The vegetables in a stew are customarily cut into small pieces, while those in a braise are in large pieces or left whole. Occasionally, beurre manié or a starch slurry is added to the juices to give the dish more substance and to improve its appearance. The thickened sauce lightly coats the vegetable, providing an attractive sheen.

Vegetable stews and braises may be composed of one main ingredient or a combination of vegetables. Braised fennel, for example, contains a single main ingredient; ratatouille is a stew that melds several different vegetables. Braises and stews generally include some aromatic ingredients, such as shallots or mirepoix.

Prepare the vegetables according to the type and the desired result. Rinse, peel, trim, and cut the vegetables, as necessary. Blanch them to remove bitter flavors or to aid in removing peels. The fat or oil chosen should have a good flavor—one that is appropriate to the dish. Vegetables that do not release a significant amount of liquid as they cook may need additional liquid, stock, wine, fumet, juice, or water, for example.

Prepare and use seasonings and aromatics such as salt and pepper, shallots, garlic, minced herbs, spices, mirepoix, or matignon. Some dishes include a pork product (salt pork, bacon, or ham) or an acid (vinegar, citrus zest or juice, or wine) to develop a complex flavor in braised and stewed vegetable dishes.

Some recipes call for an added thickener such as a slurry of arrowroot, cornstarch, potato starch, or beurre manié. Various finishing ingredients, such as reduced heavy cream, a cream sauce, butter, or a liaison, may be added to give a vegetable stew a rich flavor, some sheen, and a smooth texture. A vegetable stew or braise may be garnished with bread crumbs and cheese to create a gratin, if desired.

The main piece of equipment needed for braising is a brasier or rondeau (or other deep, wide cooking vessel) with a lid. Use a skimmer or slotted spoon to remove properly braised or stewed vegetables from the pot before finishing the sauce. Use a strainer or immersion blender to finish the sauce.

A basic formula for 10 servings of stewed or braised vegetables

3 lb to 3 lb 8 oz/1.36 to 1.59 kg prepped vegetables (weight after trimming, peeling, and cutting)

Aromatic vegetables, seasonings, herbs, and spices

Flavorful cooking liquid

Small amount of cooking fat

Finishing and garnishing ingredients

1. **Cook the aromatic vegetables in a cooking fat, beginning with members of the onion family, to develop a smooth, sweet taste in the dish.** Cook aromatic vegetables in a light-colored stew or braise just until they start to become tender and release some of their natural juices. For other dishes, cook the aromatics to the desired stage of brownness, ranging from a light golden color to a deep brown. Use enough oil to properly cook the aromatics without scorching them, and stir as needed to develop their flavor and color.

2. **Add the remaining ingredients in order, from least to most tender, stirring as necessary and adjusting the seasoning and consistency of the dish as it braises or stews.** Cook vegetable stews over gentle heat with the lid on to encourage them to release their flavor and to capture it in the cooking liquid. Braises may be cooked over direct heat or in the oven. If the cooking liquid cooks away too quickly, add more and lower the heat slightly. If the liquid does not reduce properly during cooking, remove the lid to encourage natural reduction.

3. **Stew or braise the vegetables until they are flavorful, fully cooked, and fork tender.** The stew or braise is ready to serve now, but it may be finished by preparing a sauce from the cooking liquid. To do so, remove the vegetables from the cooking liquid and thicken the liquid in one of the following ways:

- Reduce the liquid to a sauce-like flavor and consistency.

- Purée some of the aromatic vegetables and return the purée to the cooking liquid.

- Add a bit of beurre manié to the cooking liquid.

Serve as is on hot plates, or finish the vegetables with a gratin topping and brown under a salamander or broiler. Stewed and braised vegetables can be held for a longer time than other vegetables without losing significant quality. Hold them, loosely covered, in a steam table. They also may be cooled and refrigerated, then reheated as needed.

Vegetable stews and braises have deep, concentrated flavors. Stews and braises should be fork tender or, in some cases, meltingly soft.

General Guidelines for Vegetables

Each vegetable cooking technique produces specific and characteristic results and affects the flavor, texture, and nutritive value of each vegetable in different ways. The chef can take advantage of the full range of possibilities within a method to produce vegetable dishes specifically tailored to the operation's needs. Kitchens that rely on regional and seasonal produce can adapt a technique both to suit an ingredient's specific needs and to achieve an effect. For example, though acorn squash is often roasted or puréed, it can also be gently stewed in cream or grilled and served with a salsa. Cucumbers, most commonly considered a vegetable to be eaten raw, may be steamed, sautéed, or even braised. The flavor, texture, and color differences produced in one vegetable when prepared by different techniques can be quite extraordinary.

Carefully handled vegetables maintain their flavor, color, texture, and nutritional value longer. Rinse leafy or delicate vegetables carefully to avoid bruising them, and dry them thoroughly. Scrub hardier vegetables before peeling. Be sure that all traces of dirt or grit have been removed.

In all cases, from a simple dish of steamed or boiled vegetables, served seasoned but otherwise unadorned, to a complex vegetable gratin, the best overall quality is assured by properly cooking vegetables to the appropriate doneness and serving them as soon as possible. The style of service and overall volume of the kitchen determines how much advance cooking and holding is desirable just as much as the nature of the vegetable and the cooking method. Sautéed, stir-fried, pan-fried, and deep-fried dishes may be prepared just at the moment of service. Braises, stews, and purées are suited to batch cooking, since they are easier to hold and lose little, if any, of their flavor and texture when prepared in advance and reheated (and may, in fact, improve when held).

There are distinct differences in how tender a vegetable should be when it is properly cooked. Some vegetables—broccoli and green beans, for example—are not considered properly cooked until they are quite tender. Others, such as snow peas and sugar snap peas, should always retain some bite (fully cooked but still firm). Preferences regarding the correct doneness of certain vegetables may vary from one part of the world to another and from one vegetable to another. In addition, there are different standards for different cooking techniques. For example, stir-frying generally results in a very crisp texture, while baking or braising produces very tender vegetables.

Boiled Carrots

Makes 10 servings

96 fl oz/2.88 L water

salt, as needed

3 lb/1.36 kg carrots, cut into desired shape (oblique, rondelles, batonnet, julienne, etc.)

1. Bring the water to a boil in a large pot. Add enough salt to flavor the water. Add the carrots. If necessary, cover the pot to return the water to a boil as quickly as possible.

2. Boil the carrots until tender, 4 to 7 minutes, depending on the thickness of the cut. Drain immediately.

3. Serve the carrots immediately, finish as desired, or cool rapidly and refrigerate to reheat and serve later.

Boiled Edamame

Makes 10 servings

6 oz/170 g sea salt

32 fl oz/960 mL water

1 lb/454 g edamame, shelled

1. Add all but 1 tsp/5 g of the salt to the water and bring to a boil.

2. Add the edamame and simmer until tender, about 8 minutes. Drain the edamame and season with the remaining 1 tsp/5 g of salt and serve hot, or cool to room temperature.

Steamed Broccoli

Makes 10 servings

3 lb 8 oz/1.59 kg broccoli (about 4 bunches)

salt, as needed

ground black pepper, as needed

water, as needed

1. Trim the broccoli, peel the stems, and cut them into spears. Arrange the broccoli on a steamer rack or insert, and season with salt and pepper.

2. Bring water to a full boil in the bottom of a tightly covered steamer. Add the broccoli rack, replace the cover, and steam the broccoli until tender, 5 to 7 minutes.

3. Remove the broccoli from the steamer, adjust seasoning with salt and pepper, and serve immediately, or cool and store for later service.

Broccoli and Toasted Garlic: Sauté thinly sliced garlic in butter or oil until it is browned. Add the steamed broccoli and toss or roll it in the butter or oil until very hot. Adjust seasoning with salt and pepper, as necessary. Serve immediately.

Options for reheating vegetables

In simmering stock or water. Place the vegetables in a sieve or perforated basket and lower them into a pot of simmering stock or water just long enough to heat the vegetables through. Drain and immediately finish the vegetables with butter, sauce, seasonings, and so on.

In the microwave. Generally best for small amounts. Evenly space the vegetables on a flat, round, or oval plate or other microwave-safe container. Some additional liquid may be needed to keep the vegetables moist. Cover with plastic wrap and cut vents to allow the steam to escape, or cover with parchment paper. Reheat on the highest power setting for the shortest possible time, dress immediately, and serve.

By sautéing. Heat a small amount of olive oil, butter, cream, stock, sauce, or glaze in a sauté pan and add the vegetables. Toss over medium-high heat until warmed through. Add seasonings if necessary and serve.

Glazed Beets

Glazed Beets

Makes 10 servings

2 lb 8 oz/1.13 kg red or golden beets, tops trimmed, skin on

3½ oz/99 g sugar

½ fl oz/15 mL red or white wine vinegar

1½ fl oz/45 mL orange juice

8 fl oz/240 mL **Chicken Stock** (page 351)

1½ oz/43 g butter

salt, as needed

ground black pepper, as needed

1. Place the beets in a large pot and cover with water. Bring the water to a boil, reduce to a simmer, and cook the beets until they are soft when pierced with a fork, about 40 minutes.

2. Drain and cool slightly. Slice the beets into ¼-in/6-mm-thick rounds, or in wedges.

3. In a sauté pan, combine the sugar, vinegar, juice, stock, and butter and bring to a simmer. Cook gently until the glaze has the consistency of a light syrup, about 15 minutes.

4. When ready to serve, toss the cut beets in the glaze over medium heat. Season with salt and pepper. Serve immediately.

Creamed Corn

Makes 10 servings

6 oz/170 g fine-dice leeks

16 fl oz/480 mL heavy cream

salt, as needed

ground black pepper, as needed

ground nutmeg, as needed

1 lb 8 oz/680 g corn kernels, fresh or frozen

1 tbsp/3 g chopped chervil

1. Combine the leeks and the cream in a saucepan. Season with salt, pepper, and nutmeg. Simmer over medium heat until the cream has reduced by half.

2. Steam the corn over boiling water until fully cooked, 4 to 5 minutes. Add the corn to the leek mixture and simmer to reach a good flavor and consistency, 2 to 3 minutes more.

3. Adjust seasoning with salt and pepper, if necessary. Add the chopped chervil. Serve now or hold it hot for service.

Pan-Steamed Carrots

Makes 10 servings

2 lb 8 oz/1.13 kg sliced carrots (¼ in/6 mm thick)

3 oz/85 g butter

1 tsp/1 g chopped parsley

salt, as needed

ground black pepper, as needed

1. Add about 1 in/3 cm of salted water to a large pan and bring to a boil. Add the carrots to the water, adding more water if necessary to barely cover the carrots. Bring the water to a boil. Cover the pan tightly, and reduce the heat slightly.

2. Pan steam the carrots until they are fully cooked and tender to the bite, 5 to 6 minutes. When done, drain excess water from the pan. Return the carrots to the heat, add the butter and parsley, and season with salt and pepper. Stir or toss until the carrots are evenly coated and very hot. Serve immediately.

Pan-Steamed Haricots Verts: Substitute 2 lb 8 oz/1.13 kg of trimmed haricots verts for the carrots. Pan-steam the haricots verts according to the above method. To finish the haricots verts, sauté 1 tbsp/3 g shallots in 1 fl oz/ 30 mL olive oil until translucent. Add the cooked haricots verts and toss to coat. Season with salt and pepper and serve immediately.

Pecan Carrots: Prepare the carrots as directed above. In step 2, add ¾ oz/21 g minced shallots, 1½ oz/43 g honey, and 3 oz/85 g chopped toasted pecans with the butter. Substitute minced chives for the parsley.

Gingered Snow Peas and Yellow Squash

Makes 10 servings

6 fl oz/180 mL **Chicken Stock** (page 351) or **Vegetable Stock** (page 353)

2 tbsp/18 g minced ginger

½ oz/14 g minced shallots

2 tsp/6 g minced garlic

salt, as needed

ground white pepper, as needed

1 lb 8 oz/680 g snow peas

12 oz/340 g medium-dice yellow squash

2 tbsp/6 g chopped chives

1. Combine the stock with the ginger, shallots, and garlic and simmer for 2 minutes. Season with salt and pepper.

2. Add the snow peas and squash and return the stock to a simmer. Add more stock if necessary; the stock should come to a depth of about ½ in/1 cm in the pan. Cover the pan tightly and pan steam until the vegetables are tender, 2 to 3 minutes.

3. Adjust seasoning with salt and pepper. Serve hot, garnished with chives.

Green Beans with Walnuts

Makes 10 servings

2 lb 8 oz/1.13 kg haricots verts

2 oz/57 g butter

2 oz/57 g minced shallots

1 tsp/3 g minced garlic

8 fl oz/240 mL **Chicken Stock** (page 351), hot

salt, as needed

ground black pepper, as needed

1 fl oz/30 mL walnut oil

3 oz/85 g chopped walnuts

1 tbsp/3 g minced chives

1. Cut the green beans on the bias, if desired.

2. Heat the butter in a small rondeau. Add the shallots and garlic and sauté until translucent, 2 to 3 minutes. Add the green beans in an even layer and add the hot stock. Season with salt and pepper.

3. Bring the stock to a simmer, cover the pan, and pan steam the beans until tender, 15 to 18 minutes. The cooking liquid should reduce during this time and thicken slightly to coat the beans. If necessary, remove the cover and continue simmering until the liquid is almost fully reduced, 1 to 2 additional minutes.

4. Toss the green beans with the oil, walnuts, and chives. Adjust seasoning with salt and pepper and serve immediately.

Glazed Carrots

Makes 10 servings

3 oz/85 g butter

2 lb 8 oz/1.13 kg oblique-cut carrots

1½ oz/43 g sugar

12 fl oz/360 mL **Chicken Stock** (page 351) or **Vegetable Stock** (page 353), hot

salt, as needed

ground white pepper, as needed

1. Melt the butter in a large sauté pan and then add the carrots.

2. Cover the pan and lightly sweat the carrots over medium-low heat for 2 to 3 minutes.

3. Add the sugar and stock. Season with salt and pepper. Bring the stock to a simmer over medium heat.

4. Cover the pan and cook the carrots over low heat until they are almost tender, about 5 minutes.

5. Remove the cover and continue to simmer until the cooking liquid reduces to a glaze and the carrots are tender, 2 to 3 minutes.

6. Adjust seasoning with salt and pepper and serve immediately.

Grilled Shiitake Mushrooms with Soy-Sesame Glaze

Grilled Vegetables Provençal Style

Makes 10 servings

2 oz/57 g garlic cloves

8 fl oz/240 mL olive oil

2 tbsp/6 g minced rosemary

1 lb 4 oz/567 g zucchini, cut into ¾-in/2-cm-thick slices (either on an elongated bias or lengthwise)

1 lb 4 oz/567 g eggplant, cut into ¾-in/2-cm-thick slices (either on an elongated bias or lengthwise)

8 oz/227 g onion, sliced into ¾-in/2-cm rings

salt, as needed

ground black pepper, as needed

6 oz/170 g green peppers

6 oz/170 g red peppers

4 oz/113 g peeled, seeded, and medium-diced tomatoes

½ fl oz/15 mL balsamic vinegar

1 oz/28 g basil chiffonade

1. Place the garlic in a large, shallow pan and add enough oil to barely cover it. Add the rosemary and simmer over very low heat, until the garlic is cooked but not falling apart, 15 to 20 minutes. Remove from the heat and cool to room temperature. Reserve.

2. Preheat the grill or broiler. Brush the zucchini, eggplant, and onion rings with the garlic and rosemary oil and season with salt and pepper. Place them on the grill and cook on the first side until browned. Turn once and complete cooking on the second side until the vegetables are tender, about 3 minutes total or more. Remove from the grill.

3. Grill or broil the peppers until evenly charred on all sides. Remove from the grill and let the peppers cool. Remove the skin, core, seeds, and ribs. Cut into ¾-in/2 cm-thick slices and reserve until needed.

4. Put the garlic and 2 fl oz/60 mL of the oil in a large, deep saucepan and heat over medium heat. Add the grilled vegetables and concassé and stir gently to finish heating the vegetables and blending the flavors. Add the vinegar and adjust seasoning with salt and pepper. Fold in the basil or use it to garnish individual servings. Serve immediately or reserve it for service.

Marinated Grilled Vegetables: To make a marinade, combine 8 fl oz/240 mL vegetable oil, 2 fl oz/60 mL soy sauce, 1 fl oz/30 mL lemon juice, 2 tsp/6 g minced garlic, and ½ tsp/2 g fennel seeds. Marinate the vegetables for 1 hour, then allow any excess marinade to drain off before grilling.

Grilled Shiitake Mushrooms with Soy-Sesame Glaze

Makes 10 servings

SOY-SESAME GLAZE

4 fl oz/120 mL soy sauce or tamari

2 fl oz/60 mL water

2 fl oz/60 mL peanut or corn oil

2 oz/57 g tahini paste

½ fl oz/15 mL sesame oil

1 tbsp/9 g minced garlic

2 tsp/3 g minced ginger

½ tsp/1 g red pepper flakes (optional)

2 lb 8 oz/1.13 kg shiitake mushrooms

10 green onions

¾ oz/21 g toasted sesame seeds

1. Combine all the ingredients for the glaze. Keep refrigerated until ready to use. If desired, slice any large mushroom caps in half.

2. Add the mushrooms and green onions to the glaze and marinate for at least 15 minutes or up to 1 hour.

3. Remove the mushrooms and green onions from the glaze, letting the excess drain away.

4. Grill the mushrooms and green onions on a preheated grill until they are marked on all sides and cooked through, about 2 minutes on each side.

5. Scatter with the sesame seeds and serve immediately.

NOTE

Once grilled, the mushrooms can be returned to the marinade, allowed to cool to room temperature, and added to salads or other dishes as a garnish.

Butternut Squash Purée

Makes 10 servings

4 lb/1.81 kg butternut squash, halved

4 oz/113 g butter, room temperature

4 fl oz/120 mL heavy cream, hot

salt, as needed

ground black pepper, as needed

1. Pierce the squash and place it in a roasting pan, cut side down. Add enough water to create steam during the initial roasting time. Cover with a lid or foil, if desired.

2. Roast at 375°F/191°C until the squash is extremely tender, about 1 hour. To check for doneness, pierce with a kitchen fork or paring knife. There should be no resistance. Remove the cover or foil during the final 15 minutes of cooking to brown the squash.

3. Remove from the oven. As soon as the squash can be safely handled (it should still be very hot), cut it in half and remove the seeds.

4. Scoop the flesh from the skin and purée it, using a food mill, blender, or food processor. If necessary, simmer the purée to thicken.

5. Add the butter and cream and season with salt and pepper. The purée is ready to use at once, or it may be rapidly cooled and refrigerated for later service.

Spaghetti Squash

Makes 10 servings

4 lb/1.81 kg spaghetti squash

1 oz/28 g butter

salt, as needed

ground black pepper, as needed

1. Halve the squash and remove the seeds. Place the squash, cut side down, in a roasting pan. Add enough water to cover by one third. Cover with a lid or foil.

2. Roast at 375°F/191°C until the squash is extremely tender, about 1 hour. To check for doneness, pierce with a kitchen fork or paring knife. There should be no resistance.

3. When the squash is cool enough to handle, scoop out the flesh, using a fork to separate it into strands. Reheat the squash by sautéing it in butter over medium heat, and season with salt and pepper. Serve immediately.

Spaghetti Squash

Baked Acorn Squash with Cranberry-Orange Compote

Makes 12 servings

3 acorn squash

2½ oz/71 g brown sugar, honey, or maple syrup

5 oz/142 g butter

1½ tsp/7.50 g salt, or as needed

¾ tsp/1.50 g ground black pepper, or as needed

24 fl oz/720 mL **Cranberry-Orange Compote** (recipe follows)

1. Preheat the oven to 400°F/204°C. Quarter the squash and remove the seeds.

2. Place the squash, cut side up, on a baking sheet. Sprinkle the quarters with the sugar, honey, or maple syrup. Evenly divide the butter and place 1 cube on each quarter. Season with salt and pepper.

3. Cover the squash with foil and bake for 30 minutes. Remove the foil and bake for an additional 15 minutes, or until tender, basting periodically.

4. Serve each portion of the squash on heated plates topped with 2 fl oz/60 mL Cranberry-Orange Compote.

Cranberry-Orange Compote

Makes 32 fl oz/960 mL

2 lb/907 g cranberries

12 fl oz/360 mL orange juice

sugar, as needed

4 oz/113 g orange zest, blanched

salt, as needed

ground black pepper, as needed

1. Combine the cranberries, juice, and enough water to barely cover the berries in a pan. Add the sugar and simmer the berries over medium heat until they are softened and the liquid is thickened.

2. Stir in the orange zest. Season with salt and pepper. Serve hot.

Oven-Roasted Tomatoes

Makes 10 servings

4 lb 8 oz/2.04 kg tomatoes

3 fl oz/90 mL extra-virgin olive oil

½ oz/14 g minced garlic

½ oz/14 g minced shallots

2 tsp/2 g chopped basil

2 tsp/2 g chopped oregano

1 tsp/1 g chopped thyme

salt, as needed

ground black pepper, as needed

1. Remove the cores from the tomatoes and cut into the desired shape (halved, quartered, wedged, or sliced). Arrange in a single layer in a shallow pan.

2. Combine the oil, garlic, shallots, basil, oregano, and thyme. Season with salt and pepper. Drizzle this mixture over the tomatoes and turn carefully to coat them.

3. Arrange the tomatoes on racks set in sheet pans. Roast in a 275°F/135°C oven for 1 to 1½ hours, or until the tomatoes are dried and lightly browned.

4. They are ready to serve now or use as an ingredient in another dish, or they may be cooled on the racks and stored, covered, and refrigerated.

Oven-Roasted Tomatoes

Marinated Roasted Peppers

Marinated Roasted Peppers

Makes 10 servings

4 lb 4 oz/1.9 kg roasted red and yellow peppers
(page 700)

4 oz/120 mL olive oil

2 oz/57 g golden raisins

2 oz/57 g toasted pine nuts

1 oz/28 g chopped parsley

½ oz/14 g minced garlic

salt, as needed

ground black pepper, as needed

1. Cut the roasted peppers into ¼-in/6-mm slices and drain in a sieve or colander for 2 hours.

2. Combine the peppers with the oil, raisins, pine nuts, parsley, garlic, salt, and pepper.

3. Serve immediately or refrigerate for later service.

Roasted Carrots

Makes 10 servings

2 lb 8 oz/1.13 kg oblique-cut carrots

2 oz/57 g duck fat or lard

salt, as needed

ground black pepper, as needed

1. Preheat a roasting pan in a 350°F/177°C oven. Add the fat and melt it in the pan.

2. Add the carrots and season with salt and pepper. Roast the carrots until tender and golden brown.

3. Serve immediately.

Shrimp-Stuffed Mirlitons

Makes 10 servings

5 mirlitons

3 oz/85 g butter

8 oz/227 g minced onions

4 green onions, thinly sliced

2 celery ribs, small dice

2 garlic cloves, minced

8 oz/227 g peeled, deveined, and small-diced shrimp

5 oz/142 g fresh bread crumbs

hot sauce, as needed

1 tbsp/3 g minced thyme

salt, as needed

ground black pepper, as needed

1 egg, lightly beaten

1. Bring a large saucepan of salted water to a boil over high heat. Boil the mirlitons for 20 minutes or until tender when tested with a fork. Drain.

2. When cool enough to handle, cut the mirlitons in half lengthwise, remove and discard the large center seed, and scoop out the pulp using a Parisian scoop, leaving the shells intact (¼-in/6-mm sides). Coarsely chop the pulp and set aside.

3. In a large skillet, melt 2 oz/57 g of the butter over medium heat. Add the onions, green onions, celery, and garlic. Cook, stirring frequently, until the vegetables begin to soften, about 5 minutes. Add the chopped mirliton pulp and cook for 5 minutes more. Add the shrimp. Stir in 3 oz/85 g of the bread crumbs, the hot sauce, and thyme. Season with salt and pepper.

4. Remove the skillet from the heat. Let the mixture cool slightly and stir in the egg.

5. Arrange the mirliton shells on a greased half sheet tray and blot up any moisture in the shells with paper towels.

6. Spoon the stuffing into the shells, sprinkle with the remaining bread crumbs, and dot with the remaining butter.

7. Bake at 350°F/177°C, uncovered, for 30 to 35 minutes, or until the stuffing is firm and the tops are golden brown. Serve immediately.

Eggplant Parmesan

Makes 10 servings

4 lb/1.81 kg eggplant

1½ oz/43 g salt

1 tsp/2 g ground black pepper

13 oz/369 g all-purpose flour

16 fl oz/480 mL **Egg Wash** (page 1061)

1 lb 8 oz/680 g bread crumbs

26 fl oz/780 mL vegetable oil

50 fl oz/1.50 L **Tomato Sauce** (page 384)

10 oz/284 g grated Parmesan

1 lb 8 oz/680 g mozzarella cheese, sliced ⅛ in/3 mm thick (20 slices)

1. Peel the eggplant and cut it into ½-in/1-cm circles. You will need 40 slices total (4 per serving). Lay the eggplant circles on a sheet tray lined with parchment paper and lightly salt them. Set the eggplant aside for half an hour to release moisture. Drain the eggplant on paper towels.

2. Season the eggplant with pepper. Bread it using the standard breading procedure (page 458).

3. Heat the oil in a large sauté pan over medium-high heat. Working in batches, pan fry the eggplant slices until golden brown. Drain for 2 to 3 minutes on paper towels, then transfer to a rack.

4. Preheat the oven to 350°F/177°C. Lay ten 12-fl-oz/360-mL casserole dishes on a sheet tray. Spread approximately 2 fl oz/60 mL of tomato sauce on the bottom of each. Lay 2 slices of the fried eggplant on top of the tomato sauce. Sprinkle approximately ½ oz/14 g of the Parmesan over the top and lay on 1 slice of mozzarella. Top with approximately 2 fl oz/60 mL more tomato sauce and place 2 more eggplant slices on top. Evenly spread 1 fl oz/30 mL more of the tomato sauce on top and cover with the remaining slice of mozzarella and ½ oz/14 g of Parmesan.

5. Bake the eggplant until golden brown on top and the sauce is bubbling. Serve immediately.

Eggplant Parmesan

Poblanos Rellenos

Poblanos Rellenos

Makes 10 servings

4 oz/113 g dried black beans, soaked overnight

4 oz/113 g dried red kidney beans, soaked overnight

64 fl oz/1.92 L corn oil, or as needed

10 poblano chiles

2 oz/57 g small-dice onions

2 tsp/6 g minced garlic cloves

½ fl oz/15 mL olive oil

4 oz/113 g grated jalapeño Jack cheese

4 oz/113 g grated dry Jack cheese

4 oz/113 g grated queso Chihuahua

4 oz/113 g grated ancho caciotta

2 tsp/2 g chopped marjoram

1½ tsp/1.50 g epazote

1 tsp/2 g dried Mexican oregano, crushed

2 tsp/10 g salt

½ tsp/1 g freshly ground black pepper

60 **Tortilla Chips** (page 998)

10 cilantro sprigs

5 fl oz/150 mL sour cream

10 fl oz/300 mL **Summer Squash Salsa** (recipe follows)

1. Cook each type of beans separately in boiling water until completely tender, about 90 minutes for the black beans and 1 hour for the kidney beans. Drain and cool to room temperature.

2. Fill a deep rondeau with 1 to 2 in/3 to 5 cm of corn oil, or use a deep fryer. Heat the oil to 350°F/177°C. Working in batches, fry the chiles very quickly on all sides so the skin blisters, about 3 minutes per batch.

3. Place the chiles in a large bowl, cover with plastic wrap, and allow them to "sweat" for 30 minutes.

4. Using the back of a paring knife, remove the blistered skin without cutting or damaging the chiles. Cut a slit down the length of each chile. Scrape out the seeds, making sure to leave the chiles whole.

5. For the filling, sweat the onions and garlic in the oil over medium heat for 2 to 3 minutes. Combine with the beans. Add the grated cheeses, herbs, half the salt, and the pepper. Mix gently together.

6. Fill each chile with 3 oz/85 g of the filling and roll, overlapping the cut edges.

7. Heat the poblanos rellenos in a 350°F/177°C oven until the filling is very hot, 18 to 20 minutes.

8. Serve each poblano relleno with 6 tortilla chips, 1 cilantro sprig, ½ fl oz/15 mL of sour cream, and 1 fl oz/30 mL of Summer Squash Salsa.

Summer Squash Salsa

Makes 32 fl oz/960 mL

1 yellow squash, seeded, small dice

1 zucchini, seeded, small dice

1½ oz/43 g small-dice carrots

6½ oz/184 g small-dice plum tomatoes

3 oz/85 g small-dice tomatillos

3 oz/85 g small-dice red onions

½ oz/14 g minced chipotle chiles

1½ tsp/1.50 g coarsely chopped marjoram

4 tsp/4 g cilantro, chiffonade

1 fl oz/30 mL extra-virgin olive oil

1 fl oz/30 mL rice wine vinegar

½ tsp/2.50 g sugar

salt, as needed

ground black pepper, as needed

1. Blanch the squash, zucchini, and carrots, separately, in boiling salted water until just tender. Shock in an ice bath and drain.

2. Combine with the remaining ingredients and mix well. Adjust seasoning with salt and pepper.

3. The salsa is ready to serve now, or it may be refrigerated for later use.

Sautéed Arugula

Makes 10 servings

4 lb/1.81 kg arugula

2 fl oz/60 mL vegetable or olive oil

½ oz/14 g minced shallots

2½ tsp/7.50 g minced garlic

salt, as needed

ground black pepper, as needed

1. Rinse and drain the arugula, removing any tough or split stems.

2. Heat the oil in a sauté pan, add the shallots, and sauté until they begin to turn translucent, 1 to 2 minutes. Add the garlic and sauté until it begins to release its aroma.

3. Add the arugula, filling the pan (the arugula will wilt down as it sautés). Toss or turn the arugula as it cooks.

4. Sauté the arugula until it is completely wilted and tender and very hot. Season with salt and pepper and serve immediately.

Stir-Fried Shanghai Bok Choy (Qinchao Shanghai Baicai)

Makes 10 servings

2 lb/907 g baby bok choy

2 fl oz/60 mL vegetable oil

8 garlic cloves, sliced thinly

salt, as needed

sugar, as needed

1. Cut the bok choy lengthwise in half. Score the cores to promote even cooking.

2. Blanch the bok choy in boiling salted water, shock in an ice bath, and drain well.

3. Heat the oil in a wok, add the garlic, and stir-fry until aromatic and light brown.

4. Add the bok choy and stir-fry to complete the cooking process. Add a small amount of water to the wok to keep the garlic from burning, if necessary. Season with salt and sugar.

5. Serve immediately.

Stir-Fried Shanghai Bok Choy (*Qinchao Shanghai Baicai*)

Summer Squash Noodles

Makes 10 servings

1 lb/454 g yellow squash, long julienne

1 lb/454 g zucchini, long julienne

4 oz/113 g leeks, long julienne

1½ oz/43 g butter

salt, as needed

ground black pepper, as needed

¾ oz/21 g minced herbs, such as tarragon, basil, and cilantro

1. Toss the squash, zucchini, and leeks together in a large bowl.

2. Heat the butter in a sauté pan over medium heat. Add the julienned vegetables and sauté them, tossing frequently, until they are heated through and tender, about 5 minutes.

3. Season the vegetables with salt and pepper. Add the chopped herbs and serve immediately.

Belgian Endive à la Meunière

Makes 10 servings

2 lb 8 oz/1.13 kg Belgian endive

1 oz/28 g salt

1 tbsp/15 g sugar

2 fl oz/60 mL lemon juice

6 fl oz/180 mL milk

salt, as needed

ground black pepper, as needed

2¼ oz/64 g all-purpose flour

1½ fl oz/45 mL clarified butter or oil

3 oz/85 g butter

½ oz/14 g chopped parsley

1. Remove any bruised or damaged outer endive leaves. Bring a large pot of water to a boil and season with salt, sugar, and ½ fl oz/15 mL of the lemon juice. Add the endive and boil until partially cooked, about 3 minutes. Drain well.

2. Trim the endive cores with a sharp knife (there should be enough core left to hold the leaves together) and flatten each head slightly by pressing down on it with the palm of your hand.

3. To finish the endive, dip in milk, season with salt and pepper, and dredge in flour, shaking off the excess.

4. Heat the clarified butter or oil over medium-high heat in a heavy skillet. Sauté the endive until crisp and brown on both sides, 3 to 4 minutes total cooking time. Remove the endive from the pan and keep warm.

5. Pour off any excess butter or oil from the pan. Add the whole butter and cook over medium heat until it begins to brown and take on a nutty aroma. Add the remaining lemon juice and the parsley and swirl until the mixture thickens slightly, 2 to 3 minutes. Pour the pan sauce over the endive and serve immediately.

Broccoli Rabe with Garlic and Hot Crushed Pepper (Cime di Broccoli con Aglio e Pepperoncino)

Makes 10 servings

4 lb/1.81 kg broccoli rabe, washed and tough stems trimmed

2 fl oz/60 mL extra-virgin olive oil

1 oz/28 g thinly sliced garlic

1¼ tsp/2.50 g red pepper flakes

4 fl oz/120 mL **Chicken Stock** (page 351), or as needed

salt, as needed

1 fl oz/30 mL lemon juice

1½ tsp/4.50 g lemon zest, finely grated

1. Bring a large pot of salted water to a boil. Working in small batches, add the broccoli rabe and cook until tender but firm, about 3 minutes. Shock the broccoli rabe in an ice bath and drain very well. Refrigerate if it is to be finished later.

2. Heat the oil in a sauté pan over medium-high heat. Add the garlic and pepper flakes and sauté until the garlic is lightly golden, about 2 minutes.

3. Add the broccoli rabe and stock and cook over high heat, mixing the broccoli rabe thoroughly to distribute the garlic and peppers evenly. Cook until most of the liquid evaporates, 2 to 3 minutes.

4. Season with salt and lemon juice. Serve immediately, garnished with the zest.

Garden Treasures

Makes 10 servings

1 lb/454 g broccoli florets

2 lb/907 g medium-dice carrots

3 oz/85 g medium-dice celery

3 fl oz/90 mL peanut oil

4 tsp/12 g minced ginger

4 tsp/12 g minced garlic

2 oz/57 g green onions, sliced on the bias

1 lb/454 g medium-dice zucchini

1 lb/454 g medium-dice yellow squash

salt, as needed

ground white pepper, as needed

1 fl oz/30 mL sesame oil

1. Blanch the broccoli, carrots, and celery separately in boiling salted water; drain, shock in an ice bath, and drain again. Do not overcook.

2. Heat the peanut oil in a wok, add the ginger, garlic, and green onions. Stir-fry until aromatic, about 1 minute.

3. Add the broccoli, carrots, and celery and stir-fry for 2 to 3 minutes. Add the zucchini and squash and stir-fry until tender.

4. Season with salt, pepper, and sesame oil. Serve while very hot.

Jardinière Vegetables

Makes 10 servings

9 oz/255 g carrot batonnet

9 oz/255 g celery batonnet

9 oz/255 g white turnip batonnet

9 oz/255 g shelled green peas

4 oz/113 g butter

salt, as needed

ground black pepper, as needed

sugar, as needed

1 tbsp/3 g chopped parsley

1. Blanch the vegetables separately in boiling salted water; drain, shock in an ice bath, and drain again.

2. Heat the butter in a sauté pan over medium heat. Add the vegetables (by individual servings or batches) and season with salt, pepper, and sugar. Toss or stir until the vegetables are evenly coated with the butter and very hot.

3. Add parsley and serve immediately.

Vegetable Julienne

Makes 10 servings

4 oz/113 g carrot julienne

4 oz/113 g celery julienne

4 oz/113 g leek julienne

2 oz/57 g butter

salt, as needed

ground black pepper, as needed

1. Blanch the vegetables separately in boiling salted water; drain, shock in an ice bath, and drain again.

2. Heat the butter in a sauté pan over medium heat. Add the vegetables (by individual servings or batches) and season with salt and pepper. Toss or stir until the vegetables are evenly coated with the butter and very hot.

3. Serve immediately.

Macédoine of Vegetables

Makes 10 servings

2 oz/57 g butter

2 oz/57 g large-dice mushrooms

½ oz/14 g minced shallots

2 oz/57 g large-dice onions

4 oz/113 g large-dice celery

6 oz/170 g large-dice zucchini

6 oz/170 g large-dice yellow squash

6 oz/170 g large-dice carrots, steamed or boiled until tender

6 oz/170 g large-dice white turnips, steamed or boiled until tender

6 oz/170 g large-dice rutabagas, steamed or boiled until tender

2 oz/57 g small-dice red pepper

chopped chives, as needed

chopped tarragon, as needed

chopped basil, as needed

salt, as needed

ground black pepper, as needed

1. Heat the butter in a large sauté pan over medium-high heat. Add the mushrooms and shallots and cook, stirring from time to time, until the moisture is reduced, 2 to 3 minutes.

2. Add the onions and celery and sauté until the onions are translucent, about 5 minutes.

3. Add the zucchini and squash and sauté until tender, 2 to 3 minutes.

4. Add the remaining vegetables. Sauté them until heated through, 2 minutes more.

5. Add the herbs and toss to mix. Season with salt and pepper. Serve immediately or keep them hot for service.

Mushrooms with Chiles and Garlic (Hongos con Guajillos y Ajo)

Makes 10 servings

2 fl oz/60 mL olive oil

2 lb/907 g white or cremini mushrooms, quartered

5 guajillo chiles, seeded, fine julienne

3 garlic cloves, minced

6 oz/170 g minced onions

salt, as needed

ground black pepper, as needed

1. Heat the oil in a large sauté pan over medium-high heat. Add the mushrooms, chiles, garlic, and onions and sauté until the mushrooms are tender, 5 to 6 minutes.

2. Season with salt and pepper. Serve immediately.

Spinach Pancakes

Makes 10 servings

12 fl oz/360 mL milk

1 oz/28 g butter, melted

4 eggs

12 oz/340 g all-purpose flour

1 tbsp/15 g sugar

2 lb/907 g spinach, blanched, squeezed dry, coarsely chopped

1 tsp/5 g salt

½ tsp/1 g ground black pepper

¼ tsp/0.50 g nutmeg

2 fl oz/60 mL vegetable oil

1. Mix the milk, butter, and eggs until they are thoroughly combined.

2. In a large bowl, stir together the flour and sugar.

3. Make a well in the center of the bowl and pour in the milk mixture; stir until a smooth batter forms.

4. Combine the spinach with the batter and season with salt, pepper, and nutmeg.

5. Heat a small amount of oil in a sauté pan over medium heat. Ladle 2 fl oz/60 mL of the batter into the hot pan for each pancake. Cook the spinach pancakes for 2 to 3 minutes, until the undersides are golden brown.

6. Turn the pancakes and continue to cook for an additional 3 to 4 minutes. Serve immediately or transfer to a holding pan to keep them hot for service.

Pan-Fried Zucchini

Makes 10 servings

2 lb 8 oz/1.13 kg zucchini

32 fl oz/960 mL vegetable oil

½ oz/14 g salt

1 lb 10 oz/738 g **Beer Batter** (page 599)

1. Slice the zucchini on the bias, ½ in/1 cm thick. Blot dry.

2. Pour the oil into a sauté pan about 2 in/5 cm deep. Heat to 325°F/163°C.

3. Season the zucchini slices with salt and dip them into the batter to coat both sides evenly. Allow any excess batter to drain back into the bowl. Carefully lay the zucchini in the hot fat. Pan fry on the first side until browned. Turn carefully and complete cooking on the second side.

4. Remove the zucchini from the oil, blot on absorbent toweling, and adjust seasoning with salt, if necessary. Serve immediately.

Corn Fritters

Makes 10 servings

2 lb 8 oz/1.13 kg corn kernels, fresh or frozen

2 eggs, beaten

2 oz/57 g Cheddar cheese, grated (optional)

4 oz/113 g all-purpose flour

2 oz/57 g sugar

1 tsp/5 g salt

¼ tsp/0.50 g ground black pepper

8 fl oz/240 mL oil, or as needed for pan frying

1. Combine the corn, eggs, and cheese. Combine the flour, sugar, salt, and pepper in a separate bowl and make a well in the center. Add the corn mixture to the flour mixture all at once. Stir just until a relatively smooth batter forms.

2. Heat about ½ in/1 cm of the oil in a sauté pan to 365°F/185°C and ladle 1 fl oz/30 mL of batter for each fritter into the hot oil.

3. Fry on the first side until golden brown, 2 to 3 minutes. Turn once and finish frying on the second side, 2 minutes more. Blot on paper towels, adjust seasoning with salt, if necessary, and serve while very hot.

NOTE
Add diced red or green peppers to the batter and/or 1 to 2 tsp/2 to 4 g of chili powder to the dry ingredients, if desired.

Vegetable Tempura

Makes 10 servings

16 fl oz/480 mL vegetable oil

8 fl oz/240 mL peanut oil

8 fl oz/240 mL sesame oil

2 chef's potatoes, ⅛- to ¼-in/3- to 6-mm-thick strips

2 onions, ⅛- to ¼-in/3- to 6-mm-thick strips

2 carrots, ⅛- to ¼-in/3- to 6-mm-thick strips

1 lb/454 g green beans, 2 in/5 cm long

20 shiso leaves

1 lb/454 g lotus root, ⅛-in/3-mm-thick slices

8 oz/227 g all-purpose flour, or as needed

Tempura Batter (page 595), as needed

20 fl oz/600 mL **Tempura Dipping Sauce** (page 595)

1. Combine the 3 oils in a deep pan and heat to 330° to 340°F/166° to 171°C.

2. Lightly dredge the vegetables in flour, dip in the batter, and immediately fry them until crispy and white or light golden brown.

3. Drain the tempura on a rack lined with paper towels to blot the oil.

4. Serve immediately with the dipping sauce.

Boniato Fries

Makes 10 servings

2 lb 8 oz/1.13 kg boniato or sweet potatoes

32 fl oz/960 mL vegetable oil

salt, as needed

ground black pepper, as needed

1. Peel the boniato and cut them into long julienne.

2. Heat the oil to 350°F/177°C. Fry the boniato in batches until golden brown.

3. Drain the boniato on paper towels and season with salt and pepper.

NOTE
Taro root or yucca can be fried this way also.

Fried Plantains

Fried Plantains

Makes 10 servings

32 fl oz/960 mL vegetable oil, or as needed for frying

3 plantains, not too ripe

salt, as needed

1. Heat the oil to 350°F/177°C in a rondeau or deep fryer.

2. Peel the plantains and slice very thinly on the bias on a mandoline or electric slicer.

3. Fry the plantains, turning often, until they are golden brown, 4 to 5 minutes. Work in batches if necessary. Drain on paper towels and season with salt as soon as they are out of the fryer. Serve immediately.

Tostones: Slice the plantains ½-in/1-cm thick and fry as above. Press them to a thickness of about ¼ in/6 mm with a small sauteuse. Combine 1 oz/28 g salt, 4 fl oz/120 mL water, and 4 minced garlic cloves. Dip the precooked plantains in this mixture. Shake excess water off and deep fry a second time. Drain them on paper towels and sprinkle with salt. Serve immediately.

Ratatouille

Makes 10 servings

3 fl oz/90 mL olive oil, or as needed

12 oz/340 g medium-dice onions

¾ oz/21 g minced garlic

1 oz/28 g tomato paste

4 oz/113 g medium-dice green peppers

1 lb/454 g medium-dice eggplant

12 oz/340 g medium-dice zucchini

6 oz/170 g quartered or sliced white mushrooms

8 oz/227 g peeled, seeded, and medium-diced tomatoes

4 fl oz/120 mL **Chicken Stock** (page 351) or **Vegetable Stock** (page 353), or as needed

salt, as needed

ground black pepper, as needed

1 oz/28 g chopped herbs, such as basil, parsley, and oregano

1. In a large pot or rondeau, heat the oil over medium heat. Add the onions and sauté until translucent, 4 to 5 minutes. Add the garlic and sauté until soft, about 1 minute.

2. Turn the heat to medium-low. Add the tomato paste and cook until it completely coats the onions and develops a deeper color, 1 to 2 minutes.

3. Add the vegetables in the following sequence: peppers, eggplant, zucchini, mushrooms, and tomatoes. Cook each vegetable until it softens (2 to 3 minutes each) before adding the next.

4. Add the stock and turn the heat to low, allowing the vegetables to stew. The vegetables should be moist but not soupy.

5. Stew until the vegetables are tender and flavorful. Season with salt, pepper, and fresh herbs. Serve immediately.

Braised Greens

Makes 10 servings

4 lb/1.81 kg collard greens or kale

4 oz/113 g minced bacon

8 oz/227 g minced onions

3 garlic cloves, minced

5 fl oz/150 mL white wine

1 ham hock

10 fl oz/300 mL **Chicken Stock** (page 351)

salt, as needed

ground black pepper, as needed

1. Strip the leaves from the collards or kale. Cut into bite-size pieces. Blanch the greens in salted water. Shock in an ice bath, drain, and squeeze out the excess moisture.

2. In a large skillet, render the bacon over medium heat. When the bacon is a light golden, add the onions and garlic and sweat until aromatic. Add the blanched greens, deglaze with the wine, and reduce by half.

3. Add the ham hock and stock. Season with salt and pepper. Braise in a 350°F/177°C oven until tender, 30 to 45 minutes.

4. Remove the greens from the pan and reduce the liquid. Add the liquid back to the greens and adjust seasoning with salt and pepper. Serve immediately.

Braised Fennel in Butter

Makes 10 servings

4 lb 8 oz/2.04 kg fennel

6 oz/170 g butter

12 fl oz/360 mL **Chicken Stock** (page 351) or **Vegetable Stock** (page 353)

2 fl oz/60 mL lemon juice

salt, as needed

ground black pepper, as needed

4 oz/113 g grated Parmesan

1. Cut the stems from the fennel and trim the root ends. Cut from stem to root end to make halves or quarters, depending upon the size of the bulbs. Bring a pot of salted water to a boil, add the fennel, and boil until partially cooked, about 6 minutes. Drain and reserve.

2. Heat half of the butter in a rondeau. Add the fennel and turn to coat evenly with the butter. Add the stock and season with lemon juice, salt, and pepper. Bring the stock to a simmer, cover the pan, and braise the fennel in a 325°F/163°C oven until it is very tender, but still holds its shape, about 45 minutes. The liquid should be nearly cooked away; if necessary, simmer over medium heat until it has reduced.

3. Remove the cover from the pan and scatter the Parmesan in an even layer over the fennel. Dot with the remaining butter.

4. Place the fennel, uncovered, in a 450°F/232°C oven or under a broiler until the butter and cheese form a golden crust. Serve immediately.

Braised Red Cabbage

Makes 10 servings

½ fl oz/15 mL vegetable oil or rendered bacon fat

5 oz/142 g medium-dice onions

7 oz/198 g medium-dice Granny Smith apples

8 fl oz/240 mL water, or as needed

1½ fl oz/45 mL red wine

1½ fl oz/45 mL red wine vinegar

1 oz/28 g sugar

1½ oz/43 g red currant jelly

1 cinnamon stick

1 clove

1 bay leaf

2 juniper berries

1 lb 8 oz/680 g red cabbage, chiffonade

¾ tsp/2.25 g arrowroot (optional)

½ tsp/2.50 g salt

¼ tsp/0.50 g ground black pepper

1. Heat the oil or bacon fat in a large pot or rondeau over medium-low heat. Add the onions and apples and sweat until the onions are translucent and the apples are slightly soft, about 5 minutes.

2. Add the water, wine, vinegar, sugar, and jelly. The flavor should be tart and strong.

3. Make a sachet by combining the cinnamon stick, clove, bay leaf, and juniper berries. Add the sachet and cabbage. Cover and braise in a 350°F/177°C oven until the cabbage is tender, 15 to 20 minutes. Check regularly to be sure the liquids have not evaporated completely. Add more water if necessary.

4. Remove the sachet. Dissolve the arrowroot in cold water. Use this to thicken the cooking liquid slightly, if necessary. This will give additional sheen to the cabbage.

5. Season with salt and pepper. Serve immediately.

Braised Romaine

Makes 10 servings

4 lb 8 oz/2.04 kg romaine lettuce

2½ oz/71 g butter

5 oz/142 g small-dice onions

5 oz/142 g thinly sliced carrots

10 fl oz/300 mL **Brown Veal Stock** (page 352), **Chicken Stock** (page 351), or **Vegetable Stock** (page 353)

salt, as needed

ground black pepper, as needed

6 oz/170 g slab bacon, sliced ⅛ in/3 mm thick

1. Remove or trim the romaine to remove any blemishes or wilted leaves. Trim the cores. Bring a large pot of salted water to a boil. Blanch the whole heads for 1 minute, until the color turns bright and the leaves are softened. Drain the lettuce, rinse in cold water to stop the cooking, and drain again.

2. To make individual servings, cut the romaine lengthwise into 10 equal servings. Cut away the cores. Roll up each portion into a cylinder, squeezing out excess water as you roll. To make larger servings that can be sliced for service, remove the larger outer leaves and arrange them to form a large rectangle on a sheet of plastic wrap or parchment paper. Remove the cores from the heads and arrange the leaves evenly over the outer leaves. Roll up as for a jelly roll, squeezing to remove the water.

3. Heat the butter in a rondeau over medium heat. Add the onions and carrots and sweat over low heat until they are tender and starting to release their juices, 8 to 10 minutes. Add the romaine to the pan in an even layer. Add the stock and bring it to a simmer. Season with salt and pepper. Top the romaine with the slices of bacon.

4. Cover the pan and braise the lettuce in a 350°F/177°C oven for 25 to 30 minutes, or until it is very tender and the bacon is crisp. Remove the cover during the final 10 minutes of cooking time if necessary to properly reduce the cooking liquid and brown the bacon.

5. Remove the romaine from the braising liquid and keep warm. Degrease the liquid and adjust seasoning with salt and pepper.

6. Serve the romaine with the sauce on heated plates.

Braised Sauerkraut

Makes 10 servings

4 fl oz/120 mL rendered pork fat or vegetable oil

8 oz/227 g small-dice onions

7 oz/198 g grated Golden Delicious apples

6 oz/170 g grated chef's potatoes

2 lb 8 oz/1.13 kg **Homemade Sauerkraut** (page 654)

1 tsp/2 g caraway seeds

12 juniper berries

32 fl oz/960 mL **Brown Pork Stock** (page 352) or **Brown Veal Stock** (page 352)

1. Heat the pork fat or oil in a large rondeau over medium heat. Add the onions and apples and sweat until tender and translucent, 8 to 10 minutes.

2. Add the potatoes and sweat a few minutes longer. Add the sauerkraut, caraway seeds, juniper berries, and stock, and bring to a boil. Cover and braise in a 325°F/163°C oven until the stock has nearly cooked away and the sauerkraut has a good flavor, 1 to 1½ hours. If the sauerkraut has too much liquid, place it on top of the stove and reduce the liquid as necessary.

3. The sauerkraut is ready to serve now, or it may be rapidly cooled and refrigerated for later service.

French-Style Peas

Makes 10 servings

2 oz/57 g pearl onions

4 oz/113 g butter

1 lb 4 oz/567 g shelled green peas

12 oz/340 g Boston lettuce chiffonade

4 fl oz/120 mL **Chicken Stock** (page 351)

salt, as needed

pepper, as needed

3 tbsp/45 mL flour

1. Bring a large pot of water to a rolling boil. Add the pearl onions and blanch for 1 minute. Remove the onions, rinse in cool water until they can be handled, and remove the skin.

2. Heat 2 oz/57 g of the butter in a pan over low heat and add the pearl onions. Cook, covered, until they are tender and translucent, about 8 to 10 minutes.

3. Add the peas, lettuce, and stock to the onions. Season with salt and pepper. Bring the stock to a gentle simmer and return the cover to the pan. Stew the peas until fully cooked and tender, about 3 to 4 minutes.

4. Blend the remaining butter with the flour and add gradually to the peas in small pieces until the cooking liquid is lightly thickened. Adjust seasoning if necessary and serve on heated plates.

Chapter Twenty-six

Cooking Potatoes

The potato is one of the most versatile vegetables. It is found in nearly every menu category as the main component of appetizers, soups, entrées, and side dishes; it is also an important ingredient in such preparations as soufflés, pancakes, and breads.

Potato Varieties

Potato varieties differ in starch and moisture content, skin and flesh color, and shape. Sweet potatoes and yams, although not botanically related to the potato, share several characteristics with it and can be treated in the same manner. Each cooking technique produces a markedly different texture, flavor, and appearance in potatoes. Knowing the natural characteristics of each kind of potato and the ways in which a particular technique can either enhance or detract from these characteristics is important to any chef.

Low moisture/high starch

Potatoes in this category include Idaho or russet (also known as baking or bakers) and some fingerling varieties. The higher the starch content, the more granular and dry a potato is after it is cooked. The flesh is easy to flake or mash. These potatoes, desirable for baking and puréeing, are also good for frying because the low moisture content makes them less likely to splatter. Their low moisture and natural tendency to absorb moisture also make them a good choice for scalloped or other casserole-style potato dishes.

Moderate moisture and starch

Potatoes in this category include so-called all-purpose, boiling, chef's, Maine, and US 1. It also includes red-skinned, waxy yellow (e.g., Yellow Finn and Yukon Gold), and certain fingerling varieties. Potatoes with moderate amounts of moisture and starch tend to hold their shape even after they are cooked until tender. This makes them a good choice for boiling, steaming, sautéing, oven roasting, and braising or stewing. They are frequently used in potato salads and soups. Many chefs like to use waxy yellow potatoes for baking, puréeing, and casserole-style dishes because of their outstanding flavor.

High moisture/low starch

Potatoes in this category include "new" (any potato that is harvested when less than 1½ in/4 cm in diameter) and some fingerling varieties. The skin of a new potato is tender and does not need to be removed prior to cooking or eating. Their naturally sweet, fresh flavor is best showcased by simple techniques such as boiling, steaming, or oven roasting.

Boiling Potatoes

Boiled potatoes are among the simplest of preparations, with a subtle, earthy flavor. In the absence of a great number of aromatic or supporting flavors, attention must be focused on good technique and the careful selection and handling of the potato itself. Each potato variety has a unique texture and taste once boiled. Some potatoes hold their shape even when boiled until very tender and have a soft, smooth consistency. Others have a mealier consistency and a tendency to break apart when fully cooked. Both boiled and steamed potatoes can be cooked to a range of doneness: partially cooked for sautéed dishes, fully cooked for purées, and cooked and cooled for salads.

Select and prepare the ingredients and equipment

Moderate- or high-moisture potatoes are a good choice for dishes where the potatoes are presented whole, since they hold their shape when boiled. Low-moisture potatoes are preferable for purées.

Scrub the potatoes or peel them and remove the eyes and sprouts. Potatoes may be peeled before boiling; tender-skinned fingerlings or new potatoes are usually prepared unpeeled, called *en chemise* in French. If the potatoes are to be cooked whole, try to make sure the shapes are similar in size. If necessary, cut the potatoes into regular, even shapes.

Green spots in a potato must be peeled away completely. The green color indicates the presence of a toxin called solanine, which is harmful when eaten in large quantities. This same toxin is present in the potato sprouts and eyes; they should be completely removed as well.

Raw potatoes will discolor after they are peeled, first turning light pink and eventually, dark gray or black. To prevent this discoloration, submerge peeled or cut raw potatoes in cold water until time to cook. When possible, use the soaking water to cook the potatoes so any nutrients leached into it are retained.

To ensure that potatoes cook evenly, start them in a cold liquid, usually water, though some recipes specify stock or milk for a special flavor, texture, or appearance. Salt is usually added to the cooking liquid. If using salt, add enough to enhance the potato's flavor. If parcooking, add slightly more salt than if fully cooking the potatoes. Evaluate the quality of the finished boiled potatoes. A properly boiled potato has a delicate aroma and flavor and a soft texture. Boiled potatoes to be served as is should hold their shape but still be extremely tender. Seasonings added to the cooking water, as well as any additional finishing or garnishing ingredients, should be appropriate to the finished dish.

Other optional ingredients include herbs and spices, which may be added for various effects. For example, saffron or turmeric gives boiled potatoes a golden color and a special flavor. Herbs are often added to the potatoes as they are reheated in butter—parslied new potatoes are a classic example. Use butter, cream, sour cream, and sauces to dress the potatoes after they are boiled and immediately before they are served. When potatoes are held briefly before service, these finishing ingredients may be used as the medium for reheating them.

The equipment needs for boiling potatoes are simple: a cooking pot large enough to hold the water and potatoes, a slotted spoon or colander for draining the potatoes, and holding containers. Sheet pans may be used to hold the potatoes in a single layer for quick cooling or drying.

Steaming Potatoes

Steaming can be used as an alternative to boiling. To properly steam potatoes, prepare them as for boiling, taking care to make even cuts or to select like-sized whole potatoes to cook in the same batch. The potatoes should be arranged in even layers on the racks or inserts to let the steam circulate completely and encourage thorough, rapid cooking.

Convection or pressure steamers are good for steaming large quantities of potatoes. They allow for the preparation of batches as needed throughout a meal period, and they are well suited to the intense demands of a banquet or institutional feeding situation.

When using a stovetop steamer, remember that the larger the potatoes, the longer the cooking time and the more liquid that will be required. Bring the cooking liquid in the bottom of the steamer to a rolling boil before adding the potato-filled inserts or tiers. The potatoes should be arranged so that the steam can circulate around them. Do not stack the potatoes or overcrowd the tiers or inserts. Various herbs, spices, or aromatic vegetables may be added to the cooking liquid or directly to the potatoes to allow the steam to carry the flavor to the potatoes.

Tip

If you are unsure of the moisture/starch content of your potatoes, a simple test can be done to gauge the starch content. Prepare a brine of 11 parts water to 1 part salt. Place the potatoes in the brine. Those that float contain less starch.

A basic formula for 10 servings of boiled potatoes

4 lb/1.81 kg moderate- or high-moisture potatoes, weighed before peeling and cutting, or
3 lb 4 oz/1.47 kg prepped potatoes

Enough cold liquid to completely submerge the potatoes

Salt and other seasonings

Finishing and garnishing ingredients

Place the potatoes in a pot of an appropriate size and cover completely with cold water. Add salt and/or other seasonings as necessary to the cooking liquid. Starting the cooking process with cold liquid allows the heat to penetrate slowly and evenly, giving the potatoes a uniform texture without overcooking the exterior flesh. Bring to a boil and cook at a simmer or low boil until the potatoes are done.

To test for doneness, taste a piece or pierce with the tines of a fork. If there is no resistance, the potatoes are properly cooked. If the potatoes are to be only partially cooked, there should be increasing resistance as the fork is inserted deeper into the potato.

Drain the potatoes as soon as they are done and dry them to improve their flavor and texture. Potatoes can be dried by returning them to the pot and placing the pot, uncovered, over very low heat. Or spread them out in a single layer on a sheet pan and place the pan in a warm oven. Potatoes are sufficiently dried when steam no longer rises from them.

If the potatoes were cooked in the skin, remove the skin as soon as they are cool enough to handle. Use a paring knife to remove eyes or black spots. To hold potatoes for a short time (less than an hour), cover them loosely with a damp, clean cloth and keep warm.

Puréeing Potatoes

Puréed potatoes are an important basic preparation. The purée can be blended with milk and butter to make whipped potatoes, with egg yolks to make duchesse potatoes or potato croquettes, or with pâte à choux to fry as pommes lorette.

Potatoes to be puréed are first cooked by boiling, steaming, or baking in the skin. After they are puréed, the potatoes may be flavored with oil, butter, cream, garlic, or other vegetable purées.

Low- to moderate-moisture potatoes, such as russets and waxy yellow potatoes, make the best purées. Have ready boiled or steamed potatoes that have been drained and dried and that are still very hot. Hot baked potatoes may also be used. In addition to salt and pepper, which are standard seasonings for puréed potatoes, many other ingredients may be added for special flavors.

All additional ingredients should be either heated to the same temperature as the purée or at room temperature. Choices include milk or cream, soft (not melted) butter, chicken or meat broth, garlic, shallots, green onions, horseradish, mustard, cheese, or purées of other vegetables, such as parsnip or celeriac. Egg yolks or pâte à choux are needed for duchesse and lorette potatoes.

A food mill or potato ricer gives the best texture for puréed potatoes. Use a handheld potato masher for a coarser texture. Puréed potatoes may be blended with other ingredients by hand using a wooden spoon or with an electric mixer for whipped potatoes. A pastry bag with star and/or plain tips will be needed if the purée is to be decoratively piped onto plates or shaped in various ways.

A basic formula for 10 servings of potato purée

4 lb/1.81 kg low-moisture potatoes, weighed before peeling and cutting, or 3 lb 4 oz/1.47 kg prepped potatoes

12 to 16 fl oz/360 to 480 mL milk or cream

Salt, pepper, or other seasonings

1. **Cook the potatoes until very tender by boiling, steaming, or baking.** Warm the milk or cream. Potatoes may be peeled and cubed before cooking to shorten cooking and drying time when boiling (see pages 769–770) or steaming (see page 770). To bake potatoes for use in purées, leave them whole and in the skin. Season, pierce, and bake until very tender. When they are done, immediately halve them and scoop out the flesh. Use a clean side towel to protect your hands as you work.

Push hot drained and dried potatoes through a warmed food mill or ricer. For best results, the potatoes must be hot and the equipment heated. Properly cooked potatoes should pass through the food mill with no resistance. Check the bowl periodically to make sure that it is not getting overfull. Do not use a blender or food processor. The texture of the potato may become soupy, sticky, and unable to hold its shape. Large quantities of potatoes may be run through a grinder directly into the bowl of a mixer.

2. **Add seasonings and any additional ingredients, as desired or according to the recipe.** Be sure that other ingredients are at the correct temperature when added. Milk or cream should be at or near a simmer. Butter should be at room temperature. The eggs must be folded into the appareil. Season the potato purée carefully with salt and pepper. Stir or fold in such flavorings as puréed roasted garlic. Stir with a spoon by hand or use the paddle attachment of an electric mixer. Do not overwork; this will release too much starch from the potatoes, giving the purée a heavy, sticky consistency.

3. **To make Duchesse potatoes, blend potato purée and pipe even portions on parchment-lined sheet pans.** Potato purée can also be mounded or piped onto serving plates.

Puréed potatoes may be held for service over a hot-water bath or in a steam table, covered directly on the surface with plastic wrap. Do not hold purées for too long, or the quality will begin to degrade.

4. **Cook Duchesse potatoes, as shown here, until a rich golden brown.** A good potato purée is smooth, light in texture, and able to hold its shape when dropped from a spoon. It should be a consistently creamy purée, with no evidence that fat has separated from the purée.

Purées to be used in dishes that are subsequently baked, sautéed, or deep fried may be refrigerated for up to several hours. Once the final cooking is completed, they should be served immediately.

Flavoring and Seasoning Potato Purée

Basic pureed potatoes contain milk, salt, and pepper, but there are many additional ingredients that can be added or substituted to suit your needs or taste.

Milk is probably the most common liquid used for making puréed potatoes. Try substituting some or all of the milk with one of the following to create a different flavor and texture.

> **Broth (vegetable, poultry, beef, or veal)**
> **Heavy cream**
> **Stock**

Other common flavoring or seasoning ingredients include, but are not limited to:

> **Chopped fresh chives or green onions**
> **Chopped fresh herbs, such as parsley, rosemary, or sage**
> **Grated cheese**
> **Olive oil**
> **Puréed vegetables, such as carrots, butternut squash, or celeriac**
> **Roasted or sautéed garlic**
> **Sautéed onions**

Baking and Roasting Potatoes

The classic baked potato is served in its crisp skin and garnished with butter, salt, pepper, and, perhaps, sour cream and chives. When potatoes are cooked in an oven without any added liquid or steam, they develop an intense flavor and a dry, light texture. High-starch potatoes, like Idahos or russets, become mealy; the higher the moisture content of the potato, the creamier and moister the baked potato will be.

Baked potatoes are often served as is, with their skins, but there are other uses and presentations for them. The flesh can be scooped from the shell and puréed. This purée can be served on its own, or returned to the hollowed-out skin in the preparation known as stuffed or twice-baked potatoes. When oven roasting, the potatoes are cooked in oil, butter, or rendered juices from a roasted item and cooked until browned on the outside and completely tender on the inside.

Low-moisture potatoes are generally best for baking, although yellow waxy potatoes also yield good results. Low- or high-moisture potatoes may be used for oven roasting. Scrub potatoes well. For a relatively thick-skinned potato, a brush works well. For new potatoes, use a cloth. Blot the potatoes dry before placing them in a pan to prevent an excess of steam when they start to bake. Pierce the skin in a few places to allow the steam that builds up during baking to escape. Never wrap the potato in foil before baking; the result is similar to steaming. The skin will not become crisp, and there is a noticeable flavor difference. For the same reasons, baked potatoes cannot be prepared successfully in a microwave oven. Some chefs believe that baking potatoes on a bed of salt or rubbing the skin lightly with oil encourages the development of a crisp skin and a delicate, fluffy interior.

For oven-roasted potatoes, scrub or peel them and cut into the desired shape. Toss in fat (fat and drippings from roasted meats, oil, clarified butter, lard, goose fat, etc.) and season as desired with salt and pepper, fresh or dried herbs, or spices.

Equipment needs for baking potatoes are minimal. The only truly essential piece of equipment is the oven. Potatoes can be placed directly on the oven racks; they can also be arranged on sheet pans, making it easier to move them in and out of the oven, particularly when dealing with large quantities. Puréeing equipment, such as a potato ricer or a food mill, is also needed if stuffing the potatoes. Have holding and serving pieces available as necessary. For oven-roasted potatoes, sheet pans or shallow roasting pans that can hold the potatoes in a single layer are needed. Also needed are utensils for stirring the potatoes as they roast and holding and serving pieces.

Evaluate the quality of the finished baked or roasted potatoes. A properly baked potato has very crisp skin and is tender enough to mash easily when fully cooked. Serve baked or roasted potatoes as soon as they are done. This assures the best possible flavor, good texture, and optimal service temperature.

A basic formula for 10 servings of baked potatoes

10 baking potatoes (about 6 oz/170 g each) or
4 lb/1.81 kg low-moisture or yellow waxy potatoes, scrubbed

Salt or oil to lightly rub the skin of the potato (optional)

Finishing and garnishing ingredients

A basic formula for 10 servings of oven-roasted potatoes

4 lb/1.81 kg moderate- to high-moisture potatoes, weighed before peeling and cutting, or
3 lb 4 oz/1.47 kg prepped potatoes

Enough cooking fat to lightly coat the potatoes

Salt and other seasonings

Finishing and garnishing ingredients

To bake potatoes whole in the skin, scrub them, blot dry, and rub with oil or salt if desired. Pierce them with a fork to let steam escape as the potatoes bake. Whole potatoes may be placed on the oven racks or on sheet pans. If placed on sheet pans, turn the potatoes once during baking because the sides in contact with the pan may become slightly soggy.

For oven roasting, scrub, dry, peel and then cut the potatoes into a uniform shape if desired. Arrange them in a single layer on a sheet pan or in a roasting pan.

Season the potatoes, pierce, and bake or roast them until they are tender. It takes about 1 hour for a 6-oz/170-g potato to bake. To test for doneness, pierce the potato with a fork. If there is no resistance when it enters the flesh, the potato is done. Stir oven-roasted potatoes as often as necessary during the roasting time to ensure even browning. To test for doneness, taste a piece or pierce it with a fork.

Serve baked and oven-roasted potatoes immediately. If this is not possible, they can be held, uncovered, for less than an hour in a warm place. However, the steam trapped in the interior can cause the crisp skin to become soggy over time. Stuffed potatoes may be prepared in advance and held, covered, and refrigerated. Reheat and brown just prior to service.

Baking Potatoes en Casserole

Potatoes en casserole are baked in combination with cream or a custard. Scalloped, au gratin, and dauphinoise potatoes are all good examples. For dishes prepared en casserole, peeled and sliced potatoes (either raw or parcooked to speed baking time) are combined with flavored heavy cream, a sauce, or uncooked custard, and then slowly baked until the potatoes are extremely tender but set well enough to hold a shape when cut for service.

Low-moisture potatoes, because of their tendency to absorb liquid, produce casseroled potatoes that are very tender. Waxy yellow potatoes are also often prepared en casserole; these have a slightly more noticeable texture and a golden color.

Scrub and peel the potatoes and remove the eyes. Slice the potatoes thinly, or cut into an even dice or tourné. Thoroughly dry raw potatoes that have been held in water before combining them with the other ingredients. Excess water can adversely affect the flavor and final texture of the dish. Blot dry parcooked potatoes.

Have the liquid component of the dish (cream, custard, or stock, for example) hot before combining it with the potatoes. This allows the dish to reach cooking temperature more quickly, thus shortening the cooking time.

Salt and pepper are basic for any en casserole dish. Other spices are often required. Many of these dishes call for one or more grated cheeses, such as Gruyère and/or Parmesan.

Additional ingredients may be used to introduce color, flavor, and texture. Common options include herbs, mushrooms, mustard, and bread crumbs. En casserole dishes are prepared in hotel pans or similar baking pans and dishes. Liberally grease the baking pan or dish with butter or oil to prevent sticking. Additional helpful, but not necessarily essential, equipment includes a mandoline for cutting evenly thin slices of potato and a large offset spatula for serving individual servings of the dish.

A basic formula for 10 servings of potatoes en casserole

3 lb 4 oz/1.47 kg low-moisture or waxy yellow potatoes, weighed before peeling and cutting, or 2 lb 12 oz/1.25 kg prepped potatoes

24 to 30 fl oz/720 to 900 mL liquid (milk, half-and-half, stock, or sauce)

2 to 3 eggs or egg yolks (optional)

4 to 5 oz/113 to 142 g grated cheese or other topping (optional)

1. **Use a mandoline to produce very thin, even slices of potato quickly and efficiently.** Use low-moisture or waxy yellow potatoes. Parcook in the liquid called for in the recipe, if desired.

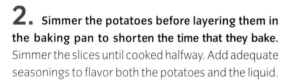

2. Simmer the potatoes before layering them in the baking pan to shorten the time that they bake. Simmer the slices until cooked halfway. Add adequate seasonings to flavor both the potatoes and the liquid.

3. Layer the potatoes evenly in a buttered baking pan. Arrange raw or parcooked potatoes in single layers, separating the slices so they will cook evenly. Add aromatic ingredients and seasonings, such as sliced garlic, cheese, or salt and pepper, to each layer for the best distribution of flavor.

4. **Pour the hot cooking liquid evenly over the potatoes.** Have cream, sauces, and drippings very hot; custards should be heated but not at a boil. Shake the pan gently to distribute the liquid evenly between the layers.

Add topping ingredients now or after baking, as necessary. Many en casserole dishes are referred to as gratins. The surface of the gratin gradually browns and forms a crust.

Bake in a warm oven (300° to 325°F/149° to 163°C) until the potatoes are just tender and the top is golden brown. The warm temperature for baking avoids curdling, especially with custards. A very creamy texture can best be achieved by baking en casserole dishes in a hot-water bath.

If the top begins to brown too quickly, reduce the oven temperature and sprinkle the dish lightly with milk or stock to moisten and cool it down. If the potatoes are done before the top browns, place the dish briefly under a salamander or broiler to brown.

5. **Evaluate the quality of the finished potatoes en casserole.** In a good potatoes en casserole, the potatoes are moist and tender; they hold their shape when cut into servings and placed on the plate.

The sauce is thick and very smooth, not runny, grainy, or curdled. The cheese should be browned and crisped for extra flavor. These dishes are particularly suitable for banquet because they are easily divided into servings.

Dishes can be held throughout a typical service period. Cover the dish loosely with foil and hold it in a warm place. If necessary, reheat the potatoes in an oven or brown them lightly under a salamander or broiler just before serving.

Sautéing Potatoes

Home fries, potatoes Anna, potato pancakes, hash browns, rösti, and Lyonnaise potatoes are prepared by sautéing. Sautéed potatoes combine a browned and crisp exterior with a tender, moist interior. The cooking fat plays a significant role in the flavor of the finished dish, and choices range from the taste of Anna-style or rösti potatoes, cooked in liberal amounts of butter, to the more rustic flavor of hash browns or home fries, sautéed in lard or goose fat. The key to successful sautéed potato dishes is in preparing the potatoes so that they become fully cooked just as the exterior has finished developing a good color and texture.

Moderate-moisture potatoes give the best texture and appearance to sautéed dishes. Scrub and peel the potatoes, and remove the eyes. Cut the potatoes into even slices, dice, julienne, tourné, or balls. If the potatoes are peeled and cut in advance, hold them submerged in cold water until it is time to cook them. Drain and blot them dry on absorbent toweling immediately before sautéing to avoid splattering. To shorten the cooking time, partially or fully cook the potatoes in advance by steaming or boiling. Drain and dry them as described on page 771.

Different kinds of cooking fat may be used, singly or in combination, for the best flavor in the finished dish. They include vegetable oil, olive oil, clarified butter, or rendered duck, goose, or bacon fat.

Season the potatoes with salt and pepper during cooking. A wide range of herbs and spices, vegetables, and meats can be combined with potatoes to produce a dish with a special flavor or appearance. Among them are onions, shallots, and green onions; diced green and red peppers; or diced bacon or ham. Finishing ingredients, such as heated cream, melted butter, heated sour cream, or grated cheese, may be added to the potatoes during the actual cooking process or after they have been cooked until tender.

Choose a sauté pan large enough to hold the potatoes without crowding. Cast-iron pans are especially good for potatoes because they can create a crust of exceptional crispness. Spatulas, serving pieces, and absorbent toweling for draining excess fat may also be necessary.

A basic formula for 10 servings of sautéed potatoes

4 lb/1.81 kg moderate-moisture potatoes, weighed before peeling and cutting, or 3 lb 4 oz/1.47 kg prepped potatoes

Cooking fat (oil, clarified butter, rendered duck, goose, or bacon fat)

Salt and other seasonings

Finishing and garnishing ingredients

1. **Scrub and peel raw potatoes and cut, slice, or grate them into the desired shape.** If the potatoes are held in water before cooking, drain and blot them dry before sautéing. Some dishes may call for the potatoes to be simmered until partially cooked either before or after they are sliced or cut.

Be sure to use enough cooking fat to coat the pan generously to prevent the potatoes from sticking and falling apart as they cook. The fat must be hot, so that the crust begins to develop immediately. This crust assures the proper color, flavor, and texture and also prevents the potatoes from absorbing too much fat. Brown the potatoes on one side evenly before flipping them over. Stir the potatoes or shake the pan occasionally as the potatoes cook, to brown evenly. In general, add garnishes or finishing ingredients when the potatoes have almost finished cooking.

For the best flavor and texture, serve sautéed potatoes immediately after they are cooked. If necessary, however, they may be held for 5 to 10 minutes, uncovered, in a warm place.

2. **Evaluate the quality of the finished sautéed potatoes. Sautéed potatoes should have a golden crisp exterior and a tender interior.** Properly sautéed potatoes have a rich flavor from the browning of the potatoes as well as from the cooking fat itself. Use seasonings to bring out the flavor of the potatoes and garnishing and finishing ingredients that further enhance the flavor by adding their own flavors, textures, and colors to the finished presentation.

Flavoring and Seasoning Sautéed Potatoes

To flavor and season sautéed potatoes, try one or a combination of any of the following:

The fat used for frying the potatoes will impart significant flavor. Any of the following are commonly used alone or in combination depending on the smoke point and desired flavor.

> Clarified butter
> Olive oil
> Rendered duck or goose fat
> Vegetable oil

The addition of certain meats is also common for seasoning sautéed potatoes:

> Bacon
> Pancetta

Herbs, spices, and aromatic vegetables, added at the proper moment will add flavor and beautiful color:

> Chopped celery
> Chopped fresh garlic
> Chopped fresh herbs such as parsley, rosemary, and chives
> Chopped fresh jalapeños
> Chopped peppers

Deep Frying Potatoes

French fries and steak fries, as well as waffle-cut, matchstick, and soufflé potatoes, are all deep-fried potatoes. They seem simple to make, but must be done carefully if excellent quality is to be achieved. Most deep-fried potatoes prepared from the raw state are first blanched in oil heated to 300° to 325°F/149° to 163°C until tender and almost translucent. They are then drained thoroughly and held until just before service. At that time, they are finished in oil heated to 350° to 375°F/177° to 191°C.

Blanching assures that the finished potato has the proper color, texture, and flavor and that it cooks thoroughly without becoming greasy or scorched. It is especially important to blanch soufflé potatoes so that they puff adequately. Potatoes cut very thinly (e.g., matchstick potatoes) can usually be cooked in a single step, without first blanching. Deep-fried potatoes, such as lorette, croquette, and dauphine, are made from a purée.

Low-moisture potatoes are best for deep frying. Scrub and peel them, and remove the eyes. Cut the potatoes into even slices, julienne, batonnet, or other cuts. If the potatoes are peeled and cut in advance of cooking, hold them submerged in cold water. Rinse the potatoes in several changes of cold water if indicated, and drain and dry them thoroughly to prevent splattering when they are added to the oil. Rinsing the potatoes in several changes of cold water removes the surface starch and helps prevent the potatoes from sticking together. Potatoes that are to be deep fried for such preparations as straw or matchstick potatoes, in particular, should be rinsed so they don't clump together as they cook. Potatoes used for deep-fried potato nests and cakes need the cohesiveness provided by the surface starch and should not be rinsed. Choose a neutral oil with a high smoke point for frying the potatoes. Deep-fried potatoes are customarily seasoned with salt after frying and prior to service. Condiments—ketchup and malt vinegar are the most common—may be served with them.

Use either a frying kettle or a deep fryer. Electric or gas deep fryers are excellent for doing a great deal of deep frying because they maintain even temperatures. They are also put together in such a way that it is relatively easy to clean them and care for the oil properly. Lacking a freestanding fryer, use a deep kettle or pot, such as a stockpot, instead. Use a thermometer to monitor and control the temperature. Once the correct frying temperature is reached, adjust the heat so that the temperature remains relatively constant. Other equipment, such as baskets, tongs, spiders, and containers lined with absorbent toweling, should also be available.

A basic formula for 10 servings of deep-fried potatoes

2 lb 8 oz to 3 lb 8 oz/1.13 to 1.59 kg potatoes, peeled and cut to shape

Enough cooking oil to completely submerge the potatoes

Salt and other seasonings

Finishing or garnishing ingredients for service

1. **Scrub, peel, cut, and hold the potatoes in cold water.** Immediately before cooking, rinse them several times in cold water, if indicated, and drain thoroughly. Blot dry. Heat the oil to 300° to 325°F/149° to 163°C. Blanch the potatoes until they are nearly cooked through but still relatively uncolored. Blanched potatoes may be held, covered, and refrigerated for up to several hours before finishing the cooking process. They may be frozen for 1 month.

2. **Just before service, reheat the oil to 350° to 375°F/177° to 191°C.** Deep fry the potatoes until golden brown on all surfaces and cooked through. Lift them from the cooking oil with a basket or spider and allow any excess oil to drain back into the fryer. Transfer to a pan lined with paper toweling to blot away excess oil. Add seasonings to the very hot fried potatoes as desired. Be sure to do this away from the oil used for frying to prolong the life of the oil.

Evaluate the quality of the finished deep-fried potatoes. Bite into one of the pieces. Very thin potatoes, such as gaufrette (waffle-cut) potatoes, should be extremely crisp, almost to the point where they shatter when bitten. Thick-cut potatoes should have a crisp exterior and a tender, fluffy interior. Deep-fried potatoes cannot be held successfully for more than a few minutes.

Variations for Deep-Fried Potatoes

Potatoes that are deep fried from the raw state may seem to be simple, but when prepared with care they can become a very important addition to textures and flavors of the plate.

Different cuts of potato will have different results. Thinner cuts will be crispy throughout, while fatter or bigger cuts will yield a crispy exterior with a creamy interior. Some of the different cuts applied to potatoes for deep frying are as follows:

Allumette or matchstick
Shoe string
Waffle cut

Salt and sometimes pepper are the most typical seasoning for deep-fried potatoes. In addition to these, try applying different ground spices or spice mixtures after frying to suit the profile of a particular dish:

Cayenne
Coriander
Cumin

Or fry sprigs of fresh herbs with the potatoes:

Rosemary
Sage

Boiled Parsley Potatoes

Boiled Parsley Potatoes

Makes 10 servings

4 lb 8 oz/2.04 kg potatoes

salt, as needed

2 oz/57 g butter

1 oz/28 g chopped parsley

ground black pepper, as needed

1. Scrub the potatoes and peel, if desired. Cut them into 2-in/5-cm cubes or wedges (hold potatoes in cold water until ready to cook to prevent discoloration).

2. Place the potatoes in a large pot with enough cold water to cover them by about 2 in/5 cm. Add salt and gradually bring the water to a simmer over medium heat. Cover and simmer until the potatoes are easily pierced with a fork, approximately 15 minutes. Drain the potatoes, return them to the pot, and let them dry briefly over low heat until steam no longer rises.

3. Heat the butter in a sauté pan over medium heat. Add the potatoes, rolling and tossing to coat them evenly with butter, and heat through.

4. Add the parsley and season with salt and pepper. Serve immediately.

Duchesse Potatoes

Makes 10 servings

4 lb/1.81 kg russet potatoes

8 oz/113 g butter, at room temperature

8 egg yolks, beaten

ground nutmeg, as needed

salt, as needed

ground black pepper, as needed

1. Scrub, peel, and cut the potatoes into large pieces. Boil or steam until tender enough to mash easily. Drain and dry them over low heat or on a sheet pan in a 300°F/149°C oven until no more steam rises from them. While the potatoes are still hot, purée them through a food mill or potato ricer into a heated bowl.

2. Add the butter and egg yolks to the potatoes. Season with nutmeg, salt, and pepper and mix well by hand or with the whip attachment of an electric mixer.

3. Transfer the mixture to a piping bag and pipe the mixture into the desired shapes on a sheet pan lined with parchment paper.

4. Bake at 375°F/191°C until the potatoes are golden brown and heated through, 10 to 12 minutes. Serve immediately.

Whipped Potatoes

Makes 10 servings

4 lb/1.81 kg russet potatoes

6 to 8 oz/170 to 227 g butter, at room temperature

12 fl oz/360 mL milk, hot

12 fl oz/360 mL heavy cream, hot

salt, as needed

ground black pepper, as needed

1. Scrub, peel, and cut the potatoes into large pieces. Boil or steam until tender enough to mash easily. Drain and dry them over low heat or on a sheet pan in a 300°F/149°C oven until no more steam rises from them. While the potatoes are still hot, purée them through a food mill or potato ricer into a heated bowl.

2. Add the butter and mix into the potatoes by hand or with the paddle or whip attachment of an electric mixer until just incorporated. Add the milk and cream, salt, and pepper and whip by hand or mixer until smooth and light.

3. Spoon the potatoes onto heated plates or transfer them to a piping bag and pipe into the desired shapes.

NOTE

Alternatively, potatoes may be baked in their skins until very tender. Halve the potatoes and scoop out the flesh while it is still very hot.

Baked Potatoes with Deep-Fried Onions

Makes 10 servings

10 russet potatoes

10 fl oz/300 mL sour cream

2 tbsp/6 g minced chives

salt, as needed

ground black pepper, as needed

10 oz/284 g deep-fried onions

1. Scrub and blot dry the potatoes. Pierce the skins in a few places with a paring knife or kitchen fork.

2. Bake on a rack in a 425°F/218°C oven until very tender and cooked through, about 1 hour.

3. Meanwhile, blend the sour cream and chives. Season with salt and pepper.

4. Pinch or cut open the potatoes, place 1 fl oz/30 mL of sour cream on the top, and top with the onions. Serve immediately.

Roasted Tuscan-Style Potatoes

Makes 10 servings

3 lb 5 oz/1.50 kg chef's potatoes

3 fl oz/90 mL olive oil

2 oz/57 g thinly sliced garlic

3 tbsp/9 g rosemary

¾ oz/21 g sage

salt, as needed

ground black pepper, as needed

1. Scrub, peel, and cut the potatoes into large dice. Starting with cold water, bring the potatoes to a boil over medium-high heat. Simmer for about 20 minutes, until the potatoes are partially cooked. Drain, being careful not to break the potatoes.

2. Heat a large sauté pan over medium heat and add the oil. Add the potatoes and brown on all sides. When they are browned, drain off all but 1½ fl oz/45 mL of the oil.

3. Add the garlic, rosemary, and sage. Cook until the garlic is lightly browned and the herbs are crispy.

4. Season with salt and pepper. Serve immediately.

NOTE
The potatoes may be tossed with 1 fl oz/30 mL olive oil, 1 tbsp/9 g minced garlic, 1 tbsp/3 g minced rosemary, salt, and pepper, transferred to an oiled sheet pan, and roasted in a 425°F/218°C oven until tender and brown, 40 to 45 minutes.

Glazed Sweet Potatoes

Makes 10 servings

4 lb/1.81 kg sweet potatoes

8 oz/227 g small-dice pineapple

2 fl oz/60 mL lemon juice

8 oz/227 g sugar

1 tsp/2 g ground cinnamon

2 oz/57 g butter

salt, as needed

ground black pepper, as needed

1. Scrub and blot dry the potatoes. Arrange in a single layer on a sheet pan. Bake in a 375°F/191°C oven until very tender and cooked through, 30 to 40 minutes.

2. Combine the pineapple, lemon juice, sugar, cinnamon, butter, salt, and pepper in a saucepan and bring to a simmer while the sweet potatoes are baking. Continue to cook until lightly thickened; keep warm.

3. As soon as the potatoes are cool enough to handle, peel them and cut into slices or large chunks. Arrange them on a sheet pan. Pour the glaze over them and bake at 350°F/177°C until very hot, about 10 minutes. Serve immediately.

Mashed Sweet Potatoes with Ginger

Makes 10 servings

3 lb/1.36 kg sweet potatoes

2 oz/57g butter

4 fl oz/120 mL heavy cream, hot

1½ tsp/4.50 g minced ginger

salt, as needed

ground black pepper, as needed

1. Scrub and blot dry the potatoes. Pierce the skins in a few places with a paring knife or kitchen fork.

2. Bake on a rack in a 425°F/218°C oven until very tender and cooked through, about 1 hour.

3. Halve the potatoes, scoop out the flesh while they are still hot, and purée them through a food mill or potato ricer into a heated bowl.

4. Combine the butter, cream, and ginger and bring to a simmer. Pour the mixture over the puréed sweet potatoes. Season with salt and pepper. Serve immediately.

Potatoes au Gratin (Gratin Dauphinoise)

Makes 10 servings

3 lb 4 oz/1.47 kg chef's potatoes

5 garlic cloves

32 fl oz/960 mL milk

ground nutmeg, as needed

salt, as needed

ground black pepper, as needed

12 fl oz/360 mL heavy cream

4 oz/113 g butter, cut into small pieces

1. Scrub, peel, and thinly slice the potatoes using a mandoline or electric slicer.

2. Put the garlic in a saucepan with the milk and bring to a boil. Season the milk with nutmeg, salt, and pepper and add the sliced potatoes.

3. Bring the milk to a simmer, and cook the potatoes for 10 to 12 minutes, taking care that the milk does not boil over. Discard the garlic cloves.

4. Transfer the potatoes and milk to a buttered hotel pan, pour the cream over the top, and dot with the butter.

5. Bake in a 375°F/191°C oven for 45 minutes or until golden brown and the milk has been absorbed.

6. Allow the potatoes to rest for 10 to 15 minutes before slicing into servings.

NOTES

Alternatively, the sliced potatoes may be shingled in the hotel pan.

Before baking, layer with 4 to 5 oz/113 to 142 g grated Cheddar cheese and then top with an additional 5 oz/142 g grated Cheddar cheese. Cover the pan with foil for 35 minutes. Uncover and allow the cheese to brown lightly.

Lyonnaise Potatoes

Makes 10 servings

4 lb/1.81 kg chef's potatoes

2 fl oz/60 mL vegetable oil

1 lb/454 g sliced onions

salt, as needed

ground black pepper, as needed

3 tbsp/9 g chopped parsley

1. Scrub, peel, and slice the potatoes. Cook them in boiling salted water until partially cooked, 6 to 8 minutes. Drain the potatoes and dry them over low heat or on a sheet pan in a 300°F/149°C oven, about 5 minutes.

2. Heat the oil in a skillet over medium-high heat. Add the onions and cook, stirring frequently, until lightly browned, 7 to 8 minutes. Remove the onions from the pan.

3. Add the potatoes to the pan and season with salt and pepper. Continue to sauté, stirring occasionally, until the potatoes are browned well on all sides and are tender to the bite, 5 to 7 minutes. Add the onions back to the pan. Garnish with parsley and serve immediately.

Château Potatoes

Makes 10 servings

4 lb/1.81 kg chef's or waxy potatoes

1 fl oz/30 mL clarified butter or oil

½ oz/14 g chopped parsley

salt, as needed

ground black pepper, as needed

1. Scrub the potatoes and peel if desired. Cut them into equal-size tourné, about the size of an olive (hold potatoes in cold water until ready to cook to prevent discoloration); rinse, drain, and dry thoroughly.

2. Heat the clarified butter or oil in a sauté pan over medium heat. Add the potatoes and sauté until tender with a golden exterior, 8 to 10 minutes.

3. Sprinkle with parsley and season with salt and pepper. Serve immediately.

Delmonico Potatoes

Makes 10 servings

5 lb/2.27 kg chef's potatoes

1 fl oz/30 mL clarified butter

2 oz/57 g butter

salt, as needed

ground black pepper, as needed

2 tbsp/6 g chopped parsley

1½ fl oz/45 mL lemon juice

1. Scrub and peel the potatoes. Use a parisienne scoop to shape the potatoes into large balls.

2. Cook the potatoes by boiling or steaming until almost tender, about 5 minutes. Drain and dry them over low heat or on a sheet pan in a 300°F/149°C oven until no more steam rises from them, 5 to 10 minutes.

3. Heat the clarified butter in a large sauté pan over high heat. Add the potatoes and sauté until cooked through and a light golden brown. Add the whole butter and melt. Season with salt and pepper.

4. Sprinkle the potatoes with parsley and lemon juice and serve immediately.

Hash Brown Potatoes

Makes 10 servings

4 lb/1.81 kg chef's potatoes

2 fl oz/60 mL clarified butter or vegetable oil

salt, as needed

ground black pepper, as needed

2 tbsp/6 g chopped parsley

1. Scrub and peel the potatoes. Cook them in boiling salted water until partially cooked, 15 to 20 minutes, depending on the size of the potatoes. Drain the potatoes and dry them over low heat or on a sheet pan in a 300°F/149°C oven, about 5 minutes. Cut the potatoes into slices, small or medium dice, or grate them.

2. Heat the butter or oil in a large sauté pan over medium-high heat. Add the potatoes and season with salt and pepper.

3. Sauté the potatoes until they are fully cooked and well browned on all sides. Garnish with parsley and serve immediately.

Hash Brown Potatoes

Potato Galettes (*Galette de Pommes de Terre Alsacienne*)

Potato Galettes (Galette de Pommes de Terre Alsacienne)

Makes 10 servings

2 lb 8 oz/1.13 kg russet potatoes

8 oz/227 g coarsely grated onions, with extra liquid squeezed out

1 tbsp/9 g crushed garlic

2 tbsp/6 g chopped parsley

2 tbsp/7 g sliced chives

3 eggs, lightly beaten

1 tbsp/7 g all-purpose flour

salt, as needed

ground black pepper, as needed

8 fl oz/240 mL vegetable oil

1. Scrub, peel, and coarsely grate the potatoes. Combine them with the onions, garlic, parsley, chives, eggs, and flour. Season with salt and pepper.

2. Heat 1½ fl oz/45 mL of oil in a large skillet over medium heat. Add a spoonful of the potato mixture to the pan and flatten with a spoon to form a galette (2 to 3 in/5 to 8 cm in diameter).

3. Cook until golden on one side, then turn to brown the other side, about 6 minutes per side.

4. Drain on absorbent paper towels, cut into servings, and serve immediately.

Potato Pancakes

Makes 10 servings

3 lb/1.36 kg russet potatoes

1 lb/454 g onions

1 fl oz/30 mL lemon juice

2 eggs, lightly beaten

1 oz/28 g bread flour

1 oz/28 g matzo meal

salt, as needed

ground black pepper, as needed

16 fl oz/480 mL vegetable oil, or as needed for frying

1. Grind or grate the potatoes and onions together with a food processor or by hand. Toss them with the lemon juice to prevent discoloration.

2. Wring the grated potatoes and onions in cheesecloth to remove excess moisture. Transfer to a bowl and add the eggs, flour, and matzo meal. Season with salt and pepper.

3. Heat ¼ in/6 mm of oil in a heavy cast-iron skillet to 350°F/177°C. Drop the potato batter into the hot oil by level serving spoonfuls. Brown on the first side for about 3 minutes. Turn them once and brown on the second side, another 2 to 3 minutes. If necessary, the pancakes may be finished in a 375°F/191°C oven until browned and crisp.

4. Blot the pancakes on absorbent paper towels and serve immediately.

Rösti Potatoes

Makes 10 servings

4 lb/1.81 kg russet potatoes

4 fl oz/120 mL clarified butter, or as needed

salt, as needed

ground black pepper, as needed

2 oz/57 g, butter, or as needed

1. Scrub the potatoes and place them in cold water to cover by 2 in/5 cm. Bring to a simmer and parcook until a fork inserted meets resistance about halfway, approximately 20 minutes. Drain and dry them over low heat or on a sheet pan in a 300°F/149°C oven until no more steam rises from them.

2. Peel the potatoes as soon as they are cool enough to handle and grate them on the coarse side of a grater.

3. Heat a rösti pan over high heat. Ladle in some of the clarified butter. Layer the grated potato in the pan. Lightly drizzle each layer with a little additional butter and season with salt and pepper. Dot the outside edge with pieces of whole butter.

4. Cook the potatoes until they are golden brown and form a cake, 4 to 5 minutes. Turn the entire cake, dot the edge with more whole butter, and cook the other side until the potatoes are fully cooked and tender and the crusts are golden brown and crisp. Turn the cake out of the pan, cut into servings, and serve immediately.

Stuffed Rösti Potatoes

Makes 10 servings

4 lb/1.81 kg chef's potatoes

1 lb/454 g leeks, julienne

2 oz/57 g butter

salt, as needed

ground black pepper, as needed

ground nutmeg, as needed

2 fl oz/60 mL white wine

16 fl oz/480 mL heavy cream

2 lb/907 g mushrooms, sliced

2 oz/57 g shallots, minced

½ oz/14 g chopped parsley

½ oz/14 g chopped chervil

4 fl oz/120 mL clarified butter, or as needed

4 oz/113 g puff pastry

1 egg, beaten

1. Scrub the potatoes and place them in cold water to cover by 2 in/5 cm. Bring to a simmer and parcook until a fork inserted meets resistance about halfway, approximately 20 minutes. Drain and dry them over low heat or on a sheet pan in a 300°F/149°C oven until no more steam rises from them.

2. Sauté the leeks in 1 oz/28 g of the butter over medium heat until soft, about 6 minutes. Season with salt, pepper, and nutmeg. Add the wine and reduce until almost dry, about 2 minutes. Add the cream and reduce until it coats the leeks and very little liquid remains, about 8 minutes. Let cool.

3. Sauté the mushrooms and shallots in the remaining butter over medium-high heat until soft, about 8 minutes. Season with salt and pepper. Let cool.

4. Peel and grate the parcooked potatoes. Mix with the parsley and chervil. Season with salt and pepper.

5. Heat a small amount of clarified butter in a rösti pan over medium to medium-high heat. Place the potato mixture in the pan and cook until the potatoes are golden brown on the bottom, 10 to 12 minutes. Flip over and brown on the second side, adding additional clarified butter, if necessary.

6. Top the potatoes with the leeks and mushrooms. Cover the vegetables with a thinly rolled puff pastry sheet. Brush the top with the beaten egg and bake in a 375°F/191°C oven until golden brown, 10 to 12 minutes.

7. Cut into wedges and serve immediately.

Stuffed Rösti Potatoes

Potatoes Anna

Makes 10 servings

4 lb/1.81 kg chef's potatoes

2½ fl oz/75 mL clarified butter, or as needed

salt, as needed

ground black pepper, as needed

1. Scrub, peel, and trim the potatoes into uniform cylinders. Thinly slice them using a mandoline or electric slicer.

2. Liberally brush a sautoir with butter. Arrange the potato slices in concentric rings. Lightly brush each layer with butter and season with salt and pepper.

3. Cover the potatoes and cook them on the stovetop over medium heat until the bottom layer is brown, about 8 minutes. Turn the potato cake upside down and brown the other side. Place it in a 400°F/204°C oven and cook until tender, 30 to 35 minutes.

4. Drain off the excess butter and turn the potato cake out onto a platter. Slice into servings and serve immediately.

Macaire Potatoes

Makes 10 servings

4 lb/1.81 kg russet potatoes

salt, as needed

2 oz/57 g butter

ground black pepper, as needed

1 egg

1 fl oz/30 mL clarified butter or vegetable oil

1. Scrub and blot dry the potatoes. Season with salt. Pierce the skins in a few places with a paring knife or kitchen fork.

2. Bake in a 425°F/218°C oven until very tender and cooked through, about 1 hour.

3. Halve the potatoes, scoop out the flesh while it is still very hot, and transfer to a heated bowl. Mash the potatoes, butter, salt, pepper, and egg together with a fork or wooden spoon until evenly blended. Shape into cakes.

4. Heat the butter or oil in a large sauté pan over medium-high heat. Working in batches, sauté the cakes until golden on both sides and very hot, 2 to 3 minutes per side. Serve immediately.

French-Fried Potatoes

Makes 10 servings

4 lb/1.81 kg russet potatoes

32 fl oz/960 mL vegetable oil, or as needed for frying

salt, as needed

1. Scrub, peel, and cut the potatoes into the desired shape (hold potatoes in cold water until ready to cook to prevent discoloration); rinse, drain, and dry thoroughly.

2. Heat the oil to 300°F/149°C. Add the potatoes, in batches, and blanch until just tender but not browned (time varies according to the size of cuts).

3. Drain well and transfer to pans lined with absorbent paper towels, scaling into servings if desired.

4. Just before service, reheat the oil to 375°F/191°C and finish the potatoes, frying until they are golden brown and cooked through. Drain well, season with salt (away from the fryer), and serve immediately.

Berny Potatoes

Makes 10 servings

4 lb/1.81 kg russet potatoes

2½ oz/71 g butter, softened

2 egg yolks, beaten

ground nutmeg, as needed

salt, as needed

ground black pepper, as needed

2 oz/57 g chopped truffles

2 oz/57 g slivered almonds

2 oz/57 g bread crumbs

egg wash, as needed

vegetable oil, as needed

1. Scrub, peel, and cut the potatoes into large pieces. Boil or steam until tender enough to mash easily. Drain and dry them over low heat or on a sheet pan in a 300°F/149°C oven until no more steam rises from them. While the potatoes are still hot, purée them through a food mill or potato ricer into a heated bowl.

2. Add the butter and egg yolks to the potatoes. Season with nutmeg, salt, and pepper and mix well by hand or with the whip attachment of an electric mixer. Fold in the truffles.

3. Combine the almonds and bread crumbs in a shallow container.

4. Shape 2-oz/57-g servings of the potato mixture into pear shapes, as desired. Dip the balls in the egg wash and then into the almond/bread crumb mixture.

5. Heat the oil to 375°F/191°C and deep fry the potatoes until they are an even golden brown, 4 to 5 minutes. Drain briefly on absorbent paper towels and serve immediately.

Sweet Potato Chips

Sweet Potato Chips

Makes 10 servings

3 lb/1.36 kg sweet potatoes

32 fl oz/960 mL vegetable oil, or as needed for frying

salt, as needed

1. Scrub, peel, and cut the sweet potatoes into circles ⅟₁₆ in/1.50 mm in diameter using a mandoline or electric slicer.

2. Heat the oil to 325°F/163°C and deep fry the potatoes in batches until golden brown, 1 to 2 minutes. Drain on absorbent paper towels and season with salt. Serve immediately, or store uncovered in a warm area.

Souffléed Potatoes

Makes 10 servings

4 lb 8 oz/2.04 kg baking potatoes

32 fl oz/960 mL vegetable oil, or as needed for frying

salt, as needed

1. Scrub, peel, and trim the potatoes into uniform cylinders. Thinly slice them using a mandoline or electric slicer.

2. Heat the oil to 300°F/149°C. Add the potato slices in small batches. Shake the basket or pot carefully to prevent the potatoes from sticking. When the slices blister, remove and drain them in a single layer on absorbent paper towels. Hold for service.

3. At service, reheat the oil to 375°F/191°C and add the blanched potato slices. Fry until puffed and golden brown. Drain well. Season with salt to taste and serve immediately.

Croquette Potatoes

Makes 10 servings

4 lb/1.81 kg russet potatoes

4 oz/113 g butter, softened

4 egg yolks, beaten

ground nutmeg, as needed

salt, as needed

ground black pepper, as needed

3 oz/85 g all-purpose flour

2 eggs, combined with 2 tbsp/30 ml milk or water for egg wash

5 oz/142 g bread crumbs

24 fl oz/720 mL vegetable oil, or as needed for frying

1. Scrub, peel, and cut the potatoes into large pieces. Boil or steam until tender enough to mash easily, 20 to 25 minutes. Drain and dry them over low heat or on a sheet pan in a 300°F/149°C oven until no more steam rises from them, 10 to 15 minutes. While the potatoes are still hot, purée them through a food mill or potato ricer into a heated bowl.

2. Add the butter and egg yolks to the potatoes. Season with nutmeg, salt, and pepper to taste and mix well by hand or with the whip attachment of an electric mixer.

3. Transfer the mixture to a piping bag and pipe it into long ropes about 1 in/2.5 cm in diameter. Cut these ropes into 3-in/8-cm lengths. Coat the potato cylinders with flour, egg wash, and bread crumbs. This can be done just before service or up to 4 hours in advance, keeping the croquettes refrigerated.

4. Heat the oil to 375°F/191°C and deep fry the croquettes until golden brown and heated through, 3 to 4 minutes. Drain briefly on absorbent paper towels and serve immediately.

Lorette Potatoes

Makes 10 servings

4 lb/1.81 kg russet potatoes

2½ oz/71 g butter, softened

2 egg yolks, beaten

ground nutmeg, as needed

salt, as needed

ground black pepper, as needed

1 lb 4 oz/567 g **Pâte à Choux** (page 1117), at room temperature

32 fl oz/960 mL vegetable oil, or as needed for frying

1. Scrub, peel, and cut the potatoes into large pieces. Boil or steam until tender enough to mash easily. Drain and dry them over low heat or on a sheet pan in a 300°F/149°C oven until no more steam rises from them. While the potatoes are still hot, purée them through a food mill or potato ricer into a heated bowl.

2. Add the butter and egg yolks to the potatoes. Season with nutmeg, salt, and pepper and mix well by hand or with the whip attachment of an electric mixer. Add the pâte à choux.

3. Transfer the mixture to a piping bag and pipe the mixture into crescent shapes on strips of parchment paper.

4. Heat the oil to 375°F/191°C and carefully lower the strips of paper into the fryer. When the lorettes have lifted off the paper, remove and discard the paper. Deep fry the lorettes until golden brown, turning if necessary to brown evenly. Remove them from the oil, blot dry on absorbent paper towels, and serve immediately.

Chapter Twenty-seven

Cooking Grains and Legumes

One of the most dramatic changes on the culinary scene in recent years has been the rediscovery of grains and legumes. Everyday grains—wheat, corn, rice—are appearing in many new forms, and beans have become more popular as well. In addition, exotic grains, such as millet and quinoa, and beans that were once rarely seen, including flageolets and borlottis, are appearing more and more frequently.

Simmering Whole Grains and Legumes

Grains and legumes are dried foods that must be properly rehydrated by cooking in stock or water before they can be eaten. Legumes and most grains are usually combined with the liquid before bringing it to a boil, but some grains (quinoa, for instance) are added to the liquid only after it has come to a boil. Some seasonings are added at the beginning of the cooking period, others at the end. (Refer to specific recipes for details.) Although grains and legumes are often referred to as boiled, they are actually simmered or steamed. The high heat of a boiling liquid tends to toughen them. When a grain completely absorbs the cooking liquid, it is often referred to as steamed. Grains may also be cooked in a quantity of liquid greater than they can absorb. Once fully cooked, the excess liquid is drained away.

Sort whole grains and legumes carefully before cooking. Spread out the grains or legumes in a single layer on a sheet pan and work from one end of the pan to the other systematically to spot and remove stones and moldy beans. Put the beans or legumes in a large pot or bowl and cover them with cold water. Any that float on the surface are too dry for culinary or nutritional purposes and should be removed and discarded. Drain the beans or legumes in a colander or sieve and then rinse them well with cold running water to remove any dust.

Most legumes and some grains are soaked prior to cooking. Whole grains, such as whole or Scotch barley and wheat and rye berries, benefit from soaking, which softens the outer layer of bran. Pearl barley, which has had the bran removed mechanically, does not need to be soaked. Imported basmati and jasmine rice should be soaked to remove excess starch from the surface and prevent clumping. Domestic basmati and jasmine rice do not need to be soaked. Steep fine- or medium-grind bulgur wheat in boiling liquid for several minutes, until the grain softens enough to be chewed easily. Like bulgur, steep instant couscous in hot stock or water. (While couscous is actually a form of pasta, it is often thought of as a grain because of its texture and appearance.)

Whether or not to soak legumes is a subject of debate among chefs. Some believe that most legumes, with a few notable exceptions (lentils, split peas, and black-eyed peas), are easier to prepare and produce a better-quality finished dish if they are soaked, because the skins soften slightly, allowing for more rapid and even cooking. Others find that soaking has no benefit beyond shortening the cooking time and that cooking legumes without soaking results in a creamier texture. If you choose to soak, there are two methods commonly used: the long soak and the short soak; except for time, there is no appreciable difference between them.

The long soak method

Place the sorted and rinsed legumes in a container and add enough cool water to cover them by 2 in/5 cm. Let the legumes soak in the refrigerator for 4 hours to overnight, depending on the type of legume.

The short soak method

Place the sorted and rinsed legumes in a pot and add enough water to cover by 2 in/5 cm. Bring the water to a simmer. Remove the pot from direct heat and cover. Let the legumes steep for 1 hour.

Whether or not to use the soaking water as the cooking liquid is also a subject of debate. In addition to softening skins, soaking the legumes causes many of the oligosaccharides (indigestible complex sugars that can cause flatulence) in the legumes to be leached into the water. At the same time, small amounts of nutrients, flavor, and color are also leached into the water. When the soaking water is used as the cooking liquid, the nutrients, flavor, and color are retained, but so are the oligosaccharides.

Water, stock, and broth are common choices for the cooking liquid. Each type of grain or legume absorbs a different amount of liquid. (See Common Ratios for Legumes and Grains, pages 1165–1166, or package or recipe instructions for details.) Grains often are cooked in an amount of liquid greater than they can actually absorb. This is especially desirable for grains that should remain separate, fluffy, and very dry after cooking. The amount of liquid required for legumes depends on the type and the age of the legume and its total cooking time. Legumes should be completely covered by liquid at all times. It is important to maintain this level throughout cooking. If the legumes are allowed to absorb all the liquid, they might break apart or scorch. Salt needs to be added to the cooking liquid at the beginning (for grains) or near the end (for legumes) of cooking time to properly enhance natural flavors. Legumes and grains have relatively subtle flavors that frequently require a boost from spices and herbs either during or after cooking.

The equipment needs for simmering grains and legumes are quite simple: a pot large enough to allow for the expansion of the grain or legume, a colander or strainer if draining will be required, and holding and serving pieces.

Evaluate the quality of the finished boiled legume or whole grains. Grains are done when they are tender to the bite. They should be fluffy, with a sweet, nutty flavor. Legumes are done when they are completely tender and creamy on the inside but still retain their shape. They should be soft and easy to mash with a fork or spoon. Undercooking legumes is a common mistake.

A basic formula for 10 servings of whole grains or legumes

Main ingredient options include:

1 lb/454 g grain

1 lb/454 g legumes

Cooking liquid options include:

Stock or water as needed to cover grains or legumes throughout cooking time

Seasoning options include:

Salt and pepper

Standard sachet d'épices or bouquet garni

Mirepoix or other aromatic vegetables

Cook the grain or legumes. Combine the grain or legumes with the cooking liquid and bring to a full boil.

Reduce the heat slightly to a simmer and cook the grain or legumes until done as desired. Legumes and some grains need to be stirred occasionally as they cook to prevent scorching. Check the level of the cooking liquid and add more as necessary to keep the legumes or grain completely covered. To check for doneness, taste a grain or legume. Salt is typically added to legumes after they have become tender. Adding salt or acidic ingredients, such as citrus juices or vinegar, earlier can toughen the skin if added at the start of cooking time.

Drain the grain or legumes or let them cool in the cooking liquid if they are to be used later. This keeps the skins tender. In many cases, the cooking liquid is an important ingredient in the finished dish. Finish and serve on heated plates or use in another preparation.

If liquid is not entirely absorbed, drain the grains in a colander and suspend it over a pot. Cover the pot and let the grain steam dry for a few minutes over low heat. Use a fork to gently fluff the grain, but do not stir; stirring may cause starch granules to burst, creating a gluey texture. Adjust the seasoning as necessary and appropriate with salt, pepper, and other ingredients. Hold the dish in a warm place, if necessary, until ready to serve.

Simmering and Boiling Cereals and Meals

Culinary grains may undergo some type of processing (milling) before they reach the kitchen to produce meals and cereals. When a whole grain is milled, it is broken down into successively smaller particles. Depending on the grain, the final result might be quite coarse (cracked wheat or groats) or quite fine (cornmeal or farina). Some grains are treated before milling. Bulgur wheat, for example, is steamed and dried before it is crushed. Cereals include various forms of oats, buckwheat groats, and rye flakes, as well as cracked grains like bulgur. Meals include grits and polenta, farina, semolina, and cream of rice. Flours are even more finely ground.

Cereals and meals vary widely according to the way in which they are processed. Meals and cereals may be ground coarsely or finely. The bran and germ may be left intact or removed. The type of grinding equipment affects both flavor and nutritional content. Coarser cereals produce a dense, porridge-like texture; finer grinds produce a smooth, even silky, texture similar to a pudding. All cereals and grains should have a fresh, appealing aroma. As they age, the natural oils can become rancid. Discard any cereals or meals that do not smell fresh. Sort the meal to remove any debris before weighing it. Some cereals and grains should be rinsed before cooking. Others must be dry so that they can be added gradually to the cooking liquid.

Water, stock, or broth may be used as the cooking liquid, depending on the grain, the dish, and the menu. Cereals and grain meals are generally cooked in just as much liquid as they can absorb; each type of cereal or meal will absorb a different amount of liquid. (Refer to package or recipe directions for details.)

Salt is generally added to the cooking water, and sometimes spices or herbs are added as well. Taste and adjust the seasoning at the end of the cooking time. Grains tend to need considerable salt; otherwise they taste flat.

The pots for cooking the cereal or meal can be small or large, depending on the amount, but, in general, they should have a heavy bottom. A colander or strainer will be necessary if draining is required. Have holding and serving pieces on hand.

A basic formula for 10 servings of cereals or meals

Main ingredient options include:

1 lb/454 g cereal or cracked or flaked grain

1 lb/454 g grain meal

Cooking liquid options include:

Stock or broth

Water

Milk

A combination of liquids

Seasoning and flavoring options include:

Salt and pepper

Bouquet garni or sachet

Aromatic vegetables, such as onions or garlic (or, for sweetened preparations, add sugar, honey, or other sweeteners)

1. **Depending on the grain, bring the liquid to a full boil and add the cereal or meal in a thin stream, stirring constantly, or combine the cereal and liquid and bring to a boil.** You may also add the cereal (polenta) to cold water like you would for a slurry and then bring it up to a simmer. This helps to prevent clumps from forming. Salt and other seasonings may be added to the liquid as it comes to a boil, along with any other desired seasonings and aromatics. Reduce the heat to establish a simmer and cook, stirring as necessary, until done. Most cereals should be stirred occasionally as they cook to prevent scorching. Drag the spoon across the bottom of the pot and into the corners to release the cereal or meal as it cooks. The mixture will thicken noticeably while cooking. Some meals or cereals may become stiff enough to pull away from the sides of the pot and are relatively heavy in texture. Others remain fluid enough to pour easily.

2. **Cook grain meals so that they are liquid enough to pour when they are still warm.** They should also have a relatively smooth creamy texture. Line a sheet pan with parchment paper and then spread hot polenta in an even layer for quick cooling.

3. **Evaluate the quality of the finished cooked meal or cereal.** Polenta, porridges, and puddings made from grain meals will be thick, with a coarse to smooth consistency, depending on the cereal.

Cold cooked meal such as polenta can be cut into a variety of shapes, then sautéed, grilled, baked, or pan fried before being served.

Pilaf

Originally from the Middle East, pilaf (also called pilau) is a grain dish in which the grain—usually rice—is first heated in a pan, either dry or in fat, and then combined with a hot liquid and cooked, covered, over direct heat or in the oven.

Pilafs may be simple dishes, composed of only the grain and cooking liquid, or they may be quite substantial and include a wide range of additional ingredients, such as meat or shellfish, vegetables, nuts, or dried fruits. In pilaf, the grains remain separate and take on a nutty flavor from the initial sautéing of the grain. The grain has a somewhat firmer texture than when it is boiled.

Rice is the grain most frequently used to prepare a pilaf, though other grains, such as bulgur or barley, can also be used. Sort and, if necessary, rinse and air-dry the grain by spreading it out in a thin layer on a sheet pan.

A neutral-flavored vegetable oil is most often used to sweat the aromatics and sauté the grain, but a cooking fat that will contribute a flavor of its own, such as butter or rendered goose fat, may also be used.

Stock is generally the preferred cooking liquid. Bring the liquid to a boil in a separate pot before adding it to the grain to help shorten the cooking time. To impart a particular flavor and/or color, substitute vegetable or fruit juice or a vegetable coulis for up to half of the liquid. If the juice is acidic (tomato juice, for instance), the cooking time may need to be increased by as much as 15 to 20 minutes.

A member of the onion family, such as finely diced or minced onions, shallots, green onions, or leeks, is usually required for a pilaf. In addition to onions, bay leaves and thyme are commonly used for flavor. Other herbs and spices may also be added. Additional vegetables may be added to sweat along with the onion. Other ingredients, including seafood, meat, vegetables, and nuts, are often added. (Refer to recipes for details.)

A heavy-gauge pot of the appropriate size, with a lid, is required to allow steaming and to prevent scorching. Holding and serving pieces are also needed.

A basic formula for 10 portions of pilaf

Main ingredient options include:

1 lb/454 g rice, quinoa, or similar whole grains

1 lb/454 g orzo or similar small pasta shapes

14 oz to 1 lb/397 to 454 g barley or lentils

Cooking liquid options include:

28 to 32 fl oz/840 to 960 mL stock, broth, or water for rice, quinoa, or similar whole grains

32 to 40 fl oz/960 mL to 1.2 L stock, broth, or water for orzo or similar small pasta shapes

40 to 48 fl oz/1.20 to 1.44 L stock, broth, or water for barley or lentils

Seasoning and flavoring options include:

Salt and pepper

Bay leaf, thyme, or other herbs

Onions or other aromatic vegetables

1. **Sweat the aromatic vegetables in fat or oil until softened.** Add the grains and sauté, stirring frequently, until they are well coated with fat.

Heating the grain in hot fat or oil, known as parching, begins to gelatinize the starches. This encourages the grains to remain separate after they are cooked. It also encourages the grains to pick up the flavor of the aromatics.

2. **Heat the liquid, add it to the grains, and bring to a simmer.** Heating the liquid before adding it speeds up the cooking process. Stir the grains once or twice as they come up to a simmer to prevent them from sticking to the bottom of the pot. Add any flavoring ingredients at this point. Cover the pot and complete the cooking in a moderate oven or over low heat on the stovetop.

3. **When done, remove the pot from the heat and let the pilaf rest, covered, for 5 minutes.** Letting the pilaf rest allows it to absorb the remaining liquid and steam. Uncover and use a fork to fluff the grains and release the steam. Adjust the seasoning.

Evaluate the quality of the finished pilaf. Test a few grains by biting into them. They should be tender but with a noticeable texture, not soft and mushy. In addition, the individual grains should separate easily. There should be no liquid visible in the bottom of the pot. Pilafs that have been overcooked have a pasty flavor; the individual grains may be mushy or soggy and may clump together. Grains that have been undercooked or cooked in too little liquid are overly crunchy.

Risotto

A classic risotto is a rich, creamy dish with a nearly porridge-like consistency, yet each grain of rice retains a distinct bite. In Italian risotto, the rice is parched as in the pilaf method, but the liquid is added and absorbed gradually while the grain is stirred almost constantly. The starch slowly releases during the cooking process, producing a creamy texture.

Grated cheese is often included, and vegetables, meats, or fish may be added to create a risotto that can be served as an appetizer or main course. Although risotto's preparation is relatively lengthy and requires constant attention, there are ways to streamline the process, making it suitable for restaurant service.

Risotto is traditionally made with special Italian varieties of medium-grain round rice. The best known of these is Arborio, but other varieties include Vialone Nano and Carnaroli. Other grains, including other long-grain or brown rices, barley, wheat berries, or small pasta shapes, may also be prepared with this method, but the quality of the finished dish is not the same as a risotto made with an Italian medium-grain rice. The cooking time will be longer for brown rice and whole grains, and the amount of liquid required may be greater.

The cooking liquid most often suggested for risotto is a high-quality stock or broth. Measure the appropriate quantity of stock or broth, season it if necessary, and bring it to a simmer before starting to cook. Wine may replace a portion of the stock or broth in some formulas. Simmering the stock first shortens the risotto's cooking time somewhat and provides an opportunity to add ingredients to infuse the broth with flavor and color. Opinions differ regarding whether the wine should be added early in the cooking time or nearer the end. Some chefs prefer to combine the stock and wine and bring them to a simmer together to cook away the harsh flavor of raw wine and improve the dish's taste.

Finely minced leeks, shallots, or onions are usually included in a risotto. Other aromatic vegetables, including mushrooms, fennel, carrots, or celery, may be added to some dishes. They should be finely cut or thinly sliced to release their flavors fully. Spices, such as saffron and fresh herbs, may also be added.

Butter contributes a sweet, rich flavor to a risotto. Other fats and oils, especially olive oil, may also be used. Cheese, usually Parmesan or Romano, should be added as close to service time as possible to assure the best flavor. Meat, fish, poultry, or vegetables may be included.

A wide, heavy-gauge saucepan is best for making risotto. Use a spoon, preferably wooden, for stirring, and if the risotto is to be cooled and finished later, use a sheet pan or similar wide shallow pan.

A basic formula for 10 portions of risotto

Main ingredient options include:

1 lb/454 g Arborio or other white or brown rice

1 lb/454 g orzo or similar small pasta shapes

1 lb/454 g fideo or similar thin noodles

Cooking liquid options include:

48 to 56 fl oz/1.44 to 1.68 L stock, broth, or water for white rices

48 fl oz/1.44 L stock, broth, or water for brown rices or pastas

(Optional: replace up to ¼ of the cooking liquid with dry white wine)

Seasoning and flavoring options include:

Salt and pepper

Bay leaf, thyme, or other herbs

Onions or other aromatic vegetables

Grated cheese

1. **Parch the rice in the oil after sweating the aromatics.** Onions or other aromatic vegetables should be given sufficient time to sweat in the hot butter or oil to fully develop their flavor. In some risottos, a cooked onion purée is used instead of chopped onions. Spices, either left whole or ground, may be added at this point as well. (If using saffron, infuse it in the cooking liquid for best flavor and color.)

Cooking the rice in the fat produces the correct finished texture in the risotto. Once a toasted aroma becomes apparent, stir in the first addition of liquid.

2. **Add the simmering liquid in parts.** Add about ¼ to ⅓ of the cooking liquid to the parched rice and stir constantly over medium heat until the liquid is absorbed. Continue adding servings of the cooking liquid in this manner. After the rice absorbs ⅓ of the liquid, the grains appear firm and quite distinct and no real creaminess is evident yet. After the rice absorbs the second addition of liquid, the grains appear more tender and they begin to adopt a creamy, sauce-like consistency.

3. **Stir constantly until the entire amount of liquid has been incorporated, the rice is fully cooked, and the risotto is creamy and thick.** The average cooking time for risotto prepared with Arborio rice is 20 minutes. Although the best risotto is prepared from start to finish just prior to service, it is possible to partially cook the dish in advance.

To do this, remove the risotto from the heat after the rice has absorbed ⅔ to ¾ of the total amount of cooking liquid. Pour the risotto onto a sheet pan and spread it in an even layer. Cool it rapidly and refrigerate. To finish risotto held in this manner, return it all or by servings to a pot and heat it over medium heat. Add the final ⅓ to ¼ of the cooking liquid and finish cooking until the risotto is creamy and the rice is fully cooked.

4. **Stir butter and grated cheese or other finishing ingredients into the risotto vigorously over low heat until well blended.** Some garnish ingredients may be added early in the cooking process so that they fully cook along with the risotto. Others may be cooked separately and added at the end. (Refer to specific recipes for details.) Add fresh herbs, if desired, adjust the seasoning to taste, and serve the risotto on heated plates.

Evaluate the quality of the finished risotto. Italians describe a properly cooked risotto as *all'onda* (wave-like), meaning that the risotto has a creamy, almost porridge-like consistency, but individual grains are slightly firm with a discernable texture. Risotto that has been cooked over high heat or too rapidly will not develop the proper consistency nor will it be adequately cooked. The finished consistency should be creamy and the risotto grains should be al dente.

Flavoring and Seasoning Risotto

There are three basic points at which flavoring and/or seasonings may be added to a risotto.

1. Before the rice is added, aromatic vegetables may be added to sautéing onion to bolster the finished flavor of a risotto. Some examples are:

> **Carrots**
> **Celery**
> **Garlic**

2. With the liquid, herbs and seasonings may be added by first adding them to the liquid to infuse. The choice of liquid will also do a lot to determine the flavor of the finished dish and should be selected carefully to complement all the other flavors. Some common herbs and seasoning are:

> **Bay leaves**
> **Saffron**
> **Water from rehydrating dried mushrooms**

3. Near or at the end of cooking, garnish ingredients may be added. The timing for the addition of these ingredients is important and will depend on the required cooking time of the individual ingredient.

> **Cut or whole vegetables, such as broccoli, peas, or asparagus**
> **Fresh herbs, such as basil, oregano, or sage**
> **Seafood, such as shrimp, scallops, or squid**

Beans from the Pot (Frijoles de Olla)

Makes 10 servings

1 lb 8 oz/680 g dried black beans

96 fl oz/2.88 L water

1 tbsp/6 g ground cumin

1½ tsp/3 g dried oregano

4 garlic cloves, minced

6 oz/170 g minced bacon

ground black pepper, as needed

salt, as needed

1. Sort the beans and rinse well with cold water.

2. Soak the beans using the long or short method. Drain the soaked beans.

3. Place the beans and water in a large saucepan with the cumin, oregano, garlic, bacon, and pepper. Cover the pot and bring to a simmer.

4. Simmer the beans for 1 hour.

5. Add salt and continue to simmer until the beans are tender to the bite, 20 to 30 minutes.

6. The beans can be drained for immediate use or rapidly cooled and refrigerated in their liquid.

Frijoles à la Charra: Heat 1½ oz/43 g lard in a sauté pan over medium-high heat. Add 8 oz/227 g chopped onion, 1 tbsp/9 g minced garlic, 1 lb/454 g medium-dice tomatoes, and 3 finely chopped serranos. Cook until the vegetables are tender, about 15 minutes. Add this mixture to the beans in the final 15 minutes of cooking.

Black Bean Mash

Makes 10 servings

2 lb/907 g dried black beans

water or **Chicken Stock** (page 351), as needed

2 bay leaves

2 tsp/4 g dried oregano

salt, as needed

4 fl oz/120 mL olive oil

8 oz/227 g medium-dice onions

4 garlic cloves, minced

1 tbsp/6 g ground cumin

2 tbsp/6 g chopped oregano

ground black pepper, as needed

1. Sort the beans and rinse well with cold water.

2. Soak the beans using the long or short method. Drain the soaked beans.

3. Combine the beans and water or stock in a medium stockpot and add the bay leaves and oregano. Simmer the beans for 1 hour.

4. Add salt and continue to simmer until the beans are tender to the bite, 20 to 30 minutes.

5. Remove the bay leaves, strain any excess liquid from the beans, and reduce it until syrupy.

6. Heat the oil in a sauté pan over medium-high heat. Add the onions and garlic and sweat until tender. Add the cumin and oregano and stir to combine.

7. Add the beans to the onion mixture and purée using a blender. If the mixture becomes too thick, add the reduced bean liquid to thin it out. Season with salt and pepper.

8. Serve immediately or hold it warm for service.

Black Beans with Peppers and Chorizo

Black Beans with Peppers and Chorizo

Makes 10 servings

12 oz/340 g dried black beans

96 fl oz/2.88 L water or **Chicken Stock** (page 351)

salt, as needed

2 fl oz/60 mL vegetable oil

3 oz/85 g minced bacon

6 oz/170 g medium-dice onions

2 tsp/6 g minced garlic

4 oz/113 g sliced chorizo

3 oz/85 g medium-dice red peppers

3 oz/85 g medium-dice green peppers

2 oz/57 g sliced green onions

1 tbsp/3 g chopped oregano

1 tbsp/3 g chopped cilantro

ground black pepper, as needed

5 oz/142 g sour cream (optional)

1. Sort the beans and rinse well with cold water.

2. Soak the beans using the long or short method. Drain the soaked beans.

3. Combine the beans and water or stock in a medium pot. Simmer the beans for 1 hour. Add salt and continue to simmer until the beans are tender to the bite, 20 to 30 minutes. Set the beans aside in their cooking liquid.

4. In a large saucepan, heat the oil and add the bacon. Cook until the bacon is rendered. Add the onions and sauté until tender and lightly browned, about 8 minutes. Add the garlic and cook 1 minute more, stirring frequently.

5. Add the chorizo and peppers and sauté, stirring frequently, until the peppers are tender, 6 to 8 minutes.

6. Drain the beans and add them with enough cooking liquid to keep them moist (the consistency should be that of a thick stew). Simmer the beans until all the flavors are developed and all the ingredients are heated through.

7. Add the green onions and herbs and season with salt and pepper. Serve the beans with sour cream, if desired.

Corona Beans (Fagioli all'Uccelletto)

Makes 10 servings

2 lb/907 g dried corona beans

8 fl oz/240 mL olive oil

½ oz/14 g crushed garlic cloves

4 oz/113 g prosciutto or pancetta

2 carrots

4 celery ribs

1 thyme sprig

1 rosemary sprig

1 bay leaf

1 gal/3.84 L water, or as needed

salt, as needed

2 tbsp/6 g chopped rosemary

½ oz/14 g chopped sage

½ oz/14 g chopped parsley

ground black pepper, as needed

1. Sort the beans and rinse well with cold water.

2. Soak the beans using the long or short method. Drain the soaked beans.

3. Heat half of the oil in a medium pot, add the garlic, and cook until lightly browned, about 2 minutes. Add the prosciutto or pancetta and cook for 1 minute. Add the carrots, celery, thyme, rosemary, and bay leaf and cook for 2 minutes more.

4. Add the beans and water. Simmer the beans for 1 hour.

5. Add salt and continue to simmer until the beans are tender to the bite, 20 to 30 minutes.

6. Remove the garlic, meat, carrots, celery, and herbs. The beans can be drained for immediate use, reserving some of the cooking liquid, or rapidly cooled and refrigerated in their liquid.

7. To finish, heat the remaining oil in a saucepot an over medium heat. Add the beans with a small amount of their cooking liquid. Stir in the rosemary, sage, and parsley, taking care not to break the beans. Season with salt and pepper.

Creamed Pinto Beans (Frijoles Maneados)

Makes 10 servings

1 lb 8 oz/680 g dried pinto beans

64 fl oz/1.92 L water

1 lb/454 g minced onions

5 ancho chiles, seeds and membranes removed

1½ tsp/3 g ground cumin

½ fl oz/15 mL tomato paste

1½ tsp/1.50 g Mexican oregano

8 fl oz/240 mL milk

2 fl oz/60 mL vegetable oil

3 garlic cloves, minced

salt, as needed

ground black pepper, as needed

8 oz/227 g grated queso chihuahua

1. Sort the beans and rinse well with cold water.

2. Soak the beans using the long or short method. Drain the soaked beans.

3. Place the beans in a large pot with the water and onions. Bring to a simmer, covered, over medium heat until tender, about 20 minutes.

4. Heat the chiles briefly under a salamander without allowing them to cook. Cut the chilies into a chiffonade and add them to the beans along with the cumin, tomato paste, and oregano.

5. Using a spoon, scoop a portion of the beans (along with a little of the cooking liquid) into a blender or food processor. Purée with about 2 fl oz/60 mL of the milk. Continue puréeing portions of the beans with the milk until all the beans are puréed.

6. Heat the oil in a rondeau over medium heat. Add the garlic and cook until aromatic. Add to the puréed beans and mix well. Season with salt and pepper.

7. Cover the pot, place in a 350°F/177°C oven, and cook for 45 minutes to 1 hour.

8. Remove the pot from the oven, top the beans with grated cheese, and serve immediately or hold them hot for service.

Middle Eastern Chickpeas

Makes 10 servings

12 oz/340 g dried chickpeas

SACHET D'ÉPICES

1½ tsp/3 g cumin seed

1 tsp/1.50 g coriander seed

¼ tsp/1 g mustard seed

½ oz/14 g sliced ginger

½ tsp/1 g cracked pink peppercorns

½ tsp/1 g cracked black peppercorns

5 cardamom pods

1 cinnamon stick

1 fl oz/30 mL vegetable oil

6 oz/170 g chopped onions

½ oz/14 g minced garlic

96 fl oz/2.88 L **Chicken Stock** (page 351), or as needed

salt, as needed

lemon juice, as needed

ground black pepper, as needed

1. Sort the beans and rinse well with cold water.

2. Soak the beans using the long or short method. Drain the soaked beans.

3. To make the sachet d'épices, combine the cumin, coriander, mustard, ginger, peppercorns, cardamom, and cinnamon in cheesecloth and tie into a pouch with twine.

4. Heat the oil in a medium pot over medium heat. Add the onions and sweat until tender and translucent, about 5 to 6 minutes. Add the garlic and cook another minute.

5. Add the chickpeas, stock, and sachet. Simmer the beans for 1 hour.

6. Add salt and continue to simmer until the beans are tender to the bite, 20 to 30 minutes.

7. Season with lemon juice, salt, and pepper.

8. The chickpeas can be drained for immediate use or rapidly cooled and refrigerated in their liquid.

Roman-Style Lima Beans

Makes 10 servings

12 oz/340 g dried lima beans

BOUQUET GARNI

2 thyme sprigs

2 oregano sprigs

1 rosemary sprig

½ tsp/1 g cracked black peppercorns

2 leek leaves, 3 to 4 in/8 to 10 cm long

1 fl oz/30 mL olive oil

4 oz/113 g diced pancetta

6 oz/170 g chopped onions

½ oz/14 g minced garlic

96 fl oz/2.88 L **Chicken Stock** (page 351), or as needed

1 Parmesan rind (optional)

salt, as needed

red wine vinegar, as needed

ground black pepper, as needed

1. Sort the beans and rinse well with cold water.

2. Soak the beans using the long or short method. Drain the soaked beans.

3. To make a bouquet garni, sandwich the herbs and peppercorns between the leek leaves, and tie into a bundle with twine.

4. Heat the oil in a medium pot over medium heat, add the pancetta, and cook until the fat has rendered. Add the onions and sweat until tender and translucent, 5 to 6 minutes. Add the garlic and cook another minute.

5. Add the lima beans, stock, bouquet, and cheese rind, if using. Simmer the beans for 1 hour.

6. Add salt and continue to simmer until the beans are tender to the bite, 20 to 30 minutes.

7. Season with vinegar, salt, and pepper.

8. The lima beans can be drained for immediate use or rapidly cooled and refrigerated in their liquid.

Southwest White Bean Stew

Makes 10 servings

2 lb/907 g **Boiled White Beans** (page 825), drained

2 tsp/10 mL vegetable oil

6 oz/170 g chopped onions

4 oz/113 g small-dice red peppers

2 oz/57 g minced jalapeños

1 oz/28 g minced garlic

2 fl oz/60 mL sherry wine vinegar

4 oz/113 g tomato concassé

2 tbsp/6 g chopped cilantro

salt, as needed

ground black pepper, as needed

1. Purée half of the cooked beans and combine with the remaining beans.

2. Heat the oil in a saucepan over medium-high heat. Add the onions, peppers, jalapeños, and garlic. Sauté until the onions are translucent, about 5 to 6 minutes.

3. Add the beans and sauté, stirring constantly, until they are heated through.

4. Add the vinegar and concassé and continue to sauté until very hot.

5. Stir in the cilantro and season with salt and pepper. Serve immediately or hold them hot for service.

Stewed Black Beans

Makes 10 servings

2 lb/907 g dried black beans

1 fl oz/30 mL olive oil

8 oz/227 g small-dice onions

1 oz/28 g thinly sliced garlic

1 ham hock

Chicken Stock (page 351), as needed

salt, as needed

3 chipotles in adobo sauce, finely chopped

3 oz/85 g small-dice sun-dried tomatoes

ground black pepper, as needed

1. Sort the beans and rinse well with cold water.

2. Soak the beans using the long or short method. Drain the soaked beans.

3. Heat the oil in a medium pot. Add the onions and garlic and sweat until translucent.

4. Add the beans, ham hock, and enough stock to cover the beans by 1 in/3 cm. Simmer the beans for 1 hour.

5. Add the salt, chipotles, and the tomatoes. Continue to simmer until the beans are tender to the bite, 20 to 30 minutes. Remove the meat from the ham hock, dice it, and add it back to the beans. Season with salt and pepper.

6. Serve immediately or hold them hot for service.

Falafel

Makes 10 servings

11 oz/312 g dried chickpeas, soaked overnight

11 oz/312 g dried fava beans, soaked 2 nights

1 bunch parsley, chopped

3 green onions, finely chopped

1 tsp/2 g cayenne

1 tbsp/6 g ground cumin

1¼ tsp/2.50 g ground coriander

6 garlic cloves, crushed with salt

1¼ tsp/3.75 g baking powder

1 tbsp/15 g salt

32 fl oz/960 mL vegetable oil, or as needed for frying

1. Drain the soaked beans. Rinse and dry them.

2. In a food processor, blend the beans, parsley, onions, cayenne, cumin, coriander, garlic, baking powder, and salt together in batches until the mixture is homogeneous. Alternatively, the mixture can be ground twice through a food mill using a small die until very smooth.

3. Form the mixture into balls 1 to 1½ in/3 to 4 cm in diameter. Slightly flatten the balls.

4. Heat the oil to 350°F/177°C in a large rondeau or fryer and deep fry the falafel until crisp and brown, about 4 minutes.

5. Remove and drain briefly on paper towels. Serve immediately.

Red Beans and Boiled Rice

Makes 10 servings

1 lb/454 g dried red kidney beans, soaked

4 oz/113 g andouille sausage, ½-in/1-cm slices

1 smoked ham hock

4 oz/113 g minced onions

2 oz/57 g small-dice celery

2 oz/57 g small-dice green peppers

4 garlic cloves, minced

1 oz/28 g bacon fat

salt, as needed

ground black pepper, as needed

hot sauce, as needed

1 lb 8 oz/680 g long-grain white rice

1 gal 64 fl oz/5.76 L water

2½ oz/71 g salt

1. Drain the soaked beans, transfer them to a medium stockpot, add the sausage and ham hock, and cover with water. Simmer the beans until they are completely tender. If necessary, add additional water to keep the liquid 1 in/3 cm above the beans as they cook. Reserve the beans in their cooking liquid.

2. In a large rondeau, cook the onions, celery, peppers, and garlic in the bacon fat until they begin to turn golden brown. Add the cooked beans and their liquid. Simmer for 30 minutes. Season with salt and pepper. The beans should remain brothy. If necessary, add additional water.

3. Remove the meat from the ham hocks, cut into a medium dice, and add to the beans. Mash the beans with the back of a spoon until they become creamy. Add the hot sauce and adjust seasoning with salt and pepper.

4. Rinse the rice under cold water in a strainer until the water runs clear. Drain the rice well before using. Bring the water to a boil and add the salt.

5. Add the rinsed rice to the boiling water and simmer until tender, 10 to 15 minutes. Stir the rice as it cooks to prevent burning.

6. Serve the beans immediately on a bed of the rice or hold everything hot for service.

Boiled White Beans

Makes 10 servings

1 lb/454 g dried white beans

1 fl oz/30 mL vegetable oil

4 oz/113 g chopped onions

1 ham hock (optional)

64 fl oz/1.92 L **Chicken Stock** (page 351)

1 **Sachet d'Épices** (page 331)

salt, as needed

1. Sort the beans and rinse well with cold water.

2. Soak the beans using the long or short method. Drain the soaked beans.

3. Heat the oil in a medium pot. Add the onions and sweat until translucent.

4. Add the beans, ham hock, if using, stock, and sachet d'épices. Simmer the beans for 1 hour.

5. Season with salt and continue to simmer until the beans are tender to the bite, 20 to 30 minutes.

6. Remove the ham hock and sachet d'épices.

7. The beans can be drained for immediate use or rapidly cooled and refrigerated in their liquid.

Vegetarian Chili

Makes 10 servings

1 lb/454 g dried black beans

salt, as needed

2 fl oz/60 mL olive oil

8 oz/227 g small-dice onions

8 oz/227 g small-dice green peppers

8 oz/227 g small-dice red peppers

8 oz/227 g small-dice yellow peppers

½ oz/14 g minced garlic

½ to 1 chipotle in adobo sauce, finely chopped, plus 1 tsp/5 mL adobo sauce

2 poblanos, roasted, seeded, and peeled, small dice

2 tsp/4 g chili powder

1 tbsp/6 g ground cumin

¾ tsp/1.50 g ground coriander

pinch ground cinnamon

2½ oz/71 g tomato paste

6 fl oz/180 mL white wine

28 fl oz/840 mL **Vegetable Stock** (page 353)

5 oz/142 g small-dice tomatoes

½ oz/14 g masa harina, diluted in vegetable stock to make a slurry

ground black pepper, as needed

sugar, as needed

8 oz/227 g grated Monterey Jack

5 fl oz/150 mL sour cream

3 tbsp/9 g chopped cilantro

1. Sort the beans and rinse well with cold water.

2. Soak the beans using the long or short method. Drain the soaked beans.

3. Simmer the beans for 1 hour. Add salt and continue to simmer until the beans are tender to the bite, 20 to 30 minutes. Drain well.

4. Heat the oil is a large saucepan over medium-high heat. Add the onions, peppers, garlic, chipotle, and poblanos and sauté until aromatic and just turning golden.

5. Add the chili powder, cumin, coriander, and cinnamon and cook until aromatic. Stir in the tomato paste, and cook for 2 minutes.

6. Add the wine and reduce by ⅔. Add the stock and tomatoes, bring to a simmer, and cook gently for 8 to 10 minutes, or until the vegetables are tender.

7. Add the drained black beans and cook an additional 5 minutes.

8. Add the masa slurry to the chili, mix well, and bring back to simmer. Season with salt, pepper, and sugar.

9. Serve immediately, garnished with cheese, sour cream, and cilantro or hold it hot for service.

Vegetarian Chili

Rice and Beans

Makes 10 servings

1 lb/454 g dried red kidney beans, soaked

4 oz/113 g diced bacon

2 garlic cloves, minced

48 fl oz/1.44 L **Chicken Stock** (page 351)

5 oz/142 g long-grain white rice

8 fl oz/240 mL coconut milk

1½ oz/43 g chopped green onions

1 tbsp/3 g chopped thyme

salt, as needed

ground black pepper, as needed

1. Drain the soaked beans. In a medium saucepan, render the bacon over low heat. Add the garlic and sweat until aromatic. Add the stock and beans. Simmer until the beans are tender.

2. Rinse the rice under cold water in a strainer until the water runs clear. Drain the rice well before using. Add the rice and coconut milk to the beans. Cover and simmer until the rice is tender, about 20 minutes, or until all the liquid is absorbed.

3. Gently fold in the green onions and thyme and season with salt and pepper.

4. Serve immediately or hold it hot for service.

Rice Pilaf

Makes 10 servings

14 oz/397 g long-grain white rice

1 fl oz/30 mL clarified butter or vegetable oil

¾ oz/21 g minced onions

24 to 28 fl oz/720 to 840 mL **Chicken Stock** (page 351), hot

1 bay leaf

2 thyme sprigs

salt, as needed

ground black pepper, as needed

1. Rinse the rice under cold water in a strainer until the water runs clear, if desired. Drain the rice well before using.

2. Heat the butter or oil in a heavy-gauge pot over medium heat. Add the onions and cook, stirring frequently, until tender and translucent, 5 to 6 minutes.

3. Add the rice and sauté, stirring frequently, until coated with butter or oil and heated through, 2 to 3 minutes.

4. Add the heated stock to the rice and bring to a simmer, stirring to prevent the rice from clumping together or sticking to the bottom of the pot.

5. Add the bay leaf, thyme, salt, and pepper. Cover the pot and place it in a 350°F/177°C oven (or leave it over low heat on the stovetop). Cook until the grains are tender to the bite, 14 to 16 minutes.

6. Allow the rice to rest 5 minutes, fluff with a fork, and serve immediately or hold it hot for service.

Short-Grain White Rice Pilaf (Valencia): Substitute an equal amount of short-grain white rice for the long-grain. Decrease the stock to between 16 and 24 fl oz/480 and 720 mL. Increase the cooking time to between 20 and 30 minutes.

Converted White Rice Pilaf: Substitute an equal amount of converted white rice for the long-grain. Use 28 fl oz/840 mL chicken stock. Increase the cooking time to between 25 and 30 minutes.

Wild Rice Pilaf: Substitute an equal amount of wild rice for the long-grain. Increase the stock to 48 fl oz/1.44 L. Increase the cooking time to 45 minutes.

Wheat Berry Pilaf: Substitute an equal amount of wheat berries for the long-grain white rice. Soak them overnight in cold water in the refrigerator and drain before cooking. Increase the stock to 38 fl oz/1.14 L. Increase the cooking time to between 1 and 1½ hours.

Pearl Barley Pilaf: Substitute an equal amount of pearl barley for the long-grain white rice. Increase the cooking time to 40 minutes.

Brown Rice Pilaf with Pecans and Green Onions

Makes 10 servings

14 oz/397 g long-grain brown rice

1½ oz/43 g butter or oil

2 oz/57 g minced onions

48 fl oz/1.44 L **Chicken Stock** (page 351), hot

1 **Bouquet Garni** (page 331)

salt, as needed

ground black pepper, as needed

2 oz/57 g toasted pecans, chopped

2 oz/57 g sliced green onions

1. Rinse the rice under cold water in a strainer until the water runs clear, if desired. Drain the rice well before using.

2. Heat the butter or oil in a heavy-gauge pot over medium heat. Add the onions and cook, stirring frequently, until tender and translucent, 5 to 6 minutes.

3. Add the rice and sauté, stirring frequently, until coated with butter or oil and heated through, 2 to 3 minutes.

4. Add the stock to the rice and bring to a simmer, stirring to prevent the rice from clumping together or sticking to the bottom of the pot.

5. Add the bouquet garni, salt, and pepper. Cover the pot and place it in 350°F/177°C oven (or leave it over low

heat on the stovetop). Cook until the grains are tender to the bite, 40 to 45 minutes.

6. Allow the rice to rest 5 minutes; uncover, and use a fork to fold in the pecans and green onions while separating the grains and releasing the steam. Serve immediately or hold it hot for service.

Short-Grain Brown Rice Pilaf: Substitute an equal amount of short-grain brown rice for the long-grain. Decrease the amount of stock to 40 fl oz/1.20 L. Decrease the cooking time to between 35 and 40 minutes.

Annatto Rice

Makes 10 servings

14 oz/397 g long-grain white rice

1 oz/28 g butter

¾ fl oz/22.50 mL annatto paste

½ Scotch bonnet, seeded and minced

3 garlic cloves, minced

1 lb/454 g small-dice **Mirepoix** (page 333)

1 bay leaf

28 fl oz/840 mL **Chicken Stock** (page 351)

salt, as needed

ground black pepper, as needed

1. Rinse the rice under cold water in a strainer until the water runs clear, if desired. Drain the rice well before using.

2. In heavy-gauge pot, heat the butter and dissolve the annatto paste.

3. Add the Scotch bonnet, garlic, mirepoix, and bay leaf. Cook over medium heat until the onions are translucent, about 10 minutes.

4. Add the rice, stock, salt, and pepper. Bring to a simmer, reduce the heat, cover, and cook in a 350°F/177°C oven for 12 to 15 minutes.

5. Allow the rice to rest for 5 minutes, fluff it with a fork, and serve immediately or hold it hot for service.

Arroz Blanco

Makes 10 servings

14 oz/397 g long-grain white rice

2 fl oz/60 mL vegetable oil

6 oz/170 g minced onions

1 garlic clove, minced

28 fl oz/840 mL **Chicken Stock** (page 351)

6 oz/170 g corn, fresh or frozen

salt, as needed

ground black pepper, as needed

1. Rinse the rice under cold water in a strainer until the water runs clear, if desired. Drain the rice well before using.

2. Add the oil to a heavy-gauge pot and heat to its smoke point. Add the rice and coat well. Cook the rice over a medium-high heat until it starts to turn a pale golden color.

3. Add the onions and garlic and continue to cook until the onions start to color. Add the stock, corn, salt, and pepper.

4. Bring to a simmer, reduce the heat, cover, and cook in a 350°F/177°C oven for 12 to 15 minutes.

5. Allow the rice to rest for 5 minutes, fluff it with a fork, and serve immediately or hold it hot for service.

Arroz Brasileiro

Makes 10 servings

1½ oz/43 g butter

4 oz/113 g minced onions

1½ tsp/4.50 g minced garlic

14 oz/397 g long-grain white rice

1 clove

36 fl oz/1.08 L water, hot

salt, as needed

ground black pepper, as needed

1. In a heavy-gauge pot, heat the butter over medium heat. Add the onions and garlic and sauté until the onions are translucent, about 5 minutes.

2. Add the rice, stirring constantly, until the rice has absorbed the butter and the grains are translucent.

3. Add the clove and the water and bring to a boil over high heat. Reduce the heat, season with salt and pepper, cover, and simmer for 20 minutes, or until the rice is tender.

4. Allow the rice to rest for 5 minutes, fluff it with a fork, and serve immediately or hold it hot for service.

Coconut Rice

Makes 10 servings

14 oz/397 g long-grain white rice

1½ fl oz/45 mL vegetable oil or melted butter

16 fl oz/480 mL water

12 fl oz/360 mL unsweetened coconut milk

salt, as needed

ground black pepper, as needed

1. Rinse the rice under cold water in a strainer until the water runs clear, if desired. Drain the rice well before using.

2. Heat the oil or butter in a heavy-gauge pot over medium heat. Add the rice and sauté, stirring frequently, until coated with butter or oil and heated through.

3. Add the water and coconut milk to the rice and season with salt and pepper. Bring to a simmer, reduce the heat, cover, and cook in a 350°F/177°C oven for 12 to 15 minutes.

4. Allow the rice to rest for 5 minutes, fluff it with a fork, and serve immediately or hold it hot for service.

Risotto

Makes 10 servings

2 oz/57 g minced onions

2 oz/57 g butter

14 oz/397 g Arborio rice

48 fl oz/1.44 L **Chicken Stock** (page 351), hot

salt, as needed

ground black pepper, as needed

1. Sweat the onions in the butter until softened and translucent, 6 to 8 minutes.

2. Add the rice and mix thoroughly with the butter. Cook, stirring constantly, until a toasted aroma rises, about 1 minute.

3. Add one third of the stock to the rice, and cook, stirring constantly, until the rice has absorbed the stock. Repeat, adding the remaining stock in 2 more portions, allowing each to be absorbed before adding the next. Cook the risotto until the rice is just tender and most of the liquid is absorbed. (The dish should be creamy.)

4. Season with salt and pepper and serve immediately or hold it warm for service.

Parmesan Risotto: Prepare the risotto, replacing up to one quarter of the stock with a dry white wine. Add the wine to the stock as it heats to a simmer for the best flavor. Finish the risotto by adding 4 oz/113 g grated Parmesan and 4 oz/113 g butter.

Wild Mushroom Risotto: Soak 3 oz/85 g dried wild mushrooms in 8 fl oz/240 mL warm water for 30 minutes to 1 hour; drain the mushrooms and add to the pan with the onions. Strain the soaking liquid through a paper filter to remove any sediment, measure it, and use it to replace an equal amount of the stock for the risotto.

Green Pea Risotto (Risi e Bisi): Fold 8 oz/227 g cooked green peas into the prepared risotto.

Risotto with Asparagus Tips: Fold 2½ oz/71 g blanched asparagus tips into the prepared risotto. Finish the risotto by adding 4 oz/113 g grated Parmesan, 4 oz/113 g butter, and 1½ oz/43 g minced parsley.

Risotto alla Milanese

Makes 10 servings

46 fl oz/1.38 L **Chicken Stock** (page 351)

¾ tsp/0.60 g saffron

salt, as needed

ground black pepper, as needed

3 oz/85 g minced onions

7 fl oz/210 mL extra-virgin olive oil

14 oz/397 g Arborio rice

2 fl oz/60 mL dry white wine

5 oz/142 g butter

6 oz/170 g grated Parmesan

1. Heat the stock over low heat. Add the saffron and season with salt and pepper.

2. Sweat the onions in 2 fl oz/60 mL of the oil until softened and translucent, 6 to 8 minutes.

3. Add the rice and mix thoroughly with the oil. Cook, stirring constantly, until a toasted aroma rises, about 1 minute. Add the wine and cook until dry.

4. Add one third of the stock to the rice, and cook, stirring constantly, until the rice has absorbed the stock. Repeat, adding the remaining stock in 2 more portions, allowing each to be absorbed before adding the next. Cook the risotto until the rice is just tender and most of the liquid is absorbed. (The dish should be creamy.)

5. Stir in the butter, cheese, and remaining oil. Adjust seasoning with salt and pepper and serve immediately or hold it warm for service.

Risotto with Mussels

Makes 10 servings

5 lb/2.27 kg mussels, cleaned and debearded

40 fl oz/1.20 L **Fish Stock** (page 353), hot

salt, as needed

ground black pepper, as needed

2 oz/57 g minced onions

2 oz/57 g butter

14 oz/397 g Arborio rice

1½ oz/43 g minced parsley

4 oz/113 g butter

1. Steam the mussels in a small amount of salted water in a covered pot until the shells open. Remove the mussel meat from the shells and reserve. Strain the cooking liquid.

2. Bring the stock and the cooking liquid from the mussels to a simmer and season with salt and pepper.

3. Sweat the onions in the butter until softened and translucent, 6 to 8 minutes.

4. Add the rice and mix thoroughly with the butter. Cook, stirring constantly, until a toasted aroma rises, about 1 minute.

5. Add one third of the stock to the rice, and cook, stirring constantly, until the rice has absorbed the stock. Repeat, adding the remaining stock in 2 more portions, allowing each to be absorbed before adding the next. Add the mussel meat and cook until the rice is just tender and most of the liquid is absorbed. (The dish should be creamy.)

6. Remove from the heat and stir in the parsley and butter. Adjust seasoning with salt and pepper and serve immediately.

Basic Boiled Rice

Makes 10 servings

14 oz/397 g long-grain white rice

96 fl oz/2.88 L water

salt, as needed

1. Rinse the rice under cold water in a strainer until the water runs clear. Drain the rice well before using.

2. Bring the water to a rolling boil and add the salt.

3. Add the rice in a thin stream, stirring it with a fork to prevent the grains from clumping as they are added. (There should be enough water to cover the rice.) When the water returns to a boil, reduce the heat to a simmer.

4. Simmer the rice until tender, about 15 minutes. Drain immediately in a colander and set the colander in the pot. Return to the heat to steam the rice dry for 5 minutes. (The rice should no longer be sticky.)

5. Fluff it with a fork and serve immediately or hold it hot for service.

Steamed Long-Grain Rice (Lo Han)

Makes 10 servings

2 lb/907 g long-grain Chinese rice

48 fl oz/1.44 L water, or as needed

1. Rinse the rice under cold water in a strainer until the water runs clear, if desired. Drain the rice well before using.

2. Place the rice in a half hotel pan and add water to cover by ¼ in/6 mm.

3. Cover and cook in a steamer or rice cooker for 45 minutes, or until the grains are tender.

4. Allow the rice to rest for 10 minutes, fluff it with a fork, and serve immediately or hold it hot for service.

Sushi Rice

Makes 10 full-sized rolls or 20 half rolls

3 lb 8 oz/1.59 kg short-grain rice

64 fl oz/1.92 L water

1 kombu square (6 in/15 cm; optional)

6 fl oz/180 mL unseasoned Japanese rice vinegar

2½ oz/71 g sugar

1¼ oz/35 g sea salt

1. Rinse the rice under cold water in a strainer until the water runs semiclear. Cover the rice with cool water and soak 1 hour. Drain well.

2. Combine the drained rice with the water in a 2-in/5-cm-deep hotel pan. Steam until the rice is almost completely cooked, about 30 minutes.

3. Allow the rice to rest at room temperature for 10 minutes.

4. If using the kombu, slash it with a knife in a few places and wipe it with a damp cloth, only to remove any sand, being careful not to remove any flavorful white powder. Combine the vinegar, sugar, salt, and kombu, in a small saucepan. Warm over low heat, stirring to dissolve the sugar and salt. Do not let the mixture boil. Cool to room temperature.

5. Transfer the rice to two 2-in/5-cm-deep hotel pans. Drizzle with the vinegar mixture. Using a wooden rice paddle, "cut" and fold the rice with horizontal strokes. Continue until the mixture has cooled and takes on a shiny appearance.

6. Combine the 2 pans of rice and serve immediately or refrigerate for later use.

Thai Sticky Rice with Mangos (Mamuang Kao Nieo)

Makes 10 servings

14 oz/397 g sticky rice, soaked overnight

22 fl oz/660 mL coconut milk

12 oz/340 g Thai palm sugar

¾ oz/21 g salt

1¼ oz/35 g sugar

1 oz/28 g rice flour

1 fl oz/30 mL water

4 mangos, peeled and sliced

1. Drain the soaked rice and place it in a steamer lined with cheesecloth. Steam until the grains are soft, 20 to 25 minutes.

2. While the rice is steaming, combine 5½ fl oz/165 mL of the coconut milk with the palm sugar and 1 tbsp/15 g of the salt in a saucepan. Warm over low heat to dissolve the salt and sugar. Mix well and set aside.

3. When the rice is done, transfer it to a bowl. While still hot, add the coconut milk and sugar mixture. Using a spatula, stir to coat the grains quickly and evenly. Cover with plastic wrap and set aside for 15 minutes, or until the rice absorbs the liquid.

4. Combine the remaining coconut milk, sugar, and salt in a saucepan. Bring to a boil and reduce the heat. Combine the rice flour and water and mix well. While the sauce is simmering, drizzle in the rice flour mixture and stir constantly. Return to a boil, immediately remove from the heat, and set aside.

5. Serve immediately with ½ to 1 oz/15 to 30 mL of the coconut topping and the mango slices or hold it hot for service.

Saffron Rice

Makes 10 servings

2 lb/907 g basmati rice

1 gal 64 fl oz/5.76 L water

1 tbsp/15 g salt

2 oz/57 g butter

2 fl oz/60 mL milk

1½ tsp/1.20 g saffron, crumbled

1. Rinse the rice under cold water in a strainer until the water runs clear. Drain the rice well before using. Bring the water to a boil and add the salt.

2. Lightly butter a medium rondeau. Prepare parchment paper and aluminum foil to use as a cover for the rondeau.

3. Melt the remaining butter in a saucepot and add the milk and saffron to steep.

4. Add the rice to the rapidly boiling water, cover, and cook for 7 minutes. Drain the rice in a colander and transfer it to the buttered rondeau.

5. Ladle the milk mixture over the rice and toss lightly with a fork to combine. Do not stir.

6. Tightly cover the rondeau with parchment paper and then aluminum foil.

7. Bake in a 400°F/204°C oven for 15 minutes.

8. Allow the rice to rest for 5 minutes uncovered, fluff it with a fork, and serve immediately or hold it hot for service.

Fried Rice with Chinese Sausage

Makes 10 servings

2½ fl oz/75 mL vegetable oil

8 oz/227 g medium-dice Chinese sausage

6 oz/170 g minced onions

8 oz/227 g medium-dice carrots, blanched

8 oz/227 g medium-dice shiitake mushrooms

8 oz/227 g roughly chopped napa cabbage

4 lb 8 oz/2.04 kg cooked long-grain rice, chilled

salt, as needed

ground black pepper, as needed

8 oz/227 g snow peas, cut into ¾-in/2-cm squares

5 eggs, beaten

2 fl oz/60 mL mushroom soy sauce (optional)

1. Heat 2 fl oz/60 mL of the oil in a wok over medium heat. Add the sausage and cook to render the fat.

2. Increase the heat and add the onions. Stir-fry until aromatic and beginning to brown.

3. Add the carrots, mushrooms, and cabbage in that order, allowing time for each ingredient to begin browning before adding the next.

4. Add the rice, salt, and pepper and stir-fry until the rice is hot and begins to brown.

5. Add the snow peas and cook until they are bright green.

6. Add the remaining oil to the sides of the wok and drizzle the egg mixture around the top of the rice. As the egg mixture cooks, fold it into the rice. Add the soy sauce, if using.

7. Adjust seasoning with salt, pepper, and soy sauce, if using. Serve immediately or hold it hot for service.

Fried Rice with Chinese Sausage

Paella Valenciana

Paella Valenciana

Makes 10 servings

20 shrimp (16–20 count)

3 fl oz/90 mL extra-virgin olive oil

2¼ tsp/1.80 g crushed saffron

72 fl oz/2.16 L **Chicken Stock** (page 351), or as needed

10 chicken legs, separated

salt, as needed

ground black pepper, as needed

6 oz/170 g large-dice onions

6 oz/170 g large-dice red peppers

6 oz/170 g large-dice green peppers

1½ oz/43 g minced garlic

6 oz/170 g dry Spanish chorizo, sliced ⅛ in/3 mm thick

1 lb 8 oz/680 g Spanish rice

6 oz/170 g peeled, seeded, and large-diced tomatoes

20 clams, cleaned

3 lb/1.36 kg mussels, cleaned and debearded

6 oz/170 g green peas, cooked

1½ oz/43 g thinly sliced green onions

4 piquillo chiles, julienned

1. Peel and devein the shrimp, reserving the shells. Sauté the shells in 1 fl oz/30 mL of the oil until they turn pink. Add the saffron and stock and simmer 30 minutes. Strain and reserve hot.

2. Season the chicken with salt and pepper. Add 1 fl oz/30 mL of the oil to a paella pan and heat to the smoke point. Add the chicken and brown on all sides. Remove from the pan and reserve.

3. Add the remaining oil to the pan with the onions and peppers. Sauté for 2 to 3 minutes, add the garlic, and sauté for 1 minute. Add the chorizo and rice, stirring to coat the rice with the oil.

4. Add the tomatoes, reserved stock, chicken, and clams to the pan. Cover, reduce the heat, and cook 5 minutes or until all the clams have opened. Do not stir the rice during the cooking process.

5. Add the mussels and shrimp to the pan. Cover and cook for 5 to 7 minutes. During the last minute, add the peas. (Add more stock during cooking, if necessary, so that the rice does not dry out.)

6. Serve immediately, garnished with green onions and piquillo chiles.

Rice Croquettes

Makes 10 servings

1 lb 8 oz/680 g **Basic Boiled Rice** (page 832) or **Risotto** (page 831)

10 fl oz/300 mL heavy **Béchamel Sauce** (page 384)

3 oz/85 g grated Parmesan

3 egg yolks

salt, as needed

ground black pepper, as needed

7 oz/198 g bread crumbs, or as needed for breading

3 oz/85 g cornmeal, or as needed for breading

4 fl oz/120 mL **Egg Wash** (page 1061), or as needed for breading

32 fl oz/960 mL vegetable oil, or as needed for frying

1. Blend the prepared rice or risotto with the béchamel, cheese, and egg yolks. Season with salt and pepper. Spread the mixture in an even layer on a buttered, parchment-lined sheet pan. Place a sheet of plastic wrap over the mixture and refrigerate for several hours or overnight to chill and firm the rice.

2. Combine the bread crumbs and cornmeal. Cut the rice in the desired shape and dip first into the egg wash, and then into the bread crumb mixture.

3. Heat the oil to 350°F/177°C and deep fry the croquettes until golden brown, 5 to 6 minutes. Drain briefly on absorbent paper towels and serve immediately.

Congee

Makes 10 servings

1 gal/3.84 L water

2-in/5-cm piece ginger, crushed

1 lb/454 g skinless chicken thighs

1 lb 12 oz/794 g long-grain white rice

½ fl oz/15 mL fish sauce

salt, as needed

CONDIMENTS

2 fl oz/60 mL soy sauce

1 fl oz/30 mL fish sauce

1 fl oz/30 mL chili sauce

2 tbsp/2 g dried shrimp

3 tbsp/9 g chopped cilantro

1 shallot, sliced

1 oz/28 g toasted peanuts, crushed

1. Place the water and ginger in a large pot and bring to a boil. Add the chicken and simmer until cooked through. Remove the chicken from the liquid, cool to room temperature, and shred into bite-size pieces.

2. Remove the ginger from the liquid and discard. Add the rice in a thin stream, stirring it with a fork to prevent the grains from clumping as they are added. When the water returns to a boil, reduce the heat to a simmer.

3. Simmer the rice until tender, about 25 minutes. Add the fish sauce and salt. Adjust the consistency with water, if necessary; the congee should be soupy.

4. Add the chicken meat to the congee. Sprinkle the condiments over the rice and serve immediately.

Basic Polenta

Makes 10 servings

120 fl oz/3.60 L water

salt, as needed

1 lb/454 g coarse yellow cornmeal

2 oz/57 g butter

ground black pepper, as needed

1. Bring the water to a boil and season with salt.

2. Pour the cornmeal into the water in a stream, stirring constantly until it has all been added. Simmer, stirring often, until the polenta pulls away from the sides of the pot, about 45 minutes.

3. Remove the pot from the heat and blend in the butter. Season with salt and pepper.

4. Serve immediately as soft polenta or hold it warm until service.

NOTES

For firm polenta, decrease the amount of water to 80 fl oz/2.40 L. After blending the butter into the polenta, spread the mixture onto a greased or plastic-lined half sheet pan, and refrigerate until cool enough to cut into desired shapes. Finish by sautéing, pan frying, grilling, or baking.

Polenta with Parmesan: Substitute Chicken Stock (page 351) for the water. Sweat ½ oz/14 g minced shallots and 1 tbsp/9 g minced garlic in 1 oz/28 g butter until aromatic, about 3 minutes. Add the stock and cook the polenta according to the above method. Remove the pot from the heat and stir in 3 egg yolks and 2 oz/57 g grated Parmesan.

Polenta with Parmesan

Green Onion–Bulgur Pilaf

Green Onion–Bulgur Pilaf

Makes 10 servings

1 lb 2 oz/510 g coarse-grain bulgur

4 fl oz/120 mL extra-virgin olive oil

10 oz/284 g sliced green onions

1 oz/28 g tomato paste

120 fl oz/3.60 L water

1½ tsp/3 g sweet paprika

1½ tsp/3 g hot paprika

salt, as needed

ground black pepper, as needed

1. Wash and rinse the bulgur in a fine-mesh sieve.

2. Heat half of the oil in a saucepan over medium-high heat. Add the green onions and sauté for 30 seconds to 1 minute.

3. Stir in the tomato paste and cook over medium heat, 30 seconds to 1 minute.

4. Add the bulgur and sauté, stirring frequently, until coated with oil and heated through, 2 to 3 minutes.

5. Add the water and bring to a boil over high heat.

6. Add the paprikas to the boiling water. Season with salt and pepper.

7. Simmer the bulgur mixture, covered, until all the water is absorbed, about 20 minutes.

8. Allow the bulgur to rest for 10 minutes, and then gently dress it with the remaining oil.

9. Serve immediately or hold it hot for service.

Kasha with Spicy Maple Pecans

Makes 10 servings

2 each egg whites, lightly beaten

14 oz/397 g kasha

24 fl oz/720 mL **Chicken Stock** (page 351) or **Vegetable Stock** (page 353)

salt, as needed

1½ oz/43 g butter

3 oz/85 g toasted pecans, chopped

2 fl oz/60 mL maple syrup

cayenne, as needed

1. Combine the egg whites and kasha in a saucepan and cook over low heat, stirring constantly, for 2 minutes.

2. Add the stock, salt, and butter to the kasha and bring to a boil over high heat. Reduce the heat to low and simmer, covered, for about 15 minutes.

3. Remove from the heat and let it steam for about 5 minutes. Uncover and fluff the kasha by lifting it gently with 2 forks to remove any lumps.

4. While the kasha steams, place the pecans, maple syrup, and cayenne in a small skillet. Heat over low heat until the pecans are well coated and the maple syrup has reduced to a very thick consistency.

5. Scatter the spiced pecans over the kasha and serve immediately or hold it hot for service.

Quinoa à la Jardinera

Makes 10 servings

14 oz/397 g quinoa

2 gal/7.68 L water

2 oz/57 g butter

2 jalapeños, seeded and minced

1 green pepper, small dice

1 red pepper, small dice

2 shallots, minced

1 tbsp/9 g finely minced ginger

1 carrot, small dice

1 celery stalk, small dice

salt, as needed

ground black pepper, as needed

4 green onions, minced

2 tbsp/6 g chopped parsley

1 tbsp/3 g chopped thyme

4 tbsp/12 g basil, chiffonade

1. Rinse the quinoa under cold water in a strainer until the water runs clear, if desired. Drain the quinoa well before using.

2. Bring the water to a simmer in a large sauce pot, add the quinoa and cook for 4 to 5 minutes, or until the quinoa is barely cooked. Pour the cooked quinoa into a strainer and drain the excess water. Transfer to a large sheet tray, spread, and allow it to cool. Fluff the quinoa from time to time.

3. Melt the butter in a large rondeau over medium-high heat. Add the jalapeños, peppers, shallots, ginger, carrots, and celery. Season with salt and pepper. Sweat the vegetables until tender.

4. Add the quinoa and continue to cook until heated through, adding additional water if necessary.

5. Serve immediately, garnished with the green onions and herbs, or hold it hot for service.

Chapter Twenty-eight

Cooking Pasta and Dumplings

The immense popularity of pastas and dumplings is not at all surprising. Nutritious and highly versatile, these foods are an important element of most cuisines. They are based on ingredients that are inexpensive and easy to store: flour, meal, and eggs. They adapt well to a number of uses and can be found on contemporary menus as appetizers, entrées, salads, and even desserts.

Making Fresh Pasta, Noodles, and Dumplings

The formula for fresh pasta may be thought of as the base recipe to produce a stiff dough that can be endlessly varied to produce myriad shapes, flavors, and colors. The general category of pasta includes both dried and fresh noodles. Pasta may be prepared fresh on the premises or purchased either fresh or dried. There are advantages to both fresh and dried pastas. Fresh pasta gives the chef freedom to create dishes with special flavors, colors, shapes, or fillings, but it has a limited shelf life. Dried pasta can be stored almost indefinitely.

Changing the ratio of flour to liquid or introducing other ingredients into a basic pasta formula produces doughs and batters that are handled and cooked differently from the base recipe. For example, the amount of liquid can be increased to create a soft batter for spätzle. This batter is cut off a spätzle board or dropped through a sieve or spätzle maker into simmering liquid rather than rolled or extruded as for a thicker pasta dough.

Adding a leavener to the basic pasta formula produces a soft batter that can be used for larger dumplings, with a bread-like texture, that are simmered in a stew or other liquid. Although the term "dumpling" may mean something very specific to an individual or a particular ethnic group, it actually is a very broad category. Some dumplings are based on doughs and batters, and others on ingredients ranging from bread to puréed potatoes. The popular Chinese dim sum, including steamed yeast doughs and fried egg rolls, is yet another category. Dumplings may be cooked in a variety of ways, according to type. They may be simmered in liquid, steamed, poached, baked, pan fried, or deep fried. A variety of ingredients can be used. See the recipes included in this chapter for specific instructions.

Because flour provides the structure in pasta, it is important to choose one that has the necessary qualities for making the best possible dough. All-purpose flours can be used successfully for most fresh pasta. Whole wheat flour, semolina, cornmeal, buckwheat flour, rye flour, ground legumes (chickpeas, for instance), and other special flours and meals can be used to replace a portion of the all-purpose flour, giving the pasta unique flavor, texture, and color. Experimentation is often the best way to determine how to use special flours. Refer to the recipes for guidance on types, ratios, and substitutions.

Eggs are frequently included in fresh pasta to provide moisture, flavor, and structure. Different formulas may specify the use of whole eggs, yolks, or whites. Because it is especially important to have the proper amount of moisture, many recipes call for water. Doughs that are too dry or too moist are difficult to roll out.

Neutral or flavored oil is often used in pasta doughs because it helps keep the dough pliable and makes it easy to work with.

Adding salt to the dough helps to develop flavor. Additional ingredients, such as herbs, vegetable purées, or citrus zest, may be added to fresh pasta dough to change its color, flavor, or texture. If these added flavoring or coloring ingredients contain a lot of moisture, it is necessary to adjust the basic formula, by either using additional flour or less water. Vegetable purées used for flavor or color are often dried slightly by sautéing them first in order to concentrate their flavors.

Equipment needs for fresh pasta are very basic, though a few special pieces of equipment can make the job even simpler. At the very least, you will need your hands, a rolling pin, and a knife. Or use an electric mixer with a dough hook or a food processor to mix the dough, and a pasta rolling machine to roll it out. Cutting attachments that result in uniform cuts of pasta are available for the rolling machines.

Fresh pasta and noodles can be covered and refrigerated for up to 2 days. If the pasta is cut in long strands, sprinkle it with cornmeal, semolina, or rice flour to keep the strands from sticking together. Hold the pasta on trays lined with plastic, and cover it with plastic as well. Filled pastas should be held on lined sheet trays, arranged so that they are not touching each other.

If the pasta is to be stored for more than 2 days, roll long strands into loose nests and arrange them on parchment-lined sheet trays. Set the trays in a warm, dry place for several days, until the pasta has hardened and dried. Once dried, pasta may be held, well wrapped, in a cool, dry place the same way as commercial dried pastas. Fresh pasta, especially filled pastas such as tortellini and ravioli, may also be frozen successfully.

A basic formula for 10 portions of fresh pasta

Main ingredient:

1 lb/454 g all-purpose flour or mixtures of flours

Tenderizing and enriching options include:

4 whole eggs

1 fl oz/30 mL oil

Ingredients to adjust seasoning and consistency:

Salt

Water

Other flavoring or garnishing ingredients as desired

1. **Mix pasta dough by hand or by machine.** For small batches, it may be just as efficient to mix the dough manually. Large batches, on the other hand, can be made much more easily with a food processor or electric mixer.

To mix the dough by hand, combine the flour and salt in a bowl or on a work bench and make a well in the center. Place the eggs, flavoring ingredients, and oil (if using) in the well. Working as rapidly as possible, gradually incorporate the flour into the liquid ingredients until a loose mass forms.

To mix in a food processor, place all the ingredients in the bowl of a food processor fitted with a steel blade. Process until blended. The dough should look like a coarse meal that will cohere when pressed into a ball. Do not overprocess.

To mix in an electric mixer, place all the ingredients in the bowl of a mixer fitted with a dough hook. Mix at medium speed until the dough forms a smooth ball that pulls cleanly away from the bowl's sides.

As the dough is mixed, adjust the consistency with additional flour or water, to compensate for the variations in ingredients, humidity in the kitchen, or the addition of optional flavoring ingredients. On very dry days, it may be necessary to add a few drops of water to reach the desired consistency.

2. **Knead until the dough is properly developed.** Let the dough rest before rolling and cutting. Once mixed, whether by hand, processor, or mixer, the dough should be turned out onto a floured work surface and kneaded until the texture becomes smooth and elastic.

3. **Gather and smooth the dough into a ball, cover, and let it relax at room temperature for at least 1 hour.** If it is not sufficiently relaxed, it will be difficult to roll into thin sheets. This resting phase is particularly important if the dough is to be rolled by hand.

Evaluate the quality of the finished fresh pasta dough. In general, pasta dough should be smooth, fairly elastic, and just slightly moist to the touch. If the dough is either tacky (from excess moisture) or crumbly (too dry), it will be difficult to roll out properly. Experience is the best guide for determining when the proper consistency has been reached.

4. **Guide the pasta through the machine at the widest setting.** Reduce the setting as you roll the pasta to create thin sheets.

Cut off a piece of dough (the amount will vary, depending on the width of the machine) and flatten it; cover the rest. Set the rollers to the widest opening and begin to guide the dough through the machine, lightly flouring the dough as necessary to prevent sticking, to form a long, wide strip.

Roll the pasta dough into thin sheets and cut into the desired shapes. Hold properly under plastic wrap if it is not to be cooked immediately. Pasta and egg noodle doughs can be rolled and cut by hand or using a pasta machine. To roll by hand, flatten a piece of dough about the size of an orange on a flour-dusted work surface. Using a rolling pin, work from the center of the dough to the edges with a back-and-forth motion to roll and stretch the dough, turning it occasionally and dusting it with flour, until it reaches the desired thickness. Once rolled into sheets, the pasta can be cut with a knife into thin strips for flat or ribbon-style pastas such as fettuccine or linguine, or stamped with cutters into squares or circles to make filled pastas such as ravioli.

5. **In this method of rolling pasta join the two ends of the sheet to roll it in one continuous loop.** Fold the strip into thirds, like a letter, and run it through the rollers again. Repeat this step 1 or 2 times, folding the dough into thirds each time. If necessary, dust the dough with flour to keep it from sticking to the rollers and tearing.

Continue to roll the pasta through the machine, setting the rollers at a narrower setting each time, until the sheet of pasta is the desired thickness. The dough should feel smooth and not at all tacky. To prevent drying, keep it covered when not working with it.

NOTE: Different machines have different methods of operation. These directions are for making pasta sheets with the common two-roller hand-operated machine. (Tube pastas, such as macaroni or ziti, are made by forcing the dough through a special die in an extrusion pasta maker.)

6. **Cut the sheets of pasta using a machine attachment, a knife, or with cutters.** The pasta may be cooked fresh as is, or may be placed on racks or loosely formed into nests and allowed to dry for storage.

Flavoring and Seasoning Fresh Pasta

Making fresh pasta is exciting not only because of its fresh and tender flavor and texture but also because it provides another opportunity for introducing flavor to a dish.

Use different flours in combination with all-purpose flour to create flavor:

> **Buckwheat**
> **Cornmeal**
> **Rice**
> **Rye**
> **Semolina**
> **Whole wheat**

Add flavor to pasta dough during mixing with the addition of herbs, spices, flavored or infused liquids, and vegetable purées:

> Flavored or infused liquids:
> **Dried herbs such as rosemary**
> **Saffron**
> **Squid ink**
>
> Herbs and spices:
> **Basil**
> **Parsley**
> **Sage**
>
> Vegetable purées:
> **Carrot**
> **Spinach**
> **Tomato**

For a dramatic effect, whole herbs and even edible flowers can be rolled between two pieces of pasta:

> **Basil leaves**
> **Chervil leaves**
> **Nasturtium flowers and leaves**
> **Parsley leaves**

Cooking Pasta and Noodles

Cook pasta and noodles, both fresh and dried, in a large amount of salted water to ensure the best flavor and an even and appealing texture. Some pastas and noodles cook very rapidly. Others take several minutes to cook properly. If you are working with an unfamiliar shape or style of pasta, be sure to consult the instructions on the packaging.

All pasta has the best flavor and texture if it is served as soon as possible after cooking. This is especially true of fresh pasta. However, there are appropriate techniques to hold cooked dried pastas to streamline cooking during service (see page 853).

Select and prepare the ingredients and equipment

Dry and fresh pasta and noodles should be chosen according to the menu or recipe requirements. Water is the most common cooking liquid, although some preparations may call for stock. Salt is added to the water as it comes to a boil.

Choose a pot that is taller than it is wide for most pasta and noodles. Filled pasta may be prepared in pots that are wider than they are tall to make it easier to remove the pasta without breaking it. For large amounts of pasta, you may use special pasta cookers, which resemble deep fryers. Place the pasta in a wire basket with a handle and drop it into boiling or simmering water until cooked, then lift the basket out of the water, allowing the pasta to drain. Have available colanders, strainers, and skimmers to drain the pasta, as well as special cutting and shaping tools, such as a ravioli press or round cutters.

A basic formula for 10 portions of dry pasta

1 lb 8 oz/680 g dry pasta

Plenty of water

1½ oz/43 g salt for every 1 gal/3.84 L water

Finishing ingredients include:

Salt and pepper

Grated cheese

Sauces

Oils

1. **Bring a large amount of water to a rolling boil.** Allow about 1 gal/3.84 L water for every 1 lb/454 g pasta. Add about 1½ oz/43 g salt to the cooking water. Taste the water before adding pasta. It should be noticeably salty, but not unpleasantly so.

Add flat or extruded pasta and noodles all at once to the boiling water. Long strands should be gently submerged in the water as they soften. Stir the pasta a few times to separate the strands or shapes to prevent them from sticking together. Lower filled pastas into the water and reduce the heat to a simmer throughout cooking time to keep the shapes from breaking apart.

Cook the pasta until it is properly cooked and tender. Drain in a colander immediately. Some pastas and noodles cook very rapidly. Fresh pasta may cook in less than 3 minutes; dried pasta may take up to 8 minutes or longer, depending on the size and shape. If you are working with an unfamiliar shape or style of pasta, be sure to consult the instructions on the packaging. The most accurate test for doneness is to bite into a piece or strand, as well as to break apart a

(continued)

strand or piece and look at the interior. As pasta cooks, it becomes translucent throughout. An opaque core or center shows that the pasta is not completely cooked.

Drain the flat or extruded pasta or noodles through a colander, shaking gently to help the cooking water drain away. Tube shapes are prone to holding water; gently stirring them with gloved hands helps to drain away as much water as possible. (Note: Reserve some of the pasta water to adjust the sauce's consistency, if desired.) Filled pastas should be lifted from the cooking water gently with a spider or slotted spoon to avoid bursting them. They may be transferred to a colander to drain or blotted briefly to remove excess water.

Fresh pasta is best served immediately. It is ready to sauce or otherwise finish and serve now. Dried pasta may be properly cooled and stored for later service.

2. **Evaluate the quality of the cooked pasta.** Properly cooked dried pasta is tender but still has texture (top) while overcooked pasta is mushy (bottom). Properly cooked dried pasta is tender, but with a discernible texture, a state known as *al dente* (Italian for "to the tooth"). Fresh pasta cooks rapidly, which makes it easy to overcook; it should be completely cooked but not raw or doughy. Pasta and noodles should remain separate and stirred once or twice as they cook. Pasta that has been cooled and held should be properly cooked once reheated. Sauces and other finishing ingredients paired with pasta and noodles should be chosen to complement the shape or texture of the pasta (see sidebar).

Holding Pasta for Service

Rapidly cool and store the pasta, if appropriate or necessary, and reheat servings or batches as needed at service. Because it takes longer to cook, dried pasta is sometimes cooked ahead of time and held for service. (Fresh pasta does not hold as well as dried pasta, and, since it cooks rapidly, it is usually feasible to cook it fresh to order during service.) If pasta is prepared in advance and held, it should be slightly undercooked, so that it will not overcook during reheating. To cool the pasta, rinse it thoroughly with cold water and drain it well.

To reheat the pasta, bring some salted water to a boil. There should be enough water to generously cover the pasta, though not so much as is required for cooking. Lower the pasta into the water using a basket or by dropping it in, and let it simmer just long enough to heat through, depending upon the thickness of the pasta. Remove the pasta from the water and drain it well before finishing it for service.

Pairing Pasta with Sauces

Sauces are customarily selected to suit a particular type of pasta. Long, flat pastas such as fettuccine or linguine are generally served with smooth, light sauces such as cream sauces, vegetable coulis, or butter and cheese combinations that will coat the strands evenly. Tube pastas, such as elbow macaroni or ziti, and twisted pastas, such as fusilli, are normally paired with more heavily structured sauces such as a meat sauce or one with a garnish of fresh vegetables because these shapes are able to trap the sauce.

A pasta's flavor is also an important consideration when choosing a sauce. The delicate flavor of fresh pasta is most successfully paired with a light cream or butter-based sauces. Heartier sauces, such as those that include meats, are usually combined with dried pastas.

Filled pastas require only a very light sauce, because the filling provides a certain amount of flavor and moisture. A sauce that will overwhelm the flavor of the filling is inappropriate.

General Guidelines for Serving Pasta

Serving fresh and dried pasta

Pasta dishes are suited to many different service styles. The speed and ease of preparing pasta makes it a good choice for à la carte restaurants; in fact, some restaurant kitchens include a separate pasta station on the hot-food line. When properly prepared, handled, and held, pasta can also be used for banquet and buffet service. Both the pasta and the accompanying sauces can be prepared in advance.

For à la carte service, cook or reheat the pasta as close to service time as possible. Since pasta loses heat rapidly, be sure to heat the bowls or plates on which it is to be served and serve it immediately.

For banquet service, use bowls or deep platters and mound the pasta to help conserve heat. Be sure to heat the serving pieces.

For buffet service, choose sturdy pastas that will hold up well. Fully preheat the steam table or heat lamps before placing the pasta on the buffet line. Cook, reheat, and/or finish the pasta as close to serving time as possible. Choose a hotel pan deep enough to contain the pasta comfortably, but not so large that the pasta is spread out in a thin layer, where it will lose heat and moisture rapidly. Even in a steam table, heat is lost rapidly. There is a limit to how long pasta dishes can be held successfully for buffet service. Holding them over heat for too long can cause the sauce to dry out and the pasta to begin to lose its texture.

Fresh Egg Pasta

Makes 1 lb 8 oz/680 g

1 lb/454 g all-purpose flour, or as needed

pinch salt

4 eggs

½ to 1 fl oz/15 to 30 mL water, or as needed

1 fl oz/30 mL vegetable or olive oil (optional)

1. Combine the flour and salt in a large bowl, making a well in the center. Place the eggs, water, and oil, if using, in the center of the well. With a fork, gradually pull the dry ingredients into the egg mixture. Stir until a loose mass forms. As the dough is mixed, adjust the consistency with additional flour or water.

2. Turn the dough out onto a floured work surface and knead until the texture has become smooth and elastic, 4 to 5 minutes. Gather and smooth the dough into a ball, cover, and let the dough relax at room temperature for at least 1 hour.

3. Roll the pasta dough into thin sheets and cut into desired shapes by hand or by using a pasta machine. The pasta is ready to cook now, or it may be covered and refrigerated for up to 2 days.

Whole Wheat Pasta: Substitute whole wheat flour for half of the all-purpose flour.

Buckwheat Pasta: Substitute 3¼ oz/92 g buckwheat flour for an equal amount of the all-purpose flour.

Spinach Pasta: Purée 6 oz/170 g spinach leaves, squeeze dry in cheesecloth, and add to the eggs; adjust the dough with additional flour as needed.

Saffron Pasta: Steep 2 to 4 tsp/1.60 to 3.20 g pulverized saffron threads in 1 fl oz/30 mL hot water and add to the eggs; adjust the dough with additional flour as needed.

Citrus Pasta: Add 4 tsp/12 g finely grated lemon or orange zest to the eggs. Substitute 1 fl oz/30 mL lemon or orange juice for the water; adjust the dough with additional flour as needed.

Curried Pasta: Add 2 to 4 tsp/4 to 8 g Curry Powder (page 463) to the flour.

Herbed Pasta: Add 2 to 3 oz/57 to 85 g chopped fresh herbs to the eggs; adjust the dough with additional flour as needed.

Black Pepper Pasta: Add 2 tsp/4 g cracked black peppercorns to the flour.

Red Pepper Pasta: Sauté 6 oz/170 g puréed roasted red pepper until reduced and dry. Cool and add to the eggs; adjust the dough with additional flour as needed.

Tomato Pasta: Sauté 3 oz/85 g tomato purée until reduced and dry. Cool and add to the eggs; adjust the dough with additional flour as needed.

Pumpkin, Carrot, or Beet Pasta: Sauté 6 oz/170 g puréed cooked pumpkin, carrots, or beets until reduced and dry. Cool and add to the eggs; adjust the dough with additional flour as needed.

Basic Boiled Pasta

Makes 10 servings

1 gal 64 fl oz/5.76 L water

2¼ oz/64 g salt, or as needed

1 lb 8 oz/680 g dry or fresh pasta

sauce or garnish (optional), as needed

oil (optional), as needed

1. Bring the water and salt to a boil in a large pot.

2. Add the pasta and stir well to separate the strands. Cook until tender, but not too soft. (Fresh pasta may cook in less than 3 minutes; dry pasta may take up to 8 minutes or longer, depending on the size and shape.)

3. Drain the pasta at once. Add any desired sauce or garnish at this point and serve. If the pasta is to be held, plunge it into a water bath or rinse thoroughly with cold water to stop the cooking. Drain the pasta immediately and toss with a small amount of oil to prevent it from sticking together. Alternately, the pasta may be drained, tossed with a small amount of oil, spread in a single layer on a parchment-lined sheet pan, and refrigerated.

Pasta alla Carbonara

Makes 10 servings

2 lb 8 oz/1.13 kg spaghetti

2 oz/57 g butter or oil

10 oz/284 g minced pancetta or bacon

8 egg yolks

12 fl oz/360 mL heavy cream

4 oz/113 g grated Parmesan, or as needed

salt, as needed

ground black pepper, as needed

2 tbsp/6 g chopped parsley

1. Bring a large pot of salted water to a rolling boil. Add the spaghetti and stir a few times to separate the strands. Cook the spaghetti until it is tender to the bite but still retains some texture.

2. Drain the spaghetti in a colander. (Note: If the spaghetti is prepared in advance, rinse it with cold water, drain well, and rub a small amount of oil through the strands. Refrigerate until ready to serve. Reheat the pasta in boiling salted water and drain well while preparing the sauce.)

3. Heat the butter or oil in a sauté pan, add the pancetta or bacon, and sauté for 3 to 4 minutes or until the meat has rendered its fat. Add the drained cooked spaghetti and sauté until the spaghetti is very hot.

4. Blend the egg yolks with the cream and Parmesan. Add the egg mixture to the pasta. Cook the mixture gently, stirring constantly, until the sauce is heated through. Do not overheat, or it will curdle. Season with salt and pepper.

5. Garnish with chopped parsley and additional Parmesan, if desired. Serve immediately.

Orecchiette with Italian Sausage, Broccoli Rabe, and Parmesan Cheese

Makes 10 servings

2 lb 4 oz/1.02 kg broccoli rabe

10 fl oz/300 mL olive oil

12 oz/340 g minced onions

9 oz/255 g tomato paste

1 lb 4 oz/567 g Italian sausage

2 lb 4 oz/1.02 kg orecchiette pasta

2 garlic cloves, sliced

¼ tsp/0.50 g red pepper flakes

1 fl oz/30 mL **Chicken Stock** (page 351) or water

2 oz/57 g chopped parsley

2 oz/57 g basil chiffonade

2 oz/57 g chopped oregano

2 oz/57 g minced chives

5 oz/142 g grated Parmesan

1. Clean the broccoli rabe by cutting off 1 in/3 cm from the bottom of each stem. Blanch the broccoli rabe in boiling salted water until 90 percent cooked, about 4 minutes. Remove and shock in ice water. Hold aside.

2. In a large sauté pan, heat 8 fl oz/240 mL of the oil over medium heat. Add the onions and cook until tender, about 4 minutes. Add the tomato paste and sausage. Crumble the sausage with a whisk in the pan. Let the mixture cook until the sausage resembles a Bolognese-style sauce, about 5 minutes. Remove from the pan and reserve.

3. Bring a large pot of salted water to a boil and cook the pasta until al dente, about 6 minutes. Remove from the water and drain.

4. While the pasta is cooking, heat a large sauté pan over medium heat with the remaining oil. Add the garlic, red pepper flakes, stock or water, and reserved sausage mixture. Cook for 1 minute, stirring to combine. Add the herbs and broccoli rabe. Add the cooked pasta and 3 oz/85 g of the Parmesan; toss to mix. Garnish with the remaining 2 oz/57 g Parmesan and serve immediately.

Orecchiette with Italian Sausage, Broccoli Rabe, and Parmesan Cheese

Pad Thai

Pad Thai

Makes 10 servings

3 lb/1.36 kg rice noodles, ¼ in/6 mm thick

2 tbsp/8 g dried shrimp

2 fl oz/60 mL Thai chili paste (*nahm prik paw*)

4 fl oz/120 mL fish sauce

2 fl oz/60 mL rice vinegar

1¾ oz/50 g palm sugar

2 fl oz/60 mL vegetable oil, or as needed

1¼ oz/35 g chopped garlic

1 leek with greens, julienned

2 lb/907 g extra-firm bean curd, pressed, ¼-in/6-mm strips

6 eggs, beaten slightly

4 green onions, shaved into 1-in/3-cm strips

1 lb/454 g bean sprouts

2¾ oz/78 g roughly chopped cilantro

10 lime wedges

5 oz/142 g peanuts, pan roasted, coarsely chopped

1. Soak the rice noodles in warm water for 30 minutes and drain well.

2. Soak the dried shrimp for 30 minutes in cool water. Drain and finely chop.

3. Whisk together the chili paste, fish sauce, vinegar, and sugar.

4. Heat the oil in a wok over medium-high heat. Add the shrimp, garlic, leek, and bean curd. Stir-fry until the leeks brighten in color and soften slightly. The garlic should begin to turn golden, but not brown.

5. Add the noodles and coat with the oil. Stir-fry for 30 seconds. Push the noodles to the upper edge of one side of the wok. Add a drizzle of oil to the space created in the wok, then add the beaten eggs and spread with a spatula to begin cooking. Allow the eggs to cook for 10 seconds before beginning to stir-fry the noodle/egg mixture again.

6. Stir in the fish sauce mixture and the green onions. Stir-fry until the noodles are soft, adding water as necessary to facilitate the rehydration of the noodles.

7. Fold in the sprouts and cilantro. Adjust seasoning with chili paste, fish sauce, and sugar, as needed.

8. Garnish with lime wedges and peanuts and serve immediately.

Stir-Fried Glass Noodles (Jap Chae)

Makes 10 servings

20 dried shiitake (oak) mushrooms

2 oz/57 g dried wood ear mushrooms

2 lb 4 oz/1.02 kg sweet-potato noodles

6 green onions, trimmed and thinly sliced

8 fl oz/240 mL light soy sauce

1 fl oz/30 mL sesame oil

1 oz/28 g sugar

8 fl oz/240 mL vegetable oil

12 oz/340 g onions, thinly sliced with the grain

1¾ oz/50 g minced garlic

8 oz/227 g red pepper julienne

1 lb 4 oz/567 g green cabbage chiffonade

12 oz/340 g carrot julienne

salt, as needed

ground black pepper, as needed

10 eggs, beaten lightly, cooked to make a ⅛-in/3-mm-thick omelet, julienned

1. Rehydrate the shiitakes in cool water overnight. Drain and reserve the rehydration water.

2. Cut off the entire stem of the shiitakes and discard (or reserve for another use). Cut the caps into ⅛-in/3-mm-wide strips.

3. Rehydrate the wood ears. Trim off the hard nodules and cut into ⅛-in/3-mm-wide strips.

4. Pour boiling water over the noodles to cover by at least 2 in/5 cm. Soak until rehydrated and elastic, 8 to 10 minutes. Drain, rinse with cool water, and reserve.

5. Whisk together the green onions, soy sauce, sesame oil, and sugar.

6. Heat the oil in a wok and stir-fry the onions and garlic until aromatic.

7. Add the mushrooms, peppers, cabbage, and carrots, and stir-fry until the vegetables are almost cooked through.

8. Add the noodles; stir-fry until heated through.

9. Stir in the soy sauce mixture. Season with salt and pepper. If the mixture appears dry, use the reserved shiitake liquid to moisten.

10. Garnish with the omelet julienne and serve immediately.

Lasagna di Carnevale Napolitana

Makes 10 servings

10 oz/284 g lasagna noodles

10 oz/284 g Italian sweet sausage

14 oz/397 g ricotta cheese

12 oz/340 g grated Parmesan

3 eggs

¾ oz/21 g minced parsley

salt, as needed

ground black pepper, as needed

ground nutmeg (optional), as needed

32 fl oz/960 mL **Tomato Sauce** (page 384), with meat

10 oz/284 g mozzarella, thinly sliced or shredded

1. Bring a large pot of salted water to a boil. Add the noodles and stir well to separate. Cook until tender but not overly soft, about 8 minutes. Drain the lasagna at once and rinse with very cold water. Drain again and reserve.

2. Poach the sausage in water until cooked through, about 15 minutes. Remove the casing from the sausage and slice thinly. Reserve.

3. To make the cheese filling, combine the ricotta, 4 oz/113 g of the Parmesan, the eggs, and parsley. Season with salt, pepper, and nutmeg, if using. Mix well.

4. Spread a small amount of sauce on the bottom of a buttered baking pan.

5. Lay in the noodles, overlapping them no more than ¼ in/6 mm. Do not allow the noodles to fold up the sides of the pan.

6. Spread the cheese filling about ¼ in/6 mm thick, then add a layer each of sausage, sauce, mozzarella, and a sprinkle of Parmesan. Continue layering the ingredients in this manner, reserving a portion of sauce and Parmesan for the top. Finish with a layer of noodles.

7. Cover with the reserved sauce and top with the remaining Parmesan.

8. Bake in a 375°F/191°C oven for 15 minutes. Reduce the heat to 325°F/163°C and bake for 45 minutes more. If the top browns too fast, cover the pan lightly with greased aluminum foil.

9. Allow the lasagna to rest for 30 to 45 minutes before cutting into servings.

Couscous

Makes 10 servings

22 fl oz/660 mL cold water

2 tsp/10 g salt

1 lb/454 g couscous

3 oz/85 g butter, melted

½ tsp/1 g turmeric

ground black pepper, as needed

1. Combine 16 fl oz/480 mL of the water with half of the salt. Soak the couscous in the salted water for 1 hour.

2. Drain the couscous in a colander or the top of a couscousière set over a pot of simmering water or stew. Cover the pot and let the couscous steam for 10 minutes.

3. Empty the couscous into a hotel pan and stir to separate the grains. Add 2 fl oz/60 mL of the water and mix it together by hand. Let it rest for 15 minutes.

4. Repeat steps 2 and 3 two more times.

5. Stir in the butter and turmeric. Season with salt and pepper. Serve immediately.

Classic Bolognese Lasagna with Ragu and Béchamel (*Lasagna al Forno*)

Classic Bolognese Lasagna with Ragu and Béchamel (Lasagna al Forno)

Makes 10 servings

2 lb/907 g **Spinach Pasta** (page 855)

40 fl oz/1.20 L **Bolognese Meat Sauce** (page 385), cold

64 fl oz/1.92 L **Béchamel Sauce** (page 384), cold

4 oz/113 g finely grated Parmesan

2 oz/57 g butter

30 fl oz/900 mL **Tomato Sauce** (page 384)

1. Roll the pasta $\frac{1}{16}$ in/1.50 mm thick. Cut the sheets of pasta into rectangles, 5 by 11 in/13 by 28 cm.

2. Bring a large pot of salted water to a boil. Add the pasta, return the water to a boil, and cook the pasta for 10 seconds. Drain the pasta and drop it into cold water. Let the pasta cool for 2 minutes, drain, and place on absorbent paper towels to dry.

3. Spread a small amount of meat sauce on the bottom of a buttered baking pan.

4. Lay in the rectangles of pasta, overlapping by no more than ¼ in/6 mm. Do not allow the pasta to fold up the sides of the pan.

5. Spread a small amount of béchamel on the pasta and sprinkle with the cheese.

6. Repeat this process until there are 5 layers of pasta, alternating between coating the layers with the meat sauce and béchamel. Top the last layer with béchamel and grated cheese, and dot with butter.

7. Bake in a 450°F/232°C oven on the top rack until golden brown, 10 to 15 minutes.

8. Allow the lasagna to rest 10 minutes before cutting into servings 3 by 4 in/8 by 10 cm. Serve each portion with 3 fl oz/90 mL of the tomato sauce.

Gnocchi di Semolina Gratinati

Makes 10 servings

50 fl oz/1.50 L milk

1 tbsp/15 g salt

8 oz/227 g semolina, medium grain

4 oz/113 g butter

2 egg yolks, beaten

4 oz/113 g grated Parmesan

1. Over medium-high heat in a large, heavy-bottomed pot, bring the milk to a boil and season with salt.

2. Turn the heat down to medium-low. Pour the semolina into the milk in a thin stream, whisking constantly until it has all been added. Simmer, stirring often, until the semolina is cooked, about 20 minutes.

3. Remove the pot from the heat and blend in 3 oz/85 g of the butter, the egg yolks, and 3 oz/85 g of the cheese.

4. Shape the gnocchi mixture into quenelles or spread it on a sheet pan to a thickness of ½ in/1 cm. Cool completely and cut as desired.

5. To serve the gnocchi, transfer them a to liberally buttered baking dish. Brush or drizzle with the remaining butter and top with the remaining cheese. Bake in a 400°F/204°C oven or brown under a broiler for 5 to 6 minutes. Serve immediately on heated plates.

Gnocchi Piedmontese

Makes 10 servings

3 lb/1.36 kg russet potatoes

1 oz/28 g butter

3 eggs

salt, as needed

ground black pepper, as needed

ground nutmeg (optional), as needed

1 lb/454 g all-purpose flour, or as needed

2 oz/57 g butter

3 oz/85 g grated Parmesan

1 oz/28 g chopped parsley

1. Scrub, peel, and cut the potatoes into large pieces. Boil or steam them until tender enough to mash easily. Drain and dry them over low heat or on a sheet pan in a 300°F/149°C oven until no more steam rises from them. While the potatoes are still hot, purée them through a food mill or potato ricer into a heated bowl.

2. Add the butter, eggs, salt, pepper, and nutmeg, if using. Mix well. Incorporate enough of the flour to make a stiff dough.

3. Roll out the dough into cylinders about 1 in/3 cm in diameter. Cut the cylinders into pieces about 2 in/5 cm long. Roll each one over the tines of a fork, pressing and rolling the dough with your thumb.

4. Cook the gnocchi in simmering salted water for 2 to 3 minutes, or until they rise to the surface. Lift the gnocchi from the water with a slotted spoon or drain in a colander.

5. Heat the butter in a sauté pan over medium-high heat, add the gnocchi, and toss until very hot and coated with butter. Add the cheese and parsley. Adjust seasoning with salt and pepper. Serve immediately on heated plates.

Shaping gnocchi using a fork

Shaping gnocchi using a gnocchi board

Gnocchi Piedmontese

Gnocchi di Ricotta

Makes 10 servings

1 lb 6 oz/624 g ricotta cheese

8 oz/227 g all-purpose flour, sifted

3 eggs

3 fl oz/90 mL olive oil

1¼ tsp/6.25 g salt

16 fl oz/680 mL **Chicken Stock** (page 351), hot

1½ oz/43 g butter

½ tsp/1 g ground black pepper

8 oz/227 g grated Parmesan

1. Place the ricotta, flour, eggs, oil, and salt in a food processor. Process until the ingredients come together to form a smooth dough, about 1 minute. Transfer the dough to a bowl.

2. Bring a large pot of salted water to a boil. Using 2 spoons, shape the dough into oval quenelles, dropping them 1 by 1 into the boiling water. When all the dough has been used, return the water to a boil for 1 minute. Remove the gnocchi to a bowl with a slotted spoon.

3. Heat the stock. Heat the butter in a medium skillet over medium heat; add the gnocchi and stock. Heat through, 1 to 2 minutes.

4. With a slotted spoon, transfer the gnocchi to a serving bowl. Garnish with the cheese and pepper. Serve immediately.

Spätzle

Makes 10 servings

6 eggs

5 fl oz/150 mL milk

8 fl oz/240 mL water

salt, as needed

ground white pepper, as needed

grated nutmeg, as needed

1 oz/28 g **Fines Herbes** (page 463; optional), **or as needed**

1 lb/454 g all-purpose flour

4 oz/113 g butter

1. Combine the eggs, milk, and water. Season with the salt, pepper, and nutmeg. Add the fines herbes, if using. Work in the flour by hand and beat until smooth. Allow the mixture to rest for 1 hour.

2. Bring a large pot of salted water to a simmer. Work the dough/batter through a spätzle maker into the simmering water. When the spätzle comes to the top of the pot, remove it with a spider. The spätzle is ready to finish now, or it may be cooled in ice water, drained, and refrigerated for later service.

3. Heat the butter in a large sauté pan over medium-high heat. Add the spätzle and sauté until very hot. Adjust seasoning with salt and pepper, garnish with more fines herbes (if using), and serve immediately.

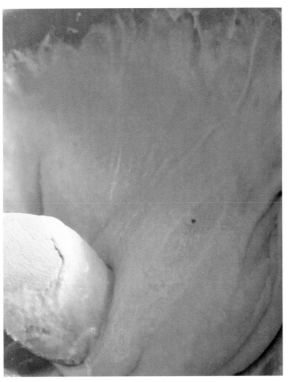

The spätzle dough should be thick but still be able to flow freely.

Move the cup slowly back and forth across the openings to produce the spätzle. Be sure that the water is at a rolling boil when the spätzle are dropped in.

The sautéed spätzle should be heated thoroughly.

Bread Dumplings

Makes 10 servings

1 lb/454 g white bread or rolls, with crust, small dice

2 oz/57 g butter

4 oz/113 g minced onions

4 oz/113 g all-purpose flour

8 fl oz/240 mL milk, or as needed

5 eggs

½ oz/14 g minced parsley

salt, as needed

ground white pepper, as needed

ground nutmeg (optional), as needed

1. Dry the bread in a 250°F/121°C oven for 20 to 30 minutes.

2. Heat the butter in a sauté pan and add the onions, sautéing until lightly browned, 8 to 10 minutes. Remove from the pan and cool.

3. Combine the dried bread, flour, and sautéed onions in a large bowl.

4. Combine the milk, eggs, parsley, salt, pepper, and nutmeg, if using, separately in another bowl.

5. Pour the liquid mixture into the dry mixture and blend together lightly. Let stand, covered, for 30 minutes. Add more milk if the bread is very dry.

6. Shape the mixture into 2-in/5-cm dumplings by hand.

7. Poach the dumplings in barely simmering salted water for 15 minutes. They are ready to serve now, or they may be lightly moistened and kept covered in a hotel pan for service. To serve, drain the dumplings with a slotted spoon or skimmer, and serve on heated plates.

Biscuit Dumplings

Makes 10 servings

8 oz/227 g all-purpose flour

2 tsp/6 g baking powder

1 tsp/5 g salt

8 fl oz/240 mL milk

1 tbsp/3 g chopped parsley (optional)

broth, soup, or stew, as needed

1. Sift together the flour, baking powder, and salt. Add the milk and parsley, if using, and mix in gently. Do not overmix. The consistency should be slightly softer than biscuit dough.

2. Drop 1 oz/28 g portions into the simmering broth, soup, or stew, about 1 in/3 cm apart. Work in batches, if necessary. Cover the pot and cook the dumplings until they have expanded and cooked completely through, about 15 minutes per batch. Return the cooking liquid to a full simmer in between batches.

3. The dumplings are ready to serve now, or they may be left in the poaching liquid to hold hot for service.

Hush Puppies

Makes 10 servings

2 eggs, beaten

8 fl oz/240 mL milk

2 fl oz/60 mL rendered bacon fat

1½ oz/43 g minced onions

12 oz/340 g white cornmeal

8 oz/170 g cake flour

2 tsp/6 g baking powder

1½ tsp/7.50 g salt

½ tsp/1 g ground black pepper

¼ tsp/0.50 g cayenne

32 fl oz/960 mL vegetable oil or lard, or as needed for frying

1. Combine the eggs, milk, fat, and onions.

2. Combine the cornmeal, flour, baking powder, salt, pepper, and cayenne. Make a well in the center and gently add the wet ingredients. Stir until just combined.

3. Form the batter into round balls, about 1 in/3 cm in diameter. Heat the oil to 350°F/177°C and deep fry the dough until crispy and brown, working in batches if necessary. Serve immediately.

Hush Puppies

Steamed Dumplings (Shao-Mai)

Makes 10 servings

8 oz/227 g ground pork, very cold

2 tsp/3 g minced ginger

2 green onions, thinly sliced

2 tsp/10 mL oyster sauce

1 tsp/5 mL light soy sauce

1 tsp/5 mL sesame oil

2 tbsp/18 g cornstarch

1 egg

½ fl oz/15 mL Shaoxing rice wine

1 tsp/5 g salt

pinch ground black pepper

4 oz/113 g shrimp (16–20 count), peeled, deveined, chopped into ¼-in/6-mm pieces

1 oz/14 g water chestnut brunoise

⅔ oz/19 g carrot brunoise

1 tbsp/3 g chopped cilantro

20 shao-mai wrappers

10 fl oz/300 mL **Ginger-Soy Dipping Sauce** (page 872)

1. Place the pork, ginger, green onions, oyster sauce, soy sauce, oil, cornstarch, egg, wine, salt, and pepper into a chilled food processor bowl. Pulse the mixture until well combined. The mixture will begin to pull together into one mass. Transfer to a chilled mixing bowl.

2. Add the shrimp, water chestnuts, carrots, and cilantro. Mix until incorporated and chill the mixture until it is very cold.

3. Using a tablespoon, place a mound of the filling mixture in the center of each wrapper. Gather the outer edges of the wrapper to form a cylinder, so the filling is exposed at the top. Wrap your pointer finger and thumb around the center "waist." Dip your thumb from the opposite hand in water (to prevent sticking) and use it to compact the filling in the dumpling. Gently tap the entire dumpling on the table to insure that it stays upright in the steamer.

4. Bring water in a steamer to a vigorous boil. Oil the steamer with sesame oil or line it with leaves or parchment paper to prevent the dumplings from sticking.

5. Arrange the dumplings in the steamer. Cover and steam for approximately 5 minutes, or until cooked through and firm.

6. Turn off the heat and let the dumplings rest for a few minutes before removing. Serve immediately with the sauce.

NOTE

For smaller, passed hors d'oeuvre, use 1 tsp/5 mL filling per dumpling.

Line up the circles of dough and place the filling in the center of each circle. Gather the dumpling dough into a cylinder around the filling, pinching together the excess dough.

Here, the dumplings are placed on top of cabbage leaves to prevent them from to sticking to the steamer.

The properly steamed dumplings

Pan-Fried Dumplings (Guo Tie)

Makes 10 servings

4 oz/113 g all-purpose flour

4 oz/113 g wheat starch

1½ tsp/5 g butter, very cold, cut into small pieces

5½ fl oz/165 mL water, boiling

6 oz/170 g ground pork

6 oz/170 g finely chopped Chinese cabbage

1 thinly sliced green onion

1 tsp/3 g minced ginger

½ fl oz/15 mL soy sauce

½ fl oz/15 mL sesame oil

1 egg

1½ tsp/4.50 g cornstarch

1 tsp/5 g salt

½ tsp/1 g ground white pepper

1½ tsp/7.50 mL sherry

½ tsp/2.50 g sugar

2 fl oz/60 mL vegetable oil, or as needed

12 fl oz/360 mL **Chicken Stock** (page 351)

10 fl oz/300 mL **Ginger-Soy Dipping Sauce** (recipe follows)

1. Place the flour and wheat starch in the bowl of a food processor. As the machine is running, pulse in the cold butter. Add the water in a slow stream; the dough should begin to come together as a solid mass.

2. Run for an additional 10 seconds to knead the dough. Remove the dough from the processor to a floured work surface and knead until it is smooth. Wrap the dough in plastic wrap and let it rest for 1 hour.

3. In a large bowl, combine the pork, cabbage, green onion, ginger, soy sauce, sesame oil, egg, cornstarch, salt, pepper, sherry, and sugar. Mix well and adjust seasoning.

4. Divide the dough into 2 pieces. Roll each piece out to a ¹⁄₁₆ in/1.50 mm thickness. Use a floured 3½-in/9-cm round cutter to cut the dough into 10 pieces. Cover the dough to prevent it from drying out.

5. Place 1 tbsp/15 mL of filling on each circle of dough and fold as desired. Transfer to a lightly floured, parchment-lined sheet pan.

6. To serve, heat a large cast-iron pan until very hot. Add 1 fl oz/30 mL of the vegetable oil and swirl to coat the sides of the pan.

7. Arrange the dumplings in concentric rings, starting from the outside of the pan.

8. Cook until the bottoms are completely browned. Release them from pan with a spatula before proceeding to the next step.

9. Add the stock to about halfway up the sides of dumplings. Bring the stock up to a simmer and cover the pan.

10. Cook until all the stock has evaporated or been absorbed. Add the remaining oil and cook until the bottoms of the dumplings are crisp. Serve immediately with the sauce.

Ginger-Soy Dipping Sauce

Makes 32 fl oz/960 mL

5 oz/142 g minced ginger

8 fl oz/240 mL light soy sauce

16 fl oz/480 mL rice vinegar

8 fl oz/240 mL water

2 fl oz/60 mL sesame oil

4 oz/113 g sugar

1. Whisk together all the ingredients until the sugar is dissolved.

2. The sauce is ready to serve now, or it may be refrigerated for later use.

Pan-Fried Dumplings (*Guo Tie*)

Potato and Cheddar–Filled Pierogi with Caramelized Onions,
Beurre Noisette, and Sage

Potato and Cheddar–Filled Pierogi with Caramelized Onions, Beurre Noisette, and Sage

Makes 10 servings

FILLING

6 lb/2.72 kg chef's potatoes

7 egg yolks

9 oz/255 g Cheddar cheese

1¾ oz/50 g green onions, halved and thinly sliced

salt, as needed

ground black pepper, as needed

nutmeg, as needed

DOUGH

1 lb 5 oz/595 g semolina flour

1 lb 5 oz/595 g all-purpose flour

9 eggs

1 oz/28 g salt

2 fl oz/60 mL **Egg Wash** (page 1061)

6 oz/170 g clarified butter

12 oz/340 g butter

¼ tsp/1.25 g salt

pinch white pepper

1 lb 12 oz/794 g onions, caramelized

2 tbsp/6 g sage chiffonade

1 lb/454 g sour cream

1. Scrub, peel, and cut the potatoes into large pieces. Boil them in salted water until tender enough to mash easily. Drain, reserving and chilling 8 fl oz/240 mL of the cooking liquid. Dry the potatoes over low heat or on a sheet pan in a 300°F/149°C oven until no more steam rises from them. While the potatoes are still hot, purée them through a food mill or potato ricer into a heated bowl.

2. Add the egg yolks, cheese, and green onions. Season with salt, pepper, and nutmeg. Set the filling aside.

3. To make the dough, place the reserved potato water, flours, eggs, and salt in a mixer fitted with a dough hook. Mix at medium speed until the dough forms a smooth ball, 3 to 4 minutes. Divide the dough into 4 sections and knead on a floured surface until the dough is barely tacky. Cover with plastic wrap, and allow it to rest for 20 minutes.

4. Roll out the dough using a pasta machine to a 1⁄16 in/1.50 mm thickness. Cut the dough into circles using a 2½-in/6-cm biscuit cutter. Lightly brush the edges with egg wash.

5. Place approximately 1 tbsp/15 mL of filling onto the center of each dough circle. Fold in half to form a half-moon and pinch the edges to seal.

6. Simmer the pierogi in boiling salted water until the dough along the edge seals are fully cooked, 4 to 5 minutes. The pierogi are ready to finish now, or they may be cooled in ice water, drained, and refrigerated for later service.

7. Heat the clarified butter in a large sauté pan over medium heat. Add the pierogi and sauté until golden brown on both sides and heated through, about 2 minutes per side.

8. Pour off the clarified butter, increase the heat to medium-high, add the whole butter, and bring it to noisette (golden brown), about 2 minutes. Add a pinch of salt and white pepper, and drizzle over the pierogi.

9. Garnish with the caramelized onions, sage, and sour cream and serve immediately.

Dim Sum

Makes 20 servings

DUMPLING SKINS

1 lb/454 g flour

8 fl oz/240 mL hot water

FILLING

12 oz/340 g ground pork

8 oz/227 g shredded Chinese cabbage

2 oz/57 g chopped green onions

1 tsp/3 g minced ginger

½ fl oz/15 mL soy sauce

½ fl oz/15 mL dark sesame oil

1 egg white

salt, as needed

white pepper, as needed

1. To prepare the dumpling skins, mix the flour and water to make a smooth batter. Let stand for 30 minutes. Divide the dough into ½-oz/14-g portions and roll out each into a thin circle.

2. To prepare the filling, combine all the filling ingredients and mix well. Check the filling consistency and seasoning by sautéing a small amount and tasting it.

3. Place 1 tbsp/15 mL of filling on a dumpling skin. Crimp and seal the edges tightly.

4. Steam the dumplings over boiling water until cooked through, about 8 minutes. Serve immediately.

Potstickers: Use prepared wonton wrappers instead of preparing the dough, if desired. Fill and seal dumplings as described above. Heat about ¼ in/6 mm of oil in a skillet. Add the dumplings in a single layer and pan fry until the bottoms are very crisp and brown. Add enough stock, broth, or water to come up to ½ in/1 cm in the pan. Cover the pan and steam the potstickers for 6 to 8 minutes, or until the wrapper is translucent and tender. Serve immediately.

Part Seven

Breakfast and Garde Manger

Chapter Twenty-nine

Cooking Eggs

Eggs can be served at virtually any meal, as part of every course. They can be cooked in the shell, poached, fried, scrambled, or prepared as omelets or soufflées. Using fresh eggs for cooking is important to ensure the best flavor and quality of the finished dish. The top grade of eggs, AA, indicates that the eggs are fresh. They will have a white that does not spread excessively once the egg is cracked and the yolk should ride high on the white's surface. Proper cooking of eggs is also essential to the quality of the finished dish. Regardless of the recipe or cooking method used, when eggs are overcooked, excessive coagulation of the proteins forces water out and the eggs become dry.

Cooking Eggs in the Shell

Although the term *boiled* may appear in the name, eggs prepared in the shell should actually be cooked at a bare simmer for best results. Eggs are cooked in the shell to make hard- and soft-cooked and coddled eggs. They may be served directly in the shell or they may be shelled and used to make another preparation, such as deviled eggs, or as a garnish for salads or vegetable dishes.

Check each egg carefully and discard any with cracked shells. Eggs should always be properly refrigerated until you are ready to cook them. To reduce cooking time for hard-cooked eggs, temper them in warm water for several minutes.

Select a pot deep enough for the eggs to be submerged in water. Have on hand a slotted spoon, skimmer, or spider to remove eggs from the water once they are cooked.

Myths and Facts about Hard-Boiled Eggs

MYTH

Piercing the shell of the egg will keep it from cracking during cooking. Or, start out with cold eggs in cold water to prevent the shells from cracking.

FACT

Maybe; maybe not. There is no evidence to support the notion that the eggshell will not break using either of these methods.

The following guidelines, however, are effective:

Use enough water to completely submerge the eggs.

Lower the eggs into the water, rather than drop them into an empty pot.

Reduce the heat under the pot once a simmer is reached.

MYTH

Cooling and peeling hard-boiled eggs immediately after they have finished cooking will prevent a green ring from forming around the yolk.

FACT

This is in fact true. The green ring is the result of an iron and sulphur interaction in the egg yolk. Extended cooking is generally the cause. Cooling and peeling of the egg releases the trapped sulphur before the interaction can take place.

A basic formula for 10 portions of eggs cooked in the shell

20 eggs (2 per portion)

Plenty of simmering water to cook coddled, soft-, medium-, or hard-cooked eggs; plenty of cold water to cover eggs if following the alternative hard-cooked method

Place the eggs in a pot with enough water to completely submerge them (the water level should be approximately 2 in/5 cm above the eggs). It is common to have the water already at a simmer when preparing coddled and soft-cooked eggs. Hard-cooked eggs may be started in simmering or cold water. In either case, lower the eggs gently into the pot so they won't crack and then bring (or return) the water to a simmer. Do not allow the water to boil rapidly. Water that is at or close to a simmer will allow the eggs to cook evenly, without toughening the whites. In addition to toughening the whites, violent boiling could cause the eggshells to crack.

Start timing the cooking only once the water reaches a simmer and cook to the desired doneness. For example, a 3-minute egg cooks for 3 minutes from the time the water returns to a simmer after the egg has been added to the water. If the timing is started when the water is cold, the egg will not be properly cooked. Simmer hard-boiled eggs for 12 to 13 minutes.

Hard-cooked eggs are easiest to peel while they are still warm. Place them under cold running water until they are cool enough to handle. Gently press down and roll the egg over a countertop to crack the shell before peeling. Peel the shell and membrane away with your fingers.

The yolks of properly cooked soft-boiled eggs are warm but still runny, while those of medium-cooked eggs are partially coagulated. Properly hard-cooked eggs are completely and evenly coagulated, with firm but tender, not tough, whites and no unsightly green ring surrounding the yolk.

The green ring is the result of a chemical reaction between the iron and sulfur naturally present in eggs, forming green iron sulfide. Heat speeds up this reaction. The best way to prevent the green ring from forming is to watch the cooking time closely and not allow the eggs to boil longer than necessary. Quick cooling also helps keep the ring from forming.

Poaching Eggs

Prepare poached eggs by slipping shelled eggs into barely simmering water and gently cooking until the egg holds its shape. The fresher the egg, the more centered the yolk, and the less likely the white is to spread and become ragged.

These tender and delicately set eggs form the basis of many dishes. Some familiar examples are Eggs Benedict or Florentine or poached eggs used as a topping for hash. They may be served in baked potatoes or on croutons, with or without a sauce, or added as a garnish to broths or hearty soups.

Poached eggs can be prepared in advance and held safely throughout a typical service period to make the workload easier during service. Slightly underpoach the eggs, shock them in ice water to arrest the cooking process, trim them, and hold them in cold water. At the time of service, reheat the eggs in simmering water.

Eggs are most often poached in water, though other liquids, such as red wine, stock, or cream, can also be used. Add vinegar and salt to the water to encourage the egg protein to set faster. Otherwise, the egg whites can spread too much before they coagulate.

Other ingredients include seasonings, garnishes, and sauces as called for by the specific recipe. Choose a pot that it is deep enough for the eggs to remain completely submerged. The size of the pan depends on the size of the batch. Have cups to hold the raw eggs, as well as a slotted spoon, skimmer, or spider for retrieving the eggs from the water, and absorbent toweling for blotting the eggs dry, a paring knife for trimming the eggs, and holding and serving pieces. An instant-read thermometer helps to accurately monitor the temperature of the water.

A basic formula for 10 portions of poached eggs

20 very fresh eggs (2 per portion), chilled until ready to poach

5 to 6 in/13 to 15 cm simmering water

1 fl oz/30 mL vinegar per 1 gal/3.84 L water

½ oz/14 g salt per 1 gal/3.84 L water

1. **Gently add the eggs one at a time to the simmering (180°F/82°C) poaching liquid.** For the most attractive shape, like a teardrop, be sure that the water is deep enough. Fill a pan with water to a depth of 5 to 6 in/13 to 15 cm and season it with just enough vinegar and salt to prevent the egg whites from spreading. The vinegar and salt should be just barely perceptible, not enough that the poached egg tastes strongly of vinegar or salt. Generally, 1 fl oz/ 30 mL of vinegar and ½ fl oz/15 mL of salt for each 1 gal/3.84 L of water are sufficient.

To reduce the chance of breaking an egg in the poaching liquid, break the eggs into cups. Discard any eggs that have blood spots on the yolks. Pour the egg from the cup into the poaching liquid.

Once added, the egg will drop to the bottom of the pot, then float to the top. The whites will set around the yolk, to create a teardrop shape. The more eggs added to the water at once, the more the temperature of the water will drop and the more time it will take to properly poach the egg. Working in smaller batches is actually more efficient. It generally takes 3 to 4 minutes to poach an egg properly.

2. **Use a slotted spoon, skimmer, or spider to gently lift the egg from the water.** Blot the egg on absorbent toweling to remove as much water as possible. A properly poached egg should have a fully coagulated egg white, a warm center that is only partially set (slightly thickened but still flowing), and should be tender with a compact oval shape. If the whites appear ragged, trim them with a paring knife to give a neat appearance. The poached egg is ready to serve now. To prepare eggs that will be chilled and held for later service, slightly undercook the eggs.

3. **Lift the eggs from the poaching liquid and submerge them in ice water until well chilled.** Trim any irregular shaping of the white around the edges and hold in ice water until service. Drain the eggs and hold them in a perforated pan until ready to reheat. To reheat the egg, lower it into simmering water for 30 to 60 seconds to finish cooking and properly reheat it. Serve the egg while still very hot.

Frying Eggs

Fried eggs call for perfectly fresh eggs, the correct heat level, an appropriate amount of cooking fat, and a deft hand.

Fried eggs American style may be served sunny side up (not turned) or over (turned once). Fried eggs may be basted with fat as they fry. Dishes like huevos rancheros, for example, feature fried eggs as part of a hearty dish of eggs, tortillas, and beans. The French prefer shirred eggs (*sur le plat*), which are cooked in the oven with various garnishes.

Using very fresh eggs is the only way to ensure a rich flavor and good appearance in the finished dish. When very fresh eggs are broken onto a plate, the yolk sits high on the white near the white's center. The white is compact and thick and it holds the yolk in place. When the egg is fried, the white holds together in a neat shape and the yolk is more likely to stay intact. As eggs age, the white and yolk weaken and thin. To prepare eggs for frying, break them into clean cups. Any eggs with broken yolks can be reserved for another use. Refrigerate the shelled eggs. (This may be done up to 1 hour in advance.)

Use oils, whole or clarified butter, or rendered animal fat for frying, even if using a non-stick surface. These cooking fats not only lubricate the pan, they can also add their own distinct flavor. Season eggs with salt and pepper as they cook for the best flavor.

Fry eggs either in a sauté pan or on a griddle. The best pan materials for frying eggs are well-seasoned black steel or nonstick surfaces. A spatula or palette knife is also needed for flipping and moving the eggs.

A basic formula for 10 portions of fried eggs

20 very fresh eggs (2 per portion), refrigerated until ready to cook

One of the following cooking media:

Whole butter

Clarified butter

Cooking oils

Rendered bacon fat

Place a frying pan over medium heat. Add the fat to the pan and continue to heat until the fat is hot. The ideal temperature range for frying an egg is 255° to 280°F/124° to 138°C—the same range at which butter sizzles without turning brown. If using a griddle, adjust its temperature and brush the surface with oil or other cooking fat. If the heat is too low, the egg will stick; if it is too high, the edges of the white may blister and brown before the rest of the egg is properly cooked.

Break the eggs into cups. Fried eggs should have intact yolks, unless the customer requests that they be broken. Slide or pour the egg out of the cup and into the pan.

Cook the egg until done as desired. Here they are sunny side up. Eggs are done once the whites have coagulated; the yolks may be soft and runny or set. For eggs cooked over easy or over hard, flip the eggs or turn them with a spatula. You may baste the eggs with hot fat to set the top instead of turning them. Or, sprinkle a few drops of water on the egg, cover the pan, and let the water steam the eggs.

Properly fried eggs have shiny, tender, fully set whites and a fairly compact shape. They are not blistered or browned. Yolks should be properly cooked, according to customer request or intended use.

Scrambling Eggs

Scrambled eggs can be made in two ways: The eggs can be stirred constantly over low heat for a soft delicate curd and a creamy texture, or stirred less frequently as they cook for a larger curd and a firm texture. Whether prepared to order or to serve on a buffet line, scrambled eggs must be served hot, fresh, and moist.

Choose eggs that are fresh, with intact shells. Adding a small amount of water or stock (about 2 tsp/10 mL per egg) to the beaten eggs will make them puffier as the water turns to steam. Milk or cream may be used to enrich the eggs. Scrambled eggs can be seasoned with salt and pepper, and/or flavored or garnished with fresh herbs, cheese, sautéed vegetables, smoked fish, or truffles.

Eggs can be scrambled in a sauté pan or on a griddle. Nonstick surfaces make it easy to prepare scrambled eggs with a minimum amount of added fat. Black steel pans are appropriate, as long as they are properly maintained and seasoned. Pans used for eggs should be reserved for that use only, if possible. A table fork, wooden spoon, or spatula is needed for stirring the eggs as they cook. Have holding and serving pieces on hand.

A basic formula for 10 portions of scrambled eggs

20 to 30 eggs (2 to 3 per portion)

Up to ½ fl oz/15 mL water, milk, or cream (optional)

Salt and pepper as needed

½ to 1 fl oz/15 to 30 mL oil, clarified butter, or rendered fats

Blend the eggs just until the yolks and whites are combined. Add liquid, if using, and seasonings. Use a fork or a whip to blend everything into a smooth, homogeneous mixture. First, heat the pan and the cooking fat over medium heat. Then pour the eggs into the pan; they should begin to coagulate almost immediately. Finally, turn the heat down to low. Use the back of a table fork or a wooden spoon to stir the eggs as they cook. Keep both the pan and the fork in motion to produce small, softly set curds. The lower the heat and the more constant the agitation, the creamier the finished scrambled eggs will be. In fact, they may be prepared by stirring them constantly over a water bath to prevent browning altogether.

Add garnishes, cheeses, or flavoring ingredients once the eggs are completely set and fold these ingredients in over low heat, just until incorporated. Remove the eggs from the heat when slightly underdone; they will continue to cook slightly from the heat they retain.

Properly prepared scrambled eggs have a moist texture, creamy consistency, and delicate flavor. Moisture weeping from the eggs indicates that they were overcooked.

Making Omelets

The rolled, or French-style, omelet starts out like scrambled eggs, but when the eggs start to set, they are rolled over. A folded, or American-style, omelet is prepared in much the same manner, though it is often cooked on a griddle rather than in a pan, and instead of being rolled, the American omelet is folded in half. There are two other styles of omelets, both based upon a beaten mixture of eggs, cooked either over direct heat or in an oven.

Flat omelets, known variously as farmer-style omelets, frittatas (Italian), or tortillas (Spanish), are a baked version. The finished dish is denser and easier to slice into servings. Souffléed or puffy omelets are made from eggs first separated into yolks and whites. The beaten whites are folded into the beaten yolks and the dish is prepared by baking the omelet in a hot oven.

Choose eggs that are fresh, with intact shells. As with scrambled eggs, the ability of the egg to hold its shape is irrelevant, but fresh eggs are preferable. Season omelets with salt, pepper, and herbs. Clarified butter or oil is the most common cooking fat.

Omelets may be filled or garnished with cheese, sautéed vegetables or potatoes, meats, and smoked fish, among other things. These fillings and garnishes are incorporated at the appropriate point to be certain they are fully cooked and hot when the eggs have finished cooking. Grated or crumbled cheeses will melt sufficiently from the heat of the eggs, and are often added just before an omelet is rolled or folded.

Start larger fritatas, as well as souffléed omelets, in a pan heated in the oven with the cooking fat before adding the eggs.

Add garnishes for flat and souffléed omelets at the start of cooking time. For rolled or folded omelets, add fillings such as cheese when the curds are barely set.

Rolled and souffléed omelets are made individually in omelet pans, which are basically small sauté pans. Omelet pans should either be well seasoned or have a nonstick surface. Treat pans carefully and avoid scratching a nonstick surface with metal. A wooden spoon, or heat-resistant rubber spatula is useful to stir the eggs as they cook.

A basic formula for 1 individual omelet

2 to 3 eggs

Up to 2 tsp/10 mL water, stock, milk, or cream (optional)

Salt

Pepper

½ to 1 fl oz/15 to 30 mL cooking fat

1. **For omelets, shell the eggs and blend with any liquid, if using, salt, pepper, and seasonings as close to cooking time as possible.** For souffléed omelets, separate the eggs into whites and yolks. Blend the yolks with seasonings and any liquid desired, then beat the whites to medium peak and fold them into the yolk mixture.

A portion-sized omelet pan should be heated over high heat. Then add the butter or oil and allow it to heat as well. The fat should appear lightly hazy, but should not be smoking. Some garnish ingredients are added to the pan before the eggs; others are added when the curds are almost completely set, depending on the desired results and recipe specifics.

Toward the beginning of cooking, stir the eggs constantly with the spatula to encourage even cooking. For individually prepared rolled and folded omelets, keep the eggs in constant motion as the omelet cooks. Cook rolled and folded omelets over brisk heat to assure that the eggs begin to set almost immediately and don't stick to the pan. If using an omelet pan, use one hand to swirl the pan over the heat source and the other to stir the eggs from the bottom and sides of the pan with the back of a fork or a heat-resistant rubber spatula. Use a flexible spatula to turn and stir an omelet cooked on a griddle.

2. **Gently shake the pan to evenly spread the eggs in the pan or use a spatula to spread the eggs flat for the best presentation.** Garnish the omelet as desired. Spread or flatten the omelet in the pan to even it out for the best-looking rolled and folded omelets. Make sure that the omelet is of a uniform thickness or it will cook unevenly.

3. **To make a rolled omelet, use the spatula to fold one third of the omelet over.** Use a rubber spatula or a fork to roll the edge of the omelet nearest the handle toward the center. Shake the pan to loosen the omelet to make it easier to roll onto the plate.

4. **Hold the plate near the pan and roll the omelet out onto the plate.** Roll the omelet out of the pan, completely encasing any filling (make sure the edges are caught neatly underneath the omelet), directly onto a heated plate. It may be necessary to shape the omelet with a clean towel.

5. **Evaluate the finished omelet.** A rolled omelet should be oval in shape and golden-yellow in color, with a creamy, moist interior. A folded omelet is a half-circle shape; the exterior is sometimes allowed to take on a very light golden color. A flat omelet should be dense but moist, able to be cut or sliced into servings, yet still hold its shape. A souffléed omelet should be light and foamy, with slight golden color on the upper surface; it starts to lose its volume rapidly after coming out of the oven, however.

Savory Soufflés

The preparation, assembly, and baking of a soufflé are not difficult tasks on their own. The tricky part is timing. Soufflés, like omelets and quiches, are not strictly for breakfast; in fact, they are more typically part of the brunch, luncheon, or even the dinner menu, where small soufflés often appear as hot appetizers, a savory course, or as a dessert.

The basic components of any soufflé, sweet or savory, are the base and beaten egg whites. A heavy béchamel, often with the incorporation of additional egg yolks, is the base for many savory soufflés. Sweet soufflés are often based upon pastry cream. Other mixtures or preparations, such as vegetable purées, can be used as the base or to flavor a base. It is important that the base mixture provide enough structure to keep the soufflé from collapsing as soon as it is removed from the oven. The base may be flavored or garnished in many ways: with grated cheese, chopped spinach, or shellfish, for example.

Egg whites give both volume and structure to the soufflé. They should be carefully separated from the yolks and beaten to soft peaks just before they are folded into the base. The yolks may be incorporated into the soufflé base, or they may be reserved for other uses. Be sure to keep eggs well chilled at all times for wholesomeness and flavor.

A variety of sauces may be served with soufflés. Cheddar Sauce (page 384) or Mornay Sauce (page 384), vegetable ragouts or coulis, or various tomato sauces are appropriate for savory soufflés. Soufflés are usually baked in ceramic or glass soufflé dishes or ramekins. For the best rise, the sides of the dish should be straight.

To prepare the molds, butter them lightly and thoroughly, dusting the sides and bottom with grated Parmesan or bread crumbs if desired. Use meticulously clean bowls and whips to beat the egg whites for the best volume in the finished soufflé.

The oven should be set to the appropriate temperature, generally 400° to 425°F/204° to 218°C for an individual portion. The temperature should be slightly lower for larger soufflés. Other equipment needs include a whisk (or electric mixer) and bowls for whipping the egg whites, a spatula for combining the soufflé mixture, and a sheet pan for baking.

A basic formula for 1 individual soufflé

A base, such as:

2 fl oz/60 mL heavy béchamel for savory soufflés

2 fl oz/60 mL pastry cream for sweet soufflés

2 fl oz/60 mL vegetable purée (consistency similar to béchamel)

A lightener

2 fl oz/60 mL egg whites, beaten to soft peaks

Seasonings, flavorings, or garnish options such as:

Salt and pepper

Vegetables

Grated cheese

1. **Make the base and blend in the flavoring. Here, spinach and Parmesan cheese are used.** The base mixture for many savory soufflés is essentially a heavy béchamel. Additional egg yolks are often tempered into the hot base to provide richness, flavor, color, and structure. The base may be prepared in advance and refrigerated. For the best rise in the finished soufflé, have the base at room temperature, or else work it with a wooden spoon until it has softened. Fold flavoring ingredients such as puréed spinach into the base until evenly blended. Prepare the molds with a light film of butter and a dusting of flour.

2. **Whip the egg whites to soft peaks and fold gently to blend the whites with the base.** Soft peaks will produce the proper rise, texture, and structure in the finished soufflé. Add the beaten whites in 2 or 3 parts. The first addition will lighten the base so that subsequent additions will retain the maximum volume.

3. **Fill the prepared molds as soon as the egg whites are folded into the base.** Spoon or ladle the batter into the mold gently to avoid knocking air out of the batter. Fill them about two thirds of the way full. Be sure to wipe the rims and outside of the mold clean for a good, even rise. Bake the soufflés as soon as the egg whites are folded into the base.

Flavoring and Seasoning Savory Soufflés

The base contains the flavoring for a soufflé. When adding flavoring or seasoning to the base, it is important that it be somewhat strong. The addition of beaten egg whites will dilute the flavor, so the base should start off very flavorful to account for this.

Some ingredients that may be used as flavoring or seasoning for a soufflé base are as follows:

Flavored liquids for preparing the base:

Broths
Stocks
Vegetable juices or purees

Ingredients added to the base after its preparation:

Finely chopped seafood or meat
Grated cheeses
Grated vegetables
Vegetable purée

4. **Place the soufflés immediately in a hot (425°F/218°C) oven and bake until risen, cooked through, and browned.** For even cooking and a good rise, place the molds on a sheet pan. The rack should be in the center of the oven. Do not disturb the soufflés as they bake. The drop in temperature when the oven door is opened could be enough to affect the soufflé. Remove individual soufflés from the oven when done, 16 to 18 minutes. To check a soufflé for doneness, shake the dish very gently. The center should be firm and set. A toothpick carefully inserted into the side of the soufflé should come out clean.

Serve the soufflé immediately. Any accompanying sauce should be hot and ready in a dish. The server should be standing by, ready to serve the soufflés as soon as they come from the oven. A properly prepared soufflé tastes of the primary flavoring ingredient and is puffy, well risen, and browned.

Hard-Cooked Eggs

Makes 10 servings

20 eggs

1. Place the eggs in a pot. Fill the pot with enough cold water to cover the eggs by 2 in/5 cm.

2. Bring the water to a boil and immediately lower the temperature to a simmer. Begin timing the cooking at this point.

3. Cook small eggs for 12 minutes, medium eggs for 13 minutes, large eggs for 14 to 15 minutes, and extra-large eggs for 15 minutes.

4. Cool the eggs quickly in cold water and peel as soon as possible. Serve the eggs now or refrigerate until needed.

NOTES

Cracking the eggs just after cooking will allow the trapped gasses inside to escape, thus reducing the amount of green discoloration around the yolk. Additionally, the eggs will peel easier if done as soon as they are cool enough to handle. If allowed to cool completely, the membrane under the skin tends to stick to the hard-cooked egg white, making them difficult to peel.

An alternative method for hard-cooking eggs is to remove the pot holding the eggs from the heat when the water reaches a boil. Cover the pot and let the eggs stand in the hot water for 20 minutes. This method is best suited for cooking large batches of eggs (2 dozen or more).

Coddled Eggs: Lower cold eggs into already simmering water and simmer for 30 seconds.

Soft-Cooked Eggs: Lower cold eggs into already simmering water and simmer for 3 to 4 minutes.

Medium-Cooked Eggs: Lower cold eggs into already simmering water and simmer for 5 to 7 minutes.

Pickled Eggs

Makes 10 servings

10 **Hard-Cooked Eggs** (preceding recipe)

2 tsp/4 g dry mustard

2 tsp/6 g cornstarch

24 fl oz/720 mL white wine vinegar

2 tsp/10 g sugar

1 tsp/2 g turmeric or **Curry Powder** (page 463)

1. Place the eggs in a stainless-steel bowl and set aside.

2. In a small saucepan, dilute the mustard and cornstarch in ½ fl oz/15 mL of cold water. Add the vinegar, sugar, and turmeric or curry powder. Bring the mixture to a boil over medium heat and simmer for 10 minutes.

3. Pour the mixture over the eggs. Cool the eggs and pickling solution to room temperature, then refrigerate overnight. The eggs are ready to serve at this point.

Red Pickled Eggs: Replace 8 fl oz/240 mL vinegar with beet juice.

Deviled Eggs

Deviled Eggs

Makes 10 servings

10 **Hard-Cooked Eggs** (page 897), **cold**

6 fl oz/180 mL **Mayonnaise** (page 936)

½ oz/14 g prepared mustard

salt, as needed

ground black pepper, as needed

1. Slice the eggs in half lengthwise. Separate the yolks from the whites. Reserve the whites separately until ready to fill.

2. Rub the yolks through a sieve or place them in a food processor bowl.

3. Add the mayonnaise, mustard, salt, and pepper. Mix or process the ingredients into a smooth paste.

4. Pipe or spoon the yolk mixture into the egg whites, garnish as desired, and serve immediately.

NOTES

The eggs can be separated and the filling mixed in advance, but if the eggs are not to be served immediately, the whites and the yolks should be held separately until just before service.

Garnishes may include chopped parsley, snipped chives, sliced green onion tops, dill sprigs, pimiento strips, chopped olives, caviar, shredded carrots, ground cumin, dried oregano, cayenne, or crushed red pepper flakes.

Substitutions for all or part of the mayonnaise include softened butter, compound butter, sour cream, puréed cottage cheese, softened cream cheese, yogurt, or crème fraîche.

Deviled Eggs with Tomato: Add 2 oz/57 g sautéed tomato concassé, ½ tsp/1 g dried herbs (basil, oregano, sage, thyme), and/or ½ tsp/1.50 g sautéed minced garlic or shallots to the yolk mixture.

Deviled Eggs with Greens: Add 1¾ oz/50 g blanched and puréed spinach, watercress, sorrel, lettuce, or other greens to the yolk mixture.

Deviled Eggs with Vegetables: Add small dice of cooked, raw, and/or marinated vegetables, such as celery, carrots, red onions, peppers, fennel, mushrooms, tomatoes, green beans, peas, corn, or eggplant to the yolk mixture.

Deviled Eggs with Peppers: Add 3 to 4 fl oz/90 to 120 mL puréed roasted red or green peppers to the yolk mixture.

Deviled Eggs with Cheese: Add ¾ oz/21 g grated hard cheese, or 2 oz/57 g soft cheese to the yolk mixture.

Deviled Eggs with Fish or Shellfish: Add 4 oz/113 g finely diced fish or shellfish (also any vegetables, if desired, see above) to the yolk mixture. Or, make a paste of fish by puréeing it with butter, mayonnaise, or heavy cream. Use smoked fish (especially small pieces or trimmings), shrimp, fresh cooked or canned tuna, salmon, crab, or lobster.

Poached Eggs

Makes 10 servings

1 gal/3.84 L water

1 tbsp/15 g salt

1 fl oz/30 mL distilled white vinegar

20 eggs

1. Combine the water, salt, and vinegar in a deep pan and bring it to a bare simmer.

2. Break each egg into a clean cup, and then slide the egg carefully into the poaching water. Cook for 3 to 5 minutes, or until the whites are set and opaque.

3. Remove the eggs from the water with a slotted spoon, blot them on absorbent toweling, and trim the edges if desired. The eggs are ready to serve now on heated plates, or they may be rapidly chilled and refrigerated for later service.

Eggs Benedict

Makes 10 servings

20 **Poached Eggs** (preceding recipe)

10 English muffins, split, toasted, and buttered

20 slices Canadian bacon, heated

20 fl oz/600 mL **Hollandaise Sauce** (page 386), warm

1. If the eggs have been poached in advance, reheat them in simmering water until warmed through. Blot on toweling and shape if necessary.

2. Top each English muffin half with a slice of Canadian bacon and a poached egg.

3. Ladle ½ to 1 fl oz/15 to 30 mL of warm hollandaise over each egg.

4. Serve immediately.

Eggs Florentine: Replace each slice of Canadian bacon with 2 oz/57 g sautéed spinach.

Poached Eggs American Style: Replace each slice of Canadian bacon with 1 sautéed slice peeled tomato and replace the hollandaise with Cheddar Cheese Sauce (page 384). Garnish with chopped, cooked bacon and parsley.

Poached Eggs with Chicken Liver Chasseur: Replace each slice of Canadian bacon with sautéed chicken livers and replace the hollandaise with Chasseur Sauce (page 361).

Poached Eggs with Smoked Salmon: Replace the English muffin with a toasted bagel and replace each slice of Canadian bacon with 1 slice smoked salmon. Garnish with chopped chives.

Eggs Benedict

Poached Eggs Mornay

Makes 10 servings

20 toast rounds or ovals

4 oz/113 g butter, melted

20 **Poached Eggs** (page 900)

16 fl oz/480 mL **Mornay Sauce** (page 384), **warm**

3 oz/85 g grated Gruyère

1. Brush the toast with butter and top with the poached eggs. Coat with the sauce and sprinkle with grated cheese.

2. Brown lightly under a broiler or salamander and serve immediately.

Poached Eggs Farmer Style: Top the toast with peeled tomato slices, boiled ham, creamed mushrooms, and poached eggs.

Poached Eggs with Mushrooms: Fill tartlets with creamed mushrooms, top with poached eggs, and coat with Hollandaise Sauce (page 386).

Poached Eggs Massena: Heat fresh artichoke bottoms and fill with Béarnaise Sauce (page 386). Top with poached eggs, coat with Tomato Sauce (page 384), and sprinkle with chopped parsley.

Poached Eggs on Hash: Top corned beef hash patties with poached eggs. Garnish with deep-fried parsley.

Fried Eggs

Makes 10 servings

20 eggs

clarified or whole butter, as needed for frying

salt, as needed

ground black pepper, as needed

1. Break the eggs into clean cups (1 egg per cup).

2. Heat the butter in a pan over medium heat. Slide the eggs into the pan and cook until the egg whites have set.

3. Tilt the pan, allowing the fat to collect at the side of the pan, and baste the eggs with the fat as they cook.

4. Season the eggs with salt and pepper and serve at once on heated plates.

Eggs over Easy, Medium, or Hard: Turn the eggs over near the end of their cooking time with a spatula and cook them on the second side until done as desired, 20 to 30 seconds for over easy, 1 minute for over medium, 2 minutes for over hard.

Scrambled Eggs

Makes 10 servings

30 eggs

1 tbsp/15 g salt

1 tsp/2 g ground white pepper

5 fl oz/150 mL water or milk (optional)

2½ fl oz/75 mL clarified butter or oil

1. For each portion, beat 3 eggs well and season with salt and pepper. Add the liquid, if using.

2. Heat a nonstick pan over medium heat and add the butter or oil, tilting the pan to coat the entire surface. The pan should be hot, but not smoking.

3. Pour the egg mixture into the pan and cook over low heat, stirring frequently with the back the back of a fork or wooden spoon until the eggs are soft and creamy. Remove the eggs from the heat when fully cooked, but still moist.

4. Serve at once on heated plates.

Scrambled Egg Whites: Substitute 60 fl oz/1.80 L egg whites for the whole eggs and omit the optional liquid. For each serving, beat 6 fl oz/180 mL egg whites well and season with salt and pepper. Heat a nonstick pan over medium heat and add the butter or oil. Alternately, a light coating of cooking spray may be used, as many contemporary, high-protein diets call for little to no fat. Pour the egg mixture into the pan. Using a rubber spatula or a wooden spoon, gently pull the egg whites into the center of the pan, being careful not to break the curds. Cook until the egg whites are soft and fluffy. Break the egg whites into curds at the end of cooking.

Scrambled Eggs with Cheese: For each portion, add ½ oz/14 g grated Gruyère or Cheddar cheese to the eggs. If desired, stir 1½ tsp/7.50 mL cream into the eggs just before removing them from the heat.

Scrambled Eggs Swedish Style: For each portion, add 1 oz/28 g sautéed smoked salmon to the eggs. Garnish with 1 tsp/1 g chopped chives.

Scrambled Eggs Hunter Style: For each portion, add ¾ oz/21 g cooked, diced bacon and ½ tsp/0.50 g chopped chives to the eggs. Prior to service, spoon 3 oz/85 g sautéed sliced mushrooms on top of the scrambled eggs.

Scrambled Eggs with Bratwurst: For each portion, top 2 sautéed slices peeled tomato with the scrambled eggs and 1 oz/28 g cooked, sliced bratwurst.

Scrambled Eggs Gratiné: For each portion, top the scrambled eggs with Mornay Sauce (page 384), sprinkle with grated Gruyère cheese, and brown lightly under the broiler.

Scrambled Eggs Greek Style: For each portion, slice a Japanese eggplant lengthwise into ½-in/1-cm slices, season with salt, and sauté in oil. Sauté 1 oz/28 g tomato concassé with garlic, salt, and pepper to taste. Spoon the scrambled eggs on top of the eggplant slices and top the eggs with the tomato concassé.

Plain Rolled Omelet

Makes 10 servings

30 eggs

1 tbsp/15 g salt

1 tsp/2 g ground white pepper

5 fl oz/150 mL water, stock, milk, or cream (optional)

2½ fl oz/75 mL, as needed clarified butter or oil

1. For each portion, beat 3 eggs well and season with salt and pepper. Add the liquid, if using.

2. Heat a nonstick omelet pan over high heat and add the butter or oil, tilting the pan to coat the entire surface.

3. Pour the egg mixture into the pan and scramble it with the back of a fork or wooden spoon. Move the pan and utensil at the same time until the egg mixture has coagulated slightly. Smooth the eggs into an even layer.

4. Let the egg mixture finish cooking without stirring.

5. Tilt the pan and slide a fork or spoon around the lip of the pan, under the omelet, to be sure it is not sticking. Slide the omelet to the front of the pan and use a fork or a wooden spoon to fold it inside to the center.

6. Turn the pan upside down, rolling the omelet onto the plate. The finished omelet should be oval shaped.

NOTES
Options for filling an omelet: A precooked filling may be added to the eggs after they have been smoothed into an even layer and before the omelet is rolled. Alternatively, the rolled omelet can be slit open at the top, and a precooked filling or sauce can be spooned into the pocket.

To give the omelet additional sheen, rub the surface lightly with butter.

Plain Rolled Egg White Omelet: Substitute 60 fl oz/1.80 L egg whites for the whole eggs and omit the optional liquid. For each serving, beat 6 fl oz/180 mL egg whites well and season with salt and pepper. Heat an omelet pan over medium heat and add the butter or oil. Alternatively, a light coating of cooking spray may be used, as many contemporary, high-protein diets call for little to no fat. Pour the egg mixture into the pan. Using a rubber spatula or a wooden spoon, gently pull the egg whites into the center

of the pan, being careful not to break the curds. Smooth the egg whites into an even layer and let them finish cooking without stirring. Finish as you would a plain omelet.

Cheese Omelet: Fill each omelet with ½ oz/14 g grated or diced cheese, such as Gruyère or Cheddar.

Cheese and Vegetable Omelet: Fill each omelet with any combination of cheese and vegetables in a similar flavor profile, such as goat cheese and sun-dried tomatoes; Gorgonzola and sautéed spinach or mushrooms; cream cheese and olives; or Gruyère and sautéed leeks.

Meat and Cheese Omelet: Fill each omelet with 1 oz/28 g cooked, diced meat (turkey, ham, or sausage) and 1 oz/28 g grated cheese.

Herb Omelet: Before rolling, sprinkle each omelet with 2 tsp/2 g finely chopped herbs, such as parsley, thyme, chervil, tarragon, basil, and oregano.

Tomato Omelet: Fill each omelet with 2 fl oz/60 mL relatively thick Tomato Coulis (page 385).

Omelet Florentine: Fill each omelet with 1½ oz/43 g sautéed spinach leaves.

Omelet Marcel: Fill each omelet with 3 oz/85 g sautéed, sliced mushrooms and 1 oz/28 g sautéed, sliced ham. Garnish the omelet with chopped chives.

Omelet Opera: Fill each omelet with 2 oz/57 g lightly sautéed chicken livers, deglazed with Madeira Sauce (page 544). Garnish each omelet with 3 asparagus tips and spoon 1 to 2 fl oz/30 to 60 mL Hollandaise Sauce (page 386) on top.

Seafood Omelet: Fill each omelet with 2 to 3 tsp/10 to 15 mL sour cream, crème fraîche, or yogurt and 2 oz/57 g cooked shrimp, smoked salmon, lobster, or other cooked and/or smoked fish, caviar, or seafood.

Shellfish Omelet: Fill each omelet with 3 or 4 oysters, clams, or mussels that have been steamed briefly in butter with wine and shallots.

Western Omelet: Fill each omelet with 1 oz/28 g each sautéed diced ham, red and green peppers, and onions. Add grated Monterey Jack or Cheddar cheese, if desired.

Spanish Omelet: Fill each omelet with 2 oz/57 g tomato concassé or sauce and 1 oz/28 g each sautéed, diced onions and green peppers.

Jelly Omelet: Fill each omelet with 2 to 3 tbsp/30 to 45 mL jelly, chutney, or other preserved fruits.

Farmer-Style Omelet

Makes 10 servings

10 oz/284 g diced bacon or 5 fl oz/150 ml vegetable oil

10 oz/284 g minced onions

10 oz/284 g diced cooked potatoes

30 eggs

1 tbsp/15 g salt

1 tsp/2 g ground white pepper

1. For each serving, render 1 oz/28 g of bacon in a skillet until crisp, or heat ½ fl oz/15 mL of the oil.

2. Add 1 oz/28 g of the onions and sauté over medium heat, stirring occasionally, until light golden brown, 10 to 12 minutes.

3. Add 1 oz/28 g of the potatoes and sauté until lightly browned, 5 minutes more.

4. Meanwhile, beat 3 eggs together with salt and pepper. Pour them over the ingredients in the skillet and stir gently.

5. Reduce the heat to low, cover the skillet, and cook until the eggs are nearly set.

6. Remove the cover and place the skillet under a broiler to brown the eggs lightly. Serve at once on a heated plate.

Souffléed Cheddar Omelet

Makes 10 servings

30 eggs

1 oz/28 g salt

1¼ tsp/2.50 g ground white pepper

5 oz/142 g grated sharp Cheddar cheese

2 tbsp/6 g minced chives

10 fl oz/300 mL clarified butter or oil

1. For each serving to order, separate 3 eggs. Beat the yolks and season with ½ tsp/2.50 g of salt and ¼ tsp/0.50 g of pepper. Add the Cheddar and chives to the beaten yolks.

2. Beat the egg whites to medium peaks and fold them into the yolks.

3. Pour the eggs into a preheated, well-oiled skillet. When the sides and bottom have set, finish the omelet in a 400°F/204°C oven until fully set and light golden on top. Serve immediately.

Spinach Soufflé

Makes 10 portions

SOUFFLÉ BASE

2 oz/57 g butter

2½ oz/71 g flour

24 fl oz/720 mL milk

salt, as needed

ground black pepper, as needed

15 egg yolks

butter, soft, as needed

3 oz/85 g grated Parmesan cheese, plus as needed for dusting molds

10 oz/284 g blanched chopped spinach

salt, as needed

ground black pepper, as needed

10 egg whites

1. To make the soufflé base, heat the butter in a pan over medium heat and stir in the flour. Cook this roux over low to medium heat for 6 to 8 minutes, stirring frequently, to make a blond roux.

2. Add the milk, whisking well until the mixture is very smooth. Add salt and pepper. Simmer over low heat, stirring constantly, for 15 to 20 minutes, or until very thick and smooth.

3. Blend the yolks with some of the hot base to temper. Return the tempered yolks to the base mixture and continue to simmer 3 to 4 minutes, stirring constantly. Do not allow the mixture to boil.

4. Adjust the seasoning with salt and pepper, and strain through a sieve if necessary. The base is ready to use now or it may be properly cooled and stored for later use.

5. To make spinach soufflé, prepare the soufflé molds by brushing them liberally with softened butter. Lightly dust the interior of each mold with grated Parmesan cheese.

6. For each portion, blend together 2 fl oz/60 mL soufflé base, 1 oz/28 g spinach, 1 tbsp/30 mL grated Parmesan, salt, and ground black pepper until the spinach is evenly distributed.

7. Beat 1 egg white for each soufflé to soft peaks. Fold about one-third of the beaten whites into the base. Add the remaining white in one or two additions.

8. Spoon the soufflé batter into the prepared molds to within ½ inch/1 cm of the rim. Wipe the rim carefully to remove any batter. Tap the soufflés gently on the counter to settle the batter. Sprinkle the soufflé tops with the remaining Parmesan.

9. Place the soufflés on a sheet pan in a 425°F/218°C oven and bake undisturbed until puffy and a skewer inserted in the center comes out relatively clean, 16 to 18 minutes. Serve immediately.

Savory Cheese Soufflé: Replace the spinach with 3 oz/85 g of grated Gruyère or Emmentaler.

Artichoke Soufflé

Makes 10 portions

10 globe artichokes

lemon juice, as needed

salt, as needed

13 eggs, separated

10 oz/284 grated Gruyère

24 fl oz/720 mL milk

2 tbsp/18 g cornstarch

ground black pepper, as needed

1. Trim the artichokes and cook in simmering water seasoned with lemon juice and salt until tender. Scrape the flesh from the leaves, discard the chokes and save the bottoms.

2. Purée the artichoke meat, egg yolks, Gruyère, milk, and cornstarch in a food processor. Season with salt and pepper.

3. Beat the egg whites to soft peaks and fold into artichoke mixture in three additions. Pour the mixture into 10 greased soufflé ramekins.

4. Bake in a preheated 400°F/204°C oven until done, about 20 minutes. Serve at once.

Warm Goat Cheese Custard

Makes 10 servings

6 oz/170 g cream cheese, room temperature

9 oz/255 g goat cheese, room temperature

½ tsp/1 g ground black pepper, plus as needed

9 eggs

24 fl oz/720 mL heavy cream

1 oz/28 g sliced chives

1 tbsp/15 g salt, plus as needed

40 seedless green grapes

1. In a food processor bowl, combine the cream cheese with 6 oz/170 g of the goat cheese, reserving the remainder for garnish. Season with the pepper and process until the mixture is very smooth.

2. Add the eggs, 8 fl oz/240 mL of the cream, half of the chives, and the salt. Pulse the processor on and off until the ingredients are just blended. Divide the mixture among 10 buttered 2-fl-oz/60-mL timbale molds and cover the molds with buttered parchment paper.

3. Place the timbale molds in a bain marie and bake in a 325°F/163°C oven until a knife inserted near the center of a timbale comes away clean.

4. Reduce the remaining cream by half and season with salt and pepper to taste. Add the remaining chives and the grapes to the cream immediately before service.

5. Unmold the timbales and coat with the sauce. Garnish with the reserved goat cheese and serve immediately.

NOTE
Replace the goat cheese with other soft cheeses, such as Boursin, Brillat-Savarin, Camembert, or Brie.

Quiche Lorraine

Quiche Lorraine

Makes 10 servings

8 oz/227 g diced slab bacon

1 oz/28 g butter or oil

6 fl oz/180 mL heavy cream

6 fl oz/180 mL milk

3 eggs

1 tsp/5 g salt

¼ tsp/0.50 g ground black pepper

pinch ground nutmeg

4 oz/113 g grated Emmentaler cheese

9 in/23 cm **Basic Pie Dough (3-2-1)** (page 1104), blind baked

1. Sauté the bacon in butter or oil until browned. Remove the bacon with a slotted spoon and drain. Discard the rendered fat, or save for another use.

2. Whisk together the cream, milk, and eggs. Season with salt, pepper, and nutmeg.

3. Scatter the bacon and cheese evenly over the crust. Add the custard mixture gradually, stirring it gently with the back of a fork to distribute the filling ingredients evenly.

4. Set the quiche pan on a sheet pan and bake in a 350°F/177°C oven until a knife blade inserted in the center comes out clean, 40 to 45 minutes. Serve hot or at room temperature.

NOTES
Quiche may also be baked without a pastry crust. Butter a shallow casserole or baking dish. Sprinkle it with grated Parmesan, if desired. Spread the filling ingredients over the casserole bottom. Pour the custard mixture on top. Bake the quiche in a bain marie until a knife inserted near the center comes out clean, about 1 hour.

Quiche may also be baked in tartlet shells, timbale molds, or custard cups.

Spinach Quiche: Substitute 1 lb/454 g spinach, blanched, squeezed dry, and coarsely chopped, for all or part of the bacon.

Tomato and Leek Quiche: Substitute 10 oz/284 g tomato concassé and 8 oz/227 g sautéed leeks for the bacon. For the leeks, sauté the white and light green parts only in butter until translucent. Add the tomato concassé and sauté until the liquid evaporates. Add 2 tbsp/6 g minced tarragon or basil.

Caramelized Onion Quiche: Substitute caramelized onions for all or part of the bacon. For 6 oz/170 g caramelized onions, cook 10 oz/284 g sliced onions in 1 fl oz/30 mL olive oil over medium-low heat until golden brown and soft, about 15 minutes. Substitute Provolone cheese for the Emmentaler.

Smoked Salmon and Dill Quiche: Substitute 4 oz/113 g diced smoked salmon for the bacon and 2 oz/57 g cream cheese, cut or broken into small pieces, for the Emmentaler. Add 2 tbsp/6 g chopped dill and 1 tbsp/3 g snipped chives.

Broccoli and Cheddar Cheese Quiche: Substitute 5 oz/142 g broccoli florets, sautéed in olive oil until tender, for all or part of the bacon. Substitute Cheddar cheese for the Emmentaler.

French Toast

Makes 10 servings

30 **Challah Bread** (page 1080) slices, cut ¼ to ½ in/6 mm to 1 cm thick

32 fl oz/960 mL milk

8 eggs

2 oz/57 g sugar

pinch salt

pinch ground cinnamon (optional)

pinch ground nutmeg (optional)

5 oz/142 g butter

1. Dry the challah slices on sheet pans overnight or in a 200°F/93°C oven for 1 hour.

2. Combine the milk, eggs, sugar, salt, and cinnamon and nutmeg, if using. Mix into a smooth batter. Refrigerate until needed.

3. Heat a skillet and grease with ½ to 1 oz/14 to 28 g of butter, or use a nonstick pan over moderate heat.

4. Dip the bread into the batter, coating the slices evenly. Fry the slices on 1 side until evenly browned, then turn and brown the other side. Work in batches if necessary.

5. Serve the French toast at once on heated plates.

NOTES
Serve with butter and maple syrup or honey.

Garnishing options include confectioner's sugar, cinnamon sugar, toasted nuts, and/or fresh or dried fruit.

French Toast

Chapter Thirty

Salad Dressings and Salads

Salads appear on the menu in so many different guises today that it is easy to imagine that they were invented by this generation of chefs. In fact, fresh concoctions of seasoned herbs and lettuces have been relished in every part of the world from the beginning of recorded culinary history.

Vinaigrette

Vinaigrettes are thought of mainly as dressings for green salads, but they are used in many other ways as well: as marinades for grilled or broiled foods; to dress salads made from pastas, grains, vegetables, and beans; as dips; as sauces served with hot or cold entrées and appetizers; or brushed on sandwiches.

A vinaigrette is a temporary emulsion, made by blending oil and other ingredients until they form a homogeneous sauce. The sauce remains an emulsion for a only a short time, quickly separating back into oil and vinegar. To add flavor and help stabilize the sauce, an emulsifier is sometimes included.

A standard vinaigrette ratio of three parts oil to one part acid works well as a starting point, but the vinaigrette needs to be tasted and evaluated whenever a change is made in the type of oil, acid, or specific flavoring ingredients.

Select the oil with an eye to both its flavor and cost. Oils used in salad dressings can be subtle or intensely flavored. Oils may serve simply to carry the other flavors in the vinaigrette, or they may have readily identifiable flavors of their own. Very strongly flavored oils are often blended with less intense oils to produce a balanced flavor in the finished sauce.

The choice of acid ranges widely as well, from vinegar, to fruit juice, to malted barley, to similar acidic liquids. Every vinegar has a different level of tartness or acidity. Both oils and vinegars can be flavored.

Additional vinaigrette ingredients include emulsifiers (egg yolks, mustard, roasted garlic, fruit or vegetable purées, or glace de viande) and such seasonings as salt, pepper, herbs, and spices. The challenge of making a good vinaigrette lies in achieving balance, a point at which the acidity of the vinegar or juice is tempered but not dominated by the richness of the oil.

Equipment needs for making vinaigrettes are minimal: measuring spoons or cups, a bowl, and a whisk or a blender, food processor, or standing mixer.

A basic formula for vinaigrette

48 fl oz/1.44 L oil

16 fl oz/480 mL vinegar

Salt, pepper, and other seasonings

Finishing and garnishing ingredients (optional)

1. **Combine the vinegar with the emulsifying and seasoning ingredients first.** Adding the mustard, salt, pepper, herbs, or other ingredients to the vinegar is the easiest way to be sure that they are evenly dispersed throughout the sauce for an even flavor before adding the oil.

Make the Vinaigrette

2. **Add the oil gradually while whisking constantly to create a thick, emulsified vinaigrette.** Whisk in the oil or, to create a more stable vinaigrette, use a blender, immersion blender, standing mixer with a whip, or food processor. Vinaigrettes made by machine hold their emulsion longer than those that are simply whipped together.

Crumbled cheese, fresh or dried fruits and vegetables, or other garnishes can be added, if desired. As the vinaigrette sits, it will begin to separate. Whip or stir the sauce before each use to recombine the oil and vinegar. Cover and refrigerate vinaigrettes when not using. For optimum flavor, make vinaigrettes in quantities that will last no longer than three days.

A well-made vinaigrette should be neither too sour nor too oily and the consistency of the sauce such that it clings nicely to the greens without looking or feeling greasy. The best way to check is to toss some of the salad with the vinaigrette, and then taste the sauce on the salad.

Flavored Oils and Vinegars

Good-quality oils and vinegars can be infused with spices, aromatics, herbs, and fruits or vegetables. Flavored oils and vinegars work well as condiments, or as a drizzle or droplets on a plated dish to add a bit of intense flavor and color. They are also excellent to use as dressings for vegetables, pastas, grains, or fruits. And of course, they can be used in vinaigrettes and other dressings for a special effect.

To infuse oils and vinegars use one of the following methods:

- Heat the oil or vinegar very gently over low heat. The flavoring ingredients, such as citrus zest or garlic, may be added to the oil or vinegar as it warms. Let the oil or vinegar steep off the heat with the flavoring ingredients until cool, then pour into storage bottles or containers. Or, you may opt to heat the oil or vinegar without any added flavorings, then pour it over the flavoring ingredients and cool. Pour the infused oil or vinegar into storage containers.

- Strain the vinegar or oil for a clearer final product, or leave the aromatics in for a more intense flavor. Add fresh aromatics after the oil or vinegar has steeped for several days to give an even more intense flavor, if desired.

- Purée raw, blanched, or fully cooked vegetables, herbs, or fruits. Bring the purée to a simmer, reducing if necessary to concentrate flavors. Add the purée to the oil or vinegar and transfer to a storage container. Leave the oil or vinegar as is and use it like a purée or strain it to remove the fiber and pulp.

- Combine room-temperature oils or vinegars with ground spices and transfer them to a storage container. Let the mixture settle until the vinegar or oil is clear and the spices have settled in the bottom of the container.

- Refrigerate the flavored oil or vinegar to rest for at least 3 hours and up to 36 hours. The time will vary according to the intensity of the flavoring ingredients and the intended use. Taste the oil or vinegar occasionally and, if necessary, strain or decant it into a clean bottle.

NOTE

Fresh or raw ingredients added to an oil or vinegar increase the risk of food-borne illness. Keep scratch-made versions refrigerated. Use within a few days for the best flavor and color.

Mayonnaise

Mayonnaise, because of its great versatility, is often included in the list of the basic, or "grand," sauces prepared in the professional kitchen.

Mayonnaise is a cold sauce made by combining egg yolks with oil to form a stable emulsion. Unlike vinaigrette, this sauce does not break as it sits. Mayonnaise and sauces made with mayonnaise as a base can be used to dress salads or as a dip or spread. Among the famous mayonnaise-based sauces are Rémoulade Sauce (page 592), Green Mayonnaise (page 936), Aïoli (garlic mayonnaise; page 936), and Tartar Sauce (page 936).

Classic recipes for mayonnaise call for 6 to 8 fl oz/180 to 240 mL of oil to each egg yolk. Egg yolks provide both the liquid, which holds the oil droplets in suspension, and an emulsifier known as lecithin. To avoid any possible food-borne illnesses (such as those caused by *Salmonella* or *E. coli*), professional chefs should use pasteurized egg yolks.

Since mayonnaise is often intended as a base sauce that can be used for a variety of purposes, it is usually best to choose an oil that does not have a pronounced flavor of its own. There are exceptions to this general rule, however. For example, a mayonnaise made with extra-virgin olive oil or a nut oil would be appropriate to serve as a dip with a platter of grilled vegetables or crudités. A small amount of mustard is often called for in mayonnaise. Though mustard is an emulsifier, its primary function in a mayonnaise is flavor. Various acids may also be used to prepare a mayonnaise, including lemon juice or wine or cider vinegars. The acid, along with water, flavors the sauce as well as provides additional moisture for the emulsification. Using white vinegar also helps to keep the mayonnaise white. Additional flavoring ingredients, such as garlic or herbs, may also be needed as indicated.

Equipment needs for making mayonnaise are minimal: measuring spoons or cups, a bowl, and a whisk are appropriate for small quantities. For large batches, use a blender or food processor. Mayonnaise sauces should be held in very clean storage containers.

A basic formula for mayonnaise

3 fl oz/90 mL pasteurized egg yolks (3 large)

24 fl oz/720 mL oil

1 to 2 fl oz/30 to 60 mL lemon juice, vinegar, or a combination

1 fl oz/30 mL water

2 tsp/4 g dry mustard (optional)

Salt, pepper, and other seasonings

1. **Blend the yolks with a bit of water and other flavoring ingredients.** Whisking the yolks with water prepares them to combine with the oil to form a good thick mayonnaise. Whisk the yolks and water together to loosen the eggs. Include lemon juice or vinegar and mustard at this point, if the recipe calls for those ingredients.

sauce will become too thick to absorb any more oil. Add any additional flavoring or garnish ingredients at the point indicated in the recipe.

Keep mayonnaise refrigerated at all times once it is prepared. Transfer it to a storage container, cover it carefully, and label it with a date. Before using mayonnaise that has been stored, stir it gently and check the seasoning carefully. If the sauce needs to be thinned, add a bit of water.

2. **Pour the oil into the egg yolks while whisking constantly.** Add the oil a little at a time, whisking it in completely. Start pouring slowly and gradually increase the amount of oil. The oil must be whipped into the egg yolks so that it is broken up into very fine droplets. Adding the oil slowly allows a good emulsion to begin to form. If the oil is added too quickly, the droplets will be too large to emulsify properly, and the sauce will appear broken. Once about ¼ to ⅓ of the oil has been properly blended into the egg mixture, start to increase the speed at which the oil is added.

When preparing mayonnaise in a mixer, add the oil in a thin stream as the machine runs. It is still true that the oil should be added more slowly at the beginning than at the end.

Adjust the thickness and flavor of the sauce by adding a bit more acid or water when incorporating the oil.

The more oil that is added to the yolks, the thicker the sauce will become. Add more lemon juice, vinegar, or a little water when the mayonnaise becomes very thick. If this step is neglected, the

Fixing a Broken Mayonnaise

Mayonnaise and similarly prepared dressings may break for a number of reasons:

- The oil was added too rapidly for the egg yolk to absorb it.

- The sauce was allowed to become too thick.

- The sauce became either too cold or too warm as it was being prepared.

A broken mayonnaise can be saved by combining 1 fl oz/30 mL pasteurized egg with 1 tsp/5 mL water and beating the mixture until foamy. Gradually add the broken mayonnaise into the diluted yolk, whisking constantly until the mayonnaise regains a smooth, creamy appearance.

3. **Continue adding the oil until the amount specified in the recipe has been added.** A finished mayonnaise should be thick enough to hold soft peaks.

By adding additional flavoring or garnish ingredients, a basic mayonnaise can be flavored to produce a different sauce. Aioli, a garlic-flavored mayonnaise, calls for a good quantity of garlic to be included in the earliest stages of mixing. However, other ingredients may be blended into the sauce once the oil is incorporated to create sauces such as Remoulade Sauce (page 592) or Green Goddess Dressing (page 934).

A properly made mayonnaise has a mild and balanced flavor, without any predominance of acidic or oily flavors. It is thick, creamy, and completely homogeneous in texture and appearance. The color is white or slightly off-white, not greenish or yellow.

Green Salads

In its most basic form, a green salad (sometimes called a tossed salad, mixed salad, or garden salad) is made of one or more tender greens tossed with a dressing. Garnishes, such as other vegetables, croutons, and cheeses, are often included as well.

The salad's character is determined by the greens selected. Greens are often grouped according to their flavors and/or textures. Commercially prepared salad blends are available today, but chefs can also create their own by combining lettuces from within one group or by selecting from among two or more groups. For more information on specific salad green varieties, see pages 248–251.

Greens and herbs used for salads are often quite sandy and gritty. Removing all traces of dirt from them is a very important part of the mise en place for the pantry and hot line. Greens that are raised hydroponically, prepared as mesclun mixes, and then prerinsed may need only a quick plunge or rinse with cool water. Other leafy greens should be cleaned by plunging them in a sink filled with cool water. Lift them from the water, drain the sink, and repeat until there are no signs of grit remaining in the water.

A key piece of equipment in salad making is the spinner. This tool, which comes in both hand-operated and large-scale electric versions, uses centrifugal force to spin the water away from the greens so that they have a better flavor and dressing clings evenly to them.

A basic formula for 10 servings of salad

30 oz/851 g salad greens

10 fl oz/300 mL vinaigrette or other salad dressing

Garnishes, as desired

Wash the greens thoroughly in plenty of cool water to remove all traces of dirt or sand. Nothing is worse than a gritty salad or one that forces the diner to use a knife to cut the lettuce.

All greens, including prepackaged salad mixes and "triple-washed" bagged spinach, must be washed before serving. Change the water as often as necessary until absolutely no traces of dirt, grit, or sand are visible in the rinsing water.

Hydroponically raised greens, prepared as mesclun mixes, may need only a quick plunge or rinse with cool water to refresh them.

Separate the lettuce or other heading greens into leaves. Loose heads and bunching greens will separate into individual leaves easily. Trim the coarse ribs or stem ends away if necessary.

To remove the core from heading lettuce, gently rap or push the core down onto a work surface. This will generally break the core away from the leaves. For tighter heads, it may be necessary to use a paring knife to cut out the core.

Dry the greens completely. Salad dressings cling best to well-dried greens. In addition, carefully dried greens last in storage longer. Use either a large-scale electric spinner for volume salad making or a hand basket for smaller batches. Clean and sanitize the spinner carefully after each use.

Store cleaned greens in tubs or other containers. Once greens are cleaned and dried, keep them refrigerated until ready to dress and serve them. Use cleaned salad greens within a day or two. Do not stack cleaned salad greens too deep; their own weight could bruise the leaves.

Cut or tear the lettuce into bite-size pieces. Traditional salad-making manuals have always called for lettuces to be torn rather than cut to avoid discoloring, bruising, or crushing the leaves. The choice to either cut or tear lettuce is primarily a matter of personal style and preference. With today's high-carbon stainless-steel knives, discoloration is not a problem. As long as the blade is properly sharpened and a good cutting technique is used, the leaves will be sliced rather than crushed or bruised.

Garnish and dress the salad. The dressing's flavor should be appropriate to the salad ingredients, because the dressing serves to pull all the flavors together. Use delicate dressings with delicately flavored greens and more robust dressings with more strongly flavored greens. Consider the weight and coating capabilities of different dressings as well. Vinaigrettes coat lightly but evenly. Emulsified vinaigrette dressings and light mayonnaise dressings, which are thicker than vinaigrettes, tend to coat the ingredients more heavily.

Choose garnishes according to the season and your desired presentation. Either toss these ingredients with the greens as they are being dressed or marinate them separately in a little vinaigrette and use them to top the salad.

To dress a salad:

- Place the greens (about 3 oz/85 g or ¾ cup per serving) in a bowl.

- Ladle a portion of salad dressing over them (2 to 3 fl oz/30 to 45 mL per serving).

- Toss the salad using tongs, spoons, or, if appropriate, gloved hands.

- Be sure each piece of lettuce is coated completely but lightly, with just enough dressing for the greens; if it pools on the plate, there is too much.

Croutons

Croutons are often used as a garnish for salads as well as soups and stews. Croustades, crostini, rusks, and bruschetta are all types of croutons. Some are cut into slices, others into cubes or disks. Some are toasted, some deep fried, some grilled, and some broiled. Large croutons made to act as the base for canapés, hors d'oeuvre, and roasted or grilled meats reflect medieval European practices when plates were actually slabs of bread intended for consumption once they had been well dampened with juices and sauces from the meal.

To make croutons:

- Cut bread (crusts removed or not) into the desired size. Rub, spray, or toss the cubes or slices lightly with oil or clarified butter, if desired. Add salt and pepper. Good croutons are light in color, relatively greaseless, and well seasoned with a crisp, crunchy texture throughout.

- To toast croutons in the oven, spread them in a single layer on a pan. Turn them from time to time to toast them evenly and check frequently to avoid scorching.

- To pan fry croutons, add the bread to hot clarified butter or oil in a sauté pan, fry until evenly browned, and drain well on absorbent toweling. Add herbs or grated cheese while still hot.

Fruit Salads

Fruits have a variety of characteristics, making some fruit salads fairly sturdy, while others lose quality very rapidly. Fruits that turn brown (apples, pears, and bananas) can be treated with citrus juice to keep them from oxidizing, as long as the flavor of the juice doesn't compete with the other ingredients in the salad.

Mixed fruit salads that include highly perishable fruits can be produced for volume operations by preparing the base from the least perishable fruits. More perishable items, such as raspberries, strawberries, or bananas, can then be combined with smaller batches or individual servings at the last moment, or they can be added as a garnish.

Fresh herbs such as mint, basil, or lemon thyme may be added to fruit salads as a garnish. Experiment to determine which herbs work best with the fruits selected for the salad.

To prepare fruit salads, you must learn how to peel, slice, or cut a variety of fruits, as shown on the following pages. Before working with any fruit, be sure it is properly rinsed. To avoid cross contamination, clean and sanitize cutting boards and tools properly. Once fruits are cut, refrigerate them until they are served.

Apples

Peel apples as thinly as possible to avoid trim loss. To prevent discoloration of the cut surfaces of apples, as well as pears, peaches, and bananas, toss them in water that has been acidulated by adding a little citrus juice. Choose a juice with a flavor that complements the fruit's flavor. There shouldn't be so much acid that it overwhelms the fruit.

To clean and peel an apple, use the tip of a paring knife to remove the stem and blossom ends. Use a paring knife or peeler to cut away the skin. Once the peel is removed, halve the apple from top to bottom and cut into quarters. To core the quarters, work from the stem end, angling your cut to the midpoint of the core, where it is deepest. Make a second cut working from the opposite direction.

To cut very even slices, use a mandoline. Working with a whole peeled apple, make slices from one side of the apple until just before the core is reached. Turn and repeat on the opposite side. When the flesh has been removed from the two wide sides, slice the flesh from the now narrow sides of the apple.

Citrus Fruits

Citrus fruits, including oranges, lemons, limes, and grapefruit, are used to add flavor, moisture, and color to dishes. They are also served as a functional garnish with some foods—for instance, a slice of lime with Cuban-style black bean soup or a wedge of lemon with broiled fish.

Before juicing citrus fruits, allow them to come to room temperature if possible. Roll the fruit under the palm of your hand on a cutting board or other work surface before juicing to break some of the membranes. This helps to release more juice. Remember to strain out the seeds and pulp before using the juice, either by covering the fruit with cheesecloth before squeezing it or by straining it after juicing. There are numerous special tools to juice citrus fruits, including reamers, extractors, and hand-operated and electric juicers.

Zesting Citrus

Citrus zest is the outer portion of the fruit's peel or rind. It is used to add color, texture, and flavor to dishes. The zest includes only the skin's brightly colored part, which contains much of the fruit's flavorful and aromatic volatile oils. It does not include the underlying white pith, which has a bitter taste. You can use the fine openings on a box grater to make grated zest, a paring knife, peeler, or zester.

Zest is often blanched before it is used in a dish to remove any unpleasant bitter flavor. To blanch zest, cook it briefly in simmering water, then drain. Repeat as often as necessary; generally two to three blanchings are best. Add sugar to the blanching water for a sweetened zest.

Making Citrus Suprêmes

Cutting the flesh away from all the connective membranes of the fruit makes citrus suprêmes, also called sections or segments.

1. After cutting away the ends of the fruit, use a paring knife to remove just the peel of the orange. Be careful to cut away as little flesh as possible.

2. To make suprêmes, use a paring knife to cut along each side of the membrane that divides the orange segments. Have a bowl ready to catch the suprêmes as you work.

Mangos

A mango has a flat seed in the center of the flesh. The peel is left on to produce a special cut, known as the hedgehog cut, or the fruit may be peeled before cutting the flesh from the pit, if desired. If cut from the stem end to the pointed end of the mango, the flesh comes away from the pit more easily.

For the hedgehog cut, the mango is not peeled before the flesh is sliced from the pit. This technique can be used to prepare mangos for salads or other uses, or it may be used for a decorative presentation on a fruit plate.

To dice the mango for puréeing or for a less decorative approach, peel it by making a series of cuts, removing as little edible fruit as possible. Cut a slice from the other side of the pit, cutting as close to the pit as possible for the best yield. Cut the remaining flesh from the two narrow sides, following the curve of the pit. Cube or slice the mango as desired.

1. Use a chef's knife to carefully slice as close to the pit as possible to remove the most flesh. If desired, the remainder of the mango can be peeled and the flesh cut away from the pit in order to improve the yield.

2. Use the tip of a paring knife or a utility knife to score the flesh in a crosshatch pattern. This may be done on the diagonal, as shown here, or using perpendicular cuts to produce cubes. The tip of the knife should not cut through the skin.

3. Turn the mango half inside out; it will look like a hedgehog. Slice the cubes away from the skin now, or present the fruit as is on a fruit plate.

Pineapples

A pineapple has a thick, spiny skin. The flesh near the skin has "eyes" that should be completely removed before using the flesh in a salad or other presentations. Slice away the pineapple top with a chef's knife, and cut a slice from the base of the pineapple.

Use a chef's knife to peel the pineapple. Make the cuts deep enough to remove the eyes but not so deep that a great deal of edible flesh is removed. For even slices or to make neat dice or cubes, slice the pineapple vertically at the desired thickness until you reach the core on the first side. Turn the pineapple, and make slices from the opposite side as well as from both ends. Cut the slices into neat julienne, batonnet, or dice as desired.

Melons

Melons are served in wedges, slices, cubes, or melon balls. The melons can be peeled before or after cutting. To make the melon more stable as you work, cut a slice from both ends. You may remove the entire rind before halving the melon and removing the seeds to streamline production of fruit plates and salads. Or you may prefer to leave the rind on.

1. After cutting the top and the bottom off of the melon, cut the rind away. Use a utility or chef's knife to follow the curve of the melon.

2. Cut the melon in half and scoop out the seeds. Be careful not to gouge the flesh of the fruit. The melon can now be made into melon balls, cut into slices, or cut into cubes or diced.

3. Scoop melon balls out of the cleaned melon half using a parisienne scoop.

Warm Salads

Warm salad, known in French as *salade tiède,* is made by tossing the salad ingredients in a warm dressing, working over medium to low heat. The salad should be just warmed through. Another approach is to use a chilled crisp salad as the bed for hot main items, such as grilled meat or fish.

Vegetable Salads

Prepare vegetables for this type of salad as required by the specific recipe. Some are simply rinsed and trimmed. Others need to be peeled, seeded, and cut into the appropriate shape. Some vegetables require an initial blanching to set colors and textures, while others must be fully cooked.

If the salad is to be served raw, combine the prepared vegetable or vegetables with a vinaigrette or other dressing and allow them to rest long enough for the flavors to marry. When the vegetable or vegetables are partially or fully cooked, there are two methods for applying the dressing. In the first method, simply drain the vegetables and combine them with the dressing while they are still warm, for faster flavor absorption. This works well for root vegetables such as carrots, beets, and parsnips, as well as leeks, onions, and potatoes. Some vegetables (especially green vegetables like broccoli or green beans) may discolor if they are combined with an acid in advance; in that case, refresh the vegetables before adding the dressing at service. Always be sure to thoroughly drain and blot dry the vegetables to avoid watering down the dressing.

Potato salads

Potatoes must be cooked completely but not overcooked. High-moisture potatoes hold their shape after cooking better than low-moisture potatoes do.

The classic American potato salad is a creamy salad, dressed with mayonnaise. Other potato salads enjoyed around the world are often dressed with vinaigrette. In some traditional European-style recipes, the dressing may be based on bacon fat, olive oil, stock, or a combination of these ingredients. The dressing may actually be brought to a simmer before the potatoes are added for the best finished flavor.

Pasta and grain salads

Grains and pastas for salads should be fully cooked. However, care should be taken to avoid over-cooking because cooked grains and pasta will still be able to absorb some of the liquid in the dressing and can quickly become soggy.

If a pasta or grain salad is held for later service, be especially careful to check for seasoning before it is served. These salads have a tendency to go flat as they sit. Salt and pepper are important seasonings, of course, but others, such as vinegars, herbs, or citrus juices, can give a brighter flavor.

Legume salads

Dried beans should be cooked until they are tender to the bite. The center should be soft and creamy, and it is even possible that the skins may break open slightly. If a salad is made of several kinds of dried beans, it is important that beans with different cooking times be cooked separately to the correct doneness before combining them.

Unlike grains and pastas, which might become too soft as they sit in a dressing, beans will not soften any further. In fact, the acid in salad dressings will make the beans become tougher, even if they are fully cooked. Bean salads, therefore, should not be dressed and allowed to rest for extended periods. If the salad is used within four hours of preparation, however, there is little significant texture change.

Composed salads

Composed salads contain carefully arranged items on a plate, rather than components tossed together. They are usually main-course salads or appetizers, rather than an accompaniment. Although there are no specific rules governing the requirements for a composed salad, the following principles should be kept in mind:

- Consider how well each of the elements combines with the others. Contrasting flavors are intriguing. Conflicting flavors are a disaster.

- Repetition of a color or flavor can be successful if it contributes to the overall dish. But generally, too much of a good thing is simply too much.

- Each element of the dish should be so perfectly prepared that it could easily stand on its own. However, each part should be enhanced in combination with the others.

- Components should be arranged in such a way that the textures and colors of the foods are most attractive to the eye.

Red Wine Vinaigrette

Makes 32 fl oz/960 mL

8 fl oz/240 mL red wine vinegar

2 tsp/10 g mustard (optional)

½ oz/14 g minced shallots

salt, as needed

ground black pepper, as needed

2 tsp/10 g sugar

24 fl oz/720 mL olive oil or canola oil

3 tbsp/9 g minced herbs, such as chives, parsley, oregano, basil, and tarragon (optional)

1. Combine the vinegar, mustard (if using), shallots, salt, pepper, and sugar. Gradually whisk in the oil.

2. Stir in the herbs, if using, and adjust the seasoning with salt, pepper, and sugar, if necessary.

3. Serve immediately or refrigerate for later service.

White Wine Vinaigrette: Substitute white wine vinegar for the red wine vinegar.

Mustard-Herb Vinaigrette: Substitute white wine vinegar for the red wine vinegar and add ½ tsp/1 g onion powder and a dash of garlic powder. Add only 2 tbsp/6 g of the chopped mixed herbs, along with 2 tbsp/6 g chopped parsley.

Roasted Garlic and Mustard Vinaigrette: Add 4 oz/113 g puréed roasted garlic.

Lemon-Garlic Vinaigrette: Substitute 6 fl oz/180 mL lemon juice for the vinegar. Add 2 tsp/6 g garlic, mashed to a paste, and 1 tsp/1 g minced rosemary.

Lemon-Parsley Vinaigrette: Substitute 6 fl oz/180 mL lemon juice for the vinegar. Add ½ to ¾ oz/14 to 21 g minced parsley.

Almond-Fig Vinaigrette

Makes 32 fl oz/960 mL

4 fl oz/120 mL balsamic vinegar

4 fl oz/120 mL red wine, such as Zinfandel or Merlot

4 shallots, minced

4 oz/113 g roasted and chopped almonds

salt, as needed

ground black pepper, as needed

12 fl oz/360 mL almond oil

16 fl oz/480 mL olive oil

5¼ oz/149 g chopped dried figs

2 lemons, juiced

Tabasco sauce, as needed

1. Combine the vinegar, wine, shallots, almonds, salt, and pepper. Gradually whisk in the oils.

2. Stir in the figs, lemon juice, and Tabasco sauce. Adjust seasoning with salt and pepper.

3. Serve immediately or refrigerate for later service.

Apple Cider Vinaigrette

Makes 32 fl oz/960 mL

16 fl oz/480 mL apple cider

6 fl oz/180 mL apple cider vinegar

1 Granny Smith apple, peeled, brunoise

2 tsp/10 g salt

¼ tsp/0.50 g ground white pepper

24 fl oz/720 mL vegetable oil

2 tbsp/6 g minced tarragon

½ fl oz/15 mL maple syrup

1. In a small saucepan, simmer the cider until it is reduced to 6 fl oz/180 mL. Allow the cider to cool.

2. Combine the cider reduction, vinegar, apple, salt, and pepper. Gradually whisk in the oil.

3. Stir in the tarragon and maple syrup. Adjust seasoning with salt and pepper.

4. Serve immediately or refrigerate for later service.

Balsamic Vinaigrette

Makes 32 fl oz/960 mL

4 fl oz/120 mL red wine vinegar

4 fl oz/120 mL balsamic vinegar

2 tsp/10 g mustard (optional)

salt, as needed

ground black pepper, as needed

½ tsp/2.50 g sugar (optional)

24 fl oz/720 mL olive oil

3 tbsp/9 g minced herbs, such as chives, parsley, oregano, basil, and tarragon (optional)

1. Combine the vinegars, mustard (if using), salt, pepper, and sugar, if using. Gradually whisk in the oil.

2. Adjust seasoning with salt, pepper, and sugar, if necessary. Mix in the herbs, if using.

3. Serve immediately or refrigerate for later service.

NOTE

The amount of sugar added to the vinaigrette will depend on the quality of the balsamic vinegar used.

Chipotle-Sherry Vinaigrette

Makes 32 fl oz/960 mL

8 fl oz/240 mL sherry vinegar

2 fl oz/60 mL lime juice

5 chipotles, canned in adobo, minced

2 shallots, minced

2 garlic cloves, minced

salt, as needed

ground black pepper, as needed

2 tbsp/28 g piloncillo or brown sugar

24 fl oz/720 mL extra-virgin olive oil

1 oz/28 g minced **Fines Herbes** (page 463)

1. Combine the vinegar, lime juice, chipotles, shallots, garlic, salt, pepper, and sugar. Gradually whisk in the oil.

2. Stir in the herbs and adjust seasoning with salt, pepper, and sugar, if necessary.

3. Serve immediately or refrigerate for later service.

Curry Vinaigrette

Makes 32 fl oz/960 mL

24 fl oz/720 mL olive oil

3 tbsp/19 g **Curry Powder** (page 463)

1 oz/28 g minced shallots

½ oz/14 g minced garlic

½ oz/14 g minced ginger

½ oz/14 g minced lemongrass (tender center portion only)

8 fl oz/240 mL cider vinegar

lemon juice, as needed

honey, as needed

salt, as needed

ground black pepper, as needed

1. Heat 3 fl oz/90 mL of the oil in a saucepan over low heat. Add the curry powder, shallots, garlic, ginger, and lemongrass. Continue to heat until the shallots are translucent. Do not brown. Remove from the heat, let cool, and combine with the remaining oil.

2. Combine the vinegar with the lemon juice, honey, salt, and pepper. Gradually whisk in the oil.

3. Adjust seasoning with lemon juice, honey, salt, and pepper, if necessary. Serve immediately or refrigerate for later service.

Honey–Poppy Seed–Citrus Dressing

Makes 32 fl oz/960 mL

2 tsp/10 mL olive oil

½ oz/14 g minced shallots

3 fl oz/90 mL ketchup

2 fl oz/60 mL red wine vinegar

2 fl oz/60 mL orange juice

2 fl oz/60 mL grapefruit juice

1 oz/28 g honey

½ tsp/1 g dry mustard

1½ tsp/4 g poppy seeds

24 fl oz/720 mL olive oil

salt, as needed

ground black pepper, as needed

1. Heat the oil in a saucepan over medium heat and sweat the shallots until translucent. Add the ketchup, vinegar, juices, honey, mustard, and poppy seeds. Bring to a simmer and cook for 1 minute. Remove from the heat and cool to room temperature.

2. Gradually whisk in the oil. Season with salt and pepper.

3. Serve immediately or refrigerate for later service.

Fire-Roasted Tomato Vinaigrette

Makes 32 fl oz/960 mL

10 plum tomatoes

16 fl oz/480 mL olive oil

6 fl oz/180 mL red wine vinegar

salt, as needed

ground black pepper, as needed

1 tbsp/3 g thyme

2 tbsp/6 g basil chiffonade

Tabasco sauce, as needed

1. Wash and core the tomatoes and lightly coat them with some of the oil. Char them over an open flame. Peel, purée, and strain the tomatoes.

2. Combine the vinegar, tomato purée, salt, and pepper. Gradually whisk in the remaining oil.

3. Stir in the herbs and Tabasco sauce. Adjust seasoning with salt and pepper.

4. Serve immediately or refrigerate for later service.

Guava-Curry Vinaigrette

Makes 32 fl oz/960 mL

4 oz/113 g guava paste

8 fl oz/240 mL red wine vinegar

2 tbsp/18 g curry powder

4 limes, juiced

1 Scotch bonnet, seeded, minced

salt, as needed

ground black pepper, as needed

24 fl oz/720 mL olive oil

3 tbsp/9 g chopped cilantro

1. Combine the guava paste, vinegar, and curry powder in a small saucepan and warm slightly until the guava paste is melted. Allow the mixture to cool.

2. Combine the guava mixture with the lime juice, Scotch bonnet, salt, and pepper. Gradually whisk in the oil.

3. Stir in the cilantro and adjust seasoning with salt and pepper, if necessary.

4. Serve immediately or refrigerate for later service.

Herb and Truffle Vinaigrette

Makes 32 fl oz/960 mL

½ oz/14 g minced garlic

4 oz/113 g minced shallots

2 fl oz/60 mL sherry vinegar

2 fl oz/60 mL lemon juice

salt, as needed

ground black pepper, as needed

8 fl oz/240 mL extra-virgin olive oil

2 fl oz/60 mL truffle oil

¾ oz/21 g chopped marjoram

¾ oz/21 g chopped parsley

4 tbsp/12 g chopped mint

1. Combine the garlic, shallots, vinegar, lemon juice, salt, and pepper. Gradually whisk in the oils.

2. Stir in the herbs and adjust seasoning with salt and pepper, if necessary.

3. Serve immediately or refrigerate for later service.

Peanut Oil and Malt Vinegar Salad Dressing

Makes 32 fl oz/960 mL

20 fl oz/600 mL peanut oil

10 fl oz/300 mL malt vinegar

2 oz/57 g dark brown sugar

2 tbsp/6 g chopped tarragon

2 tbsp/6 g chopped chives

2 tbsp/6 g chopped parsley

2 tsp/6 g minced garlic

salt, as needed

ground black pepper, as needed

1. Combine the oil, vinegar, sugar, tarragon, chives, parsley, and garlic and blend well.

2. Refrigerate the dressing to age for 24 hours before using.

3. Stir to thoroughly recombine the ingredients and season with salt and pepper. Serve immediately or refrigerate for later service.

Pesto Vinaigrette

Makes 32 fl oz/960 mL

8 fl oz/240 mL red wine vinegar

4 oz/113 g **Pesto** (page 388)

salt, as needed

ground black pepper, as needed

20 fl oz/600 mL olive or vegetable oil

1. Combine the vinegar, pesto, salt, and pepper. Gradually whisk in the oil.

2. Adjust seasoning with salt and pepper, if necessary.

3. Serve immediately or refrigerate for later service.

Vinaigrette Gourmande

Makes 32 fl oz/960 mL

5 fl oz/150 mL sherry vinegar

3 fl oz/90 mL lemon juice

salt, as needed

ground black pepper, as needed

12 fl oz/360 mL olive oil

12 fl oz/360 mL vegetable oil

½ oz/14 g minced chervil

½ oz/14 g minced tarragon

1. Combine the vinegar, lemon juice, salt, and pepper. Gradually whisk in the oils.

2. Stir in the chervil and tarragon and adjust seasoning with salt and pepper, if necessary.

3. Serve immediately or refrigerate for later service

Walnut Oil and Red Wine Vinaigrette: Substitute red wine vinegar for the sherry vinegar, walnut oil for the vegetable oil, and parsley and chives for the chervil and tarragon.

Green Goddess Dressing

Makes 32 fl oz/960 mL

2 oz/57 g spinach

2 oz/57 g watercress

1 tbsp/3 g parsley

1 tbsp/3 g tarragon

1 garlic clove, mashed to a paste

4 fl oz/120 mL vegetable oil

12 fl oz/360 mL **Mayonnaise** (page 936)

1 tbsp/15 g mustard

salt, as needed

ground black pepper, as needed

lemon juice, as needed

1. In a food processor or blender, purée the spinach, watercress, parsley, tarragon, and garlic with the oil until smooth. Combine the purée with the mayonnaise and mustard.

2. Season with salt, pepper, and lemon juice.

3. Serve immediately or refrigerate for later service.

Catalina French Dressing

Makes 32 fl oz/960 mL

3½ fl oz/105 mL pasteurized eggs

4 oz/113 g dark brown sugar

4 fl oz/120 mL apple cider vinegar

2 tsp/10 g dijon mustard

¼ tsp/0.50 g garlic powder

¼ tsp/0.50 g onion powder

dash ground allspice

salt, as needed

ground white pepper, as needed

12 fl oz/360 mL **Paprika Oil** (page 940)

1. Combine the eggs, sugar, vinegar, mustard, garlic powder, onion powder, allspice, salt, and pepper. Gradually whisk in the oil.

2. Adjust seasoning with salt and pepper, if necessary.

3. Serve immediately or refrigerate for later service.

Peanut Dressing

Makes 32 fl oz/960 mL

½ oz/14 g minced garlic

2 tbsp/6 g chopped tarragon

3 tbsp/9 g minced chives

3 tbsp/9 g chopped parsley

4 oz/113 g brown sugar

12 fl oz/360 mL malt vinegar

24 fl oz/720 mL peanut oil

8 fl oz/240 mL salad oil

4 oz/113 g peanut butter

salt, as needed

ground black pepper, as needed

Tabasco sauce, as needed

1. Combine all the ingredients.

2. Adjust seasoning with salt, pepper, and Tabasco, if necessary.

3. Serve immediately or refrigerate for later service. Allow the dressing to come to room temperature before using.

Caesar-Style Dressing

Makes 32 fl oz/960 mL

3 oz/85 g anchovy fillets

½ oz/14 g mild mustard

2 tsp/6 g garlic paste

½ fl oz/15 mL Worcestershire sauce

6 fl oz/180 mL red wine vinegar

2 oz/57 g grated Parmesan

salt, as needed

ground black pepper, as needed

18 fl oz/540 mL olive oil

1 fl oz/30 mL lemon juice, or as needed

½ tsp/2.50 mL Tabasco sauce, or as needed

1. Blend the anchovies, mustard, garlic, and Worcestershire to form a paste. Add the vinegar, cheese, salt, and pepper. Gradually whisk in the oil.

2. Add the lemon juice and Tabasco and adjust seasoning with salt and pepper.

3. Serve immediately or refrigerate for later service.

Cucumber Dressing

Makes 32 fl oz/960 mL

12 oz/340 g peeled, seeded, and thinly sliced cucumbers

2 fl oz/60 mL lemon juice

8 fl oz/240 mL sour cream

3 tbsp/9 g minced dill

1 tbsp/15 g sugar, or as needed

salt, as needed

ground white pepper, as needed

Tabasco sauce, as needed

1. Purée the cucumbers in a food processor until smooth.

2. Combine the purée with the lemon juice, sour cream, dill, and sugar. Blend until just incorporated.

3. Add the salt, pepper, and Tabasco and adjust seasoning with sugar, if necessary.

Mayonnaise

Makes 32 fl oz/960 mL

2½ fl oz/75 mL pasteurized egg yolks

1 fl oz/30 mL water

1 fl oz/30 mL white wine vinegar

2 tsp dry (4 g) or prepared mustard (10 g)

½ tsp/2.50 g sugar

24 fl oz/720 mL vegetable oil

salt, as needed

ground white pepper, as needed

1 fl oz/30 mL lemon juice

1. Combine the yolks, water, vinegar, mustard, and sugar in a bowl. Mix well with a balloon whisk until the mixture is slightly foamy.

2. Gradually add the oil in a thin stream, constantly beating with the whisk, until the oil is incorporated and the mayonnaise is smooth and thick.

3. Season with salt, pepper, and lemon juice.

4. Serve immediately or refrigerate for later service.

NOTE
Olive oil or mild peanut oil may be substituted for all or some of the vegetable oil.

Anchovy-Caper Mayonnaise: To the prepared mayonnaise, add 3 fl oz/90 mL lemon juice, 1 tbsp/15 g Dijon mustard, ¾ oz/21 g minced shallots, 1 oz/28 g minced parsley, 1 oz/28 g minced nonpareil capers, and 1 oz/28 g minced anchovy fillets. Season with salt and pepper.

Tartar Sauce: To 24 fl oz/720 mL of the prepared mayonnaise, add 12 oz/340 g drained sweet pickle relish, 2 oz/57 g minced capers, and 3 oz/85 g small diced hard-cooked eggs (page 897). Season with Worcestershire sauce, Tabasco sauce, salt, and pepper.

Green Mayonnaise: Purée 5 oz/142 g spinach leaves and 4 tbsp/12 g each chopped parsley, tarragon, chives, and dill in a blender. Mix the purée with the prepared mayonnaise and 2 fl oz/60 mL lemon juice. Adjust the consistency with water, if necessary. Adjust seasoning with salt and pepper.

Aïoli

Makes 32 fl oz/960 mL

2½ fl oz/75 mL pasteurized egg yolks

½ fl oz/15 mL water

1 fl oz/30 mL white wine vinegar

2 tsp/10 g Dijon mustard

2½ tsp/7.50 g garlic, mashed to a paste

14 fl oz/420 mL vegetable oil

10 fl oz/300 mL extra-virgin olive oil

salt, as needed

ground white pepper, as needed

lemon juice, as needed

1. Combine the yolks, water, vinegar, mustard, and garlic in a bowl. Mix well with a balloon whisk until the mixture is slightly foamy.

2. Gradually add the oil in a thin stream, constantly beating with the whisk, until the oil is incorporated and the aioli is smooth and thick.

3. Season with salt, pepper, and lemon juice.

4. Serve immediately or refrigerate for later service.

Blue Cheese Dressing

Makes 32 fl oz/960 mL

4 oz/113 g crumbled blue cheese

16 fl oz/480 mL **Mayonnaise** (page 936)

8 fl oz/240 mL sour cream

6 fl oz/180 mL buttermilk

3 fl oz/90 mL milk

½ fl oz/15 mL lemon juice, or as needed

1 oz/28 g puréed onions

2 tsp/6 g garlic paste

Worcestershire sauce, as needed

salt, as needed

ground black pepper, as needed

1. Combine the cheese, mayonnaise, sour cream, buttermilk, milk, lemon juice, onions, and garlic and mix until smooth.

2. Add the Worcestershire sauce, salt, and pepper and adjust seasoning with lemon juice, if necessary.

3. Serve immediately or refrigerate for later service.

Creamy Black Peppercorn Dressing

Makes 32 fl oz/960 mL

28 fl oz/840 mL **Mayonnaise** (page 936)

4 fl oz/120 mL milk or buttermilk

3 to 4 oz/85 to 113 g grated Parmesan, or as needed

2 oz/57 g anchovy paste

1 oz/28 g garlic paste

2 tbsp/12 g coarsely ground black pepper

salt, as needed

ground black pepper, as needed

1. Combine all the ingredients and mix well.

2. Adjust seasoning with Parmesan, salt, and pepper, if necessary.

3. Serve immediately or refrigerate for later service.

Japanese Salad Dressing

Makes 32 fl oz/960 mL

8 oz/227 g chopped carrots

4 oz/113 g chopped onions

4 oz/113 g chopped celery

1 orange, peeled and seeded

4 tsp/12 g minced ginger

1½ fl oz/45 mL light soy sauce

1½ oz/43 g ketchup

2 fl oz/60 mL rice vinegar

2 tsp/10 g sugar

1 fl oz/30 mL **Mayonnaise** (page 936)

8 fl oz/240 mL vegetable oil

salt, as needed

1. Purée the carrots, onions, celery, orange, and ginger in a blender or food processor.

2. Add the remaining ingredients and adjust seasoning with salt, if necessary.

3. Serve immediately or refrigerate for later service.

Ranch-Style Dressing

Makes 32 fl oz/960 mL

12 fl oz/360 mL sour cream

12 fl oz/360 mL **Mayonnaise** (page 936)

8 fl oz/240 mL buttermilk

1 fl oz/30 mL lemon juice

2 fl oz/60 mL red wine vinegar

2 tsp/6 g garlic, mashed to a paste

1½ fl oz/45 mL Worcestershire sauce

1 tbsp/3 g minced parsley

1 tbsp/3 g minced chives

1 tbsp/9 g minced shallots

1 tbsp/15 g Dijon mustard

1 tsp/2 g celery seed

salt, as needed

ground black pepper, as needed

1. Combine all the ingredients and mix thoroughly.

2. Adjust seasoning with salt and pepper.

3. Serve immediately or refrigerate for later service.

Thousand Island Dressing

Makes 32 fl oz/960 mL

24 fl oz/720 mL **Mayonnaise** (page 936)

6 fl oz/180 mL chili sauce

2 fl oz/60 mL ketchup

1½ tsp/7.50 mL Worcestershire sauce

1½ tsp/7.50 mL Tabasco sauce

4 oz/113 g minced onions

2¼ tsp/6.75 g minced garlic

3 oz/85 g sweet pickle relish

2 **Hard-Cooked Eggs** (page 897), finely chopped

salt, as needed

ground black pepper, as needed

½ fl oz/15 mL lemon juice, or as needed

1. Combine all the ingredients and mix well.

2. Adjust seasoning with salt, pepper, and lemon juice, if necessary.

3. Serve immediately or refrigerate for later service.

Basil Oil

Makes 16 fl oz/480 mL

3 oz/85 g basil leaves

1 oz/28 g parsley leaves

16 fl oz/480 mL olive oil

1. Blanch the basil and parsley in boiling salted water for 20 seconds. Remove from the water, shock in an ice bath, and drain well. Blot the herbs on paper towels.

2. Combine the blanched herbs with half of the oil in a blender and purée until smooth. With the blender running, add the remaining oil. If desired, strain the basil oil through cheesecloth or a coffee filter into a bottle or other clean container. (This will take approximately 15 minutes to slowly run through a coffee filter, but the result is a clear oil.)

3. Close the bottle and refrigerate. Use as needed.

NOTE

Substitute other herbs, such as chives, tarragon, or chervil for the basil. However, keep the parsley in all cases to give the oil a bright green color.

Orange Oil

Makes 16 fl oz/480 mL

12 fl oz/360 mL olive oil

6 fl oz/180 mL extra-virgin olive oil

3 oranges, zest only, cut into strips

1. Combine the oils in a saucepan and heat to 140°F/60°C. Be extremely careful not to overheat the oil. Remove the oil from the heat and add the zest.

2. Cool the oil to room temperature and infuse it overnight in the refrigerator.

3. Strain the oil into a bottle or other container.

4. Close the bottle and refrigerate. Use as needed.

Green Onion Oil

Makes 16 fl oz/480 mL

16 fl oz/480 mL vegetable oil

4 oz/113 g thinly sliced green onions

1. Combine the oil and onions in a saucepan and heat until the onions begin to sizzle. Remove from the heat and allow the mixture to cool.

2. Strain the oil through cheesecloth or a coffee filter into a bottle or other clean container.

3. Close the bottle and refrigerate. Use as needed.

Paprika Oil

Makes 16 fl oz/480 mL

16 fl oz/480 mL vegetable oil

6 oz/170 g sweet paprika

1. Combine the oil and paprika in a saucepan, warm to 120°F/49°C, and steep for 15 minutes.

2. Strain the oil through cheesecloth or a coffee filter into a bottle or other clean container.

3. Close the bottle and refrigerate. Use as needed.

Mixed Green Salad

Makes 10 servings

1 lb 9 oz/709 g mixed greens, such as romaine, Bibb, Boston, red leaf, or green leaf

5 fl oz/150 mL **White Wine Vinaigrette** (page 929)

salt, as needed

ground black pepper, as needed

1. Rinse, trim, and dry the greens and tear or cut them into bite-size pieces. Mix the greens and keep them well chilled until ready for service.

2. For each serving, place 2½ oz/71 g of the lettuce in a bowl.

3. Add ½ fl oz/15 mL of dressing to lightly coat the leaves. Season with salt and pepper. Toss the salad gently to coat evenly.

4. Mound the lettuce on a chilled salad plate and garnish as desired. Serve immediately.

NOTE
When dressing mixed greens with a vinaigrette that contains additional emulsifiers or creamy-style dressing, increase the amount to 8 fl oz/240 mL for 10 servings (1½ tbsp/22.50 mL per serving).

Table Salad

Makes 10 servings

10 red leaf lettuce leaves

1 European cucumber, skin on, julienne

6 oz/170 g bean sprouts

20 mint sprigs

30 Thai basil sprigs

30 cilantro sprigs

30 rau ram leaves

10 saw leaf herb leaves

1. Arrange the lettuce on a platter. Top with the cucumbers and bean sprouts. Garnish with the herbs.

2. Serve immediately.

Caesar Salad

Makes 10 servings

1 lb 14 oz/851 g romaine lettuce

15 oz/425 g **Garlic-Flavored Croutons** (page 676)

DRESSING

2 tsp/6 g garlic paste

5 anchovy fillets

salt, as needed

ground black pepper, as needed

3½ fl oz/105 mL pasteurized eggs (whole or yolks)

2 fl oz/60 mL lemon juice, or as needed

5 fl oz/150 mL olive oil

5 fl oz/150 mL extra-virgin olive oil

5 oz/142 g grated Parmesan, or as needed

1. Separate the romaine into leaves. Clean and dry them thoroughly. Tear or cut them into pieces if necessary. Refrigerate until ready to serve.

2. For each serving, mash about ⅛ tsp/0.60 g garlic paste, ½ anchovy fillet, salt, and pepper into a paste. Add 2 tsp/10 mL of egg and 1 tsp/5 mL of lemon juice. Blend well. Add ½ fl oz/15 mL of each oil, whisking to form a thick dressing. Add 1 to 2 tbsp/10 g of grated Parmesan and 3 oz/85 g of the romaine. Toss until coated.

3. Serve on a chilled plate. Garnish with 1½ oz/43 g of croutons.

NOTES

This salad is traditionally prepared tableside. It is important to clean and sanitize the wooden salad bowls carefully after each use. The more traditional raw or coddled egg is replaced with a pasteurized egg here, to help ensure the safety of the guest.

Caesar Salad may also be made with Caesar-Style Dressing (page 935).

Wedge of Iceberg with Thousand Island Dressing

Makes 8 servings

1 head iceberg lettuce

20 fl oz/600 mL **Thousand Island Dressing** (page 939)

8 oz/227 g cherry tomatoes, halved

8 oz/227 g bacon, crumbled

1. Clean and cut the head of lettuce into 8 wedges.

2. Place each lettuce wedge on a chilled plate and top with 2 fl oz/60 mL of the dressing. Garnish each portion with ¾ oz/21 g each of the tomatoes and bacon.

3. Serve immediately.

Chef's Salad

Makes 10 servings

2 lb/907 g mixed greens

20 roast turkey slices, rolled tightly

20 salami slices, rolled tightly

20 ham slices, rolled tightly

5 **Hard-Cooked Eggs** (page 897), cut into wedges

10 oz/284 g Cheddar cheese julienne

10 oz/284 g Gruyère cheese julienne

10 tomato wedges

3 oz/85 g thinly sliced cucumbers

3 oz/85 g thinly sliced carrots

10 fl oz/300 mL **Red** or **White Wine Vinaigrette** (page 929)

2 tbsp/6 g minced chives

1. Place the greens in a bowl or arrange them on a salad platter.

2. Arrange the meat, eggs, cheese, and vegetables on the lettuce.

3. Drizzle with the vinaigrette, top with chives, and serve immediately.

Greek Salad

Makes 10 servings

1 lb/454 g lettuce, such as romaine or green leaf, cut crosswise

30 tomato wedges

10 oz/284 g cucumbers, sliced or diced

3 oz/85 g red onion, sliced into rings

5 oz/142 g crumbled feta cheese

3 oz/85 g pitted black olives

3 oz/85 g pitted green olives

10 fl oz/300 mL **Lemon-Parsley Vinaigrette** (page 929)

1. For each serving, place 1⅓ oz/37 g of the lettuce in a bowl or arrange on a salad plate.

2. Arrange 3 tomato wedges, 1 oz/28 g of cucumbers, 3 tbsp/8.5 g of onions, ½ oz/14 g of feta, and 4 to 6 olives on top of the lettuce.

3. Drizzle with 1 fl oz/30 mL of the vinaigrette and serve immediately.

NOTE
The ingredients may be combined and tossed with the vinaigrette and then placed in a bowl or on a plate.

Endive Salad with Roquefort and Walnuts (Salade de Roquefort, Noix, et Endives)

Makes 10 servings

1 fl oz/30 mL lemon juice

1 fl oz/30 mL hazelnut oil

1½ tsp/1.50 g chopped tarragon

salt, as needed

ground black pepper, as needed

2 lb/907 g Belgian endive

2½ oz/71 g toasted walnuts, roughly chopped

4 oz/113 g crumbled Roquefort cheese

1. Whisk together the lemon juice, oil, and tarragon in a small bowl. Season with salt and pepper. Let dressing stand for 30 minutes.

2. Separate the endive into leaves and wash thoroughly. Pat dry and transfer them to a large salad bowl. Add the walnuts and cheese.

3. Add the dressing and toss until the endive is thoroughly coated. Serve immediately.

Endive Salad with Roquefort and Walnuts
(*Salade de Roquefort, Noix, et Endives*)

Cobb Salad

Cobb Salad

Makes 10 servings

6 oz/170 g vegetable oil

2 fl oz/60 mL cider vinegar

1 fl oz/30 mL lemon juice

1 oz/28 g Dijon mustard

½ oz/14 g minced parsley

salt, as needed

ground black pepper, as needed

2 lb/907 g shredded romaine lettuce

1 lb/454 g cubed roasted or smoked turkey

6 oz/170 g diced avocados

3 oz/85 g celery, sliced on the bias

2 oz/57 g green onions, sliced on the bias

10 oz/284 g crumbled blue cheese

10 bacon strips, cooked and crumbled

1. Blend the oil, vinegar, lemon juice, mustard, and parsley thoroughly in a large bowl. Season with salt and pepper.

2. Add the lettuce and toss until combined. Divide the lettuce among bowls or platters.

3. Arrange the turkey, avocados, celery, and green onions on the lettuce. Drizzle the dressing remaining in the bowl over the salad. Top with the cheese and bacon. Serve at once.

Taco Salad

Makes 10 servings

2 lb 8 oz/1.13 kg ground beef

12 fl oz/360 mL **Taco Sauce** (recipe follows), or as needed

2 lb/907 g iceberg lettuce chiffonade

10 corn or flour tortillas, fried and shaped into bowls

12 oz/340 g cooked pinto beans

12 oz/340 g cooked black beans

10 oz/284 g diced tomatoes

2 oz/57 g diced red onions

5 fl oz/150 mL sour cream

10 oz/284 g shredded Cheddar or Monterey Jack cheese

20 pitted black olives

16 fl oz/480 mL **Pico de Gallo** (page 988)

1. Brown the beef over medium heat, stirring and breaking it up until it is fully cooked and no longer pink. Remove the beef from the pan with a slotted spoon, drain well, and combine with the Taco Sauce. The mixture should hold together and be moist.

2. Lay a bed of lettuce in the bottom of each tortilla bowl. Layer with beans, beef and sauce mixture, tomatoes, onions, sour cream, cheese, olives, and salsa. Serve immediately.

Taco Sauce

Makes 32 fl oz/960 mL

2 fl oz/60 mL vegetable oil

2½ oz/71 g small-dice onions

2½ tsp/7.50 g minced garlic

4 tsp/8 g dried oregano

1¼ oz/35 g ground cumin

⅔ oz/19 g **Chili Powder** (page 463)

16 fl oz/480 mL tomato purée

21 fl oz/630 mL **Chicken Stock** (page 351)

salt, as needed

ground black pepper, as needed

cornstarch slurry, as needed

1. Heat the oil in a pan. Add the onions and cook over medium heat, stirring frequently, until the onions are brown, 10 to 12 minutes.

2. Add the garlic and continue to sauté another 1 to 2 minutes. Add the oregano, cumin, and chili powder and cook until aromatic.

3. Add the tomato purée and bring to a simmer, cooking and stirring frequently, until the mixture has reduced, 10 to 12 minutes.

4. Add the stock and simmer for 15 to 20 minutes, or until the sauce is well flavored.

5. Season with salt and pepper. Purée the sauce and strain if desired. If necessary, thicken it with cornstarch slurry. The sauce is ready to use now, or it may be rapidly cooled and refrigerated for later service.

Wilted Spinach Salad with Warm Bacon Vinaigrette

Makes 10 servings

8 oz/227 g diced bacon

1½ oz/43 g minced shallots

2 tsp/6 g minced garlic

4 oz/113 g brown sugar

3 fl oz/90 mL cider vinegar

5 to 6 fl oz/150 to 180 mL vegetable oil

salt, as needed

cracked black peppercorns, as needed

1 lb 8 oz/680 g spinach

5 **Hard-Cooked Eggs** (page 897), small dice

6 oz/170 g sliced mushrooms

3 oz/85 g thinly sliced red onions

4 oz/113 g **Croutons** (page 676)

1. To make the vinaigrette, render the bacon over medium-low heat. When the bacon is crisp, remove it from the pan, drain, and reserve.

2. Add the shallots and garlic to the bacon fat and sweat until soft. Blend in the sugar. Remove the pan from the heat. Whisk in the vinegar and oil. Season with salt and pepper.

3. Toss the spinach with the eggs, mushrooms, onions, croutons, and reserved bacon. Add the warm vinaigrette, toss once, and serve immediately.

Wilted Spinach Salad with Warm Bacon Vinaigrette

Mushrooms, Beets, and Baby Greens with Robiola Cheese and Walnuts
(*Fungetti e Barbe con Cambozola e Noci*)

Mushrooms, Beets, and Baby Greens with Robiola Cheese and Walnuts (Fungetti e Barbe con Cambozola e Noci)

Makes 10 servings

12 oz/340 g medium-sized red beets

12 oz/340 g medium-sized golden beets

salt, as needed

4 fl oz/120 mL extra-virgin olive oil

ground black pepper, as needed

2 fl oz/60 mL olive oil

5 oz/142 g cremini mushrooms

5 oz/142 g white mushrooms

11 oz/312 g assorted wild mushrooms

10 fl oz/300 mL **Herb and Truffle Vinaigrette** (page 933)

4 oz/113 g frisée hearts

2 oz/57 g baby arugula

4 oz/113 g mesclun greens

15 baguette slices, cut ¼ in/6 mm thick, on the bias

10 oz/284 g Robiola cheese

5 oz/142 g toasted walnuts, roughly chopped

truffle oil, as needed

1. Remove the tops from the beets. Place the beets in separate pots with enough cold water to cover them by about 2 in/5 cm. Add salt and cook until they are tender, 30 to 40 minutes. Drain the beets and cool.

2. Peel the beets with the back of a paring knife and cut into medium dice. Marinate them in the extra-virgin olive oil, season with salt and pepper, and reserve.

3. Heat a large sauté pan over medium heat. Add 1 fl oz/ 30 mL of olive oil to the pan. Add the cremini and white mushrooms, being careful not to overcrowd the pan. Sauté them until golden brown and tender, 4 to 5 minutes. Remove the mushrooms and cool in a half hotel pan. Repeat with the wild mushrooms. Toss the mushrooms with 7½ fl oz/225 mL of the vinaigrette and reserve.

4. Combine the frisée, arugula, and mesclun and reserve.

5. Cut each baguette slice in half lengthwise. Brush each slice with olive oil, place on a sheet pan, and bake at 400°F/204°C until golden brown on the first side, about 2½ minutes. Turn the croutons over to brown the opposite sides, about 2½ minutes more.

6. Spread 1 oz/28 g of cheese on 1 side of each crouton. Season with salt and pepper and melt under a salamander or broiler.

7. For each portion, place 2½ oz/71 g of the mushroom salad in the center of the plate. Toss 1 oz/28 g of the baby greens with 1 tsp of the vinaigrette and place on top of the mushrooms. Place 2 oz/57 g of beets around the greens and sprinkle with ½ oz/14 g of the walnuts. Place 3 croutons on the greens. Drizzle a few drops of truffle oil around the greens and serve.

Sherried Watercress and Apple Salad

Makes 10 servings

6 fl oz/180 mL vegetable oil

3 fl oz/90 mL sherry vinegar

1 oz/28 g minced shallots

1 tsp/5 g brown sugar

salt, as needed

ground black pepper, as needed

1 lb 4 oz/567 g watercress, cleaned and stemmed

10 oz/284 g Golden Delicious apple julienne

3 oz/85 g minced celery

2 oz/57 g toasted walnuts, chopped

1. Combine the oil, vinegar, shallots, sugar, salt, and pepper in a bowl and whisk until combined.

2. Add the watercress, apples, and celery to the bowl and toss until evenly coated with the vinaigrette.

3. Garnish with the walnuts and serve immediately.

Baby Spinach, Avocado, and Grapefruit Salad

Makes 10 servings

1½ avocados, sliced

3 grapefruits, cut into suprêmes

1 lb/454 g baby spinach

5 fl oz/150 mL **Balsamic Vinaigrette** (page 930)

salt, as needed

ground black pepper, as needed

1. For each serving, combine 1¼ oz/35 g of avocado with 1½ oz/43 g of grapefruit segments (about 3).

2. Toss 1½ oz/43 g of the spinach with ½ fl oz/15 mL of the vinaigrette. Season with salt and pepper.

3. Arrange the spinach on a chilled plate. Top it with the avocados and grapefruit. Serve immediately.

Celeriac and Tart Apple Salad

Makes 10 servings

DRESSING

3 fl oz/90 mL **Mayonnaise** (page 936)

2 fl oz/60 mL crème fraîche or sour cream

2 oz/57 g Dijon mustard

1 fl oz/30 mL lemon juice

salt, as needed

ground black pepper, as needed

2 fl oz/60 mL lemon juice

1 lb 8 oz/680 g celeriac

12 oz/340 g Granny Smith apples, peeled and diced

1. To make the dressing, combine the mayonnaise, crème fraîche or sour cream, mustard, and lemon juice and blend well. Season with salt and pepper.

2. Bring a large pot of salted water to a boil and add the 2 fl oz/60 mL of lemon juice. Peel and cut the celeriac into julienne. (If the celeriac is cut in advance, hold it in acidulated water to keep the celeriac from turning brown.)

3. Parcook the celeriac for about 2 minutes, then drain, and shock in an ice bath.

4. Combine the apples and celeriac and toss with the dressing. Adjust seasoning with salt, pepper, and lemon juice.

5. Serve immediately or refrigerate for later service.

Waldorf Salad

Makes 10 servings

1 lb 4 oz/567 g medium-dice apples

6 oz/170 g small-dice celery, blanched

3 fl oz/90 mL **Mayonnaise** (page 936)

salt, as needed

ground black pepper, as needed

10 oz/284 g lettuce leaves

2 oz/57 g coarsely chopped walnuts, lightly toasted

1. Combine the apples, celery, and mayonnaise. Season with salt and pepper. Refrigerate until needed.

2. Serve the mixture on a bed of lettuce. Garnish with walnuts.

Chayote Salad with Oranges (Salada de Xuxu)

Makes 10 servings

2 to 3 chayotes, peeled, seeded, julienned

8 oz/227 g jícama julienne

8 oz/227 g carrot julienne

5 oranges, cut into suprêmes, juice reserved

1½ bunches green onions, thinly sliced

3 fl oz/90 mL lime juice

1½ tsp/7.50 g sugar

salt, as needed

ground black pepper, as needed

3 fl oz/90 mL extra-virgin olive oil

1½ oz/43 g cilantro chiffonade

¾ oz/21 g mint chiffonade

1. Combine the chayotes, jícama, carrots, oranges, and green onions gently in a bowl.

2. Combine the lime juice, sugar, salt, pepper, and reserved orange juice. Gradually whisk in the oil. Pour the dressing over the chayote mixture and stir to combine. Chill the salad for 30 minutes.

3. Toss the salad and serve immediately. Garnish with the cilantro and mint.

Summer Melon Salad with Prosciutto

Makes 10 servings

1 lb/454 g cantaloupe, balls or slices

1 lb/454 g honeydew, balls or slices

1 lb 4 oz/567 g thinly sliced prosciutto

1 fl oz/30 mL aged balsamic vinegar

cracked black peppercorns, as needed

1. Arrange the melons and prosciutto on chilled plates.

2. Drizzle with the vinegar and garnish with the cracked pepper.

3. Serve immediately.

Onion and Cucumber Salad (Kachumber)

Makes 10 servings

2 lb/907 g onions, medium dice

2 European cucumbers, medium dice

1 lb/454 g plum tomatoes, seeded, medium dice

10 Thai chiles, chopped

1¾ oz/50 g chopped cilantro leaves and stems

5 lemons, juiced

salt, as needed

1. Combine the onions, cucumbers, tomatoes, chiles, and cilantro.

2. Ten minutes before service, season with salt and lemon juice. Serve immediately.

Classic Polish Cucumber Salad (Mizeria Klasyczna)

Makes 10 servings

3 lb/1.36 kg European cucumbers

½ tsp/2.50 g salt

8 oz/227 g sour cream

1¼ oz/35 g chopped dill

½ fl oz/15 mL Champagne or white wine vinegar

1 fl oz/30 mL lemon juice

salt, as needed

ground black pepper, as needed

1. Peel the cucumbers, cut in half lengthwise, deseed, and slice them into thin half moons. Place them in a bowl and mix with the salt. Allow the cucumbers to rest for 1 hour. Drain them and squeeze dry.

2. Add the sour cream, dill, and vinegar to the cucumbers and mix. Season with lemon juice, salt, and pepper.

3. Serve immediately or refrigerate for later service.

Coleslaw

Makes 10 servings

6 fl oz/180 mL sour cream

6 fl oz/180 mL **Mayonnaise** (page 936)

2 fl oz/60 mL cider vinegar

1 tbsp/6 g dry mustard

1½ oz/43 g sugar

1½ tsp/0.50 g celery seed

1½ tsp/7.50 mL Tabasco sauce

salt, as needed

ground black pepper, as needed

1 lb 8 oz/680 g green cabbage, shredded

6 oz/170 g carrots, shredded

1. Combine the sour cream, mayonnaise, vinegar, mustard, sugar, celery seed, and Tabasco together in a large bowl. Mix until smooth. Season with salt and pepper to taste.

2. Add the cabbage and carrots and toss until evenly coated.

3. Serve immediately or refrigerate for later service.

Moroccan Carrot Salad

Makes 10 servings

4 fl oz/120 mL lemon juice

½ oz/14 g chopped cilantro

½ oz/14 g sugar

4 fl oz/120 mL extra-virgin olive oil

2 lb/907 g finely grated carrots

4 oz/113 g raisins, plumped and drained

salt, as needed

ground black pepper, as needed

1. Combine the lemon juice, cilantro, and sugar. Gradually whisk in the oil.

2. Toss the dressing with the carrots and raisins. Season with salt and pepper.

3. Serve immediately or refrigerate for later service.

Corn and Jícama Salad

Makes 10 servings

1 lb 8 oz/680 g corn kernels, fresh or frozen, cooked

1 lb/454 g jícama, peeled, small dice

1 fl oz/30 mL lime juice

1 tsp/1 g chopped cilantro

pinch cayenne

salt, as needed

ground white pepper, as needed

1. Combine the corn, jícama, lime juice, cilantro, and cayenne in a bowl and toss. Season with salt and pepper.

2. Serve immediately or refrigerate for later service.

NOTE
This salad is best if prepared 30 minutes prior to serving. If held for more than 2 hours, the jícama becomes limp.

Thai-Style Green Papaya Salad

Makes 10 servings

8 garlic cloves, roughly chopped

3 Thai chiles, roughly chopped

3 tbsp/2 g dried shrimp, chopped

2 fl oz/60 mL tamarind pulp

2 fl oz/60 mL lime juice

3 fl oz/90 mL fish sauce

1 oz/28 g palm sugar

2 cups long beans, cut into 1½-in/4-cm lengths

5 cups green papaya julienne

8 oz/227 g carrot julienne

4 oz/113 g toasted peanuts, roughly chopped

10 cherry tomatoes, halved

10 green cabbage leaves

1 lb 8 oz/1.13 kg steamed sticky rice

1. Combine the garlic, chiles, and dried shrimp.

2. Add the tamarind, lime juice, fish sauce, and sugar. Stir to mix, then add the beans. Pound the mixture a few times to bruise the beans. Add the papaya, carrots, and peanuts.

3. Stir in the tomatoes and bruise lightly. Adjust seasoning with lime juice, fish sauce, and sugar, if necessary.

4. Serve the salad in a cabbage leaf with the steamed sticky rice on the side.

Jícama Salad

Makes 10 servings

1 lb 8 oz/680 g jícama, peeled, julienned

2 oz/57 g Granny Smith apples, peeled, julienned

2 oz/57 g red pepper julienne

6 fl oz/180 mL yogurt, drained well in cheesecloth

1 fl oz/30 mL lemon juice

¾ tsp/1.50 g ground cumin

salt, as needed

ground black pepper, as needed

1. Combine the jícama, apples, and red peppers in a medium bowl.

2. Mix together the yogurt, lemon juice, and cumin in a small bowl. Season with salt and pepper. Pour over the jícama mixture and toss to combine.

3. Serve immediately or refrigerate for later service.

Cucumber and Wakame Salad (Sunonomo)

Makes 10 servings

1 lb/454 g cucumbers, julienned

4 oz/113 g fine-julienne carrots

2 tsp/10 g salt

1 tbsp/3.50 g dried wakame seaweed

½ fl oz/15 mL mirin

2 fl oz/60 mL rice vinegar

½ fl oz/15 mL light soy sauce

1. Toss the cucumbers and carrots with the salt. Transfer to a perforated pan set inside a solid pan and drain in the refrigerator for 1 hour.

2. Soak the wakame in warm water for 30 minutes. Drain it in a colander and pour boiling water over it. Plunge the wakame into cold water and drain well. Trim off any tough parts and discard. Wrap the wakame in cheesecloth and twist tightly to extract the moisture. Cut the wakame into chiffonade and reserve.

3. Whisk together the mirin, vinegar, and soy sauce. Pour half of the mixture over the cucumbers and carrots. Toss gently and squeeze to remove excess salt. Drain off the liquid.

4. Pour the remaining dressing over the cucumbers and carrots. At the very last minute, add the seaweed and toss to combine. Serve immediately.

Sliced Daikon Salad (Mu Chae)

Makes 10 servings

1 lb/454 g peeled daikon

1 lb/454 g European cucumbers, sliced into half moons, ⅛ in/3 mm thick

1 tsp/5 g salt

8 oz/227 g carrots, julienne

2 fl oz/60 mL rice vinegar

¾ oz/21 g sugar

1 tsp/2 g Korean red pepper powder

½ tsp/2.50 mL sesame oil

1. Cut the daikon in half lengthwise, then into ⅛-in/3-mm-thick half moons.

2. Toss the daikon and cucumbers with the salt, cover, and set aside to drain until the daikon is pliable, about 30 minutes. Gently squeeze out any excess water and transfer to another bowl.

3. Add the carrots, vinegar, sugar, red pepper powder, and oil. Mix well, cover, and refrigerate until chilled.

4. Serve immediately.

Cucumber Salad

Makes 10 servings

4 fl oz/120 mL rice vinegar

3½ oz/99 g sugar

2 tsp/10 g salt

3 European cucumbers, halved lengthwise, cut into ⅛-in/3-mm-thick slices

1 red onion, quartered lengthwise, cut against the grain into ⅛-in/3-mm-thick slices

1 tbsp/9 g red jalapeño, halved, ⅛-in/3-mm-thick slices

4 tbsp/12 g roughly chopped or torn mint leaves

¾ oz/21 g cilantro leaves

1. Combine the vinegar, sugar, and salt in a saucepan. Warm over low heat, whisking constantly until the sugar and salt are dissolved. Do not boil.

2. Cool the mixture, pour over the cucumbers, onion, and jalapeño. Marinate for 30 minutes.

3. Drain the salad and serve immediately. Garnish with mint and cilantro.

Cucumber-Yogurt Salad (Cacik)

Makes 10 servings

1 lb 3 oz/539 g European cucumbers

½ tsp/2.50 g salt

16 fl oz/480 mL yogurt

2 garlic cloves, minced

1 oz/28 g minced green onions

2 tbsp/6 g chopped mint

½ tsp/1 g ground cumin

½ tsp/1 g ground black pepper

1. Peel the cucumbers, deseed, and cut into medium dice. Place them in a bowl and mix with the salt. Allow the cucumbers to rest for 1 hour. Drain the cucumbers and squeeze dry.

2. Transfer the cucumbers to a small bowl and combine with the remaining ingredients. Mix well.

3. Serve immediately or refrigerate for later service.

Hue-Style Chicken Salad

Makes 10 servings

3 (about 3 lb 12 oz/1.70 kg) chickens

1 tbsp/6 g coarsely ground black pepper

1 oz/28 g salt

1¾ oz/50 g sugar

8 fl oz/240 mL lime juice

3 oz/85 g onions, sliced into paper-thin rings

10 Thai chiles, thinly sliced

3½ oz/99 g torn rau ram leaves

3½ oz/99 g torn mint leaves

3½ oz/99 g torn cilantro leaves

2 fl oz/60 mL peanut oil

2 fl oz/60 mL fish sauce

2 fl oz/60 mL Vietnamese sambal

10 Boston lettuce leaves

12 oz/340 g **Steamed Long-Grain Rice** (page 832)

6 red Fresno chiles, paper-thin slices

1½ oz/43 g **Crispy Shallots** (recipe follows)

1. Bring a stockpot of salted water to a vigorous boil. Add the chickens, return the water to a boil, and simmer for 15 minutes. Turn off the heat and let the chickens sit in the pot, covered, for 45 minutes, or until they reach an internal temperature of 165°F/74°C.

2. Remove the chickens from the pot and plunge them into cool water for 10 minutes. Shred the chicken meat into thin strips. Refrigerate.

3. Season the chicken with the pepper, salt, and sugar. Add the lime juice, onions, Thai chiles, rau ram, mint, cilantro, oil, fish sauce, and sambal and toss gently.

4. Serve the salad in a lettuce leaf with the steamed rice. Garnish with 3 rings of Fresno chiles and the crispy shallots.

Crispy Shallots

Makes 4 oz/ 113 g

10 oz/284 g peeled shallots

24 fl oz/720 mL vegetable oil

1. Evenly slice the shallots ⅛ in/3 mm thick. Separate them into rings and spread them on a paper towel-lined sheet pan to air dry for 30 minutes. (This technique helps make the shallots crispy.)

2. Heat the oil to about 280°F/138°C. Add the shallots and stir often with a spider until they are golden and crisp. Remove the shallots from the oil and drain on the sheet pan. Allow the shallots to cool.

3. Serve immediately or store in a covered container for later service.

Chicken Salad

Makes 8 servings

64 fl oz/1.92 L **Chicken Stock** (page 351)

salt, as needed

1 oz/28 g crushed garlic cloves (optional)

1 lb 9 oz/709 g chicken breasts, boneless and skinless

6 fl oz/180 mL **Mayonnaise** (page 936)

2 oz/57 g roughly chopped pecans

4 oz/113 g grapes, halved

2 tbsp/6 g finely chopped marjoram

3 tbsp/9 g finely chopped chervil

3 tbsp/9 g finely chopped tarragon

2 tbsp/6 g finely chopped oregano

ground black pepper, as needed

1. Season the stock with salt and add the garlic, if desired. Poach the chicken breasts in the stock over medium heat in a sauce pot until it is fork tender and fully cooked, 30 to 35 minutes.

2. Allow the chicken to cool to room temperature. Cut it into medium dice.

3. Combine the chicken with the remaining ingredients and adjust seasoning with salt and pepper.

4. Serve immediately or refrigerate for later service.

Tuna Salad

Makes 10 servings

2 lb/907 g water-packed tuna

4½ oz/128 g small-dice celery

1½ oz/43 g small-dice red onions

¾ oz/21 g chopped dill

16 fl oz/480 mL **Mayonnaise** (page 936)

½ fl oz/15 mL lemon juice

salt, as needed

ground black pepper, as needed

1. Drain the tuna in a colander. Squeeze the excess liquid in handfuls, then flake the tuna into a large bowl.

2. Add the remaining ingredients and mix thoroughly. Adjust seasoning with salt and pepper.

3. Serve immediately or refrigerate for later service.

NOTE
Add 4 oz/113 g diced pickles or pickle relish for additional flavor.

Egg Salad

Makes 10 servings

2 lb/907 g small-dice **Hard-Cooked Eggs** (page 897)

4 fl oz/120 mL **Mayonnaise** (page 936)

6 oz/170 g minced celery

3 oz/85 g minced onions

salt, as needed

ground black pepper, as needed

½ tsp/1 g garlic powder, or as needed

1 tbsp/15 g Dijon mustard, or as needed

1. Combine the eggs, mayonnaise, celery, and onions and mix well. Season with salt, pepper, garlic powder, and mustard.

2. Serve immediately or refrigerate for later service.

Ham Salad

Makes 10 servings

2 lb/907 g diced or ground smoked ham

8 fl oz/240 mL **Mayonnaise** (page 936)

1 to 1½ oz/28 to 43 g sweet pickle relish

½ to 1 oz/14 to 28 g mustard

salt, as needed

ground black pepper, as needed

1. Combine the ham, mayonnaise, relish, and mustard and mix well. Season with salt and pepper.

2. Serve immediately or refrigerate for later service.

Shrimp Salad

Makes 10 servings

2 lb/907 g cooked shrimp, peeled and deveined

8 fl oz/240 mL **Mayonnaise** (page 936)

8 oz/227 g minced celery

3 oz/85 g minced onions

salt, as needed

ground white pepper, as needed

1. Coarsely chop the shrimp (leave small shrimp whole).

2. Combine the shrimp, mayonnaise, celery, and onions and mix well. Season with salt and pepper.

3. Serve immediately or refrigerate for later service.

Pasta Salad with Pesto Vinaigrette

Makes 10 servings

2 lb/907 g cooked penne pasta, cooled

10 oz/284 g tomatoes, diced or cut into wedges

4 oz/113 g ham, diced or julienned (optional)

2 oz/57 g olives, pitted and chopped

1 oz/28 g toasted pine nuts

3 oz/85 g diced red or sweet onions

10 fl oz/300 mL **Pesto Vinaigrette** (page 933)

salt, as needed

ground black pepper, as needed

1. Combine all of the ingredients.

2. Marinate for several hours in the refrigerator before serving.

European-Style Potato Salad

Makes 10 servings

5 oz/142 g small-dice onions

3 fl oz/90 mL red wine vinegar

8 fl oz/240 mL **White Beef Stock** (page 351)

1½ fl oz/45 mL mustard, or as needed

salt, as needed

ground black pepper, as needed

1 tsp/5 g sugar, or as needed

3 fl oz/90 mL vegetable oil

3 lb/1.36 kg cooked waxy potatoes, peeled and sliced, warm

1 tbsp/3 g chopped parsley or chives

1. Combine the onions, vinegar, and stock. Bring the mixture to a boil. Add the mustard, salt, pepper, and sugar. Stir in the oil. Immediately pour the hot dressing over the warm potato slices.

2. Sprinkle the salad with the parsley or chives. Let it stand for at least 1 hour before serving at room temperature, or properly cool and refrigerate for later service.

Potato Salad

Makes 10 servings

2 lb 8 oz/1.13 kg cooked Red Bliss potatoes, peeled and sliced

6 oz/170 g small-dice **Hard-Cooked Eggs** (page 897)

5 oz/142 g diced onions

5 oz/142 g diced celery

1 oz/28 g Dijon mustard, or as needed

16 fl oz/480 mL **Mayonnaise** (page 936)

Worcestershire sauce, as needed

salt, as needed

ground black pepper, as needed

1. Combine the potatoes, eggs, onions, and celery in a bowl. Mix the mustard with the mayonnaise and Worcestershire sauce. Gently toss with the potato mixture.

2. Season with salt and pepper.

3. Serve immediately or refrigerate for later service.

Panzanella

Panzanella

Makes 10 servings

8 oz/227 g stale or toasted Italian bread, torn into medium pieces

1 lb 8 oz/680 g large-dice tomatoes

2 tsp/6 g minced garlic

3 oz/85 g celery hearts, sliced thinly on the bias

8 oz/227 g medium-dice seeded cucumbers

6 oz/170 g medium-dice red peppers

6 oz/170 g medium-dice yellow peppers

20 anchovy fillets, thinly sliced (optional)

2 tbsp/10 g drained, rinsed capers

3 tbsp/9 g chopped basil

10 fl oz/300 mL **Red Wine Vinaigrette** (page 929), or as needed

1. Combine the bread, tomatoes, garlic, celery, cucumbers, peppers, anchovies, capers, and basil. Add the vinaigrette and toss to coat.

2. Serve immediately, or refrigerate for later service.

Eastern Mediterranean Bread Salad (Fattoush)

Makes 10 servings

2 lb 8 oz/1.13 kg **Pita Bread** (page 1073)

18 fl oz/540 mL extra-virgin olive oil

5 fl oz/150 mL lemon juice

5 fl oz/150 mL red wine vinegar

1 tbsp/9 g minced garlic

½ oz/14 g chopped thyme

1 tsp/2 g cayenne

¾ oz/21 g sugar

salt, as needed

ground black pepper, as needed

6 oz/170 g chopped green onions

2½ oz/71 g chopped parsley

2 lb/907 g plum tomatoes, seeded, medium dice

2 lb/907 g European cucumbers, peeled, seeded, medium dice

10 oz/284 g sliced radishes

6 oz/170 g small-dice yellow peppers

1. Cut the pita bread into small wedges.

2. Toss the pita wedges with 3 fl oz/90 mL of the oil, the salt, and pepper. Bake on a sheet pan in a 300°F/149°C oven for 15 minutes, turning once halfway through the baking. They should be crisp, but not brittle.

3. Combine the lemon juice, vinegar, garlic, thyme, cayenne, sugar, salt, and pepper. Gradually whisk in the remaining oil.

4. Combine the dressing with the parsley and prepared vegetables. Add the pita toasts and gently toss. Adjust seasoning with salt and pepper.

5. Serve immediately, or refrigerate for later service.

Tomato and Mozzarella Salad

Makes 10 servings

3 lb/1.36 kg sliced tomatoes

1 lb 4 oz/567 g sliced fresh mozzarella

10 fl oz/284 g **Red Wine Vinaigrette** (page 929)

salt, as needed

½ oz/14 g basil chiffonade

cracked black peppercorns, as needed

1. Place the tomatoes and mozzarella slices alternately on a plate and drizzle the vinaigrette over the top.

2. Season with salt. Garnish with the basil and pepper.

Roasted Peppers (Peperoni Arrostiti)

Makes 10 servings

4 lb 4 oz/1.93 kg roasted red and yellow peppers (see page 700)

4 fl oz/120 mL olive oil

2 oz/57 g golden raisins

2 oz/57 g toasted pine nuts

1 oz/28 g chopped parsley

½ oz/14 g minced garlic

salt, as needed

ground black pepper, as needed

1. Cut the peppers into ¼-in/6-mm slices and drain in a sieve or colander for 2 hours.

2. Combine the peppers with the oil, raisins, pine nuts, parsley, garlic, salt, and pepper.

3. Serve immediately or refrigerate for later service.

Green Lentil Salad (Salade des Lentilles du Puy)

Makes 10 servings

1 onion piqué

1 lb 8 oz/680 g French green lentils, rinsed and sorted

2 garlic cloves

1 oz/28 g finely minced shallots

½ oz/14 g Dijon mustard

1½ fl oz/45 mL red wine vinegar

salt, as needed

ground black pepper, as needed

1½ fl oz/45 mL extra-virgin olive oil

2 oz/57 g chopped parsley

1. Place the onion in a medium pot with the lentils and garlic. Cover with cold water by 1 in/3 cm. Cover the pot and bring to a boil over medium heat. Reduce the heat to low and simmer for 25 to 35 minutes until the lentils are tender, but still intact. The cooking liquid should be absorbed when lentils are cooked.

2. Discard the onion and garlic. Toss the warm lentils with the shallots.

3. Combine the mustard, vinegar, salt, and pepper. Gradually whisk in the oil. Adjust seasoning with salt and pepper, if necessary.

4. Add the dressing to the warm lentils and shallots. Mix well. Garnish with the parsley.

5. Serve immediately or refrigerate for later service.

Variation: Add 6 oz/170 g each minced green onions and chopped walnuts to the finished salad.

Mixed Bean Salad

Makes 10 servings

10 oz/284 g cooked black beans, drained

10 oz/284 g cooked pinto beans or small red kidney beans, drained

10 oz/284 g cooked chickpeas, drained

5 oz/142 g cooked red lentils, drained

6 oz/170 g small-dice red onions

4 oz/113 g minced celery

2 tbsp/6 g minced parsley

10 fl oz/300 mL **Vinaigrette Gourmande** (page 934)

salt, as needed

ground black pepper, as needed

1. Combine the black beans, pinto beans, chickpeas, lentils, onions, celery, and parsley. Gently toss with the vinaigrette.

2. Marinate in the refrigerator for 24 hours. Season with salt and pepper.

3. Serve immediately or refrigerate for later service.

Warm Black-Eyed Pea Salad

Makes 10 servings

2 rosemary sprigs

2 thyme sprigs

2 bay leaves

5 fl oz/150 mL olive oil

4 oz/113 g minced onions

2 tsp/6 g minced garlic

1 lemon, zested

12 oz/340 g dried black-eyed peas, sorted and rinsed

48 fl oz/1.44 L **Chicken Stock** (page 351), or as needed

3 fl oz/180 mL lemon juice, or as needed

3 tbsp/9 g basil chiffonade

salt, as needed

ground black pepper, as needed

1. Tie the rosemary, thyme, and bay leaf into a bundle with butcher's twine. Heat 1 fl oz/30 mL of the oil in a saucepan over high heat. Add the onions, half of the garlic, and the lemon zest and sauté until tender.

2. Add the peas, stock, and bundled herbs. Bring to a boil, reduce the heat, and simmer until the peas are tender, about 1 hour. Add more stock, if necessary, to keep the peas covered throughout the cooking time.

3. While the peas are cooking, combine the remaining oil and garlic, the lemon juice, and basil.

4. Drain the peas and remove and discard the herb bundle. Add the hot peas to the oil mixture and toss gently until evenly coated. Season with salt and pepper.

5. Serve immediately.

Curried Rice Salad

Makes 10 servings

2 lb/907 g cooked long-grain rice

8 oz/227 g cooked green peas

4 oz/113 g diced onions

4 oz/113 g diced Granny Smith apples, peeled if desired

2 oz/57 g toasted pumpkin seeds

2 oz/57 g plumped golden raisins

6 fl oz/180 mL **Curry Vinaigrette** (page 931)

salt, as needed

ground black pepper, as needed

Curry Powder (page 463; optional), **as needed**

1. Combine the rice, peas, onions, apples, pumpkin seeds, and raisins.

2. Toss lightly with the vinaigrette, adding just enough to moisten the rice. Season with salt, pepper, and curry powder, if desired.

3. Serve immediately or refrigerate for later service.

Seafood Ravigote

Makes 10 portions

½ oz/14 g minced shallots

20 shrimp (16–20 count), peeled and deveined

10 frogs leg pairs, cut in half

10 oz/284 g bay scallops, outer muscle removed

10 fl oz/300 mL white wine

14 fl oz/420 mL **Fish Stock** (page 353)

4 egg yolks

1 tbsp/15 g mustard

½ fl oz/15 mL lemon juice

8 fl oz/240 mL vegetable oil

1 tsp/2 g **Fines Herbs** (page 463)

salt, as needed

pepper, as needed

20 cooked mussels

4 oz/113 g cucumber julienne

20 leaves Boston lettuce

20 tomato wedges

10 lemon wedges

1. Combine the shallots, shrimp, frogs legs, scallops, wine, and stock and bring to a simmer. Poach the seafood until done.

2. Remove the seafood, cover, and refrigerate. Strain the poaching liquid.

3. Reduce the poaching liquid to 1½ fl oz/45 mL and transfer to a stainless-steel bowl. Add the egg yolks, mustard, and lemon juice and mix well.

4. Whisk in the oil, starting very slowly in the beginning and increasing the speed as the oil is absorbed and a thick vinaigrette forms. Add the herbs and season with salt and pepper.

5. Remove the meat from the frogs legs and clean the mussels. Combine the seafood and sauce.

6. Mix the cucumber julienne with the vinaigrette.

7. Serve the seafood ravigote on the lettuce leaves, garnished with tomato, lemon, and cucumbers.

Chapter Thirty-one

Sandwiches

Sandwiches find their place on nearly every menu, from elegant receptions and teas to substantial but casual meals. Built from four simple elements—bread, a spread, a filling, and a garnish—they exemplify the ways in which a global approach to cuisine can result in nearly endless variety.

Elements in a Sandwich

A sandwich can be open or closed, hot or cold. It can be small enough to serve as an hors d'oeuvre or large enough to serve as an entrée.

Cold sandwiches include standard deli-style versions made from sliced meats or mayonnaise-dressed salads. Club sandwiches, also known as triple-decker sandwiches, are included in this category as well.

Hot sandwiches may feature a filling, such as hamburgers or pastrami. Others are grilled, like a Reuben sandwich or a melt. Sometimes a hot filling is mounded on bread and the sandwich is topped with a hot sauce.

Breads

Bread for sandwiches runs a fairly wide gamut. Sliced white and wheat Pullman loaves are used to make many cold sandwiches. The tight crumb of a good Pullman makes it a particularly appropriate choice for delicate tea and finger sandwiches, since they can be sliced thinly without crumbling. Tea and finger sandwiches must be made on fine-grained bread in order to be trimmed of their crusts and precisely cut into shapes and sizes that can be eaten in about two average bites. Whole-grain and peasant-style breads are not always as easy to slice thinly.

Various breads, buns, rolls, and wrappers are used to make special sandwiches. The characteristics of the bread and how it will fit with the sandwich should be considered. The bread should be firm enough and thick enough to hold the filling, but not so thick that the sandwich is too dry to enjoy.

Most breads can be sliced in advance of sandwich preparation as long as they are carefully covered to prevent drying. Toasting should be done immediately before assembling the sandwich. Some breads to choose from include:

- Pullman loaves (white, wheat, or rye)
- Peasant-style breads (pumpernickel, sourdough, pain de campagne, and boule)
- Rolls (hard, soft, and Kaiser)
- Flatbreads (focaccia, pita, ciabatta, and lavash)
- Wrappers (rice paper and egg roll)
- Flour and corn tortillas

Spreads

Many sandwiches call for a spread applied directly to the bread. A fat-based spread (mayonnaise or butter, for instance) provides a barrier to keep the bread from getting soggy. Spreads also add moisture to a sandwich and help to hold it together as it is picked up and eaten. Some sandwich fillings include the spread in the filling mixture (for example, a mayonnaise-dressed tuna salad); there is no need then to add a spread when assembling the sandwich.

Spreads can be very simple and subtly flavored, or they may themselves bring a special flavor and texture to the sandwich. The following list of spreads includes some classic choices as well as some that may not immediately spring to mind as sandwich spreads.

- Mayonnaise (plain or flavored, such as aïoli and rouille) or creamy salad dressings
- Plain or compound butters
- Mustard or ketchup
- Spreadable cheeses (ricotta, cream cheese, mascarpone, or crème fraîche)
- Vegetable or herb spreads (hummus, tapenade, or pesto)
- Tahini and nut butters
- Jellies, jams, compotes, chutneys, and other fruit preserves
- Avocado pulp or guacamole
- Oils and vinaigrettes

Fillings

Sandwich fillings are the focus of a sandwich. They may be cold or hot, substantial or minimal. It is as important to properly roast and slice turkey for club sandwiches as it is to be certain that the watercress for tea sandwiches is perfectly fresh and completely rinsed and dried. The filling should determine how all the other elements of the sandwich are selected and prepared. Choices for fillings include the following:

- Sliced roasted or simmered meats (roast beef, corned beef, pastrami, turkey, ham, pâté, or sausage)
- Sliced cheeses
- Grilled, roasted, or fresh vegetables
- Grilled, pan-fried, or broiled burgers, sausages, fish, or poultry
- Salads of meats, poultry, eggs, fish, or vegetables

Garnishes

Lettuce leaves, slices of tomato or onion, sprouts, marinated or brined peppers, and olives are just a few of the many ingredients that can be used to garnish sandwiches. These garnishes become part of the sandwich's overall structure, so choose them with some thought to the way they complement or contrast the main filling. When sandwiches are plated, side garnishes may also be included. For example:

- Green salad or side salad (potato, pasta, or coleslaw
- Lettuce and sprouts
- Sliced fresh vegetables
- Pickle spears or olives
- Dips, spreads, or relishes
- Sliced fruits

Presentation Styles

A sandwich constructed with a top and a bottom slice of bread is known as a closed sandwich. A club sandwich has a third slice of bread. Still other sandwiches have only one slice of bread, which acts as a base; these are open-faced sandwiches.

Create straight-edged sandwiches by cutting into squares, rectangles, diamonds, or triangles. The yield may be lower when preparing shapes, making them slightly more expensive to produce.

Take the time to cut shapes uniformly so that they look their best when set in straight rows on platters or arranged on plates. Cut sandwiches as close to service as possible. If sandwiches must be prepared ahead of time, hold them wrapped in plastic or in airtight containers for only a few hours.

Sandwich Production Guidelines

Organize the work station carefully, whether preparing mise en place or assembling sandwiches for service. Everything needed should be within arm's reach. Maximize the work flow by looking for ways to eliminate any unnecessary movements:

- Organize the work so that it moves in a direct line.

- Prepare spreads prior to service and have them at a spreadable consistency. Use a spatula to spread the entire surface of the bread.

- Slice breads and rolls prior to service for volume production. Whenever possible, toast, grill, or broil breads when ready to assemble the sandwich. If bread must be toasted in advance, hold the toast in a warm area, loosely covered.

- Prepare and portion fillings and garnishes in advance and hold them at the correct temperature. Clean and dry lettuce or other greens in advance.

- Grilled sandwiches such as a Reuben or croque monsieur can be fully assembled in advance of service, then grilled or heated to order.

CIA Club

CIA Club

Makes 10 servings

6 fl oz/180 mL **Mayonnaise** (page 936), or as needed

30 slices white Pullman bread, ¼ in/6 mm thick, toasted

20 red leaf lettuce leaves

1 lb 4 oz/567 g thinly sliced turkey

1 lb 4 oz/567 g thinly sliced ham

20 tomato slices

20 bacon slices, cooked and cut in half

1. For each sandwich, spread 1 tsp/5 mL of mayonnaise on 1 slice of toast. Layer a lettuce leaf and 2 oz/57 g each of turkey and ham on the toast.

2. Spread ½ tsp/2.50 mL of mayonnaise on both sides of another slice of toast and place on top of the ham. Top with another lettuce leaf, 2 tomato slices, and 2 bacon slices (4 halves).

3. Spread 1 tsp/5 mL of mayonnaise on 1 more slice of toast and place it on the sandwich, mayonnaise-side down.

4. Secure the sandwich with sandwich picks. Cut the sandwich into quarters, and serve immediately.

Philly Hoagie

Makes 10 servings

7 fl oz/210 mL olive oil

3 fl oz/90 mL red wine vinegar

1 tbsp/3 g chopped oregano

salt, as needed

ground black pepper, as needed

ten 10-in/25-cm hoagie rolls

1 lb 8 oz/680 g thinly sliced prosciutto

10 oz/284 g thinly sliced sweet cappicola

10 oz/284 g thinly sliced genoa salami

1 lb 4 oz/570 g thinly sliced provolone cheese

5 oz/142 g shredded iceberg lettuce

30 tomato slices, ⅛ in/3 mm thick

30 onion slices, 1/16 in/1.50 mm thick

1. Mix together the oil, vinegar, and oregano to make a dressing. Season with salt and pepper.

2. For each sandwich, slice a roll open, leaving it hinged, and brush the inside of the roll with the dressing.

3. Divide the prosciutto, cappicola, and salami evenly between the rolls. Top with 2 oz/57 g of provolone and ½ oz/14 g of lettuce. Place 3 slices each of tomato and onions on top of the lettuce. Drizzle the sandwich with additional dressing. Close the sandwich and serve it immediately.

Chicken Burger

Makes 10 servings

2 lb 8 oz/1.13 kg ground chicken

6 oz/170 g bread crumbs

1 lb/454 g **Duxelles Stuffing** (page 556), cooled

2 tbsp/6 g chopped herbs, such as chives, oregano, basil, or parsley

1 tsp/5 g salt

½ tsp/1 g ground white pepper

10 oz/284 g thinly sliced provolone cheese

4 oz/113 g butter, melted, or as needed

10 Kaiser rolls

10 green or red leaf lettuce leaves

20 tomato slices

1. Gently mix the chicken, bread crumbs, duxelles, herbs, salt, and pepper. Form into 6-oz/170-g patties.

2. Lightly butter a sauté pan or griddle. Brown the patties on both sides. Finish in a 350°F/177°C oven to an internal temperature of 165°F/74°C.

3. Prior to service, top each burger with provolone and return to the oven to melt.

4. For each sandwich, slice a roll, leaving the bread hinged. Brush with melted butter and grill until golden. Place a burger on the roll and serve open-faced with 1 leaf of lettuce and 2 slices of tomato.

Barbecued Beef

Makes 10 servings

4 lb/1.81 kg beef brisket

1 tbsp/15 g salt

1 tsp/2 g ground black pepper

20 fl oz/600 mL **Barbecue Sauce** (page 549)

10 hoagie or Kaiser rolls

4 oz/113 g butter, melted, or as needed

1. Season the brisket with salt and pepper, place on a rack in a roasting pan, and roast in a 325°F/163°C oven for 2 hours. Cover with aluminum foil, and continue cooking until fork tender, about 3 hours more. Baste the brisket with Barbecue Sauce during the final 2 hours of roasting.

2. Cool the brisket and trim off any excess fat. Slice or shred the meat. Mix with the remaining sauce and reheat in a 350°F/177°C oven or over medium heat on the stovetop until an internal temperature of 160°F/71°C. Adjust seasoning with salt and pepper, if necessary.

3. For each sandwich, slice a roll, leaving the bread hinged. Brush with melted butter and grill until golden. Place the barbecued beef on the grilled roll and serve open-faced.

Open-Faced Turkey Sandwich with Sweet and Sour Onions

Makes 10 servings

1 lb 4 oz/567 g onion julienne

4 fl oz/120 mL clarified butter

4 fl oz/120 mL soy sauce

8 fl oz/240 mL duck sauce

4 fl oz/120 mL water

½ tsp/1 g garlic powder, or as needed

½ tsp/1 g ground ginger, or as needed

salt, as needed

ground black pepper, as needed

10 slices white Pullman bread, ¼ in/6 mm thick, toasted

2 lb 8 oz/1.13 kg thinly sliced roasted turkey

20 tomato slices

1 lb 4 oz/567 g thinly sliced Swiss cheese

1. Sauté the onions in the butter until translucent. Add the soy sauce, duck sauce, and water. Simmer until the onions are fully cooked and dry. Season with garlic powder, ginger, salt, and pepper.

2. For each sandwich, spread some of the onion mixture on a slice of toast. Cover with about 4½ oz/128 g of turkey. Spread additional onion mixture over the turkey. Place 2 slices of tomatoes on top, then cover the tomatoes with 2 oz/57 g of cheese.

3. Bake in a 350°F/177°C oven until the sandwich is heated through and the cheese is melted. Serve immediately.

Croque Monsieur

Makes 10 servings

10 oz/284 g Gruyère cheese

15 oz/425 g thinly sliced ham

20 slices white Pullman bread, ¼ in/6 mm thick

2 tbsp/30 g Dijon mustard

4 oz/113 g butter, at room temperature

1. For each sandwich, place 1 slice of Gruyère and 1 slice of ham on 1 slice of bread. Spread lightly with mustard. Place another slice of Gruyère on top and close with a second slice of bread. Butter both sides of the assembled sandwich.

2. Lightly butter a flattop or pan. Cook the sandwich until golden brown on both sides. If necessary, place in the oven and continue cooking until the cheese has melted. Serve immediately.

Eggplant and Prosciutto Panini

Eggplant and Prosciutto Panini

Makes 10 servings

8¾ oz/248 g ricotta cheese

2 tsp/2 g chopped basil

1 tsp/2 g coarse ground black pepper

1 tsp/1 g chopped oregano

1 tsp/1 g chopped parsley

salt, as needed

10 Italian hard rolls

5 fl oz/150 mL oil from marinated eggplant

1 lb 4 oz/567 g **Marinated Eggplant Filling** (recipe follows)

1 lb 4 oz/567 g thinly sliced prosciutto

1. In a bowl, combine the ricotta, basil, pepper, oregano, parsley, and salt and mix well. Cover and refrigerate overnight.

2. For each sandwich, split a roll lengthwise and brush the inside with oil from the marinated eggplant. Spread 1 oz/28 g of herbed ricotta mixture on one half of the roll and top with 2 oz/57 g each of eggplant and prosciutto. Top with the other half of the roll and serve immediately.

Marinated Eggplant Filling

Makes 1 lb/454 g

1 lb/454 g Italian eggplant

1 tbsp/15 g salt

16 fl oz/480 mL extra-virgin olive oil

3 garlic cloves, crushed

1½ fl oz/45 mL red wine vinegar

2 tbsp/12 g dried oregano

1 tbsp/6 g dried basil

1 tbsp/6 g coarse ground black pepper

pinch red pepper flakes

1. Slice the eggplant into ⅛-in/3-mm-thick slices. Layer the slices in a colander, salting each layer liberally. Allow the eggplant to sit for 1 hour.

2. Rinse off the bitter liquid and blot the slices dry with paper towels.

3. Mix the remaining ingredients together.

4. Toss the eggplant slices in the marinade; cover and refrigerate for 3 to 4 days. Stir the mixture every day.

NOTE
The eggplant is ready when the flesh has become relatively translucent and no longer tastes raw.

Three Cheese Melt

Makes 10 servings

20 slices white Pullman bread, ¼ in/6 mm thick

1 lb 4 oz/567 g thinly sliced Cheddar cheese

5 oz/142 g crumbled blue cheese

10 oz/284 g thinly sliced pepper jack cheese

4 oz/113 g butter, or as needed, at room temperature

1. For each sandwich, top 1 slice of bread with 1 oz/28 g of Cheddar, ½ oz/14 g of crumbled blue cheese, 1 oz/28 g of pepper jack, and another 1 oz/28 g of Cheddar. Top with a bread slice. Butter both sides of the assembled sandwich.

2. Lightly butter a flattop or pan. Cook the sandwich until golden brown on both sides. If necessary, place in the oven and continue cooking until the cheese has melted. Serve immediately.

Reuben Sandwich

Makes 10 servings

RUSSIAN DRESSING

10 fl oz/300 mL **Mayonnaise** (page 936)

3 fl oz/90 mL chili sauce

¾ oz/21 g prepared horseradish

1 oz/28 g minced onions, blanched

¾ tsp/3.75 mL Worcestershire sauce

salt, as needed

ground black pepper, as needed

1 lb 4 oz/567 g thinly sliced Swiss cheese

2 lb/907 g thinly sliced corned beef

1 lb 4 oz/567 g sauerkraut

20 slices rye bread, ¼ in/6 mm thick

4 oz/113 g butter, at room temperature

1. To prepare the Russian dressing, mix together the mayonnaise, chili sauce, horseradish, onions, and Worcestershire sauce. Season with salt and pepper.

2. For each sandwich, layer 1 slice of the cheese, ½ fl oz/15 mL of Russian dressing, 1½ oz/43 g of corned beef, and 2 oz/57 g of the sauerkraut on 1 slice of bread. Top with another 1½ oz/43 g of corned beef, ½ fl oz/15 mL of Russian dressing, and a second slice of cheese. Top with a bread slice.

3. Butter both sides of the assembled sandwich. Lightly butter a flattop or pan. Cook the sandwich until golden brown on both sides. If necessary, place in the oven and continue cooking until the cheese has melted. Serve immediately.

Cucumber Sandwich with Herbed Cream Cheese

Makes 10 servings

6 oz/170 g cream cheese

1 tbsp/3 g chopped dill

1 tbsp/3 g chopped chives

2 fl oz/60 mL heavy cream, or as needed

salt, as needed

ground black pepper, as needed

20 slices white Pullman bread, ¼ in/6 mm thick

12 oz/340 g thinly sliced European cucumbers

1. Blend the cream cheese and herbs with the cream to get a smooth, spreading consistency. Season with salt and pepper.

2. For each sandwich, spread 1½ tsp/7.50 mL of the herbed cream cheese on 2 slices of bread. Lay some sliced cucumbers on 1 slice of the bread and top with the second slice of bread.

3. Trim the crust off each sandwich and cut into 4 rectangles, or another desired shape.

4. Serve immediately or hold covered and refrigerated for no more than 2 hours.

Watercress Sandwich with Herb Mayonnaise

Makes 10 servings

5 fl oz/150 mL **Mayonnaise** (page 936)

½ oz/14 g minced herbs, such as chives, parsley, or dill

salt, as needed

ground black pepper, as needed

20 slices white Pullman bread, ¼ in/6 mm thick

3 oz/85 g watercress, cleaned and trimmed

1. To make the herb mayonnaise, combine the mayonnaise and herbs. Season with salt and pepper.

2. For each sandwich, spread 1½ tsp/7.50 mL of the herb mayonnaise on 2 slices of bread. Lay some watercress on 1 slice of the bread and top with the second slice of bread.

3. Trim the crust off each sandwich and cut into 4 triangles, or another desired shape.

4. Serve immediately or hold covered and refrigerated for no more than 2 hours.

TOP: **Cucumber Sandwich with Herbed Cream Cheese**
MIDDLE: **Watercress Sandwich with Herb Mayonnaise**
BOTTOM: **Apple Sandwich with Curry Mayonnaise**

Apple Sandwich with Curry Mayonnaise

Makes 10 servings

1 tbsp/6 g **Curry Powder** (page 463)

5 fl oz/150 mL **Mayonnaise** (page 936)

salt, as needed

ground black pepper, as needed

20 slices white Pullman bread, ¼ in/6 mm thick

1 lb/454 g Granny Smith apples, peeled and thinly sliced

1. In small sauté pan over medium heat, toast the curry powder. Allow the curry powder to cool and blend it into the mayonnaise. Season with salt and pepper.

2. For each sandwich, spread 1½ tsp/7.50 mL of the curry mayonnaise on 2 slices of bread. Place 1¼ oz/35 g of apple slices on 1 slice of the bread and top with the second slice of bread.

3. Using a 1½-in/4-cm round cutter, cut each sandwich into 4 circles, or another desired shape.

4. Serve immediately or hold covered and refrigerated for no more than 2 hours.

Gorgonzola and Pear Sandwich

Makes 10 servings

2 oz/57 g cream cheese

5 oz/142 g Gorgonzola

2 fl oz/60 mL heavy cream

salt, as needed

ground black pepper, as needed

2 fl oz/60 mL honey

1 fl oz/30 mL white wine vinegar

1 lb/454 g pears

20 slices raisin pumpernickel bread, ¼ in/6 mm thick

1. Blend the cream cheese and Gorgonzola with enough cream to get a smooth, spreading consistency. Season with salt and pepper.

2. Combine the honey and vinegar. Peel and thinly slice the pears and brush them with the honey-vinegar solution to prevent oxidation.

3. For each sandwich, spread the Gorgonzola mixture on 2 slices of bread. Place about 1¼ oz/35 g of the pears on 1 slice of the bread and top with the second slice of bread.

4. Cut into the desired shape. Serve immediately or hold covered and refrigerated for no more than 2 hours.

Tomato Sandwich with Oregano Sour Cream

Makes 10 servings

8 fl oz/240 mL sour cream

2 tbsp/6 g chopped oregano

salt, as needed

ground black pepper, as needed

20 slices white Pullman bread, ¼ in/6 mm thick

2 lb/907 g tomatoes, cored, sliced

1. Combine the sour cream and oregano. Season with salt and pepper.

2. For each sandwich, spread the sour cream mixture on 2 slices of bread. Place about 3 oz/85 g of tomato slices on 1 slice of the bread and top with the second slice of bread.

3. Cut into the desired shape. Serve immediately or hold covered and refrigerated for no more than 2 hours.

Chapter Thirty-two

Hors d'Oeuvre and Appetizers

The distinction between an hors d'oeuvre and an appetizer has more to do with the portion size and how and when it is served than with the actual food being served. Hors d'oeuvre are typically served as a prelude to a meal, while appetizers are usually the meal's first course.

Hors d'Oeuvre

The term *hors d'oeuvre* is from the French for "outside the meal." Hors d'oeuvre are meant to pique the taste buds and perk up the appetite. Foods served as hors d'oeuvre should be:

- Small enough to eat in one or two bites. Some hors d'oeuvre are often eaten with the fingers, while other hors d'oeuvre may require a plate and a fork. With very few exceptions, hors d'oeuvre do not require the use of a knife.

- Attractive. Because hors d'oeuvre customarily precede the meal, they are considered a means of teasing the appetite. This is partially accomplished through visual appeal.

- Designed to complement the meal that is to follow. It is important to avoid serving too many foods of a similar taste or texture. For example, if the menu features a lobster bisque, lobster canapés may be inappropriate.

Presenting hors d'oeuvre

The presentation of hors d'oeuvre can extend from the elegance of butler-style service to the relative informality of a buffet, or it may be a combination of service styles. The type of hors d'oeuvre as well as the requirements of a particular function determine how these foods are presented. These guidelines can assist the chef in hors d'oeuvre presentation:

- Keep in mind the nature of the event as well as the menu that follows when selecting hors d'oeuvre.

- Ice carvings and ice beds are often used to keep seafood and caviar very cold, as well as for their dramatic appeal. Be sure that the ice can drain properly and that heavy or large ice carvings are stable.

- Hors d'oeuvre served on platters or passed on trays should be thoughtfully presented, so that the last hors d'oeuvre on the plate is still attractively presented.

- Hors d'oeuvre that are served with a sauce require serving utensils. In order to prevent the guest from having to juggle a plate, fork, and napkin while standing, these hors d'oeuvre should ordinarily be limited to either buffet service or served as the prelude to a more elaborate meal.

- To ensure that hot hors d'oeuvre stay hot, avoid combining hot and cold items on a single platter and have chafing dishes available for buffet service.

Appetizers

While hors d'oeuvre are served separately from the main meal, appetizers are traditionally its first course. The role of the appetizer on the contemporary menu is becoming increasingly important. Although the traditional pâté, smoked trout, or escargot with garlic butter may still be found, dishes based on pasta, grilled vegetables, and grains are receiving more exposure.

The usual admonition to "build" a menu from one course to the next calls for some logical connection between the appetizer and all the courses to follow. For every rule you read about what types of foods should or shouldn't constitute an appetizer, you will find at least one good exception. What most appetizers have in common is careful attention to portioning and sound technical execution and plating. Most appetizers are small servings of very flavorful foods, meant to take just enough edge off the appetite to permit thorough enjoyment of an entrée.

Classic hors d'oeuvre can be served as appetizers by increasing the portion size slightly. Perennial favorites are perfectly fresh clams and oysters, for example, shucked as close to service time as possible and served with sauces designed to enhance their naturally briny flavor, or a classic shrimp cocktail, served with a cocktail sauce, salsa, or other pungent sauce. Smoked fish, meat, or poultry; sausages, pâtés, terrines, and galantines; air-dried ham and beef sliced paper thin—all of these can be used to create appetizer plates, on their own with a few accompaniments or garnishes, or as a sampler plate.

Salads are also served as appetizers. Portion size may be changed or a different sauce or garnish substituted to vary the salad from season to season or to showcase a range of flavors and textures from other cuisines.

Warm and hot appetizers include small servings of pasta, such as tortellini or ravioli, served on their own or in a sauce or broth. Puff pastry shells can be cut into vols au vent or made into turnovers and filled with savory ragouts or foie gras. Broiled or grilled fish, shellfish, or poultry are often featured. Crêpes, blini, and other similar dishes are popular. Meatballs and other highly seasoned ground-meat appetizers are also frequent choices.

Vegetables are more important than ever as an appetizer. They are often presented very simply—for example, steamed artichokes with a dipping sauce, chilled asparagus drizzled with a flavored oil, or a plate of grilled vegetables accompanied by an aïoli.

Preparing and presenting appetizers

In preparing and presenting appetizers, keep in mind the following guidelines:

- Keep the portion size appropriate. Generally, appetizers should be served in small servings.

- Season all appetizers with meticulous care. Appetizers are meant to stimulate the appetite, so seasoning is of the utmost importance. Don't overuse fresh herbs and other seasonings, however. It is all too easy to deaden the palate by overwhelming it with too much garlic or an extravagance of basil at the meal's start. Remember that other courses will follow this one.

- Keep garnishes to a minimum. Those garnishes that are used should serve to heighten the dish's appeal by adding flavor and texture, not just color.

- Serve all appetizers at the proper temperature. Remember to chill or warm plates.

- Slice, shape, and portion appetizers carefully, with just enough on the plate to make the appetizer interesting and appealing from start to finish but not so much that the guest is overwhelmed.

- Neatness always counts, but especially with appetizers. They can set the stage for the entire meal.

- When offering shared appetizers, consider how they will look when they come to the table. It may be more effective to split a shared plate in the kitchen, rather than leaving it to the guests to divide it themselves.

- Color, shape, and white space play a role in the overall composition of the plate. Choose the right size and shape serving pieces and provide the guest with everything necessary for the appetizer, including special utensils, dishes to hold empty shells or bones, and, if necessary, finger bowls.

Cold Savory Mousse

A cold savory mousse has many applications. Served unmolded, sliced as a loaf or terrine, or piped into a shell or as a topping, it can be featured as an hors d'oeuvre, an appetizer, or a component in other dishes.

The French word *mousse* literally means "foam" or "froth." A mousse is prepared by gently folding whipped cream or egg whites into an intensely flavored base. The light, frothy mixture is chilled enough to set before it is served. A cold mousse is not cooked after assembly since heating would deflate the mousse. A hot mousse is a small portion of a mousseline forcemeat that has been molded in a fashion similar to a cold mousse before it is cooked and served hot.

Although each base ingredient may call for an adjustment in the amount of binder and aerator, the basic formula described on page 986 is a good checkpoint. It can and should be altered depending on the type of mousse being made and the intended use of the final product.

The mousse's main, or base, ingredient may be one or a combination of the following: finely ground or puréed cooked or smoked meats, fish, or poultry; cheese or a blend of cheeses (a spreadable cheese, such as goat cheese or cream cheese, is typically used); purées of vegetables (these may need to be reduced by sautéing to intensify flavor and drive off excess moisture). All base ingredients should be properly seasoned before adding other ingredients, and the seasoning rechecked once the mousse is prepared. Be sure to test at service temperature to make adjustments if necessary.

Some base ingredients are already stable enough to give finished mousses structure (e.g., cheeses). For base ingredients that are not as dense, formulas typically include a quantity of gelatin (see sidebar, page 984). The amount of gelatin should be enough so that the mousse holds its shape. The more gelatin added, the firmer the finished mousse will be. Choose the quantity based upon presentation (a firmer mousse for slicing, a softer mousse for spooning or piping).

The lightener in a mousse can be a foam of whipped egg whites or heavy cream whipped to soft or medium peaks. If the whites or cream are overbeaten, the mousse may start to "deflate" from its own weight as it sits. Added seasonings, flavorings, and garnishes can run a wide gamut and should be chosen to suit the main ingredient's flavor.

Equipment needs for preparing a mousse include a food processor to work the main item into a purée or paste, and a whip or mixer with beaters to prepare egg whites and/or cream. Have a drum sieve on hand to strain the base if necessary. Prepare a cold ice bath to cool the mixture as well as the proper setup for weighing and handling gelatin. Prepare various molds and serving dishes, or a pastry bag, to shape the finished mousse.

Working with gelatin

Gelatin is used to make aspic, to stabilize foams, and to thicken liquid-based mixtures that will be served cold. It is added to liquid in different concentrations to get different results. The concentration of gelatin, or gel strength, in a given liquid is best described in terms of ounces per gallon (or ounces per pint). Formulas for producing a variety of gel strengths can be found in the table below.

Gel Strength Formulas

GEL STRENGTH	OUNCES PER GALLON	OUNCES PER PINT	POSSIBLE USES
Delicate gel	2	0.25	When slicing is not required; individual servings of meat, poultry, or fish bound by gelatin; jellied consommés
Coating gel	4	0.50	Edible chaud-froid; coating individual items
Sliceable gel	6–8	1	When product is to be sliced; filling pâté en croûte, head cheese
Firm gel	10–12	1.25–1.50	Coating platters for a food show or competition; cold mousse

1. **Rain or sprinkle the gelatin over a cool liquid.** If the liquid is warm or hot, the gelatin will not soften properly. Scattering the gelatin over the surface of the liquid prevents it from forming clumps.

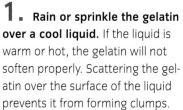

2. **Rehydrate, bloom, and then melt gelatin before use.** To bloom, soak it the amount of liquid specified in the formula, which should be approximately 8 fl oz/240 mL of a water-based liquid for every 1 oz/28 g of gelatin. An alternative method commonly used for blooming sheet gelatin is to soak it in enough cold water to completely submerge it. If this method is used, after blooming, gently squeeze and wring the sheet to force the excess water out, so as not to add additional liquid to the formula, which would change the consistency and flavor of the finished product.

3. **After it is bloomed, melt the gelatin.** To melt bloomed gelatin, place it in a pan or bowl over low heat or over a hot water bath until liquefied. As the softened gelatin warms, the mixture will clear and come liquid enough to pour easily. Then stir the melted gelatin into a warm or room-temperature base mixture.

If the base is cold, the gelatin may set up unevenly. If the base is quite warm or hot (at least 105°F/41°C), however, you may opt to add the bloomed gelatin directly to the hot base, rather than melting it separately, and allow the base's heat to melt the gelatin. Be sure to stir gelatin added this way until it is completely blended into the base.

Since the product will begin to set immediately after the gelatin is added, always prepare all molds, service containers, etc., before beginning preparation.

Some gelatin-stabilized items are served in their molds; others are unmolded before service. To unmold, dip the mold briefly into very hot water, then invert the mold onto a plate and tap it gently to release the item.

1. **Purée the main ingredients in a food processor or grind them with a meat grinder.** The base should have a consistency similar to pastry cream. It may be necessary to add a liquid or moist product such as velouté, béchamel, unwhipped cream, or mayonnaise to adjust the consistency. Cool the base over an ice bath, if the mixture is hotter than 90°F/32°C. For the best possible texture, sieve the puréed base. This removes any last bits of sinew or fiber for a very delicate end product.

Add gelatin, if necessary. Usually, a binder is necessary to produce the correct body. Hydrate the gelatin in a cool liquid. This process is known as *blooming*. Warm the gelatin to about 90° to 110°F/32° to 43°C to dissolve the granules. Stir the melted gelatin into the base. Some main ingredients, such as cheese, may be sufficiently binding without gelatin.

2. **Fold in the whipped cream and/or egg whites just until they are fully combined.** Beat the cream or egg whites to soft peaks for best results. Fold this aerator into the base carefully. Add about one third of the whipped cream first to make it easier to fold in the remaining two thirds. This technique keeps the maximum volume in the finished mousse. Stirring the whipped cream in too vigorously or for too long will cause a loss in volume and may cause the cream to become overwhipped.

3. **Pipe the smoked salmon mousse into barquettes or other containers, as desired.** There are many different ways to use a mousse. It may be piped into barquette or tartlet molds, profiteroles, or endive spears, or used as the spread for a canapé. It may be spooned or piped into portion-size molds; some presentations call for the mousse to be unmolded before service while others call for the mousse to be presented directly in the mold. A mousse can also be layered into a terrine, unmolded, and sliced for presentation. Refrigerate the mousse until needed, at least two hours if it is to be unmolded. A high-quality cold mousse should be fully flavored, delicately set, and very light in texture. The ingredients should be blended smoothly so that there are no streaks of cream or base. The color should be even and appealing.

Smoked Salmon Mousse

Makes 3 lb 9 oz/1.62 kg

1 lb 8 oz/680 g diced smoked salmon

8 fl oz/240 mL **Fish Velouté** (page 383), cold

1 oz/28 g powdered gelatin

8 fl oz/240 mL cold **Fish Stock** (page 353) or water

salt, as needed

ground black pepper, as needed

16 fl oz/480 mL heavy cream, whipped to soft peaks

1. Combine the salmon and velouté in a food processor and process to a smooth consistency. Push through a sieve and transfer to a bowl.

2. Combine the gelatin with the cold stock or water, and bloom until the gelatin absorbs the liquid. Warm the bloomed gelatin over simmering water until the granules dissolve and the mixture reaches 90° to 110°F/32° to 43°C.

3. Blend the gelatin into the salmon mixture. Season with salt and pepper.

4. Fold in the whipped cream. Shape or portion the mousse as desired. Refrigerate the mousse for at least 2 hours to firm it.

Red Pepper Mousse in Endive

Makes 30 servings

3 oz/85 g minced onions

½ tsp/1.50 g finely minced garlic

1 fl oz/30 mL vegetable oil

1 lb 4 oz/567 g small-dice red peppers

8 fl oz/240 mL **Chicken Stock** (page 351)

pinch crushed saffron threads

1 oz/28 g tomato paste

salt, as needed

ground white pepper, as needed

1 tbsp/9 g powdered gelatin

2 fl oz/60 mL white wine

6 fl oz/180 mL heavy cream, whipped to soft peaks

30 Belgian endive spears

30 red pepper slivers

1. Sauté the onions and garlic in the oil until golden. Add the diced peppers, stock, saffron, tomato paste, and salt and pepper. Simmer until all the ingredients are tender and the liquid reduces by half. Purée the mixture in a blender. Cool the base over an ice bath until it is room temperature.

2. Bloom the gelatin in the wine for several minutes and then heat to 90° to 110°F/32° to 43°C to dissolve the granules. Stir into the base and blend to combine all ingredients well.

3. Cool the mixture over an ice bath until it mounds when dropped from a spoon. Fold the whipped cream into the mixture.

4. Pipe the mousse into the endive spears and garnish each with a sliver of red pepper.

Blue Cheese Mousse

Makes 3 lb/1.36 kg

1 lb 4 oz/567 g blue cheese, crumbled

12 oz/340 g cream cheese

1 tbsp/15 g salt

½ tsp/1 g coarsely ground black pepper

12 fl oz/360 mL heavy cream, whipped to soft peaks

1. Purée the cheeses until very smooth. Season with salt and pepper.

2. Fold the whipped cream into the mousse until well blended, without any lumps.

3. Use the mousse to prepare canapés or as a filling or dip.

Goat Cheese Mousse: Substitute fresh goat cheese for the blue cheese.

Pico de Gallo

Makes 32 fl oz/960 mL

10 plum tomatoes, seeded, medium dice

8 oz/227 g small-dice onions

1 to 2 serranos or jalapeños, seeded and minced

3½ fl oz/105 mL lime juice

1 oz/28 g cilantro, chiffonade

salt, as needed

1. Combine all the ingredients. Adjust seasoning with salt.

2. The salsa is ready to serve now, or it may be refrigerated for later use.

Salsa Verde

Makes 32 fl oz/960 mL

1 lb 8 oz/680 g fresh tomatillos, husked and washed

4 serranos, stemmed

¾ oz/21 g chopped cilantro

12 oz/340 g chopped onions

2 garlic cloves, roughly chopped

½ oz/14 g lard

24 fl oz/720 mL **Chicken Stock** (page 351)

salt, as needed

1. Boil the tomatillos and serranos in salted water to cover until tender, 10 to 15 minutes. Drain.

2. Place the tomatillos and chiles in a blender, along with the cilantro, onions, and garlic. Process until almost smooth.

3. Heat the lard in a medium skillet over medium-high heat. When the skillet is hot, pour in the purée and stir constantly for 4 or 5 minutes, until the purée is darker and thicker. Add the stock, bring the sauce to a boil, reduce the heat to medium and simmer until thick enough to coat a spoon, about 20 minutes. Season with salt.

4. The salsa is ready to serve now, or it may be rapidly cooled and refrigerated for later use.

NOTE
To make a vegetarian salsa verde, substitute vegetable oil for the lard and water or vegetable stock for the chicken stock.

Papaya Black Bean Salsa

Makes 32 fl oz/960 mL

7 oz/198 g cooked black beans

7 oz/198 g small-dice ripe papaya

2 oz/57 g small-dice red peppers

2 oz/57 g small-dice red onions

½ oz/14 g minced jalapeños, or as needed

2 tbsp/6 g chopped cilantro

2 tsp/4 g dried Mexican oregano

1 oz/28 g minced ginger

2 fl oz/60 mL olive oil

1 fl oz/30 mL lime juice

salt, as needed

ground black pepper, as needed

1. Combine all the ingredients. Adjust seasoning with salt and pepper.

2. The salsa is ready to serve now, or it may be refrigerated for later use.

Grapefruit Salsa

Makes 32 fl oz/960 mL

2 fl oz/60 mL olive oil

1 tbsp/3 g chopped cilantro

4 oz/113 g finely diced red onions, rinsed

¼ to ½ tsp/0.75 to 1.50 g seeded and minced Scotch bonnet

2 tsp/2 g chopped parsley

4 Ruby Red grapefruits, segmented

salt, as needed

1. Combine the oil, cilantro, onions, Scotch bonnet, and parsley.

2. Just before service, add the grapefruit. Season with salt.

3. The salsa is ready to serve now, or it may be refrigerated for later use.

Green Papaya Salsa

Makes 16 fl oz/480 mL

2 large green papayas

2 carrots

5½ fl oz/165 mL lime juice

½ oz/14 g chopped cilantro

1 tbsp/9 g minced ginger

2 garlic cloves

1 fl oz/30 mL red wine vinegar

1 fl oz/30 mL molasses

salt, as needed

ground black pepper, as needed

1. Peel the papayas, halve them, and deseed. Grate the papayas using the large holes of a box grater. Do the same with the carrots and combine the grated papayas and carrots in a bowl.

2. Add the remaining ingredients and mix well. Season with salt and pepper.

3. The salsa is ready to serve now, or it may be refrigerated for later use.

NOTE
The papaya must be green and hard for this preparation.

Cocktail Sauce

Makes 32 fl oz/960 mL

12 fl oz/360 mL chili sauce

14 fl oz/420 mL ketchup

1 fl oz/30 mL lemon juice

1 oz/28 g sugar

2 tsp/10 mL Tabasco sauce

2 tsp/10 mL Worcestershire sauce

1½ tsp/8 g prepared horseradish

salt, as needed

ground black pepper, as needed

1. Combine all the ingredients and mix thoroughly.

2. The sauce is ready to serve now, or it may be refrigerated for later use. Stir the sauce and adjust seasoning before serving.

Cumberland Sauce

Makes 32 fl oz/960 mL

2 oranges

2 lemons

½ oz/14 g minced shallots

1 lb 4 oz/567 g currant jelly

1 tbsp/6 g dry mustard

12 fl oz/360 mL ruby port

salt, as needed

ground black pepper, as needed

pinch cayenne

pinch ground ginger

1. Remove the zest from the oranges and lemons and cut into julienne. Juice the citrus and reserve.

2. Blanch the shallots and zests for 30 seconds in boiling water. Strain immediately.

3. Combine the citrus juice, shallots, zest, and all the remaining ingredients and bring to a simmer. Simmer until syrupy, 5 to 10 minutes.

4. Chill the sauce over an ice bath. The sauce is ready to serve now, or it may be refrigerated for later use.

Asian Dipping Sauce

Makes 32 fl oz/960 mL

16 fl oz/480 mL soy sauce

8 fl oz/240 mL rice vinegar

8 fl oz/240 mL water

½ oz/14 g minced garlic

2 oz/57 g minced green onions

1 oz/28 g minced ginger

2 tsp/4 g dry mustard

1 tsp/5 mL hot bean paste

2 fl oz/60 mL honey

1. Combine all the ingredients and mix thoroughly.

2. The sauce is ready to serve now, or it may be refrigerated for later use.

Vietnamese Dipping Sauce

Makes 32 fl oz/960 mL

20 Thai chiles, red and/or green

½ oz/14 g minced garlic

4 oz/113 g sugar

16 fl oz/480 mL warm water

4 fl oz/120 mL lime juice

8 fl oz/240 mL fish sauce

1½ oz/43 g finely shredded carrots

1. Slice 5 of the chiles into thin rings and set aside for garnish. Mince the remaining chiles and transfer them to a medium bowl.

2. Add the garlic, sugar, water, lime juice, and fish sauce. Whisk to dissolve the sugar. Add the reserved chiles and carrots. Rest the sauce for 10 minutes.

3. The sauce is ready to serve now, or it may be refrigerated for later use.

Spring Roll Dipping Sauce

Makes 32 fl oz/960 mL

1 oz/28 g finely shredded carrots

2 oz/57 g finely shredded daikon

3½ oz/99 g sugar

½ oz/14 g minced garlic

½ oz/14 g minced red chiles

4 fl oz/120 mL lime or lemon juice

8 fl oz/240 mL rice vinegar

4 fl oz/120 mL Vietnamese fish sauce (*nuoc mam*)

8 fl oz/240 mL water

1. Mix the carrots and daikon with 1 oz/28 g of the sugar and let them stand for 15 minutes.

2. Combine the garlic, chiles, and the remaining sugar and purée in a food processor until smooth. Add the lime

or lemon juice, vinegar, fish sauce, and water and purée until the sugar is dissolved. Combine with the carrot and daikon mixture.

3. The sauce is ready to serve now, or it may be refrigerated for later use.

Yogurt Cucumber Sauce

Makes 32 fl oz/960 mL

16 fl oz/480 mL plain yogurt

1 lb/454 g cucumbers, peeled, seeded, small dice

1 tbsp/9 g minced garlic

2 tsp/4 g ground cumin

1 tsp/2 g ground turmeric

salt, as needed

ground white pepper, as needed

1. Place the yogurt in a cheesecloth-lined strainer. Set the strainer in a bowl and drain at least 8 hours in the refrigerator.

2. Combine the yogurt and cucumbers.

3. Add the garlic, cumin, turmeric, salt, and pepper.

4. The sauce can be served chunky or puréed until smooth. It is ready to serve now, or it may be refrigerated for later use. Stir the sauce and adjust seasoning if necessary before serving.

Guacamole

Makes 32 fl oz/960 mL

4½ oz/128 g small-dice red onions

6 avocados

5 oz/142 g small-dice plum tomatoes

½ oz/14 g jalapeños, seeded and minced

2 tbsp/6 g chopped cilantro

3 fl oz/90 mL lime juice

salt, as needed

coarsely ground black pepper, as needed

Tabasco, as needed

1. Soak the onions in cold water for 20 minutes. Drain and rinse.

2. Peel the avocados and cut roughly into a medium dice. Combine the avocados with the rest of the ingredients and mix well, smashing the avocados a little to form a rough paste.

3. Adjust seasoning with salt, pepper, and Tabasco.

4. The guacamole is ready to serve now, or it may be refrigerated for later use.

NOTE

It is best to make guacamole the same day that it is to be served.

Hummus bi Tahini

Makes 32 fl oz/960 mL

12 oz/340 g chickpeas, soaked overnight

5 fl oz/150 mL lemon juice

3 garlic cloves, crushed in salt

3 fl oz/90 mL extra-virgin olive oil

4½ oz/128 g tahini

salt, as needed

paprika, as needed

1 oz/28 g chopped parsley

1. Boil the chickpeas in water until tender, 1 to 2 hours. Drain the chickpeas, reserving the cooking liquid.

2. In a food processor, blend the chickpeas with about 4 fl oz/120 mL of cooking liquid until they become a smooth paste.

3. Add the lemon juice, garlic, oil, tahini, and salt. Process until well incorporated.

4. Adjust seasoning and consistency, if necessary. Garnish with paprika and parsley.

Baba Ghanoush

Makes 32 fl oz/960 mL

4 lb/1.81 kg (about 4) eggplants

6 oz/170 g tahini

1 oz/28 g roughly chopped garlic

6 fl oz/180 mL lemon juice

salt, as needed

ground black pepper, as needed

1½ oz/43 g chopped parsley

1. Slice the eggplants in half lengthwise. Place cut side down on a lightly oiled sheet pan. Roast in a 450°F/232°C oven, between 1 and 1½ hours, or until the skin is charred and the interior is fully cooked. Let the eggplant stand until cool enough to handle.

2. Scrape the eggplant pulp into a food processor. Add the tahini, garlic, lemon juice, salt, and pepper. Blend until the mixture is homogeneous. If it is too thick, add 1 fl oz/30 mL of water and continue blending.

3. When the mixture is smooth, add the parsley and pulse to incorporate. The consistency should be lightly spreadable, but not too loose. Adjust seasoning with salt and pepper.

4. The baba ghanoush is ready to serve now, or it may be refrigerated for later use.

Muhammara

Makes 32 fl oz/960 mL

3 oz/85 g coarsely chopped walnuts

½ oz/14 g fresh white bread crumbs

1 lb 8 oz/680 g red peppers, peeled and seeded

1 fl oz/30 mL lemon juice, or as needed

4 tsp/20 mL pomegranate molasses

¼ tsp/1.25 mL prepared red chili paste, or as needed

salt, as needed

ground black pepper, as needed

½ fl oz/15 mL olive oil

¼ tsp/0.50 g ground cumin

1. Process the walnuts and bread crumbs in a food processor until finely ground. Add the peppers, lemon juice, and molasses and purée until smooth and creamy. Add the chili paste and season with lemon juice, chili paste, salt, and pepper.

2. Refrigerate, tightly covered, 4 or 5 days or at least overnight, to allow the flavors to mellow.

3. When ready to serve, decorate with a drizzle of the oil and a light dusting of cumin.

Harissa

Makes 32 fl oz/960 mL

16 dried habaneros

4 lb/1.81 kg red chiles, seeded and stemmed

1 lb/454 g sun-dried tomatoes

1½ oz/43 g garlic, crushed in salt

1½ oz/43 g turmeric

2 tsp/4 g ground coriander

2 tsp/4 g ground cumin

2 tsp/4 g caraway seeds

2 tsp/10 mL lemon juice

2 fl oz/60 mL olive oil

1. Toast the habaneros in a sauté pan until the skin darkens and a small amount of smoke rises, about 15 seconds on each side. Hydrate the habaneros by covering them with warm water. When they are soft and hydrated, remove the stems and seeds.

2. Place the habaneros, chiles, tomatoes, garlic, turmeric, coriander, cumin, and caraway seeds in a blender and blend until smooth and homogeneous.

3. Adjust the consistency by adding the lemon juice and oil.

4. The harissa is ready to serve now, or it may be refrigerated for later use.

Tapenade

Makes 32 fl oz/960 mL

10 oz/284 g pitted green olives, rinsed

10 oz/284 g pitted black olives, rinsed

6 oz/170 g capers, rinsed

4 garlic cloves, minced

1½ fl oz/45 mL lemon juice

4 fl oz/120 mL extra-virgin olive oil

ground black pepper, as needed

2 tbsp/6 g chopped oregano

2 tbsp/6 g chopped basil

1. In a food processor, combine the olives, capers, and garlic. Blend, incorporating the lemon juice and oil slowly, until the mixture is chunky and easy to spread. Do not overmix.

2. Season with pepper and add the herbs.

3. The tapenade is ready to serve now, or it may be refrigerated for later use.

Z'hug

Makes 32 fl oz/960 mL

3 lb 4 oz/1.47 kg jalapeños

1¾ oz/50 g garlic

7 oz/198 g cilantro

3½ oz/99 g parsley

3½ oz/99 g mint

4 tsp/8 g cumin seeds, toasted

4 tsp/10 g cardamom pods, peeled, seeds toasted

16 fl oz/480 mL extra-virgin olive oil

6 fl oz/180 mL lemon juice, or as needed

salt, as needed

ground black pepper, as needed

1. Roast the jalapeños under a salamander or over an open flame. Set aside, covered. When cool enough to handle, peel the peppers.

2. Place the jalapeños, garlic, cilantro, parsley, mint, cumin, and cardamom in a food processor and pulse until finely chopped.

3. Slowly add the oil while continuing to purée. Season with lemon juice, salt, and pepper.

4. The sauce is ready to serve now, or it may be refrigerated for later use.

Wasabi

Makes 8 fl oz/240 mL

5½ oz/156 g wasabi powder

warm water, as needed

1. Place the wasabi powder in a small bowl. Add enough of the water to achieve a smooth paste. Wrap the bowl tightly with plastic wrap.

2. Allow the wasabi to sit for about 10 minutes, or until the flavors develop.

3. The wasabi is ready to serve now, or it may be refrigerated for later use.

NOTES

When mixing the wasabi powder with the water, stand back, as the fumes that rise will burn your eyes.

For a less pungent taste, substitute cold water for the warm water.

Spicy Mustard

Makes 8 fl oz/240 mL

3 oz/85 g dry mustard

pinch salt

pinch sugar

2 fl oz/60 mL cool water

1. Place the mustard in a bowl with the salt and sugar.

2. Gradually stir in the water to obtain the desired consistency. The mustard should be the consistency of a smooth, thick, heavy cream.

3. Cover the bowl with plastic wrap and allow the mustard to sit for 15 minutes before serving.

Cranberry Relish

Makes 32 fl oz/960 mL

12 oz/340 g cranberries

3 fl oz/90 mL orange juice

3 fl oz/90 mL Triple Sec

3 oz/85 g sugar, or as needed

1 oz/28 g minced orange zest

10 oz/284 g orange suprêmes

salt, as needed

ground black pepper, as needed

1. Combine the cranberries, orange juice, Triple Sec, sugar, and zest in a saucepan and stir to combine.

2. Cover the saucepan and simmer for 15 to 20 minutes, stirring occasionally.

3. When the berries burst and the liquid starts to thicken, remove the saucepan from the heat and add the suprêmes. Season with salt and pepper. Adjust the sweetness with sugar.

4. The relish is ready to serve now, or it may be rapidly cooled and refrigerated for later use.

Pickle Relish

Makes 32 fl oz/960 mL

1 lb 10 oz/737 g thinly sliced cucumber

4 oz/113 g thinly sliced onion

1½ tsp/7.50 g salt

¾ oz/21 g sugar

2 fl oz/60 mL white vinegar

1. Combine the cucumber and onion with the salt. Let stand, covered, at room temperature, for 2 to 3 hours, until the liquids have been released. Drain well.

2. Over medium-low heat, combine the sugar and vinegar in a small saucepan. Bring to a simmer. Stir well to dissolve the sugar. Cool and hold aside.

3. Pour the cooled vinegar mixture over the onions and cucumber.

4. The relish is ready to serve now, or it may be refrigerated for later use.

Spicy Mango Chutney

Makes 32 fl oz/960 mL

1 lb/454 g chopped mangos

3 oz/85 g raisins

2 tsp/6 g minced jalapeños

½ oz/14 g minced garlic

½ oz/14 g minced ginger

5 oz/142 g dark brown sugar

1 fl oz/30 mL white wine vinegar

salt, as needed

ground black pepper, as needed

1 tsp/2 g turmeric

1. Combine the mangos, raisins, jalapeños, garlic, ginger, and sugar. Refrigerate for 24 hours.

2. Transfer the mixture to a saucepan, add the vinegar, bring to a boil, and simmer for 15 minutes.

3. Season with salt and pepper. Simmer for 10 minutes, stir in the turmeric, and simmer 5 minutes more.

4. The chutney is ready to serve now, or it may be rapidly cooled and refrigerated for later use.

Roasted Red Pepper Marmalade

Makes 32 fl oz/960 mL

8 oz/227 g minced red onions

1 fl oz/30 mL extra-virgin olive oil

4 roasted red peppers, peeled and seeded, cut into brunoise

2 oz/57 g finely chopped capers

½ oz/14 g minced chives

salt, as needed

ground black pepper, as needed

1. Sweat the onions in the oil until translucent. Cool to room temperature.

2. Combine the onions, peppers, capers, and chives and season with salt and pepper. Allow the mixture to marinate for a minimum of 30 minutes.

3. The marmalade is ready to serve now, or it may be refrigerated for later use.

Curried Onion Relish

Makes 32 fl oz/960 mL

1 lb/454 g small-dice onions

¼ tsp/0.75 g minced garlic

8 fl oz/240 mL white vinegar

6 oz/170 g sugar

salt, as needed

½ oz/14 g pickling spice, tied into a sachet

1 tbsp/6 g **Curry Powder** (page 463)

1. Combine all the ingredients in a saucepan and mix well.

2. Simmer, covered but stirring often, for 30 minutes. Be careful not to scorch. Remove the sachet.

3. The relish is ready to serve now, or it may be rapidly cooled and refrigerated for later use.

Pickled Ginger

Makes 1 lb/454 g

1 lb/454 g ginger, peeled and very thinly sliced

1½ oz/43 g sea salt

16 fl oz/480 mL rice vinegar

5½ oz/156 g sugar

8 shiso leaves, chiffonade

1. Place the ginger slices in a bowl with 1 tsp/5 g of the salt for 10 minutes. Rinse in hot water and drain well.

2. Place the vinegar, sugar, shiso, and remaining salt in a small pot and bring to a boil. Pour the vinegar mixture over the ginger and cool to room temperature. Allow the ginger to pickle overnight.

3. The ginger is ready to serve now, or it may be refrigerated for later use.

Pickled Red Onions

Makes 32 fl oz/960 mL

1 habanero

1 lb/454 g thinly sliced red onions

6 fl oz/180 mL orange juice or lime juice

salt, as needed

1. Roast the habanero under a salamander or over an open flame. Set aside, covered. When cool enough to handle, peel it, remove the seeds, and finely chop.

2. Combine the onions, juice, and half of the chopped habanero. Toss well to coat. Marinate the mixture in the refrigerator for at least 2 hours.

3. Mix the onions and season with salt and additional habanero if necessary.

4. The onions are ready to serve now, or they may be refrigerated for later use.

Pineapple Raita

Makes 32 fl oz/960 mL

16 fl oz/480 mL yogurt

16 fl oz/480 mL sour cream

1 pineapple, small dice

¾ oz/21 g mint, chiffonade

10 Thai chiles, minced (optional)

salt, as needed

ground cumin, as needed

1. Place the yogurt in a cheesecloth-lined strainer. Set the strainer in a bowl and drain at least 30 minutes in the refrigerator.

2. Add the sour cream, pineapple, mint, and chiles, if using, to the drained yogurt. Season with salt.

3. The sauce is ready to serve now, or it may be refrigerated for later use. Garnish the raita with ground cumin.

Tortilla Chips

Makes 10 servings

32 fl oz/960 mL vegetable oil, or as needed for frying

¼ tsp/0.50 g cayenne

1¼ oz/35 g salt

10 blue corn tortillas, cut in wedges

10 corn tortillas, cut in wedges

1. Heat the oil to 350° F/177° C.

2. Combine the cayenne and salt thoroughly. Reserve.

3. Fry the tortilla wedges until crisp, stirring to cook evenly.

4. Drain on paper towels. Season lightly with the cayenne salt and serve.

Marinated Mackerel in White Wine

Makes 10 servings

1 lb 8 oz/680 g mackerel, drawn, head removed

MARINADE

16 fl oz/480 mL dry white wine

1 oz/28 g carrots

2 oz/57 g thinly sliced onions

salt, as needed

ground black pepper, as needed

1 thyme sprig

4 bay leaves

3 to 4 parsley stems

1. Trim the fish and rinse it to remove all traces of blood. Drain well.

2. Combine all of the ingredients for the marinade. Bring the mixture to a boil and simmer, covered, for 15 minutes.

3. Place the mackerel in a poaching vessel. Pour the hot marinade over the fish and poach at 190°F/88°C for 8 to 10 minutes. Remove the pan from the heat. Cool the fish in the poaching liquid. Refrigerate.

4. Serve the fish chilled.

Seviche of Scallops

Makes 10 servings

1 lb 4 oz/567 g sea scallops, muscle tabs removed, thinly sliced

10 oz/284 g peeled and seeded tomatoes, small dice

6 fl oz/180 mL lemon or lime juice

3 oz/85 g red onions, cut into thin rings

2 oz/57 g green onions, cut on the bias

2 fl oz/60 mL olive oil

½ oz/14 g minced jalapeños

1 tsp/3 g mashed garlic

4 tbsp/12 g chopped cilantro

1½ tsp/7.50 g salt

¼ tsp/0.50 g ground black pepper

1. Combine all of the ingredients. Marinate the scallops in the refrigerator for at least 4 hours and up to 12 hours.

2. Serve chilled.

Carpaccio of Salmon

Makes 10 servings

1 lb 8 oz/680 g salmon fillet

10 oz/284 g thinly sliced white mushrooms

1 tbsp/6 g cracked black peppercorns

4 fl oz/120 mL olive oil

20 fl oz/600 mL **Green Mayonnaise** (page 936)

1. Slice the salmon into very thin pieces, arrange them on a plate, and cover with plastic wrap.

2. Using a spoon, spread out the salmon to the edge of the plate in a thin, even layer. Remove the plastic wrap just before serving.

3. Garnish the salmon with the mushrooms and sprinkle with pepper and oil.

4. Serve Green Mayonnaise on the side.

Smoked Salmon Platter

Makes 20 servings

1 smoked salmon fillet

3 **Hard-Cooked Eggs** (page 897), whites and yolks separated and finely chopped

3 tbsp/45 mL capers, rinsed and drained

5 oz/142 g minced red onions

8 fl oz/240 mL crème fraîche

1 tbsp/3 g chopped dill

1 baguette, cut into ¼-in/6-mm slices, toasted

1. Slice the salmon very thinly on the bias, starting from the tail.

2. Arrange the salmon on a platter and garnish with separate piles of the chopped egg whites, egg yolks, capers, and onions.

3. Combine the crème fraîche and dill. Serve the salmon with the dill crème fraîche and toasted bread.

Tuna Carpaccio (Crudo di Tonno alla Battuta)

Makes 10 servings

SALSA CRUDA

11 fl oz/330 mL extra-virgin olive oil

2¼ oz/64 g red onion brunoise

4 oz/113 g salted capers, rinsed

2½ oz/71 g thinly sliced celery hearts

2 oz/57 g picholine olives, pitted and roughly chopped

2 garlic cloves, minced

1 jalapeño, deseeded, brunoise

2 oz/57 g parsley chiffonade

2 tsp/6 g lemon zest, blanched

salt, as needed

ground black pepper, as needed

1 lb 9 oz/709 g trimmed big eye or yellowfin tuna loin

CROUTONS

16 fl oz/480 mL vegetable oil, or as needed for frying

12 oz/340 g white bread, crusts removed, brunoise

salt, as needed

ground black pepper, as needed

SALAD

4 oz/113 g frisée, white parts only

4 oz/113 g arugula

4 oz/113 g endive

½ oz/14 g celery leaves

6 radishes, julienned

4 oz/113 g fennel fronds

1 fl oz/30 mL lemon juice

2 fl oz/60 mL extra-virgin olive oil

salt, as needed

ground black pepper, as needed

30 picholine olives

1. To prepare the salsa cruda, combine the oil, onion, capers, celery, olives, garlic, jalapeño, parsley, and zest. Season with salt and pepper. Reserve.

2. With a very sharp knife, cut the tuna in 2½-oz/71-g slices. Place each slice of tuna between 2 pieces of plastic wrap and pound it paper thin, being careful not to tear through the tuna. Refrigerate.

3. To prepare the croutons, heat the oil in a sauté pan over medium-high to high heat. Pan fry the bread until golden brown. Remove and drain on paper towels. Season with salt and pepper.

4. To prepare the salad, combine the frisée, arugula, endive, celery leaves, radishes, and fennel fronds. Dress lightly with ½ fl oz/15 mL of the lemon juice and 1 fl oz/30 mL of the oil. Season with salt and pepper.

5. To assemble each serving, place a piece of pounded tuna carefully in the center of each plate. Place 1½ fl oz/45 mL of the salsa cruda on the tuna and spread evenly. Sprinkle the croutons over the tuna and place a very small amount of salad in the middle of the tuna. Place 3 olives per plate around the tuna. Garnish with salt and pepper and a drizzle of the remaining lemon juice and olive oil. Serve immediately.

Tuna Carpaccio (*Crudo di Tonno alla Battuta*)

Clams Casino

Clams Casino

Makes 10 servings

4 oz/113 g diced bacon

4 oz/113 g minced onions

3 oz/85 g minced green peppers

3 oz/85 g minced red peppers

salt, as needed

ground black pepper, as needed

1 tsp/5 mL Worcestershire sauce, or as needed

8 oz/227 g butter, soft

40 littleneck or cherrystone clams

10 bacon strips, blanched and julienned

1. In a sauté pan, render the diced bacon over medium heat until it is crisp. Add the onions and peppers and sauté until tender, about 5 minutes. Remove from the heat and let cool.

2. Season with salt, pepper, and Worcestershire sauce. Add the butter and blend until evenly mixed.

3. Scrub the clams and discard any that are open. Shuck the clams and loosen the meat from the shells. Top each clam with about ½ oz/14 g of the butter mixture and 1½ tsp/5 g of the julienned bacon. Broil the clams until the bacon is crisp and serve immediately.

Poached Scallops with Tarragon Vinaigrette

Makes 10 servings

1 lb 4 oz/567 g bay scallops

16 fl oz/480 mL white wine

16 fl oz/480 mL **Fish Stock** (page 353)

1½ oz/43 g minced shallots

TARRAGON VINAIGRETTE

4 fl oz/120 mL reduced cooking liquid from scallops

1 tsp/3 g arrowroot, or as needed

4 fl oz/120 mL extra-virgin olive oil

4 fl oz/120 mL tarragon vinegar

2 tsp/2 g chopped tarragon

salt, as needed

ground black pepper, as needed

GARNISH

10 oz/284 g blanched asparagus

5 oz/142 g peeled and seeded tomatoes, medium dice

1. Shallow poach the scallops with the wine, stock, and shallots. Keep warm while finishing the vinaigrette.

2. Reduce the cooking liquid by half, and reserve the amount required for the vinaigrette.

3. To make the vinaigrette, bring the reserved cooking liquid to a simmer. Dilute the arrowroot in cold water and add as needed to lightly thicken.

4. Add the oil, vinegar, and tarragon. Season with salt and pepper and keep warm.

5. Serve the scallops with the vinaigrette, asparagus, and tomatoes.

Coconut Macadamia Shrimp

Makes 10 servings

MARINADE

1 fl oz/30 mL hoisin sauce

1 fl oz/30 mL dry sherry

½ fl oz/15 mL rice wine vinegar

½ fl oz/15 mL soy sauce

1 tsp/3 g minced garlic

1½ tsp/7.50 g salt

¼ tsp/0.50 g ground black pepper

1 lb 12 oz/794 g shrimp (16–20 count), peeled and butterflied

BATTER

3 oz/85 g all-purpose flour

2 oz/57 g ground macadamia nuts

1¼ tsp/3.75 g baking soda

5 fl oz/150 mL coconut milk

1 egg, beaten

4½ oz/128 g all-purpose flour, for dredging

3 oz/85 g freshly grated coconut

32 fl oz/960 mL vegetable oil, or as needed

10 fl oz/300 mL **Asian Dipping Sauce** (page 990)

1. To make the marinade, mix together all the ingredients. Add the shrimp, toss to coat evenly, and marinate for 1 hour. Drain away excess marinade.

2. To make the batter, combine the flour, nuts, baking soda, coconut milk, and egg. Refrigerate until needed.

3. Dredge the shrimp in flour and dip into the batter, up to the tail. Dredge the shrimp in coconut, pressing lightly to flatten the shrimp and let the coconut adhere.

4. Refrigerate for 1 hour to allow the breading to set.

5. Heat the oil to 350°F/177°C and deep fry the shrimp until golden brown and cooked through. Drain briefly on paper towels.

6. Serve immediately with the dipping sauce.

Chesapeake-Style Crab Cakes

Makes 10 servings

10 shallots, minced

1 fl oz/30 mL vegetable oil

13 fl oz/390 mL **Mayonnaise** (page 936)

2 eggs, beaten

5 fl oz/150 mL Pommerey mustard

3 tbsp/9 g chopped parsley

2 bunches chives, minced

1¼ tsp/6.25 mL Tabasco sauce

2 oz/57 g Old Bay

2 lb 8 oz/1.13 kg blue crabmeat, picked

3¾ oz/106 g saltine cracker crumbs

salt, as needed

ground black pepper, as needed

peanut oil, as needed

16 fl oz/480 mL **Roasted Red Pepper Marmalade** (page 996)

1. Sweat the shallots in the vegetable oil until translucent. Cool.

2. Combine the shallots, mayonnaise, eggs, mustard, parsley, chives, Tabasco, and Old Bay. Fold the mayonnaise mixture into the crabmeat without shredding. Fold in the cracker crumbs. Season with salt and pepper.

3. Divide the mixture into 2-oz/57-g servings and form into small cakes 1½ in/4 cm in diameter and ¾ in/2 cm thick.

4. Sauté the crab cakes in peanut oil for 2 minutes on each side, or until golden brown and cooked through.

5. Garnish each crab cake with ½ fl oz/15 mL of the marmalade and serve immediately.

Chesapeake-Style Crab Cakes

Pescado Frito

Broiled Shrimp with Garlic

Makes 10 servings

4 oz/113 g bread crumbs

½ oz/14 g minced garlic

1 tbsp/3 g chopped parsley

1 tbsp/3 g chopped oregano

6 oz/170 g butter, melted

1½ tsp/7.50 g salt

¼ tsp/0.50 g ground black pepper

1 lb 12 oz/794 g shrimp (16–20 count), peeled and butterflied

1. Combine the bread crumbs, garlic, parsley, oregano, and 4 oz/113 g of the butter. Season with salt and pepper.

2. For each serving, arrange 2 of the shrimp on a gratin dish and brush them with some of the remaining butter.

3. Place 1 to 2 tsp/4 to 8 g of the bread crumb mixture on the shrimp and broil them under a broiler until they are very hot and cooked through. Serve immediately.

Pescado Frito

Makes 10 servings

ANCHOVIES

3 garlic cloves, crushed with salt

1 tbsp/6 g sweet pimentón or paprika

4 fl oz/120 mL white wine vinegar

2 tbsp/12 g ground cumin

1 tbsp/6 g dried oregano

3 bay leaves

1 lb/454 g fresh anchovies or smelts

12 oz/340 g all-purpose flour

CALAMARES

9 oz/255 g all-purpose flour

3 oz/85 g grated Parmesan

2 tbsp/6 g minced parsley

1 lb/454 g squid, cleaned and cut into rings

salt, as needed

ground black pepper, as needed

FLOUNDER FILLETS

1 lb/454 g flounder fillets, cut on the diagonal into ½-in/1-cm-long strips

salt, as needed

ground black pepper, as needed

4 tbsp/12 g minced parsley

8 oz/227 g fresh bread crumbs

9 oz/255 g all-purpose flour

8 eggs

32 fl oz/960 mL olive oil

1 tsp/2 g red pepper flakes

20 fl oz/600 mL **Tomato Sauce** (page 384)

salt, as needed

1. Combine the garlic, pimentón, vinegar, cumin, oregano, and bay leaves. Add 16 fl oz/480 mL of cold water and mix well. Add the anchovies and carefully mix with the marinade. Marinate the anchovies in the refrigerator for at least 3 hours.

2. Remove the anchovies from the marinade, drain, and open them up like a book. Lay them flat in flour, and gently press them in the flour on both sides.

3. For the calamares, combine the flour, Parmesan, and parsley. Season the squid with salt and pepper and dredge in the flour mixture. Allow the squid to rest for 10 minutes.

4. Season the flounder with salt and pepper. Combine the parsley and bread crumbs. Bread the flounder using the standard breading procedure (see page 458). Allow the flounder to rest for 10 minutes.

5. Heat the oil to 375°F/191°C. Combine the pepper flakes and tomato sauce and reserve.

6. Working in batches, deep fry the anchovies, squid, and flounder until golden brown, 2 to 3 minutes. Drain the fried fish on absorbent paper towels to remove excess oil. Season with salt and serve immediately with the tomato sauce.

Oysters Diamond Jim Brady

Makes 10 servings

40 oysters

20 fl oz/600 mL **Royal Glaçage** (page 623)

2 oz/57 g butter

2 oz/57 g minced shallots

4 oz/113 g peeled and seeded tomatoes, medium dice

1 fl oz/30 mL crème fraîche

½ fl oz/15 mL Pernod

salt, as needed

ground black pepper, as needed

1. Rinse the oysters and discard any that are open. Shuck the oysters. Reserve the oyster liquor and stir it into the glaçage.

2. Heat the butter; add the shallots and sauté them until they are tender. Add the tomatoes and sauté until the liquid is reduced. Add the crème fraîche to bind the mixture. Add the Pernod and season with salt and pepper.

3. Place about ½ tsp/2.5 mL of the tomato mixture in the deep half of each oyster shell. Top it with an oyster and coat it with the glaçage.

4. Pass the oysters under a broiler. The edges of the oysters should be lightly curled when properly cooked. Serve immediately.

Mussels with White Wine and Shallots (Moules à la Marinière)

Makes 10 servings

4 lb/1.81 kg mussels

4 oz/113 g butter

3 shallots, minced

4 fl oz/120 mL dry white wine

1 tsp/1 g chopped thyme

salt, as needed

ground black pepper, as needed

1 tbsp/3 g chopped parsley

1. Scrub and debeard the mussels. Discard any that are open.

2. Melt 1 oz/28 g of the butter in a large skillet or saucepan over medium-high heat. Add the shallots and cook until translucent, 1 to 2 minutes.

3. Add the wine and thyme and season with salt and pepper. Allow the mixture to simmer for 2 to 3 minutes. Add the mussels, cover, and cook over high heat, shaking the pan often so that all of the mussels open at about the same time, 2 to 3 minutes. Take off the cover, remove the mussels as they open, and transfer them to a warm serving platter. When all of the mussels have opened, empty the pan and strain the cooking broth through a fine sieve.

4. Wipe out the pan and return the broth to it. Bring the liquid to a boil and cook briefly over high heat, about 1 minute, or until slightly syrupy. Remove the saucepan from the heat and whisk the remaining butter into the broth, a little at a time.

5. Adjust seasoning with salt and pepper, if necessary. Pour the broth over the mussels, garnish with the parsley, and serve immediately.

Mussels with White Wine and Shallots (*Moules à la Marinière*)

Hot Smoked Bluefish with Horseradish Cream

Makes 10 servings

2 lb 8 oz/1.13 kg bluefish fillets, cut into 4-oz/113-g servings

1¼ oz/35 g salt

½ tsp/1 g ground black pepper

lemon juice, as needed

1 fl oz/30 mL vegetable oil

HORSERADISH CREAM

1 fl oz/30 mL lemon juice

¾ oz/21 g grated horseradish, or as needed

1 tbsp/3 g chopped dill

10 fl oz/300 mL heavy cream, whipped to soft peaks

salt, as needed

ground black pepper, as needed

1. Season the bluefish generously with salt, pepper, and lemon juice. Place the fish on a rack in a pan set up for smoking. Hot-smoke the fish with high heat for 3 to 5 minutes. Let it cool in the pan.

2. When the fish is cold, rub it with the oil.

3. To make the horseradish cream, fold the lemon juice, horseradish, and dill into the whipped cream. Season with salt and pepper.

4. Serve the bluefish with the horseradish cream.

Tuna and Bean Salad (Insalata di Tonno e Fagioli)

Makes 10 servings

1 lb 8 oz/680 g white beans, soaked overnight

1 lb 4 oz/567 g thinly sliced red onions, soaked in cold water for 1 hour

1 lb 6 oz/624 g imported packed tuna

1 fl oz/30 mL red wine vinegar, or as needed

4½ fl oz/135 mL extra-virgin olive oil

salt, as needed

ground black pepper, as needed

1. Cook the beans in plenty of water over medium-low heat until tender, about 45 minutes. Drain and rinse under cold water.

2. In a large bowl, combine the beans, onions, tuna, vinegar, and oil. Season with salt and pepper and toss gently to combine.

3. Adjust seasoning with vinegar, salt, and pepper, if necessary.

4. The salad is ready to serve now, or it may be refrigerated for later use.

Stuffed Shrimp

Makes 10 servings

1 oz/28 g butter, melted

2 oz/57 g bread crumbs

CRAB STUFFING

1 oz/28 g minced onions

1½ oz/43 g minced green onions

1½ oz/43 g butter

1½ oz/43 g all-purpose flour

2½ fl oz/75 mL white wine

7 oz/198 g crabmeat, picked to remove cartilage

3 fl oz/90 mL heavy cream

salt, as needed

ground black pepper, as needed

1 fl oz/30 mL lemon juice, or as needed

1 lb 12 oz/794 g shrimp (16–20 count), peeled and butterflied

1. Combine the melted butter and bread crumbs and set aside.

2. Sauté the onions and green onions in the butter until tender. Add the flour and cook for 2 to 3 minutes. Add the wine, crabmeat, and cream and bring to a boil, stirring constantly. Cook for 5 minutes. The stuffing should be very thick. If not, simmer it longer to thicken. Season with salt, pepper, and lemon juice. Refrigerate.

3. Stuff the shrimp with the crabmeat mixture and sprinkle with the buttered bread crumbs.

4. Bake in a 420°F/216°C oven until hot and browned. Serve immediately.

Samosas

Makes 10 servings

DOUGH

12 oz/340 g all-purpose flour

1½ fl oz/45 mL vegetable oil

½ tsp/2.50 g salt

6 fl oz/180 mL water, warm

FILLING

8 oz/227 g small-dice onions

1½ oz/43 g butter

1 tbsp/9 g minced ginger

2 tsp/6 g minced garlic

2 tsp/6 g minced serranos

¾ tsp/1.50 g crushed coriander

2 tsp/4 g **Curry Powder** (page 463)

½ fl oz/15 mL tomato paste

½ fl oz/15 mL lemon juice

1 lb/454 g fine-dice shrimp

8 fl oz/240 mL **Fish Stock** (page 353)

Egg Wash (page 1061), as needed

32 fl oz/960 mL vegetable oil, or as needed

1. Mix all the ingredients for the dough until smooth. Let rest for 1 hour in the refrigerator.

2. To make the filling, sauté the onions in the butter until translucent. Add the ginger, garlic, serranos, coriander, and curry powder and sauté until the aroma is strong. Add the tomato paste, lemon juice, and shrimp. Sauté for 2 minutes without browning. Add the stock and simmer until almost all the liquid has evaporated. Transfer the filling to a bowl and refrigerate.

3. Roll the dough out in a pasta machine until very thin. Cut into strips 8 by 2 in/20 by 5 cm long.

4. Place a small amount of filling on the end of a strip of dough and fold up into a triangle as you would a flag. Seal the end with egg wash.

5. Heat the oil to 375°F/191°C. Deep fry the samosas until golden brown. Drain on absorbent paper toweling and serve while still very hot.

Spinach Crêpes with Seafood

Makes 10 servings

SPINACH CRÊPES

10 oz/284 g all-purpose flour

1½ tsp/7.50 g salt

½ tsp/1 g ground black pepper

10 oz/284 g spinach leaves, puréed

32 fl oz/960 mL milk

10 eggs, beaten

2 tsp/10 mL vegetable oil

SEAFOOD FILLING

1 tbsp/9 g minced shallots

5 oz/142 g minced mushrooms

4 oz/113 g butter

1 lb/454 g small-dice shrimp

10 oz/284 g lump crabmeat, picked

10 oz/284 g diced bay scallops

16 fl oz/480 mL **Béchamel Sauce** (page 384) or **Fish Velouté** (page 383)

5 oz/142 g red pepper brunoise (peel before cutting)

1½ tsp/7.50 g salt

½ tsp/1 g ground black pepper

½ tsp/1 g Old Bay

20 fl oz/600 mL **Mousseline Sauce** (page 386)

1. To make the crêpes, combine the flour, salt, and pepper in a large bowl. Mix the spinach, milk, and eggs together and add to the flour. Mix well until smooth.

2. Heat and oil a crêpe pan. When each crêpe browns, turn and cook the other side briefly. Stack the finished crêpes on a plate, separated with parchment paper.

3. To prepare the filling, sauté the shallots and mushrooms in the butter. Add the shrimp, crabmeat, and scallops and sauté until cooked. Add the béchamel or velouté and red pepper and bring to a simmer, reducing if necessary. Season with salt, pepper, and Old Bay. Transfer to a bowl and refrigerate.

4. Stuff and roll the crêpes, place on a sheet pan, and heat in a 350°F/177°C oven until the filling is hot.

5. Coat the crêpes with Mousseline Sauce and brown lightly under a salamander or broiler. Serve at once.

Baby Squid in Black Ink Sauce (Txipirones Saltsa Beltzean)

Makes 10 servings

20 baby squid

5 fl oz/150 mL olive oil

4 oz/113 g minced onions

4 oz/113 g minced green peppers

4 oz/113 g minced Serrano ham

2 oz/57 g bread crumbs

salt, as needed

ground black pepper, as needed

BLACK INK SAUCE

8 oz/227 g minced onions

8 oz/227 g minced green peppers

3 garlic cloves, minced

4 fl oz/120 mL tomato purée

8 fl oz/ 240 mL white wine

4 fl oz/120 mL squid ink

1. Clean the squid. Remove the tentacles and cut them into small pieces.

2. Heat 2 fl oz/60 mL of the oil over high heat. Add the tentacles and sauté briefly. Remove the tentacles from the pan with the released juices and reserve separately.

3. In the same pan, over medium heat, heat 1 fl oz/30 mL of the oil, add the onions and peppers, and cook slowly until caramelized, about 5 minutes. Add the ham and cook for 2 minutes more. Mix in the reserved tentacles and the bread crumbs. Season with salt and pepper. Remove the filling from the pan and let it rest until cool enough to handle.

4. Stuff each squid with the filling and secure it with a toothpick.

5. Heat the remaining 2 fl oz/60 mL of oil in a large sauté pan over medium-high heat. Sear the stuffed squid, about 2 minutes on each side. Remove the squid from the pan and reserve.

6. To the pan, add the onions, peppers, and garlic, and sauté until caramelized, about 5 minutes. Add the tomato purée and cook until rust colored.

7. Deglaze with the wine and reduce by half. Add the reserve juices from the sautéed tentacles and the squid ink to the sauce. Purée the sauce in a blender until smooth. Adjust seasoning with salt and pepper, if necessary.

8. Combine the squid with the sauce and simmer over very low heat for about 20 minutes, until it is tender and the sauce has slightly reduced. Serve immediately.

Octopus "Fairground Style" (Pulpo a Feira)

Makes 10 servings

2 onions, roughly chopped

1 bay leaf

2 tsp/10 g salt

4 lb/1.81 kg octopus

1 oz/28 g pimentón or paprika

8 fl oz/240 mL extra-virgin olive oil

1. Bring a large stockpot of water to a boil with the onions, bay leaf, and 1½ tsp/7.50 g of the salt.

2. Plunge the octopus tentacles in and out of the water for 5 second increments, 3 times.

3. Place the entire octopus back in the water and simmer for 90 minutes, or until the octopus is tender.

4. Remove the octopus and reserve the liquid. Allow the octopus to sit until it is cool enough to handle. Cut it into 1-in/3-cm pieces.

5. For each serving to order, submerge the octopus pieces in the reserved water for 30 seconds to reheat. Plate and sprinkle with the pimentón and salt. Drizzle with oil and serve immediately.

Grilled Shrimp Paste on Sugarcane (Chao Tom)

Makes 10 servings

2 oz/57 g pork fat

½ fl oz/15 mL peanut oil

2 shallots, minced

12 oz/340 g shrimp (31–35 count), peeled and deveined, roughly chopped

2 tsp/10 mL fish sauce

½ oz/14 g sugar

1 tsp/3 g minced garlic

1 egg

¼ tsp/0.50 g ground white pepper

½ oz/14 g cornstarch

1½ tsp/4.50 g baking powder

2 green onions, thinly sliced

10 sugarcanes, fresh or canned, cut into 4-in/10-cm lengths, no greater than ½ in/1 cm wide

5 fl oz/150 mL **Green Onion Oil** (page 939)

1. Boil the pork fat for about 10 minutes. Drain and mince. Meanwhile, heat the peanut oil over medium-high heat and sauté the shallots until translucent. Combine the pork fat and the shallots in a bowl and cool them to room temperature.

2. Add the shrimp, fish sauce, sugar, garlic, egg, pepper, cornstarch, and baking powder. Mix well to evenly coat the shrimp with the other ingredients. Transfer the mixture to the bowl of a food processor fitted with the blade attachment.

3. Pulse until the mixture is a smooth paste. Do not overmix or it will become tough. Scrape the work bowl clean and transfer to a mixing bowl. Stir in the green onions.

4. Test the mixture by pan steaming a 1-oz/28-g patty. Adjust seasoning if necessary before proceeding.

5. With wet hands, take about 1 oz/28 g of the shrimp paste and form it into a ball. Flatten the paste and place a sugarcane on top. Wrap the paste around the cane, leav-ing about ½ in/1 cm on each end for handles. Press the paste against the cane so that it will adhere (the paste should be about ½ in/1 cm thick).

6. With oiled hands, smooth the surface of the paste. Set aside on an oiled plate. Repeat the process with the remaining ingredients.

7. Steam the shrimp paste for 2 to 5 minutes. Reserve until service.

8. Preheat the grill or broiler to 400°F/204°C. Grill the shrimp paste until the outside is lightly browned, 2 to 3 minutes on each side. Brush with Green Onion Oil and serve immediately.

Mushroom Strudel with Goat Cheese

Makes 10 servings

4 fl oz/120 mL olive oil

8 lb/3.63 kg mushrooms, sliced ¼ in/6 mm thick

2½ oz/71 g finely chopped shallots

1¼ oz/35 g finely chopped garlic

8 fl oz/240 mL dry sherry

12 oz/340 g goat cheese, at room temperature

½ oz/14 g chopped chives

2 tbsp/6 g chopped thyme

2 tsp/10 g salt

1 tsp/2 g ground black pepper

20 (11 by 16-in/28 by 41-cm) phyllo dough sheets

8 oz/227 g butter, melted

14 fl oz/420 mL **Madeira Sauce** (page 544)

2 fl oz/60 mL sour cream

1. Heat ½ fl oz/15 mL of the oil over medium-high heat in a large sauté pan. In batches, sauté the mushrooms until they are golden brown. Drain any liquid that accumulates in the pan. Remove the mushrooms and set aside.

2. In the same pan, sauté the shallots and garlic until the shallots are lightly browned, about 5 minutes. Add the sautéed mushrooms back to the pan.

3. Reduce the heat to medium-low and deglaze the pan with the sherry. Cook until the liquid reduces and becomes slightly syrupy. Remove the pan from the heat and allow it to cool to room temperature.

4. Stir in the goat cheese, chives, and thyme. Season with salt and pepper.

5. For each strudel, brush 1 sheet of phyllo dough with butter. (Keep the remaining phyllo covered with plastic wrap and a damp cloth to prevent the sheets from drying.) Repeat the process to create a total of 5 layers.

6. Spread ¼ of the mushroom-cheese filling over the top sheet of phyllo, leaving a 1-in/3-cm space around the edges of the dough. Roll tightly, folding in the edges, to form a log. Place seam side down onto a half sheet pan. Repeat the process to form a total of 4 strudels.

7. Bake at 375°F/191°C for 30 to 35 minutes, or until golden brown and crisp. Slice into 10 servings and serve with the sauce and sour cream.

Black Bean Cakes

Makes 10 servings

14 oz/397 g black beans

96 fl oz/2.88 L **Vegetable Stock** (page 353) **or water**

1 fl oz/30 mL vegetable oil

3 oz/85 g minced onions

½ oz/14 g minced jalapeños

1 tbsp/9 g minced garlic

¾ tsp/1.50 g **Chili Powder** (page 463)

¾ tsp/1.50 g ground cumin

¾ tsp/1.50 g ground cardamom

1 tsp/1 g minced cilantro

1 tsp/5 mL lime juice

1 egg white

1 tbsp/15 g salt

½ tsp/1 g ground black pepper

4 oz/113 g cornmeal

1½ oz/43 g butter

5 oz/142 g sour cream

8 oz/227 g **Pico de Gallo** (page 988)

1. Cook the beans in simmering stock until tender, letting the stock reduce at the end of cooking.

2. Purée ⅔ of the beans and recombine with the whole beans.

3. Heat the oil in a sauté pan over medium heat. Add the onions and jalapeños and cook until tender and a light blond color, 8 to 10 minutes. Add the garlic, spices, and cilantro and sauté until aromatic, about 3 minutes. Add this to the bean mixture.

4. Add the lime juice and egg white to the beans and stir until blended. Season with salt and pepper, if necessary. Form into 2-oz/57-g patties.

5. Dust the patties in the cornmeal. Heat the butter in a sauté pan over medium-high heat. Add the patties and sauté on both sides until the exterior is crisp and the cake is very hot, about 3 minutes per side.

6. Remove the cakes from the pan, blot briefly on absorbent toweling, and arrange on heated plates. Serve at once, garnished with the sour cream and Pico de Gallo.

Potato Omelet (Tortilla Española)

Makes 10 servings

7 fl oz/210 mL olive oil

9 oz/255 g small-dice onions

4 oz/113 g small-dice green peppers

1 lb 11 oz/765 g medium-dice russet potatoes

salt, as needed

ground black pepper, as needed

14 eggs

1. Heat a large sauté pan or rondeau over medium heat with 3 fl oz/90 mL of the oil. Add the onions and peppers and cook, stirring frequently for about 5 minutes until both are tender and the onions are transparent.

2. Add the potatoes and season with salt and pepper. Cover and cook over medium-low to low heat until the potatoes are tender, about 15 minutes.

3. In a large bowl, whisk the eggs until smooth. Add the cooked potato mixture.

4. Heat a very large sauté pan over medium-high heat. Add 2 fl oz/60 mL of the oil to the pan and heat until close to smoking. Add half of the egg and potato mixture and lower the heat to medium-low. Cook for 3 minutes, until the eggs coagulate and begin to turn golden on the bottom. Flip the tortilla and cook for another 2 to 3 minutes until the same golden brown color is present on the underside of the tortilla and it feels firm. Repeat with the remaining oil and egg mixture.

5. Slice the tortillas into wedges and serve immediately or at room temperature.

Spring Rolls

Makes 10 servings

½ fl oz/15 mL vegetable oil

1 tsp/3 g minced ginger

½ oz/14 g thinly sliced green onions

8 oz/227 g ground pork butt

1 tbsp/7 g black mushrooms, rehydrated in warm water

8 oz/227 g napa cabbage chiffonade

8 oz/227 g bean sprouts

2 oz/57 g thinly sliced shiitake mushrooms

½ oz/14 g green onion julienne (green parts only)

1½ tsp/7.50 mL dark soy sauce

1½ tsp/7.50 mL rice wine

1½ tsp/7.50 mL sesame oil

1½ tsp/7.50 g sugar

1 tsp/5 g salt

½ tsp/1 g ground white pepper

1 tbsp/9 g cornstarch, dissolved in ½ fl oz/15 mL of water to make a slurry

10 spring roll sheets

Egg Wash (page 1061), as needed

32 fl oz/960 mL vegetable oil, or as needed

20 fl oz/600 mL **Spring Roll Dipping Sauce** (page 991)

5 fl oz/150 mL **Spicy Mustard** (page 995)

1. Heat the vegetable oil in a wok over medium-high heat. Add the ginger and green onions and stir-fry until aromatic, 30 seconds to 1 minute.

2. Add the pork and stir-fry until cooked through, 6 to 8 minutes.

3. Add the black mushrooms and stir-fry for about 2 minutes more.

4. Add the cabbage, bean sprouts, shiitakes, and green onions. Stir-fry until all the vegetables are tender, 5 to 6 minutes.

5. Add the soy sauce, wine, sesame oil, sugar, salt, and pepper. Mix them together, then push the solid ingredients to the side of the wok. Thicken the excess liquid in the bottom of the wok with the slurry.

6. Stir all the contents of the wok several times to ensure that the solids are coated with the thickened liquid. Remove from the heat and cool.

7. Place 3 to 4 tbsp/55 to 75 g of filling on each spring roll sheet with a slotted spoon (being careful to drain any excess liquid from filling), leaving a 2-in/5-cm border at each end. Brush the edges of each sheet with egg wash. Fold the corners of the long side over the filling, and roll the filling up in the wrapper, sealing the roll with more egg wash if necessary.

8. Place the finished rolls onto a parchment-lined sheet pan dusted with cornstarch until ready to fry.

9. Deep fry the rolls in the oil at 350°F/177°C until golden brown, about 2 minutes. Drain on absorbent paper toweling. Serve immediately with the dipping sauce and Spicy Mustard.

California Rolls

Makes 10 rolls

½ sheet (3½ x 9 in/9 x 23 cm) nori (seaweed)

1 fl oz/ 30 mL rice vinegar

16 fl oz/ 480 mL water

4 lb 1 oz/1.84 kg **Sushi Rice** (recipe follows)

1¼ oz/35 g sesame seeds, toasted

1 English cucumber (15 oz/445 g), peeled, cored, cut into sticks 5 in/13 cm long by ⅛ in/3 mm thick

1 avocado (7 oz/198 g), seeded, peeled, cut into slices ⅛ in/3 mm thick

7 to 8 oz/198 to 227 g surimi (imitation crab meat), split in half lengthwise

pickled ginger slices, as needed

wasabi, as needed

1. Prepare the bamboo mat by wrapping it tightly and cleanly in plastic wrap.

2. Fold a piece of nori in half lengthwise and cut along the fold. Make sure the ripples are parallel to the fold. Lay the nori on the mat at the edge closest to you.

3. Combine the rice vinegar and water. Dip your hands in the vinegar and water mixture and scoop out 6½ oz/184 g

(generous 2½ cups/600 mL) of sushi rice and spread in an even layer over the nori. If necessary, dip your hands in the vinegar and water mixture again to prevent the rice from sticking as you work.

4. Sprinkle 1 tsp/5 mL of sesame seeds on the rice and then flip the roll so that the long edge of the nori is facing you. Lay 6 sticks of cucumber, 2 slices of avocado, and 2 half sticks of surimi across the length of the roll a third of the way in from the edge closest to you. Some of the garnish should be sticking out either end.

5. Bring the edge of the mat closest to you up and over the garnish. Continue to roll tucking in and tightening the roll as you go. Gently roll the roll between your palms and the work surface. Slice into 6 even pieces. Serve immediately with a garnish of pickled ginger slices and a mound of wasabi.

Sushi Rice

Makes 5 lb/2.27 kg

3 lb 2 oz/1.42 kg short-grain rice

64 fl oz/1.92 L water

6 fl oz/180 mL rice vinegar, unseasoned

2½ oz/71 g sugar

2 tbsp/30 g kosher salt

1. Rinse the rice thoroughly (at least three times) until the rinse water is mostly clear.

2. Combine the rice and water in a pot and bring to a boil over medium heat. Cover the pot and reduce the heat to a simmer and cook until tender, about 35 minutes.

3. Spread the cooked rice out into a hotel pan, cover, and cool to room temperature.

4. While the rice is cooling, combine the vinegar, sugar, and salt in a small sauté pan and bring to a simmer over medium heat. Do not boil the mixture. Cook until the salt and sugar have completely dissolved, about 4 minutes. Cool the mixture to room temperature.

5. Once the rice and vinegar mixture has cooled, pour the vinegar over the rice and cut and toss the rice with a wooden paddle or spoon until the vinegar is thoroughly dispersed and the rice takes on a glossy sheen.

Vietnamese Salad Rolls

Makes 10 servings

5 oz/142 g fine-julienne carrots

2 tsp/10 g salt

5 oz/142 g rice noodles, cooked, shocked, and drained

1½ fl oz/45 mL lime juice

3 tbsp/9 g cilantro

3 tbsp/9 g mint

3 tbsp/9 g Thai basil

1 oz/28 g sugar

32 fl oz/960 mL water, warm

10 (6½ in/17 cm) rice paper rounds

10 green leaf lettuce leaves

10 poached shrimp (30–35 count), peeled and sliced in half lengthwise

10 fl oz/300 mL **Vietnamese Dipping Sauce** (page 991)

1. Combine the carrots and salt and let them sit for 10 minutes. Squeeze the carrots and discard any juices. Combine the carrots with the noodles, lime juice, and herbs.

2. Combine the sugar and water. Place the rice paper in the water briefly to soften. Remove the rice paper from the water and blot dry.

3. For each roll, place 1 lettuce leaf on a softened rice paper. Top with 1 oz/28 g of the noodle mixture and 1 shrimp (2 halves). Fold the paper around the filling, and roll into a cylinder.

4. Cut the rolls in half and serve immediately with Vietnamese Dipping Sauce.

Beef Carpaccio

Makes 10 servings

1½ fl oz/45 mL vegetable oil

2 lb 8 oz/1.13 kg beef sirloin, trimmed and tied

HERB RUB

1 fl oz/30 mL olive oil

1 tbsp/3 g chopped rosemary

1 tbsp/3 g chopped sage

1 tbsp/3 g chopped thyme

1 tbsp/6 g ground white pepper

½ fl oz/15 mL balsamic vinegar

14 oz/397 g salt

GARNISH

extra-virgin olive oil, as needed

grated or shaved Parmesan, as needed

20 to 30 cured black olives

2 tbsp/30 mL capers, rinsed

½ tsp/1 g ground black pepper

1. Heat 1 fl oz/30 mL of the vegetable oil in a sauté pan over medium-high heat. Add the beef and sear on all sides just until colored. Remove it from the pan and set on a large piece of plastic wrap.

2. Mix together all the ingredients for the herb rub and press and rub it into the beef, then wrap the beef securely in plastic wrap. Refrigerate until ready to slice and serve. Before service time, place the wrapped meat in the freezer for 1 hour to facilitate slicing.

3. Slice the beef very thinly on an electric slicer. Place the slices of carpaccio on a chilled plate. Rub a few drops of vegetable oil on the beef and cover with plastic. Starting from the center with a spoon, lightly push toward the outside to flatten the meat. Remove the plastic before serving the carpaccio.

4. Drizzle the carpaccio with a few drops of the olive oil and garnish with grated Parmesan, olives, capers, and pepper. Serve immediately.

Beef Satay with Peanut Sauce

Makes 10 servings

MARINADE

1½ tsp/4.50 g minced lemongrass

1 tsp/3 g minced ginger

1 tsp/3 g minced garlic

½ tsp/2.50 mL Thai chile paste

1 tsp/3 g **Curry Powder** (page 463)

1 tbsp/15 g palm sugar

1 fl oz/30 mL fish sauce

1 lb/454 g flank steak, cut 1 by 4 by ⅛ in/3 by 10 cm by 3 mm

PEANUT SAUCE

½ fl oz/15 mL peanut oil

1 tsp/3 g minced garlic

1 tbsp/9 g minced shallots

1 tsp/5 mL Thai chile paste

½ tsp/1.50 g minced lime zest

¼ tsp/0.75 g **Curry Powder** (page 463)

1½ tsp/4.50 g minced lemongrass

3 fl oz/90 mL coconut milk

½ tsp/2.50 mL tamarind pulp

½ fl oz/15 mL fish sauce

1 tbsp/15 g palm sugar

1½ tsp/7.50 mL lime juice

3 oz/85 g peanuts, roasted and cooled, ground into a paste

salt, as needed

ground black pepper, as needed

1. Combine all the ingredients for the marinade. Marinate the meat for 1 hour in the refrigerator.

2. To prepare the peanut sauce, heat the oil in a sauté pan over medium-high heat. Add the garlic, shallots, chile paste, lime zest, curry powder, and lemongrass. Stir-fry until aromatic.

3. Add the coconut milk, tamarind, fish sauce, sugar, lime juice, and peanut paste. Simmer the sauce for 15 to 20 minutes. Season with salt and pepper. Cool to room temperature.

4. Thread the beef on 6-in/15-cm bamboo skewers that have been soaked in hot water for 1 hour. Preheat the grill to 400°F/204°C. Allow any excess marinade to drain from the beef before grilling; blot if necessary. Grill the beef for 30 seconds to 1 minute on each side.

5. Serve immediately with the peanut sauce.

Vitello Tonnato

Makes 10 servings

1 lb 8 oz/680 g boneless leg of veal, tied and roasted

6 oz/170 g albacore tuna (canned), drained

4 anchovy fillets

1½ oz/43 g finely diced onions

1½ oz/43 g finely diced carrots

4 fl oz/120 mL dry white wine

2 fl oz/60 mL white wine vinegar

2 fl oz/60 mL water

1 fl oz/30 mL olive oil

2 **Hard-Cooked Eggs** (page 897; yolks only), **sieved**

1 tbsp/15 mL capers, drained and chopped

1. Slice the veal thinly, about 2 oz/57 g per serving.

2. Combine the tuna, anchovy fillets, onions, carrots, wine, vinegar, and water in a food processor. Process to a relatively smooth paste.

3. Arrange the sliced veal on chilled plates. Nappé it with the tuna sauce and drizzle with oil.

4. Garnish the veal with the egg yolks and capers and serve immediately.

Lobster Salad with Beets, Mangos, Avocados, and Orange Oil

Makes 10 servings

5 (1 lb 8 oz/680 g) live lobsters

3 to 4 red beets, cooked and peeled

3 to 4 ripe mangos

3 to 4 ripe avocados

salt, as needed

ground black pepper, as needed

10 fl oz/300 mL **Orange Oil** (page 939)

5 oz/142 g peeled and seeded tomatoes, small dice

1. Cook the lobsters by boiling or steaming until they are cooked through, 10 to 12 minutes. Remove them from the pot and cool. Remove the meat from the tail and claw sections (see pages 499–500 for more information on working with lobsters). Slice the tail sections in half lengthwise. Remove the vein from each tail section. Reserve the claw and tail meat.

2. Slice the beets about ½ in/1 cm thick. Use a round cutter to shape into circles, if desired.

3. Peel the mangos and avocados as close to service time as possible. Slice them about ½ in/1 cm thick.

4. Arrange the beets, avocados, and mangos on chilled plates and season with salt and pepper. Top with the lobster (½ tail and 1 claw section per salad). Drizzle a few drops of oil over the salad.

5. Garnish with the diced tomato. Brush the lobster with additional oil and serve immediately.

Pork and Pepper Pie (Empanada Gallega de Cerdo)

Makes 10 servings

DOUGH

1 lb 8 oz/680 g all-purpose flour

1 fl oz/30 mL white wine

1 fl oz/30 mL olive oil

1 fl oz/30 mL clarified butter

¼ tsp/1.25 g salt

¾ oz/21 g sugar

10 fl oz/300 mL water, lukewarm

FILLING

1½ fl oz/45 mL olive oil

1 lb/454 g boneless pork loin, cut into strips

10 oz/284 g small-dice onions

9 oz/255 g small-dice green peppers

2 garlic cloves, minced

1½ tsp/25 g tomato paste

3¼ oz/92 g Serrano ham, thinly sliced

¾ tsp/1.50 g sweet Spanish paprika, or as needed

¼ tsp/1.25 g salt

1 egg yolk, mixed with ½ fl oz/15 mL water

1. Sift the flour and make a well in the center. Add the wine, oil, butter, salt, sugar, and water. Mix these ingredients by pulling the flour into the wet ingredients with a fork. When a loose dough forms, knead for about 2 minutes, making a flexible dough. Refrigerate for about 30 minutes.

2. While the dough is resting, prepare the filling. Heat the oil in a sauté pan over medium heat. Add the pork and sauté until browned, about 4 minutes. Remove the pork and reserve.

3. Add the onions and peppers to the pan and cook until they begin to caramelize, about 4 minutes. Add the garlic cook for 2 minutes.

4. Add the tomato paste, stirring to incorporate. Add the ham and the reserved pork and season with the paprika and salt. Remove from the heat and set aside.

5. Divide the dough in 2 pieces. Roll each piece of dough ¼ in/6 mm thick. Line a 9-in/23-cm pie pan with 1 piece of dough. Place the filling in the pan and cover with the other piece of dough, sealing the edges with your fingers.

6. Brush the top of the pie with egg yolk and water and bake in a 350°F/177°C oven for 30 minutes, or until browned. If the top begins to become too brown, cover loosely with foil. Remove the pie from the oven and serve.

Paper-Wrapped Chicken

Makes 10 servings

STUFFING

12 oz/340 g cooked, shredded chicken breast

1 oz/28 g minced green onions

¾ tsp/3.75 g sugar

¾ tsp/3.75 mL sherry

½ fl oz/15 mL soy sauce

½ fl oz/15 mL sesame oil

¼ tsp/1.25 g salt

¼ tsp/0.50 g ground white pepper

1 egg

20 (4 by 4 in/10 by 10 cm square) rice paper sheets

32 fl oz/960 mL vegetable oil

1. Combine all ingredients for the stuffing; mix together.

2. Soak a few pieces of rice paper at a time in room temperature water to soften. Place 1 tbsp/15 mL of filling on each piece of rice paper, roll in the traditional egg roll shape and seal, or fold into a triangle.

3. Heat the oil to 350°F/177°C and deep fry the packets until golden brown. Drain on absorbent paper toweling. Serve immediately.

Corn Crêpes with Asparagus Tips and Smoked Salmon

Makes 10 servings

CORN CRÊPES

8 oz/227 g fresh or frozen corn kernels

4 oz/113 g all-purpose flour

4 eggs

8 fl oz/240 mL milk

4 fl oz/120 mL water

1½ tsp/7.50 g salt

½ tsp/1 g ground black pepper

vegetable oil, as needed

CORN SALAD

1 lb 8 oz/680 g fresh or frozen corn kernels

2 oz/57 g diced red peppers

2 oz/57 g diced green peppers

8 fl oz/240 mL **White Wine Vinaigrette** (page 929)

2 tsp/2 g chopped cilantro

2 tsp/2 g chopped parsley

10 oz/284 g smoked salmon slices

1 lb 4 oz/567 g cooked asparagus spears

16 fl oz/480 mL **Hollandaise Sauce** (page 386)

2 tbsp/6 g minced chives

1. To make the crêpes, mix all the ingredients together to form a batter, adjusting the consistency with more liquid or flour, as necessary.

2. Cook each crêpe in a heated and oiled crêpe pan. Turn and cook on the second side, then remove to a plate. Stack the crêpes with parchment paper between each one to keep separate.

3. To make the corn salad, combine all the ingredients and let the flavors marry for 1 hour.

4. Cut a slit in each crêpe, roll it into a cornucopia, and fill with the salad.

5. Arrange the crêpes, salmon, and asparagus on a platter. Warm them in the oven for 1 to 2 minutes. Combine the hollandaise and chives.

6. Garnish with the hollandaise and serve immediately.

Chapter Thirty-three

Charcuterie and Garde Manger

Charcuterie, strictly speaking, refers to certain foods made from the pig, including sausage, smoked ham, bacon, head cheese, pâtés, and terrines. Garde manger, traditionally referred to as the kitchen's pantry or larder section, is where foods are kept cold during extended storage and while being prepared as a cold plate.

Forcemeats

Forcemeat, a basic component of such charcuterie and garde manger preparations as pâtés and terrines, is prepared by grinding lean meats together with fat and seasonings to form an emulsion.

There are four types of forcemeat. A mousseline-style forcemeat consists of delicate meats such as salmon or chicken combined with cream and eggs. A straight forcemeat calls for lean meats to be ground together with fatback. Country-style forcemeats have a coarser texture than other forcemeats and usually contain liver. Gratin forcemeats are similar to straight forcemeats with the following difference: A portion of the meat is seared and then cooled before it is ground together with the other ingredients.

Once puréed or ground together, forcemeats are mixed long enough to develop a uniform and sliceable texture. All four forcemeat styles have a number of applications in the professional kitchen: to prepare appetizers, to use as stuffings, or to produce garde manger specialty items, including pâtés, terrines, and galantines.

All necessary ingredients and equipment used in preparing forcemeat must be scrupulously clean and well chilled at all times so that the lean meat and fats can combine properly. Refrigerate ingredients until they are ready to be used and hold them over a container of ice to keep the temperature low during actual preparation. Equipment can be chilled in ice water.

Forcemeats have three basic components. The main, or dominant, meat provides the forcemeat's flavor and body. Fat gives a richness and smoothness; it may be either the fat that occurs naturally in a cut of meat, or it may be in the form of fatback or heavy cream. Seasonings are critical, especially salt. Salt not only enhances the forcemeat's flavor, it also plays a key role in developing the forcemeat's texture and bind. Other seasonings may be added as desired.

An additional component is sometimes required to help bind the forcemeat together, especially if the main item is delicate or when it is not finely ground. These binders may be eggs or egg whites, heavy cream, or a liaison of cream and eggs. Pâte à choux, rice, or nonfat dry milk powder may be used as binders for forcemeats.

Panadas are also used as binders. To make a bread panada, soak cubed bread in milk, in a ratio of one part bread to one part milk, until the bread has absorbed the milk. A flour panada is essentially a very heavy béchamel enriched with three to four egg yolks per 16 fl oz/480 mL of liquid. Garnishes are often folded into a forcemeat or arranged in the forcemeat as the pâté or terrine mold is filled. Options include such items as nuts, diced meats or vegetables, dried fruits, and truffles.

A variety of liners can be used when preparing terrines and pâtés. Thin sheets of fatback, ham, prosciutto, or vegetables are commonly used for terrines. Pâtés en croûte are baked in pastry-lined molds. The dough used for pâtés is, by necessity, a stronger dough than a normal pie dough, although the preparation technique is identical. (Pâté dough may also be used to prepare barquette molds.) Herbs, spices, lemon zest, or flours other than bread flour may be added to change the flavor of the dough. For instructions for lining a pâté mold with dough, see page 1042.

Aspic is applied to foods to prevent them from drying out and to preserve their moisture and freshness. Aspic gelée is a well-seasoned, highly gelatinous, perfectly clarified stock. It is frequently strengthened by adding gelatin (see page 984). When properly prepared, aspic sets firmly but still melts in the mouth. Aspic gelée made from white stock will be clear, with practically no color. When the base stock is brown, the aspic is amber or brown. Other colors may be achieved by adding an appropriate spice, herb, or vegetable purée.

Use a meat grinder to prepare most meats, although a food processor is adequate to grind delicate meats and fish. Be sure that the blade for either the grinder or the food processor is very sharp. Meats should be cut cleanly, never mangled or mashed, as they pass through the grinder. Have an ice bath ready over which to mix and hold the forcemeat. Forcemeats can be mixed by hand over ice with a spoon, in an electric mixer, or in a food processor. Some forcemeats are pushed through a drum sieve to remove any fibers or sinew. Once prepared, forcemeats can be shaped in a variety of molds, including earthenware molds known as terrines and hinged pâté molds, as well as a variety of specialty molds.

Follow sound sanitation procedures and maintain cold temperatures at all times. Maintaining the correct temperature is important for more than the proper formation of an emulsion. Ingredients used in a forcemeat are often highly susceptible to contamination, due to handling, extended contact with equipment, and greater exposure to air. Pork, poultry, seafood, and dairy products begin to lose their quality and safety rapidly when they rise above 40°F/4°C. If the forcemeat seems to be approaching room temperature at any point in its preparation, it is too warm. Stop work and chill all ingredients and equipment. Resume work only after everything is below 40°F/4°C once more.

Grind foods properly. Both the dominant meat and fatback (if used) must be properly ground before the forcemeat can be prepared. Some garnishes are also ground along with the meat and fat.

To prepare the meat for grinding, cut it into strips or cubes that will fit easily through the grinder's feed tube. Combine it with an adequate amount of salt and the desired seasonings and let the meat marinate in the refrigerator for up to 4 hours. The salt will draw out proteins responsible for both flavor and texture development.

To prepare a grinder, choose the correct size die. For all but very delicate meats (fish and some types of organ meats, for example), begin with a die that has large or medium openings. Continue to grind through progressively smaller dies until you achieve the correct consistency. Remember to chill ingredients and equipment between successive grindings.

To use a grinder, guide the strips of meat and fatback into the feed tube. If they are the correct size, they will be drawn in easily by the worm. If they stick to the feed tray or the sides of the feed tube, they can be aided through with a tamper, but do not force the foods through the feed tube with a tamper.

To use a food processor, cut the meat into small dice before seasoning it. Chill the blade and bowl of the food processor. Run the machine just long enough to grind the meat into a smooth paste. Pulsing the machine off and on and scraping down the sides of the bowl produces the most even texture.

1. **Once the ingredients are properly ground, mix or process them, combining the ground meat with a secondary binder, if desired.** A forcemeat is more than simply ground meat. In order to produce the desired texture, the ingredients must be mixed long enough to develop a good bind. This may be done by hand over an ice bath, in a mixer, or in a food processor.

2. **Process the mixture to a smooth consistency.** This encourages the forcemeat to hold together well when sliced. Add ingredients like cold cream gradually as the processor runs for a smooth texture and to hold the ingredients together after cooking.

3. **When the forcemeat has the desired texture, push it through a drum sieve and then test for flavor and consistency.** Straight and gratin forcemeats are not typically put through a sieve. However, a mousseline forcemeat may be sieved to produce a very fine and delicate texture. Be sure that the forcemeat is very cold, and work rapidly to avoid warming the forcemeat.

Taste the forcemeat for flavor and consistency. Poach a bite-size portion of the forcemeat so that it can be evaluated (see the sidebar on quenelles, page 1029). Be sure to taste the forcemeat at serving temperature. If it is to be served cold, let the sample cool completely before tasting it. Make any necessary adjustments in the forcemeat. If it has a rubbery or tough consistency, add heavy cream; if it does not hold together properly, additional panada or egg whites may be necessary. Adjust the seasoning and flavoring ingredients as needed. Perform a new taste test after each adjustment until you are satisfied with the forcemeat.

4. **Garnish the forcemeat , if desired, and use as a stuffing or filling, or place it into a prepared mold and cook it.** Fold garnishes such as pistachio nuts, truffles, or diced ham into the forcemeat by hand, working over an ice bath. Keep the forcemeat very cold until you are ready to shape it. It may be spread, piped, or spooned into other foods as a filling, or used to fill a prepared mold.

The mold should be lined so that the pâté or terrine can be easily removed for slicing into servings. Cut sheets of liner large enough to hang over the sides and ends of the mold. These will later be folded back over the top of the pâté or terrine to form a cover. Plastic wrap is often used, but other wrappers, traditional and contemporary, may be used in addition to or in place of the plastic. One of the more elaborate garde manger preparations is pâté en croûte. Lining a mold with pastry is shown on page 1042.

5. **Smooth the forcemeat using an offset palette knife.** Once the terrine mold has been filled and the top is smooth, fold the excess pan liner over the forcemeat to seal the terrine. Cook as directed in the recipe.

A good forcemeat is well seasoned and tastes predominantly of the main meat with a rich, pleasant flavor and mouthfeel. The texture should be fairly smooth and have a uniform consistency by type, and it should hold together well when cut. Garnishes should complement the flavor of the forcemeat without overwhelming it.

Depending on the grinding and emulsifying methods and the intended use, the forcemeat can have a smooth consistency or be heavily textured and coarse. Mousseline forcemeats have a smooth, light texture that is not at all rubbery. A country-style forcemeat is less refined in texture and heartier in flavor than other forcemeats. A gratin forcemeat has quality characteristics similar to a country-style forcemeat.

Quenelles

Quenelles are poached dumplings

made from a forcemeat. They may be prepared to serve as an appetizer or as a garnish for soups. They are also the best size to check for flavor, texture, color, and consistency in a finished forcemeat to safeguard against producing terrines or pâtés that have poor quality.

1. Bring the poaching liquid to a simmer.
The liquid must not be at a rolling boil. This could cause the quenelles to fall apart as they cook.

2. Shape the quenelles.
There are many ways to shape quenelles, one of which employs 2 spoons (see photo). Other methods include using ladles or piping the mixture through a plain-tipped pastry bag.

Scoop up an appropriate amount of the forcemeat with one of the spoons, and use the second spoon to smooth and shape the mixture. Push the quenelle from the spoon into the poaching medium.

3. Poach the quenelles in barely simmering liquid.
The cooking time will vary, depending on the diameter of the quenelles. They should appear completely cooked through when broken open.

Seafood and Salmon Terrine

Makes 10 servings

SALMON MOUSSELINE

2 lb/907 g skinless salmon fillet

salt, as needed

ground black pepper, as needed

2 egg whites

16 fl oz/480 mL heavy cream

4 oz/113 g shelled crawfish tails

4 oz/113 g diced salmon

4 oz/113 g scallops

2 tbsp/6 g minced tarragon

blanched leek leaves, as needed

1. Cut the salmon fillet into strips or cubes and season with salt and pepper; chill to below 40°F/4°C. Grind the salmon in a food processor or through the fine plate of a meat grinder into a bowl set over an ice bath.

2. Purée the salmon in a food processor until it is almost a smooth paste. Add the egg whites and mix well.

3. Add the cream, 1 to 2 fl oz/30 to 60 mL at a time, until it reaches the desired consistency (run the food processor until the cream is just incorporated and scrape down the sides of the bowl to blend evenly) or gradually add the cream by hand over an ice bath.

4. Push the forcemeat through a drum sieve.

5. Test the forcemeat by poaching a small amount in simmering salted water. Adjust seasoning if necessary before proceeding. (The forcemeat is ready to use now in other applications, if desired.) Fold in the crayfish, salmon, scallops, and tarragon.

6. Line a terrine mold with plastic wrap and leek leaves. Pack the garnished forcemeat into the mold and fold over the liners to completely seal the terrine. Cover the terrine and poach in a 170°F/77°C water bath in a 300°F/149°C oven to an internal temperature of 165°F/74°C, 60 to 70 minutes.

7. Remove the terrine from the water bath and allow it to cool slightly. Weight it with a 2-lb/907-g press plate if desired. Refrigerate the terrine at least overnight or up to

2 to 3 days. Slice and serve the terrine, or wrap and refrigerate it for up to 7 days.

NOTES

This formula will produce a good texture for terrines and other items that will be sliced. For timbales or similar applications that can be softer, the quantity of cream can be almost doubled.

Flounder Mousseline: Substitute an equal amount of ground or diced flounder for the salmon in the mousseline above.

Pâté Grand-Mère

Makes 3 lb/ 1.36 kg; 18 to 20 servings

1 lb 4 oz/567 g chicken livers, sinews removed

1 oz/28 g shallots, minced

1 fl oz/30 mL brandy

1½ oz/43 g salt

1 tsp/2 g coarse ground black pepper, plus more as needed

¼ tsp/0.50 g ground bay leaf

½ tsp/1 g ground thyme

1 tsp/2.75 g tinted curing mix (TCM)

½ fl oz/15 mL vegetable oil, or as needed

1 lb 1 oz/482 g pork butt, cubed

1 tbsp/3 g chopped parsley

2½ oz/71 g crustless white bread, small dice

5 fl oz/150 mL milk

2 eggs

3 fl oz/90 mL heavy cream

¼ tsp/0.50 g ground white pepper

pinch freshly ground nutmeg

8 (¹⁄₁₆ in/1.50 mm) thin slices fatback, or as needed

6 to 8 fl oz/180 to 240 mL **Aspic Gelée** (page 984), melted

1. Sear the livers briefly in hot oil; remove them from the pan and chill. Sauté the shallots in the same pan; deglaze with the brandy and add to the livers. Mix in the salt, black pepper, bay leaf, thyme, TCM, and oil. Chill thoroughly.

2. Grind the pork butt, liver mixture, and parsley through the fine plate (⅛ in/3 mm) of a meat grinder into a bowl.

3. Combine the bread and milk; let it soak to form a panada. Add the eggs, cream, white pepper, and nutmeg. Mix with the ground meats on medium speed for 1 minute, until homogeneous.

4. Test the forcemeat by poaching a small amount in simmering salted water. Adjust seasoning if necessary before proceeding.

5. Line a terrine mold with plastic wrap and then the fatback slices, leaving an overhang. Sprinkle the fatback with black pepper, pack the forcemeat into the mold, and fold over the liners. Cure overnight in the refrigerator. Cover the terrine and poach in a 170°F/77°C water bath in a 300°F/149°C oven to an internal temperature of 165°F/74°C, 60 to 75 minutes.

6. Remove the terrine from the water bath and allow it to cool to an internal temperature of 90° to 100°F/32° to 38°C. Pour off the juices from the terrine, add enough aspic to coat and cover the terrine, and let it rest in the refrigerator for 2 days.

7. The terrine is now ready to slice and serve, or wrap and refrigerate it for up to 10 days.

Country-Style Terrine (Pâté de Campagne)

Makes 3 lb/1.36 kg; 18 to 20 servings

2 lb 8 oz/1.13 kg pork butt, cubed

8 oz/227 g pork liver, cleaned and trimmed

SEASONINGS

2 garlic cloves, minced, sautéed, and cooled

4 oz/113 g onions, finely chopped

2 tbsp/6 g finely chopped parsley

1½ oz/43 g salt

¾ tsp/2 g tinted curing mix (TCM)

½ tsp/1 g **Pâté Spice** (page 1044)

½ tsp/1 g ground white pepper, plus more as needed

PANADA

4 fl oz/120 mL heavy cream

2 eggs

2½ oz/71 g flour

1 fl oz/30 mL brandy

8 (¹⁄₁₆ in/1.50 mm) thin slices fatback, or as needed

6 to 8 oz/180 to 240 mL **Aspic Gelée**, melted (page 984)

1. Grind the pork through the coarse plate (⅜ in/9 mm) of a meat grinder. Reserve 1 lb 8 oz/680 g, then grind the remainder with the liver, garlic, onions, parsley, salt, TCM, pâté spice, and pepper through the fine plate (⅛ in/3 mm) of a meat grinder into a bowl.

2. Combine the cream, eggs, flour, and brandy in a bowl; whisk together until smooth, and then add to the ground meats. Mix, using a paddle, on low speed for 1 minute, until homogeneous. Then mix on medium speed until the mixture feels sticky to the touch.

3. Test the forcemeat and adjust seasoning if necessary before proceeding.

4. Line a terrine mold with plastic wrap and then the fatback slices, leaving an overhang. Sprinkle the fatback with pepper, pack the forcemeat into the mold, and fold over the liners. Cure overnight in the refrigerator. Cover the terrine and poach in a 170°F/77°C water bath in a 300°F/149°C oven to an internal temperature of 150°F/66°C, 60 to 75 minutes.

5. Remove the terrine from the water bath and allow it to cool to an internal temperature of 90° to 100°F/32° to 38°C. Pour off the juices from the terrine, add enough aspic to coat and cover the terrine, and let it rest in the refrigerator for 2 days.

6. The terrine is now ready to slice and serve, or wrap and refrigerate it for up to 10 days.

Pâté Maison: Substitute 3 lb/1.36 kg pork butt for the liver.

Chicken and Crayfish Terrine

Chicken and Crayfish Terrine

Makes 2 lb/907 g; 10 to 12 servings

MOUSSELINE

1 lb/454 g ground chicken breast

2 egg whites

2 tsp/10 g salt

½ tsp/1 g ground black pepper

6 fl oz/180 mL **Shellfish Essence** (recipe follows), cold

2 fl oz/60 mL heavy cream, cold

GARNISH

8 oz/227 g cooked crayfish tails, shelled and deveined

3 chipotles, seeded and minced

4 oz/113 g shiitake mushrooms, stemmed, sliced, sautéed, and chilled

2 tbsp/6 g chopped cilantro

1 tbsp/3 g chopped dill

1. Purée the chicken, egg whites, salt, and pepper in a food processor. Add the shellfish essence and cream with the machine running, and process (pulse) just to incorporate.

2. Test the forcemeat by poaching a small amount in simmering salted water. Adjust seasoning if necessary before proceeding.

3. Fold in the crayfish tails, chipotles, mushrooms, cilantro, and dill, working over an ice bath.

4. Oil a terrine mold and line it with plastic wrap, leaving an overhang of at least 4 in/10 cm on all sides. Pack the forcemeat into the lined mold, making sure to remove any air pockets. Fold the plastic wrap liner over the forcemeat to completely encase the terrine; cover.

5. Poach the terrine in a 170°F/77°C water bath in a 300°F/149°C oven to an internal temperature of 165°F/74°C, 60 to 75 minutes.

6. Remove the terrine from the water bath and allow it to cool slightly.

7. Let the terrine rest at least overnight and up to 3 days in the refrigerator, weighted with a 2 lb/907 g press plate, if desired.

8. The terrine is now ready to slice and serve, or wrap and refrigerate it for up to 7 days.

Shellfish Essence

Makes 6 fl oz/180 mL

1 lb/454 g crayfish, shrimp, or lobster shells

½ fl oz/15 mL vegetable oil

2 shallots, minced

2 garlic cloves, minced

12 fl oz/360 mL heavy cream

3 bay leaves

2 tsp/4 g poultry seasoning

1 tbsp/6 g chili powder

1 fl oz/30 mL glace de volaille or viande

1. Sauté the shells in the oil until they take on a bright red color. Add the shallots and garlic and sauté until they are aromatic.

2. Add the cream, bay leaves, poultry seasoning, and chili powder; reduce the mixture to half of its original volume. Add the glace, squeeze through a cheesecloth, and chill to below 40°F/4°C.

3. The essence is ready to use now, or to be stored under refrigeration.

Chicken Galantine

Makes 4 lb/1.81 kg; 28 to 30 servings

3 lb/1.36 kg chicken

salt and pepper, as needed

6 fl oz/180 mL Madeira wine

PANADA

2 eggs

1½ fl oz/45 mL brandy

1 tsp/2 g **Pâté Spice** (page 1044)

3 oz/85 g all-purpose flour

1 tbsp/15 g salt

¼ tsp/0.50 g ground white pepper

8 fl oz/240 mL heavy cream, hot

1 lb/454 g pork butt, cut into 1-in/3-cm cubes, cold

4 oz/113 g fresh ham or cooked tongue, cut into ¼-in/6-mm cubes

3 tbsp/25 g chopped black truffles

4 oz/113 g pistachios, blanched

½ tsp/1 g coarsely ground black pepper

Chicken Stock (page 351), as needed

1. Remove the skin from the chicken, keeping it intact. Remove the wing tips and bone out the chicken, keeping the breast whole. Separate the tenderloins from the breast and reserve.

2. Cut the chicken tenderloin into ½- to ¾-in/6-mm to 1-cm cubes. Season with salt and pepper. Refrigerate the meat in the Madeira for at least 3 hours.

3. Butterfly the chicken breast meat and pound it ⅛ in/3 mm thick, place on a sheet pan lined with plastic wrap, cover with plastic, and refrigerate.

4. Prepare the panada: Mix the eggs with the brandy, pâté spice, flour, salt, and pepper.

5. Temper the egg mixture with the hot cream. Add the cream to the egg mixture and cook over low heat until thickened.

6. Weigh the leg and thigh meat from the chicken. Add an equal amount of pork butt, or enough for approximately 2 lb/907 g of meat. Grind the chicken and pork twice, using the fine plate (⅛ in/3 mm) of a meat grinder.

7. Add the panada to the ground meat mixture. Blend well. Fold in the Madeira and the marinated chicken tenderloin, ham, truffles, and pistachios. Mix well.

Cut the skin free from the joint near the leg of the chicken. Gently remove the skin from the chicken with your hands, being careful not to puncture the skin.

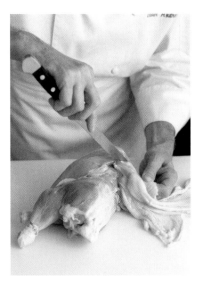

If necessary, use a knife to remove the last of the skin from the wing tips of the chicken.

Roll the chicken breast and skin around the forcemeat.

8. Lay out the reserved skin on plastic wrap and lay the pounded chicken breast on top. Season the chicken with salt and black pepper. Add the forcemeat and roll the galantine securely.

9. Poach the galantine at 170°F/77°C in enough stock to cover, to an internal temperature of 165°F/74°C, 60 to 70 minutes.

10. Transfer the galantine and the poaching liquid to a storage container. Let it cool to room temperature. Remove the galantine from the stock and wrap it in cheesecloth to firm its texture; chill at least 12 hours. To serve the galantine, unwrap and slice it.

NOTE
Classically, galantines are wrapped in cheesecloth and poached in fortified chicken stock.

Pork Tenderloin Roulade

Makes 2 lb 8 oz/1.13 kg; 16 to 18 servings

16 fl oz/480 mL **Meat Brine** (recipe follows)

3 star anise pods

2 oz/57 g roughly chopped ginger

2 tsp/4 g Szechwan peppercorns

1 lb 8 oz/680 g pork tenderloin, trimmed

MOUSSELINE

1 lb/454 g boneless chicken breast

2 tsp/10 g salt

2 egg whites, cold

2 tsp/6 g minced garlic

2 tsp/6 g minced ginger

1 fl oz/30 mL sherry, cold

10 fl oz/300 mL heavy cream, cold

6 oz/170 g sliced mushrooms

1 fl oz/30 mL glace de volaille or viande, warm

½ oz/28 g toasted sesame seeds

2 oz/57 g minced parsley

1. Mix together the Meat Brine, star anise, ginger, and peppercorns. Cover the pork with the brine mixture and use small plates to keep it completely submerged. Refrigerate for 12 hours. Rinse the tenderloin and dry well.

2. Cut the chicken into strips or dice and season with salt; chill to below 40°F/4°C. Grind the chicken in a food processor or through the fine plate of a meat grinder into a bowl set over an ice bath.

3. Mix the chicken in a food processor until it is almost a smooth paste. Add the egg whites, garlic, ginger, and sherry and mix until evenly blended.

4. Add the cream to the food processor (run until just incorporated and scrape down the sides of the bowl to blend evenly) or gradually add it by hand over an ice bath. Push the forcemeat through a drum sieve. Fold the mushrooms into the forcemeat by hand over an ice bath.

5. Test the forcemeat by poaching a small amount in simmering salted water. Adjust seasoning if necessary before proceeding.

6. Cut a large rectangle of plastic wrap. Spread half of the mousseline on the plastic. Place the tenderloin in the middle and spread the other half of the forcemeat evenly over the tenderloin. Roll tightly into a cylinder shape and secure the ends with twine.

7. Poach the roulade at 170°F/77°C in simmering water to cover to an internal temperature of 160°F/71°C. Remove the roulade from the water, and cool to below 40°F/4°C.

8. Unwrap the roulade. Cut a fresh piece of plastic wrap, brush with the glace, and scatter with the sesame seeds and parsley. Top with the cooled roulade and rewrap tightly. Refrigerate the roulade for at least 24 hours or up to 2 days before slicing and serving, or refrigerate it for up to 7 days.

Meat Brine

Makes 1 gal/3.84 L

12 oz/340 g salt

6 oz/170 g dextrose

2½ oz/71 g tinted curing mix (TCM)

1 gal/3.84 L water

Dissolve the salt, dextrose, and TCM in the water and use as needed.

Venison Terrine

Makes 3 lb/1.36 kg; 18 to 20 servings

2 lb/907 g venison shoulder or leg meat

1 lb/454 g fatback

2 fl oz/60 mL red wine

½ tsp/1 g ground cloves

1 tbsp/6 g crushed black peppercorns

1 tsp/2.75 g tinted curing mix (TCM)

1 oz/28 g minced onions, sautéed and cooled

1 oz/28 g salt

2 tsp/4 g ground black pepper

1 oz/28 g dried cèpes or morels, ground to a powder

3 eggs

6 fl oz/180 mL heavy cream

1 tbsp/3 g chopped tarragon

1 tbsp/3 g chopped parsley

GARNISH

2 oz/57 g golden raisins, plumped in 4 fl oz/120 mL brandy

4 oz/113 g mushrooms, diced, sautéed, and cooled

8 (1/16 in/1.50 mm) ham slices, or as needed

1. Dice the venison and fatback into 1-in/3-cm cubes. Marinate them with the wine, cloves, peppercorns, TCM, onions, salt, pepper, and dried cèpes and refrigerate overnight.

2. Prepare a straight forcemeat by grinding the marinated venison and fatback into a chilled mixing bowl. Mix in the eggs, cream, tarragon, and parsley on medium speed for 1 minute, or until homogeneous. Fold in the raisins and mushrooms.

3. Line a terrine mold with plastic wrap and the ham, leaving an overhang. Pack the forcemeat into the terrine mold and fold over the ham and plastic. Cover the terrine.

4. Poach terrine in a 170°F/77°C water bath in a 300°F/149°C oven to an internal temperature of 150°F/66°C, 60 to 70 minutes.

5. Remove the terrine from the water bath and allow it to cool to an internal temperature of 90° to 100°F/32° to 38°C. Let the terrine rest in the refrigerator overnight. The terrine is now ready to slice and serve, or wrap and refrigerate it for up to 10 days.

Duck Terrine with Pistachios and Dried Cherries

Makes 3 lb/1.36 kg; 18 to 20 servings

1 lb 12 oz/794 g duck meat, trimmed and cubed (from 4 to 5 lb/1.81 to 2.27 kg bird), breast meat reserved

8 oz/227 g fatback

1 tbsp/15 g salt

2 tbsp/6 g chopped sage

1 tsp/2 g ground white pepper

1 tbsp/3 g chopped parsley

¼ tsp/0.75 g tinted curing mix (TCM)

4 oz/113 g ham, small dice

2 fl oz/60 mL vegetable oil

3 oz/85 g roasted and peeled pistachios

2½ oz/71 g dried cherries

8 (1/16 in/1.50 mm) ham slices, or as needed

1. Combine 1 lb /454 g of the duck meat, reserving the breast meat for garnish, with the fatback, salt, sage, pepper, parsley, and TCM. Grind through the medium plate (¼ in/6 mm) and then the fine plate (⅛ in/3 mm) of a meat grinder.

2. Sear the duck breast meat and ham in the oil and let them cool.

3. Test the forcemeat by poaching a small amount in simmering salted water. Adjust seasoning if necessary before proceeding.

4. Fold the seared duck and ham, pistachios, and cherries into the forcemeat, working over an ice bath.

5. Line a terrine mold with plastic wrap and the ham slices, leaving an overhang, then pack with the forcemeat. Fold the ham liners over the terrine and cover the mold. Poach in a 170°F/77°C water bath in a 300°F/149°C oven to an internal temperature of 165°F/74°C, 50 to 60 minutes.

6. Let the terrine rest for 1 hour. Weight with a 2 lb/907 g press overnight, or up to 3 days in the refrigerator.

7. The terrine is now ready to slice and serve, or wrap and refrigerate it for up to 7 days.

Foie Gras Terrine

Makes 2 lb/907 g; 10 to 12 servings

2 lb 12 oz/1.25 kg foie gras, grade A

1¼ oz/35 g salt

2 tsp/4 g ground white pepper

1 tbsp/15 g sugar

¼ tsp/0.75 g tinted curing mix (TCM)

16 fl oz/480 mL white port

1. Clean the livers, remove all veins, and dry well. Combine 1 oz/28 g of the salt, 1 tsp/2 g of the pepper, the sugar, TCM, and port. Refrigerate the livers in the mixture overnight.

2. Line a 2 lb/907 g terrine mold with plastic wrap.

3. Place the foie gras on a cutting board and slice it into large pieces that will fit snugly into the mold. Place them in the mold so that the smooth sides of the foie gras pieces form the exterior of the terrine; season as needed with the remaining salt and pepper. Fill the mold up to the inner lip and press the pieces down tightly to remove any air pockets. Cover the terrine mold.

4. Poach the terrine in a hot water bath, maintaining it at a constant 160°F/71°C, for 45 to 50 minutes. The oven temperature may need to be adjusted to keep the water at a constant temperature. If it gets too hot, add cold water immediately to lower the temperature. Foie gras has the best texture and flavor when cooked to an internal temperature of 135°F/57°C. (However, be sure to check with your local and state health authorities for any regional differences.)

5. Remove the terrine from the water bath and rest it for 2 hours at room temperature, then pour off the fat. Cover the terrine with a press plate and top with a 1 to 2 lb/454 to 907 g weight. Refrigerate the terrine for at least 24 hours and up to 48 hours to mellow and mature.

6. Remove the plastic wrap and carefully remove the congealed fat. Tightly rewrap the terrine in fresh plastic wrap. Refrigerate until ready to slice and serve the terrine, or refrigerate for up to 3 days.

NOTES

To determine the amount of foie gras needed to fill any size terrine mold, simply measure the volume of water the terrine can hold. The number of fluid ounces/milliliters in volume will correlate to the number of ounces/grams in weight of foie gras necessary to fill the mold.

For easier service, slice the terrine with the plastic wrap on. Remove the plastic after the slices have been plated. A warm beveled knife works best. Save any fat removed in step 5 to use to sauté vegetables or potatoes.

Foie Gras Roulade: Prepare the foie gras as directed for the terrine. Arrange the marinated foie gras on a large sheet of plastic wrap; wrap tightly around the foie gras to form a roulade. If desired, insert whole truffles into the foie gras lobes before rolling the roulade. (Truffles must be cleaned and poached prior to use as an internal garnish. If using canned truffles, this has already been done.) Poach in a 160°F/71°C water bath to an internal temperature of 118°F/48°C. Remove from the water, cool, and rewrap. Refrigerate the roulade for at least 24 hours before slicing.

Chicken Liver Pâté

Makes 2 lb/907 g; 10 to 12 servings

1 lb 8 oz/680 g chicken livers, cleaned, sinews removed

16 fl oz/480 mL milk, or as needed for soaking

1 oz/28 g salt

¼ tsp/0.75 g tinted curing mix (TCM)

2 oz/57 g minced shallots

2 garlic cloves, minced

8 oz/227 g fresh fatback, cut into medium dice

1 tsp/2 g ground white pepper

½ tsp/1 g ground allspice

½ tsp/1 g dry mustard

1⅓ oz/37 g fresh white bread crumbs

1 fl oz/30 mL sherry

3 oz/85 g bread flour, unsifted

2 tsp/9.50 g powdered gelatin

3 eggs

6 fl oz/180 mL heavy cream

1. Soak the livers in the milk with 1½ tsp/7.50 g of the salt and the TCM for 12 to 24 hours. When ready to use, drain them well and pat dry with paper towels.

2. Purée the shallots, cloves, fatback, pepper, allspice, mustard, bread crumbs, sherry, flour, gelatin, and eggs in a blender to a smooth, loose paste.

3. Pass the mixture through a wire-mesh strainer into a stainless-steel bowl and stir in the cream. Refrigerate the mixture for 2 hours.

4. Pour the mixture into a terrine mold lined with plastic wrap, cover, and poach in a 170°F/77°C water bath in a 300°F/149°C oven to an internal temperature of 165°F/74°C, 45 minutes to 1 hour. Remove the terrine from the oven and allow it to cool at room temperature for 30 minutes.

5. Press with a 1 lb/454 g weight and refrigerate overnight before unmolding and slicing.

St Andrew's Vegetable Terrine

Makes 3 lb/1.36 kg; 18 to 20 servings

12 oz/340 g chicken breast, cubed

1 egg white

6 fl oz/180 mL heavy cream

2 tsp/10 g salt

ground white pepper, as needed

6 oz/170 g spinach, sautéed and coarsely chopped

1 roasted red bell pepper (see page 700), medium dice

8 oz/227 g yellow squash and/or zucchini, finely diced, blanched

8 oz/227 g carrots, finely diced, fully cooked

2 oz/57 g yellow turnips, finely diced, fully cooked

½ oz/14 g powdered gelatin

½ oz/14 g minced herbs, such as marjoram, dill, and/or chives

pinch grated nutmeg

½ tsp/1 g ground cardamom, roasted

salt and pepper, as needed

1. Make a mousseline-style forcemeat by processing the chicken, egg white, cream, salt, and pepper until smooth.

2. Test the forcemeat by poaching a small amount in simmering salted water. Adjust seasoning if necessary before proceeding.

3. Toss the vegetables in a bowl with the powdered gelatin, herbs, nutmeg, and cardamom. Season with salt and pepper. Fold the vegetables mixture into the forcemeat, working over an ice bath.

4. Oil a terrine mold and line it with plastic wrap, leaving an overhang of at least 4 in/10 cm on all sides. Pack the forcemeat into the lined mold, making sure to remove any air pockets. Fold the plastic wrap liner over the forcemeat to completely encase the terrine.

5. Poach the terrine in a 170°F/77°C water bath in a 300°F/149°C oven until an internal temperature of 165°F/74°C, 60 to 70 minutes. Refrigerate the terrine, weighted with a 1 lb/454 g press plate, if desired, for at least 12 hours.

6. The terrine is now ready to slice and serve, or wrap and refrigerate it for up to 4 days.

St. Andrew's Vegetable Terrine (left), Foie Gras Terrine (right)

LEFT TO RIGHT: Pork Tenderloin Roulade, Duck Terrine with Pistachios and Dried Cherries, Seafood Pâté en Croûte, Pâté Grand-Mère

Pâté Dough

Makes 1 lb 8 oz/680 g

1 lb/454 g bread flour

2 tsp/6 g baking powder

½ oz/14 g salt

1 tsp/5 g sugar

4 oz/113 g butter, cold, cubed

1 egg

2 tsp/10 mL cider vinegar

8 oz/227 g whole milk

1. Combine the dry ingredients and mix well.

2. With 2 knives or a pastry cutter, cut the butter into the dry ingredients. Work the dough until its texture becomes crumbly.

3. Mix the wet ingredients into the dough until fully incorporated. Knead the dough until smooth and not sticky.

4. Shape the dough into a 10-in/25-cm disk. Wrap and refrigerate for at least 1 hour or overnight. Pâté dough is generally used to line a rectangular pâté mold, therefore it should be shaped into an appropriate-sized rectangle prior to refrigeration.

Saffron Pâté Dough: To make the dough, infuse 2 tsp/1.60 g saffron in 5 fl oz/150 mL warm water. Replace 5 oz/150 mL of the milk with the saffron water. If desired, add 2 tbsp/6 g each chopped dill and chives in step 2.

Use round cutters to create a vent hole in the top of the pâté en croûte to prevent the top from cracking. Reinforce the vent hole and use aluminum foil to create a chimney that will prevent the dough from closing in on itself.

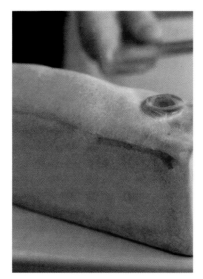

The finished pâté en croûte should be golden brown on the edges and should not have any cracks in the top of the dough.

Seafood Pâté en Croûte

Makes 2 lb 8 oz/ 1.13 kg; 18 to 20 servings

6 oz/170 g shrimp

6 oz/170 g crayfish tails

2 tbsp/6 g snipped chives

3 tbsp/9 g chopped basil

1 oz/28 g small-dice truffles (optional)

12 oz/340 g **Salmon Mousseline** (page 1030)

1 lb 8 oz/680 g **Saffron Pâté Dough** (page 1041)

Egg Wash (page 1061), as needed

dry nori sheets (optional), as needed

6 to 8 fl oz/180 to 240 mL **Aspic Gelée** (page 984)

1. Peel and devein the shrimp and crayfish tails. Cut them into dice or julienne if desired. Chill to below 40°F/4°C.

2. Working over an ice bath, fold the shrimp, crayfish, chives, basil, and truffles (if using) into the mousseline by hand.

3. Roll the dough out into a rectangle, about ⅛ in/3 mm thick. Cut pieces to line the bottom and sides of a hinged pâté mold (below); the dough should overhang on all sides. Egg wash the inside of the pâté dough liner, or add a second liner of nori sheets, if desired.

4. Pack the forcemeat into the lined mold. Fold the dough over, trim, and seal to completely encase the pâté.

5. Cut a cap piece and lay it over the pâté, tucking the sides down into the mold. Cut and reinforce vent holes in the cap piece and brush the surface with egg wash. Roll a tube of aluminum foil (known as a chimney) to fit into the vent holes and keep them from closing during baking.

6. Bake at 450°F/232°C for 15 to 20 minutes, reduce the heat to 350°F/177°C, and finish baking to an internal temperature of 155°F/68°C, about 50 minutes.

7. Remove the pâté from the oven and let it cool to 90° to 100°F/32° to 38°C. Warm the aspic to 110°F/43°C and

Use the pâté en croûte mold as a template to measure and cut the dough so that it will snugly line the inside of the mold. Cut a rectangle that will cover the bottom and 2 long sides of the mold with enough excess to cover the top of the pâté en croûte. Cut 2 smaller rectangles to cover the short sides of the mold. Be sure to grease the mold before assembling the pâté en croûte.

Gently line the pâté en croûte mold with the dough. Allow the excess dough to hang over the sides of the mold.

Use the smaller rectangles of dough to line the sides of the mold. Press the seams of the dough together firmly to create a tight seal.

ladle it through a funnel into the pâté using the chimneys. Then remove and discard the chimneys.

8. Refrigerate the pâté for at least 24 hours before slicing and serving.

NOTE
When preparing the Salmon Mousseline on page 1030, replace 12 oz/340 g of the salmon with diced shrimp, if desired.

Vegetable Terrine with Goat Cheese

Makes 3 lb/1.36 kg; 18 to 20 servings

2 lb/907 g zucchini

2 lb/907 g yellow squash

1 lb 4 oz/567 g eggplant

2 lb/907 g tomatoes

2 portobello mushrooms

MARINADE

1 fl oz/30 mL olive oil

½ oz/14 g Dijon mustard

1 tbsp/3 g chopped parsley

1 tbsp/3 g chopped chives

2 garlic cloves, minced, sautéed, and cooled

2 tsp/3 g chopped rosemary

2 tsp/6 g anchovy or olive paste (optional)

2 tsp/10 mL honey

2 tsp/10 g salt

½ tsp/1 g ground white pepper

8 oz/227 g fresh goat cheese

1 egg

1. Cut all the vegetables lengthwise into ⅛-in/3-mm-thick slices.

2. Combine all the marinade ingredients and marinate the vegetables for 1 hour.

3. Remove the vegetables from the marinade and place them in a single layer on sheet pans lined with oiled parchment paper.

4. Dry the vegetables in a 200°F/93°C oven for 1 hour, or until dry, but not brittle. Remove the vegetables from the oven and cool.

5. Mix the goat cheese with the egg.

6. Line a terrine mold with plastic wrap, leaving an overhang, and assemble the terrine by alternating layers of vegetables and the cheese mixture until the terrine is filled. Fold over the liner.

7. Cover the terrine and poach it in a 170°F/77°C water bath in a 300°F/149°C oven to an internal temperature of 145°F/63°C, about 60 minutes.

8. Remove the terrine from the water bath and allow it to cool slightly.

9. Refrigerate the terrine at least overnight and up to 3 days, weighted with a 2 lb/907 g press plate if desired. The terrine is now ready to slice and serve, or wrap and refrigerate it for up to 7 days.

Pâté Spice

Makes 14 oz/397 g

1½ oz/43 g white peppercorns

3 oz/85 g coriander seeds

1¾ oz/50 g dried thyme

1¾ oz/50 g dried basil

3 oz/85 g whole cloves

1½ oz/43 g grated nutmeg

½ oz/14 g bay leaf

¾ oz/21 g mace

1 oz/28 g dry cèpes (optional)

1. Combine all the ingredients and grind them using a mortar and pestle or a spice grinder.

2. Store any unused spice blend in an airtight container in a cool, dry place.

Gravlax

Makes 20 servings

7 oz/198 g kosher salt

1 lb/454 g dark brown sugar

¾ oz/21 g cracked white peppercorns

3 oz/85 g chopped dill

2 fl oz/60 mL lemon juice

1 fl oz/30 mL olive oil

¾ fl oz/22.50 mL brandy

3 lb/1.36 kg salmon fillet

1. Combine the salt, sugar, peppercorns, and dill to make the dry cure.

2. Combine the lemon juice, oil, and brandy. Place the salmon on a piece of cheesecloth and brush this mixture on top.

3. Pack the dry cure evenly on the salmon and wrap it tightly in the cheesecloth.

4. Place the wrapped salmon in a pan, top with a second pan, and set a weight in the second pan. Refrigerate this assembly and let it marinate for 3 days.

5. Unwrap the salmon and scrape off the cure.

6. Slice the salmon thinly on the bias to serve it.

Part Eight

Baking and Pastry

Chapter Thirty-four

Baking Mise en Place

To be successful in the baking and pastry arts, it is important to have a basic understanding of how baking ingredients function and how they react to each other. Knowledge of these principles and processes will not only help you to follow any formula and produce better quality products, but will also aid in developing formulas of your own creation.

The Functions of Baking Ingredients

The basic ingredients used in baking typically fulfill more than one function in the finished product. Eggs, for example, can act as a stabilizer, leavener, and/or thickener.

Stabilizers (tougheners, thickeners)

A stabilizer is any ingredient that helps to develop the solid structure, or "framework," of a finished product. It does this in one of two ways, either by toughening or tightening a dough or by thickening a mixture. Flour and eggs are examples of ingredients that lend structure (and nutritional value) to a finished product.

Flour acts as a binding and absorbing agent. It is the gluten (the protein component in flour) that builds structure and strength in baked goods, whereas the starch present in the flour makes a useful thickener. When starch granules suspended in water are heated, they begin to absorb liquid and swell, causing an increase in the viscosity of the mixture. This reaction, known as gelatinization, allows starches to be used as thickening agents. Different types of flours have different gluten-to-starch ratios, which will create vastly different results in the texture, appearance, and flavor of the final product used in the same formula.

Eggs lend additional stability during baking. They influence the texture and grain as well; by facilitating the incorporation and distribution of air, they promote an even-grained and fine texture. Eggs act to thicken through the coagulation of proteins. As their proteins begin to coagulate, liquid is trapped in the network of set proteins, resulting in a smooth, rather thick texture. This is known as a partial coagulation, where the proteins hold moisture; if the mixture were cooked or baked further, the proteins would fully coagulate and expel water, causing the product to curdle.

Eggs also have leavening power. As eggs (whole, yolks, or whites) are whipped, they trap air, which expands when heated, resulting in a larger and lighter product. Several other typical stabilizer/thickeners are:

Arrowroot and cornstarch

These are generally preferable for thickening sauces, puddings, and fillings where a translucent effect is desired. To dilute these thickeners before incorporating them with other ingredients, mix them with a small amount of cool liquid. Tapioca starch is also commonly used to thicken pie fillings.

Gelatin

Gelatin is used to produce light, delicate foams (Bavarian cream, mousse, stabilized whipped cream) that are firmly set. Such foams retain the shape of a mold even after unmolding and can be sliced. Available in both powder or sheets, gelatin must first be softened or bloomed in a cool liquid. Once the gelatin has absorbed the liquid, it is gently heated to melt the crystals, either by adding the softened gelatin to a hot mixture, such as a hot custard sauce, or by gently heating the gelatin over simmering water.

Pectin

Pectin is a carbohydrate derived from the cell walls of certain fruits. Some common sources of pectin are apples, cranberries, and currants. To gel, it requires the correct balance of sugar and acid.

Liquefiers (tenderizers, thinners)

Liquefiers help to loosen, or tenderize a dough or batter. Water, milk, and other liquids, fats, and sugar act as liquefiers.

Although sugar has a tendency to tighten up a mixture when it is first incorporated, its interaction with other ingredients and from the heat of baking causes it to ultimately act to loosen, or liquefy, a batter or dough.

Water acts to dilute or liquefy water-soluble ingredients such as sugar and salt. It also facilitates the even distribution of sugar, salt, and yeast in a dough if these ingredients are mixed thoroughly with the water before introducing the remaining ingredients in the formula. Water also acts in leavening as it changes to steam and expands.

Milk performs many of the same functions as water, but because of its additional components (fat, sugar, minerals, and protein), it serves a number of other functions and adds flavor as well. As the sugar (lactose) in milk caramelizes, it gives a rich color to the product's surface, and it can also aid in development of a firm crust. The lactic acid in milk has a tightening effect on the proteins in flour, which serves to increase stability, resulting in a product with a fine grain and texture.

If the total amount of fat added to a dough or batter equals no more than 3 percent of the weight of the finished dough or product, it acts to increase the elasticity of the proteins in the flour, thereby helping the product to expand during baking. In baking, fats and oils are also classified as shortening agents, a term derived from their ability to split the long, elastic gluten strands that can toughen flour-based doughs and batters. This tenderizing effect renders the strands more susceptible to breaking, or shortening, resulting in a more tender and less dense crumb.

Leaveners (biological, chemical, mechanical)

To leaven is to raise, or to make lighter. There are several ways to accomplish this in baking: with yeasts (also known as biological leaveners), with chemical agents such as baking powder or baking soda, or through steam, also known as mechanical leavening. Each method is best suited for specific applications and produces very different results. The different leavening methods may be used alone or in conjunction with one another to yield different effects.

Organic leaveners are based on yeast, a living organism that feeds on sugars, producing alcohol and carbon dioxide, the gas that lightens a dough to give it the proper texture. Unlike chemical leaveners, organic leaveners take a substantial amount of time to do their job. The yeast has to grow and reproduce sufficiently to fill the dough with air pockets. For this to take place, the temperature must be controlled carefully. Yeast will not function well below approximately 50° to 60°F/10° to 16°C, and above 140°F/60°C the yeast is destroyed.

Fresh or compressed yeast must be kept refrigerated (ideally at 40°F/4°C) to maintain its viability; it may be held for only seven to ten days, or it may be frozen for longer storage. This type of yeast comes in cake form and is usually measured by weight rather than volume.

Active dry yeast and instant yeast are two types of granular yeast. They should be kept refrigerated after opening and must be kept dry until use. Active dry or instant yeast in an unopened package is in a completely dormant stage and may be stored unopened for up to one year at room temperature.

To substitute active dry yeast for compressed yeast, use 40 percent of the amount of compressed yeast called for in the recipe. To substitute instant yeast, use 33 percent of the amount.

Sourdough starter is also a yeast-based leavener. In this case, the naturally occurring (or wild) yeast is allowed to ferment in a flour and water mixture over a period of days or weeks. With regular feedings of additional flour and water, the growing starter may be strengthened and maintained for regular use in the production of bread and other baked items indefinitely.

Baking soda and baking powder are categorized as chemical leaveners. In these leaveners, an alkaline ingredient (sodium bicarbonate or a combination of an alkali, an acid, and a starch) interacts with an acid (already present in baking powder or in an ingredient such as buttermilk, sour cream, yogurt, or chocolate). The alkalis and acids produce carbon dioxide when combined in the presence of liquid. When heated during baking, the carbon dioxide expands, giving the baked goods their characteristic texture, known as *crumb*. This process of expansion happens rapidly; hence, many items prepared with chemical leaveners are called quick breads.

Double-acting baking powder is so called because a first action occurs in the presence of moisture in the batter and a second action is initiated by the presence of heat. That is, the baking powder reacts once when it is mixed with the batter's liquids and again when the batter is placed in a hot oven.

Steam, which is produced when liquids in a batter or dough are heated, is a physical leavener. Heat causes any air pockets in a batter or dough to expand. Steam is the leavening agent in sponge cakes and soufflés. It also plays a vital role in the production of puff pastry, croissants, and Danish pastry, where the steam is trapped between layers of dough, causing them to separate and rise. Other areas in which steam helps to leaven products is when air is incorporated into a batter through either whipping or creaming an ingredient before it is incorporated into the final batter.

Preparation of Baking Ingredients

Scaling

The most accurate way to measure ingredients is to weigh them. Even liquid ingredients are often, though not always, weighed. Various types of scales are used in the bakeshop, including balance-beam, spring, or electronic scales. Other measuring tools, including volume measures, such as pints and quarts and measuring spoons, are also necessary and commonly used.

It is important to properly scale out each ingredient to prepare a baked item. It is equally important to scale out the finished dough or batter to ensure that the proper and consistent amount is used for the pan size, mold, or individual portion. Not only does this contribute to the uniformity of products, it also decreases the possibility of uneven rising or browning caused by too much or too little dough or batter.

Sifting dry ingredients

Dry ingredients used for most baked goods should be sifted before they are incorporated into the dough or batter. Dry ingredients are sifted primarily for three reasons:

- To blend
- To remove lumps or impurities
- To aerate

Sifting aerates flour and confectioners' sugar, removing lumps and filtering out any impurities. Chemical leaveners such as baking powder and some flavoring ingredients (cocoa powder, for example) are more evenly distributed after sifting. Sifting should take place after the ingredients have been properly scaled.

Cooking Sugar

When cooking sugar, all your equipment must be clean and free of any grease. The sugar must also be free of impurities, such as flour or other ingredients. Sugar is often cooked to very high temperatures and any impurities in the sugar are likely to burn or cause recrystallization before the sugar reaches the desired temperature. A copper or other heavy-bottomed saucepan should be used to ensure constant even heat.

Sugar may be cooked by one of two methods: dry or wet. The dry method is used exclusively for caramelization. The wet method may be used to caramelize sugar, but the nutty, roasted flavor characteristic of good caramel is better achieved through the dry method. The wet method is generally used when sugar must be cooked to a specific stage or temperature.

When cooking or caramelizing sugar by any method, a small amount of an acid (typically lemon juice at approximately ¼ tsp/1.25 mL for 8 oz/227 g of sugar) can be added to help prevent crystallization from occurring during cooking.

A few basic rules apply when cooking sugar:

- Use a heavy-gauge pot to prevent burning the sugar and a candy thermometer for accuracy.

- Add an acid or an invert sugar, such as corn syrup, to prevent sugar crystals from forming.

- Brush down the side of the pot with a moist pastry brush; this will also help to prevent crystallization.

- Heat milk or other liquids before adding them to caramel.

- Add all liquids carefully, away from heat. The hot caramel will foam and splatter when a liquid is added.

Caramelizing sugar by the dry method

Add a small amount of the sugar to a preheated pan set over medium heat and allow it to melt. Then add the remaining sugar in small increments, allowing each addition of sugar to fully melt before adding the next. Cook to the desired color.

When caramelizing sugar, regardless of the cooking method, stop the cooking process by shocking the pan in an ice water bath just before it reaches the desired color. Sugar retains heat and can become too dark or burn if the cooking process is not arrested.

Heat any liquids to be added to the caramel and add them carefully. Caramelized sugar is very hot and will splatter when a colder ingredient is introduced.

Cooking sugar to stages

For the wet method, the sugar is combined in a saucepan with 30 percent or more of its weight in water. Place the pan over high heat and stir constantly until the mixture comes to a boil to ensure all the sugar is melted. Once it has come to a boil, stop stirring and skim off any impurities. Using a pastry brush, wash down the sides of the pan with cool water to prevent crystals from forming. Crystallization of the cooking sugar occurs readily on the side of the pan, where crystals are deposited from evaporating liquid. These crystals, in turn, can easily act to "seed" the rest of the sugar in the pan, causing it to begin to crystallize, becoming lumpy and granular. Repeat as often as necessary to keep the sides of the pan clean until the sugar has reached the desired temperature, consistency, and/or color.

When sugar is heated, it dissolves. As the sugar continues to cook to specific temperatures, the sugar syrup changes texture. At first, the syrup will cling together enough to form threads when a utensil is dipped into the syrup and pulled away. Eventually, the syrup will start to form into balls when it is removed from the heat. Each of the following stages has different applications in baking, pastry, and candy making:

234°F/112°C	thread
238°F/114°C	soft ball
248°F/120°C	firm ball
260°F/127°C	hard ball
275°F/135°C	soft crack
310°F/154°C	hard crack

Simple syrup

Simple syrups are an indispensable preparation in every pastry kitchen. They are a mixture of water and sugar that is heated only enough to allow the sugar to dissolve completely. Various liqueurs, such as orange liqueur, brandy, rum, or coffee-flavored liqueur, may be added to the syrup for flavor after it has cooled. If desired, flavoring ingredients, such as a sachet of cinnamon and clove, a pinch of saffron, or a split vanilla bean, should be allowed to steep in the liquid. Add the flavoring to the mixture while it is hot, cover the pan, and let it stand for 15 to 20 minutes. Strain to remove any particles, if desired. Syrups of this type are used to add flavor, moisture, and sweetness to cakes before filling and finishing, act as a simple wash for puff pastry as it bakes, and serve as a poaching medium for fruits.

Whipped Cream

Heavy cream can be whipped to soft, medium, or firm peaks for use in sweet and savory applications. It may be sweetened with powdered sugar and flavored with vanilla to produce Chantilly cream. Cream to be whipped must be well chilled, as should the bowl and whip. Working with cold cream and cold equipment helps to produce a more stable foam that is easier to fold into other products.

Begin by whipping the cream at a moderate and steady speed, working either by hand or with an electric mixer. Once the cream starts to thicken, increase the speed and continue to whip until the desired thickness and stiffness is reached. The various stages of whipped cream are as follows:

Soft peak

The cream forms peaks that fall gently to one side when the beater is lifted. Soft peak cream is typically used as a sauce to pool under or spoon over desserts, or as the lightener for sweet and savory mousses with a smooth, creamy consistency.

Medium peak

As the cream passes through the soft peak stage, it becomes stiffer and holds peaks for a longer time and with less drooping when the beaters are lifted. Sugar is best added at this stage and cream whipped to medium peaks is often used to cover cakes and tortes or to use as a garnish (either a dollop dropped from a spoon or a puff piped through a pastry bag). The peaks should not stand up perfectly straight, however, because the added agitation of spreading or piping the cream might cause it to overwhip and take on an undesirable, grainy appearance.

Stiff peak

When cream is beaten to stiff peaks, the foam loses some of its flexibility. This means that there is a good chance that the cream will start to break apart, eventually becoming very grainy and finally turning into butter. As cream reaches stiff peak stage, it will lose some of its gloss and velvety texture.

Whipping Egg Whites and Making Meringues

Egg whites can be beaten into a foam to use as a leavener or lightener. Meringues are made by incorporating enough sugar to both stabilize and sweeten the foam.

There are several uses in the kitchen and bakeshop for whipped egg whites. They are the leavener for soufflés and sponge cakes and they can be used to create the light texture in some mousses and bavarians.

Egg whites must be completely free of any trace of yolk in order to whip successfully. The separated whites whip to the greatest volume when they are at room temperature. Whites taken directly from refrigeration can be tempered by warming them over a bowl of hot water.

The bowl and whip must also be completely free of any grease or fat. Some chefs rinse the bowl and whip with white vinegar, followed by a rinse with very hot water, to remove all traces of grease. The bowl should be large enough to hold the beaten egg whites, which can expand eight to ten times in volume.

Begin whipping at a slow to moderate speed, just until the whites start to loosen and become foamy. Increase the speed and continue to whip until the whites hold soft or medium peaks (see Whipped Cream, page 1055). If egg whites are overbeaten, they become dull, grainy, and dry looking. Overbeaten egg whites collapse quickly and separate as they are folded into a base or batter, adversely affecting the texture of the finished item.

Soft peak meringue barely holds its shape. The peaks tip over when the whip is lifted.

Meringue whipped to medium peak becomes stiffer and retains its shape for a longer time when the beater is lifted from the bowl.

Stiff peak meringue will hold a peak that comes to a sharp point.

Separating Whole Eggs

Eggs separate most easily when they are taken directly from refrigeration. In addition to the cold eggs, you should have four well-cleaned containers on hand for separating eggs: one to catch the white as the egg is separated, plus three more to hold the clean whites, whites with some yolk, and yolks separately.

Crack the eggshell and pull it apart into two halves. Pour the egg from one half into the other, allowing the white to fall into one of the containers. When all of the white has separated from the yolk, drop the yolk into a separate container. Examine the white in the bowl to be sure that it has no bits of yolk. If it is clean, drop it into a container that will hold only clean whites. Otherwise, put it into the container to use for other egg preparations.

Beat egg whites only if you are ready to use them immediately. For example, the whites for a soufflé are beaten and added to the base, then immediately baked for the best volume.

Adding sugar to beaten egg whites makes the foam more stable. These egg white foams are known as meringues. Meringues differ according to how the sugar is added to the whites.

To prepare a meringue, first separate the eggs carefully and be sure that the whites, the bowl, and the whip are all very clean. Different types of meringues are made in the following ways:

Common meringue

Beat the egg whites until frothy and then start to add the sugar, while whipping, in a gradual stream. Once all the sugar is added, whip the meringue to soft, medium, or stiff peaks, as required by the recipe. This type of meringue can be used to leaven angel food cakes, sponge cakes, or soufflés, top a pie, to pipe and bake into shells, or to create borders and other decorations. Because the whites in a common meringue are not heated to a safe temperature, this style of meringue should be used for applications where it will be cooked, either by poaching or baking.

Swiss meringue

To prepare a Swiss meringue, combine the whites and sugar in a mixing bowl, and warm the mixture over simmering heat until it reaches 115° to 165°F/46° to 74°C (depending on the intended use), stirring frequently to be sure that the sugar is completely dissolved into the egg whites. Once the egg whites are warmed, transfer the bowl to a mixer and whip on moderate speed until the meringue has soft, medium, or stiff peaks, as required. Swiss meringue can also be used for the same preparations as common meringue, but it may also be used for lightening mousses and creams, as a filling for cakes, and to add a decorative piped border, as well as to make buttercream.

Italian meringue

Italian meringue is produced when a hot sugar syrup is whipped into egg whites. This meringue requires more careful timing than a common meringue, but the end product has a finer grain and is much more stable. Prepare a sugar syrup and heat it to 230° to 250°F/110° to 121°C, depending on the intended use; the higher the temperature of the sugar, the firmer the resulting meringue will be. As the syrup nears this temperature, beat the egg whites to soft peaks. Once the syrup is properly cooked, pour it gradually into the whites, while the mixer is running. Continue to beat the meringue until it holds soft, medium, or stiff peaks, as required. Italian meringue can be used to prepare baked shells, cookies, or, because it is heated to a high enough temperature, it can be left unbaked to use as a filling or as the base for Italian Buttercream (page 1156).

Choosing and Preparing Pans

Many different kinds of pans are used in baking. Picking the correct shape and size of the pan is essential to ensuring the right texture and appearance. If a pan is too large, the cake or bread may not rise properly during baking and the edges may become over-baked. On the other hand, if a pan is too small, the item may not properly bake through, and the appearance will also suffer.

Pan preparation

Pans are lined with parchment paper to ease the process of removing a baked product. For batters that must be spread rather than poured, it is important to apply a thin film of butter or other fat to the pan before placing the parchment in the base of the pan. The fat will keep the paper stationary while the batter is spread. This is particularly important when using large pans. The sides of the pan should also be greased and lightly floured. Pans used for sponge cakes should be lined with parchment, but the sides of the pans should remain untreated. Angel food cakes require no pan preparation. The full rise of this cake is partially dependent on the batter being able to cling to the side of the pan as it rises during baking.

Pans should be filled approximately three quarters full with batter, unless otherwise specified in the formula's method. This should allow for sufficient room for the product to rise during baking.

Using Pastry Bags and Tips

Pastry bags and assorted tips are used to apply decorations, to add fillings to other foods, and as a portioning tool. Pastry bags have many uses in the kitchen beyond decorating cakes. They are used to portion out batters such as pâte à choux or duchesse potatoes before baking, to fill pastry shells for éclairs or profiteroles, and to apply small amounts of garnish or finish ingredients on hors d'oeuvre and canapés.

Expressing a frosting, batter, dough, or other soft mixture through a pastry bag is referred to as piping. It takes practice to develop the sure movements used to create decorative effects.

To fill a pastry bag, select the desired tip and position it securely in the pastry bag's opening or in a coupler. Fold down the bag's top to create a cuff, then transfer the buttercream to the bag with a spatula or spoon. Twist the bag to compress the mixture and to release any air pockets before beginning to pipe. Use your dominant hand to hold the bag and squeeze out the contents of the bag. Use your other hand to guide and steady the tip. Release pressure on the bag as you lift it cleanly away to avoid making tails.

Clean reusable pastry bags and tips thoroughly immediately after use by washing them carefully in warm soapy water, then rinsing thoroughly. Be sure to turn the bag inside out to clean the interior before storage. In many kitchens and bakeshops, single-use pastry bags are used for reasons of sanitation.

Borders piped using a star tip

Borders piped with a straight tip

Egg Wash

Makes 16 fl oz/480 mL

5 eggs

8 fl oz/240 mL milk

pinch salt

1. Combine the eggs, milk, and salt using a wire whip.

2. Use as needed.

NOTES
There are infinite variations possible to best suit different uses and tastes. For example, water or cream can be substituted for some or all of the milk. Egg yolks can be substituted for all or a portion of the whole eggs. Sugar can also be added.

Simple Syrup

Makes 32 fl oz/960 mL

1 lb/454 g sugar

16 fl oz/480 mL water

Combine the sugar and water in a saucepan and stir to ensure all the sugar is moistened. Bring to a boil, stirring to dissolve the sugar.

Coffee Simple Syrup: After the sugar and water comes to a boil, add 1 oz/28 g ground coffee. Remove the pan from the heat, cover, and allow to steep for 20 minutes. Strain to remove the grounds.

Liqueur-Flavored Simple Syrup: To flavor a simple syrup with a liqueur such as framboise, kirsch, or Kahlúa, add 4 fl oz/120 mL of the desired liqueur to the syrup after it has cooled completely.

NOTE
Simple syrup may be made with varying ratios of sugar to water depending on the desired use and the sweetness and flavor of the cake or pastry to which it is to be applied.

Egg Wash

Egg washes are an important component in many baked goods; they have a considerable effect on the finished appearance and may also affect the flavor, mouthfeel, and texture.

An egg wash may include whole eggs, only yolks, or only whites, which may be blended with water, milk, or cream.

Common Meringue

Makes 1 lb 8 oz/680 g

8 egg whites (about 8 fl oz/240 mL)

pinch salt

1 tsp/5 mL vanilla extract

1 lb/454 g sugar

1. Place the egg whites, salt, and vanilla in the bowl of an electric mixer fitted with a wire whip attachment and whip until frothy. (This may also be done by hand.)

2. Gradually add the sugar while continuing to whip the egg whites. Whip to the desired consistency.

Swiss Meringue

Makes 1 lb 5 oz/595 g

8 egg whites (about 8 fl oz/240 mL)

1 tsp/5 mL vanilla extract

pinch salt

1 lb/454 g sugar

1. Place the egg whites, vanilla, salt, and sugar in the bowl of an electric mixer and stir until the ingredients are thoroughly combined.

2. Place the bowl over a pot of barely simmering water and slowly stir the mixture until it reaches between 115° and 165°F/46° and 74°C, depending on use.

3. Transfer the mixture to an electric mixer and whip with a wire whip attachment on high speed until the meringue is the desired consistency.

Italian Meringue

Makes 1 lb 8 oz/680 g

1 lb/454 g sugar

4 fl oz/120 mL water

8 egg whites (about 8 fl oz/240 mL)

pinch salt

1 tsp/5 mL vanilla extract

1. Combine 12 oz/340 g of the sugar with the water in a heavy-bottomed saucepan and bring to a boil over medium-high heat, stirring to dissolve the sugar. Continue cooking, without stirring, until the mixture reaches the soft ball stage (238°F/114°C).

2. Meanwhile, place the egg whites, salt, and vanilla in the bowl of an electric mixer fitted with a wire whip attachment.

3. When the sugar syrup has reached approximately 230°F/110°C, whip the whites on medium speed until frothy. Gradually add the remaining 4 oz/113 g sugar and beat the meringue to medium peaks.

4. When the sugar syrup reaches 238°F/114°C, add it to the meringue in a slow, steady stream while whipping on medium speed. Whip on high speed to stiff peaks. Continue to beat on medium speed until completely cool.

Chantilly Cream/ Whipped Cream for Garnish

Makes 1 lb 2 oz/510 g

16 fl oz/480 mL heavy cream

2 oz/57 g confectioners' sugar

½ fl oz/15 mL vanilla extract

1. Whip the cream to soft peaks.

2. Add the sugar and vanilla and whip to desired peak.

NOTE

For plain whipped cream, omit the sugar and vanilla.

Chapter Thirty-five

Yeast Breads

Breads and rolls made from yeast-raised doughs and batters have a distinct aroma and flavor, produced by the biological process of the yeast's fermentation. The effects vary from the simplicity of a hearth-baked pizza to a delicate egg- and butter-enriched brioche.

Lean and Enriched Doughs

Relatively speaking, yeast doughs may be divided into two categories: lean doughs and enriched doughs. Lean doughs can be produced with only flour, yeast, salt, and water; in fact, those are the ingredients for a classic French baguette. Other ingredients, such as spices, herbs, special flours, and/or dried nuts and fruits, can be added to vary this dough, but they will not greatly change the basic texture.

Lean doughs contain only relatively small amounts of sugar and fat, if any. Breads made from lean dough tend to have a chewier texture, more bite, and a crisp crust. Hard rolls, French- and Italian-style breads, and whole wheat, rye, and pumpernickel breads are considered lean.

An enriched dough is produced by the addition of ingredients such as sugars or syrups, butter or oil, whole eggs or egg yolks, and milk or cream. Included in this category are soft rolls, brioche, and challah. When fats are introduced, they change the dough's texture as well as the way in which it behaves during mixing, kneading, shaping, and baking. An enriched dough is usually softer and the finished product has a more tender bite after baking than lean doughs. They may be golden in color because of the use of eggs and butter, and the crust is soft rather than crisp.

Wheat flour (all-purpose or bread flour, for instance) is the basis of yeast-raised doughs. Wheat flours contain a high percentage of protein, which gives a good texture to lean doughs. A portion of the wheat flour called for in a recipe may be replaced with other flours, such as rye, pumpernickel, or oat. Consult individual formulas and scale the flour carefully. It is generally not important to sift the flour for bread.

Yeast is a biological leavener, which must be alive in order to be effective. Bring the yeast to room temperature if necessary before preparing the dough. Water, milk, or other liquids used in a bread formula should fall within a temperature range of 68° to 76°F/20° to 24°C for compressed (or fresh) yeast. The ideal water temperature for active dry yeast is 105° to 110°F/41° to 43°C.

The viability of yeast may be tested by proofing. To do so, combine the yeast with warm liquid and a small amount of flour or sugar. Let the mixture rest at room temperature until a thick surface foam forms. The foam indicates that the yeast is alive and can be used. If there is no foam, the yeast is dead and should be discarded.

Salt develops flavor in bread and also helps to control the action of the yeast. If salt is omitted, breads do not develop as good a flavor or texture.

Pan preparation depends on the type of dough to be baked. Because of the higher browning point, lean doughs should be baked directly on the hearth. If this is not possible, either line the pan with parchment paper or dust it with cornmeal or semolina flour (cornmeal is especially well suited to free-form loaves such as baguettes or round loaves). For doughs with a higher percentage of milk, sugar, and fat, grease the pan or line it with parchment paper.

Basic yeast dough stages

There are seven stages: (1) mixing the dough, which includes the pick-up period and development period; (2) fermentation; (3) folding over; (4) scaling and preshaping; (5) final shaping; (6) resting; and (7) final fermentation.

1. First, in the *pick-up period,* the ingredients are blended on low speed until just combined. The dough is a rough mass at this point. Next, during the *clean-up period,* or preliminary development, the dough is mixed at a moderate speed and appears somewhat rough.

2. The *development period* is marked by the dough beginning to pull away from the sides of the mixing bowl, which indicates the development of the gluten's elasticity. Lastly, during *final gluten development,* the dough is smooth and elastic and leaves the sides of the bowl completely clean as the mixer runs.

3. The *first fermentation period,* known as bulk fermentation, develops the flavor of the bread. Transfer the mixed dough to a lightly oiled bowl and cover it to prevent a skin from forming on the surface.

4. Let the dough rest at room temperature (75°F/24°C) until it has doubled in size.

5. Dough is folded over during or after bulk fermentation to redistribute the available food supply for the yeast, equalize the temperature of the dough, expel the built-up fermentation gases, and to further develop the gluten in the dough. The dough should be folded over carefully to preserve the already developed structure.

6. Accurate scaling creates uniformity of size for each dough piece, which allows for uniformity in proofing and baking times.

After scaling, gently preshape the dough into a round or oblong. Preshaping gives the dough a smooth, tight skin that will help trap the gases that develop during fermentation.

Resting for 10 to 20 minutes covered with a linen cloth or plastic wrap after preshaping allows the gluten to relax, so that the dough is easier to manipulate into its final shape.

After resting, the dough is given its final shape. Brush the dough with egg wash and apply garnish, if using, after it is shaped, so that the dough is evenly coated without risk of deflating it after its final rise.

7. After shaping, the dough undergoes one more fermentation. Some doughs, such as the lean dough used to prepare boules, can simply be placed on a worktable or a board that has been dusted with flour or cornmeal. Other doughs or shapes may be placed on a linen cloth (couche) or sheet pans, in loaf pans, or in baskets (bannetons), wooden molds, or other molds. During this final rise, it is again important to ensure that a skin does not form on the surface of the dough. If you are not using a proof box for this final proof, the dough should be covered. Using the temperature and humidity controls in a proof box will prevent this from happening without the need to cover the dough.

Retarding Dough

Retarding dough means to purposely cool the dough, typically at temperatures of around 40°F/ 4°C in order to slow the fermentation process. A dough would typically be retarded during the bulk fermentation process, although fermentation can be slowed during any fermentation stage.

Retarding a dough can help to organize work to meet the needs of production and employee schedules. Retarding also effectively enhances the quality of a dough twofold. It allows the gluten to relax further, since fermentation is prolonged. This results in a dough that is easier to shape. Additionally, it gives the dough time to develop a more pronounced desirable sour flavor.

Keeping the dough fermenting for extended time at a lower temperature also requires that you use less yeast than originally called for in the recipe. Adding the full amount of yeast that was calculated for a fermentation time and rate occurring at 65°F/18°C would cause the dough to overferment if it were retarded. This would produce a flatter loaf of bread with a coarse grain and crumb.

Finishing Techniques

Scoring

1. Many breads are scored with a razor, sharp knife, scissors, or *lame* before they are loaded into the oven. Scoring helps develop a good-quality loaf with an even appearance and crumb. Scoring patterns for round loaves should be evenly distributed over the entire surface.

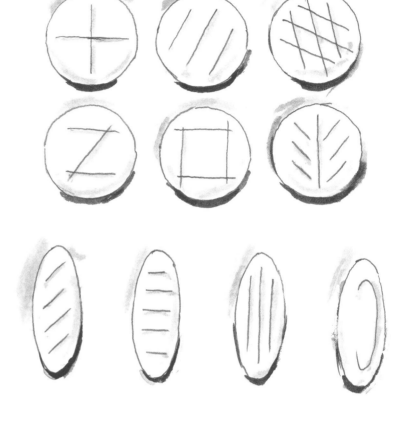

2. Some breads, like baguettes, are scored with traditional patterns that are used as a way to label the breads, making it easy for both clients and staff to identify them. Scoring patterns for oblong loaves are at the highest points on the loaf.

Washes

Use beaten eggs as a wash to create a glossy, shiny crust and seal in the moisture in the bread. Milk or cream is often used for breads baked at lower temperatures.

Baking

Lean doughs should be baked in a hot oven (400° to 450°F/204° to 232°C) with steam; enriched doughs should be baked at a slightly lower temperature (approximately 375°F/191°C). Beyond this, other things that may affect the specific baking temperature are the type of oven, the size and shape of the product, the desired crust and color development (or other such characteristics), and the length of the pan proofing.

Once the loaves are baked, it is important that they be cooled properly in order to preserve the crust and structure of the bread, as well as to allow for final development of flavor. All breads, but most importantly those made with lean doughs, should be cooled on wire racks to maintain air circulation around the entire loaf. This will prevent moisture from collecting on the bread as it cools.

Basic Lean Dough

Makes 8 lb 7¾ oz/3.85 kg dough

5 lb/2.27 kg bread flour

⅔ oz/19 g instant dry yeast

53½ fl oz/1.61 L water, warm

1¾ oz/50 g salt

1. Combine the flour and yeast. Add the water and salt and mix on low speed for 2 minutes. Mix on medium speed for about 3 minutes. The dough should be smooth and elastic.

2. Bulk ferment the dough until nearly doubled, about 30 minutes. Fold the dough gently. Ferment for another 30 minutes, and fold again. Allow the dough to ferment for another 15 minutes before dividing.

3. See pages 1064–1072 for shaping, proofing, and baking options suitable for this dough.

Baguettes

Makes 8 loaves

8 lb/3.63 kg **Basic Lean Dough** (preceding recipe)

1. Scale the dough into 1-lb/454-g pieces. For each loaf, shape the dough into an oblong. Let the dough rest, covered, until relaxed, 15 to 20 minutes. (Note: Work sequentially, starting with the first piece of dough you divided and rounded.)

2. Position the dough lengthwise, parallel to the edge of the work surface with the seam side up. Press lightly with your fingertips to stretch it into a rectangle 10 in/25 cm long, using as little flour as possible. Fold the top edge of the dough down to the center of the dough, pressing lightly with your fingertips to tighten the dough. Fold the dough lengthwise in half and use the heel of your hand to seal the 2 edges together, keeping the seam straight. Roll the dough under your palms into a cylinder 20 in/51 cm long. Keep the pressure even and hold your hands flat and parallel to the work surface. Move your hands outward from the center of the cylinder toward the ends and slightly increase the pressure as you move outward, until both ends have an even, gentle taper. Then increase the pressure at the ends of the loaf to seal them.

3. Place the loaf seam side down into a pan or onto a parchment-lined sheet pan. Proof, covered, until the dough springs back very slowly to the touch, 30 to 45 minutes. (Note: Baguettes should be slightly under-proofed when placed into the oven.)

4. Score the dough with 5 or 7 diagonal lines down the center of the loaf, overlapping each cut by ½ in/1 cm.

5. Bake in a 475°F/246°C oven until the crust is golden brown, the bread sounds hollow when thumped on the bottom, and you hear a crackle when you hold it next to your ear, 20 to 25 minutes. Cool completely on a rack.

Boules

Makes 8 loaves

8 lb/3.63 kg **Basic Lean Dough** (page 1069)

1. Scale the dough into 1-lb/454-g pieces. For each loaf, shape the dough into a round. Let the dough rest, covered, until relaxed, 15 to 20 minutes. (Note: Work sequentially, starting with the first piece of dough you divided and rounded.)

2. Cup both hands around the dough. Using your thumbs, push the dough away from you in an arc to the right, keeping a small piece of dough between the table and the edges of your palms. Using the edges of your palms as a guide, pull the dough toward you in an arc to the left. There should still be a small piece of dough that is squeezed between the table and the edges of your palms. Repeat this circular motion 2 or 3 more times, applying gentle pressure while rounding the dough, to create a tight, smooth outer skin. Place the boule seam side up in a round basket, or seam side down on a board dusted with cornmeal.

3. Proof until the dough springs back slowly to the touch, 1 to 1½ hours. Flip the dough seam side down onto a peel. Score the boule with an arc.

4. Bake in a 450°F/232°C oven until the crust is golden brown and the bread sounds hollow when thumped on the bottom, 25 to 30 minutes. Cool completely on a rack.

Focaccia

Makes 8 loaves

8 lb/3.63 kg **Basic Lean Dough** (page 1069)

olive oil, as needed

toppings, such as minced herbs, sautéed onions, sliced tomatoes, or coarse salt, as needed

1. Scale the dough into 1-lb/454-g pieces. For each loaf, shape the dough into a round. Let the dough rest, covered, until relaxed, 15 to 20 minutes. (Note: Work sequentially, starting with the first piece of dough you divided and rounded.)

2. To shape the focaccia, flatten and stretch each round of dough into a rectangle or a disk and place it on a sheet pan sprinkled with cornmeal or brushed with oil. Let the loaves rise until doubled, 30 to 40 minutes. Just before baking, dimple the focaccia with your fingertips. Brush generously with oil and scatter the desired topping over each focaccia.

3. Bake in a 450°F/232°C oven until deep in color, about 30 minutes. Cool completely on a rack.

Focaccia

Hard Rolls

Makes 3 dozen rolls

3 lb/1.36 kg **Basic Lean Dough** (page 1069)

1. Scale the dough into 36 pieces, about 1⅓ oz/38 g each. Preshape the dough into rounds. Let the dough rest, covered, until relaxed, 15 to 20 minutes.

2. Press each piece of dough lightly with your fingertips to flatten. Fold the top edge of the dough down to the center, pressing lightly with your fingertips to tighten the dough. Rotate the dough 90 degrees, fold it in half, and use the heel of your hand to seal the 2 edges together. Cup the roll in your hand and reround the dough, applying gentle pressure to create a tight, smooth ball.

3. Proof, covered, until the dough springs back slowly to the touch but does not collapse, about 30 minutes.

4. Score the rolls with a straight cut down the center of each one.

5. Bake in a 450°F/232°C oven until the rolls have a golden brown crust and sound hollow when thumped on the bottom, about 15 minutes. Cool completely on racks.

Ciabatta

Makes 7 lb 8 oz/3.40 kg dough (5 loaves)

3 lb 10 oz water (68° to 76°F/20° to 24°C)

⅓ oz/9 g compressed yeast

5 lb/2.27 kg bread flour

1¾ tsp/8.75 g salt

olive oil, as needed

kosher or sea salt

1. Combine the water and yeast in the bowl of an electric mixer and blend until the yeast is fully dissolved.

2. Add the flour and salt and mix, using the dough hook attachment, on low speed just to incorporate. Increase to medium speed and mix until the dough is smooth and elastic, 10 to 12 minutes.

3. Place the dough in a lightly oiled container, cover, and let the dough rise until doubled in volume, about 1 hour 15 minutes.

4. Turn the dough out of the bowl onto a well-floured work surface. Scale the dough into 1 lb 8-oz/680-g pieces and gently stretch each into a rectangle, about 10 in/25 cm long and 4 in/10 cm wide. Place on a lined baking sheet.

5. Bake in a 450°F/232°C oven (with steam if available) until deep in color, about 30 minutes.

6. Remove the ciabatta from the pan, and if desired, immediately brush with oil and scatter salt over the surface. Cool completely on racks.

Pita Bread

Makes 11 pitas

1 lb/454 g bread flour

1 lb/454 g whole wheat flour

¼ oz/7 g instant dry yeast

20 fl oz/600 mL water

1 fl oz/60 mL olive oil

¾ oz/21 g salt

¾ tsp/3.75 g sugar

1. Combine the flours and yeast. Add the water, oil, salt, and sugar. Mix on low speed for 4 minutes and on medium speed for 3 minutes. The dough should be slightly moist but with strong gluten development.

2. Bulk ferment the dough until nearly doubled, about 30 minutes. Fold gently.

3. Divide the dough into 4½-oz/128-g pieces. Preshape the dough into rounds. Let the dough rest, covered, until relaxed, 15 to 20 minutes. (Note: Work sequentially, starting with the first piece of dough you divided and rounded.)

4. Using a rolling pin, roll each piece of dough into a round 7 in/18 cm in diameter. Transfer them to parchment-lined sheet pans, cover, and let them relax for 10 minutes.

5. Bake the pitas in a 500°F/260°C oven until puffed but not browned, 3 to 4 minutes. Stack the pitas 5 high and wrap each stack in a cloth. Cool before serving.

Semolina Pizza Crust

Makes 8 lb/3.63 kg dough

3 lb 12 oz/1.70 kg bread flour

2 lb/907 g durum flour

½ oz/14 g instant dry yeast

48 fl oz/1.44 L water

2½ fl oz/75 mL olive oil

2 oz/57 g salt

1. Combine the flours and yeast. Add the water, oil, and salt. Mix on low speed for 2 minutes and on medium speed for 4 minutes. The dough should have good gluten development but still be a little sticky.

2. Bulk ferment the dough until nearly doubled, about 50 minutes. Fold gently. Allow the dough to ferment for another 15 minutes before dividing. Refrigerate overnight. Take out 1 hour prior to use.

3. Divide the dough in 8-oz/227-g pieces. Preshape the dough into rounds. Let the dough rest, covered, in the refrigerator, until relaxed, 1 hour. (Note: Work sequentially, starting with the first piece of dough you divided and rounded.)

4. Using a rolling pin, roll each piece of dough into a round 9 in/23 cm in diameter. Transfer the dough to parchment-lined sheet pans that have been dusted with semolina flour, or place each round on a peel before you add any topping.

5. Top the dough as desired (see the variations below), leaving a 1-in/3-cm border without garnish.

6. Bake the pizzas in a 500°F/260°C oven until golden brown around the edges, 3 to 4 minutes. Serve at once.

Margherita Pizza: Top each round of dough with 3 fl oz/90 mL Tomato Sauce (page 384). Top with 2 oz/57 g mozzarella cheese and ½ oz/14 g Parmesan.

Spinach Pizza: Top each round of dough with ½ oz/43 g Pesto (page 388), 1½ oz/43 g sautéed spinach, 1½ oz/43 g ricotta cheese, and 1 oz/28 g ricotta salata.

Naan Bread

Naan Bread

Makes 8 flatbreads

14 oz/397 g all-purpose flour

⅓ oz/9 g instant dry yeast

6 fl oz/180 mL water

2 fl oz/60 mL clarified butter, plus more as needed

2 oz/57 g plain yogurt

1 egg

1 oz/28 g sugar

1½ tsp/7.50 g salt

2 tbsp/12 g poppy seeds or black onion seeds

1. Combine the flour and yeast. Add the water, butter, yogurt, egg, sugar, and salt and mix on low speed for 4 minutes. The dough should be very elastic but still wet.

2. Bulk ferment the dough until nearly doubled, about 1 hour. Fold gently.

3. Divide the dough into 3-oz/85-g pieces. Preshape the dough into rounds. Let the dough rest, covered, until relaxed, 15 to 20 minutes. (Note: Work sequentially, starting with the first piece of dough you divided and rounded.)

4. Gently stretch each piece of dough into a round, 7 in/18 cm in diameter, so that the center is ¼ in/6 mm thick and there is a border ½ in/1 cm wide all around. Pull 1 edge out to elongate each round slightly, creating a teardrop shape.

5. Place the breads on parchment-lined sheet pans, brush them with butter, and sprinkle the seeds on top.

6. Bake the naan in a 425°F/218°C deck oven until golden brown and puffed, about 10 minutes. Cool completely on racks.

Cottage Dill Rolls

Makes 6 dozen rolls

12 oz/340 g water, at 68° to 76°F/20° to 24°C

5 oz/140 g compressed yeast

5 lb 4 oz/2.38 kg bread flour

3 lb/1.36 kg cottage cheese

4½ oz/128 g sugar

1½ oz/43 g minced onions

3 oz/85 g butter, soft

1 oz/28 g salt

1 oz/28 g chopped dill

1 oz/28 g baking soda

6 oz/170 g eggs

pinch horseradish

melted butter, as needed

kosher salt, as needed

1. Combine the water and yeast in the bowl of an electric mixer and blend until the yeast is fully dissolved.

2. Add the flour, cottage cheese, sugar, onions, butter, salt, dill, baking soda, eggs, and horseradish and, using the dough hook attachment, mix on low speed just to incorporate. Increase the speed to medium and mix until the dough is smooth and elastic, 10 to 12 minutes.

3. Place the dough in a lightly oiled container, cover, and let rise until the dough has doubled in volume, about 75 minutes.

4. Turn out onto a lightly floured work surface. Fold over the dough and scale into 6 dozen 1½-oz/43-g pieces. Round off the dough and let it rest for 15 to 20 minutes. Reshape the rolls and place on parchment-lined sheet pans.

5. Proof in a proof box or in a warm area until doubled in size, about 25 to 30 minutes. Bake in a 380°F/193°C oven until light golden in color, about 20 minutes.

6. Brush the rolls with melted butter and sprinkle very lightly with kosher salt as soon as they are taken from the oven. Let cool on the pans.

Brioche Loaf

Makes 8 loaves

5 lb/2.27 kg bread flour

1 oz/28 g instant dry yeast

16 eggs

16 fl oz/480 mL whole milk, at room temperature

2 oz/57 g salt

3 lb/1.36 kg butter, soft but still pliable

16 fl oz/480 mL **Egg Wash** (page 1061)

1. Combine the flour and yeast. Add the eggs, milk, and salt and mix on low speed for 4 minutes.

2. Gradually add the butter with the mixer running on medium speed, scraping down the sides of the bowl as necessary. After the butter has been fully incorporated, mix on medium speed for 15 minutes, or until the dough begins to pull away from the sides of the bowl.

3. Place the dough on a sheet pan that has been lined with parchment paper and greased. Cover tightly with plastic wrap and refrigerate overnight.

4. Lightly grease eight 2-lb/907-g loaf pans (8 by 4½ by 3 in/20 by 11 by 8 cm).

5. Divide the dough by hand into 64 even pieces, about 2¾ oz/78 g each.

6. Roll each piece into a ball and place it in the loaf pans to form 2 rows of 4 in each pan. Brush the loaves lightly with egg wash, cover with plastic wrap, and proof for 2 hours, or until the dough has doubled in size.

7. Brush with egg wash a second time and bake in a 400°F/204°C oven until the crust is a rich golden brown and the sides of the bread spring back fully when pressed, 30 to 35 minutes. Remove from the pan and cool completely on a wire rack.

Brioche à Tête: Divide the dough into 1¾-oz/50-g pieces (104 pieces). Roll each piece into a ball, place it in a container, and refrigerate for 15 minutes. Make a head (tête) by pinching ¼ of the dough ball with the side of your hand and rolling it back and forth on the worktable, making a depression in the dough, but not detaching it; the larger piece of dough should be about 2¾ in/7 cm long and the tête should be ¾ in/2 cm long. Gently press a hole all the way through the center of the larger piece of dough. Push the tête through the center of the larger piece of dough. Place each brioche into a greased brioche tin, with the tête on top. Brush the brioche lightly with egg wash, cover with plastic wrap, and proof for 2 hours, or until the dough has doubled in size. Brush with egg wash a second time and bake in a 400°F/204°C oven for 20 minutes, or until golden brown.

Brioche à Tête

Raisin Bread with Cinnamon Swirl

Raisin Bread with Cinnamon Swirl

Makes 6 loaves

4 lb/1.81 kg bread flour

½ oz/14 g instant dry yeast

34 fl oz/1.02 L milk, at room temperature

5¾ oz/163 g butter, soft

5¾ oz/163 g sugar

4 eggs

1½ oz/43 g salt

12 oz/340 g raisins

¾ oz/21 g ground cinnamon

Egg Wash (page 1061), **as needed**

CINNAMON SUGAR

8 oz/227 g brown sugar

1 oz/28 g ground cinnamon

1. Combine the flour and yeast. Add the milk, butter, sugar, eggs, and salt. Mix on low speed for 4 minutes and on medium speed for 4 minutes; in the last minute of mixing, add the raisins, and in the last 30 seconds of mixing, add the cinnamon, mixing just long enough to create a swirl. The dough should be slightly soft.

2. Bulk ferment the dough until nearly doubled, about 1 hour. Fold gently.

3. Scale the dough into 1 lb 4-oz/567-g pieces and pre-shape into an oblong. Let the dough rest, covered, until relaxed, 15 to 20 minutes. Lightly grease six 2-lb/907-g loaf pans.

4. Roll the dough into an even rectangle 8 in/20 cm wide by 12 in/30 cm long. Brush the dough lightly with egg wash. Combine the brown sugar and cinnamon and sprinkle 1 oz/28 g evenly over the surface. Roll the dough up along the long side under your palms into a cylinder, keeping the pressure even and holding your hands flat and parallel to the work surface to create a smooth, even loaf.

5. Place the dough seam side down in a greased loaf pan. The dough will spring back on itself slightly and fit snugly in the pan. Brush the loaf lightly with egg wash. Proof, covered, until the dough fills the pan and springs back slowly to the touch but does not collapse, 1½ to 2 hours.

6. Gently brush the bread again with egg wash. Bake in a 375°F/191°C oven until the crust is brown and the sides spring back when pressed, 25 to 30 minutes. Remove the bread from the pan and cool completely on a rack.

Challah (3-Braid)

Makes 8 loaves

4 lb/1.81 kg bread flour

½ oz/14 g instant dry yeast

32 fl oz/960 mL water

12 egg yolks

8 fl oz/240 mL vegetable oil

2 oz/57 g sugar

½ oz/14 g salt

10 fl oz/600 mL **Egg Wash** (page 1061; using yolks only)

1. Combine the flour and yeast. Add the water, egg yolks, oil, sugar, and salt. Mix on low speed for 4 minutes and on medium speed for 4 minutes. The dough should be slightly firm and smooth, not sticky.

2. Bulk ferment the dough until nearly doubled, about 1 hour. Fold gently.

3. Divide the dough into 24 pieces, about 4½ oz/128 g each. Preshape the dough into oblongs. Allow the dough to rest, covered, 15 to 20 minutes.

4. Start with the first piece of dough that you shaped and work sequentially. Starting at the center of the dough, roll each piece outward, applying gentle pressure with your palms. Apply very little pressure at the center of the dough, but increase the pressure as you roll toward the end of the dough. Roll each piece of dough into an evenly tapered strand 12 in/30 cm long. It is imperative that all of the strands be the same length. If they are not, the finished braid will be uneven.

5. Dust the tops of the strands very lightly with white rye flour. This will keep the dough dry as you braid and help maintain the overall definition of the braid.

6. Lay 3 strands of the dough vertically parallel to each other. Begin braiding in the center of the strands. Place the left strand over the center strand, then place the right strand over the center strand. Repeat this process until you reach the end of the dough. Pinch together the ends tightly. Flip the braid around and finish braiding the other side.

7. Brush the dough lightly with egg wash. Allow the dough to proof, covered, until the dough springs back lightly to the touch but does not collapse, about 1 hour.

There should be a small indentation left in the dough. Make sure that the egg wash is dry before you apply a second coat. Egg wash the dough again very gently before baking.

8. Bake in a 350°F/177°C convection oven until the braids are dark golden brown and shiny, 20 to 25 minutes. Cool completely on a rack.

Soft Dinner Rolls

Makes 12 dozen 1-oz/30-g rolls

2 1/2 lb/1.15 kg milk, at 68° to 76°F/20° to 24°C

6 oz /170 g compressed yeast

8 oz/227 g eggs

5 lb 8 oz/2.49 kg bread flour

2 oz/57 g salt

8 oz/227 g sugar

8 oz/227 g butter, at room temperature

Egg Wash (page 1061), as needed

1. Combine the milk and yeast in the bowl of an electric mixer and blend until the yeast is fully dissolved.

2. Add the eggs, flour, salt, sugar, and butter and, using the dough hook attachment, mix on low speed just to incorporate. Increase the speed to medium and mix until the dough is smooth and elastic, 10 to 12 minutes.

3. Place the dough in a lightly oiled container, cover, and let rise until the dough has doubled in volume, about 1 hour 15 minutes.

4. Turn the dough out onto a lightly floured work surface. Fold the dough over, scale into 12 dozen 1-oz/28-g pieces, and round off. Cover and let rest for 10 minutes.

5. Shape the dough into rolls (see Notes) and place them on sheet pans that have been lined with parchment. Brush lightly and evenly with egg wash. Cover and pan proof until nearly doubled, 25 to 30 minutes. Brush with egg wash again just before baking, if desired.

6. Bake in a 375°F/191°C oven until deep golden brown, about 20 minutes.

7. Let the rolls cool on the pan.

NOTES

The rolls may be shaped into knots, Parker House rolls, or cloverleaf rolls. To make knots, roll each ball of dough into a rope and then tie it into a knot or figure eight. For Parker House rolls, flatten a piece of dough, brush it with butter, and fold it in half. For cloverleaf rolls, arrange 3 small balls of dough in a triangular pattern. Place in muffin tins, if desired.

Sweet Dough

Makes 11 lb 8 oz/5.22 kg dough

64 fl oz/1.92 L milk, at 68° to 76°F/20° to 24°C

6 oz/170 g compressed yeast

1 lb/454 g eggs

1½ oz/43 g malt syrup

1 lb/454 g pastry flour

4 lb 8 oz/2.04 kg bread flour

¾ oz/21 g salt

8 oz/227 g sugar

½ oz/14 g ground cardamom

1 lb/454 g butter, soft

1. Combine the milk and yeast in the bowl of an electric mixer and blend until the yeast is fully dissolved.

2. Add the eggs and malt syrup and blend. Add the remaining ingredients and, using the dough hook attachment, mix on low speed just to incorporate. Increase the speed to medium and mix until the dough is smooth and elastic, 10 to 12 minutes.

3. The dough may be shaped now or refrigerated for later use.

Cinnamon Raisin Buns

Makes 3 dozen buns

4 lb/1.81 kg **Sweet Dough** (preceding recipe)

Egg Wash (page 1061), as needed

melted butter, as needed

raisins, as needed

cinnamon sugar, as needed

oil, as needed

apricot jam, as needed

fondant, as needed

1. Roll the dough into a rectangle; brush the long edge with egg wash and brush the remaining dough with melted butter.

2. Sprinkle the dough with raisins and cinnamon sugar, being careful not to cover the egg-washed area.

3. Roll the dough up like a jelly roll, sealing the egg-washed edge.

4. Cut into 3 dozen 2-oz/57-g slices and brush the tops with oil.

5. Place on a sheet pan, oiled side up, cover, and proof until double in size, about 20 minutes.

6. Bake in a 380° to 400°F/193° to 204°C oven until golden brown on all sides, about 25 to 30 minutes. Brush immediately with warm apricot jam. Drizzle with fondant. Let the buns cool on the pan.

Sticky Buns

Makes 32 sticky buns

CINNAMON SMEAR

10 oz/284 g bread flour

6 oz/170 g sugar

2 tbsp/12 g ground cinnamon

5 oz/142 g butter

6 egg whites

8 oz/227 g pecans, toasted and chopped

PAN SMEAR

2 lb/907 g light brown sugar

30 fl oz/900 mL dark corn syrup

30 fl oz/900 mL heavy cream

6 lb/2.72 kg **Sweet Dough** (page 1081)

8 fl oz/240 mL **Egg Wash** (page 1061)

1. To make the cinnamon smear, mix together the flour, sugar, and cinnamon. Blend them with the butter in an electric mixer using the paddle attachment on medium speed for 1 minute, or until the mixture looks like coarse meal and there are no visible chunks of butter.

2. Add the egg whites on medium speed in 2 additions, mixing to fully combine and scraping down the sides of the bowl as necessary.

3. Add the nuts and mix until just combined. Reserve until needed.

4. To make the pan smear, combine the sugar, corn syrup, and cream in a saucepan and heat to 220°F/104°C.

5. Allow the mixture to cool to room temperature before using. It may be necessary to recombine the mixture using a wire whip before using.

6. Scale the dough into four 1 lb 8-oz/680-g pieces. For each piece, roll the dough out on a lightly floured work surface into a rectangle 14 by 8 in/36 by 20 cm (approximately ½ in/1 cm thick).

7. Lightly brush each rectangle of dough with a strip of egg wash 1 in/3 cm wide along the long side of the dough.

8. Spread 8 fl oz/240 mL of the cinnamon smear evenly over the remainder of each rectangle of dough. Roll the dough up to form a log 14 in/36 cm long and seal with the egg-washed strip. Divide each piece of dough into 8 even pieces.

9. Pour 8 fl oz/240 mL of the pan smear into each of four 9-in/23-cm square baking pans. Place 4 rolls in each pan.

10. Bake in a 400°F/204°C oven for 25 to 30 minutes, or until golden brown. Immediately upon removal from the oven, invert each pan onto a plate. Serve warm or at room temperature.

Chapter Thirty-six

Pastry Doughs and Batters

Most pastry doughs and batters contain many common ingredients: flour, fat, liquid, and eggs. What makes each unique is the proportion in which each of the ingredients is used in relation to the other, the flavorings used, and the method for mixing or combining the ingredients.

Rubbed-Dough Method (Cutting-in Method)

Biscuits, scones, soda breads, and pie doughs can be prepared using a rubbed-dough, or cutting-in, method. The ingredients are not blended into a smooth batter. Instead, the fat is chilled and then rubbed into the flour to create flakes that will produce a tender flaky baked item.

Flour, a cold solid fat, and a very cold liquid are the basic components of most rubbed-dough products. All-purpose white wheat flour or a combination of wheat and other flours should be properly weighed and sifted. Any leavener should be weighed or measured and blended evenly throughout the flour either by sifting it with the flour or by blending with a whisk. Other dry ingredients (salt, spices, etc.) are typically scaled out and blended with the flour in the same manner.

Butter, shortening, and lard (or a combination thereof) are the most common fats used for this mixing method; they should be broken or cut into pieces and kept cool. Recipes using this mixing method call for a relatively small amount of liquid, and the liquid, like the fat, should be very cold to further inhibit the fat from blending completely with the flour. Water, milk, and buttermilk are all common liquid ingredients.

There are two basic types of rubbed doughs: flaky and mealy. The larger the flakes of fat before the liquid is added, the flakier and crisper the baked crust will be. If the flakes of butter or shortening are rubbed into the dough so that they remain visible, the result will be what is often referred to as "flaky" pie dough. If the butter or shortening is more thoroughly worked into the dough, until the mixture resembles coarse meal, the result will be what is sometimes referred to as "mealy" dough. Combine the liquid with the other ingredients just enough to allow the moisture to be absorbed by the flour and just until the ingredients come together, at which point the dough should be allowed to rest in the refrigerator.

Flaky pie dough is best for pies and tarts that are filled with a fruit filling and baked. Mealy dough is best suited for pies and tarts that require a fully baked shell that is filled after cooling and set until chilled, or for custard or other liquid fillings that are baked until set.

Pie pans and tart pans require no preparation because a dough of this type contains a great amount of fat. Rubbed doughs for pies or tarts should be rolled out on a lightly floured work surface to approximately ⅛ in/3 mm thick. Ovens should be properly preheated and the rack adjusted to the center position in conventional ovens. Cooling racks should be available. Scones, biscuits, and breads should be removed from baking pans and allowed to cool directly on the racks. Pies and tarts cool on racks in their pans. Tarts may be removed from their pans after they are completely cooled.

1. **Sift or blend the dry ingredients well before adding the fat.** Good results depend on working the dough as little as possible and blending the dry ingredients at the beginning to cut down on mixing time later. Have the butter or shortening cold so that it is still solid enough to be worked into the flour without blending the mixture into a smooth dough. Add the fat to the dry ingredients all at once, and rub them into the fat. Don't work the fat into the flour too thoroughly, or the end result will not be as flaky and delicate as desired.

The fat in the mixture on the left was rubbed until the pieces were the size of shelled walnuts, which will result in a flaky pie dough. The fat in the mixture on the right was rubbed until the pieces were approximately the size of peas. This will produce a mealy pie dough. Note the color difference that was achieved by rubbing the fat into the flour more thoroughly.

2. **Make a well in the center of the flour/fat mixture and add the liquid ingredients.** Slowly mix the flour together with the water, starting with the flour on the inside of the well and working to the outside.

3. **Do not overwork the dough once the liquid is added; vigorous or prolonged mixing will result in a tough product.** Knead the dough just until smooth. Divide and portion the dough for storage. Pie dough should be refrigerated after mixing and before rolling it out to the desired thickness. Use light but even pressure while rolling out the dough.

Blending Method

The blending method consists simply of making two mixtures, one with the wet ingredients and one with the dry, and then combining them. The fat, in liquid form (oil or melted butter), is incorporated with the wet ingredients. Any garnish ingredients are most typically added last. The key to a successful blending method is to not overmix the batter. The wet and dry ingredient mixtures should be blended only until just combined. Overmixing will produce too much gluten, providing a coarser grain and tougher crumb in the baked product.

This method generally requires white wheat flour, either all-purpose or pastry. Special flours, such as cornmeal, graham flour, or oat flour, also may be used to replace some or all of the white wheat flour in a recipe.

Milk, buttermilk, water, and even the moisture from vegetables like zucchini or carrots can add liquid to the recipe. Recipes typically call for the commonly used chemical leaveners baking powder or baking soda. Fats, whether oil or butter, must be liquid when added to the batter. Butter should be melted and cooled to room temperature before adding.

When adding the wet ingredients to the dry ingredients, add them all at once and blend, just until the dry ingredients are evenly moistened. If incorporating by hand, make a well in the center of the dry ingredients and add the wet into the center. Scrape the bowl down once or twice to mix the batter evenly. Mixing these batters as briefly as possible ensures a light, delicate texture to the finished product.

Specific formulas may call for adding such ingredients as fresh or dried fruits, nuts, or chocolate. Typically, they are folded into the batter just before scaling and baking. However, they may also be incorporated along with the dry ingredients.

The type of pan and its preparation will vary. For popovers, for example, popover pans or ramekins need to be buttered generously. Other baked goods may require a dusting of flour along with the butter. Use paper liners, if available, to line pans and muffin tins. See each recipe for specific pan prep instructions.

Laminated Doughs

Laminated doughs include puff pastry, croissant, and Danish. To make a laminated dough, fold and roll a previously prepared dough (the initial dough) together with a block of fat called a roll-in. Through a series of folds or turns, multiple layers of dough and fat are created that both leaven and contribute to crispness, tenderness, and lightness. The fat that separates the layers of this final dough melts during baking, providing a place for steam that is released from the dough and the fat to collect, expanding the space between the flaky layers of pastry. Proper mixing methods, rolling techniques, and temperature control are essential to producing laminated doughs that are flaky and delicate after baking.

Folding may be the most important factor in making a laminated dough, as the distinct layers of fat and dough must be maintained throughout the process. The dough must be rolled out evenly and the corners kept square throughout the lock-in of fat and all subsequent folds, to ensure proper layering.

The first fold and the step that introduces the roll-in (or lamination fat) to the dough is the lock-in. The roll-in fat and the dough must be of the same consistency. Let the roll-in stand at room temperature for a few minutes if it is too hard, or refrigerate it if it is too soft.

To administer a lock-in, divide the sheet of dough visually in half. Roll the roll-in into a rectangle that is half the size of the dough square or rectangle, and place it on one-half of the dough, then fold the other half of the dough over it and seal the edges to completely encase the roll-in fat. This type of fold doubles the number of layers in the pastry. The roll-in fat can also be added to the dough using the envelope, single-fold, or three-fold technique.

Phyllo Dough

This dough, used to prepare strudel and baklava, is a lean dough made only of flour and water and, occasionally, a small amount of oil. The dough is stretched and rolled until it is extremely thin. Butter, instead of being rolled into the dough, is melted and brushed onto the dough sheets before they are baked so that after baking, the result is similar to puff pastry.

Most kitchens purchase frozen phyllo dough. This dough needs sufficient time to thaw and come up to room temperature before it can be worked successfully. After removing phyllo from its wrapping, cover it lightly with dampened towels and plastic. Otherwise, the phyllo can dry out quickly and become brittle enough to shatter.

For the best texture, spread bread crumbs, butter, or a combination of the two evenly over the dough to keep the layers separate as they bake. Use a spray bottle or brush to apply the butter or oil in an even coat. Refrigerating phyllo pastries before baking helps the layers remain distinct and allows them to rise more as it bakes.

1. Divide the sheet of pastry visually into thirds.

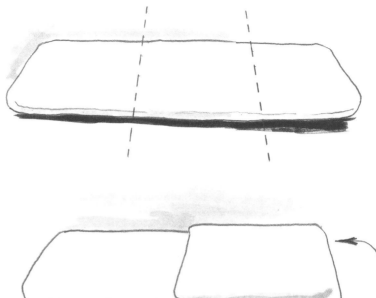

2. Fold one of the outer thirds of the dough over the middle third of the pastry.

3. Fold the remaining outer third of the dough over the folded dough. This fold triples the number of layers in the dough each time.

4. After the roll-in is added to the dough, subsequent folds are usually made with a three-fold technique. Each time, before folding and rolling the dough, brush any excess flour from its surface. When you fold the dough, the corners should squarely meet and the edges should be straight and perfectly aligned. After each fold, the dough should be refrigerated to allow it to relax and the butter to chill; the length of time the dough will need to rest will depend in large part on the temperature of the kitchen.

For each fold, turn the dough 90 degrees from the previous one to ensure that the gluten is stretched equally in all directions. Too much stress in one direction will make the dough difficult to roll, rise unevenly, and become misshapen during baking as the gluten contracts.

The Creaming Method

Muffins, cakes, quick breads, cookies, and other baked goods made with the creaming method develop their light and airy structure from the use of chemical leaveners and the incorporation of air into the batter or dough.

For the creaming method, first the fat and sugar are blended, or "creamed," until relatively smooth, light, and creamy. Then the eggs are added gradually, and finally, the sifted dry ingredients are added in one or two additions, depending on the amount of flour; if there is a liquid, the flour and liquid are added alternately, starting and ending with the flour. It is important that ingredients for a creamed batter or dough are at room temperature and the fat (butter, shortening, nut paste, etc.) is soft before beginning to mix.

The fat should be pliable so that it can aerate properly. Allow the butter or other fat to come to room temperature, or beat it with the paddle attachment of a mixer to soften it slightly. The sugar used in creaming recipes is often granulated white sugar, although brown sugar or powdered sugar may be used in some recipes. It is the act of beating the granules of sugar into the fat that produces the final texture. Eggs included in the recipe should be at room temperature to avoid breaking the creamed butter and sugar mixture. Flavorings, such as vanilla extract or chocolate, should be at room temperature. Chocolate is typically melted and allowed to cool slightly before blended into the batter. Generally, pans are greased and lightly floured or greased, lined with parchment that has been cut to size, and then greased again.

1. Cream together the fat and sugar with the paddle attachment of an electric mixer on medium speed. Scrape down the sides and bottom of the bowl occasionally as you work to ensure that all the fat is blended evenly. Continue until the mixture is pale in color and light and relatively smooth in texture.

When the butter and sugar have this appearance, it indicates that a sufficient amount of air has been incorporated into the mixture. If the ingredients are not sufficiently creamed, the final product will be somewhat dense and lack the light, tender qualities characteristic of creamed baked goods.

2. Add the eggs at room temperature, gradually, and in stages, fully incorporating them and scraping down the bowl after each addition. Scraping down the bowl is important to develop a completely smooth batter. Adding the eggs in batches will help to prevent the batter from separating.

Make the Creamed Batter

3. **Add the sifted dry ingredients all at once, or alternated with the liquid ingredient.** When adding the dry alternating with a liquid, add one third of the dry ingredients, then about one half of the liquid ingredients, mixing until smooth and scraping down the bowl after each addition. Repeat this sequence until all of the dry and liquid ingredients have been added. Increase the speed and beat the batter just until it is evenly blended and smooth. Regardless of the method of addition, after adding the dry ingredients the dough or batter should be mixed minimally, or just until incorporated.

Lastly, add any remaining flavoring or garnishing ingredients, such as nuts, chocolate chips, or dried fruit, mixing or folding until just incorporated.

Mixing a Successful Cake

There are a few things to keep in mind when making a cake, regardless of the mixing method, that will help to ensure a successful end result.

Sifting

Sift dry ingredients (flours, spices, leaveners) together to remove any lumps and to evenly distribute the ingredients. Spices are an important flavoring element and are typically used in smaller amounts (i.e., fractions of a teaspoon). It is important they be evenly mixed for proper flavor development. When leaveners such as baking powder or baking soda are not evenly distributed, the resulting baked item may have an uneven crumb with holes or hollow channels.

Temperature

Before mixing, all ingredients should be at room temperature. Ingredients not at the same temperature can inhibit proper mixing. Adding cold eggs or milk to butter can cause the batter to separate. Even when all ingredients are at the proper temperature, the liquid is often added incrementally to prevent separation and to allow for the full hydration of the flour.

Time

In many (or most) of the mixing methods used to produce cakes and quick breads, time plays an important role for two reasons. First, mixing time facilitates the development of air cells in the batter. In most of these mixing methods, air cells are important to the proper development of structure and crumb during baking. Second, it is important to restrict the mixing time after the flour has been added to prevent the development of gluten, which would make the baked item tough and chewy.

The Foaming Method

A foaming method is any method in which the eggs are whipped or beaten to incorporate air before they are folded into the rest of the batter. When using a foaming method it is vital that all ingredients and equipment are assembled and receive any preliminary treatment before beginning to mix the batter. Pans should be treated as called for in the specific recipe: greased and/or lined or dusted with flour. Butter, if called for, should be melted and slightly cooled. Dry ingredients such as flour, additional leavener, and ground spices should be sifted together.

There are three basic types of foaming methods: cold, warm, and separated. For the cold foaming method, the whole eggs are whipped with the sugar before folding into the batter. For the warm foaming method, the mixture is heated over a water bath before it is whipped, creating a more stable foam. For the separated method, the yolks and whites are whipped separately with sugar for maximum aeration.

There are, however, variations of these basic foaming methods. Two of these are the methods for making angel food cake and chiffon cake. Angel food cake is made by foaming—by making a meringue and folding in sifted flour. Chiffon cake is also made with foamed egg whites—it is made from a batter in which the sugar, fat, flour, and egg yolks are combined and then a meringue is folded in.

1. **Scale and sift dry ingredients, prepare pans, and preheat the oven before beating the eggs.** The dry ingredients must be combined with the eggs as soon as the eggs have reached their maximum volume, as they begin to lose volume after they are beaten.

For the warm foaming method, shown here, combine the eggs (whole, yolk, or whites) with sugar in a bowl and heat it to about 100°F/38°C and stir or whip to completely dissolve the sugar, increase the volume, and develop a finer grain. The eggs and sugar at the start of mixing are still a deep yellow and relatively thin. For the cold foaming method, combine the eggs and sugar in a mixing bowl.

2. **Once the eggs and sugar are combined, whip them on medium to high speed until a thick foam forms.** (This step is done on the mixer, not over the hot-water bath.) A point will come when the foam does not appear to be increasing in volume. The mixture should form a ribbon as it falls from the whip and just begin to recede after the full volume is reached. The eggs are properly beaten at that point.

Fold in the sifted dry ingredients. This is often done by hand, although some chefs add them on the machine using the lowest possible speed and turning the machine on and off, if necessary. Do not overwork the batter at this point, as the foam could start to deflate, resulting in a flat, dense cake.

If using butter or another shortening, add it after the dry ingredients have been properly incorporated. These ingredients should be warm so that they are evenly distributed throughout the batter. Temper the ingredients by blending them with a little batter to retain maximum volume. Scale off the batter into prepared baking pans and bake until done.

3. **The cake should rise evenly during baking.** When it is properly baked, it will just begin to shrink away from the sides of the pan. The surface should spring back when lightly pressed. Remove the cake from the oven and let it cool briefly in the pan. Remove it from the pan and let it cool completely on a rack. Angel food and chiffon cakes should be allowed to cool completely, upside down, in the pan before unmolding so that they retain their full volume.

Cakes prepared by the foaming method are often more spongy than other cakes, although they do have a discernible crumb. Angel food and chiffon cakes are the spongiest of these types. The limited amount of shortening used gives these cakes a slightly dry texture, which is why they are often moistened with simple syrup. Even though there is a large proportion of eggs in foamed cakes, there should not be an unpleasant egg flavor.

Cooling and Storing Quick Breads and Cakes

Quick breads and cakes should be allowed to cool slightly (just enough so they can be handled) before unmolding. Wire racks are best to use because they allow air to circulate under the pan where much heat is retained.

First, you must gently help the cake or loaf to release from the pan. Run a small metal spatula or knife around the inside edge of the pan, and press the implement to the pan to ensure that you do not cut into the cake or loaf. Invert the pan onto a cardboard cake round or wire cooling rack and gently shake and tap the bottom of the pan. Lift the pan to fully release the baked item. Peel away the parchment paper from the bottom of the cake or loaf to allow the steam to escape.

In some cases, icings may be drizzled onto items that are still slightly warm from the oven, but in most instances cakes should be completely cooled before cutting, filling, and icing or frosting.

The shelf life for quick breads and cakes is relatively limited when left exposed to the air. They can, however, be frozen for up to three weeks when tightly wrapped in plastic wrap. Before serving or use they should be allowed to thaw at room temperature.

Pâte à Choux

Pâte à choux is a precooked batter that expands from steam released from the dough to form a hollow shell when baked. It can be filled, as for profiteroles (cream puffs), or not, as for gougères.

Pâte à choux is made by cooking water, butter, flour, and eggs into a smooth batter, then shaping and baking it. The shapes expand during baking, to create a delicate shell. Pâte à choux is soft enough that a pastry bag can be used to pipe it into different shapes. Among the most common shapes are cream puffs, profiteroles, and éclairs.

All-purpose flour may be used to make a pâte à choux, but bread flour is the best choice because it has a higher percentage of protein. Flours with a higher percentage of protein are able to absorb more liquid, which will allow more eggs to be added. More eggs will result in a lighter finished pastry. The higher gluten content will make a more elastic dough, which will facilitate expansion during baking.

Before beginning a pâte à choux, sift the flour and line the sheet pans with parchment. The pot selected for cooking the batter needs to be large enough to hold the liquid, fat, and flour, with enough room to stir vigorously with no spillage. Assemble a mixer fitted with a mixing bowl and paddle attachment before the cooking process begins.

1. **Bring the liquid and butter to a full boil.** Add the flour and cook, stirring constantly. Be sure to have the liquid at a rolling boil before adding the flour all at once. As pâte à choux is stirred and cooked, a film starts to develop on the bottom of the pan. Cook until the mixture pulls away from the pan, forming a ball. Transfer the mixture to a mixing bowl. Using the paddle attachment, mix the dough for a few minutes to cool it slightly. This will prevent the heat of the dough from curdling the eggs as they are worked into the mixture.

The eggs should be added gradually, in three or four additions, working the dough until it is smooth each time. Scrape down the sides and bottom of the bowl as necessary. Continue until all the eggs are incorporated.

2. **Pipe the dough onto prepared sheet pans according to the desired result.** Bake until the dough is puffed and golden brown, with no beads of moisture on the sides. Begin by baking at a high temperature (375° to 400°F/191° to 204°C). Reduce the heat to 325°F/163°C once the dough begins to take on color. Continue to bake the pâte à choux until it is completely dry. Remove the pâte à choux from the oven.

3. **Evalutate the baked pâte à choux.** When properly prepared and baked, pâte à choux has a definite golden color because of the high proportion of eggs. This color does not change drastically during baking. Properly baked pâte à choux appears perfectly dry, without moisture beads on the sides or top. It will swell to several times its original volume during baking.

Proper baking produces a dry, delicate texture. Remove the moist interior before adding filling for éclairs or puffs of any kind. Eggs should be the predominant flavor of pâte à choux.

Pâte à Choux: Water or Milk?

Water and milk are the two most common liquids used for making pâte à choux. Each produces significantly different results, each best suited for different uses depending on your needs.

For pâte à choux made with water, the temperature of the oven should be reduced during baking. Start with a higher temperature when you first put it in the oven. This will encourage greater expansion of the dough. After the dough is fully puffed, lower the temperature to dry out the pastry completely, for a very light and crisp result.

Milk will cause the pastry to brown more quickly before the pastry has a chance to completely dry out. The result is that pâte à choux made with milk will be slightly moist and tender; the solids present in milk will also impart more flavor.

Depending on your needs, you can also try making pâte à choux with half water and half milk for a result somewhere in between the two.

Guidelines for Shaping and Baking Cookies

Cookies are prepared in many different ways: piped, scooped, sliced, and molded, to name just a few. They are often served at receptions, as part of a dessert buffet, or with ice cream or sorbet. An assortment of cookies might be presented at the end of a meal, as an appealing extra. Cookies contain a high percentage of sugar, so the oven temperature must be carefully regulated during baking. Convection ovens, which produce evenly baked items, are especially good for baking many kinds of cookies. Cookie doughs and batters can be prepared using different mixing methods. Some must be shaped and baked as soon as the batter or dough is prepared. Others need to be chilled before they are shaped. Prepare the dough or batter as directed in the recipe and assemble the tools needed to shape and bake the cookies.

Drop cookies typically spread as they bake, so allow enough room for them to expand without touching each other. Arrange the cookies in even rows for even baking. Bake drop cookies at 325° to 350°F/163° to 177°C until the bottoms are golden brown and the cookies are baked through but still moist. Cool on racks and store in tightly wrapped containers at room temperature, or freeze for longer storage.

Rolled and cut cookies are made from stiff doughs that are often allowed to chill thoroughly before rolling. While the dough chills, line sheet pans with parchment. Roll out the dough on a lightly floured work surface, using the same technique as described for rolling pie dough. Lightly dust the rolling pin as you work. For some cookies, the work surface and rolling pin can be dusted with powdered sugar. Very rich and delicate cookie batters can be rolled out between two sheets of parchment. When you have finished rolling, the dough should be even and generally no more than ⅛ to ¼ in/3 to 4 mm thick. Be sure that the dough is not sticking to the work surface as you roll it out. Cutters of various shapes and sizes can be used, or the dough can be cut into shapes with a knife. As you work, dip the cutter or knife blade into a small amount of flour or powdered sugar to keep it from sticking to the dough. Transfer the cookies to the baking sheet and bake in a 350°F/177°C oven until the edges of the cookies just start to turn golden. Immediately transfer them to a cooling rack to prevent overcooking them. Store these cookies well wrapped or in airtight containers at room temperature. Shaped cookies are often glazed or iced. These coatings should be applied after the cookie is completely cooled. If the cookies are to be frozen for longer storage, freeze them plain and decorate or ice them after they have thawed.

Biscotti or twice-baked cookies are a type of molded and sliced cookie. They are made into a half moon–shaped log directly on lined baking sheets and then baked. Once baked, the biscotti are sliced to make individual cookies. They are returned to the oven on parchment-lined sheet pans to lightly toast and dry.

Piped cookies are shaped as soon as the dough is completed, so you should assemble all your equipment before starting to mix the batter. Pastry bags and tips should be assembled and the sheet pans should be greased or lined with parchment. When the dough is properly mixed, transfer it to the pastry bag with a rubber spatula and twist the top of the bag to express any air pockets. Squeeze the pastry bag to form a cookie and release the pressure on the bag once it is the desired size. Arrange the cookies in neat, even rows and leave some room for the cookies to spread as they bake.

1. Since drop cookies are often shaped and baked as soon as the dough is mixed, prepare baking sheets by lining them with parchment before mixing the dough. Most drop cookie doughs are prepared by the creaming or the foaming method. For the professional baker or chef, there are a variety of scoop sizes commonly used to portion cookie dough. To portion drop cookies using a scoop, fill a scoop of the appropriate size with dough and level it off, then release it onto the parchment-lined sheet pan. If indicated in the formula, flatten the mounded dough for a more even spread.

2. The dough for most drop cookies can also be portioned by slicing rather than scooping; this method is very efficient for volume production. To portion dough by this method, scale it into manageable portions and shape each one into a log. Wrap the dough in parchment paper or plastic wrap, using it to compress the dough into a compact cylinder, and refrigerate or freeze until firm. Slice the dough into uniform slices.

3. **Stenciled cookies are made from a very soft batter.** The batter can be prepared and held while assembling the tools for shaping and baking. Stencils can be purchased, made of heavy flexible plastic, or you can cut them from sturdy cardboard. Line sheet pans with silicone baking mats, or use an inverted sheet pan that has been greased, floured, and then frozen. Freezing the pan helps the grease and flour to stick to the pan rather than coming off onto the cookie as it is stenciled.

Lay the stencil on the prepared sheet pan and drop a spoonful of batter into the stencil. Spread it into an even layer with a small offset spatula or the back of a spoon.

4. **Remove the stencil and repeat until the sheet is filled.** These cookies do not spread, but be sure to allow enough room so that the stencil will not disturb any already shaped cookies. Bake carefully, keeping a close eye on the cookies.

5. Quickly press the hot cookies into a concave mold or over a rolling pin to shape them into tuiles. Alternatively, the tuiles may be shaped over a glass or a PVC pipe to make them into cups. Tuiles may be used to hold a scoop of ice cream, mousse, or as a decorative garnish.

Molded Cookies

Cookies may be molded in a variety of ways. Classic tuile cookies may be stenciled and molded into various shapes and filled, or they can be used as containers for ice cream, mousse, or compote for a plated dessert.

Shortbread cookies may be baked in a mold or stamped before baking to achieve a decorative design.

Elaborate stamps are pressed into springerlie and gingerbread doughs before baking. These molds were traditionally carved out of wooden blocks or into wooden rolling pins. Today replicas of these molds are available in resins for a fraction of the price. These cookies can be left plain, or for an even more elaborate finish they can be painted.

Madeleines, another traditional molded cookie, are made of a delicate foamed batter that is piped into scallop-shaped molds. Because their delicate structure deteriorates quickly, they are best when eaten immediately after baking.

Basic Pie Dough (3-2-1)

Makes 6 lb 6 oz/2.89 kg

3 lb/1.36 kg all-purpose flour

1 oz/28 g salt

2 lb/907 g butter, cut into pieces, cold

16 fl oz/480 mL cold water

1. Combine the flour and salt thoroughly. Gently rub the butter into the flour using your fingertips to form large flakes, or walnut-size pieces for an extremely flaky crust, or until it looks like a coarse meal for a finer crumb.

2. Add the water all at once and mix until the dough just comes together. It should be moist enough to hold together when pressed into a ball.

3. Turn the dough out onto a floured work surface and shape into an even rectangle. Wrap the dough with plastic and chill for 20 to 30 minutes. The dough is ready to roll out now, or it may be refrigerated for up to 3 days or frozen for up to 6 weeks. (Thaw frozen dough in the refrigerator before rolling it out.)

4. Scale the dough as necessary, using about 1 oz/28 g of dough per 1 in/3 cm of pie pan diameter.

5. To roll out the dough, work on a floured surface and roll the dough into the desired shape and thickness using smooth, even strokes. Transfer the dough to a prepared pie, tart, or tartlet pan. The shell is ready to fill or bake blind now.

Buttermilk Biscuits

Makes 40 biscuits

3 lb 8 oz/1.59 kg all-purpose flour

4 oz/113 g sugar

3 oz/85 g baking powder

¾ oz/21 g salt

1 lb/454 g butter, cold

8 oz/227 g eggs

24 fl oz/720 mL buttermilk

Egg Wash (page 1061), **as needed**

1. Line a sheet pan with parchment paper.

2. Combine the flour, sugar, baking powder, and salt.

3. Add the butter and rub together until the mixture has the appearance of a coarse meal.

4. Combine the eggs and buttermilk. Add to the flour mixture, tossing to combine.

5. Roll out the dough on a lightly floured work surface to a thickness of 1 in/3 cm and, using a 2-in/5-cm cutter, cut out the biscuits.

6. Place the biscuits on the prepared pans and lightly brush them with egg wash.

7. Bake at 425°F/218°C until golden brown, about 15 minutes.

8. Transfer the biscuits to racks and allow them to cool completely.

Buttermilk Biscuits

Cream Scones

Makes 5 dozen scones

5 lb 10 oz/2.55 kg bread flour

1 lb 5 oz/595 g sugar

5¼ oz/149 g baking powder

2¼ oz/64 g salt

72 fl oz/2.16 L heavy cream, cold

6 fl oz/180 mL milk

6 oz/170 g coarse sugar

1. Combine the flour, sugar, baking powder, and salt and mix on medium speed with a paddle attachment until well blended, about 5 minutes. Add the cream and mix until just combined.

2. Scale the dough into 2 lb 5-oz/1.05-kg portions and pat each portion by hand into a cake pan or ring that is 10 in/25 cm in diameter. Remove the dough from the ring, place it on a parchment-lined sheet pan, and freeze thoroughly.

3. Cut each disk into 10 equal wedges and place the wedges on parchment-lined sheet pans. Brush with the milk and sprinkle with the coarse sugar.

4. Bake in a 350°F/177°C oven until golden brown, 20 to 25 minutes.

5. Cool the scones on the pans for a few minutes, then transfer them to racks to cool completely.

Raisin Scones: Add 3 lb/1.36 kg raisins to the dough just before blending in the wet ingredients.

Ham and Cheddar Scones: Omit the milk and coarse sugar. Add 3 lb/1.36 kg diced ham, 3 bunches of chopped green onions, and 1 lb 8 oz/680 g diced Cheddar cheese just before blending in the wet ingredients.

Buttermilk Pancakes

Makes 10 servings

1 lb 5 oz/595 g all-purpose flour

1 oz/28 g baking powder

1 tsp/7 g baking soda

1 tsp/5 g salt

4½ oz/128 g sugar

8 eggs

32 fl oz/960 mL buttermilk

4 oz/113 g butter, melted

1. Sift the dry ingredients into a large bowl and make a well in the center.

2. Combine the eggs with the buttermilk and mix well. Pour all at once into the center of the dry ingredients. Slowly mix using a whisk in a controlled circular motion.

3. Add the butter when about ¾ of the dry ingredients are moistened. Continue to mix only until the butter is worked in. Do not overmix.

4. Keep the batter cool, if making large batches, by holding it over an ice bath, or dividing and keeping the extra batter in the refrigerator.

5. Heat a large skillet or griddle pan over medium heat, lightly greased with vegetable oil or clarified butter.

6. Ladle approximately 2½ fl oz/75 mL of batter onto the pan. When bubbles break and the bottom is golden brown, 1 to 2 minutes, turn over. Finish cooking on the second side, about 1 minute. Serve immediately.

Basic Waffles: Replace the whole eggs with separated eggs. Mix the egg yolks with the buttermilk, and continue with steps 2 and 3. Beat the egg whites to medium-stiff peaks. Fold the beaten egg whites into the finished batter. Preheat a waffle iron to 350°F/177°C and grease lightly with oil. Ladle the batter into the waffle iron, close it, and cook the waffles until golden brown and cooked through, about 3 to 4 minutes. (Amount of batter required will vary according to the size of the waffle iron.)

Banana Pancakes: Omit 5 fl oz/150 mL of the buttermilk. Add 8 oz/227 g chopped bananas.

Chocolate Chip Pancakes: Fold 8 oz/227 g chocolate chips and 2½ oz/71 g toasted pecans or walnuts into the finished batter.

Blueberry Pancakes: Fold 8 oz/227 g blueberries into the batter just before making the pancakes.

Oatmeal Pancakes: Replace 2½ oz/71 g of the flour with 4 oz/113 g oatmeal, 1 tsp/2 g ground cinnamon, ¼ tsp/0.50 g grated nutmeg, and a pinch of ground cloves.

Irish Soda Bread

Makes 4 loaves

2 lb 8 oz/1.13 kg all-purpose flour

2½ oz/71 g baking powder

6 oz/170 g sugar

1¼ tsp/6.25 g salt

5½ oz/156 g butter

6 oz/170 g currants

½ oz/14 g caraway seeds

26 fl oz/780 mL milk

1. Sift together the flour, baking powder, sugar, and salt.

2. Gently rub the butter into the dry ingredients using your fingertips, until it is the consistency of cornmeal.

3. Add the currants and caraway seeds and toss together with the mixture.

4. Add the milk and blend until it forms a shaggy mass.

5. Turn the dough out onto a lightly floured work surface and knead for 20 seconds.

6. Scale into 1-lb/454-g portions and round. Place on a parchment-lined sheet pan. Dust the tops of the loaves lightly with flour and, using a paring knife, press an X gently onto the top surface of each loaf.

7. Bake in a 425°F/218°C oven until browned and baked through, 45 to 60 minutes. To test for doneness, insert a wooden skewer into the thickest part of the loaf. The skewer should not have any crumbs clinging to it.

8. Remove the loaves from the pan and let them cool completely on wire racks before slicing and serving.

Johnny Cakes

Makes 10 servings

6¼ oz/177 g all-purpose flour

6¼ oz/177 g cornmeal

1 tsp/5 g salt

3 oz/85 g sugar

¾ oz/21 g baking soda

½ oz/14 g baking powder

25 fl oz/750 mL buttermilk

6 eggs, lightly beaten

1¾ oz/50 g butter, melted

5 oz/142 g corn kernels, cooked (optional)

1½ fl oz/45 mL vegetable oil

1. Sift together the flour, cornmeal, salt, sugar, baking soda, and baking powder into a large bowl.

2. In a separate bowl, whisk together the buttermilk, eggs, and half of the melted butter.

3. Add the wet ingredients to the dry ingredients. Add the remaining butter. Stir with a wooden spoon to combine. The batter will be slightly lumpy.

4. Add the corn, if using, and mix well.

5. Heat a large cast-iron skillet or griddle until moderately hot and brush lightly with oil.

6. Drop the batter onto the griddle, using a 2-fl-oz/60-mL ladle, leaving about 1 in/3 cm of space between the cakes.

7. Cook the cakes until the undersides are brown, the edges begin to dry, and bubbles begin to break the surface of the batter, 3 to 5 minutes. Turn the cakes and cook them until the second sides are brown, about 2 minutes. Repeat using the remaining batter.

8. Serve the cakes immediately or keep them warm, uncovered, in a low oven. Do not hold the cakes longer than 30 minutes, or they will become tough.

Fried Bread (Puri)

Makes 10 servings

1 lb 8 oz/680 g all-purpose flour

1 tbsp/15 g salt

1½ fl oz/45 mL vegetable oil, plus as needed for frying

8 fl oz/240 mL water, warm

1. Place the flour in a bowl, sprinkle with the salt, and add 1½ fl oz/45 mL of the oil.

2. Gradually add the water and knead the dough until it is firm, about 5 minutes. Cover the dough with a moist cloth and let it rest for 15 minutes.

3. Roll the dough into a cylinder 12 in/30 cm long and portion it into 12 equal balls. Using a little flour for dusting, roll each piece of the dough into a 5-in/13-cm round.

4. Fry each piece of dough, 1 at a time, in oil heated to 350°F/177°C until it puffs up and becomes light brown, about 40 seconds.

5. Serve immediately.

Crêpes Suzette

Makes 10 servings

3 oz/85 g sugar

12 oz/340 g butter, cubed

3 oz/85 g orange zest, grated

6 fl oz/180 mL orange juice

30 **Dessert Crêpes** (page 1109)

6 fl oz/180 mL Grand Marnier

6 fl oz/180 mL brandy or cognac

1. Sprinkle sugar evenly across the bottom of a preheated suzette pan without allowing the spoon to touch the bottom (which can cause the sugar to crystallize).

2. As the sugar begins to caramelize, add the butter to the outside edges of the pan and gently shake the pan; this allows the butter to evenly temper and blend with the sugar.

3. Add the zest and shake the pan gently to thoroughly blend all the ingredients and become a light orange caramel color.

4. Pour the juice on the outside edges of the pan slowly, allowing it to temper and blend with the sugar.

5. Shake the pan gently, incorporating all the ingredients and allowing the sauce to thicken.

6. Sandwich 1 crêpe between a fork and a spoon and place it into the sauce. Flip the crêpe over to coat the other side. Set it aside on a parchment-lined sheet pan.

7. Repeat with the remaining crêpes, moving quickly so the sauce does not become too thick.

8. Remove the pan from the réchaud and add the Grand Marnier. Do not flame it. Return the pan to the réchaud and shake gently.

9. Slide the pan back and forth over the front edge of the réchaud, allowing the pan to get hot.

10. Remove the pan, add the brandy or cognac, and tip the pan slightly to flame. Shake the pan until the flame dies.

11. Plate 3 crêpes per portion, shingling one over the other, and coat with sauce.

Dessert Crêpes

Makes 20 to 30 crêpes

4 eggs

16 fl oz/480 mL heavy cream

8 oz/227 g milk

½ oz/14 g vegetable oil

8 oz/227 g all-purpose flour

2 oz/57 g confectioners' sugar

1 tsp/5 g salt

1½ tsp/7.50 mL vanilla extract

1. Combine the eggs, cream, milk, and oil and beat just until blended.

2. Sift the flour, sugar, and salt into a bowl.

3. Add the wet ingredients and mix until smooth, scraping down the bowl as necessary.

4. Add the vanilla. Stir just until the ingredients are blended into a relatively smooth batter. (The batter may be prepared in advance to this point and refrigerated for up to 12 hours. Strain the batter if necessary before preparing the crêpes.)

5. Add a small amount of batter to a preheated buttered crêpe pan, swirling the pan to coat the bottom with batter.

6. Cook over medium heat. When set, turn over and finish on the other side. The crêpes may be cooled, then stacked between parchment paper, and wrapped and refrigerated or frozen. Thaw frozen crêpes before filling and folding.

7. Fill as desired, roll or fold, or use in other desserts (see Crêpes Suzette, page 1108).

Ladle the crêpe batter while swirling it to evenly coat the entire surface of the bottom of the pan. Be sure that the crêpe is of a uniform thickness or it will cook unevenly.

Once the edges of the crêpe have turned golden brown, flip the crêpe to finish cooking it.

Puff Pastry Dough

Makes 8 lb 12 oz/3.97 kg

1 lb 10 oz/737 g bread flour

6 oz/170 g cake flour

4 oz/113 g butter, soft

20 fl oz/600 mL water

¾ oz/21 g salt

ROLL-IN

2 lb 4 oz/1.02 kg butter, pliable (60°F/16°C)

4 oz/113 g bread flour

1. To prepare the dough, sift together the flours. Blend in the butter on low speed with a dough hook attachment until pea-size nuggets form. Combine the water and salt; add them all at once to the dough and mix on low speed until smooth, about 3 minutes. Shape the dough into a rough rectangle. Transfer it to a sheet pan lined with parchment, wrap the dough in plastic wrap, and allow it to relax in the refrigerator for 30 to 60 minutes.

2. To prepare the roll-in, blend the butter and flour on low speed with a paddle attachment until smooth, about 2 minutes. Transfer it to a sheet of parchment paper. Cover with a second sheet and roll into a rectangle 8 by 12 in/20 by 30 cm. Square off the edges, cover with plastic wrap, and refrigerate until firm but still pliable. Do not allow the roll-in to become cold.

3. To lock the roll-in into the dough, turn the dough out onto a lightly floured work surface and roll it into a rectangle 16 by 24 in/41 by 61 cm, keeping the edges straight and the corners square. Set the roll-in on half of the dough and fold the remaining half of the dough over the roll-in. Seal the edges, turn the dough 90 degrees, and roll it into a rectangle 16 by 24 in/41 by 61 cm, making sure the edges are straight and the corners are square.

4. Administer a three-fold. Cover the dough in plastic wrap and allow it to rest for 30 minutes in the refrigerator.

5. Turn the dough 90 degrees from its position before it was refrigerated and roll it out into a rectangle 16 by 24 in/41 by 61 cm, making sure the edges are straight and the corners are square. Administer a second three-fold.

Cover the dough in plastic wrap and allow it to rest for 30 minutes in the refrigerator. Repeat this process 2 more times for a total of 4 folds, turning the dough 90 degrees each time before rolling and allowing the dough to rest, covered in plastic wrap, in the refrigerator for 30 minutes between each fold.

6. After completing the final fold, wrap the dough in plastic wrap and allow it to rest in the refrigerator for 30 minutes before using.

Blitz Puff Pastry Dough

Makes 5 lb/2.27 kg

1 lb/454 g cake flour

1 lb/454 g bread flour

2 lb/907 g butter, cubed, cold

¾ oz/21 g salt

18 fl oz/540 mL water, cold

1. Combine the flours in the bowl of a stand mixer. Add the butter and toss with your fingertips until the butter is coated with flour. Combine the salt and water and add to the flour all at once. Mix on low speed with a dough hook attachment until the dough forms a shaggy mass.

2. Tightly cover the mixture with plastic wrap and allow it to rest in the refrigerator until the butter is firm, but not brittle, about 20 minutes.

3. Place the mass on a lightly floured work surface and roll it out into a rectangle that is ½ in/1 cm thick and approximately 12 by 30 in/30 by 76 cm.

4. Administer a three-fold, roll out the dough to the same dimensions, and administer a second three-fold. Tightly wrap the dough in plastic wrap and allow it to rest in the refrigerator for 30 minutes.

5. Repeat this process 2 more times for a total of 4 three-folds, refrigerating and turning the dough 90 degrees each time before rolling. After completing the final fold, wrap the dough in plastic wrap and allow it to firm in the refrigerator for at least 1 hour. (The dough can be held refrigerated or frozen.)

Basic Muffin Recipe

Makes 1 dozen muffins

13 oz/369 g all-purpose flour

1 tbsp/9 g baking powder

10½ oz/298 g sugar

2¾ oz/78 g butter, soft

1½ tsp/7.50 g salt

5 oz/142 g eggs

5 fl oz/150 mL buttermilk

½ fl oz/15 mL vanilla extract

2¾ fl oz/83 mL vegetable oil

2 oz/57 g coarse sugar

1. Coat the muffin tins with a light film of fat or use appropriate paper liners.

2. Sift together the flour and baking powder.

3. Cream together the sugar, butter, and salt on medium speed with the paddle attachment, scraping down the bowl periodically, until the mixture is smooth and light in color, about 5 minutes.

4. Whisk the eggs, buttermilk, vanilla, and oil together. Add them to the butter-sugar mixture in 2 to 3 additions, mixing until fully incorporated after each addition and scraping down the bowl as needed.

5. Add the sifted dry ingredients and mix on low speed until evenly moistened.

6. Scale about 3 oz/85 g of batter into each prepared muffin cup, filling them ¾ full. Gently tap the filled tins to release any air bubbles and sprinkle with coarse sugar.

7. Bake at 375°F/191°C for 30 minutes, or until a skewer inserted near the center of a muffin comes out clean.

8. Cool the muffins in the tins for a few minutes, then unmold and transfer them to racks to cool completely.

Cranberry-Orange Muffins: Fold in 11 oz/312 g cranberries (fresh or frozen) and 1½ oz/43 g orange zest after adding the dry ingredients.

Blueberry Muffins: Fold in 12 oz/340 g blueberries (fresh or frozen) after adding the dry ingredients.

Bran Muffins

Makes 1 dozen muffins

12 oz/340 g bread flour

1 oz/28 g baking powder

8 oz/227 g sugar

4 oz/113 g butter, soft

1½ tsp/7.50 g salt

4 eggs

8 fl oz/240 mL milk

2 oz/57 g honey

2 oz/57 g molasses

4 oz/113 g wheat bran

1. Coat the muffin tins with a light film of fat or use appropriate paper liners.

2. Sift together the flour and baking powder.

3. Cream together the sugar, butter, and salt on medium speed with the paddle attachment, scraping down the bowl periodically, until the mixture is smooth and light in color, about 5 minutes.

4. Combine the eggs and milk and add to the butter mixture in 3 additions, mixing until fully incorporated after each addition and scraping down the bowl as needed. Add the honey and molasses and blend until they are just incorporated.

5. Add the sifted dry ingredients and the bran and mix on low speed until evenly moistened.

6. Scale 3½ oz/99 g of batter into each prepared muffin cup, filling them ¾ full. Gently tap the filled tins to release any air bubbles.

7. Bake at 375°F/191°C for 20 minutes, or until a skewer inserted near the center of a muffin comes out clean.

8. Cool the muffins in the tins for a few minutes, then unmold and transfer them to racks to cool completely.

Corn Muffins

Makes 1 dozen muffins

11 oz/312 g all-purpose flour

5 oz/142 g cornmeal

2 tsp/10 g salt

1 tbsp/9 g baking powder

4 eggs

8 fl oz/240 mL milk

6 fl oz/180 mL vegetable oil

1 fl oz/30 mL orange juice concentrate

8 oz/227 g sugar

1. Coat the muffin tins with a light film of butter and a light dusting of cornmeal, or use appropriate paper liners.

2. Combine the flour, cornmeal, salt, and baking powder in a bowl and stir together using a wire whisk.

3. Combine the eggs, milk, oil, orange juice concentrate, and sugar and mix on medium speed with the paddle attachment for 2 minutes, until light in color and smooth.

4. Add the dry ingredients to the egg mixture and blend on medium speed just until combined, scraping down the bowl as necessary.

5. Scale about 3 oz/85 g of batter into each prepared muffin cup, filling them ¾ full. Gently tap the filled tins to release any air bubbles.

6. Bake at 400°F/204°C for 20 minutes, or until a skewer inserted near the center of a muffin comes out clean.

7. Cool the muffins in the tins for a few minutes, then unmold and transfer them to racks to cool completely.

Corn bread: Coat a 9 by 9 in/23 by 23 cm pan with a light film of butter and a light dusting of cornmeal. Pour the batter into the pan and bake at 400°F/204°C for 50 minutes, or until a skewer inserted near the center comes out clean. Allow the bread to cool, and cut into desired shapes.

Pumpkin Bread

Makes 4 loaves

2 lb/907 g all-purpose flour

2 tsp/6 g baking powder

¾ oz/21 g baking soda

1 tbsp/15 g salt

2 tsp/4 g ground cinnamon

14 fl oz/420 mL oil

2 lb 12 oz/1.25 kg sugar

2 lb/907 g pumpkin purée

8 eggs

13 fl oz/390 mL water

7 oz/198 g chopped toasted pecans

1. Coat four loaf pans with a light film of fat or use appropriate pan liners. Sift together the flour, baking powder, baking soda, salt, and cinnamon.

2. Combine the oil, sugar, pumpkin purée, eggs, and water in the bowl of an electric mixer. Using the paddle attachment, blend on low speed until fully incorporated.

3. Add the sifted dry ingredients to the oil mixture and blend until just incorporated, scraping the sides of the bowl as necessary. Blend in the nuts.

4. Scale 1 lb 14 oz/851 g of batter into each pan. Gently tap the filled pans to burst any air bubbles.

5. Bake in a 350°F/177°C oven until a skewer inserted near the center of each loaf comes out clean and the centers spring back when gently pressed, 1 to 1½ hours.

6. Cool the bread in the pan for a few minutes. Remove them from the pans and cool on a rack before slicing and serving or wrapping for storage.

See photo on page 1113.

Pumpkin Bread, Blueberry Muffins, and Banana-Nut Bread

Banana-Nut Bread

Makes 6 loaves

4 lb 4 oz/1.93 kg bananas, very ripe

½ fl oz/15 mL lemon juice

2 lb 13 oz/1.28 kg all-purpose flour

2 tsp/6 g baking powder

¾ oz/21 g baking soda

1¼ tsp/6.25 g salt

2 lb 13 oz/1.28 kg sugar

6 eggs

14 fl oz/420 mL oil

8 oz/227 g pecans

1. Coat loaf pans with a light film of fat.

2. Purée the bananas and lemon juice together.

3. Sift together the flour, baking powder, baking soda, and salt.

4. Combine the sugar, banana purée, eggs, and oil and mix on medium speed with a paddle attachment until blended. Scrape the bowl as needed.

5. Add the sifted dry ingredients and mix until just combined. Mix in the pecans.

6. Scale 1 lb 14 oz/851 g of the batter into each prepared loaf pan. Gently tap the filled pans to release any air bubbles.

7. Bake at 350°F/177°C until the bread springs back when pressed and a tester inserted near the center comes out clean, about 55 minutes.

8. Cool the loaves in the pans for a few minutes, then unmold and transfer them to racks and cool completely.

See photo on page 1113.

Pound Cake

Makes 4 cakes

1 lb 4 oz/567 g butter

1 lb 8 oz/680 g sugar

1 oz/28 g lemon zest (grated)

1½ tsp/7.50 g salt

1 lb 8 oz/680 g cake flour

5 oz/142 g cornstarch

¾ oz/21 g baking powder

2 lb/907 g eggs

1. Grease four loaf pans and line with parchment paper.

2. Cream together the butter, sugar, lemon zest, and salt on medium speed with the paddle attachment, scraping down the bowl as needed, until the mixture is smooth and light in color.

3. Sift together the flour, cornstarch, and baking powder.

4. Add the eggs alternately in 3 stages with the sifted dry ingredients on low speed.

5. Scale 1 lb 10 oz/737 g of batter into prepared pans.

6. Bake in a 375°F/191°C oven until a skewer inserted near the center of the cake comes out clean, about 45 minutes.

Devil's Food Cake

Makes 6 cakes (8 in/20 cm each)

3 lb 13 oz/1.73 kg sugar

2 lb 5 oz/1.05 kg cake flour

1¼ oz/35 g baking soda

2½ tsp/7.50 g baking powder

12 eggs

1 lb 9 oz/709 g butter, melted and kept warm

50 fl oz/1.50 L water, warm

1 fl oz/30 mL vanilla extract

15 oz/425 g cocoa powder, sifted

1. Coat six 8-in/20-cm pans with a light film of fat and line them with parchment circles.

2. Combine the sugar, flour, baking soda, and baking powder.

3. Blend the eggs and add them in 3 additions, using the paddle attachment on medium speed. Mix until fully incorporated after each addition and scrape down the bowl as needed.

4. Add the butter and mix until evenly blended. Add the water and vanilla and mix, scraping down the bowl periodically, until a smooth batter forms. Add the cocoa powder and mix until evenly blended.

5. Scale 2 lb 3 oz/992 g of batter into each prepared pan.

6. Bake at 350°F/177°C until a skewer inserted near the center of a cake comes out clean, about 45 minutes.

7. Cool the cakes in the pans for a few minutes, then transfer to racks to cool completely.

Angel Food Cake

Makes 5 tube cakes (8 in/20 cm each)

2 lb 8 oz/1.13 kg sugar

½ oz/14 g cream of tartar

15½ oz/439 g cake flour

1½ tsp/7.50 g salt

40 egg whites

½ fl oz/15 mL vanilla extract

1. Sprinkle the insides of five 8-in/20-cm tube pans lightly with water.

2. Combine 1 lb 4 oz/567 g of the sugar with the cream of tartar. Sift together the remaining 1 lb 4 oz/567 g sugar with the flour and salt.

3. Whip the egg whites and vanilla to soft peaks using the whip attachment on medium speed.

4. Gradually add the sugar and cream of tartar mixture to the egg whites, whipping on medium speed until medium peaks form.

5. Gently fold the sifted sugar and flour mixture into the egg whites until just incorporated.

6. Scale 15 oz/425 g of batter into each prepared tube pan.

7. Bake at 350°F/177°C until a cake springs back when lightly touched, about 35 minutes.

8. Invert each tube pan onto a funnel or long-necked bottle on a wire rack to cool. Alternatively, for each cake, invert a small ramekin on top of a wire rack and prop the cake pan upside down and at an angle on the ramekin. Allow the cakes to cool completely upside down.

9. Carefully run a palette knife around the sides of each pan and around the center tube to release the cake. Shake the pan gently to invert the cake onto the wire rack.

Vanilla Sponge Cake

Makes 6 cakes (8 in/20 cm each)

9 oz/255 g butter, melted

1 fl oz/30 mL vanilla extract

13 eggs

13 egg yolks

1 lb 11 oz/765 g sugar

1 lb 11 oz/765 g cake flour, sifted

1. Coat six 8-in/20-cm pans with a light film of fat and line them with parchment circles.

2. Blend the butter with the vanilla.

3. Combine the eggs, egg yolks, and sugar in an electric mixer bowl. Set the bowl over a pan of barely simmering water and whisk constantly until the mixture reaches 110°F/43°C.

4. Put the bowl on the mixer and whip with the whip attachment on high speed until the foam is 3 times its original volume and no longer increasing in volume.

5. Fold in the flour. Fold the butter and vanilla into the batter.

6. Scale 1 lb/454 g of batter into each prepared cake pan.

7. Bake at 375°F/191°C until the tops of the cakes spring back when lightly touched, about 30 minutes.

8. Cool the cakes in the pans for a few minutes, then transfer to racks to cool completely.

Chocolate Sponge Cake: Replace 4 oz/113 g of the flour with Dutch-process cocoa powder. Sift the cocoa powder together with the flour.

Cheesecake

Makes 6 cheesecakes (8 in/20 cm each)

15 oz/425 g **Graham Cracker Crust** (recipe follows)

7 lb 8 oz/3.4 kg cream cheese

2 lb 4 oz/1.02 kg sugar

½ oz/14 g salt

16 eggs

5 egg yolks

15 fl oz/450 mL heavy cream

1½ fl oz/45 mL vanilla extract

1. Coat six 8-in/20-cm cake pans with a light film of fat and line them with parchment circles.

2. Press 2½ oz/71 g of the crust mixture evenly into the bottom of each pan.

3. Combine the cream cheese, sugar, and salt and mix on medium speed with the paddle attachment, occasionally scraping down the bowl, until the mixture is completely smooth, about 3 minutes.

4. Whisk the eggs and egg yolks together. Add the eggs to the cream cheese mixture in 4 additions, mixing until fully incorporated after each addition and scraping down the bowl as needed.

5. Add the cream and vanilla and mix until they are fully incorporated.

6. Scale 2 lb 8 oz/1.13 kg of batter into each prepared pan. Gently tap the pans to release any air bubbles.

7. Bake in a hot water bath at 325°F/163°C until the centers of the cakes are set, about 1 hour 15 minutes.

8. Cool the cakes completely in the pans on wire racks. Wrap the cakes, in the pans, in plastic wrap and refrigerate overnight to fully set.

9. To unmold, apply the gentle heat of a low, open flame to the bottom and sides of each cake pan. Run a knife around the side of the pan. Place a plastic wrap–covered cake circle on top of the cake, invert, and tap the bottom of the pan to release the cake if necessary. Remove the pan, peel off the paper from the bottom of the cake, and turn it onto a cake circle or serving plate.

Graham Cracker Crust

Makes 1 lb 4 oz/567 g

10 oz/284 g graham cracker crumbs

4 oz/113 g brown sugar

6 oz/170 g butter, melted

1. Process the crumbs, sugar, and butter in a food processor just until crumbly, about 5 minutes.

2. The crust is ready to be pressed into prepared pans and baked.

Chocolate XS Cake

Makes 6 cakes (8 in/20 cm each)

24 fl oz/720 mL water

2 lb 11½ oz/1.23 kg sugar

1 lb 13 oz/822 g semisweet dark chocolate, chopped

2 lb 2 oz/964 g bittersweet chocolate, chopped

2 lb 11 oz/1.22 kg butter, melted

3 lb 10 oz/1.64 kg eggs

1 fl oz/30 mL vanilla extract

1. Brush the insides of six 8-in/20-cm cake pans with softened butter and line with parchment circles.

2. Combine the water and 1 lb 13 oz/822 g of the sugar in a heavy-bottomed saucepan and bring to a boil. Remove from the heat and add both chocolates; stir until the chocolates are melted. Stir in the butter. Let the mixture cool to room temperature.

3. Whip the eggs, the remaining 14½ oz/411 g sugar, and the vanilla using the whip attachment on high speed until light and fluffy, about 4½ minutes.

4. Gently fold the chocolate mixture into the egg mixture.

5. Scale 2 lb 5 oz/1.05 kg of batter into each prepared pan.

6. Bake in a water bath at 350°F/177°C until the tops of the cakes feel firm, about 1 hour.

7. Cool, then wrap in plastic wrap and refrigerate overnight in the pans before unmolding.

Pâte à Choux

Makes 6 lb 8 oz/2.95 kg

16 fl oz/480 mL milk

16 fl oz/480 mL water

1 lb/454 g butter

1½ tsp/7.50 g sugar

1½ tsp/7.50 g salt

1 lb 8 oz/680 g bread flour

2 lb 4 oz/1.02 kg eggs

1. Bring the milk, water, butter, sugar, and salt to a boil over medium heat, stirring constantly. Remove from the heat, add the flour all at once, and stir vigorously to combine. Return the pan to medium heat and cook, stirring constantly, until the mixture pulls away from the sides of the pan, about 3 minutes.

2. Transfer the mixture to the bowl of a stand mixer and beat briefly on medium speed with a paddle attachment. Add the eggs 2 at a time, beating until smooth after each addition.

3. The pâte à choux is ready to be piped and baked. See pages 1097–1098.

NOTE
For a drier and deeper blond pâte à choux, substitute an equal amount of water for the milk.

Gougères (Gruyère Cheese Puffs): Before piping the pâte à choux, add ¼ tsp/0.50 g cayenne and 1 lb/454 g grated Gruyère cheese to the dough. Continue mixing for 1 minute. Transfer the dough to a pastry bag with a plain tip and pipe into domes ¾ in/2 cm in diameter. Bake for about 35 minutes in a 350°F/177°C oven. Serve warm or store in airtight containers.

Profiteroles

Profiteroles

Makes 1 dozen profiteroles

1 lb/454 g **Pâte à Choux** (page 1117)

Egg Wash (page 1061), as needed

2 oz/57 g sliced almonds

1 oz/28 g sugar

12 oz/340 g **Pastry Cream** (page 1133)

9 oz/255 g **Chantilly Cream** (page 1062)

confectioners' sugar, as needed

1. Pipe the pâte à choux into bulbs, 1½ in/4 cm in diameter, onto parchment-lined sheet pans using a No. 5 plain piping tip. Lightly brush with egg wash.

2. Stick several almond slices into the top of each bulb so that they protrude from the top and then sprinkle each lightly with the sugar.

3. Bake at 360°F/182°C for 50 minutes, or until the cracks formed in the pastries are no longer yellow. Allow them to cool to room temperature. Slice the top off each of the baked pastries.

4. Pipe the pastry cream into the bases using a No. 5 plain pastry tip, being careful not to overfill them.

5. Pipe a double rosette of Chantilly cream on top of the pastry cream using a No. 5 star tip.

6. Place the tops of the pastries on the Chantilly cream, and lightly dust with confectioners' sugar.

Ice Cream-Filled Profiteroles: Substitute Vanilla Ice Cream (page 1136) for the pastry cream. Omit the almonds, sugar, Chantilly cream, and confectioners' sugar. Slice the tops off each profiterole. Scoop the ice cream using a No. 50 scoop, and place it into the bases. Place the tops on the pastries and serve with Chocolate Sauce (page 1160), if desired.

Éclairs

Makes 1 dozen éclairs

1 lb/454 g **Pâte à Choux** (page 1117)

Egg Wash (page 1061), as needed

1 lb/454 g **Pastry Cream** (page 1133)

8 oz/227 g **fondant** (see pages 1149–1150)

3 oz/85 g dark chocolate, melted

light corn syrup, as needed

1. Pipe the pâte à choux into cylinders, 4 in/10 cm long, on parchment-lined sheet pans, using a No. 8 plain piping tip. Lightly brush with egg wash.

2. Bake at 360°F/182°C for 50 minutes, or until the cracks formed in the pastries are no longer yellow. Allow them to cool to room temperature.

3. Pierce each end of the éclairs using a skewer or similar instrument.

4. Fill the éclairs with the pastry cream from each end using a No. 1 plain piping tip.

5. Warm the fondant over a hot water bath, add the chocolate, and thin to the proper viscosity using the corn syrup.

6. Top the filled éclairs with the chocolate fondant either by dipping the tops or by enrobing them using the back of a spoon.

Chocolate Éclairs: Substitute Chocolate Pastry Cream (page 1133) for the pastry cream.

1-2-3 Cookie Dough

Makes 6 lb/2.72 kg

2 lb/907 g butter, soft

1 lb/454 g sugar

½ fl oz/15 mL vanilla extract

8 oz/227 g eggs

3 lb/1.36 kg cake flour, sifted

1. Cream together the butter, sugar, and vanilla on medium speed using a paddle attachment, scraping down the bowl periodically, until smooth and light in color. Add the eggs gradually, a few at a time, scraping down the bowl and blending until smooth after each addition. Add the flour all at once and mix on low speed until just blended.

2. Turn the dough out onto a lightly floured work surface. Scale the dough as desired. Wrap tightly and refrigerate for at least 1 hour before rolling. (The dough can be refrigerated or frozen.)

Almond-Anise Biscotti

Makes 32 biscotti

10 oz/284 g bread flour

1 tsp/4 g baking soda

3 eggs

6½ oz/184 g sugar

1¼ tsp/6.25 g salt

1 tsp/5 mL anise extract

7 oz/198 g whole almonds

2 tbsp/12 g anise seeds

1. Line a sheet pan with parchment paper.

2. Sift together the flour and baking soda.

3. Whip the eggs, sugar, salt, and extract using a wire whip attachment on high speed, until thick and light in color, about 5 minutes. On low speed, mix in the dry ingredients until just incorporated. Add the almonds and anise seeds by hand and blend until evenly combined.

4. Form the dough into a log 16 by 4 in/41 by 10 cm and place it on the prepared sheet pan.

5. Bake at 300°F/149°C until light golden brown and firm, about 1 hour. Remove the pan from the oven and cool for 10 minutes. Lower the oven temperature to 275°F/135°C.

6. Using a serrated knife, cut each strip crosswise into slices ½ in/1 cm thick. Place them on sheet pans and bake, turning the biscotti once halfway through the baking time, until golden brown and crisp, 20 to 25 minutes. Transfer them to racks and cool completely.

Almond-Anise Biscotti

Chocolate Chunk Cookies

Makes 12 dozen cookies

4 lb 5 oz/1.96 kg all-purpose flour

1½ oz/43 g salt

1 oz/28 g baking soda

2 lb 14 oz/1.30 kg butter, soft

1 lb 14 oz/851 g sugar

1 lb 6 oz/624 g light brown sugar

9 eggs

1¼ fl oz/38 mL vanilla extract

4 lb 5 oz/1.96 kg semisweet chocolate chunks

1. Line sheet pans with parchment.

2. Sift together the flour, salt, and baking soda.

3. Cream the butter and sugars on medium speed with a paddle attachment, scraping down the bowl periodically, until the mixture is smooth and light in color, about 5 minutes.

4. Combine the eggs and vanilla. Add to the butter-sugar mixture in 3 additions, mixing until fully incorporated after each addition and scraping down the bowl as needed. On low speed, mix in the sifted dry ingredients and the chocolate chunks until just incorporated.

5. Scale the dough into 1½-oz/43-g portions and place them on the prepared pans. Alternatively, the dough may be scaled into 2-lb/907-g portions, shaped into logs 16 in/41 cm long, wrapped tightly in parchment paper, and refrigerated until firm enough to slice. Slice each log into 16 pieces and arrange on the prepared sheet pans in even rows.

6. Bake at 375°F/191°C until golden brown around the edges, 12 to 14 minutes. Cool them completely on the pans.

Cherry–Chocolate Chunk Cookies: Add 2 lb/907 g chopped dried cherries along with the chocolate.

Mudslide Cookies

Makes 12½ dozen cookies

10½ oz/298 g cake flour

1 oz/28 g baking powder

1¾ tsp/8.75 g salt

4 fl oz/120 mL espresso, brewed

½ fl oz/15 mL vanilla extract

1 lb 4 oz/567 g unsweetened chocolate, chopped

4 lb/1.81 kg bittersweet chocolate, chopped

10½ oz/ 298 g butter, soft

22 eggs

4 lb/1.81 kg sugar

1 lb 5 oz/595 g walnuts, chopped

4 lb 8 oz/2.04 kg semisweet chocolate chips

1. Line sheet pans with parchment.

2. Sift together the flour, baking powder, and salt.

3. Blend the espresso and vanilla.

4. Melt the chocolates together with the butter. Stir to blend.

5. Beat the eggs, sugar, and coffee mixture with a whip attachment on high speed until light and thick, 6 to 8 minutes. Blend in the chocolate mixture on medium speed. On low speed, mix in the dry ingredients until just blended. Blend in the walnuts and chocolate chips just until incorporated.

6. Scale the dough into 2-oz/57-g portions and arrange them on the prepared sheet pans in even rows. Alternatively, the dough may be scaled into 2-lb/907-g portions, shaped into logs 16 in/41 cm long, wrapped tightly in parchment paper, and refrigerated until firm enough to slice. Slice each log into 16 pieces and arrange them on the prepared sheet pans in even rows.

7. Bake at 350°F/177°C until the cookies are cracked on top but still appear slightly moist, about 12 minutes. Allow them to cool slightly on the pans. Transfer them to racks and cool completely.

Oatmeal-Raisin Cookies

Makes 12 dozen cookies

2 lb 4 oz/1.02 kg all-purpose flour

1 oz/28 g baking soda

½ oz/14 g ground cinnamon

½ oz/14 g salt

3 lb/1.36 kg butter, soft

1 lb 3 oz/539 g sugar

3 lb 8 oz/1.59 kg light brown sugar

10 eggs

1 fl oz/30 mL vanilla extract

3 lb 3 oz/1.45 kg rolled oats

1 lb 8 oz/680 g raisins

1. Line sheet pans with parchment.

2. Sift together the flour, baking soda, cinnamon, and salt.

3. Cream the butter and sugars on medium speed with a paddle attachment, scraping down the bowl periodically, until the mixture is smooth and light in color, about 10 minutes. Blend the eggs and vanilla and add to the butter-sugar mixture in 3 additions, mixing until fully incorporated after each addition and scraping down the bowl as needed. On low speed, mix in the sifted dry ingredients and the oats and raisins until just incorporated.

4. Scale the dough into 2-oz/57-g portions and arrange them on the prepared sheet pans in even rows. Alternatively, the dough may be scaled into 2-lb/907-g portions, shaped into logs 16 in/41 cm long, wrapped tightly in parchment paper, and refrigerated until firm enough to slice. Slice each log into 16 pieces and arrange them on the prepared sheet pans in even rows.

5. Bake at 375°F/191°C until the cookies are light golden brown, about 12 minutes. Allow them to cool slightly on the pans. Transfer them to racks and cool completely.

Nut Tuile Cookies

Makes 25 cookies

2 oz/57 g almonds

3 oz/85 g hazelnuts

6 oz/170 g sugar

2½ oz/71 g all-purpose flour

pinch salt

4 egg whites

1. Line sheet pans with parchment paper or silicone baking mats. Have stencils and an offset spatula nearby, as well as shaping implements such as cups, dowels, or rolling pins, depending on the desired shapes.

2. Combine the almonds, hazelnuts, and sugar in a food processor and pulse to grind to a fine powder. Add the flour and salt and pulse several times to combine. Transfer to a large bowl.

3. Whip the egg whites on high speed using the whip attachment until medium peaks form. Using a rubber spatula, fold gently into the nut mixture in 3 additions.

4. Using the offset spatula and desired template, spread the batter on the prepared sheet pans.

5. Bake at 375°F/191°C, until an even light brown, about 10 minutes. Remove the tuiles from the oven and immediately shape them. If they begin to get too firm, put them back in the oven for a few seconds to soften and then form immediately.

Fudge Brownies

Makes 1 whole sheet pan or 60 brownies
(2 by 3 in/5 by 8 cm each)

1 lb 8 oz/680 g unsweetened chocolate

2 lb 4 oz/1.02 kg butter

1 lb 14 oz/851 g eggs

4 lb 8 oz/2.04 kg sugar

1 fl oz/30 mL vanilla

1 lb 8 oz/680 g cake flour, sifted

1 lb 2 oz/510 g nuts (pecans or walnuts)

1. Line a sheet pan with parchment.

2. Melt the chocolate and butter carefully over a pan of simmering water. Do not exceed 110°F/43°C. Remove from the heat and cool to room temperature.

3. Combine the eggs, sugar, and vanilla and whip on high speed until thick and light in color.

4. Add the chocolate and butter to the egg mixture using a liaison.

5. Blend ⅓ of the egg mixture into the chocolate to temper it, then fold in the remaining egg mixture. Gently fold in the sifted flour.

6. Fold in 1 pound of nuts. Pour onto the prepared sheet pan and sprinkle the remaining nuts on top.

7. Bake at 350°F/177°C for 30 minutes or until firm to the touch.

Chapter Thirty-seven

Custards, Creams, and Mousses

When baked, eggs, milk, and sugar result in a smooth and creamy baked custard. When stirred together over gentle heat, these same ingredients become vanilla sauce. Starches or gelatin can be included to produce textures that range from thick but spoonable to a sliceable cream. Folding meringue or whipped cream into the custard or cream produces a cold mousse, Bavarian, or Diplomat cream. For a soufflé, meringue is folded into a base and baked until it rises high, for one of the most dramatic of all desserts.

Baked Custards

A simple baked custard calls for blending eggs, a liquid such as milk or cream, and sugar and baking until set. Mascarpone, cream cheese, or another soft fresh cheese may be substituted for part of the cream to yield a richer and firmer result, such as for a cheesecake. The proportion of eggs also may be varied, as may the choice of whole eggs, yolks only, or a combination of the two. Using all whole eggs gives more structure to a custard that is to be served unmolded. There are two basic methods for combining the ingredients to make a baked custard: warm and cold.

For the cold method of mixing a custard base, the ingredients are simply stirred together, then poured into molds and baked. This method is effective for small batches.

To mix a custard base using the warm method, heat the milk or cream and some of the sugar, stirring with a wooden spoon, until the sugar is completely dissolved. Add the flavorings at this point and allow them to steep, if necessary, off the heat and covered, long enough for them to impart a rich, full flavor.

Blend the eggs and the remaining sugar to make a liaison and bring the milk or cream to a boil. Whisking constantly, slowly add about one-third of the hot milk, a few ladlefuls at a time to the liaison, to temper it. Once the liaison is tempered, you can add the rest of the hot milk more rapidly without scrambling the egg mixture.

Ladle the custard into molds (they can be coated with a light film of softened butter if you intend to unmold the custard) and bake them in a hot water bath. The water bath keeps the heat constant and gentle, resulting in a smooth texture in the baked custard. To check the custard for doneness, shake the mold gently; when the ripples on the surface move back and forth, rather than in concentric rings, the custard is properly baked.

Carefully remove the molds from the water bath and wipe the ramekins dry. Place them on a cool sheet pan, allow them to cool, and then refrigerate them. For crème caramel, an overnight resting period (optimally 24 hours) is essential, not only to completely set the custard so it can be unmolded, but also to allow the caramel to liquefy into a sauce.

Stirred Custards, Creams, and Puddings

Custard that is prepared on the stovetop (such as vanilla sauce) must be cooked by stirring constantly, until the stage of nappé (it coats the back of a spoon).

Creams and puddings that are thickened with starch and prepared on the stovetop must be cooked, stirring constantly, until they come to a full boil, both so the starch is heated sufficiently to thicken the mixture and to remove any undesirable flavor and mouthfeel that the uncooked starch contributes.

Some recipes for stirred custards, creams, and puddings may include whole milk, while others call for heavy cream, light cream, or a combination of cream and milk. Some recipes use only egg yolks; others use whole eggs or a blend of whole eggs and egg yolks.

It is especially important to have all the necessary equipment assembled before beginning, including a heavy-bottomed pot or a bain-marie, a fine-mesh sieve or conical sieve, and containers to hold the finished sauce during cooling and storing. To cool the custards, creams, or puddings rapidly and safely, have an ice bath prepared.

Hot Water Bath

A hot water bath, or bain-marie, ensures gentle heat at a constant temperature, allowing for even baking or cooking. Using a hot water bath for baking custards also prevents both the formation of a crust and rapid expansion that would lead to cracking of the custard's surface.

Select a pan with sides at least as high as the sides of the molds. Set the molds in the pan as they are filled, leaving about 1 in/3 cm around each mold so it will be surrounded by hot water. Set the pan securely on the oven deck or rack. Add enough very hot or boiling water to the pan to come to about two thirds of the height of the molds. Be careful not to splash or pour any water into the custards.

After custards are properly baked and removed from the oven, they should also be removed from the hot water bath. This will stop the cooking process and allow the custards to cool. Custards will continue to cook after they are removed from the oven if they are left in the hot water bath, which may cause them to become overdone.

1. **Combine the milk with half of the sugar (and a vanilla bean, if using) and bring it to a simmer.** Combine the egg yolks or eggs with the remaining sugar in a stainless-steel bowl.

Heating the milk or cream with the sugar dissolves the sugar for a smoother, silkier finished texture. If a vanilla bean is used to flavor the sauce, add the seeds and the empty pod to the milk (or cream) and sugar as it heats. (If desired, vanilla extract may be used instead of vanilla beans. Add the extract just before the sauce is strained.) Heat just to the boiling point. Keep an eye on the milk as it heats since it can easily boil over as it nears the boiling point.

Beating the eggs and sugar together prevents the eggs from scrambling when they are combined with the hot milk or cream. Blend the ingredients well, using a whip, for long enough to dissolve the sugar into the eggs.

2. **Temper the hot milk into the egg mixture to produce a smooth sauce.** Ladle the hot milk into the egg mixture a little at a time, stirring constantly, until about ⅓ of the milk or cream mixture has been blended into the eggs. Return the tempered egg mixture to the pot. Continue to cook the sauce over low heat until it begins to thicken. Stir the sauce constantly to prevent it from overcooking. Do not let the sauce come to a boil, because the egg yolks will coagulate well below the boiling point. The sauce is cooked when it has thickened enough to coat the back of a wooden spoon. The temperature of the sauce should not go above 180°F/82°C, or it will begin to curdle.

3. **Evaluate the finished vanilla sauce.** The finished vanilla sauce should coat the back of a wooden spoon and hold a line that is drawn through it. When it reaches this stage, strain it immediately through a fine-mesh sieve into a container. Cool the sauce in an ice water bath if it is to be held for later storage or served cold, stirring frequently as it cools, and refrigerate it immediately. Placing a piece of plastic wrap on the surface prevents a skin from forming.

A good vanilla sauce is thick and glossy and coats the back of a wooden spoon. It shows no signs of curdling. This sauce should have a smooth, luxurious mouthfeel, with a well-balanced flavor.

Ice Cream

Custard, or French, ice cream is made with a base of stirred egg custard (essentially vanilla sauce). This type of base should be allowed to mature in the refrigerator (at approximately 40°F/4°C) for several hours before freezing. This will result in a smoother ice cream. To churn the ice cream, run the chilled base in an ice cream freezer only to soft-serve consistency and then extract it from the machine, pack it into containers, and place it in a freezer for several hours to allow it to firm to a servable temperature and consistency.

All of the ingredients add flavor to the ice cream, but each one also plays a part in determining consistency and mouthfeel. The eggs make it rich and smooth. The milk and cream allow for incorporation of air during freezing, giving the final product a smoother mouthfeel and lighter body. However, too much incorporated air will diminish the flavor, make the ice cream too soft, and make it melt quickly. For best results, use a mixture of milk and cream, to avoid having too much butterfat in the mix.

Sugar both adds sweetness and reduces the freezing point of the base, keeping the ice cream from freezing too hard.

Simple Flavorings for an Ice Cream Base

There are a number of different methods for adding flavorings to ice creams. Flavorings such as vanilla bean, tea, coffee, or spices can be infused into the milk and cream as they are heating. Then cook the ice cream base as usual, with the flavorings, and strain them out before freezing. Purées can be blended into the custard after it has cooled, or folded into still-soft, just-churned ice cream for a swirled effect. Melted chocolate can be added to the still-warm, just-cooked ice cream base, while nut pastes, such as peanut butter and praline paste, can be added to the milk and cream and cooked into the base mixture.

Some fruit juices or frozen concentrates, such as lemon, orange, or passion fruit, have a very intense flavor. Add up to 8 fl oz/240 mL of these juices or frozen concentrates to the same amount of base as you would purée, using just enough to give the proper flavor. It is not necessary to reduce the volume of liquid in the base; adding this amount of additional liquid to a 48-fl-oz/1.44-L batch will not noticeably affect the ice cream's texture (or volume).

Mousse

The name for this delicate dessert comes from the French; the word translates literally as "frothy, foamy, or light." To make a mousse, an aerating ingredient, such as whipped cream and/or meringue, is folded into a base such as a fruit purée, vanilla sauce, cream, pudding, curd, sabayon, or pâte à bombe (cooked whipped egg yolks). The base should be light and smooth so the aerating ingredient can be incorporated easily.

To make an egg-safe mousse, use pasteurized egg whites or a Swiss or Italian meringue. Stabilizers such as gelatin may be used in varying amounts, depending on the desired result. If a mousse is stabilized with gelatin, it will begin to set immediately, so prepare all molds and serving containers before beginning preparation.

Whatever the flavoring ingredient used, it should be at room temperature and liquid enough to fold together with whipped cream and/or egg whites without deflating those foams. To prepare chocolate, chop it into small pieces and melt it properly over simmering water or in the microwave. Let it cool to room temperature, when it should still be pourable.

Eggs, both yolks and whites, are called for in some mousse recipes. Consult the recipe and prepare the eggs as directed. Separate yolks and whites carefully, keeping whites free of all traces of yolk. Whites generally whip to a greater volume if they are at room temperature. Use a very clean bowl and whip to beat egg whites.

Cream should be kept very cold and whipped just to soft or medium peaks. Keep whipped cream very cold if it is prepared in advance. For the best volume in the whipped cream, chill the bowl and beaters before whipping the cream.

Have a simmering water bath ready to cook egg yolks and sugar together. Use a rubber spatula to fold the mousse together. Have molds arranged to fill with the finished mousse.

Beat the egg whites with the remaining sugar to stiff peaks in a completely clean and dry bowl. Beat the eggs at medium speed at first to begin to separate the protein strands. Add the sugar in small increments with the mixer on high speed until the peaks of the beaten whites remain stiff and do not droop when the beater is pulled from the bowl. The whites should still appear shiny, not dry. Gently fold them into the yolk mixture to keep the maximum amount of volume. Some chefs like to add the whites to the yolks in 2 or more additions, so that the first addition lightens the base. That way, less volume is lost from subsequent additions.

Use a lifting and folding motion to avoid deflating the mousse. The finished mousse should be well blended but still retain as much volume as possible. At this point, the mousse is ready for service or may be refrigerated, covered, for a short period of time before service. The mousse may be scooped or piped into molds or containers for presentation.

1. Prepare the flavor ingredients for the mousse and cool them, if necessary. Some mousse flavorings are made from puréed fruit, sweetened as necessary and strained to remove any fibers or seeds. Chocolate, one of the most popular mousse flavors, is prepared by chopping the chocolate. A quantity of butter is added to the chocolate and they are melted together over simmering water. Take care to avoid dropping any water into the chocolate as it melts. Adding butter to the chocolate makes it easier to melt. The flavor base should be soft enough to stir easily with a wooden spoon, and very smooth. Blend the ingredients together using a wooden spoon. Let them cool to room temperature before use.

Heat the egg yolks and sugar to 145°F/63°C for 15 seconds, whisking constantly. Combine the egg yolks and sugar in a saucepan over a hot water bath. Whip them together until thick and light. The mixture will fall in ribbons from the whip when the base has reached the correct consistency. At this time, flavoring ingredients should be added by folding them in. It is important that the flavorings be liquid enough to blend easily. Continue to fold in the flavorings just until there are no streaks in the mixture.

2. **Evaluate the finished mousse.** A well-made mousse should have an intense, identifiable flavor, with added smoothness and richness from the cream. The color should be even throughout each portion. Mousses have a light, foamy texture due to the addition of both beaten egg whites and whipped cream. When the whites and cream are beaten properly, the texture is very smooth and fine.

Making the Perfect Mousse

There are a few simple rules to remember that will help your mousse be a success every time:

- Flavor the base well—The base of the mousse is all that provides flavor. Once the aerators (whipped cream and egg whites) are folded in, the flavor of the base will become diluted, so make sure the base is very flavorful to ensure the amount of flavor you desire is carried to the finished product.

- Keep the cream cold and only whip to soft peaks—To maintain its structure during and after whipping, keep the cream cold before and after whipping. Only whip the cream to soft peaks. After whipping, the cream will be folded into the remaining ingredients for the mousse. If it is whipped beyond soft peaks, this folding will overwhip the cream, giving the mousse a grainy appearance.

- Use a rubber spatula for folding—The use of a rubber spatula or another tool with a broad surface for folding ensures the retention of volume.

- Lighten the base with one third of the aerator—Quickly fold approximately one third of the aerator into the base to lighten it before folding in the remainder of the aerator; this will help retain the volume.

- Portion immediately after preparation—Whether your mousse has gelatin or not, you should have all portioning equipment and receptacles ready before you begin the preparation. A mousse will begin to set as soon as it is complete, and it should be portioned immediately to ensure the best texture and appearance.

Vanilla Sauce

Makes 32 fl oz/960 mL

16 fl oz/480 mL milk

16 fl oz/480 mL heavy cream

1 vanilla bean, split and scraped

8 oz/227 g sugar

14 egg yolks

1. Heat the milk, cream, vanilla bean pod and seeds, and half the sugar until the mixture reaches the boiling point.

2. Combine the egg yolks and the rest of the sugar and temper the mixture into the hot milk.

3. Stirring constantly, heat slowly to 180°F/82°C.

4. Remove the milk mixture immediately from the stove and strain it through a fine-mesh sieve, directly into a container set in an ice bath.

NOTES
This sauce can be made over a water bath for more control of the heat source.

Substitute ½ fl oz/15 mL vanilla extract for the vanilla bean. Add it just before straining the sauce.

All milk or light cream can be used in place of heavy cream.

Pastry Cream

Makes 32 fl oz/960 mL

32 fl oz/960 mL milk

8 oz/227 g sugar

3 oz/85 g cornstarch

6 to 8 eggs

½ fl oz/15 mL vanilla extract

3 oz/85 g butter

1. Combine the milk with half the sugar in a saucepan and bring it to a boil.

2. Combine the remaining sugar with the cornstarch, add the eggs, and mix until smooth.

3. Temper the egg mixture into the hot milk and bring it to a full boil, stirring constantly.

4. Remove it from the heat and stir in the vanilla and butter. Transfer it to a clean container, place a piece of plastic wrap directly on the pastry cream, and let it cool.

5. The pastry cream is ready to use now, or it may be thoroughly cooled and stored for later use.

Chocolate Pastry Cream: Add 8 oz/227 g Hard Ganache (page 1160) to the finished pastry cream.

Pastry Cream for Soufflés

Makes 2 lb 2 oz/964 g

21 fl oz/630 mL milk

6½ oz/184 g sugar

4 oz/113 g all-purpose flour

2 eggs

3 egg yolks

1. Combine approximately 6 fl oz/180 mL of the milk with half of the sugar in a saucepan and bring to a boil, stirring gently with a wooden spoon.

2. Meanwhile, combine the flour with the remaining sugar. Stirring with a wire whisk, add the remaining 15 fl oz/450 mL of milk. Add the eggs and egg yolks, stirring with a wire whisk until the mixture is completely smooth.

3. Temper the egg mixture by adding about ⅓ of the hot milk, stirring constantly with a wire whisk. Return the mixture to the remaining hot milk in the saucepan. Continue cooking, vigorously stirring with the whisk, until the pastry cream comes to a boil and the whisk leaves a trail in it.

4. Pour the pastry cream onto a large shallow container or bowl. Cover it with plastic wrap placed directly against the surface of the cream, and cool it over an ice bath.

5. Refrigerate the pastry cream, covered.

Crème Brûlée

Makes 10 servings

32 fl oz/960 mL heavy cream

6 oz/170 g sugar

pinch salt

1 vanilla bean

5½ oz/156 g egg yolks, beaten

5 oz/142 g sugar

4½ oz/128 g confectioners' sugar

1. Combine the cream, 4 oz/113 g of the sugar, and the salt and bring to a simmer over medium heat, stirring gently with a wooden spoon. Remove from the heat. Split the vanilla bean, scrape the seeds from the pod, add both the pod and scrapings to the pan, cover, and steep for 15 minutes.

2. Return to the heat and bring the cream to a boil.

3. Combine the egg yolks and the rest of the sugar and temper the mixture into the hot milk. Strain the custard and ladle it into 6-fl-oz/180-mL crème brûlée ramekins, filling them ¾ full.

4. Bake in a water bath at 325°F/163°C until just set, 20 to 25 minutes.

5. Remove the custards from the water bath and wipe the ramekins dry. Refrigerate until fully chilled.

6. To finish the crème brûlée, evenly coat each custard's surface with a thin layer (1/16 in/1.50 mm) of sugar. Use a propane torch to melt and caramelize the sugar. Lightly dust the surface with confectioners' sugar and serve.

Crème Caramel

Makes 10 servings

2 fl oz/60 mL water

5¾ oz/163 g sugar

23 fl oz /690 mL milk

6 oz /170 g sugar

2 tsp/10 mL vanilla extract

4 eggs, lightly beaten

3 egg yolks

1. To prepare the caramel: add the water and a small amount of the sugar to a pan set over medium heat. Allow the sugar to melt.

2. Add the remaining sugar in small increments, allowing it to melt before each new addition. Continue this process until all the sugar has been added. Cook the caramel to the desired color.

3. Divide the caramel equally among ten 4-fl-oz/120-mL ramekins, swirling the caramel to coat the bottoms. Place the ramekins into a deep baking dish and reserve.

4. To prepare the custard, combine the milk and half of the second measure of sugar and bring to a simmer over medium heat, stirring gently with a wooden spoon. Remove from the heat and add the vanilla. Return to the heat and bring the milk to a boil.

5. Blend the eggs and egg yolks, combine with the rest of the sugar, and temper the mixture into the hot milk.

6. Strain the custard and ladle it into the caramel-coated ramekins, filling them ¾ full. Bake the ramekins in a water bath at 325°F/163°C until fully set, about 1 hour.

7. Remove the custards from the water bath and wipe the ramekins dry. Allow the custards to cool.

8. Wrap each custard individually and refrigerate them for at least 24 hours before unmolding and serving.

9. To unmold the custards, run a small sharp knife between the custard and the ramekin, invert each one onto a serving plate, and tap it lightly to release.

Crème Caramel

Diplomat Cream

Makes 32 fl oz/960 mL

16 fl oz/480 mL heavy cream

¼ oz/7 g gelatin

2 fl oz/60 mL water

16 fl oz/480 mL **Pastry Cream** (page 1133), **warm**

1. Assemble and prepare the desired pastries, containers, or molds that are to be used in the application of the cream before beginning preparation.

2. Whip the cream to soft peaks. Cover and refrigerate.

3. Bloom the gelatin in the water and melt.

4. Temper the melted gelatin into the freshly prepared and still-warm pastry cream. Strain, then cool the pastry cream over an ice bath to 75°F/24°C.

5. Gently blend approximately ⅓ of the reserved whipped cream into the pastry cream mixture. Fold in the remaining whipped cream, thoroughly incorporating it.

6. Immediately pipe the diplomat cream into the prepared pastries or containers. Cover and refrigerate until completely set.

Vanilla Ice Cream

Makes 48 fl oz/ 1.44 L

16 fl oz/480 mL milk

16 fl oz/480 mL heavy cream

1 vanilla bean, split and scraped

7 oz/198 g sugar

1 oz/28 g glucose syrup

¼ tsp/0.50 g salt

15 egg yolks

1. Combine the milk, cream, vanilla bean pod and seeds, half of the sugar, syrup, and salt in a saucepan.

2. Bring the mixture to a simmer over medium heat, stirring constantly, 7 to 10 minutes.

3. Remove the saucepan from the heat, cover the pan, and allow it to steep for 5 minutes.

4. Meanwhile, blend the egg yolks with the remaining sugar.

5. Remove the vanilla pod and return the mixture to a simmer.

6. Temper ⅓ of the hot mixture into the egg yolks, whisking constantly.

7. Return the tempered egg mixture to the saucepan with the remaining hot liquid, stirring constantly over medium heat until the mixture is thick enough to coat the back of a spoon, about 3 to 5 minutes.

8. Strain the ice cream base into a metal container over an ice bath, stirring occasionally until it reaches below 40°F/4°C, about 1 hour.

9. Cover and refrigerate for a minimum of 12 hours.

10. Process the base in an ice cream machine according to the manufacturer's directions.

11. Pack the ice cream in storage containers or molds as desired, and freeze for several hours or overnight before serving.

Chocolate Ice Cream: Before straining the ice cream base, stir 6 oz/170 g melted bittersweet chocolate into the mixture.

Coffee Ice Cream: Substitute 2 oz/57 g coarsely ground coffee for the vanilla bean.

Raspberry Ice Cream: Omit the milk from the recipe. After refrigerating the ice cream base, stir in 16 fl oz/480 mL raspberry purée.

Chocolate, Coffee, and Vanilla Ice Cream

Raspberry Mousse

Raspberry Mousse

Makes 88 fl oz/2.64 L

1 oz/28 g gelatin

10 fl oz/300 mL water

14 fl oz/420 mL heavy cream

24 fl oz/720 mL raspberry purée

5 egg whites

9 oz/255 g sugar

1. Assemble and prepare the desired pastries, containers, or molds that are to be used in the application of the mousse before beginning preparation.

2. Bloom the gelatin in the water.

3. Whip the cream to medium peaks. Cover and refrigerate the whipped cream.

4. Warm half of the fruit purée in a saucepan. Remove it from the heat. Melt the gelatin. Add the melted gelatin and stir to incorporate. Blend in the remaining purée.

5. Combine the egg whites and sugar in a mixer bowl over a pot of simmering water and heat, stirring constantly with a wire whip, until the mixture reaches 145°F/63°C. Transfer the bowl to the mixer and whip at high speed with the whip attachment until stiff peaks form. Continue beating until the meringue has completely cooled.

6. Cool the raspberry mixture to 70°F/21°C.

7. Gently blend approximately ⅓ of the meringue into the raspberry mixture to lighten it. Fold in the remaining meringue, thoroughly incorporating it. Fold in the reserved whipped cream.

8. Immediately pipe or ladle the mousse into molds.

Chocolate Mousse

Makes 10 servings

10 oz/284 g bittersweet chocolate

1½ oz/43 g butter

5 eggs, separated

1 fl oz/30 mL water

2 oz/57 g sugar

8 fl oz/240 mL heavy cream, whipped

rum (optional), as needed

1. Combine the chocolate and butter and melt over a hot water bath.

2. Combine the egg yolks with half of the water and half of the sugar and whisk over a hot water bath to 145°F/63°C for 15 seconds. Remove from the heat and whip until cool.

3. Combine the egg whites with the remaining sugar and whisk over a hot water bath to 145°F/63°C. Remove the whites from the heat and beat to full volume. Continue beating until cool.

4. Using a large rubber spatula, fold the chocolate mixture into the egg yolks.

5. Fold the egg white mixture into the egg yolk-chocolate mixture.

6. Fold in the whipped cream and add the rum, if desired.

Chocolate Soufflé

Makes 10 servings

3 oz/85 g butter

10 oz/284 g bittersweet chocolate, chopped

2 lb 2 oz/964 g **Pastry Cream for Soufflés** (page 1133), cooled

3 egg yolks

12 egg whites

5 oz/142 g sugar

1. Coat the inside of ten 4-fl-oz/120-mL ramekins with a film of softened butter, making sure to coat the rims as well as the insides, and dust with sugar.

2. To prepare the soufflé base, melt the butter and chocolate together in a bowl over a pan of barely simmering water, gently stirring to blend. Blend the chocolate mixture into the pastry cream. Blend in the egg yolks and set aside.

3. Whip the egg whites to soft peaks using the whip attachment.

4. Gradually sprinkle in the sugar while continuing to whip, then whip the meringue to medium peaks.

5. Gently blend approximately ⅓ of the meringue into the chocolate base. Fold in the remaining meringue, thoroughly incorporating it.

6. Portion the soufflé mixture into the prepared ramekins.

7. Bake at 350°F/177°C until fully risen, about 20 minutes. Serve immediately.

Bread and Butter Pudding

Makes 10 servings

3 oz/85 g raisins

4 fl oz/120 mL rum

9 oz/255 g **Brioche Loaf** (page 1076) or **Challah** (page 1080)

3 oz/85 g butter, melted

32 fl oz/960 mL milk

6 oz/170 g sugar

6 eggs, beaten

4 egg yolks, beaten

½ tsp/2.50 mL vanilla extract

½ tsp/1 g ground cinnamon

½ tsp/2.50 g salt

1. Place the raisins in a bowl and add the rum. Set them aside to plump for 20 minutes, then drain.

2. Cut the bread into ½-in/1-cm cubes. Place them on a sheet pan and drizzle with the butter. Toast in a 350°F/177°C oven, stirring once or twice, until golden brown.

3. Combine the milk and 3 oz/85 g of the sugar in a saucepan and bring them to a boil.

4. Meanwhile, blend the eggs, egg yolks, vanilla, and the remaining 3 oz/85 g of sugar to make the liaison. Temper by gradually adding about ⅓ of the hot milk, whipping constantly. Add the remaining hot milk and strain the custard into a bowl.

5. Add the bread, cinnamon, salt, and drained raisins to the custard. Soak over an ice bath for at least 1 hour to allow the bread to absorb the custard. Lightly brush ten 6-fl-oz/180-mL ramekins with softened butter.

6. Ladle the mixture into the prepared ramekins, filling them ¾ full. Bake in a water bath at 350°F/177°C until just set, 45 to 50 minutes.

7. Remove the custards from the water bath and wipe the ramekins dry. Refrigerate them until fully chilled.

Chapter Thirty-eight

Fillings, Frostings, and Dessert Sauces

There are many options for assembling and finishing a cake or for creating the finishing touches to a plated dessert. In adding these elements the chef should always be mindful of marrying all the flavors and textures, so that they blend, complement, and enhance each other. In addition to their role as a dessert adornment, they are also used as a basic component of other items. Fillings, frostings, and sauces can be prepared in a variety of consistencies to complement a range of dessert items. They can be pooled on the plate, drizzled, spooned, or spread over the main item, cake, or pastry.

Buttercream

Buttercreams are made by blending softened butter into an egg and sugar base. Buttercreams help to make elegant cakes and tortes. The manner in which the eggs and sugar are combined, as well as whether whole eggs, egg yolks, or egg whites are used, produces a variety of icings.

To make a buttercream, measure and assemble all the ingredients. Refrigerate eggs to keep them safe until you separate them. Sift the sugar if necessary to work out any lumps. The butter should be cut or broken into small pieces and softened before it is added to the buttercream. Flavorings, such as chocolate or fruit purées, should be prepared in advance, according to the recipe, and kept at the appropriate temperature.

Use an electric mixer with a whip attachment to mix the buttercream. Use a candy thermometer to check the temperature of the sugar solution as it is heated. Have a plastic or rubber scraper at hand, as well as storage and service items as necessary.

 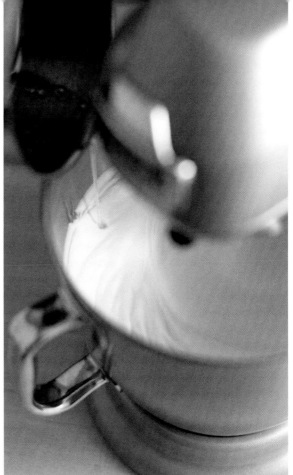

1. **To make an Italian buttercream, use an Italian meringue as the base.** To prepare the meringue, combine the sugar and water in a saucepan and bring them to a boil. Continue to boil the sugar syrup, without stirring, until the temperature reaches 240°F/116°C. Use a wet pastry brush to wipe down the sides of the pan to dissolve any sugar crystals that splashed onto the sides. If the crystals remain, they will act as "seeds" and cause the syrup to crystallize. Use a candy thermometer to check the temperature of the syrup. This stage is also known as the soft ball stage. When the syrup reaches the correct temperature, it should be immediately added to the egg whites.

2. **As the sugar syrup cooks, whip the egg whites on medium speed.** The ideal is to have the egg whites reach soft peaks at the same time that the syrup reaches 240°F/116°C. With the machine still running, gradually pour the hot sugar syrup in a thin stream into the whites. Add the syrup so that it pours down the side of the bowl rather than onto the whip, to prevent splattering. Continue to beat the mixture until a firm meringue forms and the mixture cools to room temperature. If the meringue is too hot, it will melt the butter as it is added. Check the temperature by feeling the side of the bowl. It should be cool to the touch.

3. **Gradually add softened butter to the base and beat the mixture until a smooth, light buttercream forms.** As the butter is first added, the meringue will fall and the mixture may appear broken. Continue to add the butter in small amounts with the mixer running and the buttercream will become smooth and light.

At this point, it is ready to apply to a prepared cake, or it may be refrigerated for later use. Buttercream takes on other flavors and odors readily and must, therefore, be tightly wrapped before storing for up to 7 days, or frozen for 2 to 3 months. Allow chilled buttercream to return to room temperature and beat it using the paddle attachment until very smooth and light before using it to fill or frost a cake.

Buttercreams should be perfectly smooth and soft. They should be sweet, but not overly sweet. There should be no detectable grains or pieces of sugar or any lumps of butter.

Cake Layering Basics

Cake layers should be allowed to cool completely before cutting them into layers. Cut the cakes into layers. Cakes that are made of more and thinner layers are preferable than those with fewer and thicker layers, because they end up with a more uniform flavor and texture. Fillings that are spread onto layers should generally be less than ½ in/1 cm thick.

Before slicing a cake into layers, trim any uneven areas from the sides and top. For the best results, use a cake-decorating turntable and a knife with a long, thin, serrated blade. Set the cake on a cake round and then on the turntable. First, divide the cake by eye into the desired number of layers. Then insert the knife into the side of the cake at the appropriate level and, holding the knife steady and level and slowing rotating the turntable, move the blade of the knife into the cake to cut the layer. Remove the layer and set it aside; repeat as necessary.

Before assembling the cake, brush any loose crumbs from the layers. Cake layers are often moistened with a variety of syrups, from plain simple syrup to one infused with spices or a liqueur. The syrup adds moisture to drier layers, such as sponge cakes, and adds flavor as well. Brush the syrup evenly over the cut surface of each layer before it is assembled. The layers should be moistened but not sodden.

1. **Use a turntable for icing a cake.** A turntable allows the cake to be easily rotated, which aids in the application of a smooth even layer of icing. Use either a straight or an offset metal spatula to ice the cake. The appropriate length of the spatula depends on the size of the cake and personal preference. After filling the cake, place a generous amount of buttercream on top. While spinning the cake stand, hold a spatula steady and at a slight angle to apply a smooth even layer of buttercream on top of the cake. Allow the excess buttercream to fall down the sides of the cake.

2. **To ice the sides of the cake, apply a generous amount of icing to the sides to ease smoothing and ensure a clean finish.** To smooth the sides of the cake after applying the icing, hold a spatula vertically against the cake at a 45-degree angle, with the edge of the spatula touching the icing, and rotate the cake against the spatula; the tip of the spatula should just touch the surface of the turntable. This will not only smooth the icing, but will also cause some of the excess icing from the sides to rise above the top of the cake, making a lip or ridge.

3. **Work from the edges of the cake toward the center.** Hold the spatula parallel to the top of the cake at a 45-degree angle, smooth the lip of icing over and across the top to create a perfectly smooth top and a sharp angled edge.

4. **Mark the cake into portions if desired, using a straight-edged knife or long, straight metal spatula.** Alternatively, garnish may be applied by treating the cake top as a whole (this is typically done to smaller cakes or to special occasion cakes). A variety of simple garnishes can also be applied (such as a shell border or rosettes), with or without additional garnishes, such as chocolate cutouts, fresh berries, jam, and the like.

Fillings and Icings for Layered Cakes

FILLING	AMOUNT FOR 8-IN/20-CM CAKE	AMOUNT FOR 10-IN/25-CM CAKE	
Buttercream	12 oz/340 g	1 lb/454 g	
Lemon curd	12 oz/340 g	1 lb/454 g	
ICING			
Ganache (for glazing)	12 oz/340 g	1 lb/454 g	
Buttercream	12 oz/340 g	1 lb/454 g	

Ganache

Ganache has many uses. It may be used as a sauce or to glaze a cake, or it may be whipped and used as a filling and/or icing. Ganache can also be made with a stiffer consistency, chilled, and rolled into truffles.

Light ganache is sometimes used as a chocolate sauce. There are a number of different recipes for this all-time favorite dessert sauce, and by varying the proportions in the recipe so that there is more chocolate in relation to the amount of milk or cream, a harder ganache can be made. This hard ganache can be paddled and used for icing or filling. Adding an even greater amount of chocolate will produce the heavy ganache used to prepare chocolate truffles.

Chocolate for ganache should be cut into very small pieces, which facilitates even melting. One of the most efficient ways to chop chocolate is to use a serrated knife; the serration causes the chocolate to break into small shards as it is cut. Use the best-quality chocolate available to be sure of a smooth, richly flavored sauce. Place the chopped chocolate into a heatproof bowl. Place the cream and butter in a saucepan and bring to a boil.

Tempering Chocolate

Chocolate contains two distinct types of fat, which melt at different temperatures. In order to ensure that the chocolate will melt smoothly and harden evenly with a good shine, it must be tempered. This particular method of tempering is sometimes known as the seed method.

1. Chop the chocolate with a serrated knife and put it in a stainless-steel bowl. Place the bowl over very low heat or barely simmering water, making sure that no moisture comes in contact with the chocolate. Stir the chocolate occasionally as it melts to keep it at an even temperature throughout.

2. Continue to heat the chocolate until it reaches a temperature between 105° and 110°F/41° and 43°C. Use an instant-read thermometer for the most accurate results.

3. Remove the chocolate from the heat. Add a large piece of unmelted chocolate (the seed) and stir it until the temperature drops to 87° to 92°F/31° to 33°C. If the chocolate drops below 85°F/29°C, it will be necessary to repeat the steps described here to gently reheat it to 92°F/33°C. If the chocolate scorches or becomes grainy, it can no longer be used. If any moisture comes in contact with the chocolate as it is being tempered, it will seize.

Tempered chocolate will evenly coat the back of a spoon and then harden into a shiny shell. Dried or fresh fruit or baked items can be dipped directly into the tempered chocolate with a dipping fork, or rolled in the tempered chocolate, or placed on a rack over a clean sheet pan and have the chocolate poured over it.

1. **Combine the cream and chocolate.** Heat the cream and pour it over the chopped chocolate. Allow the mixture to stand, undisturbed, for a few minutes.

2. **Stir the ganache until the cream is fully incorporated and the mixture is completely smooth.** At this point, add any desired flavoring (e.g., flavored liqueurs, extracts, or purées). The ganache is ready to be used now, or it may be refrigerated for later use.

Ganache should be intensely flavored, with the chocolate flavor enriched and smoothed by the addition of cream. The texture should be completely smooth and dense. The more chocolate in the ganache, the thicker the texture will be. Ganache is very glossy when warmed and used as a glaze. When cooled and whipped, it becomes more opaque and matte, lightening in color somewhat. Ingredients added to flavor or garnish the sauce should be appropriate to the sauce without masking or overwhelming the chocolate's flavor.

Glazing Cakes, Cookies, or Pastries

Set a cake that is to be glazed on a cardboard round and apply a seal coat of buttercream or jam, if necessary, and chill until set prior to glazing. A seal coat is vital if the cake being glazed has been trimmed or cut and layered, as it prevents crumbs from incorporating into the glaze. Place the cake or cakes on a wire rack resting on a clean sheet pan. Have the glaze tepid so that it does not melt the crumb coating (if applied). It should not be so thin as to run off the cake completely. Pour or ladle the glaze over the cake. Using an offset spatula, quickly spread the glaze to completely enrobe the sides of the cake. This step must be done quickly, before the glaze begins to set up, to avoid leaving marks of the spatula on the surface. Gently tap the wire rack on the sheet pan to facilitate the flow of any excess glaze off the cake.

1. **Fondant is used as the traditional glaze for many pastry items such as petit fours, éclairs, and doughnuts.** For fondant to gain its glossy finish, it must be properly warmed until it is liquid enough to flow readily. Properly thinned fondant should be shiny and slightly transparent. This procedure is known as tempering.

Most kitchens and bakeshops use purchased fondant. To prepare fondant so that it may be used for glazing, place it in a stainless-steel bowl and melt it over a hot water bath. Do not let the fondant exceed 105°F/41°C. Thin the fondant to the desired consistency with warm water, corn syrup, or a liqueur.

2. Once it has been melted, plain fondant can be flavored and/or colored as desired with coloring pastes, purées, concentrates, or chocolate. If using chocolate, for example, stir the melted chocolate into the fondant to flavor it. The fondant may need to be thinned again after the chocolate has been added.

3. Keep the fondant warm as you work and be sure to have a complete glazing setup ready. Small items, such as éclairs, are typically dipped into fondant. Larger items are set on racks on sheet pans and the glaze is poured, ladled, spooned, or drizzled over the item.

Dip the top of an éclair into the bowl of thinned fondant and hold it vertically to allow the excess fondant to drip off. Use your finger to gently remove any excess fondant that still remains at the bottom of the éclair before placing it on a sheet pan.

Making a Pie or Tart

Fruit fillings are used for many pies and tarts. They are usually prepared with sliced and peeled fresh fruit. The fruit is typically combined with sugar and a starch (flour, arrowroot, cornstarch, or tapioca) to produce a flavorful filling with enough body to slice into neat portions. Cooked cream or pudding fillings should be prepared only after the pie or tart shell has been completely prepared, baked, and cooled, so that when the filling is ready it may be immediately poured into the shell. Hold all fillings at the correct temperature for the best flavor and consistency in the finished pie or tart.

There are a wide variety of toppings commonly used for pies and tarts, including crumb or streusel, pastry crust, meringue, or glazes, such as melted chocolate ganache or apricot jam. Egg wash is often applied to double-crust pies or tarts and should be blended in advance and applied in an thin, even layer with a pastry brush. Pies and tarts should be baked on sheet pans to catch any drips. Cool pies on cooling racks.

Lining a pie or tart pan

Always work with thoroughly chilled dough. Chilling allows the dough to relax, the fat to firm up, and the starches present in the flour to completely absorb the liquid.

To roll out dough, turn it onto a floured work surface. Lightly dust the surface of the dough with additional flour. Using even strokes, roll the dough into the desired thickness and shape. Turn it occasionally to produce an even shape and to keep it from sticking to the work surface. Work from the center toward the edges, rolling in different directions.

1. **Line the pie or tart pan with pastry dough.** Carefully transfer the rolled dough into the pan. Position the dough so that it completely covers the entire pan. Settle the dough into the pan, pressing the dough gently against the pan. Use a ball of scrap dough to gently press the pie dough into the pie pan. Trim the excess dough from the rim, leaving enough to seal a top crust in place, if necessary, or to prepare a fluted or raised edge for a single-crust pie or tart.

2. **Finish and fill the pie crust as desired.** Some pies and tarts are filled, then baked. Others call for the crust to be baked separately, either baked blind or fully baked (see Blind Baking, page 1153). To add a fruit filling to an unbaked pie shell, combine the filling ingredients and mound them in the shell. Custard-type fillings should be carefully poured into the shell to just below the rim of the pan.

Some pies, especially fresh fruit pies, have a top crust as well as a bottom crust. Roll out the top crust in the same manner as for the bottom crust. Cut vents in the top crust to allow steam to escape, and carefully lay the top crust over the pie. Press the dough in place around the rim to seal the top and bottom crusts. Trim away excess overhang, and pinch or crimp the edges. Pies and, less frequently, tarts may be finished with a lattice crust, made by cutting strips of dough and laying them on top of the filling to make a grid. Seal and crimp the edges as for a double-crusted pie. Crumb toppings should be applied in an even layer over the surface of the filling. Another frequent pie topping is meringue, which is piped onto the pie in a decorative pattern or simply mounded and peaked. The meringue is then quickly browned in a very hot oven or with a torch.

3. **Bake the pie or pie crust.** For a double-crusted pie, brush the top crust very lightly with egg wash and bake the pie on a sheet pan in a hot oven (425°F/218°C) until done. In general, pies and tarts are baked until the crust is a rich golden brown. The dough should appear dry. If the dough has been rolled out unevenly, the thicker portions may appear moist, indicating that the dough is not fully baked. Fruit fillings should be bubbling. Custard fillings should be just set, but not cooked to the point at which the surface cracks or shrinks away from the crust.

Blind Baking Pie and Tart Shells

To *blind bake* **means** to bake an unfilled pie or tart shell, partially or fully, before adding the filling. Pastry shells are partially prebaked when the time required to bake the filling will not be long enough to fully bake the crust. Shells are completely prebaked when they are to be filled with a precooked filling or one that does not require cooking or baking.

To blind bake a pie or tart shell, line the dough with parchment paper and fill it with pie weights or dry beans or rice. The weights will prevent the bottom of the crust from bubbling up and the sides from collapsing or sliding down the sides during baking.

Place the pan in the preheated oven. The parchment and weights need only stay in the pan until the crust has baked long enough to set. Once the crust has baked long enough so that it has set and will maintain its form (generally 10 to 12 minutes for a 9-in/23-cm pan), remove the parchment and weights to allow for even browning of the crust. Return the pan to the oven and bake the crust until it reaches the desired color. If the crust is to be baked again with a filling, bake it just until light golden. For a fully baked crust, bake it until it reaches a deep golden brown, about 20 minutes.

Brush fully prebaked pastry shells with a light coating of softened butter or melted chocolate and allow them to set fully before filling. This will prevent moisture in the filling from seeping into the crust and making it soggy, or causing it to lose its crisp texture. Apply a thin coating to the shell using a pastry brush. Place the shell in the refrigerator so that the butter or chocolate will harden, then fill the shell.

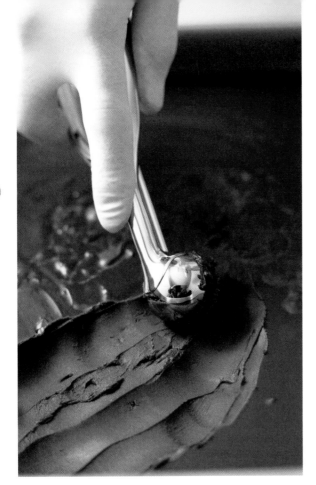 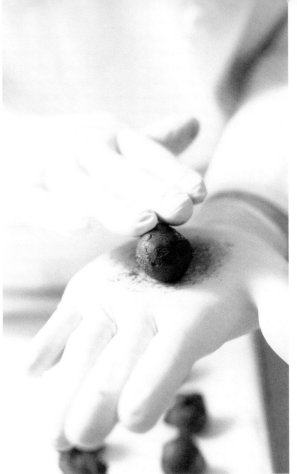

1. **Hard ganache (page 1160) has a stiffer consistency and, when chilled, it can be shaped and rolled into truffles.** Scoop the hard ganache using a smooth motion to create uniform truffles, place them on a parchment-lined sheet pan, and refrigerate for 10 to 15 minutes, or until the ganache becomes firm again.

2. **Roll the scoops of ganache into smooth balls using only your fingertips.** Refrigerate them one more time to be sure that the truffles are firm before rolling them in chopped nuts, cocoa powder, or confectioners' sugar. Truffles can also be coated with tempered chocolate to give them a glossy coating, as well as to give them a longer shelf life.

3. **This station is set up for working from right to left.** The unfinished truffles are on the right, the bowl of tempered chocolate is in the center, and the coated truffles are on the left. As you work, place the coated truffles on the farthest side of the sheet tray, to prevent having to pass over them and possibly dripping chocolate onto them that could ruin their finish.

When coating truffles with tempered chocolate, they must not be cold from the refrigerator. They should be allowed to set so they lose their chill before coating. This will prevent the hard chocolate shell from cracking. To coat truffles with tempered chocolate, smear a small amount of the chocolate into the palm of your hand, roll the truffle to coat in a thin even layer, and place it on a clean, parchment-lined sheet pan. Allow the truffle to set until the chocolate has completely hardened and repeat the process.

4. **After the tempered chocolate coating sets up, the truffles should be shiny, without any cracks.** After the coating has set, truffles should be stored in a cool dry environment. If they are dipped in tempered chocolate, make sure they do not touch; if handling, wear gloves and do so carefully. The surface of tempered chocolate is easily marred and the appearance of the truffles will be destroyed by scratches and/or fingerprints.

Italian Buttercream

Makes 3 lb 4 oz/ 1.47 kg

1 lb/454 g sugar

4 fl oz/120 mL water

8 egg whites

2 lb/907 g butter, cut into medium chunks, soft

½ fl oz/15 mL vanilla extract

1. Combine 12 oz/340 g of the sugar with the water in a heavy-bottomed saucepan and bring to a boil over medium-high heat, stirring to dissolve the sugar. Continue cooking, without stirring, to the soft ball stage (238°F/114°C).

2. Meanwhile, place the egg whites in the bowl of an electric mixer fitted with the wire whip attachment.

3. When the sugar syrup has reached approximately 230°F/110°C, whip the egg whites on medium speed until frothy. Gradually add the remaining 4 oz/113 g of sugar and beat the meringue to medium peaks.

4. When the sugar syrup reaches 238°F/114°C, add it to the meringue in a slow steady stream while whipping on medium speed. Whip on high speed until the meringue has cooled to room temperature.

5. Add the butter in small batches, mixing until fully incorporated after each addition and scraping down the sides of the bowl as necessary. Blend in the vanilla. The buttercream is now ready for use or it may be tightly covered and refrigerated.

Coffee Buttercream: Add ½ oz/14 g coffee paste, ½ fl oz/ 15 mL brandy, and 1 tsp/5 mL vanilla extract to 1 lb/454 g prepared buttercream.

Mocha Buttercream: Add ½ fl oz/15 mL of melted and cooled bittersweet chocolate to 1 lb/454 g coffee buttercream.

Chocolate Buttercream: Add 3 oz/85 g melted and cooled bittersweet chocolate to 1 lb/454 g prepared buttercream.

Apple Pie

Makes one 9-in/23-cm pie

1 lb 4 oz/567 g **Basic Pie Dough** (page 1104)

1 lb 8 oz/680 g Golden Delicious apples, peeled, cored, and sliced

5 oz/142 g sugar

½ oz/14 g tapioca starch

¾ oz/21 g cornstarch

½ tsp/2.50 g salt

½ tsp/1 g ground nutmeg

½ tsp/1 g ground cinnamon

½ fl oz/15 mL lemon juice

1 oz/28 g butter, melted

1. Prepare the pie dough according to the recipe directions. Divide the dough in 2 equal pieces. Roll half of the dough ⅛ in/3 mm thick and line the pie pan. Reserve the other half wrapped tightly and refrigerated.

2. Toss the apples with the remaining ingredients. Fill the pie shell with the apple mixture.

3. Roll out the remaining dough ⅛ in/3 mm thick and place it over the filling.

4. Crimp the edges to seal, cutting several vents in the top of the pie.

5. Bake at 375°F/191°C until the filling is bubbling, about 45 minutes to 1 hour.

6. Cool to room temperature before serving.

Cherry Pie

Makes 5 pies (9 in/23 cm)

11 lb 4 oz/5.10 kg cherries (pitted, frozen)

1 gal 12 fl oz/4.20 L cherry juice

10 oz/284 g cornstarch

1 lb 4 oz/567 g granulated sugar

1 oz/28 g salt

10 fl oz/300 mL lemon juice

10 fl oz/300 mL **Egg Wash** (page 1061)

1. Allow the cherries to thaw overnight in a sieve so the juice drains away. Catch and reserve the juice in a bowl. Use the reserved cherry juice and supply additional if the cherries did not yield enough.

2. Combine 20 fl oz/600 mL of cherry juice with the cornstarch and stir to dissolve, making a slurry.

3. Combine the remaining 120 fl oz/3.60 L of cherry juice with the sugar and salt in a saucepan and bring to a boil to dissolve.

4. Slowly add the slurry to the hot cherry juice, stirring constantly with a whisk. Bring the mixture back to a boil and stirring constantly cook for 1 minute, or until clear.

5. Fold in the cherries and lemon juice. Scale 2 lb 12 oz/1.25 kg of the filling into a 9-in/23-cm pie shell, top with a second piece of pie dough, and seal the edges. Prick some holes in the top of the pie shell and brush with the egg wash.

6. Bake in a 450°F/232°C oven for 40 minutes, or until the top of the pie is golden brown and you can see the filling bubbling inside.

Pecan Pie

Makes 5 pies (9 in/23 cm)

1 lb 4 oz/567 g pecans

3½ oz/99 g sugar

3½ oz/99 g bread flour

5 lb/2.27 kg corn syrup

14 eggs

1 oz/28 g salt

1 fl oz/30 mL vanilla extract

6 oz/170 g melted butter

1. Scale out 4 oz/113 g of the pecans for each 9-in/23-cm pie and spread them in an even layer in the bottom of each unbaked pie crust.

2. Place the sugar and flour in a large stainless-steel bowl and whisk to combine. Add the corn syrup and blend.

3. Add the eggs, salt, and vanilla and stir until they are fully combined.

4. Blend in the butter.

5. Scale 1 lb 12 oz/794 g of mixture into each prepared pie shell.

6. Bake in a 400°F/204°C oven until the filling has set and the crust is a golden brown, about 40 minutes.

7. Let cool completely before serving.

Cranberry-Pecan Pie: Spread 2 oz/57 g cranberries in an even layer in the bottom of each unbaked pie crust before filling as above.

Lemon Meringue Pie

Lemon Meringue Pie

Makes 5 pies (9 in/23 cm)

64 fl oz/1.92 L water

2 lb/907 g sugar

½ oz/14 g salt

10 fl oz/300 mL lemon juice

1 oz/28 g grated lemon zest

6 oz/170 g cornstarch

8 oz/227 g egg yolks

4 oz/113 g butter

1. Combine 48 fl oz/1.44 L of the water and 1 lb/454 g of the sugar with the salt, lemon juice, and zest in a saucepan and bring to a boil.

2. Combine the remaining sugar and the cornstarch and mix thoroughly.

3. Combine the egg yolks with the remaining water and mix thoroughly. Combine the sugar-cornstarch mixture with the egg yolk-water mixture and blend well.

4. When the lemon mixture comes to a boil, temper in the egg yolk mixture.

5. Return the mixture to a boil. Boil for 1 minute, stirring constantly.

6. Stir in the butter. Scale 1 lb 8 oz/680 g into a prebaked 9-in/23-cm pie shell. Refrigerate overnight before topping with meringue.

Pumpkin Pie

Makes 5 pies (9 in/23 cm)

80 fl oz/2.40 L pumpkin purée

1 lb 2 oz/510 g sugar

5 oz/142 g dark brown sugar

½ oz/14 g salt

2½ tsp/5 g ground cinnamon

2½ tsp/5 g ground ginger

2½ tsp/5 g ground nutmeg

1¼ tsp/2.50 g ground cloves

20 fl oz/600 mL milk

20 fl oz/600 mL evaporated milk

15 eggs

1. Combine the pumpkin, sugars, salt, and spices and mix until smooth.

2. Mix together the milk, evaporated milk, and eggs. Combine with the pumpkin mixture.

3. Scale 1 lb 14 oz/851 g into each prebaked 9-in/23-cm pie shell.

4. Bake in a 375°F/191°C oven for 50 minutes, or until the filling is set and the filling and crust are golden brown on top.

Frangipane Filling

Makes 3 dozen tartlets (3 in/8 cm)

8 oz/227 g almond paste

1¼ oz/35 g sugar

2 eggs

4 oz/113 g butter

1½ oz/43 g cake flour

1. Cream together the almond paste and sugar and add 1 of the eggs to be sure there are no lumps. Add butter and cream well.

2. Gradually add the remaining egg.

3. Add the flour and mix just until combined.

4. Use as a filling for tart shells.

Pecan Diamonds

Makes 100 pieces (1 in/3 cm each)

2 lb/907 g **1-2-3 Cookie Dough** (page 1120)

PECAN FILLING

1 lb/454 g butter, cubed

1 lb/454 g light brown sugar

4 oz/113 g sugar

12 oz/340 g honey

4 fl oz/120 mL heavy cream

2 lb/907 g pecans, coarsely chopped

1. Roll out the dough to a rectangle 14 by 18 in/36 by 46 cm and ⅛ in/3 mm thick. Lay it gently in a half sheet pan so that it completely lines the bottom and sides. Dock the dough with a pastry docker or the tines of a fork.

2. Bake at 350°F/177°C until light golden brown, about 10 minutes.

3. To make the filling, cook the butter, sugars, honey, and cream in a heavy-bottomed saucepan over medium-high heat, stirring constantly, until the mixture reaches 240°F/116°C. Add the nuts and stir until fully incorporated. Immediately pour into the prebaked crust and spread into an even layer.

4. Bake at 350°F/177°C until the filling bubbles or foams evenly across the surface and the crust is golden brown, 25 to 30 minutes. Cool completely in the pan.

5. Using a metal spatula, release the sheet from the sides of the pan and invert the slab onto the back of a half sheet pan. Transfer it to a cutting board, carefully flipping it over so it is right side up. Trim off the edges. Cut into 1-in/3-cm diamonds.

Hard Ganache

Makes 5 lb/2.27 kg

4 lb/1.81 kg dark chocolate, finely chopped

32 fl oz/960 mL heavy cream

1. Place the chocolate in a stainless-steel bowl.

2. Bring the cream just to a simmer. Pour the hot cream over the chocolate, allow it to stand for 1 minute, and stir until the chocolate is thoroughly melted.

3. The ganache can be used immediately, or it can be covered and refrigerated, then rewarmed.

Chocolate Sauce

Makes 32 fl oz/960 mL

10 oz/284 g sugar

16 fl oz/480 mL water

4½ oz/128 g light corn syrup

4 oz/113 g cocoa powder, sifted

1 lb/454 g bittersweet chocolate, melted

1. Combine the sugar, water, and syrup in a heavy-bottomed saucepan and bring to a boil over medium-high heat. Remove from the heat.

2. Place the cocoa in a bowl and add enough of the hot sugar syrup to make a paste, stirring until smooth. Gradually add the remaining syrup and mix until fully incorporated.

3. Add the chocolate and blend until fully incorporated.

4. Strain the sauce through a fine-mesh sieve.

5. Serve warm or chilled.

Classic Caramel Sauce

Makes 32 fl oz/960 mL

24 fl oz/720 mL heavy cream

13 oz/369 g sugar

10 oz/284 g glucose syrup

2¼ oz/64 g butter, soft, cubed

1. Place the cream in a saucepan and bring to a boil over medium heat. Leave the pan over very low heat to keep warm.

2. Prepare an ice bath. Combine the sugar and syrup in a heavy-bottomed saucepan and slowly cook over medium heat, stirring constantly, until all the sugar has dissolved. Stop stirring and continue to cook to a golden caramel. Remove from the heat and shock the saucepan in the ice bath to stop the cooking.

3. Remove from the ice bath and stir in the butter. Carefully stir in the hot cream, mixing until fully blended.

4. Serve warm or chilled.

Raspberry Coulis

Makes 32 fl oz/960 mL

2 lb/907 g raspberries (fresh or frozen)

8 oz/227 g sugar, or as needed

1 fl oz/60 mL lemon juice, or as needed

1. Combine the raspberries, 8 oz/227 g of the sugar, and 1 fl oz/30 mL of the lemon juice in a saucepan over medium heat. Simmer, stirring, until the sugar has dissolved, about 10 minutes.

2. Strain the coulis through a fine-mesh sieve.

3. Add additional sugar and/or lemon juice, if necessary.

NOTE
An equal amount of another fruit, such as strawberries or chopped mangos, can be substituted for the raspberries.

Sabayon

Makes 32 fl oz/960 mL

18 egg yolks

12 oz/340 g sugar

12 fl oz/360 mL white wine

1. Combine the egg yolks, sugar, and wine in the bowl of an electric mixer and whisk together until thoroughly blended. Place the bowl over a pot of simmering water and heat, whisking constantly, until the mixture is thickened and very foamy and has reached 180°F/82°C.

2. Transfer the bowl to the electric mixer fitted with a wire whip attachment and whip until cool.

3. Transfer the sabayon to a container and cover it with plastic wrap placed directly against the surface to prevent a skin from forming. Sabayon may be served warm or at room temperature.

NOTE
If desired, whip 24 fl oz/720 mL heavy cream to medium peaks and fold it into cooled sabayon.

Zabaglione: Substitute Marsala for the white wine.

Apricot Glaze

Makes 1 lb 9½ oz/723 g

9 oz/255 g apricot jam

6 fl oz/180 mL water

9 oz/255 g corn syrup

1½ fl oz/45 mL liquor, such as rum or brandy

1. Combine all the ingredients in a saucepan, bring to a boil, and stir the mixture until smooth.

2. Use the glaze while it is still warm, applying it to the items with a pastry brush.

Apple Butter

Makes 32 fl oz/960 mL

7 lb/3.18 kg apples

24 fl oz/720 mL apple cider

1 lb/454 g sugar

1 tbsp/6 g ground cardamom

2 tsp/4 g ground cinnamon

1 tsp/3 g lemon zest, grated

¼ tsp/1.25 g salt

1. Peel, core, and slice the apples. Combine them with the cider in a large heavy-bottomed saucepan, cover, and bring to a simmer. Simmer until the apples are a soft pulp, about 30 minutes.

2. Pass the apple pulp through a food mill and transfer it to a saucepan.

3. Add the sugar, spices, zest, and salt and simmer, stirring frequently, until very thick, about 2 hours.

4. Cool completely.

Pear Frangipane Tartlets

Makes 1 dozen tartlets

1 lb 4 oz/567 g **1-2-3 Cookie Dough** (page 1120)

9 oz/255 g **Frangipane Filling** (page 1159)

12 **Poached Pears** (page 1164), halved

Apricot Glaze (page 1162), warm, as needed

3 oz/85 g sliced almonds, toasted and chopped

1. Roll out the dough to a thickness of ⅛ in/3 mm. Using a 4½-in/11-cm cutter, cut 12 rounds from the dough.

2. Place the rounds in 3-in/8-cm tart rings.

3. Dock the bottoms of the tartlet shells with a pastry docker or the tines of a fork. Using a pastry bag fitted with a No. 5 plain pastry tip, pipe ¾ oz/21 g of the frangipane filling into each shell, filling them halfway. Slice the pears and fan them on top of the frangipane.

4. Bake at 375°F/191°C until the shells and filling are golden brown, about 45 minutes. Cool the tartlets to room temperature.

5. Brush the tops of the tartlets with the glaze. Arrange a thin border of toasted almonds around the edge of each tartlet. Serve.

Pear Frangipane Tartlets

Poached Pears

Makes 12 poached pears

12 small pears

POACHING LIQUID

16 fl oz/480 mL red or white wine

8 fl oz/240 mL water

8 oz/227 g sugar

1 cinnamon stick (optional)

6 cloves (optional)

1. Peel the pears. They may be left whole with the stem intact, or halved and cored.

2. Combine all the poaching ingredients in a saucepan and bring to a simmer, stirring to dissolve the sugar.

3. Place the pears in the poaching liquid and simmer until they are tender. Let the pears cool in the poaching liquid, drain, and serve as desired.

Fruit Salsa

Makes 1 lb 14 oz/851 g

5 oz/142 g papaya, small dice

5 oz/142 g mangos, small dice

5 oz/142 g honeydew melon, small dice

5 oz/142 g strawberries, small dice

1 fl oz/30 mL passion fruit juice

1 tbsp/3 g mint, finely chopped

3 fl oz/90 mL amaretto liqueur

8 fl oz/240 mL orange juice

3 oz/85 g sugar

1. Combine the fruit, passion fruit juice, and mint. Set aside to macerate.

2. Combine the amaretto, orange juice, and sugar and bring to a boil. Boil until reduced. Gently blend the reduced liquid into the fruit.

3. Refrigerate until needed.

Dried Cherry Sauce

Makes 1 lb 10 oz/737 g

3 oz/85 g sugar

13 fl oz/390 mL red wine

6 fl oz/180 mL water

1 fl oz/30 mL orange juice

1 fl oz/30 mL lemon juice

1 vanilla bean

4 oz/113 g dried cherries

½ oz/14 g cornstarch

1. Combine the sugar, 12 fl oz/360 mL of the red wine, the water, orange juice, and lemon juice in a saucepan. Split the vanilla bean, scrape the seeds into the pan, add the pod, and bring the mixture to a boil. Remove from the heat and add the cherries.

2. Refrigerate overnight, covered.

3. Strain the sauce, reserving the cherries. Pour the sauce into a saucepan and bring to a boil.

4. Meanwhile, make a slurry with the cornstarch and the remaining 1 fl oz/30 mL of red wine. Gradually whisk the slurry into the sauce and bring back to a boil, whisking until the sauce thickens enough to coat the back of a spoon.

5. Allow the sauce to cool to room temperature.

6. Add the reserved cherries and serve at once.

Appendix

TYPE	SOAKING TIME	COOKING TIME
Adzuki beans	4 hours	1 hour
Black beans	4 hours	1½ hours
Black-eyed peas*	—	1 hour
Chickpeas	4 hours	2 to 2½ hours
Fava beans	12 hours	3 hours
Great Northern beans	4 hours	1 hour
Kidney beans (red or white)	4 hours	1 hour
Lentils*	—	30 to 40 minutes
Lima beans	4 hours	1 to 1½ hours
Mung beans	4 hours	1 hour
Navy beans	4 hours	2 hours
Peas, split*	—	30 minutes
Peas, whole	4 hours	40 minutes
Pigeon peas*	—	30 minutes
Pink beans	4 hours	1 hour
Pinto beans	4 hours	1 to 1½ hours
Soybeans	12 hours	3 to 3½ hours

*Soaking is not necessary

Cooking Ratios and Times for Selected Grains

TYPE	RATIO OF GRAIN TO LIQUID (CUPS)	APPROXIMATE YIELD (CUPS)	COOKING TIME
Barley, pearled	1:2	4	35 to 45 minutes
Barley groats	1:2½	4	50 minutes to 1 hour
Buckwheat groats (kasha)	1:1½ to 2	2	12 to 20 minutes
Couscous*	—	1½ to 2	20 to 25 minutes
Hominy, whole[†]	1:2½	3	2½ to 3 hours
Hominy grits	1:4	3	25 minutes
Millet	1:2	3	30 to 35 minutes
Oat groats	1:2	2	45 minutes to 1 hour
Polenta	1:3 to 3½	3	35 to 45 minutes
Rice, Arborio (for risotto)	1:3	3	20 to 30 minutes
Rice, Basmati	1:1½	3	25 minutes
Rice, converted	1:2	4	25 to 30 minutes
Rice, long-grain, brown	1:3	4	40 minutes
Rice, long-grain, white	1:1½ to 1¾	3	18 to 20 minutes
Rice, short-grain, brown	1:2½	4	35 to 40 minutes
Rice, short-grain, white	1:1 to 1½	3	20 to 30 minutes
Rice, wild	1:3	4	30 to 45 minutes
Rice, wild, pecan	1:1¾	4	20 minutes
Wheat berries	1:3	2	1 hour
Wheat, bulgur, soaked[‡]	1:4	2	2 hours
Wheat, bulgur, pilaf[‡]	1:2½	2	15 to 20 minutes
Wheat, cracked[§]	1:2	3	20 minutes

*From 1 cup of uncooked grain.

[†] Grain should be soaked briefly in tepid water and then drained before it is steamed.

[‡] Grain should be soaked overnight in cold water and then drained before it is cooked.

[§] Grain may be cooked by covering it with boiling water and soaking it for 2 hours or cooking it by the pilaf method.

Weight Measure Conversions

U.S.	METRIC
¼ ounce	7 grams
½ ounce	14 grams
1 ounce	28.35 grams
4 ounces	113.4 grams
8 ounces (½ pound)	226.8 grams
16 ounces (1 pound)	453.6 grams
32 ounces (2 pounds)	907.2 grams
40 ounces (2¼ pounds)	1.134 kilograms

Volume Measure Conversions

U.S.	METRIC
1 teaspoon	4.93 milliliters
1 tablespoon	14.79 milliliters
1 fluid ounce (2 tablespoons)	29.58 milliliters
2 fluid ounces (¼ cup)	59 milliliters
8 fluid ounces (1 cup)	236.64 milliliters
16 fluid ounces (1 pint)	473.28 milliliters
32 fluid ounces (1 quart) (0.95 liter)	946.56 milliliters
128 fluid ounces (1 gallon)	3.79 liters

Temperature Conversions

DEGREES FAHRENHEIT (°F)	DEGREES CELSIUS (°C)*	DEGREES FAHRENHEIT (°F)	DEGREES CELSIUS (°C)*
32°	0°	325°	163°
40°	4°	350°	177°
140°	60°	375°	191°
150°	66°	400°	204°
160°	71°	425°	218°
170°	77°	450°	232°
212°	100°	475°	246°
275°	135°	500°	260°
300°	149°		

*Celsius temperatures have been rounded.

1 gallon = 4 quarts = 8 pints = 16 cups (8 fluid ounces) = 128 fluid ounces

1 fifth bottle = approximately 1½ pints or exactly 25.6 fluid ounces

1 measuring cup holds 8 fluid ounces (a coffee cup generally holds 6 fluid ounces)

1 egg white = 2 fluid ounces (average)

1 lemon = 1 to 1¼ fluid ounces of juice

1 orange = 3 to 3¼ fluid ounces of juice

To convert ounces and pounds to grams: multiply ounces by 28.35; multiply pounds by 453.59

To convert Fahrenheit to Celsius: $\dfrac{(°F - 32)}{1.8} = °C$

To convert ounces and pounds to grams:

Multiply ounces by 28.35 to determine grams; divide pounds by 2.2 to determine kilograms

To convert grams to ounces or pounds:
Divide grams by 28.35 to determine ounces; divide grams by 453.59 to determine pounds

To convert fluid ounces to milliliters:
Multiply fluid ounces by 30 to determine milliliters

To convert milliliters to fluid ounces:
Divide milliliters by 30 to determine fluid ounces

Metric prefixes
kilo = 1,000

hecto = 100

deka = 10

deci = 1/10

centi = 1/100

milli = 1/1000

Converting to common unit of measure
To convert measurements to a common unit (by weight or volume), use the following chart.
This information is used both to convert scaled measurements into practical and easy-to-use recipe measures and to determine costs.

Common Unit Conversions

(U.S.) WEIGHT TO VOLUME

1 pound	N/A	16 ounces
1 gallon	4 quarts	128 fluid ounces
1 quart	2 pints	32 fluid ounces
1 pint	2 cups	16 fluid ounces
1 cup	16 tablespoons	8 fluid ounces
1 tablespoon	3 teaspoons	½ fluid ounce

Weights and Measures Equivalents

Dash	less than ⅛ teaspoon
3 teaspoons	1 tablespoon (½ fluid ounce)
2 tablespoons	⅛ cup (1 fluid ounce)
4 tablespoons	¼ cup (2 fluid ounces)
5⅓ tablespoons	⅓ cup (2⅔ fluid ounces)
8 tablespoons	½ cup (4 fluid ounces)
10⅔ tablespoons	⅔ cup (5⅓ fluid ounces)
12 tablespoons	¾ cup (6 fluid ounces)
14 tablespoons	⅞ cup (7 fluid ounces)
16 tablespoons	1 cup
1 gill	½ cup
1 cup	8 fluid ounces (240 milliliters)
2 cups	1 pint (480 milliliters)
2 pints	1 quart (approximately 1 liter)
4 quarts	1 gallon (3.75 liters)
8 quarts	1 peck (8.8 liters)
4 pecks	1 bushel (35 liters)
1 ounce	28.35 grams (rounded to 30)
16 ounces	1 pound (453.59 grams, rounded to 450)
1 kilogram	2.2 pounds

Glossary

A

abalone: A mollusk with a single shell approximately 6 in/ 15 cm long and a large, edible adductor muscle. Abalones are generally cut and pounded into steaks before being sautéed or grilled and have a chewy texture with a mild flavor.

aboyeur: Expediter or announcer; a station in the kitchen brigade system. The aboyeur accepts orders from the dining room, relays them to the appropriate stations of the kitchen, and checks each plate before it leaves the kitchen.

acid: A substance that tests lower than 7 on the pH scale. Acids have a sour or sharp flavor. Acidity occurs naturally in many foods, including citrus juice, vinegar, wine, and sour-milk products. Acids also act as tenderizers in marinades, helping to break down connective tissues and cell walls.

adulterated food: Food that has been contaminated to the point that it is considered unfit for human consumption.

aerobic bacteria: Bacteria that require the presence of oxygen to function.

aïoli: Garlic mayonnaise often used as a condiment with fish and meat. Also, in Italian, *allioli*; in Spanish, *aliolio*.

à la carte: A menu in which the patron makes individual selections from various menu categories; each item is priced separately.

à l'anglaise: French term for foods that have been prepared "in the English way." Refers to foods that have been breaded and fried or boiled or poached.

albumen: The egg white. Makes up about 70 percent of the egg and contains most of the protein in the egg.

al dente: Literally, "to the tooth"; refers to an item, such as pasta or vegetables, cooked until it is tender but still firm, not soft.

alkali: A substance that tests at higher than 7 on the pH scale. Alkalis are sometimes described as having a slightly soapy flavor and can be used to balance acids. Olives and baking soda are some of the few alkaline foods.

allumette: Vegetable cut usually referring to potatoes cut into pieces the size and shape of matchsticks; ⅛ in by ⅛ in by 1 to 2 in/3 mm by 3 mm by 3 to 5 cm. Also called *julienne*.

amandine: Garnished with almonds.

amino acids: The building blocks of proteins. Of the 20 amino acids in the human diet, 9 are called "essential" because they cannot be produced by the body and must be supplied through a person's diet.

amuse-gueule: French for "appetizer." Chef's tasting; a small portion (1 or 2 bites) of something exotic, unusual, or otherwise special that is served when the guests in a restaurant are seated. The amuse is not listed on a menu and is included in the price of an entrée.

anaerobic bacteria: Bacteria that do not require oxygen to function.

angel food cake: A type of sponge cake that is made without egg yolks or other fats. Beaten egg whites give it its light and airy structure; typically baked in a tube pan.

antioxidants: Naturally occurring substances that retard the breakdown of tissues in the presence of oxygen. May be added to food during processing or may occur naturally. Help to prevent food from becoming rancid or discolored due to oxidation.

antipasto: Literally, "before the pasta." Typically, a platter of hot or cold hors d'oeuvre that includes meats, olives, cheeses, and vegetables.

apéritif: A light alcoholic beverage consumed before the meal to stimulate the appetite.

appareil: A prepared mixture of ingredients used alone or in another preparation.

appetizer: Light food served before a meal or as the first course of a meal. These may be hot or cold, plated or served as finger food.

aquaculture: The farm raising of fish or shellfish in natural or controlled marine tanks or ponds.

Arborio: A high-starch, short-grain rice traditionally used in the preparation of risotto.

aromatics: Ingredients, such as herbs, spices, vegetables, citrus fruits, wines, and vinegars, used to enhance the flavor and fragrance of food.

aromatized wine: Fortified wine infused with any of a wide variety of aromatic plants or bitter herbs, roots, bark, or other plant parts (e.g., vermouth).

arrowroot: A powdered starch made from the root of a tropical plant of the same name. Used primarily as a thickener. Remains clear when cooked.

aspic: A clear jelly made from stock (or occasionally fruit or vegetable juices) thickened with gelatin. Used to coat foods or cubed and used as a garnish.

as-purchased (AP) weight: The weight of an item as received from the supplier before trimming or other preparation [as opposed to edible-portion (EP) weight].

B

bacteria: Microscopic organisms. Some have beneficial properties; others can cause food-borne illnesses when contaminated foods are ingested.

baguette: A loaf of bread that is of French origin, made with 12 to 16 oz/340 to 454 g of dough that is shaped into a long skinny loaf that ranges from 2 to 3 in/5 to 8 cm in diameter and 18 to 24 in/46 to 61 cm in length. The dough, made of flour, water, salt, and yeast, yields a paper-thin crisp crust and a light and airy crumb.

bain-marie: The French term for a water bath used to cook foods gently by surrounding the cooking vessel with simmering water. Also, a set of cylindrical nesting pots used to hold foods in a water bath or with a single, long handle used as a double boiler. Also, steam table inserts.

bake: To cook food by surrounding it with dry heat in a closed environment, as in an oven.

bake blind: To partially or completely bake an unfilled pastry crust by lining with parchment and filling with weights, which are removed after or during baking.

baking powder: A chemical leavener made with an acid and an alkaline ingredient; most commonly these are sodium bicarbonate (baking soda) and cream of tartar. When exposed to liquid, it produces carbon dioxide gas, which leavens doughs and batters. Double-acting baking powder contains ingredients that produce two leavening reactions: one upon exposure to liquid, the second when heated.

baking soda: Sodium bicarbonate, a leavening agent that, when combined with an acidic ingredient and moisture, releases carbon dioxide gas and leavens baked goods.

barbecue: To cook food by grilling it over a wood or charcoal fire. Usually some sort of marinade or sauce is brushed on the item during cooking. Also, meat that is cooked in this way.

bard: To cover a naturally lean meat with slabs or strips of fat, such as bacon or fatback, to baste it during roasting or braising. The fat is usually tied on with butcher's twine.

barquette: A boat-shaped tart or tartlet, which may have a sweet or savory filling.

baste: To moisten food during cooking with pan drippings, sauce, or other liquid. Basting prevents food from drying out.

batch cooking: A cooking technique in which appropriately sized batches of food are prepared several times throughout a service period so that a fresh supply of cooked items is always available.

baton/batonnet: Items cut into pieces somewhat larger than allumette or julienne; ¼ in by ¼ in by 1 to 2 in/6 mm by 6 mm by 3 to 5 cm. French for "stick" or "small stick."

batter: A mixture of flour and liquid, sometimes with the inclusion of other ingredients. Batters vary in thickness but are generally semi-liquid and thinner than doughs. Used in such preparations as cakes, quick breads, pancakes, and crêpes. Also, the liquid mixture used to coat foods before deep frying.

Bavarian cream, bavarois: A mousse-like dessert made from vanilla sauce that is flavored with a fruit purée or juice and then lightened with whipped cream and stabilized with gelatin.

béarnaise: A classic emulsion, similar to hollandaise, made with egg yolks, a reduction of white wine, shallots, and tarragon. Also, butter finished with tarragon and chervil.

béchamel: A white sauce made of milk thickened with a light roux and flavored with white mirepoix. One of the "grand" sauces.

bench-proof: In yeast dough production, to allow dough to rise after it is panned and just before it is baked.

beurre blanc: Literally, "white butter." A classic emulsified sauce made with a reduction of white wine and shallots thickened with whole butter and possibly finished with fresh herbs or other seasonings.

beurre fondue: Melted butter.

beurre manié: Literally, "kneaded butter." A mixture of equal parts by weight of whole butter and flour, used to thicken gravies and sauces.

beurre noir: Literally, "black butter." Butter that has been cooked to a very dark brown or nearly black. Also, a sauce made with browned butter, vinegar, chopped parsley, and capers. It is usually served with fish.

beurre noisette: Literally, "hazelnut butter" or "brown butter." Whole butter that has been heated until browned to a hazelnut color.

binder: An ingredient or appareil used to thicken a sauce or hold together another mixture of ingredients.

bisque: A soup based on crustaceans or a vegetable purée. It is classically thickened with rice and usually finished with cream.

bivalve: A mollusk with two hinged shells. Examples are clams, scallops, oysters, and mussels.

blanc: A preparation containing water, flour, onion, cloves, a bouquet garni, salt, and lemon juice. Used to cook vegetables such as mushrooms, celeriac, salsify, or cauliflower to keep them white.

blanch: To cook an item briefly in boiling water or hot fat before finishing or storing it. Blanching preserves the color, lessens strong flavors, and helps remove the peels of some fruits and vegetables.

blanquette: A white stew, usually of veal but sometimes of chicken or lamb with white onions and mushrooms. It is served with a sauce that has been thickened with a liaison.

blend: A mixture of two or more flavors combined to achieve a particular flavor or quality. Also, to mix two or more ingredients together until combined.

blini: A silver-dollar-sized, yeast-raised buckwheat pancake originating in Russia.

bloom: To hydrate gelatin in liquid before dissolving. Also, the light gray film on the skin of apples, blueberries, grapes, and prunes. Also, streaks of white/gray cocoa fat that appear on solid untempered chocolate.

boil: A cooking method in which items are immersed in liquid at or above the boiling point (212°F/100°C).

borscht: A soup originating in Russia and Poland, made from fresh beets and garnished with sour cream. May include an assortment of vegetables and/or meat, and may be served hot or cold.

botulism: A food-borne illness caused by toxins produced by the anaerobic bacterium *Clostridium botulinum*.

boucher: French for "butcher."

bouillabaisse: A hearty fish and shellfish stew flavored with tomatoes, onions, garlic, white wine, and saffron. A traditional specialty of Marseilles, France.

bouillon: French for "broth."

boulanger: Baker, specifically of breads and other unsweetened doughs.

bouquet garni: A small bundle of herbs tied with string. It is used to flavor stocks, braises, and other preparations. Usually contains bay leaf, parsley, thyme, and possibly other aromatics wrapped in leek leaves.

braise: A cooking method in which the main item, usually meat, is seared in fat, then simmered at a low temperature in a small amount of stock or another liquid (usually halfway up the meat item) in a covered vessel for a long time. The cooking liquid is then reduced and used as the base of a sauce.

bran: The outer layer of a cereal grain and the part highest in fiber.

brandy: Spirit made by distilling wine or the fermented mash of fruit. May be aged in oak barrels.

brazier/brasier: A pan, designed specifically for braising, that usually has two handles and a tight-fitting lid. Often is round but may be square or rectangular. It is also called a *rondeau*.

bread: Food product made of flour, sugar, shortening, salt, and liquid leavened by the action of yeast. Also, to coat food with flour, eggs, and crumbs before fying or baking.

brigade system: The kitchen organization system instituted by Georges-Auguste Escoffier. Each position has a station and well-defined responsibilities.

brine: A solution of salt, water, and seasonings, used to preserve or moisten foods.

brioche: A rich yeast dough traditionally baked in a fluted pan with a distinctive topknot of dough.

brisket: A cut of beef from the lower forequarter, best suited for long-cooking preparations such as braising. Corned beef is cured beef brisket.

broil: To cook by means of a radiant heat source placed above the food.

broiler: The piece of equipment used to broil foods.

broth: A flavorful, aromatic liquid made by simmering water or stock with meat, vegetables, and/or spices and herbs.

brown sauce: A sauce made from a brown stock and aromatics and thickened by roux, a pure starch slurry, and/or a reduction; includes sauce Espagnole, demi-glace, jus de veau lié, and pan sauces.

brown stock: An amber liquid produced by simmering browned bones and meat (usually veal or beef) with vegetables and aromatics (including caramelized mirepoix and tomato purée).

bruise: To partially crush a food item in order to release its flavor.

brunoise: Dice cut of ⅛-in/3-mm cubes. For a brunoise cut, items are first cut in julienne, then cut crosswise. For a fine brunoise, 1/16-in/1.50-mm cube, cut items first in fine julienne.

butcher: A chef or purveyor who is responsible for butchering meats, poultry, and occasionally fish. In the brigade system, the butcher may also be responsible for breading meat and fish items and other mise-en-place operations involving meat.

butter: A semisolid fat made by churning cream; must contain at least 80 percent milk fat.

buttercream: An icing made of butter, sugar, and eggs or custard, used to garnish cakes and pastries. The four types are Italian, Swiss, French, and German.

butterfly: To cut an item (usually meat or seafood) and open out the edges like a book or the wings of a butterfly.

buttermilk: A dairy beverage with a slightly sour flavor similar to that of yogurt. Traditionally, the liquid by-product of butter churning, now usually made by culturing skim milk.

C

Cajun: A hearty cuisine based on French and southern influences; signature ingredients include spices, dark roux, pork fat, filé powder, green peppers, onions, and celery. Jambalaya is a traditional Cajun dish.

cake: A sweet product containing flour, sugar, salt, egg, milk, liquid, flavoring, shortening, and leavening agent. Also, a patty, such as a fish cake.

calorie: A unit used to measure food energy. It is the amount of energy needed to raise the temperature of 1 kilogram of water by 1°C.

calzone: Pizza dough that is stuffed with meats, vegetables, or cheese, folded over to resemble a large turnover, then baked or deep fried.

Canadian bacon: Smoked eye of the pork loin. Referred to as back bacon in Canada, Canadian bacon is leaner than slab bacon and purchased precooked.

canapé: An hors d'oeuvre consisting of a small piece of bread or toast, often cut in a decorative shape, garnished with a savory spread or topping.

caramelization: The process of browning sugar in the presence of heat. The caramelization of sugar occurs between 320° to 360°F/160° to 182°C.

carbohydrate: One of the basic nutrients used by the body as a source of energy. Types include simple (sugars) and complex (starches and fibers).

carbon dioxide: A colorless, tasteless, edible gas obtained through fermentation or from the combination of soda and acid, which acts to leaven baked goods.

carry-over cooking: Heat retained in cooked foods that allows them to continue cooking even after removal from the cooking medium. Especially important to roasted foods.

casing: A synthetic or natural membrane (if natural, usually pig or sheep intestines) used to enclose sausage forcemeat.

casserole: A lidded cooking vessel that is used in the oven; usually round with two handles. Also, food cooked in a casserole, often bound with a sauce and topped with cheese or bread crumbs.

cassoulet: A stew of white beans baked with pork or other meats, duck or goose confit, and seasonings.

caulfat: A fatty membrane from a pig or sheep intestine that resembles fine netting; used to bard roasts and pâtés and to encase sausage forcemeat.

cellulose: A complex carbohydrate; it is the main structural component of plant cells.

cephalopod: Marine creatures whose tentacles and arms are attached directly to their heads, such as squid and octopus.

chafing dish: A metal dish with a heating unit (flame or electric) used to keep foods warm and to cook foods tableside or during buffet service.

Champagne: A sparkling white wine produced in the Champagne region of France using three grape varieties: Chardonnay, Pinot Noir, and Pinot Meunier. The term is sometimes incorrectly applied to other sparkling wines.

charcuterie: The preparation of pork and other meat items, such as hams, terrines, sausages, pâtés, and other forcemeats.

charcutière: The person who prepares charcuterie items. À la charcutière, meaning "in the style of the butcher's wife," refers to items (usually grilled meat) that are served with Sauce Robert and finished with a julienne of gherkins.

chateaubriand: A cut of meat from the thick end of the tenderloin. Traditionally cut thick and served with chateau potatoes and bearnaise sauce.

chaud-froid: Literally, "hot-cold." A food that is prepared hot but served cold as part of a buffet display, with a coating of brown or white sauce and glazed with aspic.

cheesecloth: A light, fine mesh gauze used for straining liquids and making sachets.

chef de partie: Station chef. In the brigade system, these are the line-cook positions, such as saucier, grillardin, and so forth.

chef de rang: Front waiter. The waiter responsible for properly set tables, proper delivery of foods to a table, and meeting the guests' needs. A demi-chef de rang is a back waiter or busboy.

chef de salle: Headwaiter. Responsible for service throughout the restaurant. May be covered by the maitre d' or captain.

chef de service: Director of service.

chef de vin: Wine steward. Responsible for purchasing the restaurant's wine, helping guests make wine selections, and serving the guests' wine. Also known as the *sommelier*.

chef's knife: An all-purpose knife used for chopping, slicing, and mincing; its blade is usually between 8 and 14 in/20 and 36 cm long.

chef's potato: All-purpose potato with a thin, speckled skin and a waxy flesh. It is used mainly for sautéing and boiling.

chemical leavener: An ingredient or combination of ingredients (such as baking soda or baking powder) whose chemical action produces carbon dioxide gas, which is used to leaven baked goods.

cherry stone: A medium-sized (less than 3 in/8 cm across the shell), hard-shell clam indigenous to the East Coast of the United States; may be served raw or cooked.

chiffon: A cake made by the foaming method; contains a high percentage of eggs and sugar and relatively little, if any, fat to produce a light and airy cake.

chiffonade: Leafy vegetables or herbs cut into fine shreds; often used as a garnish.

chile: The fruit of certain types of capsicum peppers (not related to black pepper), used fresh or dry as a seasoning. Chiles come in many types (e.g., jalapeño, serrano, poblano) and varying degrees of spiciness.

chili: A stewed dish flavored with chili powder, meat, and beans (optional).

chili powder: Dried chiles that have been ground or crushed, often with other ground spices and herbs added.

chine: Backbone. A cut of meat that includes the backbone. Also, to separate the backbone and ribs to facilitate carving.

chinois: A conical sieve used for straining foods through a fine wire mesh.

cholesterol: A substance found exclusively in animal products such as meat, eggs, and cheese (dietary cholesterol) or in the blood (serum cholesterol).

chop: To cut into pieces of roughly the same size. Also, a small cut of meat including part of the rib.

choucroute: Sauerkraut cooked with goose fat, onions, juniper berries and white wine. *Choucroute garni* is sauerkraut garnished with various meats.

chowder: A thick soup that may be made from a variety of ingredients but usually contains potatoes.

***ciguatera* toxin:** A toxin found in certain fish, harmless to the fish, that causes illness in humans when eaten. The poisoning is caused by the fish's diet and is not eradicated by cooking or freezing.

cioppino: A fish stew usually made with white wine and tomatoes, believed to have originated in Genoa and popularized by Italian immigrants in San Francisco.

clarification: The process of removing solid impurities from a liquid (such as butter or stock). Also, a mixture of ground meat, egg whites, mirepoix, tomato purée, herbs, and spices used to clarify broth for consommé.

clarified butter: Butter from which the milk solids and water have been removed, leaving pure butterfat. Has a higher smoking point than whole butter but less butter flavor.

coagulation: The curdling or clumping of proteins, usually due to the application of heat or acid.

coarse chop: A type of preparation in which food is cut into pieces of roughly the same size. Used for items such as mirepoix, where appearance is not important.

cocoa: The pods of the cacao tree, processed to remove the cocoa butter and ground into powder. Used as a flavoring.

cocotte: Casserole. A cooking dish with a tight-fitting lid for braising or stewing. Also, a small ramekin used for cooking eggs. *En cocotte* is often interchangeable with *en casserole*.

coddled eggs: Eggs cooked briefly in simmering water (about 30 seconds), in their shells or in ramekins or coddlers, until set.

colander: A perforated bowl, with or without a base or legs, used to strain or drain liquids from foods.

collagen: A fibrous protein found in the connective tissue of animals, used to make glue and gelatin. Breaks down into gelatin when cooked in a moist environment for an extended period of time.

combination method: A cooking method that involves the application of both dry and moist heat to the main item (e.g., meats seared in fat then simmered in a sauce for braising or stewing).

commis: Apprentice. A cook who works under a chef de partie to learn the station and its responsibilities.

communard: The kitchen position responsible for preparing staff meals.

complete protein: A food source that provides all of the essential amino acids in the correct ratio so that they can be used in the body for protein synthesis. May require more than one ingredient (such as beans and rice together).

complex carbohydrate: A large molecule made up of long chains of sugar molecules. In food, these molecules are found in starches and fiber.

composed salad: A salad in which the items are carefully arranged on a plate, rather than tossed together.

compote: A dish of fruit—fresh or dried—cooked in syrup flavored with spices or liqueur. Also, a type of small dish.

compound butter: Butter combined with herbs or other seasonings and usually used to sauce grilled or broiled items, vegetables, or steamed dessert puddings.

concasser: To pound or chop coarsely. *Concassé* usually refers to tomatoes that have been peeled, seeded, and chopped.

condiment: An aromatic mixture, such as pickles, chutney, and some sauces and relishes, that accompanies food. Usually kept on the table throughout service.

conduction: A method of heat transfer in which heat is transmitted through another substance. In cooking, when heat is transmitted to food through a pot or pan, oven racks, or grill rods.

confiserie: Confectionery or candy. A *confiseur* is a pâtissier specializing in, and responsible for, the production of candies and related items, such as petits fours.

confit: Meat (usually goose, duck, or pork) cooked and preserved in its own fat.

consommé: Broth that has been clarified using a mixture of ground meat, egg whites, and other ingredients that trap impurities, resulting in a perfectly clear broth.

convection: A method of heat transfer in which heat is transmitted through the circulation of air or water.

convection oven: An oven that employs convection currents by forcing hot air through fans so it circulates around food, cooking it quickly and evenly.

converted rice: Rice that has been pressure-steamed and dried before milling to remove surface starch and retain nutrients. Also known as *parboiled rice*.

coquilles St. Jacques: Scallops. Also, a dish of broiled scallops with a creamy wine sauce that is gratinéed and served in the shell.

coral: Lobster roe, which is red or coral-colored when cooked.

cornichon: A small, sour, pickled cucumber. Often an accompaniment to pâtés and smoked meats.

cornstarch: A fine, white powder milled from dried corn; used primarily as a thickener for sauce and occasionally as an ingredient in batters.

cottage cheese: A fresh cheese made from the drained curd of soured cow's milk.

coulis: A thick purée of vegetables or fruit, served hot or cold. Traditionally refers to the thickened juices of cooked meat, fish, or shellfish purée or certain thick soups.

country-style: A term used to describe forcemeat that is coarse in texture, usually made from pork, pork fat, liver, and various garnishes.

court bouillon: Literally, "short broth." An aromatic vegetable broth that usually includes an acidic ingredient, such as wine or vinegar; most commonly used for poaching fish.

couscous: Pellets of semolina or cracked wheat usually cooked by steaming, traditionally in a couscoussière. Also, the stew with which this grain is traditionally served.

couscoussière: A set of nesting pots, similar to a steamer, used to cook couscous.

couverture: Fine semisweet chocolate, used for coating and decorating, that is extremely glossy and smooth. Chocolate containing a minimum of 32 percent cocoa butter.

cream: The fatty component of milk; available with various fat contents. Also refers to a mixing method for batters and doughs in which the sugar and fat are beaten together until they are light and fluffy before the other ingredients are added.

cream cheese: Soft, unripened cheese derived from cow's milk, which must contain 33 percent milk fat and 55 percent or less moisture. Used as a spread, a dip, in confections, and in dressings.

cream of tartar: A salt of tartaric acid used extensively in baking, found in wine barrels after fermentation. Used to give stability and volume in whipping egg whites and often as the acid component in baking powder.

cream puff: A pastry made with pâte à choux, filled with crème pâtissière, and usually glazed. Also called *profiterole*.

cream soup: Traditionally a soup based on a béchamel sauce. Loosely, any soup finished with cream, a cream variant such as sour cream, or a liaison.

crème anglaise: A stirred custard made with cream and/or milk, sugar, eggs, and vanilla. May be served as a sauce or used in pastry preparations such as bavarian cream and ice cream. Also known as *vanilla sauce*.

crème brûlée: Literally, "burnt cream"; a baked custard topped with sugar that is caramelized before service. The caramelized sugar creates a dual-textured dessert with a soft, creamy custard and a brittle sugar topping.

crème fraîche: Heavy cream cultured to give it a thick consistency and a slightly tangy flavor. Used in hot preparations since it is less likely than sour cream or yogurt to curdle when heated.

crème pâtissière: Literally, "pastry cream." A stirred custard made with eggs, flour or other starches, milk, sugar, and flavorings, used to fill and garnish pastries or as the base for soufflés, creams, and mousses.

Creole: This sophisticated type of cooking is a combination of French, Spanish, and African cuisines; signature ingredients include butter, cream, tomatoes, filé powder, green peppers, onions, and celery. Gumbo is a traditional Creole dish.

crêpe: A thin pancake made with egg batter; used in sweet and savory preparations.

croissant: A pastry consisting of a yeast dough with a butter roll-in, traditionally formed into a crescent shape.

cross contamination: The transference of disease-causing elements from one source to another through physical contact.

croustade: A small baked or fried edible container for meat, chicken, or other mixtures; usually made from pastry but may be made from potatoes or pasta.

croûte, en: Encased in a bread or pastry crust and baked.

crouton: A bread or pastry garnish, cut into bite-size pieces and toasted or sautéed until crisp.

crumb: A term used to describe the texture of baked goods; for example, an item can be said to have a fine or coarse crumb.

crustacean: A class of hard-shelled arthropods with elongated bodies, primarily aquatic, which include edible species such as lobster, crab, shrimp, and crayfish.

cuisson: Shallow poaching liquid, including stock, fumet, or other liquid, which may be reduced and used as a base for the poached item's sauce.

curd: The semisolid portion of milk once it coagulates and separates. Also, a sweet, creamy, pudding-like preparation that is made of fruit juice (typically citrus), sugar, eggs, and butter.

cure: To preserve a food by salting, smoking, pickling, and/or drying.

curing salt: A mixture of 94 percent table salt (sodium chloride) and 6 percent sodium nitrite, used to preserve meats. Also known as *tinted curing mixture* or *TCM*.

curry: A mixture of spices, used primarily in Indian cuisine. May include turmeric, coriander, cumin, cayenne or other chiles, cardamom, cinnamon, clove, fennel, fenugreek, ginger, and garlic. Also, a stew-like dish seasoned with curry.

custard: A mixture of milk, beaten egg, and possibly other ingredients, such as sweet or savory flavorings, cooked with gentle heat, often in a bain-marie, double boiler, or water bath.

D

daily values (DV): Standard nutritional values developed by the Food and Drug Administration for use on food labels.

danger zone: The temperature range from 40° to 140°F/4° to 60°C; the most favorable condition for rapid growth of many pathogens.

Danish pastry: A pastry consisting of rich yeast dough with a butter roll-in, possibly filled with nuts, fruit, or other ingredients, and iced. This pastry originated in Denmark.

daube: A classic French meat stew braised in red wine, vegetables, and seasonings and traditionally cooked in a daubière, a specialized casserole with a tight-fitting lid and indentations to hold hot coals.

debeard: To remove the shaggy, inedible fibers from a mussel. These fibers anchor the mussel to its mooring.

deck oven: An oven in which the heat source is located underneath the deck or floor of the oven and the food is placed directly on the deck instead of on a rack.

deep fry: To cook food by immersion in hot fat; deep-fried foods are often coated with bread crumbs or batter before being cooked.

deep poach: To cook food gently in enough simmering liquid to completely submerge the food.

deglaze, déglacer: To use a liquid, such as wine, water, or stock, to dissolve food particles and/or caramelized drippings left in a pan after roasting or sautéing. The resulting mix then becomes the base for the accompanying sauce.

degrease, dégraisser: To skim the fat off the surface of a liquid, such as a stock or sauce.

demi-glace: Literally, "half-glaze." A mixture of equal proportions of brown stock and brown sauce that has been reduced by half. One of the "grand" sauces.

dépouillage: To skim the impurities from the surface of a cooking liquid, such as a stock or sauce. This action is simplified by placing the pot off center on the burner (convection simmer) and skimming impurities as they collect at one side of the pot.

deviled: Meat, poultry, or other food seasoned with mustard, vinegar, and possibly other hot and spicy seasonings, such as red pepper and Tabasco.

dice: To cut ingredients into evenly sized small cubes (¼ in/ 6 mm for small, ½ in/1 cm for medium, and ¾ in/2 cm for large is the standard).

die: The plate in a meat grinder through which foods pass just before a blade cuts them. The size of the die's opening determines the fineness of the grind.

digestif: A spirit usually consumed after dining as an aid to digestion. Examples include brandy and cognac.

direct heat: A method of heat transfer in which heat waves radiate from a source (e.g., an open burner or grill) and travel directly to the item being heated with no conductor between heat source and food. Examples are grilling, broiling, and toasting. Also known as *radiant heat*.

dock: To cut the top of dough before baking to allow steam to escape and control the expansion of the dough and/or to create a decorative effect.

doré: Coated with egg yolk or cooked to a golden brown.

drawn: Describes a whole fish that has been gutted but still has its head, fins, and tail. Also refers to clarified butter.

dredge: To coat food with a dry ingredient such as flour or bread crumbs prior to frying or sautéing.

dressed: Prepared for cooking. A dressed fish is gutted and scaled, and its head, tail, and fins are removed (same as pan-dressed). Dressed poultry is plucked, gutted, singed, trimmed, and trussed. Also, coated with dressing, as in a salad.

drum sieve: A sieve consisting of a screen stretched across a shallow cylinder of wood or aluminum. Also known as a *tamis*.

dry cure: A combination of salts and spices used to preserve meats; often used before smoking to process meats and forcemeats.

dry sauté: To sauté without fat, usually using a nonstick pan.

dumpling: Any of a number of small soft dough or batter items, which are steamed, poached, or simmered (possibly on top of a stew), baked, pan fried, or deep fried; may be filled or plain.

durum: A very hard wheat typically milled into semolina, which is primarily used in the making of pasta.

dusting: Distributing a film of flour, sugar, cocoa powder, or other such ingredients on pans or work surfaces, or on finished products as a garnish.

Dutch oven: A kettle, usually of cast iron, used for stewing and braising on the stovetop or in the oven.

Dutch process: A method for treating cocoa powder with an alkali to reduce its acidity.

duxelles: An appareil of finely chopped mushrooms and shallots sautéed gently in butter, used as a stuffing, garnish, or as a flavoring in soups and sauces.

E

éclair: A long, thin shell made of pâte à choux, filled with crème patissière, and glazed with chocolate fondant or ganache.

edible-portion (EP) weight: The weight of an item after trimming and preparation [as opposed to the as-purchased (AP) weight].

egg wash: A mixture of beaten eggs (whole eggs, yolks, or whites) and a liquid, usually milk or water, used to coat baked goods to give them a sheen.

émincer: To cut an item, usually meat, into very thin slices.

emulsion: A mixture of two or more liquids, one of which is a fat or oil and the other of which is water based, so that tiny globules of one are suspended in the other. This may involve the use of stabilizers, such as egg or mustard. Emulsions may be temporary, permanent, or semipermanent.

endosperm: The largest portion of the inside of the seed of a flowering plant, such as wheat; composed primarily of starch and protein. This is the portion used primarily in milled grain products.

entrecôte: Literally, "between the ribs." A very tender steak cut from between the ninth and eleventh ribs of beef.

entremetier: Vegetable chef/station. The position responsible for hot appetizers and often soups, vegetables, starches, and pastas; may also be responsible for egg dishes.

escalope: A *scallop* of meat; this cut of a small boneless piece of meat or fish of uniform thickness is most often sautéed.

Espagnole sauce: Literally, "Spanish sauce." Brown sauce made with brown stock, caramelized mirepoix, tomato purée, seasonings, and roux.

essence: A concentrated flavoring extracted from an item, usually by infusion or distillation. Includes items such as vanilla and other extracts, concentrated stocks, and fumets.

estouffade: A French stew with wine-moistened pieces of meat. Also, a type of rich brown stock based on pork knuckle and veal and beef bones that is often used in braises.

ethylene gas: A gas emitted by various fruits and vegetables; ethylene gas speeds ripening, maturing, and eventually rotting.

étouffée: Literally, "smothered." Refers to food cooked by a method similar to braising, except that items are cooked with little or no added liquid in a pan with a tight-fitting lid. (Also *étuver, à l'étuvée*.) Also, a Cajun dish made with a dark roux, crayfish, vegetables, and seasonings over a bed of white rice.

evaporated milk: Unsweetened canned milk from which 60 percent of the water has been removed before canning. It is often used in custards and to create a creamy texture in food.

extruder: A machine used to shape dough into various shapes. The dough is pushed out through perforated plates rather than rolled.

F

fabrication: The butchering, cutting, and trimming of meat, poultry, fish, and game (large pieces or whole) into a variety of smaller cuts to prepare them to be cooked.

facultative bacteria: Bacteria that can survive both with and without oxygen.

farce: Forcemeat or stuffing; means "stuffing" in French.

farina: A fine flour or meal that can be eaten as a breakfast cereal when cooked in boiling water, used in puddings, or used as a thickener.

fat: One of the basic nutrients used by the body to provide energy. Fats also carry flavor in food and give a feeling of fullness.

fatback: Pork fat from the back of the pig, used primarily for barding, but is also used to make lard and cracklings.

fermentation: The process of yeast acting to break down sugars into carbon dioxide gas and alcohol, which is essential in bread leavening and beer, wine, and spirit making. Also, the period of rising in yeast doughs.

fiber, dietary fiber: The structural component of plants that is necessary to the human diet and is indigestable. Also referred to as roughage.

filé: A thickener made from ground dried sassafras leaves; used primarily in gumbos.

filet mignon: The expensive, boneless cut of beef from the small end of the tenderloin.

fillet, filet: A boneless cut of meat, fish, or poultry.

fines herbes: A mixture of herbs, usually parsley, chervil, tarragon, and chives that lose their flavor quickly. They are generally added to the dish just prior to serving.

first in, first out (FIFO): A fundamental storage principle based on stock rotation. Products are stored and used so that the oldest product is always used first.

fish poacher: A long, narrow pot with straight sides and possibly a perforated rack, used for poaching whole fish.

five-spice powder: A mixture of equal parts ground cinnamon, clove, fennel seed, star anise, and Szechwan peppercorns.

flat fish: A type of fish characterized by its flat body and having both eyes on one side of its head (e.g., sole, plaice, flounder, and halibut).

flattop: A thick plate of cast iron or steel set over the heat source on a range; diffuses heat, making it more even than an open burner.

fleurons: Garnishes made from light puff pastry cut into oval, diamond, or crescent shapes and served with meat, fish, or soup.

Florentine, à la: Dishes prepared in the style of Florence, Italy; denotes the use of spinach and sometimes mornay sauce or cheese.

foaming mixing method: A method of producing batters where the main structural component is a foamed egg (whole and/or yolk and whites)–sugar mixture.

foie gras: The fattened liver of a duck or goose that has been force-fed and fattened over a four- to five-month period.

fold: To gently combine ingredients (especially foams) so as not to release trapped air bubbles. Also, to gently mix together two items, usually a light, airy mixture with a denser mixture. Also, the method of turning, rolling, and layering dough over on itself to produce a flaky texture.

fond: The French term for stock. Also describes the pan drippings remaining after sautéing or roasting food. It is often deglazed and used as a base for sauces.

fondant: A white paste made from sugar and liquid, usually water or corn syrup, that has been dissolved, heated, and agitated during cooling. Used as a filling and glaze for pastries and confections.

food-borne illness: An illness in humans caused by the consumption of an adulterated food product. For an official determination that an outbreak of food-borne illness has occurred, two or more people must have become ill after eating the same food, and the outbreak must be confirmed by health officials.

food cost: Cost of all food purchased to prepare items for sale in a restaurant.

food mill: A strainer with a crank-operated, curved blade. It is used to purée soft foods while straining.

food processor: A machine with interchangeable blades and disks and a removable bowl and lid separate from the motor housing. It can be used for a variety of tasks, including chopping, grinding, puréeing, emulsifying, kneading, slicing, shredding, and cutting into julienne.

forcemeat: An emulsion of chopped or ground meat, fat, and a binder, used for pâtés, sausages, and other preparations. The four types are mousseline, straight, country-style, and gratin.

fork-tender: Degree of doneness in braised foods and vegetables; fork-tender foods are easily pierced or cut by a fork, or should slide readily from a fork when lifted.

formula: A recipe in which measurements for each ingredient may be given as percentages of the weight for the main ingredient.

fortified wine: Wine to which a spirit, usually brandy, has been added (e.g., Marsala, Madeira, port, or sherry).

free-range: Refers to livestock that is raised unconfined.

frenching: The process of cutting and scraping meat from rib bones before cooking.

fricassée: A stew of poultry or other white meat with a white sauce.

fritter: Sweet or savory food coated or mixed into batter and deep fried. Also called *beignet*.

friturier: Fry chef/station. The position responsible for all fried foods; it may be combined with the rôtisseur position.

fructose: A simple sugar found in fruits. Fructose is the sweetest simple sugar.

fumet: A type of stock in which the main flavoring ingredient is allowed to cook in a covered pot with wine and aromatics. Fish fumet is the most common type.

G

galantine: Boned meat (usually poultry) that is stuffed with forcemeat, rolled, poached, and served cold, usually in aspic.

ganache: A preparation made of chocolate, heavy cream, and sometimes butter, sugar, and other flavorings. Among other things, it may be used as a sauce, a glaze, a filling, or to make confections. Can range from soft to hard, depending on the ratio of chocolate to cream used.

garbure: A thick vegetable soup, usually containing beans, cabbage, and/or potatoes.

garde manger: Pantry chef/station. The position responsible for cold food preparation, including salads, appetizers, pâtés, and so forth.

garni: Garnished. Used to describe dishes accompanied by vegetables and potatoes.

garnish: An edible decoration or accompaniment to a dish or item.

gazpacho: A cold soup made from vegetables, typically tomatoes, cucumbers, peppers, and onions.

gelatin: A protein-based substance found in animal bones and connective tissue. When dissolved in hot liquid and then cooled, it can be used as a thickener and stabilizer.

gelatinization: A phase in the process of thickening a liquid with starch in which the starch molecules swell to form a network that traps water molecules.

génoise: A light cake containing flour, sugar, eggs, butter, vanilla, and/or other flavorings that is made using the foaming mixing method.

germ: The portion of the seed of flowering plants, such as wheat, that sprouts to form a new plant; the embryo of the new plant.

gherkin: A small pickled cucumber.

giblets: Organs and other trim from poultry, including the liver, heart, gizzard, and neck, used to flavor stocks and soups.

glace: Reduced stock; ice cream.

glacé: Glazed or iced; icing.

glaze: To give an item a shiny surface by brushing or otherwise coating it with sauce, aspic, icing, or another appareil. For meat, to coat with sauce and then brown in an oven or salamander.

glucose: A simple sugar found in honey, some fruits, and many vegetables. It has about half the sweetness of table sugar and is the preferred source of energy for the human body.

gluten: A protein present in wheat flour that develops through hydration and mixing to form elastic strands that build structure and aid in leavening.

grand sauce: One of several basic sauces that are used in the preparation of many other small sauces. The grand sauces are Espagnole, velouté, béchamel, hollandaise, and tomato. Also called *"mother" sauce.*

gratin: Cheese or bread crumb topping browned in an oven or under a salamander (*au gratin, gratin de*). Gratin can also refer to a forcemeat in which some portion of the dominant meat is sautéed and cooled before it is ground.

gravlax: Raw salmon cured with salt, sugar, and fresh dill. A dish of Scandinavian origin often accompanied by mustard and dill sauce.

griddle: A heavy metal cooking surface, which may be either fitted with handles, built into a stove, or heated by its own gas or electric element. Cooking is done directly on the griddle.

grill: A cooking technique in which foods are cooked by a radiant heat source placed below the food. Also, the piece of equipment on which grilling is done. Grills may be fueled by gas, electricity, charcoal, or wood.

grillardin: Grill chef/station. The position responsible for all grilled foods; may be combined with the position of rôtisseur.

grill pan: A skillet with ridges that is used on the stovetop to simulate grilling.

grissini: Thin, crisp breadsticks.

griswold: A pot, similar to a rondeau, made of cast iron; may have a single short handle rather than the usual loop handles.

gumbo: A Creole soup/stew thickened with filé or okra, flavored with a variety of meats and fishes and dark roux.

H

haricot: Literally, "bean." Haricots verts are green beans.

hash: Chopped, cooked meat, usually with potatoes and/or other vegetables, that is seasoned, bound with a sauce, and sautéed. Also, to chop into small, irregular pieces.

Hazard Analysis Critical Control Point (HACCP): A monitoring system used to track foods from the time that they are received until they are served to consumers, to ensure that the foods are free from contamination. Standards and controls are established for time and temperature, as well as safe handling practices.

Heimlich maneuver: First aid for choking, involving the application of sudden, upward pressure on the upper abdomen to force a foreign object from the windpipe.

high-ratio cake: A cake in which the batter includes a high percentage of sugar in relation to other ingredients.

hollandaise: A classic emulsion sauce made with a vinegar reduction, egg yolks, and melted butter flavored with lemon juice. It is one of the "grand" sauces.

hollow-ground: A type of knife blade made by fusing two sheets of metal and beveling or fluting the edge.

hominy: Corn that has been milled or treated with a lye solution to remove the bran and germ. Ground hominy is known as grits.

homogenization: A process used to prevent the milk fat from separating out of milk products. The liquid is forced through an ultrafine mesh at high pressure, which breaks up fat globules, dispersing them evenly throughout the liquid.

hors d'oeuvre: Literally, "outside the work." An appetizer.

hotel pan: A rectangular metal pan in any of a number of standard sizes, with a lip that allows it to rest in a storage shelf or steam table.

hydrogenation: The process in which hydrogen atoms are added to an unsaturated fat molecule, making it partially or completely saturated and solid at room temperature.

hydroponics: A technique that involves growing vegetables in nutrient-enriched water rather than in soil.

hygiene: Conditions and practices followed to maintain health, including sanitation and personal cleanliness.

I

induction burner: A type of heating unit that relies on magnetic attraction between the cooktop and metals in the pot to generate the heat that cooks foods in the pan. Reaction time is significantly faster than with traditional burners.

infection: Contamination by a disease-causing agent, such as bacteria.

infusion: Steeping an aromatic or other item in liquid to extract its flavor. Also, the liquid resulting from this process.

instant-read thermometer: A thermometer used to measure the internal temperature of foods. The stem is inserted in the food, producing an instant temperature read-out.

intoxication: Poisoning. A state of being tainted with toxins, particularly those produced by microorganisms that have infected food.

inventory: An itemized list of goods and equipment on hand, together with the estimated worth or cost.

invert sugar: A sugar that is a mixture of dextrose and fructose, which will not easily crystallize. These sugars can occur naturally or be created by boiling sucrose with an acid.

J

jardinière: A mixture of vegetables.

julienne: Vegetables, potatoes, or other items cut into thin strips; ⅛ in by ⅛ in by 1 to 2 in/3 mm by 3 mm by 3 to 5 cm is standard. Fine julienne is ¹⁄₁₆ in by ¹⁄₁₆ in by 1 to 2 in/1.5 mm by 1.5 mm by 3 to 5 cm.

jus: Juice. Refers to fruit and vegetable juices as well as juices from meats. *Jus de viande* is meat gravy. Meat served *au jus* is served with its own juice or jus lié.

jus lié: Meat juice thickened lightly with arrowroot or cornstarch.

K

kasha: Buckwheat groats that have been hulled and crushed and roasted; usually prepared by boiling.

knead: To work or mix a dough by hand to soften to working consistency or to stretch and expand gluten in yeasted doughs.

kosher: Prepared in accordance with Jewish dietary laws.

kosher salt: Pure, refined salt used for pickling because it does not contain magnesium carbonate and thus does not cloud brine solutions. Also used to prepare kosher items. Also known as *coarse salt* or *pickling salt*.

L

lactose: The simple sugar found in milk. This disaccharide is the least sweet among the natural sugars.

laminate: To fold and roll a dough together with a roll-in fat to create alternating layers of fat and dough; used to create puff pastry, Danish, and croissants.

lard: Rendered pork fat used for pastry and frying. Also, to insert small strips of fatback into naturally lean meats before roasting or braising. The process is done using a larding needle.

lardon/lardoon: A strip of fat used for larding; may be seasoned. Also, bacon that has been diced, blanched, and fried.

leavener: Any ingredient or process that produces gas and causes the rising of baked goods. Can be chemical (baking powder), mechanical (folding in air in whipped egg whites), or biological (yeast).

lecithin: An emulsifier found in eggs and soybeans.

legume: The seeds of certain pod plants, including beans and peas, which are eaten for their earthy flavors and high nutritional value. Also, the French word for vegetable.

liaison: A mixture of egg yolks and cream used to thicken and enrich sauces. Also loosely applied to any appareil used as a thickener.

liqueur: A spirit flavored with fruit, spices, nuts, herbs, and/or seeds and usually sweetened. Also known as *cordials*, liqueurs often have a high alcohol content, a viscous body, and a slightly sticky feel.

littleneck: Small, hard-shell clams often eaten raw on the half shell; smaller than a cherrystone clam and less than 2 in/5 cm in diameter.

low-fat milk: Milk containing less than 2 percent fat.

lox: Cold, smoked, salt-cured salmon.

lozenge cut: A knife cut in which foods are cut into small diamond shapes ½ in by ½ in by ⅛ in/1 cm by 1 cm by 3 mm thick.

Lyonnaise: Food cooked in the Lyons style. Refers to a sauce made with onions and usually butter, white wine, vinegar, and demi-glace. Lyonnaise potatoes are sautéed with onions and butter.

M

macaroon: Small cookies of nut paste (typically almond or coconut), sugar, and egg white.

Madeira: A Portuguese fortified wine that is treated with heat as it ages, giving it a distinctive flavor and brownish color.

Maillard reaction: A complex browning reaction that results in the particular flavor and color of foods that do not contain much sugar, including roasted meats. The reaction, which involves carbohydrates and amino acids, is named after the French scientist who first discovered it. There are low-temperature and high-temperature Maillard reactions; the high-temperature reaction starts at 310°F/154°C.

maître d'hôtel: Dining room manager or food and beverage manager, informally called maître d'. This position oversees the dining room or front of the house staff. Also, a compound butter flavored with chopped parsley and lemon juice.

mandoline: A slicing device of stainless steel with carbon-steel blades. The blades may be adjusted to cut items into various shapes and thicknesses.

marbling: The intramuscular fat found in meat that makes it tender and juicy.

marinade: An appareil used before cooking to flavor and moisten foods; may be liquid or dry. Liquid marinades are usually based on an acidic ingredient, such as wine or vinegar; dry marinades are usually salt based.

mark on a grill: To turn a food (without flipping it over) 90 degrees after it has been on the grill for several seconds to create the cross-hatching associated with grilled foods.

marzipan: A paste of ground almonds, sugar, and sometimes egg whites that is used to fill, cover, and decorate pastries.

matelote: A French fish stew traditionally made with eel or other freshwater fish and flavored with wine and aromatics.

matignon: An edible mirepoix that is often used in poêléed dishes and is usually served with the finished dish. Typically, matignon includes two parts carrot, one part celery, one part leek, one part onion, one part mushroom (optional), and one part ham or bacon.

mayonnaise: A cold emulsion of oil, egg yolks, vinegar, mustard, and seasonings used as a dressing, a spread, or a base for additional sauces.

mechanical leavener: Air incorporated into a batter or dough to act as a leavener.

medallion: A small, round scallop of meat.

meringue: Egg whites beaten with sugar until they stiffen. Types include regular or common, Italian, and Swiss.

mesophilic: A term used to describe bacteria that thrive in temperatures between 60° and 100°F/16° and 38°C.

metabolism: The sum of chemical processes in living cells by which energy is provided and new material is assimilated.

meunière, à la: French for "in the style of the miller's wife." Refers to a cooking technique in which the item, generally fish, is dusted with flour, sautéed, and served with a sauce of beurre noisette, lemon juice, and parsley.

microwave oven: An oven in which electromagnetic waves (similar to radio waves) generated by a device called a magnetron penetrate food and cause the water molecules in it to oscillate. This rapid molecular motion generates heat, which cooks the food.

mie: The soft part of bread (not the crust); *mie de pain* is fresh white bread crumbs.

millet: A small, round, glutenless grain that may be boiled or ground into flour.

milling: The process by which grain is separated into germ/husk, bran, and endosperm and ground into flour or meal.

mince: To chop into very small pieces.

mineral: An inorganic element that is an essential component of the diet. Provides no energy and is therefore referred to as a noncaloric nutrient. The body cannot produce minerals; they must be obtained from the diet.

minestrone: A hearty vegetable soup that typically includes dried beans and pasta.

minute, à la: Literally, "at the minute." A restaurant production approach in which dishes are not prepared until an order arrives in the kitchen.

mirepoix: A combination of chopped aromatic vegetables—usually two parts onion, one part carrot, and one part celery—used to flavor stocks, soups, braises, and stews.

mise en place: Literally, "put in place." The preparation and assembly of ingredients, pans, utensils, and plates or serving pieces needed for a particular dish or service period.

mode, à la: Literally, "in the style of" (often followed by *de* plus a descriptive phrase). Boeuf à la mode is braised beef; pie à la mode is served with ice cream.

molasses: The dark brown, sweet syrup that is a by-product of sugarcane and sugarbeet refining. Molasses is available as light (the least cooked but sweetest), dark, and blackstrap (the most cooked and most bitter).

mollusk: Any of a number of invertebrate animals with soft, unsegmented bodies usually enclosed in a hard shell; mollusks include gastropods (univalves), bivalves, and cephalopods. Examples include clams, oysters, snails, octopus, and squid.

monosodium glutamate (MSG): A flavor enhancer derived from glutamic acid, without a distinct flavor of its own; used primarily in Chinese and processed foods. It may cause allergic reactions in some people.

monounsaturated fat: A fat with one available bonding site not filled with a hydrogen atom. Helpful in lowering the LDL cholesterol level (the bad cholesterol). Food sources include avocados, olives, and nuts.

monté au beurre: Literally, "lifted with butter." Refers to a technique used to finish sauces, thicken them slightly, and give them a glossy appearance by whisking or swirling whole butter into the sauce until melted.

mousse: A foam made with beaten egg whites and/or whipped cream folded into a flavored base appareil. May be sweet or savory.

mousseline: A mousse. Also, a sauce made by folding whipped cream into hollandaise. Also, a very light forcemeat based on white meat or seafood lightened with cream and eggs.

N

napoleon: A pastry traditionally made of layered puff pastry rectangles filled with pastry cream and glazed with fondant.

nappé: To coat with sauce; thickened. Consistency of a sauce that will coat the back of a spoon.

nature: French for "ungarnished" or "plain." Pommes natures are boiled potatoes.

navarin: A French stew, traditionally of lamb, with potatoes, turnips, onions, and possibly other vegetables.

new potato: Any small young potato that is less than 1½ in/4 cm in diameter, usually prepared by boiling or steaming and is often eaten with its skin. The new potato has not yet converted its sugar into starch, creating a waxy potato with a thin skin.

noisette: Hazelnut or hazelnut colored. Also, a small portion of meat cut from the rib. Pommes noisette are tournéed potatoes browned in butter. Beurre noisette is browned butter.

nonbony fish: Fish whose skeletons are made of cartilage rather than hard bone (e.g., shark, skate). Also called *cartilaginous fish*.

nouvelle cuisine: Literally, "new cooking." A culinary movement emphasizing freshness and lightness of ingredients, natural flavors simply prepared, and innovative combinations and presentation.

nutrient: A basic component of food used by the body for growth, repair, restoration, and energy. Includes carbohydrates, fats, proteins, water, vitamins, and minerals.

nutrition: The process by which an organism takes in and uses food.

O

oblique cut, roll cut: A knife cut used primarily with long, cylindrical vegetables such as carrots. The item is cut on a diagonal, rolled 180 degrees, then cut on the same diagonal, producing a piece with two angled edges.

offal: Edible entrails and extremities; variety meats, including organs (brains, heart, kidneys, lungs, sweetbreads, tripe, tongue), head meat, tail, and feet.

offset spatula: A hand tool with a wide, bent blade set in a short handle, used to turn or lift foods from grills, broilers, or griddles.

oignon brûlé: Literally, "burnt onion." A peeled, halved onion seared on a flattop or in a skillet and used to enhance the color of stock and consommé.

oignon piqué: Literally, "pricked onion." A whole, peeled onion to which a bay leaf is attached, using a clove as a tack. It is used to flavor béchamel sauce and some soups.

omega-3 fatty acids: Polyunsaturated fatty acids that may reduce the risk of heart disease and tumor growth, stimulate the immune system, and lower blood pressure; they occur in fatty fish, dark green leafy vegetables, and certain nuts and oils.

omelet: Beaten egg that is cooked in butter in a specialized pan or skillet and then rolled or folded into an oval. Omelets may be filled with a variety of ingredients before or after rolling.

organic leavener: Yeast. A living organism acting to produce carbon dioxide gas, which will cause a batter or dough to rise through the fermentation process.

organ meat: Meat from an organ, rather than the muscle tissue, of an animal. Includes kidneys, heart, liver, sweetbreads, and the like.

oven spring: The rapid initial rise of yeast doughs when placed in a hot oven. Heat accelerates the growth of the yeast, which produces more carbon dioxide gas and also causes this gas to expand.

P

paella: A dish of rice cooked with onion, tomato, garlic, vegetables, and various meats, including chicken, chorizo, shellfish, and possibly other types. A paella pan is a specialized pan for cooking paella; it is wide and shallow and usually has two loop handles.

paillard: A scallop of meat pounded until thin; usually grilled or sautéed.

palette knife: A small, long, narrow metal spatula with a rounded tip. May be tapered or straight, offset or flat.

pan broiling: A cooking method similar to dry sautéing that simulates broiling by cooking an item in a hot pan with little or no fat.

pan dressed: Portion-size whole fish with the guts, gills, and scales removed. The fins and tail may or may not be trimmed or removed.

pan frying: A cooking method in which items are cooked in fat in a skillet; this generally involves more fat than sautéing or stir frying but less than deep frying.

pan gravy: A sauce made by deglazing pan drippings from a roast and combining them with a roux or other starch and additional stock.

pan steaming: A method of cooking foods in a very small amount of liquid in a covered pan over direct heat.

papillote, en: Refers to a moist-heat cooking method similar to steaming, in which items are enclosed in parchment and cooked in the oven.

parchment: Heat-resistant paper used in cooking for such preparations as lining baking pans, cooking items en papillote, and covering items during the process of shallow poaching.

parcook: To partially cook an item before storing or finishing.

parisienne scoop: A small tool used for scooping balls out of vegetables or fruits and for portioning truffle ganache and other such preparations. Also called a *melon baller*.

par stock: The amount of stock (food and other supplies) necessary to cover operating needs between deliveries.

pasta: Literally, "dough" or "paste." Noodles made from a dough of flour (often semolina) and water or eggs that is kneaded, rolled, and cut or extruded, then cooked by boiling.

pasteurization: A process in which milk products are heated to kill microorganisms that could contaminate the milk.

pastry bag: A bag—usually made of plastic, canvas, or nylon—that can be fitted with plain or decorative tips and used to pipe out icings and puréed foods.

pâte: Noodles or pasta. Also, dough, paste, or batter (as in pâte brisée).

pâté: A rich forcemeat of meat, game, poultry, seafood, and/or vegetables, baked in pastry or in a mold or dish and served hot or cold.

pâte à choux: Cream puff batter, made by boiling a mixture of water or milk, butter, and flour, then beating in whole eggs. When baked, pâte à choux puffs to form a hollowed pastry shell that can be filled.

pâte brisée: Short pastry used to create crusts for pie crusts, tarts, and quiches.

pâté de campagne: Country-style pâté, with a coarse texture made of pork butt, chicken livers, garlic, onion, and parsley, flavored with brandy.

pâté en croûte: Pâté baked in a pastry crust.

pâte feuilletée: Puff pastry.

pâte sucrée: Sweet short pastry used for pies, tarts, and filled cookies.

pathogen: A disease-causing microorganism.

pâtissier: Pastry chef/station. This station is responsible for baked items, pastries, and desserts. This is often a separate area of the kitchen.

paupiette: A fillet or scallop of fish or meat that is rolled up around a stuffing and poached or braised.

paysanne or fermier cut: A knife cut in which ingredients are cut into flat, square pieces; ½ in by ½ in by ⅛ in/1 cm by 1 cm by 3 mm.

peel: A paddle used to transfer shaped doughs to a hearth or deck oven. Also, to remove the skin from a food item.

pesto: A thick, puréed mixture of an herb, traditionally basil and oil. Used as a sauce for pasta and other foods and as a garnish for soup. Pesto may also contain grated cheese, nuts or seeds, and other seasonings.

petit four: A fancy bite-sized layered cake covered in fondant. Also, more generally can refer to bite-sized pastries and cookies.

pH scale: A scale with values from 0 to 14 representing degree of acidity. A measurement of 7 is neutral, 0 is most acidic and 14 is most alkaline. Chemically, pH measures the concentration of hydrogen ions.

phyllo/filo dough: Pastry made with very thin sheets of a flour and water dough layered with butter and/or bread or cake crumbs; similar to strudel.

physical leavener: The leavening that occurs when steam is trapped in a dough through the introduction of air (vs. a chemical leavener), expanding and causing the cake or bread to rise.

phytochemicals: Naturally occurring compounds in plant foods that have antioxidant and disease-fighting properties.

pickling spice: A mixture of herbs and spices used to season pickles. Often includes dill weed and/or seed, coriander seed, cinnamon stick, peppercorns, bay leaves, and others.

pilaf: A technique for cooking grains in which the grain is sautéed briefly in butter, then simmered in stock or water with various seasonings until the liquid is absorbed. Also called *pilau, pilaw, pullao, pilav*.

pincé: Refers to an item caramelized by sautéing; usually refers to a tomato product.

pluches: Whole herb leaves connected to a small bit of stem; often used as a garnish. Also called *sprigs*.

poach: To cook gently in simmering liquid that is 160° to 185°F/71° to 85°C.

poêlé: Refers to food cooked in its own juices (usually with the addition of a matignon, other aromatics, and melted butter) in a covered pot, usually in the oven. The technique is also called *butter roasting*.

poissonier: Fish chef/station. The position responsible for fish items and their sauces; may be combined with the saucier position.

polenta: Cornmeal mush cooked in simmering liquid until the grains soften and the liquid absorbs. Polenta can be eaten hot or cold, firm or soft.

polyunsaturated fat: A fat molecule with more than one available bonding site not filled with a hydrogen atom. Food sources include corn, cottonseed, safflower, soy, and sunflower oils.

port: A fortified dessert wine. Vintage port is high-quality unblended wine aged in the bottle for at least twelve years. Ruby port may be blended and is aged in wood for a short time. White port is made with white grapes.

pot-au-feu: A classic French boiled dinner that typically includes poultry and beef, along with various root vegetables. The broth is often served as a first course, followed by the meats and vegetables.

prawn: A crustacean that closely resembles shrimp; often used as a general term for large shrimp.

presentation side: The side of a piece of meat, poultry, or fish that will be served facing up.

pressure steamer: A machine that cooks food using steam produced by heating water under pressure in a sealed compartment, allowing it to reach temperatures higher than boiling (212°F/100°C). The food is placed in a sealed chamber that cannot be opened until the pressure has been released and the steam properly vented from the chamber.

primal cuts: The large portions produced by the initial cutting of an animal carcass. Cuts are determined standards that may vary by country and animal. Primal cuts are further broken down into smaller, more manageable cuts.

printanière: A garnish of spring vegetables.

prix fixe: Literally, "fixed price." A type of menu in which a complete meal is offered for a preset price. The menu may offer several choices for each course.

proof: To allow yeast dough to rise. A proof box is a sealed cabinet that allows control over both temperature and humidity.

protein: One of the basic nutrients needed by the body to maintain life, supply energy, build and repair tissues, form enzymes and hormones, and perform other essential functions. Protein can be obtained from animal and vegetable sources.

Provençal(e), à la Provençale: Dishes prepared in the style of Provence, France, often with garlic, tomatoes, and olive oil. May also contain anchovies, eggplant, mushrooms, olives, and onions.

pulse: The edible seed of a leguminous plant, such as a bean, lentil, or pea. Often referred to simply as legume.

purée: To process food by mashing, straining, or chopping it very finely in order to make it a smooth paste. Also, a product produced using this technique.

Q

quahog/quahaug: A hard-shell clam larger than 3 in/8 cm in diameter, usually used for chowder or fritters.

quatre épices: Literally, "four spices." A finely ground spice mixture containing black peppercorns, nutmeg, cinnamon, cloves, and sometimes ginger. Used to flavor soups, stews, and vegetables.

quenelle: A light, poached dumpling based on a forcemeat (usually chicken, veal, seafood, or game), bound with eggs, and shaped in an oval by using two spoons.

quick bread: Bread made with chemical leaveners, which work more quickly than yeast because they require no kneading or fermentation. Also called *batter bread*.

R

raft: A mixture of ingredients used to clarify consommé. The term refers to the fact that the ingredients rise to the surface and form a floating mass.

ragoût: Stew of meat and/or vegetables.

ramekin/ramequin: A small, ovenproof dish, usually ceramic.

reach-in refrigerator: A refrigeration unit, or set of units, with pass-through doors. They are often used in the pantry area for storage of salads, cold hors d'oeuvre, and other frequently used items.

reduce: To decrease the volume of a liquid by simmering or boiling; used to provide a thicker consistency and/or concentrated flavors.

reduction: The product that results when a liquid is reduced.

refresh: To plunge an item into, or run it under, cold water after blanching to prevent further cooking. Also known as *shock*.

remouillage: Literally, "rewetting." A stock made from bones that have already been used for stock. Weaker than a first-quality stock, it is often reduced to make glaze.

render: To melt fat and clarify the drippings for use in sautéing or pan frying.

rest: To allow food to sit undisturbed after roasting and before carving; this allows the juices to seep back into the meat fibers.

rich dough: A yeast dough that contains fats such as butter or egg yolks. May also contain sweeteners. Rich doughs tend to produce more tender breads with a darker crust than lean doughs.

rillette: Potted meat, or meat that is slowly cooked in seasoned fat, then shredded or pounded with some of the fat into a paste. The mixture is packed in ramekins and covered with a thin layer of fat and often used as a spread.

ring top: A flattop with removable plates that can be opened to varying degrees to expose the food to more or less heat.

risotto: Rice that is sautéed briefly in butter with onions and possibly other aromatics, then combined with stock, which is added in several additions and stirred constantly, producing a creamy texture with grains that are still al dente.

roast: A dry-heat cooking method where the item is cooked in an oven or on a spit over a fire.

roe: Fish or shellfish eggs.

roll-in: Butter or a butter-based mixture that is placed between layers of pastry dough, which is then rolled and folded repeatedly to form numerous layers. When the dough is baked, the layers remain discrete, producing a very flaky, rich pastry.

rondeau: A shallow, wide, straight-sided pot with two loop handles often used for braising.

rondelle: A knife cut that produces round or oval flat pieces; used on cylindrical vegetables or items trimmed into cylinders before cutting.

rôtisseur: Roast chef/station. The position is responsible for all roasted foods and related sauces.

roulade: A slice of meat or fish rolled around a stuffing. Also, filled and rolled sponge cake.

round: A cut of beef from the hind quarter that includes the top and bottom round, eye, and top sirloin. It is lean and usually braised or roasted. Also, in baking, to shape pieces of yeast dough into balls. This process stretches and relaxes the gluten and ensures even rising and a smooth crust.

round fish: A classification of fish based on skeletal type, characterized by a rounded body and eyes on opposite sides of its head. Round fish are usually cut by the up and over method.

roux: An appareil containing equal parts of flour and fat (usually butter) used to thicken liquids. Roux is cooked to varying degrees (white, blond, or brown), depending on its intended use. The darker the roux, the less thickening power it has but the fuller the taste.

royale: A consommé garnish made of unsweetened cooked custard cut into decorative shapes.

rub: A combination of spices and herbs applied to foods as a marinade or flavorful crust. Dry rubs are generally based upon spices; wet rubs (sometimes known as *mops*) may include moist ingredients such as fresh herbs, vegetables, and fruit juice or broth, if necessary, to make a pasty consistency. The rubs absorb into the meat and create a greater depth of flavor.

S

sabayon: Wine custard. Sweetened egg yolks flavored with Marsala or other wine or liqueur, beaten in a double boiler until frothy. In Italian, *zabaglione*.

sachet d'épices: Literally, "bag of spices." Aromatic ingredients, encased in cheesecloth, that are used to flavor stocks and other liquids. A standard sachet contains parsley stems, cracked peppercorns, dried thyme, and a bay leaf.

salt cod: Cod that has been salted, possibly smoked, and dried to preserve it.

saltpeter: Potassium nitrate. A component of curing salt, used to preserve meat. It gives certain cured meats their characteristic pink color.

sanitation: The maintenance of a clean food-preparation environment by healthy food workers in order to prevent food-borne illnesses and food contamination.

sanitize: To kill pathogenic organisms by chemicals and/or moist heat.

sashimi: Sliced raw fish that is served with such condiments as a julienne of daikon radish, pickled ginger, wasabi, and soy sauce.

saturated fat: A fat molecule whose available bonding sites are entirely filled with hydrogen atoms. These tend to be solid at room temperature and are primarily of animal origin, though coconut oil, palm oil, and cocoa butter are vegetable sources of saturated fat. Animal sources include butter, meat, cheese, and eggs.

sauce: A liquid accompaniment to food, used to enhance the flavor of the food.

sauce vin blanc: Literally, "white wine sauce." Sauce made by combining a reduced poaching liquid (typically containing wine) with prepared hollandaise, velouté, or diced butter.

saucier: Sauté chef/station. The chef de partie responsible for all sautéed items and their sauces.

sausage: A forcemeat mixture shaped into patties or links, typically highly seasoned; originally made to preserve the meat and use edible scraps. Sausage is made from ground meat, fat, and seasonings. Sausage varies in size, shape, curing time, degree of doneness, and type of casing.

sauté: To cook quickly in a small amount of fat in a pan on the range top.

sauteuse: A shallow skillet with sloping sides and a single, long handle. Used for sautéing. Referred to generically as a sauté pan.

sautoir: A shallow skillet with straight sides and a single, long handle. Used for sautéing. Referred to generically as a sauté pan.

savory: Not sweet. Also, the name of a course (savory) served after dessert and before port in traditional British meals. Also, a family of herbs (including summer and winter savory) that tastes like a cross between thyme and mint.

scald: To heat a liquid, usually milk or cream, to just below the boiling point. May also refer to blanching fruits and vegetables.

scale: To measure ingredients by weighing, or to divide dough or batter into portions by weight. Also, to remove the scales from fish.

scaler: Tool used to scrape scales from fish. Used by scraping against direction in which scales lie flat, working from tail to head.

scallop: A bivalve whose adductor muscle (the muscle that keeps its shells closed) and roe are eaten. Also a small, boneless piece of meat or fish of uniform thickness. Also, a side dish where an item is layered with cream or sauce and topped with bread crumbs prior to baking.

score: To cut the surface of an item at regular intervals to allow it to cook evenly, allow excess fat to drain, help the food absorb marinades, or for decorative purposes

scrapple: A boiled mixture of pork trimmings, buckwheat, and cornmeal compressed into a loaf, chilled, and sliced. It is often fried after chilling and served for breakfast.

sear: To brown the surface of food in fat over high heat before finishing by another method (e.g., braising or roasting) in order to add flavor.

sea salt: Salt produced by evaporating seawater. Available refined or unrefined, crystallized or ground. Also known as *sel gris* (French for "gray salt").

seasoning: Adding an ingredient to give foods a particular flavor using salt, pepper, herbs, spices, and/or condiments. Also, the process by which a protective coating is built up on the interior of a pan.

semolina: The coarsely milled hard durum wheat endosperm used for gnocchi, some pasta, and couscous. Semolina has a high gluten content.

shallow poach: To cook gently in a shallow pan of simmering liquid. The liquid is often reduced and used as the base of a sauce.

sheet pan: A flat baking pan, often with a rolled lip, used to cook foods in the oven.

shelf life: The amount of time in storage that a product can maintain its quality.

shellfish: Various types of marine life consumed as food, including mollusks such as univalves, bivalves, cephalopods, and crustaceans.

sherry: A fortified Spanish wine varying in color and sweetness.

shirred egg: An egg cooked with butter (and often cream) in a ramekin until the whites are set.

sieve: A container made of a perforated material, such as wire mesh, used to drain, rice, or purée foods.

silverskin: The tough connective tissue that surrounds certain muscles. This protein does not dissolve when cooked and must be removed prior to cooking.

simmer: To maintain the temperature of a liquid just below boiling. Also, to cook in simmering liquid. The temperature range for simmering is 185° to 200°F/85° to 93°C.

simple carbohydrate: Any of a number of small carbohydrate molecules (mono- and disaccharides), including glucose, fructose, lactose, maltose, and sucrose.

simple syrup: A mixture of water and sugar (with additional flavorings or aromatics as desired), heated until the sugar dissolves. Used to moisten cakes or to poach fruits.

single-stage technique: A cooking technique involving only one cooking method—for example, boiling or sautéing—as opposed to more than one method, as in braising.

skim: To remove impurities from the surface of a liquid, such as stock or soup, during cooking.

skim milk: Milk from which all but 0.5 percent of the milk fat has been removed.

slurry: A starch such as arrowroot, cornstarch, or potato starch dispersed in cold liquid to prevent it from forming lumps when added to hot liquid as a thickener.

small sauce: A sauce that is a derivative of any of the "grand" sauces.

smoker: An enclosed area in which foods are held on racks or hooks and allowed to remain in a smoke bath at the appropriate temperature.

smoke roasting: A method for roasting foods in which items are placed on a rack in a pan containing wood chips that smolder, emitting smoke, when the pan is placed on the range top or in the oven.

smoking: Any of several methods for preserving and flavoring foods by exposing them to smoke. Methods include cold smoking (in which smoked items are not fully cooked), hot smoking (in which the items are cooked), and smoke roasting.

smoke point: The temperature at which a fat begins to break (and smoke) when heated.

smother: To cook in a covered pan with little liquid over low heat. The main item is often completely covered by another food item or sauce while it braises.

sodium: An alkaline metal element necessary in small quantities for human nutrition; one of the components of most salts used in cooking.

sommelier: Wine steward or waiter. This person helps diners select wine and serves it. They are responsible for the restaurant's wine cellar.

sorbet: A frozen dessert made with fruit juice or another flavoring, a sweetener (usually sugar), and beaten egg whites, which prevent the formation of large ice crystals.

soufflé: Literally, "puffed." A preparation made with a sauce base (usually béchamel for savory soufflés, pastry cream for sweet ones), whipped egg whites, and flavorings. The egg whites cause the soufflé to puff during cooking.

sourdough: A yeasted bread dough leavened using a noncommercially produced fermented starter. Also refers to a naturally leavened bread that contains no commercial yeast.

sous chef: Literally, "underchef." The chef who is second in command in a kitchen; usually responsible for scheduling, filling in for the executive chef, and assisting the chefs de partie as necessary.

spa cooking: A cooking style that focuses on producing high-quality, well-presented dishes that are nutritionally sound and low in calories, fat, sodium, and cholesterol.

spätzle: A soft noodle or small dumpling made by dropping bits of a prepared batter into simmering liquid.

spice: An aromatic vegetable substance from numerous plant parts, usually dried and used as seasoning.

spider: A long-handled skimmer used to remove items from hot liquid or fat and to skim the surface of liquids.

spit-roast: To roast an item on a large skewer or spit over, or in front of, an open flame or other radiant heat source.

sponge: A thick yeast batter that is allowed to ferment and develop a light, spongy consistency and is then combined with other ingredients to form a yeast dough.

sponge cake: A sweet batter product that is leavened with beaten egg foam. Also called génoise.

springform pan: A round, straight-sided pan whose sides are formed by a hoop that can be unclamped and detached from its base. Primarily used for cheesecakes and mousse cakes.

stabilizer: An ingredient (usually a protein or plant product) that is added to an emulsion to prevent it from separating (e.g., egg yolks, cream, or mustard). Also, an ingredient, such as gelatin or gum, that is used in various desserts to prevent them from separating (e.g., Bavarian creams).

standard breading procedure: The assembly-line procedure in which items are dredged in flour, dipped in beaten egg, then coated with crumbs before being pan fried or deep fried.

Staphylococcus aureus: A type of facultative bacteria that can cause food-borne illness. It is particularly dangerous because it produces toxins that cannot be destroyed by heat. Staph intoxication is most often caused by transfer of the bacteria from infected food handlers.

steak: A portion-size (or larger) cut of meat, poultry, or fish made by cutting across the grain of a muscle or a muscle group. May be boneless or bone in.

steamer: A set of stacked pots with perforations in the bottom of each pot. They fit over a larger pot that is filled with boiling or simmering water. Also, a perforated insert made of metal or bamboo that can be used in a pot to steam foods.

steaming: A cooking method in which items are cooked in a vapor bath created by boiling water or other liquids.

steam-jacketed kettle: A kettle with double-layered walls, between which steam circulates, providing even heat for cooking stocks, soups, and sauces. These kettles may be insulated, spigoted, and/or tilting. The latter are also called *trunnion kettles*.

steel: A tool used to hone knife blades. It is usually made of steel but may be ceramic, glass, or diamond-impregnated metal.

steep: To allow an ingredient to sit in warm or hot liquid to extract flavor or impurities, or to soften the item.

stew: A cooking method nearly identical to braising but generally involving smaller pieces of meat and hence a shorter cooking time. Stewed items also may be blanched, rather than seared, to give the finished product a pale color. Also, a dish prepared by using the stewing method.

stir-frying: A cooking method similar to sautéing in which items are cooked over very high heat, using little fat. Usually this is done in a wok, and the food is kept moving constantly.

stock: A flavorful liquid prepared by simmering meat bones, poultry bones, seafood bones, and/or vegetables in water with aromatics until their flavor is extracted. It is used as a base for soups, sauces, and other preparations.

stockpot: A large, straight-sided pot that is taller than it is wide. Used for making stocks and soups. Some have spigots. Also called *marmites*.

stone ground: A term used to describe meal or flour milled between grindstones. Because the germ of the wheat is not separated, this method of grinding retains more nutrients than other methods.

straight: A forcemeat combining lean meat and fat by grinding the mixture together.

straight-mix method: The dough-mixing method in which all ingredients are combined all at once by hand or machine.

strain: To pass a liquid through a sieve or screen to remove particles.

suprême: The breast fillet and wing of chicken or other poultry. *Sauce suprême* is chicken velouté enriched with cream.

sweat: To cook an item, usually vegetables, in a covered pan in a small amount of fat until it softens and releases moisture but does not brown.

sweetbreads: The thymus glands of young animals, usually calves, but also lambs or pigs. Usually sold in pairs. Sweetbreads have a mild flavor and smooth texture. They must be soaked in acidulated water prior to cooking and the outer membrane must be removed.

swiss: To pound meat, usually beef, with flour and seasonings; breaking up the muscle fibers and tenderizing the meat.

syrup: Sugar that is dissolved in liquid, usually water, possibly with the addition of flavorings such as spices or citrus zests.

T

table d'hôte: A fixed-price menu with a single price for an entire meal based on entrée selection.

table salt: Refined, granulated salt. May be fortified with iodine and treated with magnesium carbonate to prevent clumping.

table wine: Still red, white, and rosé wines containing between 7 and 14 percent alcohol; served with a meal.

tart: A shallow straight-sided pastry crust (may be fluted or plain) that is filled with a savory or sweet, fresh and/or cooked filling. Also, describes something that is very acidic or sour.

temper: To heat gently and gradually. May refer to the process of incorporating hot liquid into a liaison to gradually raise its temperature. May also refer to the proper method for melting chocolate.

tempura: Seafood and/or vegetables that are coated with a light batter and deep fried, usually accompanied by a sauce.

tenderloin: A boneless cut of meat, usually beef or pork, from the loin. Usually the most tender and expensive cut.

terrine: A loaf of forcemeat, similar to a pâté, but cooked in a covered mold in a bain-marie. Also, the mold used to cook such items, usually an oval shape made of ceramic.

thermophilic: Heat-loving. A term used to describe bacteria that thrive within the temperature range from 110° to 171°F/43° to 77°C.

thickener: An ingredient used to give additional body to liquids. Arrowroot, cornstarch, gelatin, roux, and beurre manié are examples of thickeners.

tilting kettle: A large, relatively shallow, tilting pot used for braising, stewing, and occasionally steaming.

timbale: A small pail-shaped mold used to shape rice, custards, mousselines, and other items. Also, a preparation made in such a mold.

tomalley: Lobster liver, which is olive green in color and used in sauces and other items.

tomato sauce: A sauce prepared by simmering tomatoes in a liquid (water or broth) with aromatics. One of the "grand" sauces.

total utilization: The principle advocating the use of as much of a product as possible in order to reduce waste and increase profits.

tournant: Roundsman or swing cook. A kitchen staff member who works as needed throughout the kitchen.

tourner: To cut items, usually vegetables, into barrel, olive, or football shapes. Tournéed foods should have five or seven sides or faces and blunt ends.

toxin: A naturally occurring poison, particularly those produced by the metabolic activity of living organisms, such as bacteria.

tranche: A slice or cut of meat, fish, or poultry cut on a bias in order to visually increase the appearance of the cut.

trash fish: Fish that have traditionally been considered unusable. Also called *junk fish* or *underutilized fish*.

Trichinella spiralis: A spiral-shaped parasitic worm that invades the intestines and muscle tissue. Transmitted primarily through infected pork that has not been cooked sufficiently.

tripe: The edible stomach lining of a cow or other ruminant. Honeycomb tripe comes from the second stomach and has a honeycomb-like texture.

truss: To tie up meat or poultry with string before cooking it in order to give it a compact shape for more even cooking and better appearance.

tuber: The fleshy root, stem, or rhizome of a plant, able to grow into a new plant. Some, such as potatoes, are eaten as vegetables.

tuile: Literally, "tile." A thin, wafer-like cookie (or food cut to resemble this cookie). Tuiles are frequently shaped while warm and still pliable by pressing them into molds or draping them over rolling pins or dowels.

tunneling: A fault in baked goods that may occur due to overmixing, or by not fully incorporating a chemical leavener, among other reasons. The finished product will contain large holes or tunnels.

U

umami: Describes a savory, meaty taste; often associated with monosodium glutamate (MSG) and mushrooms.

univalve: A single-shelled, single-muscle mollusk, such as abalone and sea urchin.

unsaturated fat: A fat molecule with at least one available bonding site not filled with a hydrogen atom. These may be monounsaturated or polyunsaturated. They tend to be liquid at room temperature and are primarily of vegetable origin.

V

vanilla sauce: A stirred custard made with cream and/or milk, sugar, eggs, and vanilla. May be served as a sauce or used in pastry preparations such as bavarian cream and ice cream. Also known as *crème anglaise.*

variety meat: Meat from a part of an animal other than the muscle; for example, organ meats. Variety meats include tongue, liver, brains, kidneys, sweetbreads, and tripe. Also called *offal.*

vegetable soup: A broth- or water-based soup made primarily with vegetables; may include meats, legumes, and noodles and may be clear or thick.

vegetarian: An individual who has adopted a specific diet (or lifestyle) that reduces or eliminates animal products. Vegans eat no foods derived in any way from animals. Lacto-ovo-vegetarians include dairy products and eggs in their diet. Ovo-vegetarians include eggs in their diet.

velouté: A sauce of white stock (chicken, veal, seafood) thickened with white roux. One of the "grand" sauces. Also, a cream soup made with a velouté sauce base and flavorings (usually puréed) that is usually finished with a liaison.

venison: Meat from large game animals in the deer family, but often used to refer specifically to deer meat.

vertical chopping machine (VCM): A machine, similar to a blender, that has rotating blades used to grind, whip, emulsify, or blend foods.

vinaigrette: A cold sauce of oil and vinegar, usually with various flavorings. It is a temporary emulsion. The standard proportion is three parts oil to one part vinegar.

virus: A type of pathogenic microorganism that can be transmitted in food. Viruses cause such illnesses as measles, chicken pox, infectious hepatitis, and colds.

vitamins: Any of various nutritionally essential organic substances that do not provide energy but usually act as regulators in metabolic processes and help maintain health.

W

waffle: A crisp, pancake-like batter product that is cooked on a specialized griddle that gives the finished product a textured pattern, usually a grid. Also a special vegetable cut that produces a grid or basket-weave pattern. Also known as *gaufrette.*

walk-in refrigerator: A refrigeration unit large enough to walk into. It is occasionally large enough to maintain zones of varying temperature and humidity to store a variety of foods properly. Some have reach-in doors as well. Some are large enough to accommodate rolling carts as well as many shelves of goods.

wasabi: Root of an Asian plant similar to horseradish. It becomes bright green when mixed with water and is used as a condiment in Japanese cooking.

whey: The liquid left after curds have formed in milk.

whip/whisk: To beat an item, such as cream or egg whites, to incorporate air. Also, a special tool for whipping, made of looped wire attached to a handle.

white chocolate: Cocoa butter flavored with sugar and milk solids. It does not contain any cocoa solids, so it does not have the characteristic brown color that regular chocolate has.

white mirepoix: Mirepoix that does not include carrots and may include chopped mushrooms or mushroom trimmings and parsnips. It is used for pale or white sauces and stocks.

white stock: A light-colored stock made with bones that have not been browned.

whole grain: An unmilled or unprocessed grain.

whole wheat flour: Flour milled from the whole grain, including the bran, germ, and endosperm. *Graham flour* is a whole wheat flour named after Sylvester Graham, a nineteenth-century American dietary reformer.

wok: A round-bottomed pan, usually made of rolled steel, that is used for nearly all cooking methods in Chinese cuisine. Its shape allows for even heat distribution and easy tossing of ingredients.

Y

yam: A large tuber that grows in tropical and subtropical climates; it has starchy, pale-yellow flesh. The name yam is also used for the (botanically unrelated) sweet potato.

yeast: Microscopic fungus whose metabolic processes are responsible for fermentation. It is used for leavening bread and in the making of cheese, beer, and wine.

yogurt: Milk cultured with bacteria to give it a slightly thick consistency and sour flavor.

Z

zest: The thin, brightly colored outer part of citrus rind. It contains volatile oils, making it ideal for use as a flavoring.

Readings and Resources

Food History

American Food: The Gastronomic Story. Evan Jones. Overlook, 1992.

Cod: A Biography of the Fish That Changed the World. Mark Kurlansky. Walker and Co., 1997.

Consuming Passions: The Anthropology of Eating. Peter Farb and George Armelagos. Houghton Mifflin, 1983.

Culture and Cuisine: A Journey Through the History of Food. Jean-François Revel. Translated by Helen R. Lane. Doubleday, 1982.

The Deipnosophists (Banquet of the Learned). Athenaeus of Naucratis. Translated by C. D. Yonge. Henry G. Bohn, 1854.

Eating in America: A History. Waverley Root and Richard de Rochemont. Ecco, 1995.

Fabulous Feasts: Medieval Cookery and Ceremony. Madeleine Pelner Cosman. Braziller, 1976.

Food and Drink Through the Ages, 2,500 B.C. to 1937 A.D. Barbara Feret. Maggs Brothers, 1937.

Food in History. Reay Tannahill. Crown Publishers, 1989.

Gastronomy: The Anthropology of Food and Food Habits. Margaret L. Arnott, ed. The Haughe: Mouton, 1976.

Kitchens and Table: A Bedside History of Eating in the Western World. Colin Clair. Abelard-Schuman, 1965.

Much Depends on Dinner: The Extraordinary History and Mythology, Allure and Obsessions, Perils and Taboos, of an Ordinary Meal. Margaret Visser. GrovePress, 1987.

Our Sustainable Table. Robert Clark, ed. North Point Press, 1987.

The Pantropheon: or, A History of Food and Its Preparation in Ancient Times. Alexis Soyer. Paddington Press, 1977.

Platine on Right Pleasure and Good Health: A Critical Edition and Translation of De Honesta Voluptate et Valetudine. Mary Ella Milham, ed. MRTS, 1998.

The Rituals of Dinner: The Origins, Evolution, Eccentricities, and Meanings of Table Manners. Margaret Visser. Viking Penguin Books, 1992.

The Roman Cookery of Apicius: A Treasury of Gourmet Recipes and Herbal Cookery. Translated and adapted by John Edwards. Hartly & Marks, 1984.

The Travels of Marco Polo. Maria Bellonci. Translated by Teresa Waugh. Facts on File, 1984.

Why We Eat What We Eat: How Columbus Changed the Way the World Eats. Raymond Sokolov. Simon & Schuster, 1992.

A Woman's Place Is in the Kitchen: The Evolution of Women Chefs. Ann Cooper. Wiley, 1998.

Sanitation and Safety

Applied Foodservice Sanitation Textbook. 4th ed. Educational Foundation of the National Restaurant Association, 1993.

Basic Food Sanitation. The Culinary Institute of America, 1993.

HACCP: Reference Book. Educational Foundation of the National Restaurant Association, 1993.

Chemistry of Cooking

CookWise: The Secrets of Cooking Revealed. Shirley Corriher. Morrow/Avon, 1997.

The Curious Cook. Harold McGee. Macmillan, 1992.

The Experimental Study of Food. 2nd ed. Campbell Penfield Griswold. Constable and Co., 1979.

Food Science. 3rd ed. Helen Charley. Prentice Hall Professional, 1994.

On Food and Cooking: The Science and Lore of the Kitchen. Harold McGee. Scribner, 2004.

Equipment and Mise en Place

The Chef's Book of Formulas, Yields and Sizes. 2nd ed. Arno Schmidt. Wiley, 2003.

Food Equipment Facts: A Handbook for the Foodservice Industry. 2nd ed. Carl Scriven and James Stevens. John Wiley & Sons, 1989.

The New Cook's Catalogue: The Definitive Guide to Cooking Equipment. Emily Aronson, Florence Fabricant, and Burt Wolf. Knopf, 2000.

The Professional Chef's Knife Kit. 2nd ed. The Culinary Institute of America. Wiley, 1999.

The Williams-Sonoma Cookbook and Guide to Kitchenware. Chuck Williams. Random House, 1986.

General Product Identification

Dictionaries and Encyclopedias

Asian Ingredients: A Guide to the Foodstuffs of China, Japan, Korea, Thailand, and Vietnam. Bruce Cost. Perenial Currents, 2000.

The Cambridge World History of Food. Kiple, Kenneth F. and Kriemhild Coneè Ornelas, editors. Cambridge University Press, 2000

The Chef's Companion: A Concise Dictionary of Culinary Terms. 2nd ed. Elizabeth Riely. Wiley, 2003.

A Concise Encyclopedia of Gastronomy. André Louis Simon. Overlook Press, 1983.

The Cook's Ingredients. Philip Dowell and Adrian Bailey. Cookbooks, 1990.

The Encyclopedia of American Food and Drink. John F. Mariani. Lebhar-Friedman, 1999.

The Encyclopedia of Asian Food and Cooking. Jacki Passmore. Hearst, 1991.

The Ethnic Food Lover's Companion, Understanding the Cuisines of the World. Eve Zibart. Menasha Ridge Press, 2001.

Food. André Simon. Horizon Press, 1949.

Food: An Informal Dictionary. Waverley Root. Simon and Schuster, 1980.

Food Lover's Companion. 4th ed. Sharon Herbst. Barron's Educational Series, 2001.

Gastronomy. Jay Jacobs. Newsweek Books, 1975.

Gastronomy of France. Raymond Oliver. Translated by Claud Durrell. Wine & Food Society with World Publishing, 1967.

Gastronomy of Italy. Anna Del Conte. Pavillion Books, 2004.

Hering's Dictionary of Classical and Modern Cookery. Walter Bickel. French and European Publications, 1981.

Knight's Foodservice Dictionary. John B. Knight and Charles A. Salter, eds. John Wiley & Sons, 1987.

Larousse Gastronomique. Jenifer Harvey Lang, ed. Potter, 2001.

The Master Dictionary of Food and Wine. 2nd ed. Joyce Rubash. John Wiley & Sons, 1996.

The Oxford Companion to Food. Alan Davidson. Oxford University Press, 1999.

Patisserie: An Encyclopedia of Cakes, Pastries, Cookies, Biscuits, Chocolate, Confectionery and Desserts. Aaron Maree. HarperCollins, 1994.

The Penguin Atlas of Food, Who Eats What, Where, When, and Why. Erik Millstone and Tim Lang. Penguin Books, 2003.

Tastings: The Best from Ketchup to Caviar: 31 Pantry Basics and How They Rate with the Experts. Jenifer Harvey Lang. Crown, 1986.

The Von Welanetz Guide to Ethnic Ingredients. Diana and Paul von Welanetz. Warner, 1987.

The World Encyclopedia of Food. Patrick L. Coyle. Facts on File, 1982.

Meats, Poultry, and Game

The Meat Buyers Guide. National Association of Meat Purveyors, 1992.

The Meat We Eat. 13th ed. John R. Romans. Prentice Hall, 2000.

Fish and Shellfish

The Complete Cookbook of American Fish and Shellfish. 2nd ed. John F. Nicolas. John Wiley & Sons, 1990.

The Encyclopedia of Fish Cookery. A. J. McClane. Henry Holt & Co., 1977.

Fish and Shellfish. James Peterson. Morrow, 1996.

McClane's Fish Buyer's Guide. A. J. McClane. Henry Holt, 1990.

Fruits and Vegetables

The Blue Goose Buying Guide for Fresh Fruits, Vegetables, Herbs and Nuts. 9th ed. Castle and Cook, 1990.

The Foodservice Guide to Fresh Produce. Produce Marketing Association. Produce Marketing Association, 1987.

Rodale's Illustrated Encyclopedia of Herbs. Random House, 1998.

Uncommon Fruits and Vegetables: A Commonsense Guide. Elizabeth Schneider. Morrow/William, 1998.

Cheeses

Cheese: A Guide to the World of Cheese and Cheese-Making. Bruno Battistotti. Facts on File, 1984.

Cheese Buyer's Handbook. Daniel O'Keefe. McGraw-Hill, 1978.

The Cheese Companion: The Connoisseur's Guide. Judy Ridgway. Running Press, 1999.

Cheese Primer. Steven Jenkins. Workman Publishers, 1996.

Cheeses of the World. U.S. Department of Agriculture. Peter Smith, 1986.

The World of Cheese. Evan Jones. Knopf distributed by Random House, 1976.

Nonperishable Goods

The Book of Coffee and Tea. 2nd ed. Joel Schapira, David Schapira, and Karl Schapira. St. Martin's, 1996.

The Complete Book of Spices: A Practical Guide to Spices and Aromatic Seeds. Jill Norman. Viking, 1995.

Spices, Salt and Aromatics in the English Kitchen. Elizabeth David. Penguin, 1970.

General and Classical Cookery

The Art of Making Sausages, Pâtés, and Other Charcuterie. Jane Grigson. Knopf, 1968.

The Chef's Compendium of Professional Recipes. 3rd ed. John Fuller, Edward Renold, and David Faskett. Butterworth-Heinemann, 1992.

Classical Cooking the Modern Way. 3rd ed. Eugene Pauli. John Wiley & Sons, 1999.

Cooking Essentials for the New Professional Chef. The Food and Beverage Institute. Mary D. Donovan, ed. John Wiley & Sons, 1997.

Cooking for the Professional Chef. Kenneth C. Wolfe. Delmar, 1982.

Cuisine Actuelle. Victor Gielisse. Taylor Publications, 1992.

Culinary Artistry. Andrew Dornenberg and Karen Page. John Wiley & Sons, 1996.

Culinary Olympics Cookbook: U.S. Team Recipes from the International Culinary Olympics. Ferdinand E. Metz and the U.S. Team. Steve M. Weiss, ed. Cahners, 1983.

Dining in France. Christian Millau. Stewart, Workman Pub Co., 1986.

Escoffier: The Complete Guide to the Art of Modern Cookery. Auguste Escoffier. John Wiley & Sons, 1997.

Escoffier Cook Book. Auguste Escoffier. Crown, 1976.

The Essential Cook Book. Terence Conran, Caroline Conran, and Simon Hopkinson. Steward, Tabori & Chang, 1980.

Essentials of Cooking. James Peterson. Artisan, 2003.

Garde Manger: The Art and Craft of the Cold Kitchen. The Culinary Institute of America. John Wiley & Sons, 2004.

The Grand Masters of French Cuisine. Selected and adapted by Celine Vence and Robert Courtine. Putnam, 1978.

Great Chefs of France. Anthony Blake and Quentin Crewe. Harry N. Abrams, 1978.

Guide Culinaire: The Complete Guide to the Art of Modern Cooking. Auguste Escoffier. Translated by H. L. Cracknell and R. J. Kaufmann. John Wiley & Sons, 1979.

Introductory Foods. 11th ed. Marion Bennion. Prentice-Hall, 2004.

Jacques Pepin's Art of Cooking. Jacques Pepin. 2 vols. Knopf, 1987.

James Beard's Theory and Practice of Good Cooking. Running Press Book Publishers, 1997.

Jewish Cooking in America. Joan Nathan. Alfred A. Knopf, 1998.

La Technique. Jacques Pepin. Pocket, 1989.

Le Répertoire de la Cuisine. Louis Saulnier. Barron's, 1977.

Ma Gastronomie. Ferdinand Point. Translated by Frank Kulla and Patricia S. Kulla. Lyceum Books, 1974.

Pâtés and Terrines. Frederich W. Elhart. Hearst, 1984.

Paul Bocuse's French Cooking. Paul Bocuse. Translated by Colette Rossant. Pantheon, 1987.

The Physiology of Taste, or Meditations on Transcendental Gastronomy. Jean-Anthelme Brillat-Savarin. Counterpoint, 2000.

Soups and Sauces

Sauces: Classical and Contemporary Sauce Making. James Peterson. John Wiley & Sons, 1998.

The Saucier's Apprentice: A Modern Guide to Classic French Sauces for the Home. Raymond A. Sokolov. Knopf, 1980.

Soups for the Professional Chef. Terence Janericco. John Wiley & Sons, 1993.

Splendid Soups. James Peterson. John Wiley & Sons, 2001.

Fruit and Vegetable Cookery

Charlie Trotter's Vegetables. Charlie Trotter. Ten Speed Press, 1996.

Jane Grigson's Fruit Book. Jane Grigson. Atheneum, 1982.

Jane Grigson's Vegetable Book. Jane Grigson. Viking Penguin, 1981.

Roger Vergé's Vegetables in the French Style. Roger Vergé. Artisan, 1994.

Vegetables. James Peterson. Morrow, 1998.

Vegetarian Cooking for Everyone. Deborah Madison. Broadway, 1997.

Nutrition and Nutritional Cookery

Choices for a Healthy Heart. Joseph C. Piscatella. Workman, 1988.

Food and Culture in America: A Nutrition Handbook. Pamela Goyan Kittler and Kathryn P. Sucher. Wadsworth, 1997.

Handbook of the Nutritional Value of Foods in Common Units. U.S. Department of Agriculture. Dover, 1986.

In Good Taste. Victor Gielisse. Simon & Schuster, 1998.

Jane Brody's Good Food Book: Living the High-Carbohydrate Way. Jane Brody. Bantan, 1987.

The Mediterranean Diet Cookbook: A Delicious Alternative for Lifelong Health. Nancy Harmon Jenkins. Bantam, 1994.

The New Living Heart Diet. Michael E. DeBakey, Antonio M. Gotto Jr., Lynne W. Scott, and John P. Foreyt. Simon and Schuster, 1996.

Nutrition: Concepts and Controversies. 8th ed. Eleanor R. Whitney and Frances S. Sizer. CT: Brooks/Cole, 2003.

The Professional Chef's Techniques of Healthy Cooking. 2nd ed. The Culinary Institute of America. Jennifer Armentrout, ed. John Wiley & Sons, 2000.

American Cookery

An American Bounty: Great Contemporary Cooking from the CIA. The Culinary Institute of America. Mary Donovan, ed. Rizzoli, 1995.

Charlie Trotter's. Charlie Trotter. Ten Speed Press, 1994.

Chef Paul Prudhomme's Louisiana Kitchen. Paul Prudhomme. Morrow, 1984.

Chez Panisse Cooking. Paul Bertolli with Alice Waters. Peter Smith, 2000.

City Cuisine. Susan Feniger and Mary Sue Milliken. Morrow, 1994.

Epicurean Delight: The Life and Times of James Beard. Evan Jones. Knopf, 1990.

I Hear America Cooking. Betty Fussell. Viking Penguin, 1997.

Jasper White's Cooking from New England. Jasper White. Biscuit Books, 1998.

Jeremiah Tower's New American Classics. Jeremiah Tower. Harper & Row, 1986.

License to Grill. Chris Schlesinger and John Willoughby. Morrow, 1997.

The Mansion on Turtle Creek Cook Book. Dean Fearing. Grove-Atlantic, 1987.

The New York Times Cook Book. Craig Claiborne. Harper & Row, 1990.

Saveur Cooks Authentic American. The editors of *Saveur Magazine.* Chronicle, 1998.

The Thrill of the Grill: Techniques, Recipes & Downhome Barbecue. Chris Schlesinger and John Willoughby. Morrow, 1997.

The Trellis Cookbook. Marcel Desaulniers. Simon and Schuster, 1992.

International Cookery

Latin and Caribbean

The Art of South American Cooking. Felipe Rojas-Lombardi. Harper, 1991.

The Book of Latin American Cooking. Elizabeth Lambert Ortiz. HarperCollins, 1994.

The Essential Cuisines of Mexico. Diana Kennedy. Crown, 2000.

Food and Life of Oaxaca. Zarela Martínez. Wiley, 1997.

Food from My Heart: Cuisines of Mexico Remembered and Reimagined. Zarela Martínez. Macmillan, 1995.

Rick Bayless's Mexican Kitchen. Rick Bayless. Scribner, 1996.

The Taste of Mexico. Patricia Quintana. Stewart, Tabori & Chang, 1986.

European and Mediterranean

The Art of Turkish Cooking. Neset Eren. Hippocrene Books, 1993.

The Belgian Cookbook. Nika Hazelton. Athenum, 1977.

The Best of Southern Italian Cooking. Jean C. Grasso. Barron's, 1984.

Bistro Cooking. Patricia Wells. Workman Publishing, 1989.

A Book of Mediterranean Food. Elizabeth David. New York Review of Books, 2002.

Classical and Contemporary Italian Cooking for Professionals. Bruno Ellmer. John Wiley & Sons, 1997.

Classical French Cooking. Craig Claiborne, Pierre Franey, et al. Time-Life Books, 1970.

The Classic Food of Northern Italy. Anna Del Conte. Pavilion, 1995.

The Classic Italian Cookbook. Marcella Hazan. Knopf, 1976.

Classic Scandinavian Cooking. Nika Hazelton. Galahad, 1994.

Classic Techniques of Italian Cooking. Bugiali, Giuliano. Simon and Schuster, 1982.

The Cooking of the Eastern Mediterranean. Paula Wolfert. HarperCollins, 1994.

The Cooking of Italy. Waverly Root, et al. Time-Life Books, 1968.

The Cooking of Provincial France. M. F. K. Fisher, et al. Time-Life Books, 1968.

The Cooking of South-West France: A Collection of Traditional and New Recipes from France's Magnificent Rustic Cuisine. Paula Wolfert. Harper, 1994.

Couscous and Other Good Food from Morocco. Paula Wolfert. Perenial Currents, 1987.

Croatian Cuisine. Ruzica Kapetanovic and Alojzije Kapetanovic. Associated, 1993.

The Czechoslovak Cookbook. Joza Brizova et al. Crown, 1965.

The Food and Cooking of Russia. Lesley Chamberlain. Viking Penguin, 1989.

The Food of Italy. Waverly Root. Athenum. 1971.

The Food of North Italy: Authentic Recipes from Piedmont, Lombardy, and Valle d'Aosta. Luigi Veronelli. Tuttle Pub., 2002.

The Food of Southern Italy. Carlo Middione. William Morrow, 1987.

The Foods and Wines of Spain. 11th ed. Penelope Casas. Knopf, 1982.

La France Gastronomique. Anne Willan. Arcade Pub, 1991.

French Provincial Cooking. Elizabeth David. Perguin Books, 1999.

French Regional Cooking. Anne Willan. Stoddart Publishing, 1995.

George Lang's Cuisine of Hungary. George Lang. Wings, 1994.

The German Cookbook. Mimi Sheraton. Random House, 1965.

Giuliano Bugialli's Classic Techniques of Italian Cooking. Giuliano Bugialli. Fireside, 1989.

Greek Food. Rena Salamon. Harper, 1994.

Italian Food. Elizabeth David. Penguin, 1999.

Italian Regional Cooking. Ada Boni. Bonanza Books, 1969.

Lidia's Italian American Kitchen. Lidia Matticchio Bastianich. Alfred A. Knopf, 2001.

A Mediterranean Feast. Clifford Wright. William Morrow and Company, Inc., 1999.

Mediterranean Grains and Greens. Paula Wolfert. Harper-Collins, 1998.

The New Book of Middle Eastern Food. Claudia Roden. Knopf, 2000.

Pasta Classica: The Art of Italian Pasta Cooking. Julia Della Croce. Chronicle, 1996.

Paula Wolfert's World of Food: A Collection of Recipes from Her Kitchen, Travels, and Friends. Paula Wolfert. HarperCollins, 1995.

Pierre Franey's Cooking in France. Pierre Franey and Richard Flaste. Knopf, 1994.

Please to the Table: The Russian Cookbook. Anya Von Bremzen. Workman, 1990.

The Polish Cookbook. Z. Czerny. Vanous, 1982.

Regional French Cooking. Paul Bocuse. Flammarion, 1991.

Roger Vergé's Cuisine of the South of France. Roger Vergé. Translated by Roberta Smoler. Morrow, 1980.

Simple Cuisine. Jean-Georges Vongerichten. Wiley, 1998.

The Taste of France: A Dictionary of French Food and Wine. Fay Sharman. Houghton Mifflin, 1982.

A Taste of Morocco. Robert Carrier. Clarkson Potter, 1987.

Asian

Classic Indian Cooking. Julie Sahni. Morrow/Avon, 1980.

The Cooking of Japan. Rafael Steinberg and the editors of Time-Life Books. Time-Life Books, 1969.

Cracking the Coconut: Classic Thai Home Cooking. Su-Mei Yu. Morrow/Avon, 2000.

Cuisines of India: The Art and Tradition of Regional Indian Cooking. Smita Chandra and Sanjeev Chandra. Ecco Press, 2001.

Essentials of Asian Cuisine: Fundamentals and Favorite Recipes. Corinne Trang. Simon & Schuster, 2003.

The Food of Asia: Featuring Authentic Recipes From Master Chefs in Burma, China, India, Indonesia, Japan, Korea, Malaysia, The Philippines, Singapore, Sri Lanka, Thailand, and Vietnam. Forewords by Ming Tsai and Cheong Liew; introductory essays by Kong Foong Ling. Periplus Editions, 2002.

Food Culture in Japan. Ashkenazi, Michael and Jeanne Jacob. Greenwood Press, 2003.

The Food of Korea: Authentic Recipes From the Land of Morning Calm. Texts by David Clive Price. Periplus Editions, 2002.

The Foods of Vietnam. Nicole Routhier. Stewart, Tabori, & Chang, 1999.

Growing up in a Korean Kitchen: A Cookbook. Hi Soo Shin Hepinstall. Ten Speed Press, 2001.

The Indian Cookbook. Shehzad Husain. Lorenz Books, 2002.

Japanese Cooking: A Simple Art. Shizuo Tsuji. Kodansha, 1980.

The Joy of Japanese Cooking. Kuwako Takahashi. C. E. Tuttle, 2002.

Madhur Jaffrey's Far Eastern Cookery. Madhur Jaffrey. Perennial, 1992.

Madhur Jaffrey's Indian Cooking. Madhur Jaffrey. Barron's, c1982.

The Modern Art of Chinese Cooking. Barbara Tropp. Hearst Co., 1996.

The Noon Book of Authentic Indian Cooking. G. K. Noon. Periplus Editions, 2002.

Pacific and Southeast Asian Cooking. Rafael Steinberg and the editors of Time-Life Books. Time-Life Books, 1970.

A Taste of Japan. Jenny Ridgewell. Raintree Steck-Vaughn, 1997.

A Taste of Madras: A South Indian Cookbook. Rani Kingman. Interlink Books, 1996.

Terrific Pacific Cookbook. Anya Von Bremzen and John Welchman. Workman, 1995.

Traditional Korean Cooking. Chin-hwa Noh. Weatherhill, 1985.

Baking and Pastry

The Baker's Manual. 4th ed. Joseph Amendola. John Wiley & Sons, 2002.

The Bread Bible: Beth Hensperger's 300 Favorite Recipes. Beth Hensperger. Chronicle, 2004.

Flatbreads and Flavors: A Culinary Atlas. Jeffrey Alford and Naomi Duguid. Morrow/Avon, 1995.

Great Dessert Book. Christian Teubner and Sybil Schonfeldt. Hamlyn, 1995.

Nancy Silverton's Breads from the La Brea Bakery: Recipes for the Connoisseur. Nancy Silverton with Laurie Ochoa. Villard, 1996.

The New International Confectioner. 5th ed. Wilfred J. France. Virtue, 1981.

Nick Malgieri's Perfect Pastry. Nick Malgieri. Macmillan, 1998.

The Pie and Pastry Bible. Rose Levy Beranbaum. Scribner, 1998.

Practical Baking. William J. Sultan. John Wiley & Sons, 1996.

The Professional Pastry Chef. 3rd ed. Bo Friberg. John Wiley & Sons, 2002.

Swiss Confectionery. 3rd ed. Richemont Bakers and Confectioners Craft School, 1991.

Understanding Baking. 2nd ed. Joseph Amendola and Donald E. Lundberg. John Wiley & Sons, 2002.

Wines and Spirits

Exploring Wine: The Culinary Institute of America's Complete Guide to Wines of the World. 2nd ed. Steven Kolpan, Brian H. Smith, and Michael A. Weiss. John Wiley & Sons, 2001.

Great Wines Made Simple: Straight Talk from a Master Sommelier. Andrea Immer. Broadway, 2000.

Hugh Johnson's Modern Encyclopedia of Wine. 4th ed. Hugh Johnson. Simon & Schuster, 1998.

Larousse Encyclopedia of Wine. Christopher Foulkes, ed. Larousse, 1994.

Windows on the World Complete Wine Course: 2001 Edition. Kevin Zraly. Sterling, 2000.

Business and Management

At Your Service: A Hands-on Guide to the Professional Dining Room. The Culinary Institute of America. John Fisher. John Wiley & Sons, 2005.

Becoming a Chef: With Recipes and Reflections from America's Leading Chefs. Andrew Dornenburg and Karen Page. John Wiley & Sons, 1995.

Cases in Hospitality Marketing and Management. 2nd ed. Robert C. Lewis. John Wiley & Sons, 1997.

Culinary Math. Linda Blocker, Julie Hill, and The Culinary Institute of America. John Wiley & Sons, 2002.

The Discipline of Market Leaders: Choose Your Customers, Narrow Your Focus, Dominate Your Market. Michael Treacy and Fred Wiersma. Perseus Books, 1995.

Food and Beverage Cost Control. Donald Bell. McCutchen, 1984.

Foodservice Organizations. 4th ed. Marion Spears. Prentice-Hall, 2004.

Lessons in Excellence from Charlie Trotter. Charlie Trotter. Ten Speed Press, 1999.

The Making of a Chef: Mastering the Heat at the CIA. Michael Ruhlman. Henry Holt, 1997.

Math Principles for Food Service Occupations. 3rd ed. Robert G. Haines. Thomson, 1995.

Math Workbook for Foodservice and Lodging. 3rd ed. Hollie W. Crawford and Milton McDowell. John Wiley & Sons, 1997.

Principles of Food, Beverage & Labor Cost Controls. Paul Dittmer. John Wiley & Sons, 2002.

Principles of Marketing. 7th ed. Philip Kotler and Gary Armstong. Prentice-Hall, 2005.

Professional Table Service. Sylvia Meyer. Translated by Heinz Holtmann. John Wiley & Sons, 1997.

Recipes into Type: A Handbook for Cookbook Writers and Editors. Joan Whitman and Dolores Simon. HarperCollins, 1993.

Remarkable Service. The Culinary Institute of America. Ezra Eichelberger and Gary Allen, eds. John Wiley & Sons, 2001.

The Resource Guide for Food Writers. Gary Allen. Routledge, 1999.

The Successful Business Plan: Secrets and Strategies. 2nd ed. Rhonda Abrams. Planning Shop, 2003.

What Every Supervisor Should Know. Lester Bittle and John Newstrom. McGraw-Hill, 1992.

Periodicals and Journals

American Brewer

Appellation

Art Culinaire

The Art of Eating

Beverage Digest

Beverage World

Bon Appétit

Brewer's Digest

Caterer and Hotelkeeper

Chef

Chocolate News

Chocolatier

Cooking for Profit

Cooking Light

Cook's Illustrated

Culinary Trends

Decanter

Eating Well

Food and Wine

Food Arts

Food for Thought

Food Management

Foodservice and Hospitality

Foodservice Director

Food Technology

Fresh Cup

Gastronomica

Gourmet

Herb Companion

Hospitality

Hospitality Design

Hotel and Motel Management

Hotels

IACP Food Forum

Lodging

Meat and Poultry

Modern Baking

Nation's Restaurant News

Nutrition Action Health Letter

Pizza Today

Prepared Foods

Restaurant Business

Restaurant Hospitality

Restaurants and Institutions

Saveur

Wine and Spirits

Wines and Vines

Wine Spectator

Culinary Associations

American Culinary Federation (ACF)
180 Center Place Way
St. Augustine, FL 32095
(800) 624-9458
www.acfchefs.org

The American Institute of Wine & Food (AIWF)
1303 Jefferson Street, Suite 110-B
Napa, CA 94559
(800) 274-2493
www.aiwf.org

Chefs Collaborative
262 Beacon Street
Boston, MA 02116
(617) 236-5200
www.chefscollaborative.org

Chefs de Cuisine Association of America
155 East 55th Street, Suite 3028
New York, NY 10022
(212) 832-4939

The International Council on Hotel, Restaurant and Institutional Education (CHRIE)
2810 North Parham Road, Suite 230
Richmond, VA 23294
(804) 346-4800
www.chrie.org

International Association of Culinary Professionals (IACP)
304 West Liberty Street, Suite 201
Louisville, KY 40202
(502) 581-9786
www.iacp.com

The James Beard Foundation
167 West 12th Street
New York, NY 10011
(212) 675-4984
www.jamesbeard.org

Les Dames d'Escoffier (LDEI), DC Chapter
P.O. Box 2962
Reston, VA 20195
(202) 973-2168
www.members.aol.com/lesdamesdc/

National Restaurant Association (NRA)
1200 17th Street, NW
Washington, DC 20036
(202) 331-5900
www.restaurant.org

Oldways Preservation Trust
266 Beacon Street
Boston, MA 02116
(617) 421-5500
www.oldwayspt.org

Roundtable for Women in Foodservice
3022 West Eastwood Avenue
Chicago, IL 60625
(312) 463-3396

Share Our Strength (SOS)
1730 M Street, NW, Suite 700
Washington, DC 20036
(800) 969-4767
www.strength.org

Women Chefs and Restaurateurs (WCR)
304 West Liberty Street, Suite 201
Louisville, KY 40202
(502) 581-0300
(877) 927-7787
www.womenchefs.org

Recipe Index

Subject Index

quality of, 276
whole, 323
Buttercream, 1142–1143, 1146
Buttermilk, 276, 277
Butternut squash, 246, 247

C

Cabbage, 243
Cabbage (brassica) family, 242–243
Cabrales cheese, 141
Cabrero cheese, 141
Caciotta cheese, 282, 283
Cajun cuisine, 42
Cake flour, 294, 295
Cake pans, 165
Cakes
    buttercream for, 1142–1144
    to cool and store, 1095
    creaming method, 1090–1092
    foaming method, 1093–1095
    to glaze, 1149–1150
    icing procedure, 1145–1146
    layering procedure, 1144
Calaspara rice, 297
Calcium, 22
Caloric intake, recommended, 20
Camembert cheese, 280, 281
Cameo apple, 228, 229
Canary beans, 306, 308
Cannellini, 308
Canola oil, 323
Cantal cheese, 285
Cantaloupe, 235, 236
Capellini, 303, 304
Capon, 198
Captain, 9
Caramelization, 23, 25, 1053
Caraway, 313, 314
Carbohydrates, 20, 25
Carborundum stones, 151
Cardamom, 313, 314
Cardinal sauce, 365
Career opportunities, 7–10
Carême, Marie-Antoine, 110
Caribbean cuisine, 46
Carrots, 262, 263, 332
Carry-out food service, 8
Carving, 518–520
Casaba melons, 236
Casareccia, 304
Cashews, 310, 311
Cassava, 264, 265
Cassava flour, 339
Casseroled potatoes, 778–781
Cast-iron pans, 160, 161, 782
Catalan cuisine, 138–139
Catering, career opportunities in, 8
Catfish, 214
Cauliflower, 243
Caviar, 127
Cayenne, 314
Cazuela, 141
Celery, 266, 267, 332
Celery root, 262, 263
Celery seed, 313, 314
Central European cuisine, 133–135
Cèpe mushrooms, 255
Cephalopods, 215, 220–221
Cereals and meals, simmering and boiling, 809–811
Chakki (spice mill), 72
Champagne grapes, 234
Chanterelle mushrooms, 254, 255
Chapati, 64
Charcuterie, 1024–1029
Charcutière sauce, 361
Chard, 252, 253
Chasseur sauce, 361
Châteaubriand, 472
Chawan mushi, 80
Chayote, 244, 245
Cheddar cheese, 284, 285
Cheeks, veal, 185
Cheese

in Mediterranean cuisine, 121
Parmigiano-Reggiano, 116, 286, 287
production of, 277
in Spanish cuisine, 141
types and culinary uses, 278–289
Cheesecloth, 159
Chef de cuisine, 8
Chefs. See also Culinary profession
    in brigade system, 8–9
    uniform of, 34
Chef's knife, 149, 681
Chef's potatoes, 264, 265, 768
Chemical contaminants, 28
Cherries, 238
Cherry sauce, 361
Cherry tomatoes, 268, 269
Chervil, 270, 272
Chestnuts, 311
    to peel, 701
Chèvre (goat cheese), 278, 279
Chevreuil sauce, 361
Chicken. See also Poultry
    classes of, 196, 197–198
    doneness of, 461
    to halve and quarter, 489
    sûpremes, 486–487, 611
    to truss, 488
Chickpeas, 307, 308
Chiffonade cut, 683
Chiffon cake, 1093
Chiles
    to cut and seed, 699
    dried, to rehydrate, 705
    dried, varieties of, 259
    to peel, 700
    varieties of, 258–259
Chili powder, 316
Chinese cabbage (Napa), 243
Chinese cuisine, 54–61
    equipment and tools, 58, 60
    history and tradition, 60–61
    ingredients, 57, 59
    meals, 56
    regional, 54–56
    techniques, 55, 56
Chinese five-spice, 316
Chinese long beans, 260, 261
Chinese white cabbage (bok choy), 243
Chives, 271, 272, 682
Chivry sauce, 366
Chocolate
    in creamed batter, 1090
    fondant, 1150
    ganache, 1147–1148
    mousse, 1131
    production of, 325
    sauce, 1147
    storage of, 325
    tempered, 1147, 1155
    truffles, 1154–1155
Cholesterol, 21
Cho'lim, 85
Chopping vegetables, 682
    garlic, 694
Chops, bone-in, to cut, 475
Chopsticks, 58, 80, 101
Choron sauce, 376
Chowder, 410–413
Chuck cuts
    beef, 177, 179, 180
    veal, 185
Chula, 72
Cilantro, 270, 272
Cinnamon, 313, 314
Cipollini onions, 256, 257
Citrus fruits
    to juice, 923
    sûpremes, 924
    varieties of, 232–233
    to zest, 924
Clams, 216, 218
    to clean and open, 504

doneness, 461
Clarified butter, 323, 337–338
Cleaning
    copper pans, 161
    grills and broilers, 717
    mushrooms, 701
    salad greens, 919, 920
    sanitizing procedures, 29, 33
    vegetables, 681, 708
Cleaver, 150, 151
    Chinese, 58, 60
Cloves, 313, 314
Coagulation, 23
Cockles, 218
Coconut, 239, 240
Coconut milk, 97–98
Coconut oil, 323
Coconut rice, 99
Cod, 204, 205
Coffee, 326
Colander, 159
Cold-foods chef, 8
Collard greens, 243
Combi oven, 167
Commis (apprentice), 9
Communard, 9
Composed salads, 928
Concassé, tomato, 697–698
Conch, 217
Concord grapes, 234
Condensed milk, 275
Condiments
    in Chinese cuisine, 55, 59
    in Indian cuisine, 71
    in Japanese cuisine, 79
    in Korean cuisine, 84, 87
    pantry basics, 325
Conduction method of heat transfer, 23
Confectioner's sugar, 319, 321
Confiseur, 8–9
Confucianism, food customs of, 83
Conical sieve, 159
Consommé, 395–399
Contamination, food, 28
    cross contamination, 29, 30
Convection method of heat transfer, 23–24
Convection oven, 167
Convection steamer, 166
Cookies
    creaming method, 1090–1092
    drop, 1099, 1101
    to glaze, 1149–1150
    molded, 1103
    piped, 1100
    rolled and cut, 1099–1100
    stenciled, 1102
Cooking fats. See Fats and oils
Cooking liquids
    for boiling, 708, 709, 769, 809
    for braising, 634
    in Chinese cuisine, 59
    to cool, 31, 615
    in Indian cuisine, 71
    in Japanese cuisine, 79
    in Korean cuisine, 87
    for pan-steaming, 714, 715
    for pilaf, 812, 813
    for poaching (deep), 613, 614
    for poaching (shallow), 608
    for poaching eggs, 882, 883
    for risotto, 815, 816
    for simmering grains and legumes, 807, 809
    for steaming, 602, 711, 770
    for stewing, 642
Cooking methods
    barbecuing, 41
    beef, 178–179
    boiling, 708–710, 769–771
    braising, 25, 634–639, 733–735
    cereals and meals, 809–811
    in Chinese cuisine, 55, 56

custards, 1126–1129
deep frying, 570–571, 730–732, 785–787
eggs, 880–896
grains, 807–808, 812–818
grilling and broiling, 508–511, 717–718
hot water bath, 1127
in Indian cuisine, 70, 72
in Japanese cuisine, 80
in Korean cuisine, 85–86
lamb, 192–193
legumes, 806–808
in Middle Eastern cuisine, 95–96
pan frying, 567–569, 728–729
pan steaming, 714–716
en papillote, 605–607
pasta, 850–852
poaching (deep), 613–615
poaching (shallow), 608–612
pork, 188–189
potatoes, 769–787
poultry, 197–198
puréeing, 772–775
roasting, 512–520, 719–721, 776, 777
sautéing, 562–566, 723–725, 782–784
simmering, 613–615
steaming, 602–604, 711–713, 770
stewing, 640–643, 733–735
stir-frying, 562, 726–727
veal, 184–185
vegetables, 708–735
Cooking process, scientific principles in, 23–26
Cookware. See Pots and pans
Cooling foods, 31
Copper pans, 160, 161
Cordials, 326
Coriander, 313, 314
Corn, 260, 261, 298, 702
Cornish hens, 198, 489
Cornmeal, 298
Corn oil, 323
Cornstarch, 298
    as thickener, 339, 1048
Corn syrup, 319, 321
Cortland apple, 228, 229
Cost
    as-purchased, 15–16
    butcher's yield test, 18
    edible portion, 17
Cottage cheese, 279
Cottonseed oil, 324
Count measurement, 12
Country-style forcemeats, 1024
Couscous, 302, 305
Couscoussière, 123
Cox orange pippin, 228, 229
Crab, 222, 224
    doneness, 461
    soft-shelled, to clean, 502
Crabapple, 229
Cracked wheat, 293
Cranberries, 230, 231
Cranberry beans, 261, 307, 308
Crayfish, 223, 503
Cream
    in custard, 1126, 1127
    forms of, 274, 275
    in ganache, 1148
    in liaisons, 340–342
    in mousse, 1130, 1132
    whipped, 1055
Cream cheese, 279
Creamed batters, 1090–1092
Cream soup, 404–409
Crème fraîche, 277
Cremini mushrooms, 254, 255
Crenshaw melons, 236
Creole cuisine, 42
Crêpe pan, 163

Tava (iron pan), 72
Tea, 326
Tea ceremony, Japanese, 74, 75
Teaching opportunities, 9
Teff, 300, 301
Temperature
  deep frying, 571
  meat, poultry, and fish doneness,
      460–461
  poaching, 614
  roasting, 513, 514–515
  storage, 30, 200
  for stuffings, 457
Tempered chocolate, 1147, 1155
Tempering, 340
Tempura, 80
Tenderloin
  medallions, 472
  pork, 186, 189
  to trim, 471
Teriyaki, 80
Terrine mold, 165
Terrines, forcemeat for, 1024–1028
Tetch'im, 85
Tetilla cheese, 141
Thai chiles, 258, 259
Thai cuisine, 100
Thali (serving trays), 72
Thawing frozen foods, 32
Thermometers, 158, 515, 570
Thickeners. See also Roux
  in baking, 1048–1049
  in bisques, 418
  in braise sauce, 639
  in chowders, 410
  in cream soups, 404, 409
  ingredients, 326
  liaisons, 340–342
  slurries, 339, 356
  in stews, 335–342, 733
Thompson seedless grapes, 234
Thyme, 271, 272
Tian, 123
Tilapia, 214
Tilefish, 207
Tilting kettle, 166
Timbale mold, 165
Time management, 6–7
Tomatillos, 268, 269
Tomatoes
  to peel and cut, 697–698
  sauce, 367–370
  varieties of, 268–269
Tongue
  beef, 179
  lamb, 193
  preparation of, 480
  veal, 185
Tools. See Equipment and tools
Toppings, for pies and tarts, 1151,
    1152
Tourné cuts, 686, 691
Tournedos, 472

Tourné knife, 150, 151
Training. See Education and training
Tranche, 497
Tripe, 179
Trout, 208, 209
Truffle, black and white, 255
Truffles, chocolate, 1154–1155
Trussing poultry, 488
Tube pans, 165
Tubers, 52, 264–265
Tubetti, 302, 305
Tuile cookies, 1102
Tuna, 208, 209–210
Turbinado sugar, 319, 321
Turbot, 202, 203
Turkey, 198, 461
Turmeric, 313, 316
Turnip greens, 243
Turnips, 262, 263

U

Udon noodles, 304
Umani, 80
Uniform, chef's, 34
Uniq (Ugli fruit), 232, 233
United States, regional cuisine in.
    See American cuisine
United States Department of
    Agriculture (USDA), 173, 226
Usable trim, value of, 17
Utility knife, 149, 150

V

Vanilla sauce, 1129
Variety meats
  beef, 179
  lamb, 193
  pork, 189
  preparation techniques, 480–481
  storage of, 172
  veal, 185
Veal. See also Meat
  cuts of, 182–185
  doneness of, 461
  grades of, 182
Vegetable chef, 8
Vegetable oil, 324
Vegetables. See also specific veg-
    etables
  as appetizers, 981
  aromatic. See aromatic vegeta-
      bles
  boiling, 708–710
  boiling potatoes, 769–771
  to cut. See Cutting vegetables
      and herbs
  deep frying, 730–732
  deep frying potatoes, 785–787
  doneness in, 710, 736
  dried, rehydrating, 705
  grilling and broiling, 717–718
  in hearty broths, 403

hydroponically grown, 226
locally grown, 226
mise en place for, 680–706
pan frying, 728–729
pan steaming, 714–716
to purée 722
to reheat, 737
roasting and baking, 719–721
roasting and baking potatoes,
    776–777
salads, 927–928
sautéing, 723–725
to shock, 710
steaming, 711–713
steaming potatoes, 770
stir-frying, 726–727
storage of, 30, 226–227
varieties of, 242–269
yield percentage for, 16–17
Vegetables in world cuisines
  American, 39, 40, 42, 43, 44, 45
  Chinese, 59
  Eastern European, 126, 128, 131
  French, 106–107
  Indian, 62, 71
  Italian, 118–119
  Japanese, 76–77
  Korean, 87
  Latin American, 52
  Mediterranean, 121
  Middle Eastern, 89
  Portuguese, 143
  Southeast Asian, 100
  Spanish, 138
Vegetarian diet
  Chinese, 61
  Indian, 62, 67
  protein in, 20
Velouté, 362, 366
Velvetting, 56
Venison, cuts of, 194
Vermicelli, 303, 304
Vermillion snapper, 206, 207
Véron sauce, 366
Vertical chopping machine (VCM),
    169
Vietnamese cuisine, 98, 100, 102
Villeroy sauce, 366
Vinaigrette, 26, 912–914
Vin blanc sauce, 366, 612
Vinegar, 325
  balsamic, 116
  flavored, 914
  in vinaigrette, 912
Viruses, 28
Vitamin A, 22
Vitamin B-complex, 22
Vitamin C, 22
Vitamin D, 22
Vitamin E, 22
Vitamin K, 22
Vitamins and minerals, 21, 22
Volume measurement, 13, 14

W

Wabi sabi (food presentation), 75
Waffle cuts, 689
Wait staff, 9
Walk-in refrigeration, 170
Walleyed pike, 206, 207
Walnut oil, 324
Walnuts, 310, 311
Water, in cooking, 26
Water activity scale, 29
Watercress, 250, 251
Watermelon, 234, 235
Weakfish, 207
Weight measurement, 13, 15
Western cuisine (U.S.), 44
Wheat, 293
Wheat berries, 293
Wheat bran, 293
Wheat flour, 294–295
Wheat germ, 293
Whelk, 217
Whipping cream, 275, 1055
Whipping egg whites, 1056
Whips and whisks, 157
White sauce, 362–366
White stock, 344
Whole grains, 292
Whole wheat flour, 294, 295
Wild rice, 296, 297
Wine, culinary uses of, 326
Wine steward, 9
Wok, 58, 81, 86
Wolf fish, 204, 205, 214
Workplace
  orderly, 7
  safety in, 33–34
World cuisines. See American cui-
    sine; Asian cuisine; European
    cuisine; Latin American cui-
    sine; Middle Eastern cuisine

Y

Yeast, 325, 1050
Yeast dough, 1064–1068
Yellow squash, 244, 245
Yellowtail snapper, 206, 207
Yield
  butcher's yield test, 18
  percentage, 16–17
  recipe conversion factor (RCF),
      14
Yogurt, 96, 275, 276, 277
Yuca, 264, 265

Z

Zakusky (appetizers), 127
Zest, citrus, 924
Zingara sauce, 361
Zucchini, 244, 245